3444 ⌐ 20∽

KU-482-783

Bearing
the Cross

Martin Luther King, Jr
and the
Southern Christian
Leadership Conference

David J. Garrow

976

R.T.C. LIBRARY LETTERKENNY

JONATHAN CAPE
THIRTY-TWO BEDFORD SQUARE LONDON

R.T.C. LIBRARY LETTERKENN.

First published in Great Britain 1988
Copyright © 1986 by David J. Garrow
Jonathan Cape Ltd, 32 Bedford Square, London WC1B 3EL

Quotations from the works of Martin Luther King, Jr reprinted
by permission of Joan Daves. Copyright © 1963, 1967 and 1968
by Martin Luther King, Jr and the Estate of Martin Luther King, Jr.
Quotations from the records of the Ford Foundation by written
permission of the Ford Foundation. Quotations from the
correspondence of Daniel P. Moynihan by permission of
the Hon. Daniel P. Moynihan.

A CIP catalogue record for this book
is available from the British Library

ISBN 0-224-02603-8

Printed in Great Britain by Richard Clay Ltd, Bungay, Suffolk

This is the cross
that we must bear
for the freedom of our people.

—MARTIN LUTHER KING, JR.
  October 26, 1960
  Reidsville State Prison,
  Tattnall County, Georgia

The cross we bear
precedes the crown we wear.
To be a Christian one must take up his cross,
with all of its difficulties and agonizing
and tension-packed content
and carry it until that very cross
leaves its marks upon us and redeems us
to that more excellent way which comes
only through suffering.

—MARTIN LUTHER KING, JR.
  January 17, 1963
  National Conference on Religion & Race,
  Chicago, Illinois

When I took up the cross,
I recognized its meaning. . . .
The cross is something that you bear,
and ultimately that you die on.

—MARTIN LUTHER KING, JR.
  May 22, 1967
  Penn Community Center,
  Frogmore, South Carolina

To JDB, DLC, MMK, JHC, and SFN

Bearing the Cross

Contents

1

The Montgomery Bus Boycott, 1955–1956

R.T.C. LIBRARY, LETTERKENNY

Thursday had been busy and tiring for Mrs. Raymond A. Parks. Her job as a tailor's assistant at the Montgomery Fair department store had left her neck and shoulder particularly sore, and when she left work at 5:30 P.M. that December 1, 1955, she went across the street to a drugstore in search of a heating pad. Mrs. Parks didn't find one, but she purchased a few other articles before recrossing the street to her usual bus stop on Court Square. The buses were especially crowded this cold, dark evening, and when she boarded one for her Cleveland Avenue route, only one row of seats—the row immediately behind the first ten seats that always were reserved for whites only—had any vacancies. She took an aisle seat, with a black man on her right next to the window, and two black women in the parallel seat across the way.

As more passengers boarded at each of the two next stops, the blacks moved to the rear, where they stood, and the whites occupied their exclusive seats at the front of the bus. At the third stop, more passengers got on, and one, a white male, was left standing after the final front seat was taken. The bus driver, J. F. Blake, looked back and called out to Mrs. Parks and her three colleagues, "All right you folks, I want those two seats." Montgomery's customary practice of racial preference demanded that all four blacks would have to stand in order to allow one white man to sit, since no black was allowed to sit parallel with a white. No one moved at first. Blake spoke out again: "You all better make it light on yourselves and let me have those seats." At that, the two women across from Mrs. Parks rose and moved to the rear; the man beside her rose also, and she moved her legs to allow him out into the aisle. She remained silent, but shifted to the window side of the seat.

11

Blake could see that Mrs. Parks had not arisen. "Look, woman, I told you I wanted the seat. Are you going to stand up?" At that, Rosa Lee McCauley Parks uttered her first word to him: "No." Blake responded, "If you don't stand up, I'm going to have you arrested." Mrs. Parks told him to go right ahead, that she was not going to move. Blake said nothing more, but got off the bus and went to a phone. No one spoke to Mrs. Parks, and some passengers began leaving the bus, not wanting to be inconvenienced by the incident.

Mrs. Parks was neither frightened nor angry. "I was thinking that the only way to let them know I felt I was being mistreated was to do just what I did—resist the order," she later recalled. "I had not thought about it and I had taken no previous resolution until it happened, and then I simply decided that I would not get up. I was tired, but I was usually tired at the end of the day, and I was not feeling well, but then there had been many days when I had not felt well. I had felt for a long time, that if I was ever told to get up so a white person could sit, that I would refuse to do so." The moment had come, and she had had the courage to say no.

Blake returned from the phone, and stood silently in the front of the bus. After a few minutes, a police squad car pulled up, and two officers, F. B. Day and D. W. Mixon, got on the bus. Blake pointed to Mrs. Parks, said he needed the seat, and that "the other ones stood up." The two policemen came toward her, and one, in Mrs. Parks's words, "asked me if the driver hadn't asked me to stand. I said yes. He asked, 'Why didn't you stand up?' I said I didn't think I should have to. I asked him, 'Why do you push us around?' He said, 'I don't know, but the law is the law, and you are under arrest.' So the moment he said I was under arrest, I stood up. One picked up my purse, one picked up my shopping bag, and we got off the bus." They escorted her to the patrol car, and returned to talk to Blake. The driver confirmed that he wanted to press charges under Montgomery's bus segregation ordinance, and the officers took Mrs. Parks first to police headquarters and then to the city jail. By then Mrs. Parks was tense, and her throat was uncommonly dry. She spied a water fountain, but was quickly told that she could not drink from it—it was for whites only. Her processing complete, Mrs. Parks was allowed to call home and tell her family what had transpired.[1]

Word of Mrs. Parks's arrest began to spread even before that phone call. One passenger on the bus told a friend of Mrs. Parks's about the event, and that friend, Mrs. Bertha Butler, immediately called the home of longtime black activist E. D. Nixon, a past president of Montgomery's National Association for the Advancement of Colored People (NAACP) chapter and the most outspoken figure in the black community. Nixon was not at home, but his wife, Arlet, was, and she phoned his small downtown office. Nixon was out at the moment, but when he returned a few moments later, he saw the message to call home. "What's up?" he asked his wife. She told him of Mrs. Parks's arrest, but couldn't tell him what the charge was. Nixon hung up and immediately called the police station.

The desk officer rudely told Nixon that the charges against Mrs. Parks were none of his business. Determined to pursue the matter, but knowing that Montgomery's principal black lawyer, Fred Gray, was out of town, Nixon called the home of a white lawyer, Clifford Durr, one of the city's few racial liberals. Durr agreed to call the station and learn the charges, and after doing so he immediately called Nixon back and related the details. Nixon told Durr that he would go down and sign the $100 bond to secure Mrs. Parks's release, and Durr told him to stop by and that he would go along. When Nixon pulled up in front of the house, both Durr and his wife, Virginia, hurried out to meet him, and the three set off for the city jail.

Mrs. Parks, Mr. Nixon, and the Durrs all had known each other for a number of years. Mrs. Parks, forty-two years old at the time of her arrest, had been an active member and occasional officer of Montgomery's NAACP chapter since 1943, and had worked with Nixon on a number of voter registration efforts. Nixon, a Pullman porter whose job regularly took him to Chicago and other northern cities, had been a stalwart member of A. Philip Randolph's Brotherhood of Sleeping Car Porters, as well as a local activist, since the 1920s. The Durrs, Alabama natives who had returned to the state several years earlier following Clifford's service on the Federal Communications Commission, had become friendly with Nixon through his political activism. Needing a good seamstress to help with her children's clothes, Mrs. Durr had asked Nixon if he could recommend anyone, and Nixon told her he knew just the person: his NAACP colleague, Mrs. Rosa Parks. Beginning in 1953 or 1954, Mrs. Parks was a regular visitor to the Durrs' home.

Over the years, the Durrs had heard distressing stories of how Montgomery bus drivers regularly insulted black passengers. Mrs. Parks once told them about how she had been physically thrown off a bus some ten years earlier when, after paying her fare at the front of the bus, she had refused to get off and reenter by the back door—a custom often inflicted on black riders.

On their way to the jail Nixon and the Durrs discussed the possibility of Mrs. Parks being a test case. They knew how strong her character was, and they had seen a strengthened self-confidence in her the past few months, following a two-week interracial conference that the Durrs had arranged for her to attend at Tennessee's Highlander Folk School in late July. At the jail, the desk officer instinctively handed the bond papers to Clifford Durr for signature. Durr told him, no, Mr. Nixon, a property owner, would be the man to sign. Mrs. Parks was released, and they all headed to the Parks's home to discuss the matter over coffee.

Clifford Durr listened to Mrs. Parks's description of her arrest on the bus, and explained how, under the precise terms of Montgomery's segregation ordinance, she could not be convicted for refusing to get up, since no other seat had been available for her to move to, as the law required. Nixon, however, emphasized that this was just what they had been waiting for. *"This is the case.* We can boycott the bus lines with this and at the same time go to the Supreme Court." Mrs. Parks was not immediately convinced that her arrest could be the spark for all of that, but Nixon's enthusiasm soon persuaded her. Although her husband was extremely fearful of possible white reprisals, Mrs. Parks told Nixon, "If you think it is all right, I'll go along with you."[2]

Meanwhile, Fred Gray had returned to town and learned of Mrs. Parks's arrest. He immediately called Mrs. Jo Ann Robinson, president of the Women's Political Council (WPC) and a key community activist who had moved to Montgomery in 1949 to teach English at Alabama State College. At Christmas of that year, Mrs. Robinson had boarded a bus on her way to the airport to visit relatives in Cleveland. She sat toward the front, but suddenly was roused from her holiday thoughts when the driver angrily ordered her to the rear. "He was standing over me, saying, 'Get up from there! Get up from there,' with his hand drawn back," she later recalled. Shaken and frightened, Mrs. Robinson fled from the bus. "I felt like a dog. And I got mad, after this was over, and I realized that I was a human being, and just as intelligent and far more trained than that bus driver was. But I think he wanted to hurt me, and he did . . . . I cried all the way to Cleveland."

That experience had convinced Mrs. Robinson that the Women's Political Council, which her friend and colleague Mrs. Mary Fair Burks had founded in 1946, ought to target the bus situation. "It was then that I made up . . . my mind that whatever I could add to that organization that would help to bring that practice down, I would do it," Mrs. Robinson explained. "When I came back, the first thing I did was to call a meeting . . . and tell them what had happened." Only then did she learn that her experience was far from unique, that dozens of other black citizens, primarily women, had suffered similar abuse. "Everyone would look the other way. Nobody would acknowledge what was going on," Mrs. Burks remembered. "It outraged me that this kind of conduct was going on," and that so far no black community organizations had done anything about it.

Throughout the early 1950s the Women's Political Council, sometimes in conjunction with Nixon or Nixon's chief rival for active leadership in the black community, businessman and former Alabama State football coach Rufus Lewis, who headed the Citizens Steering Committee, repeatedly complained to Montgomery's three popularly elected city commissioners about how the municipally chartered Montgomery City Lines mistreated its black customers. The commissioners politely, but consistently, brushed aside the WPC's entreaties concerning drivers' behavior and how blacks had to stand while whites-only seats remained vacant. In early 1954 Mrs. Robinson suggested to the commissioners "a city law that would make it possible for Negroes to sit from back toward front, and whites from front toward back until all seats are taken," so that no one would have to stand over a vacant seat, but again the officials were unresponsive.

Then, on May 17, 1954, the U.S. Supreme Court handed down its widely heralded school desegregation decision in *Brown* v. *Board of Education of Topeka,* which explicitly held that the segregationist doctrine of "separate but equal" was unconstitutional. Her spirits lifted, Mrs. Robinson four days later sent a firm declaration to Montgomery Mayor W. A. Gayle. The WPC was "very grateful" for their previous meeting, she said, but the black community was insistent that the bus situation be improved, and white officials had best remember that "three-fourths of the riders of these public conveyances are Negroes. If Negroes did not patronize them, they could not possibly operate." Her letter continued:

> There has been talk from twenty-five or more local organizations of planning a city-wide boycott of buses. We, sir, do not feel that forceful measures are necessary in bargaining for a convenience which is right for all bus passengers. We . . . believe that when this matter has been put before you and the commissioners, that agreeable terms can be met in a quiet and unostensible manner to the satisfaction of all concerned.

Other Alabama cities, such as Mobile, were using the front-to-back and back-to-front seating policy without any problems, Mrs. Robinson reminded Gayle. Why could not Montgomery do the same? "Please consider this plea," she wrote him, "and if possible, act favorably upon it, for even now plans are being made to ride less, or not at all, on our buses. We do not want this."[3]

Robinson's hints about a boycott were not supported by any unified sentiment in the black community. One mid-1954 meeting of community leaders had found a majority opposed to any boycott at that time. The stalemate continued into early 1955 as Nixon and the WPC privately discussed the possibility of mounting a legal challenge to Montgomery's bus seating practices. Then, on March 2, 1955, an incident occurred that galvanized the long-smoldering black sentiments. A fifteen-year-old high school student, Claudette Colvin, refused a driver's demand that she give up her bus seat, well toward the rear of the vehicle, to allow newly boarding whites to sit down. Policemen dragged Colvin from the bus, and word spread quickly. Mrs. Robinson and Nixon thought they might have an ideal legal test case. Colvin had been active in the NAACP Youth Council, and the group's advisor, Mrs. Rosa Parks, along with her friend Virginia Durr, began soliciting contributions toward the legal fees. Almost immediately, however, problems developed. First, Colvin's resistance to the arresting officers had resulted in her being charged with assault and battery as well as violating city and state segregation statutes. Second, both Robinson and Nixon learned in independent interviews with Colvin and her family that the young unmarried woman was several months pregnant. Both leaders concluded that Colvin would be neither an ideal candidate for symbolizing the abuse heaped upon black passengers nor a good litigant for a test suit certain to generate great pressures and publicity. Colvin was convicted of both charges, but when her attorney appealed, the prosecutor pressed only the assault count. That conviction was affirmed and the black leadership chose not to pursue the case.

In the wake of the Colvin incident, Mrs. Robinson and a delegation of black leaders, including Nixon and Mrs. Parks, met with one city commissioner and bus company manager James H. Bagley to point out that Montgomery's segregation ordinance specified that a rider could be compelled to surrender a bus seat only if another one was available—and not if the rider would be forced to stand. Nothing came of the session, and three months later Mrs. Robinson, attorney Fred Gray, and other black representatives met with Bagley, Gayle, city attorney Walter Knabe, and bus company attorney Jack Crenshaw to reiterate that the city ordinance required no one to give up a seat on an already full bus, and that nothing in either the ordinance or state law barred Montgomery from adopting the front-to-back, back-to-front seating arrangement that Mobile and other Alabama cities employed. The whites disagreed, and there the matter rested until Mrs. Parks's arrest.

When Mrs. Robinson learned of the arrest late that Thursday night from Fred Gray, she immediately phoned Nixon, who had just gotten home from Mrs. Parks's house. Together they agreed that this was just what they had been waiting for. "We had planned the protest long before Mrs. Parks was arrested," Mrs. Robinson emphasized years later. "There had been so many things that happened, that the black women had been embarrassed over, and they were ready to explode." Also, "Mrs. Parks had the caliber of character we needed to get the city to rally behind us." Robinson told Nixon that she and her WPC colleagues would begin producing boycott leaflets immediately, and the two agreed that the flyers would call on all black people to stay off the buses on Monday, the day of Mrs. Parks's trial. They also agreed that the black community leadership should assemble on Friday. Nixon would organize that meeting, while Robinson would see to the leafletting.

Robinson alerted several of her WPC colleagues, then sat down and drafted the leaflet. She called a friend who had access to Alabama State's mimeograph room, and they rendezvoused at the college and began running off thousands of copies. They worked all night, and when morning came, WPC members, helped by some of Robinson's students, began distributing the announcements to every black neighborhood in Montgomery. The leaflets read:

> Another Negro woman has been arrested and thrown into jail because she refused to get up out of her seat on the bus for a white person to sit down.

It is the second time since the Claudette Colbert *[sic]* case that a Negro woman has been arrested for the same thing. This has to be stopped. Negroes have rights, too, for if Negroes did not ride the buses, they could not operate. Three-fourths of the riders are Negroes, yet we are arrested, or have to stand over empty seats. If we do not do something to stop these arrests, they will continue. The next time it may be you, or your daughter, or mother.

This woman's case will come up on Monday. We are, therefore, asking every Negro to stay off the buses Monday in protest of the arrest and trial. Don't ride the buses to work, to town, to school, or anywhere on Monday.

You can afford to stay out of school for one day if you have no other way to go except by bus.

You can also afford to stay out of town for one day. If you work, take a cab, or walk. But please, children and grown-ups, don't ride the bus at all on Monday. Please stay off all buses Monday.

The long-discussed boycott was about to get under way.[4]

After a fitful night, E. D. Nixon arose early Friday morning to begin assembling the black leadership. Nixon knew that a mass boycott of Montgomery's buses could not be accomplished simply by the WPC and the few regular activists such as himself. Although the women had been the driving force behind all of the black community efforts of the last few years, a mass protest would succeed only if they could obtain the enthusiastic support of Montgomery's black ministers. With that in mind, Nixon made his first call to one of the youngest and most outspoken of the city's pastors, Ralph D. Abernathy.

Abernathy, the secretary of the Baptist Ministers' Alliance, told Nixon he would support the effort. Nixon queried Abernathy about when and where the black leadership should meet, and they agreed that a meeting that evening at a central, downtown location would be good. Abernathy recommended that they call the meeting in the name of the Baptist Ministers' Alliance, and that Nixon call the elderly president of the group, the Reverend H. H. Hubbard, to secure his blessing. Abernathy also advised Nixon to phone one of Abernathy's best friends, the Reverend M. L. King, Jr., pastor of Dexter Avenue Baptist Church, and ask if the meeting could be held there. In the meantime, Abernathy would begin contacting other ministers.

Nixon quickly secured Hubbard's approval. He then called King. Nixon related the events of the previous evening, told King of the emerging consensus to begin a boycott on Monday, and asked if the young pastor would join in supporting the effort. King hesitated. He had a newborn daughter, less than one month old, and heavy responsibilities at his church. Only a few weeks earlier he had declined to be considered for president of the local NAACP chapter because of these other demands on his time. He wasn't sure he could handle any additional responsibilities. "Brother Nixon," he said, "let me think about it awhile, and call me back." Nixon told King that he and Abernathy already were telling people to meet at King's church that evening. "That's all right," King replied. "I just want to think about it and then you call me back." Nixon agreed.

King hadn't had long to mull over Nixon's request before Abernathy called. Abernathy had heard from Nixon about his friend's hesitation, and wanted to stress to King the opportunity that the Parks arrest represented. King acknowledged that Abernathy was correct; he had no quarrel with the boycott plan. So long as he did not have to do the organizational work, he would be happy to support the effort and host the evening meeting at Dexter church. Satisfied, Abernathy turned his efforts to contacting additional ministers.

Both Nixon and Abernathy had good success in asking individuals to attend the Friday night meeting at King's church. Nixon would have to miss the session, since his railroad job required a weekend run to Chicago, but he and Abernathy discussed how they wanted a strong endorsement of the Monday boycott. Nixon spoke with the Reverend L. Roy Bennett, president of the Interdenominational Ministerial Alliance (IMA), and recommended that Bennett preside at the Friday night session, a recommendation with which Reverends Abernathy and Hubbard also concurred.

Early Friday evening, as Mrs. Robinson's leaflets circulated throughout Montgomery, some seventy black leaders assembled in the basement meeting room of Dexter Avenue Baptist Church. After a brief prayer by Hubbard, Bennett took the floor and told the influential group that he did not see much need for any extended discussion because he, Bennett, knew full well how to organize a boycott.

Bennett lectured on. As the minutes passed, more and more people became frustrated and angry. Despite repeated requests, Bennett refused to yield the floor. When Bennett's monologue reached the half-hour mark, some people began walking out. Among those to leave was Alabama State Professor James E. Pierce, one of Nixon's closest allies. Earlier that day Pierce had tried to dissuade his friend from the boycott plan on the grounds that many black citizens might not support it. This session had only strengthened Pierce's doubts about the effort, and his fear that many individual leaders, like Bennett, would be unable to put aside their rivalries and desires for self-advancement long enough to agree on a unified community effort. Heading out the door, Pierce paused and whispered to King, "This is going to fizzle out. I'm going." King was unhappy too, and told Pierce, "I would like to go too, but it's in my church."

Finally, Ralph Abernathy stood up and took over the meeting from Bennett, insisting that all of the twenty or so people who remained be given an opportunity to speak. Jo Ann Robinson seconded Abernathy's demand, and proposed that all present endorse the Monday boycott. A mass meeting would be called for Monday night at the large Holt Street Baptist Church to determine whether community sentiment would sup-

3444 230

port extending the boycott beyond Monday. A new version of Robinson's leaflet would be prepared, adding the news about the mass meeting. Some ministers, hesitant about even a one-day boycott, went along so that some unity would emerge despite Bennett's performance. It was agreed that those who remained would meet again Monday afternoon, after Mrs. Parks's trial, to plan the mass meeting.

Abernathy and King stayed at Dexter church until almost midnight, mimeographing the new leaflets. Early Saturday the distribution began, with two hundred or more volunteers giving out the handbills in door-to-door visits. Meanwhile, a taxi committee headed by Rev. W. J. Powell was winning agreement from all the black cab firms to carry riders on Monday for only the standard bus fare of ten cents. Then, Saturday evening, King, Abernathy, and others visited nightclubs to spread further the news of the upcoming boycott.[5]

Montgomery's white leadership also was gradually learning about the blacks' plans for Monday. Friday afternoon, one bus driver brought company manager Bagley a copy of the Robinson leaflet he had found on his bus. Bagley, assuming only a small number of the leaflets existed, immediately told drivers to check their buses and gather up any that they found. Also on Friday afternoon, before leaving for his Chicago run, E. D. Nixon called *Montgomery Advertiser* reporter Joe Azbell and confidentially alerted him to what was happening. It would be a great story, Nixon told him, if Azbell could acquire one of the leaflets and write a story for Sunday's paper about the upcoming protest.

The first public word of the impending boycott appeared, however, in the Saturday afternoon edition of Montgomery's smaller paper, the *Alabama Journal*. It quoted the bus company's Bagley as saying he was "sorry that the colored people blame us for any state or city ordinance which we didn't have passed," and reported that he had discussed the news with company attorney Jack Crenshaw. Montgomery City Lines, Bagley stressed, felt it had no choice in the matter. "We have to obey all laws."

Just as Nixon had hoped, Sunday morning's *Advertiser* featured an Azbell story headlined NEGRO GROUPS READY BOYCOTT OF CITY LINES. Quoting from the leaflet, Azbell noted how the Monday boycott would be followed by the community meeting at Holt Street church. Precisely who was sponsoring the boycott, or the meeting, was unclear, however; Holt Street pastor A. W. Wilson declined to say who had scheduled the meeting for his church, and Azbell named no other sources.

The prominent news story had two immediate effects. First, Montgomery's white community was informed of the blacks' challenge. City Police Commissioner Clyde Sellers, a rabid racist, went on local television to denounce the effort and to say that Montgomery policemen would stand ready on Monday to assist those black citizens who wanted to ride the buses. Black "goon squads," Sellers claimed, were being organized to intimidate the many blacks who otherwise would keep right on riding.

Second, the *Advertiser* story, plus Sellers's television pronouncement, reached many of Montgomery's black citizens, including some who had missed both the door-to-door leaflets and the Sunday morning pulpit announcements in most black churches. Nixon, who returned Sunday morning from his train run, and the other organizers were overjoyed at the unwitting assistance the whites were giving them.

Although happy with the public coverage, the black leaders discussed Bennett's disastrous performance and the need to move the protest out from under the mantle of his Interdenominational Ministerial Alliance. There were few options. The leadership of the Women's Political Council knew that any public revelation of their central role would cost many of them their jobs at publicly controlled Alabama State. No other existing organization, including the NAACP chapter, had sufficient breadth of membership to represent all those who already had taken a hand in organizing the boycott. A new organization, with freshly chosen leaders, would have to be formed.

Abernathy and King agreed that creating a new organization would be the best way to oust Bennett without openly insulting him. Abernathy thought that Nixon would be the obvious choice for president of the new group, but King had doubts, arguing that Rufus Lewis would be better suited for the job. Only one month earlier King had tried to persuade Abernathy to take the NAACP presidency, but he had said no. He was thinking of returning to graduate school. Abernathy knew that King also had declined the NAACP post.

In addition to King and Abernathy, several other central figures pondered what to do at the Monday meeting. Nixon and J. E. Pierce discussed the need both to oust Bennett and to block Nixon's longtime rival, Lewis, from winning control. They discussed other possible candidates, and recalled how favorably impressed they both had been when the young Reverend King had spoken to a meeting of the NAACP chapter four months earlier.

Much like Nixon and Pierce, Rufus Lewis and one of his closest friends, P. E. Conley, spent the weekend discussing what they could do. They also wanted to be rid of Bennett, and Lewis felt that the unschooled Nixon would be equally unacceptable. An ideal candidate who should be acceptable to all the different groups, Lewis told Conley, was his own pastor, Reverend King. True, Lewis conceded, the twenty-six-year-old King did look "more like a boy than a man," but he was extremely well educated and an articulate speaker. Those qualities would appeal strongly to the wealthier, professional segment of the black community, people who otherwise might be ambivalent about conditions on public buses that they rarely patronized. Likewise, the fact that King was a minister, and a Baptist minister, should help to draw the more conservative clergy into what had begun as a secularly led effort. Additionally, King's ministerial status also would appeal to the many regular churchgoers in the black community. Lewis himself might be a passive church member, and one from the "classes," but he recognized that the strength of the black church and its "masses" would be essential to a successful boycott. King, he told Conley, would be an ideal choice; both men agreed to put him forward at the Monday meeting.[6]

Early Monday morning the attention of the black leadership shifted to the question of how successful the boycott would be. Nixon, Robinson, King, and others arose early to begin their own individual surveys of bus ridership. King watched several nearly empty buses pass his South Jackson Street home and then set out by car to observe others. In one hour's worth of driving, King spied only *eight* black riders. Hundreds of others could be seen headed toward their jobs on foot, or gathering for rides with friends and acquaintances. The black leaders were pleased; the first hours of the boycott represented a grand success.

At 9:00 A.M Mrs. Parks's trial got under way before City Court Judge John B. Scott. Although Mrs. Parks initially had been charged with violating Montgomery's segregation ordinance, prosecutor Eugene Loe, aware of how the ordinance specified that a rider could be compelled to surrender one seat only if another were available, dropped the charge and substituted in its place one based upon a 1945 *state* law. That law lacked the limiting clause of the city statute. It simply mandated segregation and awarded drivers unlimited power to enforce it. Loe placed driver Blake on the stand to describe the incident, followed by two white women riders who supported the driver's account. Defense attorney Fred Gray challenged the validity of the segregation law, but Judge Scott immediately announced his verdict: guilty, with a $10 fine. Gray stated he would appeal. The entire proceeding took barely five minutes.

Several hundred blacks had gathered at the courthouse, an unprecedented event, to show their support for Mrs. Parks. Among them were Nixon, Abernathy, and another young minister, Rev. Edgar N. French of Hilliard Chapel AME Zion Church. At the conclusion of the trial, as they headed out of the courthouse, Nixon suggested to the other two men that perhaps they should take a few minutes to discuss the upcoming leadership meeting. The three men agreed that a detailed plan of action should be presented both to the mass meeting that night, and to the afternoon leadership gathering. First off, the almost unanimous mass support that morning suggested the black community was ready for more than a one-day boycott. Second, blacks should demand some specific concessions from the bus company before they returned to the buses. Number one, of course, would be the ridership plan that Robinson and her colleagues had long been arguing for: Blacks would seat themselves from the rear forward, and whites from the front backward. No one would ever have to surrender a seat to someone else, and no one would ever have to stand over a vacant seat. First come, first served would be fair to all, the three men agreed. Number two, drivers would have to show proper courtesy to all bus patrons at all times. The company, as Robinson and Gray had demanded a year earlier, should discipline any driver who insulted or assaulted a black passenger. Number three, Nixon said, blacks, who constituted 75 percent of the ridership, should be able to apply for jobs as drivers. Together, the men agreed on these three points, and on Abernathy's suggestion that the new organization be called the Montgomery Improvement Association (MIA).[7]

That afternoon, several dozen black leaders assembled at Reverend Bennett's Mt. Zion AME Church. Bennett immediately took charge. "'We are not going to have any talking. I am not going to let anybody talk; we came here to work and to outline our program.'" As Ralph Abernathy recalled the scene, "I tried to get the floor, but he said, 'Well, Ab, although you're my good friend, I'm not going to even let you talk—so sit down.'" At that point, an objection was raised that some "stool pigeons" representing city officials might be present, and that a smaller group should meet in private to map their course of action. That idea was adopted, and a committee of eighteen persons was chosen to meet in the pastor's study. As they walked in, Abernathy reproved Bennett for his stubbornness and asked for the floor when the group convened. "After much needling, he agreed reluctantly and promised that as soon as we got the meeting under way he might recognize me," Abernathy remembered.

> Then I dropped back and started talking to Reverend King. I told him that we had worked out a proposal for permanent organization of the movement which included the election of the officers and a state-ment of aims and objectives. He was very happy to hear this. "But who will be the president?" King asked.

Abernathy voiced his preference for Nixon, and King replied that "'Lewis might make the better man.' Well, there we were trying to de-cide whether to elect Lewis or Nixon. By this time Bennett opened the meeting and was calling for me to say what I had to say. I presented Nixon who in turn asked Reverend French to read the proposal. The committee adopted it verbatim."

The group also accepted Abernathy's recommendation of "Montgomery Improvement Association" as a name for the new organi-zation. Then Bennett called for nominations for officers, beginning with president. Without a moment's pause, Rufus Lewis's voice rang out. "Mr. Chairman, I would like to nominate Reverend M. L. King for presi-dent." P. E. Conley, Lewis's friend, immediately seconded it. No other candidates were put forward, and King was asked if he would accept the position. Abernathy, seated beside him, fully expected King to decline. Instead, after a pause, King told his colleagues, "Well, if you think I can render some service, I will," and accepted the presidency. Bennett was quickly and unanimously chosen as vice-president, Nixon as treasurer, Reverend French as corresponding secretary, and Rev. U. J. Fields as recording secretary. An executive committee of twenty-five persons, in-cluding all of those present, was proposed and approved.

Discussion then shifted to the boycott. The first issue was whether the effort would be continued beyond its one-day success. Most of the leaders were in favor of continuing the protest, but some of the older ministers argued that their leverage would be maximized if they now returned to the buses while warning the city that the boycott would resume if changes were not made. After some debate, it was decided to present the option to the mass meeting, and let the people decide. Reverend Wilson reported that press photographers would be at the rally, and some ministers seemed reluctant to volunteer as speakers in light of that fact. E. D. Nixon angrily rebuked them. "Somebody in this thing has got to get faith. I am just ashamed of you. You said that God has called you to lead the people and now you are afraid and gone to pieces because the man tells you that the newspaper men will be here and your pictures might come out in the newspaper. Somebody has got to get hurt in this thing and if you preachers are not the leaders, then we have to pray that God will send us some more leaders." The ministers responded positively to Nixon's exhortation, and a committee headed by Abernathy was appointed to present the resolutions. If the mass meeting was enthusiastic, the protest would go forward; if the sentiment was less than enthusiastic, the leadership would pause to plan their next step.[8]

The newly chosen president returned home less than an hour before the meeting at which he would deliver the major speech. Martin King pondered what he could tell the people at the rally. Realizing he could not adequately prepare any remarks, he "became possessed by fear" and "obsessed by a feeling of inadequacy," as he later wrote. He turned to prayer, and felt reassured, but still worried about how to "combine two apparent irreconcilables," militancy and moderation, in his address.

As 7:00 P.M. approached, the area around Holt Street Baptist Church became increasingly crowded with cars and people. Thousands of Montgomery's black citizens were intent upon attending the mass meeting. The building itself was full to capacity long before seven, but Reverend Wilson quickly arranged for loudspeakers to be set up outside. King and Abernathy had to make their way slowly through the growing crowd, which was solemn and dignified almost to the point of complete silence. Though perhaps unwieldy, the number of people was gratifying to the leaders, and answered the question that had been left open that afternoon. As King put it, "my doubts concerning the continued success of our venture" were dispelled by the mass turnout. "The question of calling off the protest was now academic."

When the program got under way, one thousand people were inside the church and four thousand were gathered outside for at least a block in every direction. Contrary to E. D. Nixon's desire, no speakers were introduced by name as one pastor led a prayer and a second read a selection of Scripture. Then King stepped forward to tell the people why and how they must protest the arrest and conviction of Mrs. Parks and the continuing indignities that hundreds of them regularly suffered on

Montgomery's buses. King gave a lengthy testimonial to Mrs. Parks's character, and reminded his listeners that she, and they, suffered these insults only on account of their race. "First and foremost we are American citizens," he continued. "We are not here advocating violence. We have overcome that. . . . The only weapon that we have . . . is the weapon of protest," and "the great glory of American democracy is the right to protest for right." He referred twice to the commands of the U.S. Constitution, and once to the Supreme Court's prior vindication of blacks' demands for truly equal rights. But protest and legal demands were only part of what was required, King went on. "We must keep God in the forefront. Let us be Christian in all of our action." The protesters must not hate their white opponents, but be guided by Christian love while seeking justice with their demands. "Love is one of the pinnacle parts of the Christian faith. There is another side called justice. And justice is really love in calculation." But the protest was not simply a matter of convincing the white officials of Montgomery of the justice of the MIA's cause, King indicated. "Not only are we using the tools of persuasion, but we've got to use tools of coercion. Not only is this thing a process of education, but it is also a process of legislation." Then King closed, reminding the audience to protest courageously but with dignity and Christian love. Rising to their feet, the people applauded heartily.

Mrs. Parks was introduced to the crowd, and was greeted with equal enthusiasm. Then Ralph Abernathy rose to read the three-page resolution calling for everyone to remain off the buses until "some arrangement" was worked out between the black community and white officials. Asked for their approval, the people unanimously roared an endorsement of the boycott. In a post-rally caucus, the MIA leadership resolved to go forward. Afterward, King and Abernathy placed in the mail to city and bus company officials an unsigned copy of the MIA's three demands, plus a statement indicating the protesters' readiness to negotiate a settlement.[9]

White Montgomery was astonished by both the boycott and the headlined accounts that the local papers gave of the Monday night mass meeting. Bus company attorney Jack Crenshaw told reporters Tuesday morning that he had no objection to meeting with black representatives, but the bus company had no discretion on the matter of seating.

On Tuesday, Reverend King met with reporters at Fred Gray's office to explain the MIA's demands. He detailed the request for a first-come, first-served seating policy, and stressed, "We are not asking for an end to segregation. That's a matter for the legislature and the courts. We feel that we have a plan within the law. All we are seeking is justice and fair treatment in riding the buses. We don't like the idea of Negroes having to stand when there are vacant seats. We are demanding justice on that point." King said that the MIA stood ready to meet with the bus company, but that the protest would continue "until we gain concrete results." Hardly a black person was seen on any bus Tuesday, but by the end of the day the company had not contacted the MIA.[10]

Wednesday morning at 10:00 A.M. the MIA's executive board assembled for its first full meeting. The principal order of business was to appoint several committees to supervise the burgeoning protest. Most essential was a transportation committee that could examine the alternatives people were using to avoid the buses, and what the MIA could do to assist them. The MIA made no move to contact city or company officials, and attorney Crenshaw indicated that their stance had not changed. "If they don't like the law we have to operate under, then they should try to get the law changed, not engage in an attack upon the company."

That same day the semiannual meeting of the board of the Alabama Council on Human Relations (ACHR) was taking place in Montgomery. Board member Thomas R. Thrasher, a Montgomery minister, and Executive Director Robert E. Hughes discussed whether they should take the lead in bringing the two sides together. Thrasher, who knew King and other MIA officials from past ACHR business, contacted the black leadership and secured their agreement to sit down with city and bus company officials. Thrasher then called Bagley and Crenshaw from City Lines, but their private position was the same as their public one: "They were merely 'obeying the law.' They said further there was no sense in negotiating unless the city was willing to interpret the law in a manner other than" the way Crenshaw interpreted it. Frustrated there, Thrasher tried to call Mayor W. A. Gayle, a member of Thrasher's congregation. After some delay, he reached Gayle, who suggested that a meeting be called for Thursday morning. Robert Hughes relayed this proposal to King, who accepted.[11]

The next morning the different parties assembled. King, Abernathy, Fred Gray, Jo Ann Robinson, and eight others represented the MIA. The three commissioners—Gayle, Clyde Sellers, and Frank Parks—and several attorneys were present for the city; Bagley and Crenshaw represented the bus company. Thrasher and Hughes served as intermediaries, and several reporters sat on the sidelines. Gayle stated that the meeting had been requested by ACHR, and Thrasher emphasized that he and Hughes were not on either side, but simply had wanted to bring everyone together for discussion. Then King spoke, explaining "that we are not out to change the segregation laws" and that the MIA had "a plan that can work within the laws of the state"—namely the back-to-front and front-to-back seating arrangement that the black community had presented previously. King also stated the MIA's requests for "better treatment and more courtesy" toward riders, and for the hiring of black drivers. "We are merely trying to peacefully obtain better accommodations for Negroes." Crenshaw was the first to respond. The MIA seating plan simply did not comport with state law, Crenshaw asserted. The bus company would reprimand discourteous drivers if specific complaints were registered; that was not a matter of disagreement. Lastly, the time was not right for black drivers, even on a virtually all-black route, as King had suggested. Instead, the bus company would offer that every other bus on that one route would be an all- black "special," with no white riders, on which blacks could occupy all the seats. Gray and King pointed out how other Alabama cities, such as Mobile, were using the same format that the MIA was proposing—the front to back for whites, and back to front for blacks—and did not violate the state segregation provision, for it was simply a more courteous form of segregation than Montgomery presently was using. But none of the city or company representatives indicated any flexibility on the matter. The wrangling went on for close to two hours.

Finally, Mayor Gayle called a halt and suggested that a smaller group—King and Gray, Sellers and Parks, Bagley and Crenshaw—discuss the matter in private. "'You all go in the conference room and settle this,'" Crenshaw recalls Gayle instructing him. But Crenshaw believed there was nothing he could do. "I tried to tell him, 'Look, we can't settle it. We can't change the law . . .' But he said, 'Go in there and see what you can do.'" No progress was made by the smaller group, however, and the negotiating session broke up after four hours of unproductive discussion.[12]

The black representatives were surprised by the whites' uncompromising stance, and for the first time realized that they might have a lengthier boycott on their hands than they had anticipated. "We thought that this would all be over in three or four days," Ralph Abernathy later remembered. Since "our demands were moderate," King recalled, "I had assumed that they would be granted with little question." The MIA's new concern was reflected in a Thursday letter they mailed to the bus company's parent firm, National City Lines of Chicago, asking that it "send a representative to Montgomery to arbitrate."

Whites also were growing more concerned. Several near-empty buses had been fired upon, and the home of a black policeman had been shot into. Police Chief G. J. Ruppenthal announced that armed officers would trail many buses. Company manager Bagley, admitting that ridership had declined 75 percent since Monday, warned that service might be halted on routes drawing few riders. The editors of the leading newspaper, the *Advertiser,* quoted approvingly King's published remark that the MIA was not seeking to end segregation, just modify its terms. "If the grievance is confined to that, then attention should be given to it promptly," the paper recommended.

The editorial also noted that an obscure section of state law made all boycotts illegal. Another threat was broached by Commissioner Sellers in the morning meeting. He mentioned that a city ordinance required all taxis to charge a certain minimum fare. The boycott's main alternative transportation system might suddenly be priced out of most people's range.

King took Sellers's threat to heart and wondered what other alternative means of transportation the black community could create. One person who could advise him was an old family friend, the Reverend Theodore J.

Jemison of Baton Rouge. Two years earlier, in June, 1953, the black community of Baton Rouge had undertaken a ten-day boycott of that city's buses. Though the effort had not eliminated segregated seating, the Baton Rouge activists had mobilized their community to stay off the buses. Jemison told King how the blacks of Baton Rouge had organized "Operation Free Lift," a car pool system. The key, Jemison stressed, was having one set of gathering points in the morning, where people beginning their day could be picked up, and another, different set of gathering points in the evening rush hour, for people headed home. If enough citizens with cars could volunteer to drive, and if adequate communications between the different "stations" could be coordinated by some central facility so that cars could properly be apportioned, a totally volunteer transportation system could meet the needs of the Montgomery black community.

The MIA's second mass meeting took place Thursday night at St. John AME Church. King described the conference with city officials, the letter to National City Lines, and the advice he had gotten from Jemison. King explained how they could organize their own transportation system if enough cars and drivers were available. Sign-up sheets were passed around, and the response was heavy. There was no slackening of mass support now that a longer protest seemed in store. King also asked the crowd not to allow the regrettable acts of violence against the buses.[13]

Friday morning, while the MIA's transportation committee was starting to organize its volunteers and map out a car pool system, the city commissioners met with J. H. Bagley. Afterward, the commissioners "expressed regret" that the Thursday session had produced no solution.

Also, as expected, the city announced it would enforce the minimum fare for cabs. At the same time, Bagley stated that as of 6:00 P.M. Saturday, bus service would be halted on two routes that were drawing few riders. King, in a Saturday response, reiterated the MIA's position that under the state segregation law the method of seating is "left entirely to the transportation companies themselves." Since the Mobile plan did not conflict with the state statute, there was no legal obstacle to the company's accepting the MIA's proposal. "We feel that there is no issue between the Negro citizens and the Montgomery City Lines that cannot be solved by negotiations between people of good will. . . . There is no legal barrier to such negotiations."

On Monday, December 12, the MIA marked the first week of the boycott with a mass meeting at Bethel Baptist Church. Working hard on the car pool system, MIA leaders announced that it would begin functioning in earnest the next day, with forty-two morning "stations" and forty-eight evening ones. More than two hundred volunteer drivers had been recruited. A downtown parking lot manned by transportation committee volunteers would serve as a central command post. Mass support of the protest remained strong, but the cancellation of some bus routes compelled even the hesitant to continue the boycott. "The decision to slash bus runs in Negro sections," one local black historian wrote several months later, "did more to crystallize the movement than any act thus far."[14]

The MIA leadership continued to be surprised that city and company officials were unwilling to compromise with the blacks' modest demands. "We felt that in a week's time, the city would give in," Mrs. Robinson remembered. "That was the longest, we thought." White public opinion seemed more ready to accept racial change than did the white officials, the black leaders noted. Several white citizens wrote to the *Advertiser* in support of the blacks' complaints about the buses. One, Mrs. I. B. Rutledge, stated that "I have yet to find one white person who feels that it is right that a Negro be made to stand that a white person may sit." A second white woman asked why Montgomery could not operate its buses in the fashion of Mobile and other southern cities. A third, Miss Juliette Morgan, told of how she had heard drivers call black women "black apes" and commended the protesters, comparing their boycott to Mohandas K. Gandhi's Indian salt march. "Passive resistance combined with freedom from hate is a power to be reckoned with," she wrote.

The MIA was buoyed by such expressions of support, but was puzzled by the lack of official action. In his first interview with a national newspaper, King—identified as "Rev. J. R. King"—described the failure of the Thursday meeting and stressed that "we merely wanted them to follow a policy of having the colored passengers fill the bus from the rear and the whites fill the bus from the front." Reserving seats for whites "didn't make sense to us," King added.[15]

The arrival of two outsiders added new elements to the situation. On Tuesday morning, W. C. Patton, the NAACP representative in Alabama, arrived in town to study the situation. He met with Fred Gray, Mrs. Parks, and then King, and queried them all about the public reports that the group was seeking only a better form of segregation. "King assured me," Patton informed NAACP Executive Secretary Roy Wilkins, that the MIA's "ultimate goals are the same as those of the NAACP, but that they were working to solve some immediate crisis" with the first-come, first-seated plan. "Gray made it clear that this is only a tentative arrangement"—one put forward because the black leadership expected the white officials to find it acceptable.

On Thursday evening, Kenneth E. Totten, a representative of National City Lines, arrived in Montgomery "for talks with any group anxious to discuss the boycott." Early Friday, Totten joined Bagley for a meeting with Mayor Gayle. Upon learning of Totten's presence, King and his MIA colleagues were perturbed that the Chicago man had made no effort to speak with them despite the letter the MIA had sent to the Chicago office. King told local reporters that the MIA and its car pool could continue the protest for a year with 75 percent black cooperation. The city responded by warning taxi drivers they could be arrested for failing to charge the minimum forty-five-cent fare, and that overloaded private autos—such as those in the car pool—would be halted by police.

At Thursday night's mass meeting at the First Baptist Church, Transportation Committee Chairman Rufus Lewis reported that the first three days of the car pool had been a success. Some 215 volunteer drivers already had taken part, and the "station" system—many of which were black churches—had proven effective. King spoke and contrasted the MIA to the segregationist White Citizens Councils. "We are for truth and justice, they are for injustice; we believe in love and fair play, they believe in hate and inequality; we work with the tools of love, not the weapons of violence." In one interview, though, King said he had urged MIA members to observe a "sacrificial Christmas" and not shop downtown, so that further economic pressure could be brought upon white Montgomery.[16]

By late Friday, Thrasher and Hughes of the ACHR, aware of the MIA's disappointment with Totten's quietude, set up a second meeting of all the parties for Saturday morning at the Chamber of Commerce. Gayle invited a number of representatives from the white community, and hence the Saturday session was considerably larger than the earlier one. Gayle stated that "I want to see it settled as soon as possible," asked Thrasher to speak briefly, and then recognized King to speak for the MIA. King reviewed the three basic points, but indicated that the MIA executive board had modified one of them as a showing of flexibility. They would not demand the immediate hiring of black drivers, but merely the acceptance of job applications from interested blacks. King also pointed out another legal wrinkle that Fred Gray had suggested earlier in the week: even if Crenshaw continued to insist that the state statute did prohibit a Mobile-like seating plan, perhaps the state law should be read as covering only intercity, and not intracity buses. If that interpretation were acceptable, then all the city commission had to do was abide by its own already existing ordinance, which would allow for the MIA's Mobile-like plan.

Those suggestions of compromise, however, had no softening effect on Crenshaw. He reiterated his previous stand, and Totten joined in, endorsing what Crenshaw said. Totten's remarks, coming before he had had any conversations with the MIA, infuriated King, who volunteered that Totten's statements were unfair and inaccurate. Gayle then called upon several of the white citizens, including segregationist pastor G. Stanley Frazer of St. James Methodist Church. Frazer offered some paternalistic remarks about how ministers should stay out of political affairs, and King responded. "I can see no conflict between our devotion to Jesus Christ and our present action. In fact I see a necessary relationship. If one is truly devoted to the religion of Jesus he will seek to rid the earth of social evils. The gospel is social as well as personal."

Gayle then moved to appoint a special "citizens' committee" to discuss the issues and report back to the city commission. He named eight of the whites already in attendance, plus two blacks not connected to the MIA whom he had invited to the meeting and who were suspect in the others' eyes. He offered the MIA three representatives on the committee, but Jo Ann Robinson immediately broke in, stating that if it had eight whites, it should have eight blacks. Gayle conceded the point, and six MIA leaders—King, Abernathy, Robinson, Reverend Hubbard, and attorneys Gray and Charles Langford—joined the eight whites and two suspect "Toms"—P. M. Blair and Dungee Caffey—as all the other participants departed.

The special committee was able to agree upon a resolution calling for everyone on the buses to show courtesy toward others, but made no other headway. Reverend Frazer suggested a seating plan in which ten seats at each end of the bus would be reserved exclusively for each race, unless all the passengers on board were of one race, in which case no seat would be reserved. The MIA rejected it. White businessman James J. Bailey suggested that the boycott be postponed until January 15 on account of the Christmas holiday, but that motion failed on a tie vote along racial lines. Then the group adjourned, agreeing to reassemble on Monday morning.

At 9:00 A.M. Monday, when the committee members arrived at the Chamber of Commerce office, the MIA representatives spied a new face—Luther Ingalls, secretary of the Montgomery chapter of the White Citizens Council. No one said anything initially, but some minutes into the meeting, Ingalls started to speak and King immediately questioned his role. Committee Chairman Rev. Henry A. Parker explained that Gayle had added Ingalls to the group, and that a white woman member now would become a nonvoting secretary. King strenuously objected. "The mayor has been very unfair to add to the committee without consulting us. He has not appointed a representative committee of whites." Looking at Ingalls, King added that some whites had "preconceived ideas" and their "minds already made up."

King's statement angered the whites. One, Mrs. Logan A. Hipp, told King, "I resent very deeply the statement that we have come here with preconceived ideas. I most certainly did not." Another, businessman Bailey, added that "I came here prepared to vote for liberalization of interpretation of the city's laws with certain conditions. We have some whose minds are made up and I think Reverend King is one of them." King, taken aback by the criticisms, said he had been speaking only about certain whites, not all of them. He objected only to those who clearly were biased. Chairman Parker was quick to retort that "if that's true, then *you* should not be here. Your stand has been made clear." Ingalls joined in, claiming that Gayle had appointed him to the committee initially, but he had not been able to attend the Saturday meeting. King was momentarily speechless in the face of the onslaught, and no one spoke. "For a moment," King wrote later, "it appeared that I was alone. Nobody came to my rescue" until Ralph Abernathy spoke up, saying that King was speaking not just for himself but for all the black representatives. After Abernathy's interjection, Parker brought the discussion back to the topic of bus seating. Reverend Frazer tried again to sell the blacks on his idea of unreserved seating on single-race buses, but the MIA was not interested. King and Gray again argued that their first-come, first-seated policy was legal, but city attorney Walter Knabe, sitting in with the whites, flatly contradicted Gray and said it was not. On that note the meeting broke up, with no plans for another session.[17]

After that second failed meeting, the MIA reconsidered its strategy. To white reporters, Gray reiterated that the MIA was not asking "for an abolition of segregation at this time." The best-informed correspondent on the scene, black editor Emory O. Jackson of the *Birmingham World,* reported in the wake of the Monday session that "plans are being made for a 12-month campaign" by the MIA.

On Thursday, December 22, the MIA executive board held a lengthy meeting to discuss the protest. Although no minutes survived, editor Jackson, privy to the discussion, reported that "the leadership originally felt that City Hall and the bus company officials would work with them in trying to improve the services to a point of rider equality." The two meetings, however, had disabused them of that hope. "They came away disgusted and with a feeling that they had placed too high an estimate in certain places." Now they resolved, Jackson said, to continue the protest until "the company grants major proposals. No more conferences will be held with company or City Hall officials unless they have something to offer in the way of accepting the three-point program." The MIA leadership decided to present their side of the dispute to the people of Montgomery, and prepared a detailed brochure, which also appeared as a paid ad in the Christmas day *Advertiser.* Issued in the names of the MIA and three ministerial alliances, it reviewed many past instances of mistreatment on the buses and explained that the protest was not simply over Mrs. Parks, "but is the culmination of a series of unpleasant incidents over a period of years." It went on to explain the seating policy the MIA was advocating. "When seats become vacant in the rear, Negro passengers will voluntarily move to these vacant seats and by the same token white passengers will move to vacant seats in the front of the bus. . . . At no time, on the basis of this proposal, will both races occupy the same seat," the MIA reassured white Montgomery.

White officials made no reply to the MIA's statement. K. E. Totten left town on Thursday, December 22, after concluding he could not settle the problem. That same day, after further reducing the number of routes in service, the commission canceled all bus service for several days over the Christmas-New Year's period. They also warned that the lack of riders might necessitate a fare increase early in 1956.[18]

While these developments were taking place, King was becoming the focus of more attention from the black community. His remarks at the continuing series of Monday and Thursday night mass meetings were drawing growing attention. One observer noted how King increasingly made reference to Mohandas K. Gandhi. "In reminding the followship that love will win," editor Jackson wrote, "he often tells the story of how Mahatma Gandhi, the emaciated emancipator, liberated India with his nonviolence campaign. . . . What he," King, "seems to be trying to do is to find a suitable adaptation of the Gandhi philosophy and method and apply it to the Montgomery problem." One of King's favorite devices in those early meetings was to tell stories about the many black Montgomerians who had to walk to and from work every day, about the sacrifices that every member of the black community was making. But King's message stressed action, not passivity. "Our weapons are protest and love," he told one meeting, and "we are going to fight until we take the heart out of Dixie."

King's MIA colleague and subsequent biographer, L. D. Reddick, later observed that "during this early period, King's philosophy of nonviolent resistance was only gradually taking form. When he made his debut as president of the MIA at the initial mass meeting, December 5, he did not mention Gandhi or anything directly relating to the Mahatma's theory or practice of social change. His speech was just one more appeal to principles of Christianity and democracy, to fair play and compassion for those in the opposite camp." By Christmas, however, an emerging emphasis on nonviolence was clear. The statement of the MIA position, set forth in the mimeographed brochure, observed that "this is a movement of passive resistance, depending on moral and spiritual forces. We, the oppressed, have no hate in our hearts for the oppressors, but we are, nevertheless, determined to resist until the cause of justice triumphs." Though "*passive* resistance" was a misnomer, the conscious desire to combine Gandhian precepts with Christian principles was growing in both King and the MIA.[19]

Martin Luther King, Jr., was only twenty-six years of age and had lived in Montgomery for hardly fifteen months when he emerged as the MIA's preeminent leader during the boycott's early weeks. However, King had great resources of experience and training upon which to draw as his leadership role became more and more challenging as the boycott continued. The experience was a long personal heritage in the traditions of the black church. The training was academic, indeed scholarly, consisting of three college degrees, including a doctorate in systematic theology. He was at home in the pulpit, and at ease with abstract ideas. Both in the church and in the academy, he had been schooled in the expressive use of language.

Young King's tradition in the black Baptist church went back not only to his father, the well-known pastor of Atlanta's Ebenezer Baptist Church, but also to his maternal grandfather, A. D. Williams, who had founded Ebenezer. King's father, Martin Luther King, Sr., had come to the big city as a young man, worked his way through high school, and in 1926 married Alberta Williams, daughter of Ebenezer's pastor. Known to his friends as "Mike," King, Sr., and his wife lived with her parents on Auburn Avenue just one block east of the church. Auburn was the hub of black Atlanta, and Mike King moved up fast. He enrolled at Morehouse College, became assistant pastor at Ebenezer, and celebrated the birth of his first child, daughter Christine. A year later, on January 15, 1929, a second child, Martin Luther, Jr., or "little Mike," was born. In July, 1930, just after Reverend King's graduation from Morehouse, a second son, Alfred Daniel, or "A.D.," joined the family.

Both relatives and friends recall the King-Williams household as being close and warm. In 1931, when little Mike, or "M.L.," as his father called him, was two, Grandfather Williams died. Reverend King took over the full pastorship of Ebenezer, and Grandmother Williams—"Mama" to young Mike—continued to live with the family. With three young children in the home, both Mrs. King and Mama Williams were kept busy.

Reverend King's pastorship at a large and growing church meant that the family suffered no privation even in the worst years of the Depression. The Ebenezer community provided a multitude of friends and play-mates, and all of the King children, but especially little Mike, seemed precocious. When Christine was scheduled to begin elementary school, her five-year-old brother insisted that he, too, would go along. For a while the trick worked, but then little Mike erred and told his teacher his true age. He was sent home and told to wait a year.

As King recalled it fifteen years later, his early childhood years were spent in "a very congenial home situation," a family "where love was central and where lovely relationships were ever present." Only one incident, he later said, marred those early childhood years. That came at age six, just after he had begun his actual first grade education at Yonge Street Elementary. For several years one of his close playmates had been a white child whose father owned a small grocery near the King home. After they began attending separate schools, they saw much less of each other. As King later described it:

This was not my desire but his. The climax came when he told me one day that his father had demanded that he would play with me no more. I never will forget what a great shock this was to me. I immediately asked my parents about the motive behind such a statement. We were at the dinner table when the situation was discussed, and here, for the first time, I was made aware of the existence of a race problem. I had never been conscious of it before.

That painful discovery aside, young M.L. clearly enjoyed school, doing well both at Yonge Street and then later at David T. Howard, where he finished his elementary years. M.L. spent seventh and eighth grades at the Laboratory High School of Atlanta University. Its closure forced him to transfer to the regular public high school, Booker T. Washington, which, like all others, was totally segregated.

In each of his environments—at home and in church with his family, in the neighborhood with his friends, and in school—young M.L. appeared to be a happy and well-adjusted child. In the King home, he was especially fond of his grandmother, Mama Williams. Even thirty years later, King would tell people of his special relationship with his loving and "saintly" grandmother, and how he never had forgotten the good biscuits she had made for him. "Mother Dear," as M.L. called Mrs. King, was a strong but quiet figure in the household, usually taking a backseat to her forceful and outspoken husband. "Daddy" King, as he came to be called, let no one, especially his children, forget that he was boss of the King household. If they did forget, King, Sr., was quick to remind them, and whippings were frequent. One neighbor who lived next door to the Kings in the early 1940s, after the family had moved from Auburn to a larger brick house several blocks away, remembered one whipping M.L. received. Watching from next door, Howard Baugh saw Daddy King give thirteen-year-old M.L. a vigorous spanking, telling him "that he was going to make something out of him if he had to beat him to death, meaning that he really wanted him to become a real man." Baugh, sixteen or seventeen himself, couldn't keep from laughing at the sight. King, Sr., spied him, took umbrage, and asked the young man's mother to send him over for some similar instruction. She agreed, and Reverend King whipped Baugh too. All in all, the forcefulness of his father was the most striking aspect of King's school-age years. "Whippings must not be so bad," he joked in later years, "for I received them until I was fifteen."[20]

King's closest teenage friend, Larry Williams, an Ebenezer church member who was four years his senior, never forgot how angrily King, Sr., erupted when he once caught Williams and M.L. dancing with girl friends at a church social. Shouting furiously, Reverend King told the two young men to leave the YWCA where the social was being held. King, Sr., was "a strict disciplinarian," Williams recalled. "M.L. was real frightened of his daddy."

M.L. participated fully in his father's church, even singing as a very young soloist at several church functions with his mother as the accompanist. As he grew up in the church, M.L.'s attitude toward it and its teachings slowly began to change. Initially he participated without a great deal of reflection. "I joined the church," he said in later years, recalling his decision to step forward for baptism, "not out of any dynamic conviction, but out of a childhood desire to keep up with my sister." By his early high school years, however, he began to question the literal interpretation of the Bible that his father's church taught. Once M.L. shocked his Sunday school teacher by denying the bodily resurrection of Jesus.

Among his neighborhood playmates M.L. was a typical young man. They played ball, rode their bicycles, and occasionally threw stones at each other. Young King suffered his share of scrapes—getting struck in a baseball game, having his bike hit by a car, jumping or falling from the second floor of the Auburn Avenue homestead—but came out of each with little more than scratches. If anything distinguished him from the others, it was his ability to use words. Younger brother A.D., boyhood friends, and other neighbors all recalled in later years that M.L. "had the gift of talking himself out of unpleasant situations." He resorted to fisticuffs only infrequently, but he certainly did not seek to avoid the rough-and-tumble of everyday teenage activities.

M.L. suffered only a few truly painful incidents. One came on May 18, 1941, a Sunday, when Mama Williams died of a heart attack. Twelve-year-old M.L. had been playing down on Auburn Avenue and learned of her death only several hours later. The news sent him to pieces, and made him so distraught that he took another leap from the second story of the home. Again he suffered no injury, and his parents consoled his sorrow by explaining the doctrine of spiritual immortality.

Another distressing occurrence took place two years later, when King and his high school teacher, Miss Sarah Bradley, traveled to a South Georgia town for an oratorical contest sponsored by the black Elks. M.L. did well, delivering his speech on "The Negro and the Constitution" without either manuscript or notes, but on their way back a white bus driver insisted that the two surrender their seats to newly boarding white riders. M.L. resisted at first, but his teacher finally encouraged him to get up, and the young man had to stand for several hours as the bus made its way to Atlanta. "It was," King recalled twenty years later, "the angriest I have ever been in my life."[21]

That was the most traumatic encounter with segregation that young King suffered. He had seen his father refuse to accept second-class service in stores, tell white policemen that a forty-year-old black minister should be addressed as "Reverend," not "boy," and himself had been called "nigger" by a hostile white in a downtown store. Looking back on these experiences a decade later, King recalled that he had never fully gotten over the shock of his initial discovery of racial prejudice as a six-year-old. "From that moment on," he remembered, "I was determined to hate every white person. As I grew older and older, this feeling continued to grow," even though "my parents would always tell me that I should not hate the white man, but that it was my duty, as a Christian, to love him."

Reminders of the problem were not that frequent for young M.L., however, because his daily life took place in an almost all-black environment: at home, at church, at school, and in the neighborhood. Also, there were occasional reminders that not all white persons displayed racial prejudice; one of his favorite junior high instructors, Miss Beatrice Boley, a biology teacher at the Laboratory High School, happened to be white.

The race problem aside, M.L. was a happy young man and a good student. At Booker T. Washington High, he skipped two grades–ninth and twelfth. Some of his friends began to tease him about his new taste for good clothes, and one of them, Emmett Proctor, coined a nickname for M.L.—"Tweed." Even though he was rather short, he played regularly on both intramural and YMCA basketball teams. He had a newspaper route, delivering the afternoon *Atlanta Journal,* and in time became an assistant to one of the district distribution managers. All in all, M.L. was a "happy-go-lucky" guy, "just another one of the boys" in the Auburn neighborhood, as one contemporary later recalled. Even though he graduated from high school at the tender age of fifteen, he struck most of his friends as just "an ordinary person. . . . Nobody ever figured that he would become anything more than a good preacher."[22]

There was never much question that M.L. would follow in his father's footsteps and attend Morehouse College, located on the west side of downtown Atlanta, a mile or so from the King family home. It was *the* school for the children of Atlanta's black middle class, and Reverend King was a particular fan of Morehouse President Benjamin E. Mays, a well-known scholar of black religion. World War II had reduced Morehouse's student body to under five hundred, and President Mays was willing to experiment with unusually young but promising freshmen.

It was September of 1944 when M. L. King, Jr., began his classes at Morehouse. He continued to live at home and commuted by bus to school. Some of his classmates, such as Oliver "Sack" Jones and Rial Cash, were old friends from Auburn Avenue. M.L. quickly and easily made new friends, like Walter McCall, a South Carolinian five years older than King, Robert Williams, a singer two years ahead of King, Charles Morton, and Philip Lenud. Some of these young men, such as McCall, thought that M.L. was very much under the thumb of his father. Though he would take part in their parties, M.L. betrayed some hesitation about enjoying things that would be frowned upon by his strict Baptist upbringing. Nonetheless, young King overcame such self-doubts and joined the regular social whirl, dating women he knew from town, like Juanita Sellers and Betty Milton, or students at neighboring Spelman College, like Madeline Knight, with whom he was "very thick" for almost a year. Close friend Larry Williams, who entered Morehouse as an older student two years after King, later recalled that "M.L. could get involved with girls, and most of the girls he got seriously involved with were light," "very fair-skinned." Williams and King socialized together regularly, and kiddingly called themselves "Robinson and Stevens, the wreckers." When old chum Emmett Proctor asked why, King smiled and replied, "We wreck girls." Robinson and Stevens, Williams laughingly later explained, was the name of an Atlanta wrecking company, a name he and King adapted for a different usage. "We wreck up all the women. We're the wreckers." Although he was only sixteen halfway through his freshman year, M.L. King, Jr., was growing up fast.

If starting college had presented a new series of social challenges and activities, it also rudely awakened King to the fact that his accelerated education in Atlanta's segregated schools had not been of high quality. An early exam, he later recalled, showed him reading at only an eighth-grade level, and his freshman composition course indicated that his spelling and punctuation skills left a good deal to be desired. Professor G. L. Chandler found King to be a B− or C+ student who was "quiet" and "humble," and whose grades could have been higher had he mastered spelling and elementary grammar. Professor Melvin Kennedy, King's freshman advisor and history teacher, recalled that M.L. was "not particularly impressive" when he first arrived at Morehouse. He was "quiet, introspective, and very much introverted" that first year; "he had a tendency to be withdrawn and not to participate."

King's fellow students did not view him as an introvert, and in later years some recalled the "fancy sportcoat and wide-brimmed hat" that made him a recognizable figure on campus. Most found King to be a quiet and reserved young man, "just a regular student," who always sat in the back of classrooms. If he did not make much of an impact on his classmates or most of his instructors, he did impress two important men, religion professor George D. Kelsey and Morehouse President Mays. Each weekday of the school term began with a thirty-minute assembly in the school chapel, and attendance was required. Mays spoke every Tuesday morning, and he regularly noticed that young King was one of the most attentive listeners. "As I recall," Mays said years later, "he took copious notes."

M.L., or Mike, as some of his close friends still called him, had realized for several years that nothing would please his father more than for him to follow his dad's footsteps into the ministry. M.L., however, was decidedly ambivalent about that course. Much black religion, he believed, emphasized emotion rather than ideas and volume rather than elocution. Furthermore, many ministers preached only about the after-life, rather than about what role the church could play in improving present-day society. In his first year at Morehouse, King had thought of either law or medicine as careers that would allow him to make a meaningful contribution to society. His difficulties with science courses suggested medicine would be a poor choice, and as a sophomore King chose sociology as his major, and thought increasingly of a legal career. The exposure to new bodies of knowledge also heightened King's doubts about the religious teachings he had learned at Ebenezer. His sophomore year witnessed what King later called "a state of skepticism" on his part toward religion. This problem persisted, he said, "until I studied a course in Bible in which I came to see that behind the legends and myths of the Book were many profound truths which one could not escape." At Morehouse, "the shackles of fundamentalism were removed" from his mind.[23]

If his college experience altered his attitude toward the church, it also affected his thoughts about race. Although King's academic record remained mediocre, he still took the time to participate in numerous college activities: the glee club and chorus, a student-faculty discipline committee, the NAACP chapter, and the annual oratorical contests, in which he once won second prize. One endeavor, however, left a more lasting mark: participation in several intercampus, interracial organizations with white students from other Atlanta schools. M.L. had not forgotten the pain and insult of those earlier childhood encounters with prejudiced whites, and the question had remained in his mind, he said later, "how could I love a race of people who hated me and who had been responsible for breaking me up with one of my best childhood friends? This was a great question in my mind for a number of years," and "I did not conquer this anti-white feeling" until he got to know white students through these interracial groups.

Much of King's thinking, though, concerned his own career choice: law or the ministry. The examples of Professor Kelsey and President Mays, two ministers who were erudite men, increasingly reminded M.L. that intellectual excellence could be combined with preaching and the pastoral role. Also, one summer King and several friends traveled to Connecticut to earn some money picking tobacco in a farming area outside of Hartford. It was King's first trip north and his first extended time away from home. The group chose King as their devotional leader, and King was struck by how positively the others responded to him. Finally, early in the summer of 1947, M.L. made his decision for the ministry. He delivered a trial sermon at Ebenezer that was a grand success, and the church's board of deacons licensed him to preach. He began serving as assistant pastor to his father, and early in the fall semester of his senior year started applying to several seminaries to seek a divinity degree after his graduation from Morehouse.[24]

King's parents were pleased by his decision to pursue the ministry. Along with President Mays and two Morehouse professors who were close family friends, Samuel Williams and Lucius Tobin, Daddy King presided at his son's ordination at Ebenezer on February 25, 1948. In a recommendation letter to M.L.'s first-choice seminary, Crozer Theological, King, Sr., called his nineteen-year-old son a "very conscientious" young man with a "very pleasing personality" who "makes and holds friends easily, among youth and adults." M.L. also had the aptitude for further study. "He has always been a very steady child, quite scholarly. From childhood he always wanted to possess scholarship." M.L.'s Morehouse references spoke less glowingly. President Mays, in a letter recommending both King and another undergraduate, said they had "good minds" and were capable of "substantial B work" but were "not brilliant students." Dean B. R. Brazeal explained that King's 2.48 GPA, a C+ average, stemmed from "a comparatively weak high school background." Professor Kelsey admitted that King's record was "short of what may be called 'good,'" but asked that King's application be given "serious consideration" because "King is one of those boys who came to realize the value of scholarship late in his college career. His ability exceeds his record at Morehouse."

Kelsey also informed Crozer that he viewed King as "quite serious about the ministry and as having a call rather than a professional urge." Speaking for himself on his Crozer application, King said he had chosen the ministry because of "an inescapable urge to serve society" and "a sense of responsibility which I could not escape." In a longer explanation, written just a few years later, King spoke of his decision as follows:

> I had felt the urge to enter the ministry from my latter high school days, but accumulated doubts had somewhat blocked the urge. Now it appeared again with an inescapable drive. My call to the ministry was not a miraculous or supernatural something; on the contrary, it was an inner urge calling me to serve humanity. I guess the influence of my father also had a great deal to do with my going in the ministry. This is not to say that he ever spoke to me in terms of being a minister, but that my admiration for him was the great moving factor. He set forth a noble example that I didn't mind following.[25]

By mid-April King had accepted Crozer's offer of admission, and several months after his June graduation from Morehouse, King left Atlanta to begin three years of study in Chester, Pennsylvania. Crozer was a very small school, with fewer than one hundred students, including more than half a dozen blacks. King lived in the main dorm and spent most of his time coping with a heavy work load.

King's academic performance at Crozer was far superior to that at Morehouse. Although his first-year average suffered because of several Cs, principally in two public-speaking courses, King made consistent progress, getting nothing below a B in his second year and straight As in his third. He impressed his instructors and fellow students both in the classroom and out. He made many friends, among them two white students from Georgia, DuPree Jordan and Francis Stewart, and an older black classmate, Horace "Ed" Whitaker. In his spare time, King played billiards, cardgames, or went bowling with his old friend from Morehouse, Walter McCall, who had come to Crozer one semester after him. A good friend of the King family, the Reverend J. Pius "Joe" Barbour, a Morehouse graduate who had attended Crozer and first recommended the school to King, lived only two miles from campus, and M.L. was a frequent visitor. He enjoyed the cooking, the opportunity to argue about politics and race, and the chance to listen to prizefights. Barbour took an interest in all the black students at Crozer, and frequently counseled "little Mike" on a variety of topics. Barbour "was like a father to all of us," Ed Whitaker recalled, and the intellectual jousting with Barbour was an "enriching experience. King in particular would challenge him and they would have quite a debate." Barbour's dialogues, Whitaker thought, were more stimulating than their classes, and for King they "sharpened his philosophical views in many ways, over and above being at seminary."

Only a few troubles marred King's three years at Crozer. Several months after arriving, he and Jordan went into nearby Philadelphia together. "We went to the Stouffer's restaurant right there in downtown," Jordan later remembered, "and he was ignored there for twenty or thirty minutes. . . . Finally we demanded service, and we got service . . . unfortunately, in one or more of his vegetables that he was served, he had sand on his plate." Jordan and King "were both just outraged by that," but King's overall reaction seemed "surprisingly subdued" to Jordan. "He took it rather quietly," and "did not want to make demands that would make a scene."

King also reacted relatively coolly a few months later when a southern white student, Lucius Z. Hall, Jr., who had been victimized by a dorm-room prank, blamed King for the trick and threatened him with a pistol. Hall and King had previously had "some little clashes," Marcus Wood, an older black student, later recalled, but on this occasion Hall burst into King's room, gun in hand. "I was in the room," Wood explained. "I saw the gun," and "King was scared." Wood intervened and tried to calm Hall down. "I got him out of the room," and back to his own. King declined to bring any charges, and no disciplinary action was taken against Hall, who left Crozer at the end of that academic year. King's calm reaction to the incident was respected by his fellow students. That emotional maturity, plus King's superior academic record, heavily influenced King's subsequent election as student-body president.

Toward the end of King's first year at Crozer, another incident involving a gun took place. King, McCall, and their dates had traveled from Chester into nearby New Jersey and stopped at a restaurant in Maple Shade, outside of Camden. The white proprietor refused to serve the foursome, and they chose to remain seated. The owner became furious, pulled a gun, threatened them, and finally ran outside, firing the pistol once in the air. With that, the group chose to leave, and McCall sought out a policeman, with whom they returned to the establishment. McCall pressed charges, and three white student witnesses initially agreed to testify against the owner. Parental pressure later changed their minds, and to King's and McCall's dismay the matter had to be dropped.

King dated regularly during his Crozer years, but one of his companions, a white girl of German origin whose mother worked for Crozer, raised concern in the eyes of Barbour and other friends. Barbour heard about the couple's serious romantic involvement, and told King in no uncertain terms of the difficulties an interracial relationship would face. King refused to reconsider the liaison; he and the girl were in love with each other, and even had talked about marriage. King's closest friends, like Ed Whitaker, knew the couple was "very serious" and considered the girl a "lovely young woman," but seconded Barbour's stern advice. If King wanted to return south to pastor, as he often said, an interracial marriage would create severe problems in the black community as well as the white. Another black student, Cyril Pyle, put it more bluntly. "I told him it was a dangerous situation and it could get out of hand and if it did get out of hand it would affect his career." Barbour insisted to King that marrying the young woman would be a tremendous mistake, and urged both of them to reconsider. Finally, after a six-month involvement, the couple took the advice of King's friends and ended their relationship on amicable but painful terms. King, Barbour said years later, "was a man of a broken heart—he never recovered."

Neither love affairs nor the two pistol incidents interrupted M.L.'s new commitment to academic excellence and intellectual curiosity. Walter McCall observed that "the dramatic change came in him when he entered the seminary. He began to take his studies more seriously . . . he devoted time to his books night and day." DuPree Jordan agreed. "He was very studious; he spent a lot more time on his lesson assignments than most of us did." King also pursued intellectual topics outside the classroom, such as attending a lecture that well-known pacifist A. J. Muste gave at Crozer in early November, 1949. Muste and King got into "a pretty heated argument," Francis Stewart later remembered. "King sure as hell wasn't any pacifist then."

Stimulated by a philosophy course he was taking at the University of Pennsylvania, Mike devoted much of his Christmas holiday that year to a close reading of Marx. Regarded as a "gifted speaker" by his classmates, King chose "Christianity and Communism" as his subject when Stewart invited him to address a white Baptist women's group at a Chester church. "'Most of us are not capitalists, we're just potential capitalists,'" King told his audience.[26]

King particularly blossomed during his third and final year at Crozer, 1950–1951. Professor George W. Davis, with whom King took 34 of his 110 course hours, was especially impressed with King's development. In a December 1950 evaluation, Davis wrote:

1. Exceptional intellectual ability—discriminating mind;
2. Very personable;
3. Makes good impression in public in speaking and discussion. Good speaking voice;
4. A man of high character;
5. Should make an excellent minister or teacher. He has the mind for the latter.

King made a similarly positive impression on a young instructor with whom he studied, Kenneth L. Smith, who lived on the same dorm floor as King. Smith, like others, felt that Mike had "a certain reserve about him, which made him difficult to get close to," but the two men talked regularly about intellectual subjects.

King's "reserve" and intellectual focus hindered him in the bimonthly student pastorship assignment he held during the fall of 1950 at the First Baptist Church of East Elmhurst in Queens, New York. Assigned to the church because its senior deacon was a King family friend and because its newly called pastor, Rev. William E. Gardner, needed an interim assistant, King drove up from Chester on Saturdays and returned on Sunday evening. Although church ladies such as Mrs. Matilda Sims found him "marvelous" and "brilliant," Pastor Gardner gave King a B for "pulpit ability" and highlighted several shortcomings in an evaluation requested by Crozer: "an attitude of aloofness, disdain and possibly snobbishness which prevent his coming to close grips with the rank and file of ordinary people. Also, a smugness that refuses to adapt itself to the demands of ministering effectively to the average Negro congregation."

At Crozer, however, King's intellectual focus was most appropriate. Beginning with his first courses under George Davis, King was impressed with the writings of Walter Rauschenbusch, the "social gospel" theologian of the early twentieth century. Rauschenbusch, a social reformer who held pastorates in New York City, had argued that religion must be relevant to real world problems and that the church should be actively involved. His writings also emphasized a very optimistic view of society's chances for progress and man's possible perfectability. King, attracted to Rauschenbusch's call for social activism, had wholeheartedly adopted his optimism as well. That attraction, King admitted, was not simply a matter of abstract preference; "it is," he wrote at the time, "quite easy for me to lean more toward optimism than pessimism about human nature mainly because of my childhood experiences." It is "quite easy," he added, "for me to think of the universe as basically friendly."

King held those views until he encountered the writings of Reinhold Niebuhr during his two senior-year courses with Kenneth Smith. Niebuhr was a favorite of Smith's and one of the sharpest critics of Rauschenbusch's optimism. Niebuhr believed that Rauschenbusch's emphasis upon the power of Christian love to advance the cause of social justice was misplaced and naïve, that "it did not measure adequately the power and persistence of man's self-concern." Man's selfishness, Niebuhr had stressed in a 1932 book, *Moral Man and Immoral Society*, was the major barrier to justice in society, and men in privileged groups were the most persistent in obstructing any efforts to improve society. "Disproportion of power in society is the real root of social injustice," Niebuhr argued, and "economic power is more basic than political power." Because of these persistent inequalities, "relations between groups must therefore always be predominantly political rather than ethical." Social-gospel thinking was blind to these painful truths about modern society.

The arguments of Niebuhr and the friendly prodding of Smith moved King away from his earlier blind attachment to the optimism that pervaded not only Rauschenbusch's social gospel but indeed all of the evangelical liberalism that George Davis had suffused him with. Looking back, King later confessed that he had become "absolutely convinced of the natural goodness of man and the natural power of human reason." Niebuhr's more persuasive realism, however, showed him "the complexity of human motives and the reality of sin on every level of man's existence." Clearly Christian love alone could not defeat injustice and achieve social change.

King pondered just what greater social justice might entail. One key area was economics, and Mike was becoming increasingly hostile toward capitalism and its reliance on the profit motive. In Smith's fall class, King presented an excellent and positive report on R. H. Tawney's classic Marxist study, *Religion and the Rise of Capitalism.* In another paper, King spoke about "my present anticapitalistic feelings." Reverend Barbour, recalling his long conversations with King at the time, said that King "thought the capitalistic system was predicated on exploitation and prejudice, poverty, and that we wouldn't solve these problems until we got a new social order." King, Barbour added, "believed that Marx had analyzed the economic side of capitalism right."[27]

King wondered how improvements could be made. He had heard Muste urge the pacifist approach, and several months later he heard Howard University President Mordecai Johnson, just back from a trip to India, describe how the nonviolent *satyagraha* of Mohandas K. Gandhi had brought about revolutionary changes in Indian society. However, King had serious doubts about pacifism and nonviolence, even though the Johnson lecture spurred a new interest in Gandhi. In the fall of 1950, at the same time that he was debating Rauschenbusch and Niebuhr with Smith, King read extensively on Gandhi in George Davis's psychology of religion course. King's doubts were expressed clearly in a paper he submitted to Smith. Picking up on a recent article in the *Crozer Quarterly* by political theorist John H. Hallowell which attacked Muste's pacifism, King argued that Gandhi's success in India did not mean that the pacifist approach would work everywhere. Reflecting his new exposure to Niebuhr, King stated that pacifists "fail to recognize the sinfulness of man." Though they focus upon the problem of war and violence, they do not appreciate that those are merely symptoms of man's sinfulness. "Since man is so often sinful," King wrote, "there must be some coercion to keep one man from injuring his fellows." Aggression and injustice must be resisted, not tolerated, though the respondents "must not seek revenge." An active stance, not a passive one, must be adopted in the face of injustice. Seven years later, looking back upon the evolution of his thought, King remarked that "when I was in theological school I thought the only way we could solve our problem of segregation was an armed revolt."

King's commitment to the life of the mind, plus his superb academic record, led his professors to suggest that he pursue doctoral studies in theology. They wrote enthusiastic recommendations for King, with Dean Charles E. Batten terming him "one of the most brilliant students we have had at Crozer," someone who was "interested in social action" and "a real leader" while possessing "a keen mind which is both analytical and constructively creative." Another instructor called King "the outstanding student in his class," and Morton S. Enslin, perhaps Crozer's most illustrious professor, recommended King without qualification as a "very competent student, conscientious, industrious, and with more than usual insight." Enslin noted King's success as student-body president despite Crozer's "largely southern" population, and observed that "he is entirely free from those somewhat annoying qualities which some men of his race acquire when they find themselves in the distinctly higher percent of their group." Enslin added that "so far as his moral character is concerned there is no need of any qualification, at least so far as I know, and I think that very few details of that sort escape me."

King was accepted by several doctoral programs—Yale, Edinburgh in Scotland, and Boston University's School of Theology—and after pondering the choice, decided upon Boston. One of the major professors there was Edgar S. Brightman, a man George Davis highly recommended and whose book, *A Philosophy of Religion,* had been a main text in two courses King had taken with Davis.

When King graduated from Crozer in 1951, he was valedictorian of the class and received the school's major annual prize, a $1,200 award to support his further study. His father was pleased, although he hinted that seven years of higher education was plenty for a young man who would be coming back sooner or later to join his father as co-pastor. M.L., who had learned long before that no one ever won an argument with Daddy, simply nodded and uttered his standard noncommittal remark: "Oh yes." M.L. once again spent the summer back at Ebenezer assisting his father before setting out in September for Boston and his next challenge in a new green Chevrolet, a present from his parents for his success at Crozer.[28]

M.L. found a small apartment on St. Botolph Street in Boston and began the rigor of a full load of graduate courses. Both Professor Brightman and other principal members of the Boston faculty, such as L. Harold DeWolf and Peter Bertocci, were advocates of a theological view known as "personalism," which King had been introduced to at Crozer by George Davis. Personalism, as the name suggested, held that the human personality, i.e. all individual persons, was the ultimate instrinsic value in the world. Some of King's own strong attraction to that philosophy was rooted in one of its major corollaries: if the dignity and worth of all human personalities was *the* ultimate value in the world, racial segregation and discrimination were among the world's ultimate evils.

In his first year at Boston, M.L. continued to wrestle with the questions Niebuhr had raised for him a year earlier. Looking back on Crozer, King realized that he still accepted much of Davis's optimistic liberalism as well as Smith's Niebuhrian realism. If he could trace his attraction to optimism back to his familial setting, his attraction to realism might be similar, for

"The balanced Christian," King stated, "must be both loving and realistic
. . . As an individual in complex social relations he must realistically meet
mind with mind and power with power." The answer should not be an
"either—or" choice, it should be "both—and." The love ethic could
work well in direct relationships, but in the larger social setting coercive
power was necessary to increase social justice. "Whereas love seeks out
the needs of others, justice . . . is a check (by force, if necessary) upon
ambitions of individuals seeking to overcome their own insecurity at the
expense of others." Liberal theology and the social gospel, he believed,
confuse "the ideal itself with the realistic means which must be employed
to coerce society into an approximation of that ideal. . . . Men are controlled by power, not mind alone." Despite the attractions of balance and
inclusivity that the dialectical combination offered, King still leaned
toward Niebuhr's analysis. Niebuhr was "unqualifiedly pessimistic about
the future of things," but "his analysis of the complexity of the social
situation is profound indeed, and with it I would find very little to disagree."[30]

Late in 1952, King's parents came to Boston for a visit. The purpose of
the trip was to end the blossoming relationship between Martin and Coretta Scott, and the visit was filled with tension. Daddy King wanted Martin to finish his schooling, return to Ebenezer fulltime, and marry an
Atlanta girl. Several women there, and one in particular, were interested
in Martin. They came from fine families, Daddy King pointedly told Coretta, families he himself had known for years. She bluntly told him that
she, too, came from a fine family, while Martin, with a nervous grin, sat
silently under his father's assault. Later, Martin told his mother that it
was his intention to marry Coretta. Though he said nothing to his father,
two days later Daddy King, just before leaving for the return trip to
Atlanta, told the young couple that if they were going to "court" full
time, they might as well get married.

Martin returned home at Christmas, and Daddy King indicated his acceptance of his son's decision. Coretta, however, stayed in Boston, and
Martin saw an old girlfriend over the holiday. When he returned north,
he and Coretta seriously discussed marriage, and he confessed his Atlanta
indiscretions. They had an intense argument, but it passed. They made
plans to announce their engagement that spring, and planned a June wedding.

King continued his doctoral work and prepared for his comprehensive
exams. He tried hard to impress his professors with both his personal
bearing and academic ability. Harold DeWolf, who was King's principal
supervisor after Brightman's death, recalled that the young man "always
impressed me as being especially well prepared for every conference he
had with me." King was "scholarly, well-groomed, invariably courteous."
He was both "very self-contained, and resourceful. He always came in
with a list of questions. He knew exactly what he wanted to ask." King's
"immaculate dress and his very fine, thoughtful courtesy" also stood out.

He was not as active in the life of the theology school as he had been at Crozer, but the regular meetings of the "Dialectical Society" at his apartment gave him many chances for social exchange.

In June, 1953, Martin and Coretta were married by Daddy King in the garden of Coretta's parents' home in rural Perry County, Alabama. It was a small ceremony; A.D. served as his older brother's best man. The couple spent their wedding night in nearby Marion at the home of an undertaker who was a Scott family friend. In later years, Martin would sometimes joke about having spent his honeymoon in a funeral parlor. Two days later they returned to Atlanta for the summer. Daddy King had obtained a job for Coretta at a local bank, and the young couple lived with Martin's parents in the family home.

When Coretta and Martin returned to Boston in the fall, they rented a four-room apartment on Northampton Street and resumed their studies. DeWolf and other instructors tried to persuade King to pursue a university teaching career, but Martin was firmly committed to the ministry. "He told me, fairly early, that he was not a scholar, and that he wasn't interested, really, in the academic world," one Boston friend, Cornish Rogers, later remembered. "He said, 'I like people too much. I want to work with people.'" Martin made the same points to Coretta. "He had this strong feeling for the masses," she recalled. "He said to me, 'I'm going to be a pastor of a church, a large Baptist church in the South. . . . I'm not going to be on a college campus . . . I'm going back South. I'm going to live in the South because that's where I'm needed.'" Perhaps he might do some part-time teaching, but the black church in the South would be his deepest commitment.[31]

Daddy King was happy to a point with that decision, but he pressed Martin hard to return to Atlanta and join him as co-pastor at Ebenezer. Daddy enlisted the help of Benjamin Mays, and Morehouse offered Martin a faculty position he could combine with the Ebenezer appointment. Martin, however, declined the offer and began exploring pastorships in other cities. One attractive possibility was the First Baptist Church of Chattanooga, Tennessee. Martin arranged to preach there during the Christmas holiday. A few days before he was to deliver that sermon, King learned from a family friend in Atlanta that Montgomery's prominent Dexter Avenue Baptist Church was in search of a minister. Dexter recently had dismissed its well-known and outspoken pastor, the Reverend Vernon Johns, and Robert D. Nesbitt, clerk of the church, was in Atlanta on business. A meeting was arranged, and Nesbitt, impressed with the young man, asked King to come take a look at Dexter before making any decision about other possible pastorships. King agreed to visit Montgomery and preach at Dexter before he returned to Boston.

Daddy King warned M.L. that Dexter had a reputation for being a "big-shots church" that was very tough on its pastors. Thomas Randall, the chairman of the deacons, had a well-deserved nickname: the "preacher killer." King heard similar warnings when he met Vernon

Johns, but he received a warm welcome to Montgomery from the young pastor at First Baptist Church, Ralph D. Abernathy, whom he had met briefly once before. King also was pleased by his first exposure to the people of Dexter. He chose to preach his favorite sermon, "The Three Dimensions of a Complete Life."

Dexter's worshipers were more restrained than those at Ebenezer, but they were attentive. After the service, King met with Dexter's lay leaders, who were as pleased with King's humble personality as they were with his first-rate preaching skills.[32]

King returned to Boston and considered his options. Coretta, or "Corrie," as he called her, would graduate from the conservatory in June. He would take his comprehensive exams in a few weeks, and he already was well along with reading for his dissertation topic, an examination of the differing conceptions of God held by two prominent theologians, Paul Tillich and Henry Nelson Wieman. He could write the dissertation anywhere he chose to live.

Other job leads came in from churches in New York, Massachusetts, and Michigan. In late February, Martin flew to Detroit to preach a guest sermon. A week after he returned, a telegram arrived from Dexter: The church had voted to offer its pastorship to King and wanted him to return to Montgomery in two weeks to discuss the details. King postponed the visit for two more weeks and pondered his options. Both his dad and Coretta vocally opposed his accepting Dexter's offer. The new Mrs. King, whose childhood home was only fifty miles from Montgomery, did not want to leave the North and a career in music to return to the rigid segregation of the Deep South. But M.L. made up his own mind; he wanted to return to the South, he wanted independence from Dad, he wanted to be in a good-sized city, and he wanted a church that would appreciate intelligent preaching. Dexter fit the bill on every count. In early April, King returned to Montgomery to discuss the details of the offer with Dexter's officials, and on April 14, he formally accepted the position. He would start in September.

Since Dexter had no interim pastor, King spent much of the summer commuting to Montgomery to preach. Coretta graduated in June, and after Martin passed his exams in August, the couple loaded their possessions in the Chevrolet and headed for Montgomery by way of Atlanta.

Dexter was still in the process of refurbishing its parsonage at 309 South Jackson Street when the Kings arrived on September 1, so they stayed for several weeks with a hospitable church member. King set about implementing at Dexter the lessons he had learned while watching his father's stewardship of Ebenezer. His top priorities were to establish the pastor's authority over the lay leadership, and to increase the congregation's active participation in—and contributions to—the activities of the church. He especially wanted to involve more young adults. Just a few weeks after his arrival, King presented his blueprint to the members. "Recommendations to the Dexter Avenue Baptist Church for the Fiscal

Year 1954–1955," as he titled the document, was blunt and straightforward. King wanted to make it "crystal clear that the pastor's authority is not merely humanly conferred, but divinely sanctioned . . . Leadership never ascends from the pew to the pulpit, but it invariably descends from the pulpit to the pew." The pastor, he added, "is to be respected and accepted as the central figure around which the policies and programs of the church revolve."

King also appointed a host of new committees and made clear that the membership of every church board depended upon his choices. Neither deacons nor trustees, he decreed, could consider an issue unless the pastor placed it before them. King also placed special emphasis upon a new social and political action committee. "This committee," he instructed, "shall keep before the congregation the importance of the NAACP. The membership should unite with this great organization in a solid block. . . . Every member of Dexter," he added, "must be a registered voter."

The new pastor threw himself into his preaching. Each week he would devote hours to writing out and memorizing the complete text of his Sunday sermon. His young pulpit assistant, John Thomas Porter, was always impressed by how King would bring that text with him, but would leave it in his chair and ascend to the pulpit without any notes. The results impressed almost all. "He was fantastic," Porter recalled, both silvertongued and substantively challenging. "That first year was just super. . . . He talked about love a lot," and how to deal with everyday human problems. Porter, who remained a friend of King and his family for many years thereafter, felt that it was clearly King's "greatest year of preaching." King himself, looking back a decade later, also agreed; having time to prepare a sermon made one a much better preacher.

When not working on his sermons, King was writing his dissertation. He traveled to Boston that fall to present DeWolf with a complete draft, and delivered the final version the following spring. An exceedingly academic piece of work, the dissertation argued that neither Tillich nor Wieman possessed adequate conceptions of God, and that a synthesis of their viewpoints, plus a large dose of personalist theology, would be superior. Again the dialectical method proved attractive to King. In early June, 1955, he was awarded his Ph.D. by Boston University.[33]

King preached at Dexter almost every Sunday from the fall of 1954 through the fall of 1955. Despite his superior preaching, Dexter remained a quiet church where the sanctuary was never full for Sunday services. The middle-class and upper-middle-class membership were independent people who required little pastoring, and for whom Alabama State College, rather than the church, was the social center of their lives. King's extensive efforts to activate the congregation met with only modest success.

King had barely put the finishing touches on his dissertation when Coretta informed him that she was pregnant, and they began making preparations for the happy event. Home, church, and writing left King little time for other endeavors. He joined the Montgomery chapter of the NAACP, and also attended meetings of the only interracial organization in the city, the Alabama Council on Human Relations. When the Colvin incident occurred in March, 1955, King was one of the sizable group that met with white officials. In early August he spoke at a meeting of the NAACP chapter, and it was the first time that many local citizens had the opportunity to hear the young pastor of the "rich folks'" church speak. King made a positive impression on many of the activists who heard him, and two weeks later he received a letter from the secretary of the NAACP chapter, Mrs. Rosa Parks, telling King he had been named to the group's executive committee. Three months later, when the presidency of the chapter was proffered, King felt compelled to turn it down because of his church and family responsibilities.

The Kings' first child, Yolanda Denise, was born on November 17. They accepted the delights and demands of parenthood eagerly; their quiet social life easily adapted to the duties of child rearing. Frequently they would spend an evening with Ralph and Juanita Abernathy, and often they talked about race. Ralph Abernathy later recalled that "we had no particular program in mind when we talked about the social ills of society . . . except for the fact that Dr. King felt his training demanded that he bring to the Dexter Avenue congregation the greatest social gospel and action program it had ever experienced."

When the MIA's presidency unexpectedly was thrust upon him on December 5, King was uncertain of his ability to lead a community he had resided in so briefly, but he was able to draw upon the same strong convictions that had inspired his leadership at Dexter. The pressures upon him had grown as the boycott continued, and by the time the protest entered its third week, the white community focused upon King as the effort's principal spokesman. In the wake of the angry meeting of December 19, white city leaders tried to paint King as the major obstacle to a settlement of the protest. Whites hinted to black acquaintances that King no doubt had his hand in the MIA's till, and asked why the older, long-established leaders of black Montgomery had ceded their authority to this young newcomer. Word of these efforts to divide the MIA leadership reached many ears, including King's. The young pastor, shaken by the attacks on him at the December 19 meeting, and feeling what he called "a terrible sense of guilt" about his verbal outbursts that day, was further laid low by the whispering campaign being mounted against him. "I almost broke down under the continual battering of this argument," and at one emotional meeting of the MIA board, King volunteered to step down as president. The board quickly rejected his offer and vowed to stand behind him. Editor Jackson, well-informed as always, wrote that "an attempt was made to try to get one of the major spokesmen for better treatment purged and isolated. Instead of doing this, the Montgomery leadership built a solid phalanx around this leader and told the upper-hand [white] leadership that he would never be deserted or shelved."[34]

The twenty-seven-day-old protest entered the New Year quietly. In New York, NAACP chief Wilkins instructed W. C. Patton, his Alabama representative, that the organization could not at present assist in any appeal of Mrs. Parks's conviction on account of the MIA's seating proposal. The NAACP could not join in "on any other basis than the abolition of segregated seating on the city buses." The organization already was pursuing a case to desegregate the city buses of Columbia, South Carolina, and hence "could not enter an Alabama case asking merely for more polite segregation." In Montgomery, the *Advertiser* ran a long and pointed story about how numerous southern cities, including Mobile, Huntsville, Nashville, and Macon, already employed the first-come, first-seated policy the MIA was advocating.

After the New Year's holiday, bus company official Totten returned from Chicago. The following day, Montgomery City Lines announced that it was losing twenty-two cents for every mile one of its buses traveled, and applied to the city commission for a fare increase from ten to twenty cents. Even the company conceded that the black boycott was nearly 100 percent effective. One day later, the commission granted the company half of what it sought, raising the adult fare to fifteen cents. King, asked for comment, said that the MIA would meet with anyone interested in settling the protest, but that he knew of no circumstances in which the three demands would be dropped. MIA Secretary Rev. Uriah J. Fields, in an unauthorized letter to the *Advertiser,* went even further, and appeared to bare some disagreements within the group. "The Negroes of Montgomery have no desire to compromise," he stated. Regarding the three demands, "this is a compromise to begin with. We should have demanded complete integration." Fields was strongly reprimanded for speaking out of turn.

On Friday, January 6, two significant events took place. Montgomery attorney Fred Ball wrote to the *Advertiser* and to solicitor William Thetford suggesting that the MIA's protest violated the state's antiboycott law. That evening a 1,200-person White Citizens Council rally took place at the city auditorium. Halfway through the program, city Police Commissioner Clyde Sellers took the podium and announced that he was joining the ardently segregationist group. As the *Advertiser* noted, "In effect, the Montgomery police force is now an arm of the White Citizens Council."

In the wake of those two threats, King contacted Gayle and requested another meeting between city officials and MIA leaders. It took place Monday afternoon, January 9, and the MIA again presented its first-come, first-seated policy, emphasizing how the different races would never share a common seat. "Our request is not a request for the abolition of segregation on buses but for a fair and reasonable seating of passengers so as to assure all passengers equal treatment," or "separate but equal," as the infamous 1896 Supreme Court decision in *Plessy* v. *Ferguson* had labeled it. Once again the city said no. "We are going to carry out the law as we see it," Gayle declared.[35]

As the boycott moved into its sixth week, bus company officials became more worried as revenues slipped further despite the fare increase. One published estimate stated the company was losing more than $3,000 a day. Attorney Crenshaw, sounding a new note, told reporters that the company "will do anything that Mayor Gayle suggests." King, speaking with out-of-town black reporters, indicated confidence. "Either the bus company will have to meet our demands or fold up." Citing letters to the editor supporting the protest, King argued that "the white citizens are solidly behind us" on the courtesy and seating demands, and only recalcitrant officials were blocking a settlement. King also indicated that the MIA would retain its demand for black drivers. "We say that if we have to pay the fares, that we have the right to be employed." Queried again about the desirability of the MIA's seating proposal, King responded that the negotiations were separate from the conviction of Mrs. Parks, which was being appealed. "We are fighting the question of segregation in the courts."

As the week of January 9 wore on, an increasing number of threats and harassing phone calls were received by MIA leaders. Reverend Robert Graetz, the white pastor of a black church and the only white visibly active in the protest, had his car vandalized. The MIA executive board, meeting on January 12, concluded that "it seems that it is now a test as to which side can hold out the longer time, or wear the other down." To keep up the spirits of boycott supporters, King announced on the fifteenth that the mass meetings would be expanded from two nights a week to six. White harassment continued apace, and Police Commissioner Sellers, speaking to the Junior Chamber of Commerce on the seventeenth, vowed that "we must at all cost strive to preserve our way of life." Many whites whispered that the boycott was not the action of local blacks, but that "outside agitators" had put them up to it. Most Montgomery blacks would return to the buses were it not for the "goon squads" of MIA people that threatened any who tried to ride. As one MIA leader noted, "The white man in this town just does not want to believe that this is a people's movement." Meanwhile, further attention focused on attorney Ball's contention about the antiboycott law, and one letter writer pointedly inquired, "Doesn't the solicitor know his job? Why does he have to be reminded of his duty?"[36]

By the third week of January, the press began to focus upon King as the principal spokesman for the movement. He struck reporters as very mature for someone who had celebrated his twenty-seventh birthday on January 15. "He looks and acts older," one wrote. "Most people would guess him to be about 35." King conceded to reporters that the MIA's seating proposal was modest and had cost the protesters the active support of the NAACP. "We began with a compromise when we didn't ask for complete integration," he admitted. "Frankly, I am for immediate integration. Segregation is evil, and I cannot, as a minister, condone evil." King's feelings about the white officials remained strong. "They appear determined not [to] settle this protest in our favor even though it appears that we are right. It seems that the mayor is used to having colored people coming to him begging for things; well, we are demanding our rights. . . . Our demands are simple. They can be met. Until they are met we will continue to protest."

Asked about the wider meaning of the boycott, King proclaimed: "It is part of a world-wide movement. Look at just about any place in the world and the exploited people are rising against their exploiters. This seems to be the outstanding characteristic of our generation."

Within the private councils of the MIA, there was growing appreciation both for King's ability as the boycott's principal public spokesman and for his skillful leadership of the executive board. "King knew how to get along with all types and classes of people. He also persuaded them to get along with each other," MIA historian Lawrence Reddick later recalled. King's "democratic, patient and optimistic" approach to things impressed everyone. The growing closeness of King's friendship with Ralph Abernathy surprised some participants who expected competition for the spotlight, but King treasured Abernathy's loyalty. Abernathy acknowledged King as "the spiritual and philosophical leader of the movement," while viewing himself as "the most effective leader of the movement in respect to strategies and operational tactics."[37]

On Saturday, January 21, the city commission made a different attempt to stifle the boycott. Mayor Gayle met with three little-known black ministers who were not members of the MIA, the Reverends William K. Kind, Benjamin F. Mosely, and D. C. Rice, and announced to the press late that evening that a settlement had been reached. With the active complicity of the *Montgomery Advertiser,* the commissioners' erroneous story claimed that the "prominent Negro ministers" had agreed to a plan whereby ten front seats would be reserved exclusively for whites and ten rear ones for blacks. Saturday night, as the *Advertiser* went to press, the wire services began distributing the story on the reported settlement.

One man who heard the report was a black correspondent in Minneapolis, Carl T. Rowan, who had visited the MIA leaders briefly two weeks earlier. Puzzled by the settlement terms and by the lack of any names, Rowan called King in Montgomery. King knew nothing about any settlement or supposed meeting. Rowan then called Gray, who also had heard nothing. After contacting the Associated Press to question the truthfulness of their story, Rowan called Montgomery Police Commissioner Sellers, who parried Rowan's queries about the identities of the black representatives before conceding that they may not have been members of the MIA. Rowan called King back, informed him of Sellers's comments, and efforts to warn the black community of the falsity of the city's claim began.

By late Saturday night, the MIA had asked all black ministers to tell their congregations the next morning that the protest was not at an end despite the headlines in the *Advertiser*. Other representatives were sent out to pass the word at Saturday nightspots. Acting on the clues Sellers had given Rowan, King and the other MIA principals managed to identify and track down Kind, Mosely, and Rice, all of whom claimed they had made no deal with the commission concerning the buses. A denial in their names was issued to the press, and by Sunday afternoon it was clear that the city's effort at deception had failed miserably.

The embarrassment of that flop only made the city commissioners more determined to best the MIA. On Monday, Mayor Gayle announced that the city was adopting a new, tougher stance. Calling the MIA "a group of Negro radicals who have split asunder the fine relationships" between Montgomery's blacks and whites, Gayle declared that "we have pussyfooted around on this boycott long enough." No further negotiations would take place while the protest remained in force. "Until they are ready to end it, there will be no more discussions." White people, Gayle emphasized, must realize that far more was at stake in the MIA's demands than merely the question of seating practices. "What they are after is the destruction of our social fabric."

The meaning of the new city policy quickly became clear. Sellers ordered policemen to disperse groups of blacks waiting for car pool rides on street corners, and Gayle asked white housewives to stop giving rides to their black domestic workers. Giving a lift to any black person would merely aid "the Negro radicals who lead the boycott." City police also began tailing drivers from the MIA car pool, issuing tickets for trivial or nonexistent traffic violations. The official harassment made some protest supporters pause. "The voluntary pick-up system began to weaken," one MIA leader reported, and "for a moment the protest movement seemed to be wavering."[38]

One of the first motorists to fall victim to this new policy of traffic enforcement was King himself. On Thursday, January 26, King left Dexter church in midafternoon, accompanied by one of his best friends, Robert Williams, and his church secretary, Mrs. Lillie Thomas. Before heading home, King stopped at the MIA's central transportation point to give three other persons a lift. When King pulled out, two motorcycle officers began tailing him. After several blocks, King stopped to drop off the riders. The officers pulled up beside him and told him he was under arrest for going thirty miles per hour in a twenty-five-MPH zone. King stepped out of the car, was frisked and told that he would have to go to the city jail until bond was arranged. King told Williams to take the car home and alert Coretta and the others. Then King himself was placed in a patrol car and driven to the dingy city jail, a long and somewhat fearful ride to a desolate section of northern Montgomery.

King was placed in a filthy group cell with various black criminals. Several minutes later he was taken out and fingerprinted. It was the first time King had been locked in a jail, and the first time he had been fingerprinted. It was not pleasant. In less than thirty minutes, Ralph Abernathy arrived to bail King out. The jailer told Abernathy that for release on a signature bond, he had to have a certified statement showing he owned sufficient property. It was too late in the evening to secure that, the jailer noted, and King would have to stay in jail overnight. Abernathy then asked if cash would be accepted. Reluctantly, the jailer said yes, and Abernathy rushed off to collect the necessary money.

Meanwhile, word of King's arrest had spread rapidly through the black community. Even before Abernathy returned, several dozen others—members of Dexter, MIA colleagues, and friends—began arriving at the jail. The growing crowd worried the white jailers, and while the fingerprinting ink was still being wiped from King's hands, the chief jailer told him he was free to leave upon his own signature. His trial would be Saturday morning. In hardly a moment's time, King was escorted out and driven back to town.

The emotional trauma of the arrest heightened the growing personal tensions King was feeling. He had not wanted to be *the* focal point of the protest in the first place, and he had erroneously assumed that a negotiated settlement would be obtained in just a few weeks time. With no end in sight, and more attention coming his way, King wondered whether he was up to the rigors of the job. He stressed to everyone that he as an individual was not crucial to the protest, that if something happened to him, or should he step aside, the movement would go on. "If M. L. King had never been born this movement would have taken place," the young minister told one mass meeting. "I just happened to be here. You know there comes a time when time itself is ready for change. That time has come in Montgomery, and I had nothing to do with it."

But others thought King had everything to do with it. The obscene and threatening phone calls continued apace, and they took their toll. "I felt myself faltering and growing in fear," King recalled later. Finally, on Friday night, January 27, the evening after his brief sojourn at the Montgomery jail, King's crisis of confidence peaked. He returned home late after an MIA meeting. Coretta was asleep, and he was about to retire when the phone rang and yet another caller warned him that if he was going to leave Montgomery alive, he had better do so soon. King hung up and went to bed, but found himself unable to sleep. Restless and fearful, he went to the kitchen, made some coffee, and sat down at the table. "I started thinking about many things," he recalled eleven years later. He thought about the difficulties the MIA was facing, and the many threats he was receiving. "I was ready to give up," he said later. "With my cup of coffee sitting untouched before me I tried to think of a way to move out of the picture without appearing a coward," to surrender the leadership to someone else. He thought about his life up until that moment. "The first twenty-five years of my life were very comfortable years, very happy years," King later said, reflecting back on that moment in the most remarkable and self-revealing utterances he ever made publicly:

> I didn't have to worry about anything. I have a marvelous mother and father. They went out of their way to provide everything for their children . . . I went right on through school; I never had to drop out to work or anything. And you know, I was about to conclude that life had been wrapped up for me in a Christmas package.
>
> Now of course I was religious, I grew up in the church. I'm the son of a preacher . . . my grandfather was a preacher, my great grandfather was a preacher, my only brother is a preacher, my daddy's brother is a preacher, so I didn't have much choice, I guess. But I had grown up in the church, and the church meant something very real to me, but it was a kind of inherited religion and I had never felt an experience with God in the way that you must, and have it, if you're going to walk the lonely paths of this life.

That night, for the first time in his life, King felt such an experience as he sought to escape the pressures the MIA presidency had placed upon him.

He thought more about how trouble-free his life had been until the movement began.

> Everything was done [for me], and if I had a problem I could always call Daddy—my earthly father. Things were solved. But one day after finishing school, I was called to a little church, down in Montgomery, Alabama. And I started preaching there. Things were going well in that church, it was a marvelous experience. But one day a year later, a lady by the name of Rosa Parks decided that she wasn't going to take it any longer. . . . It was the beginning of a movement, . . . and the people of Montgomery asked me to serve them as a spokesman, and as the president of the new organization . . . that came into being to lead the boycott. I couldn't say no.
>
> And then we started our struggle together. Things were going well for the first few days but then, about ten or fifteen days later, after the white people in Montgomery knew that we meant business, they started doing some nasty things. They started making nasty telephone calls, and it came to the point that some days more than forty telephone calls would come in, threatening my life, the life of my family, the life of my child. I took it for a while, in a strong manner.

But that night, unable to be at peace with himself, King feared he could take it no longer. It was the most important night of his life, the one he always would think back to in future years when the pressures again seemed to be too great.

"It was around midnight," he said, thinking back on it. "You can have some strange experiences at midnight." The threatening caller had rattled him deeply. "Nigger, we are tired of you and your mess now. And if you aren't out of this town in three days, we're going to blow your brains out, and blow up your house."

I sat there and thought about a beautiful little daughter who had just been born. . . . She was the darling of my life. I'd come in night after night and see that little gentle smile. And I sat at that table thinking about that little girl and thinking about the fact that she could be taken away from me any minute.

And I started thinking about a dedicated, devoted and loyal wife, who was over there asleep. And she could be taken from me, or I could be taken from her. And I got to the point that I couldn't take it any longer. I was weak. Something said to me, you can't call on Daddy now, he's up in Atlanta a hundred and seventy-five miles away. You can't even call on Mama now. You've got to call on that something in that person that your Daddy used to tell you about, that power that can make a way out of no way.

And I discovered then that religion had to become real to me, and I had to know God for myself. And I bowed down over that cup of coffee. I never will forget it . . . I prayed a prayer, and I prayed out loud that night. I said, 'Lord, I'm down here trying to do what's right. I think I'm right. I think the cause that we represent is right. But Lord, I must confess that I'm weak now. I'm faltering. I'm losing my courage. And I can't let the people see me like this because if they see me weak and losing my courage, they will begin to get weak.'

Then it happened:

And it seemed at that moment that I could hear an inner voice saying to me, 'Martin Luther, stand up for righteousness. Stand up for justice. Stand up for truth. And lo I will be with you, even until the end of the world.' . . . I heard the voice of Jesus saying still to fight on. He promised never to leave me, never to leave me alone. No never alone. No never alone. He promised never to leave me, never to leave me alone.

That experience gave King a new strength and courage. "Almost at once my fears began to go. My uncertainty disappeared." He went back to bed no longer worried about the threats of bombings. The next morning he went down to the Montgomery courthouse and was convicted of the Thursday speeding charge. He was fined $10, plus $4 in court costs. Fred Gray filed notice of appeal.[39]

As the city's stance became increasingly hostile, the MIA considered two further courses of action. Some MIA members discussed whether the organization should apply to the city for a franchise to operate its own jitney transportation system on six formalized routes using a fleet of station wagons. Such a legalized status would allow drivers to collect fares from passengers, something not allowed in the informal free-lift car pool system. Paying for gas, oil, and tires for the many volunteer drivers was costing the MIA a hefty sum each week, which so far had been met by collections taken up at each of the mass meetings. Though some meetings, like the one on January 23, produced collections of $2,000, a more regular system for producing income was needed. Perhaps naïvely, some MIA members believed the city might assist them in this effort. Unsurprisingly, the effort came to naught.

The MIA's application did bring accusations that its real goal was to put City Lines, which was in the middle of renegotiating its own franchise with the city, out of business. King denied any such intention. "We aren't interested in putting them out of business. We want them to comply with our demands." To emphasize further the continuing moderation of its position, the MIA took out another ad in the local paper, stressing its own limited desires and castigating the city's conduct. "At no time have we raised the race issue in the movement, nor have we directed our aim at the segregation laws."

Though that was the MIA's public stance, in private discussions the leadership had considered since mid-January launching a direct attack on the bus segregation laws. White attorney Clifford Durr had continued to provide behind-the-scenes advice to the MIA's young lawyers, Fred Gray and Charles Langford. Durr stressed that if the black community wanted to make a legal challenge to the segregation provisions, the appeal of Mrs. Parks's conviction would not be a sufficient vehicle. First of all, since the appeal would have to be made through Alabama's state courts before it could reach the U.S. Supreme Court, it would be vulnerable to extensive delaying tactics. Second, given the specific circumstances involved, where another seat had not been available to Mrs. Parks, the conviction might well be voided without the issue of segregation itself being resolved. If the MIA really wanted to eliminate segregated seating, Durr advised, it should file its own suit in federal court alleging that segregated public transportation was unconstitutional in light of the earlier Supreme Court decision in *Brown* about public schools. E. D. Nixon supported Durr's suggestion, and Gray and Langford, with further counsel from New York NAACP attorney Robert L. Carter, began drafting the necessary documents.[40]

On the evening of January 30, the MIA held its regular Monday night mass meeting, this time at Abernathy's First Baptist Church. Two members of the Dexter congregation, Roscoe Williams and Richmond Smiley, stopped by the parsonage to give King a ride to the meeting. Since his speeding arrest, the young men of Dexter had provided him with regular accompaniment. Williams's wife, Mary Lucy, had come along to stay with Coretta and two-month-old Yoki. Later that evening, the two women heard an unusual noise, like the sound of a brick striking the concrete floor of the front porch. Footsteps sounded outside the house as Coretta suggested they move out of the front room. Just as they darted into the guest bedroom, an explosion rocked the house, filling the front room with smoke and shattered glass. Frightened and shaken, the two women retreated to the rear of the house, where Yoki was safely sleeping. Coretta started to call the Montgomery police, but realized they were not the best people to call. She thought to call Winston Craig, a Dexter member who was Governor James Folsom's chauffeur, but couldn't find his number. A neighbor, Mrs. Euretta Adair, called to ask if they were all right and said she already had called the police. Other people began arriving at the house. Coretta called the First Baptist Church and told the woman who answered that the home had been bombed.

At the church, King was on the platform, supervising the collection, when the call came. He saw Abernathy, E. N. French, and others reacting to whispered messages, but none came to him. Finally, he asked Abernathy about the commotion, and he informed King of the bombing. King stepped back to the podium, informed the crowd about the report, said that he must leave immediately, and asked that they also go quickly to their homes. Those watching King were surprised by his calm and steady demeanor. Looking back on it, King agreed that he had "accepted the word of the bombing calmly. My religious experience a few nights before had given me the strength to face it."

By the time King arrived home, a crowd of several hundred black onlookers had gathered at the scene. Numerous policemen also had arrived, and Mayor Gayle, Police Commissioner Sellers, and Fire Chief R. L. Lampley all were on the porch, inspecting the broken windows and the two-inch by four-inch hole in the concrete porch floor that the bomb had left. King made his way through the crowd and entered the house, where he found Coretta, Yoki, and Mrs. Williams unharmed. Commissioner Sellers took King aside and expressed his condemnation of the attack. "I do not agree with you in your beliefs," reporters heard him say, "but I will do everything within my power to defend you against such acts as this." King nodded his appreciation, but one Dexter member bluntly told Sellers that the bombing was a direct outgrowth of the heated rhetoric and "get tough" policy that officials like him had been championing. Sellers did not reply.

The crowd outside grew larger and angrier as word of the bombing spread. White reporters on the scene were fearful as police efforts to disperse the throng were ineffective. One officer told Sellers that a calming influence was needed, and the police commissioner asked King if he would say a few words to reassure the onlookers. King agreed, and stepped onto the porch, where, flanked by Sellers and Gayle, he told the crowd that his wife and child had not been injured. "Everything is all right. It is best for all of you to go home. The police are investigating, nobody has been hurt, and everything is under control." He emphasized that everyone in the protest should remain peaceful, and not retaliate against the white community.

We are not advocating violence. We want to love our enemies. I want you to love our enemies. Be good to them. Love them and let them know you love them. I did not start this boycott. I was asked by you to serve as your spokesman. I want it to be known the length and breadth of this land that if I am stopped, this movement will not stop. If I am stopped, our work will not stop. For what we are doing is right, what we are doing is just.

Sellers and Gayle each spoke to the crowd, promising to spare no effort to solve the crime. Then King stepped forward again, and asked everyone to disperse. "Go home and sleep calm. Go home and don't worry. Be calm as I and my family are. We are not hurt and remember that if anything happens to me, there will be others to take my place."

After the crowd and officials departed, the Kings were driven to the home of Dexter members Mr. and Mrs. J. T. Brooks to spend the night. M.L. had trouble falling asleep, and several hours later there was a knocking at the door. He and Coretta peered out, but couldn't tell who it was and decided not to answer. The visitor disappeared, but shortly thereafter the phone rang. It was Daddy King, who, along with Christine and A.D., had driven over from Atlanta upon hearing of the bombing. He had been the person at the door, and he quickly returned. At almost the same time, Coretta's father, Obie, who also had heard of the bombing, arrived from nearby Marion.

Daddy King told M.L. that he and all the family should leave Montgomery and return to Atlanta. Bombers who had tried once might well try again. Martin said no, that he could not desert his colleagues in the MIA. Daddy King, his temper flaring, told his son, "It's better to be a live dog than a dead lion." Martin again refused, and then Obie Scott said that if Martin would not take the family to Atlanta, he would take Coretta and Yoki with him back to Marion. Coretta also refused, saying she would stay with her husband. Daddy King pushed Martin harder. "He very strongly insisted on Martin's coming home for a while and getting away from things," Coretta later recalled. "He really wanted him to get completely out of the Movement." The young couple maintained their resistance, and finally the early-morning argument broke up. M.L., Coretta, and Yoki all would remain in Montgomery.[41]

The following morning, the MIA executive board met to discuss their next step. The white violence, coming on the heels of eight weeks of official obstinacy, convinced the black leadership that the time had come for a direct attack upon the segregation statutes. The next day, February 1, Fred Gray filed suit in federal court in the names of five black women plaintiffs. The suit sought an injunction against segregated bus seating, and also a halt to the harassment of the car pool. No longer was the MIA seeking simply a more polite form of "separate but equal"; now the challenge would be total.

King and the MIA had practical as well as strategic concerns in the wake of the bombing. Sellers's promise aside, and a city-sponsored reward of $500 for information on the bombing notwithstanding, the MIA did not believe that the Montgomery police could be trusted to protect the protest leaders. While repair work on the parsonage got under way, the men of Dexter organized themselves into three four-hour shifts of two people each to guard King's home from 8:00 P.M. to 8:00 A.M. each night. Robert Williams vowed to keep watch with a shotgun, while King and Abernathy decided to take up sidearms. "We felt we ought to be ready," Abernathy later explained. "I asked King if he had any means of protection for him and his family. He said the only weapon he had was a butcher knife. He asked, 'What do you have?' I said, 'The only thing I have is a razor.' We decided that we should go downtown together and buy some weapons for our protection." Accompanied by Reverend Hubbard, King and Abernathy appeared at the county sheriff's office on Wednesday afternoon, February 1, to request pistol permits. King stated that he wanted a gun so that the watchmen at his home could be armed, but the application was denied. That very night the bombers struck again at the home of E. D. Nixon. The device, apparently thrown from a passing car, landed some twenty feet from the house and did no substantial damage. Nixon was out of town at the time, and did not learn of the attack until his train from Chicago pulled into Birmingham the next day.

The two bombings in forty-eight hours led King and four other MIA representatives to call on a potential ally, Alabama Governor James E. Folsom. Reviled by many whites for having entertained black New York Congressman Adam Clayton Powell, "Big Jim" Folsom was as liberal on race as any white politician in the South. Folsom told the black visitors that he deplored the bombings and hoped the situation would not deteriorate further. He asked King how long the protest would continue. "Until our demands are granted," the young minister told the governor. "What we really want to ask of you, is protection of the state. We have no confidence in the city police affording us such protection." Folsom said he would have state officers keep an eye on King's home, and that he also would speak to the county sheriff. But King wanted something else. "What we would like to have, is to have you issue a permit to keep a gun in my car," he told Folsom. The governor responded that he would have to discuss that with the sheriff too.

King returned home from the state capitol to find Roscoe Williams installing floodlights around the parsonage, and Daddy King back in town again to persuade his son to return to Atlanta. M.L. once more said no to his father's entreaties, but one observer who watched him that day wrote that King's "nervous pacing reveals he is under a tremendous strain." Coretta appreciated her husband's burden, supported his refusals of Daddy King's pleas, and talked with him about their likely fate. "We realized that our lives were in danger. I did a lot of soul-searching . . . we were right in what we were doing, and if we were going to stand up for a cause, we had to be willing to face that which may be the inevitable consequences."

Within the MIA leadership, the filing of the federal court suit led some to wonder whether the boycott should be continued or whether the black community should return to the buses while awaiting legal vindication. On February 7, King admitted that the MIA's thinking had "changed somewhat" because it was now clear that negotiations would not bring an end to the protest. Only the suit could do that, and since the litigation might take a "long time," King was not certain whether the boycott would continue until the suit was decided. "We are now depending on the courts to give the final answer." The following day, however, King said that his previous comments had been "misunderstood," and the MIA announced there would be no change in its stance.[42]

While the bombings led the black community to take a stronger stand against segregation, they also motivated some of Montgomery's white business leaders to try to resolve the protest. The "Men of Montgomery," a businessmen's group, announced on February 8 that it stood ready to mediate a settlement. Over the next five days, two representatives of that group, Joe Bear and C. T. Fitzpatrick, held discussions with the city commission. The officials were willing to guarantee courtesy, to promise that all passengers could board through the front door, and that the adult fare would return to ten cents. They were not, however, willing to surrender in principle the idea of ten reserved seats for each race at opposite ends of each bus. They did concede, though, that "whenever the condition exists that there is no probability of any additional white passengers boarding a bus, or any colored passengers as the case may be, in that event the bus operator shall assign such seats as may be required in the reserved sections." In other words, no one would have to stand over a vacant "reserved" seat.

King left town for several days to visit his parents in Atlanta and to travel to Chicago for a previously scheduled preaching engagement. During his Chicago stay King also met with interested leaders of the United Packinghouse Workers to discuss pressuring National City Lines' Chicago headquarters and to seek outside support to boost the boycotters' morale. While King was in Chicago, Montgomery's newspapers reported that Circuit Judge Eugene W. Carter had instructed solicitor William Thetford and the current grand jury to consider whether the MIA's protest was a violation of Alabama's antiboycott statute. Asked about the report, King told Chicago reporters, "I don't doubt that they will indict some of us." He emphasized that the protest "is a movement of passive resistance," and acknowledged that the litigation to resolve the problem would take at least several months. "I am not sure that the people will want to continue the boycott that long." He also stressed that Montgomery was not an isolated incident. "The oppressed people of the world are rising up. They are revolting against colonialism, imperialism and other systems of oppression," including American segregation.

When King returned to Montgomery, there were rumors of indictments looming against the MIA leadership. On February 18 the grand jury indicted MIA attorney Fred Gray on a trumped-up charge of having named as a plaintiff in the MIA's federal court suit a woman who actually had not authorized him to use her name. That same day King left on a speaking trip to Atlanta and Nashville.

Among the white leadership there was less than complete agreement on what steps to take next. The Men of Montgomery were pressing both the city commissioners and the bus company to authorize one last approach to the MIA before proceeding with mass indictments. Solicitor Thetford was ambivalent about pressing criminal charges, and instead wanted the bus company to seek an injunction against the MIA's car pool on the grounds that it infringed upon the bus line's exclusive municipal transportation franchise. Company attorney Crenshaw, however, opposed having the company take any legal initiative against the MIA, and also objected to the idea of criminal indictments. By this time Crenshaw, Bagley, and the company were willing to accept a negotiated settlement on the MIA's terms in order to save the franchise from financial ruin. They waited for city officials to take the lead. The three commissioners, however, remained as staunchly opposed as ever.

On Monday morning, February 20, the Men of Montgomery won agreement from both the commissioners and the bus company to have the newest version of the reserved seating plan presented to the MIA. That afternoon the proposal was conveyed to Abernathy, who promised to present it to the leadership and to that evening's mass meeting. Some of the leaders contended privately that maintaining the car pool system until the court case was resolved would be too difficult a task, but their argument failed. When the seating plan was described to several thousand people gathered that night at St. John AME Church, only L. Roy Bennett and his assistant pastor voted publicly to accept it. After the meeting, Abernathy contacted the Men of Montgomery, informed them of the outcome, and thanked them for their effort. Commenting on the meeting's action, one MIA leader stated that "the morale of the masses, once again, revived the morale of the leaders."[43]

The next morning the grand jury returned indictments against almost one hundred MIA members under the state antiboycott law. "We are committed to segregation by custom and by law," the jury's report stated, and "we intend to maintain it." Abernathy called King in Nashville to give him the news. King promised to return to Montgomery the next morning, after stopping in Atlanta to pick up Coretta and Yoki, who had stayed with Daddy and Mama King.

Daddy King was more insistent than ever that Martin not return to Montgomery. The dangers were just too great, he argued. His son should know full well that the trial would be far from just. Who knew how long he might be confined in some Alabama penitentiary?

Martin told his parents he simply could not desert his colleagues in Montgomery. While he and his father argued vehemently in the kitchen, Coretta took Yoki and went upstairs. Martin, already angry at his father, became furious with Coretta for leaving his side at such a crucial moment. "Martin told me that I had run out on him," she admitted later. Even the next morning, Daddy King was unwilling to give up the fight. After Martin agreed to remain in Atlanta one more day, his father assembled most of Atlanta's black leadership at the King home to get them to persuade M.L. not to return. AME Bishop Sherman L. Green, drugstore owners L. D. Milton and C. R. Yates, newspaper publisher C. A. Scott, attorney A. T. Walden, educators Benjamin E. Mays and Rufus E. Clement, and businessman T. M. Alexander all gathered to hear King, Sr., ask them to endorse the argument he was giving his son. At first, the group expressed support for Daddy King's contentions. Then Martin forcefully told them he could not abandon his friends in Montgomery, no matter what the consequences. "I would rather go back and spend ten years in jail than not go back." That convinced Morehouse president Mays. "You're right," he declared, and newspaperman Scott agreed. Their support strengthened Martin's resolve, and his father gave up the fight. In tears, Daddy King admitted that his son had to go back. Before the session broke up, attorney Walden phoned NAACP chief counsel Thurgood Marshall in New York to obtain his promise that King would be afforded the best possible defense. Marshall, who had already been called by E. D. Nixon, told Walden to assure the Kings of that commitment. The next morning Daddy King drove Martin and Coretta back to Montgomery.

The black community, prepared in advance for the mass indictments, responded with a new demonstration of strength. As the names of those being sought spread through town, the MIA organized a mass gathering at the courthouse to show that blacks would not be intimidated. "We made a special effort to get every one of them to go down at one time" to be booked, Rufus Lewis recalled. "Reverend Hubbard just made the suggestion that we dress for the occasion and go down en masse, so that it would appear that we were together." The plan was a marvelous success. Those who had been indicted showed up in their Sunday best, and those who had not came down to sign bonds for the others. The atmosphere, one local white reporter said, was like "old home week."

By the time King returned the following morning, the MIA had organized a special mass rally for Thursday night, followed by a "carless" Friday, when the arraignments of those arrested would take place. King, accompanied by his father, surrendered himself for booking at the courthouse shortly after his return. Early that afternoon the MIA leadership met with attorney Arthur D. Shores and his assistant, Peter Hall, whom the NAACP had sent in from Birmingham, to discuss legal strategy. Although the rally was not scheduled to begin until 7:00 P.M., people began gathering in the afternoon. They sang hymns as the crowd grew to some five thousand. When the program got underway, King spoke about how the protest was motivated not simply by Mrs. Parks's arrest, but by many events that go deep down into the archives of history. We have known humiliation, we have known abusive language, we have been plunged into the abyss of oppression. And we decided to rise up only with the weapon of protest. It is one of the greatest glories of America that we have the right of protest.

There are those who would try to make of this a hate campaign. This is not a war between the white and the Negro but a conflict between justice and injustice. This is bigger than the Negro race revolting against the white. We are not just trying to improve the Negro of Montgomery but the whole of Montgomery.

If we are arrested every day, if we are exploited every day, if we are trampled over every day, don't ever let anyone pull you so low as to hate them. We must use the weapon of love. We must have compassion and understanding for those who hate us. We must realize so many people are taught to hate us that they are not totally responsible for their hate.

The mass indictments drew more national attention to the Montgomery protest than had any earlier events, even the bombing of King's home. For the first time, major newspapers such as *The New York Times* and the *New York Herald Tribune* carried front-page stories on the boycott, and King's Thursday night speech was his first to receive extensive national press coverage. Even network television began covering events there, with one ABC commentator comparing the protesters to Gandhi and the bankruptcy of white Montgomery's position to that of the British in India.[44]

Reporters were not the only people whose attention was drawn to the protest movement. In New York other race activists besides the NAACP took a growing interest in the events in Alabama. One who had a special curiosity was Bayard Rustin, a longtime advocate of nonviolent protest, who was a close associate of A. Philip Randolph, president of the Brotherhood of Sleeping Car Porters and the most noted national black leader. Rustin had taken part in a 1947 bus protest, the "Journey of Reconciliation," which had attempted to desegregate interstate bus facilities in the South. Rustin was intrigued with the Montgomery protest, and spoke with Randolph and other activists—Norman Thomas, James Farmer, and A. J. Muste—about his desire to take a firsthand look. With proper advice, he argued, the Montgomery movement could be expanded into a regionwide effort that would implement a boycott of segregated buses throughout the South. Randolph and the others shared his interest in Montgomery, but some cautioned against Rustin making a visit there. His public record, they pointed out, included a brief membership in the Young Communist League, a prison term for draft resistance, and a conviction three years earlier for homosexual activity with two other men in a parked car. Any or all of those could be used to smear the Montgomery leadership should Rustin become associated with them publicly.

Rustin, with the support of Randolph and Muste, won out over those objections. He arrived in Montgomery on Tuesday, February 21, just as the indictments were being issued. Carrying letters of introduction to King and Abernathy, he found the Kings out of town, but located Abernathy and Nixon. He discussed the protest with them, mingled with people Wednesday as those who had been indicted crowded around the courthouse, and attended the Thursday night mass meeting. On Friday he attended a transportation committee meeting, and on Saturday met with ACHR Executive Director Robert Hughes. On Sunday morning he heard King preach a decidedly optimistic sermon at Dexter, "Faith in Man." White southerners should not be hated, King said. "Believe that the most prejudiced mind in Montgomery, in America, can become a living mind—a mind of goodwill." The MIA would triumph in its effort, and the consequences "will be world-shaking," he stated. "But our victory will not be a victory for Montgomery's Negroes alone. It will be a victory for justice, a victory for fair play and a victory for democracy." With a "spirit of love and protest," the boycott would go forward. "Don't get weary. Don't lose faith in me. My faith in man is, at bottom, a faith in God."

The arrival of Rustin and other outside visitors made many of the MIA leaders wary. Holt Street pastor A. W. Wilson pointedly told reporters that the protest was a local movement and not for outside agitators. Birmingham editor Jackson observed that some of the visitors "are offering services which if accepted by the protest group could obviously damage and set back their program." In private, Jackson insisted that it would be best for everyone if Rustin left town quickly, and many MIA activists agreed. "We had almost a paranoia about anybody getting involved who was related to any kind of a subversive or questionable organization. We were just on our guard constantly," Robert Graetz remembered. Graetz and others spoke freely with a local air force officer who kept a regular eye on boycott developments, and Graetz didn't think twice when an FBI agent introduced himself and said, "If you don't mind, I'll be checking in with you occasionally."

Although outside contributions had increased dramatically, including a $500 check from the national NAACP, the MIA was leery of many of its new friends. The organization welcomed a call for federal action from the bishops of the AME church, but voted against sending a representative to a scheduled New York rally called by Adam Powell to highlight a planned one-hour nationwide work stoppage in support of the boycott. Martin King, though friendly toward Rustin, appreciated his colleagues' fears. "We have to be very careful that no one exploits this movement," he told Rustin and his Dexter congregation that Sunday morning. "We need money, but we're not going to do anything and everything to get it. No one is going to get fat on this, and no one is going to get any handouts."

Sunday evening Rustin had his first lengthy conversation with King, at the parsonage. Over coffee in the kitchen, they chatted about nonviolence, or what King, in his public remarks, increasingly was calling "passive resistance." That stance was not chosen "by any single person," King said that weekend. "It was the spontaneous movement of the people," and he and other spokesmen simply "have attempted to give leadership to it." Jo Ann Robinson, whose teaching job forced her to remain in the background, gave a similar description to one black reporter:

> The amazing thing about our movement is that it is a protest of the people. It is not a one man show. It is not the preachers' show. It's the people. The masses of this town, who are tired of being trampled on, are responsible. The leaders couldn't stop it if they wanted to.[45]

On Monday morning, February 27, a second representative of the New York pacifist and racial progress groups joined Rustin in Montgomery. He was Rev. Glenn E. Smiley, a white official of the Fellowship of Reconciliation (FOR), whose top officials, Charles Lawrence and John Swomley, had argued against Rustin's trip. Not wanting to appear in competition with his friend Rustin, Smiley visited several southern cities before arriving in Montgomery to meet with King. A native of Texas and a devout believer in Gandhian nonviolence, Smiley was deeply touched by their first meeting. He took along an armful of books on nonviolence and asked King about his familiarity with the doctrine. "I said to Dr. King," Smiley recalled, "'I'm assuming that you're very familiar and have been greatly influenced by Mahatma Gandhi.' And he was very thoughtful, and he said, 'As a matter of fact, no. I know who the man is. I have read some statements by him, and so on, but I will have to truthfully say'—and this is almost a direct quote . . .—'I will have to say that I know very little about the man.'" King emphasized that he nonetheless admired Gandhi, and Smiley described to him how the essence of nonviolence was a refusal to retaliate against evil, a refusal based on the realization that "the law of retaliation is the law of the multiplication of evil." King expressed interest in the point, and told Smiley they would have to talk further.

Overjoyed at King's receptivity, Smiley wrote to several friends, describing King's limitless potential. Their conversation had been "one of the most glorious, yet tragic interviews I have ever had. . . . I believe that God has called Martin Luther King to lead a great movement here and in the South. But why does God lay such a burden on one so young, so inexperienced, so good? King can be a Negro Gandhi, or he can be made into an unfortunate demagogue destined to swing from a lynch mob's tree." Smiley asked his friends to pray for King's becoming the former, not the latter. Smiley also dispatched a note to King, telling him how he had asked for those prayers. In closing, he quoted Gandhi: "'If one man could achieve the perfect love it is enough to neutralize the hatred of millions.' Who knows? Maybe in Montgomery someone may achieve this perfect love! I am at your service."

King was grateful for Rustin's and Smiley's support, but other MIA leaders worried about what roles the outsiders might seek to play in the protest. On Monday evening one black leader, apparently E. D. Nixon, called A. Philip Randolph in New York to ask some searching questions about why Rustin had been sent to Montgomery. Randolph defended his assistant to the caller, but alerted his New York colleagues to the concerns the Montgomerian had expressed. To some, there was the intimation that Rustin was claiming a significant role in the movement's deliberations, even though he had been there only a week. On Tuesday, Randolph convened a group of some twenty people to consider the question of Rustin's presence in Montgomery. "It was the feeling of this group," John Swomley of FOR immediately wrote to Smiley, "that Bayard should be urged to leave Alabama and return to New York. They felt that there were very serious elements of danger to the movement there for Bayard to be present." Randolph, Farmer, and the others felt that the New York leadership should concentrate on organizing potential national support for the protest, such as that expressed by Powell, the AME church, and the National Council of Churches. "It was the conviction," Swomley said, "that we should not try from the North to train or otherwise run the nonviolent campaign in Montgomery, as Bayard had hoped to do, but rather to expect them to indicate ways in which we could be of help. . . . Phil Randolph indicated that the Montgomery leaders had managed thus far more successfully than any 'of our so-called nonviolence experts' a mass resistance campaign and we should learn from them rather than assume that we knew it all."

Swomley advised Smiley to stay free from any association with Rustin in the eyes of both the MIA and local whites. On Wednesday, February 29, however, Smiley by chance encountered Rustin, along with black reporter William Worthy, at King's MIA office. They exchanged greetings. Smiley mentioned the encounter in a subsequent phone call to FOR's New York office, and was reprimanded for letting it occur. In a subsequent letter, Smiley stressed that no MIA officials other than King knew that he and Rustin were acquaintances.

That same afternoon, Randolph informed Rustin by phone that the New York group advised that he move on. Some of the New York people feared that Rustin would hesitate, and Swomley informed Smiley that he and James Farmer had discussed what ought to be done. "There are some here," Swomley said, "who feel the local leaders ought to know about Bayard's personal problem but dare not mention it over the phone. They ought to know the risks that are being taken and if they are prepared to accept those risks then it is not our responsibility." Rustin and Worthy left for Birmingham on Wednesday evening.

Smiley in the meantime was having a joyful time familiarizing himself with the operations and leadership of the MIA. The organization was overwhelmed, he wrote Swomley, with the flood of outside contributions since the mass indictments. About $12,000 had arrived from out of state within the last two weeks, a great change from the eight weeks prior to the bombing of King's home, when there had been little national interest or support. Smiley felt the black leadership was responsive to his message of nonviolence, and King gave him a personal introduction at the Thursday evening mass meeting, March 1. The response of the 2,500 people warmed the white minister deeply. "Religious fervor is high and they are trying to keep it spiritual," Smiley reported to New York. "Not once was there an expression of hatred towards whites, and the ovation I received when I talked of Gandhi, his campaign, and then of the cross, was tremendous. They do want to do the will of God, and they are sure this is the will of God."

Smiley's advice to those in New York paralleled the thoughts of Randolph and Farmer. "We can learn from their courage and plain earthy devices for building morale, etc., but they can learn more from us, for being so new at this, King runs out of ideas quickly and does the old things again and again. He wants help, and we can give it to him without attempting to run the movement or pretend we know it all." So long as all the outside volunteers understood that, there would be a supporting role for them to play in the Montgomery protest.

Smiley's white face and southern voice allowed him to sample white opinion in Montgomery as well as black. The city's white liberals were in a powerless position, and community tension was increasing as whites feared the MIA would expand its boycott to other enterprises, such as the downtown stores. "Whites are scared stiff and Negroes are calm as cucumbers," Smiley observed. He also appreciated white Montgomery's desire to attribute the protest to some outside influence or subversive force. "'If it's not you,'" some suspicious whites asked him, "'who is it, because we know the niggers are not that smart.'" Many seemed unwilling or unable to view the boycott as an indigenous protest; "they really believed . . . that it had to be some white guy or some New Yorker" orchestrating the entire movement.[46]

Northern reporters, who were arriving in Montgomery in increasing numbers, assessed the situation similarly. "Neither side is yielding an inch to the other," and "there is very little middle ground left." Many of the correspondents emphasized two major themes: the tactical ineptitude exhibited to date by the city officials, and the MIA's talk about loving one's enemies. A chronicling of the whites' errors was straightforward and rather lengthy: the refusal to entertain seriously the initial arguments from Gray and King about a Mobile-style seating plan, the "get tough" policy which ended with the bombing of King's home, and, most egregiously, the mass indictments of the MIA leadership. In private, MIA activists were still puzzled over the city's stubborn refusal to negotiate the modest initial demands, and they quietly rejoiced at how the "get tough" arrests and the bombings had reinvigorated the black community's commitment just when some were beginning to wonder whether a long-term boycott could be sustained. The indictments were yet another tonic.

As Mrs. Durr told a friend, "to arrest all of their leaders was the very thing that was needed to make them more determined."

The reporters found the "boyish-looking" King and his talk of love especially intriguing. "What we are preaching is best described by the Greek word 'agape,'" King told one correspondent, referring to an analysis of different types of love he had read in a graduate school textbook. "Agape" really meant "good will, a redemptive sort of love. That is what we are trying to get our people to feel," King explained. "I don't know that they fully understand it yet, but they are making progress." Whites as well as blacks were victims of racism and segregation. "While I will fight him to get out from under his subjugation, I will also try to understand him and I will not try to defeat him," King said. Montgomery was not really a racial conflict; "the fight here is between light and darkness," not blacks and whites. "The job of us leaders is to make that clear to our people."

King's sense of history and the broader meaning of the protest was striking. "Whether we want to be or not, we are caught in a great moment of history," King told one mass meeting. "It is bigger than Montgomery. . . . The vast majority of the people of the world are colored. . . . Up until four or five years ago" most of them "were exploited by the empires of the west. . . . Today many are free. . . . And the rest are on the road. . . . We are part of that great movement." The target was larger than just segregation. "We must oppose all exploitation. . . . We want no classes and castes. . . . We want to see everybody free."

On a more mundane level, King's principal concern as the boycott entered its fourth month was the upcoming trials and how the legal bills would be paid. The MIA had formalized an agreement with Birmingham attorney Arthur Shores to represent all ninety-odd people at a fee of $100 per person, but no one was sure where that $9,000 would come from. Although contributions continued to pour in, the car pool system was now costing $3,000 per week, and several paid employees manned the MIA's busy office at Lewis's Citizens Club. The national office of the NAACP had been publicizing heavily its legal support of the movement, but the MIA was not fully happy. In early March King wrote Roy Wilkins to voice the concern:

> One of the problems which we are confronting in raising funds is that so many people are giving through mass meetings sponsored by the NAACP [across the country] with the impression that the total legal expense is being defrayed by the National Office. Since this money is being raised in the name of our movement,

King pointedly observed, "we are hoping that the bulk of it will come to support us in our legal struggle."

Wilkins moved quickly to reassure King and repair any breach before it could widen. "It was our intention from the first news of the indictments and mass arrests to assume the entire cost of the defense for those persons arrested and indicted and thus to relieve the MIA of any burden in that respect," Wilkins stated. Beyond that, "we expect also to bear the major part, if not the entire cost, of the bus segregation case challenging the state law," which would be quite expensive and likely to end only at the U.S. Supreme Court. The NAACP also would pay the bills for the appeal of Mrs. Parks's conviction, but could contribute toward the MIA's own operating expenses only in an emergency. Wilkins ended his message to King with a clear warning: "At this time it would be fatal for there to develop any hint of disagreement as to the raising and allocating of funds."[47]

While preparations proceeded for the trial, both Smiley and Rustin continued to advise King. Smiley remained in Montgomery through March 10, and worked to persuade local white ministers to open lines of communication with their black counterparts. Meanwhile, Rustin, who was operating out of Birmingham, intensified his efforts with King. In several lengthy discussions in early March, some in Birmingham rather than Montgomery, the two men reached an accord on how Rustin's New York sponsors best could assist the Montgomery movement. King "is very happy to receive outside help," Rustin notified Randolph on March 7, but was "sensitive" to the southern white notion

> that New Yorkers, northern agitators and communists are in reality leading the fight. It was his view therefore that all communications, ideas, and program that can be developed, as they directly pertain to activities in Montgomery, come through him or Mr. Nixon rather than directly to the Improvement Association. *It was agreed that this was a wise and necessary procedure.* . . . The Improvement Association must give the appearance of developing all of the ideas and strategies used in the struggle.

There were many types of practical assistance that could be given King and the MIA: bicycles for the protesters; "ghostwriters for King, who cannot find time at present to write articles, speeches, etc., himself"; and "keeping an eye on their news coverage and suggesting ideas on what is important and when to emphasize certain elements in the struggle."

Much of Rustin's time was spent discussing nonviolence with King. In one report to his New York colleagues, Rustin asserted that King "is developing a decidedly Gandhi-like view. . . . He is eagerly learning all that he can about nonviolence." In private, though, Rustin, like Smiley, was among the first to admit that King's acceptance of the philosophy was far from complete. "He didn't even use the word at first," Smiley later stressed. "He used 'passive resistance' almost entirely." The point was underscored one day when Rustin and Worthy visited King at the parsonage. Rustin took a seat on the living room couch and Worthy started to sit down in an armchair. Rustin looked over and saw a pistol on the seat. "Watch out, Bill, there's a gun in that chair." Worthy put the pistol aside, and when King came in, Rustin queried him about whether the gun was compatible with a nonviolent movement. Yes, King said, they intended to harm no one unless violently attacked. That night they sat up late as Rustin attempted to persuade King that even the presence of guns was contrary to the philosophy that he was increasingly articulating.

Philosophy aside, Rustin's primary interest remained the creation of a southwide movement to spread the message of Montgomery throughout the region. To Randolph, in early March, he recommended "the establishment of a workshop on nonviolent resistance to be held in June or July in Atlanta to which would be invited *leaders* from many areas of tension in the Deep South." They would discuss the theory and practice of nonviolence, and he hoped the meeting would produce an "ad hoc committee" for ongoing intercity contacts. "King is all for bringing this off," Rustin reported. Perhaps King, Sr., or Morehouse President Mays could host it, for a strong affiliation with the southern black church would be the key to its success, as Montgomery showed. The movement there, Rustin appreciated, "is strong because it is religious as well as political. It has been built upon the most stable institution of the southern Negro community—the Church." Any expansion would have to rely upon that same base.

Just after Rustin's long meeting in Birmingham with King, the *Montgomery Advertiser* ran a front-page story, accompanied by an unidentified photo of Rustin, asserting that some unnamed Negro had been masquerading as a correspondent for several European publications while visiting Montgomery. Those papers denied sending anyone to Alabama, and the *Advertiser* wondered who the man seen associating with the MIA might really be. The headlines sent new fears through the black leadership, but King was not overly perturbed. Rustin assured him that he had not misrepresented himself as a staff writer for anyone, and sent him the text of an article Rustin had written for publication under King's name. It argued that the Montgomery story clearly refuted the standard, negative stereotypes about blacks, and King approved it with hardly any alterations. It appeared in the April issue of *Liberation,* the first item ever published under King's name.[48]

With the antiboycott trials scheduled to begin on Monday, March 19, solicitor Thetford and the defense lawyers reached agreement that the first of the ninety-odd defendants to be tried would be the MIA president, King. The prosecution's intent, made clear early the first morning, was to prove that the MIA had instigated and maintained the boycott without "just cause or legal excuse," that illegal black violence had helped enforce the boycott, and that King had led the MIA's effort—all in violation of the state antiboycott statute. Although prosecutor Thetford had had two city detectives looking into the MIA's early activities, and though several members, including Rufus Lewis, had been called to testify before the grand jury, the prosecution had little real evidence about how the protest had originated. Thetford called bus manager Bagley, Holt Street's Reverend Wilson, and MIA Financial Secretary Erna Dungee in an unsuccessful effort to trace the start of the movement. Wilson could not recall who had set up the first mass meeting at his church, and had an equally fuzzy recollection of when the MIA had been established. Thetford had considerably more success in proving through the MIA's subpoenaed financial records that the organization had put together and funded the car pool system. Mayor Gayle testified that the MIA had negotiated with him over ending the protest, further evidence that they had conspired to boycott the buses. Lastly, in the second day of prosecution testimony, Thetford mounted a weak attempt to link the MIA to the December incidents of shooting at buses.

The defense, fully expecting that Judge Eugene W. Carter would find King guilty no matter what the evidence, concentrated its efforts on giving a full and accurate portrayal of both the abuse suffered by black bus riders and the peaceful character of the MIA's protest. Mrs. Thelma Glass of the Women's Political Council testified about her group's long and unsuccessful efforts to improve the buses, and others of the twenty-eight defense witnesses described the humiliations they had been subjected to on the buses. Then, Arthur Shores called King to the stand. He asked about King's speeches at the various mass meetings, and King testified he had never urged people not to ride the buses, but just "to let your conscience be your guide." He commented on the car pool, the negotiations, and described how the MIA firmly opposed violence. Prosecutor Thetford, on cross-examination, asked if King had called the initial Monday boycott, or if he knew who had. King said no. He queried King about his own experiences on the buses, and King stated he had ridden them only once since he had lived in Montgomery.

On Thursday, March 22, with all testimony complete, Judge Carter immediately announced the verdict: guilty as charged. He would fine King $500, plus $500 court costs. Alternatively, King could choose 386 days in jail. King's attorneys announced they would appeal, and King was freed on a $1,000 bond. Shores indicated he expected the appeal to take more than a year, and the prosecution announced that the other trials would be held in abeyance until King's conviction was reviewed by higher courts.

Trial sessions had been crowded, with MIA spectators wearing cloth crosses on their lapels reading "Father, Forgive Them." When King exited the courthouse that Thursday afternoon following his conviction, a crowd of more than three hundred people cheered him. "We will continue to protest in the same spirit of nonviolence and passive resistance, using the weapon of love," King told them and the dozens of newsmen. That evening, to the three thousand people gathered at Holt Street church for the mass meeting, he urged the people to keep up their spirits despite his conviction. "Let us not lose faith in democracy. For with all of its weaknesses, there is a ground and a basis of hope in our democratic creed."

King's conviction made front-page news across the country and increased the amount of press coverage the Montgomery protest was receiving. Once again, white Montgomery's efforts to stifle the boycott had backfired, and correspondents reported another renewal of the protesters' determination. King himself held a press conference the day after his conviction, and one reporter asked him if his role in the protest ever at times made him afraid. King answered:

No, I'm not. My attitude is that this is a great cause. This is a great issue that we are confronted with and the consequences for my personal life are not particularly important. It is the triumph for the cause that I am concerned about, and I have always felt that ultimately along the way of life an individual must stand up and be counted and be willing to face the consequences, whatever they are. If he is filled with fear, he cannot do it. And my great prayer is always that God will save me from the paralysis of crippling fear, because I think when a person lives with the fear of the consequences for his personal life, he can never do anything in terms of lifting the whole of humanity and solving many of the social problems that we confront.

The strength and freedom he had found that Friday night eight weeks earlier, sitting at his kitchen table, remained with him, as it always would.[49]

The following weekend, King traveled to New York for his first northern speaking engagements since he had become a front-page figure. Addressing 2,500 at Brooklyn's Concord Baptist Church, King spoke for eighty-five minutes on how black Montgomery was fighting injustice by means of "passive resistance." In India, Gandhi had used it "to break loose from the political and economic domination by the British and brought the British Empire to its knees. . . . Let's now use this method in the United States." To one black interviewer, though, King stressed that the Montgomery method was not principally a derivative from India. "I have been a keen student of Gandhi for many years. However, this business of passive resistance and nonviolence is the gospel of Jesus. I went to Gandhi through Jesus."

Upon King's return to Montgomery, the MIA began to tackle two new efforts: a block-by-block canvassing of black Montgomery aimed at increasing the number of registered black voters, and an expansion of the car pool system into a more extensive jitney bus service, using station wagons bought with contributions from the many new national supporters. For a second time, the MIA applied to the city commission for a transportation franchise, and again the application was rejected. At the same time, however, the existing difference of opinion between the commission and the City Lines bus company broke into the open when National City Lines President Roy Fitzgerald told California reporters that his company was caught "in the middle of a situation we can do nothing about. . . . We would be tickled if the law were changed."

Mid-April was a relatively quiet time for the protest, and King took the opportunity to enjoy a brief vacation with his family. He also traveled to Birmingham, Chicago, Columbus, and Dallas for a series of speaking engagements, and enjoyed a four-day visit with his old Crozer friend J. Pius Barbour. The older man was astounded by the changes the young minister had undergone. "King practically lived with me for three years," he remarked, "but he is not the King I knew. He has grown twenty years in about five. He is almost to a fault exceedingly retiring; he wanders around in a daze asking himself: Why has God seen fit to catapult me into such a situation."

Then, on April 23, newspapers reported that the U.S. Supreme Court had affirmed a federal appellate court ruling striking down segregated seating on the municipal buses of Columbia, South Carolina. Upon receipt of the news, Montgomery City Lines announced that its drivers would no longer enforce segregation, effective immediately. For a moment, it seemed that the boycott would be over. Then, Montgomery Mayor Gayle angrily announced that the city would continue to enforce segregation, and that any bus drivers who failed to do so would be subject to arrest. National City Lines' legal vice-president, B. W. Franklin, responded by saying that the company would stand behind any drivers whom the city tried to prosecute.

King and the MIA looked on with bemusement as the internecine warfare broke out among their opponents. King announced on the twenty-fourth that the boycott would continue, pending clarification of the legal situation, and at the Thursday night mass meeting on April 26, some three thousand people unanimously affirmed a resolution calling for the protest to continue at least until May 11, when the federal court suit Gray had filed would be tried in Montgomery. King declared that "we are grateful to the bus company for their stand," and stated that the MIA would consider its number three demand satisfied whenever the bus company promised to give equal consideration to both black and white driver applicants.

The legal maneuvering continued as the city commission filed suit in state court, seeking a temporary restraining order against the bus company to maintain segregation. Company manager Bagley suffered a serious heart attack, and company attorney Crenshaw resigned from his role. State Judge Walter B. Jones granted the city's request for the order against the company, and King stated that the MIA was simply "waiting and hoping. Our whole strategy is based on the May 11 trial."

That hearing, in front of Federal Judges Richard T. Rives, Seybourn H. Lynne, and Frank M. Johnson, Jr., took only one day. The four black female plaintiffs, plus Gayle and Sellers, were among the few witnesses called. The panel reserved their decision, and the MIA was uncertain that a majority of those three Alabama white men would vote to strike down segregation.[50]

The MIA also was troubled by two festering internal problems. First, many participants had realized that·the reimbursement system for car pool expenses was extremely vulnerable to abuse. King resolved that the transportation committee required a full-time supervisor, and the board chose Alabama State Professor Benjamin J. Simms for the new role. Simms instituted tighter controls, and the problems all but vanished.

Second, some voices within the organization also were complaining that only a few officers, principally King, were filling the MIA's speaking invitations. Those criticisms remained private, but some, like Treasurer Nixon, wondered whether all of the honorariums were making their way to the MIA's treasury.

In public, King increasingly talked of how the MIA needed to move beyond simply bus segregation. To one mass meeting, he stated that "until we as a race learn to develop our power, we will get nowhere. We've got to get political power and economic power for our race." King went beyond exhortation, recommending to the MIA executive board that "a strong emphasis . . . be placed on increasing our political power through voting and increasing our economic power through the establishment of a bank." A banking committee was appointed to seek a federal charter for a building and loan association, and King moved to put further resources behind the voter registration effort, led by Rufus Lewis. "The key to the whole solution of the South's problem," King asserted in early May,

> is the ballot. Through the ballot many of the other problems will be solved. Until the colored man comes to this point he will have a hard struggle. When he gets the ballot, he can wield political power and come into his own. . . . The chief weapon in our fight for civil rights is the vote.

The bus boycott "might possibly last several more months," and "the present relaxed phase" of it afforded the MIA an opportunity to plan ahead for other initiatives.[51]

In early June, as the relative quietude continued, the Kings and Abernathys decided to seek a brief respite from the tensions of Montgomery. Together, the four of them set out by car on a two-week vacation to California and the Southwest. They hoped it would be an opportunity to relax and see a part of the country none of them had visited before. However, even after they got out of the Deep South and into Texas and the Southwest, the two couples had a difficult time finding motels that would accept black guests. "It spoiled the trip for him and for all of us," Coretta recalled, "because we had looked forward to seeing the beauty of the west and then having to go through all of this."

Just as they set out, the good news reached them that the three-judge federal court had voted two to one to strike down the segregated seating practices. However, the city vowed to appeal the ruling to the U.S. Supreme Court, and the boycott remained in place. Then, just after the couples reached Los Angeles, the MIA's office called to report that Rev. Uriah J. Fields, who had recently been replaced as the organization's recording secretary, had alleged at a mass meeting, with reporters present, that the MIA had misused funds and that some of its officers had been lining their pockets. Leaving Coretta and the Abernathys in Los Angeles, King flew back to Montgomery.

Fury at Fields was running high in the black community. His church, Bell Street Baptist, voted to fire him as pastor, and many threats were being voiced. Although E. D. Nixon, for one, felt privately that there was more than some truth to Fields's charges, substantial pressure was placed upon the young minister to retract his allegations. One week after he had voiced his claims, Fields appeared before a derisive crowd at another mass meeting to recant and apologize. He asserted that his outburst had been based upon personality clashes with others, not King, and that there had been no financial misconduct. King asked the crowd to forgive Fields, and grudgingly they accepted his call. The crisis passed, and King rejoined his wife and the Abernathys for the conclusion of their trip.[52]

At the end of June, King traveled to San Francisco to give a major address at the NAACP's annual convention. In that speech, as in other appearances before northern audiences, King combined a description of the Montgomery protest with an exposition of his religious beliefs. He argued that Montgomery showed there was a "new Negro," someone who no longer would accept the depersonalizing experiences of segregation. Montgomery also indicated that rank-and-file blacks themselves could act to advance the race's goals, rather than relying exclusively on lawyers and litigation to win incremental legal gains. King stated that one should avoid both "extreme optimism" and "extreme pessimism" about the struggle for integration, and adopt a "realistic attitude" about the future, but he also asserted, "I have no doubt that by 1963 we will have won the legal battle." King also denounced "the madness of militarism" and "an economic system which takes necessities from the masses to give luxuries to the classes," but reminded each of his audiences that in all its efforts, the black movement would remain nonviolent.

Although the NAACP convention accorded King an honored place, Executive Secretary Wilkins and other officials made it clear that the organization had grave doubts about whether nonviolent mass resistance in the Montgomery style could really add much to the pursuit of civil rights, which they viewed as principally a legal struggle. King, who privately believed that the NAACP put too exclusive an emphasis on the legal route, studiously avoided any public disagreements.[53]

In Montgomery the boycott continued with a steady effectiveness. By midsummer, with twenty-two station wagons in full-time service, the car pool system had achieved a new level of efficiency. King continued to keep a busy speaking schedule, and wrote to Smiley in early July to decline several possible appearances because of "the strain under which I am working." My doctor, he explained, "is insisting that I slow up and stop living such a rushed schedule." Just a few days later, on July 11, King went to the Montgomery railroad station to take a train northward to Nashville, for Fisk University's annual race relations institute. Coretta and Robert Williams were with him as he started to enter the main waiting room. A Montgomery policeman stepped in front of King, barring the door, and told him that the room was for white people only. King spoke back, and for upwards of five minutes, the two men debated the practice that the officer was attempting to enforce. Finally, with King's train ready to depart, the policeman allowed the three of them to pass through the room without pausing. If King ever tried it again, though, the officer promised to "let me have it." Like the car trip to Los Angeles, it was one more reminder of how regularly racial distinctions impeded everyday life.

King spent most of late July and much of August on the road. His many speaking engagements were repetitive and tiring work, but the appearances helped keep the MIA's bank accounts in the black. Old Crozer friend Ed Whitaker, whom King visited in northern New York in late July, could see the effects. "He was weary, very much weary because of the stress and strain which the movement had put him under." King talked about the constant anonymous threats, and how his early morning communication with God six months earlier had enabled him to persevere. That experience, Whitaker sensed, was "the key to how he could endure and face what was the reality of the situation."

Late in August, Montgomery's bombers struck again, this time damaging the home of white pastor Robert Graetz. Then, on September 8, while King was on a speaking tour in Denver, the insurance policies on seventeen of the MIA's station wagons suddenly were canceled. Without the coverage, the vehicles could not be used in the car pool, and private autos had to be employed to fill the void. Several weeks passed before new coverage was obtained.

With the insurance problem solved, the car pool resumed normal operations as the MIA awaited word of when the U.S. Supreme Court might rule on the appeal that Montgomery had made of the June federal court decision. Weekly expenses had risen to $5,000, due to increased auto repair expenses, and outside contributions had declined substantially. Nevertheless, the protest was in fine shape, King told Rustin, and "the people are just as enthusiastic now as they were in the beginning." He expected the Supreme Court to affirm the earlier decision by Christmas or January at the latest, and he and the other Montgomery leaders were working hard "to instill within the minds of the people the great implications of the bus protest. We are seeking to show that it is much larger than a bus situation . . . that it is just one aspect of the total question of integration in the South."[54]

King received yet another reminder of that point on September 27, while flying to speak at Virginia's Hampton Institute. When his flight northward from Atlanta was delayed, the airline gave each passenger a voucher for a free meal in the terminal restaurant. King, the only black person, was refused a seat in the main room of the Dobbs House restaurant. King resisted the manager's order to eat in a rear room, and told the man that he was an interstate passenger, and that previous court rulings barred such discrimination in interstate commerce. His argument had no effect on the manager, who cited state and local ordinances. Passenger King remained hungry.

October began as a quiet month. King was on the road a good deal, and apologized for it in his annual report to the Dexter congregation: "I have often lagged behind in my pastoral duties." Then, on October 26, two rabid segregationists, attorney John P. Kohn and labor leader Jack D. Brock, suggested to the city commission that an injunction be obtained to halt the MIA's car pool as an infringement on the bus company's franchise. The commission indicated it would consider the move. King, in Boston for a speech, hurried home when word of the impending action reached him. On October 30 the city filed its request for such an order with State Judge Carter. Three days later the MIA asked Federal Judge Frank Johnson to bar Carter from issuing such an order, but Johnson declined to intervene, and set a hearing for November 14, the day after Carter was scheduled to rule on the city's request.

On Tuesday, November 13, King and the other MIA leaders assembled in Carter's courtroom for a daylong hearing on the city's request to ban the car pool. The outcome was not in doubt, and King was depressed at the thought of losing their system. "I was faltering in my faith and my courage," he recalled, and the MIA was uncertain if the protest could be sustained. Then, during a brief late-morning recess, Associated Press reporter Rex Thomas came up to King and handed him a brief teletype story. Datelined Washington, it announced that hours earlier the Supreme Court had affirmed the lower court decision ending bus segregation in Montgomery. In their darkest hour, the protesters had triumphed. Joyfully, King passed the word to his colleagues. They sat through the remainder of the hearing, and, as expected, Carter immediately issued the order the city had requested. Nonetheless, King and the MIA were jubilant. They announced that the black community would return to the buses whenever the Supreme Court's order formally was delivered to Montgomery, which King guessed would take only a few days. "The universe is on the side of justice," he declared.

The following day, Federal Judge Johnson again declined to intercede in the state court proceeding, and bus manager Bagley announced that segregation would be enforced until the May injunction the city had obtained against the company was dissolved. The MIA executive board met, planned two simultaneous mass meetings for that evening, and voted to terminate the protest, but delay any actual return to the buses until the Supreme Court order actually took effect. The joyous crowds at the mass meetings endorsed that decision.

Only a day or two later did the MIA learn that the Supreme Court order would not be so quick in reaching Montgomery. The losing party, the city, had the option of petitioning the high court for a reconsideration, and had done so. Until that last-gasp effort was dismissed, the order would not take effect. With the car pool now banned, the MIA scrambled to institute a neighborhood-based "share a ride" system, with Rev. Solomon S. Seay as informal coordinator. On November 19, the MIA petitioned Supreme Court Justice Hugo L. Black to make the Court's order of the thirteenth effective immediately, but Black rejected the request the following day.[55]

While the Montgomery black community anxiously awaited the arrival of the Court's final order, the MIA made preparations for a weeklong "Institute on Nonviolence and Social Change" that had been scheduled for December 3–9. Although some noted outsiders, such as Mahalia Jackson, Lillian Smith, and Rev. J. H. Jackson of the National Baptist Convention, would be in attendance, many of the sessions were designed to prepare black Montgomerians for riding on integrated buses. Most of the visitors from outside Montgomery were other young black southern ministers who headed up protest organizations or civic leagues in their own cities: Joseph E. Lowery of Mobile, Theodore Jemison from Baton Rouge, C. K. Steele, who was leading a successful but little-heralded bus protest in Tallahassee, and Fred L. Shuttlesworth of Birmingham, who had founded a new local protest group, the Alabama Christian Movement, when state legal harassment had closed down the NAACP in Alabama several months earlier. Though most of the men had known each other through church functions, the Montgomery meetings gave them a better opportunity to get acquainted and share ideas.

King delivered the opening address on Monday night, December 3, at Holt Street Baptist Church, where, almost exactly one year earlier, he had given his first speech as the newly chosen president of the MIA. "In my little way and with my stumbling words," King told the crowd of 1,500, "I would like to express my deepest appreciation to each of you for following my leadership." The success and determination of the Montgomery protest signified a "revolutionary change in the Negro's evaluation of himself," and the triumph had shown how valuable mass nonviolent resistance could be. The real goal, however, was not to *defeat* the white man, but "to awaken a sense of shame within the oppressor and challenge his false sense of superiority. . . . The end is reconciliation; the end is redemption; the end is the creation of the beloved community" where all men would treat each other as brothers and equals. "There are great resources of goodwill in the southern white man that we must somehow tap," King asserted, and we must work to "speed up the coming of the inevitable."

After the institute week, preparations continued for the desegregation of Montgomery's buses. Two staff members of the Southern Regional Council who visited the city found an atmosphere of calm and widespread agreement that the change would take place peacefully. They visited with a number of MIA leaders, including King, who told them that "things are quiet. . . . The power structure of Montgomery is concerned about this situation. They seem more alert than they have in the past. . . . The Mayor has said quietly that he would not permit violence." Other sources endorsed King's perception, and many praised him as being primarily responsible for the air of calmness.

Finally, on December 17, the Supreme Court rejected the city's last appeal. The actual order arrived in the city on Thursday, December 20, and U.S. marshals served the writs on the white officials shortly before noon. That night the MIA held two mass meetings, one at Holt Street and one at St. John AME, and King again reminded the crowds to follow the "Integrated Bus Suggestions" that had been distributed to all. Drafted by Glenn Smiley, they recommended "a calm and loving dignity" and more specifically instructed: "Do not deliberately sit by a white person, unless there is no other seat." The time had come, King said, to "move from protest to reconciliation."

The next morning, Montgomery City Lines resumed full service on all of its routes. At 5:45 A.M., Abernathy, Nixon, Mrs. Parks, and Smiley gathered at the King home on South Jackson. Ten minutes later, when the first bus of the day pulled up at a nearby corner, Martin Luther King, Jr., was the first passenger to the door. He paid his fare and selected a seat toward the front of the bus. Glenn Smiley, the white Texan, sat down next to him. As news photographers snapped pictures, the bus pulled away from the curb. Black Montgomery, after 382 days of mass effort, had achieved its goal.[56]

2

The Birth of SCLC, 1957–1959

The first two days of Montgomery's integrated bus service were without incident. Then, at 1:30 A.M. on Sunday morning, December 23, a shotgun blast ripped through the front door of King's home. The floodlights were on, but no watchman was present. King, Coretta, and Yoki were asleep, and no one was injured. King chose not to call the police, but he did announce the incident to his Dexter congregation later that morning. "It may be that some of us may have to die," he solemnly remarked. That evening, at a mass meeting, he declared that "I would like to tell whoever did it that it won't do any good to kill me" and announced that the MIA was looking beyond bus integration. "We have just started our work. . . . We must have integrated schools. . . . That is when our race will gain full equality. We cannot rest in Montgomery until every public school is integrated." It marked the first occasion any MIA officer had publicly articulated that goal.

Christmas passed peacefully, but on the evening of December 28, two buses were fired upon by snipers. One black rider suffered a minor wound. Police Commissioner Sellers immediately halted bus service, and the next morning the commission resolved that no buses would run after 5:00 P.M. One more bus was fired upon that day, and Sellers then announced that Montgomery would hire twenty additional policemen to protect the vehicles. Meanwhile, anonymous leaflets urging blacks to run King out of town began to appear around the city.[1]

Martin and Coretta were on their way to Baltimore, where King was to speak at an Omega Psi Phi fraternity convention banquet and receive their "Citizen of the Year" award. Bayard Rustin met them at the airport, and introduced three white friends who were with him. Harris and Clare Wofford were a young couple who had traveled to India and written a book on Gandhian nonviolence. Wofford had been the first white man to graduate from Howard University Law School, had spent time in

Alabama, and, in November, 1955, had given an address at Hampton Institute that the black press reported with headlines such as GANDHI METHODS URGED FOR CIVIL RIGHTS FIGHT. King had heard E. D. Nixon speak of Wofford, and was pleased to meet him. Rustin's third white companion, Stanley D. Levison, was a white New York attorney who had been active in a group called "In Friendship" that had been raising funds for southern activists since early 1956. Coretta had met him several weeks earlier at a New York benefit the group had sponsored for the MIA, and King had heard Rustin speak of how Levison and another leader of In Friendship, Ella Baker, were among his closest New York friends. Rustin had told both Wofford and Levison that he would like to secure funds for King to travel to India and Africa, and they chatted about the possibilities as they drove to Baltimore.

After King had delivered his address, a black reporter asked if the new spate of violence in Montgomery made him fearful. No, King said. "Once you become dedicated to a cause, personal security is not the goal. It is greater than that. What will happen to you personally does not matter. My cause, my race, is worth dying for." King and his party headed back to Washington in the Woffords' car. Rustin and Levison told King that they and Baker had spent a recent evening discussing Rustin's idea of using the Montgomery movement as the basis for a wider civil rights initiative across the South. The attendance at the recent Institute on Nonviolence and Social Change clearly showed that other southern activists shared King's desire for more interaction, and with the Montgomery boycott complete, now was a propitious time for calling a southwide meeting. Levison and Rustin had drafted a memo detailing the merits and broader possibilities of a "Southern Leadership Conference on Transportation," and King agreed with their suggestions. Rustin promised to draw up an agenda while King contacted other southern leaders and prepared a call for a meeting.

At one point, someone joked about how the white opposition, given its many blunders during the past year, might give the movement another boost by actually jailing King at some point. Coretta quickly halted the laughter by remarking that no southern jail was a joke, and how she had a recurring fear that her husband would be killed. Her comments left a frosty silence, and the tension was broken only when King himself spoke up. "If anybody had asked me a year ago to head this movement," he said, "I tell you very honestly that I would have run a mile to get away from it. I had no intention of being involved in this way." King paused, and then went on:

As I became involved, and as people began to derive inspiration from their involvement, I realized that the choice leaves your own hands. The people expect you to give them leadership. You see them growing as they move into action, and then you know you no longer have a choice, you can't decide *whether* to stay in it or get out of it, you *must* stay in it.[2]

From Washington, Martin and Coretta traveled to Atlanta for the New Year's holiday. At noon on January 1, King spoke to an Emancipation Day crowd of seven thousand at Big Bethel AME church, praising the NAACP and describing how the Congress and president needed to activate themselves on the subject of racial justice. He articulated the same themes in an evening address in Birmingham, and then returned to Montgomery.

Preparations moved ahead for the southwide meeting Rustin had long been hoping for. King and his colleagues chose January 10 and 11 as the dates, and King, Sr., agreed to host the sessions at Ebenezer church. Rustin, in New York, was busy drafting seven "working papers" that would serve as the basis for discussions. He talked about them with Levison and Baker, never hiding his belief that "the movement needed a sustaining mechanism that could translate what we had learned during the bus boycott into a broad strategy for protest in the South." It was "vital," Rustin asserted, "that we maintain the psychological momentum Montgomery had generated."

In the actual papers to be presented to those attending the meetings, Rustin was more reserved. In the first one, he said there were two initial questions that had to be addressed: "Do we need a coordinating group for advice and council among the present protest groups?", and "Should such a council try to stimulate bus protests in other areas of the South?" He made little secret that he thought the answer to each question should be yes.

Although officially entitled the "Southern Negro Leaders Conference on Transportation and Nonviolent Integration," Rustin's agenda had a wide sweep. True, bus integration across the South was the initial focus, but one principal lesson of Montgomery, Rustin stressed, was an economic one: "The bus companies are not prepared to lose money to save segregation." City Lines had been a bit slow in coming around, but Rustin's scenario was an accurate analysis: "The political leadership and the bus officials part company. The opposition is divided. The bus companies may be prepared to make common cause with protest leaders."

Buses, however, would be only the first step toward a wider struggle. "We must understand," Rustin wrote, "that our refusal to accept jim crow in specific areas challenges the entire social, political and economic order that has kept us second class citizens. . . . Those who oppose us, understand this." As the struggle expanded, Rustin explained, there would be two principal methods to employ: voting power and mass direct action. In regard to the first, there would have to be an extensive effort to increase black voter registration across the South. But "until the Negro votes on a large scale, we shall have to rely more and more on mass direct action as the one realistic political weapon." Montgomery showed that "the center of gravity has shifted from the courts to community action," and the leaders should realize that the people, and not simply their lawyers, could win their own freedom. The question then would be what forms of mass action should be employed. Should local communities go beyond the MIA's tactics and adopt "extra-legal mass action?" Also, "under what circumstances are mass arrests strategically desirable or necessary?" Finally, should the leadership try to establish a "small, disciplined group of nonviolent shock troops" to lead such efforts? "Can the movement proceed through the next stages without such a group?" Rustin asked.[3]

King, Abernathy, Rustin, and Baker were still polishing Rustin's handiwork in Atlanta the evening before the meetings were to commence. Back in Montgomery, however, a different group had something else in mind. At 1:55 A.M. on Thursday morning, January 10, a bomb demolished the home of Rev. Robert S. Graetz. The family fled uninjured, only to find a second, defective explosive lying in the yard. Moments later, another bomb struck the Abernathys' parsonage. Then, in rapid succession, four additional explosions rocked Montgomery as a series of black churches, including Abernathy's, were heavily damaged. Juanita Abernathy immediately telephoned her husband at the King family home in Atlanta, and Abernathy and King were on the phone throughout the early morning hours, learning further details of the bombings. They reluctantly concluded that they had no choice but to return home and give help to their shaken community.

In their absence, Fred Shuttlesworth and Coretta King, who remained in Atlanta, presided at the sessions, with Rustin and Baker looking on. The meetings were closed to the press, and some participants objected when a white man, Will D. Campbell of the National Council of Churches, sought admittance. Rustin ascertained his credentials, reassured the others, and thus ensured at least token integration. The discussions were lively and loud, but with King and Abernathy absent, Rustin's working papers did not exert the formative influence they otherwise might have.

On Friday, the conference participants, almost all of whom were ministers, approved "A Statement to the South and Nation." In midafternoon, King returned for the final hours of the gathering, was named temporary chairman of the group, and held a press conference to announce the statement and other initiatives. The statement extolled the virtues of nonviolence, but the tangible actions consisted of three telegrams the group dispatched to President Dwight D. Eisenhower, Vice-President Richard M. Nixon, and Attorney General Herbert Brownell. The one to Eisenhower, saying that "a state of terror prevails" in the South, asked him to make a speech advocating compliance with the *Brown* decision. Nixon was asked to make a tour of the South and familiarize himself with violence against blacks. The message to Brownell asked him to meet with black representatives to discuss possible federal protective actions.

King also told reporters that the group would be a continuing body, and that it would next meet in New Orleans on a date yet to be chosen. One questioner asked if King thought all southern buses would be integrated by 1960, and King responded, "I hope sooner than that." He emphasized that the group would tackle other forms of segregation, such as in schools, but that no specific plans had been formed. Change at the local level, he said, could best be won through interracial negotiations. "Wherever it is possible, we want to avoid court cases in this integration struggle."[4]

In the wake of the bombings, the Montgomery City Commission suspended all bus service indefinitely. Governor Folsom announced a $2,000 reward for information on the attacks, and many white Montgomerians condemned the violence. The black community was angry at the bombings and fearful that the commission might use the violence as an excuse for permanently halting bus service, thus denying the MIA the victory it had won. Privately, Federal District Judge Frank M. Johnson voiced the same fears to U.S. Deputy Attorney General William Rogers in Washington, and told FBI officials that the city was not doing all it could to prevent the violence. When King called the local FBI office to ask for federal help and complain that blacks had no confidence in the city police, however, he was informed that no investigation had been authorized.

King was growing tired from the travels and tensions, and was troubled by the new wave of violence. "I began to feel a personal sense of guilt for everything that was happening," he later wrote. That Monday evening, King presided at a mass meeting at Bethel Baptist Church. While leading the prayer, he became caught up in "an emotion I could not control." Speaking to God, and with an emotional crowd responding, King spoke of the violent dangers the protesters still faced, saying, "If anyone should be killed, let it be me." He "got much more emotional than he ever got with his speeches," one MIA colleague remembered, and "it was obvious that he was at the point of exhaustion. . . . He was going to probably just pass out if he kept on going." King was unable to continue, and E. D. Nixon and another friend helped him to a chair. Reporters who were present immediately publicized the event, one writing that King had "collapsed at the rostrum."

The next day, meeting with the press to criticize a white initiative to set up a private, segregated bus line, King was at some pains to deny that he had collapsed the evening before. He asserted that he had halted the prayer because of too much emotion throughout the audience. "It was simply a matter of people breaking down. I decided it was time to stop the prayer because the audience had gone almost to pandemonium. I shed no tears nor was I overcome with emotion. To the contrary, I was calm and balanced throughout." In subsequent years, when the incident was more distant in time, King admitted the accuracy of the eyewitness accounts and abandoned his denial.[5]

The collapse at Bethel church was merely one public indication of the increasing strain that both King and the MIA were experiencing. The aftermath of the boycott had brought not celebration, but a run of violence. King, who had looked forward to a respite, found instead that the pace of engagements had quickened. One of his friends observed that King "was noticeably tiring," and believed he was especially troubled by a new series of disagreements within the MIA.

The principal problem was one that had quietly existed for many months: resentment over the considerable personal fame that had come to King because of the protest. E. D. Nixon was the most bitter, but, reflecting back on the Fields incident, he chose not to pick a personal quarrel. Instead, the issue became one of how the MIA would pursue its voter registration efforts. Nixon, whose enthusiasm for the rhetoric of nonviolence was limited, argued for a partisan format. If the MIA would announce an effort to win representation within the Democratic party, perhaps the national committee would lend its support. King and others found such hopes fanciful, and blocked Nixon from soliciting any registration funds in the name of his Progressive Democrats organization. Virginia Durr, who regularly heard Nixon's side of the dispute, noted at the time that Nixon "suffers from the same fate of all old leaders that see a young man come on and take the leadership away from him, and do what he has not been able to do, which is to unite the people around him." Nixon's resentment was especially strong, she felt, because "he feels the boycott was his idea" to begin with. Nixon was not alone in thinking that the MIA of early 1957 was not as democratic as it had been twelve months earlier. Another board member acknowledged that the MIA office had become "a closed operation," and one where "if people outside had been aware of what was going on . . . they could have found all kinds of things to criticize." Further dissension developed over the organization's continued refusal to put Mrs. Parks, a Nixon ally who had lost her seamstress job long before, on the payroll, but that dispute, like the "blazing row" over Nixon's disagreements, stayed behind closed doors. Mrs. Parks "is very, very disgruntled with MLK and really quite bitter," her friend Mrs. Durr wrote, but no incidents were allowed to break the public front of unity.

The increasing conflict took a toll on King. One sympathetic friend stated:

It was almost unbelievable to King that the very people who, a few months ago, were shouting his praises were now asking him for justification for every proposal he put forward. He felt deserted and alone. He told some of his close friends that perhaps he had outlived his usefulness in Montgomery and should leave.

As this supporter acknowledged, "King's colleagues felt that he was taking too many bows and enjoying them," that "he was forgetting that victory . . . had been the result of collective thought and collective action."[6]

Private tribulations and criticism were not King's only ongoing problems. The continued existence of bus service remained in jeopardy, and even when daytime service was resumed, the troublesome 5:00 P.M. curfew on bus runs remained. Also, King received a telegram from the White House informing him that the president would not speak out for desegregation in the manner the Atlanta conference had requested. That was followed by a Justice Department letter saying that the attorney general would not see them because a meeting would "not be helpful or appropriate."

Sunday, January 27, marked the anniversary of King's experience in the kitchen one year earlier. This Sunday morning, Montgomery awoke to learn that twelve sticks of dynamite, with a fuse which had smoldered out, had been found on the porch of the Dexter parsonage. Though King and his family had not been spending the night in the house for several weeks, the murder attempt affected King deeply. In his sermon that morning, King spoke about the experience he had had one year earlier and how it had prepared him to deal with the question of his own fate. "I realize that there were moments when I wanted to give up and I was afraid but You gave me a vision in the kitchen of my house and I am thankful for it." He explained to his listeners how, early in the boycott, "I went to bed many nights scared to death." Then,

> early on a sleepless morning in January, 1956, rationality left me. . . . Almost out of nowhere I heard a voice that morning saying to me, 'Preach the gospel, stand up for truth, stand up for righteousness.' Since that morning I can stand up without fear.
>
> So I'm not afraid of anybody this morning. Tell Montgomery they can keep shooting and I'm going to stand up to them; tell Montgomery they can keep bombing and I'm going to stand up to them. If I had to die tomorrow morning I would die happy because I've been to the mountaintop and I've seen the promised land and it's going to be here in Montgomery.

As before, the vision in the kitchen was a source of inner strength when times were difficult.[7]

Four days later much of Montgomery breathed a sigh of relief as seven young white men were arrested in connection with the series of bombings. King remained tied to a busy travel schedule, speaking in New Orleans one week and traveling to Oberlin College the next. At Oberlin, theologian Harvey Cox, who had invited King, introduced him to James M. Lawson, Jr., a black graduate student who had just returned from spending three years in India. At dinner that night, February 7, King questioned Lawson about his experiences in India. Lawson was a strong and well-informed believer in Gandhian nonviolence, and the two men agreed to keep in touch.

On February 10, King announced that the second meeting of the Atlanta transportation conference group would take place in New Orleans on February 14. In telegrams to those who had attended the first session, King outlined the cold refusals received from Eisenhower and Brownell and advised that the New Orleans gathering issue a further statement. The response was gratifying, and ninety-seven persons gathered at Rev. A. L. Davis's New Zion Baptist Church for the meeting. Officers were elected: King, president, Steele of Tallahassee, first vice-president, Davis, second vice-president, Samuel Williams of Atlanta, third vice-president, Jemison of Baton Rouge, secretary, Medgar W. Evers, an NAACP activist from Jackson, Mississippi, assistant secretary, and Abernathy, treasurer. Shuttlesworth, three representatives of the United Packinghouse Workers, ministers, and a few attorneys from across the South also were in attendance.

The group also resolved to adopt the name Southern Leadership Conference in place of the previous Southern Negro Leaders Conference. More important, King announced that the group would sponsor a pilgrimage to Washington if the president continued to refuse to speak out in support of desegregation in the South. "This will not be a political march," King said. "It will be rooted in deep spiritual faith."

Immediately after the New Orleans meeting, King's portrait appeared on the cover of *Time* magazine. The laudatory profile sketched King's biography and summarized the success of the Montgomery movement. In Montgomery, however, the story received a mixed reception, even in the black community. "There was among some of the Negro leadership," a well-informed black reporter wrote, "an element of resentment and jealousy, a feeling that the article gave King too much credit at the expense of other leaders." The tensions remained strong between E. D. Nixon and King, and Nixon considered resigning from MIA and turning his efforts toward a partisan political effort, but hesitated at a public break. The arrest of the bombers was followed by a halt in the violence against buses, and on February 19, evening service was restored.[8]

Invitations continued to pour in to King, including one from Kwame Nkrumah inviting him to attend the March 5 independence ceremonies of the new West African nation of Ghana. Both the MIA and Dexter offered to help with the travel expenses. King and Coretta flew first to New York, and joined other black American notables—A. Philip Randolph, Adam Powell, Ralph Bunche—who also were going. The long flight gave everyone a chance to get better acquainted. Upon arrival, King was impressed by the modern facilities of the city of Accra. The independence ceremony itself, a moving event, took place at midnight on March 5. There were many dinners and receptions, and King also enjoyed a private lunch with Nkrumah. At one reception, King encountered U.S. Vice-President Richard M. Nixon, the senior American representative at the celebration. King, troubled by the Eisenhower administration's continuing coolness, seized the opportunity. "Mr. Vice-President, I'm very glad to meet you here, but I want you to come visit us down in Alabama where we are seeking the same kind of freedom Ghana is celebrating." Nixon shook his hand, nodded, and said King should come speak with him in Washington sometime.

The Kings' socializing was cut short when they both came down with serious fevers. Nonetheless, his first trip outside the United States, and his first visit to Africa, made a deep impression upon King. It helped him realize, he told one companion, that "there is no basic difference between colonialism and racial segregation"—both were based on the notion of white supremacy. Describing it weeks later, King remarked that American blacks could learn some important lessons from the freedom struggles that Africans had waged against European colonialists. "The oppressor never voluntarily gives freedom to the oppressed. . . . Privileged classes never give up their privileges without strong resistance. . . . Freedom comes only through persistent revolt, through persistent agitation, through persistently rising up against the system of evil."

From Accra, Martin and Coretta traveled to Nigeria, and then to Rome, Geneva, Paris, and London for sightseeing. A highlight in London was lunch with black intellectual C.L.R. James, who marveled at King's description of the Montgomery protest. After two weeks in Europe, King flew back to New York, where he met with A. Philip Randolph and Roy Wilkins to discuss the Washington Pilgrimage.[9]

Five weeks had passed since the Southern Leadership meeting had announced the Pilgrimage. Rustin had ensured that Randolph would respond positively to the proposal, but Wilkins was cool to the idea of mass action. Increasingly he was troubled by what the Southern Leadership organization might mean for the NAACP's own branches in the South. Wilkins knew that Medgar Evers, the NAACP's Mississippi representative, had been elected assistant secretary, and he ordered Evers to "quietly ease out" of the new group. "The NAACP does wish to cooperate with the ministers group," and wanted nothing to arise "to suggest that we are at odds with them," but Wilkins still did not want his subordinates helping to build up this new organization and its young leader.

Less personally, Wilkins also was troubled by King's emphasis on mass action and his criticism of a purely legal approach to change. Wilkins stressed the "limitations" of mass, direct action, and believed that "the particular form of direct action used in Montgomery was effective only for certain kinds of local problems and could not be applied safely on a national scale." King, on the other hand, acknowledged the value of *Brown,* and the need for civil rights statutes, but contended that blacks "must not get involved in legalism [and] needless fights in lower courts." King felt that was "exactly what the white man wants the Negro to do. Then he can draw out the fight. . . . Our job now is implementation. . . . We must move on to mass action . . . in every community in the South, keeping in mind that civil disobedience to local laws is civil obedience to national laws."

The references to civil disobedience were new and infrequent for King, but his emphasis upon such mass actions as the Pilgrimage bothered the NAACP's chief. Nonetheless, Wilkins agreed to another planning session on April 5 in Washington. More than seventy representatives of various groups attended that meeting, and chose May 17, the third anniversary of the *Brown* decision, as the Pilgrimage date. Randolph, Wilkins, and King announced the plans to the press, and stated they expected a minimum of fifty thousand people to participate. The "Prayer Pilgrimage for Freedom" had five objectives: to demonstrate black unity, provide an opportunity for northerners to demonstrate their support, protest ongoing legal attacks on the NAACP by southern states, protest violence in the South, and urge the passage of civil rights legislation. New York Congressman Adam Clayton Powell, who opposed the march, secretly boasted to White House aides that he had prevented any anti-Eisenhower emphasis from emerging, but King and his colleagues had never had such an intent.

In their public remarks, both King and Wilkins underscored that the Pilgrimage was "not a protest march, nor is pressure a dominant factor," as the NAACP chief put it. King spoke of how the Pilgrimage would be an appeal to the nation, and the Congress, to pass a civil rights bill that would give the Justice Department the power to file law suits against discriminatory registration and voting practices anywhere in the South. King told one audience that "I've come to see more and more" the importance of voting rights, but the purpose of the Pilgrimage, he stated, is "to register our protest with Congress, not to make any threats."[10]

Rustin and other organizers spent the balance of April and early May preparing for the Pilgrimage and working to encourage a large turnout. In addition, Rustin and Stanley Levison each prepared drafts for King of the remarks he would make at the Pilgrimage's main event, a rally on the steps of the Lincoln Memorial. Levison's draft emphasized the common interests of black people and the labor movement. Rustin, however, did not like Levison's tone and emphasis. "There is not sufficient spiritual content," he told King. "There is not a clear statement on nonviolence. . . . I hope you will consider using this occasion to call upon Negroes north and south to adhere to nonviolence in work, thought and deed."

King would have only ten minutes, Rustin reminded him, and he should speak about voting, labor cooperation, and, of course, nonviolence. King's primary responsibility, though, was to issue a call for action, and stress

the need to expand the struggle on all fronts. Up to now we have thought of the color question as something which could be solved in and of itself. We know now that while it [is] necessary to say 'No' to racial injustice, this must be followed by a positive program of action:

the struggle for the right to vote, for economic uplift of the people. A part of this is the realization that men are truly brothers, that the Negro cannot be free so long as there are poor and underprivileged white people. . . .

Equality for Negroes is related to the greater problem of economic uplift for Negroes and poor white men. They share a common problem and have a common interest in working together for economic and social uplift. They can and must work together.

Having returned to the same argument he had criticized Levison for emphasizing, Rustin advised King to use his Pilgrimage speech, his first truly national address, to propose such an effort. The Southern Leadership Conference should announce a major meeting for several months hence where southern black leaders and white unionists would "discuss the role of organized labor in the struggle for freedom, and a proposal that labor implement the struggle for Negroes to vote freely." If King was serious about mass action in the South, he had best come up with a program for moving forward. "The question of where you move next," Rustin told him, "is more important than any other question Negroes face today." In spite of such a warning, King accepted only part of Rustin's and Levison's suggestions. King focused his text on the demand for action by the federal government to protect blacks' right to vote in the South. No call for a direct role for white labor in the Deep South was included.

When King boarded his flight to Washington early on May 16, he carried with him a letter to the White House requesting a personal meeting with President Eisenhower. It mentioned that King would be seeing Vice-President Nixon sometime in the near future, as a result of the Ghana conversation, but emphasized that that "can in no way substitute for the necessity of my talking directly with the head of our great government." Such a meeting, "if it does nothing else, . . . would at least give persons of goodwill in general and Negro Americans in particular a feeling that the White House is listening to the problems which we confront," King stated. Perhaps, in the wake of the Pilgrimage, the president would be more responsive to black people than he had been in the past.

At noon on May 17, a smaller than anticipated crowd gathered at the Lincoln Memorial. Although the sponsors' predictions had ranged from 50,000 to 75,000, estimates of the actual number varied from only 15,000 to 27,000. Of the different speakers, however, the young minister from Montgomery received by far the most enthusiastic ovation. King's call for the right to vote included strong criticism of both major political parties, the Congress, and President Eisenhower. "The executive branch of government is all too silent and apathetic," King stated. His peroration— "Give us the ballot"—supplied the headline for news accounts of the Friday rally.

While some of the press coverage noted the modest turnout, accounts in the black news media heralded King's new national stature. *Ebony* magazine pronounced that King "emerged from the Pilgrimage as the No. 1 Negro leader of men." An influential New York *Amsterdam News* columnist, James Hicks, also proclaimed King "the number one leader." The Pilgrimage had been King's idea, Hicks said, and King deserved the credit for its success. "No other Negro leader in America was enthusiastic about it," and "at no time did either Mr. Randolph or Mr. Wilkins throw the full weight of their offices and their organizations completely behind the Pilgrimage," Hicks asserted. "Many among that leadership did a good job of dragging their feet . . . with the direct hope that the March would fail, and that the threat of King's leadership would thus die aborning." The elders were not happy. The young minister from the South represented a direct and personal challenge to "the so-called Negro leadership" which had previously received the headlines.

The Pilgrimage notwithstanding, President Eisenhower continued to avoid any meeting with the black leadership. In late May, however, King announced that Vice-President Nixon had formally invited King to a private meeting on June 13. Increasingly, Martin Luther King, Jr., appeared to be the new point man for black Americans.[11]

Before his trip to Washington, King had several less pleasant tasks to attend to in Montgomery. First was the trial of Sonny Kyle Livingston and Raymond C. Britt, two of the seven men arrested for the January bombings. Both men initially had confessed their involvement to police, saying they had planned the series of explosions in a meeting at Britt's home. Later, they recanted those confessions and requested a jury trial. On May 29, the men's attorney, John Blue Hill, summoned King as a *defense* witness, and asked the MIA president a long series of insulting and offensive questions. Had not King plotted the bombings in order to stimulate contributions to the MIA? What about rumors that King once had been intimate with a white woman? None of it had anything to do with Livingston's and Britt's guilt, and not many were surprised when the all-white jury on May 30 declared the men not guilty, despite their earlier confessions.

King also had to contend with continuing tensions within the MIA. Some members were discomforted by King's continuing close relationship with Rustin, who effectively served as King's New York-based assistant while on the payroll of the War Resisters League. Robert Graetz, the white minister, resented the assertive Rustin, who seemed to have King's ear more than Glenn Smiley. Both men had contributed to the MIA's adoption of nonviolence, but "most of the credit for giving form and substance to this principle must go to Glenn Smiley," not anyone else. Smiley, Graetz pointedly noted, "did not come in with a program for us to adopt and put into practice." Although certain members expected King to resolve the rivalry between the two advisors, he declined to act.

King also faced the continuing problem of E. D. Nixon. Although his actual role in the MIA had decreased greatly, Nixon still remained treasurer in name. In early June, he sought to resign this last remaining tie, saying he did not care for the small clique that now ran the organization. "I resent being treated as a newcomer to the MIA . . . I do not expect to be treated as a child." King refused to accept the resignation, and efforts to repair the breach continued.[12]

In preparation for the scheduled June 13 meeting with Vice-President Nixon, Rustin prepared a long briefing memo for King that emphasized six points he should articulate to the vice-president: that *neither* political party had done enough on civil rights; that problems in the South could be solved only with federal action; that most white southerners could cope with racial change, but needed prodding; that Eisenhower should speak out for civil rights; that Nixon should speak out for the pending civil rights bill, and do so in the South; and that the administration had to stop pondering and start acting.

Thus advised, King, along with Ralph Abernathy, arrived at Nixon's Capitol office at 3:30 P.M. that Thursday for what was scheduled as a one-hour meeting. Labor Secretary James P. Mitchell joined Nixon to hear King and Abernathy describe the numerous acts of racial violence that black people across the South had been subjected to. Nixon spoke up in defense of the Eisenhower administration, stating that its civil rights bill would pass the House and faced an even chance of success in the Senate. King proposed that Nixon come South and make a speech in support of law and order, but Nixon responded noncommittally. Secretary Mitchell pointed out that a presidential committee charged with eliminating racial bias from government contracts soon would be holding hearings in the South, and perhaps Nixon could speak before them. Nixon appeared to endorse the idea. Then, at the conclusion of what had become a two-hour meeting, the vice-president hinted that he might be able to arrange the personal meeting with Eisenhower that King had requested.

King and Abernathy held an early-evening press conference on the meeting at a local hotel. Both men indicated that they felt Nixon and Mitchell genuinely were interested in racial problems, but that no firm commitments had been won. King talked about how the SLC wanted to undertake voter registration drives in some ten southern cities, but said that specific plans had not yet been made.

The Washington reporters, however, were more interested in whether King had actually obtained any promises from the vice-president. In contrast to the commentaries on the Pilgrimage, some black reporters questioned King's performance in the meeting with Nixon. The young Alabama minister was "not yet ready for the political big time," one commentator opined.

In the wake of the Nixon conference, King set off on another round of speeches in Texas and California. At the end of June, he had the special honor of receiving the NAACP's foremost award, the Spingarn Medal, at the association's annual convention in Detroit. King took the opportunity to return the NAACP's compliment, and combat the earlier news reports of tensions, by praising Roy Wilkins and calling on everyone to double their contributions to the NAACP. The appearance received extensive and positive coverage in the black press.[13]

Back in Montgomery in early July, King found a number of different issues confronting him. Foremost was a spate of reports that he would be leaving Montgomery for a more attractive position elsewhere. The initial story had King under serious consideration for the presidency of Fisk University, but King also had been approached about the deanship of Howard University's School of Religion. While he found the idea of teaching attractive, he decided not to pursue either offer. "My work in the South," he wrote Howard President Mordecai Johnson, "is not quite complete, or at least I have not been able to do several things that I would like to see done before leaving. The vast possibilities of a non-violent, noncooperation approach to the solution of the race problem are still challenging indeed. I would like to remain a part of the unfolding development of this approach for a few more years." Ten months later, when another attractive offer arrived from the Garrett Biblical Institute in Illinois, King cited the same reasons in "reluctantly" saying no.

Another aspect of King's life was also provoking gossip. Many people whispered about the intimate details of his private life, even though Coretta was expecting their second child in October. Then in one of the most widely read national black newspapers, the *Pittsburgh Courier*, there appeared the most blatant sort of warning. A "prominent minister in the Deep South, a man who has been making the headlines recently in his fight for civil rights, had better watch his step," the paper announced. Detectives hired by white segregationists, it claimed, were hoping "to create a scandal by catching the preacher in a hotel room with a woman other than his wife, during one of his visits to a Northern city." True, it did not call him by name, but no one could mistake who it was. Even though most of King's Montgomery friends and civil rights colleagues knew nothing of the uninhibited life-style King had pursued during his theology school days, such rumors only added to King's burdens.

Then there was still E. D. Nixon to deal with. King, Abernathy, and Nixon had a showdown meeting on July 8 in which Nixon voiced his complaints about the MIA's financial procedures and about the cliquishness he felt had grown up around King. "Money was mishandled in some instances," Nixon later said, and more complete records of income and expenses could have been kept. "There was general knowledge among a number of us at least that there were some things that were happening financially that were less than ideal," another board member subsequently acknowledged, but the tough questions were never raised at board meetings because of how divisive it would have been. Nixon had complained that MIA officers—i.e. King—should not be allowed to incur unlimited telephone and telegram charges, but the board had rejected his points. King and Abernathy, now aiming for a peaceful compromise, conceded there was some truth to Nixon's complaints. Improvements would be made, and Nixon should not resign from the MIA. His hurt assuaged, Nixon agreed to stay on.[14]

After a New York trip, which included an appearance at one of Billy Graham's "crusades," King turned his attention to organizing a third meeting of the SLC on August 8 and 9 in Montgomery. King had recruited a full-time MIA executive secretary to ease his own administrative burdens. The new man, Mose Pleasure, Jr., who had been alumni secretary at Dillard University, helped King ensure that this SLC gathering would have a more tangible payoff than the first two. Its focus, King announced, would be the same as that of his Pilgrimage speech: registration and voting. "Ways and means through which we may increase the number of Negro voters in the South at this particular time will be our most important concern in this meeting."

When well over one hundred persons assembled at Holt Street church, King was ready with some specific program proposals. First, he wanted to change the name of the organization to Southern *Christian* Leadership Conference (SCLC), to emphasize that most of its participants and its potential popular base came from the black church. Rustin had tried to dissuade King from the idea, arguing that the new word might discourage nonreligious supporters of civil rights, but King had held firm.

After winning assent to that, King detailed a plan for a large-scale voter registration effort that he, Rustin, and Levison had prepared. The "Crusade for Citizenship" would have a central office in Atlanta and a budget of $200,000. The Crusade would have several goals: to establish voting clinics, to provide educational materials to local voter registration efforts, to collect evidence of discriminatory election practices, and "to arouse the conscience of the nation through radio, T.V., newspapers, [and] public appearances of southern leaders as to conditions that exist, progress being made, and the responsibility of the entire nation to help ensure for Negro citizens these elementary rights." First and foremost, however, the Crusade would seek "to arouse the masses of Negroes to realize that, in a democracy, their chances for improvement rest on their ability to vote."

Some in attendance had doubts about so grand an undertaking. First, where would they find $200,000? Russell Lasley of the Packinghouse Workers said that his union would contribute $11,000, but that alone would not finance what King had in mind. Some also wondered if the effort would not place the nascent group in direct competition with the NAACP. King said no, but several questioners reiterated that a cooperative effort with the NAACP would be preferable to SCLC attempting to go it alone. King parried the criticisms, saying that the details of implementation would be agreed upon at the SCLC's next meeting, sometime in the fall, in Memphis.

When news of the Montgomery meeting reached Roy Wilkins, he became furious. Several NAACP loyalists told him what King had in mind, and one supporter furnished him a detailed account of the Montgomery discussions. It observed, editorially, that "we need only one national organization to speak for Negroes and all other organizations and leadership should rally around the NAACP." Wilkins immediately instructed his assistants to send copies of that missive to all NAACP staff members, and to tell them that they must check with the national office before participating in any conferences called by groups other than the NAACP.[15]

During the rest of August, King again was on the road: New Orleans, Wisconsin, Detroit, and Washington. To newsmen, King spoke in expansive terms about the soon-to-begin voter registration effort. Total black registration across the South was estimated at barely 1,250,000 at present, but his new effort, King said, had a goal of five million *new* minority voters.

On Labor Day weekend King and Abernathy went to Tennessee for the twenty-fifth anniversary celebration of the Highlander Folk School, the interracial institution that Mrs. Parks had attended two years earlier. There were new people to meet; songs were being sung, and a photographer was snapping pictures. King and Abernathy had an appointment in Louisville, and had to leave the celebration after only a three-hour stay. A white activist from Louisville, Anne Braden, offered to give them a lift. They accepted, and as they drove north, both Braden and King commented on one of the songs they had each heard for the first time when Pete Seeger had sung it that afternoon. King kept humming it, and recalled its name—"We Shall Overcome." "There's something about that song that haunts you," he told the others.

When the first federal Civil Rights Act since the Reconstruction era passed the Congress in September, King, like other black leaders, found little to celebrate. The act did establish a civil rights commission and allowed the Justice Department to file voting rights suits against discriminatory southern registrars, but neither provision promised much in the hands of the somnolent Eisenhower administration. The pending crisis in Arkansas over the integration of Little Rock's Central High School all but demanded presidential intervention, but instead it was a federal district judge who took the lead in demanding obedience to federal authority. Also, two days after the civil rights bill was passed, King's close Birmingham ally, Fred Shuttlesworth, was brutally beaten by a white mob when he attempted to enroll one of his children in a previously all-white school. Again there was no federal action or presidential statement, and black leaders' ongoing efforts to obtain an audience with Eisenhower remained unsuccessful.

By early October, Coretta was only a few weeks away from the expected birth of the couple's second child. King had begun to write a new column, "Advice for Living," in *Ebony* magazine. The format was a familiar one: answering letters from the troubled and forlorn. In his initial columns, King advised a woman not to marry a man twenty-five years younger, stated that "the primary obligation of the woman is that of motherhood," and remarked that "almost every minister has the problem of confronting women in his congregation whose interests are not entirely spiritual."[16]

Serious problems continued to exist in the MIA. Executive Secretary Pleasure found himself frozen out of major influence by an old-timers' clique that viewed even King as a newcomer. Office secretaries Hazel Gregory and Erna Dungee effectively dominated the MIA operations, and King was away so much that he had little idea of the full dynamics of the situation. Pleasure was amazed at the "tremendous resentment" over King's personal fame, and was disappointed that he lacked the time to give any serious attention to preparing substantive MIA program initiatives. "Martin was being . . . pulled in so many directions by so many forces that he couldn't manage them. . . . It caused him some real pain in terms of what his life was all about and where he was going and what he wanted to do." Torn between a desire to minimize his MIA and Dexter obligations and guilt over doing so, King avoided facing any tough choices. Some black news reporters had begun writing about the estrangement of Nixon and Mrs. Parks from King. Nixon finally had accepted outside money for his own voter registration plans, but Mrs. Parks, whom he had intended to hire, had already taken a job at Virginia's Hampton Institute. Executive Secretary Pleasure issued a new ten-point program in the MIA's name, "Looking Forward," but what it listed were hopes, not concrete activities. An individual membership drive was launched to replenish the group's coffers, but all could see that the MIA was gradually becoming moribund.

By October, King had served three years as pastor of Dexter Avenue Baptist Church. The past ten months had been a frustrating period, and in his annual report to the members, King told them frankly about "the all too many dark moments of leadership." He had preached at Dexter only thirty Sundays out of the last twelve months, and complained that "I have not scratched the surface in doing the things at Dexter that I had hoped to do by this time." He was far too busy, yet his busyness had no focus or tangible achievements. "Almost every week—having to make so many speeches, attend so many meetings, meet so many people, write so many articles, counsel with so many groups—I face the frustration of feeling that in the midst of so many things to do I am not doing anything well." While King was presenting the report at an evening meeting on October 23, word came that Coretta had just given birth to a son, their second child. King had been hoping for a boy who could be named Martin Luther King, III. Although Coretta argued against it, she could not dissuade her husband.

Four days later, on Sunday afternoon, King was at Dexter for a live, thirty-minute NBC interview program, *Look Here,* that would be seen across the country. King told host Martin Agronsky that nonviolence was an active stance, and not simply another name for pacifism. A purely pacifist approach, King said, was defeatist. When the broadcast was complete, King and Agronsky received a shock: An act of sabotage by local whites had damaged the transmitting tower of the local TV station just as they went on the air. Although the broadcast had been seen by much of the nation, south Alabama viewers had missed it. The local blackout had brought quite a crowd to Dexter, wondering what had happened. The anxious black community was relieved when word spread that only the transmitter, and not King, had been put out of action.[17]

At the end of October, King announced that the SCLC would hold its fourth meeting on Tuesday, November 5, at Mt. Olive CME Cathedral in Memphis. When the group gathered that morning, King explained how they would push ahead with the Crusade for Citizenship. Simultaneous rallies in twenty different southern cities would mark a January 20 kickoff. The proposed budget remained $200,000, and King envisioned an executive director based in Atlanta, plus two traveling field staff members. A special effort would be made to get the black press to publicize the January rallies.

Just as in Montgomery three months earlier, some delegates questioned whether any money was in hand, or if there were precise plans for how to raise it. Had anyone yet been hired to coordinate these rallies? No, though King did have a committee at work on selecting an executive director. What about the problem of competition with the NAACP? "No conflict exists between this organization and the NAACP," King replied. He had met with Roy Wilkins, and A. Philip Randolph, in New York on October 16, and they agreed that the SCLC's and NAACP's efforts would not duplicate or compete with each other, and that the two groups soon would undertake a joint fund-raising drive in the North. Although King's reassurances were spoken strongly, some doubted that Wilkins envisioned any such arrangement, even if King had been told so.

That afternoon, SCLC voted to send a telegram to President Eisenhower. It commended him for his eventual action in Little Rock, but pointedly stated that the events there indicated how the president needed to speak personally with black leaders from across the country. Additionally, Eisenhower was asked to appoint quickly the new Civil Rights Commission, authorized two months earlier, and to name at least two blacks to the panel. That evening King spoke to a 1,500-person rally. Telegrams like the one to Eisenhower, he told the crowd, "will be effective according to the political activity of the masses of Negroes at the local level."[18]

Less than a week later, Roy Wilkins moved to show the young upstarts who was boss. The NAACP announced a two-day meeting in Atlanta to plan its own southern voter registration effort. Though Wilkins invited King to speak briefly at the opening session, the message was clear. King pledged SCLC's cooperation, but when Wilkins met reporters to announce a goal of three million new black registrants, not one mention was made of King or SCLC. Some hostile southern white reporters began to write about the friction between the two groups.

For King, the problems with Wilkins were especially enervating. King was even more tired than usual, having just come through a bout with the flu. One morning at Dexter, he apologized for preaching the same sermon, "Loving Your Enemies," for the third time in three years to the same congregation. A week earlier he had repeated the exact same text to an audience at Howard University. On both occasions he had told his listeners that "each of us is something of a schizophrenic personality. We're split up and divided against ourselves. There is something of a civil war going on within all our lives." He felt exhausted and troubled, and wondered what he could do with a life that made more demands upon him than he wanted, a life that kept him always busy but also tense and frustrated. "Within the best of us there is some evil, and within the worst of us there is some good," he told the congregation.

In December the Montgomery black community celebrated the second anniversary of the boycott. Attendance at the MIA's annual institute on nonviolence was down from the year before, and the widening divisions within the MIA made for an uneasy atmosphere. While visiting northern reporters focused on the integrated buses, and what they were told was a new level of courtesy toward black people, the MIA leadership was gloomy. Some criticized the final settlement that had been reached with solicitor Thetford. The charges against all the MIA leaders except King had never been resolved, and King's appeal of his conviction was thrown out on the grounds that his lawyers had not filed the proper papers in time. Thetford proposed a deal: King would pay his long-standing $500 fine, all the other charges would be dropped, and the state also would dismiss the charges against the remaining bombers who had not been brought to trial after the first two acquittals. With great reluctance, the MIA accepted, and King paid his fine.

In the meantime, E. D. Nixon had finally resigned as MIA treasurer. As he pursued his voter registration effort, the MIA suddenly put much greater life into its own, directed by Nixon's old rival, Rufus Lewis. Mrs. Durr felt that "there is a good deal of bitter feeling" in the black community, and believed that the preboycott factionalism was reemerging. "It is the old class split coming to the fore again," the division between mass and elite that had existed before both Nixon and Lewis had united behind King.

Nevertheless, King tried to strike a positive tone in his opening speech at the institute. "I believe firmly that there are many more white people of good will in the South than we are able to see on the surface." He apologized again for neglecting his responsibilities at Dexter, even though no one had complained. King stated: "I speak as one who has to live every day under the threat of death, ... I believe in the future because I believe in God." No matter how strong his belief, however, King could not salvage a conference that even the MIA publicly admitted "was a flop." Soon after, the MIA board fired Executive Secretary Pleasure. One of King's friends wrote that these events left King "quite distraught. Again, he wondered if he had lost his touch in Montgomery."[19]

King had little time for remorse about the institute, because the problems of the Crusade for Citizenship loomed ever larger. He had spoken repeatedly with Rustin and Levison about the obstacles, and Levison drafted a letter for him to send to black leaders and sympathetic whites, asking for financial assistance and moral support. The letter, which went out on December 16, emphasized that "in no sense are we in conflict with the NAACP or any other group." SCLC sought to implement at the local level through nonviolence, the legal advances which the NAACP had won in the courts. The Crusade would be its first major project for three particular reasons: Blacks' right to vote per se was not openly opposed by even the worst segregationists; black voting strength could aid in achieving other rights; and "the right to vote does not raise the issue of social mixing to confuse the main concern." The Crusade aspired to double the number of black voters in the South, to approximately two and a half million within one year's time—not the *five* million new voters King had been speaking of four months earlier.

Even before there was a response to the letter, King and his colleagues realized they had to get moving. On Thursday, December 19, an executive group of SCLC met at Ebenezer church in Atlanta. King and several others had been in touch with a man whom they hoped to hire as executive director, young educator Lucius H. Pitts, but Pitts had been putting them off, saying he could not give a final answer until April. The scheduled rallies were now one month away, and they had no one to organize them. Accordingly, two decisions were reached: First, the kick-off date would be moved back from January 20 to February 12, Lincoln's Birthday. Second, Bayard Rustin would be hired to coordinate the rallies. Some had decidedly mixed feelings about Rustin, but none questioned his organizational ability.

Over the Christmas holidays, King remained in Montgomery to rest. He started to draft some chapters of an autobiographical account of the boycott that Stanley Levison had arranged for Harper & Brothers to publish. Some days King was able to sneak away to the home of some friends, where there were fewer interruptions than at Dexter or his MIA office. Coretta was happy to see more of him, and it gave him a greater opportunity to spend time with his children.

After the first of the year, 1958, King had several northern speaking engagements. On January 8 he was in Rochester, New York, where reporters pressed him about the reports of conflict between the SCLC and NAACP. King denied them, saying they were "so erroneous I shouldn't even comment. . . . I have always had the warmest relationship with the NAACP." To prove it, King said he soon would purchase an NAACP life membership.

From Rochester, King flew to New York to meet with Levison and Rustin. Levison and the other New York activists had urged that Rustin not go south to work on the Crusade. If he assumed any public role in the effort, segregationists could smear King with the publicly documented facts about Rustin's homosexuality, early flirtation with communism, and conscientious objection during World War II. Reluctantly, King agreed. However, if Rustin would not be going south, someone else had to, or the Crusade would never get off the ground. Levison and Rustin promised King that Ella Baker, who had been serving as executive secretary of In Friendship, could be counted on to take Rustin's place.

King had been talking about opening an SCLC office in Atlanta ever since the August meeting in Montgomery. It had not happened, however, and Baker arrived in Atlanta without any quarters out of which to organize the February 12 rallies. Initially she worked out of a room in the Savoy Hotel on Auburn Avenue, and with no word from King. Then, Samuel Williams, the Morehouse professor and Atlanta pastor who was one of SCLC's officers, offered his help and found her office space. With a phone, a typewriter, and little more, Baker got to work making contacts in different southern cities. If the various ministers who had attended the previous SCLC meetings could be activated now, the series of rallies might succeed.

Baker found only modest enthusiasm in many of the cities she contacted. In some, local NAACP representatives were attempting to sandbag SCLC's efforts. Medgar Evers, the Mississippi staff member whom Wilkins had ordered to cut his SCLC ties, now needed no prompting. He kept his NAACP superiors closely informed of SCLC's effort to set up a rally in Jackson. As Evers reported in late January, "We have naturally discouraged, 'tactfully,' any such movement here in Jackson. It will be our design through the NAACP . . . to control the present state of affairs." When Baker tried to make plans for a rally, Evers wrote, "the person who was contacted to arrange such a meeting came immediately to our office for advice. We immediately halted those plans." With allies like the NAACP, SCLC's effort had little chance of success.

In late January SCLC's executive committee met at Ebenezer church to assess the situation. Things did not look encouraging; however, they had little choice but to forge ahead. To call attention to the rallies, King issued a press release, implicitly worded to reassure local leaders who might worry about this apparent intrusion. SCLC, King said, "will function as a service agency to help further registration and voting in communities where such efforts are already underway, and to stimulate other communities into action."

All in all, the rallies received little advance publicity. Their actual occurrence received even less. King spoke at the Miami rally about the value of the franchise. Most of the Lincoln's Birthday rallies did take place. but little effort was made to use them as the kickoff for local registration campaigns. Although Baker, surveying the scene several weeks later, could identify a number of cities where local registration efforts were making headway, an Associated Press survey of cities listed for SCLC rallies found that "only a handful" of black applicants came to registration offices in the weeks following the rallies. White officials in some cities, like Montgomery and Birmingham, took special glee in telling reporters that black applicants were even fewer in number than usual. Headlines such as DRIVE LAGS FOR NEGRO REGISTRATION were about all that SCLC garnered from its effort. On February 16, four days after the rallies, Baker returned to New York, her temporary assignment complete.[20]

The SCLC was moribund. The discussions with Lucius H. Pitts were stymied, although King still wanted to hire him. On March 20, Ella Baker returned south to staff the Atlanta office. She spoke several times with Pitts, but got no firm answer. Baker knew that since she was a woman, and not a minister, King and his colleagues would not consider appointing her as executive director. Despairing of Pitts, she contacted an old college friend, Rev. John L. Tilley of Baltimore. She had discussed the vacancy with Tilley, who had led a very successful voter registration effort in Baltimore a year or so earlier. Perhaps he would be interested in the job, and SCLC in him. Tilley replied that he was, so Baker notified King and others of this new candidate. King wanted Levison's judgment of the man, and in mid-April Tilley accompanied Baker to New York. The three of them met in an ice cream parlor on 125th Street, and Levison later told King that his judgment was favorable. On April 30 the SCLC executive board met and appointed Tilley executive director and named Baker associate director. Finally, after fifteen months of existence, and several name changes, the organization had the beginnings of a staff.

King spent much of the spring working on the book manuscript, often at the west Montgomery home of close friends Elliott and Genevieve Finley. He addressed an Easter Sunday demonstration organized by the MIA to protest the electrocution of a young black man convicted of rape, a rally whose planning the FBI monitored through its unwitting informant in the MIA. King's travel schedule was still hectic, but writing became his top priority. King's personal advice column remained a regular monthly feature in *Ebony*, and his comments ranged widely. He told one questioner that the "development and use of nuclear weapons of war should be banned" and advised another that gospel music and "rock n' roll" were "totally incompatible" because rock music "often plunges men's minds into degrading and immoral depths." When a woman asked what to do about her husband's extramarital affair, King told her to think of what the other woman might have to offer that she did not. What faults of her own might make her husband look elsewhere? "Do you nag?" King asked her. Answers that King offered to other questions had application to both personal and societal problems: "People fail to get along with each other because they fear each other. They fear each other because they don't know each other."

As King sent each chapter of his book manuscript north, Levison and Rustin proved to be tough critics. Levison objected to King's rather self-centered narration of the Montgomery protest. Many of the chapters, he said, gave the impression "that everything depended on you. This could create unnecessary charges of an egocentric presentation of the situation and is important to avoid even if it were the fact." When the concluding chapter, entitled "Where Do We Go From Here?" arrived in the mail, Levison again was harsh. The material was poorly organized and repetitive. Significant subjects had been skipped over, even ones that King regularly spoke about: "On voting and registration you mention nothing, which is a serious omission." Other subjects that King had emphasized simply should be left out, Levison advised. In particular, "the section on Negro self-improvement is undesirable. . . . The goal should be to activate, and organize people toward the main objective rather than appeal for change of character separated from the pursuit of social goals."

King appreciated and welcomed Levison's assistance, even when it was sharply critical. Though Levison was seventeen years older than King, and though their backgrounds had little in common, King found two rare qualities in the outspoken New Yorker. First, he was one of the few people who would assist King without seeking anything, even informal favors, in return. Second, Levison was one of the few people willing to criticize King to his face. When Levison recommended revisions in the book manuscript, they were made. When Levison, despairing at times of the slow pace of the book's progress, simply wrote out his own material and inserted it into the text, King accepted the contributions and thanked Levison for them. Between Levison and Rustin, the minutiae of King's life were attended to and the book manuscript kept on the road to publication.[21]

On May 29 the fifth meeting of SCLC, and the first under the new administration of Tilley and Baker, convened in Clarksdale, Mississippi. The ninety-seven delegates spent the morning listening to reports on voter registration efforts in various cities. The speakers emphasized the positive, and one jaundiced observer, NAACP Registration Director John M. Brooks, wrote that "75% of this time was spent by ministers praising themselves, the conference and Rev. King, Jr. . . . 95% of the reports made on voting and civil rights activities were projects of the NAACP. The representatives, however, left the impression that these projects were being carried out by the SCLC." Many of those in attendance however, were far less sanguine. "The group is having a hard time getting anything more than lip service from leading ministers," Brooks reported to Roy Wilkins. "Rev. King, Sr., was very bitter about this fact."

In the afternoon session, the delegates ratified the selection of Tilley as executive director and approved a strongly worded message to President Eisenhower expressing "shock and dismay" over a recent presidential statement that enforcement of the law should not be allowed to create hardship or injustice. Such a backhanded slap at *Brown* was totally inappropriate, they said. A telegram to Eisenhower from King conveyed the resolution and renewed the long-standing request that the president meet with black leaders. That telegram was the only tangible product of the meeting; no firm plans for any voter registration initiatives were adopted.

At the White House, King's telegram received serious attention. One week after the Clarksdale meeting, presidential assistant Rocco C. Siciliano called King. If King was going to be in Washington anytime soon, Siciliano would be happy to talk with him. King said he would check his schedule, and several hours later had his secretary call back to say that he would come to Washington on Monday, June 9. A 2:00 P.M. meeting was set.

At the appointed time, Siciliano, Deputy Attorney General Lawrence E. Walsh, and black presidential assistant E. Frederic Morrow met with King to discuss the requested audience with the president. Morrow asked King if a twosome of King and A. Philip Randolph would be sufficient. King said no, Roy Wilkins would have to be invited also. The three men asked King what he would propose for an agenda, and he indicated that the "subject matter would be largely confined to some potential problems of school integration which might occur this fall." What was important, King emphasized, was not the agenda for the meeting but the mere fact of it. Eisenhower, who had been in the White House five years, had yet to hold such an audience, and "the Negro community is beginning to feel that the President would not or could not see Negro leaders." Siciliano thanked King for coming by, and said he would be back in touch by the end of the week. He, Walsh, and Morrow huddled briefly, and unanimously agreed to recommend that Eisenhower see the three black leaders "as soon as possible." Presidential chief of staff Sherman Adams approved the recommendation, and Siciliano called King to say that a meeting would be scheduled in the near future, and that a fourth black leader, Lester B. Granger of the National Urban League, might be invited as well. King was pleased, and three days later Siciliano called again, to say that the appointment had been set for Monday, June 23.[22]

With one week to prepare, King and the other three men traded thoughts about what to say to Eisenhower. They agreed that a written statement should be presented to the president, and several quick drafts were circulated. They met in Washington at 8:00 P.M. Sunday night to prepare a final version. King vetoed use of the word "angry" to describe blacks' attitudes toward the administration, but the four leaders harmoniously hammered out a statement that made nine points. The principal ones called upon Eisenhower to declare that the law, i.e. *Brown*, would be enforced, to call a White House conference to promote peaceful desegregation, to support the enactment of stronger federal civil rights laws, to order the Justice Department to become more active concerning voting discrimination, and to recommend an extension of the temporarily established Civil Rights Commission. The four men agreed that Randolph would make an opening statement for them, with King, Wilkins, and Granger each then speaking about three of the nine specifics.

The four leaders met at the White House forty-five minutes in advance of their appointment. After they were ushered into the Oval Office, and greetings were exchanged, Randolph began the scheduled thirty-minute meeting by reading the nine points in their prepared statement. Then, he called on King to expand upon the first three: that Eisenhower should call for obedience to the law, call a White House conference, and offer federal aid to help communities adjust to integration. Using a standard line from his speeches, King told the president that it was true, as Eisenhower himself had said, that morals could not be legislated. However, laws did constrain people's behavior, and civil rights laws thus could combat discrimination. Wilkins and Granger each added their comments. Eisenhower expressed dismay at Granger's observation that black bitterness had reached a new height, especially if that meant bitterness toward his administration. Granger, Randolph, and Wilkins all spoke up to say that it was bitterness toward the overall racial situation, not Eisenhower. Then, Eisenhower addressed the nine points: "I don't propose to comment on these recommendations. I know you do not expect me to. But I will be glad to consider them. There may be some value to your idea of a conference. But I don't think anything much would really come of one." Randolph, seizing the only opening, pressed the point about the conference. Eisenhower made a remark or two about voting, and the meeting was at an end. It had lasted fifteen minutes longer than scheduled, but the black leaders were not pleased. King and Granger in particular felt that Eisenhower had seemed very poorly informed, as well as totally noncommittal. The White House staffers were more pleased, though they expressed some concern about the attitude of "the most militant of the group," Roy Wilkins.[23]

The summer of 1958 was by far the most relaxed time in King's life since the beginning of the Montgomery protest. The MIA remained largely somnolent. King was troubled by the group's internal divisions, which increasingly pitted the lay people against most of the ministers, but King's frequent absences limited his ability to improve matters. A petition seeking desegregation of Montgomery's recreational facilities was presented to and rejected by the city commission, but one report described the MIA's weekly mass meetings as having descended to a "state of lethargy." Ella Baker was busy planning a major SCLC conclave in Norfolk for early October, while warning King that "we are losing the initiative in the Civil Rights struggle in the South mainly because of the absence of a dynamic philosophy, or spiritual force." King acknowledged that more ought to be done, but in mid-July he and Coretta left for a two-week vacation on the coast of Mexico. Coretta enjoyed this first real holiday since their marriage, but Martin was disturbed by the extreme poverty in which many Mexicans lived.

A. Philip Randolph pressed his three compatriots to unite with him in putting public pressure on Eisenhower to hold the White House conference on integration, but nothing was done. On August 1, Randolph wrote Eisenhower to repeat the request. More than a month later Siciliano responded that the time was not good. King spent much of August relaxing in Montgomery, while Stanley Levison, who had been overseeing the progress of King's book, *Stride Toward Freedom*, kept him apprised of plans for its September publication.[24]

The quiet of Montgomery was broken on Friday night, August 29, when Ralph Abernathy was assaulted at his church office by a man who alleged that Abernathy had an intimate relationship with the man's wife. Abernathy spent several days in the hospital, and the trial of his assailant was set for Wednesday, September 3. When the Abernathys and Kings arrived at the courthouse that morning, two white policemen sought to prevent them from entering the courtroom. Abernathy attempted to explain their purpose, and King sought to summon Fred Gray from inside, but the two officers would hear none of it. When King paused a moment longer, the two policemen, O. M. Strickland and J. V. Johnson, grabbed King and began hustling him toward the jail. One held King's arm tightly behind King's back, paying no attention to a photographer who was taking pictures of the scene. Within minutes, King was frisked and thrown into a cell.

Hardly ten minutes passed before ranking officers came and released King. The charge against him was loitering, they said, and he was allowed to sign a $100 bond. His hearing would be Friday, September 5. Reporters immediately began to spread the story of the incident, and King described to them how the cops "tried to break my arm; they grabbed my collar and tried to choke me, and when they got me to the cell, they kicked me in." He said he would continue to "stand up for what I think is right, even if it means further arrest, or even physical death."

King resolved to contest the fictitious charge filed against him. After talking with his colleagues, and "a night of meditation and soul-searching," he decided that he would pay no fine if convicted. Instead, he would serve the equivalent jail sentence. When his trial opened, the prosecution changed the charge to refusing to obey an officer. King was quickly found guilty, and Judge Eugene Loe set the penalty at a $10 fine and $4 court costs, or fourteen days in jail. He said he could see no evidence of excessive force by the police. Fred Gray immediately announced that King would serve the time, and King presented a prepared statement to both Loe and newsmen. In it, King explained his unwillingness to acknowledge the validity of the charges or the proceedings. Serving the time instead of paying the fine was an expression of this, and not simply "some histrionic gesture or publicity stunt, for moral convictions never stem from the selfish urge for publicity. Neither am I motivated by a desire to be a martyr." The court proceeding complete, King was led away, and his colleagues left the courthouse in a one-hundred person procession for the seven-block walk to Dexter church.

Police Commissioner Clyde Sellers was angry at how King had been able to turn one more Montgomery blunder into a national news story. Now, the matter would remain alive for two more weeks while King served his time. As King waited in a detention room, Sellers took out the cash and paid King's $14 fine. Even before his friends had reached Dexter, King was told he was free to leave.

King was visibly dismayed when told that his fine had been paid. Free to walk away, he went back to the courtroom and found Loe's chambers. King told the judge that he wanted to serve his time, and protested the payment of the fine. Loe said there was nothing he could do. Disconsolate, King left the courthouse. A passing motorist gave him a ride to Dexter, and a crowd gathered as word spread of King's strange release. King spoke to them for ten minutes, talking about how "the Negro must come to the point of refusing to cooperate with evil," but without ever hating the evildoers. "I have no malice toward anyone, not even the white policeman who almost broke my arm, who choked and kicked me. Let there be no malice among you."

The Abernathy incident provoked one longtime King family friend, Los Angeles pastor J. Raymond Henderson, to remind young M.L. that he had to avoid even the "appearance of evil. . . . You are a 'marked man.' All sorts of subtle attempts will be made to discredit you. Some Negroes right in Montgomery would be glad to witness your downfall. . . . One of the most damning influences is that of women. They themselves too often delight in the satisfaction they get out of affairs with men of unusual prominence. Enemies are not above using them to a man's detriment. White women can be lures. You must exercise more than care. You must be vigilant indeed."[25]

In early September, after Eisenhower's rebuff about the integration conference, A. Philip Randolph announced that a coalition of civil rights groups would make their own statement in support of educational desegregation in an October 11 "Youth March for Integrated Schools" in Washington. King would be the "honorary chairman." In mid-September King traveled to New York to speak at several churches to stimulate interest in the Youth March. That same week his book was published, and King made a number of appearances to help promote it. One of those was a Saturday autographing session at Blumstein's department store in Harlem. King, surrounded by friends and admirers as he sat on a chair in the book department, was suddenly approached by a middle-aged black woman who asked, "Is this Martin Luther King?" King looked up and replied, "Yes, it is." Quickly, the woman pulled a sharp, seven-inch Japanese letter opener from her handbag and slammed it into King's upper left chest. The shocked onlookers grabbed the woman, and the store security officer handcuffed her. King was fully conscious and remained calmly seated in the chair until an ambulance arrived. With the weapon protruding from his chest, King was driven to nearby Harlem Hospital. As a team of doctors prepared for surgery, police officials brought the assailant, Mrs. Izola Ware Curry, to the hospital for King to make a positive identification. A loaded pistol had been found in her purse, and her incoherent comments indicated severe mental illness. After King identified her, she was taken away to a mental hospital.

In Montgomery, Coretta had been awaiting her husband's return that evening. Shortly after the stabbing, Rev. O. Clay Maxwell called her from New York with the news. Maxwell reported that surgery had not begun, but the wound was serious. Coretta, along with Ralph Abernathy and Robert Williams, arranged to fly to New York that night. Martin's sister Christine would join them when they changed planes in Atlanta.

At Harlem Hospital, a team of surgeons began the operation to remove the weapon. Many notables, including A. Philip Randolph, Roy Wilkins, and New York Governor Averell Harriman, gathered at the hospital to await word along with dozens of reporters. Finally, after hours of work, the surgery was completed. The senior surgeon emerged from the operating room to say King would recover, but would remain hospitalized for at least two weeks. His full convalescence would take three months. It had been an extremely close call; the sharp blade of the letter opener had been found resting right alongside the aorta. Had that been punctured, by any movement or even a sneeze, King would have died almost immediately from massive internal bleeding. He was a very lucky man.

Early Sunday morning Coretta and her companions arrived in New York and were driven to the hospital. She spoke briefly with the chief surgeon before seeing her heavily sedated husband. After a brief visit, Coretta made arrangements to stay in New York.

On Monday, King took "a sudden turn for the worse" when he developed pneumonia. "Prognosis is guarded," his doctors announced. By the next morning, however, the pneumonia had begun to clear, and King was more active. He sat up in bed, walked ten yards, and looked through the growing pile of get-well cards. One in particular made an impression on him that he never forgot. It was from a young girl in White Plains who had seen the news accounts of how even a sneeze would have been fatal. She was glad King had not sneezed, she said. As he thought about it, King was too.

The deluge of telegrams, phone calls, and letters, many of which contained unsolicited contributions, led Ella Baker and Coretta King to set up a temporary SCLC office right at Harlem Hospital as King's recovery continued at a good pace. Six days after the stabbing, doctors announced that he was out of danger. By the next day, the pneumonia had vanished and the external stitches were removed. King would have a scar, in the shape of a cross, right over his heart, but otherwise would suffer no lingering ill effects. On October 3, as a crowd of five hundred people gathered outside, King was released from the hospital. He began a three-week rest at the Brooklyn home of Rev. Sandy F. Ray, a longtime friend of Daddy King. King had little contact with the press, but he did issue one statement before he left Harlem Hospital: "I feel no ill-will toward Mrs. Izola Curry." He also volunteered that he was "immensely impatient" to get back to work.[26]

King's wounding and convalescence threw plans for the Youth March and SCLC's major fall gathering into disarray. Randolph postponed the former from October 11 to October 25, and Ralph Abernathy took King's place at the SCLC convention in Norfolk on October 1 and 2. In King's absence, no substantive program initiatives were proposed. Reverend Tilley, who rather than give up his pastorship was commuting to Atlanta on a weekly basis from Baltimore, prepared a planning document, but it called for few tangible actions other than the formation of state or sectional councils composed of pastors who had attended previous SCLC gatherings. Miss Baker, when not answering King's New York mail, was assigned to promote the sales of *Stride Toward Freedom*, a task she found unpleasant and demeaning. Voter registration work was all but abandoned, and SCLC's hope of raising substantial sums through direct sales of the book met with little success.[27]

If *Stride Toward Freedom* did not enrich SCLC, it did generate a host of enthusiastic reviews. Commentators found the book both informative and uplifting, and devoted more space to evaluating the Montgomery protest than to judging King's account of it.

Most of the book was a straightforward narration of the Montgomery protest, with great care taken to identify the contributions of others. King pulled no punches in discussing black Montgomery before the boycott, declaring there had been a "crippling factionalism" and "an appalling lack of unity among the leaders." He also admitted that the rhetorical emphasis upon nonviolence and Gandhi had emerged only as the boycott matured; "in the first days of the protest none of these expressions was mentioned."

The intellectual heart of the volume was Chapter Six, an autobiographical account of King's philosophical development entitled "Pilgrimage to Nonviolence." It received much comment in book reviews and in later analyses, even though the chapter was in part a poorly organized and at times erroneous hodgepodge of contributions from a number of King's editorial advisors: Rustin, Levison, and Harris Wofford, who by then was on the staff of the newly formed Civil Rights Commission.

The chapter purported to sketch out the different scholars and writers from whom King had drawn intellectual succor during his theological education. However, the discussion of Reinhold Niebuhr's criticisms of nonviolence was, as one sympathetic King scholar charitably put it, "a caricature." Whether King's misreading of Niebuhr was accidental or intentional cannot be definitely established. It did indicate, however, how carelessly that chapter, and other parts of the manuscript, had been put together.

Problems of accuracy pale beside another one that was not discovered until the 1970s. A lengthy unpublished study by Professor Ira Zepp has identified a series of King passages that reflect "exact reproduction or paraphrasing" from other works. The two books that were the major sources for such selections—Paul Ramsey's *Basic Christian Ethics* and Anders Nygren's *Agape and Eros*—both had been assigned reading in Kenneth Smith's Christianity and Society course which King took in the spring of 1951, his last year at Crozer. Phrases, sentences, even large parts of paragraphs from *Stride Toward Freedom* can be traced back directly to Ramsey and Nygren. As Zepp's detailed analysis points out, *Stride Toward Freedom* made no acknowledgment of, or reference to, its heavy and direct use of Ramsey's and Nygren's writings.

Although *Stride Toward Freedom* could not withstand a careful textual exegesis, the book competently performed its intended function of spreading the story of the Montgomery protest. Mass action by everyday black people was just as powerful a tool for social change as the lawsuit, and maybe more so. If King could symbolize that lesson, even better. The basic moral of the boycott could be conveyed in print, even if SCLC as an organization had not been doing a competent job of propagating it by action.[28]

It was that topic, far more than the strengths and weaknesses of *Stride,* which occupied Martin King's thoughts as he spent the first three weeks of October recuperating at Sandy Ray's home. Many old friends wrote to wish him a speedy recovery. One was J. Pius Barbour from Chester, who teased King about his past at Crozer:

I was not concerned about your stabbing as I always felt that you would not die. The only thing that bothered me was the thought that perhaps one of your Old Girl Friends had decided to take vengeance on you. If that woman had been white, I would have fainted, unless I had seen her name.

Most simply wished him well, and King tried to acknowledge some of the letters. He told his colleagues in the MIA that he was eager to rejoin them, and that "through this whole experience I can't remember one moment that I became excited or even upset." On October 17, King interrupted his rest to testify about the stabbing before a grand jury, which then indicted Curry for attempted murder. Eventually she was found insane, unable to stand trial, and committed to a state hospital.

On October 24, three weeks after leaving the hospital, King returned to Montgomery. The very next day the Youth March for Integrated Schools took place in Washington, and Coretta stood in for him. Some ten thousand people, mostly college students, walked down Constitution Avenue to the Lincoln Memorial, led by Randolph, singer Harry Belafonte, former baseball star Jackie Robinson, and Coretta. Notably absent were Roy Wilkins and other NAACP officials. At the Memorial, Randolph and the other leaders spoke, with Coretta delivering Martin's prepared remarks.[29]

Throughout November and early December, King remained on a quiet schedule and traveled little. Levison prodded him to make SCLC more active and to establish systematic fund-raising. The reaction to the stabbing had shown that many people were interested, and direct-mail appeals might bring in substantial funds.

In mid-November, King presented his fourth annual report to the Dexter congregation, and the record showed that he had preached there on only twenty eight Sundays over the past year. Again he apologized. The bitterness of E. D. Nixon was still a problem for the MIA, and tensions also had arisen between Fred Gray and others. On the boycott's third anniversary King announced that the MIA soon would challenge the segregation of Montgomery's schools. Several days later a federal suit was filed seeking the desegregation of all Montgomery parks and recreation facilities. The city responded by closing all public parks, and the black plaintiffs petitioned the court to force their reopening. There the matter languished.

Things were no better with SCLC. The executive board met in Atlanta on December 10, and agreed that Reverend Tilley, who was still commuting from Baltimore, would be assigned to work full time as director of a citywide voter registration effort in Atlanta. Miss Baker would continue to assist registration drives in other cities.[30]

Talk continued between King, Rustin, Levison, and Wofford over the long-discussed idea of King taking a major trip to India. It had been put off previously, but by late December, Wofford had arranged for an American foundation to meet most of the travel expenses and for India's Gandhi National Memorial Fund to send King a formal invitation. After a restful January, King and Coretta, along with MIA colleague Lawrence D. Reddick, who had just completed a biography of King, left Montgomery on February 2. The next day the three flew from New York to Paris, where Reddick introduced King to expatriate black novelist Richard Wright. After another stopover in Switzerland, the Kings and Reddick arrived in Delhi and began a thirty-day tour of cities and villages all across the vast country.

The Gandhi Fund had set a busy schedule for King, and assigned two escorts, Swami Vishwananda and James E. Bristol, to help him stick to it. Immediately upon arrival there was a crowded press conference at King's hotel; the following evening he delivered a major speech. Then, on February 13, the heavy traveling began. The pace took its toll; King spent March 1 and 2 ill in Ahmedabad. Once he recovered, they went on to Agra to see the Taj Mahal, and then spent the final five days of their visit back in Delhi.

They met many of Gandhi's closest surviving disciples, and most of India's leading political officials. King was deeply impressed by their desire to transform a country in which millions still lived in frightful poverty, a condition that pained King greatly. Still, India had had more success in eliminating caste discrimination, he believed, than had the United States in combating racial discrimination. There was much that might be learned, and conversations with people he met convinced him that India might lead the way in persuading both the United States and the Soviet Union to declare unilateral disarmament. He made that hope the focal point of his farewell statement when he, Coretta, and Reddick departed Delhi on March 9.

From Delhi, the three flew to Karachi, and then on to the Middle East, where the Kings visited Lebanon and the Holy Land. In Jerusalem they secured a car and drove the biblical route to Jericho. On March 21, exhausted from the constant traveling, they returned to Montgomery.

Back in the United States, King spoke out strongly in support of extensive U.S. assistance to India. Only if continued progress against hunger and poverty could be made by India's democratic government would Communist or military rule be averted there, King warned. Privately, it was clear that the visit had widened King's vision, and had given him a more sophisticated view of how social injustice and evil could be combated by the method of nonviolence. No longer were India and Gandhi simply rhetorical reference points, and no longer would it be possible to presume that Gandhi and his method had eliminated all of India's serious problems. Reddick, Virginia Durr wrote, "thinks the trip was a great experience for King and made him see that 'Love' alone will not cure poverty and degradation." It "is much more likely now," Reddick guessed, that King will "try and make a big pitch for political activity and participation."

The India visit also deepened King's understanding of Gandhi the man. There were three things about Gandhi, King told his Dexter congregation the day after his return, that were especially commendable. First was his great capacity for self-criticism. Second was his all but total avoidance of material possessions. Third was the "absolute self-discipline" that Gandhi had exhibited in his private as well as in his public life, so that "there was no gulf between the private and the public," King noted in admiration. Gandhi had steadfastly refused to use any of the large amounts of money that people sent him. Once, King remarked, Gandhi had even criticized his wife in public for using such donations for their own benefit.[31]

Coretta was only one of several people who sensed the deep personal appeal that Gandhi's individual example held for King. Later she recalled how, in speaking of the unsolicited funds that regularly came in, he had said, "'I'm not going to take this money for myself.'

He didn't like the attitude of his father wanting money. His whole attitude toward money—he completely divorced himself from it—from the desire for money. He finally came to the point of where he, after going to India, especially, he said, 'I don't want to own any property. I don't need any property. I don't need a house.'. . . He said, 'A man who devotes himself to a cause, who dedicates himself to a cause doesn't need a family.' He had a family and he loved his family and he wanted a family but he said, 'But man doesn't need a family' because he had this terrific conflict about the duty to his family and the duty to his fellow man, and he really recognized that he had this obligation to both. But if you are going to serve humanity you've got to neglect your family to some extent.

When King returned from India, he had no time to rest. As Coretta recalled it, he said, "'You know, I just can't stop because we don't have enough money to pay the salaries, so I have to get right out as soon as I get into Atlanta and make some speeches.'" Tilley was helping the Atlanta drive, and Ella Baker had traveled to Shreveport to assist a local registration effort there, but SCLC Treasurer Ralph Abernathy apologized to both individuals for being weeks behind in paying their salaries. Money was available to pay the phone bill, and the rent on the Auburn Avenue office, but that was all.

Even so, Tilley and Baker had prepared outlines of how SCLC might increase black voter registration. King still talked of doubling the number of black registered voters by 1960, but two staffers certainly could not achieve that goal. Baker continued to stress that SCLC had to get its many ministerial supporters involved in registration efforts in their different locales, but no mechanism for doing so had been created. In the first issue of *Crusader,* a new SCLC newsletter, Baker spoke of the organization as "a service agency to facilitate coordinated action by local protest groups and to assist in their sharing resources and experiences." So far, however, there had been little facilitation and few resources.

SCLC's inaction troubled those board members who wanted to unite all of the different municipal protest groups behind one common plan of action. After his return from India, King heard those complaints from several colleagues. There were two specific bones of contention. First, John Tilley had not proved to be an effective executive director. SCLC was just as moribund now as when Tilley had arrived. Second, King would have to put more of his own time and energy into SCLC if the organization was to thrive.

On April 2, SCLC's administrative committee met in Montgomery to consider the monetary plight and Tilley's status. They decided that firing Tilley was both financially desirable and justified on its merits. The next day, King wrote to inform him. King stressed "the financial crisis confronting the organization," how "our treasury is almost empty and we are now operating in the red." The budget, he said, "must be cut immediately. This automatically means cutting the staff." Reaching the heart of the matter, King reported:

It was the feeling of the committee that the organization has not had a dynamic program commensurate with the amount of money that it is spending. It was also felt that the Executive Director had not been able to achieve the public response expected. We had hoped that our program would be well developed by now.

King lowered the boom quickly. Tilley's resignation was requested immediately, to take effect twelve days later. As soon as money was available, they would send a check paying Tilley's salary through that date. Baker would stay on as interim director.

The proponents of a more active SCLC were still dissatisfied. Birmingham's Fred Shuttlesworth wrote a strong letter to King in advance of the major spring meeting in Tallahassee in mid-May. Not enough was being done to combat segregationist forces in Alabama, Shuttlesworth said. Local groups across the state had to unite for organized protests. A mid-January gathering of Alabama activists in Montgomery had not been enough. "When the flowery speeches have been made, we still have the hard job of getting down and helping people." SCLC "must move now, or else [be] hard put in the not too distant future, to justify our existence." The Tallahassee meeting would be crucial, Shuttlesworth said. He hoped that this time "we can really lay some positive plans for action. . . . Now is the time for serious thinking and practical resulting actions."[32]

King understood the complaints. However, his schedule was still more than he could handle. If it were not for Bayard Rustin and Stanley Levison in New York, dozens of small but important tasks never would get done. Rustin was receiving a salary of $50 a week as King's executive assistant, but the well-to-do Levison refused any compensation and continued to do a myriad of jobs: preparing King's tax returns, drafting articles and speeches, and keeping an eye on Harper's promotion of *Stride Toward Freedom*. Only on the rarest occasions did Levison ask anything of King. One exchange was especially revealing. "A couple of years ago," Levison wrote, "I loaned you my top-coat. If you had a use for it I am delighted, but if it is sitting in a closet somewhere, I would appreciate it if it could be sent back to me."

King was deeply embarrassed at his forgetfulness, and wrote to say that the coat would be mailed back immediately. Furthermore, he insisted, Levison should bill him for the many hours he had been devoting to King's affairs. It was wrong that Levison was getting no compensation for his extensive work.

Levison was not surprised by King's overreaction. King at that time, Levison said later, was

very thoughtful, quiet, and shy—very shy. The shyness was accented, I felt, with white people. And even in his relations with me in the early period, there was not always a relaxed attitude, but one of carefully listening to every word that he was saying so that he might not offend me, and that I might not offend him. There was a—a certain politeness, a certain arm's length approach, and you could feel the absence of relaxation. As the years went on this vanished.

Levison responded quickly to King's letter of apology. "It is out of the question" for King to pay him, Levison said. "My skills," he explained,

were acquired not only in a cloistered academic environment, but also in the commercial jungle. . . . Although our culture approves, and even honors these practices, to me they were always abhorrent. Hence, I looked forward to the time when I could use these skills not for myself but for socially constructive ends. The liberation struggle is the most positive and rewarding area of work anyone could experience.

King accepted Levison's position, and their relationship grew closer.[33]

In early April, A. Philip Randolph announced that a second Youth March for Integrated Schools would take place in Washington on April 18. The October March had been only a modest success, and Randolph hoped that April weather and King's presence would make for a larger turnout. When the day came, Randolph's hopefulness proved justified: A crowd of 26,000, two and one-half times that of October, gathered at the Washington Monument. The principal speakers were King, Kenyan leader Tom Mboya, visiting in the United States, and Roy Wilkins of the NAACP. In his remarks King again placed primary emphasis upon the right to vote. After the speechmaking, when a delegation of student representatives approached the White House gate, presidential assistant Gerald Morgan received them and explained that Eisenhower shared their desire to eliminate racial discrimination. Although the Youth March received only moderate national press coverage, it was distinctly more successful than the earlier one.

The White House was not the only part of the government interested in civil rights protests. The Federal Bureau of Investigation had warned the White House that the American Communist party had taken a special interest in both Youth Marches. The FBI was particularly curious about the role that an inactive party member, Stanley Levison, had played in the two events. Randolph had publicly commended Levison for his work on the October March, and the acknowledgment had aroused the FBI's curiosity.[34]

After the Youth March, King had two major engagements prior to the crucial SCLC gathering in Tallahassee. One was in Washington, where Vice-President Nixon had invited King to speak to a conference on racial discrimination in employment called by the President's Committee on Government Contracts. Nixon, who had taken the lead role in this effort against job bias, told the audience of four hundred that "there is a vital need for Americans to recognize that this is basically a moral problem." That declaration, which pleased King greatly, was exactly the sort of statement he and others long had been seeking from Eisenhower but never could obtain. King told the gathering that the church in particular should take a strong role in supporting fair employment practices. "Love and persuasion are virtues that are basic and essential," King said, "but they must forever be complemented by justice and moral coercion."

Two days later, SCLC held an "African Freedom Dinner" in Atlanta for Kenyan leader Tom Mboya, who had appeared at the Youth March with King. "I am absolutely convinced," King told him, "that there is no basic difference between colonialism and segregation. They are both based on a contempt for life, and a tragic doctrine of white supremacy. So our struggles are not only similar; they are in a real sense one."

At the Tallahassee gathering, many of the principals openly pressed King to put "maximum time" into SCLC's affairs. No true plan of action was adopted, and no search for a successor to Tilley was instituted. The meeting's only material result was adoption of a statement calling on President Eisenhower to take action against a growing number of violent assaults on black people across the South. The recent lynching of Mack Charles Parker in Poplarville, Mississippi, was but the best-known case, and a federal antilynch law was needed. If nothing was done, SCLC warned, it "might be necessary and expedient to appeal to the conscience of the world through the Commission on Human Rights of the United Nations."[35]

In late May, much of King's time was devoted to giving commencement speeches at black colleges across the South. Such a schedule left him little time for responding to Shuttlesworth's prodding to move him and SCLC into more meaningful activity. "The times are far too critical for us to get good solid ideas on what should be done in certain situations, and then take too long a time to put these ideas into action," Shuttlesworth warned.

During the summer months, Ella Baker attempted without success to stimulate voter registration in Columbia, South Carolina. She also initiated contacts in Birmingham and Montgomery, where the MIA remained dormant. No efforts to pursue school desegregation had been taken, largely because many MIA leaders opposed King's idea. "There was nothing he could get going," one member recalled. "When he began to talk about school desegregation—and he's talking to black teachers primarily . . . nobody was willing to go out on the limb on that." The MIA was torn by "a great deal of rivalry and jealousy," and "Martin became disgusted," she explained.

King's political opinions sometimes surprised his Montgomery friends. One evening he and Coretta had dinner with Clifford and Virginia Durr and Aubrey Williams, three of the very few Montgomery whites who openly supported the MIA. All were shocked when King said black voters viewed Richard Nixon as the one potential 1960 presidential candidate with an interest in civil rights. King described how friendly Nixon had been to him and related Nixon's comments at the Washington conference a month earlier. No other possible nominee had made contact with him, King said. Under the Durrs' questioning, King admitted he thought well of Adlai Stevenson, but had never met him. King conceded he still had some doubts about Nixon, but his conversations with the vice-president had reduced those worries, King told one correspondent. Nixon seemed "absolutely sincere" about civil rights. King also believed that

> Nixon would have done much more to meet the present crisis in race relations than President Eisenhower has done. . . . Much of the tension in the South and many of the reverses we are now facing could have been avoided if President Eisenhower had taken a strong, positive stand on the question of civil rights and the Supreme Court's decision as soon as it was rendered. . . . Nixon, I believe, would have done that.

The vice president, King added, was "very personable . . . one of the most magnetic personalities that I have ever confronted . . . his personality will carry him a long, long way politically." King had found him a very persuasive man. "Nixon has a genius for convincing one that he is sincere . . . he almost disarms you with his apparent sincerity," King observed. "If Richard Nixon is not sincere, he is the most dangerous man in America."[36]

In his public speeches, King repeatedly denounced President Eisenhower. What American politican had done the most to promote integration the last five years? King asked. It certainly was not Eisenhower. Instead, King said, it was Arkansas Governor Orval Faubus, who had instigated the crisis at Little Rock. "His irresponsible actions brought the issue to the forefront of the conscience of the nation" as nothing else had, "and allowed people to see the futility of attempting to close the public school." For Eisenhower, though, King expected the verdict to be even more harsh:

> I fear that future historians will have to record that when America came to its most progressive moment of creative fulfillment in the area of human relations, it was temporarily held back by a chief executive who refused to make a strong positive statement morally condemning segregation.

Hypocritical northern Republicans, he added, were more dangerous than bigoted southern Democrats. "The Negro must make it palpably clear that he is not inextricably bound to either political party. . . . We will not blindly support any party that refuses to take a forthright stand on the question of civil rights."[37]

At the end of August, the MIA asked the local school board to make a "reasonable start" toward desegregation of the public schools. King stated the MIA would go to court if the board did not act, but nothing happened. The organization also began another voter registration drive, again under Rufus Lewis's direction.

At the same time, Ella Baker began exploring whether SCLC could improve its voter registration efforts by stressing adult education. She traveled to the Highlander Folk School, which had developed a citizenship education program out of the ideas of two black South Carolinians, Esau Jenkins and Septima P. Clark. No firm plans were made, but Baker told the SCLC delegates when they gathered in Columbia, South Carolina, at the end of September for the major fall meeting that the organization needed to look further in this direction.

Citizenship education, however, was not the primary focus of the strongly worded report Baker gave to the SCLC board in Columbia. Instead, she took up the cudgel Shuttlesworth had been wielding for the previous six months. "Have we been so busy doing the things that *had* to be done," just to keep the organization in existence, "that we have failed to [do] what should be done?" she asked. "Have we really come to grips with what it takes to do the job for which SCLC was organized; and are we willing to pay the price?" Too much of her own time, and too much of SCLC's resources had been taken up with busywork, Baker said. The organization should commit itself to three aims. First, it should "facilitate *coordinated* action by local groups," as it always had hoped to. Second, "While serving existing leadership, SCLC seeks to *develop potential leaders.*" However, both of those were intermediate steps toward the third and most important goal: "developing a vital movement of nonviolent direct mass action against racial discrimination." To do that, Baker said, "a corps of persons" would be needed, much as Rustin had envisioned three years earlier.

SCLC needed more thinking, more strategy, more planning, Baker argued, and an expanded staff. It also needed to seek out indigenous leaders more aggressively. As soon as possible the executive board should meet to reflect "on how the crusading potential of SCLC might be realized," with working papers and an agenda prepared in advance.

Baker was not the only one who felt that SCLC's two and a half years of existence had produced only meager accomplishments. King in his remarks to the board essentially agreed. The emphasis had to be upon programmatic achievement, and not merely organizational maintenance. A second professional staff member should be hired, to fill Tilley's vacancy, and only one full convention, rather than two in the spring and fall, should be held each year. On the substantive matter of voter registration, King admitted that "we have not yet really scratched the surface in this area." SCLC also needed to draw more press and public attention, King stated, and a third staff member should be hired for that purpose. However, "the greatest channel of publicity for the organization is the existence of a positive, dynamic, and dramatic program," which SCLC did not have. A committee to define that "Future Program" was in order, and King announced he was naming Abernathy, Shuttlesworth, Reddick, Samuel Williams and Joseph Lowery to serve on it.

The SCLC board agreed with Baker's and King's positions, and they mandated that Baker meet with the Future Program committee within three weeks to make plans for 1960. They also adopted a resolution that addressed King himself. The members of the board, it read, "urgently request that he seriously consider giving the maximum of his time and energies to the work" of SCLC. Their previous request in May had not met with sufficient response from King. Now they chose to act publicly.[38]

In the wake of the Columbia meeting, several items appeared in black publications noting SCLC's weaknesses and the board's message to King. In *Jet* magazine, correspondent Simeon Booker highlighted SCLC's lack of achievement on voter registration, and claimed the group had raised only $25,000 over three years. King was furious, and suspected John Tilley was the source of the aspersions. King immediately called Booker and tried to rebut the items. He did concede, in a subsequent note to Booker, that SCLC was "quite conscious of the fact we have not scratched the surface in the South in this all-important area of voting." In correspondence with a friend, black trade unionist Theodore E. "Ted" Brown, King was less charitable. "Almost everything he says in the article is false," King complained. SCLC had raised more than $25,000, even though "we have never really seriously developed a fund raising program." In regard to voter registration, "SCLC has done much more than the NAACP," King claimed. But even in his closing comment, King's defensiveness and strenuous desire to put a good face on a bad situation shone through: "We are really planning to rise up more aggressively."

Ella Baker continued to press her effort for just that. In preparation for the upcoming meeting on the Future Program, she prepared a memorandum simply titled "SCLC as a Crusade." The organization, she argued, had to turn some effort toward leadership training and citizenship education. She envisioned identifying a total of a thousand ministers and other local leaders who could then recruit and stimulate others. "The word CRUSADE connotes for me a vigorous movement, with high purpose and involving masses of people," Baker said. SCLC must "map out a program for developing action teams in nonviolent direct action."

King also increasingly thought about what had to be done. Several things required quick action, he told his colleagues. First, intensive voter drives had to be held in cities where there would be no active resistance, so that a tangible achievement could be shown. Second, King had to see Roy Wilkins, to "clear up what appears to be seeds of dissension." Third, Bayard Rustin, who had been in Ghana for a short time, should be called home and added to the staff as the public relations person. "I make this recommendation not unmindful of the possible perils involved," King conceded. "We may employ him for a period on a trial basis, with the understanding that if any undue criticism that would prove embarrassing to him or the organization [arose], he would quietly resign." But last, and most important, thought had to be given to moving beyond a program of simply assisting voter registration. Just what that might be, King did not say—and probably did not yet know.[39]

Throughout the first two weeks of November, King pondered his options. On November 2, he returned to Chester to accept an alumni award from Crozer. His close friend J. Pius Barbour was happy to see him, and observed that Mike had

not changed his outrageous eating habits. I gave a steak supper one night, and he gulped down a great big sirloin steak swimming in hot sauce. Where does he put all that food, I wondered.

One of his "old flames" came up to shake hands. "Great God, Barbour," said Mike, "she looks like she fell into a concrete mixer."

With Barbour, with Stanley Levison in New York, with Abernathy and other close friends in Montgomery, and with Daddy and Mother King in Atlanta, King discussed one particular question: Had the time come for him to leave Montgomery and Dexter? Two particular concerns forced him to address that question. First, his colleagues in SCLC had made clear their demand that he make that organization the primary focus of his activities. If he did so, he almost certainly would have to move to Atlanta. Second, he was increasingly plagued by guilt about the quality of his pastorship at Dexter. No one had voiced complaints openly, but King knew, as one close friend stated it, that "he was really getting into trouble" with the congregation because of his frequent absences and greatly overburdened work load. The church, he himself felt, deserved better than he could give it.

Coretta also recognized the growing pressures upon her husband. Once he had taken such pride in his preaching, in the precisely memorized sermons that he sometimes practiced in front of the bathroom mirror. Now, for several years, he had not had "time to memorize," she said. "He didn't have time to even write his sermons out. He didn't have time to adequately plan and prepare" most of them, and would find himself preaching familiar sentences with no more preparation than a quickly scrawled outline. Later, she reflected on it:

The demands of the movement were getting so great, and he really didn't feel that he was doing an adequate job of pastoring. That's when he decided to move to Atlanta. He realized that his responsibilities wouldn't get any less, but he just felt that it was not fair to the congregation to give them so little of his time.

The pressure from his SCLC colleagues, and his guilt about Dexter, each pushed the decision upon him. Dexter's lay leadership told him that he could stay and preach only once a month, but King knew that was not fulfilling the pastoral responsibility. In addition, he feared the state would take economic reprisals against Dexter members who were public school teachers in retaliation for his desire to pursue school integration. Daddy King, who had pressed his son for years to leave the dangers of

Montgomery and rejoin him in Atlanta, also urged the move. M.L. could be co-pastor with him at Ebenezer, where he had belonged all along, and the co-pastorship would allow him plenty of time for SCLC while still permitting him to retain a ministerial role. All the arguments pointed in one direction, but the decision was painful and one King was reluctant to make. Five years earlier, King had come to Montgomery in search of a quiet but socially relevant pastorship. Then, through no initiative of his own, he had been caught up in something larger than he had ever imagined. The vision in the kitchen had given him the courage and faith to accept that, but even when the protest ended, he realized that he was not free, that he could not and would not escape from the responsibility of the larger role into which he had been cast. After almost three years of struggling against himself, he realized that this decision, just like the one he had described to Stanley Levison and Harris Wofford during that trip to Washington three years earlier, was not really his to make. It was made for him, whether he wanted it or not.

By the middle of November King was ready to act. He wrote to Levison, asking when Rustin would return from Africa. King wanted Levison's and Rustin's advice about how to announce his resignation to the public. Rustin's return was delayed, and King realized he could not keep the news out of the press once he announced it to his congregation. On Sunday morning, November 29, he told the Dexter membership that he was submitting his resignation, effective the end of January, 1960. The prepared statement that he issued stressed that the shift was motivated by new plans for SCLC:

> The time has come for a broad, bold advance of the Southern campaign for equality. . . . Not only will it include a stepped up campaign of voter registration, but a full-scale approach will be made upon discrimination and segregation in all forms. . . . We must employ new methods of struggle involving the masses of our people.

Across the nation, news reports noted his decision.[40]

A number of tasks confronted King in advance of the move. The day after his announcement, he flew to New York to see Roy Wilkins and to try to arrange a joint accommodation between SCLC's and the NAACP's voter registration plans. They agreed to hold a larger meeting in Atlanta at the end of December. Back in Montgomery, King gave his annual address at the rally commemorating the fourth anniversary of the boycott. Only nine hundred people, a relatively small crowd, attended. He defended, at some length, the MIA's handling of its own finances, and the actions it had taken concerning Montgomery's parks, which remained closed despite a favorable court ruling. Three months had passed since the MIA publicly had raised the school desegregation issue, but nothing had transpired. For over a year, he said, the time had been "ripe for expanded militant action across the South," but it had not occurred. All in all, it was a decidedly downbeat performance. In one sidelight, seven incumbent members of the MIA board stood for reelection. Six were returned to office, and one was defeated: E. D. Nixon. King was leaving, and his old protagonist was being booted out.

In early December, several SCLC matters required King's attention. He traveled to Washington to discuss the lagging desegregation of interstate transportation facilities with representatives of several federal regulatory commissions. He also had remained in touch with Kenya's Tom Mboya, and had asked SCLC to sponsor a scholarship for a selected African student at a black American college. Mboya's choice, twenty-five-year-old Nicholas W. Raballa, visited with King in December, and King used the publicity to call for others to sponsor such exchanges with Africa. "There is a growing feeling that our struggles are a common struggle," he remarked.

On December 8 the SCLC hierarchy met in Birmingham to discuss plans for the upcoming year. King wanted to move beyond a voter registration program, but the desire remained unfocused. "This is the creative moment for a full scale assault on the system of segregation," he told his colleagues. "We must practice open civil disobedience. We must be willing to go to jail en masse. That way we may be able to arouse the dozing consciences of the South . . ." and reach what King called "the conscience of the great decent majority." Just what form this assault would take remained unspecified.

At the end of December, King, Abernathy, and Shuttlesworth met with Roy Wilkins and four NAACP staff members to discuss cooperative endeavors on voter registration. No concrete plans were announced, but they did tell reporters that their goal was to increase black registration across the South from its current level of 1.4 million to 2.5 million before the 1960 fall elections. The newsmen, however, were more interested in pressing King on the implications of his upcoming move to Atlanta. He told them that SCLC hoped to expand its staff, that Atlanta had fine black leadership, and that his emphasis would not be upon taking an active role in local Atlanta affairs. "King said he is coming here merely to devote more time to his SCLC activity," the black *Atlanta Daily World* observed. Nonetheless, many of the older men in Atlanta's black elite made no secret of their distaste for this new development. Daddy King might be their equal, but his thirty-year-old son certainly was not, even if the press presumed him to be their superior. "Jealousy among Negro leaders is so thick it can be cut with a knife," the *Pittsburgh Courier* commented.[41]

On January 1, King flew to Virginia, where Wyatt T. Walker, an energetic young Petersburg minister whose outspokenness had impressed King at several SCLC meetings, had organized an Emancipation Day march in Richmond to protest the state's decision to close the public schools in Prince Edward County, rather than integrate them. King led the procession to the state capitol, and then spoke to the crowd. It was another positive indication of Walker's abilities, that he could bring off what he promised to bring off. Tilley's old job of executive director was still vacant, and no leading candidates had emerged. After the rally, King broached the subject to Walker. Would he be interested in considering the position? Walker said yes. They chatted about it some, about how Walker would have to leave his pastorship at Petersburg's historic Gillfield Baptist Church and move his family to Atlanta. King promised to get back to him about it.

Back in Montgomery, and busy with preparations for the move to Atlanta, King worried about getting SCLC off the ground. Rustin still had not returned, and King continued to press Levison for news: "Please keep me informed about Bayard's possible return. We really need his services as soon as possible." A mid-January trip took King to Washington to join other black leaders for meetings with congressional leaders—Lyndon B. Johnson, Sam Rayburn, Everett M. Dirksen—to lobby for civil rights legislation in this presidential election year. Supplication was not what the leaders had in mind, and one week later A. Philip Randolph, with King at his side, publicly announced at a New York rally that blacks would march on both the Democratic and Republican National Conventions to urge both parties to adopt strong stands on civil rights. Then, for one last time, King went home to Montgomery.

The farewell ceremony at Dexter took place on Sunday evening, January 31. The next night, King spoke at an MIA meeting that formally inaugurated Ralph Abernathy as the group's new president. King hoped that his new life in Atlanta would be more restful and less frustrating. "I have been under extreme tension for four years," he confided to one questioner, "because of my multiple duties. The time has long since come for me to shift gears." In many ways, he was relieved, for the move would signify a break from what had become an increasingly troubled existence. In other ways, though, he realized that the move placed before him an uncertain future, yet one from which he could not retreat. His own contemporaneous account put it most strikingly:

> For almost four years now I have been faced with the responsibility of trying to do as one man what five or six people ought to be doing. . . . I found myself in a position which I could not get out of. This thrust unexpected responsibilities my way. . . .
>
> What I have been doing is giving, giving, giving and not stopping to retreat and meditate like I should—to come back. If the situation is not changed, I will be a physical and psychological wreck. I have to re-organize my personality and reorient my life. . . .
>
> I have a sort of nagging conscience that someone will interpret my leaving Montgomery as a retreat from the civil rights struggle. Actually, I will be involved in it on a larger scale. I can't stop now. History has thrust something upon me from which I cannot turn away.[42]

3

SNCC, the Kennedys, and the Freedom Rides, 1960–1961

On February 1, 1960, four young black men who were students at North Carolina A & T College sat down at the lunch counter in a Greensboro F. W. Woolworth's store and refused to leave when they were denied service. Only white patrons were served at the counter. Word of their act spread among fellow students, and the next day, more than two dozen occupied the lunch counter, doing schoolwork when they also were refused service. Over the following four days the numbers grew larger and larger. A few white participants joined in, while other whites heckled the protesters. The effort spread to other Greensboro lunch counters until, by the end of the week, all such facilities were closed. With those spontaneous actions, the "sit-ins" began.

By Monday, February 8, the sit-in protests had spread to Durham and Winston-Salem. Within the following two days, they spread to Charlotte, Raleigh, Fayetteville, and Elizabeth City. By the end of the week they had reached Norfolk and Portsmouth, Virginia, and Rock Hill, South Carolina. With no prompting from any of the existing civil rights organizations or black adult leadership, a new stage in the black freedom struggle had been launched.

As the sit-ins spread across North Carolina and into other southeastern states, several young adult activists moved to the fore. In Durham, Rev. Douglas E. Moore, a young minister who had been attending SCLC meetings for two years, began calling friends in other cities, including Rev. James M. Lawson in Nashville. Lawson and other young black activists in Nashville had been discussing nonviolent protest and preparing for just such an initiative. The technique itself was not original to Greensboro; other black protesters had employed it in 1957 and 1958 in Oklahoma and Kansas, though with little press coverage. As the phone calls and other contacts spread, so did the sit-ins. By February 13, protests had begun in Nashville and Tallahassee, and a New York staff member of the Congress of Racial Equality (CORE), Gordon Carey, was dispatched to aid the various North Carolina efforts.[1]

Martin King spent the first ten days of February getting situated in Atlanta. He and his family—Yoki was now four, and Marty two—had rented from Ebenezer church the house in which King had grown up as a young boy. Mrs. Maude Ballou, King's secretary from Montgomery, came and lived with them on a temporary basis until he could find a new secretary in Atlanta. King told reporters that his first task in Atlanta would be to work on a book of sermons, and Daddy King pronounced that "he's not coming to cause trouble. Instead of that, he had chosen the pulpit." On February 7, the new co-pastor preached his first sermon to a crowd of 1,200 at Ebenezer. Daddy King introduced him, remarking, "He's not little M.L. anymore, now. He is 'Dr. King' now."

Besides his work at Ebenezer, King tried to develop SCLC's program. In one formulation, he identified four tasks facing the organization. The joint voter registration effort with the NAACP should be pursued, and workshops should continue to be held to discuss nonviolence. He felt "there is need for carrying out some dramatic campaign at both political conventions in order to mobilize more support for strong civil rights legislation in the future." Randolph had already announced that, and Rustin and Levison were at work on it. Most important, King said, "There is need to mobilize the masses of our people in the South for implementation" of desegregation. SCLC hoped "to work through the churches in order to develop this type of mass action."

King's first direct contact with the sit-ins was a phone call from Durham's Doug Moore during the week of February 8. Moore wanted to convene a meeting on February 16 to establish formal contacts between the sit-in protests in different North Carolina cities. Would King come to Durham and speak to the gathering? King readily said yes.

On Tuesday morning, February 16, King flew to Durham. Moore gave him and Abernathy a tour of the downtown lunch counters and then took them to an afternoon strategy meeting of the representatives from the different cities. King told the student leaders not to forget that the struggle was justice versus injustice, not black versus white, and reminded them always to be open to compromise with local whites. He particularly stressed the idea of "jail, not bail" and described his own 1958 decision to serve time rather than pay a fine for his arrest at the Montgomery courthouse. Even if his attempt had not succeeded, it was the morally correct stance to take toward an unjust use of the law to support segregation.

King suggested to the student representatives that they form a coordinating council of members from each of the different schools and cities. He also recommended that they tell store owners that if lunch counters were not opened on an integrated basis, the protesters would recommend that people of goodwill boycott the entire store. King's remarks were well received, and the group established a coordinating council with three representatives from each locale. Although some competition for leadership was visible between supporters of the NAACP, CORE, and SCLC, "many student leaders expressed the desire to keep the movement as much 'student-led' as possible," one observer noted.

That evening, King spoke to a rally of more than one thousand at Durham's White Rock Baptist Church. He was in top form, buoyed by what he could see developing. "What is new in your fight is the fact that it was initiated, fed, and sustained by students." He promised that "you have the full weight of the SCLC behind you in your struggle," and emphasized that his audience appreciate how they stood at a crucial point in the freedom movement. "At a certain point in every struggle of great importance, a moment of doubt or hesitation develops," King remarked, thinking back to Montgomery four years earlier. "If there is one lesson experience has taught us . . . it is that when you have found by the help of God a correct course, a morally sound objective, you do not equivocate, you do not retreat—you struggle to win a victory." The personal cost might be high, but one must resolve to bear it. The goal was not simply integration, but true personal freedom, for "freedom is necessary for one's selfhood, for one's intrinsic worth."[2]

By noon the next day, King was back in his office at Ebenezer Baptist Church. Without notice, two local deputy sheriffs arrived in midafternoon and asked to see him. They had a warrant for his arrest, they told King, a warrant from the state of Alabama seeking his extradition. The charge? Two counts of perjury, a felony, for falsely swearing to the accuracy of his 1956 and 1958 Alabama state tax returns. Accompanied by Dad and brother A.D., King went downtown for arraignment and was released on a $2,000 bond. Reporters indicated that King "reacted with no outward show of concern to his arrest," but internally he was devastated. Alabama news reports indicated that renegade MIA official U. J. Fields had testified before a Montgomery grand jury several weeks earlier, and that the income tax charges against King were based on allegations he had failed to report money that he had improperly acquired from the treasuries of the MIA and SCLC. King vigorously denied those claims. "I have never misappropriated any funds. I have never had the need nor the desire to do so. Such an act would betray my moral instincts and the teachings of a lifetime." Stories that he lived in a lavish house or owned a fancy car were total fiction, he noted. "I don't even wish it were true. . . . I own just one piece of property, a 1954 Pontiac . . . I am renting the home I live in." King added that he had "no pretense to absolute goodness," but that if he had "one virtue, it's honesty."

The following day King waived extradition, saying he would return to Alabama voluntarily to face the charges. "I have nothing to hide." Asked to explain how he thought the matter had arisen, King detailed the destructive role of U. J. Fields. King had thought the tax question was resolved, he explained, when he had met sometime earlier with the Alabama agent who was auditing him, Lloyd Hale. The agent had claimed that King's income in both 1956 and 1958 was greater than King had reported, by a total of some $27,000, and King with great reluctance had given Alabama officials a check for $1,600 to end the dispute. Apparently it had not.

In public King put forward a strong face, but in private he was overwhelmed. "I had never seen Martin affected so deeply," Coretta wrote. The tax charges "caused Martin more suffering than any other event of his life up to that point." He was deeply worried that people who knew him only from a distance would presume the allegations were true, and lose faith in him. Stanley Levison and other close friends explained that King could prove that he had done nothing wrong by showing at the trial, with the best possible defense, that the allegations had no basis in fact. King should not let the matter worry him to death, for his New York friends would raise the money for a first-rate legal defense.

Still deeply troubled, King flew west for some SCLC fund-raising appearances. Then, on February 29, he arrived in Montgomery for his Alabama arraignment. The sit-in protests had reached King's former hometown on February 25, when a small group of Alabama State students, after consultation with Ralph Abernathy, had attempted to gain service at the segregated snack bar in the Montgomery County courthouse. The protests had grown over the following three days, and King spoke to two enthusiastic rallies after his arraignment. It was the most enlivened Montgomery had been in over three years. Within a week's time Alabama State expelled the leaders of the protests, and a mass prayer march to the state capitol was organized. Policemen broke it up, and King, back in Atlanta, said he was sending a telegram to President Eisenhower demanding federal action. No response was forthcoming.

In early March, King's New York friends announced the creation of a "Committee to Defend Martin Luther King" and a fund-raising goal of $200,000 for King's legal defense and SCLC's voter registration plans. A. Philip Randolph would serve as chairman, and Rustin was named publicly as executive director. Solicitation of contributions began, and a legal team was assembled. Hubert Delaney of New York and William Robert Ming of Chicago, two noted black attorneys, would head it up, along with Fred Gray, Charles Langford, Arthur Shores, and S. S. Seay, Jr., from Alabama.[3]

The sit-in protests finally reached Atlanta on March 15. A group of students from the black colleges had begun planning soon after word of Greensboro reached them, but the college presidents and other black adults urged them to move carefully. The presidents recommended that the student leaders draw up a statement of their grievances, and two of them, Roslyn Pope and Julian Bond, drafted the document. It was entitled "An Appeal for Human Rights," and Atlanta University President Rufus Clement arranged to have it appear as a full-page ad in all three Atlanta daily newspapers on March 9. That same afternoon the student leaders met with Atlanta Mayor William B. Hartsfield at Clement's office. Hartsfield urged negotiations with white business leaders before protests were begun. A group of white ministers recommended the same course, but on the fifteenth some two hundred black students sat in at numerous establishments. Over seventy were arrested, and slow-paced negotiations with white businessmen began. In the span of six weeks, the sit-in protests had become a southwide effort.

One of the most enthusiastic observers of the student protests was Ella Baker. She knew that her time with SCLC was limited, that many of the ministers resented having an outspoken woman as chief of staff, and that King had discussed the executive directorship with Wyatt T. Walker. Nonetheless, the students should be encouraged, and she had welcomed Douglas Moore's initiative in calling the February 16 meeting. In its aftermath, she had spoken with King, Abernathy, Moore, and James Lawson about convening a second and larger gathering, one that would bring together sit-in protesters from all across the South. The idea was applauded, and by the second week of March she was working on plans for such a meeting to be held on April 15 and 16 at her alma mater, Shaw University in Raleigh. On March 16 she flew to Raleigh to finalize the arrangements, and ran into both Moore and Glenn Smiley at the airport. They chatted about the plans, and about their common desire that the student protest remain student led and not be taken over by any established civil rights organization. Baker reported her arrangements with Shaw to King and Abernathy, and pointedly stressed to them the content of her discussion with Moore and Smiley: "They agreed that the meeting should be youth centered, and that the adults attending would serve in an advisory capacity, and should mutually agree to 'speak only when asked to do so.'" The adults who would be there, Baker recommended, should meet in advance so that that rule would be clear to all.

By the end of March the fund-raising efforts of the Committee to Defend Martin Luther King were in full swing. The committee placed a full-page ad in *The New York Times*, headlined HEED THEIR RISING VOICES, detailing the prosecution of King and the repression of the Montgomery protests. Alabama officials took great offense at some of the assertions, and demanded a retraction. They were not the only people angered by the appeals being issued by the committee; the NAACP was irritated about the claims being made for SCLC's voter registration achievements. Program Director James Farmer told Wilkins: "I think it is a thoroughly dishonest and deceptive appeal but if this is deceptive you should hear the oral appeals being made publicly, although not put in writing. . . . Should not Randolph and/or King be privately taken to task?" Wilkins chose to bide his time.[4]

On April 5, Baker issued the first public announcement of the Shaw meeting. The release explained how student representatives from across the South had been invited, and that James Lawson would be the keynote speaker. The three-page statement made no mention of King, who was keeping to a quiet schedule in Atlanta and was preoccupied with his impending trial. On April 10, he spoke at Spelman College, and the next day talked with reporters about the upcoming Shaw conference. King "predicted a Southwide council of students will come out of the meeting," one wrote. "He said he would serve in an advisory capacity only, and any future direction in the protest actions would come from the students themselves." Baker's pressure appeared to have taken hold.

Some two hundred students, twice the number Baker expected, gathered at Shaw University on Friday, April 15. King spoke to the press and students at the beginning of the meeting, emphasizing "the need for some type of continuing organization." He hoped that the students would weigh a nationwide selective buying campaign, and that they also "seriously consider training a group of volunteers who will willingly go to jail rather than pay bail or fines.

> The youth must take the freedom struggle into every community in the South without exception. . . . Inevitably this broadening of the struggle and the determination which it represents will arouse vocal and vigorous support and place pressures on the federal government that will compel its intervention.

That evening James Lawson delivered a well-received keynote speech on the importance of nonviolence. Later, as additional delegates continued to arrive, King spoke privately with a number of people about his expectations for the conference. Some, like Wyatt Walker and Bernard Lee, the student leader of the Montgomery protesters from Alabama State, pressed King to ask the delegates to align themselves formally with SCLC. Others, like Lawson, reminded King of the need to let the students make their own decisions. Meanwhile, Baker continued to fear that King, Abernathy, Walker, and others were plotting an SCLC takeover, and she warned some participants to assert their independence when the time came.

Lawson in particular knew how strongly Baker felt about blocking any adult takeover of the students. He and King had discussed the subject in advance of the gathering, and did so again that Friday night:

> We made an explicit decision that the students . . . would proceed as they wanted to proceed, and that . . . we would not try to impose upon them our analysis or our own determination of how they should go. . . . Both King and I in our personal conversations had reached that conclusion. . . . If he and I decided we should establish an SCLC student arm, boom, it could have been done . . . we had the votes from the students to do that. But we agreed . . . after we got on the scene

and got involved in the whole process, he and I agreed that we should pretty much let the process of the conference direct itself.

Bernard Lee had a similar encounter with King that same evening when he voiced his own sentiment that SCLC "was the logical place to house such an effort." King acknowledged that the idea had much to recommend it, but made clear that Baker's opposition was too great and potentially embarrassing an obstacle to overcome:

I discussed it very candidly with Dr. King and Wyatt that evening and I remember Dr. King almost verbatim saying that as much as he would like to see the students identify with SCLC, he thought that because of the events taking place, the way the conference was structured . . . that that would not be in the best interests of the students or SCLC. . . . He chose to let it become independent. . . . That was a little disappointing, but still I understood exactly what he was saying and I knew the players at that point.

King thus made up his mind not to fight a battle that he could win but which would exact too high a price—an open break with the increasingly unhappy Baker. On Saturday, as the delegates split up into discussion groups to talk about nonviolent protest and the next steps for the student movement, conversations about the issue spread and many student representatives received the impression that the organizational allegiance question might be posed formally at a later session. King and Walker, however, backed away from pressing the issue. "They did not lobby the students" that morning, Bernard Lee recalled. As of then the disagreement with Baker "was not very visible but it was definitely there," and to press the issue of forming an SCLC youth arm "would have been a little destructive. . . . He did not want that to spew over into a public thing between he and Ella Baker," Lee noted. So, "King and Wyatt Walker kept their preferences to themselves; Ella Baker [and] Jim Lawson made their preferences publicly known to the students." Open controversy was avoided, though Baker's bitterness ripened.

When the delegates assembled on Saturday afternoon, King spoke to them, praising Lawson's speech and explaining that he would be leaving that evening, in advance of Sunday's decision-making session, to appear on *Meet the Press*. He answered questions about nonviolence, and no organizational squabbles developed. That evening he, Walker, and Abernathy all spoke at a mass rally, and then departed. When the student delegates held the final plenary meeting on Sunday, there was no battle over the question of organizational ties. A "temporary" Student Nonviolent Coordinating Committee (SNCC) was approved, to be headquartered in Atlanta, with King and Lawson each serving as advisors. The only controversy was over whether only southern students, and not northern ones, would be represented on that committee. A compromise solution was agreed upon, and the delegates departed from what almost all agreed had been an encouraging conference.[5]

King found the Raleigh meeting enervating. Instead of demonstrating unity behind the students' efforts, the adults had devoted much of their energy to a debilitating dispute over the structure that the student movement should adopt. He was depressed enough about the tax indictment; he did not need additional problems with Ella Baker. There seemed to be no respite, and his appearance on *Meet the Press* the following morning supplied further aggravation. Instead of a friendly reception, the reporters bombarded him with hostile questions. They focused in particular upon a statement by former President Harry S. Truman that Communists were behind the sit-in protests. King said he was "very disappointed" and that Truman ought to make a public apology. He strongly defended the sit-in tactic, explaining that "sometimes it is necessary to dramatize an issue because many people are not aware of what is happening. . . . The sit-ins serve to dramatize the indignities and the injustices which Negro people are facing all over the nation." He further explained that the principal focus of the movement would remain the right to vote, and that "ultimately the federal government should set forth a uniform pattern of registration and voting."

Back in Atlanta, King had no opportunity to relax. While the Raleigh conference had averted any public controversy about Ella Baker's attitude, it did lead to more reports of a split between SCLC and the NAACP. Several news stories had highlighted a line from Lawson's speech criticizing the NAACP's tactics as too exclusively legalistic, and had labeled Lawson "a leading disciple" of King. Roy Wilkins was furious and let King know it. He said he was "puzzled and greatly distressed" by the news stories about "this unwarranted attack." King certainly must share his "determination not to have a break between our groups," Wilkins remarked. "I am hopeful that you can help clarify the situation. I know you will want to. There are some other disturbing elements in the picture which I would not care to go into here, but which I feel you and I should discuss privately as soon as possible." King moved to avoid further offending the sensitive Wilkins. Prior to the Shaw conference, he had considered adding Lawson, and Doug Moore, to SCLC's staff if funds could be raised. Moore was no favorite of NAACP loyalists, and hiring either man would be taken by Wilkins as another slap. King chose to postpone any action, and Lawson was disappointed. "He did not want to alienate Roy Wilkins," Lawson later stated. "He did not want to appear to be battling the NAACP. Rightly or wrongly he backed off a number of things for that very reason."

King felt drained by the unending series of turmoils—the tax case, Baker, and now Wilkins again. It seemed as if he had no time to renew his energy. He told one friend that "I have felt terribly frustrated over my inability to retreat, concentrate, and reflect." The move to Atlanta had not provided the expected respite. "I felt that by coming here I would have more time to meditate and think through the total struggle ahead," but instead the past ten weeks had been more hectic than life in Montgomery. He knew that he had to slow down, and on some occasions the possibility of withdrawing into a more restful existence seemed especially attractive. Then, however, he would think back four years, to that night in the kitchen, and resolve to go on. "I must admit," he noted that April,

> that at times I have felt that I could no longer bear such a heavy burden, and was tempted to retreat to a more quiet and serene life. But every time such a temptation appeared, something came to strengthen and sustain my determination. . . . . God has been profoundly real to me in recent years. In the midst of outer dangers I have felt an inner calm.

No matter how resolute that inner strength, these past few months had been enervating. "I know that I cannot continue to go at this pace," he wrote one friend.[6]

While the tax trial loomed on the horizon, the period from mid-April to mid-May brought King more tribulations. While King was in Nashville for a speech at Fisk, a bomb threat interrupted the rally and caused a forty-five-minute delay. Back in Atlanta, a cross was burned on the lawn of King's home one night. Authorities attributed it to youthful pranksters. Then, a nationally syndicated black columnist lambasted King for his remarks on *Meet the Press,* claiming the young minister had an "uncanny knack of muffing his big opportunities to show qualities of leadership on a national scale." Perhaps this one was Wilkins's revenge.

While King tried to turn his attention to SCLC's program, legal difficulties continued to interfere. SCLC, he told one questioner, was planning "to use nonviolent techniques in the area of voter registration," with masses of people descending upon election offices. "We've never attempted this on a grand scale." A more pressing problem, however, was the Alabama authorities' continued objections to the ad which King's defense committee had placed in *The New York Times.* Montgomery's commissioners not only had sued the newspaper for libel, but also had filed actions against the four Alabama residents who had signed the ad, Abernathy, Fred Shuttlesworth, Joseph Lowery, and S. S. Seay, Sr. SCLC would have to assist them.

Then, on the night of May 4, King had a direct encounter with the law. He and Coretta had entertained white Georgia writer Lillian Smith at dinner, and afterward King drove Smith back to Emory University Hospital, where she was undergoing treatment. Near the university, police spied the car with the black man and white woman and pulled King over. King had borrowed the car, and the plates on it were expired. Furthermore, King had only an Alabama driver's license, while Georgia law required new residents to obtain a Georgia license within ninety days.

King's deadline had passed. The officer issued a citation, and allowed King and Smith to go on their way.

Several days later King went to New York for a luncheon with labor leaders who were contributing to the defense committee. More important, the trip gave him an opportunity to bring Rustin, Levison, and Wyatt Walker together, and for his two old friends to draw their own impressions of the man King was proposing as the new executive director. Levison and Rustin were both impressed with Walker, and the four men spent the better part of two days discussing program, salary, and staff. Walker had two close assistants in his Petersburg Improvement Association (PIA) whom he wanted to bring with him, and the others gave their assent. They also settled on a salary of $8,000, and a firm agreement that Walker would be *the* chief of SCLC's staff—and not anyone in New York. The public announcement would come shortly, and Walker would begin his work by midsummer.

In Atlanta the student movement's temporary coordinating committee held its first meeting on May 13 and 14. King, Lawson, and Baker attended, and the students ratified a statement of purpose and voted to hire a temporary staff member whom SCLC offered to house in its office. Atlanta's student protesters also had remained active, and on May 17 organized a march of two thousand students from Morehouse to the state capitol to commemorate the sixth anniversary of *Brown*. King spoke to them before they set off, and again at the conclusion of the march, after police had diverted the procession from the capitol itself. The students gave King a thundering ovation.[7]

Finally, after three months of incessant worry, the time for the tax trial arrived. It was the first time Alabama had ever prosecuted someone for perjury on a tax return. Testimony began in Montgomery on May 25 with the prosecution putting state tax agent Lloyd Hale on the stand. Under cross-examination, Hale came close to admitting that the state's claim that King had misreported his 1956 income was without foundation. King had stated an income of $9,150—$5,040 from Dexter and $4,110 in honorariums—and Alabama's claim was that his true income was $16,162, the total deposits made in King's accounts for that year. The difference, cross-examination quickly showed, was simply payments reimbursing King for expenses he had incurred in his travels—in other words, not money that constituted income. The defense put Mrs. King, Maude Ballou, and Benjamin Mays on the stand along with an accountant and a black former IRS agent, Chauncey Eskridge. After three days of testimony, the case went to the jury of twelve white men on Saturday morning, May 28. King waited pessimistically for the verdict. No matter how foolish the evidence had shown the state's charge to be, a black civil rights leader was unlikely to receive justice at the hands of an all-white, Deep South jury.

Three hours and forty-five minutes after they began deliberations, the jury returned to the courtroom. Their verdict: not guilty. Daddy and

Mother King both cried with joy, but King remained calm—"emotion-less" to one observer, "a little stunned" in the words of another. Report-ers crowded around, and King told them that the acquittal strengthened his faith in white southerners' ability to do justice. Then he hurried back to Atlanta to preach at Ebenezer the next morning. He titled the sermon, "Autobiography of Suffering," and told the congregation how difficult the last four and a half years had been. The tax case had been the most painful burden of all, and now justice had lifted that from his shoulders.

The same Sunday, Wyatt T. Walker made the announcement in Pe-tersburg that he would become executive director of SCLC on August 1. Three days later King visited Petersburg to speak to a PIA rally. His acquittal had lifted a huge weight from King's mind, and he felt more relaxed than he had in months. Still, news reporters pressed him with financial questions. Patiently, he explained that he had no big house, no big car. His house rental was $110 a month; his book, *Stride Toward Freedom*, had earned less than $20,000, and much of that he had donated to SCLC and Morehouse. "I have no desire to live a big life, to drive a Cadillac, to live in the finest home, to be the best dressed and things like that," he explained to one questioner. Then, after the rally and the news-men, he enjoyed dinner at Walker's home with the PIA activists, and met for the first time the two colleagues whom Walker wished to bring to SCLC—Dorothy F. Cotton and James R. Wood. Cotton found King to be attentive, unhurried, and thoughtful, unusual traits for one who spent so much time in the public eye. He was "quiet and unassuming, yet at the same time a dynamic kind of presence," she thought.[8]

In June the controversy with the NAACP heated up once more. Two magazine articles set off the uproar. In one, "The Negro Revolt Against 'the Negro Leaders,'" black journalist Louis Lomax asserted that the spring protests showed that younger blacks had bypassed the older, adult leadership signified by the NAACP. The second, in *Commonweal*, di-rectly quoted an unnamed King "lieutenant" as saying that "the courts are secondary to direct action by the masses. The NAACP is not a mass movement. . . . We have sometimes had to force it into cooperating with us on mass action." Even more threateningly to Wilkins, it went on to say that "King admits privately that [SCLC] may soon become a national organization with membership open to individuals as well as affiliate groups." SCLC long had eschewed recruiting individual members so as to avoid competition with the NAACP's favorite means of marshaling its forces.

As the articles were passed around, some whispered that James Law-son was one of the sources behind them. The NAACP's anger got hotter, and was expressed strongly on June 8 and 9 when Ella Baker, Wyatt Walker, Bernard Lee, and the chairman of the Student Nonviolent Coor-dinating Committee, Marion Barry of Nashville, visited the NAACP in New York. King tried to downplay the disagreements, but no longer was he willing to greet the NAACP's insults with the same equanimity he had displayed in the past. He told baseball great Jackie Robinson, who earlier had warned King about the defense committee's assertions, that "I have never seen any conflict between the two organizations." More frankly, King stated:

> I have been so concerned about unity and the ultimate victory that I have refused to fight back or even answer some of the unkind statements that I have been informed that NAACP officials said about me and the Southern Christian Leadership Conference. Frankly, I hear these statements every day, and I have seen efforts on the part of NAACP officials to sabotage our humble efforts.

He could not turn the other cheek completely, however, and felt compelled to rebut one particular rumor: "I have no Messiah complex."

King visited New York on June 9 to make a joint announcement with A. Philip Randolph of the "massive nonviolent picketing" that was planned for the Democratic and Republican National Conventions. Although one month earlier Congress had passed the Civil Rights Act of 1960, the two men rightly asserted that that weak measure "does not meet the needs of abolishing second-class citizenship." Stronger legislative measures were needed, and the "March on the Conventions Movement for Freedom Now" would bring the demand home to each of the major parties. Both in Los Angeles in early July, and in Chicago at the end of that month, the Democratic and Republican delegates would be greeted by "more than 5,000" protesters, Randolph stated.

In truth, recruitment of protesters was running many thousands behind Randolph's optimistic claim. This exaggeration, however, did not dissuade one opponent of the protests, black New York Congressman Adam Clayton Powell, from launching a personal assault on King and Randolph. In Buffalo on June 19 to speak to a church conference that King had addressed the previous day, Powell denounced both Randolph and King for being "captives" of what the press called "behind the scenes interests." More specifically, Powell alleged that King was controlled by Bayard Rustin, and that Randolph, as the *Pittsburgh Courier* phrased it, "is the captive of socialist interests and . . . is guided principally by one Stanley Levinson [sic]."

King was about to leave for a vacation in South America, but he immediately dispatched a telegram to Powell asking for a public correction of the "malicious things" Powell had said about him and Randolph. Both of them had supported Powell in past scrapes, and King could see no reason for him to turn on them now. King hoped for a retraction, and said he would make no public rejoinder.[9]

Before he departed on his South America trip, King had one final engagement: a June 23 breakfast meeting in New York with one of the Democratic presidential candidates, Massachusetts Senator John F. Kennedy. Even though his friend Harris Wofford had joined Kennedy's campaign staff a month earlier, King was not impressed by Kennedy's Senate record. He particularly recalled an important vote Kennedy had cast on a provision of the 1957 Civil Rights Act, a vote against the position supported by the black leadership. That had won Kennedy friends among segregationist senators, but to King it seemed that Kennedy "was so concerned about being President of the United States that he would compromise basic principles to become President." Hence King had "very little enthusiasm for Mr. Kennedy when he first announced his candidacy."

Their meeting changed King's feelings. At that two-man breakfast, King emphasized that strong presidential leadership was needed on civil rights, and that initiatives to protect the right to vote and to eliminate racial discrimination in federally assisted housing were two areas for immediate action. Kennedy agreed that strong executive leadership was important, and that voting rights were especially crucial. King was pleased. In a letter written the next day, King called the ninety-minute conversation "fruitful and rewarding. . . . I was very impressed by the forthright and honest manner in which he discussed the civil rights question. I have no doubt that he would do the right thing on this issue if he were elected President."

King hoped that his South America vacation would be an escape from the tensions of the movement. That hope was soon dashed. He had been in Brazil only a day or two when word reached him through a close friend of Adam Powell's that the congressman's unhappiness over the King-Rustin relationship had not blown over. Instead, Powell intended to renew his assault in an even more devastating manner. If King did not dismiss Rustin, and cancel the convention protests, Adam would make public the most damaging sort of information against King and Rustin, Powell's messenger told King. A huge scandal would ensue.

King took the threat with the utmost seriousness, and was deeply worried. Immediately he called Rustin in New York. King explained that Powell was still on the warpath, and that the intermediary, a woman with a strong dislike of her own for Rustin, had conveyed the most vile threats. Given that, he thought that they should not go ahead with the convention protests. Rustin was puzzled and upset, and pressed King about the specifics of the threat. King didn't want to mention the details over the phone, but said the protests should be canceled. Rustin demurred, and said he would have Randolph phone King in South America.

Rustin spoke with Randolph and argued that they should not allow King to be intimidated by Powell. Randolph agreed and called King. He said he was certain King had good reasons for feeling as he did, reasons they could discuss when King returned, but that he, Randolph, was committed to going ahead with the convention protests. Powell could not prevent him from sponsoring those demonstrations and, given that, King should not pull out. King reluctantly agreed.

When King returned, the entire matter was discussed in detail. As Rustin recounts it, King explained frankly just what Powell's threat was:

The story is that he has some information that he will have to reveal to the press unless Martin drops out. And what is that information? That he has some evidence that Martin and I are sleeping together. Well, he couldn't possibly have that kind of information. Martin knew god damn well he couldn't have that kind of information; you can't sleep with a guy without his knowing it.

Rustin, Randolph and others all told King that to knuckle under to that sort of threat was wrong.

Still, King was worried. "What are we going to do if he puts out stories that are not true?" he asked. Randolph responded, "We simply deny them and go on doing our business." For King, however, that was not good enough. He asked several intermediaries to speak with Powell. They reported back that they thought it best for Rustin to resign from his multiple roles with King and Randolph. Rustin waited for King to decide, but King procrastinated, so Rustin took matters into his own hands. "I decided that the best thing to do under these pressures, since I knew Dr. King was distressed, was to say, 'Well, I resign.'" King had not requested the resignation, and Rustin expected King to reject it. To Rustin's bitter disappointment, however, King accepted it. Many people close to the intense discussions felt King's decision reflected insufficient courage; peace activist A. J. Muste wrote that he was "personally ashamed of Martin." Early in July the press reported Rustin's departure as special assistant to King and director of SCLC's New York office. Rustin's statement noted Powell's public attack and opposition to the convention protests.[10]

The demonstrations at the two conventions went forward even in Rustin's absence. In Los Angeles, King spoke at a Sunday kick-off rally, but Monday's picketing drew only sixty-five participants; their effort attracted little attention. King kept a low profile, hiding in a hotel room and talking politics with Michael Harrington, the young activist who had organized the picketing. King surprised Harrington with "how intellectually serious he was, that he was radical on all kinds of economic issues, and as far as I was concerned he was a socialist, although he didn't use the word and I was much too discreet to pose" it. Two weeks later in Chicago, the demonstrations at the Republican convention were limited to a single protest rally led by King, Randolph, and Roy Wilkins calling for a strong civil rights plank in the party's platform. Even a turnout of five thousand people failed to draw much attention to the March on the Conventions, and the nation's interest turned to the upcoming presidential contest between John F. Kennedy and Richard M. Nixon.[11]

Back in Atlanta, Wyatt T. Walker arrived for his first day as SCLC's executive director on August 3. Wood and Cotton were not far behind him, but what they found in the "dinky little room" at 208 Auburn Avenue was a very small operation. There were two secretaries, Lillie Hunter, who had been with the MIA, and Ernestine Brown, but only one field-worker was on the payroll—Rev. Harry Blake, a member of Shreveport, Louisiana's United Christian Movement, an SCLC affiliate. In one corner were SNCC's sole employee, Jane Stembridge, and a SNCC volunteer, Robert Moses. "Very honestly, it wasn't any organization; no real program," Walker later recalled. Walker vowed that under his leadership, SCLC would grow in both staff and accomplishments.

Walker's first task was to coordinate another institute on nonviolence that the departing Ella Baker had arranged at Atlanta's Butler Street YMCA just prior to the small August meeting of the Student Nonviolent Coordinating Committee. The workshop itself went well, with both King and Walker among the speakers, and SNCC made plans for a larger conference in Atlanta in mid-October. Baker's departure, however, left a legacy of strained feelings in its wake. She had never held King or Abernathy in high regard, and once she had formally left the organization, she made no secret of her attitude. Baker had found them unwilling to discuss substantive issues with her as an equal, and unreceptive to any critical comments she might offer. To James Lawson, the root of the problem was simple: "Martin had real problems with having a woman in a high position." Baker also did not support a "leader-centered" approach to organizing a movement, and felt no special awe for King. "I was not a person to be enamored of anyone," she noted. The ministers of SCLC, on the other hand, thought Baker was haughty and aloof, with what they felt was a disdain for anyone who was a black male preacher. The resulting bitterness would not mellow with time.

August was a generally quiet time for King himself. On the nineteenth he and his brother, A.D., performed the ceremony as their sister, Christine, married Isaac Farris. A.D. was pastoring a church in Newnan, Georgia, and had a young family of his own, but relatives and close friends were aware that he was a troubled man. One very close acquaintance thought the problem was twofold. First, A.D. was forced to live in his famous brother's shadow. Second, and more important, A.D. had never devised a means for coping with their very demanding father. "They had a running battle. They fought daily. There was never peace between them," this friend observed. Daddy demanded excellence and decorum, and A.D. "did not represent what the old man wanted." Instead of learning to ignore and brush off King, Sr.'s constant instructions, A.D. fought back. "He rebelled, and he lost, because the old man was too strong. . . . He would break you. . . . M.L. would say, 'Aw, Dad,' and walk away. But A.D. couldn't walk away." It was painful for all.[12]

In Atlanta, tensions surrounded the ongoing student protests. In late May the local black adult leadership had organized a committee "to examine and better understand" the student movement, as one adult put it, and on June 24 they arranged a meeting between the student leaders and Richard H. Rich, owner of downtown Atlanta's largest department store, a store with thoroughly segregated facilities. Rich was a reputed liberal, but he offered no concessions and demanded that the protests be halted.

The students said no, threatened a complete boycott of the store, and Rich angrily walked out. On August 8, the student chairman of the Committee on the Appeal for Human Rights (COAHR), Lonnie C. King, Jr., wrote Rich to suggest another negotiating session. Rich declined, saying that the earlier one had "made our views perfectly clear to you" and that a further one "would not be productive." Three weeks later, Jesse Hill, Jr., the young chairman of the black adults' Citizens' Negotiations Committee, wrote to Rich to request another session. Rich again refused, saying such meetings were "fruitless" but leaving the door open to personal contact with Hill. As the fall semester opened, picketing and sit-ins at various Atlanta businesses continued on a modest basis.

King remained silent about the Atlanta situation, but in his public remarks in other cities he continued his criticisms of the civil rights records of both major political parties. He also continued to make reference to massive "stand-ins" by prospective black voters at registration offices, and on September 14 he and Wilkins joined forces to announce a "Nonpartisan Crusade to Register One Million New Negro Voters." Those in the know recognized this as a convenient nonpartisan cover for a last-minute Democratic party registration effort.[13]

In mid-September King met for a second time with Senator Kennedy. The Democratic presidential nominee had a better grasp of civil rights issues than he had three months earlier, King thought, but the senator expressed strong concern about where he stood with black voters. Advisors like Wofford were suggesting that Kennedy appear with King and make a strong speech on civil rights. King was not amenable to such a plan, or to an SCLC rally or dinner for Kennedy. SCLC was a nonpartisan organization and would not endorse a candidate, but perhaps it could invite both Kennedy and Nixon to appear before it. King emphasized that he would not endorse either candidate. Kennedy expressed no interest in a joint appearance, and mentioned that that troublesome 1957 vote still counted against him in the minds of many blacks. King agreed, and parted from Kennedy, telling him that "something dramatic must be done to convince the Negroes that you are committed on civil rights."

Even after meeting with Kennedy, King had no strong feelings about the upcoming election. "I did not feel at that time that there was much difference between Kennedy and Nixon," he later recalled. "I could find some things in the background of both men that I didn't particularly agree with," and even though he had known Nixon longer, he feared that the Republican nominee was "an opportunist at many times who had no real grounding in basic convictions." On balance King leaned toward Kennedy simply because Wofford and other personal acquaintances whom he respected, such as Chester Bowles, strongly vouched for him.

On September 23, King had to attend to a small piece of unfinished business. Accompanied by a black Decatur lawyer whom Daddy King had hired, Charles M. Clayton, King appeared before Judge J. Oscar Mitchell of DeKalb County Civil and Criminal Court to resolve his May traffic ticket. King sat in the back of the courtroom while Clayton spoke with Mitchell. Mitchell noted the two counts: the expired plates on the borrowed car, and King's failure to obtain a Georgia license within ninety days. King heard Mitchell dismiss the first charge, and impose a fine of $25 on the second. King immediately paid the fee, and headed back to the office. He did not see the sentence form that Mitchell filed and that Clayton was privy to: It specified the $25 fine, plus twelve months probation, requiring that King "shall not violate any Federal or State penal statutes or municipal ordinances" for one year's time.[14]

Throughout late September, King and Walker directed their efforts toward organizing registration stand-ins. SCLC announced that the coordinated protests would take place on October 3 in more than a dozen cities, but when Walker's "D Day" arrived, newsmen counted only fifty people in Atlanta, a few dozen in Tallahassee and several other cities, and none at all in Nashville or Durham. King told reporters that this had been only a "pilot project," and that SCLC planned "to develop it on a much larger scale."

On October 11, the SCLC board met in Shreveport for its semiannual session. King emphasized that the organization "must do something creative this year," and Walker promised to meet just that need. The board members were pleased by their first exposure to the new executive director and his commitment to establish a "dynamic program." The reality of the problems they all were up against was brought home once again the evening after the final meeting, when shots from a passing car were fired at SCLC's local field representative, Harry Blake. He escaped uninjured.

From Shreveport, King returned to Atlanta for the first large SNCC conference since the gathering in Raleigh. He and Lawson spoke to the students, with Lawson arguing strongly for the doctrine of "jail, not bail."[15] The Atlanta student protest leaders were growing impatient. They decided that the time had come to resume intensive sit-ins, targeted principally against the store of hostile Richard H. Rich. On Tuesday, October 18, three of the student leaders—Lonnie King, Herschelle Sullivan, and Julian Bond—contacted King to ask if he would accompany their troops in the first assault on Rich's. King was hesitant, and the small group went to see him in person at Ebenezer. Lonnie King put the request bluntly, Bond recalls: "Martin, you've got to come with us." King hesitated again, and Lonnie King pushed harder. "I indicated to him that he was going to have to go to jail if he intended to maintain his position as one of the leaders in the civil rights struggle." How could King speak of "filling the jails," and "jail, not bail," if he was unwilling to join a sit-in? Reluctantly, King agreed to meet them outside of Rich's.

The next morning the sit-ins resumed with a bang. King and thirty-five others, including one white man, were arrested for violating an antitrespass law when they refused to leave Rich's restaurant after being declined service. They were taken to the county jail, and King made one brief phone call home. Reporters were allowed in for a short time, and

King told them that he, like the students, would not make bond, and that he would serve his time if convicted. He had begun a fast and explained to newsmen that the protest was not something he had instigated. "I did not initiate the thing. . . . Last night they called me and asked me to join in it. They wanted me to be in it, and I felt a moral obligation to be in it with them." To a black reporter, he put it more succinctly: "I had to practice what I preached." That night was the first King ever had spent in jail.

While King and the other protesters were in the Fulton County jail, twenty-six more demonstrators were arrested on Thursday. More picketing but fewer sit-ins took place on Friday, and Atlanta's black and white adult leadership began discussing how to resolve the new wave of protests as quickly as possible. Meanwhile, DeKalb County officials filed notice with their Fulton counterparts that they also were interested in King because his arrest at Rich's violated the terms of the probation Mitchell had imposed in September.

On Saturday morning, Atlanta Mayor William B. Hartsfield convened a meeting with sixty black representatives in the city council chamber. At the same time, King friend and Kennedy campaign official Harris Wofford, who had seen news reports of King's imprisonment, got an idea at his home in Virginia. He phoned an Atlanta friend and Kennedy supporter, attorney Morris Abram, who was also an acquaintance of Atlanta Mayor Hartsfield. Wofford mentioned King's jailing, and made a suggestion: "I want you to get him out and claim the credit for Senator Kennedy." Abram asked how, explaining that Hartsfield was meeting with the black leadership. Wofford recommended that Abram see Hartsfield himself, and Abram promised he would inform the mayor of Wofford's interest. He was able to reach Hartsfield, and told him of the call. The mayor replied that the meeting was still in progress and that Abram should come over at once.

By the time Abram arrived at City Hall, Hartsfield had announced to the press an agreement with the black leadership. Demonstrations would be suspended for thirty days, and all of the jailed protesters would be released. The city would drop its charges and ask the merchants to do the same. Hartsfield would serve as an intermediary in further discussions between the students and the merchants, and would furnish the students with weekly progress reports on his efforts. Hartsfield also told reporters that a Georgia representative of Kennedy, meaning Abram, had expressed an interest in securing King's release.

While Abram called Wofford to warn him of Hartsfield's public comment about Kennedy's interest, and Hartsfield in turn sought to reassure a worried Wofford that the story would redound to Kennedy's advantage, two snags developed in the settlement. First, store owner Rich was hesitant about having the state charges dropped; he feared a white backlash for doing so. Second, King and the other jailed protesters conveyed word that they would not leave jail unless all charges were dropped.

Late Saturday evening, Abram and Mayor Hartsfield went to Richard Rich's home to ask his support. After much pleading, Rich agreed to go along if Fulton County solicitor John I. Kelley would also. Sunday morning Abram, Hartsfield, and Rich all called on Kelley, who had no objections to the plan. Abram called Atlanta Police Chief Herbert Jenkins, and by late Sunday afternoon all of the jailed protesters were released—except one.

Shortly after his arrest, King had learned of the DeKalb complication and was prepared to stay behind after the students were released. As the students emerged, word spread that everyone would gather at Paschal's restaurant to celebrate. Few people were aware that King would not be with them, and Jesse Hill phoned Coretta to tell her of the Paschal's gathering. Only when she arrived there was she told that King was still being held.

On Monday morning, DeKalb Judge Mitchell explained to reporters why King was still in custody. A hearing on whether King's arrest at Rich's violated his September probation would be held at 11:00 A.M. the next morning, Mitchell said. Authorities tried to move King from the Fulton jail to the DeKalb jail, but the Fulton sheriff insisted upon maintaining custody. Early Tuesday morning, while A. D. King and Bernard Lee stood watching outside the Fulton jail, a DeKalb sheriff's car picked up King for delivery to Mitchell's hearing. With handcuffs on his wrists, King sat quietly in the backseat. A large German shepherd sat at attention on the seat beside him.[16]

King's new attorney, Donald L. Hollowell, moved into action by filing an appeal of King's September license conviction. The thirty-day opportunity had not quite passed, and the pendency of such an appeal allowed Hollowell to contend at the Tuesday hearing that King could not be imprisoned in the matter until the conviction had been upheld. Mitchell responded that Hollowell's argument was irrelevant, that the question was whether King had violated the terms of his probation. King took the stand to explain that he had not been aware of the probation. Then Hollowell put four members of Atlanta's black elite on the stand to testify to King's good character. Mitchell again found the defense arguments irrelevant, and gave King a four-month sentence for violating probation. Hollowell argued further that in a misdemeanor case such as this, the judge was required to release the defendant on an appeal bond while the probation issue was appealed, but Mitchell denied his request. He ordered King's probation revoked immediately and said King could be transferred to a state prison to begin serving his four months. Mitchell did grant Hollowell's request for a further hearing Wednesday morning on the appeal-bond argument.

Coretta, Daddy King, Christine, and Roy Wilkins were all in the audience during the hearing. Both Coretta and Christine broke into tears when Mitchell pronounced the four-month sentence, and Daddy King was upset by their loss of composure. He and Coretta were allowed a brief visit with King in a holding cell behind the courtroom. King was calm and sought to comfort his wife. "Corrie, you have to be strong. I've never seen you like this. You have to be strong for me." Then he was taken to the county jail.

News reports spread the word of King's sentencing. In Washington, Deputy Attorney General Lawrence E. Walsh considered making a move in court, but instead prepared a statement for President Eisenhower, who did not issue it. Nixon campaign officials had been kept posted since Saturday by black Atlanta Republican John H. Calhoun, but White House aide E. Frederic Morrow, traveling with the vice-president, could not convince Nixon's advisors to send telegrams to Mrs. King and Georgia officials. Nixon press secretary Herb Klein pocketed Morrow's drafts, saying that to send them would be poor election strategy.

Coretta was still shaky when she returned home from the hearing. She was six months pregnant and frightened about what might happen to Martin in a remote state prison. The bad dream she had had about southern jails seemed to be coming true. Still upset, she called Harris Wofford, having heard about his Saturday intercession.

"They are going to kill him, I know they are going to kill him," she cried to Wofford. The young lawyer did his best to comfort her, but after they had hung up he still was troubled by Coretta's appeal for assistance. Wofford and fellow campaign staffer Louis E. Martin already were drafting a public statement for Kennedy to issue, but its release had been delayed by a promise from Georgia Governor Ernest Vandiver's office that he would resolve the matter without the Democratic presidential nominee becoming publicly involved. Wofford and Martin talked about what else they might do, and Wofford thought of asking Kennedy to call and reassure Coretta King. They tried for several hours to reach the traveling candidate, without success. Wofford then asked his friend Chester Bowles, a prominent Democratic politician who had met the Kings, to make such a call in Kennedy's stead. Bowles did so on Tuesday evening, and Coretta found the expression of support heartwarming.[17]

Wednesday morning at 3:30 A.M., King was asleep in the DeKalb County jail. Suddenly he was awakened by a voice. "Get up, King—Did you hear me, King? Get up and come on out here. And bring all your things with you." The jailers were saying it was time for a trip—in the middle of the night. King asked where they were headed, and they did not reply. At 4:05 A.M., in handcuffs and leg irons, King was placed in the backseat of a car with two deputies up front. They drove for over two hours, but King had no idea where they were going. At dawn, as they passed through Dublin, he realized their destination was the Georgia state prison at Reidsville. At 8:00 A.M. the car pulled into the prison. King was taken out, the irons were removed, and he was handed a blue and white striped prison uniform. Then he was placed alone in a cell.

At approximately the same time that King was arriving at Reidsville, attorney Hollowell arrived at the DeKalb courthouse to discover that his client had been taken away. Word spread quickly, and A. D. King called Coretta with the news. Again she was distraught, and spoke with both Wofford and Daddy King. Wofford tried to comfort her, but he wanted to do something more. He called Kennedy in-law Sargent Shriver in Chicago and asked him if Kennedy might call Mrs. King. Shriver said he would go over to Kennedy's hotel and put the question to him in person. When he got there, he had to wait for several staffers to leave. Then he explained the situation to John Kennedy. Would he call her? "That's a wonderful idea," Kennedy responded. Shriver had the Kings' number, and Kennedy picked up the phone.

Coretta received the call just as she was leaving to meet Daddy King at Morris Abram's office to discuss possibly asking the state parole board to release King. John Kennedy told her of his concern about her husband's imprisonment, and how this must be extremely difficult for her. If there was anything he could do to ease her burdens, she should not hesitate to let him know. Coretta thanked him and he wished her well.

Coretta told Daddy King of Kennedy's phone call as they prepared to see Morris Abram. King, Sr., was ecstatic, and said that this was enough to shift his traditionally Republican presidential preference and vote instead for Kennedy, the man who had called his daughter-in-law. He told Abram the same thing while they discussed the parole possibility, and Abram immediately called Wofford. It was the first the Kennedy staffers had heard of the call, and Wofford was deeply pleased. The candidate's younger brother and de facto campaign manager, Robert F. Kennedy, was not pleased, however. Earlier he had reprimanded Wofford for his weekend intercession with Abram and Hartsfield, and now he was furious that the staff workers had managed to align his brother publicly with a national symbol of black activism. Did Wofford and Martin realize what that would do to John Kennedy's chances of carrying the white South? Robert asked heatedly. He stalked out and headed for the airport to catch a plane to New York.

Unbeknownst to Wofford and Martin, Robert Kennedy, despite his electoral protestations, was also infuriated at what Judge Mitchell had done to King. He thought about it on the plane, and when he landed in New York he called the DeKalb courthouse, and asked for Judge Mitchell. When Mitchell came on, Kennedy identified himself and said he was calling simply as a lawyer to express to the judge his belief that all defendants had a right to release on bond while they appealed. Mitchell said it was good to talk with him, and thanked him for his interest.[18]

Locked deep inside Reidsville prison, King knew nothing of the efforts being made to win his release. He had been alone in his cell since early morning. He could speak with other prisoners in the same cell block, and notes could be passed, but it gave him little solace. The convicts were astounded by the identity of their new compatriot, and told King they were ready to stage a strike to protest his imprisonment. Quietly he dissuaded them from that idea.

King found the loneliness of prison difficult to bear. At one point, as he later told Coretta, "He just broke down and cried and then he felt so ashamed of himself." By late afternoon, however, he had conquered that "enormous anxiety," as Daddy King later called it. He simply had to accept that he would be in prison for four months, and that he had to make the best possible use of that time. He wrote a letter to Coretta, telling her that visitors were allowed every other Sunday. He asked that she and the children come down the next weekend, and that she bring him several books, a reference dictionary, and a good number of his sermon texts. At least he could make some progress on the book of sermons he had been thinking about for over a year. He also asked that she bring him a radio, and that Wyatt Walker also come along.

Beyond the incidental requests, however, he asked her to make an effort, like his, to allow their common faith to carry them through the most difficult moments they had yet encountered. She must believe, as he did, that one's suffering is not in vain, and that in the end it contributes to the betterment of all. "I know this whole experience is very difficult for you to adjust to," King wrote, "but as I said to you yesterday, this is the cross that we must bear for the freedom of our people." The struggle is difficult, but "I am asking God hourly to give me the power of endurance." He had the faith to believe that he could survive, and asked the family "not to worry about me. I will adjust to whatever comes in terms of pain." He signed it, "Eternally yours, Martin."[19]

On Thursday morning, Judge Mitchell held another hearing at which Hollowell argued once more for King's release on bond while the original traffic charge was appealed. Hollowell had marshaled his precedents carefully, and this time Mitchell agreed: King should be released pending final judgment. Bond would be $2,000, and Hollowell had it posted immediately. Mitchell signed the release order, and Hollowell arranged to charter a plane. In early afternoon he flew to Reidsville, handed over the order, and King was released. Coretta, Christine, and A.D. were among the small crowd at the airport to welcome him home. King told reporters that he was "deeply indebted to Senator Kennedy," then the family group headed for a celebration rally at Ebenezer. There, Daddy King openly proclaimed his change of heart and announced that he would be voting for John Kennedy for president, even if he was a Catholic and King a Baptist. King also spoke warmly of the Democratic nominee, saying that he held him "in very high esteem," but stopping short of an explicit endorsement.

Abram and Wofford each wondered if it might be possible to secure King's formal endorsement of Kennedy before Election Day. King chose not to, saying that as president of SCLC it would not be proper to express a partisan preference. Nonetheless, on November 1 he issued a statement that stopped just short of an endorsement. "I want to make it palpably clear," King said, "that I am deeply grateful to Senator Kennedy for the genuine concern he expressed. . . . [He] exhibited moral courage of a high order." In private, he added that the contrast between Kennedy's call and Nixon's inaction was very real to him. Even though Nixon had known him longer, he had done nothing. "I really considered him a moral coward," King remarked.

Even lacking a formal endorsement, the Kennedy staffers made full use of King's comments and Daddy King's change of heart. They prepared a small flyer, " 'No Comment' Nixon versus a Candidate with a Heart, Senator Kennedy: The Case of Martin Luther King," and saw to it that hundreds of thousands of copies were distributed in black precincts before the election. Although neither of the Kennedys' phone calls "became a major story in the white media or an issue in the campaign," they very definitely made a difference when the votes were tallied on November 8. Several weeks later, President Eisenhower complained to reporters that Nixon had lost simply because of a "couple of phone calls."

In the wake of his release, King told one friend that the eight days he had spent in jail had had at least one positive effect. "I think I received a new understanding of the meaning of suffering," he wrote Harold De-Wolf, "and I came away more convinced than ever before that unearned suffering is redemptive." The imprisonment had not been pleasant, but he did feel that his faith had benefited from the experience.[20]

By mid-November SCLC had two new initiatives under way. In the first, James Wood was following up on Ella Baker's earlier interest in leadership training and the contacts she had made at the Highlander Folk School. Wood visited the Tennessee facility in mid-November and talked at length with Director Myles Horton and Program Coordinator Septima P. Clark. Wood was extremely impressed by their four-year record of achievement, and he reported to King and Walker Horton's suggestion that SCLC think about taking over the training program because of ongoing legal harassment by Tennessee state authorities that threatened Highlander's existence. If the school did not win a pending appeal in a state court, Highlander would be closed and its facilities seized. At Highlander, Wood also met L. B. Moore, a representative of the Field Foundation, who expressed his organization's interest in supporting a continuation of the leadership training program, under whomever's auspices. Field would be willing to fund the effort if SCLC assumed sponsorship of it. "I urge and recommend very strongly the future consideration and adoption of this plan," Wood advised King.

The second new SCLC effort was the formation of a Virginia state conference of local groups that had been affiliated with SCLC. Many of the fifty people who attended the Petersburg session were former colleagues of Walker, and a local pastor, Rev. Milton Reid, was elected the new unit's president. Walker announced that the group was part of SCLC's "bold new program with an increased staff and an emphasis on state-by-state organizations which will ultimately function as units in a southwide attack on some specific area of segregation."

In Atlanta, Hartsfield's promise to the student protesters proved to be one on which he could not follow through. On November 23, at the end of the thirty-day moratorium on student demonstrations, the mayor met with the students to admit that he had had no success in persuading Atlanta's downtown merchants to desegregate their stores. He asked for thirty days more in which to try further; the students responded that they would give him three. The student leadership held a late-night strategy meeting the following day which King attended. They decided to resume picketing, but not the sit-ins.

On November 25 a three-day meeting of SNCC's executive committee took place in Atlanta. On the second day, the group paused to watch a nationally televised debate between King and segregationist newspaper editor James J. Kilpatrick. The two men argued about segregation and the sit-ins, with Kilpatrick contending that "the key thing that is involved are questions of property rights." King responded that "any law that degrades human personality is an unjust law," and morally should not be obeyed. The SNCC members viewed the telecast in the company of the embittered Ella Baker, and some of them came to the conclusion that King was "no match" for Kilpatrick. Certainly that was Baker's view, and she made no secret of it. "It was almost in the cards that he would muff it, for he had not forced himself to analytically come to grips with these issues," Baker told a later questioner. "The students were sitting there in front of the TV, waiting for him to 'take care' of Kilpatrick. Finally, some got up and walked away." It was, Baker said, the first occasion when the students' unhappiness with King "finally broke openly to the surface."[21]

During the winter months, Atlanta's black leadership continued its efforts to mediate a solution to the city's ongoing desegregation struggle, and King spoke to a large student rally on December 19. The chairman of the black Student-Adult Liaison Committee, Rev. William Holmes Borders, told reporters with some exasperation that both the students and the merchants realized that eventual desegregation was inevitable, and the battle was simply about *when*. King looked forward expectantly to John Kennedy's inauguration, and told one Chattanooga crowd that Kennedy ought to be reminded "that we are expecting him to use the whole weight of his office to remove the heavy weight of segregation from our shoulders." More personally, King phoned the president-elect to wish him well and to suggest Morris Abram as a superb candidate for U.S. solicitor general. Black newsmen asked King if he was under consideration for any position in the new administration, and King replied that he had "had some discussion" with members of Kennedy's staff. "They were sort of feeling me out." However, King added, "I made it clear that I had no interest in a government post, for I am too much involved in the civil rights fight to add anything else." King also rejected feelers about whether he would like to become national director of the Congress of Racial Equality.

By mid-January, Jim Wood's effort to get SCLC to take over Highlander Folk School's training program had picked up speed. Highlander

had been considering changing the program from one in which all participants went there for training, to one in which citizenship teachers were
trained at a central place and then sent back to instruct others in their
own locales. It was an alteration that Wood strongly endorsed. Training
such a cadre of teachers would allow SCLC to set up citizenship instruction centers throughout the South, hosted by SCLC's many affiliates.
Dorothy Cotton would coordinate the recruitment of students, and Septima Clark would direct the training. Over sixteen months, the program
could train 240 prospective teachers, each of whom could then start
classes in his or her own hometown. Such an effort would invigorate
SCLC's entire program. "The need for a program through which affiliates
may become active in other than fund-raising capacities is very evident,"
Wood argued, "and will create a much needed action device." King and
Walker agreed, and in early February SCLC's and Highlander's new joint
endeavor was announced to the press. At the same time, a request for a
$30,000 grant to fund the project was submitted to the Field and Taconic
foundations.[22]

In late January, King was guest of honor at a large celebrity gala in
New York's Carnegie Hall, organized by Stanley Levison and a young
aide, Maya Angelou, which raised over $20,000 for SCLC. Three days
later, Coretta gave birth to the Kings' third child and second son, whom
they named Dexter in honor of the Montgomery church. Within a week,
the Atlanta student protests heated up for a third time when the students
initiated a new sit-in and "jail-going" effort. As the number of jailed
demonstrators increased day by day, Atlanta's black and white leadership
tried to resolve the controversy. King remained in the background, but
other distractions crossed his path, such as younger brother A.D.'s arrest
for drunken driving. King also was lobbying an Atlanta church to offer its
pastorship to Ralph Abernathy, so that his Montgomery colleague could
rejoin him. On February 15, though, King appeared in local court to lend
moral support to a group of young ministers, including his friend Walter
McCall, now pastoring in Atlanta, who had joined the students and been
arrested. That night King spoke to a large rally, and endorsed the students' vows that the sit-ins would continue until the white merchants
agreed to desegregate.

Behind the scenes, one of black Atlanta's oldest leaders, attorney A.
T. Walden, initiated discussions with Richard Rich's lawyer, Robert
Troutman, Sr. Together, the two men approached Ivan Allen, Jr., the
new president of Atlanta's powerful Chamber of Commerce. Allen knew
that many in the business community wanted the matter resolved, and he
also felt that "the national publicity was running us crazy" and harming
the city's reputation. Allen met with white business leaders, and found a
consensus: "Go ahead and work something out. Get us off the hook,
even if it means desegregating the stores." Allen talked with Walden and
other black adult representatives until they reached agreement on a basic
principle: The desegregation of the lunch counters, rest rooms, and other

store facilities would be tied to the desegregation of Atlanta's public schools, scheduled to begin in September. Within thirty days of school desegregation, the store facilities would be desegregated. In return, the students would end their demonstrations and all charges would be dropped. The black and white adult representatives summoned the two principal student leaders, Lonnie King and Herschelle Sullivan, to a meeting at the Chamber of Commerce on Monday, March 6. The adults tried to persuade the two students to accept the settlement plan. Lonnie King did not want to endorse it, but Daddy King, Reverend Borders, and Walden pressed him very hard. Finally, the students gave in. The next morning Allen announced the agreement to the public. As word of its terms spread, however, the student community grew angry and spoke of rejecting it.

Friday evening, March 10, a mass meeting was called at Warren Memorial Methodist Church for the negotiators to defend the settlement to the black community. Many people were upset that the agreement did not specify a precise date for desegregation. The adults' explanation that the stores would be desegregated no matter what happened with school integration was not persuasive, and the crowd turned hostile. Walden, Borders, Samuel Williams, Jesse Hill, and Daddy King all received boos and hisses when they went to the pulpit to defend the agreement. It looked as if the meeting would repudiate the negotiators' work.

Martin King stood in the rear and watched the crowd of a thousand shout down his father and the other speakers. The throng remained noisy and restless as King made his way to the pulpit. He stood there silently for a moment, waiting for everyone to quiet. Lonnie King could see tears in King's eyes, tears over how the crowd had humiliated his father. As Martin stood there, they all quieted. Then he began to speak. Calmly and forcefully he defended the efforts of the negotiators. "If I had been on that committee that met Monday afternoon, I wouldn't mind anybody saying, 'Martin Luther King, Jr., you made a mistake.' I wouldn't mind anybody saying, 'Martin Luther King, Jr., you should have thought it over a little longer.' I wouldn't have minded anybody saying to me, 'Martin Luther King, Jr., maybe we made a tactical blunder.' But I would have been terribly hurt if anybody said to me, 'Martin Luther King, Jr., you sold us out!' I would have been hurt by that." In a tone that had "both warmth and authority," King declared that the black community must remain united, and must not repudiate what its leaders had agreed to. As he spoke, the crowd grew calm. "When King sat down," one observer wrote, "the mood of the crowd had been transformed, and the opposition to the agreement was silenced." Many in the audience thought it was the best and most powerful oration they had ever heard King deliver. Lonnie King said that it was "probably the greatest speech of his life." Only King's words, he said, kept "that meeting from really turning into a riot." King left quickly, and "after the singing of a spiritual the crowd dispersed . . . the agreement was saved." Integration of Atlanta's schools began peacefully and on schedule, and a month later facilities in the downtown stores were desegregated.

Though he supported his father and the other negotiators in public, King's personal sentiments strongly favored the students. He had purposely limited his role in the Atlanta protests as much as possible, so as to avoid offending jealous adults already troubled by his return to Atlanta. Though his stance caused many of the students to hold an ambivalent attitude toward King, he privately criticized the failure of the city's black middle class to give the protesters greater support. "They're conservatives. Their unhappiness with the sit-in demonstrations is largely economic," he told one person.[23]

The increasing cost of running SCLC forced King to make fund-raising one of his top priorities. King and Walker told the board's administrative committee that expenses were now $7,000 a month, and to meet those outlays, King continued to speak all around the country. The pace was draining. Some days he delivered as many as five speeches, and some nights he slept for only four hours. King had hired a personal secretary, Dora McDonald, to take Maude Ballou's place in organizing his schedule. Meanwhile, SCLC planned intensive voter registration drives in selected locales, and Walker expanded their contacts in other regions of the country. A regional support group, the *Western* Christian Leadership Conference, was established in California, principally to aid in fund-raising. Walker also engaged an old school friend then pastoring in Washington, Walter Fauntroy, to serve as SCLC's representative in the District of Columbia.

SCLC's effort to join Highlander in an expanded citizenship training program also gradually moved forward, and the school began searching for a new staff member to handle the program's administration. By late March, Highlander had found a candidate for the job, a young black minister, Andrew Young, who was working for the National Council of Churches in New York. Young was inclined to accept the job, but thought first he would inquire about the school and the program from someone he had spent an evening with four years earlier: Martin King. To Young it had been a memorable event, but King did not remember him when he received Young's letter seeking advice about Highlander. King was uncertain what to tell Young. He asked Stanley Levison to make inquiries about Young, but without waiting for Levison's response, wrote Young and advised that he not take the job, that the uncertainties of Highlander's legal situation were too great. Young decided otherwise, and made plans to move south in September.[24]

King was also trying hard to secure an appointment with the newly inaugurated president through the persistent efforts of Harris Wofford, now Kennedy's special assistant for civil rights. King had written a magazine article calling for more aggressive support of civil rights by the new administration, and he pointedly sent several copies of it to another acquaintance on the White House staff, Frank D. Reeves. In the article

King noted three areas in which the president should take the initiative. First, Kennedy ought to introduce a broad legislative program in Congress, especially a bill on voting rights. Second, the president should employ moral persuasion in his public remarks to rally support for civil rights. Third, Kennedy could issue executive orders eliminating much racial discrimination in federally assisted programs without having to wait for Congress to act. Overall, King said, "a recognition of the potentials of federal power is a primary necessity if the fight for full racial equality is to be won." In his accompanying letter to Reeves, King added that preparing the article had left him "amazed" at "the powerful things that the President can do" through executive orders.

Three weeks later, King wrote to Kennedy formally requesting a conference within the next month. Both Wofford and Reeves saw the letter, and each recommended to Kennedy's appointments secretary, Kenneth O'Donnell, that King's request be granted quickly. Some staffers thought the president should see King and Roy Wilkins together, but Wofford and Reeves advised against that, pointing out the long-reported rivalry between the two men. They ought to receive separate appointments, and soon. Wofford knew that the administration had decided not to make any major civil rights initiatives during its first year in office. Administration strategists believed that there was insufficient congressional support for any proposals that might be made. "Such a meeting with King is important now," Wofford wrote in mid-March, "to lay the groundwork for his understanding why there will be no substantial civil rights legislation this year."

O'Donnell saw no such urgency in the matter, and replied to King that the president's schedule would be too busy for such a meeting for at least a month. Try again in late April, he recommended. In the meantime, King did secure a brief mid-April meeting with the new attorney general, Robert F. Kennedy, to discuss possible Justice Department initiatives to secure the desegregation of interstate transportation facilities throughout the South. Then one week later, on April 21, King stopped by the White House to visit Harris Wofford. Word of King's presence reached John Kennedy, and the president stopped by to chat with King for five minutes. Kennedy was preoccupied with the Bay of Pigs fiasco in Cuba that had occurred two days earlier, and "we didn't even discuss civil rights," King later recalled. His request for a formal meeting remained pending.[25]

Five days after King's encounter with the president, the new national director of CORE, James Farmer, who had been program director at the NAACP, wrote to both of the Kennedy brothers to inform them of a new initiative, a "Freedom Ride," that CORE would undertake in one week's time. Beginning in early May in Washington, Farmer said, a small, integrated group would begin a bus trip through the South to New Orleans, where they hoped to arrive on May 17, the seventh anniversary of *Brown*. "We propose to challenge . . . every form of segregation met by the bus passenger," Farmer told them. Neither the White House nor the Justice Department paid any attention to Farmer's announcement.

The group of thirteen travelers set out from Washington on May 4. The pace was intended to be slow, with as many stops as possible to test facilities in bus terminals in each town. Only minor incidents marred their nine-day journey through Virginia and the Carolinas. When they arrived in Atlanta on May 13, the trip so far had drawn little national publicity.

While the Freedom Ride was beginning, King and Walker were busy with SCLC's affairs. King was personally troubled by a request from white activist Anne Braden, whom he had met at Highlander in 1957, that he sign a clemency petition for her husband. Carl Braden had been convicted of contempt of Congress for refusing to answer questions before the House Un-American Activities Committee. King hesitated to add his name to the petition, and told Braden he would have to think about it. Several weeks passed, and Braden heard nothing. Her husband was scheduled to begin his one-year jail term on Monday, May 1, and Braden wanted to release the petition when he surrendered. On Saturday night she made one last attempt, and called the Kings' home. Coretta said that Martin was not in, and Braden decided to give up her efforts. Early Sunday morning her phone rang. It was King. "Anne, I want you to put my name on that petition. I prayed about this most of last night, and I want you to put my name on it." Braden was immensely pleased. King had nothing to gain from taking such a controversial stand, nor did the other SCLC leaders who signed with him. King "came down on the right side, although it may have taken him a while to get there," Braden observed.

The spring meeting of SCLC's board took place in Montgomery on May 10 and 11. Walker reported that SCLC's finances were in great shape: A mail appeal overseen by Stanley Levison in New York had raised $37,000 in the wake of King's Georgia imprisonment, on top of the $20,000 produced by the January benefit at Carnegie Hall. In addition, the Field Foundation was contributing $26,000 to the citizenship training program. Walker also explained that he intended to use King's speaking engagements for better SCLC fund-raising, and had scheduled seven appearances for this purpose over the next eight weeks. With this healthier bankroll, Walker advised that SCLC could expand its staff and take a direct hand in voter registration drives in several cities. The board agreed, and Walker soon hired a student liaison and field secretary, Bernard Lee, who had been active in SNCC while attending college in Atlanta during the 1960–1961 school year. All in all, the board was pleased with the changes that had taken place in the first nine months of Walker's directorship. They also discussed the Montgomery commissioners' ongoing suits against the signers of the *New York Times* ad, and held a nighttime rally at Holt Street church. It marked King's first return to Montgomery since his tax acquittal one year earlier.[26]

Upon returning to Atlanta, King and Walker met with the Freedom Riders before they headed on to Birmingham and Mississippi. Walker gave them the names of SCLC's contacts in various towns and arranged for Fred Shuttlesworth's group to meet the riders in Birmingham. Some of the participants expressed surprise at what little difficulty they had had so far, but Walker cautioned them that the remainder of their journey would be no lark. To some, Walker's warning was good rather than bad news. Their top priority was to draw national attention to racial discrimination in interstate travel and to force the federal government to combat it. James Farmer later explained:

We planned the Freedom Ride with the specific intention of creating a crisis. We were counting on the bigots in the South to do our work for us. We figured that the government would have to respond if we created a situation that was headline news all over the world, and affected the nation's image abroad. An international crisis, that was our strategy.

On May 14 the riders encountered what Farmer had hoped for. Just outside Anniston, Alabama, one of the two buses was attacked by a mob. As windows were broken, an incendiary device was tossed into the bus, and a fire broke out. The passengers fled, and police arrived belatedly. Meanwhile, local toughs boarded the other bus at the Anniston station, and seriously beat several of the riders. Cars dispatched by Shuttlesworth brought the riders on the first bus to Birmingham, while the second vehicle was set upon by yet another mob when it arrived at Birmingham's bus terminal. Once again, local police were slow in appearing. Pictures of the burning bus and bloodied riders flashed around the world showing the true temper of the white South.

The next day, the riders discovered that no bus drivers were willing to take them on the rest of their trip. After deliberations with a Justice Department representative dispatched by Robert Kennedy, the riders decided to fly from Birmingham to New Orleans so as to conclude their planned journey on schedule. That decision, however, marked the end of only the first Freedom Ride, for two of the riders, John Lewis and Henry Thomas, quickly vowed that the effort would continue. They returned from New Orleans to Nashville, where other student activists who had participated in SNCC's early meetings volunteered to join them. On Wednesday, May 17, this new group of ten riders set out from Nashville for Birmingham. Upon their arrival in Birmingham, Police Commissioner Eugene "Bull" Connor promptly arrested them. Three of the ten were released, and late on the night of May 18, Commissioner Connor personally drove the remaining seven to the Alabama-Tennessee border and left them on the roadside. After several harrowing hours, the group found a sympathetic black resident and contacted their friends in Nashville. They wanted to continue on, and Diane Nash, one of the Nashville leaders, dispatched a car to take them back to Birmingham. Once there, they found that again no bus driver would take them to Montgomery. The riders spent the night in the bus station, while the Justice Department and the White House sought to resolve this problem with Alabama officials.

The riders finally set out for Montgomery early the next morning on a Greyhound bus heavily guarded by state troopers. In Montgomery local police were supposed to continue the protection. When the vehicle pulled into the Montgomery station, however, no officers were anywhere to be seen. As the riders left the bus, a white mob attacked them with clubs and chains. Ralph Abernathy and other MIA activists rescued the riders, but three were beaten severely and the Justice Department representative, John Seigenthaler, was knocked unconscious. Fifteen minutes after the attack began, the first local police arrived. An official of the Anti-Defamation League concluded several days later, after making careful inquiries, that "Police Commissioner L. B. Sullivan had conspired with mob leader Claude Henley to allot the mob ten minutes to do with the Freedom Riders as they saw fit."[27]

In Washington an infuriated Robert Kennedy, who believed that state and local officials had broken their promises to protect the riders, ordered federal marshals into Montgomery and obtained a federal court injunction barring the Ku Klux Klan and other hoodlums from harassing the riders. King was in Chicago when he learned of the attack, and on Sunday, May 21, he flew to Montgomery, where the riders were being housed by the MIA. They decided to hold a rally at Abernathy's First Baptist Church, and by early evening over one thousand people were crowded into the large church.

King had prepared his remarks during his flight south. He told the audience that primary responsibility for the violence lay with Alabama Governor John Patterson, who was "consciously and unconsciously aiding and abetting the forces of violence." Officials' failure to halt the mob attacks in Birmingham and Montgomery indicated that the time for federal intervention and for a more massive attack on segregation by the movement had come:

> Among the many sobering lessons that we can learn from the events of the past week is that the Deep South will not impose limits upon itself. The limits must be imposed from without. Unless the federal government acts forthrightly in the South to assure every citizen his constitutional rights, we will be plunged into a dark abyss of chaos.

The present crisis, King said, called for "a full scale nonviolent assault on the system of segregation in Alabama," which would include

> an intensified voter registration drive, a determined effort to integrate the public schools, lunch counters, public parks, theaters, etc. In short, we will seek to mobilize thousands of people, committed to the method

of nonviolence, who will physically identify themselves with the struggle to end segregation in Alabama. We will present our physical bodies as instruments to defeat the unjust system.

Much to everyone's unpleasant surprise, the opportunity to present their bodies to the forces of segregation was more immediately at hand than King had expected. First Baptist was located in downtown Montgomery, and a hostile white mob had gathered outside the church. Federal marshals were using tear gas against the crowd, but the mob was totally out of control. They set fire to a car belonging to Clifford and Virginia Durr that a friend, writer Jessica Mitford, had driven to the rally. It seemed possible that the mob might storm the church and try to burn it.

Inside, the crowd remained calm, with "not a sign of panic," Mitford said. They continued to sing hymns, and King told them about the disorder outside. Shortly after 10:00 P.M. King went to the basement office to call Attorney General Kennedy in Washington. To Kennedy, and to Assistant Attorney General for Civil Rights Burke Marshall, King displayed little of the calm that he had shown the church audience. Marshall found King "panicky" and "scared" that the mob would set the church afire. The federal officials told him that national guardsmen were on their way to reinforce the marshals, but that promise did not lessen King's concern.

Robert Kennedy was worried about what the mob might do, but he tried to lessen the tension by using humor with King. As Kennedy later recalled it:

> I said that our people were down there and that as long as he was in church, he might say a prayer for us. He didn't think that that was very humorous. He rather berated me for what was happening to him at the time. I said that I didn't think he'd be alive if it hadn't been for us, that we were going to keep him alive, and that the marshals would keep the church from burning down.

In the early morning hours, the contingent of guardsmen led by General Henry V. Graham arrived at the church to reinforce the marshals. King stepped outside for the only time that night to discuss the situation with Graham, and returned inside to tell the trapped protesters that things were under control, although the mob had not been dispersed. Attorney General Kennedy twice called the church to check on developments, and found King still angry about the situation. Kennedy called Alabama Governor Patterson to seek further promises that the black community would be protected, then phoned King to voice more reassurances. At about 3:00 A.M., General Graham decided that everyone in the church had best remain there for the night. Once the mob melted away, those who were trapped in the church would be given escorts home. Finally, between 5:00 and 6:00 A.M., the mob had dispersed sufficiently for the protesters to be escorted home by the guardsmen.[28]

Later that day the Nashville contingent of Freedom Riders told King that they were committed to continuing the ride into Mississippi. At the same time, Deputy Attorney General Byron White, whom Robert Kennedy had sent to take command of the Montgomery situation, made clear the strong federal preference that the rides not continue. If Montgomery, generally a quiet town, had experienced mass white violence, the students could expect much worse in far tougher places in Mississippi.

In private, the Nashville students also told King that he should feel morally obligated to come along with them. King held back, however, telling them that any new arrest might get him into deeper trouble with his Georgia probation. The students were disappointed, and some were angry at what they felt was King's reluctance and indecisiveness. His claim about the probation problem was unpersuasive.

These private conversations continued on Tuesday morning. National guardsmen continued to protect the movement people, and more volunteer riders, including several contingents of northern whites, arrived in Montgomery. Tuesday afternoon, King, Abernathy, CORE's James Farmer, and Nashville student leaders John Lewis and Diane Nash held a press conference in Abernathy's backyard. They announced that the Nashville riders would continue on from Montgomery to Jackson, Mississippi.

Early the next morning the heavily guarded riders ate breakfast at the Montgomery bus station and boarded a special bus for Jackson. King stood beside it, waving good-bye and wishing them well. What looked to reporters like a supportive gesture, however, was viewed by the riders with considerable ambivalence. John Lewis later noted that "it was a big criticism that he came to the bus station and saw the people off and he refused to go." A second bus set out later in the morning, carrying more riders. Accompanied by police cars, each bus made a peaceful and uneventful trip to Jackson. Once there, however, the riders were arrested when they attempted to use the facilities of the Jackson bus station.[29]

That same afternoon, Robert Kennedy called for a temporary halt in the rides. Several hours later the attorney general phoned King in Montgomery to argue for such a "cooling-off period." King told Kennedy that the heavy protection given the two buses had made the ride to Jackson meaningless. Kennedy said that he was seeking to get the arrested riders out of Jackson, but King interjected that the protesters had vowed to remain in jail as "part of the philosophy of this movement. It's a matter of conscience and morality. They must use their lives and their bodies to right a wrong. Our conscience tells us that the law is wrong and we must resist, but we have a moral obligation to accept the penalty."

Kennedy took King's exposition of the nonviolent method as a thinly veiled threat: If the administration did not back the riders, the movement would exacerbate the crisis. Kennedy responded with some heat. "That is not going to have the slightest effect on what the government is going to do in this field or any other. The fact that they stay in jail is not going to have the slightest effect on me."

King in turn was offended by Kennedy's tone. "Perhaps it would help if students came down here by the hundreds—by the hundreds of thousands," he told the attorney general. Kennedy shot back: "The country belongs to you as much as to me. You can determine what's best just as well as I can, but don't make statements that sound like a threat. That's not the way to deal with us."

King moved to lower the temperature of the exchange. "It's difficult to understand the position of oppressed people. Ours is a way out—creative, moral and nonviolent. It is not tied to black supremacy or Communism, but to the plight of the oppressed. It can save the soul of America. You must understand that we've made no gains without pressure and I hope that pressure will always be moral, legal and peaceful."

Kennedy replied, "But the problem won't be settled in Jackson, Mississippi, but by strong federal action." King responded, "I'm deeply appreciative of what the administration is doing. I see a ray of hope, but I am different than my father. I feel the need of being free now!" Kennedy answered, "Well, it all depends on what you and the people in jail decide. If they want to get out, we can get them out." King said, "They'll stay," and the two men hung up.

The next morning King returned to Atlanta and told reporters that the rides would resume "in full force" on either May 29 or 30. That same morning, Abernathy, Walker, Shuttlesworth, and Lee accompanied a group of new riders, professors from Yale and Wesleyan, to the Montgomery bus terminal. The integrated group asked for service at the station coffee shop and were arrested by the Montgomery County sheriff. Several days later they were released on bail.[30]

Back in Atlanta, King convened a meeting of representatives from SCLC, CORE, SNCC, the Nashville movement, and the National Student Association to discuss the future of the Freedom Rides. The group agreed that they should continue the Freedom Rides until all interstate travel was both integrated and safe. The immediate objective would be to "intensify the Freedom Ride so that national public attention can be brought to examine the denial of legal rights of interstate travellers" and "to fill [the] jails of Montgomery and Jackson in order to keep a sharp image of the issues before the public." Some tensions had emerged between CORE people, who had initiated the rides, and SCLC adherents who had helped sustain it. The group thus decided to set up a temporary four-person "Freedom Ride Coordinating Committee." Both SCLC and CORE would contribute $1,000 to the committee, and all agreed "that publicity would clearly establish CORE as the originator of the Freedom Ride."

To interested reporters, King voiced a more restrained tone than the private declarations agreed upon by the strategy meeting. He said there would be "a temporary lull but no cooling off" in the rides, with a "large-scale" resumption sometime the following week. He pointed out that "a victory has been won in the sense that the issue has been placed squarely before the conscience of the nation." More interestingly, King said he was hopeful that something would be done which would make any continuation of the rides unnecessary, such as a federal order banning racial segregation in bus terminal facilities.

On Monday, May 29, Robert Kennedy made precisely the move that King had hoped for. The attorney general announced that he had requested the Interstate Commerce Commission, a separate body with direct responsibility for interstate travel facilities, to issue regulations banning all segregation in such facilities. With that, King's interest in any continuation of the rides declined sharply. Although CORE continued small-scale recruitment of riders for bus trips into Jackson, where all protesters were jailed immediately, SCLC exhibited little interest. Some black activists called on King to join the jailgoers, but neither he nor SCLC took any further action. The Freedom Ride brought national attention to the southern movement, but it also exacerbated both student distrust of King's personal commitment and organizational competition among the civil rights groups.[31]

In June, King resumed his heavy speaking schedule. New York State's black Baptist churches organized a series of fund-raising rallies for SCLC, and King appeared at them all. At several, he emphasized an idea that had been put forward four months earlier by the U.S. Civil Rights Commission: the issuance of a "Second Emancipation Proclamation" by the president, "declaring all forms of racial segregation illegal" by executive order. While the idea had rhetorical appeal, not even the most fervent civil rights advocates within the Kennedy administration thought that the proposal had *any* practical possibilities. Although King continued to speak of the idea, it won few supporters in Washington.

During the summer, two major program issues faced SCLC. First, there were discussions with Highlander about citizenship training. The Field Foundation had awarded a $26,000 grant to the project, but federal tax laws required that the money be disbursed to an organization that was tax exempt, which SCLC was not. Jim Wood, working in conjunction with Maxwell Hahn from Field and Myles Horton from Highlander, began discussions with two officials of the United Church of Christ (UCC), Herman Long and Wesley Hotchkiss, about the UCC's Board of Home Missions serving as the formal recipient of the grant. A "Citizenship School Committee" comprised of Wood, Horton, and Long would direct the program, with Andrew Young overseeing the recruitment of students by Dorothy Cotton of SCLC and their teaching by Septima Clark. A former UCC facility at Dorchester in Liberty County, Georgia, near Savannah, was selected as the instructional site. Although Young would not move south until September, all the other personnel were in place.[32]

The second major initiative facing SCLC was a proposal, an offspring of the Kennedy administration, for an intensive southern voter registration effort. Robert Kennedy felt that "voting was at the heart of the problem," as he once put it. "If enough Negroes registered, they could obtain redress of their grievances internally, without the federal government being involved in it at all." Justice Department civil rights chief Burke Marshall shared Kennedy's belief, and in conversations with outgoing Southern Regional Council Executive Director Harold C. Fleming and wealthy young philanthropist Stephen R. Currier, devised a plan for the establishment of a privately funded, nonpartisan, region-wide registration drive that would coordinate the efforts of all the interested civil rights organizations. The Justice Department, of course, could not finance voter registration, but a well-funded private initiative would mesh neatly with the Kennedy-Marshall idea that filing federal voting rights suits would be more effective than pursuing legislative battles with an unresponsive Congress.

Fleming's proposal gained strength throughout the summer. At an informal retreat on June 9 in Capahosic, Virginia, civil rights representatives responded enthusiastically to the idea. A week later, a second meeting was held at the Justice Department to discuss the plan further. Robert Kennedy attended the session, and according to some who were present, stated that the government could lend far more support to voter registration than to protests such as Freedom Rides or sit-ins. Some SNCC members worried that the attorney general wanted to dissuade movement activists from demonstrations, and was pushing voter drives in order to do so. Others thought Kennedy endorsed federal protection for movement staffers engaged in registration activities, protection that would not be given for demonstrations.[33]

While Walker, Cotton, and Wood were working on those projects, King was on the road. Walker had brought a new level of sophistication to King's increasing number of speaking engagements; they now were structured to reap a substantial financial harvest for SCLC's treasury. Appearances in Albany with New York Governor Nelson Rockefeller, in Los Angeles with California Governor Edmund G. Brown, and in other cities raised thousands of dollars for SCLC while enabling King to reach white northerners with his message of civil rights reform and racial brotherhood.

In late July, Martin and Coretta went to Martha's Vineyard for a family vacation. Outside demands, however, repeatedly interrupted King's holiday. His father broke his ankle, and M.L. had to fly to Atlanta several times to take his place in Ebenezer's pulpit. There also were previously scheduled commitments to preach at New York's Riverside Church, and at a Lutheran Church convention in Miami Beach. To an audience of fourteen thousand Lutherans, and to other gatherings, King voiced newly strengthened criticisms of President Kennedy, who still had not granted him an appointment after seven months in office. John Kennedy, King said, has "failed to come through with certain promises made prior to his election" concerning both legislative proposals and executive actions. Kennedy had broken his word to the black voters who had given him his victory margin and that failure would not be forgotten.[34]

By the end of the summer progress had been made on both the citizenship training program and plans for southwide voter registration. SNCC had resolved its internal debate about a voter registration effort in a heated meeting at Highlander in mid-August. Some members feared that a registration emphasis would mean turning away from "direct action" demonstrations. Ella Baker resolved the split by suggesting that SNCC informally could have two wings, one aimed toward voting, the other toward protests. She already realized something that younger movement workers would learn quickly: In the rural Deep South, local whites were just as hostile toward "outside agitators" who canvassed door to door seeking prospective black registrants as they were toward activists who sat in. Robert Moses, a young worker who went to McComb, Mississippi, in late July under joint SNCC-SCLC sponsorship, was one of the first to perceive that the dichotomy between voter registration and direct action was false. By early August Moses also had decided that his joint sponsorship was untenable, and wrote to Wyatt Walker to return the first paycheck SCLC had sent him. "You can understand that I feel closer to the students." Moses' unease was but one more sign of the student ambivalence toward SCLC and King that now was over a year old.

Represented by its chairman, Charles McDew, SNCC on August 23 joined representatives of the other four major civil rights groups— Wilkins from the NAACP, Farmer from CORE, Whitney Young from the National Urban League, and Walker, standing in for the vacationing King—at a climactic meeting at the Taconic Foundation's New York office to ratify the "Voter Education Project" (VEP) that Fleming, Currier, and the Kennedy representatives had worked out. Sheltered under the wing of the tax-exempt Southern Regional Council, the VEP would have its own director and would parcel out registration responsibilities and funds to local representatives and affiliates of civil rights organizations throughout the South. The program would satisfy all of its participants: philanthropic foundations that wanted to support civic progress, a Democratic administration eager for more southern black voters, and civil rights groups anxious for financial subventions for efforts they wanted to undertake in any case.

Wyatt Walker hoped to use VEP as a platform for expanding SCLC. He proposed that SCLC hire a voter registration director and five field secretaries, and seek responsibility for all of Alabama, most of Louisiana, and metropolitan Atlanta when the VEP assigned areas to different organizations. SCLC also could be active in Virginia and some parts of Tennessee. Walker estimated the cost at almost $100,000 a year, but SCLC with its ministerial orientation was well suited to take *the* leading role in the new effort. "Any successful voter registration drive," Walker emphasized, "must be church-oriented," just like SCLC itself.

King and Walker hoped that VEP could work hand-in-hand with the citizenship training program. Although Myles Horton of Highlander wanted the Citizenship School Committee, rather than SCLC, to direct the program, it was clear even before Andrew Young moved south that he and Walker envisioned the training schools as an integral part of an expanded SCLC program. Young stressed how SCLC had to publicize the training to its affiliates, and pointed out the long-range benefits for the organization. "A trained local leadership would be on hand to coordinate a wide variety of SCLC programs in the future."[35]

While Walker was occupied in early September with a tense civil rights situation in Monroe, North Carolina, King made plans for his first venture as a teacher. King had agreed to teach a senior philosophy seminar at Morehouse in conjunction with his good friend Professor Samuel Williams of the college. Atlanta student activist Julian Bond was enrolled in the course, and most sessions ended with discussions of the civil rights movement. King enjoyed the teaching, and it reminded him of the opportunities for thought and relaxation that a college position would offer. Although he was far too busy to give the Morehouse course the time he would have liked to, it allowed him to think about what his future might hold. "I know I will not always be a leader," King remarked in one conversation. "I will not always be in the public eye and in the news . . . I feel that there are many things just as important ahead for me, and I have almost an eagerness to give the rest of my life to the pursuit of the cultural, intellectual and aesthetic ideas I've been pulled away from by this struggle. Not now, of course," King added after a pause, "but some day."

In the eighteen months that King had lived in Atlanta, Coretta and others close to him had seen some changes take place. Both Coretta and Walker thought that King was less concerned about his clothes and personal appearance than he once had been. Coretta felt that that was just part of a larger change, a pronounced selflessness that had emerged after the India trip and that had grown stronger since then. King felt comfortable in the old frame house at 563 Johnson Avenue that they rented, and wanted nothing more. "At times he has even talked seriously," Coretta commented then, "about whether or not he should even own anything that's not absolutely necessary for the rest of the family." It was an attitude she did not share, but one to which King increasingly became attached.

King and those around him realized that he had grown more relaxed but also more reserved, indeed solemn, since his return to Atlanta. The changes had occurred simultaneously with his growing acceptance of the role into which he had been cast. That acceptance, once so grudging, now made him less fearful about meeting a sudden end. As that tension abated, it was replaced by an awareness of the responsibilities that came with his leadership role. It made King seem even more formal to those who were only modest acquaintances. "I'm sure I've become more serious," King admitted to one questioner who asked him about these impressions. "I don't think I've lost my sense of humor, but I know I've let many opportunities go by without using it. I seldom joke in my speeches anymore. I forget to." In private, King still could be the outspoken joker and mimic that his closest friends had long known him to be, but very few people were exposed to him in circumstances where he felt free enough to relax his serious public self. It puzzled many who met him for the first time, expecting a charismatic leader. Instead, they found the great symbol of the southern movement to be "remote" and "bland." They wondered if they had encountered him at an unusual time, but the reserved King *was* the real man on all those occasions when the mantle of leadership lay heavily upon his shoulders.

The many responsibilities of that public leadership role continued to make King a sometime father and husband. Early in September Coretta was trying to decide what school Yoki should attend when she began the first grade. She sought unsuccessfully to interest Martin in the question. "I spoke to my husband about it," she recalled later, "and he said he would leave it up to me because those were the things that I had to deal with and he was very busy and so on." He was not intentionally uncaring, but sometimes it seemed that way. All of that selflessness might be commendable in a famous public figure, but King's version brought no pleasure to his own family.[36]

In early September, King was involved in several unpleasant incidents. The most regrettable was an internal controversy involving SCLC's number two staff member, Jim Wood. Tensions which had developed between Wood and Wyatt Walker worsened when Walker's secretary told him that Wood had made uncomplimentary comments about both King and Walker. King called Wood in, told him that such remarks were unacceptable, and asked for his resignation. Wood denied the allegations and refused to resign. King told him he had no choice. Distraught, Wood returned home and wrote King a letter denying the supposed statements. "As I sat there" with you this afternoon, Wood told King, "I thought of all the things that have been said to me about SCLC and the men who lead it. Things I have not chosen to repeat nor even accept as truth. . . . As I listened to the things I was charged with saying I recognized them as things I've heard many times in many places here in Atlanta, Petersburg and others." The accusations made it seem "that I have been involved in some vulgar plan to discredit SCLC and the men in it." Wood insisted he had not been; "with God as my witness I did not say these things." He ended by saying that he wished "there was something I could do about" the situation, but King made it plain there was not. It was one of the most painful situations King ever had been involved in.

Less than one week later, a public controversy enveloped King. For three years King had served as a vice-president of the nation's largest organization of black Baptists, the National Baptist Convention (NBC). The group's autocratic president, the Reverend Joseph H. Jackson of Chicago, had spoken out against the student sit-ins, and many younger ministers felt he was insufficiently supportive of all civil rights initiatives. Jackson was up for reelection at the September convention, and the young progressives nominated an alternate candidate, the Reverend Gardner C. Taylor of Brooklyn, who actively supported civil rights. King was a friend of Taylor's and endorsed his candidacy. A tumultuous uproar characterized the climactic election session on September 6. At the height of the commotion, one Jackson supporter, Rev. Arthur G. Wright, collapsed and died of a heart attack. Jackson triumphed in the election, and then tried to lay the blame for Wright's death on those who had supported his opponent. Jackson claimed the Taylor candidacy had been masterminded by King, and that King should bear some of the responsibility for Wright's passing. Jackson's supporters on the NBC board removed King from his vice-presidency.

Jackson's statements set off a huge uproar within the black church community. Letters and telegrams denouncing Jackson for his "vicious and unChristian attack" upon King were dispatched by many notables. Some close observers felt that an insecure and envious Jackson had lost control and lashed out at King, a younger man whose fame far exceeded Jackson's. Much as King was seen as a threat to the "old order" in civil rights, namely Roy Wilkins and the NAACP, he was also perceived as a personal threat by this tradition-bound leader of the NBC, the religious equivalent of the "NAA." King was shocked by Jackson's outburst, but rejected the advice of many that he sue Jackson for libel concerning the death allegations. His "basic philosophy," King told one friend, would not allow him to do that. "This unjust attack is just another cross that I must bear." In short order, Taylor's supporters split from the Jackson group and set up their own organization, the *Progressive* National Baptist Convention. Similarly, several Jackson supporters ended their active involvement in SCLC.[37]

Hardly had the Jackson controversy passed when tensions heightened between SNCC and SCLC. In the wake of SNCC's August meeting at Highlander, several members decided to join Robert Moses' organizing effort in McComb, Mississippi, rather than return to college. While the intense white harassment brought home Baker's point about the false debate between voter registration and direct action, the creation of a SNCC field staff led to a more pressing need for funds. SCLC had made repeated gifts of $250 and $500 early in 1961, but many SNCC members believed that SCLC owed them a good deal more. SCLC's direct-mail appeals generated considerable amounts from northerners, but many who sent contributions, the students claimed, thought they would be assisting the initiatives the students had undertaken over the past eighteen months. They contended that they had done more than SCLC to bring about change. They had begun the sit-ins, had persuaded a reluctant King to join the Atlanta sit-ins, and had kept the Freedom Rides going after the first CORE contingent flew on to New Orleans. King might be a well-known symbol to northerners, but it was the students who had taken the initiative. If SCLC were to be fair, it would share some of the northern contributions with the students.

In mid-September SNCC acquired a new executive secretary, James Forman, a somewhat older Chicagoan. A relentless worker and superior administrator, Forman brought a firm hand to the SNCC organization. Along with Julian Bond and several others, including Ella Baker, Forman arranged a meeting with King and Ralph Abernathy to discuss funds. The SNCC delegation outlined its plans for an expanded Mississippi project that would require $25,000. Although King and Abernathy were enthusiastic about the project, King responded that that sum was beyond SCLC's means. He said he would be happy to give SNCC one third of what had been raised at a recent rally sponsored by a New York union. The students understood that the total had been $11,000, and that King thus was promising them more than $3,500.

Then Baker broached a touchier issue. As Forman described it, Baker raised "the question of other organizations having allegedly received funds marked by the donors for the student movement. [King] asked for specific examples and one was raised, but the circumstances were truly complicated and vague so we were unable to clarify the situation much," Forman recalled. "Mrs. Baker was also critical of certain public relations techniques of SCLC, suggesting that their techniques could be sharpened up so as not to suggest that they were really more involved in certain situations than they really were." The meeting ended without any resolution of that issue, and shortly afterward SCLC gave SNCC $1,000. After waiting awhile for the anticipated balance, Forman approached King and asked for at least another $500 toward SCLC's pledge. King put him off and Forman went away empty-handed. Even after that rebuff, however, the students' anger was directed more toward Walker than King. "We somehow never associated King except peripherally," Julian Bond explained later, "with what we thought was some corruption in SCLC, not corruption in the sense of them taking the money for themselves, but that they were corrupting the movement" by taking for SCLC contributions really intended for SNCC. "We had the feeling that King knew it but he was too nice a guy to do anything about it."[38]

Early September was a draining time for King. Andrew Young recalled that when he arrived in Atlanta, he "got the impression [that King] was a guy that was pretty harried by the administrative responsibilities of running an organization." The small office was becoming cramped, and the staff spoke about moving to larger quarters. Preparations also were under way for SCLC's annual convention in Nashville in late September. Then, on September 22, came the first piece of good news in several months, an announcement by the Interstate Commerce Commission (ICC) that all interstate transportation facilities must be desegregated. The order would be effective November 1, and was exactly the federal initiative that the Freedom Riders had been hoping for. Robert Kennedy's request to the ICC had been honored, and King and Walker were extremely pleased.

When SCLC's convention opened in Nashville on September 27, King and Walker presented an optimistic report to their several hundred colleagues from across the South. Walker told the board how the first citizenship training sessions had taken place at Dorchester, and that Young, Cotton, and Clark all were working hard to ensure that more students would come their way. SCLC's affiliates should encourage their members to take the training course, and then return home to set up citizenship courses under the affiliate's sponsorship. King was excited about what the VEP would do for voter registration across the South, and both men told the board how the past twelve months had been the most successful financial period in SCLC's history. Almost $200,000 had been raised, not counting the citizenship grants; $60,000 of that amount had come from rallies at which King had appeared. The biggest financial breakthrough, Walker said, was the productive direct-mail effort overseen by Stanley Levison and a young black man whom Levison had recruited as administrator of SCLC's two-person New York office, Jack O'Dell. The new man had also sent King several memos on voter registration, but 90 percent of the New York office's work concerned fund-raising. "There is no way to calculate," Walker told the board, "what Stanley Levison and Jack O'Dell have meant to SCLC in this regard." Their efforts had produced a list of nine thousand proven contributors, individuals who could be counted on to support SCLC at least twice a year. Their hope was to increase that list to 25,000.

Walker told the board that he had bright hopes for SCLC's future. The past twelve months had been "a challenging and exciting year," and now SCLC ought to consider two major additions to its program. First, James Lawson should be added to the staff to focus on direct-action projects. By hiring Lawson, "SCLC will be provided with the opportunity of organizing 'nonviolent teams' to service communities where direct action is desired," Walker said. "The possibilities of development of a Southwide mass movement are tremendous." King agreed and told the board that "we intend to do even more in the area of direct action than we have done in the past. We will have to carry the struggle more into South Carolina, Mississippi and Alabama." Once again the details for implementing this idea were vague, and curious reporters asked Lawson just what SCLC had in mind. The plan, Lawson told them, was for SCLC to recruit a ten thousand-person "nonviolent army," individuals ready to oppose segregation with their bodies and willing to endure lengthy jail stays. Reporters asked King if he agreed with Lawson's intent, and King said he did. Those day and night stand-ins at voter registration offices he had talked of in the past had still not been tried, and Lawson could implement them. Wyatt Walker by contrast tried to downplay Lawson's figure of 10,000 people, and said that 100 or 150 over the next year was a more practical goal for Lawson's recruiting effort.

In addition to the proposal for expanded direct action, Walker also urged that the board contemplate changing SCLC from an organization made up of affiliated local groups to one that would enroll individual members. He recommended that they "seriously consider national organization to embrace the many people who wish to be identified with us." The idea had previously been rejected for fear of provoking competition with the NAACP, but Walker urged that "the business of us becoming a 'membership' organization ought to be carefully reconsidered." Over the past year "our growth has not been as great as it might have been," and the ability to sell individual memberships would exploit the opportunities for expansion. One board member, Rev. Dearing E. King of Louisville, asked if consideration also could be given to changing the organization's name to the *National* Christian Leadership Conference, and King responded that several people had raised the question. Both that issue and the membership recommendation were referred to the administration committee for "further study."

In the wake of the Nashville gathering, Walker and Lawson, now called SCLC's "Special Projects Director," turned their attention to fleshing out the "nonviolent army" idea. Some three hundred volunteers would be recruited and trained in the methods of nonviolent action. Each person had to be willing to spend at least six months in jail, and once the training was complete, would remain "on call" until the time came for SCLC to deploy this "army." Lawson's recruitment efforts were to begin by mid-November.[39]

King again was trapped in a heavy schedule of far-flung speaking appearances. On top of that, a minor tempest arose over an offer from movie director Otto Preminger that King play the role of a Georgia senator in a production of the well-known Washington novel *Advise and Consent*. King initially consented because it would pay $5,000 to SCLC. Newspapers got wind of the scenario, however, and a bizarre public debate arose over the propriety of a black civil rights leader appearing as a Deep South senator. King had little patience for the controversy, and withdrew his acceptance.

Throughout the summer and early fall, King's friend Harris Wofford had continued to press the White House for a formal meeting between King and President Kennedy. Wofford told appointments secretary Kenneth O'Donnell that King had been "somewhat hurt by the long delay" in arranging an audience, but that he was "resilient and has faith in the President." Finally, an appointment was scheduled for October 16, nine months after John Kennedy had entered the presidency. King met first with Robert Kennedy before having a one-hour audience with the president. King took the initiative in both conversations, and pressed upon John Kennedy his idea that the president ought to issue a "Second Emancipation Proclamation" declaring all segregation illegal in light of the Fourteenth Amendment. He also asked the president why he had not issued an order banning segregation in federally assisted housing, something that Kennedy during his campaign had repeatedly promised to do as soon as he took office. Kennedy replied that he would be happy to see a written explanation of the "Second Emancipation" proposal, and noted that his brother had taken the initiative in getting the ICC to mandate the desegregation of all airport, train station, and bus terminal facilities, an order that would take effect two weeks hence. Kennedy went on to explain that the political climate in Congress was not supportive enough of civil rights to warrant any administration proposal of civil rights legislation or the long-promised housing order. The backlash on Capitol Hill would be too great, and would make either effort counterproductive. King did not contest the president's political analysis. The conversation ended in a friendly fashion, and Kennedy offered to give King a tour of the White House's private rooms. They encountered Kennedy's wife, Jacqueline, and together the first family showed King the second-floor living quarters. King was touched by the gesture and told the president he would quickly submit a detailed explanation of the "Proclamation" idea.

Outside, King told reporters about the suggestions he had made to the president, and stated that Kennedy had "listened very sympathetically, and said that he would certainly take all of these things under consideration." That evening King went to the Woffords' home for dinner, and chatted about the afternoon meeting, which Wofford had not attended. King had enjoyed seeing Kennedy but was unhappy with the lack of civil rights initiatives in the administration's first nine months in office. In a sad tone, he told Wofford:

> In the election, when I gave my testimony for Kennedy, my impression then was that he had the intelligence and the skill and the moral fervor to give the leadership we've been waiting for and do what no other President has ever done. Now, I'm convinced that he had the understanding and the political skill but so far I'm afraid that the moral passion is missing.

Wofford did not argue with King, for his own sentiments were similar. Within the White House, other staff members viewed Wofford as the civil rights community's representative to them, rather than *their* ambassador to the black leadership. Wofford knew well how long it had taken for him even to secure an appointment for King, and how both the president and his brother often discounted Wofford's advice. Neither of the Kennedys felt comfortable with King's moralizing and his emphasis on the idealistic rather than practical, political considerations.

Civil rights issues promised only headaches and political losses. If Wofford could keep the civil rights leadership quiet and reasonably content, the entire problem could be kept on a back burner. "What Kennedy liked best in my role, and I liked least," Wofford later wrote, "was my function as a buffer between him and the civil rights forces pressing for presidential action. . . . I got tired of his accosting me with a grin and asking, 'Are your constituents happy?'" So long as Wofford's "constituents" were happy, presumably the South would be relatively quiet.[40]

After that day in Washington, King returned to Atlanta and SCLC's affairs. One positive development was the decision of Atlanta's West Hunter Street Baptist Church to offer the pastorship to Ralph Abernathy. King's friend accepted and made plans to move to Atlanta by mid-November. SCLC also decided to move to larger quarters in a downtown building at 41 Exchange Place, some distance from the traditional black business district on Auburn Avenue. Walker also wanted to hire a voter registration staffer and a person to assume Jim Wood's duties as public relations director. King mentioned both vacancies to Levison, and Stanley wrote from New York to advise him that "Jack [O'Dell] and I are contacting candidates."

At the end of October, King flew to London to appear on an English television program. King's visit to the British capital included one incident that stunned him: During a speech, some racists in the audience heckled and booed throughout King's remarks. It was the first time he had ever encountered any hostility while speaking. The television appearance included no such problems, and the interviewer succeeded in getting King to speak more freely than usual. Asked about his feelings toward his role in the movement, King explained how "I had no idea that I would be catapulted into a position of leadership in the civil rights struggle" and alluded to how the vision in the kitchen had given him the strength to conquer his doubts. "I don't think anyone in a situation like this can go through it without confronting moments of real fear," King explained. "But I have always had something that gave me an inner sense of assurance, and an inner sense of security. . . . I have always felt a sense of cosmic companionship."

Although that companionship gave King an inner security, still "there are those moments when I feel a sense of inadequacy as a symbol. It is never easy for one to accept the role of symbol, without going through constant moments of self-examination," and for King his increasing realization that he could not escape that role was extremely painful. The more he realized it, the more he felt trapped. If he could not jettison it, however, he was determined to bear the burden as productively as possible. "I must confess," he said, "that there are moments when I begin to wonder whether I am adequate or whether I am able to face all of the challenges and even the responsibilities of this particular position."[41]

Still, the strength to go forward had always been there. His first eighteen months in Atlanta had been much more satisfying than his final two years in Montgomery. The student movement had resolved the debate about civil rights methods in favor of direct action, and had thrust King to new prominence as the principal symbol of the southern movement. The sit-ins, his stay in Reidsville prison, and the Freedom Rides had given King a greater understanding of the challenges the movement faced and the efforts needed to overcome them. Nonviolence could not be simply a tool of persuasion for convincing southern whites of the evilness of segregation, it had to be a political strategy, a means by which the movement could defeat the forces of evil by rallying greater support to its own side. That lesson had been brought home by the Freedom Rides, by the forced activation of a reluctant Kennedy administration, and by the triumph—the ICC order—that eventually emerged from the crisis brought on by the rides. King detailed his understanding of it in a letter written at the end of October:

> Public relations is a very necessary part of any protest of civil disobedience. The main objective is to bring moral pressure to bear upon an unjust system or a particularly unjust law. The public at large must be aware of the inequities involved in such a system. In effect, in the absence of justice in the established courts of the region, nonviolent protesters are asking for a hearing in the court of world opinion. Without the presence of the press, there might have been untold massacre in the South. The world seldom believes the horror stories of history until they are documented via mass media. Certainly, there would not have been sufficient pressure to warrant a ruling by the ICC had not this situation been so well-publicized.

On November 1, as the ICC order took effect, the students of SNCC once again took the lead in pursuing the true mass action that King had spoken of for over four years. Just as they had set the movement's pace throughout 1960 and 1961, the students led King forward to the first real mass direct action that the movement had seen: Albany, Georgia.[42]

4

Albany and Lessons for the Future, 1961–1962

Charles Sherrod was twenty-two years old when he became SNCC's first field secretary in the summer of 1961. A native of Petersburg, and a graduate of Virginia Union University, he had joined Robert Moses in July for SNCC's first explorations in southwest Mississippi. In August he made a brief visit to southwest Georgia, a rural region where one of the most repressive counties, Terrell, had been the target of the first federal voting rights suit filed under the 1957 Civil Rights Act. The only city of any size in the area was Albany—"All-*BENNY*," most pronounced it—and if SNCC hoped to start an outpost in southwest Georgia, the 26,000-person black community of Albany—one third of the city's population—appeared a safer refuge than the small hamlets of counties like Terrell. Some young Albany residents encouraged Sherrod to organize a SNCC voter registration drive in their city, and Sherrod briefed his SNCC colleagues on Albany's prospects at the mid-August Highlander meeting. Then Sherrod went back to Mississippi and the intense white harassment in McComb. After several weeks there, he returned to Atlanta. A few days later, Sherrod and another SNCC staffer four years his junior, Cordell Reagon, took the long bus ride south to Albany to see if a SNCC voter registration effort could be mounted.

Sherrod and Reagon had few contacts in Albany, especially among black adults. Local black leaders were not uninterested in civil rights advancement, but they were suspicious about the two young outsiders and what they might do. An NAACP chapter had existed for several decades, and dentist E. D. Hamilton and businessman C. W. King had been among its leaders since the late 1930s. There also was an organization of black professional men, the Criterion Club, which took an interest in civic affairs and numbered both the older leaders and a younger generation of more aggressive men—osteopath William G. Anderson, businessman Thomas Chatmon, and two brothers from the King family, attorney Chevene B. and insurance agent Slater—among its members. Many of these younger professionals lived in a newer section of Albany, Lincoln Heights, and had repeatedly complained to city officials about poor drainage, unpaved streets, and lack of sewer lines in their subdivision. Along with the older men, they had also taken an interest in one of Albany's most glaring examples of segregation, the use of racially separate polling places each election day. Black interest in racial progress clearly existed, but local acceptance of Sherrod and Reagon was something else. Sherrod initially stayed at the home of C. B. King, and then lived for two weeks at Dr. Hamilton's. Sherrod could see the hostility of many of the black adults, but he and Reagon worked hard to persuade people to discuss civil rights. Hamilton and the King brothers explained to the two newcomers the recent history of black initiatives in Albany: the Lincoln Heights complaints, the requests to integrate the polling places, and an unsuccessful effort earlier that year to boycott the *Albany Herald* after its segregationist editor, James H. Gray, had written a distasteful February 6 editorial dismissing the appeals that black representatives had voiced to the city.

Sherrod and Reagon determined that focusing on organizing black youngsters would be more productive than on black adults, and the local leadership did not quarrel. Dr. Hamilton thought Sherrod disdainful of the adults' efforts, and was disappointed that Sherrod seemed unwilling to pursue his organizing efforts in conjunction with the local NAACP and the long-existing Dougherty County Voters' League.[1]

Largely writing off the adults, Sherrod and Reagon concentrated their efforts on black high school students and on the 650 students at all-black Albany State College. They found that many of the college students were interested in organizing for civil rights, and the two young men drew small groups of students together each evening for workshops on the movement. They continued to approach black adults, and won permission to hold their meetings in area churches. After uncertainty about where they would live, Sherrod and Reagon found semipermanent lodgings with a young couple, Emanuel "Bo" and Eliza "Goldie" Jackson, and won support from several young professionals. Many blacks remained reluctant to have anything to do with them, however. "People would see us walking down the street," Reagon later recalled, and "they'd cross over to the other side. . . . They were extremely afraid of us, because we represented something that had never been done." Still, Sherrod and Reagon made headway and secured a tiny office near the black business district.

By late October they had organized an eighteen-person "central committee" for their student group despite efforts by black administrators at Albany State to banish them from the campus. They hoped to use the students to canvass for voters, but college officials warned students to have nothing to do with Sherrod and Reagon. A core group continued to meet each evening, some motivated by the refusal of college and city officials to halt the harassment of black coeds by marauding whites. The SNCC men also planned to test desegregation of Albany's transportation terminal facilities on November 1 when the ICC order took effect.[2]

Albany's black adult leadership also was active. Albany Mayor Asa D. Kelley, Jr., wanted to secure federal funding for urban renewal. With some diffidence, he invited Dr. Anderson and Albany State President William H. Dennis, Jr., to serve in an adjunct capacity on a citizens' advisory committee. Black leaders took the invitations as a hopeful sign, and appeared at the city commission's October 24 meeting to repeat their requests for action in Lincoln Heights. "We have filed three petitions . . . over a period of approximately eight years requesting paving and sewage in our area," their spokesman reminded the commission. "We have attempted to be very patient . . . but one's patience grows short when we can find no other reason for this systematic denial except race." Kelley responded that race had nothing to do with the matter, that sewer construction would begin within the next month, and that a serious drainage problem was the reason that no curbs, gutters or paving could be installed until more funds became available. The rejection dashed black leaders' hopes for a meaningful relationship with white officials.[3]

Sherrod and Reagon had planned daily tests of Albany's airport, train station, and bus terminal facilities beginning on November 1, but these efforts were interrupted when they were called back to McComb to stand trial for previous arrests. While they were in Mississippi, word reached them that the NAACP had moved to cancel any facilities testing in Albany. They hurried back to Georgia and made plans for their own bus ride from Atlanta to Albany early on November 1. A white SNCC volunteer, Salynn McCollum, went along to observe, and when their bus pulled into Albany at 6:30 A.M. city Police Chief Laurie Pritchett, alerted by his sources in the black community, had a dozen officers waiting at the station. Blocked from access to the white waiting room, Sherrod and Reagon postponed the challenge until a more opportune moment. They returned to the black community, contacted their young supporters, and at 3:00 P.M. nine volunteers went to the bus station and sat down in the white area while McCollum looked on. Police ordered them to leave, and threatened them with arrest if they did not. Since the objective was to test compliance with the ICC order, rather than initiate a jail-going campaign, the group departed. McCollum's report on how segregation was being enforced in Albany despite the ICC mandate was forwarded to federal officials by the SNCC office in Atlanta.

In the wake of that first test, Sherrod and Reagon, who now had been joined by SNCC's Charles Jones, continued to organize the students. NAACP loyalists such as Dr. Hamilton took increasing offense at the SNCC workers' refusal either to defer to established organizations or to acknowledge the NAACP Youth Council as the only organizational vehicle needed for student activism. Many black ministers in town shared Dr. Hamilton's sentiments toward the three young men from SNCC.

As these strains between the student activists and the older black leadership became more pronounced, the young black professionals moved to heal the breach and assert their own influence. They preferred a more aggressive stance than Dennis or Hamilton took, yet the SNCC workers' success with the students threatened to place those youngsters at the forefront of the black community. Dr. Anderson and the King brothers decided to act. "This thing was evolving to the extent that it was going to become community wide," Anderson recalled, "and we said, 'Well, we better get together and do something.'"[4]

A community rally was held on November 9. Four days later Albany Mayor Kelley was reelected to a second term over a more conservative opponent. Three quarters of Albany's black voters supported Kelley, and the outcome was interpreted as a victory for the more progressive part of the white community. A second rally took place on November 16, and the following evening Slater King and the other young professionals scheduled a small meeting to discuss what new approaches the black community might make in the wake of Kelley's reelection. It was to be a gathering of half a dozen people, but word spread and about twenty individuals gathered, including the three young SNCC workers, several student leaders, Dr. Hamilton, and several ministers. Dr. Anderson opened the meeting by noting that everyone was committed to breaking down segregation, but that any effort to win compliance with the ICC order was almost certain to lead to arrests. The bus and train stations would be their first targets, but segregation of Albany's municipal facilities—the library, the parks, the hospital, and the city buses—was also intolerable. Then there were other ongoing problems: incidents of police brutality, the lack of employment opportunities for blacks in city government, blacks' exclusion from juries, and the meager job opportunities with private businesses.

Everyone present had worked on those problems through the organizations they represented: the Criterion Club, the Voters' League, the Ministerial Alliance, the NAACP, the Federated Women's Clubs, and the Youth Council. As Sherrod later described it, "The real issue immediately took the floor in the form of a question" posed by Dr. Anderson and Slater King: "Would the organizations involved be willing to lose their identity as separate groups and cooperate under the name of 'The Albany Movement'?" The representatives of each organization caucused, and all but one agreed. Dr. Hamilton explained that the local NAACP would have to consult with Regional Director Ruby Hurley and state Field Secretary Vernon Jordan before it could endorse the new organization. Hamilton's hesitation did not dissuade the others, and the decision to create the Albany Movement was made. Anderson was elected president and Marion S. Page, an older man and postal employee, was elected secretary. Along with Slater King, they were named as a three-man committee to attempt new contacts with city officials.

NAACP officials Hurley and Jordan were familiar with Albany and the relative inactivity of its NAACP branch over the past few years. They also knew that Sherrod had created a SNCC-oriented student group that was well on the way to replacing the NAACP Youth Council as the major focal point for young black people in Albany. They advised Hamilton that in any new civil rights initiatives in Albany, the NAACP should take the lead. Hamilton agreed, and made plans for a legal attack upon Albany's defiance of the ICC order. Three members of the Youth Council, with their parents' permission, were selected to test the segregated waiting room at the Albany bus station. Their arrest was expected, and Hamilton promised to bail them out quickly. Hurley instructed that there be no more than three so that costs would be minimized.

On Wednesday, November 22, the three high school students entered the station, purchased interstate tickets, sat down in the white waiting room, and attempted to patronize the lunch counter. Albany Police Chief Pritchett promptly arrested them. Hamilton and Youth Council advisor Thomas Chatmon secured their release, and notified Hurley in Atlanta. "I didn't do anything without letting the authorities in Atlanta know," Hamilton later commented. Word of the test spread quickly in Albany. That afternoon hundreds of Albany State students, heading home for the Thanksgiving holiday, descended upon the bus station. College Dean Charles Minor went to the station and beseeched the students to abide by the rules of segregation. Many obeyed, but two who were active in Sherrod's group, Bertha Gober and Blanton Hall, insisted upon using the white facilities and were arrested. Unlike the NAACP-sponsored protesters, Hall and Gober remained in jail until Saturday, and Dean Minor suspended them from college.

The day after those arrests the young adults moved to head off any further split between the NAACP and SNCC. Dr. Anderson convened a meeting of all the parties, including Sherrod, Reagon, and Vernon Jordan. Jordan explained that he wanted no conflict between the two groups, implying that the SNCC workers were encouraging such. Slater King said that if problems existed, they were caused by the NAACP, whose supporters had undertaken a whispering campaign against Sherrod, Reagon, and Jones. Though no one was satisfied, there the matter was left.[5]

On Saturday evening, a mass meeting of four hundred persons was held at Mt. Zion Baptist Church. This was a larger crowd than the previous rallies, and it generated a more intense community spirit. The following day, Albany State's students returned to town from their holiday. The trials of all five students began Monday morning at the downtown courthouse. A large crowd of about four hundred black people gathered outside the courthouse to protest. C. B. King represented Hall and Gober, while Hurley and Chatmon, who felt King was too supportive of SNCC, secured Atlanta attorney Donald Hollowell to defend the three Youth Council members. The trial was interrupted by the appearance of Charles Sherrod, who sat on the white side of the segregated courtroom.

Sherrod refused police efforts to move him, and Judge Abner Israel stopped the proceedings and summoned King and Hollowell to the bench. After the conference, the two black attorneys spoke to Sherrod, who left. Segregation also won out in the trial; Judge Israel sentenced each of the five students to fifteen days probation and a $100 fine.

At the trial's end, Charles Jones led the crowd of four hundred from downtown to the Union Baptist Church, where everyone signed a petition to Albany State President Dennis protesting Dean Minor's suspension of Hall and Gober. Then the procession moved to the college, where Dennis refused to meet with them. The group dispersed, but Monday's mass march marked a new student commitment to protest segregation.

The following night Dr. Anderson appeared at the regular meeting of the city commission. He asked Mayor Kelley if the city had any response to the Albany Movement's request for desegregation of city facilities. The mayor replied that the commissioners felt "there would be no advantage in a general discussion" of the subject since they "could find no area of agreement in the petition for discussion." Anderson was disappointed at the white officials' refusal to open a dialogue, especially after the harbinger of Monday's mass march. Their refusal, he said, was "regrettable, unfortunate, and not in the best interests of Albany," and he walked out of the council chamber. Wednesday's *Albany Herald* gave prominent coverage to Dr. Anderson's statement, and thoughtfully printed his home and office addresses for anyone who might be interested.

While Anderson was appearing at the commission meeting, Albany State President Dennis was swearing out trespass warrants for the arrest of Sherrod, Reagon, and Jones. Sherrod was arrested that evening and spent the night in jail, but the next morning, before Jones and Reagon could be located, state education authorities ordered Dennis to withdraw the warrants. The incident widened the split between the more conservative black adults and the SNCC-oriented students.[6]

On November 29, the day after his appearance before the city commission, Anderson went to Atlanta to talk with Hurley and Jordan about NAACP financial support for the Albany Movement. They made it clear that "there was no need for two separate organizations when you have an NAACP branch in the community." If Anderson wanted NAACP backing, he had better "play down the Albany Movement and direct everything through the Branch." Otherwise, the NAACP would pay the bills only for the three youths arrested in the bus station test. Hurley and Jordan also suggested that Dr. Anderson could be made president of the NAACP branch. When he left to return to Albany, the two NAACP staffers had the erroneous impression that Anderson was interested in going along with their suggestions.

On December 1, another mass meeting was held, where speakers decried false charges appearing in the *Albany Herald* that the black community was plotting a write-in effort against white officials in the December 4 municipal general election. The charges fed white fears that the new activism of the black community meant that full-scale conflict was just around the corner. On Election Day, the white turnout exceeded that of a month earlier, while the black turnout declined almost 50 percent, to 750.

SNCC staffers made plans for a new initiative while Albany's young black adult leadership tried to mute the competition between SNCC and the NAACP. Vernon Jordan adopted a more passive stance, and black leaders planned to boycott stores that advertised in the *Herald*, protesting the newspaper's fictional election story. Attorney C. B. King and Albany State student leaders tried without success to contest the dismissals of Hall and Gober, and to protest letters that Dennis had sent to dozens of students threatening expulsion unless their activism ceased.

At another mass meeting on December 6, Anderson told the modest crowd about the movement's boycott plans. A dispirited Vernon Jordan, listening to Anderson's remarks, concluded that his and Hurley's hopes of enlisting Anderson to remake the Albany Movement into an NAACP effort had been unrealistic. The Albany Movement was likely to remain a permanent organization, Jordan decided, and Anderson was "unreliable". The next day a disappointed Jordan flew back to Atlanta. Beside him on the plane was one of the local leaders, Mrs. Irene Wright, a former dean at Albany State who had resigned in protest over Dennis's accommodationist policies. Jordan talked of his unhappiness with the organizational situation, and Wright explained that Hamilton's conservatism had mandated the creation of the Albany Movement. She expressed sympathy for Jordan's desire for a reinvigorated NAACP branch, and said she would mention it to Slater King and to Marion Page when she returned to town. "This gave Jordan some hope," an NAACP staffer noted, "of getting everything under the control of the NAACP."

By December 6, SNCC worker Charles Jones in Albany and SNCC Executive Secretary James Forman in Atlanta had laid plans for a new Freedom Ride from Atlanta to Albany on Sunday, December 10. An integrated group of eight volunteers would take the train southward. Reporters would be notified in advance. The time had come, as Jones phrased it, for the black community to "take the legal guarantees on thin paper and turn them into thick action of implementation."

Albany Police Chief Pritchett knew well in advance what was being planned for Sunday afternoon. The SNCC workers worried that their office phone was tapped, but most of Pritchett's information came from secondhand reports volunteered by black adults. Sunday morning the eight riders, four black and four white, gathered in Atlanta. Wyatt Walker supplied the money for the train tickets. The young president of the Albany Youth Council, Bobby Burch, also was in Atlanta. He asked Vernon Jordan's advice about whether to join the eight riders. "Jordan advised Burch not to go," an NAACP memo noted, "because he didn't want him . . . getting involved with anything initiated by SNCC."

The railroad was obeying the ICC order, and the eight volunteers all rode south in the traditionally white car. Pritchett and his men were waiting at the Albany train station, along with one hundred black citizens who had gathered to greet the Freedom Riders. Across the street, a hostile crowd of white hecklers also looked on. When the train pulled in, the riders got off and mingled with their friends while the police watched. They entered the white waiting room and were discussing a motorcade to a local church for a rally when Pritchett suddenly ordered everyone out, telling them they would be arrested if they did not move quickly. The group moved outside and prepared to enter the cars waiting to take them to the church. Then Pritchett arrested them for blocking the sidewalk and obstructing traffic. All eight riders, plus Jones and two others who had come to greet them, were taken to jail. The entire group refused bail. As word of their arrest spread through the black community, support for SNCC's activism reached new heights. Pritchett claimed he had had no intention of arresting anyone, and that the action was necessary because of the presence of the two opposing crowds. Independent observers agreed, however, that there had been no danger of a clash, and that Pritchett had made a strategic error by arresting the riders and further inflaming the black community.[7]

The trial of the eleven began at 10 A.M. Tuesday, and more than 250 black students marched to City Hall in a driving rain. After they had circled the block twice, the police herded the protesters into an alley behind the building and told them they were under arrest. As the youngsters, and some adults, were processed and taken inside, authorities set a cash bond of $200 for each person. The entire group of 267 remained in jail, and at an emotional mass meeting that evening, the black community voted to continue the protests on Wednesday.

The next morning, Slater King led a group of eighty marchers to City Hall just as the trial of the Freedom Riders was about to resume. Mayor Kelley asked them to disperse, but King said no. Police arrested them and charged King with contempt of court. The riders' trial was postponed while Slater King was brought before the court on the contempt charge. Found guilty, he was sentenced to five days and sent off to jail. Later in the day, two additional groups of demonstrators marched downtown and likewise were arrested. By the end of the day, a total of 471 people were in custody.

While the protests mushroomed, the Albany Movement leadership asked its followers to boycott the major white stores, and invited outside notables to come to Albany to assist the protesters. Dr. Anderson took the first step in that direction by contacting SCLC's Ralph Abernathy on Tuesday to ask if he and Martin King could come. Abernathy put the request to King, who spoke with Anderson sometime late Wednesday or early Thursday. He agreed to come down on Friday afternoon, and asked only that there be a formal invitation to him from the Albany Movement. Thursday morning Anderson dispatched a telegram: WE URGE YOU TO COME AND JOIN THE ALBANY MOVEMENT. King felt that he could not refuse.

Anderson's invitation to King led some in the Albany Movement to suggest that similar requests be made to representatives of the other major civil rights organizations, and that was done. SNCC's representatives, however, questioned the idea of importing outside leaders to assist the movement. Some people argued that it would bring more national attention, but the two days of mass arrests already had put Albany on front pages across the country. One network television commentator offered his ironic congratulations to the Albany police for their "brilliant action" of imprisoning protesters who had not been "disturbing the peace." Instead, he observed, the photographs conveyed a "deeply moving picture of American citizens rising up with devastating orderliness and good manners . . . to demand their simple constitutional rights." Albany's police tactics had "dramatized the story to the country of the Negroes' courage." Nonetheless, SNCC staffers argued that the local community could direct its own efforts. The younger adults disagreed, and Anderson pointed out that the Albany Movement had neither the money nor the lawyers for sustaining a lengthy effort. If their protest was to be all-out, external assistance had to be summoned.

Late Wednesday the movement leadership, upset that the protesters had been moved to jails in neighboring rural counties, told city officials that the demonstrations would stop if transportation terminals were desegregated and charges dropped against all those who had been arrested. Albany's white commissioners, however, were adamant that they would begin no dialogue with the black community. "At this point," Mayor Kelley said late Wednesday, "it is the feeling of the City Commission that there is no area of possible agreement."[8]

Thursday morning sizable contingents of Georgia state police and local national guardsmen were readied for possible use. Mayor Kelley met with Georgia Governor Ernest Vandiver, and together the two men spoke by phone with Attorney General Robert Kennedy in Washington. Albany, they told him, had no race problem; the entire uproar was the work of outside agitators in the form of the SNCC workers. At much the same hour, Kennedy's civil rights assistant, Burke Marshall, phoned Dr. Anderson. Later that morning, Marion Page conferred privately with Kelley, and at a noontime press conference the mayor sounded a different tune than he had the previous day. "I am ready and have always been ready to sit down and discuss all problems with responsible local Negro leadership."

Thursday afternoon white Rev. J. Frederick Wilson, acting under the auspices of the Albany Ministerial Association, succeeded in creating a quasi-secret and informally sanctioned biracial negotiating committee with three black and three white representatives. The six men—Rev. H. C. Boyd, insurance agent Solomon Walker, and photographer Benny Frank Cochran from the black community, plus Reverend Wilson, hotel owner Horace Caldwell, and department store owner Joe Rosenberg from the white community—met for the first time that afternoon. They discussed the most pressing issues, and reached agreement that in exchange for a halt in the demonstrations, the train and bus stations would be desegregated and a formal biracial committee created to continue discussions of desegregation. They hit a snag, however, on what should be done about the jailed protesters; the black representatives insisted that all be released immediately, and the whites declined, knowing that the city commission would not allow it. Late in the evening there was a report that Charles Sherrod had been severely beaten in the Terrell County jail, and the negotiations were halted until Friday morning. The story turned out to be exaggerated, as Sherrod was not seriously injured. Both Reverend Boyd and movement secretary Marion Page expressed optimism when questioned that a settlement might be reached on Friday. White officials were willing to release local demonstrators without bail, but were set on treating out-of-towners—the Freedom Riders—less kindly. The black representatives, Boyd said, would continue to insist that everyone be released without bond. If that was not agreed to on Friday, demonstrations would resume. The two thousand enthusiastic citizens massed at that night's rally at Shiloh Baptist Church indicated that the warning was not an empty one.

As the discussions resumed on Friday morning, Burke Marshall at the Justice Department continued to lobby Mayor Kelley by phone to resolve the crisis quickly. By early afternoon the six negotiators had made no headway on the release of the riders without bond, but agreed to report back to their respective sponsors to see if either side could devise a way around this last impasse. Instead, the two sides adopted firmer stances and moved farther apart. The Albany Movement was troubled by several points in the negotiating committee's proposal. First, the agreement indicated that the bus and train stations would be desegregated in thirty days time—not immediately. Second, the convictions of the five young people arrested November 22, and the contempt sentence against Slater King, were not dropped. Further, the agreement did not address the two suspensions from Albany State, and Dennis's threat of additional ones. The movement wanted to hear from the city on all those points, as well as the release of the riders, before agreeing to any settlement.

The Albany City Commission began backing away from the tentative settlement even before those queries from the movement reached them. Although Mayor Kelley concurred with what the negotiating committee had recommended, a majority of his fellow commissioners insisted that they would not make concessions to what *Albany Herald* editor James Gray called "professional agitators." On each of the three basic points, the city's Friday evening response to the movement was less than the negotiators and the black community wanted. On the bus and train stations, the city stated only that "it will continue to be our purpose to preserve peace and tranquility according to our laws and in compliance with the ICC ruling." That might well mean that black patrons would be charged with "disturbing the peace" if they attempted to use previously all-white facilities. Second, the city would release those currently jailed only upon payment of a $100 cash bond or $200 security bond per person, quite a sum when multiplied by 471. Third, no commitment was offered to continue biracial discussions. If there was an "absolute halt" to all protests for thirty days, the commission at that time "will consider the formation of a committee of representative white and colored citizens." Lastly, the city said that it had no control over the convictions of the November 22 students or Slater King, nor any power concerning Albany State's suspensions.[9]

That response from the city reached the Albany Movement leadership just as two mass rallies were getting under way at Shiloh and Mt. Zion Baptist churches. Martin King, Ralph Abernathy, and Wyatt Walker had driven down from Atlanta to speak at both meetings. When Dr. King entered Shiloh church, the crowd came to its feet cheering, and spontaneously launched into a joyous song of greeting, "Free-dom, Free-dom, Free-dom," one of the many musical expressions of hope and commitment that the people of Albany brought forth to sustain themselves. Martin King found the spontaneity of that enthusiastic greeting reminiscent of the early weeks of the Montgomery protest. Ralph Abernathy spoke first, and then King. For him, the speech was a standard one, comments he had made many times before in many different towns. To the people of Albany, though, it was new and inspiring, a further encouragement to go forward. When King concluded, Dr. Anderson stepped to the pulpit and told the crowd that no settlement had been reached with the city and that demonstrations would resume early the next day. "Be here at 7 o'clock in the morning. Eat a good breakfast. Wear warm clothes and wear your walking shoes."

After the conclusion of the rally, the movement leadership held a long strategy meeting. The leaders resolved to make one more request to city officials for a more positive answer to the negotiating committee's recommendations before resuming the demonstrations. Dr. Anderson sent Mayor Kelley a telegram saying that the movement would "prayerfully await an acceptable response by 10:00 A.M. this morning." Kelley received the wire at about 9:30 A.M., and reacted negatively to the implicit threat. He called the commission into private session, and all agreed that they would make no concessions. The ten o'clock hour came and passed, and just before noon Kelley told reporters that the city was refusing the movement's request. He dispatched a letter by hand to Dr. Anderson and Marion Page, informing them of the refusal and rebuking the movement both for the additional requests and the telegram. Instead, he claimed, the movement should have continued to work through the six-man negotiating committee. "We feel that you are not acting in good faith and until you can do so we can give no response to your demand."

Upon receiving Kelley's hostile missive, Anderson and Page hurried to City Hall to try to persuade the city to begin an ongoing dialogue with its black citizens. For well over an hour the two men met with Mayor Kelley, and then returned to Shiloh church, where they again appealed to Kelley by phone. The mayor said he would ask his fellow commissioners if they would meet as a group with movement representatives. Kelley had no doubt about his colleagues' attitude, and soon called back to say there would be no meeting and no concessions. With that, the local leaders and King, Abernathy, and Walker huddled in the pastor's study at Shiloh church. The final choice, one they had been striving hard to avoid, was now before them. The time to march had come, and it could not be postponed. King and his SCLC colleagues had been in town just twenty-four hours and had a far from complete understanding of the issues and internal tensions that had predominated during the preceding six weeks. Still, King knew that he could not desert this movement at its most pressing moment. Shortly before 4:00 P.M., the leadership emerged, and Dr. Anderson announced that the march downtown would begin. "The talks have been broken off and they will not be resumed."

Side by side at the head of a double-file column of more than 250 marchers, and with Albany police detectives walking alongside, King and Anderson led the procession toward City Hall and downtown Albany. They moved quietly for several blocks, to the intersection of Jackson and Oglethorpe, the symbolic dividing line between black Albany and white Albany. There Police Chief Pritchett and dozens of officers blocked the line of march. While Dr. Anderson gently repeated "God bless you" to the surrounding policemen, Pritchett told the marchers that they must disperse or they would be arrested for parading without a permit, congregating on the sidewalk, and obstructing traffic. The entire group stood their ground, and Pritchett announced that they were under arrest. While the hundreds of new prisoners were processed and placed in custody, King, Anderson, and Abernathy were driven to the Sumter County jail in Americus for special safekeeping. Bond of $200 cash or $400 security was set for each marcher, and King and Anderson vowed to remain in custody until concessions were made by the city. Late Saturday Abernathy accepted bond so that he could return to Atlanta to rally outside support for this movement in which SCLC had become deeply involved literally overnight.[10]

When King, Anderson, and Abernathy entered jail late Saturday, the leadership passed to Marion Page for the Albany Movement and to Wyatt Walker for SCLC. There were no announcements of what the movement would do next, and Sunday morning's newspapers indicated that the next steps in the crisis were uncertain. In one story, however, the headline account in the *Atlanta Journal and Constitution*, reporter Gordon Roberts indicated that SCLC's Wyatt Walker "took over leadership" after Saturday's arrests. That phrase might have seemed innocuous to most readers, but it infuriated Marion Page and focused all of the distaste for outside civil rights organizations and their representatives that had been growing within Albany's black leadership since the earliest stages of the SNCC-NAACP rivalry. While Ralph Abernathy was issuing a call for a nationwide pilgrimage of civil rights supporters to Albany, Page called a press conference to say that the Albany Movement was an effort "by and for local Negroes," period. The movement was under the direction of no outsiders, he emphasized, and was being led by a six-person executive committee of local people for whom he was the spokesman. Page added that he expected negotiations with city officials to resume shortly, and that there would be no demonstrations in the interim. In a further comment, not directly attributed to Page, an Albany Movement leader was quoted as saying, "Why can't these national organizations understand that this is a local movement? This is not a national thing. It is only for and by Albany Negroes. We do not want to make a national movement out of it."

Sixty miles away in the Americus jail, Martin King had no knowledge of these events. When a wire service reporter inquired about his role, King explained he had not anticipated this deep an involvement. "I had just intended to give an address, but seeing that negotiations were broken between Negro and white, I felt I had to join the pilgrimage." In light of Albany's refusal to respond to its black citizens, King expected no early end to the crisis or his imprisonment. "I will not accept bond. If convicted I will refuse to pay the fine. I expect to spend Christmas in jail. I hope thousands will join me."[11]

On Monday, King and Anderson were brought to Albany for trial. The proceedings were postponed, however, because a new round of negotiations had gotten under way that morning with Mayor Kelley and Chief Pritchett representing the city, and Page plus attorneys C. B. King and Donald Hollowell speaking for the Albany Movement. Within several hours time, the small group reached a tentative settlement. It involved only two substantive issues. First, all local citizens still being held in custody would be released from jail without any cash bonds having to be paid. Second, if there were no more protests during the next thirty days, the city commission would appoint an eight-member biracial committee. The draft specified that the commission "will activate such a committee" sometime after that first thirty days but before the passage of *sixty* days, "provided there are no further demonstrations or parades. Four members of this committee shall be selected from those recommended by the Albany Movement."

The three black representatives then left to meet with Goldie Jackson, Irene and Thomas Wright, and the recently freed Slater King from the local leadership, Walker from SCLC, Hurley and Jordan of the NAACP, and Ella Baker and Charles Jones representing SNCC. They explained what the city had offered, and Hollowell pointed out that agreement did not firmly guarantee that negotiations would take place even at the end of sixty days. The Atlanta attorney asked the others what they thought, and whether the movement should accept the city's offer.

Some thought the top priority was to secure the release of all who were still being held in custody as quickly as possible. Page took that position, as did Ruby Hurley. Charles Jones and the Wrights opposed accepting the city's offer, saying that halting all demonstrations for sixty days was too much to give up simply for the release of the jailed protesters, who still would have charges hanging over their heads. The NAACP's two representatives disagreed, and Hurley "advised them not to be too demanding because they don't have any political power." Finally, the group voted to accept the settlement so as to secure everyone's release, but agreed informally that the moratorium on demonstrations would be binding only until January 1. No one was happy, but Page in particular felt that the release of their jailed colleagues was of primary importance. Furthermore, he was hopeful that city officials would institute more reforms than they would formally commit themselves to. With the decision made, Hollowell returned to City Hall.[12]

Martin King and Dr. Anderson spent the morning and part of the afternoon sitting in the City Hall courtroom as traffic cases were presented for trial. They were aware that further negotiations were under way, but knew no details of what was transpiring. A black reporter got within whispering distance of King, and asked about his arrest and imprisonment. King explained why his Saturday involvement had been unavoidable. "The people wanted to do something they would have done with or without me, but having preached the effectiveness of going to jail for one's rights, I could hardly do less than they." King said he had suffered no ill treatment in jail, but that the Sumter County sheriff, who repeatedly addressed him as "boy," was "the meanest man I have ever met."

King's and Anderson's courtroom sojourn ended when Donald Hollowell informed them of the leadership group's decision to accept a settlement. Hollowell detailed the situation, explaining that there was a gentlemen's understanding that none of the jailed demonstrators would be brought to trial, although their release would not include dropping charges. He also explained Page's anticipation that additional reforms soon would be forthcoming. C. B. King was hesitant because the settlement did not provide for a written agreement signed by both sides, but Hollowell indicated that such a document was not absolutely necessary, for these were honorable men they were dealing with. Martin King shared C. B. King's concern, and "was reluctant to accept the agreement," Anderson recalled. "'I want that in writing,'" King told Hollowell, but he responded that Kelley and Pritchett would not agree to formal recognition of the black community. As an alternative, King suggested the movement issue a public statement detailing its understanding of the agreement. The other men concurred. Hollowell left to notify Kelley and Pritchett that the Albany Movement would accept the release of the demonstrators in exchange for a moratorium on demonstrations.

That afternoon Martin King and Dr. Anderson were called before Judge Abner Israel. Anderson signed $400 security bonds for both of them, and they were released from custody. As the freeing of the seven hundred other jailed protesters got under way, King and Anderson were driven to Shiloh church, where Page and Hollowell had prepared a statement for the press detailing the settlement. Page went to the pulpit and told the crowd of reporters and local citizens that the settlement included not only the release of the protesters, but also promises that the terminal facilities would be open to everyone, and that a movement spokesman would be allowed to present all of the black community's requests to the city commission at its first meeting of the new year.

Reporters badgered Page, Anderson, and King for comments on the agreement. Page conceded that "this may not be exactly all that we wanted, but it is a beginning." Some wondered if King and Anderson regretted the settlement terms. King said that that was not the case, and indicated that while he was less than satisfied, the movement's negotiators had not betrayed his and Anderson's trust. "While there was some reluctance" on his and King's part to accept the settlement, Anderson later said, "Nobody in our camp sold us down the river by making an agreement that we didn't know about." Asked by reporters why he had left jail despite his pledge to remain imprisoned through Christmas, King answered that his release was a necessary part of the agreement. "I would not want to stand in the way of meaningful negotiations." Newsmen pointed out that many items were not covered by the settlement, whereupon Page responded, "Our primary concern was with putting every last Albany citizen who was in jail back upon the streets of Albany." The agreement was "nothing to shout to the rafters about," one leader noted, but it did free seven hundred people from confinement and provide for further dialogue between the movement and the city.[13]

Monday evening King spoke at Shiloh church and then flew to Atlanta. Attorney General Robert Kennedy phoned Mayor Kelley to congratulate him on resolving the crisis, and Albany city officials treated all the white members of the press to an impressive dinner at a segregated restaurant. When newsmen queried the officials about the settlement, it quickly became clear that the whites' version of the agreement bore no resemblance to that offered by Marion Page. Pritchett and Kelley told reporters that they had not made any concessions to the black protesters, and that there was no formal agreement of any sort. True, the blacks were being released from jail, but that was because they were posting the necessary bonds. The ICC order already applied to the bus and train stations, and any citizen could attend a city commission meeting and present requests. The city had promised nothing more; hence all the commotion had won no gains at all for the "outside agitators."

Tuesday's news reports all across the United States portrayed the cessation of the Albany protests as a clear defeat for the black demonstrators. One New York newsman called it "a devastating loss of face" for Martin King, and many national accounts gave credit for the white victory to Albany Police Chief Pritchett. His policy of mass arrests and nonviolent police work, the reporters said, had meant that no federal intervention was necessary. Unlike the Freedom Rides, where white violence had led to federal action on behalf of the black protesters, the Kennedy administration had seen no need to assist Albany's black protesters and had congratulated Kelley for the city's success.

Even sympathetic newsmen observed that it was "difficult to see how the local Negroes gained much of anything" from the protests. Albany's black citizens were disappointed at the lack of tangible accomplishments, but movement leaders like Page responded to the critical news stories by insisting that there had been a formal agreement and that concessions had been promised for the near future. Page admitted that at least thirty days would have to pass before further biracial discussions could take place, but he asserted that the commission's willingness to hear the movement's demands in public was "our greatest gain."

By Wednesday, December 20, it was clear that the city had no intention of granting anything to the movement. The greatest dispute arose over the city's supposed promise to exchange cash bonds for property bonds. Black leaders complained that no money was being released. In retaliation, they said, the movement's boycott of Albany's white stores would resume. Kelley told newsmen there had been no agreement about bonds, but Chief Pritchett did concede that he would not call any of the released demonstrators' cases for trial for at least sixty days as long as no new protests took place.

While news accounts highlighted the "defeat" suffered by the civil rights forces, some reporters suggested that it was caused by the competition between different black organizations. Newsmen like Claude Sitton of *The New York Times* were well aware of the disparaging remarks that SNCC's Charles Jones and advisor Ella Baker would make "off the record" about Wyatt Walker and King, and about SCLC's supposed taking of contributions really intended for the students. Those comments led to headlines such as RIVALRIES BESET INTEGRATION CAMPAIGNS, and stories that a SNCC-SCLC rivalry had led to the puzzling settlement. Missing from almost all accounts was any understanding of the longer-standing SNCC-NAACP rivalry, and of what was more important, the dislike of all the outside organizations that had grown up among some of Albany's black leaders.[14]

Martin King was thankful to get out of Albany. Andrew Young, then SCLC's newest staff member, had the distinct impression that King had found himself in a situation that he did not really want to be in. King had not anticipated either his arrest or his association with the dubious settlement, and he was not pleased by SNCC's efforts to convince reporters that local blacks had settled with the city in order to get King and Wyatt Walker out of town. King asked Walker what had created the public controversy about SCLC "taking over," and Walker replied that the problem had been Jones and Baker, who had encouraged Marion Page to speak out in defense of local autonomy. King accepted the explanation without quarrel. Seeking to put Albany behind him, King spent the Christmas holiday at home with his family and made plans for a meeting of SCLC's board and staff to map plans for 1962.

When the group convened January 4 and 5 in Atlanta, little attention was given to Albany. Instead, three organization-building topics dominated the discussions. First, SCLC needed to acquire a field staff. In conjunction with strengthened ties to SCLC's local affiliates, these full-time workers could make SCLC into "a southwide 'grass roots' organization" that could take advantage of the voter registration funds that would soon be available from the Voter Education Project. The idea of individual memberships again was discussed and rejected, but the board recommended that King take a more active role in strengthening relationships between SCLC and its local affiliates. The president of the organization, they indicated, "should function more as an advisor, remaining in communities a few days for consultation with leaders."

Second, the meeting also concluded that SCLC needed to encourage youth participation in the organization, something that could be done by adding younger people to the board and by approaching SNCC members who were not hostile to King—John Lewis, Bob Moses, Diane Nash, and James Bevel—about the possibility of signing on with SCLC as field staffers. Third, SCLC needed to give greater attention to publicity. The board approved Walker's recommendation to hire a young man, Gould Maynard, as the new public relations director, replacing Jim Wood, and discussed the idea of organizing a demonstration in Washington at the end of the year to mark the one hundredth anniversary of the Emancipation Proclamation. An all-night vigil at the Lincoln Memorial on New Year's Eve could be followed by a march to the White House on January 1, 1963, with a petition asking President Kennedy to take an initiative reminiscent of Lincoln's. King was pleased to learn that Kennedy's forthcoming State of the Union address would include support for a federal ban on state poll taxes and for legislation mandating that anyone with at least a sixth grade education did not have to take a literacy test in order to register to vote in a federal election. This was "encouraging," King wrote several days later, but it was "unfortunate" that Kennedy had not gone further and demanded "strong, vigorous civil rights legislation to speed up school desegregation as well as guaranteeing the right to vote."[15]

While King and SCLC turned their attention to a new agenda, SNCC and the NAACP remained in close contact with Albany's black leadership. People like Page and Anderson were deeply disappointed at how the community enthusiasm of three weeks earlier had been transformed into a feeling of defeat. They now realized their error in accepting an unwritten settlement and recognized they had been naïvely optimistic in their interpretations of the whites' disingenuous comments. "I was a naïve little boy," Page commented later. "They put things over on me." Dr. Anderson felt likewise. "We felt as though they were good faith negotiations. We had no reason to think that there was any subterfuge." That belief had been wrong. "I should never have come out of jail until there was a written agreement," Anderson reflected. "We were guilty of being inexperienced."

Albany's black leadership looked forward to the opportunity to present its requests at the first meeting of the commission, which was scheduled for January 11. Two strategy meetings were held to discuss the presentation, and the NAACP sought to reassert its influence. One of Roy Wilkins's principal assistants in New York, Gloster Current, told Regional Director Ruby Hurley that "a program of action listing the wants and desires of Negroes . . . should be presented by the NAACP leadership." Field Secretary Vernon Jordan took an active role in drafting the statement, along with a number of outside volunteers, including Paul Rilling of the Southern Regional Council, Arthur Levin of the Anti-Defamation League, and Frances Pauley of the Georgia Council on Human Relations, all of whom were trying to act as behind-the-scenes interracial mediators. Just prior to the scheduled session, the commission announced that it would be postponed until January 23. Preparations for the presentation went forward, along with the boycott of the city's major stores. The black leadership knew that the boycott was costing white merchants a high price for the city's obstinacy. SNCC's staff was preoccupied by problems at Albany State, where President Dennis had suspended forty students for participating in the December demonstrations. SNCC, the students, and some of their parents had no success in persuading Dennis to reverse his action, but more than a dozen of them decided to occupy their time by conducting a "read-in" at the segregated city library. Somewhat to their surprise, they were not arrested.

On Friday, January 12, an eighteen-year-old black student, Ola Mae Quarterman, was arrested for refusing to move to the rear of an Albany city bus and for allegedly saying "damn" to the driver after he had issued his order. The incident sparked the movement to enlarge its boycott to include the city bus line, which relied very heavily upon black patronage. SNCC's staffers organized a car pool system, and sponsored small tests of various public facilities. Although the bus station was supposedly desegregated, its lunch counter continued to refuse service to black patrons. On January 18, Charles Sherrod and Charles Jones were arrested for "loitering" when they were unable to obtain service. That same week the movement extended the boycott to several businesses with heavy black patronage that refused to hire black employees.[16]

On Tuesday, January 23, the Albany Movement's leaders finally appeared before the full city commission. Police Chief Laurie Pritchett introduced Anderson and Page, and the two men read to officials a detailed statement that began in conciliatory tones. They described previous black appeals, and noted that the mass protests had begun only in response to the arrests at the train station on December 10. "This testing of the railroad's compliance," they said, "has been laid at our doors. Actually, we had absolutely nothing to do with this." The crisis had been brought on by Pritchett, not the Albany Movement. Anderson and Page then asked the commissioners "to reaffirm in writing your oral agreement of December 18" that the bus and train stations would be desegregated, that cash bonds would be refunded in exchange for security bonds, and that a biracial committee would be established. They noted that the stations were not open to all equally, that the bonds had not been exchanged, and that the time had come to appoint the biracial committee.

When Anderson and Page concluded, Mayor Kelley stunned the movement representatives by adjourning the meeting without allowing any discussion. He said only, as the official minutes phrased it, that "there are many areas of discussion presented by the petition and assured the leaders of the movement that serious consideration would be given by the City Commission. He advised that Chief Laurie Pritchett . . . would contact them within the next ten days."

Kelley's hasty termination of the long-awaited appearance of Anderson and Page represented not personal opposition to the movement's requests, but was an effort to avoid any public airing of the divisions which had developed within the commission. Even before the mass protests on December 11, Kelley had argued in private for a more conciliatory stance. Of his six fellow commissioners, however, only one, Buford Collins, even partially shared Kelley's belief that moderation would serve Albany better than ignoring the protesters' appeals, as advocated by hard-line Commissioners Allen Davis, C. B. "Bunny" Pritchett (no relative of the police chief), and W. C. Holman. Kelley's attitude had been clear to his colleagues during his sponsorship of the negotiations convened by Reverend Wilson. He had no objection to accepting all of the terms worked out by that six-member committee, plus release of the Freedom Riders, but the commission majority refused to consider such concessions. The hard-liners were not pleased by even the indirect negotiations, and insisted they would not acknowledge the existence of the Albany Movement. Privately, they made it clear to Kelley that he would have to accede to the majority position, or face a public condemnation supported by the *Albany Herald*'s vituperative editor, James H. Gray. Kelley did not want a public break, and accepted Laurie Pritchett's argument that they maintain a united stance no matter how strong their private disagreements.

Despite his public advocacy of the hard-line attitude, Kelley exhibited a more responsive attitude in private with the black representatives. This response, combined with a similar tone from Laurie Pritchett, had led the black negotiators to expect city officials to deliver more than they were promising. The black representatives did not detect the growing tensions among the white officials, and failed to understand that Asa Kelley's attitude was something different from city policy.[17]

In the wake of the January 23 meeting, the bus boycott and the need for some written city response to the movement's petition finally brought the division within the white ranks into public view. As the store boycott gained strength, increasing numbers of merchants indicated a preference for Kelley's moderation rather than the "segregation at all costs" stance advocated by the other commissioners. The movement's bus boycott was so successful that on January 26, the Cities Transit president, Charles L. Carter, informed the commission that a lack of revenue would force the company to suspend operations on January 31 unless the city was willing to purchase the buses or subsidize the firm until the boycott ended. The commissioners met in a special closed session on January 27 and agreed to explore the subsidy option. Kelley also asked his colleagues how they wanted to respond to the movement's petition and the group appointed its three most conservative members—Davis, Pritchett, and Holman—to prepare an answer.

The next day city attorney Grady Rawls advised the commission that Albany could not legally subsidize a private company. Both company officials and Albany business leaders wanted to preserve bus service. On Monday, January 29, representatives of the Albany Movement met with bus company officials and offered to halt the boycott if the company would promise in writing to desegregate the buses and accept job applications from blacks.

Company officials responded that they could promise nothing without first ascertaining whether the city would stop enforcing its segregation ordinances. Company President Carter phoned Kelley to explain that the company would rather grant the movement's request than go out of business. Kelley convened a special meeting of the commission at which all six of his colleagues refused to allow the bus company to desegregate. With only the mayor dissenting, the group approved a brief statement: "As in the past the City Commission has refused to negotiate under duress and we recommend that the bus company officials follow the same policy." That action was too much for an exasperated Asa Kelley. "There is no harm in the City Commission allowing the bus company to operate as they wish," he told his colleagues. "It is more important to save the buses and avoid continued turmoil and strife than to refuse to allow the company to operate the way they desire."

News of the commission's rebuff brought more merchants into the struggle on the side of the bus company. Some business leaders advised the company to submit a written request to the commission so that the question could be reconsidered after the businessmen had an opportunity to make their views known. Company President Carter dispatched a letter on Tuesday, asking the city for a written statement that it would not interfere with integration of the buses. If not, bus service would end at midnight Wednesday.

The city commission met twice on Wednesday morning. At the first session, the bus company's letter was put aside until after a discussion of the commission's response to the movement's petition. The answer drafted by the three conservatives denied that any concessions had been agreed to on December 18, and rebuked Kelley for the discussions he had held with the movement's representatives. The only commitment that had been made was that Chief Pritchett would "follow his usual procedure with reference to the taking of appearance bonds for persons in custody for violations of city ordinances," and would "use his discretion as to when the cases will be presented" for trial. "This was the complete statement and the only statement," the hard-liners told the movement. "Anything construed by you to the contrary could only have been caused by misinterpretation of statements by unauthorized persons. . . . No individual citizen—no single elected official can speak for this body."

Asa Kelley criticized the proposed response as an "evasion of the basic issue" of "whether governmental authority will establish lines of communication with the Albany Movement." That dialogue was "absolutely necessary" for Albany's municipal good. His colleagues disagreed, and approved the draft.

Hardly an hour later the commission met in a second public session to consider the request from Cities Transit. Many local merchants were in attendance to speak in favor of the city giving the bus company a written guarantee of noninterference. Commissioner Holman responded that the basic issue was not buses, but whether the city would knuckle under to the Albany Movement. Bunny Pritchett felt likewise. "It's not a segregation–integration struggle anymore," he put it in a revealing statement. "This is the struggle to decide who makes the policy of this city." With only Kelley voting no, the commission approved a motion informing the bus company that it would not make the requested statement. Late that night, bus service came to an end.[18]

Albany Movement leaders announced at a mass meeting on Friday, February 2, that the boycott of city stores would be expanded to a larger number of establishments. The movement's car pool system would continue to operate, and no mass demonstrations would be mounted. In the white community, businessmen's condemnations of the commission increased. Faced with such criticism, the six who had voted against the bus company's request issued a statement saying they were "reasonable men" who were willing to hear "entreaties" from responsible local Negroes. Albany Chamber of Commerce President R. E. McTigue announced that white businessmen would discuss ways of reestablishing bus service, and intimated that his organization would open a dialogue with the Albany Movement. Mayor Kelley gave his endorsement to the businessmen's initiative and said he was "very hopeful" that private efforts would lead to a resumption of bus service "with or without commission action, because the commission is not going to change its attitude." Throughout the next two weeks, private discussions about a reinstatement of bus service continued.[19]

While the Albany situation continued to percolate, Martin King was trying to implement the decisions made at SCLC's conference. After several weeks of preparation, he convened a February 2 meeting in Atlanta of the heads of many of SCLC's local affiliates across the South. King told them of the organization's plans for the year and its desire to increase the involvement of affiliates in SCLC's program. Over one hundred people already had attended the citizenship training program at Dorchester Center, and the Field Foundation had committed another $15,000, ensuring that classes could continue through June. Some thirty people per month would receive training, and SCLC hoped that these individuals would become leaders in the intensified voter registration effort that would get under way once the Voter Education Project formally came into existence on April 1. King also explained that he and James Lawson would be undertaking several "People-to-People" tours that spring in different areas of the South, tours aimed at recruiting volunteers for an SCLC "Freedom Corps." These members of the now-renamed "nonviolent army" would be used in both voter registration and direct action projects.

Accompanied by Wyatt Walker and Dorothy Cotton, King began his first "People-to-People" tour on February 7 in the Mississippi Delta town of Clarksdale. In three days time, he delivered more than a dozen speeches at churches and schools in seven different Delta towns. While King was busy delivering those addresses, Cotton and Walker took the names of prospective Freedom Corps volunteers and teacher training candidates for the Dorchester program.

From the People-to-People tour, King flew to Puerto Rico to visit the Inter-American University. While he was away, the tensions that had existed in SCLC's home office for several months grew stronger. While the two newest members of the staff, Andrew Young and Public Relations Director Gould Maynard, were popular with almost everyone, many employees found Executive Director Wyatt Walker difficult to put up with. One who viewed Walker very critically was King's secretary, Dora McDonald. She thought Walker immature and petulant, a man who behaved imperiously toward his subordinates. For instance, when Valentine's Day came, Maynard presented each female staffer with a rose. The gesture infuriated Walker, McDonald wrote King, because he thought Maynard's kindness made him look bad by comparison. "Wyatt will never reach his full potential because he is so very childish and narrow," she told King.

February marked the start of a new venture for King, a fortnightly newspaper column in the New York *Amsterdam News*. Often written in collaboration with Wyatt Walker, several of the early articles lashed out strongly at the Kennedy administration's quiescence on civil rights. The president had still not issued the long-promised order banning discrimination in all federally assisted housing, and had given no sign of putting forward any notable civil rights legislative proposals. "The new administration has failed to give the strong leadership . . . that is necessary to grapple with the enormity of the problem," King stated.[20]

While King continued his criticism of the administration, the Kennedys were in private consternation about FBI reports that American Communist party leaders were claiming that old ally Stanley Levison nowadays was *the* number one advisor to Martin Luther King. In fact, the reports said, word in the party had it that Levison was writing many of King's most important speeches, such as one he had given in December to an AFL-CIO convention in Miami. Though the FBI's informants had no dependable information that Levison was still loyal to the party's commands, they did know that he continued to give it modest financial support even after severing direct ties. The FBI suspected that Levison's 1955 departure from party activity might have been a cover, and that Levison's friendship with King might be a secret assignment undertaken at the behest of American Communists and their Soviet sponsors. International communism, through the shadowy figure of Levison, might be exerting influence over this new leader of the civil rights movement. While the Bureau said nothing to the Kennedys about how incomplete its information on Levison was, its reports gave loud voice to the Bureau's worst fears about the Levison-King relationship.

The FBI's assertions provoked fear in Robert Kennedy and his closest assistants. Within several weeks time, two courses of action were decided upon. First, electronic surveillance of Levison would be instituted to monitor both his advice to King and any telephone contacts with Soviet or Communist agents. Second, those in the Kennedy administration who had some personal acquaintance with King—Harris Wofford, Burke Marshall, John Seigenthaler, and the attorney general himself—all would warn the civil rights leader that he ought to end his relationship with Levison immediately. King would also be warned about Jack O'Dell, the man Levison had brought in to manage SCLC's New York office. O'Dell had been involved with the Communist party throughout the 1950s, and his public record of such associations could be used against King and SCLC.

On several occasions during the spring, Robert Kennedy and his assistants warned King about Levison and O'Dell, without being specific about the allegations. Anything too detailed, the FBI told the Justice Department, might lead to the exposure of the Bureau's top secret sources within the Communist netherworld, sources the FBI would not identify even to Robert Kennedy. Each time the warnings were voiced to King, he listened quietly, thanked the speaker for his concern, and said that he was not one to question the motives of people in the movement, certainly not one so selfless as Stanley Levison. As King explained to Harris Wofford, how could he give credence to such vague allegations, coming from who knew where, when Levison had a proven track record of five years of honest counsel? If the administration had anything more specific to offer, King would gladly listen, but until then, he would not doubt one of his closest friends.[21]

King and Ralph Abernathy returned to Albany on February 27 to stand trial for their December 16 arrest. In the three weeks before his return, Albany's white businessmen had continued their attempts to re-establish bus service and to persuade the movement to give up its boycott of the buses and white stores. Service on largely white routes had resumed on February 19, but Albany Movement leaders insisted that their boycott would not end until seating was integrated and black drivers hired. Their boycott of Albany's stores would not end until the terms of the December 18 agreement were implemented by the city.

King's day in court represented the first trial to emerge from December's mass arrests. Hollowell and C. B. King represented him, and the prosecution put only one witness on the stand, Chief Pritchett. After more than two hours of haggling about whether the procession King led had constituted a "parade" within the meaning of the statute, Recorders' Court Judge A. N. Durden, Sr., recessed the proceeding and announced that he would issue a verdict within sixty days.

While King returned home to Atlanta, Albany remained unsettled. Within the movement, tensions continued to exist between SNCC's staff and more conservative members of the black leadership. Several black ministers who had been active only on the fringes of the protest suggested that SNCC was improperly handling the finances of the car pool operation. This allegation raised personal animosities to new heights, but Anderson and Slater King resolved the controversy without it becoming public.

On March 2, Albany's bus company tried to end the boycott by importing a single black driver from its sister firm in Tallahassee in the hope that this action would bring black riders back to Albany's buses. The movement refused to end the protest and reiterated its demand for integrated seating. Bus service ended again on March 6, this time for good. Four days later, in an intensified effort to enforce the downtown boycott, movement leaders announced that "Vigilante Committees" would identify blacks who were shopping in those stores. At the same time, Anderson, Slater King, and several others set up their own picket line to publicize the boycott. "Our objectives," they stated in a leaflet they distributed, "do not include the destruction of any business." What they sought to accomplish, it said, was to "prevail upon you to see the wisdom of urging the City Commission to abandon its intransigency and to take such steps as will lead to a settlement of all issues." After twenty-five minutes the picketers were arrested for disorderly conduct. Despite their efforts and those of many white businessmen, the hard-line majority on the commission gave no sign that it would begin negotiations with the black community.[22]

In mid-March, representatives of all the major national civil rights organizations met in Greenwich, Connecticut, to discuss their groups' interactions and rivalries. Albany was a primary topic of conversation, and SNCC representatives James Forman and Charles McDew strongly defended the formation of organizations like the Albany Movement into which the national groups' local affiliates would be combined. Roy

Wilkins of the NAACP quarreled with that position, and rejected a suggestion King made that all of the groups consider a unified fund-raising effort. King spoke strongly in favor of unity without uniformity, and received a polite response. Nevertheless, SNCC's delegates came away from the session believing that both the NAACP and Whitney Young of the Urban League were hostile toward their group.

On March 27, King undertook the second of SCLC's People-to-People tours, this time in southside Virginia. King and his colleagues went from door to door in Petersburg to encourage a voter registration drive, and also visited Lynchburg and Hopewell. Upon their return to Atlanta, word awaited them that the Field Foundation had decided to commit an additional $94,000 to the citizenship training program, a sum that would continue the program from July, 1962, through June, 1963.

Early in April, King announced that SCLC was undertaking its first major expansion since Wyatt Walker had arrived twenty months earlier. James Bevel and Herbert Coulton would become field secretaries for Mississippi and Virginia, respectively. Longtime Atlanta Republican activist John Calhoun would join the staff to assist voter registration efforts in Georgia, as would former Atlanta student leader Fred C. Bennette. Harry Blake remained SCLC's representative in Louisiana, and Bernard Lee continued to function as a field secretary at large and informal liaison to SNCC. Unannounced to the press was the appointment of Jack O'Dell as voter registration director. Once he arrived in Atlanta, O'Dell quickly made contact with the director of the newly inaugurated Voter Education Project, Wiley Branton, as efforts began to apportion responsibility for different parts of the South to the various civil rights organizations.[23]

On April 7, King commenced a three-day visit to Washington. Several rallies had been planned to launch the creation of an SCLC affiliate in the District of Columbia. King had appointments on Monday, April 9, with both Robert Kennedy and Vice-President Lyndon B. Johnson. Nonetheless, he voiced strong criticism of the Kennedy administration's record on civil rights. "Forthright, vigorous leadership" was needed, and John Kennedy had not given it, King said. Accompanied by Walker, Shuttlesworth, and several others, King met with Robert Kennedy and Burke Marshall on Monday afternoon. The federal officials heard SCLC's call for greater government action to protect black voting rights, and promised to act on any specific complaints. In private, Marshall warned King about his continued association with Stanley Levison. The FBI's secret wiretaps on Levison were now in place, and regular Bureau reports informed the attorney general of what transpired between King and Stanley. In one intercepted conversation, for instance, Wyatt Walker remarked that SCLC had to adopt a more critical stance toward John and Robert Kennedy. "By being nice we haven't gotten anything," he observed. Once again, however, King brushed Marshall's warning aside.[24]

Back in the South, King undertook a third People-to-People tour, this time visiting Charleston, Orangeburg, and Manning, South Carolina. Although he had not returned to south Georgia since his February trial, King kept up with news from Albany. Movement leaders had continued to picket the downtown stores, and in early April several sit-in protests at store lunch counters resulted in thirty arrests. A brief flurry of new negotiations followed, then on April 16, Anderson and Page handed a fresh statement of movement demands to Police Chief Pritchett. A few hours later Pritchett responded that the city had not been harassing blacks at the bus and train stations, that the police department would not interfere with bus service if it resumed, and that cash bonds would be refunded if the picketing and boycott were ended. He offered no answer to a request for a biracial committee, and said that no disposition of the hundreds of arrest charges would be made until Judge Durden ruled on the King and Abernathy cases. The movement considered these answers unacceptable, and the boycott and the picketing continued. Internal tensions remained high in both the black and white communities. The Georgia Council on Human Relations found little enthusiasm among prominent whites for an Albany human relations group, and the business community made no progress in influencing the commission's hard-liners. Within the Albany Movement, ministers and more conservative members increasingly complained about Anderson's leadership. In early May, he offered to resign, but received a strong vote of confidence.[25]

In mid-May, SCLC held its spring board meeting in Chattanooga, Tennessee. With fewer than half the members in attendance, King reported on his People-to-People trips, and Jack O'Dell explained the new voter registration program. King also spoke of plans that had been under way since early February to set up an adjunct tax-exempt organization that would serve as a channel for sizable contributions to support SCLC's programs. This idea had come from white New York attorney Harry H. Wachtel. Wachtel and King had met in New York to discuss the plan, and King had given Wachtel authority to proceed. In conjunction with black attorney Clarence B. Jones and another New York lawyer, Theodore W. Kheel, Wachtel made the arrangements for establishing what King decided to call the "Gandhi Society for Human Rights." A kick-off dinner was scheduled for May 17, and Jones began functioning as the organization's executive director.

King told the board that the Gandhi Society would bring new funds to SCLC, larger gifts than those brought in by the successful mass mail program run by the New York office. Two board members, Roland Smith and Dearing E. King, took the opportunity to suggest that President King should receive a salary from SCLC. King declined the offer, and explained that what he kept from his speaking fees and royalty income—some $6,000 per year—was sufficient to supplement his salary from Ebenezer Baptist Church. "I think I get along fairly well by speaking and writing. . . . I must never give people the impression that I am out for big money. . . . All of us have our shortcomings. I always ask God to help me. One of my shortcomings, I feel, is not in the realm of money."

The second day of board meetings was dominated by a discussion of organizational competition within the civil rights movement. One columnist for a national black newspaper had claimed that "King and his group are out to take over the NAACP's area in the Deep South," and had cited King's three tours and the Freedom Corps recruitment as evidence. He also complained that SCLC kept funds raised at local rallies sponsored by its far-from-wealthy affiliates. The board had heard all this before, and was more concerned about improving relations with SNCC. Hiring field secretaries who had come out of the student movement, like James Bevel, would be helpful. Some suggested that SCLC make a sizable annual contribution to SNCC to halt the complaints about financial competition. That idea was rejected, but King's nomination of some younger members for the board, including John Lewis of SNCC, was accepted.

King announced at the Gandhi Society's formal kickoff that a 115-page brief recommending a "Second Emancipation Proclamation" was being delivered to the White House that same day by SCLC's Washington representative, Walter Fauntroy. The time for presidential action had more than come, and King criticized the administration's passivity during the recent Senate rejection of its sixth grade literacy bill. "I do not feel that President Kennedy has given the leadership that the enormity of the problem demands." Nonetheless, King was optimistic about the movement. "I have the feeling that within the next ten years desegregation will be a reality all over the South." He added that he believed "segregation will end in my lifetime."[26]

While Albany experienced a peaceful May, movement activity increased in two other southern cities. The first was Birmingham, where students at Miles College, in cooperation with Shuttlesworth's Alabama Christian Movement, had launched a boycott of downtown stores in mid-March. Thirty-one-year-old student Frank Dukes led the effort, and received strong private support from Miles's president, Lucius H. Pitts, whom SCLC had tried to woo as executive director four years earlier. The boycotters sought desegregation of the stores' facilities, the hiring of black sales clerks, and a general upgrading for black employees. Their effort was extremely effective; white merchants conceded privately that their stores were hurting badly. As in Albany, however, the Birmingham businessmen said they could not desegregate without acquiescence from the city commission. And as in Albany, the city officials were hard-line segregationists, and Birmingham Public Safety Commissioner Eugene "Bull" Connor, the leader of the three-man board, was an outspoken racist. The commission cut off the city's surplus food distribution program in an effort to punish the black community, and made clear to the merchants that city ordinances requiring segregation would be enforced. Despite widespread dislike in the black community for Shuttlesworth's autocratic leadership style, the boycott drew loyal support and remained in force. The city's stance, Martin King remarked early in June, showed that Birmingham was the "most difficult big city in the United States in race relations."

The second trouble spot was Shreveport, Louisiana, where the home of Dr. C. O. Simpkins, president of SCLC's affiliate, had been bombed three months earlier. Simpkins had since left town, and local efforts were now being led by SCLC Field Secretary Harry Blake. King, Walker, and Bernard Lee made plans to fly in for a rally, only to be warned that death threats had been made against SCLC's president. Such warnings did not faze King, and the rally took place as scheduled. Local police managed to arrest Walker and Blake on charges of "loitering," and Bernard Lee remained behind to direct ongoing voter registration efforts.

King returned from Shreveport to Atlanta, where an SCLC benefit concert by Harry Belafonte was scheduled on June 6. Belafonte's integrated troupe received the usual rebuffs from several Atlanta hotels and restaurants, and King joined Belafonte in an unsuccessful attempt to secure lunch at one city eatery. That experience served as a reminder of the difficulties that SCLC staffers had in obtaining service at many neighboring shops, and in particular of how the restaurant on the ground floor of their own office building continued to refuse them equal service despite a sit-in protest several months earlier. On June 9, King wrote building owner Ben Massell that SCLC would be moving back to the more hospitable environs of Auburn Avenue. Just a few days earlier his daughter, Yoki, had asked for some ice cream, then had run into the restaurant and sat down. King had coaxed her out, saying it was not a good time. King's letter to Massell was "longer than any I have written in the last few years. . . . I cannot begin to express in words the agonizing and frustrating hours I have spent as a result of this situation."[27]

Other painful problems arose. A prominent church magazine, *Christian Century,* for which King had written several short articles, attacked the Gandhi Society, saying the name was un-Christian. King complained, and told the embarrassed editors that their appreciation of God's word was insufficiently ecumenical. "I believe that in some marvelous way, God worked through Gandhi, and the spirit of Jesus Christ saturated his life. It is ironic, yet inescapably true that the greatest Christian of the modern world was a man who never embraced Christianity." Appropriately reprimanded, the editors printed an apology.

The FBI kept up its round-the-clock electronic surveillance of Stanley Levison throughout the spring and summer. The wiretaps detected no contacts with Communist agents, but they did allow the Bureau to furnish Attorney General Robert Kennedy with a continuing flow of reports on Levison's phone conversations with King. Most of these were mundane, but in mid-June, King told Levison that the recent resignation of public relations assistant Gould Maynard meant that King would have to hire a new administrative aide. Levison suggested that King consider Jack O'Dell, but warned King about O'Dell's record of past involvement with the Communist party. "No matter what a man was, if he could stand up now and say he is not connected, then as far as I am concerned, he is eligible to work for me," King told Levison. King understood that O'Dell's ties to the party were all in the past, but the FBI told Robert Kennedy that not only was O'Dell still a member, he had been elected to the party's national committee under a pseudonym less than three years earlier. Although O'Dell returned to SCLC's New York office instead of taking the Atlanta post, Levison's recommendation of him for a job close to King led to intensified FBI suspicion about Levison's motives.

In early July, King gave the major address at an important NAACP fund-raising dinner. King praised the association, decried what he called the "borderline slander" that movement leaders had engaged in against each other, and said that "ego battles and trivial organizational conflicts" could only harm the movement. His comments about SCLC's voter registration efforts, however, led some critical observers to question whether SCLC's accomplishments lived up to King's claims. Birmingham editor Emory O. Jackson, who had followed King since Montgomery, had his doubts. "Is this merely visionary oratory unmatched by action," he asked rhetorically. "At the moment there is little more than the press releases from Dr. King's publicists." Local movements could do a better job of voter registration than SCLC, he argued, especially when SCLC had someone with an "entangled background"—a veiled reference to O'Dell—heading up its registration efforts. "An itinerant leadership which floats in and flows out of a city is not the correct approach. There must never be allowed to develop a let-King-do-it attitude. . . . No exotic leadership with a medicine show type of exhibition is likely to get the job done."[28]

Two days after King's NAACP appearance, Albany Judge A. N. Durden, Sr., announced that he would issue his decision in King's and Abernathy's cases the following Tuesday, July 10. Albany Movement leaders had spoken with Laurie Pritchett throughout June, but no progress had been made on establishing a biracial committee or resolving the charges still pending from December's demonstrations. Furthermore, while Pritchett claimed that the bus and train stations were available to all on equal terms, a four-member Albany Movement delegation went to Washington to complain to Justice Department attorney John Doar that Albany's police were enforcing segregation in the two terminals in clear violation of the ICC order. They also asked why the federal government could not protect the movement's First Amendment right to picket in downtown Albany, where most participants quickly were arrested. Doar heard them out, while eight other Albany Movement members picketed outside the Justice Department, and then sent them away without satisfaction. "I explained to them," he informed Burke Marshall, "that the Department of Justice had no authority to seek injunctions in this field." The movement issued further press releases condemning the department's inaction, and small-scale picketing continued intermittently in downtown Albany.

On Tuesday morning King and Abernathy appeared before Judge Durden. They had committed themselves to serve prison terms rather than pay fines if Durden found them guilty. King had reached the decision only after much thought, because the loneliness of jail going was very trying. As Coretta explained it, "He didn't like to be alone. Jail going wasn't easy for him because he never liked to be alone. . . . He could never stay away from people for long periods because he liked company." That distaste, however, was more than outweighed by his long-standing advocacy that nonviolent protesters should serve time rather than pay their fines into the state's coffers. A year earlier he had been painfully aware that many of the students thought his hesitancy to put his own body on the line did not measure up to the rhetorical standards he had set. Off the record, SNCC member Julian Bond bluntly voiced the growing student perception of King:

He has been losing since he left Montgomery. He lost when he didn't go on the Freedom Ride when the students begged him to go on the Freedom Ride and he didn't go. I think he's been losing for a long time. And I think eventually that more Negroes and more white Americans will become disillusioned with him, and find that he after all is only another preacher who can talk well.

Such criticism had increased after King's sudden departure from Albany in December, just hours after his public vow to remain imprisoned over Christmas. Longtime SNCC activist Diane Nash, who had married SCLC Field Secretary James Bevel, circulated a long memo that spring to movement activists, explaining her decision to serve a lengthy jail sentence in Mississippi. She also discussed the need for the movement's senior leaders to do a better job of practicing what they preached:

I believe that the time has come, and is indeed long past, when each of us must make up his mind, when arrested on unjust charges, to serve his sentence and stop posting bonds. I believe that unless we do this our movement loses its power and will never succeed.

We in the nonviolent movement have been talking about jail without bail for two years or more. It is time for us to mean what we say. . . . If we do not do so, we lose our opportunity to reach the community and society with a great moral appeal and thus bring about *basic* changes in people and in society. . . .

I think we all realize what it would mean if we had hundreds and thousands of people across the South prepared to go to jail and stay. There can be no doubt that our battle would be won. . . . We have faltered and hesitated. . . .

King recognized the painful truths in Nash's argument, and vowed that this time he would do better.

Judge Durden read a prepared statement announcing that King and Abernathy were guilty of the charges against them, and sentencing them to forty-five days in jail or a $178 fine. The two defendants chose imprisonment, and were led away. The Albany Movement convened a daytime rally at Shiloh Baptist Church, and both Coretta King and Juanita Abernathy spoke to the crowd. Burke Marshall and Robert Kennedy were on the phone to many people in Albany, seeking to avert a new round of mass arrests, and Marshall called Mrs. King to reassure her about the federal government's interest in her husband's safety. A demonstration was announced for Wednesday, and late Tuesday two police cars were stoned by unidentified assailants near Shiloh church.[29]

On Wednesday only thirty-two people, many of them high school students, volunteered to take part in a march downtown, which ended in their arrests. Wyatt Walker returned to Atlanta, and Wednesday evening a hostile crowd of black citizens jeered police officers near Shiloh church. Chief Pritchett spoke with movement leaders at the church, was introduced to the mass meeting, and the threat of violence passed. President Anderson announced that he hoped negotiations with the city would resume, and Mayor Kelley stated that he would present any movement requests to the full commission.

King and Abernathy spent Wednesday in the city jail, assigned to a clean-up detail. Early Thursday morning, a jailer came and told them to get dressed because Chief Pritchett wanted to see them. Then, to King's puzzlement, ninety minutes passed before the officer returned and took them to see the chief. Pritchett said that their fines had been paid, and that now they had to leave. King protested strongly; he had authorized no such action, and they could not be thrown out against their will. Pritchett politely disagreed, and claimed that an "unidentified, well-dressed Negro man" had come into the police station and given the desk sergeant $356 in cash as payment of their fine. One did not have to present identification to make such payments, and since the payment had been made, the city could not continue to hold them.

In an extremely unhappy mood, King and Abernathy were driven to Shiloh church by two detectives. King described the odd event to startled newsmen, and stated that "this is one time that I'm out of jail and I'm not happy to be out . . . I do not appreciate the subtle and conniving tactics used to get us out of jail." If the involuntary release were an effort to get him out of Albany, King said, it was an effort that would fail. This time he would remain in Albany until city officials met the movement's demands.

Speculation spread as to who had been behind the appearance of the "well-dressed Negro man." Some thought it could well be conservative Albany blacks, eager to be rid of King and SCLC. Others wondered if it was a misguided effort by Daddy King, once again seeking to protect his son from the perils of movement leadership. Many more argued that Robert Kennedy and the Justice Department had engineered the release so as to avert demonstrations over King's imprisonment. Some believed that made particular sense in light of the ongoing Georgia gubernatorial race, in which the Kennedys were supporting moderate Carl Sanders. Any racial uproar would play into the hands of virulent segregationist Marvin Griffin.

Such theories amused the few people in Albany who actually knew what had happened. While reporter after reporter pressed Pritchett for a more detailed description of the supposed "well-dressed Negro," Asa Kelley and his closest confidants—law partners J. W. "Taxi" Smith and B. C. Gardner, and department store owner Joe Rosenberg—knew that the man never existed. When pressed hard, Chief Pritchett admitted that he had not seen the supposed visitor. In truth, Pritchett knew full well that Asa Kelley had ordered King's release. Kelley had no desire for a new round of mass demonstrations, which would put Albany back in the nation's headlines. Keeping Martin Luther King in jail for a month and a half would bring every civil rights leader in the country to Albany, and that was the last thing that the city's mayor and his strongest supporters in the business community wanted to see. If tossing King and Abernathy out of jail would avoid that, it was his duty to do it. The hard-liners would scream that Kelley was soft on those dangerous agitators if the release was done openly, but this way all they could do was grouse about their suspicions in private. The plan had worked well, and no one leaked the truth to any reporters.[30]

Events took another sudden turn the afternoon of King's release when he, Abernathy, Anderson, and C. B. King returned to Chief Pritchett's office for a renewed discussion of the movement's demands. Pritchett told them that the city would desegregate the two stations and the city buses, whenever service resumed, and would refund all cash bonds. The movement representatives appeared willing to compromise on a timetable for the creation of a biracial committee, and Pritchett sounded more flexible about dropping the hundreds of arrest charges without bringing the protesters to trial. When the meeting adjourned, King was optimistic. "Definite progress" had been made, he said, and the negotiations would resume on Friday. At that night's mass meeting, King told the crowd that "victory is ours."

King and his three movement colleagues met for ninety minutes with Pritchett and city manager Stephen Roos on Friday afternoon. Pritchett was less flexible than he had seemed the day before, and no progress was made. That evening the city commission met, and the hard-line majority reiterated that there would be no biracial committee and no dismissal of the arrest charges. King's tone at that night's rally also was more restrained. He repeated his pledge to remain in Albany until the city capitulated. On Saturday morning, Chief Pritchett phoned Anderson to report that the commission would not dismiss the charges.

On Sunday afternoon the movement leadership met to discuss Pritchett's response. A consensus quickly emerged that the movement was getting nowhere negotiating with the commission through Pritchett. Their experience on Thursday and Friday, when a resolution of the charges had seemed possible, led them to wonder whether Pritchett was a sufficiently forthright intermediary. Martin King had agreed before his Saturday night departure to Atlanta that a demand for direct talks with the commissioners was a desirable next step. The gathering adopted a "position paper" or "manifesto," drafted earlier by Wyatt Walker, that requested face-to-face discussions with the commission. The document was issued to the press Sunday evening, and in Atlanta King told newsmen that the civil rights forces would resume demonstrations if the city did not respond favorably to the request within a week. Further negotiations through Pritchett were unacceptable, King stated. "He says one thing behind closed doors and another when he meets the press."[31]

A copy of the "Albany Manifesto" was delivered to city officials on Monday, just as King returned to town. The commission wasted no time in announcing that it would not accede to the request for a face-to-face meeting. We "will not deal with law violators," they proclaimed. A mass meeting that evening drew a larger crowd than any since December.

The next day several groups of students tried to patronize the all-white city library, and word spread that movement attorneys were planning to file an omnibus federal court suit seeking the desegregation of all city facilities. Movement leaders sent a telegram to the commission repeating their request for a face-to-face meeting, and the city once more refused. Mayor Kelley announced that no further discussions involving King or Abernathy would take place, and King again addressed an enthusiastic evening rally. The Justice Department's concern about the situation increased, and Albany's six resident FBI agents were reinforced by an additional half-dozen.

Wednesday brought more sit-ins at lunch counters, public park facilities, and the bus terminal's grill by teams of young demonstrators organized by SNCC's Charles Jones and SCLC's Wyatt Walker. Arrests were avoided, and King left town for Washington to speak at the National Press Club's Thursday luncheon. Seven movement "testers" were arrested for a Thursday sit-in, and Mayor Kelley and city attorney Grady Rawls went secretly to Atlanta to consult with Georgia Governor Ernest Vandiver about the desirability of seeking a federal court injunction to block the mass marches that Kelley expected would resume within the next few days. On Thursday evening, movement President Anderson had the unprecedented opportunity to speak for thirty minutes on local television in response to a vitriolic attack on the black community that station owner and *Herald* editor James H. Gray had delivered two nights earlier. Anderson emphasized that the Albany Movement "did not begin through the instigation of any outside persons," and was "a basically indigenous expression of aspirations of the Negroes of Albany." He outlined the racial reforms the black community was seeking, and emphasized that "our great desire is to establish new bridges of honest communication."

City manager Stephen Roos received written notification on Friday morning that the movement planned to conduct a Saturday march from

Shiloh church to City Hall for a one-hour prayer service. Only when the commission was summoned to consider this news did some members learn of Kelley and Rawls's unannounced trip, which had taken them from Atlanta to Columbus, where they met with Federal District Judge J. Robert Elliott at his home. The commission voted unanimously to "express its deep concern" about Kelley's failure to consult with them. When Martin King returned to Albany from Washington late Friday afternoon, he told reporters that he would take part in Saturday's march and was willing to be arrested again. That evening he spoke to an enthusiastic rally of 1,200 movement supporters, telling them of the rumor that the city might obtain an injunction against the movement. The city's refusal to negotiate, King said, indicated that the time had come for the movement to rely upon actions rather than words.[32]

Kelley and Rawls were successful in securing an injunction against the movement. Early Saturday morning, Judge Elliott issued a temporary restraining order against King, Abernathy, Anderson, and others active in the movement, barring any mass demonstrations in Albany and setting a hearing for July 30 to consider making the restraint permanent. King and his colleagues huddled in Albany while attorney Donald Hollowell flew from Atlanta to New Orleans to request that the Fifth Circuit Court of Appeals immediately overturn Elliott's action. Gandhi Society attorney Clarence Jones and a fellow New York lawyer, William M. Kunstler, flew with Wyatt Walker to Albany and found an angry Martin King reluctantly admitting that he had no choice but to obey the order. King spoke by phone with the Justice Department's Burke Marshall, and asked angrily why a federal judge who was a recent Kennedy appointee was colluding with city officials to crush the Albany Movement. Marshall replied that the movement's lawyers must seek a reversal of Elliott's order by the appeals court, and that until such a decision was won, King would have to abide by the restraining order. King realized that the movement could not defy a federal court order after years of arguing that segregationists were obligated to obey federal judicial rulings that they often sought to avoid.

Federal marshals spent several hours trying to serve King with Elliott's order, but not until King, Abernathy, and Anderson voluntarily appeared at Pritchett's office were they officially presented with the court decree. The proposed march was scrapped, but an alternative plan evolved in discussions with the visiting lawyers. While those named in Elliott's order could be prosecuted for federal contempt if they marched, people not so named could be charged only with the standard city offense of parading without a permit. That night King, Coretta, and the others went to Shiloh church where a mass rally was under way, and watched from a back room as a local minister, not named in Elliott's order, called for volunteers to join him in a march downtown. Over one hundred persons joined the procession headed toward City Hall. "King was jubilant," attorney Kunstler later recalled. " 'They can stop the leaders,' he exulted, 'but they can't stop the people.'" The column moved toward downtown, and one block from City Hall Pritchett arrested all the participants. A smaller group followed soon after and was also arrested. King returned to Anderson's home for the night, ending the long day by joining the other leaders in candlelight around the piano, singing songs of hope.

King was deeply troubled by Elliott's order forcing him into a passive role, and he felt especially bitter toward Burke Marshall and Robert Kennedy, whom he unfairly held at fault for the court decree. He wondered out loud if the order had really been arranged simply to help gubernatorial candidate Carl Sanders by quelling the protests. He had several more heated phone discussions with Kennedy and Marshall on Sunday. Andrew Young later recalled that those conversations were the angriest he ever had seen King. Though King implied to Kennedy and Marshall that he might well violate Elliott's order, at a Sunday afternoon press conference he announced that he felt compelled to abide by the decree even though he considered it "unjust and unconstitutional." Burke Marshall felt the same way. In private, he told Robert Kennedy that "there is serious doubt whether the court had any jurisdiction and whether the restraining order is constitutional."[33]

Although King was willing to obey the injunction, the SNCC staff argued vociferously that the movement should defy the unjust decree. King's passive acceptance of the situation, they contended, was just one more example of his excessive moderation and was dampening the enthusiasm the black community had generated over the preceding week. On Sunday evening, King and Wyatt Walker met with SNCC workers Charles Sherrod, Cordell Reagon, Charles Jones, and a new white arrival, Bill Hansen. The SNCC representatives complained that SCLC had supplanted the local black adults as the real decision-makers over the preceding ten days. King and Walker denied the allegation, and the three-hour session ended without any firm resolutions. The frank exchange of views had cleared the air, however, and in private the SNCC staffers admitted that SCLC was in control of the situation because Anderson and other local people were deferring to King.

Visiting attorneys Jones and Kunstler spent Sunday with C. B. King drafting a document to persuade Elliott or another federal judge to void the restraining order. Donald Hollowell had been unsuccessful in his effort to secure weekend action by the court of appeals, and early Monday morning the attorneys learned that Elliott was now traveling out of state. Kunstler and C. B. King drove to Macon in search of another federal jurist, William A. Bootle. He also was away and, when reached by phone, refused to act on their petition. Growing more anxious, the two attorneys called the Atlanta office of Chief Federal Appellate Court Judge Elbert P. Tuttle. He offered to see them immediately, and they drove to Atlanta and handed him the request. Graciously, Tuttle set a formal hearing on the motion to vacate for 10:00 A.M. the next morning, and notified Albany Mayor Kelley to have an attorney present.

Back in Albany, King and Anderson met privately with Police Chief Pritchett on Monday. They explained that the movement's primary goal was to obtain face-to-face negotiations with the city commission, and that if their request was granted, King would return to Atlanta. Pritchett replied that he doubted the commission would accept such a tradeoff, and the session ended.

Many of the demonstrators arrested in July remained in custody in small-town jails outside of Albany, and movement supporters regularly visited them to check on their well-being. Late Monday afternoon, Slater King's wife, Marion, drove south to Camilla to visit the Mitchell County jail. Two officers gave her a hostile reception. While her three small children looked on, Mrs. King, who was pregnant, was knocked to the ground and kicked by the policemen. Not badly injured, but fearful that the brutality had endangered her pregnancy, Mrs. King returned to Albany, where word of her experience spread. A furious Martin King called Burke Marshall to demand Justice Department action, and seven persons led by Rev. Vincent Harding, a visiting black clergyman who had been trying to mediate the crisis, staged a late-night prayer protest at City Hall and were arrested.[34]

In Atlanta the movement's attorneys spent most of Monday night in Donald Hollowell's office. In addition to preparing for the hearing, they drafted two complaints challenging Albany's segregated city facilities and its policy of arresting peaceful protesters. The two suits would open a new, legal front in the movement's assault on Albany. Some people wondered why civil rights forces had been so slow to file suit, but now the movement was finally taking the legal initiative. King flew to Atlanta for the hearing, where he sat in the front row as city attorney Rawls and state lawyer Freeman Leverett tried to convince Judge Tuttle that Albany was not enforcing segregation and that movement protests would be a threat to public safety. Tuttle found their contentions unpersuasive, and agreed with movement attorneys that Elliott's action had been improper. He dissolved the order, effective immediately. King was pleased that that obstacle to his involvement had been removed. Asked by reporters about Albany's claim that it was not enforcing segregation, King said, "I must admit I had to smile. . . . We were laboring under the impression they were."

While King headed back to Albany, movement leaders sent yet another message to city officials asking for face-to-face contact at that night's scheduled commission meeting. The city offered no written response, and the commissioners quietly canceled the planned session. King arrived in time to speak to the evening mass meetings at Mt. Zion and also across the street at Shiloh. Afterward, a group of forty marchers formed a procession and began walking downtown. A crowd of several hundred onlookers gathered to watch. At the corner of Jackson and Oglethorpe, the symbolic dividing line between black Albany and downtown, Pritchett's officers halted the marchers and began arresting them.

The black onlookers who had followed the column became angry and began throwing rocks and bottles at the policemen. One city officer was struck by a bottle, one state trooper by a rock. The disorder continued for some time before gradually dying out. National news reports the next day emphasized that black violence had followed Tuttle's voiding of Elliott's order. "Marchers Hurl Rocks at Police After Protest Ban is Voided," the *Atlanta Constitution* stated.

King was deeply upset by the disorder, and held a Wednesday morning press conference to explain to newsmen that the violence had come not from the marchers but from "onlookers who were not a part of our movement." The incident ran counter to all that the protesters desired, King explained, and a twenty-four-hour moratorium on all demonstrations, a "day of penance," would be instituted as a symbolic apology for what had happened. King told newsmen that henceforth the movement would follow a four-pronged program, with direct action, the new lawsuits, and the ongoing boycott being joined by a voter registration drive. Everyone realized that it was the combination of the boycott and the downtown protests that was exacting a toll on white Albany for the city government's continued intransigence. One white merchant admitted to Pritchett that "our business is at present suffering an approximate 50% decrease" because of the black boycott and white customers' avoidance of downtown. While movement leaders appreciated the effectiveness of this two-pronged effort, they also realized that no amount of economic pressure upon the merchants would be enough to make the hard-line commissioners compromise.[35]

Tuesday night's violence magnified a problem that movement leaders had been aware of since December. Police Chief Pritchett had become a special favorite of white reporters covering the protests. He combined a good ol' boy's friendliness with a sophistication that northern reporters found impressive for a Deep South lawman. In December, and again in July, several influential newspapers and news magazines carried glowing descriptions of Laurie Pritchett. The chief told reporters that he had studied Martin Luther King's nonviolence, and that he believed in nonviolent law enforcement. Civil rights workers would find no police brutality in Albany, he emphasized.

Pritchett's relationship with the newsmen served white Albany's interests in more ways than one. Local black leaders, and some whites, feared that their telephones were being tapped. Pritchett's information on their plans often was too good to have come simply from the pair of detectives who often parked near Dr. Anderson's home to keep track of King and other movement principals. SNCC's staffers wondered if someone in the post office was providing the chief with copies of their mail, but over time it became clear that neither the phone nor the mail was the principal source of leaks. The problem was human informants, some paid, some not, whom Pritchett had recruited within the black community. Initially he had purchased the services of a young black man, a stock clerk in a liquor store, to keep an eye on Sherrod's and Reagon's efforts to organize the young people. By late spring, as a number of the older, more conservative black leaders became increasingly unhappy with both SNCC's influence and Anderson's attachment to SCLC, at least two of these men began sharing their thoughts and complaints with the personable police chief, whom they viewed as a moderate, even a liberal. Neither NAACP loyalist E. D. Hamilton nor movement Secretary Marion Page thought their conversations with Pritchett, or their frequent chats with the FBI, were traitorous to the black community. For Pritchett they were invaluable sources of information on the plans and internal conflicts of the black community. In Pritchett's judgment, neither man wanted to lose his individual entrée with the white leadership. Page, he later said, "was talking both sides of the street. He'd talk to them and then he'd come to me."

While Pritchett learned much from these contacts in the black community, he learned an equal if not greater amount from his friends the newsmen. The reporters would let him listen to their tape recordings of the black leaders' statements at the mass meetings, or to recordings of interviews with movement figures. At the outset, many local activists had been quite willing to share their thoughts with newsmen, the crucial link to the wider world. Only in time did movement officers realize that many reporters were conveying information to Pritchett. The chief found the press extremely helpful, for while he had to pay his young movement informant, "the information I was getting from the media was free." Every night, he said, "the tapes would come to me after the mass meetings." Once the situation became clear to movement leaders, newsmen were barred from an increasing number of movement sessions.[36]

In the wake of Tuesday night's disorder, press stories again portrayed Pritchett as the "white knight." If the black community was as committed to peaceful protest as he was to professional law enforcement, Pritchett remarked to newsmen, what did King and his colleagues have to say about those "nonviolent rocks" that had been thrown at his officers? The movement leaders realized the image problem that Tuesday night's events had created, and King took reporters along on a Wednesday afternoon walking tour of black hangouts while he preached the virtues of nonviolence and explained the need for he day of penance. "One thing about the movement is that it is nonviolent," he told the habitués of one poolroom. "As you know, there was some violence last night. Nothing could hurt our movement more. It's exactly what our opposition likes to see."

At Wednesday night's mass meeting King said that Thursday might witness renewed demonstrations, but things remained quiet as movement leaders tried once more to persuade city officials to open direct talks. They had no more success than before, and by Thursday evening King was so busy pondering the movement's next step that Anderson took his place at that night's rally. Anderson hinted that the movement might issue a call for all civil rights supporters across the nation to make a mass pilgrimage to Albany.

Late Friday morning King phoned Asa Kelley with one more request for direct negotiations. The mayor said no, and shortly after 2:00 P.M., King, Abernathy, Anderson, Slater King, and a local black minister appeared outside City Hall. As reporters looked on and Wyatt Walker distributed a prepared statement, King told Laurie Pritchett that they had come to see the commissioners. Pritchett responded that the next meeting was not until August 7, and that the group would be under arrest if they did not depart within three minutes. They knelt in prayer, and after the allotted time passed, Pritchett arrested them. Several hours later, SNCC workers Charles Jones and Bill Hansen led a second group of protesters to City Hall, where they, too, were arrested.[37]

King and his colleagues had chosen a return to jail in the hope that it could mobilize another round of mass protests sufficient to force the hand of the recalcitrant city commissioners. That night's mass meeting suggested that the tactic would fail. While reporters looked on, Andrew Young and Charles Sherrod were able to induce only fifteen of the five hundred people to volunteer for jail going. It was a depressing turn of events, indicative of a growing sentiment throughout black Albany that protests would not succeed and that without federal intervention no tangible concessions would be won.

In the city jail, King and Abernathy were placed in the same cell they had left involuntarily two weeks earlier. They held a brief worship service and sang some songs, and at about 9:00 P.M. Pritchett sent word that he wanted to see King. Suspicious, King refused to leave the cell and told the jailer the chief could come see him. Pritchett did, saying that it was no trap but that a highly agitated Lawrence Spivak, host of *Meet the Press,* insisted upon speaking with King by phone to find out whether his arrest meant that he would not be able to make his scheduled appearance on Sunday's program. King took the call, told Spivak he would have to think about the problem, and then asked that Wyatt Walker and C. B. King come to the jail. When they arrived, they agreed that Martin King should not leave jail for the television appearance. Instead, it was suggested that Dr. Anderson appear in his place. On Saturday morning the Albany Movement president was released.

Both Walker and Coretta visited Martin King in jail on Saturday. Two small groups of picketers arrived at City Hall in midafternoon and were arrested. In a separate incident, C. B. King, visiting the county courthouse across the street from City Hall, was struck by a cane and badly bloodied by cantankerous Dougherty County Sheriff D. C. Campbell. Chief Pritchett criticized the attack as "regrettable," and personally told Martin King what had happened. King summoned Walker and asked him to contact Justice Department officials about the brutality.

While King and Abernathy spent a quiet Sunday in jail, Dr. Anderson appeared on television. He explained that the movement sought "an opportunity to talk face to face with the City Commission concerning the issues." He expressed disappointment that "the Kennedy Administration has not done as much as it can do to alleviate this situation."

A Sunday afternoon mass meeting at Mt. Zion reinforced the fact that the common people of Albany, the necessary foot soldiers of the movement, had lost their stomach for jail going. No visible gains were resulting from their self-sacrifice. Wyatt Walker tried to recruit volunteers for another prayer demonstration downtown, but only three listeners stepped forward. In private, movement leaders realized that their ability to put pressure on white Albany was fast slipping from their hands.[38]

Monday morning marked the start of Judge Elliott's hearing on the city's request for an injunction against all further protests. Even though Judge Tuttle had voided his earlier, temporary decree, Elliott made clear that he would give the city's petition his most respectful consideration and denied the movement attorneys' requests that the proceeding be dismissed. King was allowed to attend the hearing, held at the Albany federal building several blocks from the jail, but the testimony was uneventful. In New York, two ministerial allies of SCLC, Thomas Kilgore and George Lawrence, announced that a group of ministers would soon go to Washington to demand federal action in Albany. That evening, sixteen more praying protesters were arrested outside City Hall, despite an earlier movement promise to Pritchett that no demonstrations would disrupt his wedding anniversary night.

Elliott's hearing continued on Tuesday, with Pritchett on the stand most of the day. King told reporters that he would be happy to leave Albany if that would lead the city to negotiate with the movement. In Washington ten senators met with Burke Marshall to ask for Justice Department action in Albany. The following day President Kennedy, when asked about Albany at a press conference, said:

> I find it wholly inexplicable why the city council of Albany will not sit down with the citizens of Albany, who may be Negroes, and attempt to secure them, in a peaceful way, their rights. The U.S. government is involved in sitting down at Geneva with the Soviet Union. I can't understand why the government of Albany . . . cannot do the same for American citizens.

In private, the president pressed his brother and Marshall for federal action to solve the impasse. As Marshall later admitted, "He found it difficult to believe that there wasn't something the Department of Justice should do about Albany." Kennedy's criticism of the city's intransigence won quick praise from King and condemnation from Asa Kelley. King said he was "very grateful" that the president had spoken "so forthrightly," and wired Kennedy that he hoped "you will continue to use the great moral influence of your office to help this crucial situation." Mayor Kelley branded the presidential comment "inappropriate" because "this is a purely local problem." We "will never negotiate with outside agitators," he said.

King and his movement colleagues recognized Kennedy's comment as their best opportunity yet to resolve a situation in which their followers were unwilling to make further personal sacrifices. In a public statement, King reiterated that "I have always indicated publicly and privately that I would go so far as to leave Albany temporarily as long as there were begun good faith negotiations." The movement followed up that assertion with a telegram to the city commissioners, asking for a face-to-face meeting and that "we earnestly desire reconciliation in the Albany community, not victory." Asa Kelley responded that there would be no negotiations until the "outsiders" left.[39]

Thursday night, seven civil rights representatives—Melvin Wulf of the American Civil Liberties Union, Richard Haley of CORE, Roy Wilkins and two NAACP colleagues, and William Kunstler and Walter Fauntroy representing SCLC—met in Washington with Robert Kennedy and Burke Marshall to discuss Albany. The movement representatives asked the Justice Department to join the two civil suits that movement lawyers had filed against the city. If the department doubted its authority to intervene legally, then the administration ought to take some symbolic action in support of the movement, something more than the president's statement. Marshall and Kennedy said that their immediate goal was to establish direct negotiations between local blacks and local whites. The movement representatives did not dissent when Kennedy indicated that King would have to leave Albany as part of any agreement to begin face-to-face talks. While King's departure would be desirable, everyone agreed that any decision to leave "must be his alone," as Wulf put it. If King departed and the commission refused to begin negotiations, then the Justice Department would be morally obligated to "take bold steps," the movement delegation said. Although no firm promises were made, both sides left the meeting with a shared understanding of how the Albany situation could be resolved.

Elliott's hearing recessed on Friday, and Martin King and Ralph Abernathy celebrated the anniversary of their first week back in jail. On Saturday, August 4, the city commission issued a public statement saying it stood ready to talk with "responsible, law-abiding" local blacks. As hard-line Commissioner C. B. "Bunny" Pritchett explained, that excluded anyone who had been arrested—in other words, anyone active in the Albany Movement. The hard-line whites realized that the black community was losing interest in protests, and visiting white reporters sensed no mood for compromise among influential whites. Those reporters continued to praise what one New York Times story termed "the remarkable restraint of Albany's segregationists and the deft handling by the police of racial protests," and they asked movement leaders whether the absence of mass protests reflected blacks' disinterest in continuing the struggle.

On Sunday Coretta brought the Kings' three children to visit their imprisoned father. This was the first time he had seen them in three weeks. King and Abernathy spent most of their time reading the newspaper or listening to the radio, although King also worked on his long-planned book of sermons. It was a relaxed setting, though one white reporter thought it incongruous that King was wearing blue silk pajamas in a stifling south Georgia jail.[40]

Elliott's hearing resumed once more, and King spent Monday and Tuesday sitting in the hot courtroom. On Wednesday morning the Kennedy administration filed a "friend of the court" brief opposing the city's effort to win an injunction against the movement. The federal brief also supported the two suits filed by the movement, noting that city ordinances mandated segregation in all phases of Albany life, and that the city had followed a policy of closing "all avenues of demonstrative protest, however few the persons involved or however restrained their conduct."

Wednesday afternoon King took the stand as the final witness before Elliott recessed the hearing without setting a date for its resumption. King's testimony was simply a narration of his involvement in the Albany protests, but after eleven enervating days in captivity even that proved to be too much. "I was so exhausted and sick," he said later, that Dr. Anderson had to be called to administer medical treatment.

Although no contacts had been arranged between the city and the movement, Mayor Kelley continued his efforts to find some middle ground despite his anger at President Kennedy's public slap. Kelley's close friend and law partner J. W. "Taxi" Smith began private conversations with three blacks who were not active in the Albany Movement. It was hoped that this might lead to direct talks between blacks and the commission without King and SCLC leaving town, but on August 8 the hard-liners learned what had been developing. They denounced the mayor's efforts, saying that no conversations had been authorized and that "we will never deal with law violators or outside agitators." Kelley initially responded that no one had been representing the city, but the next day he spoke more frankly, saying that "the majority of the commission is absolutely wrong in condemning responsible business and religious leaders for discussing problems now facing this community."[41]

Following the recess of Elliott's hearing, local officials announced that King and Abernathy would be tried Friday morning for their July 27 arrest in front of City Hall. King took the stand during the brief proceeding and volunteered that he would be "happy to leave . . . if I stand in the way of any negotiations which would be held in good faith." Judge A. N. Durden, Sr., rendered his decision with no delay, finding the defendants guilty but suspending their sixty-day sentences and $200 fines. King was free, and he admitted later that Durden's decision "did not come as a complete surprise." Friday night King spoke at three different mass meetings, announcing that he and Abernathy would be returning to Atlanta for the weekend to attend to their church responsibilities. He hoped that their temporary absence would lead city officials to adopt a less intransigent stand toward the black community. He promised to return on Monday if no progress was made.

Before King left for Atlanta, Dr. Anderson notified the city commission that statements made by Judge Durden and city attorney Grady Rawls during King's trial had been interpreted by the movement to mean that officials would no longer enforce segregation statutes. In exchange, Anderson said, the movement would cancel a mass march scheduled for Saturday. SNCC's Charles Jones announced that he and others would test various city facilities over the weekend to see if enforcement of segregation had actually been halted.

Asa Kelley responded to Anderson's message by telling reporters that nothing said in court represented any change in the city's position, and that King's weekend departure did not mean a settlement had been reached. On Saturday morning the full commission issued a statement expressing pleasure over King's leaving town and hope that "a new and responsible voice for the colored citizenry of Albany will be heard." They added that "all valid laws and ordinances of the city and state will be enforced," and that they remained ready to "hear any responsible law-abiding citizens at any Commission meeting." This pronouncement signaled to all that King's departure had not changed the views of the hard-liners. The city's stance was reiterated when Jones found that the city library and all park facilities had suddenly been closed so as to protect "public safety."42

King was "visibly angry" when he learned of those developments. He would return to Albany the next morning and "keep on marching until victory is completely ours." On Monday, King joined Dr. Anderson to announce that the movement would strengthen its boycott of white businesses. Anderson said that his daughter would apply to the all-white high school to begin school desegregation, and that a black candidate would run for a city commission seat in the November elections. King told a mass rally that a movement delegation would appear at the commission's Wednesday evening meeting. The delegation was led by Marion Page, who never had been arrested. Called upon by Kelley as "Marion," Page read a statement asking for clarification of all the issues pending since last December: the bus and train stations, the arrest bonds, the local buses, the right to picket, and the disposition of hundreds of arrest charges still pending. With nary a pause, the mayor responded that the commission could not act or comment because of the ongoing litigation. "Every area covered tonight now rests with the federal courts, where it should be." Rebuffed once again, movement representatives returned to Shiloh church for a mass meeting.

The next morning Dr. Anderson announced that there would be no more protests, and that the movement would turn its attention to voter registration. Anderson said, "It seems tactically wise to let up on our mass demonstrations," because the movement realized it was "settling down for the long haul. And in the long haul you can't be sending two hundred people to jail every day." The leadership had conceded that there was no way to change the city commission's stance, and that the movement would have to give up its hope of establishing direct negotiations with the city.[43]

King returned to Atlanta Thursday morning, as eight SCLC staff members gathered in Albany to aid the newly intensified voter registration effort. Fred Bennette and John Calhoun helped local leaders like Rev. Samuel Wells organize the black community for door-to-door canvassing, while Dorothy Cotton and a new staff member, Annell Ponder, began to set up citizenship training classes. Dr. Anderson, with SCLC's help, contacted Voter Education Project Director Wiley Branton and obtained $4,000 to support the Albany drive. Within two weeks time over five hundred new black voters were added to the city's rolls.

After a quiet week of rest in Atlanta, King returned to Albany on Monday, August 27. That same day, two groups of white northern ministers from New York and Chicago arrived in Albany. Encouraged by Dr. Anderson and other local leaders, the visitors hoped to serve as mediators and reach out to the white community. However, Albany's white ministers announced they would not speak with the outsiders. On Tuesday afternoon, seventy-five visiting preachers were arrested after conducting a prayer vigil at City Hall, and eleven of them chose to stay in jail. King used their arrest as an opportunity to call again for federal action, stressing blacks' disappointment with John Kennedy's failure to move more strongly on Albany. Later that week, he wired President Kennedy to ask that the administration mediate the conflict by inviting both city officials and movement representatives to Washington. King's telegram went unacknowledged, even though seven U.S. senators visited Burke Marshall to urge federal action. Marshall expressed no interest in taking any further steps; with tranquillity returning to Albany, the Kennedy administration did not want to intervene in a situation it had been trying to quiet since the preceding December.[44]

Many newsmen took the late August halt in Albany's demonstrations as a final sign that the movement had ended in failure. One national news magazine observed that "not a single racial barrier fell" and that Albany remained "just as segregated as ever." Some journalists attributed the segregationist success to Laurie Pritchett's sagacity. There had been virtually no violence committed against demonstrators during the entire nine months of protests, either by lawmen or white toughs. Taking into account the night of disruption in July, Pritchett and the proponents of segregation appeared more nonviolent than segregation's opponents. "In the movement," SCLC Field Secretary James Bevel told *Newsweek,* "you generally just set up a situation and wait for your adversary to make a mistake. But these are very shrewd people." Pritchett had enforced segregation in every phase of Albany's life, and had won widespread praise in the national media for his success.

It was a painful irony to movement activists, who concluded accurately that the national public had taken little offense at Albany's establishment of what one observer termed "an efficient police state." So long as the Laurie Pritchetts of the South succeeded in maintaining segregation in a fashion that eschewed public violence and brutality, it seemed that the Kennedy brothers would be content to leave civil rights on the back burner.

Both King and Wyatt Walker blamed the Kennedys for the unsatisfactory developments in Albany. They believed that the absence of federal pressure on Albany's white officials accounted for the lack of city concessions. They thought that the Kennedys had been behind Judge Elliott's order, and that that moratorium had broken the momentum and diminished the black community's enthusiasm for continued protests. "We thought the Kennedy administration worked against us," Andrew Young remembered. It seemed that significant federal action would be forthcoming only when violent crises such as the Freedom Rides erupted. Pritchett's ability to keep Albany's opposition to racial justice nonviolent should not have made segregation any more palatable to the Kennedys or other Americans, but the administration and the nation's response to Albany had shown that peaceful segregation stirred little of the outrage that had greeted the racist assaults upon the Freedom Riders.

The SCLC leadership knew that Pritchett's professionalism and the Kennedys' preference for order over justice did not fully account for the Albany Movement's failure to win tangible gains. When King and his colleagues had arrived in town in mid-December, the movement seemed to have an enthusiasm, and perhaps a naïveté, that King had not seen since the Montgomery boycott. It was a spirit that had come through powerfully in the songs and fervor of those early mass meetings, but it had been dampened as people realized that the federal government would not aid them and that the movement was riven by petty organizational conflicts. The narrow-minded self-interestedness of the NAACP had most offended the local black leadership, but the open hostility of Charles Jones and Ella Baker of SNCC had equally irritated Wyatt Walker and Martin King. If the local black community had been unified, if SNCC had not tried to turn the local leaders against SCLC and Walker's supposed takeover, there would not have been the embarrassing "settlement" in December and a true victory might have been won. "There was a time," King later remembered, "that we had Albany really almost to the point of having to give in." That opportunity for a triumph had come and gone in December, and both Walker and Andrew Young had had private doubts about the wisdom of SCLC's July return to a city where the black community's divisions were still unresolved. Yet they had gone back, and the absence of federal action and the high personal costs had led the black community to conclude that their faith had been naïve, that nothing would be gained by their own additional sacrifices. Unfortunately, King and his colleagues had been unable to convince them that they were wrong. The spirit had drained out of the movement.[45]

In explaining the failed effort, Wyatt Walker thought King had been too tolerant of the internal tensions and backbiting. He believed that if King had exercised his leadership more firmly, many of the tensions would have been eliminated. Other participants, such as Samuel Wells and Vincent Harding, thought that the entire effort had become too involved in questions of money and publicity, and in activating the Kennedy administration; the movement had forgotten that the real emphasis in nonviolent protest was upon changing the hearts and minds of one's oppressors, the white officialdom of Albany. Harding had invested much time in talking with hard-line whites for just this purpose, and felt that the movement's leadership had given insufficient attention to making private appeals to Albany's whites, appeals that might persuade them to admit the justice of the movement's goals. Though philosophically correct, practical experience in Albany had shown that belief to be wrong. Harding's efforts, and those of other intermediaries such as Frances Pauley of the Georgia Council on Human Relations, had had little impact. Reverend Wells was only one of those who was disappointed by white Albany's intransigent stance:

> The white church, the white community, let us down. The white community was without a heart, without a conscience. My sole reason for demonstrating was to reach the better people—who hadn't thought about injustice before. I don't know what happened. We were depending on the white community. We had faith.

That one statement, "We had faith," summed up the beauty and the pain of Albany. It was a faith that white obstinacy and federal disinterest had proved naïve and misplaced. Although the national press emphasized that there had been no tangible gains, local black leaders correctly argued that black Albany nonetheless had benefited from the experience. There was more self-confidence, more self-esteem, less fear of the white man's jail, and a more widespread commitment to eventual equality than had existed a year earlier. While the experience had been disappointing and depressing, it had also been a strong step forward.

For SCLC's leader the disappointments of Albany underscored the fact that they had had no prior intention of going there, that Martin King had been drawn into a situation not of his own making after both the contentious NAACP and hypercritical SNCC were already on the scene. "We got dragged into" it, Wyatt Walker groused later, and neither Martin King nor his SCLC colleagues had foreseen the consequences when King had headed south for that Friday night speech in December. Albany had been the first opportunity for Andrew Young to get to know King well. "At that time it was clear to me," Young later recalled, "that he was a man thrust into a situation that he really didn't want to be in." In fact, as King knew then and as Young later realized, Albany in one respect was just like the Montgomery boycott, just like the Atlanta sit-ins, just like the Freedom Rides. It was not an involvement that Martin King had sought out, not a protest he had instigated or planned, not an event that he was eager to be involved in. As in those earlier instances, Albany had started out as a situation King knew in good conscience he could not avoid; it was his responsibility because of the role into which he had been cast and from which he had found no escape. For six and a half years, that responsibility had lain upon his shoulders, and there was no indication it would be lifted from him anytime soon. It was his to bear, and he had known ever since that Friday night in the kitchen in Montgomery that it could not be shirked.[46]

Back in Atlanta the first week of September, King told Benjamin Mays he could not teach the Morehouse philosophy seminar as he had done the previous year. His time-consuming involvement in Albany had left him well behind in raising funds for SCLC. He also had to put much more time than he had expected into the pastoral duties he shared with his father at Ebenezer. "I had hoped that my responsibility at the church would be limited to the preaching ministry," King said, but it had not turned out that way. In all his activities over the past year, King confessed, "I failed to do what I had hoped to do," and with the seminar in particular he had let too many of the responsibilities fall upon his partner, Sam Williams. "The demands on my time grow greater and greater," King wrote. "The job . . . takes unbelievable tolls on my time and physical strength. I can see no let-up in the coming year. In fact, I can see nothing but deeper and deeper involvement." Although he could foresee no escape from those responsibilities in the immediate future, his decision not to teach the seminar was no indication that teaching had proven unpleasant, King told Mays:

> I hope that it will be possible for me to return to such a challenging responsibility sometime in the future. I certainly have my moments of intellectual nostalgia—moments when I long to leave the arena of endless activity, and spend creative moments in the world of ideas.

After that week in Atlanta, King plunged back into that "endless activity." There were two speeches and a Gandhi Society board meeting in New York, and then a trip back to south Georgia, where two black churches in rural counties near Albany had been torched by white arsonists. King wired John Kennedy to call for an all-out federal investigation, and told newsmen that the pace of the FBI's initial inquiries "has been all too slow." King was joined at a New York dinner by Governor Nelson Rockefeller, who privately had contributed $5,000 to SCLC in August and who pledged an additional gift of $10,000 toward rebuilding

the burned churches. In his dinner speech, King voiced his strongest public criticism of John Kennedy to date. "No President can be great, or
even fit for office," King intoned, "if he attempts to accommodate to
injustice to maintain his political balance." Some wondered if King was
implying that Rockefeller's support of the movement meant that he now
would rank more highly in the eyes of civil rights leaders than his potential 1964 presidential opponent, an incumbent who had not kept his campaign promises to black Americans.[47]

By mid-September, preparations were under way for SCLC's annual
fall convention, scheduled to begin September 25 in Birmingham. Fred
Shuttlesworth had urged Birmingham as the site so that SCLC's presence
there might further prod the city's white merchants, who still were refusing to desegregate their store facilities despite the ongoing black boycott.

Shuttlesworth spread the word that Birmingham would see demonstrations during the SCLC convention if concessions were not made by the
merchants. Throughout the first three weeks of September the city's business leadership, represented by real estate executive Sidney Smyer, spoke
with local black leaders, such as college president Lucius H. Pitts and
wealthy businessman A. G. Gaston, in an effort to avert mass protests.
Many moderate whites wanted to prevent demonstrations because of an
upcoming November plebiscite on replacing the existing three-member
city commission, dominated by Bull Connor, with a mayor-council form
of government that they hoped would be more temperate. Any protests,
they argued, would play into Connor's hands.

Pitts was eager to win desegregated facilities without demonstrations.
He skillfully recruited two other interested parties to his side: the liberal
white officials of the Alabama Council on Human Relations and its parent body, the Southern Regional Council, and the U.S. Justice Department. Pitts met with Robert Kennedy and Burke Marshall in Washington
the second week of September, then consulted with his black leadership
colleagues and the Alabama Council. Accompanied by two liberal whites,
Pitts paid a Sunday call on Sidney Smyer to say that demonstrations could
be avoided only if the downtown stores removed their segregation signs
from rest rooms and water fountains before the SCLC convention began
ten days hence. Pitts also asked that whites commit themselves to biracial
discussions of further integration. Smyer thought Pitts's suggestions were
sensible; several days later a group of merchants met with the black leaders and reluctantly agreed to paint over their segregation signs. In return,
Shuttlesworth made clear that SCLC's gathering would not be marked by
public protests.

King spent mid-September raising funds. His appearances at a series of
rallies in New York City produced substantial sums before he headed
south to Birmingham for the SCLC convention. Speaking to reporters the
first day, King said that SCLC would focus its efforts on Alabama in the
not-too-distant future. He commended the Kennedys for their support of
black applicant James Meredith in the growing crisis over his admission

to the University of Mississippi, and suggested that SCLC would seek out other black applicants for Alabama's segregated state universities.

Until the final day, the convention sessions were uneventful. Wyatt Walker explained that the past twelve months had given SCLC a more specific set of goals than the organization had had one year earlier. He identified the key turning point as the joint meeting of the staff and board in Atlanta in early January. Jack O'Dell reported that voter registration efforts had been more productive than ever before, and that the ongoing drive in Albany had added 1,200 new black voters in just six weeks time. Walker contended that Albany had been a positive experience for the organization, that "SCLC came of age in Albany." He pointed out the value of the four-pronged strategy—direct action, lawsuits, boycotts, and voter registration—that SCLC and the Albany Movement had adopted only at the end of July. He did not amplify King's cryptic comment about SCLC's future plans for Alabama, and the spate of resolutions adopted by the convention were limited to exhortations for stronger federal action.[48]

Late Friday morning, September 28, King addressed the convention's final session from the stage of the L. R. Hall Auditorium. During his remarks, a young white man who had been sitting in the sixth row rose suddenly and approached King. Without warning, the man punched King in the face. A shocked stillness came over the crowd, which watched in amazement as King stood his ground and accepted several blows. As one eyewitness described it, King made no move to strike back or turn away. Instead, he looked at his assailant and spoke calmly to him. Within seconds, several people pulled the attacker away. While others led the crowd in song, King and his colleagues spoke with the assailant at the rear of the stage. Then King returned to the podium to tell the audience that the man, Roy James, was a twenty-four-year-old member of the Nazi party from Arlington, Virginia. King said he would not press charges against him. Birmingham police arrived and insisted that the city would press charges even if King chose not to. Without delay, James was hustled before a local court judge, convicted of assault, and sentenced to thirty days in jail and a $25 fine. Birmingham's segregationist mayor, Art Hanes, visited the courtroom to tell James to his face never again to set foot in Birmingham. The entire incident, from assault to sentencing, took barely four hours. It left most onlookers stunned and impressed by King's lack of fear when confronted by direct physical violence.[49]

King spent the first ten days of October in Atlanta, trying to make progress on his book of sermons. Then he was back to that "endless activity," with speaking engagements at several colleges and an audience in New York with Algerian leader Ahmed Ben Bella. One week later he was in Montgomery for a meeting of SCLC's Alabama affiliates, telling one reporter that SCLC intended to launch a major assault on segregation in Alabama in six weeks time. It would begin, King said, with another People-to-People tour to gain new recruits for the "nonviolent army," which would then tackle voter registration throughout the state and desegregation of public facilities in Alabama's major cities. Lunch counters would be an initial target. Though King did not mention it, Birmingham's white merchants had reinstituted the segregation of their store facilities shortly after SCLC's convention. The owners told angry Birmingham black leaders that Public Safety Commissioner Connor had forced the reversal upon them, threatening harassment through building and fire code inspections if they refused to comply. The black leaders knew that the merchants had been far from enthusiastic about desegregation in the first place, and the boycott of the stores was renewed. Some white businessmen offered to finance a legal test case if the blacks would initiate a single arrest for use of a segregated rest room, but the black leadership spurned the offer, saying that the white merchants should take on Connor themselves. Although the white moderates triumphed in the early November plebiscite on changing Birmingham's form of government, the black boycott remained in effect and no progress was made toward desegregation.[50]

Late in October King addressed a large New York dinner sponsored by the National Maritime Union. The gathering generated $30,000 as a nest egg for the Gandhi Society, which had gotten off to a slow start in its first five months of existence. Three days after that dinner, serious controversy broke when several conservative newspapers ran almost identical front-page stories detailing the Communist party ties of SCLC staff member Jack O'Dell. The FBI-planted stories reported that the thirty-nine-year-old O'Dell not only had a public record of past association with the "CP," but in fact still served as "a concealed member" of the party's national committee. The Bureau hoped that this exposé would so embarrass King that the supposed Communist mole would be purged. Although the planted stories got several details wrong, such as an assertion that O'Dell was SCLC's "acting executive director," this smear definitely was embarrassing.

After several days, King issued a statement saying that O'Dell had resigned from SCLC and claiming that his role had been much more tangential than the news reports indicated. "Ninety per cent" of O'Dell's work, King asserted, had involved responsibility for SCLC's mail appeals, which meant that he had "functioned purely as a technician." Although this announcement ended public discussion of the matter, movement insiders knew that not only was King's description of O'Dell's job far from the truth, but that the resignation was fictional. While King's statement carefully noted that SCLC had accepted the resignation, "pending further inquiry and clarification," those in the know, including the FBI, were aware that O'Dell remained with SCLC as head of its New York office. He was taken off the payroll briefly in order that King's statement would not prove to be a lie if the subject later reemerged. The FBI reasoned that King's deceptiveness in retaining O'Dell indicated that the civil rights leader was insensitive to the dangers of Communist subversion, as well as dishonest.[51]

At the same time, the Voter Education Project (VEP) began querying SCLC about its failure to submit adequate reports on its spending of VEP's grants. Jack Minnis of the VEP complained to Andrew Young that SCLC was not living up to its responsibilities. He had thought O'Dell was in charge, and then Young, but neither man had responded to requests for fuller documentation of SCLC's registration work in different areas of Georgia, Louisiana, Alabama, and Virginia. The few memos SCLC had submitted, Minnis warned Young, were "wholly inadequate," consisting of "vague generalities which convey little or no information about what is actually being done by SCLC field staff." "Unless we can get SCLC to understand that we require more than vague generalities," Minnis told VEP Director Wiley Branton, "I suggest we consider terminating or reducing their participation in VEP."

While SCLC was trying to remedy those problems, it was also launching a new project called "Operation Breadbasket." This program sought better employment opportunities for black workers at companies whose products were purchased by black consumers. If a company failed to hire black employees and treat them fairly, black consumers would take their business elsewhere. The original "selective patronage" idea had come from Philadelphia ministers Leon Sullivan, Alfred Dunston, and Joshua Licorish. In the fall of 1962, several Atlanta pastors active in SCLC's local affiliate suggested that the organization apply this principle to Atlanta businesses so as to win better jobs for their parishioners. Reverend Sullivan was invited to Atlanta to explain the program. He told the ministers how to select target firms, request statistics on black employment from them, and recommend specific improvements to the companies if their opportunities for blacks were inadequate. He also stressed that the ministers should ask their constituents to boycott the firm if those recommendations were not accepted. Sullivan told the pastors to have properly skilled applicants ready to take the jobs that were won. By early November, the Atlanta ministers, with Ralph Abernathy in the lead, had begun negotiations with two food-processing firms.[52]

Throughout early November King tried to work as much as possible on his book of sermons. He set rigid work hours for himself and often spent his nights "across town," as he called it, rather than return home to the distractions and interruptions created by a wife and three young children. On November 16, he took time out to attend Yoki's seventh birthday party, then headed to south Georgia for the first time in two months to speak at a rally commemorating the first anniversary of the Albany Movement. Few contacts had taken place between city officials and local black leaders since August, and no steps toward desegregation had been taken. The movement's two suits languished in Judge Elliott's court, and a somewhat weakened boycott of the downtown stores remained in effect. At the rally, SCLC's president exhorted the crowd to keep their spirits high and their commitment strong, and then flew off to a Sunday preaching engagement in New York.[53]

In mid-November, King commended John Kennedy for finally issuing the long-promised executive order banning racial discrimination in federally assisted housing. King's praise was tempered, however, not only by the twenty-two-month delay in issuing the order, but also by the fact that its scope was narrower than many specialists had expected, especially in its lack of a clause providing for retroactive application. Blacks would have to seek aggressive enforcement of the order, King said, if its provisions were to have an effect upon housing discrimination.

King also made a special effort to attend a private forum convened by the American Negro Leadership Conference on Africa (ANLCA). Headed by labor activist Theodore "Ted" Brown, whom King had known for several years, the ANLCA's purpose was to establish closer ties between black African leaders and American civil rights proponents. King understood colonialism and economic imperialism's close links to racism and segregation. They all shared a "failure to respect the dignity and worth of all human personality." The parallel between the American South and black Africa could be carried further, King said, if one examined the role of the U.S. government. "The very same set of complex politico-economic forces are operative in both instances. There seems always the choice between political expediency and that which is morally compelling." The Kennedy administration had done no better when faced with "the choice between advantageous economic aid and military alliances, versus the establishment of racial and political justice," in South Africa than it had in dealing with Albany. The American black freedom struggle had much in common with Africa's.[54]

After another stint of work in Atlanta on his book of sermons, King began his Alabama People-to-People recruitment tour. The trip started on Wednesday, December 5, in Anniston, and took King to Gadsden, Talladega, Tuscaloosa, then to Montgomery for a rally celebrating the seventh anniversary of the boycott. The next day King and his colleagues drove to Selma and were almost attacked by white toughs, who were angry at the civil rights leader's presence in their thoroughly segregated little city. From Selma the SCLC delegation went on to Uniontown, then headed back to Montgomery, where King preached a Sunday morning sermon at Dexter Avenue church.

Sunday afternoon, King drove north to address the installation ceremony of Rev. John Thomas Porter, King's ministerial assistant at Dexter eight years earlier, at Birmingham's Sixth Avenue Baptist Church. King also needed to talk with Fred Shuttlesworth about the Alabama Christian Movement's desire for SCLC to help them protest the still-segregated facilities of Birmingham's downtown stores. Though the merchants gave no indication of a willingness to desegregate, white moderates and influential blacks argued that any protests should be delayed until after the early March mayoral election, which had been mandated by the successful November plebiscite, and in which Bull Connor would be the segregationist candidate. Protests would work to Connor's advantage, and King agreed that the subject of direct action would have to be discussed carefully in January.

A few days after King's visit, bombers struck Birmingham's Bethel Baptist Church, site of many of the Alabama Christian Movement's mass rallies. King dispatched a telegram to John Kennedy calling for federal action and decrying "the Gestapo like methods" of Connor's city police. Birmingham, he said, "is by far the worst big city in race relations in the United States." Two days later, King joined Ted Brown and five other prominent black leaders—Randolph, Wilkins, James Farmer, Whitney Young of the National Urban League, and Dorothy Height of the National Council of Negro Women—for a White House meeting at which they presented the president with several resolutions about American-African relations adopted at the ANLCA meeting three weeks earlier. After that session, King met privately with Kennedy to discuss the Birmingham bombing and the need for a stronger administration stance on civil rights. Kennedy made no promises, and said that opposition in Congress would doom any legislative proposal on civil rights. Later King told a reporter that "we still have not had a strong voice from the White House dealing with the moral issues" in civil rights.[55]

While King's thoughts turned increasingly toward Birmingham, SCLC's daily affairs continued to press upon him. The Gandhi Society's fund-raising prospects remained in limbo because of federal inaction on its application for tax-exempt status. SCLC's fund-raising continued to depend heavily upon the direct-mail appeals overseen by Jack O'Dell in New York. Andrew Young assumed supervision of SCLC's disjointed voter registration efforts, while Dorothy Cotton took charge of his previous responsibilities for the citizenship education program. One week before Christmas, Young assembled all the SCLC field secretaries in Atlanta in an effort to bring more order to their fragmented assignments. Each worker detailed the obstacles they had encountered, and Young reported to King that definite improvements had to be made in SCLC's efforts in Louisiana, Georgia, and eastern Alabama.

King's holiday schedule took him to North Carolina, Tennessee, and Oakland, California, where he told a New Year's Day Emancipation rally that black people should come together in a national boycott of firms with discriminatory employment policies. On January 3, King returned to Atlanta to tell his SCLC colleagues that the time had come for them to focus on Birmingham. King proposed that SCLC's inner circle gather at Dorchester in eastern Georgia for a two-day meeting beginning Thursday, January 10.[56]

The discussions in that group of twelve to fifteen people marked the first time that King, Walker, Abernathy, and Young had sat down to analyze the lessons of Albany. To King, such an analysis was imperative before launching any effort in Birmingham, so that they could "see where mistakes were made" in Albany and "determine what could be done in Birmingham to offset them." King's reflections and the two days of intensive conversations, he later explained, led him to conclude that two principal errors had been made in Albany. First, the Albany Movement

> was centered on segregation in general, and no form of segregation in particular, and I think it would have been greater and would have been wiser, from a strategic and tactical point of view to say, "now we are going to attack segregated lunch counters," or "we are going to attack segregated buses," . . . in other words, center it on something. . . .
>
> I think the main tactical error was that the leadership did not center this marvelous revolt on some particular phase of segregation so that you could win a victory there and give the people the kind of psychological lift, a morale lift that they needed.

In the Dorchester discussions of Birmingham, King said, "one of the things we decided was that we would center this on . . . certain aspects of segregation and aspects and areas where we could win a victory."

Second, King explained, in Albany the civil rights forces had not appreciated how little leverage they could exercise on the city commission, a weakness that the Dorchester talks traced to the minimal voting power of the black community prior to the August registration drive.

Albany would have had greater success if from the start the movement had targeted Albany's business leaders, rather than the city's elected officials. The boycott of downtown stores had been an effective but limited tactic, King decided, because the movement's direct action efforts had not been combined with the boycott so as to inflict a maximum penalty upon those business leaders. "All of our marches in Albany," King related,

> were marches to the city hall trying to make them negotiate, where if we had centered our protests at the stores, the businesses in the city, [we could have] made the merchants negotiate. . . . If you can pull them around, you pull the political power structure because really the political power structure listens to the economic power structure.

If the black community did possess substantial voting strength, King expounded, "you *can* center your conflict on the political power structure— you can march to the city hall. . . . When you don't have this, you ought to center it on the economic power structure—you've got to center in the area where you have power." From what Shuttlesworth and others said about Birmingham, it was clear that in Birmingham also the civil rights forces should adopt an economic rather than political focus. "In Birmingham we knew in the beginning," King later explained, "that Negroes did not have enough votes to move the political power structure, but we knew that Negroes had enough money, enough buying power to make the difference between profit and loss in almost any business. So we decided to center it on the economic power structure."

The key to Birmingham would be to select an initial goal that could be won from the economic leadership and that would give the black community a morale-boosting victory.

King, Walker, and the others at the Dorchester retreat knew there were several other important ways in which Birmingham would differ from Albany. First, Shuttlesworth's affiliation with SCLC, and his unchallenged status as the principal leader of Birmingham's only indigenous protest group, the Alabama Christian Movement for Human Rights (ACMHR), meant that SCLC's efforts would not be hindered by destructive wrangling with other civil rights organizations and their local adherents. Shuttlesworth's role should make for a unified local leadership, and neither SNCC nor the NAACP was as active in Birmingham as it had been in Albany. Shuttlesworth's several hundred loyal supporters would supply a core, and the congregations of four young pastors new to the city and ready for direct action—Martin King's brother A.D., John Thomas Porter, Nelson H. Smith, and John Cross—also could be counted on. With that base, Birmingham's black community ought to give sustained support for ongoing protests.

King and Walker also believed that Birmingham's reputation as a strongly segregationist city would give those protests, and any victories that were won, a southwide if not national symbolic value. In particular, both men knew that one of the greatest obstacles in Albany had been the sagacious way Laurie Pritchett had defended segregation and won national newsmen to his side. Southern racism was a brutal experience for blacks, but Albany had conveyed little of that brutality to either the nation or those in Washington whose lack of moral sensitivity had been expressed by their preference for order over justice. In Birmingham, however, the city's defense of segregation—at least until the upcoming municipal election in March—would be led by Public Safety Commissioner Bull Connor, who was infamous for his hair-trigger temper and heavy-handed advocacy of segregation. Shuttlesworth knew Connor's proclivities at close hand, and believed that Birmingham's "Bull" would give southern segregation a more graphic portrayal than had Pritchett. To Shuttlesworth, Connor was "the symbol of brutality, police brutality in the South," a man who could be counted on to show the entire country how the white South treated black people. "The idea of facing Bull Connor was the thing," Shuttlesworth said later. "We knew that we would have at least the spotlight," and that between Connor, a committed local black community, and SCLC's experience with Pritchett, "we had at least something that we might make a confrontation which would bring the nation to its conscience to recognize the injustice."[57]

If Shuttlesworth knew Connor best at close range, no one appreciated Connor's potential for aiding the movement more than Wyatt Walker. Looking back, Walker said, "We knew that when we came to Birmingham that if Bull Connor was still in control, he would do something to benefit our movement. We didn't want to march after Bull was gone." But Birmingham's potential reached beyond Connor himself, Walker knew. Describing it a few years later, Walker explained that SCLC "decided that Birmingham would be our target because we felt that after Albany we had to take on what represented the symbol of the inflexible South." We "knew that there had been no real dramatization to the nation of what segregation was like and Birmingham would provide us with that kind of platform." At Dorchester, he said, "we decided on Birmingham with the attitude that we may not win it, we may lose everything. But we knew that as Birmingham went, so would go the South. And we felt that if we could crack that city, then we could crack any city."

King, Walker, and the others at Dorchester also knew that there was a third element, besides the local black community and the white opposition, which would be crucial to success in Birmingham: the Kennedy administration. As King put it, "The key to everything is federal commitment." Two years earlier, the administration had responded to the heavily publicized violence that marked the Freedom Rides with federal intervention and a commitment to desegregate interstate travel facilities. In Albany, however, where there had been no photos of burning buses or beaten protesters, the Kennedys had shown no interest in bolstering the movement's cause. Indeed, the administration had seemed more supportive of the city's efforts to keep municipal peace and quiet than of the Albany Movement's efforts to win desegregation and simple human recognition from elected officials. Everyone at the Dorchester retreat realized the importance of the Kennedys' response to whatever developed in Birmingham. The Kennedy brothers, the Dorchester group concluded, would respond if their hand was forced by demonstrations that evoked the true character of southern segregation.

King believed that protests in Birmingham would lead to "the *surfacing* of tensions already present." Those tensions and great underlying injustices were present in Birmingham and countless other places whether SCLC chose to act or not, and the existence of those injustices supplied a moral imperative *to act,* King argued. "To cure injustices," he later explained, "you must expose them before the light of human conscience and the bar of public opinion, regardless of whatever tensions that exposure generates. Injustices to the Negro must be brought out into the open where they cannot be evaded." The moral requirement, in short, was to "set out to precipitate a crisis situation that must open the door to negotiation," and to use that crisis so that "the pressure of public opinion becomes an ally in your just cause," King said later. If that could be done, those meeting at Dorchester agreed, the power of the federal government and the moral influence of the American presidency could be brought to the movement's side in a way they never had before.

Although most of the two-day discussions were devoted to analyzing

Albany and devising a better strategy for Birmingham, their tenor was not dry or studious. The atmosphere in the small group was emotional, with a gravity appropriate to the importance of the decisions that were being made. Everyone realized there was no certainty that Birmingham would turn out better than Albany, and no guarantee that things would not be far worse.

"Perhaps the most dramatic moment in the planning meeting," Stanley Levison later said,

> was at the close, . . . when I thought it would be useful to point out that Bull Connor had an ugly history with the labor movement and had fought it for years to keep it out of Birmingham . . . and the use of forced brutality and all kinds of devices were employed to defeat what was then a powerful movement; that we were not *as* powerful as the labor movement had been in its organizing days; and consequently, we had to realize that we were facing a rough adversary . . .

Then, Levison remembered, King spoke up:

> 'I want to make a point that I think everyone here should consider very carefully and decide if he wants to be with this campaign.' He said, 'There are something like eight people here assessing the type of enemy we're going to face. I have to tell you that in my judgment, some of the people sitting here today will not come back alive from this campaign. And I want you to think about it.'

Andrew Young never forgot that moment. In later years, he thought that Martin King had no more eagerness to go to Birmingham than he had had to step forward in Montgomery, to join the Atlanta sit-ins, to participate in the Freedom Rides, or to be dragged into Albany. As in those earlier situations, the decision to go to Birmingham was thrust upon him, a responsibility King felt he could not avoid. Perhaps this time SCLC was making its own plans, rather than simply responding to the initiatives of the students, CORE, or SNCC. But at Dorchester it was Fred Shuttlesworth, not Martin King, who emphasized that Birmingham was a challenge that SCLC had to confront. "He went to Birmingham," Young said of King, "because Fred Shuttlesworth pleaded with him to do it," and Martin King "knew, more than anybody else, that every time he made a commitment to something like this he was committing his life. . . . He thought in everything he did it meant his death. He would never say it that way. He would always say it in terms of us. He would say for instance, 'Now Andy, Bull Connor doesn't play.' He said," with a touch of hyperbole, " 'They've had fifty bombings in the last year, and you might not come back. You better let me know what kind of eulogy you want.' And even though he was talking about me, I knew he was talking about himself."

On that somber note the discussions came to an end. Young drove Levison into Savannah to catch the train northward, and early Saturday morning Martin King and his Atlanta colleagues flew back home. King's mood was solemn as he thought about what lay ahead of him. It was, in many ways, just like the time when he had come to Savannah two years earlier, and had spoken to others what he really was saying to himself:

> We must rise above our fears. . . . There is nothing to be afraid of if you believe and know that the cause for which you stand is right. You are ready to face anything and you face it with a humble smile on your face, because you know that all of the eternity stands with you and the angels stand beside you and you know that you are right.

No matter how dangerous Birmingham was, no matter how vicious Bull Connor was, Martin King knew that his God would stand beside him, would speak to him, and would watch over him, come what may.[58]

5

Birmingham and the March on Washington, 1963

The Dorchester discussions established that SCLC would make a major commitment to Birmingham, but set no precise timetable for the protests. On January 23, SCLC's executive staff met to discuss Birmingham in detail. The city election was scheduled for March 5, and King knew that Birmingham's black leaders wanted no protests before that time. SCLC settled on a target date of March 14. King said that jail going would be a necessary part of the campaign and that as many SCLC board members as possible should be recruited to join the effort. Wyatt Walker described how he would proceed with reconnoitering Birmingham's segregated facilities, especially the lunch counters and other whites-only facilities in the downtown department stores that had reneged on their fall agreement with Shuttlesworth. King said that a larger session with Shuttlesworth and his Birmingham associates would be scheduled for early February.

In Birmingham word of the planned protest was very tightly held, although the principal black leaders and white liberals associated with the Alabama Council on Human Relations understood that something was in the offing. Few if any knew the target date King had selected. There was considerable concern that no protests be launched prior to the crucial mayoral election in which Connor would oppose two relative moderates, former Lieutenant Governor Albert Boutwell and the somewhat more liberal Tom King. The city's business leadership rallied behind Boutwell as the strongest alternative to the dangerous Connor. They hoped that a Boutwell victory would lead to some agreement that would end the boycott, which continued to exact a high toll from the white stores.

To many Birmingham residents, black and white, expelling Connor from public office represented an opportunity to eliminate the segregationist violence that had long troubled Birmingham and stained its national reputation. In 1960 *The New York Times* had created a municipal furor by detailing how extremist white violence against anyone who spoke up for desegregation had frightened virtually every white, and most blacks, into timid silence. By early 1963 the climate had changed little. One national magazine article, written by a native Birmingham white, labeled it "A City in Fear." Years of unsolved bombings had led to one neighborhood of upper-class black homes being called "Dynamite Hill," and jokes about "Bombingham" abounded. Well-informed observers decried the lack of moderate and courageous white leaders. Only a defeat of Connor would allow some official dialogue to begin between blacks and whites. Leaders of both races hoped that SCLC would not complicate their task.[1]

In late January, King spoke to a thousand members of the Chicago Sunday Evening Club gathered at Orchestra Hall. Just before he began, King saw in the audience the young Nazi who had assaulted him in Birmingham four months earlier. This time the fascist had five compatriots with him. King was disturbed, but proceeded with the speech, betraying no obvious nervousness. Later he admitted he had wondered if this would be the last speech he ever made. The address ended without incident, and King's hosts escorted him to a reception line. King spied the Nazi and his friends approaching, and beckoned a nearby policeman to stop them. "You're the one who attacked me," King called out to the young assailant. With that statement and the policeman's presence, the fascists left quietly and no incident occurred. King, however, found the encounter frightening; one witness said he appeared "quite upset" by the men's presence. When King returned to Atlanta he related the experience to Coretta and several friends. His SCLC staff advised him to travel with an aide, but King objected to any suggestion that he should have an armed companion. That was an overreaction, he felt, and would not necessarily do any good. "Most of the time," Coretta said, "Martin doesn't think about the possibility of anything happening," but King lived with the certainty that at some point something *would* happen, and that there was nothing he could do to avoid it. "He just always talked about the fact that he didn't expect to have a long life," Coretta said later. "Somehow he always felt that he would die early," and he saw no need always to be on guard against the inevitable.

King's fatalistic attitude did not sit well with his friends. Early in February he described the Chicago incident to labor activist Ted Brown over lunch in New York. Brown insisted that King should be receiving protection. King demurred, but several days later Brown called Burke Marshall, told him King's story, and asked Marshall to see if Justice and the FBI could arrange for local police to give King protection during his travels. "You are more useful to the cause alive than dead," Brown lectured King after his conversation with Marshall.[2]

While Walker concentrated on plans for Birmingham's March 14 kickoff, Andrew Young, Ralph Abernathy, and Dorothy Cotton moved forward with other projects. The citizenship education program at Dorchester now had more applicants for teacher training than it could accommodate. The Field Foundation had promised an additional $250,000 to support the project for at least two more years after mid-1963. In Atlanta the ministers of Operation Breadbasket had chosen the baking industry as their first target for black employment gains. By mid-February, they had won formal agreements with five different bakeries that provided for several dozen new jobs and more than forty promotions.

Friction persisted, however, between SCLC and the VEP staff, who remained dissatisfied with SCLC's voter registration reports. Jack Minnis and Wiley Branton had pressed Andrew Young for the proper documents throughout December and January without satisfaction. Consequently, VEP withheld payment of the scheduled second half of SCLC's grant. Early in February, Branton raised the issue with King, explaining that "the VEP staff considered SCLC as being in a state of suspension in so far as their right to receive the unpaid balance of their grant was concerned." King expressed surprise that such shortcomings had arisen, and promised to remedy the problem immediately.

In fact, Branton knew that SCLC's voter registration shortcomings went beyond a lack of reporting. As Minnis and others could document, SCLC had done nothing in many of its assigned areas. In five northern Louisiana parishes around Shreveport, there was no evidence of activity. The same was true in Tallahassee, Chattanooga, and five counties in northeastern North Carolina. Herbert Coulton's work in Virginia deserved praise, but in nineteen Georgia counties assigned it, "SCLC either has not tried to or has failed to stimulate local leadership," Minnis observed. Even in Montgomery, supposedly an SCLC stronghold, Young admitted that voter registration was "floundering in confusion." Surveying the entire SCLC situation in mid-February, Branton observed that "it appears that they simply have not been carrying on a registration program during this period consistent with the terms of the grant and the objectives of the project."

On Thursday, February 28, Leslie Dunbar of the Southern Regional Council and Branton met with King and his assistants to discuss SCLC's problem. King admitted that SCLC had not met its obligations. He promised that the organization would do better in the future, and explained that SCLC was hiring a new Louisiana field secretary, Major Johns, plus a full-time staffer in eastern North Carolina, Golden Frinks. Young promised that the organization would conform to the reporting requirements in the future. The meeting ended on an upbeat note, and Branton released the check for the second half of the grant.[3]

That evening two events distracted King and Walker from their discussions of Birmingham. First, there were news reports that the Kennedy administration had sent to Congress a modest voting rights message calling for legislation to authorize speedier trials of voting discrimination cases. King greeted the move with ambivalence, subsequently telling Stanley Levison that this half-hearted initiative was further evidence of the administration's "schizophrenic tendency" on civil rights. They acted friendly, but they appointed segregationist judges like Elliott, and they had shown no desire to press for congressional action. "Kennedy has often said to me," King told Stanley, that "there is no point in introducing strong civil rights legislation because you can't get it through."

Hours later word came from Greenwood, Mississippi, that a car carrying two SNCC workers, Robert Moses and Jimmy Travis, plus VEP staffer Randolph T. Blackwell, had been shot up by white night riders. Travis had suffered serious wounds but was expected to recover. SNCC staffers immediately converged on Greenwood, and movement activists were again reminded that the possibility of being shot down was always present.

Two days before the mayoral election, King slipped into Birmingham to speak with several young ministers whom Wyatt Walker had contacted during trips back and forth from Atlanta. Walker had selected three downtown stores—Loveman's, Pizitz's, and Britt's—as primary targets for direct action. A group of federal buildings near the post office was a secondary target, and a suburban shopping center, Atlantic Mills, was a third possibility. Once the election was over, training of prospective demonstrators could begin. Tuesday night's election results, however, threw a sudden obstacle in SCLC's path. None of the three candidates won a majority, and a runoff between the two top finishers, Boutwell and Connor, would be held on April 2.

King and Walker wondered whether the protests should be postponed until after the runoff. Birmingham's black leaders advised them to wait, and King agreed. The local leaders breathed a sigh of relief. They worried that Connor might arrange a staged racial incident in advance of the runoff in order to stimulate segregationist voters. Shuttlesworth publicly announced that the ACMHR would undertake no demonstrations prior to the contest.[4]

While things remained on a back burner in Birmingham, King traveled north for a series of appearances to improve SCLC's finances before the protests got under way. In New York at the apartment of black entertainer Harry Belafonte, King described SCLC's Birmingham plans to a group of wealthy potential contributors, all of whom had been sworn to secrecy. He explained that when protests began, mass arrests would be all but certain, and that substantial monies for bail bonds would be needed. Many who were present pledged their help. Meanwhile, Fred Shuttlesworth pressed King for more detailed planning of the demonstrations and for more first-string targets beyond Walker's three department stores. "I am concerned that we have not clearly defined areas of action, points of emphasis, the degree of commitment, and the time and methods by which other groups will be allowed to participate," Shuttlesworth complained. He also asked King to think about "a broader scope of activities than just lunch counters. My feeling is that we should cover the waterfront—including Parks implementation (golf, Kiddie-Land), Roving squads to ride Taxis, Buses, etc.; Picketing if necessary, Marches, and even a Prayer meeting at City Hall." King and Walker, who appreciated the lessons of Albany better than Shuttlesworth did, stuck to their narrower focus. They also paid little attention to Shuttlesworth's understated warning that "some few Negroes are not for D. A. [direct action] at this time." In King's and Walker's minds, Birmingham's black community was ready for a concentrated protest campaign as soon as the mayoral election was past.[5]

Besides Birmingham, King was concerned with two other issues. First was the problem of Jack O'Dell's and Stanley Levison's alleged Communist affiliations and the firm warnings that continued to emanate from the Justice Department about them. Gandhi Society counsel Clarence Jones, upon whom King increasingly relied for assistance, pressed King several times in early 1963 to create a documentary record to explain O'Dell's continued affiliation with SCLC should the matter again appear in the press. At King's request, O'Dell prepared a private letter explaining his political past. O'Dell stated in the letter that while he had previously supported the Communist party program, "quite awhile before" joining SCLC, he had concluded that his prior belief that a "democratic reformation of the South . . . required a Communist movement in the South" was incorrect and "mistaken. . . . I no longer hold such a viewpoint, and neither do I have any Communist affiliation," O'Dell told King. Satisfied with that statement, Jones advised King that O'Dell's supposed "interim resignation" could be set aside, and that O'Dell could remain with SCLC because he "has no present communist affiliation whatsoever."

Although little is known about precisely what Stanley Levison told King concerning his Communist ties, come mid-March, Levison and several of his New York friends decided that the time had come to break their final connection to the American Communist party. On March 19, Levison arranged to have lunch with a longtime acquaintance, Communist financial functionary Lem Harris, to tell Harris that he and his friends were through with the CP. In a memorandum reporting that conversation, secretly furnished to the FBI by its two invaluable double agents in the Communist hierarchy, Jack and Morris Childs, Harris stated that "a whole group, formerly closely aligned to us, and over many years most generous and constant in their support, are now disenchanted." "The group had been continuing support out of habit and sentiment alone," but now they had decided that "the CP is 'irrelevant' and ineffective," and that they would give no further support to it. Levison, the FBI's wiretaps indicated, was pleased with the firm position he articulated to his unhappy old friend. "I was tough, and I think I established my firm view, firm position," Stanley told his twin brother, Roy Bennett, the next day. Though his ties to the party were now in the past, such evidence of his final disengagement did not persuade FBI officials, who continued to suspect that Stanley Levison might be a Soviet agent exerting substantial influence on the civil rights movement through his close friendship with Martin King.[6]

O'Dell and Levison aside, King also was nervous about his family life. He was spending nearly half his time away from home, and he was painfully aware that Coretta resented both his absence and his belief that it was his wife's job to remain home and take care of the family while he sacrificed his life to a cause many times more important than any one man's or one family's personal life. He tried to spend important holidays and the children's birthdays at home, but sometimes it was impossible. Even when he did get home, he was often exhausted from the unending stream of demands made of him. "Sometimes he would come home and say," Coretta recalled, " 'You know, I have at least twenty phone calls to make and most of them are long distance calls and they're from important people and I just can't get to them.' " And if he was not on the phone making calls, it was rare for more than a few moments to pass without an incoming call for him. "There was just no way for him to meet all of the demands," Coretta explained. "I tried to carry on the family as best I could and not bother him about many of the problems," but that lack of sharing resulted in tensions and resentments. Yolanda King, looking back on her childhood, remembered "a household where my mother basically called the shots because Daddy was away *so* often. She was running the house, she made all the decisions," because "he was not there to actively participate in those." By mid-March of 1963, Coretta was expecting their fourth child, and King was worried that Birmingham and other obligations might interfere with his being there for the birth. As it happened, King arrived back in Atlanta one day before Coretta gave birth to their second daughter, whom they christened Bernice Albertine.[7]

On April 2, Birmingham's voters went to the polls and gave Albert Boutwell a decisive eight thousand-vote victory over Bull Connor. Walker and Shuttlesworth made final plans for launching the first department store sit-ins the next morning, and King, busy in Atlanta with meetings about SCLC's voter registration troubles, planned to fly in the next afternoon. While Wednesday's *Birmingham News* celebrated Boutwell's win with a huge headline proclaiming NEW DAY DAWNS FOR BIRMINGHAM, two dozen protesters, many of them students from Miles College, initiated lunch-counter sit-ins at four stores. Bull Connor, still the public safety commissioner, announced that the demonstrators would be arrested only upon complaints by store managers, and by the end of the afternoon, over twenty had been taken into custody. That evening King and Ralph Abernathy joined Shuttlesworth at a mass meeting, where they told the crowd that it was the merchants' failure to keep their fall promises that necessitated protests now. "If you create enough tension you attract attention to your cause" and "get to the conscience of the white man," King explained. About seventy-five members of the audience volunteered to join future demonstrations. The volunteers then went into a back room with Walker, A.D. King, and James Lawson for training in nonviolence. The next morning another group of demonstrators descended on the downtown stores, and a handful were arrested. Puzzled reporters wondered why the protests were getting off to such a quiet start.

King asserted at a press conference that the small scale of activity had been planned. He denied rumors that the lack of larger demonstrations was because few Birmingham blacks wanted to join a jail-going protest. The key element in the movement's effort, he said, was a tight boycott of the white downtown stores, whose traditionally strong sales during the Easter season depended in good part upon black consumers. "The Negro has enough buying power in Birmingham," King stated,

> to make the difference between profit and loss in a business. This was not true in Albany . . . I think this is a real advantage and I think we must use this buying power to its most constructive ends in terms of withdrawing our economic support from businesses that will not respect our persons.

The boycott would be an inducement to Birmingham to grant the movement's six specific goals: desegregation of the store facilities; adoption of fair hiring practices by those stores; dismissal of all charges from previous protests; equal employment opportunities for blacks with the city government; reopening on a desegregated basis of Birmingham's closed municipal recreation facilities; and establishment of a biracial committee to pursue further desegregation. Although those goals received little coverage in news accounts of the campaign's debut, King emphasized the importance of the boycott at that evening's mass rally. Fifty more volunteers came forward, and ten were arrested during sit-ins the next morning. King stressed the boycott again at Friday's mass meeting, and thirty people agreed to join Shuttlesworth in a Saturday morning march to City Hall. To no one's surprise, the small band was arrested after moving only a few blocks.[8]

By that time it was clear to King that he had made several miscalculations about Birmingham. Despite public statements to the contrary, SCLC was finding it difficult to recruit the large number of potential demonstrators it had anticipated. The problem was rooted in Fred Shuttlesworth's controversial stature among Birmingham blacks, and the reluctance of many black citizens to help launch protests in the immediate wake of Boutwell's victory over Connor.

King had long known that many people found Shuttlesworth excessively autocratic. Some cited his often-expressed conviction that his civil rights activism was a mission given to him directly by God. As one sympathetic friend described him then, "Shuttlesworth sees himself as taking orders only from God who speaks to him and through him." Hence, he was "difficult for more sophisticated people to appreciate." Among Birmingham's black leaders, respect for Shuttlesworth's courage was universal, but respect for his judgment and emotional stability was not.

Although many tolerated his fanaticism, influential men like Pitts, Gaston, and ministerial conference President Rev. J. L. Ware were not willing to put up with Shuttlesworth's insistence that he alone was the leader of black Birmingham. As King's friend John Thomas Porter learned upon his arrival, Birmingham's civil rights movement, the ACMHR, "was a one man show. It was Fred all the way. He made decisions . . . he was just a dictator. That was his style." It was a style that grated on almost everyone in Birmingham's black middle class, people who never criticized Shuttlesworth publicly but kept their distance from ACMHR. His several hundred regular followers were individuals from less advantaged backgrounds who looked up to him as an exemplar of the fiery black southern preacher. Other ministers and most of the black professionals agreed that Shuttlesworth simply "could not work with people," as John Porter put it. "He told me once, 'Porter, this is *my* movement. You get in line or get out.'" It was an experience that many others had had, and it meant that Birmingham's black leaders had no enthusiasm for joining in an SCLC campaign that would put Fred Shuttlesworth forward as the black community's spokesman.[9]

Black antipathy toward Shuttlesworth was not the only problem King had failed to anticipate. Even more pressing was the feeling among several important constituencies—the black ministers, some of the professional people, the most sympathetic local whites, and the Kennedy administration—that Boutwell's victory was a compelling reason to delay the protests. These groups shared the hope that once a moderate administration took office, both the merchants and the city government would grant some of the movement's requests without demonstrations being necessary. A further consideration was that Birmingham momentarily was in the odd situation of having two competing city governments. Connor and his two fellow commissioners vowed that they would not surrender control until the terms to which they had been elected prior to the change of government plebiscite expired several years hence. It would take at least a month for the Alabama Supreme Court to resolve that claim, and until a decision was rendered, lame-duck Connor would remain in day-to-day control of the police.

While local blacks made that case to King in private, some ostensibly moderate Alabama whites were less circumspect. Father Albert S. Foley, chairman of the U.S. Civil Rights Commission's Alabama advisory committee, publicly criticized King's entry into Birmingham, asserting that voluntary desegregation of downtown facilities would have taken place shortly if blacks had been willing to wait. *Birmingham News* publisher Vincent Townsend phoned Burke Marshall to ask that federal officials intercede with King and request a postponement. Marshall reluctantly made the call, repeating to King the argument that Boutwell's election eliminated the need for protests. To Marshall, and to others who voiced similar contentions, King replied that he failed to see what there was to welcome about the polite advocacy of continued segregation that Boutwell had offered during his campaign. "We feel Mr. Boutwell will never desegregate Birmingham voluntarily," King said at his Thursday news conference, and Boutwell's victory "does not appear to materially affect the life of the Negro."[10]

Vowing to remedy what he admitted was the "tremendous resistance" of many local black leaders to mass demonstrations, King made personal pleas to influential figures. He also organized two important meetings for Monday and Tuesday, April 8 and 9, the first with more than one hundred of the city's black pastors and the second with a number of black business and professional leaders. In the meantime, the nightly mass rallies and SCLC's efforts to recruit additional demonstrators continued. King appeared at Saturday evening's mass meeting dressed in a pair of overalls, announced another march for Sunday, and vowed that he would be going to jail in the near future. The next day his brother A.D., led a small march, and for the first time, Bull Connor displayed one of the weapons that Walker had been hoping for: a squad of snarling police dogs. A large crowd gathered as police arrested the two dozen marchers. One black bystander lunged at a dog with a large knife. As *The New York Times* described it, "The dog immediately attacked and there was a rush of other Negroes toward the spot where the dog had pinned the man to the ground. Policemen with two more dogs and other policemen who were congregated in the area quickly rushed against the crowd, swinging clubs." The black onlookers dispersed, but the crowd's presence and the officers' use of the dogs and clubs had given Walker the sort of incident he had been looking for. Just a day or two earlier, King had said to him, "Wyatt, you've got to find some way to make Bull Connor tip his hand" and show the movement and the press the kind of brutal tactics local blacks knew he was capable of. Although Walker had taken to calling the Birmingham campaign "Project C," for "confrontation," he had told King, "I haven't found the key yet, but I'm going to." Now, the chance gathering of that late-afternoon crowd, and one man's unrestrainable anger toward the police dogs, had suddenly given the movement the national coverage King and Walker had been seeking. Walker thought that their problems in recruiting demonstrators were solved, that crowds of black bystanders could give the protests the "mass" quality that staff recruiters had not yet been able to produce. He reached King by phone, and informed him excitedly, "I've got it. I've got it." From now on, if demonstrations took place when the black populace was present and ready to look on, press reports would portray mass community support for the protests even if no more than a few dozen marchers had been recruited. SNCC's James Forman encountered Walker and Dorothy Cotton at the SCLC headquarters, the Gaston Motel, soon after Walker made that realization, and was appalled at their joy over the day's events. They "were jumping up and down, elated," Forman later wrote. "They said over and over again, 'We've got a movement. We've got a movement. We had some police brutality. They brought out the dogs. We've got a movement.'" To Forman, this celebration "was a disgusting moment . . . for it seemed very cold, cruel and calculating to be happy about police brutality coming down on innocent people, bystanders, no matter what purpose it served." Walker's enthusiasm was soon tempered, however, when he realized that these "helpful" events were dependent upon the movement having at least some protesters, a problem made no less pressing by Sunday's violent clash.[11]

King took a major step toward surmounting that obstacle with a persuasive appearance before the large group of black ministers on Monday. He apologized for not having consulted with them earlier about the protests, but explained that the need for secrecy had been paramount. He argued that the time for protests had come, and that the black community should not allow internal disunity to halt the movement. He repeated those contentions the next day to the gathering of black professionals, who also responded positively. The crowds at both the Monday and Tuesday night mass meetings were larger and more enthusiastic. Late Tuesday, following the arrest of another small group of protesters, word spread that Reverend Ware's Baptist Ministers' Conference had voted unanimously to support the protests and that wealthy businessman A. G. Gaston also was ready to declare his support.

King's ability to bring the black leadership to his side, and his declarations at the evening rallies that he intended to get arrested, led the white business community to launch one more effort to forestall large-scale protests. Sidney Smyer, the key white negotiator, arranged to meet secretly with Shuttlesworth, who had been released from jail the day before. Believing he was in a position of strength, Shuttlesworth told Smyer that whites would have to grant all of the movement's requests, plus commit themselves to prompt school desegregation, in order to avoid mass demonstrations. Smyer demurred and emphasized that the merchants could not speak for Boutwell or the city. Given the governmental confusion, there was no way that any official negotiations could be undertaken, he explained.[12]

Although the Wednesday issue of Birmingham's black newspaper, the World, decried direct action as "both wasteful and worthless," that editorial evaluation was outweighed by Gaston's declaration of support. King told the Wednesday night mass meeting that on Friday, "Ralph Abernathy and I will make our move. I can't think of a better day than Good Friday for a move for freedom," and a move toward jail. At virtually the same moment, two city attorneys asked State Circuit Court Judge William A. Jenkins, Jr., to issue a temporary injunction against King and other movement leaders barring all marches or other protests. Jenkins signed the request at 9:00 P.M., and four hours later the court order was served on King, Abernathy, and Shuttlesworth.

King was not surprised by the court order. In private, King had often lamented how Elliott's order had defused Albany's summer protests, and he vowed that it would not happen again. If a state court injunction were issued in Birmingham, he would defy it, and even another federal order would not halt the movement. The only question was whether King himself should march in defiance of the court's ban, or whether others should lead the protests. King wanted to march, so after a brief night's sleep he told a Thursday press conference that he and Abernathy would lead a Good Friday procession to City Hall in defiance of Jenkins's injunction. Seventeen more sit-in protesters were arrested during the day, bringing the total for the campaign to 160. In a chance encounter with Shuttlesworth, Public Safety Commissioner Connor remarked that the city would work him "real hard" if he gave them the opportunity. Shuttlesworth responded that he would wear his overalls to save Birmingham the cost of a set of jail work clothes.

At Thursday night's mass meeting Daddy King exhorted the crowd to put their bodies on the line for the movement. Miles College's sole white professor, Robert Brank Fulton, told the audience he would be marching with King on Friday, and Abernathy said that the time for jail had come. He joked about how the "doohickey," the small electronic transmitter that state agents had placed in the pulpit, would not help Bull Connor much, and the crowd responded with an enthusiasm that had marked few if any of the previous rallies. New volunteers stepped forward, among them a large young man who had graduated from Parker High School, James Orange, who now would help recruit others.[13]

King did not speak at the Thursday rally. He remained closeted at the Gaston Motel, where word had reached him that the movement's bail-bond funds were all but depleted. If those accounts were not replenished, there would be no way to reassure prospective demonstrators that they would not have to spend weeks or perhaps months in jail. Even of those who were willing to undergo arrest, few could afford lengthy imprisonment. King spoke with Clarence Jones and Harry Belafonte in New York, but there was no guarantee that the money could be raised overnight. It might be necessary for King to return north in order to generate those funds, and if so, he had better not get arrested for violating Jenkins's order. King pondered his options throughout Thursday night, then asked the SCLC staff and the local leaders to meet with him the next morning to discuss the situation. At 8:30 A.M. Friday, some two dozen people gathered in King's room. King sat at the head of the bed and outlined the problem to his colleagues. There were protesters in jail who had been promised they would be bailed out in less than a week, and for whom there were no monies to secure their release. Anyone else arrested would be in a similar fix. King felt he had a responsibility to keep the promises the movement had made to these people. However, there were other considerations. He had been telling everyone for a week now that he would be arrested. The campaign had not caught fire, and King hoped that his arrest would inspire black citizens who had not yet made a commitment to the movement. Then King sat back to listen to his colleagues' opinions. As the discussion progressed, a consensus emerged: No matter whether King got arrested or stayed out, the movement was in trouble. If he backed off, it would look like Albany. Any judge willing to sign an order could stop King in his tracks and immobilize the campaign. Perhaps that would allow him to raise the funds, but there might not be a Birmingham movement left in which to use them if the protests came to an end because of Jenkins. Alternatively, if King did submit to arrest, there was no guaranteeing when he would be released, and he would be cut off from contact with movement colleagues. Either way, his choice might result in disaster. He was uncertain what to do, and later remarked that "a sense of doom began to pervade the room."

Deeply troubled, King told his colleagues he would pray over the decision alone in another room. He left, and the others waited for his return. Thirty minutes later, King reappeared wearing a new pair of blue-denim overalls. The group quieted, and King spoke with firmness. "The path is clear to me. I've got to march. I've got so many people depending on me. I've got to march." The injunction would have to be disobeyed. "If we obey it, then we are out of business." As some remembered it, Daddy King was one of the first to speak up. "Son, I've never interfered with any of your civil rights activities, but I think at this time my advice would be to you to not violate the injunction." King let his father finish, then said no, there were other things more important than the injunction.With a downcast look, Dad acquiesced.

It was well past noon, and King and Abernathy hurried to Sixth Avenue Zion Hill Baptist Church, where the march would begin. Only fifty movement supporters stood ready to join the Good Friday pilgrimage. The group set out for City Hall in a double-file column, the two SCLC leaders at the front. They moved at a moderate pace, with curious onlookers bringing up the rear and Wyatt Walker striding alongside, camera in hand, ready to photograph whatever transpired. Four and a half blocks from their starting point they met a squad of Connor's officers ready to block their advance. A paddy wagon pulled up, the marchers were placed under arrest, and within moments they were on their way to the downtown city jail. Photos showing an apprehensive-looking King, clad in his blue overalls and being led to the wagon, were flashed around the world.[14]

At that evening's mass meeting, Wyatt Walker called for student supporters to rally on Saturday morning and for volunteers to "test" segregated white churches on Sunday. Earlier that day, he noted, just hours before King's arrest, some of Birmingham's most liberal white churchmen had condemned the protests as "unwise and untimely" and had urged "our own Negro community to withdraw support from these demonstrations." They had lashed out at "outsiders," and had asserted that black demands "should be pressed in the courts and in negotiations among local leaders, and not in the street." The ministers failed to mention that almost every white church in Birmingham refused to admit black worshipers, and also omitted any reference to the undependable track record of white negotiators over the past year. It was hard to believe that the white churchmen were being anything other than disingenuous by publicly reprimanding the *black* leadership for Birmingham's lack of biracial negotiations.

At the city jail, King was placed in solitary confinement, cut off from contact even with Abernathy. He expected some word from the movement's lawyers, but the long night passed without news from anyone on the outside. Jail going had always been extremely difficult for King, even when Abernathy accompanied him, but the loneliness of solitary confinement and absence of outside contact made it considerably more painful. King said later that first night in the Birmingham jail represented some of "the longest, most frustrating and bewildering hours I have lived . . . I was besieged with worry."[15]

Unbeknownst to King, movement attorney Norman Amaker tried to see him at the jail Friday evening. The jailers told Amaker he could meet with King only with guards present. Amaker had protested this denial of a private conversation and refused to accept a monitored one. At about 11:00 P.M., Amaker told Wyatt Walker what had transpired, and Walker was infuriated. Near midnight, Walker called Burke Marshall at home to ask for federal help. Marshall promised to make inquiries, and later in the morning Walker sent a telegram to President Kennedy: WE ASK THAT YOU USE THE INFLUENCE OF YOUR HIGH OFFICE TO PERSUADE THE CITY OFFICIALS OF BIRMINGHAM TO AFFORD AT LEAST A MODICUM OF HUMAN TREATMENT to King and Abernathy. John Kennedy had heard news reports of King's imprisonment and called Marshall to inquire about the Birmingham situation. Marshall explained to the president, as he had to reporters, that no grounds existed for federal action. By late Saturday afternoon, movement attorneys made contact with King, but questions of further access and of King's opportunity to speak by phone with people on the outside remained unresolved. Wyatt Walker knew a good issue when it was placed in his lap, so on Sunday morning he told a concerned Coretta King that they should take additional steps to draw attention to the troubling conditions under which her husband was being held. Coretta suggested she issue a statement, but Walker recommended that she call President Kennedy instead. Mrs. King demurred, saying they should get a note to her husband asking his judgment before they tried that. Walker consented but had no success in getting the message through. Later in the day he called Coretta back, reported that he had been unable to make any contact with King, and encouraged her to phone the White House. She agreed, calling both there and at Vice-President Lyndon Johnson's office without getting through to anyone. Finally, an operator connected her with presidential press secretary Pierre Salinger, who was in Florida with his boss. Salinger promised to pass along her message, and forty-five minutes later Attorney General Robert Kennedy phoned

Mrs. King. He expressed the administration's concern and said that the Justice Department would make inquiries in Birmingham about the conditions of her husband's imprisonment.

At the time those phone calls were taking place, King's brother, A.D., tried to lead a small march from Sixteenth Street Baptist Church to the jail. The thirty participants were arrested before getting very far, but just like one week earlier, an angry crowd gathered while the police were waiting for their paddy wagons to arrive. Officers arrested one onlooker, and were showered with rocks by other bystanders. The police moved in with clubs, and the crowd dispersed. Once again those police tactics received prominent coverage in Monday's national newspapers.

Although Bull Connor personally blocked movement attorneys from seeing King at midafternoon Sunday, by the end of the day lawyers Arthur Shores and Orzell Billingsley were allowed to meet with him. They told King that there was no good news yet on the financial front, but that Clarence Jones would be arriving from New York on Monday. King was worried about the movement's lack of bail money when he was arraigned in court the next morning but later that afternoon Jones arrived at the jail to report that Belafonte and other supporters had obtained sufficient funds for SCLC to meet all the bail costs. King was relieved, and relaxed for the first time since his arrest. His faith that Friday's decision would somehow prove correct had been justified. Meanwhile, movement attorneys filed an application to dissolve Jenkins's injunction banning all protests, and the city's lawyers petitioned the judge to hold King and his colleagues in contempt for defying that edict.[16]

On Monday afternoon, without warning, came just the event Walker had been hoping for ever since Friday's arrests: John Kennedy phoned Coretta King to express his concern about her husband's imprisonment and to assure her that FBI agents had ascertained he was safe. Furthermore, Kennedy said, it had been arranged for King to phone her, and she should await his call. Thirty minutes later, a somewhat puzzled King was told by his jailers that he could call home. He was pleased, but surmised correctly that the phone was tapped and that whatever he and his wife said would not be private. After initial greetings, he assured Coretta that he was doing "pretty good," and she eagerly told him what had transpired. "I just got a call from the President and he told me you were going to call me in a few minutes." Yoki and Marty came on the line, interrupting at that point, and King spoke with them before asking Coretta about her earlier comment.

"Who did you say called you?"

"Kennedy, the president."

"Did he call you direct?"

"Yes, and he told me you were going to call in a few minutes. It was about thirty minutes ago. He called from Palm Beach. I tried to phone him yesterday."

"Is that known?"

"It's known here; I just got it."

"Let Wyatt know."

"The executive in Birmingham?"

"Yes, do that right now."

King was elated at John Kennedy's gesture and wanted to be certain that news of it was disseminated quickly. He asked his wife about their new baby, Bernice, and reassured her that his own spirit was "all right." Coretta told him of the FBI inquiries, which King had not heard about, and mentioned her phone conversation with Robert Kennedy the night before. She thought he might call back today, but instead "it was the President himself, and he assured me of his concern. He asked if we had any complaints and said if we did to be sure and let them know." King responded:

"Be sure and get that to the Reverend. I think it will make a very good statement."

"He's very sympathetic and kept saying, 'How are you, I understand you have a little baby.' He said things might get better with the new [city] administration. This is a problem."

"Is it being carried well [by the press]?"

"Not too well here, still not too well. There was a good program today with Dick Arnell."

"What about the *Constitution*? . . ."

"They have been carrying articles. Yesterday they had something. . . . The *[Atlanta Daily] World* has had front page about every day recently, but it was not accurate. They said the boycott was not effective. There was something this morning about yesterday. It's been carried pretty good. They had a picture last night of A.D. [King]. I think with the national it's been pretty good; it's been pretty good today."

"When you get this over it will help."

Coretta explained she would travel to Birmingham on Thursday, and King asked her to give his greetings to his parents. He assured his wife that the jail food was "all right," and told her there was nothing she needed to bring him. "I'll probably come out in the next day or so. Be sure to get in touch with the Reverend. I think this gives it a new dimension."

Coretta notified Wyatt Walker of these developments, and Walker announced the news of John Kennedy's phone call to that evening's mass rally. Newsmen reported it, and Birmingham police officials denied there had been federal pressure to allow King to make his call. The decision, they claimed, had been entirely their own. Walker also announced that the Birmingham campaign would move into its second phase, with primary efforts being directed toward voter registration. Asked by reporters to explain the shift from integrating lunch counters to voting, Andrew Young said that "this is the only way we can get the Justice Department in on this."[17]

On Thursday afternoon Coretta King and Juanita Abernathy visited their husbands. They found them in good spirits. King explained he had been spending much of his time composing a response to the criticisms of the protests voiced by local white religious leaders a week earlier. Attorneys Shores, Billingsley, and Jones had been visiting King daily, and had been passing the handwritten sheets to Walker, who would go over them each evening and then have them typed up by his secretary, Willie Pearl Mackey. The typescripts would be sent back to King for editing. Shortly after Coretta's visit, Walker phoned Burke Marshall to say that the black leadership would like him to meet with Fred Shuttlesworth the next morning in Washington. Marshall granted the appointment but reiterated both to Shuttlesworth and SCLC's Walter Fauntroy that no grounds for federal action existed. Shuttlesworth returned to Birmingham in time for Friday night's mass meeting, and announced to the crowd that King and Abernathy would be leaving jail voluntarily on Saturday. When they were released, the two men were blocked from holding an impromptu press conference at the jail, but told reporters afterward that although they would be heading to Atlanta that night in order to preach at their respective churches the next morning, they would return to Birmingham almost immediately and the protest campaign would go forward.[18]

Monday morning, April 22, King and fourteen others went on trial before Judge Jenkins on the charge of violating his injunction. The proceedings continued through Wednesday afternoon, with defense attorneys winning dismissal of the charges against four defendants on the grounds that they had never been served with the order. Otherwise, Jenkins gave short shrift to the lawyers' efforts to set forth the constitutional infirmities of his injunction. When not in court, King and his colleagues spent much of their time discussing the best avenues for appealing Jenkins's decision once the expected guilty verdicts were announced, and how to continue the protests in the wake of that outcome. King told one midweek mass meeting that he expected to be sent back to jail, and that he was prepared for that burden. "I would rather stay in jail the rest of my days than make a butchery of my conscience. . . . I'm ready to go to jail with my colleagues; I will die there if necessary." James Bevel of SCLC and Isaac "Ike" Reynolds from CORE were training youths for future demonstrations, and on Thursday, white intermediary Sidney Smyer and two young lawyers, David Vann and Erskine Smith, indicated to the local black leadership that meaningful biracial negotiations might soon be in the offing. That same day, King had an unsatisfactory meeting with several local white ministers. He felt that their criticism of the movement was one more indication of the southwide failure of white clergy to play a positive role in reforming the region's morally repulsive racial practices. These Birmingham clergy had asserted that black leaders were not interested in negotiating, but King pointed out that the disinterest in meaningful talks lay with the whites. "The purpose of . . . direct action is to create a situation so crisis-packed that it will inevitably open the door to negotiation. . . . We who engage in nonviolent direct action are not the creators of tension. We merely bring to the surface the hidden tension that is already alive. We bring it out in the open where it can be seen and dealt with." The movement's efforts to do just that, King made clear at that Thursday session, would go forward aggressively.[19]

On Friday morning, Judge Jenkins announced that all eleven defendants were guilty of criminal contempt. He sentenced each of them to five days in jail and a $50 fine. The sentences would be held in abeyance while appeals were pursued. King told the crowd at that evening's mass meeting that they must continue the boycott of the downtown stores and expand their efforts to integrate worship services at Birmingham's white churches. King had a Sunday preaching engagement in Little Rock, Arkansas, but Walker and Bevel continued to recruit more young demonstrators for future protests. Saturday's rally marked the twenty-fifth consecutive night on which the movement had held a mass meeting, but this time the crowd was small and showed little promise of furnishing the numbers of protesters Walker had hoped for. Black "testers" were admitted to nine of thirty-eight white churches on Sunday morning, and King canceled a speech in Houston to return to Birmingham on Monday. Movement leaders met that day to discuss their next steps, and to hear Bevel and Reynolds argue that the movement's shortage of demonstrators could be remedied if organizers enlisted the hundreds of black high school students who were eager to participate in direct-action protests. Several local black adults who sat on the advisory board, or "central committee," that had been set up as part of King's entreaties earlier in the month opposed the use of teenagers, but Bevel was more persuasive. National news coverage of Birmingham had all but vanished over the past few days, and King was worried that national newsmen would leave town. "You know, we've got to get something going. The press is leaving, we've got to get going," King told John Thomas Porter, who was astounded by King's emphasis on pragmatic rather than spiritual considerations. "'We've got to pick up everything, because the press is leaving.' And I looked at him," Porter recalled, "and really couldn't believe my ears to hear him say that we need the press." King spoke with some urgency, and his SCLC associates agreed that "the press is losing interest. We've got to do something to get their attention again." Bevel's plan for using the high school students would do just that, and Walker endorsed it enthusiastically. "We needed more troops. We had run out of troops. We had scraped the bottom of the barrel of adults who could go," Walker later explained. "We needed something new," and Bevel's proposal fit the bill. Though King held back from giving authorization for the use of student demonstrators, he endorsed the suggestion that interested students be told to gather at Sixteenth Street church at noon Thursday.[20]

By midday Tuesday, scores of leaflets were circulating in Birmingham's black high schools urging students to join Thursday's gathering. Worried local FBI agents warned the city's police intelligence squad commander, Maurice House, and two white detectives who attended that evening's mass rally reported that Bevel had given clear indications that some big plans were on tap for Thursday. Although King, Walker, Shuttlesworth, and Abernathy left town overnight for a fund-raising rally in Memphis, Bevel, Reynolds, Dorothy Cotton, and Andrew Young spent all of Tuesday and Wednesday spreading the word about the Thursday action. Shortly before noon on Thursday the leaders gathered. Sixteenth Street church was packed with hundreds of eager youngsters. Connor's forces were deployed alongside Kelly Ingram Park, a square-block expanse of greenery marking the symbolic dividing line between the black district and white downtown. An effort by officials at Parker High School to detain their pupils backfired as scores jumped over fences to head for Sixteenth Street. Although King was hesitant about unleashing the untrained teenagers, especially when black adults were arguing that children should not be used as the shock troops of the movement, Bevel and Walker knew it was no time for hesitation. Shortly after noon, while King remained closeted at the Gaston Motel, the first wave of youngsters headed out the door of Sixteenth Street church in a brave pilgrimage to City Hall. Singing and laughing, the several hundred teenagers willingly submitted to arrest at the hands of Birmingham's police. After the first wave of students had been taken into custody and driven away, a second group marched out of Sixteenth Street church, and then a third. James Bevel was in direct command of the young troops, although Wyatt Walker served as overall field general, coordinating tactical moves with Bevel, Young, and others through a system of walkie-talkies. Walker was optimistic that the young masses, and the attendant interest of black adults, would be just what was needed to evoke segregationist brutality from the trigger-tempered Connor. Walker wanted to mount as strong an effort as possible, and did not shy from employing a wide variety of tactics, some of which he did not reveal to King. One example, Walker said later, was dispatching "eight or ten guys to different quarters of the town to turn in false alarms." Connor was trying to mass both the police and the hoses of the city's fire companies in the area between the protesters and downtown, and Walker's tactics were aimed at depleting Connor's forces. Very few had knowledge of such efforts, but in subsequent years Walker made no apologies for employing tactics he felt would be effective for revealing to the entire nation the racist brutality of Connor and the system he represented. "I had to do what had to be done," Walker explained. "At times I would accommodate or alter my morality for the sake of getting a job done . . . I did it consciously. I felt I had no choice. I wasn't dealing with a moral situation when I dealt with a Bull Connor." "We did with design precipitate crises, crucial crises in order to expose what the black community was up against," Walker said. "There was premeditation and calculated design in that for which I don't think we ever made any apologies." King and Walker were reticent about their pragmatism, even in private, and Walker purposely kept some of the specifics from his boss. "Dr. King never knew that I sent people to turn in false alarms . . . that's one thing I was very guarded about, because I knew he would not want to do that." Thursday afternoon, while King continued to ponder using the children, Walker and Bevel proved within several hours that the decision had been one of the wisest SCLC had made.[21]

By Thursday night more than five hundred young marchers had been taken into custody, and Birmingham was again in the headlines. More than two thousand people crowded into that evening's mass meeting. King and his colleagues met late into the night discussing more youth marches for Friday. The next morning King told reporters that Friday afternoon's demonstrations would be even more massive than Thursday's. "We intend to negotiate from strength. If the white power structure of this city will meet some of our minimum demands, then we will consider calling off the demonstrations, but we want promises, plus action." In midafternoon, another column of young demonstrators marched out of Sixteenth Street church and headed east toward Connor's officers. At the front of the ranks stood fire fighters equipped with high-pressure hoses, ready to repulse any protesters who attempted to evade the blockade. Black onlookers gathered along the fringes of Kelly Ingram Park, and some hurled verbal taunts at the white officers. Connor was on the scene, and ordered six police dogs deployed to force the crowd back. The sight of the snarling dogs further roused the hostility of the onlookers, and rocks and bottles began to sail out of the crowd toward the police and firemen. Then Connor ordered the dogs into action, and instructed that the powerful hoses be used to drive the demonstrators and bystanders from the park. "I want to see the dogs work. Look at those niggers run," one newsman quoted Connor as yelling. Firemen used the hoses to chase protesters out of the park and away from nearby buildings; the high-pressure water literally tore the clothes off some victims' backs. After a half hour of this brutal and uneven combat, no black faces remained in Ingram Park. The movement's foot soldiers retreated to the church, and the hundreds of onlookers scattered.

Even before the ground in Ingram Park was dry, Burke Marshall was on the phone to King and others in Birmingham. He had called King that morning to question the wisdom of any further mass demonstrations, and now he remonstrated over the disorder that had erupted that afternoon. Marshall spoke also with *Birmingham News* publisher Vincent Townsend, black businessman A. G. Gaston, and Jefferson County Sheriff Mel Bailey. From all of them he heard that there were no ongoing biracial discussions, and that Birmingham's white leadership had no idea what concessions the blacks would require in order to halt the protests. Marshall later said he had found King rather vague on the movement's precise goals, but in addressing that evening's mass meeting, King stressed to the crowd and the many reporters present the protests' four principal aims: desegregation of the downtown stores, better job opportunities for blacks in those stores, dismissal of all charges against demonstrators, and establishment of a biracial negotiating committee to discuss school desegregation and other aspects of Birmingham life. King also announced that new demonstrations would take place on Saturday, and noted that Connor had one weapon in reserve behind his dogs and hoses: an armored military vehicle called the "tank," which appropriately was painted white.

Friday's clash made Saturday headlines across the country. Striking photographs of the snarling dogs and the high-pressure hoses appeared everywhere. One popular picture depicted a Birmingham officer holding a black citizen with one hand and a police dog's leash in the other while the dog attempted to sink its teeth into the man's stomach. News reports stated that three people had been treated at hospitals for dog bites, that five black children had been injured by the fire hoses or police clubs, and that one black woman bystander had accused police of knocking her down and kicking her in the stomach intentionally. Reactions to such images were strong, and members of one group that visited President Kennedy Saturday morning stated that the chief executive had said the photos made him "sick." Kennedy also mentioned that although he had no power to intervene, Burke Marshall and Assistant Deputy Attorney General Joseph Dolan were on their way to Birmingham to mediate.[22]

King was leery about Marshall coming to Birmingham. Perhaps, as in Albany, the Kennedy administration was interested not in winning greater racial justice, but in quieting racial trouble and getting those scenes of violence out of the national and international media. When Marshall arrived, however, King's worries dissipated. Marshall immediately met with Smyer, David Vann, Erskine Smith, and several of the downtown merchants to press for biracial talks and meaningful concessions. He told them he would not advise them what to do but would endeavor to be helpful. Marshall believed the black leadership would settle for less than it was demanding. He also understood that there was no possibility of persuading the local black leadership to break away from King and Shuttlesworth, as the whites hoped. Reputable lawmen explained that the involvement of black bystanders meant that the demonstrations were only loosely under SCLC's control, and that unrestrained combat could break out at any time. Additionally, the city's jails were full and it appeared likely that Connor would pursue a policy of violently dispersing the demonstrators rather than arrest people he could not imprison. The movement's long-proclaimed desire to "fill the jails" had become a reality. Faced with those circumstances, the white representatives felt that they had little choice but to take a step forward. They agreed that a larger, more representative group would meet with Marshall on Sunday to consider new negotiations with black representatives.

While Marshall had been prodding those moderate whites, James Bevel brought another column of young protesters up against Bull Connor's men on Saturday afternoon. The atmosphere was even tenser than on Friday, and a large crowd of onlookers taunted the police. Connor kept the police dogs in their kennel trucks, but the high-pressure fire hoses drove the throng out of Kelly Ingram Park. Angry members of the crowd threw rocks, and Bevel and other organizers used bullhorns to ask the black citizenry to disperse before further violence erupted. Photographs in Sunday papers across the country showed club-wielding officers pursuing drenched black citizens as they fled the scene.[23]

King and Walker were overjoyed at Connor's tactical stupidity and hoped it would continue. As Walker commented later:

> Bull Connor had something in his mind about not letting these niggers get to City Hall. I prayed that he'd keep trying to stop us. . . . Birmingham would have been lost if Bull had let us go down to the City Hall and pray; if he had let us do that and stepped aside, what else would be new? There would be no movement, no publicity. But all he could see was stopping us before we got there. We had calculated for the stupidity of a Bull Connor.

While Connor's allies in city government, outgoing Mayor Arthur Hanes and Police Chief Jamie Moore, thought he had lost his head, movement strategists such as Walker wondered if Connor was intentionally using such tactics to bolster his reputation with segregationist voters in preparation for a statewide political race. Chief Moore thought Connor did not care if his actions were winning sympathy and support around the globe for Birmingham's protesters. Connor's only priority was teaching those good-for-nothing agitators who was boss. Walker, on the other hand, presumed that Connor, like the movement's leaders, was more calculating than his public image indicated:

> He was a perfect adversary. Connor wanted publicity, he wanted his name in the paper. He believed that he would be the state's most popular politician if he treated the black violently, bloodily, and sternly. We knew that the psyche of the white redneck was such that he would inevitably do something to help our cause.[24]

King returned to Atlanta to preach at Ebenezer on Sunday. He was optimistic that Marshall's involvement would produce concessions from Birmingham's white leadership. "In a few days we will have everything we are asking and maybe more," he told his congregation. That afternoon, while Marshall continued his conversations with white businessmen, another mass march took place. This time, to the astonishment of participants and onlookers alike, Connor's men allowed the column, led by local minister Charles C. Billups, to pass through their lines without either dogs or hoses being used. James Bevel announced that there would be another protest on Monday, and speakers at Sunday night's mass rally reassured the crowd that the arrested teenagers were safe and that no one should engage in open hostility against Connor's officers.

Birmingham's merchants spent much of Sunday discussing how to resolve the crisis. At an afternoon meeting, the entire group reluctantly agreed that they had no choice but to make contact with the black leadership and try to halt the protests. "The idea of negotiation," one participant indicated, "was offensive to all present," but "the prospect of continued violence" was "an unpleasant and even more disastrous alternative." They emphasized to each other that they could negotiate only matters involving their own stores, and not city government issues, but they instructed Smyer and Vann to contact black businessman A. G. Gaston and ask for a meeting that night with black representatives. Gaston assented and the session was arranged. It began, one participant said, with "a free interchange of counter accusations of bad faith" between the two sides. Then the black representatives presented a brief document entitled "Points for Progress," which specified the movement's minimum demands. These were:

1. Immediate desegregation of all store facilities including lunch counters, rest rooms, and fitting rooms.

2. Immediate upgrading of store employees and a program of nondiscriminatory hiring.

3. Merchant pressure on city government to drop all charges against arrested demonstrators.

4. Merchant pressure on city government to establish [a] biracial committee to deal with future problems and to develop specific programs for the hiring of Negro policemen, removal of voter registration obstacles, school desegregation, reopening of all municipal facilities, and the desegregation of movies and hotels.

The white representatives declared that points three and four were not negotiable. They "absolutely refused to deal in any way with matters before the courts, or prerogatives of city government." Additionally, the representatives of some stores claimed they had already removed some segregation signs and begun upgrading their black employees. Furthermore, the whites said they could do nothing until the question of which administration was the real city government had been settled. On that negative note the session ended.[25]

Monday morning, Burke Marshall met with King for two hours to discuss the whites' position. Further conversations between the various parties continued throughout the day, and early in the afternoon more protesters confronted Connor's forces at the edge of Kelly Ingram Park. The police and firemen used neither dogs nor hoses, but arrested all the marchers. Wave after wave of young protesters willingly submitted to arrest, and by the end of the afternoon more than one thousand had been taken into custody. Birmingham no longer had any facilities in which to house them, so hundreds were placed into an uncovered outdoor pen with no protection from a chilly rain. SNCC's James Forman, trying to assume a role in the protests despite SCLC's hostility, argued to King that the leadership had to do something about that. After some angry words, King, Forman, and Bevel went to the stockade, after which King called Marshall to complain. Later, at the mass meeting, he reassured the crowd that the prisoners were being moved indoors.

The black and white negotiators met again Monday night. The merchants said they had five or six black employees who could be promoted to sales jobs immediately, and that stores with fitting rooms would integrate them. The whites wanted to delay desegregation of lunch counters and rest rooms until the federal courts compelled the city to begin desegregating its schools, but the blacks rejected this suggestion and argued that the counters be integrated right away *if* Boutwell's administration won the legal battle over which was the true city government. The discussion bogged down at that point, and both sides agreed to talk further on Tuesday.

Late Monday evening, after the black negotiators reported back, the movement's leaders began making plans for an intensification of demonstrations on Tuesday morning. Walker, Bevel, Dorothy Cotton, and Forman developed a scenario for replacing the standard pattern of several sequential waves of afternoon marchers with fifteen separate groups of protesters who would strike simultaneously at noontime, when most of the police were on their lunch break, in an effort to get a substantial number of young demonstrators into the heart of downtown Birmingham. With so many different groups heading downtown by a variety of routes, some no doubt would succeed in getting there.[26]

Tuesday morning, May 7, the white merchants met with Smyer, Vann, and Erskine Smith to mull over where they stood in the negotiations. The merchants believed they could satisfy the demand for upgraded jobs in the stores, but most remained opposed to lunch-counter integration before school desegregation began. More important, they felt that they could do nothing concerning the arrest charges or further biracial discussions about city government policies unless a larger group of white notables was drawn into the negotiations. If the merchants could offer nothing on those latter points to the black representatives, it was clear that no hope existed of ending the protests through negotiations. If there was no settlement, no one could predict what might happen. "Continued use of force on the demonstrators" would "aggravate the situation further," but the police could not make more arrests, for "there was no room in the jails," as one white negotiator explained. With considerable exasperation, the store owners agreed that they would have to ask all seventy-odd members of the "Senior Citizens Committee," a Chamber of Commerce-sponsored group established eight months earlier to push the change of government referendum, to meet that afternoon to discuss what to do. Sidney Smyer informed Burke Marshall, who immediately got on the phone to Washington to be certain that Kennedy administration officials would contact their acquaintances among Birmingham's Senior Citizens to urge that the white leadership authorize a comprehensive settlement.

By noontime Tuesday, movement staffers had six hundred young demonstrators ready to invade downtown Birmingham. King told newsmen that "demonstrations will go on until some progress has been made," and when the noon hour came, SCLC made good on King's promise. Catching the police off guard, the groups of protesters made it into the heart of the city without one person being arrested. Dozens of youngsters scampered through the business district, causing no damage but shattering whites' presumption that the protesters were not their problem and could be kept in check by lawmen. NEGRO MOBS BREAK THROUGH POLICE screamed that afternoon's edition of the *Birmingham News*. Anxious members of the Senior Citizens Committee worried what would come next as they assembled for the early-afternoon meeting. Sidney Smyer introduced Jefferson County Sheriff Mel Bailey, who explained that the day's events were evidence that the police had been stretched to the breaking point. He told them that another clash was now under way in Kelly Ingram Park between Connor's men and a second wave of protesters whom SCLC had attempted to send downtown. Smyer also introduced Burke Marshall, who recommended a negotiated peace. Several men spoke in favor of pursuing an agreement, and a reluctant consensus emerged that a settlement would have to be negotiated unless the city wanted to bring in state troopers or national guardsmen. "None of the Senior Citizens were anxious to urge a settlement," one participant later indicated, "but only a few preferred an apparently imminent declaration of martial law." The merchants asked that the larger body vote its consent for their negotiators to pursue a comprehensive settlement with the black leaders, and the eighty people did so with only two or three dissents. Everyone present understood that they were committing themselves to the desegregation of downtown facilities as soon as Boutwell's administration was victorious in the courts, and to support ongoing biracial discussions.[27]

Burke Marshall left the meeting extremely pleased. He called the White House to report that he expected a settlement could be won in a day or so's time. That sounded all the better in light of the continuing brutality Connor's forces had demonstrated that afternoon. After the successful noontime breakthrough into downtown Birmingham, King and Walker ordered a second attempt several hours later. This time, however, the police and firemen were waiting. An angry James Forman went to the Gaston Motel to ask King to call it off, since serious injuries seemed certain to result. King was on the phone; he had changed into his pajamas and was eating a steak for lunch. Forman took one look and gave up. He felt again how wide the gap had grown between the style of SNCC's field-workers and that of King's SCLC.

When the young demonstrators ventured toward Connor's men, the hoses were unleashed and black onlookers began to pelt the officers with bricks and bottles. The firemen used the high-powered water to drive the blacks back toward Sixteenth Street church, and movement staffers asked their troops to pull back. Fred Shuttlesworth was slammed against a wall by a blast from one hose and was carried away on a stretcher. Newsmen quoted Bull Connor expressing regret that Shuttlesworth had left in an ambulance and not a hearse. While many reporters distinguished between the movement's peaceful protesters and the violent bystanders, almost all observers could see that SCLC's staff had no way of maintaining control of the situation. Some accounts of the Tuesday afternoon clash bore headlines such as RIOTING NEGROES ROUTED BY POLICE, and King and his aides knew that that sort of national portrayal could harm the movement's cause.

Tuesday evening four white negotiators—Smyer, Vann, Edward Norton of Royal Crown Cola, and Roper Dial of Sears—met privately with L. H. Pitts, Arthur Shores, and SCLC's Andrew Young. Burke Marshall and Billy Hamilton, Boutwell's chief aide, also were present. In several hours time the small group reached agreement on the desegregation of the downtown stores, the upgrading of black employment opportunities, and the establishment of a committee for ongoing biracial discussions. Although total accord was not reached on the precise wording with which to announce those points, a fourth topic remained a serious obstacle: By what means would the hundreds of arrested demonstrators be released and the charges against them dropped? The whites were adamant that they could not arrange an amnesty, and the blacks were reluctant to concede this point and be faced with the massive financial obligations that the bonding and defense of some 2,600 people would entail. Though everyone present felt that the group was close to a settlement, the session broke up with no firm commitment except a promise to talk again on Wednesday.

A smaller circle of negotiators continued chatting late into the night at the home of black businessman John Drew. Andrew Young wanted the employment agreement to call for more than a few token black sales clerks, and to establish firm figures on future black representation in the stores' work forces. The actual debate, however, came down to a much narrower question: Would *each* of the stores agree to hire at least one black clerk, or would the stores *as a group* add a black employee or two? While the blacks wanted a firm agreement, the whites were frightened at the thought of Bull Connor's reaction to any black triumph. As one participant explained the dilemma, "How could a settlement be announced in terms specific enough for the Negroes to know that their demands were being fairly met, and yet vague enough so that white leaders would not be subject to attacks and their stores not subject to demonstration from the other side?" It was a difficult problem, but each side's representatives wanted to find a solution to the crisis.[28]

Midmorning Wednesday, the entire advisory committee of local blacks assembled to hear a progress report from the negotiators and movement leaders. Fred Shuttlesworth remained hospitalized, so in his absence King and L. H. Pitts framed the terms of the discussion. King believed that the

progress in the negotiations, and Tuesday's near riot, argued for a one-
day truce in demonstrations. Such a halt would signify the blacks' good
faith to the white negotiators, and perhaps hasten a settlement. If an
agreement was not won, demonstrations could resume Thursday, with
movement staffers better prepared to keep a tight rein on them. Pitts
agreed, and endorsed both the truce and the emerging terms of the settlement. Pitts recommended that the negotiators present the whites with a
detailed text for an agreement, then wait for their response. It would
specify desegregation of the stores immediately after Boutwell assumed
power, one new black clerk per store, and a firm commitment to ongoing
biracial discussions. "It is my candid opinion that if a truce is called with
the above beginnings of change and with a definite time schedule on desegregating of all store facilities and upgrading of employment practices
that we would be in a good position to effect continual change in the
community." Those present agreed, and King announced the one-day
moratorium on protests while the black negotiators resumed discussions
with their white counterparts. Release of the jailed demonstrators remained the principal topic. The black representatives also raised the
question of whether school authorities would seek administrative sanc-
tions against the many teenagers who had skipped classes in order to join
the protests. The conversations continued through the afternoon and into
the evening. In Washington, President Kennedy told reporters that he
welcomed the new developments, and added that the turmoil was
"damaging the reputation of both Birmingham and the country."[29]

One person who was not pleased by the truce was Fred Shuttlesworth,
who had left the hospital but remained under sedation at the Gaston
Motel. Early Wednesday afternoon, Shuttlesworth went to meet King at
the home of John and Addine Drew. Shuttlesworth was livid because
King had halted the demonstrations without notifying him. ACMHR's
fiery leader had always been more suspicious of Marshall's and the Kennedys' priorities than was his SCLC colleague. Now it appeared that
while Shuttlesworth had been hospitalized, King had caved in to pressure
from Marshall to accept dubious promises from the white negotiators.
Already unhappy with Marshall's role, and irritated that King had not
visited him in the hospital, Shuttlesworth erupted when King told him
that Wednesday's demonstrations had been called off. "'Say that again,
Martin,'" Shuttlesworth later recalled asking.

"Did I hear you right?" He said, "We have decided to call off the
demonstrations." I said, "Well, Martin, *who* decided?" He said, "Well,
we just decided that we can't have negotiations with all this going on."
I said, "Well, Martin, it's hard for me to see . . . how anybody could
decide that without me. . . . We're not calling anything off. . . ." And
he said, "Well, uh—" And I said, "Well, Martin, you know they *said* in
Albany that you come in, get people excited and started, and you leave
town." I said, "But I live here, the people trust me, and I have the

responsibility after SCLC is gone, and I'm telling you it will not be called off."

King interrupted, " 'Now Fred, you ought not to say it like that.' I said, 'Well, Martin, I have to say what's on my mind and speak the truth.' " He went on to lambast King for having disregarded their agreement that King, Abernathy, and Shuttlesworth would discuss developments at least once a day. " 'Where you spend your time and how, I haven't bothered, and it's gone on. . . . Maybe that's why you're in the predicament you're in now. . . . You're in a hell of a fix, young man.' " Someone interrupted to remind King he had scheduled a press conference. Shuttlesworth mocked him. "Oh, you've got a press conference? I thought we were to make joint statements. Well, I'll tell you what to do: you go ahead, I'm going home. You go ahead and do it."

Mrs. Drew tried to intervene, but Shuttlesworth cut her off. "Now Martin, you're mister big but you're soon to be mister nothing. You're going to fall from up here to down here, and you're dead. . . . Let me make it plain to you . . . I'm going back home . . . I'm going to wait until I see it on TV and hear it on the radio that you've called it off." Then Shuttlesworth said he would go to Sixteenth Street church and lead the youngsters back into the streets.

King looked hurt. Ralph Abernathy told Shuttlesworth he was ill and should go back to the hospital, but he would have none of it. Burke Marshall, who had watched in silence, feared the situation was unraveling and said, " 'We made promises to these people.' " Shuttlesworth shot back, "What promises did you make to what people? . . . Any promises that you made to anybody that I didn't approve . . . are not any good. I did not make any agreement that we're going to call off the demonstrations."

Through a doorway Shuttlesworth could hear one of Marshall's assistants on the phone, relaying word of the problem to Washington. "Tell President Kennedy he doesn't live down here, and I live down here, and the people trust us, and we're not calling the demonstrations off, no matter who calls you. Tell him King can't call it off, tell him he can't call it off, tell him I ain't going to call it off . . . I'm going home." King struggled to salvage the situation. " 'Wait a minute, Fred.' " Turning to Marshall, King said, " 'We got to have unity, Burke. We've just got to have unity.' " Shuttlesworth's feelings were not assuaged. "I'll be damned if you'll have it like this. You're mister big, but you're going to be mister S-H-I-T. I'm sorry, but I cannot compromise my principles and the principles that we established." With that, Shuttlesworth walked out.[30]

Another important figure who was not pleased with the truce was Bull Connor. Faced now with the likely loss of both his city post and his personal crusade to keep Birmingham segregated, Connor struck hard in a last-ditch effort to derail the talks. Late Wednesday afternoon, with no warning, Connor's officers confronted King and Abernathy with the news that the required value of the bonds on which they had been released three weeks earlier had been increased to $2,500 per person. The two men could pay up or return to custody. King and Abernathy declined to comply, and were taken to jail. That further enraged Fred Shuttlesworth. He announced that protests would resume immediately, and headed for Sixteenth Street church. Burke Marshall's subordinate, Joseph Dolan, physically waylaid the Birmingham leader and persuaded him to speak by phone with Robert Kennedy before returning to the streets. Meanwhile, Marshall and local black leaders quickly decided that the best way to blunt Connor's thrust was to post the money for King's and Abernathy's release. Within minutes businessman A. G. Gaston wrote out the checks, and King and Abernathy returned to the motel.

While the negotiations continued into Wednesday evening, King, under pressure from Shuttlesworth, told reporters that demonstrations would resume on Thursday if an agreement was not reached by 11:00 A.M. Thursday morning. The hour came and passed with no settlement and no marches. King told the news media that the truce had been extended while the talks continued. He acknowledged that tentative agreement had been reached on desegregating the stores and continuing the biracial discussions, but that neither the details of the employment accord nor the terms for the release of the jailed protesters had been finalized. The major obstacle was securing the several hundred thousand dollars that would be necessary to meet bail costs for the jailed demonstrators. The white representatives refused to budge on this point, and by midday Thursday both the black negotiators and Marshall realized that the movement would have to come up with the money. Gaston was willing to guarantee some of it, but Marshall and Robert Kennedy had to lend their assistance to secure the remainder. Contact was made with United Auto Workers President Walter Reuther and with the UAW's Washington attorney, Joseph L. Rauh, and four different labor organizations promised to supply $40,000 each to help meet the costs. With those commitments in hand, Rauh wired a guarantee for $160,000 to white Birmingham attorney Erskine Smith. That settled, David Vann, Andrew Young, and several others worked late into Thursday night finalizing the text of a "Birmingham Truce Agreement." The whites' fears dictated that the document not be released publicly, but all agreed that King could announce the general terms of the settlement sometime Friday.[31]

The completed document intentionally papered over one specific demand that the negotiators had not resolved: the number of black sales clerks to be hired by the downtown stores. In their effort to reach an agreement, both sides had chosen to ignore that particular problem. However, the agreement did give the movement some of what it had been seeking on three of the four principal points: store desegregation, upgraded employment, and ongoing biracial talks. The movement's concession to pay the bail costs to secure the release of its protesters was not a part of the formal text. In full, the accord provided that:

1. Within three days after the close of demonstrations, fitting rooms will be desegregated.

2. Within thirty days after the city government is established by court order, signs on wash rooms, rest rooms and drinking fountains will be removed.

3. Within sixty days after the city government is established by court order, a program of lunchroom counter desegregation will be commenced.

4. When the city government is established by court order, a program of upgrading Negro employment will be continued and there will be meetings with responsible local leadership to consider further steps.

Within sixty days from the court order determining Birmingham's city government, the employment program will include at least one sales person or cashier.

Within fifteen days from the cessation of demonstrations, a Committee on Racial Problems and Employment composed of members of the Senior Citizens Committee will be established, with a membership made public and the publicly announced purpose of establishing liaison with members of the Negro community to carry out a program of upgrading and improving employment opportunities with the Negro citizens of the Birmingham community.

After a final meeting of the negotiators Friday morning, it was announced that King would meet with the press at noon. True to the many inside jokes about how the movement in general and King in particular operated on "CPT," or "colored people's time," meaning several hours late, it was not until 2:30 P.M. that King, Abernathy, Shuttlesworth, and Wyatt Walker appeared in the courtyard of the Gaston Motel. Shuttlesworth, carefully accorded the lead role by the SCLC contingent, read a prepared statement detailing the settlement. King then read a statement of his own, praising Shuttlesworth's courageous leadership, calling the white negotiators "men of good will," and characterizing the accord as "a great victory" for the movement. King and Abernathy added that SCLC would launch an intensive voter registration drive in Birmingham. As King spoke, an exhausted Shuttlesworth collapsed. Then the press conference continued, and later that afternoon Sidney Smyer released a statement acknowledging that the white business leadership had agreed to the settlement in the interest of restoring civic peace.[32]

That night at a celebratory rally King pledged that the agreement would be enforced and that biracial discussion of school desegregation, the reopening of city parks, and the hiring of black policemen would commence within two weeks. Although he and Abernathy would return to Atlanta over the weekend to preach in their churches, King promised that they would be back in Birmingham on Monday and that SCLC would not be leaving town; SCLC staff workers would launch the new voter registration effort the next week. This time, King suggested, he and his organization would not leave themselves open to charges that they abandoned local communities as soon as the headline events had passed.

Saturday morning, King chatted with several interviewers at the Gaston Motel before returning to Atlanta. While many press commentators and some movement activists were questioning whether SCLC had settled for too little in the negotiated accord, King reiterated his view that the settlement was a commendable one. Most of his colleagues in the Birmingham leadership agreed. Just before King left Birmingham, he offered SCLC's Joseph Lowery the use of his motel room. Lowery accepted, since he had a speaking engagement the next day in north Alabama and planned to stay in Birmingham rather than return home to Nashville.

That evening, while the movement's regular rally was taking place at A. D. King's First Baptist Church in suburban Ensley, the Ku Klux Klan gathered outside the city. Some conscientious city and state police investigators were thankful that the Klan had kept its distance from the daily demonstrations. Some of the investigators, aware of Bull Connor's close personal ties with several Klan activists, believed the Klan's restraint was not accidental, and that word had gone out to the white terrorists in April that they should stay clear of local racial events. Unlike previous periods of racial tension in Birmingham, the past six weeks had witnessed no terror bombings.

Late Saturday night, after Connor's earlier efforts to derail a settlement had failed, the terrorist lull suddenly ended. Shortly before midnight, a powerful bomb destroyed the front portion of A. D. King's home in Ensley. Luckily, the family was in the rear of the house and no one was injured. Friends had gathered on the Kings' lawn when a second loud explosion sounded from the direction of downtown. Immediately members of the crowd guessed the second target: the Gaston Motel. A powerful explosive had been detonated directly under and outside of King's room. In another stroke of good fortune, no one was injured by the motel blast. Joseph Lowery had changed his mind and decided to take the night train home to Nashville rather than stay over in King's room.

Police and firemen hurried to the motel, as a large crowd of angry black citizens gathered. Wyatt Walker and other activists moved through the crowd urging calm and reassuring everyone that there had been no injuries. Among themselves, however, the movement staffers were furious at what they perceived as an intentional setup. Until just hours earlier, the area around the motel and Ingram Park had been heavily patrolled by Alabama state troopers under the command of Colonel Al Lingo, a close ally of Connor's and a trusted confidant of Governor George C. Wallace. Then, as suddenly as they had withdrawn, Lingo's troopers returned to downtown Birmingham after the bombings. Some bystanders threw bricks and bottles at the officers, and the call went out for Connor's dogs and the white armored car. A full-scale riot was soon under way. Angry blacks overturned a passing car and set it afire, and brutal state troopers used their billy clubs on anyone within reach. Movement staffers had little success trying to halt the growing disorder. Violence flared in the area until after dawn. News stories the next day reported that one policeman had been stabbed during the lengthy melee, and many papers featured a photo of a heavily bloodied Birmingham police inspector who had been brained by a rock.[33]

Martin King preached his Sunday morning sermon in Atlanta before hurrying back to Birmingham. He told his congregation that he had had no more than two hours sleep in one night for almost a week, but that he was happy with the accord and that the movement would not allow Saturday night's violence to destroy it. After church he spoke by phone with Robert Kennedy, whose Justice Department aides were pondering what federal action might be appropriate. While King flew into Birmingham and huddled with Joseph Dolan, Kennedy, Burke Marshall, and other administration strategists discussed whether federal troops should be sent into the city to restrain both potential black rioters and the state troopers. Kennedy was especially worried that any more white bombings might beget a black response of greater magnitude than Saturday night's clash. Kennedy dispatched two more assistants, Ramsey Clark and John Nolan, to Birmingham, and early that evening he and Marshall went to the White House to discuss the Birmingham situation with the president.

John Kennedy shared his brother's concerns about the provocative conduct of the Alabama state troopers and the black violence the lawmen might provoke. "This could trigger off a good deal of violence around the country" by blacks in other cities, the attorney general warned, and recommended the president act strongly to show blacks "that the federal government is their friend." John Kennedy agreed, emphasizing that everything should be done to save the Birmingham accord. "If the agreement blows up, the other remedy that we have . . . is to send legislation up to the Congress this week as our response to that action. . . . We may have to do that anyway, but at least that would be our public response . . . if the agreement blows up." The men discussed the possible use of soldiers in Birmingham, and Marshall stepped out to phone King to get his opinion of the situation. "He says he thinks that if there are no other incidents, like no other bombings, that he can control his people," Marshall reported back to Kennedy. The president decided he would federalize the Alabama National Guard to block any use of it by Governor Wallace, and would also move regular federal troops into position near Birmingham so that they would be available if needed. Later that night John Kennedy appeared on nationwide television to announce those steps and to pledge that violence would not be allowed to sabotage the Birmingham settlement. King spoke to a Sunday night meeting at one Birmingham church and tried to calm the volatile black community. Local white moderates lobbied hard to get Lingo's troopers withdrawn from town. On Monday, Sidney Smyer held a press conference to reiterate the business community's support for Friday's agreement. He noted pointedly that he had never met Martin Luther King during the negotiations, and that he understood the settlement would require only one black sales clerk somewhere among the downtown stores. Early in the afternoon King and a sizable press contingent took to the sidewalks for a pool-hall-by-pool-hall effort to sell nonviolence to black Birmingham. At the New Home Billiard Parlor, Ralph Abernathy quieted the players and introduced King to the ambivalent crowd. King spoke briefly, emphasizing that black violence hurt the movement's cause. "Bull Connor is happy when we use force." After a rendition of "We Shall Overcome," the group moved on to a similar establishment and repeated the procedure. Then Lingo's troopers moved in and halted the procession on the grounds that the walking tour obstructed Birmingham's sidewalks. A disappointed King retreated to the Gaston Motel.[34]

King spoke at that night's mass meeting and then left for a fund-raising appearance in Cleveland. All of Birmingham hoped there would be no repetition of Saturday's bombings and riots. Burke Marshall, back in town from Washington, worked hard to consolidate white support for the agreement. Tuesday afternoon twenty Alabama newspaper editors met with Robert Kennedy at the Justice Department, where the attorney general praised King's leadership and recommended that southern officials allow protests rather than suppress them. King's greatest virtue, Kennedy said, was his relative moderation and his commitment to nonviolence. "If King loses, worse leaders are going to take his place." In a subsequent "background briefing" for national newsmen on his session with the Alabamans, Robert Kennedy repeated his views and admitted that the primary reason the federal government had considered sending troops into Birmingham had been concern about Lingo's state troopers rather than about the black citizenry.

While Birmingham remained quiet throughout the week, pressure grew within the white community for a full airing of just who had agreed to the settlement, which so far had only Sidney Smyer's name publicly attached to it. On Thursday, May 16, Smyer finally released a list of the seventy-seven men who had authorized the white negotiators to proceed at the crucial session on May 7. Smyer again stated, with only a little stretching of the truth, that the white representatives had never dealt with any SCLC officials or out-of-towners, and stressed that the accord called only for one black salesclerk to be employed in a downtown store.

Smyer's statement led to new media reports that "King won little or nothing" in the settlement. The stories also harped on what one reporter called "King's exaggerated version of the concessions." Thursday afternoon King held a press conference to rebut those assertions and to repeat that the movement expected one black clerk to be hired in each of seven different downtown stores. King also, mistakenly, stated that Smyer had erred in saying lunch-counter and rest-room desegregation was pegged to the legal vindication of Boutwell's election rather than to the date of the agreement itself. He added that he had faith in the whites, but that the employment problem had to be resolved. The next morning a letter was dispatched over Shuttlesworth's signature to the white negotiators stating that "it is our understanding that at least one clerk in each of the major stores was the point of agreement." The letter made no reference to the purposely vague text of the agreement, and there was no response from the whites before King flew to Chicago for a weekend speech.[35]

The first week's anniversary of the two bombings passed without incident, but at midday Monday, another conservative white effort to derail the settlement occurred. Birmingham school authorities expelled 1,100 students for having skipped classes to demonstrate. Local black leaders were outraged and issued an immediate call for a total boycott of all schools and white businesses. King was notified of this new problem and hurried back to Alabama. In a hastily called strategy meeting, he argued that the expulsions were simply one more Connor-style effort to destroy the agreement, and that the black leadership should go to court to win the students' reinstatement rather than react in a way that hostile whites would welcome. On reflection, the black leaders agreed, and at that night's meeting King announced that the boycott call had been scrapped. The next morning, movement attorneys went into federal court seeking an order reinstating the pupils, and within thirty-six hours, Chief Judge Elbert P. Tuttle of the Fifth Circuit Court of Appeals issued the necessary command. One day later the finishing touch was placed upon the Birmingham accord when the Alabama Supreme Court ruled in Boutwell's favor and ordered Connor and his fellow commissioners to surrender their offices posthaste.[36]

The apparent resolution of the many successive crises threatening the Birmingham accord gave King and his assistants their first real opportunity to reflect upon the events of the last seven weeks. In retrospect, they could see that they had prevailed despite their having begun with several misconceptions. First, they had not appreciated the depth of the split that existed within the Birmingham white community. Their expectations of how Bull Connor would react to mass protests had been fulfilled, and they had also correctly assumed that the segregationist preferences of the white business leadership would buckle under the economic pressure of a boycott. As Walker put it, "what I did in Birmingham I learned in Albany." SCLC had not fully understood, however, that white Birmingham lacked an effective civic leadership when the demonstrations began. Everyone appreciated the legal complexities arising from the two competing city administrations, but the movement had not perceived the deep-seated fear that kept Birmingham's economic elite impassive until the threat of citywide turmoil forced them into action on May 7. No matter how great an economic price the movement exacted from the downtown merchants, that price would seem insignificant if those merchants refused to follow their self-interest or if they were unable to influence the wielders of official power. Although the boycott had been effective, only the widespread disorder of that Tuesday afternoon had convinced the city's business leadership to settle. Masses of unrestrained black teenagers had convinced the downtown businessmen in a way that peaceful picketing or sit-ins never had that segregation was not worth the price they would have to pay.

At the outset King had misjudged the black community as well as the white. Fred Shuttlesworth had had neither the troops nor the adult peer support that SCLC had anticipated. Neither ACMHR nor the Miles College student body had been able to supply enough demonstrators, and only the recruitment of the eager high school students had given SCLC the foot soldiers it needed to reveal Connor's true colors to the nation. King's decision to go to jail despite the financial crisis had been the emotional high point of the campaign, but Walker's accidental discovery of how black bystanders could contribute to the movement's cause had been the principal strategic breakthrough. The teenagers and onlookers could not have contributed so well had it not been for Connor's tactical stupidity in repeatedly using police dogs and fire hoses. Walker had been sagacious and pragmatic in his efforts to use the protests to evoke those reactions from Connor's men. Walker appreciated the huge amount of sympathetic national news coverage those police excesses had garnered for the civil rights cause, and in private he made no excuse for his tactics. "I didn't believe in provocation—unless the stakes were right." In Birmingham the stakes had been right, and Connor had complied perfectly by attempting to keep the protesters from reaching City Hall. "We didn't really want to get down there," Walker admitted; the news coverage of Connor's efforts to block them was far more valuable. "In essence," Andrew Young commented, "we were consciously using the mass media to try to get across to the nation what our message was," that southern segregation was far more vicious than most white Americans had ever realized. "The movement was really about getting publicity for injustice . . . the injustice was there under the surface and as long as it stayed below the surface, nobody was concerned about it. You had to bring it out in the open." As Walker later boasted, "There never was any more skillful manipulation of the news media than there was in Birmingham." SCLC had succeeded in bringing the civil rights struggle to the forefront of the national consciousness. This success far outweighed the narrower question of whether the settlement provided for speedy enough desegregation of Birmingham's stores or an acceptable number of black sales clerks.[37]

Martin King spent the final week of May traveling around the country to address a series of hugely successful fund-raising rallies in Los Angeles, St. Louis, Chicago, and Louisville. Over $50,000 was raised in one day in Los Angeles alone, and King realized that the movement now had achieved a central position in American public life. Funds flowed in to SCLC by the thousands. The impact of Birmingham gradually became clearer, and King considered what the movement should do now to take advantage of this new national interest in an issue that both the white South and the Kennedys had hoped to keep under wraps. At various fund-raising rallies, King repeated his year-old call for an executive order prohibiting all segregation, and in several late-night phone conversations, he asked Stanley Levison where the movement should turn. Levison agreed that the current moment was a special one, and that King should move beyond his call for an executive order by asking for a personal meeting with John Kennedy to discuss the situation. The two men agreed that the Kennedys were sensitive to the international impact of the Birmingham photos, and that that embarrassment, coupled with the domestic outpouring of support for the movement, might push the administration into more aggressive support of civil rights than it had been willing to risk so far. If a face-to-face meeting were granted, King could ask for a clear policy shift. If President Kennedy refused to see him, the movement would have to adopt Birmingham's tactics in other cities. That way, King said, so much pressure would be placed upon the president that he would have no choice but to sign an executive order declaring segregation unconstitutional.[38]

On Thursday, May 30, King sent a telegram to the White House requesting a conference with both the president and the attorney general. The following day the FBI, which had monitored King's telephone comments by means of its wiretap on Stanley Levison, notified Robert Kennedy of what the civil rights leader and Levison had discussed. The attorney general asked that the FBI furnish an account of the crucial conversation to his brother, and within hours it was done. The next day presidential assistant Lee C. White notified King that John Kennedy's busy schedule would not allow for any meeting for at least a week, and that he, White, would be in touch in the near future. In the wake of that rebuff, King discussed the situation with Levison in two more lengthy wiretapped conversations. Stanley reiterated his advice that "the Birmingham pattern" could be used in other cities, such as Atlanta, and King agreed. "We are on the threshold of a significant breakthrough and the greatest weapon is the mass demonstration. . . . We are at the point where we can mobilize all of this righteous indignation into a powerful mass movement." He told Levison that they ought to announce a mass "March on Washington," for "the threat itself may so frighten the President that he would have to do something." Both he and Levison knew that other movement activists, particularly Bayard Rustin and A. Philip Randolph, had been talking about such an idea for months. Levison reminded King that they had best secure unanimity among all the movement's groups before anyone made a public announcement. Levison asked King to consider whether more pressure upon Kennedy would be generated by a single mass March on Washington or by a series of Birmingham-like protests across the country. King said that simultaneous demonstrations all across the country were just what he had in mind, and that those protests could be combined with a nationwide work stoppage. He asked Levison if the time was right, and he replied yes, "the time is now." Levison indicated that he or Clarence Jones would discuss the matter with Randolph, and that King should hold his ideas in abeyance until it was known how both Randolph and Roy Wilkins felt about it.[39]

Several days later Levison told King that Jones had conferred with Randolph, who was eager to combine King's desire with the plans that he and his associates had been making for a Washington pilgrimage in early October. Randolph asked Jones to have King get in touch with him, and King agreed to make the call. King's interest in mass action in the nation's capital stemmed in part from an idea that had circulated among some of the movement's younger staff workers, such as Jim Bevel and Ike Reynolds, during the later stages of the Birmingham demonstrations.

Randolph's associates had been discussing such a March since late in 1962. At the end of January, 1963, Rustin and two associates, Norm Hill and Tom Kahn, had prepared a three-page memo for Randolph that proposed a two-day "mass descent" upon Washington in May, 1963. They suggested a target figure of 100,000 marchers, and argued that mass action was necessary to draw public attention to "the economic subordination of the American Negro," the pressing need for "the creation of more jobs for all Americans," and the wider goal of "a broad and fundamental program of economic justice." "Integration in the fields of education, housing, transportation and public accommodations will be of limited extent and duration so long as fundamental economic inequality along racial lines persists," the planning document argued. On the first day of the pilgrimage there would be a "mass descent" upon Congress, blocking all legislative business, while a smaller delegation visited the White House. Both Congress and the president should be presented with specific legislative demands, demands that could be drafted if Randolph approved the project and gave his staffers permission to approach other civil rights activists and liberal sympathizers in organized labor and religious groups. The second day of the March would be devoted to "a mass protest rally."

In early March, Randolph approved his aides' recommendation and suggested that they consider a target date of June 13 and 14. The national executive board of Randolph's Negro American Labor Council (NALC) met in New York on March 23 to be briefed on the project. Plans now called for one day of lobbying on Capitol Hill. A second day would feature a mass procession down Pennsylvania Avenue culminating in a rally at the Lincoln Memorial that President Kennedy would be invited to address. Randolph wanted his board's approval before he approached other organizations, and it was given enthusiastically. Several days later Randolph contacted National Urban League Executive Director Whitney M. Young, Jr., to ask that his organization endorse and help finance the plan. Randolph made a similar approach to the NAACP's Roy Wilkins. Randolph and his aides now were scheduling the March for early October instead of June, but even a more realistic schedule could do little to persuade Young or Wilkins, both of whom reacted coolly to Randolph's initiative. Young wrote Randolph at the end of April to say that although his organization felt "great sympathy and emotional support for the effort," it could not participate formally. Young stated that the October date would conflict with other Urban League plans, and that his organization's tax-exempt status barred it from direct involvement in a legislative lobbying effort. He explained that the Urban League's close working relationships with many federal officials might be damaged if the organization took part in an open protest against those officials' policies. Wilkins delivered a similar rebuff. Randolph attempted to interest King and SCLC in the plan but received little response, since the organization was totally preoccupied with bringing the Birmingham protests to their climax. Although Randolph and Rustin kept their fall plans on the front burner, and succeeded in interesting influential black trade unionist Cleveland Robinson of New York's District 65 in the march idea, they made little progress toward their goal. The events in Birmingham were the focus of everyone's attention, and the New York activists were devoting their energy to organizing demonstrations of support for the Birmingham protesters rather than working on plans for Washington. Thus, when Jones notified Randolph in early June that King was ready to consider mass action in Washington, the grand old man of the black movement seized the opportunity and turned his energies to a plan that had threatened to die aborning.[40]

Only after Birmingham did King and his aides consider how the national impact of those protests might be used to pave the way for new federal legislative initiatives on civil rights. In both his public and private comments, King focused upon how Birmingham had made clear the pressing need for unilateral executive action on civil rights, and how John Kennedy's record was "inadequate." He "has not furnished the expected leadership and has not kept his campaign promises," King said during one interview. If Kennedy did not speak to the country about the moral imperative of integration, the movement might sponsor an interracial March on Washington that could include sit-ins on Capitol Hill. It was King's first public reference to such a possibility, and news reports gave prominent coverage to his comments about Kennedy. "Dr. King Denounces President on Rights," *The New York Times* proclaimed. In a late-night conference call on June 9, King told Levison and Jones that the Washington protest ought to be scheduled for sometime in August, and that special pressure should be placed upon Congress to pass a civil rights bill. King said he would get in touch with Randolph immediately to coordinate plans, and contemplated making a quick public announcement of the March in order to compel NAACP support. Thirty-six hours later Jones and New York pastor George Lawrence, a frequent supporter of SCLC efforts, informed newsmen that such a pilgrimage, perhaps employing disruptive, civil disobedience tactics, would take place later that summer if the federal government did not act quickly to aid black Americans.[41]

While King pondered how best to take advantage of Birmingham in pressing the Kennedys for stronger support of civil rights, the administration was intensively discussing what should be done. Both John and Robert Kennedy, plus Justice Department aides like Marshall and Ramsey Clark, understood that new initiatives had to be taken. Birmingham had set off a string of public-accommodations protests across the South, and another crisis threatened in Alabama, where Governor Wallace was vowing to disobey a federal court order requiring admission of black students to the University of Alabama at Tuscaloosa. Robert Kennedy met with influential southern whites to urge their support for peaceful desegregation, but he, like his Justice Department aides, realized that persuasion alone could not integrate the South. Ramsey Clark had returned from Birmingham convinced that the administration had to propose a comprehensive civil rights bill to Congress. Marshall also realized that much of the frustration the Justice Department felt over its inability to do anything except mediate in Birmingham was caused by a lack of federal statutes authorizing intervention. The only action open to the executive branch was the use of military troops in the event the president proclaimed a state of civil unrest. John Kennedy limited his public comments to a strong defense of blacks' right to protest segregation, saying that their demonstrations are "in the highest traditions of American freedom." As early as May 24, however, Robert Kennedy conceded in a private interview that "further legislation is needed. Unless it is passed, I don't think we can do any more than is now being done."

Later that same day, May 24, Robert Kennedy's growing emotional involvement with the civil rights issue was heightened considerably by an angry meeting in New York with black writer James Baldwin, black psychologist Kenneth Clark, Clarence Jones, Harry Belafonte, and a number of other outspoken individuals from the civil rights movement and black cultural community who believed passionately that the Kennedy administration was ignorant of the pressing moral need for the federal government to get behind the movement. Robert Kennedy left the session furious at the lack of appreciation shown by the other participants for the government's efforts concerning civil rights. The more lasting impact of the encounter was to sensitize him more deeply than ever to the fact that what the federal government had done still fell short of what was morally necessary. On Saturday, June 1, the same day that the White House refused King's request to meet with the president, Robert Kennedy convened a meeting of the administration's key legal and political strategists to discuss civil rights. The attorney general declared that the government had to take the lead in proposing broad legislation that would strike at racial segregation and discrimination. Others in the meeting, relying upon the accepted wisdom of two years, replied that the congressional mood still argued against any administration push for a comprehensive civil rights bill that would have only a modest chance of passage. Robert Kennedy's insistence that the government's proposal had to provide for the desegregation of all public accommodations drew heavy flak, but both

John Kennedy and Lyndon Johnson came down on the attorney general's side. The president instructed his aides to draft promptly a broad-gauged proposal, and asked everyone involved to be careful not to reveal the administration's plans.[42]

Martin King knew little about the government's decision to propose comprehensive civil rights legislation until Tuesday, June 11. That morning, Alabama Governor Wallace barred the door of the University of Alabama's administration building to Deputy Attorney General Katzenbach and two black students seeking to enroll under the provisions of the federal court order. Wallace's effort was symbolically effective but practically futile, and later that day President Kennedy federalized the Alabama National Guard. Wallace stood aside when the commanding general returned with the students at the end of the day. That evening President Kennedy went on nationwide television and for the first time in his presidency issued a clear moral call to the American people to banish segregation and racism from the land. Although he provided few details, Kennedy stated that he soon would propose to Congress a civil rights bill that would include a public-accommodations title among its provisions; only by moving forward with federal legislative remedies could this crisis be resolved. The depth of the problem, and the potential price to be paid by those who tried to solve it, was brought home to the entire country just hours after Kennedy's remarks. Mississippi NAACP leader Medgar Evers was shot from ambush and killed outside his home in Jackson.

Martin King was overjoyed by John Kennedy's speech. "He was really great," King remarked over the phone to Stanley Levison the next day, and in a telegram King told the president that his remarks had constituted "one of the most eloquent, profound and unequivocal pleas for justice and the freedom of all men ever made by any president." King told Levison that this meant that their March on Washington must be aimed at the Congress rather than the president, and Levison agreed. King also wanted to take some action in response to Medgar Evers's assassination; he called Roy Wilkins of the NAACP to suggest that they jointly announce a national day of mourning and establish a memorial fund in Evers's name. The ever-prickly Wilkins, perceiving one more supposed effort by King and SCLC to challenge what he thought were the NAACP's unique prerogatives, told King to mind his own business. When the two men met at Evers's funeral in Jackson, Wilkins warned King that SCLC should drop any idea of moving in to assist the Jackson protests that Evers's NAACP forces had led. In subsequent days Wilkins complained about King's alleged presumptuousness and self-promoting to anyone who would listen. Within less than a week, major newspapers and magazines carried a new spate of stories describing intense organizational conflict within the movement.

To a number of close observers, Wilkins's anger and the growing appearance of interorganizational competition were rooted basically in the heightened financial stakes that had resulted from the Birmingham crisis. That event had elevated King to the indisputable civil rights top spot in the American public's mind. It also meant that King's SCLC, rather than the long-established NAACP, would be the chief financial beneficiary of this new interest in civil rights. Evers's death offered an opportunity to correct that imbalance, and Wilkins had no intention of missing it. Between these financial tensions, and the equally strong divisions over Randolph's and King's commitment to mass action in Washington, the movement was threatening to split apart in public just as it reached its highest level of potential influence.[43]

Two interested onlookers who were worried by this threat were Taconic Foundation President Stephen R. Currier and his principal staff member, Jane Lee Eddy. In the immediate wake of the Evers killing, they decided that something had to be done to ensure unity within the movement and to eliminate the growing competition for potential contributions. After consultations with Whitney Young, Roy Wilkins, and NAACP Legal Defense and Educational Fund Director Jack Greenberg, Currier asked all of the black leadership to gather in New York eight days after Evers's death for a breakfast discussion.

The afternoon before the breakfast with Currier, King, Abernathy, Shuttlesworth, and Levison met at Randolph's New York office with Rustin, Cleveland Robinson, L. Joseph Overton of NALC, Bill Mahoney of SNCC, and Norman Hill from CORE for the first group discussion of the March on Washington. Rustin suggested that they aim for a target date sometime between August 10 and 24, and recommended that Robinson and George Lawrence be named temporary coordinators of the effort. He asked that each organization choose one representative who would sit on a policy-making committee for the March, and suggested that that group convene six days hence on June 24. Rustin said he hoped that Roy Wilkins or some other NAACP representative would attend that meeting.

At the Currier-sponsored breakfast the next morning, the Taconic Foundation's president recommended that the black leadership establish the Council for United Civil Rights Leadership (CUCRL) which, under Currier's auspices, would serve as a clearinghouse for dividing large contributions among all the organizations. Everyone present knew of Currier's great personal wealth, as well as his remarkable ability to generate funds from other well-to-do friends. No one dissented from his plan. The arrangement could lessen the growing internecine conflict before serious damage was done, and it was all but certain to provide each of the organizations with funds they otherwise would not receive.[44]

King flew to Birmingham from New York. He had returned there at least once a week since the crisis had passed, and so far the white merchants had lived up to the agreement. A core group of high school students had remained committed to SCLC's work after the demonstrations ended, and had helped mount an effective voter registration drive in black neighborhoods throughout the city. Notwithstanding less than eager white registration officials, the young SCLC workers were adding some four hundred new black registrants to the polling books each week.

Despite this success, painful tensions had arisen between ACMHR and SCLC concerning the two organizations' intertwined financial relationship. ACMHR Treasurer William E. Shortridge complained to Fred Shuttlesworth that their organization was not receiving a fair share of the monies that SCLC was reaping in the wake of the protests. Because Shuttlesworth gave little heed to his repeated complaints, Shortridge took them to SCLC Treasurer Abernathy, explaining that ACMHR had received little income since late May and bills were piling up, especially those from the attorneys and bonding companies that had helped secure the release of the hundreds of demonstrators. Shortridge acknowledged that SCLC had passed along two checks totaling $14,000, but ACMHR was in the red and required further support. King also listened sympathetically to Shortridge during his June 20 visit, but the issue remained a problem throughout the summer.

At that evening's ACMHR mass meeting, King talked about the upcoming pilgrimage to the nation's capital and how it would put pressure on Congress to pass the civil rights bill that John Kennedy had sent to Capitol Hill just the day before. "As soon as they start to filibuster," King declared, "I think we should march on Washington with a quarter of a million people." The next morning, March coordinators Cleveland Robinson and George Lawrence announced plans for the protest to the New York press. The purpose of the mass demonstration, Robinson emphasized, would be to draw national attention to the problem of black unemployment and the need for thousands of new jobs, and not simply to lobby for civil rights legislation.[45]

Within hours of Robinson's announcement the Kennedy White House summoned the black leadership to a meeting the following day with the president. When the session convened, John Kennedy explained what it would take to win congressional approval of the administration's bill. The most difficult hurdle would be to obtain cloture in the Senate; for that, the votes of many midwestern Republicans who usually took little interest in racial issues would be necessary. The proposed March on Washington might hinder rather than help the effort to gain those votes. "We want success in Congress," Kennedy stated,

> not just a big show at the Capitol. Some of these people are looking for an excuse to be against us. I don't want to give any of them a chance to say, "Yes, I'm for the bill but I'm damned if I will vote for it at the point of a gun." It seemed to me a great mistake to announce a march on Washington before the bill was even in committee. The only effect is to create an atmosphere of intimidation—and this may give some members of Congress an out.

Philip Randolph spoke out in defense of black demonstrations in general and the March in particular, but the president was not swayed from his position:

> . . .Now we are in a new phase, the legislative phase, and results are essential. The wrong kind of demonstration at the wrong time will give those fellows a chance to say that they have to prove their courage by voting against us. To get the votes we need we have, first, to oppose demonstrations which will lead to violence, and, second, give Congress a fair chance to work its will.

Vice-President Johnson endorsed Kennedy's remarks, and said that the administration's entire civil rights initiative hinged upon some twenty-five swing votes in the Senate. "To get those votes we have to be careful not to do anything which would give those who are privately opposed a public excuse to appear as martyrs."

Both James Farmer of CORE and King defended the need for demonstrations. King argued that the March on Washington "could serve as a means through which people with legitimate discontents could channel their grievances under disciplined, nonviolent leadership. It could also serve as a means of dramatizing the issue and mobilizing support in parts of the country which don't know the problems at first hand. I think it will serve a purpose. It may seem ill-timed. Frankly, I have never engaged in any direct action movement which did not seem ill-timed. Some people thought Birmingham ill-timed."

John Kennedy interrupted, saying, "Including the Attorney General." Then the president expressed a sentiment that both he and his brother strongly shared, a sentiment that said much about their political and emotional evolutions over the preceding six weeks. "I don't think you should all be totally harsh on Bull Connor. After all, he has done more for civil rights than almost anybody else."

With his wry remark about Connor, John Kennedy brought the meeting to a close. Then, while the other guests departed, Kennedy took King aside for a brief private conversation, and invited him out into the Rose Garden. The president was worried that the FBI's increasing concern about King's relationship with Stanley Levison and Jack O'Dell's continuance on SCLC's payroll posed an even greater threat to the civil rights program than did the proposed March on Washington. "You've read about Profumo in the papers?" the president asked, referring to the current scandal rocking the British government. King nodded. "That was an example of friendship and loyalty carried too far," Kennedy went on. "Macmillan is likely to lose his government because he has been loyal to his friend. You must take care not to lose your cause for the same reason." Then he named O'Dell and Levison. "They're Communists. You've got to get rid of them." The president emphasized that any public revelations by newsmen or the FBI's friends in Congress about the backgrounds of the two men would harm not just King, but the entire movement and the Kennedys' civil rights bill. "If they shoot *you* down, they'll shoot us down too—so we're asking you to be careful." Kennedy also warned King that opponents of civil rights would have him under close surveillance. King nodded again and indicated that he would not quarrel with Kennedy about O'Dell. But Levison was different. "I know Stanley," King told the president, "and I can't believe this. You will have to prove it." Kennedy said he would have Burke Marshall convey proof of the allegations to King. With that, the brief conversation ended.[46]

King and his fellow civil rights leaders emerged from the White House with differing responses to the president's remarks. While Kennedy had not explicitly asked that the March be canceled, Roy Wilkins was noncommittal about NAACP participation and stressed that "I am not involved at the present moment." King defended the March and stated that "we feel a demonstration would help the President's civil rights legislation." Afterward, UAW President Walter Reuther hosted a luncheon meeting for the black leadership, one purpose of which, Wilkins later admitted, "was to talk Dr. King out of trying to apply the model of Birmingham to Washington." Wilkins argued that only "quiet, patient lobbying tactics" should be employed to aid the Kennedys' bill. King reassured Wilkins that the entire question of tactics would be discussed when the full March on Washington committee met in New York two days later, a meeting Wilkins agreed to attend.

King was concerned about Kennedy's fear and Wilkins's hesitancy over the March, but he was both troubled and bemused by the president's warning about O'Dell and Levison. King jokingly asked Andrew Young why the president had taken him outdoors before raising the subject. Did Kennedy suspect that someone was bugging his office? King was concerned that the administration took the problem so seriously as to have the president convey a personal warning, but he was no more moved to sever his ties with Levison or O'Dell by Kennedy's admonition than he had been by the half-dozen cautionary notes sounded by Robert Kennedy, Burke Marshall, Harris Wofford, and John Seigenthaler.

In private, King was preoccupied with the rapidly accelerating pace of black activism. "The Negro is shedding himself of his fear," he had said some weeks earlier, "and my real worry is how we will keep this fearlessness from rising to violent proportions." King realized that he was "running into more and more bitterness because things haven't moved fast enough. . . . The Negro in the South can now be nonviolent as a stratagem, but he can't include loving the white man. . . . Nonviolence has become a military tactical approach." King had come to appreciate that it was the coercive direct action of Birmingham, and not persuasive moral appeals aimed at winning over the hearts of southern whites, that the movement would have to pursue. Only through confrontation could the nation be shown the true essence of segregation and racism. "We are merely bringing to the surface the tension that has always been at the heart of the problem," King told one audience. Demonstrations "may be peaceful and nonviolent, but you make people inflict violence on you, so you precipitate violence."

Throughout the Birmingham protests, both King and Walker had been more attuned to the potentiality of federal executive intervention than to the distant possibility of obtaining strong congressional legislation. The goal, Walker admitted in early June, had been one of "creating a crisis so severe that government—the federal administration—has to grapple with it and do something immediately." Both he and King had been deeply pleased by the forthright stance that John Kennedy had taken on June 11, but neither man had high hopes for the passage of Kennedy's legislative proposal. Walker volunteered publicly that "I personally don't believe it has a prayer of passing," and contended that what was needed to prevent more Birminghams and more terrorist assassinations was "strong executive action. It may be that we will have to see martial law declared in several areas throughout the South." King stopped far short of saying that in public, admitting that "I do not think civil rights legislation will solve all of the problems that we now face," while adding "but I do think it will solve many."[47]

The day after the meeting at the White House, King flew to Detroit to appear at a 125,000-person civil rights rally, one of an increasing number of sympathy demonstrations all across the country. Then he went to New York for the crucial March on Washington meeting. Roy Wilkins was in attendance, and Philip Randolph took pains at the outset to emphasize that "we are working on the principle of nonviolence, not civil disobedience." That pronouncement did not please some who were present, such as SNCC's Bill Mahoney, nor was it enough to satisfy the reluctant Wilkins, who inquired how the March would be designed to help pass the Kennedy legislation. A procession with a "tinge of Harlem" to it, Wilkins said, would be harmful. The NAACP's executive director also volunteered that he did not want his organization to have to pick up the tab. "Someone asked him if the March wasn't worth the cost," one participant recalled. "Wilkins said, 'Not when someone else gets the publicity.'" Despite that sourness, NAACP participation was grudgingly promised, and the group settled upon a one-day pilgrimage and a firm date of Wednesday, August 28.

Announcement of the date generated some worries among sympathetic observers. Black Detroit Congressman Charles C. Diggs, Jr., wrote to King to express "increasing concern" about the movement's plans. Diggs complained that many members of Congress would respond positively only if they had direct contact with their own constituents. He also voiced concern over whether movement leaders could assure "that disciplinary problems will be minimized." The announcement of the March had made "a lot of people nervous," and Diggs hoped that King and his colleagues would rethink their plans.[48]

Diggs's worries were not King's only immediate problem. On the morning of June 30, the *Birmingham News,* relying upon information leaked by the FBI, revealed that Jack O'Dell was still on SCLC's payroll and working in its New York office despite King's claim that O'Dell had resigned. Burke Marshall again pressed King to cut all ties with O'Dell and Levison. Reluctantly, King gave in and acted on the first request. He wrote to O'Dell, in a letter primarily intended for Marshall's consumption, that the "temporary resignation" of the preceding November now was being made permanent. Although SCLC had not discovered "any present connections with the Communist party on your part," the continuing allegation that O'Dell was a secret member of the CP's national committee was a damaging one, and "in these critical times we cannot afford to risk any such impressions."

Although King reluctantly accommodated the administration on O'Dell, he refused to end his friendship with Levison. Burke Marshall, acting at John Kennedy's direction, spoke to Andrew Young about the specific evidence against King's advisor, but all Marshall was able to offer were vague allegations of Levison's unspecified Soviet contacts. Not surprisingly, King again refused to act when Young relayed the information to him.

Levison took a different view of the situation. Fully aware of the notions that the Kennedys possessed about him, Levison insisted to King that they make the break that for eighteen months King had refused to initiate. Hearings on the administration's civil rights bill were about to begin, and the O'Dell leak was evidence that the movement's opponents were ready to use all their ammunition. Moreover, it also was clear that the Kennedys' newly strengthened support for civil rights would be held back in King's case so long as Levison remained a presence. Thus Stanley insisted that their direct contact end. "I induced him to break," Levison later explained. "The movement needed the Kennedys too much. I said it would not be in the interests of the movement to hold on to me if the Kennedys had doubts." King unwillingly agreed to the break, but arranged to keep in touch with Levison through black New York attorney Clarence Jones. The two men would be able to pass news and advice to each other while abiding by the Kennedys' demand.[49]

Another problem for the movement was the growing national attention being paid to the Nation of Islam, the "Black Muslims," whom the white press negatively portrayed as being just one step away from a violent "hate whitey" onslaught. The normally mild-mannered King had lashed out strongly against the Muslims in several public comments, and Wyatt Walker had almost gotten into a fistfight with Muslim activist Malcolm X after a joint television appearance. King feared that the extensive news coverage of the Muslims and their rhetoric would dissuade sympathetic whites from supporting civil rights. While movement leaders always stressed the nonviolent nature of their protests, the Muslims repeatedly suggested that only physical violence could defeat American racism. These provocative statements deeply angered King. "What gets me is that these people don't have the nerve, nor are they irrational enough, to advocate the alternative of violence. If they're for violence, why don't they say so?" Comments like these further heightened the Muslims' antipathy toward King, and one late June night in Harlem the group threw eggs at King as he arrived to speak at a church rally. For King, it was one of "those moments when you think about what you are going through and the sacrifices and suffering you face, that your own people don't have an understanding—not even an appreciation" of one's efforts. For the moment it left King "feeling sorry for myself and rejected."[50]

On July 2, just as the black leadership was gathering for a further discussion of CUCRL and the March on Washington, *The New York Times* reported that SCLC intended to become a membership organization throughout the South. Wyatt Walker wanted to expand SCLC's network of local affiliates, and each affiliate would recruit members for the parent organization. Annual dues of $2 per person, Walker explained, would help SCLC while also providing funds for the state conferences of affiliates that Walker hoped to organize.

That news was one more provocation to the NAACP's Roy Wilkins, who now saw SCLC taking aim at his organization's greatest source of strength, its thousands of local, dues-paying members. This time his anger did not make the public press, but Wilkins was in an uncooperative mood when the black leadership assembled to discuss the March and announce that CUCRL had raised $800,000 to distribute among movement organizations. Bayard Rustin presented a detailed document on plans for the March that listed several economic goals as primary targets: more and better jobs, a stronger minimum wage, a fair employment practices commission, etc. Support for the civil rights bill, and protests against the upcoming segregationist filibuster in the Senate, were listed as secondary aims. Rustin anticipated a budget of $65,000, and said 100,000 participants would be expected. The six major black leaders—Randolph, King, Wilkins, Young, James Farmer of CORE, and newly elected SNCC Chairman John Lewis—would serve as co-chairmen, and each would designate one subordinate as his administrative coordinator. A primary task would be to get local groups across the country to organize their members to come to Washington for the one-day gathering, which was only eight weeks away. Also, Rustin noted, a director for the March would have to be chosen.

Wilkins, who realized he had been roped into participating, moved to block the appointment of Rustin, the one logical candidate, as director. With Randolph prodding him to make his objections explicit, Wilkins referred to the three problems that dogged Rustin's reputation: his prison sentence for refusing to serve in the armed forces, his early flirtation with communism, and his arrest record for homosexuality. Randolph asked the others what they thought, and both King and Farmer spoke up in Rustin's defense, saying that none of those issues had ever created serious public relations problems in the past. Wilkins indicated that those sorts of reassurances would not lead him to drop his objection, and that segregationists looked ready to mount a dirtier fight now than at any time in the past. SNCC's John Lewis thought that the entire discussion was "petty politics," but Whitney Young of the Urban League moved to heal the division by suggesting that Randolph be named director of the March, and that he pick whomever he wanted as his deputy. Wilkins was in no position to object to Randolph, and consented. Randolph also agreed, and announced he was designating Rustin as his deputy. Wilkins's effort had failed, and Rustin would run the March in fact if not in name. The leaders emerged from the meeting to announce their unity, and to emphasize that no sit-ins or civil disobedience would be a part of the March. Now that a grudging internal unity had been won, the organizers could get on with the actual plans for the August 28 pilgrimage.[51]

While the March on Washington announcements were the focus of national headlines, much of King's time over the summer months was devoted to encouraging nascent local protest movements across the South. The most notable of these had emerged in the southern Virginia city of Danville. King had made a brief visit in March, and in late May, when local activists began mass demonstrations that met with police violence, the local black leadership appealed for SCLC's assistance. In mid-June, Wyatt Walker and Virginia Field Secretary Herbert Coulton arrived to aid the protesters, and Justice Department officials began working behind the scenes to end the demonstrations. In early July a federal judge briefly halted the protests, but when King came to Danville on July 11 to address a 1,200-person rally, SCLC was giving serious consideration to making Danville its "next Birmingham." Coulton organized an intensive voter registration drive, but mass protests did not develop.[52]

King also continued to keep in touch with the situation in Birmingham. He visited the city three times in July, and told an ACMHR mass meeting during his second trip that "things have gone well as far as the agreement goes." The first meeting of the official biracial committee took place on July 16, and one week later the new city council that had been elected with Mayor Boutwell repealed all of Birmingham's segregation ordinances. SCLC put out a press release heralding the city for living up to the agreement. The settlement, King declared, "is being implemented in good faith and on schedule."[53]

The March on Washington, however, remained King's major preoccupation throughout July, and he canceled a planned trip to Europe so as to stay in close touch. Bayard Rustin arranged a Washington meeting in which the March coordinators came together with representatives of the D.C. police and the executive branch to discuss logistical questions. Rustin reassured the group that there would be no civil disobedience or blocking of transportation, and that a large contingent of black police officers from New York City would serve as parade marshals. Lobbying visits to Capitol Hill would be closely overseen by March leaders, and the pilgrimage down Pennsylvania Avenue to the Lincoln Memorial would be solemn, with all placards and banners being produced by the March's staff. Rustin stated that he thought press estimates of 300,000 participants were far too high, and expressed hope that federal authorities could protect the busloads of southern marchers against terrorist violence. The Justice Department's representative explained that that would be impossible, but otherwise the tone of the meeting reflected official eagerness to help the March's organizers bring it off in the smoothest possible fashion. Rustin and his colleagues were pleased by that receptiveness.[54]

By mid-July the widespread concern about the March that had existed four weeks earlier had begun to dissipate. John Kennedy publicly endorsed the rally at a July 17 press conference, and in a chance encounter a day earlier, King found that previously nervous Congressman Diggs also felt better. The reassurances about no civil disobedience and no mass lobbying had fallen upon receptive ears. Movement leaders uttered reassuring comments in public. In a joint appearance on national television, each of the men, including Wilkins and Young, enthusiastically called for mass participation.

While King stressed that the March sought "to arouse the conscience of the nation over the economic plight of the Negro," Young and Wilkins emphasized that the rally was principally to support John Kennedy's civil rights bill, which was encountering rough sailing in the Senate. "We see this as an all-inclusive demonstration of our belief in the President's program," Young remarked.

Although one national news magazine ran a prominent story reporting that King was held in higher esteem than Roy Wilkins or other leaders by rank-and-file black citizens, and by one hundred black notables, all of the "big six" offered at least public lip service to the movement's internal unity. CUCRL announced its first apportionment of $565,000 among movement organizations, and no public criticisms were voiced when the NAACP and the Urban League received $125,000 each while SCLC and SNCC were awarded only $50,000 and $15,000, respectively. Although King explained that SCLC needed less money in light of its post-Birmingham financial windfall, SNCC's leaders knew that they were receiving far less than their due. "We always felt that we got the short end," John Lewis recalled. Nonetheless, SNCC's representatives pledged to abide by the rules for the March.[55]

Throughout the mid-July Senate hearings on the civil rights bill, segregationist spokesmen such as Mississippi Governor Ross Barnett repeatedly made wild accusations that the civil rights movement was a Communist conspiracy, allegations that were reported under headlines such as BARNETT CHARGES KENNEDYS ASSIST RED RACIAL PLOT. Several senators asked the FBI and Justice Department to respond to these claims, and on July 25, Attorney General Robert Kennedy released a carefully worded statement to the effect that no civil rights leaders were "Communists or Communist-controlled." That same day, the *Atlanta Constitution,* aided by another FBI leak, revealed that Jack O'Dell had continued to frequent SCLC's New York office even after his "permanent" resignation four weeks earlier. King was caught in a major public embarrassment, made all the worse when an SCLC secretary innocently told one newsman that O'Dell was still the head of the New York office. King's Atlanta headquarters corrected this misstep, but not before the national wire services had a field day with the checkered series of claims that King had made concerning O'Dell over the past nine months.[56]

Hardly a week later, the movement suffered a more painful blow at Robert Kennedy's own hands. On August 9, with the March less than three weeks away, the Justice Department announced the federal criminal indictments of nine Albany activists on charges of perjury and conspiring to injure a juror. At issue was the April picketing of an Albany food store whose proprietor, Carl Smith, had served on a federal jury that several days earlier had found notorious Baker County Sheriff L. Warren Johnson not guilty of shooting black prisoner Charles Ware. Among those charged were five leaders of the Albany Movement: Dr. Anderson, Slater King, Thomas Chatmon, Mrs. Eliza "Goldie" Jackson, and Rev. Samuel B. Wells.

The irony of criminal charges being brought against movement leaders by a Kennedy Justice Department that had stayed out of court when Marion King was beaten at the Mitchell County jail and when C. B. King was bloodied by Dougherty County Sheriff Campbell was a demoralizing blow to the already frustrated black community. Two movement appeals for the establishment of a biracial committee had been rejected by city officials in February, and internal tensions increased within the Albany Movement's leadership. Rumors circulated that Dr. Anderson would move to another city. Some of the recriminations were aimed at SCLC, but the Kennedy administration and Kennedy-appointed Federal Judge J. Robert Elliott, who was ruling against black Albany's suits at every turn, were more favored targets. Early in March the city commission repealed Albany's segregation ordinances, but the cosmetic change represented no triumph for the movement. The Johnson acquittal and the subsequent picketing of Smith's store, which movement leaders attributed to Smith's reneging on a promise to promote black employees to cashier positions to serve his heavily black clientele, was followed by more downtown picketing in early May.

A new spate of Albany protests began in mid-June under the prodding of SNCC activists. Within several days, more than one hundred demonstrators were arrested, including all the SNCC staffers the police could locate. The Justice Department dispatched federal attorney Jerome K. Heilbron to try to prod city officials to open biracial talks, but the commission again said no. One reporter stated that "anger, frustration and despair" characterized the black community, and another that "Albany remains a monument to white supremacy . . . the triumph of sophisticated segregation. . . . Not one of the expectations aroused by the demonstrations of late 1961 and mid-1962 has been realized."[57]

Outside of southwest Georgia, most movement activists, including Martin King, put aside the infuriating news from Albany to concentrate on the upcoming March. Early in August, A. Philip Randolph announced that the six-man black leadership had been supplemented by four white figures—UAW President Walter Reuther, Protestant notable Rev. Eugene Carson Blake, Jewish leader Rabbi Joachim Prinz, and Catholic layman Mathew Ahmann—and that the group would seek an audience with President Kennedy on the day of the March. Randolph also emphasized that the March was a nonpartisan undertaking, and welcomed white participation, as the addition of the white co-chairmen signified. However, as Bayard Rustin's initial *Organizing Manual* stated, some people would not be welcome. "We expressly reject the aid or participation of totalitarian or subversive groups of all persuasions. Organizational participation is invited from only the established civil rights organizations, from major religious and fraternal groups, and from labor unions." Although the major labor federation, the AFL-CIO, and its powerful president, George Meany, no fan of Reuther's, had refused to endorse the March, substantial white support seemed assured.

Randolph, King, and the other leaders were not the only parties concerned about making the pilgrimage a biracial success and keeping it free from any taint of leftist infiltration. Once John and Robert Kennedy realized that the event was inevitable, they assigned one of the attorney general's principal assistants, John Douglas, to keep a close eye on March preparations. Robert Kennedy was greatly relieved to learn from FBI reports that the Communist party was having little success in infiltrating planning groups. King was concerned that segregationists might try to smear the effort with histrionics about Rustin's leftist affiliations and homosexual proclivities, and that either the total number of marchers or the white contingent might be disappointingly small. He, Coretta, and the children took a ten-day vacation in the middle of August, relaxing at Clarence Jones's home in New York. King hoped to get started on his third book, an account of the Birmingham campaign that Stanley Levison had suggested to him three months earlier. King's second volume, *Strength to Love,* the collection of sermons on which he had labored for several years, had enjoyed modest sales following its June publication. Levison advised that a book on Birmingham, especially one incorporating the increasingly heralded letter that King had written in jail in response to criticisms by the white clergy, would receive more attention. King spent part of each day working with black ghostwriter Al Duckett, who had been hired to do much of the work on the book, but King used a good deal of the New York sojourn for family outings to the Empire State Building and the Staten Island Ferry. Those ten days were a rare opportunity to spend substantial time with his family, and King enjoyed the break. Unbeknownst to him, the FBI was happy about it too. Wiretaps had been placed on Jones's phones several weeks earlier so as to monitor his role as intermediary between King and Levison, and the taps gave the

Bureau considerable knowledge about King's private affairs during that ten-day period. Accounts of King's telephone comments were passed on to Robert Kennedy, and, on at least one occasion, from him to his brother.[58]

In the days immediately preceding the March, King and the other leaders worked to ensure a large and orderly turnout. King and Roy Wilkins appeared on *Meet the Press,* and along with others contributed articles to *The New York Times Magazine* detailing "What the Marchers Really Want." Although most press commentary continued to link the March's purpose to the passage of John Kennedy's civil rights bill, King emphasized that the goals went beyond antidiscrimination legislation. Full equality, King said, would require not merely the elimination of legal segregation, but the far broader achievement of "untrammeled opportunity for every person to fulfill his total individual capacity." For black Americans, that goal would require more than just John Kennedy's bill. "Housing and employment opportunities seem most critical—if any priority can be assigned to the many ills the Negro suffers," King stated.

The program for Wednesday's March called for the leaders to walk to the Lincoln Memorial at the head of the crowd, and for each of them to speak there as part of a mass program that also would feature other movement notables and entertainers. Afterward, the leadership would see President Kennedy at the White House. Although the schedule required all the speakers to have prepared texts of their remarks ready for advance distribution to the press Tuesday afternoon, August 27, King arrived in Washington late that evening without the necessary text. At his hotel, he sketched an outline, and shortly after midnight, wrote out his remarks in longhand. After finishing this, he had time for a few hours sleep while the draft was typed and mimeographed for distribution to newsmen on Wednesday morning.[59]

Even before King's arrival in Washington, controversy had arisen over SNCC Chairman John Lewis's text, which had been prepared and distributed in advance. Robert Kennedy's assistants, who had been keeping an eye on everything concerning the March, had collected the advance texts and passed them on to the attorney general and Burke Marshall for careful scrutiny. There was much in Lewis's remarks, which had been drafted with substantial assistance from Tom Kahn, one of Rustin's top assistants, that was not acceptable to the Kennedys. First, the speech said that SNCC could *not* support the administration's civil rights bill because it was "too little, and too late." Second, it seemed like a leftist ideological tract, with passages such as "We are now involved in a serious revolution. This nation is still a place of cheap political leaders who build their careers on immoral compromises and ally themselves with open forms of political, economic and social exploitation." Lewis went on to attack the federal indictments in Albany, and to contrast them with the lack of action against attacks on movement workers, and Kennedy's appointment of "racist judges." SNCC asked, "Which side is the federal government on?" Third, the advance text contained rhetorical statements certain to outrage many civil rights supporters. "The revolution is at hand," it declared. "We will take matters into our own hands and create a source of power, outside of any national structure that could and would assure us a victory. . . . If any radical social, political and economic changes are to take place in our society, the people, the masses, must bring them about." And, Lewis vowed, in the southland SNCC *would* bring them about. "We will march through the South, through the Heart of Dixie, the way Sherman did. We shall pursue our own 'scorched earth' policy and burn Jim Crow to the ground—nonviolently. We shall crack the South into a thousand pieces and put them back together in the image of democracy." Robert Kennedy and Burke Marshall agreed that Lewis's comments should not be allowed a place at this March. They made certain that a number of sponsors and program participants were aware of the text. Both men spoke with Patrick Cardinal O'Boyle, the Catholic prelate of Washington who was scheduled to deliver the invocation. O'Boyle's reaction was exactly what the Justice Department expected. "When I read it, I said I could not give the invocation or sit on the platform because it would be equivalent to approving a speech of this kind," the cardinal recalled. O'Boyle was especially upset about the reference to Sherman's march, inappropriate rhetoric for a nonviolent movement. Walter Reuther also was greatly displeased when he learned of Lewis's language. Word of the controversy and O'Boyle's threatened withdrawal was passed to Rustin, who called a meeting and went to Lewis's hotel room to ask that he change the offending passages. Lewis refused, despite pleas voiced at the hastily called late-night strategy session.

The dispute continued Wednesday morning. Lewis insisted he would deliver the speech without any changes, and O'Boyle reiterated his stance to Burke Marshall, who promised that the necessary changes would be made. Tens of thousands of March participants were pouring into Washington, and by shortly after noon a huge mass of people had set off from the Washington Monument toward the Lincoln Memorial without waiting for the leaders to take their place at the head of the column. Crowd estimates placed the number of participants at twice the predicted hundred thousand, and movement leaders were pleased that nearly 25 percent were white.

With the program only minutes away, the leadership arrived at the Lincoln Memorial with the controversy over Lewis's text still unresolved. Rustin promised O'Boyle that the necessary changes would be made, and the cardinal agreed to appear on the platform and deliver the invocation, so long as he was handed a copy of the revised Lewis text at least ten minutes before the SNCC chairman's appearance. O'Boyle told Rustin that if it were unsatisfactory, or if Lewis delivered the original draft, he and other religious leaders would get up and leave.

Meanwhile, in a small room just behind Lincoln's statue, Lewis, James

Forman, and Courtland Cox from SNCC were huddling with Randolph, Wilkins, King, Eugene Carson Blake, and other March leaders, plus the harried Rustin and his assistant, Tom Kahn. Many of those present had gone over the advance text closely, and Burke Marshall had personally delivered a revised draft by getting through to the Lincoln Memorial in the sidecar of a police motorcycle. At the outset of the huddle, it was clear to the outnumbered SNCC contingent that everyone else supported changes in the text. As Lewis remembered it later, Martin King firmly advised him to make the alterations. "'John, I know who you are. I think I know you well. I don't think this sounds like you.'" Wilkins and Blake also spoke in favor of changes, and complained about the usage of words like "masses" and "revolution." Randolph spoke up in support of those words, remarking that he used them himself. But, he told Lewis, he also felt the modifications should be made for the sake of unity. Then both Rustin and Kahn, who also favored the changes, pointed out that the specific deletions being requested had originally come not from Lewis's pen but from Kahn's. With that, the SNCC threesome gave in and agreed that Lewis would deliver the revised text. The meeting broke up, and everyone took their places near the podium. A copy was passed to Cardinal O'Boyle, and the program commenced without incident. Two Kennedy aides stood ready to "pull the plug" on the public address system in case anything went amiss.[60]

The massive rally was a powerful and joyous scene, with both speeches and musical presentations evoking fervent emotional responses. The program was well along before King's turn came to speak, and he moved forward carrying his prepared text. "I started out reading the speech," he recalled in a private interview three months later, and then, "just all of a sudden—the audience response was wonderful that day—and all of a sudden this thing came to me that I have used—I'd used it many times before, that thing about 'I have a dream'—and I just felt that I wanted to use it here. I don't know why, I hadn't thought about it before the speech." So he dispensed with the prepared text and went on extemporaneously. He had used the same peroration previously—at a mass meeting in Birmingham in early April, and in a speech at Detroit's huge civil rights rally in June—but on this warm August afternoon, standing before tens of thousands of people, the words carried an inspirational power greater than many of those present ever had heard before:

I say to you today, my friends, so even though we face the difficulties of today and tomorrow, I still have a dream. It is a dream deeply rooted in the American dream. I have a dream that one day this nation will rise up and live out the true meaning of its creed—we hold these truths to be self-evident, that all men are created equal.

I have a dream that one day on the red hills of Georgia, the sons of former slaves and the sons of former slave-owners will be able to sit down together at the table of brotherhood.

I have a dream that one day, even the state of Mississippi, a state sweltering with the heat of injustice, sweltering with the heat of oppression, will be transformed into an oasis of freedom and justice.

I have a dream that my four little children will one day live in a nation where they will not be judged by the color of their skin but by the content of their character. I have a dream today!

I have a dream that one day, down in Alabama, with its vicious racists, with its governor having his lips dripping with the words of interposition and nullification, one day, right there in Alabama, little black boys and black girls will be able to join hands with little white boys and white girls as sisters and brothers. I have a dream today!

I have a dream that one day every valley shall be exalted, every hill and mountain shall be made low, the rough places will be made plain and the crooked places will be made straight and the glory of the Lord shall be revealed and all flesh shall see it together.

This is our hope. This is the faith that I go back to the South with. With this faith we will be able to hew out of the mountain of despair a stone of hope. With this faith we will be able to transform the jangling discords of our nation into a beautiful symphony of brotherhood. With this faith we will be able to work together, to pray together, to struggle together, to go to jail together, to stand up for freedom together, knowing that we will be free one day.

The fervor and applause of the massive crowd rose with each new passage, and King spoke forcefully to make himself heard over the growing roar. "Let freedom ring," he said, from every mountainside in the East, from every peak in the West, even from those in the South.

When we allow freedom to ring, when we let it ring from every village and every hamlet, from every state and every city, we will be able to speed up that day when all of God's children—black men and white men, Jews and Gentiles, Protestants and Catholics—will be able to join hands and sing in the words of the old Negro spiritual, 'Free at last, free at last; thank God Almighty, we are free at last.'

Dripping with sweat, King stepped back as the audience gave him a thundering ovation. Although he did not know it, the speech had been the rhetorical achievement of a lifetime, the clarion call that conveyed the moral power of the movement's cause to the millions who had watched the live national network coverage. Now, more than ever before, even more than when the footage of Bull Connor's Birmingham had horrified thousands, white America was confronted with the undeniable justice of blacks' demands. Then, as the crowd slowly quieted, Bayard Rustin stepped to the podium and presented to the audience for their verbal ratification the specific goals of the "March on Washington for Jobs and Freedom": passage of Kennedy's civil rights bill, a $2 minimum wage, desegregation of schools, a federal public-works job program, and federal action to bar racial discrimination in employment practices. The crowd roared approval after each demand was read. As the last act of an incredible drama, Morehouse College President Benjamin E. Mays, who fifteen years earlier had had such an influential effect on Martin King, came forward and gave the benediction. As the crowd slowly broke up, the March's leaders headed for the White House.[61]

The exultant euphoria over King's remarkable performance was plain all around him. However, Coretta King's pleasure with the event was replaced by fury when she learned that her husband would not be taking her along to the audience with John Kennedy. She retreated to their hotel room, and King and his colleagues went on to the White House. John Kennedy was as happy as anyone over the joyous and peaceful tone of the March. He was pleased that no disruptive incidents had marred an event that had begun as a protest but had ended as a celebration and public relations bonanza for both the movement and for Kennedy's civil rights program. Robert Kennedy's and Burke Marshall's efforts to influence the March toward moderation and away from angry condemnations, toward a legislative focus and away from an economic one, had been an overwhelming success. The president understandably was in a jovial mood when King and the others arrived, and he immediately ordered sandwiches from the White House kitchen when Roy Wilkins mentioned that everyone had missed lunch. The leaders reported on the success of the day's events and the president congratulated them. Wilkins said that the marchers wanted not only passage of the civil rights bill, but "a change in climate that will affect their daily lives." Wilkins, Randolph, and Reuther all stressed the importance of a fair employment practices provision in the new legislation, but the president responded by emphasizing the difficult congressional future that faced the administration's civil rights bill. Urban League Director Whitney Young was struck by Kennedy's strong and excessive pessimism. Then photographers were invited in to snap pictures of the smiling group.

From the White House, the ten principal leaders of the March—six black and four white—were driven to a Washington television studio to tape an hour-long nationwide interview program. Moderator Jay Richard Kennedy was a longtime friend of both A. Philip Randolph and James Farmer's; unbeknownst to any of the leaders, he was also the Central Intelligence Agency's principal source of domestic political information on the civil rights movement and an old enemy of Stanley Levison's. To Martin King, Kennedy was simply one more interviewer; to the audience, Kennedy was introduced as an award-winning novelist. All the leaders were eager to use the program to spread the message of the March, and Randolph stressed how "the mood of the Negro today is one of impatience and anger, frustration if not desperation." Wilkins told how their group had informed the president that his civil rights bill should be strengthened further, and that Kennedy "made it plain to us that he felt we ought to take our case to the Congress." King added that movement forces would do just that, because "this is a revolution to get in . . . a revolution of rising expectations . . . a quest to get into the mainstream of American society." The taping complete, King headed back to his hotel.

King was extremely happy, in one of his most buoyant moods in some time, when he arrived back at the hotel that night. It had been a memorable day, perhaps the most gratifying event since the income-tax acquittal more than three years earlier. It had shown that he and the movement's small band of activists were far from alone, that hundreds of thousands of people were willing to support the civil rights cause. It was a moment of supreme pleasure, but one that Martin King knew would be short-lived. It had reinvigorated his faith that the movement could redeem the soul of America, as SCLC's official slogan put it, his faith that Georgia and Mississippi and Alabama could be transformed in the ways he had described to tens of thousands earlier that afternoon. But now, he knew, the time would soon be at hand when the southern struggle would have to be picked up and pursued once again. The dream was still far from fruition, and the obligation to see it realized remained as pressing as ever. With his faith renewed, the mission now, as Martin King had said that afternoon, was to "go back to the South."[62]

6

The Alabama Project,
St. Augustine,
and the
Nobel Peace Prize,
1963–1964

The March on Washington generated an emotional and political glow in which the civil rights movement could bask for weeks. The pilgrimage was the culmination of a summer during which the race issue had finally moved to the front of the American political agenda. In some circles the realization of that achievement was followed by a letdown. The principal leaders, however, aware of that danger and hopeful that the March could inaugurate a period of intensified activism, pushed ahead, intent on not allowing an attitude of self-satisfaction to develop. Martin King told reporters the day after the pilgrimage that SCLC would launch a direct-action campaign in one of four southern towns—Albany, Montgomery, Gadsden or Danville—and plans were made for a three-day retreat at Dorchester to discuss the organization's next move.

No one was more committed to keeping up the pressure and capitalizing on the success of the March than Bayard Rustin. The March, he emphasized, was "not a climax but a new beginning," and the movement now had to advance quickly to exploit the new support it had won. At one level, this support had to be used to put pressure on the Congress as soon as the anticipated Senate filibuster against the civil rights bill was launched. Rustin recommended that one thousand demonstrators a day descend upon Washington when the filibuster began and constitute themselves into a "People's Congress" to conduct their own hearings on the need for civil rights legislation. "It is hoped that [that] program could be made so exciting that the news media usually covering Congress would, in the face of a boring filibuster, shift much of its attention to *our* Congress," Rustin argued. Additionally, he hoped those efforts in Washington would be paralleled by simultaneous demonstrations in scores of other cities nationwide. Both Rustin and Tom Kahn argued that passage of a strong civil rights bill should not be the only goal. They stressed that the movement must articulate economic goals, explain to people that "the roots of discrimination are economic," and draw attention to the economic goals of the March which had received little public attention. Kahn noted that "the news media have conspicuously downplayed the ten demands," especially the economic demands that gave the March a "radical character" by intimating that "there can be no political or social freedom without economic security." "Reading popular accounts of the March," Kahn added, "it is hard to resist the notion that an effort is under way to expropriate a revolution."

It was true that few viewers of the March pictured it as the first step toward an economic revolution, but Rustin and Kahn believed that an economic emphasis would do more than simply draw the movement toward the real problems which underlay race in America. It also would contribute significantly toward winning valuable white support for the cause. "The civil rights revolution," Rustin proclaimed, "will succeed to the degree that we succeed in moving this country to the left." The movement had to avoid any suggestion that the struggle was one of black versus white, or any violent disorders that would make the cause less compelling to potentially sympathetic whites. The March had been a first step toward drawing new white allies to the movement's cause, and the emphasis now had to be upon creating an interracial coalition that could pursue those economic goals. "The civil rights movement," Rustin explained,

> has now to face the fact that it has to go deeper into the economic and social questions, because there is no way to put Negroes back to work through a purely Negro movement. . . . The civil rights movement itself cannot put Negroes back to work. What is required now is an alliance between the trade union movement and the civil rights movement and the unemployed to face this problem of jobs directly.

The movement had to enter a new phase. "I am against the present economic and social structure in this country," Rustin declared. "What I want people to do is accept the fundamental ideals of American society, democracy and equality, and try to work out an economic and social system which fits them."[1]

While Rustin and Kahn were concerned with those broad issues, Martin King and his SCLC colleagues assembled at Dorchester to reflect upon the past eight months and discuss where the organization should turn next. As Andrew Young realized, those months had witnessed some important changes in King. Before Birmingham, and ever since Montgomery, King had become aware of the increasingly prominent public leadership role into which he was being cast, but he had been less than eager to assume all the responsibilities that came with it. "After

Montgomery, I think he tried to run from it, especially after he was stabbed," Young observed. "And my notion of it is that it was almost Birmingham . . . before he took up the mantle of leadership, that from '57 to '63 he was being dragged into one situation after another that he didn't want to be in. . . . He didn't see himself as being the leader of everything black people wanted to do. He resisted as long as he could the responsibilities and burdens of taking on a whole movement for social change."

King lamented the flood of requests that constantly inundated him. "About three or four months after Montgomery got underway, numerous demands came in for speaking commitments, and I don't think I've been free from these demands since then." He told another interviewer of how "I dream of the day when the demands presently cast upon me will be greatly diminished." Young thought that King's lack of personal ambition was a key both to his integrity and to the trust that tens of thousands of people felt for him. Jim Bevel humorously made the same point in a Chicago talk. "King ain't after nothing. Most of the time you see him he's trying to get somewhere to sleep. [Audience laughter] Seriously, that's what he's doing most of the time, scheming up ways to get out of doing some work, off hiding so nobody will bother him."

Ralph Abernathy recalled that "we knew that we had developed into symbols." Others could see that realization in King too, and once King expressed his dismay about it to his old Crozer mentor, J. Pius Barbour. "'I am conscious of two Martin Luther Kings. I am a wonder to my-self. . . . I am mystified at my own career. The Martin Luther King that the people talk about seems to me somebody foreign to me,'" Barbour remembered. "He couldn't understand his career, all the publicity and things he'd gotten . . . with no effort of his own. . . . He said, 'There's a kind of dualism in my life'. . . . He always said that that Martin Luther King the famous man was a kind of stranger to him."

Nonetheless, King knew he could not flee from his role, no matter how much he might dislike its daily burdens. "I think that Martin always felt that he had a special purpose in life and that that purpose in life was something that was given to him by God, that he was the son and grand-son of Baptist preachers, and he understood, I think, the scriptural no-tion of men of destiny," Young observed. "That came from his family and his church, and basically the Bible."

Dorothy Cotton and other close colleagues also saw it. "People are predestined . . . to play special roles in life, if they're open to it, and I think Dr. King eventually became quite open to it. I don't think it was a conscious decision necessarily, but he found himself in that position." Albany's Dr. Anderson agreed. "He literally felt as though this was a divine calling. . . . This was not a job for him, this was a life's commit-ment." Glenn Smiley felt the same. "Eventually Martin came to accept the fact that this was his destiny." However, "it was not a mantle that fell on him lightly."

By mid-1963 Walter Fauntroy felt that King "was fairly comfortable with his mission, and the need to suffer to carry it out." King occasionally gave explicit voice to that awareness. "I pray that recognizing the necessity of suffering we will make of it a virtue," he remarked one tense evening. "To suffer in a righteous cause is to grow to our humanity's full stature. If only to save ourselves, we need the vision to see the ordeals of this generation as the opportunity to transform ourselves and American society."

King thought often about "this challenge to be loyal to something that transcends our immediate lives." "We have," he told one audience, "a responsibility to set out to discover what we are made for, to discover our life's work, to discover what we are called to do. And after we discover that, we should set out to do it with all of the strength and all of the power that we can muster."

The revelation in the kitchen seven years earlier had fundamentally eased his acceptance of that responsibility, for the tangible experience of a transforming faith is a profoundly strengthening and liberating event. "There are certain spiritual experiences that we continue to have," King stated, "that cannot be explained with materialistic notions." One "knows deep down within there is something in the very structure of the cosmos that will ultimately bring about fulfillment and the triumph of that which is right. And this is the only thing that can keep one going in difficult periods."

SCLC's early September Dorchester discussions focused on narrower and more immediate considerations, however. Wyatt Walker had given increasing thought to how southern protest campaigns should be mounted. The contrast between SCLC's experience in Albany and that in Birmingham suggested several important lessons, Walker said. First, the Birmingham effort had benefited from better planning and calculation, preparations that had not been made in advance of SCLC's sudden involvement in Albany. Second, Albany had demonstrated that internal divisions were one of the most dangerous threats to any protest campaign, and such problems had been far better contained in Birmingham. Third, the two campaigns had shown that selection of specific goals both aided public understanding of the protests' purpose *and* allowed participants a firm sense of victory when some gains, no matter how minor, were won. The two efforts also had demonstrated the potential power of economic boycotts and the utility of activating youthful protesters. Jim Bevel and Walker had both been impressed by how spontaneous participants—"people who have nothing to lose—unemployed, students, people off the streets"—could form the backbone of a movement in cities where more prosperous black citizens were reluctant to participate in demonstrations.

The group agreed upon several towns as possible targets. Internal divisions would be a serious obstacle to working with Savannah's highly active black community, and the combination of police and judicial repression made Danville formidable. Voter registration efforts were moving forward in some areas of Louisiana and Georgia, and SCLC's representative in northeastern North Carolina, Rev. F. H. LaGarde, described an ongoing local campaign in Williamston. No firm choices were made but by the end of the three-day retreat it was agreed that Bevel and newly hired Affiliates Director C. T. Vivian would look into Williamston.[2]

During the Dorchester gathering, word arrived from Birmingham of new racist violence. On the same day that two black students desegregated a previously all-white city school, a bomb demolished the home of black attorney Arthur Shores, and shortly thereafter a black man was killed in what appeared to be a random racist shooting. Some local leaders wondered if the victim's physical resemblance to Fred Shuttlesworth explained why he had been shot down. King decried the violence in a telegram to John Kennedy, and told reporters that Alabama Governor George C. Wallace had to bear moral responsibility for what was happening.

King had many demands on his time. SCLC's New York office was in need of a director after Jack O'Dell's departure. The FBI listened in as King held several long phone conversations with Clarence Jones to discuss whether Rustin's successful leadership of the March on Washington meant that he could be placed in charge of SCLC's New York operations without the issue of his sexual preference becoming a subject of public gossip. King wanted to discuss that and other questions with Levison, but Jones reminded King that his promise to the Kennedys barred SCLC's president from making contact with his old friend. "I'll discuss it with our friend and get his feelings about it," Jones reassured King. "He understands why I haven't called him," King asked. "Yes, absolutely. In fact, he would be a little upset if you did," Jones responded. "I'm trying to wait until things cool off—until this civil rights debate is over—as long as they may be tapping these phones, you know—but you can discuss that with him," King explained. Jones made contact with Levison, and the FBI promptly informed Robert Kennedy that the King-Levison connection remained intact despite King's promise. That news, plus reports that Jack O'Dell had been seen at SCLC's New York office, strengthened the administration's suspicion that King was being less than frank with it and intensified its fear that any public revelation of King's associations could scuttle the civil rights bill.[3]

King's worries about those matters were swept aside on Sunday morning, September 15, when a powerful dynamite blast devastated Birmingham's Sixteenth Street Baptist Church and killed four young black girls who were attending Sunday school. It was the greatest human tragedy that had befallen the movement. The rage and desperation felt by black Birmingham exploded on the city's streets as hundreds of furious citizens pelted police with rocks and other debris. Officers tried to disperse the crowds by firing shotguns over their heads, and one black youth was struck in the back and killed. Another young black man was murdered in a racial shooting incident just outside of town, and a half-dozen other people, black and white, were injured during the disturbances. After King arrived in town Sunday evening, he realized that tangible federal action was necessary to reassure the black community of its physical safety. "We feel that Birmingham is now in a state of civil disorder," an "emergency situation," King told reporters Monday morning. The U.S. Army, he said, "ought to come to Birmingham and take over this city and run it, because Negroes are tired now, tireder than ever before." King spoke by phone to Clarence Jones in New York, and explained how "something dramatic has to be done by the federal government to reestablish a sense of hope in the Negro people here. . . . Unless some kind of national pressure is brought to bear on the President to do something, it's just going to lead to an even deeper night of bitterness . . . I think the main thing is to try to get that kind of pressure on the President to have federal intervention here." Later that day King sent Kennedy a telegram requesting an audience for himself and half a dozen Birmingham black leaders as soon as possible. If the federal government failed to act meaningfully, he warned, "we shall see the worst racial holocaust this nation has ever seen."

Monday morning John Kennedy issued a statement decrying the bombing and implicitly pointing the moral finger at Alabama Governor Wallace. "Public disparagement of law and order," the president declared, "has encouraged violence which has fallen on the innocent." Justice Department aides bemoaned "the dismal lack of leadership" in white Birmingham, and considered developing "an intelligence program separate and apart from the FBI" for better information on extremists.

Movement activists discussed more decisive responses. Jim and Diane Nash Bevel were in Williamston, North Carolina, when word of the killings reached them. They decided immediately that massive nonviolent action should be mounted against the state of Alabama, and especially its government in Montgomery, in response to the multiple deaths. Diane conferred in Atlanta on Monday with SCLC's C. T. Vivian, and by the time she arrived in Birmingham on Tuesday, she had prepared a "Proposal for Action in Montgomery" that called for movement supporters to close down completely Alabama's capital city. What the proposal envisioned was the actual creation of the "nonviolent army" that James Lawson first had spoken of two years earlier. The effort, she said, would have two principal objectives: "removal of George Wallace from the governorship of Alabama," and registration of every Alabama citizen twenty-one years of age or older as a certified voter. The plan of action would follow a military motif:

Immediately recruit Alabama students and adults who will be trained intensively in nonviolent discipline. A school and headquarters for this should be set up in Montgomery. The program must include:

a. Nonviolent workshops—general & specific

b. Marching and drills in command and coordination of battle groups

c. Instruction in jail know-how; cooperation or noncooperation with jail procedures and trial

d. Group morale while imprisoned

e. Drill in dealing with fire hoses, dogs, tear gas, cattle prods, police brutality, etc.

f. Practice in blocking runways, train tracks, etc.

g. Elementary politics including an analysis of this program.

Then, when the forces were ready, "a written case against George Wallace" would be made public, along with "a declaration that within our consciences his government is null and void." After that would come the climactic step:

REVOLUTION. Severing communication from state capitol bldg. and from city of Montgomery by:

1. Surrounding the capitol building in such a way as to allow no vehicles to enter or leave the bldg. and preferably in such a way that pedestrians may not enter or leave also.

2. Keeping busy all the telephones in the capitol bldg. by calling and talking about freedom.

3. Lying on railroad tracks, runways, and bus driveways cutting off train, bus, and plane transportation.

4. Organize a general work strike.

5. Study the tax set up and refuse to pay taxes in the most feasible manner.

6. Wear overalls and something black at all times (armbands, maybe).

7. Establish instructive mass meetings several times a week in several towns.

8. Demonstrations aimed at federal government to insure our right to vote.

9. Demonstrations at the United Nations to secure the vote.

And, Diane Bevel indicated, there could be much more. "This is an army," she stressed. "Develop a flag and an insignia or pin or button. Use candlelight and kerosene lamps and close down the power companies." Additionally, there were "many other such possibilities," some far more drastic. "Ask Kennedy not to recognize Wallace's government and cut off federal funds." Right now, however, movement activists had to agree to this plan and then move into action. "Start recruiting Birmingham students to train and then to demonstrate and also to be used to recruit students in Montgomery and other cities." The youngsters whom SCLC had organized back in May, and who had worked in the voter registration efforts, could form a core for this new army.[4]

Diane Bevel explained her plan to Fred Shuttlesworth upon her arrival in Birmingham, and he recommended a strategy meeting with King before any steps were taken. The funeral of one bombing victim—Carole Robertson—was held on Tuesday, and on Wednesday King preached at the joint service for the other three young girls—Cynthia Wesley, Denise McNair, and Addie Mae Collins. Diane Bevel was one of thousands of people who crowded into or around Sixth Avenue Baptist Church, and it was clear to her that the mood of the crowd cried out for effective leadership. "People were highly aroused, frustrated, and sad, eager to do something, but no one knew what to do," she wrote several days later. "You can tell people not to fight *only* if you offer them a way by which justice can be served without violence."

That evening, September 18, after the joint funeral, Shuttlesworth arranged the strategy meeting with King, several SCLC staffers, and local activists. Diane Bevel presented her Proposal for Action in Montgomery, explaining that the angry mood of black Birmingham called out for effective channels of action into which this boiling energy could be directed. Her plans for Alabama's capital city would provide that type of channel. As Birmingham pastor John Thomas Porter later described King's response, he simply "looked at her and laughed . . . because she suggested we go out and throw ourselves under trains and the wheels of airplanes, and he just chuckled. He said, 'Oh, Diane. Now wait, wait. Now, let's think about this.'" In King's eyes the whole idea "was a joke, really," Porter said, but Diane Bevel, "she was for real." Many of the others present shared King's response, and Bevel was told that the idea would have to be considered carefully before any action could begin. That was King's, as well as Shuttlesworth's, gentle way of saying no, but Bevel's enthusiasm for the plan remained strong. King did not explicitly reject the idea, so she remained optimistic that other activists' ardor for such action would bring King around. Word of her initiative spread rapidly in movement circles, and SNCC was solidly behind it. Jim Bevel, C. T. Vivian, and even Wyatt T. Walker—no favorite of many younger activists—were also positively disposed. Some of the SCLC contingent knew that King had been considering a suggestion from Clarence Jones that the black leadership call for a brief nationwide work stoppage and a moment of silence to commemorate the victims of Birmingham's bombers. Ralph Abernathy had spoken publicly about organizing a "march on Montgomery," and Jim Bevel was committed to finding some admixture of his wife's initiative and Abernathy's suggestion that could win King's support and focus upon George Wallace and the right to vote. "'What do we need to do to bring Alabama to a direct breaking point?'" young Birmingham CORE activist William "Meatball" Douthard told his superiors Diane

Bevel was asking. "'What will it take to really break the back of segregation in Alabama?'" The answer, according to Bevel and a number of young activists, was "a series of demonstrations in Montgomery which would be composed of upwards of 20–40 thousand students and adults," Douthard reported. "The demonstrators who would converge on Montgomery, putting the issue directly in Wallace's lap, would be protesting only one issue—the right of Negroes to vote." If organizing started soon, the climactic protests could take place in March or April, 1964.[5]

Intensive debate about those possibilities dominated the movement's agenda throughout the week following Birmingham's tragic deaths. Meanwhile, John Kennedy agreed to meet with King, Abernathy, Shuttlesworth, L. H. Pitts, A. G. Gaston, influential Baptist leader Rev. J. L. Ware, and CME Bishop H. I. Murchison. Kennedy expressed to the group his sorrow and concern about the Birmingham developments, but King told him that federal action, not just words, was necessary. The Birmingham situation, King said, was "so serious that it threatens not only the life and stability of Birmingham and Alabama, but of our whole nation." The city had reached "a state of civil disorder," and "the Negro community is about to reach a breaking point. . . . I am convinced that if something isn't done to give the Negro a new sense of hope and a sense of protection, there is the danger that we will face in that community the worst race riot that we've ever seen in this country. I think it's just at that point. I don't think it will happen if we can do something to save the situation, but I do think . . . that something dramatic must be done at this time to give the Negro in Birmingham and Alabama a new sense of hope and a good sense of protection."

King had several specific recommendations that Birmingham's black leaders had endorsed. Although "the problem in the South cannot be ultimately solved with federal troops," soldiers were temporarily needed to protect black citizens from the state troopers because "unfortunately Alabama has a madman for its governor." Also, federal punishment of government contractors who discriminated against black employees was necessary. Those two steps, King said, "can lead us out of this dark moment," and would reassure both blacks and white moderates that the federal government was supporting them.

John Kennedy acknowledged that federal action was needed, but said no grounds for dispatching troops presently existed. Instead, he would send two special representatives, former Army Secretary Kenneth Royall and former West Point football coach Earl "Red" Blaik, to Birmingham as presidential mediators. Additionally, Kennedy had summoned a group of white Birmingham leaders to the White House for a meeting to encourage their support for racial justice. In the meantime, black retaliatory violence had to be avoided, the president emphasized. "I can't do very much, Congress can't do very much, unless we keep the support of the white community throughout the country. Once that goes, then we're pretty much down to a racial struggle." No one could guarantee that this bombing was the last, but "I think you've just got to tell the Negro community that this is the very hard price which they have to pay to get this job done."

King told reporters after the session that Kennedy's statements represented "the kind of federal concern needed." Several days later Kennedy told Birmingham's white leaders to live up to their May accord and be thankful that King, not SNCC, was leading the opposition. "SNCC has got an investment in violence," the president asserted. "They're sons of bitches." King may have been reassured by Kennedy's comments to him, but administration officials were worried about the Montgomery "mass action" plan. Burke Marshall had assigned a young black Justice Department attorney, Thelton Henderson, to keep a close eye on King and developments in Birmingham. Within days of the drafting of Diane Bevel's plan, Henderson had sent Marshall a complete copy. The content of the plan created consternation in the Kennedy Justice Department, and Marshall warned that this new movement stance was "revolutionary." Henderson could not confirm whether the plan would be implemented, modified, or discarded, and the administration remained acutely concerned.[6]

When SCLC's annual convention opened in Richmond on September 24, informal discussions focused on the Montgomery issue, and several prominent news stories detailed for the first time some of the plan's specific recommendations. King brushed off press queries about the Montgomery plan, and volunteered that it was more likely that SCLC would launch a campaign in Danville and/or resume mass demonstrations in Birmingham. Action also was possible in Shreveport, Gadsden, Savannah, Macon, Greenwood, and Nashville. King preferred SCLC to concentrate its forces in Danville, as he told SCLC's Board of Directors. An active discussion ensued, with some members, such as Rev. Benjamin Hooks of Memphis, arguing that the March on Montgomery should be a top priority, and others, like King's old Montgomery colleague L. D. Reddick, contending that SCLC had to focus on Birmingham. King admitted that Alabama was "more tense now than ever before," and that some SCLC staff would have to remain there. Rev. Major Jones, who had known King since his days at Boston University, pressed hard to make Alabama and the Montgomery plan SCLC's top priority, but Ralph Abernathy warned that some elements in the local black community might not give the Montgomery action their full support. Fred Shuttlesworth asserted that "demonstrations may have to start again in Birmingham," but Virginia's Rev. Milton Reid said that the situation in Danville was equally urgent. Reverend Hooks and Professor Reddick moved that SCLC declare Birmingham its first priority and meet with the Montgomery community to discuss mass action. Finally, King put a halt to the discussion by suggesting that they postpone the choice between Alabama and Danville until more information could be gathered and evaluated by SCLC's top leadership a week or two hence in Atlanta. His colleagues acquiesced, and he agreed to Abernathy's suggestion that the board endorse the idea of a March on Montgomery while deferring any decisions.

Another major issue confronting the board was King and Abernathy's desire to expand Operation Breadbasket. The Atlanta effort to win more and better jobs for blacks was making good progress, and King hoped that a southwide and eventually a national expansion could be launched. King pointed out that one aspect of this expansion could be a call for nationwide boycotts of those industries and businesses whose black employment policies were especially poor. Such a plan would be more effective than black comedian Dick Gregory's idea that the movement promote a Christmas boycott as a national protest against the Birmingham murders.

Wyatt Walker favored "a national program of economic withdrawal" and believed that the spring boycott in Birmingham had played a crucial role in moving the city's business leadership toward a settlement. Speaking to a public session of the convention, Walker declared that "the 'Freedom Now' forces must devise a way to command the attention of the national community in order that all the emoluments of citizenship are secured once, now and forever." Ways to do that, Walker indicated, included "a nationwide work stoppage" or a day "when major transportation centers will be strangled by mass acts of civil disobedience" that would "literally immobilize the nation." His own preference, however, was for economic action. "A massive refusal to buy on the part of the Negro community and others of good will would throw the business world into shock." The movement's ability to affect the "flow of dollars" was potentially one of its most powerful weapons, he emphasized. "Maybe then, and only then, will the nation's financial leaders exert some initiative in eliminating the evils of segregation and discrimination."

Walker's call for action received prominent news coverage across the country. Reporters said that the atmosphere at the convention was one of "bitterness and disappointment" over the Birmingham deaths, with "a steadily mounting deep sense of urgency and widespread frustration." King sensed the growing despair and a particular bitterness toward the Kennedys. Again the question voiced by John Lewis with reference to the Albany indictments was asked: Which side was the federal government on? Most who attended the SCLC convention felt that the administration's response to the Birmingham tragedy had been inadequate, and King realized that his acceptance of the president's token action had disappointed many people. In his major address to the Richmond convention, SCLC's president criticized Kennedy's failure to do more than appoint two mediators. Just three days earlier King had stated that Danville should be the site of SCLC's next campaign, but now, realizing that many of those at the convention felt the need for direct action in Alabama, King sounded a different note, asserting that both the economic action and SCLC's protest staff should focus upon Birmingham.

King's call to action was a more decisive position than he had taken in the SCLC board meeting forty-eight hours earlier. "Starting with Christmas and continuing for as long as it is necessary, we will withhold economic support from any product produced in Birmingham, any service or product whose source comes from Birmingham or benefits Birmingham," he declared. There was no reference to tying the boycott to a Breadbasket strategy, and although Danville remained high on SCLC's agenda, Birmingham, King said, was the number one challenge confronting the movement. "Birmingham is the symbol, the beginning of the revolution. We knew, when we went into Birmingham, . . . that this was the test, the acid test of whether the revolution would succeed." In early May, the success had seemed real, but the modest changes called for by the settlement, and the deaths at Sixteenth Street church raised the question of how much the spring protests had actually achieved and how much Birmingham had really changed. Now, four months later, "we are faced with an extreme situation and therefore our remedies must be extreme." King stated that he would return to Birmingham to lead new demonstrations unless the city government promptly met four conditions: hire Birmingham's first black policemen, issue a public call for law and order, demand the withdrawal of the provocative Alabama state troopers, and institute good-faith negotiations with the black community. If those actions were not taken, King said, Birmingham would see mass demonstrations on a scale larger than those of May.

As King's varied public pronouncements indicated, SCLC wanted to take immediate action, but was uncertain about exactly what to do. An atmosphere of hectic irresolution was intensified by the comments of guest speakers at the convention and by the disparate reactions of other movement observers to SCLC's strategic debates. Roy Wilkins spoke to one session and made clear his distaste for any national economic action but sounded supportive of possible SCLC action in Alabama or Danville. New York Congressman Adam Clayton Powell, on the other hand, explicitly called for SCLC to become a national organization and expand its programs to the North. Powell coupled this with a stinging attack on the NAACP and the Urban League, and offered King a co-pastorship at his own Abyssinian Baptist Church in New York as an aid in building a nationwide movement. King politely declined the offer, and assured Wilkins that CUCRL, the "unity council," could discuss the boycott plan before SCLC launched it. Additionally, while Wilkins predicted that the Kennedy civil rights bill would be approved by Congress, Powell asserted that it had no chance of passage. King handled that disagreement by vowing another March on Washington if the measure encountered serious problems. "If something is not done quickly, if Congress filibusters the civil rights bill and does not pass the public accommodations section, Negroes will have to engage in massive civil disobedience," he declared. "It would be a massive uprising, and all we would be able to do would be to try to channel it into nonviolent lines."[7]

Although King and his colleagues left Richmond without agreement on what to do next, others moved to reduce SCLC's options. In Birmingham, A. G. Gaston and Arthur Shores stated that "there is no need for any additional outside help at this time, and we would hope that there would not be any additional outside interference that would disturb our present negotiations." Meanwhile, Wilkins and other moderate figures worked behind the scenes to ensure that SNCC and SCLC's national boycott idea would be rebuffed at the next meeting of CUCRL in New York on October 4. King backed away from the idea in the interests of unity once Wilkins, Whitney Young, and others had expressed their opposition. Bayard Rustin, usually dispirited by King's unwillingness to argue with the sharp-tongued NAACP chief, felt this time that the choice was a wise one. Rustin insisted that the coalition that had mounted the March on Washington had to be kept intact, and that the movement's diversity had to be prevented "from becoming disunity." This meant no open conflict between King and Wilkins, and hence no "nationalization" of SCLC. Thus, "the big, broad questions that are crying for attention," as L. D. Reddick termed them, would have to be addressed by King and SCLC in terms of renewed direct action in the South.

As King considered how SCLC should proceed, new tensions developed involving Wyatt Walker. SCLC's talented chief of staff never had been satisfied with his modest salary of $10,000, but the Board of Directors, some of whom bristled at Walker's outspokenness, were not eager to grant him a raise. Also, Walker, who was a firm administrator, felt that the kind-hearted King, who always searched for the good in all people, was undercutting his efforts to bring order to SCLC's operations. In particular, King had not backed Walker's attempts to exert authority over Jim Bevel. Then, in a move that added insult to injury, King and the board changed Walker's title from executive director of SCLC to executive assistant to King. They insisted that the title change signified no loss of status, but Walker rejected this explanation. "That was a demotion," he later explained. "They tried to tell me, 'No, that's more,'" and "I said, 'Look, lack of sense I don't have. Don't tell me that I haven't been demoted.'" Angry and insulted, Walker wrote a letter of resignation to King, warning that he planned to leave at the end of December. "The conditions under which I work have become completely intolerable. I am willing to reconsider this step only in the light of an immediate solution to the conditions which have prompted this action." Walker wanted a raise to $12,000, to meet the costs of raising four children, plus a more impressive title, executive vice-president. On those points the board would not budge, but King reassured Walker that he would strive to be more supportive of Walker's administrative authority. Walker withdrew his resignation, but the underlying tensions remained.[8]

Another pressing concern was the Birmingham book manuscript. Ghostwriter Al Duckett had made considerable progress, but King was worried about the project. He pressed Clarence Jones to arrange a meeting with Levison, in violation of King's promise to the Kennedys. The meeting took place at the New York Park Sheraton on October 5, and Levison reluctantly agreed to take an active role in overseeing the work of a new ghostwriter, Nat Lamar. A troubled Levison explained over his wiretapped phone to one of his oldest friends, businesswoman Alice Loewi, that allowing King to violate his pact with the Kennedys was "a very annoying thing. I don't want to maintain contact and yet this was an obligation I took—and you can't just let it go." Apprised of these developments through its electronic surveillance of Levison and Jones, the FBI trumpeted to the attorney general the news that King and Levison were in direct, surreptitious contact despite King's promise not to do so.

King remained preoccupied with the question of where SCLC should turn next in the South. During the first few days of October, King tried to resolve the competing considerations about Birmingham, Danville, and Montgomery that had been raised in Richmond. To him, the top priority was indisputable. "We cannot leave the Birmingham situation until we emerge with a clear cut victory . . . it would be a great setback for the whole movement if we fail to sustain the victory achieved last spring." King felt that two weighty considerations required that SCLC launch "a new action program" in Alabama's largest city. First was "the failure of the merchants to carry out every aspect of the agreement. . . . They have backed up on their promise to hire Negro clerks. This means that some pressure tactic will have to be brought to bear on the merchants to dramatize this broken promise." Second was the "sense of hopelessness and frustration in large segments of the Negro community" generated by the September violence. Together, these factors meant that SCLC had three tasks to undertake in Birmingham:

1. We must put pressure on the merchants to carry out all aspects of the agreement;

2. We must press the city council and mayor to make immediate good faith steps to restore a sense of hope and protection in the Negro community;

3. We must keep alive the great hope that Birmingham brought to Negroes all over the nation by making it palpably clear that we are still on the job in Birmingham, and will remain firm in a determination to see conditions changed for the better.

An immediate goal was a city commitment to hire Birmingham's first black policemen, a demand that Fred Shuttlesworth had been voicing since 1956.

King explained to his colleagues that it was the *threat* of demonstrations, rather than the protests themselves, that he hoped would move Birmingham forward. "The city does not want to see demonstrations renewed, if for no other reason than that the city's economy can't afford it. I must hasten to say that I would hope that demonstrations will not have to be resumed," King stressed. "If they are resumed they will be effective only if they are bigger and more determined than before. This would be no minor undertaking." Though SCLC was in the best financial shape of its life—with income of $735,000 and expenses of only $383,000 for the twelve months ending in August, 1963—hundreds of thousands of dollars were tied up in the bail bonds that had been obtained to secure the release of the hundreds of demonstrators arrested in May. The wealthiest supporters had already given more than their due for the year, and King believed that "all available resources are pretty well exhausted." Therefore, "we must realistically recognize that demonstrations must be an absolute last resort on our part. Our challenge now is to be ingenious enough to keep the threat of demonstrations alive so as to give the local and national public a picture of our determination and continued militancy and yet constantly find face saving retreats in order to avoid demonstrations if possible." It was a pragmatic yet sagacious strategy, and one he thought would succeed.

King's first step in implementing this plan would be to go to Birmingham on October 7 to announce SCLC's plans. He would declare that "if a certain number of Negro policemen are not hired in two weeks, we will have no alternative but to resume demonstrations." Depending upon the city's response, King might suggest that Birmingham set a time when black officers would be hired, but if no positive reply was made by October 22, SCLC would announce demonstrations for the near future. If that threat did not prod the whites, protests would begin on November 1.

King was optimistic that Birmingham would respond affirmatively. If so, SCLC would turn its full attention toward Danville, where "the arrogant refusal of the city officials to grant any of the demands of the Negro community is an affront to the whole civil rights movement." By late October, SCLC's staff could "develop a genuine nonviolent army" in Danville, and mass demonstrations could begin in early November. Religious leaders, celebrities, and other "symbols" would be invited to participate, and if wholesale arrests followed, SCLC could step up the pressure by calling for "a nationwide and possibly world-wide boycott of Dan River Mill products," Danville's dominant corporation. Then, sometime in early 1964, SCLC could proceed with the "Alabama Project" that Jim and Diane Nash Bevel were promoting.[9]

On October 7, King put his Birmingham blueprint into action. He announced that unless the city hired twenty five black officers within two weeks, and unless city officials opened face-to-face negotiations with local black leaders over the additional hiring of black employees, demonstrations would resume. This time, he warned, "we will bring many people in from other communities," stage larger protests than those in May, and perhaps call a nationwide march on Birmingham. The threat of the new demonstrations loomed large after Birmingham Mayor Albert Boutwell and the city council decreed on October 9 that there would be no new talks about hiring black police.

After a trip home, King returned to Birmingham on October 14 to press the demand for black policemen and to call upon the black community to reinstitute its boycott of Birmingham's downtown stores. "Last May," he told over one thousand listeners at an ACMHR rally, "we had an agreement with the downtown merchants to desegregate luncheon counters, fitting rooms, and take down the white and colored signs and also to hire Negro clerks. Some of these agreements have taken place, but some of them are still not being done. The only way to remedy this is to boycott. Don't forget that we have enough buying power to make the difference between profit and loss." Fred Shuttlesworth warned the crowd that some black "leaders" might be talking to Mayor Boutwell behind their backs, and King realized that a resumption of protests would not draw support from all segments of the black community. Nonetheless, King felt that he and SCLC could not avoid the challenge that Birmingham represented. "God has told me that he wants freedom for us," he told the crowd at John Porter's Sixth Avenue Baptist Church. "I'm not going to run from the responsibility. It may mean going through the floods and going through the waters, but I'm going if it means that. It may mean going through the storms and through the winds, but I'm going if it means that. It may mean going to jail, but I'm going if it means that. It may even mean physical death, but if it means that I will die standing up for the freedom of my people—" and the thundering roar of the crowd drowned out his final words.

The following day King went to Selma to address a community rally. He had been invited by Mrs. Amelia P. Boynton, a local activist who had sought both SNCC's and SCLC's help in confronting the heavy-handed racism of Dallas County Sheriff James G. Clark, Jr. Ten months had passed since King's earlier visit to Selma, ten months that had witnessed significant black efforts to build a local movement. In April, SCLC had considered supporting protests in Selma, but Birmingham's events had foreclosed that possibility. Since then, local youngsters had mounted a series of mid-September sit-in demonstrations, and SNCC had organized a massive "Freedom Day" turnout at the county courthouse to protest discriminatory voter registration practices. Jim Bevel wondered if Selma's grass-roots activism could be combined with his Alabama Project idea, but King's speaking visit was just another "one night stand."[10]

In his appearances across the country, King emphasized that the movement had to achieve a clear-cut victory in Birmingham. He spoke out against the Kennedys' efforts to persuade liberals in the House of Representatives not to strengthen the administration's civil rights bill in ways that might reduce the chances for moderate Republican support on the House floor and in the Senate. He declared again that protests would resume in Birmingham unless twenty-five black policemen were hired. On October 21 he returned to Birmingham to witness a standing vote at the evening's mass meeting in favor of new demonstrations. The next day the city council again rejected the demand, and King went into a five-hour huddle with two dozen local black leaders. Many of those present had little enthusiasm for resuming direct action, and King realized he would have to change his plans. He emerged from the session to tell reporters that he was withdrawing the demand for black policemen in order to allow the city council to save face. He claimed that only his public deadline had led the council to refuse the idea, and that he believed Birmingham would take the initiative once the formal threat was removed. King asserted there would still be "a full scale assault in Birmingham," but knowledgeable observers knew that most black leaders would not support further protests even though King and Fred Shuttlesworth wanted to proceed.

King was disappointed at the lack of local support and brooded about how the movement's inaction, combined with the Kennedys' ambivalent stance toward strong legislation, had dissipated the civil rights momentum that had existed after the March on Washington. The national political climate appeared to be turning more conservative, and King feared the effects that the emergence of conservative Arizona Senator Barry Goldwater as front-runner for the 1964 Republican presidential nomination would have on John Kennedy's civil rights position. Andrew Young mused to King about how the Kennedy brothers' moderate stand on civil rights legislation reflected their fears about Goldwater. Their efforts to limit the House bill, Young said, seem "to indicate the Kennedys are trying to assure the nation that they are still 'white.' This effort to attain a more moderate image could do us a great deal of harm between now and the '64 elections." The best way for the movement to counterbalance this trend, Young said, would be for voter registration efforts to be intensified across the South and expanded to major northern cities. A growing field staff was making substantial contributions to voter registration drives in Georgia, some parishes of Louisiana, several counties in eastern North Carolina, and southern Virginia. These efforts would continue, but Young told King that the movement should give greater attention to the possibilities of registering thousands of new black voters in crucial "swing states" in the North and Midwest. Such a drive would help "counter this conservative swing within our nation," might incline Republicans to name a more moderate standard-bearer than Goldwater, and would remind the Kennedys to tend their left flank as well as their right. "This kind of move in this election," Young said, "can be much more important than pushing the economic emphasis, and would receive much wider support."[11]

Stanley Levison and Bayard Rustin shared King's and Young's thoughts. Levison pressed Clarence Jones to convey to King the absolute necessity of emerging victorious from Birmingham before SCLC moved on to Danville or any other city. FBI officials focused upon Levison's ongoing involvement in King's and SCLC's affairs, and in early October renewed their entreaties to Robert Kennedy about the serious security threat represented by Levison's role and King's refusal to sever the relationship. Their warnings received a sympathetic hearing by the attorney general, and Robert Kennedy felt compelled to take the step that the FBI had been recommending since midsummer: the wiretapping of King's home and office in Atlanta. If Levison were a Communist agent, as the Bureau led Kennedy to believe, and if King was dissembling about his ties to the man, such direct surveillance was warranted. Given the fact that any public leak about the King-Levison allegations by the Bureau or its congressional friends might torpedo the civil rights bill, granting the FBI its wiretaps would serve a political as well as a "national security" purpose. Kennedy also approved an FBI request to wiretap Bayard Rustin.

Rustin felt strongly that the movement needed "to achieve a genuine break-through in the integration struggle" rather than "mere 'token' achievements." The leadership should not sit back and celebrate the events of the spring and summer, because "progress, if measured against the goal to be reached, has been minimal." Like Andrew Young, Rustin believed that opposition to racial change was growing, not declining, and that the movement had to combat this trend with "a more militant as well as astute counter-strategy." The Kennedys' civil rights stance was weaker than it ought to be, and the black leadership should force their hand. "The change which the integration movement seeks in various aspects of American life is . . . a 'revolutionary' one," and "a new dimension of Direct Action" ought to be employed to pursue it. Birmingham had symbolized for millions the moral rightness of the movement's cause, and it was there that SCLC again should focus its energies. Rustin argued that a new protest effort would help win passage of the civil rights bill and strengthen the Kennedys' position:

> It will be precisely in the degree that action takes place outside Washington that Congress will act on legislation. To assume that in the absence of such pressure one can 'trust Congressmen to vote right,' is the height of folly and weakness. By the same token it will be the continuance of action, which admittedly brought the President to the point of introducing legislation, which will convince him that he must abandon any thought of compromise with the hard-line Dixiecrats, any attempt to hold the Democratic Party together on the basis of alliance with or toleration of them.[12]

King shared Rustin's desire to keep the pressure on the federal government, but he knew better than his New York friends that the local situation in Birmingham no longer represented a vehicle for launching that sort of campaign. When King returned to Birmingham on November 4 for a one-night appearance, he recognized that SCLC would have to turn its attention toward Danville and not Birmingham. While he had little enthusiasm for shifting the entire focus from Alabama to Virginia, he believed he had made a commitment he could not ignore. Fred Shuttlesworth understood King's reluctant decision, but emphasized that

SCLC must not "lose the initiative" in the Deep South. "Unless we can plan some people-to-people meetings in Alabama . . . . with a view towards building up massive numbers of committed persons for spring demonstrations, we will have failed the movement."

Like Young, Levison, and Rustin, Shuttlesworth also wanted King not to be too slow about pushing forward immediately in some nationally significant way. "You, as the Symbol of the Movement, must lead in planning and stirring up people in the South," Shuttlesworth lectured his longtime friend in early November. "Writing and speaking in the North," he added pointedly, "may be less crucial at the moment." Even though the "so called Negro moderates in Birmingham" had blocked any new SCLC protests there, King must not allow his commitment to direct action in Alabama to lessen. "However painful it may be, we must give thought to adding new dimensions to our Mass Actions, namely, some forms of effective Civil disobedience . . . we must set some guidelines and timetables for action in Alabama." The boycott remained in force in Birmingham, and Shuttlesworth was planning his own arrest in order to strengthen his troops' resolve. "The masses are with us," he told King, "but we can lose them by inaction and indecisiveness."

Shuttlesworth did not oppose a short-term SCLC push in Danville, but he insisted that King not forget the need for drastic mass action in the Deep South, much like Jim and Diane Nash Bevel had been recommending. "We should plan a concerted drive not later than Spring in Birmingham," he wrote King, "with the second step of going from Birmingham to Montgomery, with about 35–40,000 people. If such is needed, we will have to think in terms of tying up telephones, and effectively immobilizing Birmingham and Montgomery. Most of your staff members think this way," Shuttlesworth reminded King, "and many people in other parts of the country also.

> I have come to understand that we must either keep leadership or give it over to more active elements.
>
> I hope I am not frightening you, but some immediate thought, action and planning are necessary, for many people in many parts of the country think that we are in a period of vacuum. I think we should exert all efforts toward the 'one man, one vote' ideal in Alabama before the National Conventions

of the two major parties eight months hence.[13]

King agreed that there should be no lull, but the absence of black unity in Birmingham was a serious obstacle that could not be overcome simply by Shuttlesworth's enthusiasm. Danville looked like the next best alternative, but the local black community was not completely supportive of new protests. SCLC Affiliates Director C. T. Vivian and several other staff members headed there the first week of November, but the local NAACP leadership did not agree with SCLC's affiliate, the Danville

Christian Progressive Association (DCPA), that outside assistance was desirable. Fitful negotiations with city representatives had been unproductive, and those talks collapsed soon after the SCLC staff contingent arrived in town. Wyatt Walker announced on November 9 that SCLC would enter Danville "in full force within the next seven days," and that King would arrive on November 15. Initially, Walker said, SCLC would conduct an "Operation Dialogue" in an effort to confront Danville whites with the immorality of racism. If such persuasive appeals did not succeed, demonstrations would be launched and a nationwide boycott of Dan River Mills would be considered.

Faced with that threat, Danville officials moderated their position. Five city council members met with NAACP and DCPA representatives on November 12, and agreement was reached on a written city policy of nondiscrimination in hiring and on future biracial discussions. When King arrived three days later, he proclaimed that demonstrations might be necessary, but that SCLC would not launch any protests so long as negotiations were progressing. Reporters were surprised when only four hundred black citizens turned out to hear King at an evening rally, and special notice was taken of the absence of local NAACP President Rev. Doyle Thomas. Some speculated that the campaign would not get off the ground, but Andrew Young, after a careful weekend survey, informed King on November 18 that "things seem to be picking up." Several hundred young people were ready for voter registration work and nonviolent training sessions, and expert staffers like James Bevel and James Orange believed that many willing protesters could be recruited. "It looks like we may yet work up on a Movement," Young told King.[14]

While the Danville situation remained unsettled, other problems tugged at King's attention. Segregationist officials in Selma were doing their utmost to embarrass the Justice Department and King with public revelations that a federally rented car, borrowed from attorney Thelton Henderson by a Birmingham pastor, had been used to transport King to and from Selma during his October visit. A hostile young racist assaulted King on an airplane until physically restrained by flight attendants, and SCLC staffers resolved that King never should travel alone. In south Georgia, the Albany Movement was celebrating its second anniversary and preparing for the federal trials of its leaders. Acting President Slater King had run an unsuccessful race for mayor in the October election, garnering 2,500 votes, but the pending criminal charges dominated the atmosphere when Martin King spoke to 1,500 people at the anniversary rally. "We thought we had friends in the federal government," he told the crowd. "But when the federal government through the Justice Department came down on Albany with a heavy hand, we knew different." King volunteered to bring SCLC back to town whenever invited, but his own aides were recommending that Williamston, North Carolina, where SCLC field staffer Golden Frinks had been jailed for leading demonstrations, would be a more fruitful target than Albany if Danville did not pan

out as a major protest effort. At the same time, major editing problems
continued to plague King's book on the Birmingham campaign. The publisher was worried about its falling behind schedule, and King was unhappy with portions of the text. Stanley Levison, working to remedy the
problems, arranged a discreet rendezvous to discuss the issues with King
and Clarence Jones at a New York airport hotel. The FBI, fully aware of
the get-together through its wiretaps, sent agents to the hotel to snap
secret photos of King and his companions when they emerged from the
meeting. Bureau officials would show the Kennedys this incontrovertible
evidence of King's deceptive ongoing contact with the supposed Soviet
agent.[15]

Two days later Martin King was home watching television when the
first news reports from Dallas flashed on the screen. He called downstairs
to his wife, who was on the phone. "Corrie, I just heard that Kennedy
has been shot, maybe killed." She joined him in front of the TV, and
together they awaited more news. "While we were waiting and sitting,"
Coretta later recalled, Martin said, "Oh, I hope that he will live, this is
just terrible. I think if he lives, if he pulls through this, it will help him to
understand better what we go through." Then came the news that Kennedy was dead. King was quiet for a few moments, Coretta remembered,
"but finally he said, 'This is what is going to happen to me. This is such a
sick society.'"

King was deeply disturbed by John Kennedy's death. He believed the
assassination reflected not just one man's deed but a larger and more
tragic national climate of violence. King was especially pained that Kennedy had been cut down just as he was making a stronger commitment to
civil rights than he had during the first two years of his administration. "I
really think we saw two Kennedys," King explained some months later,
one prior to Birmingham and another afterward. King had been touched
by Kennedy's June speech on civil rights. Even though the administration's handling of its civil rights bill had left much to be desired, King had
hoped that Kennedy "was getting ready really to throw off political considerations and see the real moral issues." Now there would be no opportunity to see that hope fulfilled.

Sick in bed for several days, a weary King arose only to attend John
Kennedy's funeral in Washington. He went on to New York for a
CUCRL meeting and a speech at the Waldorf-Astoria. Returning to Atlanta, King had to confront how the president's death had disrupted
SCLC's immediate plans just as it had much of American life. The Danville effort had come to a halt, and staff members were looking for a new
focus and ways to rekindle their emotional energy. Serious tensions
abounded in SCLC's headquarters, and King felt so overcommitted that
he could not even keep up with the news summaries and brief book reviews that staff members prepared to keep him up to date on public issues that newsmen often asked him about. Wyatt Walker was dissatisfied,
feeling that because King was so burdened, SCLC was not receiving the

leadership it required. New administrative aide Harry Boyte shared those feelings despite his deep respect for King. "He gives me a lot of responsibility, but very little authority to execute it, and this is frankly very frustrating," Boyte complained in one off-the-record interview. King conceded that "we've had our growing pains," and acknowledged that "so many things are happening that it's difficult to keep up." He turned increasingly to Clarence Jones in New York for daily counsel and assistance with myriad obligations, but the pressure remained constant. Even at home the air was not free of tension, as Coretta, now burdened with four youngsters, increasingly felt left out of much of her husband's life. "I've never been on the scene when we've marched," she commented to one reporter. "I'm usually at home, because my husband says, 'You have to take care of the children.'"[16]

Just days after Kennedy's murder, two right-wing columnists, writing in several obscure newspapers, warned that new President Lyndon Johnson and Attorney General Robert Kennedy would have to confront "evidence obtained by tapping telephones" which indicated that a black leader who had been discussing voter registration plans for 1964 with the Democrats was linked with a Soviet agent. Warned of the column by Levison, Clarence Jones contacted King, who said he was "horrified" by the item and its allusion to his discussions about the 1964 election with Democratic National Committee official Louis Martin. Especially frightening was the columnists' warning that "if this close association isn't ended, the new administration faces public disclosures of this individual's RED ties in the midst of the coming congressional debate on civil rights legislation."

Although Jones pressed King to contact Robert Kennedy about the matter, King declined to follow up. He was due at the White House in three days time for an audience with Lyndon Johnson, and he resolved to pursue the 1964 voter registration discussions without being distracted by the FBI's indirect threats. On December 3, King met with Johnson and presidential civil rights advisor Lee White for forty-five minutes. Johnson made no allusions to Communist links, and displayed to King a convincing commitment to both the pending civil rights bill and to black voter registration efforts. King emerged from the session to tell reporters he was "impressed by the President's awareness and depth of understanding," and labeled their conversation "very fruitful." Then he headed to New York for another black leadership meeting.[17]

Several serious problems would not go away. Burdened with almost daily speaking engagements across the country, King learned from Clarence Jones that administration representatives were raising new questions about another supposed subversive in SCLC's ranks, New York attorney Arthur Kinoy, who had helped his partner, William Kunstler, represent Danville's protesters on behalf of the Gandhi Society. Jones and Wachtel were already furious with Kunstler for incurring greater legal expenses than they thought were warranted, and King agreed that it should be made clear that Kinoy had no affiliation with SCLC and that Kunstler should be reined in. On top of that, things were not going smoothly with the final editing of King's book manuscript, and he had to fly to New York to move matters along.

Most serious, however, were the continuing tensions among SCLC staffers. Citizenship training supervisor Septima Clark, nearly two generations older than most of SCLC's youthful staff, complained to King that the organization's energies were being misdirected. Too many employees, she charged, were interested only in protests and not in the equally valuable gains that could be achieved through the Citizenship Education Program (CEP). Even though the Dorchester teacher training classes had continued regularly, "many states are losing their citizenship schools because there is no one to do follow-up work" with the new teachers, Clark told King. Although Andrew Young and Dorothy Cotton were supposed to assist in this work, "it seems as if Citizenship Education is all mine, except when it comes time to pick up the checks," Clark complained. Apparently the others felt "that the work is not dramatic enough to warrant their time," she stated. "Direct action is so glamorous and packed with emotion that most young people prefer demonstrations over genuine education."

King accepted Mrs. Clark's comments, but Andrew Young felt compelled to defend himself. He conceded that he and other staff members had focused too heavily upon protests at the expense of other work. Like most others in SCLC, Young was physically exhausted and emotionally drained by the events of the last nine months. "Frankly, I need a breather . . . I have really been struggling along just content to survive since the summer." Martin King shared that sentiment, and recommended that the staff and his New York advisors would all benefit from a three-day retreat at a church conference center in the North Carolina mountains soon after the first of the year.[18]

King spent Christmas and New Year's at home with his family, and Coretta found it an unusually pleasant time. A preholiday speech to an Atlanta protest rally marked one of King's rare public forays in his hometown, but he spent as much time as he could playing with his children. One of their favorite activities was jumping off the refrigerator into their father's arms, despite Coretta's warnings. King found it a relatively relaxing time, even though the phone rarely stopped ringing. Two days before New Year's, King learned that *Time* magazine had chosen him its "Man of the Year" for 1963. Movement supporters were overjoyed, but King was upset by some of the comments in the magazine's cover story. It characterized his style in clothes as "funereal conservatism," because of his preference for black suits, and wrongly commented that King "has very little sense of humor." Additionally, in sketching a brief biography, *Time* referred to King's two childhood jumps by remarking that "twice, before he was 13, he tried to commit suicide."

King shook off his disappointment and plunged back into SCLC's work. Direct-mail fund-raising had fallen off, in part because King had not decided whether to ask Bayard Rustin to fill Jack O'Dell's vacancy as director of the New York office. Discussion of that issue and the continuing difficulties with King's manuscript was postponed until after King returned from a trip to Washington for the penultimate Supreme Court oral arguments over the libel suit that Montgomery authorities had brought against *The New York Times* and King's SCLC colleagues almost four years earlier on account of the controversial fund-raising advertisement.

King's stay at Washington's Willard Hotel offered the FBI just the chance it had been looking for. Ever since the wiretaps on King's own home and office were added in November, the supervisors of the King-Levison investigation had been turning their attention more and more to King's private life and away from their previous fixation on his supposed Communist ties. At a mid-December conference, Bureau officials discussed in detail how they could gather further evidence of what they felt were King's serious personal and moral shortcomings, and had resolved that if they could, they would use such material to expose King "as an immoral opportunist" and "clerical fraud." Domestic intelligence chief William C. Sullivan recommended placing surreptitious microphones, or "bugs," in King's hotel rooms, and when the wiretaps revealed his upcoming visit to D.C., agents from the FBI's Washington field office were mobilized. Listening devices were secretly planted in King's room at the Willard, and fifteen full reels of tape recorded what transpired during his two-day stay. The bugs picked up a lively, drunken party involving King, several SCLC colleagues, and two women from Philadelphia. FBI personnel were immediately put to work transcribing the recordings for dissemination to the White House. A few days later, when King made his trip to New York, Bureau agents observed his rendezvous at a midtown hotel with Jones and Levison. Word of that contact also was passed to the White House and the attorney general.[19]

On Friday night, January 17, Lyndon Johnson summoned King, Roy Wilkins, Whitney Young, and James Farmer to a Saturday meeting to seek their support for his new war on poverty initiative. King was supportive of Johnson's plans, and hoped that the president would make his assault full-scale. "Some kind of compensatory crash program," King told one interviewer, was needed "to bring the standards of the Negro up and bring him into the mainstream of life." Johnson's effort might do that for blacks as well as for needy whites, and extend the gains achieved by the movement. "We are making progress but it is in the middle classes," King acknowledged. "The masses remain about the same," and civil rights forces had to pay increased attention to improving black employment opportunities and job training. Voter registration would be one focus for 1964, but expanded use of Breadbasket-style consumer boycotts would be another. "The innovation for this year," King asserted, "will be large-scale selective buying programs aimed at the giants in the consumer industry."[20]

Extended discussions of how the movement could confront those economic issues were a principal focus of the three-day SCLC retreat at Black Mountain, North Carolina, that began on January 20. New York advisors Jones and Wachtel joined the Atlanta staff for the sessions, where Jones spoke about how any advocacy of compensatory treatment for black people would have to include a call for similar assistance to disadvantaged whites. King agreed, and explained that he intended to incorporate such an argument into the final chapter of his book. Wyatt Walker proposed a national "selective withdrawal" campaign against General Motors Corporation to win more jobs for blacks in the automotive industry, but it received little support.

Between breaks for Ping-Pong and softball games, King and his colleagues wrestled with a host of questions. They talked about the continuing allegations of Communist influence, and of having Jones maintain regular contact with Levison, without reaching a decision on the matter. Walker and others spoke of how the SCLC staff had expanded substantially over the past five months, but that the organization had accomplished little during that time. King acknowledged that they had been in a period of "inevitable pause," but said nothing about the major stumbling block posed by SCLC's internal tensions. Walker was unhappy that King had dismissed his idea of mounting a Birmingham-style campaign in Atlanta, and still complained about King's unwillingness to rein in James Bevel. Along with his wife, Bevel continued to talk up a massive spring assault on Alabama. No decision was made at Black Mountain, but the antagonism between Bevel and Walker remained constant. Others reported that some people in SNCC were becoming increasingly vocal in their criticisms of SCLC, King, and especially Walker, and that those attitudes were promoted by Ella Baker, who had become a trusted advisor to the younger activists.

After the retreat, King's party was ready to board their Atlanta flight at the Asheville airport when an anonymous caller threatened to bomb the plane. The message was dismissed as a crank call, and passengers went on board. When the plane had taxied onto the runway, the pilot suddenly announced that everyone had to evacuate immediately. The passengers were directed to walk back to the terminal, and King, Coretta, and Dorothy Cotton set out as a group. Quiet at first, Martin suddenly spoke up, his wife remembered. "'I've told you all that I don't expect to survive this revolution; this society's too sick.' And of course Dorothy said, 'Oh, Martin, don't say that.' And he said, 'Well, I'm just being realistic.'" Coretta recalled that she "had heard him say it several times before. . . . He had an awareness of what could happen to him, and he . . . was not able to forget about it because he lived with this constantly." The bomb threat against his plane—the first one he had encountered—was just another reminder of what King believed awaited him in the not-too-distant future.[21]

King resumed a hectic travel schedule with both SCLC's problems and the FBI nipping at his heels. Ever since its productive surveillance of King in Washington, the Bureau's domestic intelligence division had intensified its efforts to obtain recordings of King's private life. When attempts to monitor King in Milwaukee failed to turn up anything interesting, the FBI office there explained to headquarters that it was because local police had given King close protection. Director J. Edgar Hoover expressed disappointment, and dissented from Milwaukee's hypothesis for King's supposed restraint. "I don't share the conjecture. King is a 'tom cat' with obsessive degenerate sexual urges."

Back in Atlanta for a brief visit home, King apologized to one old friend for the delays in answering even personal correspondence. He was traveling 90 percent of the time, and felt deeply drained by "the problems and the pressures under which I must work every day. The problems have risen to almost unmanageable proportions." He hoped to spend more time in the South, and more time at home, but he knew he had made and broken similar vows many times before.

In the wake of the Black Mountain discussions, Clarence Jones urged King to complete his book manuscript. The publishing firm with whom King's literary agent, Joan Daves, had contracted the book, New American Library, was aiming for early June publication, but neither King nor free-lance editor Hermine Popper had finished the final chapter yet. Ghostwriters Al Duckett and Nat Lamar had written most of the text, but the crucial last chapter remained unformed. Jones and Levison each drafted some passages, and Jones gave them to King, emphasizing that the text "must give greater emphasis to the alleviation of economic and cultural backwardness on the part of the so-called 'poor white.'" King, already persuaded by the Black Mountain conversations, instructed Popper to integrate Jones's material. "Any 'Negro Bill of Rights' based upon the concept of compensatory treatment as a result of the years of cultural and economic deprivation resulting from racial discrimination," King wrote her,

> must give greater emphasis to the alleviation of economic and cultural backwardness on the part of the so-called "poor white." It is my opinion that many white workers whose economic condition is not too far removed from the economic condition of his black brother, will find it difficult to accept a "Negro Bill of Rights," which seeks to give special consideration to the Negro in the context of unemployment, joblessness, etc. and does not take into sufficient account their plight (that of the white worker).

King's instructions followed Jones's recommendations to the letter, and the new material was added to the concluding chapter.[22]

The FBI's monitoring of King continued as agents observed him meeting with Jones, Rustin, and Levison at a New York hotel to discuss the book manuscript and SCLC's northern office. King was looking forward to a brief vacation in Puerto Rico and a longer trip to Hawaii later in February, but his comments in New York reflected that there still was no focus for SCLC's efforts. He noted the long-announced voter registration plans, the need to ensure Senate passage of a strong civil rights bill despite the threatened segregationist filibuster, and the importance of taking new steps in the economic arena. Passage of a potent version of the Kennedy bill by the House of Representatives was only a few days away, but securing the two-thirds Senate vote several months hence to cut off the filibuster would be nip-and-tuck. King announced that SCLC was promoting D.C.-area regional representative Walter E. Fauntroy to full-time head of a new Washington office in order to lobby for the bill. Dramatic protests would be used to build opposition to a filibuster, and federal executive authority would be expected to help protect any lawful demonstrations.

Accompanied by Bernard Lee, King spent four relaxing days in Puerto Rico, returned to Atlanta for less than twenty-four hours, and then flew to the West Coast with Wyatt Walker for visits to San Francisco and Los Angeles, and then to Honolulu. He was busy with speaking engagements and private fund-raising affairs. However, the real purpose of the trip was rest and relaxation. On February 18, King and Walker, along with Baltimore pastor Logan Kearse and two California lady friends, headed to Honolulu. Thanks to its New York and Atlanta wiretaps, the FBI had anticipated King's Hawaiian holiday, and a special five-man squad of agents armed with sophisticated electronic and photographic surveillance gear was dispatched to monitor his actions. Bugs were planted in his hotel room, but King and his friends suspected they were under surveillance. They kept the air conditioners and televisions turned on when they were in their rooms, and made plans to return early to Los Angeles. The expensive surveillance venture produced nothing at all because, as the squad chief explained, any bug is "ineffective no matter where it is placed if the TV is blasting away." A hurried Bureau effort to install microphones in King's Los Angeles hotel rooms did not succeed, and King returned east without the FBI having added any new highlights to what King and his friends jokingly called J. Edgar Hoover's "golden record club."

King's western vacation was moderately restful, but his long absence in the face of SCLC's many pressing problems made more urgent the need to resolve them. Levison complained to Jones in one wiretapped phone call that "it would be wonderful if someone could convince King to pay some attention to detail, and also to come across with some of the promises he makes." When King returned, Jones pressed him to decide whether or not to name Bayard Rustin as SCLC's northern representative. King admitted that he was leaning heavily against the idea, at least while the civil rights bill was pending in the Senate. It made no sense to give the segregationists "one more weapon in their arsenal, however false these things are," he told Jones. Levison and Jones also complained to

King that SCLC's lack of activity was allowing SNCC to supplant it as the movement's leading organization in the eyes of many northern civil rights supporters. King reassured them that SCLC was just about to announce a major statewide summer project for Alabama, and to form an affiliate organization which would cover all of Florida.[23]

While King was preoccupied with his busy schedule and endless problems, James Bevel had been refining his plan for "a prolonged nonviolent campaign" that would "eventually lead to the education and enfranchisement of nearly all people in Alabama." He wanted to launch the program at a meeting of SCLC's Alabama affiliates on March 4 and 5, even though aside from ACMHR, "the affiliates by and large are not action oriented." They could, however, endorse the plan and lend their assistance in what Bevel foresaw as the most crucial part of the enterprise: "Past experience has taught us that students are the ones who usually provide manpower," and hence "our main responsibility is reaching, organizing and preparing the students in Alabama for action." SCLC field secretaries would work with high school and college youth, while King, Abernathy, and Shuttlesworth would undertake People-to-People tours aimed at black adult leaders in different towns and counties. A letter would go out to Alabama Governor George C. Wallace "and all appropriate state officials asking that all laws be repealed and tactics stopped that tend to discourage and disenfranchise any citizen who is 21 years of age. An effort to contact these officials and talk with them personally [also] should be made."

This would prepare for the real action of the campaign: physical protests. "There are two types of demonstrations that we probably should consider: mass demonstrations in one city, and demonstrations in many places simultaneously," Bevel told King.

The advantages of concentrating in one city are:

1. The romance of leaving home to go demonstrate would attract more Negro males.

2. The news media would cover more thoroughly and effectively one city than many.

3. Extensive coverage would tend to prevent brutality, or if it occurred it would be well covered.

4. Because we lack many well trained leaders it would also help in maintaining discipline.

5. It would be more dramatic to have 5 or 6 thousand people in jail in one city than in many cities across the state in smaller numbers.

The advantages of demonstrations in many places are:

1. They would directly involve more communities.

2. They would keep the brunt of the entire resources of the state from falling on one place; it would split their forces.

3. They would help keep the state off balance in trying to anticipate what will happen next and where.

4. More leaders would probably be developed.

Bevel noted that "both these approaches can be used at different times," and that in any event "the results will probably be jail-ins." Therefore, "it is important to involve large numbers of people who are committed to staying in jail for at least 4 or 5 months" and to be certain that northern supporters would be ready with funds and sympathy protests. Bevel recommended that an Alabama headquarters be opened in Montgomery or Birmingham immediately, and predicted that the campaign would take at least eight months. "The objective of this particular battle," he stressed in conclusion, "is enfranchisement of Negro people in Alabama." Thus, "the most important part of this battle is to actually see that obstacles are removed and to get numbers of Negroes in Alabama registered. . . . Unless we can in fact get Negroes registered, we cannot stop bombings of churches, unjust court proceedings, police brutality, etc."[24]

King found Bevel's plan, with its increased emphasis on voter registration, worthy of pursuit, and he considered combining it with Fred Shuttlesworth's desire to resume direct action in Birmingham. Three of the downtown stores had hired black salespeople, but two major ones had not, and a boycott of those stores remained in effect. The White Only signs were gone, and four public schools had undergone token desegregation peacefully, but no progress had been made on the issue of black policemen. Black businessman John Drew, a close friend of King's, told reporters that the Boutwell government and the downtown merchants had been less active than the black leadership had expected. "The new administration is a complete disappointment to us," Drew said. "It is a do-nothing administration. The mayor is a weak, sick, old man," and the merchants' failure to implement the 1963 agreement "has been quite a letdown." When SCLC's Alabama affiliates gathered in Montgomery on March 4, King stated that mass demonstrations would resume in Birmingham within thirty days.

King made clear at the Montgomery conference that SCLC was ready to pursue Bevel's plan and to target it on Birmingham. The two hundred representatives of SCLC's local affiliates were enthusiastic about the plan, and a five-point program was endorsed with only one idiosyncratic dissent. The program called for (1) intensified voter registration efforts; (2) initiation of "a state-wide coordination of [the] masses in direct action to secure in fact the right of the ballot" by employing "whatever techniques [are] necessary to implement the 'one man—one vote' concept"; (3) patronizing only those businesses that practiced equal employment; (4) implementation of the civil rights bill's public-accommodations provisions all across Alabama if and when Congress passed the bill; and (5) petitioning for a reduction of Alabama's representation in the Congress until the state's black citizens were allowed to vote freely. Along with a similar statewide summer effort that SNCC intended to undertake in Mississippi, the Alabama Project promised an intensification of civil rights activity in the Deep South beyond anything that 1963 had witnessed.[25]

King left the Montgomery session early in order to lead a ten-thousand-person civil rights march in the Kentucky capital of Frankfort, and meet with Governor Edward T. Breathitt. Then, after a quick visit home, King went to Orlando for a statewide meeting aimed at forming a Florida affiliate for SCLC. Although the groundwork had been laid through longtime supporters like Tallahassee's C. K. Steele, the most important development came out of a conversation between Affiliates Director C. T. Vivian and several local activists from St. Augustine—Robert B. Hayling, Goldie Eubanks, and Henry Twine—who had driven to Orlando to ask that SCLC lend its assistance to their racially troubled community. Although Vivian made no commitment, he told Hayling that he knew of the outrages in their town, and of their previous efforts to interest King and SCLC in the situation, and he promised to visit before the end of March. Vivian authorized them to designate themselves an SCLC affiliate, and encouraged them to press forward with efforts they had been pursuing for more than a year.

The fight against segregation in St. Augustine dated to the late 1950s, and had grown significantly during 1963. Proud of its status as the first European place of settlement on the North American continent, St. Augustine looked forward to the 1965 quadricentennial of the Spanish settlement and was seeking federal money to finance the observance. St. Augustine's NAACP branch was outraged that government dollars might go to a city that maintained rigidly segregated facilities and discriminated against black employees. Led by Robert B. Hayling, a dentist who was advisor to the NAACP Youth Council, black citizens tried to enlist Vice-President Lyndon B. Johnson, who visited St. Augustine in March, in their cause. Neither federal officials nor national NAACP leaders responded favorably, and in mid-June the *St. Augustine Record* revealed the blacks' efforts to block federal funding. The activists braced for white retaliation, and the paper quoted Hayling as saying that "I and others of the NAACP have armed ourselves and we will shoot first and ask questions later." That statement outraged local whites, and city officials rejected a black request for biracial discussions. Picketing commenced, and white toughs harassed Hayling and his colleagues. One night, bricks and gunfire struck Hayling's home. Armed blacks returned the fire, wounding several night riders, and lawmen arrested participants on both sides.

Hayling twice called SCLC headquarters in Atlanta seeking King's help. King dispatched a letter to Vice-President Johnson questioning the possible use of federal funds, and Wyatt Walker made inquiries in Washington. Local demonstrations and arrests continued throughout the summer. In September, Hayling and three associates were badly beaten while trying to observe a Ku Klux Klan rally on the outskirts of town. St. Johns County Sheriff L. O. Davis, widely viewed as a KKK sympathizer, arrested several Klansmen but also charged the four black victims with assault on their attackers. Protest telegrams went out to Attorney General Robert Kennedy, but FBI officials notified their superiors that local lawmen had matters completely in hand. "Police in St. Augustine," one report said, "have been doing a good job of controlling demonstrations and have not permitted violence."

Four weeks later an armed white night rider was shot and killed as he and several companions drove through a black residential neighborhood late at night. St. Augustine police charged that the fatal shot had come from the home of black activist Goldie Eubanks, and he and three other men were indicted for murder. Hayling again called SCLC, then went unsuccessfully to federal court to seek judicial intervention. Florida Governor C. Farris Bryant dispatched state highway patrolmen to town, and a special grand jury was impaneled to study the situation and make recommendations. Burke Marshall told Robert Kennedy that conditions were "quite bad," but "I do not see what we can do." NAACP executives, while admitting that Hayling had been "the moving force that sparked St. Augustine into motion," decided to remove him as Youth Council advisor. When the grand jury report criticized Hayling and called for biracial talks, the courageous dentist and Eubanks quit the NAACP, but no negotiations ensued. White terrorists torched the car of one black family, and the home of another, whose children were in newly integrated schools, and four shotgun blasts ripped through the front door of Hayling's house. No one was injured, and conservative St. Augustine Mayor Joseph Shelley condemned the attacks, but Hayling contacted the governor's office to request state protection.[26]

There matters stood when Hayling, Eubanks, and Henry Twine conferred with C. T. Vivian in Orlando on March 6 and received his encouragement to affiliate with SCLC. Within five days, using SCLC's name and Vivian's recommendations, Hayling sent letters to movement supporters at northern colleges inviting campus clergymen and students to come to St. Augustine during spring vacation to protest segregation and Klan terrorism. SCLC supporters in Massachusetts responded to the plea, and began arriving in town on March 23. SCLC staffers Hosea Williams and Bernard Lee appeared soon thereafter, and on March 26 a large demonstration was conducted at a local high school. The presence of the outside volunteers brought new enthusiasm to St. Augustine's black community, and on Saturday, March 28, twenty-six sit-in participants were arrested by city police. Nine more were taken into custody the next day, and an additional thirty-nine on Monday. More northern supporters arrived, including Mrs. John Burgess, wife of a well-known Episcopal bishop, and Mrs. Malcolm Peabody, socially prominent mother of the Massachusetts governor. Mrs. Burgess and Dr. Hayling were taken into custody on Monday for attempting to gain service at the Ponce de Leon Motor

Lodge, and the next morning 150 black students marched to the motel. Over half of them were arrested, and early that afternoon Mrs. Peabody and an interracial group of seven colleagues were charged while attempting to patronize the Ponce de Leon.

That night, with some two hundred movement supporters in jail, an enthusiastic mass meeting ratified eleven comprehensive demands put forward by the St. Augustine SCLC chapter. In addition to calling for the desegregation of all public facilities and public accommodations, and establishment of a biracial committee, the demands included immediate release of the arrested protesters and no school or employment retaliation against them. Additional demonstrations by local students took place the following morning, and Mrs. Peabody was arraigned before a local magistrate as national publicity descended upon St. Augustine for the first time. The next day Hayling and Mrs. Peabody were bailed out and testified in Jacksonville before U.S. District Judge Bryan Simpson in support of a petition filed by movement attorneys seeking transfer of the protesters' cases to federal court. Simpson denied the request, and as northern students headed home for the resumption of classes, the week of protests came to an end. Although the heavy publicity, including Mrs. Peabody's appearance on the *Today* show, brought unwelcome notoriety to their town, St. Augustine's white leadership made no move to open a dialogue with local blacks.[27]

King had things other than St. Augustine on his mind during this time. SCLC's internal troubles remained, and relations between Walker and Bevel had reached a breaking point. Bevel lost his temper and cussed Walker out in front of others; Walker charged him with insubordination and demanded that King fire him. Bevel apologized for his outburst, but Walker refused to accept the apology or retract his demand, despite requests from King. Before long, Walker announced his intention of leaving SCLC as soon as he located a suitable opportunity. Since King, Jones, and Levison remained undecided about Bayard Rustin taking over SCLC's northern responsibilities, Rustin lost interest as the matter dragged on. Some consideration was given to having Walker, who was considering a job with a New York publishing firm, take charge of SCLC's New York office, but Levison and other advisors felt that his hard-driving style would work no better there than in Atlanta. Levison and Jones thought that C. T. Vivian would make an excellent replacement for Walker in the top staff job, but King had two other candidates in mind: D.C. bureau chief Walter Fauntroy and Voter Education Project official Randolph T. Blackwell.

As King maintained his usual busy travel schedule throughout March, the FBI kept close tabs on his activities. Agents watched as Stanley Levison traveled to Atlanta for a daylong meeting with King on March 9, and the Bureau monitored King's travels as he went from Tuscaloosa to Hartford to Bridgeport to Savannah and then back to New York. The FBI's Detroit office bugged King's hotel room when he and Bernard Lee went to that city for a religious speaking engagement, and the two men were overheard discussing Wyatt Walker's idea that King begin a "hunger strike" whenever the segregationist filibuster against the civil rights bill was launched in the Senate. This information was forwarded to the attorney general and the White House.

While King traveled the country, he and SCLC made little headway with plans for direct action. King admitted to one reporter that SCLC hoped to launch the Alabama campaign in late April or early May with some 10,000 protesters mounting demonstrations in four or five different cities across the state. He also contended that SCLC would follow through on its northern voter registration proposal and launch a nationwide "selective buying" effort to improve minority job opportunities. He suggested that "more massive demonstrations than ever" in Alabama might coincide with the Senate's civil rights debate. At the end of March he met in Washington with two dozen black ministers to discuss how SCLC could help win the bill's passage. If the segregationist filibuster seriously threatened to weaken or block the bill, "we will engage in some type of direct action here in Washington," King told reporters. He also went to Capitol Hill to discuss strategy with Senators Humphrey, Kuchel, Hart, Douglas, and Javits, and had a friendly chance encounter with Black Muslim leader Malcolm X as news photographers snapped away.[28]

While King pondered the legislative situation, James Bevel was becoming increasingly unhappy about SCLC's lack of interest in his Alabama campaign. Along with his wife, Diane, and James Orange, Bevel moved from Atlanta to Montgomery in the hope of prodding King. "It is important that an adequate number of staff people be engaged in the preparation and building of the nonviolent project in Alabama," he told King, because enthusiasm for mass action was dissipating as local activists saw SCLC remaining inactive. "People are losing faith . . . in the nonviolent movement," Bevel warned, and SCLC would have to accomplish "tangible change for the masses of poor people" in order to win grass-roots support. Bevel was recruiting volunteers for a statewide "Freedom Army," but it would require more staff than the five presently assigned. The Alabama workers were asking students to commit one full year to the "army," and explaining the necessity of personal sacrifice. "In a regular war people leave home, leave their families and jobs, leave school, or whatever they are doing and go off to fight. We must do the same thing if we are ever going to be free." To muster a sizable force, however, King would have to devote more resources to the campaign.

One serious obstacle to Bevel's plans was SCLC's deteriorating finances. With a monthly budget that had grown to $50,000 in expenditures, and with fewer contributions coming in, SCLC's resources were stretched. "We're about to go out of business," King exclaimed to Clarence Jones in early April. Jones warned him that the financial decline was merely one symptom of how the movement in general, and SCLC in particular, had allowed momentum to lag and leadership to pass from its hands in the eight months since the March on Washington. Another factor was the strong support that Alabama Governor Wallace was receiving in Democratic presidential primaries in states such as Wisconsin and Indiana, and the growing evidence that Arizona Senator Barry Goldwater, rather than a more moderate figure, would be the Republican presidential nominee. Civil rights forces, Jones told King, were confronted "by a substantial and growing counter-revolutionary movement" that had been aided by "a total collapse of effective civil rights leadership." All segments of that leadership, Jones said, had "underestimated the consequences of their failure to clearly chart out programs of activity to carry forward the gains achieved after Birmingham . . . and the March on Washington. . . . The failure of the civil rights movement to come forward with an effective program" had created a vacuum that anti-civil rights candidates like Wallace and Goldwater had "been able to take advantage of." It also had opened the way for tactically foolish spin-offs, such as the threat by a Brooklyn CORE chapter to block access to the upcoming World's Fair by having civil rights sympathizers obstruct bridges and highways. "In the absence of any constructive alternative," Jones added, "these distortions of nonviolent direct action will continue to gain a great deal of public attention and continue to have a negative effect on the possibilities of building a forceful political alliance between the Negro revolution, the progressive forces from the white community, and certain political allies of both within the Congress." King and SCLC must develop "an effective program of mass action" to meet the current situation, and the entire black leadership should consider "another mass, more militant protest to Washington, as well as programs of mass direct action and agitational work" in a dozen other cities. The present time called for not only "an immediate consideration of ways to exercise national moral leadership," but also "the implementation of programs designed to bring about mass political action."

King thought Jones's recommendations fit in well with Bevel's Alabama Project and the symbolic fast that Walker had suggested as a response to the Senate filibuster. King felt a pressing need to speak out about the deteriorating national political climate on civil rights. He told a Philadelphia audience that the prospect of Goldwater's nomination was making him rethink his policy of never taking sides in political campaigns, but he explained to another group that he did not yet feel he could endorse Lyndon Johnson. "I will not throw my full support to him until I see how he acts during a crisis, like Kennedy did."[29]

When SCLC's board convened in Washington in mid-April for its semiannual meeting, much of the discussion concerned the Senate and the civil rights bill. Wyatt Walker explained the lull in direct action by emphasizing how John Kennedy's assassination had brought the Danville effort to an unexpected end, but noted that SCLC had more than doubled its number of affiliates and intended to expand Breadbasket's selective patronage approach nationwide. Then he recommended that sometime in early May, King should "remove himself from the public scene and announce that because of negative efforts directed toward the civil rights bill, that he would go on a fast for an indefinite period of time for the purposes of mobilizing the silent good people." The board members turned expectantly toward King, who explained what he had in mind:

> I have made the decision that if there is a determined filibuster to water down the civil rights bill, that I will engage in a fast and refuse to eat, but I have not decided how far I will go—whether unto death, but this is a decision that I have not made.
>
> Two main things will be at the center of my mind: one, to appeal to the Negro to remain true to nonviolence during this period and, two, to appeal to the forces of good will—the silent good people—to rise out of their apathetic slumber. Most revolutions are based on hope and hate. We are faced with the fact that the problem is so great that the Negro cannot fight it alone.

The board members, as they did with virtually all of King's initiatives, expressed their assent. The two days of talks closed with Walker's announcement that he would be leaving as of mid-June, but would be willing to direct the New York office if needed. Ralph Abernathy asked the board to wish Walker well, saying that both he and King had tried unsuccessfully to talk him into staying. Daddy King interjected pointedly that they should leave it up to Walker, period.[30]

Just as that two-day board meeting began, King and his advisors were embarrassed by another public warning about subversive influence in the movement. This time the statements came from widely read Washington commentator Joseph Alsop, well-known for his close ties to the highest offices in government. In a column that appeared in *The Washington Post*, the *New York Herald Tribune,* and other papers, Alsop noted that there had been much official headshaking about how King had dispensed with Jack O'Dell only after repeated public disclosures and private warnings. However, Alsop wrote, there was greater federal concern about a more serious problem:

> Official warnings have been given to King about another, even more important associate who is known to be a key figure in the covert apparatus of the Communist Party. After the warning, King broke off his open connections with this man, but a secondhand connection nonetheless continues.

Alsop's remarks created consternation among King's advisors, who knew about his contacts with Stanley Levison. Jones spoke with Levison, and both agreed that King had to explain the situation to Burke Marshall. Jones insisted that King see Marshall, but King did not feel that the problem was so serious. He was unconvinced that anything had to be done.

An angry Levison instructed Jones to tell King bluntly that Alsop was simply a vehicle by which the administration was publicly calling him a liar. King continued to procrastinate, and not until four days later did he ask SCLC Washington representative Walter Fauntroy to reassure Marshall that King had no ongoing contacts with Levison. Then the next morning, newspapers reported secret testimony that FBI Director Hoover had given to a House subcommittee in January alleging that Communist influence was present within the civil rights movement. Jones told King that he could not allow that to pass without public response, and drafted a statement for King to issue the next day. It accused Hoover of aiding right-wing extremists in smearing the civil rights movement, and said King found it particularly "difficult to accept the word of the FBI on communistic infiltration in the civil rights movement when it has been so completely ineffectual in protecting the Negro from brutality in the Deep South." King's statement received nationwide attention when he released it at an April 23 press conference. King was pleased at the positive coverage his denial of Communist influence received. He had wanted to even the score with Hoover, King remarked in one FBI-wiretapped phone call, and believed he had. "I want to hit him hard—he made me hot and I wanted to get him."[31]

The subversion controversy passed from the headlines after a few days. King was still uncertain about where the movement should turn next. He complained to his staff that he felt he was becoming largely a fund-raiser and did not like it. He continued to talk up the Alabama plans to reporters, saying that summer demonstrations would take place in five or six cities, with a "real possibility" that the campaign would culminate with a mass march on Montgomery. He made progressively less mention of a national voter registration effort or selective buying campaign. Voter Education Project officials criticized the big urban registration drive that SCLC had mounted that spring in Atlanta. On the national scene, the black leadership publicly denounced the disruptive "stall-in" tactics that the small band of New York activists had announced for the World's Fair. King declined to join a condemnation, and wrote a long memo to his colleagues expressing his views. The stall-in idea, he acknowledged, was "a tactical error. I would only advocate such a drastic program of civil disobedience when persistent attempts at good faith negotiations have completely failed." Nonetheless, the movement should not emphasize its disagreements in public, for such a course would only assist those who, like Alabama Governor Wallace, "a merchant of hate," were "peddling the ugly commodity of racism." Clearly echoing Clarence Jones's views, King said that civil rights leaders must realize they were "confronted by a substantial and growing counter-revolutionary movement," and that mass action, not timidity, was the proper response:

Frankly, I have gotten a little fed-up with the lectures that we are now receiving from the white power structure, even when it comes from such true and tried friends as Humphrey and Kuchel, Javits and Keating. Somewhere along the way someone has forgotten that demonstrations have been sacred when they were engaged in by white Americans. . . . They always become wrong and ill-timed when they are engaged in by the Negro.

King was disappointed that his fellow leaders wanted to denounce the stall-in as "revolutionary." To do that would betray a misunderstanding of the nature of the movement:

Indeed, we are engaged in a social revolution, and while it may be different from other revolutions, it is a revolution just the same. It is a movement to bring about certain basic structural changes in the architecture of American society. This is certainly revolutionary. My only hope is that it will remain a nonviolent revolution. . . .

It was true, King said, that the movement should avoid tactics that needlessly offended potential allies, but, he emphasized, "we do not need allies who are more devoted to *order* than to *justice*. . . . Neither do we need allies who will paternalistically seek to set the time-table for our freedom. . . . If our direct action programs alienate so-called friends. . . . they never were real friends."[32]

Throughout the latter half of April, King was caught up in a hectic schedule of speaking engagements and fund-raising trips. The FBI continued to follow him, installing bugs in his hotel rooms in Sacramento and Las Vegas. Following King's Las Vegas visit, local investigators gave the Bureau a graphic memorandum reporting the alleged activities that a prostitute who doubled as a police informant had engaged in with King. FBI officials passed the titillating thirdhand story on to Lyndon Johnson and Robert Kennedy.[33]

As of early May, King was still uncertain about what SCLC should do next. Both Bevel in Montgomery and black leaders in Birmingham were ready to launch the Alabama Project at the end of the month, but Hosea Williams and Bernard Lee suggested that SCLC consider mounting a full-scale campaign in St. Augustine. Assistant Program Director John Gibson was sent to explore the possibilities further. Gibson was aware that some local blacks found Hayling too aggressive, but he quickly concluded that the town offered substantial opportunities for a successful protest campaign. Gibson sketched out a plan for direct action beginning in late May that would use imported demonstrators, big downtown marches, and "jail-ins." Hayling and fellow activist Henry Twine were enthusiastic, and on Sunday, May 3, Gibson met with fifty black citizens to explain SCLC's interest and hear their thoughts. "Everyone voted to work together and to start immediately to solidify the Negro community behind an all out push in early June," Gibson wrote the next morning. He and Hayling made plans for training workshops and small-scale picketing to take place in the three weeks before their anticipated kickoff.

Even before Gibson returned to Atlanta from St. Augustine with his strong recommendation that SCLC take action, King was considering making a commitment there. White House aide Lee White had responded to an SCLC telegram about federal involvement with the quadricentennial celebration by writing King that the Johnson administration was "gravely concerned with recent developments." King mused to Clarence Jones that that unique federal link to St. Augustine might augur well for obtaining a strong presidential response to a new southern protest campaign. SCLC's executive staff convened in Atlanta on May 4, and although Gibson had not yet made his report, King told his aides that St. Augustine was one of several issues they must consider. Another was SCLC's extremely poor financial situation. King said they might be forced to postpone any action in order to do fund-raising.

The staff meeting concentrated on summer action plans. SNCC's Bob Moses described the Mississippi Summer Project that his organization and the new Freedom Democratic party intended to launch with the help of several hundred northern volunteers. Jim Bevel spoke about how the voting rights effort in Alabama would complement SNCC's effort in Mississippi, and explained that the Alabama Project should confront both state and federal governments with the fact that black citizens were excluded from Alabama's electoral process. King pointed out that the plan had to be sufficiently specific, and "suggested that action revolve around one more concrete goal in Montgomery. Developments from this would lead to [the] larger voter registration goal." Then King spoke about the more immediate choice he faced, whether to undertake efforts in the nation's capital concerning the pending civil rights bill, and/or make a serious commitment to protests in St. Augustine. As the minutes of the meeting put it, "the President will take ten days to decide whether there will be action in Washington or St. Augustine. If Washington, St. Augustine goes on. Keep some staff in St. Augustine; move most staff to Alabama to prepare for action the middle of June."

John Gibson returned to Atlanta and briefed Wyatt Walker on St. Augustine while King was considering his options. Walker was not persuaded by Gibson's pitch for action, so Gibson tried a different tactic. "I kind of bypassed Wyatt one day and went in to see Dr. King." He gave King the memo he had prepared, "and just asked him to read it. The next day he called Wyatt, Andy, myself, Bernard Lee [and] Reverend Abernathy in and said, 'John's got a proposal and I think it's all right. Let's talk about it.'" They discussed Gibson's idea and reached a consensus that it was a good plan. Making the commitment to St. Augustine would mean postponing a full-scale push in Alabama until sometime in June or July, but only Jim Bevel objected. Everyone else agreed that St. Augustine might be what SCLC had been looking for to get the nonviolent movement back on track.[34]

In his public remarks in mid-May, King placed principal emphasis upon the importance of the civil rights bill and SCLC's plans for a "massive,

. . . full-scale assault on the system of segregation," in Alabama some-time in midsummer. He stressed that Senate civil rights supporters should not trade away vital sections of the House-passed bill, especially the sweeping public-accommodations and fair employment titles, in order to win the support of midwestern Republicans. "I would rather see no bill at all than a bill devoid of these sections," King declared. Even if the mea-sure did make it through the Senate unscathed, the movement would maintain its pressure on the federal government and both major political parties as the national conventions and fall elections approached. There was "a possibility" that King would endorse a candidate, and "a real pos-sibility that we will have a march on both of these conventions calling for strong civil rights enforcement." He all but ruled out demonstrations in Washington, and lashed out at Hoover and the FBI whenever questions about Communist involvement in the movement were raised by report-ers. The Bureau kept up its reports on King to the attorney general and White House, and Robert Kennedy dispatched a memo to Lyndon Johnson warning of SCLC's aggressive Freedom Army plans for Ala-bama.[35]

On May 18 King made his first visit to St. Augustine, where he told an enthusiastic crowd at an evening mass meeting that he and SCLC's "nonviolent army" were committed to demonstrations in their "small Bir-mingham." As one listener emphasized, "Just listening to him speak gave you the courage to go on." Hosea Williams was already working with St. Augustine's local activists, and a tentative kick-off date of May 26 was set for mass demonstrations. King returned to town on the evening of May 25, the same day that notorious racist J. B. Stoner arrived in St. Au-gustine, and local Klansmen rallied to vow their opposition to the pro-tests. The next evening, at Williams's suggestion, Dr. Hayling led a column of marchers to the downtown slave market and held a rally at that symbolic site. Hostile Klansmen harassed the participants, but local law-men kept the groups apart, and SCLC's new campaign got off to a suc-cessful start.

Wyatt Walker accompanied King to St. Augustine to bring greater order to SCLC's typically free-wheeling efforts. "Our operation appears to be raggedy," Walker told King, adding that staff workers were not following any "actual prescribed schedule." That first night march, Walker thought, had not reflected sufficient discipline among the partici-pants, and SCLC had to be aware of the "danger that our demonstrations will keep or assume the character of a minstrel show," with noisy pro-testers taunting lawmen and unsympathetic bystanders.

Walker also told King there needed to be greater discipline among SCLC's staff. "You must clearly establish what the chain of command is here in St. Augustine. It appears to be vague in the minds of several staff members," Walker complained.

At a broader level, Walker advised King that SCLC had to appreciate the crucial significance that St. Augustine had for the short-term future of the entire civil rights movement. SCLC should focus public attention on how "America's oldest city" was also America's oldest bastion of segregation. With the town so committed to its quadricentennial celebration and its tourist-dependent economy, SCLC should remember that "one of our chief levers is to mount national opinion so greatly that either the Federal monies are withheld or the city fathers [are] faced with the prospect of the tremendous loss of commerce and industry." Birmingham and Albany had taught SCLC that the most direct path to local political concessions was through pinching the pocketbooks of powerful economic interests.

Walker explained to King that nationally, St. Augustine's "nonviolent campaign symbolically could be the 'beautiful' prelude for the long, hot summer" many politicians and commentators had been predicting. "Care must be taken that we do not miss. The issue . . . must be joined in the area of public accommodations. Much must be made of the fact that this is a tourist resort, supported by tourists *from the North*." Additionally, SCLC had to realize how "the St. Augustine movement must visually pull the nonviolent thrust of the Negro back on center. The national press calls *every* activity of the Negro community, whether it be picketing or throwing rocks, 'demonstrators.' Somehow, we must recapture the moral offensive so that it cannot be suggested that the nonviolent revolution has become surly, irresponsible, and undisciplined. *This is an absolute must!*"

For specific strategy, SCLC had to remember the lessons of Birmingham. Authorities might not arrest demonstrators initially, and Williams's innovation of night marches offered a new tactical tool. Walker recommended a regular schedule of such marches reaching into early June, then "stepped up demonstrations" to increase the movement's pressure, followed by protests featuring "outside names or clergy," and finally a "*big* push" around June 14. Walker's battle plan won quick acceptance, and another downtown evening march took place the night of May 27. One hundred and fifty hostile whites heckled the demonstrators, but police prevented a clash.[36]

With Walker's program on track, King left St. Augustine for a speech in New York and a six-day western fund-raising trip. In both his formal and informal remarks, King laid new emphasis on how the movement needed to concentrate upon economic issues and reach out to deal with northern urban problems. "The economically deprived condition of the Negro," he told the NAACP Legal Defense and Educational Fund, "will remain unless the Negro revolution builds and maintains alliances with the majority white community, alliances with a basic goal: the elimination of the causes of poverty." Millions of whites suffered similarly, and the movement should initiate "a massive assault upon slums, inferior education, inadequate medical care, [and] the entire culture of poverty." Although he said SCLC's summer focus would be Alabama and implementing the public-accommodations guarantees of the civil rights bill there if and when the measure became law, the act alone "will not be a panacea" and "will not solve all of the problems," especially outside the

South. King said he had "come to the conclusion that the whole problem of segregation is so deeply rooted in the entire nation that I will have to give more attention to the struggle in the North." Tactics would have to be found to expose the evils of such problems as substandard housing, and a nationwide selective-buying program aimed at eliminating employment discrimination would have to become reality, not just rhetoric. All the attention given George Wallace's northern electoral successes, and the supposed "white backlash" against the civil rights gains of 1963, should not obscure the fact, King said, that "we have more support for the civil rights struggle from the white community now than ever before."[37]

During King's long western trip, which took him from San Diego to San Francisco, Los Angeles, and Fresno, and to Tempe, Arizona, a succession of problems occurred in the South. Back in St. Augustine, a third successive night march through downtown took place on May 28. It was after 11:00 P.M. when the 200 marchers reached the slave market and were greeted by 250 hostile whites. Law officers protected the participants from the angry crowd, but several white toughs savagely attacked white newsmen who were covering the protest. The demonstrators made it back to the black neighborhood unharmed, but several hours later rifle shots ripped through a cottage that SCLC had rented for King when he was in town. At much the same time, another bullet shattered the rear window of Harry Boyte's car at a local motel. This happened less than twelve hours after Boyte and Andrew Young had met secretly with powerful local banker Herbert E. Wolfe in an unsuccessful effort to get St. Augustine's business leaders to open negotiations with the black community. Movement leaders denounced the attacks, and King telegrammed Lyndon Johnson from California, asserting that "all semblance of law and order has broken down in St. Augustine" and requesting immediate federal protection for the black community.

The next evening, local law officers turned back a night march, and movement lawyers petitioned Federal Judge Simpson to intervene to protect the protesters' constitutional rights. Increasing complaints also were voiced about the close relationship between local lawmen such as County Sheriff L. O. Davis and area Klan leader Holstead "Hoss" Manucy, who had been seen in the company of Davis and several different deputies. Some local blacks wondered if Davis, too, was a Klan member, but the sheriff denied that, as well as the repeated suggestions that he and Manucy's forces were working in concert. Manucy, however, later remembered it differently. "We worked with the city police and the sheriff's department. . . . It was just like everybody here was working together—the mayor, the city police, sheriff's department, [and the] Ancient City Hunting Club," the public name for the St. Augustine Klan. Local FBI agents, who were pressing headquarters to give approval to electronic surveillance of Hayling's home, King's bullet-ridden cottage, and Manucy's residence, also knew Davis's real orientation:

No information is available indicating Sheriff L. O. Davis is or was [a] member of [the] Klan. He has currently indicated he would rely on Klan members for assistance in controlling any demonstrations. Davis is quite close to Holstead Manucy, Exalted Cyclops of the Klan at St. Augustine. Davis also was instrumental in helping the Klan hide out . . . a Klansman [who was] responsible for the bombing of the residence

of an activist in nearby Jacksonville.

Despite public concern, the Klan presence in St. Augustine increased, and a Saturday night, May 30, rally outside of town drew three hundred people. Rumors spread that the terrorists were plotting to kill King when he returned to town, and a warning was telephoned to King in California. He brushed off that threat as he had many earlier ones, but he did have two lengthy Saturday phone conversations with Burke Marshall and White House aide Lee White in which he argued that local lawmen were not doing their jobs in good faith and that federal intervention was necessary to protect the black community from the Klan. Marshall urged the FBI to keep a close eye on developments, and White contacted Florida Governor C. Farris Bryant to discuss the situation.[38]

If the new violence and Klan death threat did not upset King, a Sunday phone conversation from Los Angeles with his wife in Atlanta did. All spring Coretta had been telling him that she was extremely dissatisfied with his frequent long absences from home, but generally she restrained her anger about the apparently low priority her husband gave their family and personal life. This time, however, her complaints were more pointed and far more strongly voiced. King was exhausted by his schedule and other unrelenting pressures, and had little patience for Coretta's criticisms. They exchanged angry words, and the argument left King even more drained. FBI executives were happy to add that wiretap recording to their growing collection of King tapes, and Florida agents told state officials they were welcome to borrow one. "They had this very lurid tape recording," and Florida "could use it as a weapon if we wanted to run King out of St. Augustine by threatening to expose him." The offer was rejected.[39]

Saturday and Sunday witnessed a few small, peaceful movement demonstrations in St. Augustine. On Monday, June 1, the federal court hearing on the movement's complaint against Sheriff Davis, City Police Chief Virgil Stuart, and Mayor Shelley began in Jacksonville. Judge Bryan Simpson took testimony from movement activists and local officials all day Tuesday and Wednesday, and pressed Sheriff Davis hard about whether some of his volunteer "special deputies" might be Klan members. The FBI had made inquiries into the local Klan situation, and had notified both the governor's office and Judge Simpson of the close ties between the terrorists and lawmen. That confidential information proved especially helpful to the judge when he questioned Sheriff Davis, and on the final day of the hearing, Simpson pointed out to the sheriff that one name on his list of special deputies was that of Holstead Manucy, once convicted of bootlegging in Simpson's court. An abashed Davis promised to screen his volunteers more carefully in the future.

While Simpson's hearing was in progress and large demonstrations were in abeyance, Justice Department attorney Joseph Dolan came to town to speak with the different parties and the judge to see what action Burke Marshall and Robert Kennedy could take to resolve the situation. He found St. Augustine's white leadership not at all interested in opening a dialogue with the black community. A disappointed Dolan told Marshall "it would not be helpful for the executive branch of the federal government to be active as a mediator at this point." Judge Simpson would try to use his position to advance some settlement, but the public-accommodations demands would probably not be resolved until the civil rights bill, still awaiting its long-pending cloture vote in the Senate, actually became law.

When the federal court hearing ended on June 3, Simpson asked movement attorneys William Kunstler and Tobias Simon if they and their clients—represented by Hayling and Young—would suspend any night marches until he handed down a ruling in the near future. Young and the others agreed to the request. When Martin King returned to town the next day, he found that the movement's mass protest plans were on hold awaiting Simpson's decision. That night King addressed a large mass meeting, telling them about the Klan death threats, and vowing that the St. Augustine campaign would be expanded unless the city proved responsive. After huddling with his aides and local activists, King appeared before reporters the following day to put forward in conciliatory language five "suggestions" he hoped city officials would consider: desegregation of all hotels and restaurants within thirty days; hiring of twelve new blacks as city employees within ninety days; establishment of a biracial committee to which SCLC could name two thirds of the black representatives; dropping of all arrest charges; and a promise that all city businesses would accept job applications from black citizens. If the city did not act, King said, demonstrations would resume "on a massive scale," because of all the cities in which SCLC had been active, "we have never worked in one as lawless as this."[40]

After that twenty-four-hour return visit, King headed north for two college commencement speeches, a meeting with his New York advisors, and a *Today* show appearance to plug the publication of his third book, *Why We Can't Wait*. He was scheduled to return on June 10 to St. Augustine, where only a few small, intermittent daytime protests took place as activists abided by their pledge to await Simpson's ruling. While King was away, a suspicious fire gutted the cottage SCLC had rented for him. Wyatt Walker phoned the FBI, and Daddy King contacted Burke Marshall to voice concern about Martin's safety when he returned. Dr. Hayling, who believed in armed self-defense, strengthened the black community's security by deploying weapons among several trusted followers. "We were not totally nonviolent," he later acknowledged. "This got back to Martin," who was "totally unhappy because he was totally committed to nonviolence." Nonetheless, armed guards watched over King every night that he spent in St. Augustine.

Several local whites pressed Mayor Shelley to respond to King's five suggestions and appoint a biracial committee, but no answer was forthcoming. Then, late Tuesday afternoon, June 9, Judge Simpson handed down his order upholding the movement's complaint that local officials were infringing upon protesters' rights by preventing their night-time marches. "No circumstances even slightly justifying prior restraint of orderly demonstrations were present" when city and county officers implemented their policy on May 29, Simpson declared. Law enforcement officials would have to protect, not obstruct, the marchers whenever they conducted such protests in the future. SCLC and its local allies were overjoyed by the judge's endorsement of their position, and later that evening Andrew Young led some marchers into downtown St. Augustine. The white toughs were waiting, and this time about twenty of them broke through police lines to attack the demonstrators. No serious injuries were suffered, but the renewed white violence allowed King to repeat his call for federal intervention when he returned to St. Augustine the next morning. Besides requesting U.S. marshals, he sent a telegram to Lyndon Johnson asking that the president intervene "personally."

Presidential aide Lee White conferred several times with Florida Governor Bryant to encourage better police protection for the night marches. "He gave his flat assurance that the situation would be under control," White recorded. The administration notified King and Hayling that "sufficient state law enforcement officers are present in St. Augustine to preserve law and order" and that no federal action was required. King, buoyed by that day's successful 71–29 Senate cloture vote on the civil rights bill, encouraged the crowd at that evening's mass meeting to join in another downtown procession. A column of four hundred people headed into the old slave market area as two hundred law officers attempted to hold back six hundred angry whites. Rocks rained down upon the demonstrators, some of whom were attacked by whites who broke through police lines. The officers, mainly Florida highway patrolmen, responded forcefully and used tear gas against the rioting whites, some of whom retaliated against the lawmen. When the smoke cleared and the white crowd had dispersed, the protesters returned to the black section of town without anyone suffering serious injury.

The next morning, in line with a suggestion he had made the previous day, King decided to intensify the campaign by submitting to arrest. Shortly after noontime, King, Ralph Abernathy, Bernard Lee, and seven others appeared at the restaurant of the Monson Motor Lodge and sought service. Owner James Brock, a relative moderate among St. Augustine businessmen who nonetheless refused to serve blacks, asked King and his party to leave. King declined, and engaged Brock in conversation about his segregationist practices for more than fifteen minutes. Brock became increasingly exasperated, and when City Police Chief Virgil Stuart arrived on the scene and King refused to depart, Brock asked for his arrest. King and his colleagues were taken away. News reports headlined his incarceration as other movement leaders organized a third successive night-time march.[41]

Movement representatives and some local whites renewed their efforts to make progress behind the scenes. Wyatt Walker phoned administration officials to ask for federal mediators, and voiced concern about King's safety in Sheriff Davis's St. Johns County jail, but Judge Simpson informed Joseph Dolan that he saw no need for federal intervention. State circuit attorney Dan Warren announced that he would ask the grand jury to reexamine the situation and make further recommendations to supplement its December presentment.

The next day two groups of marchers made uneventful forays into downtown while King was arraigned before a local judge. Immediately after his arraignment, King was whisked into a three-hour appearance before the grand jury to give secret testimony on the St. Augustine situation. State attorney Warren hoped to persuade the grand jury to appoint a biracial committee and either end the crisis or leave the onus on King for refusing to halt protests despite satisfaction of the movement's principal demand. After his testimony King was bundled into the backseat of a police car and driven north to spend the night at Jacksonville's Duval County jail, which state officials considered safer than Sheriff Davis's. King was irritated by the rude treatment he received from the Duval jailers, who showed particular interest in his collection of pills—diet pills. Greeted in a friendly manner by one black jail employee, an exasperated King voiced a pointed response. "Hello, sister. I've been in fifteen jails, but this is the first time that I have been treated like a hog." King spent the night in solitary confinement in "a very lonely, dark and desolate cell by myself, cut off from everybody." That night's downtown march was without incident, but several hours later white racist leader J. B. Stoner led two hundred whites on a well-guarded late-night march through black residential neighborhoods. Refusing to be intimidated by the Klan's show of force, black citizens turned out to line the streets, sing, and applaud.[42]

King was bonded out of custody on Saturday, June 13, in time to deliver Sunday and Monday commencement addresses at two northern colleges. Presidential aide Lee White, encouraged by Warren's grand jury initiative and the active support that moderate State Senator Verle Pope was giving to Warren, told Lyndon Johnson and Wyatt Walker that he was "rather hopeful" about peaceful progress. With King out of town until Tuesday evening, it appeared that the crisis might move toward a solution.

Friends who saw King on his trip north found him "tired" and "a little haggard." St. Augustine was eating up much of his time. He had given little attention to the Alabama Project or to choosing a successor to Wyatt Walker. He had asked Andrew Young to take over some of Walker's tasks, but that shift of responsibility would merely create another vacancy. Young and Bevel still intended to pursue voter registration efforts in some Alabama cities, and King spoke of testing public accommodations in the same cities once the civil rights bill won final congressional approval and was signed into law, but the larger plan had been put on a back burner because of St. Augustine. Feeling more and more overburdened, King asked New York friends like Jones, Rustin, Harry Wachtel, and Cleveland Robinson, along with other advisors such as Lawrence Reddick and white trade unionist Ralph Helstein, to meet with him once a month to discuss the questions confronting the movement. Rustin advised King of one issue that was of the utmost importance. The grassroots effort by SNCC's Mississippi staffers and the Mississippi Freedom Democratic Party (MFDP) was becoming a full-scale challenge to the seating of the state's all-white delegation at the Democratic National Convention in late August. Some of the Freedom Democrats wanted to organize aggressive demonstrations for the Atlantic City convention site, and for several weeks Rustin had been alerting a wide range of movement leaders to the danger that the SNCC-MFDP strategy might be counterproductive to the movement's broader goals and anticipated coalitions. MFDP's national representatives knew that Rustin and others were worried about their plans. They understood Rustin's intention when he asked MFDP representatives Walter Tillow and Ella Baker to attend a June 15 meeting with Norman Hill, James Farmer, and King. The group agreed that Rustin and Hill would draw up a statement explaining the MFDP effort to the wider movement and Democratic party audience. Before the end of the month Rustin recommended that movement leaders convene to discuss a comprehensive strategy for the Democratic convention.[43]

Back in St. Augustine, Sunday, June 14, was marked by three dozen arrests as movement supporters tried to desegregate religious services at several white churches. Dr. Hayling and Henry Twine went to Washington to meet with Burke Marshall, and opinion grew in both the white and black communities that a solution based upon establishment of a biracial committee was within reach, so long as SCLC would suspend demonstrations and not insist that Dr. Hayling, a particular anathema to local whites, be one of the black representatives. On Monday, Governor Bryant moved to end the rising tensions between state and local lawmen by placing Sheriff Davis, Police Chief Stuart, and their men under the authority of the Florida Highway Patrol and instructing that all laws be strictly enforced.

On Tuesday more white and black witnesses appeared before the grand jury as word spread that most local officials, aside from Mayor Shelley, would support a biracial committee in exchange for a halt in the protests. King returned to town to speak at Tuesday night's mass meeting, and one more downtown march transpired uneventfully. By Wednesday reports indicated that the grand jury would call for a truce and a biracial committee the next day, and hoped for city commission endorsement of that recommendation despite the mayor's opposition. SCLC officials told newsmen they would accept such a tradeoff, and a secret meeting of town businessmen endorsed the plan. An evening prayer march by three hundred persons, including seventeen newly arrived rabbis, to the Monson Motor Lodge was held without incident, and everyone awaited Thursday's announcement.[44]

The situation took a turn for the worse Thursday afternoon when an integrated group of seven protesters jumped into the Monson Motor Lodge's outdoor pool and initiated the "swim-in" as a new tactic of desegregation, while Martin King looked on from across the street. Monson owner Brock was enraged by the demonstrators' audacity and poured gallons of pool-cleaning chemicals into the water to scare away the demonstrators. That maneuver failed, and only when an off-duty city policeman jumped in and physically forced the demonstrators out of the pool did the protest end. Law enforcement officers took the wet group into custody for trespassing.

White leaders who had supported a biracial committee were outraged by what they regarded as the movement's duplicity in intensifying protests before the release of the grand jury report. They also were angered by a reported King statement that "we are going to put the Monson out of business." Word of the imbroglio spread quickly, and the grand jury went back into session to hear testimony from witnesses to the swim-in. The new comments led the jury to change its draft, and at the end of the afternoon the report was finally made public. It claimed St. Augustine possessed "a solid background of harmonious race relations" and "a past history of non-discrimination in governmental affairs." The grand jury asserted that the real question was whether King and SCLC "truly desire the problem solved here in St. Augustine," and that if they did, the grand jury asked King "and all others to demonstrate their good faith by removing their influences from this community for a period of 30 days" and by a thirty-day cessation of all protests. If King and his allies accepted the request, at the end of thirty days the grand jury would name a biracial committee of five whites and five blacks, "whose members have tentatively agreed to serve."[45]

That presentment outraged King. SCLC had been led to believe that appointment of a biracial committee would take place when the demonstrations stopped, and one news report indicated that a late-afternoon grand jury vote to recommend just that had fallen barely short of a majority. King reacted strongly to the weaker recommendation. "This is an absolute contradiction of everything they had talked about in the last few days." He also denied assertions that the evening vigil and midday swim-in at the Monson had been intended to sharpen the struggle. "We don't have any desire to prolong this. We'd like to see it settled tomorrow morning but it's got to be a good-faith settlement."

Friday morning King offered a further response to the grand jury's proposal. He said the movement was "greatly disappointed at what we consider an unwise, unfair, and unreasonable position." The grand jury had made the "false assumption" that St. Augustine had had good race relations until SCLC's arrival, and had failed to realize that "there will be neither peace nor tranquility in this community until the righteous demands of the Negro are fully met." The movement would halt demonstrations for one week in exchange for the immediate appointment of a biracial committee, but would not accept a longer moratorium. White officials and grand jury foreman Aubrey Davis rejected the counterproposal, and in midafternoon a group of protesters made a peaceful foray to a traditionally segregated beach for a "wade-in." That evening, as four hundred whites gathered in the old slave market, two hundred demonstrators marched downtown, where patrolmen arrested Andrew Young, C. T. Vivian, and Hosea Williams for trying to approach the white crowd.

That tactical effort angered white officials even more, and the next morning white leaders met to discuss how the potentially deadly nighttime protests could be halted despite Judge Simpson's two previous refusals. They contacted Governor Bryant, and early that evening, after a vicious Klan attack on a small band of movement beachgoers, Bryant issued an executive order banning all protests between 8:30 P.M. and sunrise. King had left town several hours earlier to speak at a civil rights rally in Chicago, and movement leaders agreed to abide by the edict while challenging it in Judge Simpson's court. Klansmen staged a Sunday march into the black community, and twice on Monday, movement protesters attempting to use the public beaches were attacked by whites while highway patrolmen struggled to drive them back. Simpson set a Friday hearing on the movement's petition against Bryant's order.[46]

King returned on Wednesday, June 24, and repeated his request for a federal mediator. Behind the scenes, an old King friend, Boston University Professor L. Harold DeWolf, along with three academic colleagues, were working to open lines of communication with local whites, who were still furious over the swim-in. DeWolf and his friends briefed King on the situation, then renewed their conversations with State Senator Verle Pope the next morning. That same day there was another confrontation between movement protesters and whites at the beach, and the highway patrolmen were more forceful than ever in repelling the whites' attacks. One white man was clubbed on the head, further increasing local antipathy. Then, early that evening, as Klansmen gathered at the slave market to hear racist orators J. B. Stoner and Connie Lynch, some two hundred movement marchers headed downtown toward the rally. Inflamed by the racist rhetoric, and angry at the state lawmen as well as the black protesters, the white toughs ferociously attacked the demonstrators. When the highway patrolmen moved to protect the marchers, the Klansmen attacked the officers, and a pitched battle developed as the lawmen tried to direct the marchers back toward the black residential area. Nineteen demonstrators were taken to the hospital for treatment of injuries, and one state trooper was shot in the arm. Governor Bryant's representative on the scene, former FBI agent Elmer H. Emrick, concluded that only martial law could cope with the violence. King told newsmen that troops would be necessary if a sizable force of federal marshals were not sent to St. Augustine immediately. King spoke by phone with a noncommittal Burke Marshall, then complained to Clarence Jones in New York that the Klan "is making a showdown down here and the federal government has not done a thing." King suggested to Jones that SCLC stage a march on the White House to protest the administration's inaction in St. Augustine and the recent disappearance of three young civil rights workers in Mississippi. He was pessimistic that any concessions would be forthcoming from St. Augustine's leaders so long as the Klansmen maintained effective control there.[47]

Thursday night's violence, however, stimulated a number of parties in renewed efforts toward a settlement. Judge Simpson, whose hearing opened the next morning, indicated that he might hold Governor Bryant in contempt of court for his executive edict banning the night marches. However, a secret late-night meeting between the two men at a mutual friend's home in Jacksonville just prior to the hearing defused the confrontation. Simpson appreciated Bryant's concern about maintaining the peace, and the governor promised to do all he could to create the local biracial committee that the judge, like many others, felt was the most practical way of ending the crisis. Friday morning, Simpson's hearing began with testimony from highway patrol officers that uncontrollable violence would result from a resumption of night marches. Simultaneously, Governor Bryant huddled in St. Augustine with banker Herbert Wolfe, and King's four Boston professors met in Jacksonville with the state's attorney, Dan Warren. Meanwhile, Florida Senator George Smathers, a close acquaintance of Lyndon Johnson's, called both Bryant and Wolfe to impress upon them Washington's desire that the controversy be resolved by establishing a biracial committee. Thus prodded by both the governor and a U.S. senator, Wolfe agreed to call together the town's white leadership on Monday for a secret meeting to seek support for such a solution. Dan Warren was still upset at King's rejection of the grand jury initiative, but when Harold DeWolf and his colleagues, working through a local newsman, asked Warren to meet secretly with King, the state attorney readily agreed. King told Warren that the grand jury's offer to appoint a biracial committee only after King's departure and if a thirty-day moratorium on protests was declared, was unacceptable because it would make King appear to be deserting his local allies without having won anything tangible. If Warren and other white officials truly wanted to reach an accord and stop the demonstrations, King said, they must get Hoss Manucy and the Klan under control and appoint without delay a biracial committee with a specified agenda. Warren replied that King had to appreciate how difficult it had been to persuade the grand jury to offer to appoint any sort of biracial committee, and that the past week's events left him little hope that he could extract any better proposal from the jury. King stressed to Warren that he had absolutely no desire to prolong the protests. "'I want out of St. Augustine. . . . But I must come out of St. Augustine with honor. . . . I must come out of here with a victory.'" Immediate appointment of a committee would satisfy that requirement. Warren agreed that that was fair, and King went to Atlanta for the weekend while local white leaders made plans to achieve consensual agreement on a biracial committee at Wolfe's Monday meeting.

Throughout the weekend both sides worked toward mutual approval of the individuals who would compose the four-member committee of two whites and two blacks. By Sunday night newsmen reported agreement on three of the four, and that there was "reasonable optimism on both sides" about a Monday agreement. Hosea Williams announced a suspension of the downtown marches and King prepared to return to town, feeling that a settlement and a victory were close at hand. At the eleventh hour, however, the negotiations threatened to collapse when Wolfe and another banker, Frank Harrold, were unable to persuade their fellow civic leaders to support a biracial committee. Mayor Shelley, who consistently opposed such negotiations, would not budge from his position. He called Governor Bryant to reiterate his opposition to granting any concessions to the protesters. By Monday night it appeared as if the accord might collapse, and on Tuesday morning, local officials filed charges against Hayling, King, SCLC's Gibson, and another local activist for having contributed to the delinquency of minors by recruiting them for demonstrations. King arrived back in town, surrendered at the courthouse for arraignment, and was quickly released. It seemed likely that a new round of protests was in the offing.[48]

Suddenly, with no advance warning, Governor Bryant announced Tuesday evening that a biracial committee of four unnamed men had been appointed to mediate the situation. Bryant told newsmen that this group would serve for thirty days, at which time he expected the grand jury to name a larger body. He also told them that each of the individuals had assured either Bryant or State Attorney General James Kynes of his willingness to serve. Enterprising reporters said the four were rumored to be white bankers Wolfe and Harrold, Florida Memorial College President R. W. Puryear, and black high school principal Richard Murray, but no confirmations were forthcoming. King learned of the news, caucused with Hayling, then told that night's mass meeting that the leadership welcomed the development and would suspend all demonstrations for two weeks to see what progress the committee could obtain.

Mayor Shelley was furious when he learned of Bryant's announcement. He did not hide his anger from reporters and called Bryant for an explanation. Gently but directly, Bryant explained that this initiative was a necessary step, whether the biracial committee had official approval or ever actually met. Unsatisfied, Shelley asked just what Bryant meant. "'I'll tell you something, Dr. Shelley, if you'll give me your word you won't reveal it.' I said, 'What's that?' 'Well, there is no committee.' He said, 'I've told everybody including the nigras that I've appointed a committee, but I have not.'" Shelley was livid, but kept his word for several months time. In this situation, where all parties were looking for a face-saving way out, such a step offered a convenient cover that everyone could put to good use, even if the committee amounted to nothing at all.

After a long night of further talks and phone conversations, Martin King also realized exactly what the score was. Like many whites, he, too, wanted to bring the crisis to an end, even if doing so meant participating in an accord that actually amounted to almost nothing. He was scheduled to leave for Washington in less than twenty-four hours to attend the ceremony in which President Johnson would sign the newly passed Civil Rights Act of 1964 into law. The immediate applicability of those new provisions meant that SCLC could turn its attention to the Alabama plans that had been sidetracked for almost two months by the unexpected eruption of St. Augustine. When King met with reporters the next day, he asserted he was hopeful about St. Augustine and said SCLC would turn its attention to obtaining full implementation of the Civil Rights Act's public accommodations provisions throughout Alabama. Demonstrations would resume in St. Augustine if progress was not made, but SCLC was withdrawing its complaint against Bryant and other officials from Judge Simpson's court. Behind the scenes, Harold DeWolf was in touch with state attorney Dan Warren in an effort to convince Herbert Wolfe to make something real out of the governor's sudden sleight-of-hand. At the same time that King was offering reporters his prognostications, eighty St. Augustine businessmen were meeting privately to discuss how to respond to the desegregation provisions of the new law. With considerable unease, though with only five actual dissents, the group voted to abide by the statute, and Monson owner James Brock announced the action to the press. In private, Brock and his colleagues feared Klan retaliation once they put their new policy into effect, and Brock wrote Judge Simpson to ask that U.S. marshals protect them from "the mob action that will undoubtedly occur." Simpson, however, was optimistic that the crisis had passed and sought to reassure Brock that state and local officers had the situation well in hand. "Developments over the last twenty four hours," Simpson wrote Brock, "make me extremely hopeful that the trouble you anticipate will not materialize."[49]

King was happy to leave St. Augustine because of the many other issues demanding action. The Alabama Project stood at the top of the list, with SCLC's internal organization a close second. Wyatt Walker had announced his departure to join a new publishing venture, the Negro Heritage Library, and King was pressing Andrew Young to reorganize the staff to take up the slack. Both men wanted to bring Hosea Williams into a more central place on the staff. King also worried about SCLC's talented but troubled public relations director, Ed Clayton, whose long-time problem with alcohol was growing worse. Citizenship teacher supervisor Septima Clark remained unhappy with Young's minimal contribution to that program, and pressed him and King to give the citizenship education effort the attention it deserved. Young responded that perhaps Williams or VEP's Randolph Blackwell could be persuaded to take a central role, and apologized for how his hectic schedule, coupled with Walker's departure, had left SCLC at loose ends. "Last year was perhaps the most confused and complicated year of my life," Young wrote. "There were many days when I thought I might be on the verge of cracking up." The tensions that troubled most SCLC staffers could be lessened only when the incredible and seemingly constant burdens somehow decreased.

Martin King felt even more of those tensions, and the lack of focus in SCLC and the movement detracted from the sense of joy that the formal presidential signing into law of the Civil Rights Act of 1964 brought with it. King had worried for months about SCLC's unfulfilled obligations in Albany, and the St. Augustine situation also left him unhappy. He had had little chance to give any thought to how testing of the new federal public accommodations statute should be combined in Alabama with Bevel's grand ideas for a statewide action program, and the question remained unsettled when he flew to Washington for the July 2 signing ceremony. He remarked to one newsman that the act "will bring a great deal of practical relief to Negroes in many southern communities," but tempered that comment with a prediction that "it will probably take five years to see the civil rights bill fully implemented in the South." For the short term, the act would whet black appetites for further progress, and in the Deep South, "the scope of direct action this summer will depend on the scope of compliance" with the bill.[50]

Lyndon Johnson, only four months away from an election in which conservative Republicans threatened to tie the Democratic incumbent to the least popular aspects of civil rights protests, had very different ideas about how black America should respond to the new law. The president used the signing ceremony not only to congratulate those who had contributed to the passage of one of the legislative milestones in modern American history, but also to caution the black leaders about how they should greet this new achievement. After the public ceremony, the president spoke in private with King, Wilkins, Whitney Young, and other black representatives. He told them that there had to be "an understanding of the fact that the rights Negroes possessed could now be secured by law, making demonstrations unnecessary and possibly even self-defeating." Johnson suggested they would be self-defeating for the movement, but most of those in attendance, King included, knew that the president's real fear was that protests would play into the hands of Republican candidates seeking to convince fearful whites that someone other than Lyndon Johnson should be in the White House to preserve public order throughout America. Although no one countered the president's comments, King and his colleagues left knowing that the chief executive wanted the next four months to be quiet ones on the civil rights front.

King's concern about how the movement should press forward was matched by substantial tensions in his personal life. Coretta was still angry at his slighting of family responsibilities, and she was particularly disappointed that he had forgotten to call home as promised on the night of the signing ceremony in Washington. She had taken their sons, Marty and Dexter, to the hospital to have their tonsils removed, and had reminded her husband to call Atlanta to check on the children. King had forgotten to call, and this forgetfulness symbolized a neglect of family that Coretta found extremely painful. Then, on top of that, Harold DeWolf wrote to Martin and Coretta warning them of a development he had been alerted to by a Methodist Church executive in Washington. A number of bishops, DeWolf said, "have been receiving some mail seeking to undermine any favorable views they might have concerning you, both politically and morally." He recommended that King look into this, but, as with the earlier warnings about Levison and FBI surveillance, King chose to leave unpleasant matters well enough alone.[51]

The top item on King's agenda was Alabama, and on Monday, July 6, SCLC's staff and the officers of local affiliates met in Birmingham to discuss their plans. With passage of the new law, emphasis had shifted away from Jim Bevel's focus on voter registration. King told them that "our main goal this summer is to see that the civil rights law is implemented in all its dimensions all over the state of Alabama." Just days earlier, King had told a newsman that SCLC's testing of the public accommodations provisions would take place "mainly in Alabama since we anticipate a great deal of resistance there," but surprisingly, the first three days of testing for desegregated facilities at various restaurants, hotels, and theaters found almost complete compliance in Montgomery, Birmingham, Mobile, Huntsville, and Gadsden. Noncompliance was widespread in Tuscaloosa and especially in Selma, where daily demonstrations by local youths got under way on July 3. King said SCLC would seek federal action to ensure complete desegregation, and if that were not forthcoming, massive protests would take place. In private, King made clear his hope that SCLC would not have to return to St. Augustine, while Bevel continued to stress that the Alabama program ought to be expanded to encompass mass action on voter registration and political education, in addition to efforts to desegregate public schools.[52]

King flew to San Francisco to appear before the platform committee of the Republican National Convention. It was all but certain that the Republicans would nominate conservative Arizona Senator Barry Goldwater, who had voted against the Civil Rights Act. King had been saying for weeks that passage of the Civil Rights Act did not mean that the movement would relax its efforts, and he stressed that "there is still the need for stronger action from the federal government," particularly in protecting civil rights advocates in places like St. Augustine and Mississippi. "There will be no tranquility or cessation of demonstrations until every vestige of racial injustice is eliminated from American society," King told the Republicans on July 7. "The necessity for a vigorous and creative use of the power of the executive branch of government to protect federal rights in locally hostile environs" had not decreased because of the Civil Rights Act. King called upon Democrats as well as Republicans to support creation of "a special panel of United States marshals to serve as field observers in the offices of the local voting registrars in any area where there is a claimed denial or deprivation of a right to vote." He also renewed his call for a "bill of rights for the disadvantaged" that would compensate both blacks and poor whites for past injuries and provide financial support to any family with an annual income under $3,000. The conservative-dominated Republican convention showed little interest in King's proposals. He went to Los Angeles for several days of relaxation while his San Francisco proposals were forgotten. His West Coast trip did, however, demonstrate at least one "vigorous and creative use of the power of the executive branch"—a team of FBI agents bugged King's Los Angeles hotel room for two days. Bureau executives were pleased with the tapes, and another set of transcripts was passed around throughout the upper reaches of the executive branch.

By the time King returned from the West Coast, it was apparent that compliance with the public accommodations provisions of the Civil Rights Act was so widespread throughout Alabama that no statewide action campaign could be built around continued segregation in public establishments. A state court injunction, which a federal judge refused to void, blocked any protests in Selma, the principal locus of noncompliance. On July 10, Andrew Young told the Mississippi Summer Project's executive committee that the absence of any need to demonstrate in Alabama cities would allow King to make a People-to-People swing through Mississippi to aid the MFDP's recruitment efforts in advance of its own convention to choose an integrated delegation to go to the Democratic National Convention. The SNCC and MFDP activists accepted SCLC's offer, and plans for a tour got under way.[53]

When the Republican convention chose Barry Goldwater as its presidential candidate on July 15, King denounced the "unfortunate and disastrous" nomination. Goldwater, he said, "articulates a philosophy which gives aid and comfort to the racist," and urged all supporters to vote against the Republican nominee and other Republican candidates who did not disassociate themselves from him. Then King made his first return trip in two weeks to a "very tense" St. Augustine, where Manucy's Klansmen had launched some "direct action" of their own to intimidate white businessmen into resegregating their establishments. Although the first week of desegregation had been relatively uneventful, beginning on July 9, Klan members under Manucy's direction had picketed businesses like the Monson Motor Lodge that were reluctantly accepting black customers. Racist agitators Lynch and Stoner joined the protesters, and within several days most establishments in St. Augustine had buckled under and resegregated. SCLC protested to federal officials, and King told an evening rally that demonstrations would resume unless all public accommodations were desegregated once and for all. Civil rights attorneys moved to have Judge Simpson order the businesses to abide by the new act, and presidential aide Lee White asked Governor Bryant that local businessmen be protected against white terrorist attacks. The atmosphere was extremely tense during King's twenty-four-hour visit. After the evening rally King discussed his Mississippi tour with the SCLC staff. Everyone knew the possibility of assassination loomed large in Mississippi, and King was not eager to make the trip. Several staffers told him he had no choice but to go, and King became so irritated he walked out. An hour later he returned, admitting that he could not shirk the tour. "'I want to live a normal life,'" King told one aide, but "the staff was trying to tell him that 'you have no normal life. You are not an ordinary man.'"[54]

After a weekend trip to New York, King began his five-day Mississippi tour amid repeated warnings that the Klan had vowed to kill him during the visit. Friends begged him to reconsider. Harold DeWolf, in Atlanta to oversee the shipment of King's earliest papers to Boston University's archives, was astounded by how "quietly and calmly" Martin and Coretta spoke "about the possibility that he might never come back." King "really did not have that kind of fear which most people are subject to," DeWolf thought. Burke Marshall called King the morning of his departure, July 21, to reiterate the danger of the Klan's threat, but he went ahead and flew into Greenwood for his first speaking engagement that night. Lyndon Johnson, alerted to the threats against King, instructed FBI Director Hoover to make sure that King was protected in Greenwood, and an unhappy Hoover, who decried ever having his agents protect notables, reluctantly acceded to Johnson's order.

King largely ignored the hubbub and began his Greenwood visit by helping MFDP workers canvass local residents door-to-door, and by speaking to surprised black citizens in a series of downtown nightspots. The trip was King's first return to Mississippi since Medgar Evers's funeral, and he repeatedly took the opportunity to voice his support for MFDP's challenge to the "regular" Mississippi Democrats' all-white delegation. He also spoke about the plan for "voting rights marshals" that he had laid out to the Republican platform committee two weeks earlier, and that he hoped to present the proposal personally to President Johnson. On Thursday, July 23, King caucused at Tougaloo College with SNCC's James Forman, CORE's James Farmer, Mississippi activists Robert Moses, David Dennis and Edwin King, plus Bayard Rustin. The disagreements that had developed since May over what strategy MFDP should pursue at Atlantic City were widening as Rustin, who had enlisted support for the challenge in many quarters, argued that obstructive demonstrations at the convention would harm the movement, no matter what the outcome of MFDP's petition to have its delegation seated. The Tougaloo session clarified but did not resolve these differences. King then went on to make other appearances in Vicksburg and Meridian on Friday. North of Meridian, he toured the small city of Philadelphia, where an interracial team of three movement workers—James Chaney, Michael Schwerner, and Andrew Goodman—had disappeared six weeks earlier. The young men's burned-out car had been found in a swamp, but there was no trace of the victims, despite a presidentially ordered FBI investigation. While everyone presumed the three workers were dead, no arrests had been made and a palpable fear hung over Philadelphia. King stopped in a small poolroom as Ralph Abernathy and other aides gathered a crowd to greet him. King, who had fancied himself something of a pool shark in his northern college days, challenged a youngster to a game of eight-ball while seventy onlookers assembled; King managed to laugh when the young man convincingly defeated him. After urging the residents to have courage and faith, King's party visited the ruins of a church burned by the Klan, then headed to Meridian for an evening rally. A carload of FBI agents made certain King would not suffer the same fate as the three young workers who had visited Philadelphia, and the emotional tour concluded with a final Saturday rally in Jackson.[55]

King intended to take a brief respite in Atlanta, but he was confronted with a request from New York Mayor Robert Wagner that he help quell rampant rioting that had broken out on July 18 after the fatal shooting of a black youth, James Powell, by a white policeman two days earlier. King was hesitant to become involved, but felt he could not refuse Wagner's request. Both Clarence Jones and Bayard Rustin cautioned him to check with New York's black leaders and to maintain his ability to criticize the mayor's response to the disorders. Rustin consulted Harlem Unity Council leader Livingston Wingate, a close associate of Congressman Adam Clayton Powell, and on Monday evening, July 27, King flew to New York to meet briefly with Wingate before hurrying to a session with Mayor Wagner that stretched into the early-morning hours. Some local black activists questioned why King was involving himself at the mayor's behest, and criticism appeared in the press the next morning. King stressed to reporters that he wanted not only to end black violence, but to identify the underlying causes of the disorders and appeal "to the white power structure to give us some concrete victories." In his second meeting with Mayor Wagner on Tuesday afternoon, King proposed that a civilian review board be appointed to examine complaints about police conduct, and that the officer who shot Powell be suspended. Wagner's police commanders unalterably opposed these steps, and the mayor refused to act on King's proposals. King was disappointed. He feared that Harlem blacks would accuse him of being an "Uncle Tom," as he remarked to

Rustin. Meeting again with Wagner on Wednesday, King found him still unresponsive, and then declared publicly that "profound and basic changes" concerning "jobs, housing and quality integrated schools" would be necessary if urban disorders were to be avoided.[56]

Being caught in the middle between an inflexible mayor and angry community leaders was not the only serious problem King encountered in New York. The NAACP's Roy Wilkins, picking up on the suggestion Lyndon Johnson had made several weeks earlier, called a meeting of black leaders for July 29 to propose that they publicly ask all movement supporters "to observe a moratorium of all mass marches, picketing, and demonstrations until after Election Day" so as not to make white voters more susceptible to Barry Goldwater's anti-civil rights appeals. Whitney Young of the National Urban League was prepared to endorse it, but James Farmer of CORE and John Lewis of SNCC were opposed. Farmer argued that protests would not strengthen the much-touted "white backlash," but Bayard Rustin said Wilkins was correct. Farmer and Lewis looked to King for support, but as was usually the case, SCLC's president had no desire for confrontation with the combative Wilkins. "Martin was not an arguer at all or a debater," Farmer later recalled. As Rustin observed, "When it came to doing battle within the movement, he was at a loss. . . . He simply couldn't stay in a room where he had to contend with Wilkins. He had no ability for this." Combat with people outside the movement was one thing, but head-to-head unpleasantness was something King avoided consistently, be it disciplining SCLC subordinates or confronting an equal like Wilkins. "He never was able to infight," Rustin remembered. "He always took a neutralist position, and let the decision be made." King adopted that passive stance as the argument about the moratorium swirled around him, acknowledging, as he often did, the validity of both sides' contentions. Farmer's and Lewis's vociferous dissents, and veiled threats that their organizations would ignore any ban, forced Wilkins to modify the proposal so as to maintain an image of unity. When issued to the press, the resolution urged "a broad curtailment, if not total moratorium of all mass marches, picketing and demonstrations"—a notable if not substantial change from what Wilkins, and Lyndon Johnson, had wanted.[57]

As the moratorium debate ended, King found himself trapped in a no-win situation in New York. He met with the Harlem Unity Council in an effort to mute any further public criticism of him by local blacks, and then saw Mayor Wagner for a fourth and final session. The mayor remained unresponsive, and King left the meeting to give newsmen a strongly worded statement Rustin had helped him prepare. It emphasized New York's need for "a swift and constructive program for the removal of the causes of violence and conflict," and urged Wagner to begin round-the-clock negotiations with local black leaders. King said a major part of the problem was Wagner's police commissioner, Michael J. Murphy, whom King termed "utterly unresponsive to either the demands or the aspirations of the Negro people. He . . . has little understanding of the urgency of the situation."

Nonetheless, King emphasized, the problem was larger than police insensitivity toward blacks, for "social peace must spring from economic justice." Reflecting Rustin's tutelage, King's statement concluded that "the major problem remains one of economics . . . the need for millions of dollars *now* for full employment and for the elimination of slums." The next day, as King returned to Atlanta, Wagner announced his rejection of all black demands, including the police review board. King told reporters that northern cities were "potentially more explosive" than any place in the South, and that his five days in New York had left him more optimistic about the South than the North.[58]

King returned to St. Augustine on August 5 for his second visit since the end of the protests. Two weeks earlier, at the urging of Judge Simpson and Monson owner James Brock, St. Augustine's motels and restaurants had reintegrated their facilities despite the Klan's threats. The next day, two firebombs were thrown into the Monson's restaurant. Judge Simpson issued an injunction barring continued segregation, but the Klan's message was more persuasive than Simpson's, and many facilities continued to deny service to blacks. While SCLC's Harry Boyte directed a voter registration effort, Simpson and local officials such as state attorney Dan Warren tried again to devise a lasting settlement. Early on August 5, Simpson issued a comprehensive order barring Hoss Manucy and his followers from discouraging desegregated service in business establishments. Several hours later the local grand jury named a ten-person biracial committee to assume the central role in future discussions. Unfortunately, the committee quickly collapsed as four of the five white members resigned, complaining that the grand jury had not checked with them before announcing their selection. That collapse left matters at a tense standstill, and compliance with the desegregation decree remained fitful throughout August as Simpson continued his behind-the-scenes efforts and as the movement turned its attention toward voter registration.[59]

Martin and Coretta had hoped to spend much of August in New York, touring the city with their children and enjoying a holiday from the demands of the movement, but problems concerning the Mississippi Freedom Democrats' convention challenge impinged upon King almost daily. Bayard Rustin pressed King not to commit himself to participate in any Atlantic City protests. Rustin was unsure whether SNCC's and CORE's troops would abide by the controversial "moratorium" agreement, which James Farmer had publicly repudiated. King had come to think the moratorium a wise course, but he told Rustin he felt compelled to support the MFDP's effort to get seated at the Democratic convention. A good compromise, King said, would be for him to fast for the duration of the convention. Rustin did not argue, and the two men agreed King would seek an audience with Lyndon Johnson to talk about the moratorium and the MFDP's challenge. King sent a telegram to the White House, stressing the moratorium but making no reference to the challenge. Rustin phoned presidential aide Lee White to press for a meeting before King left on August 15 for a three-day trip to Europe. White said Johnson's schedule was full, and a disappointed King told Rustin to refuse White's offer of a telephone conversation with the president. His real hunch, King told Rustin, was that Johnson did not want to see him because of the impact that news coverage of their meeting might have on southern white voters. King told Rustin to press White harder, reminding him that "Lyndon Johnson needs the Negro vote. He feels that we have nowhere to go, but we can certainly stay home."

The New York sojourn that had started out as a family vacation turned out to have little time for such activities, although King did take a VIP day trip to the World's Fair with Coretta and the children. Escorted from exhibit to exhibit, son Marty asked why they did not have to stand in line like other tourists. King was embarrassed by the question, for it was an uncomfortable reminder that despite his many burdens, his life nonetheless was privileged. Being taken to the head of the line struck his son as wrong, and it should have struck him that way too, King acknowledged. "Martin himself realized that there was something wrong about this," Coretta remembered.[60]

By the time King left for Europe, Rustin and Lee White had agreed upon a meeting of all the black leadership with Johnson on August 19, the day after King's return. SCLC's affairs were well in hand under the supervision of new Program Director Randolph T. Blackwell, a former VEP administrator. That change freed Andrew Young to lead a brief peacemaking foray of six SCLC staffers into Rochester, New York, another city that had suffered summer disorders. Rustin continued his behind-the-scenes contacts during King's absence, and compared notes almost daily with longtime Democratic activist Joseph L. Rauh, Jr., a Washington lawyer serving as the MFDP's chief convention strategist. Rustin had cleared the request for the presidential meeting with Rauh, who had close ties to Minnesota Senator, and vice-presidential front-runner, Hubert H. Humphrey, as well as to United Auto Workers President Walter Reuther, another influential party figure. Rauh had endorsed the initiative, and had warned Rustin that the president was likely to press the black leaders to mute their support for the MFDP's challenge. Johnson's fear of losing white votes, and perhaps many southern states, to Goldwater if the Democratic convention ousted Mississippi's all-white "regulars" in favor of the MFDP appeared to outweigh any sympathy the president might have for the MFDP's documented charges that the state's regular Democratic party openly excluded black citizens. Rauh advised that only if King pushed Johnson forcefully, warning of a direct-action explosion if the MFDP was rebuffed, would there be any chance of the president supporting the joint seating of both contending Mississippi delegations.

Rauh's warning about Johnson's position and the fact that King's private meeting with the president had been transformed into a session with the entire black leadership, led Rustin to wonder if King should participate at all in what would likely be an unproductive discussion. It seemed that the dangers of King's being trapped in an apparent presidential embrace outweighed the possibility that he could persuade Johnson to endorse the MFDP's legitimacy. Rustin briefed King on his concerns, explained Rauh's worry that Johnson might refuse to discuss the MFDP issue at all, and then concurred with King's decision that it would be better for him to skip the meeting. While the FBI, privy to these many phone conversations thanks to its taps on both King and Rustin, was busy furnishing these details to the White House, a telegram was dispatched expressing King's regrets that he would be unable to attend the meeting. King's message called on the president to support the MFDP, but when the August 19 meeting opened, Johnson immediately informed the other black leaders that he would not talk about the convention. He devoted most of the session to a lecture on the civil rights accomplishments of his administration. None of the black leaders brought up the MFDP issue. After hearing Philip Randolph's account of the meeting, Rustin pronounced it a "fiasco," and a thankful King—right there in Washington to testify before the convention's platform committee—kept silent about why he stayed away. News reports speculated that King's absence meant the president could forget any moratorium on demonstrations during the fall election campaign if the MFDP delegation was not seated at the convention.[61]

The credentials committee hearing of the MFDP's challenge began on Saturday, August 22, with testimony from Freedom Democratic Party leaders Aaron Henry, Mrs. Fannie Lou Hamer, and white Rev. Edwin King. There was also a strong endorsement by Martin King and the presentation of a lengthy legal brief by Rauh detailing the discriminatory and exclusionary practices of the "regulars." Mrs. Hamer's powerful testimony—a vivid account of the brutalities she had suffered as a grass-roots activist in Mississippi—shocked a nationwide television audience until coverage was suddenly shifted to a quickly called presidential press conference. Mrs. Hamer's appeal, however, could not make up for the fact that Lyndon Johnson's henchmen were working at full strength to defeat a challenge that the president viewed as a serious obstacle to his defeating Barry Goldwater.

Much of the pressure was focused upon Joseph Rauh, whose friendships and loyalties were being pulled in opposite directions. More than a week before the convention, both UAW President Reuther, for whom Rauh served as Washington counsel, and several of Senator Humphrey's staffers had warned Rauh that failure to achieve MFDP acceptance of whatever the Johnson forces offered might prove costly to Rauh's friend

Humphrey when the president finally chose a running mate. Rauh proposed to National Chairman John Bailey and Pennsylvania Governor David Lawrence, chairman of the credentials committee, that each of the Mississippi groups be seated. Initially both men, plus Humphrey, seemed supportive of the idea, but another Democratic National Committee operative with closer ties to the inner Johnson circle, future Federal Appeals Judge Harold Leventhal, suggested that such an egalitarian solution was unacceptable. MFDP strategists stuck to their guns, but by the time that MFDP representatives went before the credentials committee on Saturday, it was clear that the integrated Mississippians would be able to muster only minority support, and would have to pin their hopes on having sufficient votes in the committee for a minority report to the full convention, which then would have an opportunity to reverse the committee's recommendation and vote to seat the MFDP delegation. Like others, Martin King stayed up late into the night lobbying credentials committee members on behalf of the MFDP.

On Sunday, MFDP supporters met twice and amid heated discussion endorsed a proposal advanced by Oregon Congresswoman Edith Green that the convention seat all members of either Mississippi delegation who would take an oath of loyalty to the Democratic party and presidential ticket, a step that many of the white Mississippians would likely decline in favor of supporting Goldwater. Estimates were that seventeen credentials committee members, six more than needed for a minority report, would support the Green initiative, and that proposal became the movement's position. Phone calls flew back and forth between the MFDP headquarters at the Gem Motel, King's room at the Claridge Hotel, and MFDP supporters among the delegates and credentials committee members. A special squad of FBI agents under the personal direction of the Bureau's powerful White House liaison, C. D. "Deke" DeLoach, listened in on many of the conversations thanks to electronic surveillance of the MFDP office and of King's and Rustin's rooms. The Bureau forwarded important information hourly to presidential aides Walter Jenkins and Bill Moyers. Johnson's assistants, fearing a nationally televised MFDP victory should a credentials committee minority report get to the convention floor, pulled out all the stops to reduce the number of dissenting votes to below the necessary eleven. Congresswoman Green remembered that Minnesota Attorney General Walter Mondale, a Humphrey protégé, was the administration's point man in its efforts to get delegates to abandon the MFDP. "I have never seen such just really blatant use of power" as the Johnson forces used to keep her proposal from the convention floor.[62]

As the two camps fought hard for the crucial votes, Senator Humphrey moved into the fray with a Johnson-sponsored plan that he presented privately at a meeting with King, Rauh, and other MFDP supporters. Two members of the sixty-four-person MFDP delegation would be given individual "at-large" votes as convention delegates; the remainder of the group would be admitted to the hall and seated as guests of the convention; only those Mississippi "regulars" who would take a Democratic loyalty oath would participate in casting the state's complement of votes; and the national Democratic party would promise to eliminate all racial discrimination in state party-delegate-selection procedures in advance of the 1968 convention. The MFDP reaction was cool, and Johnson allies tried to convince MFDP supporters of the wisdom of that settlement while continuing their hardball tactics with the credentials committee. Less than twelve hours before the credentials question would come to the convention floor, DeLoach phoned presidential aide Jenkins to report that MFDP support had fallen to thirteen votes; Jenkins replied that administration loyalists were working hard to reduce it further. Late Tuesday morning, the MFDP delegation listened to a description of the administration compromise, and decided to accept nothing less than the Green loyalty-oath proposal.

The MFDP rejection of Johnson's compromise infuriated once sympathetic power brokers like Walter Reuther. An angry Reuther told the harried Rauh that he should accept the two-vote offer at that afternoon's final credentials committee meeting or otherwise forget about future employment with the UAW. "He got very tough about my job," Rauh remembered. Reuther curtly dismissed Rauh's explanation that he, as counsel, had no authority to accept anything without checking with MFDP Chairman Aaron Henry. Careful nose-counting indicated that MFDP support within the committee had fallen to fewer than the necessary eleven, but there was no opportunity for the MFDP to caucus before the credentials committee meeting. Governor Lawrence, the committee chairman, ignored Rauh's efforts to win an adjournment, and the formal recommendation of the Johnson-backed two-vote compromise was voted through the committee without Rauh's endorsement. A last-ditch effort by Rauh and seven MFDP supporters to bring the Green plan to the floor of the full convention failed.

By late Tuesday afternoon it was clear that the MFDP and its supporters faced an unpalatable choice: surrender their pride and accept the two token at-large votes, or reject the Johnson offer and condemn the blatant hypocrisy of a president and a party that professed a commitment to civil rights but refused to seat an integrated group of delegates fully supportive of the policies that president and party claimed to advocate. Martin King had kept abreast of all the discussions and had supported the MFDP throughout, but now the choice was more difficult. Bayard Rustin believed that it was in the movement's interest to accept the proposal, and to signal that the South's activists understood the necessities of compromise and coalitions in electoral politics just as well as they appreciated the value of protest demonstrations. Andrew Young agreed and argued that the situation was analogous to that in Birmingham fifteen months earlier: The settlement was far from what the movement sought, but it represented a tangible gain.[63]

Many of the MFDP leaders, however, felt the Johnson offer was little more than an insult, and found it particularly offensive that the president's forces had specified the two MFDP delegates who should assume the seats: party Chairman Henry and white college chaplain Ed King. "Lyndon made the typical white man's mistake," Aaron Henry later observed. "Not only did he say you've got two votes, which was too little, but he told us to whom the two votes would go."

Late Tuesday afternoon, Rauh and the seven remaining MFDP supporters from the credentials committee met with King, Rustin, SNCC's Jim Forman, and the MFDP leaders at a church that served as the movement's strategy center. Rauh, torn between his obligation to the MFDP and his loyalty to Reuther and Hubert Humphrey, was uncertain what to do. He asked for King's advice to the group. "I said to Dr. King, 'I'd like your recommendation.'" Almost immediately, Bayard Rustin interrupted. "'Joe, you've done something you will know someday was wrong. You tried to take your responsibility and give it to Dr. King.'" Emotionally drained, Rauh realized his error. "I almost burst into tears because he was right. I shouldn't have done that, and I was looking for help that I wasn't entitled to." Rustin continued his reprimand. "'Dr. King cannot take your responsibility; this is your responsibility—you and the other seven delegates here. It is your responsibility to decide what you want to do.'" Rustin's effort to deflect the choice away from King succeeded, and Rauh apologized. Nonetheless, the decision rested not with the eight credentials committee members, but with the MFDP's leadership. Rauh indicated he saw many reasons for accepting the compromise, and Rustin did likewise. However, when it came King's turn to speak, he explained that he could see valid grounds both for accepting and for rejecting the offer. He appreciated Rustin's argument that the movement was beginning to undergo a shift "from protest to politics," as Rustin later termed it, and that unattractive compromises were unavoidable in the political arena. Accepting the compromise would mean more help for the movement from Lyndon Johnson and important presidential friends like Reuther, men who could encourage substantial contributions which, in situations like Birmingham, were crucial to the movement's survival. However, King also appreciated why the MFDP, after hard work and visions of triumph in Atlantic City, would judge the Johnson offer unacceptable. On balance, King suggested that accepting it was the better choice, but "he did not pressure us strongly to take it," Tougaloo chaplain Ed King recalled. "His position, as he told me, was that he wanted to see us take this compromise because this would mean strength for him, help for him in Negro voter registration throughout the South and in the North. . . . He said, 'So, being a Negro leader, I want you to take this, but if I were a Mississippi Negro, I would vote against it.' So he understood."

Efforts continued to design an agreement the MFDP could accept. Some Freedom Democrats unjustly suspected that Rauh was proving disloyal, but by mid-evening, Rustin had arranged for MFDP leaders Henry, Ed King, and Robert Moses, along with King and Andrew Young, to meet face-to-face with Hubert Humphrey and Reuther to try to work out some agreement. The discussion made clear that the MFDP's distaste for the Johnson offer was based not upon the two votes per se, but upon the issue of by whom those votes would be cast. Aaron Henry thought the problem could be solved if all sixty-four members of the MFDP delegation were given floor seats and $\frac{1}{32}$nd of a vote apiece. Ed King pressed Humphrey and Reuther to allow four MFDP members—Henry and King plus two black women, Mrs. Hamer and Victoria Gray—to cast one-half vote per person. Humphrey's refusal strengthened Ed King's belief that the real presidential motive was to keep the electrifying Mrs. Hamer out of the spotlight. A television set had provided coverage of the convention's floor activities during the discussions, and all of sudden, the group saw Rhode Island Senator John Pastore, the convention chairman, announce that the two-vote compromise had been accepted by all. A stunned Robert Moses walked out of the meeting, telling Humphrey, "You cheated." The session collapsed, and King and the other movement representatives returned to the MFDP's church headquarters to discuss what could be done with the public *fait accompli* that Lyndon Johnson had handed them.

More administration pressure was exerted on movement leaders to persuade the MFDP to accept the Johnson offer. Roy Wilkins and Whitney Young recommended that the compromise be accepted. Rustin and Andrew Young advised King to speak out more strongly in favor of the proposal, and on Wednesday King joined other national movement figures at the MFDP's church headquarters to speak in favor of acceptance. Many in the MFDP delegation whispered that Rauh, Rustin, and King had sold them out. "Tension was very high," one participant recalled, as speaker after speaker pleaded with the delegates to accept the Johnson offer. Rauh called it "a great victory for civil rights" to have won the two seats, but neither he nor any other national figure could persuade the black Mississippians to accept Johnson's proposal. An ambivalent Martin King said that the two-vote offer was a good proposal, but that the decision was the Mississippians', not his. "He made no effort to persuade," Andrew Young remembered, and the MFDP delegation voted overwhelmingly to reject the compromise. That evening, after announcing his choice of Hubert Humphrey for vice-president, Lyndon Johnson was awarded the presidential nomination of a convention that he and his supporters had controlled and manipulated with remarkable thoroughness. The next morning, as the MFDP delegation wrestled with their anger and disillusionment, a tired and disappointed Martin King left Atlantic City without waiting to hear Humphrey's and Johnson's acceptance speeches.[64]

The Atlantic City convention left the movement more shaken and divided than at any prior time. The suspicion and bitterness that some of

SNCC's young activists felt toward Martin King could be traced back to Atlanta four years earlier, to his refusal to join the Freedom Rides, and to the tensions of Albany, but now the demoralization was greater than ever before. "We went to Atlantic City with all of this hope," Mrs. Hamer later explained. "We went there because we believed that America was what it said it was." They had learned the hard way that it was not, and had discovered what Ed King later called "the emptiness of traditional liberalism." Like the grass-roots people of the MFDP, SNCC's workers also "went to Atlantic City with a great deal of optimism," Chairman John Lewis explained. They came away "disappointed, disillusioned," rather than victorious, and looking back they marveled at their naïveté. "It now seems foolish that the FDP could have ever expected the President to be either on their side or neutral," SNCC's Frank Smith wrote in the aftermath. The real problem, however, was not the movement's failure to understand American politics, as Rustin had suggested, but American politics' failure to understand the moral justice of the movement's cause. That was a realization as painful as it was profound, a realization suggesting that the problems the movement confronted had deep roots outside of Mississippi and the South as well as within. That realization suggested some deep and perhaps fatal flaw in Rustin's coalition politics argument. When the time for choice had come, old friends and allies had deserted the cause and forgotten there were some compromises a moral crusade could not make. "Some people," John Lewis reflected, "lost respect for Dr. King and for people like Bayard."

Although many in the MFDP had harsh words for King, Andrew Young, Rauh, Rustin, and Reuther, no one ascribed an ignominious role to King, and he felt comfortable with the stance he had taken. Birmingham had shown that even small tangible gains could represent extraordinary symbolic victories, even if those people closest to the struggle could not appreciate it at the time.[65]

King had no angry words for his critics as he rested in Atlanta, then prepared for a mid-September European tour. Accompanied by Coretta and Ralph Abernathy, King flew to West Berlin for a two-day visit sponsored by Mayor Willy Brandt. King's schedule was overbooked as usual. In one day he appeared at a memorial service for President Kennedy, an afternoon service in a stadium packed with 25,000 worshipers, and an evening church appearance on the other side of the Wall in East Berlin. He spoke warmly of the promise that John Kennedy had held, of how southern racial violence would be eliminated only when federal authorities intervened, and how Barry Goldwater's presidential candidacy was ripe with the "danger signs of Hitlerism."

Then it was on to Rome, for a personal audience with Pope Paul VI that Atlanta Archbishop Paul J. Hallinan had arranged. With Abernathy at his side, King was granted a twenty-five-minute conversation on September 18. The pope endorsed America's nonviolent civil rights movement, and promised he would issue a statement condemning racial segregation and discrimination. King was deeply pleased, and offered reporters an optimistic view of the American civil rights picture. "Progress is faster than we thought it would be," and the future appeared bright. "If the tide of racial prejudice continues to recede to the present rate, there would be no reason why a Negro could not be elected" president within twenty-five years, King volunteered. In the South, he opined, the winter months might bring protests in "some of the most difficult areas . . . where the civil rights bill is not being enforced, or we may work on the wider front of voter registration." King again voiced his belief that the North would be "even a bigger problem than the South," but even that awareness did not undercut his optimism. "My hope is that the American racial situation will become such that I can return full time to my first and still intended work, that of being pastor of a church," King said in a rare admission of his hope that someday he could retire from the movement.

From Rome, Martin, Coretta, and Ralph flew to Madrid for a two-day vacation. Then they went on to London for a day's worth of events marking the English publication of *Why We Can't Wait*. When reporters there asked him the same questions he had answered in Rome, King again voiced his hopefulness. "I'm optimistic. Since the civil rights bill got through, the South has complied quite surprisingly." Difficult issues concerning housing, school integration, and jobs lay ahead, but "we are not far from the day when the barriers of segregation will be completely destroyed in the South."[66]

While King and Abernathy were in Europe, SCLC's staff discussed future plans with other movement groups and prepared for the organization's annual convention, scheduled for Savannah in September. Many tensions were developing in the wake of Atlantic City, and some of them sprang to the surface at a September 18 intergroup meeting in New York. Gloster Current of the NAACP expressed unhappiness about all the criticism of his group, and SNCC's Courtland Cox hotly replied that Current and fellow NAACPer John Morsell ought to be more careful about some of the accusations they had been aiming at SNCC and the MFDP. Robert Spike of the National Council of Churches pointed out that mutual distrust had to be eliminated if different groups were to work together cooperatively. SCLC's Andrew Young, sounding Bayard Rustin's theme, said that passage of the Civil Rights Act meant the movement would no longer pursue public accommodations protests, but had to seek electoral change. First on the agenda, Young said, was reestablishing a focus on the right to vote. Joseph Rauh explained the need for federal legislation authorizing federally assigned registrars for those southern counties where less than one third of the black voting-age population was registered. Young agreed, observing that experience had shown "gradual voter registration doesn't work" and that a "more creative approach" was needed in Mississippi and Alabama.

At the top of the SCLC agenda were the Savannah convention and an October get-out-the-vote tour which King hoped would mobilize blacks to vote against Barry Goldwater on November 3. SCLC's staff responsibilities had been clarified by hiring Blackwell as program director, and also by the installation of Hosea Williams as head of voter registration and James Bevel as "director of direct action." Andrew Young was free to function as King's executive assistant, and the New York office's mail appeals had been going smoothly for six months under the direction of newly hired Adele Kanter. SCLC's annual accounting showed that $626,000 had been received since the Richmond convention a year earlier, and that expenses had exceeded that amount by about $50,000. Even so, the organization seemed on more solid footing than at any time since the departure of Wyatt Walker. King's optimism was as visible during the Savannah gathering as it had been on his European trip. He told the board about his July experiences in New York, about the brief explorations that staffers had made in Rochester and in Philadelphia, and explained that SCLC had to give increasing thought to the North and to expanding its program into cities like Washington and Newark that had black-majority populations. "It is a question of whether SCLC can move out from its southern base," King said. The need to stress political action and to address economic issues meant that SCLC had to adopt a more national perspective and seek out white allies who would join in pursuing those broader goals. Profoundly influenced by Rustin's analyses, King set out his view of the future in an annual report he read to the convention on October 1:

> Tactics are to be used only so long as they are effective in achieving specific goals. They should be subjected to frequent analysis, review and evaluation. Tactics must be modified in response to the ever changing situations that confront us.
>   In the past our demonstrations against public accommodations have been highly successful precisely because they were unique in doing three things: first, they called attention to the evil; second, they aroused the conscience of the community; third, they eliminated the evil *itself* when men, women and children stood firm and accepted what came.

In this phase of protest, the movement had to keep those evils in the national news. "When we are idle, the white majority quickly forgets the injustices which started our movement and only think of the demands for progress as unreasonable requests from irresponsible people," a perception that candidate Goldwater was attempting to capitalize upon.

However, as the movement's agenda shifted from southern segregation to nationwide economic issues, protest tactics could no longer fulfill that third function of eliminating the evil itself, King said. These new national issues required not just protest, but "political action, for we are now facing basic social and economic problems that require political reform." For a real "War on Poverty," one far larger in scope than what Lyndon Johnson yet envisioned, substantial federal funds would be necessary, and the movement would have to see to "creating political power to in-duce Congress to appropriate such a sum of money." To do that, new methods and allies would be needed. "Each day it becomes clearer," King emphasized, "that the solution to our full citizenship, political and economic, cannot be achieved by the Negro or civil rights forces alone." A broader coalition would be required, and the movement would have to shift from protest to politics.[67]

King's political vision had undergone a sizable expansion since mid-summer, but he was still a prisoner of his heavy speaking schedule. An early October trip took him from a speech in Philadelphia to fifteen thou-sand persons, to three Sunday speaking engagements in Newark and New York, and then to two Monday speeches at a church convention in St. Louis. He returned to Atlanta on Tuesday fatigued almost to the break-ing point, and took Coretta's and his doctor's advice to check into an Atlanta hospital for an examination and some desperately needed rest. Dr. Asa G. Yancey found he was twenty pounds overweight and suffering from a severe virus and high blood pressure. Coretta pronounced him "completely exhausted, tired and empty."

Wednesday morning King was asleep at St. Joseph's Infirmary when Coretta called to tell him that the wire services had just notified her that King had been awarded the 1964 Nobel Peace Prize. The news did not come as a complete surprise to the Kings, for they both had known of his nomination for the award by eight Swedish legislators and of the prize committee's request for copies of his books and speeches. Just one week earlier, Oslo sources had termed King a "heavy favorite" for the Peace Prize, but Coretta's initial reaction to the notification was not simply joyous. At the moment, Martin badly needed several days of rest, and the announcement was certain to interrupt that. On the other hand, the news of the prize was a perfect cure for the depression that accompanied his exhaustion. "I realized that this was exactly the sort of lift Martin desperately needed," and as her groggy husband realized that his wife's call was neither a dream nor a practical joke, his mood became quiet and serious. Nine months earlier he had told Stanley Levison that *Time*'s "Man of the Year" award was nothing special, that he had two hundred plaques at home, and "what's one more?" but the Nobel Peace Prize was different. This was not simply a personal award, but the most significant international endorsement possible of the civil rights struggle. This was not a prize being given to one individual, King thought, but the "foremost of earthly honors" being accorded the movement that he had come to symbolize. They should celebrate it not as a personal triumph, King told Coretta and his closest aides—Bernard Lee, Andrew Young, and Dora McDonald—when they gathered in his hospital room, but as a victory of moral recognition for the cause of justice. Intensely serious, he asked them to join him in prayer, for this symbolic award meant that he and they, too, would have to redouble their efforts and intensify their commitment. "It was a great tribute, but an even more awesome burden," Coretta said. It meant there might be no escape from this life and this role, from the responsibilities and burdens that had been so constant ever since that night in the kitchen more than eight years earlier in Montgomery. The prize might mean there would never be any respite, never any retreat to a quiet pastorship or seminary professorship. More than anything else, the prize made the cross loom larger. "History has thrust me into this position," King told the reporters who gathered at St. Joseph's that Wednesday morning. "It would both be immoral and a sign of ingratitude if I did not face my moral responsibility to do what I can in this struggle."[68]

7

Selma and the Voting Rights Act, 1965

At thirty-five, King was the youngest person ever to be awarded the Nobel Peace Prize, and newsmen marveled at the "spartan-like simplicity" of the rented home he and his family lived in, and how the only family car was a 1960 Ford with seventy thousand miles on the odometer. Although King remained in St. Joseph's Infirmary through the weekend despite the deluge of publicity, he told reporters he was eager to end his rest and begin a fifteen-city northern "get out the vote" tour in advance of the presidential election. The prize carried with it a financial award of $54,000, and King conferred with his advisors as to what he should do with the funds. He asked Bayard Rustin to make the arrangements for the December trip to Europe to accept the prize, and Coretta suggested that some of the financial windfall should be used to pay the transportation costs to Oslo for relatives and friends who wanted to accompany King to the ceremonies. She also argued that he ought to put aside at least $5,000 for each of their children's college education, but Martin resisted. He felt that the prize was an award to the movement in general, rather than to him individually, and that the entire amount should be used in the struggle and not for the benefit of his family.

Congratulations flowed in from around the world, but Coretta was disappointed there was no greeting from Lyndon Johnson. King explained that the president was no doubt trying to avoid anything that would offend southern white voters just two weeks before the election. On October 21, after a week of rest, King set out on a nationwide voter turnout crusade. Chicago, Cleveland, and Los Angeles were the first stops, and King encouraged black pastors to urge their church members to vote on November 3. Then it was back to Chicago for a hectic day of nonstop appearances at sixteen street-corner rallies. The following day witnessed a similar pattern in Detroit, and the day after that a tour through Baltimore. King emphasized the dangers of the Republican nominee more than the virtues of Lyndon Johnson, telling one Baltimore rally that "Goldwater is a threat to freedom." He received enthusiastic receptions, and after ten days of constant travel returned home to Atlanta to await the returns. A Republican dirty trick forced him to make a public appearance the day before the election to denounce anonymous leaflets urging write-in votes for King that were circulating in several cities.[1]

Lyndon Johnson's massive victory pleased King deeply because the Democratic landslide represented a clear repudiation of the opposition to civil rights that Republican Goldwater had voiced. This, he told friends, was the same sort of crucial national indicator that passage of the Civil Rights Act had been, and was an event the movement should capitalize on. The day after the election, King said that SCLC "will probably have demonstrations in the very near future in Alabama and Mississippi, based around the right to vote." The one principal shortcoming of the 1964 act had been the absence of a provision authorizing the assignment of federal registrars to aid southern blacks who faced blatant discrimination when they attempted to register with local officials. SCLC wanted federal action to protect the right to register and vote. After that, King explained, he wanted to focus upon northern cities, where "progress for the Negro . . . has been relatively insignificant, particularly in terms of the Negro masses. What little progress has been made . . . has applied primarily to the middle-class Negro." Many Americans lived in "abysmal ignorance" of how pervasive racial discrimination was throughout the country. "America today is an extremely sick nation," and "the truth is that deep prejudices and discriminations exist in hidden and subtle and covert disguises." In the near future SCLC would tackle the issues of jobs, schools, and housing in the North's biggest and worst cities; "on a longer-range basis, the physical ghetto itself must be eliminated."[2]

One week after the election King convened an SCLC staff retreat at Birmingham's Gaston Motel "to assess the era through which we have come . . ., to assess the structure and program of SCLC," and "to chart our course in the nonviolent movement over the next six months." King spoke about "the real needs in large northern and western cities," and about the need to "instill the philosophy of nonviolence in the North," but the primary issue on the agenda was voting rights in the Deep South. Hosea Williams spoke about possible registration efforts, and King interjected that SCLC ought to give "special attention to areas where there are structural obstructions," such as Alabama and Mississippi. "Our entire method must be changed or broadened. We must have Federal registrars or other drastic measures for voter registration." Williams recommended they concentrate on counties where white opposition to registration efforts would be relatively low, but C. T. Vivian reminded them that "we must have a rallying point around which we can stir the whole nation." Jim Bevel, who had never stopped advocating a statewide Alabama Project, emphasized that the time had come for SCLC to pursue his plan for a comprehensive attack on black disfranchisement.

SCLC's Alabama affiliates were ready to move, and "will send a letter of invitation to SCLC so that there is no question of why we are there," he reported. Bevel explained that one opportune target would be to challenge the seating of Alabama's all-white state legislature when it convened on May 4, 1965, and the staff debated how public they should be about their plans. "Dr. King felt," the minutes recorded, "that a general press release should be issued now, and when he moves into the state [that] this too should be widely publicized. This is necessary since arousing the national conscience and winning allies is more difficult in the absence of facts."

The first day's discussion left unsettled the questions of how much direct action would be used, and where the initial efforts would center, but the next morning both issues were clarified. Mrs. Amelia Boynton, the Selma activist whom King and his SCLC colleagues had known for several years, spoke about how SNCC's commitment to Selma was diminishing, and how blacks had been unable even to hold a mass meeting since July, when State Judge James Hare had issued an injunction banning all gatherings in the wake of local efforts to desegregate public accommodations after the Civil Rights Act became law. If SCLC were serious about launching an Alabama movement against political repression, there would be no better place to begin than Selma. Ralph Abernathy stated that Mrs. Boynton's suggestion was an excellent one, and that no further discussion of the starting point was necessary: They should go to Selma and break the injunction.

After lunch, the group talked in detail about Selma's possibilities. Eric Kindberg, a young white staffer who worked for Bevel, was assigned to research Selma, while Bevel would plan direct action across the state. C. T. Vivian would visit Selma and meet with the local black leadership, the Dallas County Voters League (DCVL), to "show them our concern and convince them of our interest in helping them to build a mass movement. Selma should make an effective testing ground since an attitude of defiance has been so strongly demonstrated." An initial mass meeting featuring King would be set for January 2, 1965, and SCLC would be ready if lawmen tried to enforce Hare's order and keep the rally from taking place.[3]

The Birmingham retreat gave SCLC a more specific programmatic focus than the organization had had in over a year. Looking back at that time, King confessed that he and others had "failed to assert the leadership the movement needed," but that he would correct the error. Then he headed off for a series of speeches in North Carolina, some meetings in Atlanta to discuss the Nobel Prize trip, and a brief vacation at Adam Clayton Powell's island retreat on Bimini.

At the same time, Affiliates Director Vivian made his exploratory trip to Selma. He met with the Voters League leadership one evening at Mrs. Boynton's home, and listened as Frederick D. Reese, a Selma minister and schoolteacher, talked about how SNCC's effort had "just about run its course." The black community "needed some rejuvenation," and hoped SCLC would provide it. Vivian was impressed by the Selma activists' interest in mobilizing the entire community to protest the discriminatory registration practices which had kept all but several hundred Dallas County blacks from becoming registered voters. If SCLC wanted to launch a voting rights crusade, Selma seemed like "an ideal place to do it," Vivian remembered. SCLC "knew what we wanted to do," he explained. "We wanted to raise the issue of voting to the point where we could take it outside of the Black Belt [counties]. . . . We were using Selma as a way to shake Alabama . . . so that it would be no longer a Selma issue or even an Alabama issue but a national issue." To Vivian, SNCC's remaining presence "was the only real negative" in a situation that featured a unified black community and lawmen who exemplified the worst of the Deep South. Boynton, Reese, and other Selma activists like Mrs. Marie Foster pointed out that Dallas County Sheriff James G. Clark, Jr., was infamous for his racial hostility and violent temper. Vivian knew that Clark and his men had shown their true colors at SNCC's 1963 protest and during the short-lived July efforts to desegregate Selma's public accommodations. "We really didn't know what Jim Clark was like per se," Vivian recalled, "but we didn't have any doubt about the police reaction" if voting rights demonstrations or "tests" of downtown desegregation were launched. "It wasn't a matter of *that person* as much as the general police reaction" that led Vivian to expect responses similar to those SCLC had experienced in St. Augustine. Impressed by Selma's possibilities, Vivian returned to Atlanta as preparations were made for the January 2 kick-off rally.[4]

Martin King's Bimini vacation was interrupted on Wednesday, November 18, by word that FBI Director J. Edgar Hoover had labeled him the "most notorious liar" in America in an interview earlier that day with a group of women journalists. Hoover asserted that the basis for his name-calling was King's public complaint two years earlier that native southern FBI agents in Albany had done an inadequate job investigating civil rights complaints; the truth of the matter, Hoover said, was that four of the five Albany agents were northerners. Hoover added off the record that King was "one of the lowest characters in the country." Well-informed observers did not doubt that Hoover's outburst was based upon more than an obscure two-year-old complaint. King's response, in both a brief public statement and a longer personal telegram, addressed Hoover's attack at face value. Publicly, King expressed pity for the FBI director:

> I cannot conceive of Mr. Hoover making a statement like this without being under extreme pressure. He has apparently faltered under the awesome burden, complexities and responsibilities of his office. Therefore, I cannot engage in a public debate with him. I have nothing but sympathy for this man who has served his country so well.

In the telegram, King said he was "appalled and surprised" by Hoover's "irresponsible accusation" and offered to meet with the director to discuss the Bureau's "seeming inability to gain convictions in even the most heinous crimes perpetrated against civil rights workers." No charges had been filed over Albany's incidents of brutality, no arrests had been made for the bombing of Birmingham's Sixteenth Street Baptist Church, and no arrests had taken place in the murders of Chaney, Schwerner, and Goodman in Mississippi. The FBI's shortcomings in the South seemed to more than justify his complaints, King suggested.

Hoover's outburst and King's rebuttals received front-page coverage across the country, and FBI agents in Atlanta and New York monitored the wiretapped phones of King's aides and advisors to learn what responses King's supporters might make. They overheard King tell his secretary, Dora McDonald, that Hoover was "too old and broken down" to continue as director, and they eavesdropped on a subsequent conversation in which King told C. T. Vivian that Hoover "is old and getting senile" and should be "hit from all sides" with criticism in a concerted effort to get President Johnson to censure him. One day after the story broke, all of the major black leaders except King, who was still in the Caribbean, attended a previously scheduled White House meeting and expressed their support for King to Lyndon Johnson. The president, Roy Wilkins told newsmen afterward, "simply listened and gave no comment and no opinion."

Lyndon Johnson, like King and his closest aides, knew that underlying Hoover's attack was the potentially damaging material about King's personal life and his relationship with Stanley Levison that the Bureau had collected. Although the wiretaps on Levison never had confirmed that his closeness to King was motivated by adherence to the Soviet Union or to the American Communist party, the FBI could show that one of King's closest advisors, with whom he kept in contact despite many warnings, had been once intimately involved in the Communist party's financial dealings. More important, through the hotel buggings that had continued irregularly for ten months, and through the wiretaps on King's home and office, Bureau officials knew more about King's private life than Coretta or most of his friends did. The many reports that the Bureau had circulated throughout the executive branch about Levison's affiliations and King's liaisons had made many people privy to the underside of the public controversy. Widespread suspicion of the true root of Hoover's animus increased when he attacked "pressure groups" headed by "Communists and moral degenerates" in a November 24 speech in Chicago.[5]

King's advisors were divided on whether a counterattack should be launched on Hoover, or whether King's vulnerability required caution and conciliation instead. Clarence Jones and Kenneth Clark recommended a forceful response; Bayard Rustin and Harry Wachtel also advised King to adopt a somewhat combative stance. As Rustin remembered it, however, the first suggestion of a different approach came from Stanley Levison, who counseled that King follow through on his initial offer to Hoover that they meet and discuss the situation. Such a course would avoid the danger of inviting the FBI to wage full-scale combat. Further discussions ensued after King's return from Bimini, and support for making a conciliatory approach to Hoover grew as rumor after rumor suggested that Bureau officials were telling reporters privately of the extensive ammunition the FBI could use against King. Acting Attorney General Nicholas deB. Katzenbach, who had replaced Robert Kennedy two months earlier when Kennedy resigned to run for a New York Senate seat, was warned of the FBI's efforts and traveled with Burke Marshall to Lyndon Johnson's Texas ranch in an unsuccessful effort to obtain presidential intervention. Other civil rights leaders such as Roy Wilkins and James Farmer also heard the rumors from newsmen, and each made private appointments with high-ranking FBI officials to ask about the reports and demand that the leaks be halted.

King was deeply disturbed by the controversy and the rumors. He found it hard to concentrate on the text of his Nobel lecture that he had started writing in Bimini. On the evening of November 30, he met with CORE's James Farmer at New York's Kennedy Airport for a private discussion of the FBI's whispering campaign. Farmer explained he had heard three different charges against King: rumors of financial misconduct, allegations about being the tool of Communists, and claims that he had participated in group sex orgies. King denied each charge, and said he could remember no such sexual incidents. Farmer volunteered to drop the entire matter, saying, "I'll forget it." King replied, "'Don't forget it. No, let's do what we can to stop it. If something like this comes out, even if it isn't true, it will damage all of us in the whole movement.'" Farmer agreed and promised to keep an appointment with the FBI's C. D. "Deke" DeLoach that he had made for the next day.[6]

Although King did not mention it to Farmer, extensive behind-the-scenes efforts were under way to arrange a meeting between King and an unwilling J. Edgar Hoover. The morning after the King-Farmer discussion, Attorney General Katzenbach recommended to the Bureau that such a meeting take place, and soon after that Andrew Young called and obtained DeLoach's agreement that King could see Hoover that afternoon. Young, Ralph Abernathy, and Walter Fauntroy accompanied a nervous King, while DeLoach sat alongside Hoover. Greetings were exchanged, and Abernathy offered some positive comments about the FBI and its director. Then, according to a detailed recounting of the conversation by DeLoach that SCLC aides later said was accurate:

> Reverend King spoke up. He stated it was vitally necessary to keep a working relationship with the FBI. He wanted to clear up any misunderstanding which might have occurred. He stated that some Negroes had told him that the FBI had been ineffective; however, he was inclined to discount such criticism. Reverend King asked that the Direc-

tor please understand that any criticism of the Director and the FBI which had been attributed to King was either a misquote or an outright misrepresentation. He stated this particularly concerned Albany, Georgia. He stated that the only time he had ever criticized the FBI was because of instances in which Special Agents who had been given complaints in civil rights cases regarding brutality by police officers were seen the following day being friendly with those same police officers.

King added that he always had encouraged movement activists to cooperate with the Bureau, and volunteered that he held a strong personal dislike of communism.

Following King's statement, Hoover launched into a meandering description of the FBI's work in the South that went on almost without interruption for nearly an hour. King interjected at one point that SCLC was planning voter registration protests in Selma, and Hoover detailed prior investigations the FBI had made there as part of several discrimination suits the Justice Department had filed against Dallas County Sheriff Clark and other local officials. When the time was up, DeLoach told the SCLC contingent that the FBI would make no statement about the meeting to reporters, but King told newsmen waiting outside Hoover's office that the conversation had been "very friendly, very amicable." King said that he and Hoover had reached "new levels of understanding," and added, "I sincerely hope we can forget the confusions of the past and get on with the job."

King's aides were far from satisfied with the meeting, however, for there had been no explicit discussion of the real issues that underlay the conflict. "We never really got around to the disagreements that were going on between them," Young recalled later, terming it "a completely nonfunctional meeting." King's advisors were pleased at the efforts other civil rights leaders had made to warn the Bureau and the administration about the serious repercussions any FBI leaks against King would have, but the danger of such revelations was not eliminated by the unproductive session. King was extremely vulnerable, and his heightened status as the moral symbol of the American civil rights struggle could vanish overnight, Nobel Prize or not, if the FBI succeeded in getting its tawdry leaks into the press. The face-to-face meeting did not end the FBI's efforts— one newsman had been offered incriminating material on King while he waited outside Hoover's office during the meeting—and secondhand reports indicated that the smear campaign was going forward at full tilt as journalists and church leaders told friends of being offered embarrassing material on King by FBI representatives.[7]

"I only wish that there was nothing there that did undermine the morality," Harry Wachtel told Bayard Rustin as King's advisors discussed the troubling situation that confronted them on the eve of King's departure for what was to have been a triumphal trip to accept the Nobel Prize.

King was worried and depressed, preoccupied with the FBI problem, and essentially disinterested in the European tour that his family and closest friends had been looking forward to. Coretta, his parents, his two siblings, the Abernathys, Rustin, Wachtel, Wyatt Walker, and SCLC associates Bernard Lee, Andrew Young, Dorothy Cotton, Carole Hoover, Dora McDonald, Lillie Hunter, and Lawrence Reddick, among others, gathered for a December 4 departure from New York, but what should have been a joyous time found King in a state of "complete exhaustion." Bayard Rustin apologized to newsmen when King was late for a press conference, explaining, "He's just worn out—exhausted." King confessed that doctors had told him he needed "a long period of rest," but he spoke about how pleased he was by the previous day's federal arrests in the three Mississippi killings. "I must commend the Federal Bureau of Investigation for the work they have done in uncovering the perpetrators of this dastardly act."

On the long flight to London, an unhappy King talked haltingly to Wachtel about his fears of what could happen should the FBI succeed in leaking its material about his personal life. He had thought long and hard about this for two weeks now, and he admitted to himself that there were many instances in which he had sinned, instances that called out for him to do better in the future. In public appearances in London he betrayed little of his inner turmoil. On Sunday, December 6, King preached to thousands at St. Paul's Cathedral, and kept a hectic schedule of meetings and dinners with Anglican church leaders, visiting Indian dignitaries, and English peace advocates. Asked about South Africa, King responded that "more and more I have come to realize that racism is a world problem," not simply an American one, and the following evening, at his last public appearance in London before heading on to Oslo, he called for a "massive economic boycott" of the apartheid state by all other nations.[8]

The first night at Oslo's Grand Hotel, the King entourage held a late-night birthday party for New York financial supporter Marian Logan. *Ebony* magazine reporter Charles Sanders played the piano as people sang. At the end of the evening Daddy King spoke about the deep pride that his son's honor had brought to the family. His remarks moved many of the group to tears. The next day King met the Norwegian press and said he viewed the trip as an educational opportunity for him and his colleagues. "We feel we have much to learn from Scandinavia's democratic socialist tradition and from the manner in which you have overcome many of the social and economic problems that still plague a far more powerful and affluent nation." King was able to conceal his depression during his public appearances; he beamed as widely as ever when the Peace Prize was presented to him by Nobel officials and Norwegian royalty in a lavish ceremony at Oslo University on December 10. King told the audience that he accepted the prize on behalf of an entire movement, which he represented merely as a trustee. His brief acceptance speech

was optimistic as he professed "an abiding faith in America and an audacious faith in the future of mankind." That night the guest of honor
was toasted at a grand formal dinner, and the following day he delivered
the second of the two official addresses expected of him, the lengthier
Nobel lecture which King and his aides had worked on for nearly a
month.

King used the occasion to link the domestic nonviolence of the American civil rights movement with the entire globe's pressing need for disarmament and world peace. Many times in past years he had identified war
and international violence as evils that must be combated just like racial
segregation, but King used the Nobel platform to issue his strongest call
for the extension of nonviolent resistance to issues beyond racial injustice. The most notable aspect of the American movement, he stressed,
was the "direct participation of masses in protest, rather than reliance on
indirect methods which frequently do not involve masses in action at all."
He seemed to suggest that mass action be used to let all world leaders
know that people across the globe were committed to ending war.
Beyond racial justice, and beyond economic justice, the attainment of a
lasting world peace was the great goal that lay before them, King emphasized. Pursuing it would be personally taxing, but they could not retreat
from such a moral necessity. "Those who pioneer in the struggle for
peace and freedom will still face uncomfortable jail terms, painful threats
of death; they will still be battered by the storms of persecution, leading
them to nagging feelings that they can no longer bear such a heavy burden," King remarked in a personally revealing statement. There would
always be "the temptation of wanting to retreat to a more quiet and serene life," but one could not surrender to it. One must go forward bearing the weight of one's burden, whether one wanted to or not.[9]

The pleasures of Oslo were interrupted by word from the United States
that the nineteen Mississippi whites taken into custody for the three June
killings had been released on a procedural technicality. Although the situation was remedied quickly, King spoke out strongly, warning that "a
complete boycott of Mississippi products" would be necessary if justice
was not enforced. This depressing news reminded King of the upcoming
plans for Selma, and the portrait of the city Vivian had painted after his
trip there. "It was on his mind," Coretta recalled, since he alluded to it
several times in contrasting their present circumstances with what lay
ahead. "He made a comment about the fact that things were going to be
very difficult in Selma and that . . . those of us who were on this trip
should enjoy ourselves, because somebody was going to get killed in
Selma; he didn't expect us to get out of Selma without bloodshed."
Thinking ahead also sparked his deep-seated worries about the FBI, a
more painful threat than anything that might await him in Selma. Privately, those worries pervaded his thinking throughout the trip. As Coretta later confessed:

Only Martin's family and close staff members knew how depressed he was during the entire Nobel trip. It was a time when he ought to have been happy. . . . But he was worried that the rumors might hurt the movement and he was concerned about what black people would think. He always worried about that. . . . This was on his mind while we were in Europe and we had to work with him and help him out of his depression. Somehow he managed all the official functions, the speeches, the whole trip and the public never knew what he was going through.

King's depression was not the only problem for his friends and family. Ralph Abernathy and his wife, Juanita, caused a major scene by insisting that Abernathy deserved the same official perquisites as King. Even in Montgomery some of King's closest companions had been troubled by how Ralph was "very jealous of Martin, very jealous." Among SCLC's staff, many had grown to dislike Abernathy's self-importance and superior attitude toward others, especially women. Although Wyatt Walker had viewed Abernathy's role as "tangential," and while King's northern advisors joked about Abernathy's propensity to fall asleep during meetings, the Alabama field staff had resented his opposition to SCLC activity in the rural counties where his relatives lived. "I do not want anyone bothering with my family," he instructed, recommending that the staff stick to urban areas. "If you are not able to locate any of these cities I will be very pleased to send you a list of them." Similarly, Septima Clark had tired of Abernathy's constant complaints that he deserved treatment and respect identical to King's. "He was just a spoiled little boy," who "never . . . had a chance to grow up and be a real man." Many aides were puzzled by King's infinite tolerance for Abernathy's faults, especially since few could see any tangible contributions Abernathy made to SCLC despite his long association with King. To others, however, Abernathy's presence at King's side, going all the way back to the tense early days of the Montgomery boycott, was *the* crucial resource that allowed King to endure the emotional burdens of his role. "Abernathy was the glue for Martin King's soul," one put it. "Every Christian has to have a pastor," and Abernathy was King's—"he gave him counsel, he gave him solace, he gave him perspective." Some thought Abernathy's failings stemmed less from his desire to share King's limelight than from Juanita's hunger to be first lady of the movement, an interpretation that gained support the day after the Abernathys' public rebuff by Nobel officials. Mrs. Abernathy then became ill, and spent two days in a hospital recovering. Coretta stayed with her as the rest of the party went on from Oslo to Stockholm, where the two women rejoined them.

Some members of the group took advantage of all the possible pleasures that the trip and their lush lodgings offered. One late evening, Dora McDonald, upset by the goings-on, awakened Bayard Rustin with a phone call to ask that he, as the group's coordinator, put a stop to some of the wilder activities. Rustin, already aware of what he later termed "absolutely unbelievable behavior in that hotel," opened his door and "two guys come running down the hall chasing a woman and they're stark naked." One was A. D. King, pursuing a new female acquaintance who was attempting to steal his money and watch. Security men, alerted by Rustin, halted the group in the lobby and prepared to take several scantily clad women into custody for attempted robbery. Quickly assessing the situation, Rustin firmly recommended to the officers that the women not be arrested, for such charges would embarrass the government by indicating it had not afforded King's party adequate "protection" from local criminals. The officers complied, and started to give Rustin the women's loot so that it could be returned to its owners. Rustin had a different idea. "I said, 'No, I don't want these girls talking, let them have it. As far as I'm concerned, they've earned it. And get them out.'" The unhappy victims went back to their rooms, grousing at Rustin's costly settlement of the possible scandal.

King's two-day visit to Stockholm was sponsored by the Swedish Peace Council, and his schedule featured a sermon at the city's cathedral and an address to a nighttime gathering celebrating the independence of Kenya. King renewed his condemnation of South African racism, and afterward was in a happy enough mood to dance a waltz with Coretta; this was the first time they had taken to a dance floor since their days in Boston. Then they enjoyed a late-night visit to the home of famous Swedish social scientists Gunnar and Alva Myrdal. They planned to go on from Stockholm to Copenhagen, but King was not up to it. Instead, they went directly to Paris, their last stop before returning to a welcome-home celebration in New York.[10]

King received a hero's welcome in New York. The mayor and city council presented him with a special award. He told the crowd, "I am returning with a deeper conviction that nonviolence is the answer to the crucial political and moral questions of our time." His realization of America's need for "economic justice" had been reinforced by his visit to Scandinavia, where the countries "have no unemployment and no slums" and better educational and medical systems than in the United States. "There is a deep but unnecessary economic malady in our country which must be healed here and now." He called for "a broad alliance"—what in Oslo he had termed "a grand alliance"—"of all forces, Negro and white, dedicated to the achievement of economic justice." King's remarks indicated that the combination of the Nobel award and the FBI's private threats had left him with a deeper commitment to a life of personal sacrifice, and a clearer realization that some individuals are chosen for special roles they did not want but nonetheless had to fulfill. "They will hold the torch firmly for others," King told his New York audience, "because they have overcome the threat of jail and death. They will hold this torch high without faltering because they have weathered the battering storms of persecution and withstood the temptation to retreat to a more quiet and serene life."

After the City Hall ceremony, King met with reporters to announce that all of his Nobel Prize money would be given to the movement—$12,000 to SCLC, $17,000 to the other organizations making up CUCRL, and the remaining $25,000 to a special fund established several months earlier and closely linked to SCLC. He repeated his warning that there might be a nationwide economic boycott of Mississippi, and also mused about his desire to make a tour of Africa "in the near future." Then, after an early-evening cocktail party at the Waldorf-Astoria, which Vice-President-Elect Humphrey attended, King headed uptown to the Harlem Armory to address an enthusiastic crowd of eight thousand. The Nobel trip, he said, had been a mountaintop experience, but now the time had come to return to the valley. Alluding to SCLC's Selma plans, and to an Atlanta, strike by black employees of the Scripto Company just a few blocks from his home that had begun several weeks earlier, King said that serious challenges lay just ahead of him.

First, however, there was one more honor. Although the FBI, thanks to its wiretap on the outspoken Rustin, was furnishing the White House secondhand details of the most lively incidents that had occurred on the Nobel trip, Lyndon Johnson arranged to give King, his parents, and Coretta a brief personal welcome home. Flown from New York to Washington on Governor Nelson Rockefeller's private jet, the Kings were whisked to the White House for a formal greeting that was followed by a brief one-on-one conversation between the two principals. The president spoke of how beneficial his "war on poverty" effort would be for American blacks, and how they would have to play a leadership role in the program. King reminded Johnson that there were still serious civil rights problems in the South, and that the need for federal legislation to ensure blacks' voting rights was great. "Martin, you're right about that. I'm going to do it eventually, but I can't get a voting rights bill through in this session of Congress," King later recalled Johnson telling him. It was less than six months since the Civil Rights Act had become law, the president pointed out, and he would need southern congressmen's votes for other "Great Society" initiatives. He would lose these votes if he pressed for a voting rights measure. The time would come, Johnson said, but not in 1965.[11]

Afterward, reporters asked King whether the FBI dispute had come up during his chat with the president. No, King answered, it had not; that was a "dead issue" and "a matter of the past." Arriving in Atlanta, King found another welcoming party, this one composed of young people from Ebenezer Baptist Church who greeted him with Christmas carols. Local newsmen besieged him with questions about the Nobel journey and his upcoming plans as church members escorted him to a final ceremony at Ebenezer. The strike by black workers, many of whom attended Ebenezer, against Scripto's racially discriminatory wages was a serious civil rights issue that SCLC would support by backing a boycott of the company's products, King said. Voting rights in Alabama would be the main upcoming focus, but "more and more the civil rights movement must identify itself more closely with the forces of labor," and the Scripto conflict offered a perfect opportunity for joinder. Then, after a joyous ceremony in the same church into which he had been born almost thirty-six years earlier, the world's youngest Nobel Peace Prize winner went home to the rented frame house on Johnson Avenue.

The Christmas season was a time of rest for King, who was physically exhausted from nonstop travels and emotionally drained by the schizophrenic roller-coaster of worldwide honors and frightful worry about the FBI. He struggled to shift his attention from the public praise and private warnings to the Scripto strike and the upcoming campaign in Selma. His family and closest aides knew he was deeply disturbed, and one night King's mother, concerned about her son's mood and unannounced departure from the house, called his old childhood friend, Howard Baugh, by then Atlanta's highest-ranking black police officer. "'He was very depressed,'" Mama King told Baugh, who realized how unusual this was. "That frightened me to death because he'd never done that before," Baugh explained. He described how he set out to look for King on the streets of Atlanta. It was nearly midnight, the Scripto strike was still on, so Baugh went by the plant. There, standing silently by himself on the sidewalk, waiting for the midnight shift change, so that he could speak to the workers, was Martin Luther King, Jr. "He was disturbed about Scripto," Baugh remembered, recalling how King's support of the strikers troubled Atlanta's older power brokers of both races who had made it clear that King had better stage no protests in their city. King seemed fine, so Baugh left him to his late-night work before reassuring Mama King that her son was all right.[12]

Aside from the Scripto strike, which ended in a successful settlement shortly before Christmas, the major issue on SCLC's agenda was Selma. White staffer Harry Boyte spent a week reconnoitering the city in the wake of Vivian's encouraging visit, and had a detailed analysis ready by the time King returned home. Selma had just elected a new, young, and relatively moderate mayor, Joseph T. Smitherman, who had turned city law enforcement over to a well-experienced professional, Wilson Baker. As Selma's public safety director, Baker would have to work in concert with the volatile Sheriff Clark, an accord that many local observers expected would be difficult to maintain. Smitherman, Baker, and another mayoral advisor, local newspaperman Arthur Capell, had met after the election with SNCC worker John Love and Selma's top three black leaders, Rev. C. C. Brown, Ed Moss, and Rev. F. D. Reese, and had offered to get together on an ongoing basis. Another meeting had not yet taken place, but Reverend Reese, one of the key people who had met with Vivian, explicitly warned Public Safety Director Baker that SCLC would be coming to town. City and county officials were well aware of what lay ahead, and a number of influential whites—Capell, bank executives Rex Morthland, Frank Wilson, and Roger Jones, and school board President

Edgar Stewart—met privately to help support Baker and Smitherman's course of moderation. Boyte recommended some initial approaches to these white leaders to establish communication in advance of demonstrations.

In Selma's black community, Boyte reported, Rev. Reese, though a young man, was emerging as the central leader. Brown and Moss, men of an older generation, had long struggled between themselves for a preeminent role, and younger activists suspected both of being too moderate. Many blacks identified Mrs. Boynton closely with SNCC, but SCLC's greatest immediate need, Boyte said, was to reassure all the local black leaders, particularly Reese, that a firm organizational commitment had been made to Selma. Despite his own and Vivian's promises, Boyte said, local leaders "do not seem to understand that a commitment has been made by SCLC to stay in Selma and see a program through; they are worried that we will come into town and leave too soon. It seems urgent that assurances must be made to these men."

Although Vivian and Boyte had been SCLC's pathfinders in Selma, the overall Alabama Project was under the direction of Jim Bevel, based in Montgomery. While King was in Europe, Bevel convened a meeting of activists from several organizations, including SNCC's John Love and David Dennis and Ike Reynolds of CORE, to brief them on the Alabama effort. As Dennis characterized Bevel's presentation, "It was proposed that all projects be done under SCLC and that all efforts be done through a central office in Montgomery which will be an SCLC office." That suggestion received negative responses. Love argued that such an approach would do little to stimulate local black communities to organize and make their own decisions, as SNCC's projects sought to. CORE's Dennis agreed, telling his superiors that he "did not feel that there was any real effort on the part of those who planned the program to really involve indigenous leadership." Bevel's initial foray seemed to have done more harm than good, Boyte reported to Atlanta, and recommended that "a meeting for purposes of clarifying some misunderstandings or disagreements," especially between Love and Bevel, be held "as soon as possible."[13]

King acted on Boyte's recommendation immediately after Christmas, calling a meeting of all Alabama Project participants for December 28 in Montgomery. Some representatives from other organizations, such as SNCC's Robert Moses and Ivanhoe Donaldson from Mississippi, argued that the focus should be on MFDP's challenge to the seating of Mississippi's representatives by the U.S. Congress. They also spoke out against SCLC's Alabama plans, but almost all of the one hundred local activists and SCLC staffers voiced support for Bevel's idea. King announced that the formal kickoff would take place at the January 2 mass meeting in Selma. Bevel and Eric Kindberg distributed copies of the blueprint, entitled "Project for Alabama—Political Freedom Movement," and explained how they expected the campaign to develop. Disfranchisement was "the cause of most of the problems that face Negroes," the document stated, and the Alabama Project would organize people from all across the state to protest that denial. Selma's injunction and racial climate meant that arrests might begin at that first rally, and mass efforts to stimulate black citizens' interest in winning the ballot would continue. A statewide steering committee of local representatives would petition Governor Wallace to remove the discriminatory barriers to blacks' participation, and if no satisfactory response was forthcoming, a "freedom registration" and "freedom election," just like Mississippi activists had had fifteen months earlier, would be undertaken to protest the exclusion. This effort would produce representatives who would contest the validity of Alabama's all-white state legislature when the 1965 session opened on May 4, much as MFDP's delegates had attempted to challenge Mississippi's convention delegation. As the project built to this climax, direct-action tactics, particularly in Selma, and a purposeful arrest of Dr. King, would fuel popular interest. "Arrests should continue over months to create interest in the Freedom Registration and Freedom Vote," the outline specified. "After Dr. King is in jail, a letter dealing with bombings, violence, not being represented, etc. should be widely distributed." Then, on May 4, "with the opening of the Alabama legislature, the seating of present legislators and senators will be challenged and action will shift from Selma and other similar towns and counties to Montgomery." The December 28 session approved that game plan and the initial emphasis upon Selma. Although SCLC's leaders were aware that the discussions had not resolved the tensions with SNCC, their attention turned to the Saturday kick-off rally in Selma.[14]

While Bevel, Vivian, and Blackwell concentrated on those plans, King continued to be dogged by worries and depression. Although he kept up his public schedule and was able to hide his turmoil from audiences, his closest acquaintances became increasingly worried about him as his depression failed to abate. The FBI listened in as Coretta, Dora McDonald, and Andy Young discussed Martin's problems and what could be done to relieve them. Young knew that King was deeply distressed by the rumors about his private life, so on December 31, he called the Bureau's ubiquitous Deke DeLoach. SCLC, Young said, wanted to be sure the FBI knew of King's plans to be in Selma for the January 2 rally; additionally, Young thought that he and DeLoach ought to get together for a discussion in the near future.

In Selma on New Year's Day, Jim Bevel met with the steering committee of the Dallas County Voters League to finalize preparations for the town's first public civil rights event in six months. Public Safety Director Baker, no one's fool, announced that he had no intention of enforcing Judge Hare's injunction by arresting everyone who showed up for the rally. King's appearance drew a crowd of seven hundred people to Brown Chapel AME Church. King told the audience—including state and local lawmen and numerous reporters—that SCLC had chosen Selma because the city "has become a symbol of bitter-end resistance to the civil rights movement in the Deep South." If Selma rebuffed SCLC's registration drive, "we will appeal to Governor Wallace. If he refuses to listen, we will appeal to the legislature. If they don't listen, we will appeal to the conscience of the Congress in another dramatic march on Washington." After the rally, King caucused at Mrs. Boynton's home with SCLC's and SNCC's Selma staff members. He encouraged them to work together co-operatively in urging local blacks to attempt to register on the few days per month that Alabama statutes required county registration boards to accept applicants. SCLC's first objective, Andrew Young said, would be to get prospective registrants to assemble at the Dallas County courthouse in downtown Selma on those days. "We want to establish in the mind of the nation that a lot of people who want to register are prevented from doing so. We hope this will lead to a revision of the voter registration laws in this state."[15]

While King returned home, the Selma workers got down to business. The day after King's visit, Bevel and SCLC's staff met with the three SNCC staffers and E. L. Doyle, representing the local citizens. Also sitting in was Rev. Ralph E. Smeltzer, a white representative of the Church of the Brethren who had been working behind the scenes in Selma for more than a year to improve race relations. Bevel explained that the two staffs would work together on voter registration, operating under the direction of a "Committee of Fifteen," local black citizens who would make the basic decisions. The first step would be to recruit supporters in all of the city's wards and begin a door-to-door canvass of all black residents in preparation for the first registration day, January 18. Although Bevel warned that SCLC might keep all of its Alabama field staffers in Selma for only a month before shifting some of them elsewhere, there would be a continuing commitment to the city for the duration of the Alabama Project, he promised. Initial meetings were held in each of Selma's wards within several days, and scores of black citizens turned out to support the movement.

The two staff sessions on January 2 and 3 went a long way toward minimizing the interorganizational conflict that SCLC and the local activists feared might harm the Selma movement. The SNCC workers welcomed SCLC's appearance on the scene, and Jim Bevel seemed ready to run a campaign in which all participants would have input. If SNCC's distaste for SCLC's media-oriented protests and King's supposed indecisiveness could be neutralized, and if the enthusiasm of Selma's black leadership could be translated into community support for mass action, SCLC might have just the staging ground for the Alabama Project it had hoped for.[16]

Despite the bright prospects in Selma, Martin King was depressed. He told Ralph Abernathy during their January 2 trip to Selma that he should be prepared to take over as president of SCLC, since he, King, might meet his own end before the campaign concluded. Then, two days after

he returned home, Coretta found and opened a thin box containing a reel
of tape that had been received at SCLC headquarters a month earlier.
Staff members had assumed it was a recording of one of King's speeches
and put it aside for Coretta, who collected them, but upon playing it, she
realized that this was not a speech. On some of the tape was her husband's voice, but his remarks certainly had not been delivered to any
public audience. Furthermore, the box also contained an anonymous
threatening letter:

KING,
   In view of your low grade . . . I will not dignify your name with
either a Mr. or a Reverend or a Dr. And, your last name calls to mind
only the type of King such as King Henry the VIII. . . .
   King, look into your heart. You know you are a complete fraud and
a great liability to all of us Negroes. White people in this country have
enough frauds of their own but I am sure they don't have one at this
time that is anywhere near your equal. You are no clergyman and you
know it. I repeat you are a colossal fraud and an evil, vicious one at
that. You could not believe in God. . . . Clearly you don't believe in
any personal moral principles.
   King, like all frauds your end is approaching. You could have been
our greatest leader. You, even at an early age have turned out to be
not a leader but a dissolute, abnormal moral imbecile. We will now
have to depend on our older leaders like Wilkins [,] a man of character [,] and thank God we have others like him. But you are done.
Your "honorary" degrees, your Nobel Prize (what a grim farce) and
other awards will not save you. King, I repeat you are done.
   No person can overcome facts, not even a fraud like yourself. . . . I
repeat—no person can argue successfully against facts. You are finished. . . . Satan could not do more. What incredible evilness. . . .
King you are done.
   The American public, the church organizations that have been helping—Protestant, Catholic and Jews will know you for what you are—
an evil, abnormal beast. So will others who have backed you. You are
done.
   King, there is only one thing left for you to do. You know what this
is. You have just 34 days in which to do (this exact number has been
selected for a specific reason, it has definite practical significant [sic]).
You are done. There is but one way out for you. You better take it
before your filthy, abnormal fraudulent self is bared to the nation.

Surprised and shocked, Coretta called her husband, and King summoned
several confidants—Abernathy, Young, Joseph Lowery, and Chicago
lawyer Chauncey Eskridge—to listen to the tape and examine the
frightening letter.
   King and his aides had little doubt about the origin of the package: J.
Edgar Hoover's FBI. The material on the tape—dirty jokes and bawdy
remarks King had made a year earlier at Washington's Willard Hotel,

plus the sounds of people engaging in sex—had obviously been acquired by bugging King's hotel rooms. Their surmise was correct: The embarrassing recording, and the threatening letter that seemed to suggest King commit suicide, had been prepared at the behest of Assistant FBI Director William C. Sullivan just two days after Hoover's public attack on King in mid-November. Sullivan had instructed the Bureau's laboratory to prepare a tape containing the "highlights" of the many recordings of King that the Bureau had garnered over the preceding ten months. Then Sullivan composed the threatening letter, and directed one of his agents to fly to Miami with it. On November 21—thirty-four days before Christmas—the agent arrived in Miami, phoned Sullivan for further instructions, and was ordered to mail the package to King at SCLC headquarters.[17]

The FBI's frightening threat sent King into an even worse state of mind. He became so nervous and upset that he could not sleep, and was certain that the Bureau would do anything to ruin him. "They are out to break me," he told one close friend over a wiretapped phone line. "They are out to get me, harass me, break my spirit." The most intimate details of his personal life, King said, ought to be no business of the FBI's. "What I do is only between me and my God." Neither his relatives nor his aides pressed him about the contents of the tape, but their reserve could not relieve the severe emotional tension King was experiencing. Coretta later laughed off questions about the tape, saying, "I couldn't make much out of it, it was just a lot of mumbo jumbo," but on one occasion she revealed more clearly why she had not confronted her husband with angry questions about the tape:

> During our whole marriage we never had one single serious discussion about either of us being involved with another person. . . . If I ever had any suspicions . . . I never would have even mentioned them to Martin. I just wouldn't have burdened him with anything so trivial . . . all that other business just didn't have a place in the very high-level relationship we enjoyed.

Unfortunately, Martin King, as a small number of close friends knew, had certain compelling needs that could not be satisfied within a "very high-level relationship." Serious marital differences already existed over King's insistence on giving away the Nobel money, his demand that the family live in the most modest circumstances possible, and his belief that Coretta's primary role was to stay home and raise the children. Outweighing them all, however, was the fact that there were some things Martin King badly needed that he could not find at home. Now that King faced the threat of having his personal life exposed in excruciating detail to the entire nation, the inner pressures were worse than ever.

King already realized that his private life was no secret. Many movement activists were aware of his various sexual involvements with a number of different women, and James Farmer was not the only person who had cautioned King about the serious damage that the proliferating stories could do. CUCRL Director Wiley Branton raised the problem directly one day. "'I think you ought to know what it is some people have come to me with and have said, and I feel obligated to at least tell you what's being said.'" Movement colleagues "did not want to see King hurt in any way, and they were trying in some way to get him to come to grips with whatever those problems were." Branton did not ask King for any response, and King had little to say. Another friend broached the subject of his compulsive sexual athleticism with him after being prompted by a worried mutual acquaintance. "'I'm away from home twenty-five to twenty-seven days a month,'" King answered. "'Fucking's a form of anxiety reduction.'"

Three particular relationships had flowered to the status of something more than occasional one-night stands, and for almost the past two years King had grown closer and closer to one of those women, whom he saw almost daily. That relationship, rather than his marriage, increasingly became the emotional centerpiece of King's life, but it did not eliminate the incidental couplings that were a commonplace of King's travels. Some longtime friends viewed it as "a natural, human concomitant" of the tense, fast-paced life King had led for almost a decade. Others thought of it as standard ministerial practice in a context where intimate pastor-parishioner relationships long had been winked at, and where King and theology school classmates joshed openly about their success in "counseling" attractive women. Some activists considered King's pattern typical of the overall movement—"this was not at all a sour-faced, pietistic" endeavor, Michael Harrington remembered. "Everybody was out getting laid." King's opportunities, however, were virtually limitless, as one staffer learned at a suburban New York fund-raising party. "I watched women making passes at Martin Luther King. I *could not believe* what I was seeing in white Westchester women. . . . It was unbelievable. . . . They would walk up to him and they would sort of lick their lips and hint, and [hand him] notes. . . . After I saw that thing that evening, I didn't blame him."

King's closest friends accepted and indeed respected his attitude toward women. "He loved beautiful women," one longtime family intimate remembered. "The girls he 'dated' were just like models . . . the girls were tall stallions, all usually were very fair, never dark. He was really a Casanova . . . but [with] a quiet dignity. He would give the girls respect." At home and at the office, however, King operated on very traditional assumptions. Coretta openly complained about her husband's insistence that she take care of the home and family and not become involved in movement activities. "I wish I was more a part of it," she told one interviewer. "Martin didn't want her to get too active," Andrew Young recalled. Bernard Lee put it more bluntly. "Martin . . . was absolutely a male chauvinist. He believed that the wife should stay home and

take care of the babies while he'd be out there in the streets." Dorothy
Cotton saw it regularly. "He would have had a lot to learn and a lot of
growing to do" concerning women's rights. "I'm always asked to take the
notes, I'm always asked to go fix Dr. King some coffee. I did it, too," but
she fully realized "the male chauvinism that existed within the movement." "They were sexist male preachers" and "grew up in a sexist
culture. . . . I really loved Dr. King but I know that that streak was in
him also."

King's sexual behavior stood at great distance from his professed beliefs about sexuality, and the contradictions created painful and at times
overwhelming guilt. "What God creates is good and . . . must be used
properly and not abused," King told one interviewer:

> Sex is basically sacred when it is properly used and . . . marriage is
> man's greatest prerogative in the sense that it is through and in mar-
> riage that God gives man the opportunity to aid him in his creative
> activity. Therefore, sex must never be abused in the loose sense that it
> is often abused in the modern world.

King's pronouncements on sexuality could be harsh: "Modern man has
strayed to the far countries of secularism, materialism, sexuality and racial injustice." He spoke of "the psychological problems that bring the
looseness into being," and decried "the causal basis of sexual promiscuity, the deep anxieties and frustration and confusion of modern life
which lead to the abuses." Sex might indeed be anxiety-reducing, but
King considered himself a sinner for being unable to ward off those
needs. "Each of us is two selves," he told his Ebenezer congregation:

> And the great burden of life is to always try to keep that higher self in
> command. Don't let the lower self take over. . . . Every now and then
> you'll be unfaithful to those that you should be faithful to. It's a mix-
> ture in human nature. . . . Because we are two selves, there is a civil
> war going on within all of us. . . ."

Two days after discovering the FBI's threatening letter and embarrassing
tape, King preached at Atlanta University. He spoke about "disarming
the whole world," and how war, along with racism and poverty, was one
of the three basic evils that man must eliminate. But, King warned,
"When you stand up against entrenched evil, you must be prepared to
suffer a little more. I cannot promise you that if you stand up against the
evils of our day, you will not have some dark and agonizing moments,"
moments that King knew all too well.

By Friday, January 8, King and his closest aides had decided that
something must be done about the FBI's threat. He had tried resting at a
private hideaway known to just two other people, only to have Atlanta

fire trucks turn up at the door in response to a false alarm that King correctly surmised had been turned in by the FBI so as to upset him further. Andrew Young phoned Deke DeLoach to ask for a Monday appointment for himself and Ralph Abernathy. Then, Young and Bernard Lee accompanied King on a flight to New York, where the three men holed up at the Park Sheraton to discuss how that Monday conversation should be handled. Though they anticipated greater privacy in New York, FBI agents watched them arrive at Kennedy airport. "King and [his] party [were] extremely security conscious" as they made their way to the hotel, the agents observed, where the Bureau had installed listening devices in the rooms reserved for King. As a deeply depressed King and his two assistants discussed the FBI situation, the Bureau garnered a verbatim record of their remarks. The conversation revealed how greatly disturbed King was, and the bugs, in the words of one summary, "recorded King characterizing the mailing of the tape as, 'God's out to get you,' and as a warning from God that King had not been living up to his responsibilities in relation to the role in which history had cast him." Once again, however, King summoned up the strength to carry out his public duties, giving two Sunday addresses in Boston and a Monday speech in Baltimore. He told one Boston audience that he would return in April because "there is a need for a strong and vigorous movement against 'slumlordism.'"[18]

While King was in Baltimore, Young and Abernathy met in Washington with DeLoach to ask that the FBI halt its leaks. Young explained that he had heard many rumors about the FBI's interest in Communists around King, in SCLC's finances, and in King's personal life. DeLoach responded that the Bureau could not offer any comments about Communists, but did deny that the FBI had any interest in SCLC's finances or King's private life. Young and Abernathy knew that DeLoach's assertions were false, and Young was extremely disappointed that the meeting had not produced a frank exchange about what everyone knew was going on. Its only value, Young explained later, was to show him how FBI executives like DeLoach had "almost a kind of fascist mentality. It really kind of scared me. . . . There really wasn't any honest conversation." While Young and Abernathy reported their frustration to King, DeLoach gloated to his superiors that he had tried to make the talk as unpleasant and embarrassing as possible for King's two aides. Meanwhile, the Bureau kept its campaign on full throttle. Assistant Director Sullivan tried to derail a dinner honoring King that white Atlanta community leaders were organizing, and two prominent Georgia newsmen—Eugene Patterson and Ralph McGill—were contacted to offer them tidbits on King's personal life. Derogatory memos continued to circulate to officials throughout the federal executive branch. One FBI letter to Attorney General Katzenbach reported that King "has recently become emotionally upset and once became extremely violent." Although the Bureau made no mention how its anonymous package had contributed heavily to that state of affairs, it did tell Katzenbach that "King fears public exposure."[19]

King returned to Selma on January 14. Bevel reported that efforts to activate city youths and rural residents were going well, and that daily meetings of the SCLC and SNCC staffs had "cut down on the friction between the organizations." King told the audience at that evening's rally that mass action would get under way in four days, with potential registrants gathering at the courthouse and other movement supporters "testing" the desegregation of Selma's restaurants and other businesses. He also said Selma would be the base for voter registration efforts in ten rural counties.

While the movement was preparing for its first direct action, Selma's white leadership was working to assure a calm and unified response to the protests. Art Capell of the *Selma Times-Journal* ran two prominent editorials praising Public Safety Director Wilson Baker's handling of the January 2 rally. A number of leading bankers were encouraging Sheriff Clark and Judge Hare to support Baker's tactical stance. City attorney W. McLean Pitts worked out a written agreement, signed by Clark, Baker, and Mayor Smitherman, giving Baker full authority for all Selma law enforcement except "in and around the courthouse," where Clark's county deputies would be in charge. Reverend Smeltzer continued his behind-the-scenes contacts, and at the urging of the Justice Department's Burke Marshall, Baker had welcomed two other white mediators, Andrew M. Secrest and J. Kenneth Morland, from the new federal Community Relations Service (CRS). Created by a provision of the Civil Rights Act that had been of special interest to Lyndon Johnson, and headed by moderate former Florida Governor LeRoy Collins, the CRS had a mandate to conciliate community racial tensions wherever an outbreak seemed possible. Selma represented one of its first focal points, and former newspaperman Secrest immediately perceived the subtle conflict between his agency's mission and the movement's goals when he and college professor Morland arrived in town on Sunday, January 17. "If the CRS seeks to help Selma make steady progress in complying with the Civil Rights Act and to avoid lawsuits, violence and arrests, this may run counter to Dr. King's objective of creating a kind of confrontation which will lead him to Montgomery and Governor Wallace." As SCLC moved forward with its plans, the two mediators contacted leaders of both races.

Monday morning, King and SNCC Chairman John Lewis led four hundred black citizens from Brown Chapel to the county courthouse. Clark blocked their entry to the courthouse and instructed the applicants to wait in an alley for the county registrars to call them one at a time to take Alabama's difficult voter registration literacy test. Also waiting outside the courthouse were American Nazi party leader George Lincoln Rockwell and several followers, plus fellow racist J. B. Stoner, whom SCLC knew from St. Augustine. Rockwell and another man engaged King in conversation, and King offered to let them speak at that evening's mass meeting. Then, after an outdoor wait of several hours during which not one applicant was registered, King and his aides went to Selma's Albert Hotel to register as its first black guests. Although the "tests" of seven other establishments had been successful and peaceful, King was attacked without warning as he stood with Dorothy Cotton at the hotel desk. James Robinson, a young Nazi from out of town, landed two firm punches to King's right temple before John Lewis pulled him away and Public Safety Director Baker placed Robinson under arrest. King was stunned but not injured, and spoke at that night's rally from which Baker wisely barred the other invited fascists.[20]

After the rally King and the SCLC staff caucused to evaluate the day's events. As one participant later explained, they were surprised and disappointed that Sheriff Clark's demeanor had been so mild. Aside from the assault at the Albert Hotel, there had been no picturesque incidents of racial hatred for the sizable corps of newsmen to bring to the nation's attention. If Baker and Smitherman were successful in keeping Clark from behaving as he had in the past, SCLC ought to turn its attention to some other Black Belt town, such as Marion or Camden, in search of the police conduct toward blacks that pervaded the region. They would march to the Selma courthouse the following day, but if Clark adopted the style of Laurie Pritchett rather than that of Bull Connor, SCLC would shift its efforts to other locales.

While SCLC mapped its strategy, white officials hoped that their first day's luck would hold. Baker had a new informant—a young white SCLC staffer who would face immediate charges of sexual misconduct with underage black youngsters if he did not cooperate—from whom he learned of SCLC's discussions, but Baker and Smitherman knew that Sheriff Clark was chafing at the tactics of restraint.

Tuesday morning the marchers refused to move into the alley where Clark had directed them the previous day. Angered, Clark ordered them off the courthouse sidewalk. When the column was slow to move, Clark lost his cool. Seizing Mrs. Amelia Boynton, he "grabbed her by the back of her collar and pushed her roughly for half a block into a patrol car," as one national newspaper described the scene in a front-page story. Watching from across the street, King told reporters that the incident was "one of the most brutal and unlawful acts I have seen an officer commit." More than sixty marchers were arrested, and that night, after a mass rally at which Ralph Abernathy pronounced the sheriff an honorary SCLC member for his day's work, the staff celebrated their success in getting Clark to show his true colors. Unhappy city officials groused that Clark was "out of control," and movement workers planned another march to the courthouse for the next morning while King left to give two speeches in Pennsylvania.

Three successive waves of black marchers made their way to the courthouse on Wednesday. The sheriff told the first group to wait outside one specific door, but John Lewis said they preferred another one, the one that black people regarded as the *front* door. Clark placed them under arrest, and did the same with a second group that was equally insistent. When the third wave reached the courthouse, Wilson Baker told them they could use the front entrance as long as they did not obstruct the sidewalk. Clark objected, and for several moments he and Baker glared at each other as assistants shuttled back and forth. Finally, Clark told the marchers they had one minute to move, and then took them into custody. By the end of Wednesday—the final day that the registrars would be at the courthouse—a total of some 226 demonstrators were in jail.[21]

Selma's white leadership was unhappy that Clark's hot-headedness had placed their city on the front pages of the nation's newspapers. That disappointment notwithstanding, CRS mediators Secrest and Morland found little receptivity from white officials. "Once Baker and Mayor Smitherman learned that CRS would not and could not persuade Dr. King to leave Selma," Secrest reported, "they lost interest in what CRS could do for them." Smitherman, who was "noticeably apprehensive and tense," "quite simply told us to go home." White business leaders were very poorly informed about the black community, and appeared interested only in keeping the peace, not in abetting any real changes. "We uncovered no white integrationists. . . . There is no real commitment to racial reform, and Selma, moderate or segregationist, will take no steps they are not forced to take." Wilson Baker had initially led them to believe that Selma was committed to change, but they had found out otherwise. Relative moderates such as school board President Stewart and attorney Sam Hobbs advised that they saw no chance of forming a biracial committee. Smitherman, who had met with local black leaders two months earlier, vowed that he would not see King or any "troublemaking" Selma people.

In the black community, Secrest and Morland found a different spirit. They listened as Reese, Boynton, Foster, and Doyle "emphasized that their first goal was to secure the right to vote, for until they could vote no real progress could be made. . . . Consequently they ha[ve] not planned any program beyond voting." Although King made clear that his "primary interest was to challenge the Alabama voter registration law and that Selma was a symbol and a tool for this purpose," the local activists looked at SCLC's presence in terms of how it could help rectify their own disfranchisement. "At present," Morland wrote, "the grievances of the Negroes are not so great that they could not be dealt with by reasonable whites. In fact I was surprised that the Negroes were as limited as they appear to be in their immediate goals."

For the local leaders, the campaign was a way to change Selma, but for King and SCLC, it was a way to challenge the entire structure of racial exclusion in Alabama politics and to force Lyndon Johnson's hand on a federal voting statute. Washington news reports indicated that Justice Department attorneys were drafting a constitutional amendment barring literacy tests, the primary tool for black disfranchisement in the South, but passage and ratification of such a proposal would be slow and uncertain. A bill that would provide for federal registrars was being considered as a stopgap measure until such an amendment took effect, but the administration seemed in no hurry and congressional observers predicted a rocky path for such an initiative. Nonetheless, SCLC was pleased with Clark's conduct on Tuesday and Wednesday, and it seemed possible Selma might become the voting rights symbol that the movement needed. "Jim Clark," one staffer said, "is another Bull Connor. We should put him on the staff."[22]

More marches to the courthouse were planned when registration resumed, but on Friday, January 22, an event occurred that was so unusual that Andrew Young exaggerated only moderately when he termed it "the most significant thing that has happened in the racial movement since Birmingham." Over one hundred black Selma teachers, led by Voters League President Reese, marched to the courthouse to protest the unfair voter registration system that had denied many of them the ballot. School officials tried unsuccessfully to persuade them to leave, and only after Sheriff Clark and his deputies began prodding them with billyclubs did the column turn around and return to Brown Chapel.

King came back to Selma for Friday night's mass meeting, and the next day U.S. District Judge Daniel H. Thomas, acting in response to a petition filed by movement lawyers, issued a temporary restraining order barring Selma and Dallas County officials from hindering voter registration applicants as they had that preceding week.

Thomas's order did not change the pattern when movement efforts resumed on Monday, January 25. Another column of applicants marched to the courthouse, and Sheriff Clark, again seeking to demonstrate his authority, pushed several participants. As King watched from across the street, one hefty woman, fifty-three-year-old Mrs. Annie Lee Cooper, gave the sheriff a powerful punch to the head. Three deputies pounced on her as photographers clicked away. "She put up quite a battle as the officers seized her and threw her to the ground," one newsman reported. "'I wish you would hit me, you scum,' she snapped at the sheriff. He then brought his billyclub down on her head with a whack that was heard throughout the crowd gathered in the street." Eventually she was subdued, but a wire-service photo showing Clark with his billyclub over her head ran in Tuesday's newspapers across the country.[23]

Tuesday morning, as another band of movement marchers made their way to the courthouse and were arrested, King returned to Atlanta to prepare for the Wednesday evening banquet that Atlanta notables had organized to honor their Nobel Peace Prize winner. He was still troubled by the FBI rumors, and became especially upset when his father spoke to him after being warned by Atlanta Police Chief Herbert T. Jenkins that Hoover, in a personal conversation with him, had expressed incredible antipathy for King. The Bureau had kept up its efforts—even listening in on a January 15 phone conversation with Lyndon Johnson in which King urged Whitney Young's appointment to a Cabinet post. Assistant Director Sullivan was disappointed that his contacts with newspaper editors Patterson and McGill and Atlanta Archbishop Paul Hallinan had not derailed King's banquet. All of the 1,500 tickets were sold in advance, and the evenly integrated crowd joined in a stanza of "We Shall Overcome" after King, perennially late, accepted their gift of a Steuben bowl and told them he still had "faith in America" and "the conscience of the great decent majority." Then King retreated to New York for a weekend of rest in a secluded hotel room, which the FBI once again had wired for sound.[24]

Jim Bevel and SCLC's Selma staff decided in late January that the time had come for King to submit to intentional arrest to give the movement a publicity boost. Monday, February 1, was chosen as the date, and King returned to Selma on Sunday for one more strategy session. The next morning several hundred volunteers gathered at Brown Chapel and were told that this time, the column would *not* split up into smaller groups to avoid running afoul of Selma's parade ordinance. Their arrests were necessary, King told them. Then the column set out. It moved only a few blocks before Wilson Baker brought it to a halt, informed King that they were violating the law, and arrested 260 marchers. King and his companions were herded to the jail, where the leaders refused to accept release on bail and were led away to a special cell. Newsmen pressed King to explain his choice. "I must confess this is a deliberate attempt to dramatize conditions in this city, state, and community," he acknowledged. Later in the day another seven hundred movement marchers were arrested by Sheriff Clark outside the courthouse, and in the town of Marion, fifty miles distant, SCLC staffers led six hundred Perry County residents in the first protest march held in one of the outlying communities.

Prepared for a jail stay of several days, King and Ralph Abernathy shared a cell with white SCLC field staffer Charles Fager. A trusty offered the group a bowl of turnip greens and a ham steak, but King shook his head, explaining that he and Abernathy always fasted their first two days in jail. The next morning King struck up a conversation with Fager about how difficult it would be to win true freedom. King's vision was more far-reaching than his public remarks would indicate. It was an unforgettable realization, Fager recalled years later. "I remember the words exactly, 'If we are going to achieve real equality, the United States will have to adopt a modified form of socialism.'"

Even from jail, King passed strategic instructions to Andrew Young, who was allowed several brief visits a day with King. Marches had continued Tuesday morning, with several hundred more arrests taking place, but King felt strongly that SCLC had to take other initiatives, as he instructed Young in a detailed note:

Do [the] following to keep national attention focused on Selma:

1. Make a call to Governor Collins [of the Community Relations Service] and urge him to make a personal visit to Selma to talk with city and county authorities concerning speedier registration and more days for registering.

2. Follow through on suggestion of having a congressional delegation to come in for personal investigation. They should also make an appearance at mass meeting if they come.

3. Make personal call to President Johnson urging him to intervene in some way (send a personal emissary to Selma; get Justice Department involved; make plea to Dallas [County] & Selma officials in press conference).

4. Urge lawyers to go to 5th circuit [court of appeals] if Judge Thomas does not issue an immediate injunction against continued arrest[s] and speeding up registration.

5. Keep some activity alive every day this week.

6. Consider a night march to the city jail protesting my arrest (an arrest which must be considered unjust). Have another night march to court house to let Clark show [his] true colors.

7. Stretch every point to get teachers to march.

8. Immediately post bond for staff members essential for mobilization who are arrested.

9. Seek to get big name celebrities to come in for moral support.

10. Get Wyatt [Walker] to contact Gov. Rockefeller and other Republican big names to come out with strong statements about the arrests, the right to vote and Selma.

11. Call C. T. [Vivian] and have him return from Cal. in case other staff is put out of circulation.

12. Local Selma editor [Roswell K. Falkenberry of the *Times Journal*, earlier that morning] sent [a] telegram to [the] President calling for [a] congressional committee to come and study true situation of Selma. We should join in calling for this. By all means don't let them get the offensive. They are trying to give the impression that they are an orderly and good community because they integrated public accommodations. We must insist that voting is the issue and here Selma has dirty hands.

"Let me hear . . . on all of this tomorrow morning," King told Young.[25]

King's instructions altered the movement's plans. Earlier that morning Young had sounded a conciliatory note, suggesting that SCLC might shift its focus elsewhere. "If the Mayor and local officials would get together with the Dallas County Voters League and work out some program, maybe a public statement backing us on the voting issue, we might be able to stop demonstrations." Now, however, word went out that the pressure would be stepped up, and newsmen were told that SCLC expected to remain in Selma for "some time to come." Orders went out to other aides to follow through on King's instructions, and Walker pursued the Republican contacts while Walter Fauntroy organized a visit by sympathetic congressmen. Attorneys petitioned Judge Thomas for a further order to speed up registration, and Young spoke with Clarence Jones about recruiting celebrity visitors.

Wednesday morning the mass marches continued for a third straight day, and more than three hundred protesters were arrested. In Marion more than seven hundred were taken into custody. Word circulated in Washington that a delegation of congressmen would travel to Selma on Friday, and Young contacted presidential aide Lee White to urge the White House initiatives King had mentioned. As White recorded Young's points in a memo to Lyndon Johnson, SCLC wanted the president to

1. Send a personal emissary to Selma to evaluate the situation and report back to the President.

2. Make a specific statement supporting the right to register and vote in Dallas County and Selma, Alabama.

3. Through appropriate legislative and executive action secure the right to register and vote in all elections including those controlled by the individual states.

White advised Johnson that Young should be told the Justice Department was following the situation, that any press queries would draw a strong endorsement of the right to vote from the president, and that unspecified legislative proposals on the subject would be submitted to Congress as soon as the administration was ready. More immediately, White told Johnson, Attorney General Katzenbach believed that Federal Judge Daniel H. Thomas, with whom Katzenbach had secretly been in contact, could resolve the Selma conflict. Meanwhile, presidential press secretary George Reedy said that the White House would take no action on editor Falkenberry's request for a congressional investigating committee.

Young told King of these developments, of his expectation of a further order from Thomas, and suggested that the movement greet that initiative with a temporary halt in demonstrations. Once again, however, King had a detailed set of instructions for Young. First, Young or Hosea Williams ought to speak at that night's rally in Marion. Second, Young should call entertainer Sammy Davis, Jr., and request that he do an Atlanta benefit show for SCLC in March or April.

"These fellows respond better when I am in jail or [there is] a crisis. You should try to get him tonight." Third, King would be coming out of jail by the weekend and returning to Atlanta. Young should call Dora McDonald "and tell her to get word to my church secretary that I will preach Sunday morning" at Ebenezer. Additionally, King had planned SCLC's agenda for the following week. "Our program for Monday should be as follows: (1) Come to Selma in the morning and spend most of day encouraging registration (2) Set up meeting for Lyons [Lowndes] County," a tough rural area east of Selma, "at 6:00 P.M. (3) Set meeting for Montgomery at 8:00. This will give continuity to [the] Alabama drive and demonstrate that we aren't stopping with one community. Send at least three or four staff members into Lyons [Lowndes] by Saturday to set up meeting." That was not all. "Speak to lawyers about filing suit in Marion to speed up registration and get students and jailed persons released. We must let Marion know that we are concerned." Concerning Selma, King said, "Insist on seeing me before there is an official call-off of demonstrations. . . . Chief Baker will bend [and allow another visit] if you insist that a settlement cannot be reached without such consultation. Be sure to brief me on all aspects of the pending order from Judge Thomas." Then, once the order was issued and the sympathetic congressmen had arrived in town, Young should have King and Abernathy bonded out of jail. "Prepare the kind of statement that I should read to the press on release from jail. When it is definite that we are coming out let the press know the time so they will be on hand at the jail for our release."[26]

On Thursday Judge Thomas issued a wide-ranging order instructing the Dallas County registrars to stop using Alabama's difficult registration test, to not reject applicants because of minor errors on their forms, and to process at least one hundred applications each day the registrars met. Monthly reports would go to the judge, and Justice Department officials told newsmen that Thomas's decision "was as favorable to the Negro community as could be obtained." SCLC staffers expressed disappointment that the order was not more far-reaching, but nevertheless suspended the day's scheduled marches.

Fast on the heels of Thomas's action came a statement from Lyndon Johnson that was precisely what King and Young had asked for. "All Americans," the president declared,

> should be indignant when one American is denied the right to vote. The loss of that right to a single citizen undermines the freedom of every citizen. This is why all of us should be concerned with the efforts of our fellow Americans to register to vote in Alabama. The basic problem in Selma is the slow pace of voting registration for Negroes who are qualified to vote. . . . I hope that all Americans will join with me in expressing their concern over the loss of any American's right to vote. . . . I intend to see that that right is secured for all our citizens.

Johnson's words were an explicit endorsement of SCLC's efforts in Selma, public support far stronger than he had given during St. Augustine.

In the Selma jail, however, King learned of Thomas's decree before he heard Johnson's pronouncement, and he told Young that the moratorium on marches was a mistake and that further legal initiatives were necessary. He instructed Young to call Jack Greenberg of the NAACP Legal Defense Fund, which had been coordinating the Selma movement's courtroom efforts, "and let him know that we don't feel that they are moving fast enough. Thomas' restraining order is far from clear. . . ." King stressed, "Please don't be too soft. We have the offensive. It was a mistake not to march today. In a crisis we must have a sense of drama. Don't let Baker control our movement. We may accept the restraining order as a partial victory, but we can't stop."

Friday morning the protests resumed as five hundred marchers were arrested at the courthouse by Sheriff Clark. At the same time, two other carefully planned SCLC initiatives came off. First, a prominent advertisement, headlined A LETTER FROM MARTIN LUTHER KING FROM A SELMA, ALABAMA JAIL, appeared in *The New York Times*. Designed by SCLC to remind readers of King's Birmingham missive and to coincide with his incarceration, the paid appeal showed how well-refined King's fund-raising efforts had become. "Dear Friends," the ad began:

> When the King of Norway participated in awarding the Nobel Peace Prize to me he surely did not think that in less than sixty days I would be in jail. He, and almost all world opinion will be shocked because they are little aware of the unfinished business in the South.
>
> By jailing hundreds of Negroes, the city of Selma, Alabama, has revealed the persisting ugliness of segregation to the nation and the world. When the Civil Rights Act of 1964 was passed many decent Americans were lulled into complacency because they thought the day of difficult struggle was over.
>
> Why are we in jail? Have you ever been required to answer 100 questions on government, some abstruse even to a political science specialist, merely to vote? Have you ever stood in line with over a hundred others and after waiting an entire day seen less than ten given the qualifying test?
>
> THIS IS SELMA, ALABAMA. THERE ARE MORE NEGROES IN JAIL WITH ME THAN THERE ARE ON THE VOTING ROLLS. . . .

The printed plea asked supporters to make their contribution to the Selma effort by writing a check to SCLC.[27]

Friday afternoon fifteen supportive congressmen arrived in Selma. King left jail to meet the delegation, and told newsmen he would be going to Washington to ask President Johnson for voting rights legislation while SCLC accelerated the Selma campaign. Andrew Young asked Harry Wachtel to notify presidential aide Lee White of King's desire for an appointment on Monday, but White House staffers bridled at the news that King had announced his intentions before making the necessary contacts. Wachtel tried to convince White that Johnson should hear about King's Selma experiences at first hand, but White remained cool. "My own personal reaction," he told the president after the phone discussion, "is to avoid seeing King. You've gone that 'extra mile' with him quite a few times. In addition," White reported, "Nick Katzenbach has the impression that the city of Selma has acted pretty responsibly and that King and his people should be quite content with Judge Thomas' order." If King insisted upon coming to Washington, either Katzenbach or Vice-President Humphrey should see him, White advised.

King headed to New York, then returned to Atlanta for a weekend of rest. In Washington presidential press secretary George Reedy, questioned about King's request for a meeting to discuss voting rights, said Johnson would be making "a strong recommendation" to Congress for such legislation in the near future. "Mr. Reedy's statement," *The New York Times* commented, "provided the first official confirmation of reports that President Johnson would definitely press for Congressional action this year to strengthen Federal laws against racial discrimination" in voting. Since that legislation would be prepared by the Justice Department, King's recommendations would best be directed to Attorney General Katzenbach, Reedy pointed out. Wachtel kept lobbying Lee White throughout the weekend. White told him on Saturday that Johnson's Monday schedule could not accommodate another appointment, but on Sunday White said that something might be worked out for Tuesday if King would abide by a detailed White House scenario. King would meet with Katzenbach and Humphrey at the latter's office next to the White House. After that session the vice-president would take King over for a brief meeting with the president, but only if King refrained from any prior announcement that such a meeting had been arranged. Wachtel apprised King of the arrangement, and King agreed to go along with Johnson's game plan. Wachtel and Clarence Jones drafted a press release saying King would speak in Montgomery on Monday and then meet Humphrey and Katzenbach Tuesday to discuss voting rights.[28]

In Selma the week began with a dispute that threatened the movement's unity. Judge Thomas's order had prompted local officials to propose an "appearance book" that prospective registrants could sign at the courthouse that would guarantee them first-come, first-served processing by the county registrars without a lengthy wait in line. Voters League President Reese had accepted the format, but on Monday SCLC's Jim Bevel denounced it as a delaying tactic with which the movement would not cooperate. "We've changed our minds," he told reporters as he led a small group of potential registrants to the courthouse for an ostentatious rejection of the "appearance book" An agitated Sheriff Clark arrived on the scene. "Shaking with anger," reporters said, Clark jabbed Bevel with a billyclub and grabbed him to force him out of the courthouse. Newsmen watched as the scene developed. "'You're making a mockery out of justice,' Sheriff Clark told him, his voice so tense it was barely audible. 'I have a constitutional right—' Mr. Bevel began. 'You get out of here,' Sheriff Clark said, punching him repeatedly with his club." When Bevel refused to be dragged away, Clark placed the entire group under arrest.

King, alerted in Montgomery about these developments, sent Fred Shuttlesworth to Selma to patch up the disagreement before the local black leadership took offense at Bevel's reversal of them.

On Tuesday King led a small march to Montgomery's courthouse before making a late departure for his Washington appointment with Katzenbach and Humphrey. Accompanied by Wachtel, Fauntroy, and other aides, King conferred for over an hour with Katzenbach and Humphrey about voting rights legislation. Lee White had advised Wachtel—and Wachtel, King—that Johnson would phone Humphrey during the meeting to invite the vice-president and his guest to the Oval Office. Worried about whether the president would follow through as planned, King waited anxiously for Humphrey's phone to ring as Katzenbach briefed them on legislative possibilities. Finally, after what seemed an eternity, the phone rang. Humphrey told Johnson he would be right over, and then, forgetting the script, started out for the White House without King. Lee White caught up with the vice-president and reminded him of the game plan. Without missing a beat, Humphrey turned to King and asked him to "come on with me." The entire group trooped to Johnson's office for a quick greeting, and then King and the president, joined by White, spoke privately for ten minutes. Afterward, King told reporters that the discussions had been "very successful. . . . The president made it very clear to me that he was determined during his administration to see all remaining obstacles removed to the right of Negroes to vote." Johnson had said a voting rights proposal would go to Congress "very soon," and King had special praise for the president's "deep commitment to obtaining the right to vote for all Americans." King had explained to the president's advisors that new legislation was needed to eliminate discriminatory literacy tests and provide federal registrars in areas like Selma where local officials treated black applicants unfairly. Johnson and his colleagues had not endorsed these recommendations, King said, but they had promised to consider them.[29]

King returned to Alabama, pleased at how the discussions had gone but knowing that additional public pressure would be necessary to move the administration forward with the sort of comprehensive voting rights legislation that would be essential for a voter registration breakthrough in the rural Deep South. On Wednesday another dramatic scene occurred in Selma when Sheriff Clark and his men used nightsticks and cattle prods to drive a group of 165 protesters out into the countryside on a forced march at a runner's pace. Many angry black citizens turned out for the two evening mass meetings that King addressed. Later, King convened a late-night meeting of the SCLC and SNCC staffs to discuss strategy. Three questions confronted them, King said: "Where are we going in Selma?", "How far can Selma take us on the right to vote," and "What do we do in reference to the rest of the state?" Selma had become the focal point, and hence everything undertaken there needed to be well planned, as the contradictory responses to the "appearance book" had not. King said an appropriate solution would be a strategy committee of representatives of SCLC, SNCC, the DCVL, and younger protesters that would resolve such issues. Second, he stated, there was the question of moving beyond Selma, whose citizens were tired after carrying the entire Alabama campaign for almost a month. Lyndon Johnson had promised him a voting rights bill, King told his colleagues, a bill attributable to their work in Selma, but "the question is, how do we wrap up Selma and what are we pushing for from now on?" They discussed how to bring Selma to a successful conclusion and how to shift the focus to Lowndes County, one of the most hard-core rural areas in the Alabama Black Belt. "We should settle on two or three points," King said, "so that the local people of Selma will feel that they have some kind of victory, because the pressure of the movement cannot continue for another four months." Rev. Reese agreed, remarking that "we should, at this point, shape a victory," and Andrew Young explained that one important advantage of Lowndes was that it lay in a more desirable federal court district than did Dallas. "We should look to Congress or the courts to fight against discrimination in the right to vote. Judge [Frank M.] Johnson in Lowndes can be better dealt with than Judge Thomas in Dallas County. This is why SCLC wants to work Lowndes County first." King endorsed that shift. "You should not only know how to start a good movement, [you] should also know when to stop. . . . In order to get [the forthcoming voting rights] bill passed, we need to make a dramatic appeal through Lowndes and other counties because the people of Selma are tired." The others present agreed. Selma had "reached a state of fatigue," and the campaign now faced a "transitional period."[30]

King left Selma the next day for a speaking engagement in Michigan. Then he returned to Atlanta, where his doctor ordered him hospitalized for the weekend because of "exhaustion." Selma was relatively quiet as news reports focused upon how SCLC's imprisoned James Bevel had been chained to an infirmary bed while being treated for a fever, and how Sheriff Clark had also been hospitalized for exhaustion. In Washington civil rights advocates from the House and Senate pressed Katzenbach and President Johnson for details and quick action on the legislative proposals the administration had announced it was preparing to send to Capitol Hill. Justice Department and White House aides, however, remained close-mouthed about just what they had in mind.

When white leaders in Selma learned of SCLC's plan to turn its attention elsewhere, they acceded to a Community Relations Service (CRS) request for a joint meeting with the city's black leadership on Saturday, February 13. DCVL activists such as Rev. Reese, E. L. Doyle, and Rev. L. L. Anderson attended; white leaders included Public Safety Director Baker, lawyer Sam Hobbs, City Council President Carl Morgan, and school board President Edgar Stewart. Reese and his colleagues explained the movement's goals. What the CRS termed an "open, candid, [and] respectful" discussion followed, with the blacks stressing that local people, not outsiders, were in charge of the protests. In response the whites promised to seek speedier voter registration for all. That offer was pursued further after the meeting when registration board Chairman Victor B. Atkins notified the CRS intermediaries that his office would work with local black leaders on mutually agreeable registration procedures.

Those developments, conveyed to King when he returned to Selma Monday morning, reinforced a point that the events of the preceding week had illuminated: The three different groups within the movement had different goals for the Alabama campaign. SNCC's staffers, though ostensibly working in tandem with SCLC, had grown resentful of how SCLC made decisions and then expected everyone to comply. King complained to Clarence Jones that the SNCC-SCLC "animosity" had reached the point where it reminded him of Albany. King hoped that Harry Belafonte would speak with SNCC about the problem, for he did not want the press to highlight the irresponsibility that characterized some SNCC staffers' actions.[31]

Additionally, there were obvious tensions between SCLC and its local allies in Selma. The DCVL leadership had invited SCLC in to improve local conditions, a context within which developments like the "appearance book" proposal represented tangible progress. SCLC, however, had chosen Selma as part of a larger strategy. "Just as the 1964 civil rights bill was written in Birmingham," Andrew Young told one newsman, "we hope that new federal voting legislation will be written here." Selma, though, had turned out to be less aggressively racist than SCLC had anticipated. Selma authorities, and Judge Thomas, had made considerable efforts to ease the local registration process, but a local accord on voting rights was not all that SCLC was seeking. "SCLC leaders admitted to us," CRS representative Morland noted in mid-February, "that if Selma Negroes gained these things under special court order or through community agreement that this would not satisfy SCLC. Such orders or agreements might require SCLC to change its tactics in Selma or even to move into another Alabama county, but these things would not meet SCLC objectives." Those national objectives explained SCLC's interest in shifting into the more hostile outlying counties.

On Monday King led a march to the Dallas County courthouse, where the movement's prospective registrants peacefully signed the "appearance book." Then he headed to the small town of Camden, the seat of Wilcox County, to witness a similar procession. Later he went to Marion in Perry County before returning to Selma for a late-night strategy session in which it was decided to continue mass action in Selma while branching out into other locales. Such multiple bases, the group agreed, would be the best preparation for the eventual climax of the campaign in Montgomery. "We are considering," King told a reporter Tuesday morning, "the possibility of a large group from throughout the state going to Montgomery." His own health was still too poor to allow him to lead that day's procession to the courthouse through a steady rain. C. T. Vivian directed the column to the building's door and beseeched Clark to allow the group into the building and out of the weather. The sheriff refused and stood glowering in the doorway along with two deputies as the sharp-tongued Vivian criticized Clark and compared him to Hitler. Vivian was hardly two feet away from Clark, and he kept up his heckling for some time, eventually daring the infuriated sheriff to hit him. Suddenly, while the deputies tried to restrain Clark, a fist struck Vivian in the face, send-ing him reeling backward down the steps as cameramen recorded the scene. Vivian was placed under arrest while news reports went out high-lighting the dramatic confrontation. The film "made vivid television," one commentator noted, and newspaper headlines reported how TAUNTED SHERIFF HITS RIGHTS AIDE. "Every time it appears that the movement is dying out," one SCLC staffer told the press, "Sheriff Clark comes to our rescue." Asked by newsmen why he had thrown the punch, a grinning Clark said he had no memory of it. Only years later did Vivian admit that it was one of Clark's deputies who had punched him. "Clark didn't, but he wanted to take credit for it," and Vivian had no reason to contest it. "He was the symbol, not the guy standing beside him."[32]

King's poor health forced him to rest in bed much of the next two days, although he told a Wednesday night audience at Brown Chapel which had voted to boycott all of downtown Selma that the time may have come for nighttime protests. His closest aides, knowing how sick King was, encour-aged him to get away from Selma for a few days vacation. King agreed and instructed that a thousand-person march on Governor Wallace's Montgomery office, which some had been discussing for the forthcoming Monday, be postponed indefinitely. Evening marches could get under way in Marion, where a contingent of Alabama state troopers had rein-forced Perry County lawmen. King returned to Atlanta Thursday while SCLC staffers finalized plans for a demonstration that night in Marion.

That evening, after a rally in a downtown church, C. T. Vivian led a procession out of the building toward the Perry County courthouse. State troopers halted the column before its first ranks were a block from the church and instructed the marchers to turn around. Suddenly, the street-lights went out, and the detachment of lawmen began assaulting the dem-onstrators with billyclubs. The terrified protesters scattered, while across the street white toughs attacked the contingent of national newsmen. NBC's Richard Valeriani suffered a serious head wound, and a short dis-tance away, inside a small café, a trooper shot a young black man who was attempting to shield his mother from the lawmen's blows. The victim, Jimmie Lee Jackson, bleeding heavily from a stomach wound, was taken to a Selma hospital.

The state troopers' violent onslaught brought renewed national press coverage to the Alabama campaign and stimulated new calls for federal action. One Alabama newspaper decried the incident as "a nightmare of State Police stupidity and brutality," and Selma's Wilson Baker, fearing a similar scene, blocked an SCLC attempt to stage a Friday night march to the Dallas County courthouse. King, bedridden in Atlanta, dispatched a telegram to Attorney General Katzenbach denouncing the violence, and Alabama Governor Wallace issued a ban on all nighttime marches and labeled SCLC "professional agitators with pro-Communist affiliations."[33]

Somewhat recuperated, King returned to Selma on Monday, February 22. He led a peaceful march to the courthouse, visited the hospitalized Jimmie Lee Jackson, and made a brief afternoon visit to Marion. When he returned, he received an unusual phone call from Attorney General Katzenbach. The Justice Department had just learned of a dangerous plot against King. The conspirators, Katzenbach said, had intended to shoot him from ambush one week earlier during his visit to Marion, but had been unable to get a clear shot. SCLC's staff had heard several such reports, but this warning from the attorney general carried the utmost credibility. King should take the greatest care with his personal safety, Katzenbach advised. King made reference to the warning when he spoke to that night's mass rally at Brown Chapel, but he focused his remarks on how the movement would use night marches whether Governor Wallace granted permission or not, and on how SCLC would send "carloads" of disfranchised Alabama blacks directly to Wallace's doorstep. King did not mention that the death-threat warnings had come just twenty-four hours after the assassination of Malcolm X in a hail of gunfire in a Harlem ballroom.

King spent Tuesday conferring with the SCLC staff before speaking at that night's rally and heading home to Atlanta. He told newsmen that the motorcade to the Alabama state capitol would take place on March 8, after which night marches would take place in Selma. He had to undertake a four-day West Coast fund-raising trip, and much of SCLC's leadership got some badly needed rest.[34]

King's long flight to Los Angeles afforded him the luxury of uninterrupted time to reflect on Malcolm X's assassination. The two men had met only once—eleven months earlier in Washington—and had spoken to each other for no more than a minute, but Malcolm's death troubled King.

In the fall of 1964, as Malcolm's schism with the mainline Black Muslim leadership of Elijah Muhammad had grown more visible, King had felt optimistic that in time this dynamic orator would forsake the "hate whitey" rhetoric that the Nation of Islam emphasized. "I look forward to talking with him," King told a black newsman shortly after the Nobel Peace Prize announcement. Subsequent events—Malcolm's utterance of anti-Semitic statements—had cooled King's ardor. In early February, while King was in jail, Malcolm made a quick visit to Selma after a speech in Tuskegee. Malcolm's sudden appearance at Brown Chapel threw Andy Young and Jim Bevel into a tizzy. They summoned Coretta King to help keep the unwanted visitor within bounds. Malcolm spoke reassuringly to her about his presence in Selma before addressing the crowd. He told her he was "trying to help," Mrs. King remembered, that "he wanted to present an alternative; that it might be easier for whites to accept Martin's proposals after hearing him." Coretta's fears had not been wholly allayed, but she was struck by how "he seemed rather anxious to let Martin know he was not causing trouble or making it difficult, but that he was trying to make it easier." Malcolm's restrained remarks to the audience bore out his professed intentions. "He seemed sincere," Coretta later observed, and she told Martin about the encounter during her jail visit to him the same afternoon. "He didn't react too much one way or the other," she later recalled.

Now, with Malcolm's death apparently the deed of black rivals, King's reactions were more intense. Internecine black violence, even among the Muslims, was particularly obscene, and he vowed to see it brought to a quick end, even if he had to intervene as a mediator in a complicated and dangerous situation. Additionally, the death raised personal questions for King, questions that newsmen put to him upon his arrival in Los Angeles. Did Malcolm's shooting make King more fearful of his own end? As usual, he responded with a disinterest bordering on nonchalance. "I get threats quite often. This is almost a daily and weekly occurrence." Had he designated a successor should he meet a similar fate? Ralph Abernathy, King replied. Did not all these threats deeply disturb him? "I have learned now to take them rather philosophically. . . . One has to conquer the fear of death if he is going to do anything constructive in life and take a stand against evil." What was his own reaction to Malcolm's passing? "It is even more unfortunate that this great tragedy occurred at a time when Malcolm X was re-evaluating his own philosophical presuppositions and moving toward a greater understanding of the nonviolent movement and toward more tolerance of white people." Malcolm's death reminded King again that black liberation in America would require much more than a civil rights act or a voting bill.[35]

That evening King was in a world where few people would remember Malcolm X—a dinner party for eighty at the home of a Beverly Hills physician. The next day King spoke to an 1,800-person luncheon and attended a gala film premiere whose proceeds would go to SCLC. Fund-raising trips were an economic necessity to keep SCLC operating, but King disliked the crush such appearances entailed and retreated to his heavily guarded room at the Statler Hilton in Los Angeles whenever possible. He learned on Friday that Jimmie Lee Jackson had died and spoke repeatedly to his different audiences about how more outside help was needed in the South. SCLC soon would launch a nationwide boycott of all Mississippi products. "Changes in Alabama and Mississippi will not come from within," he explained. "I cannot see the changes coming short of massive federal action." Progress might be made on voting rights with the Johnson administration bill due for introduction in the near future. "My hope is that we can get it through in the next few weeks," King said. But the Deep South was not the only thing on his mind. "Some of our most nagging problems in the future will be in the big cities in the North on the area of jobs and schools and housing," he warned. On Sunday, the last day of the trip, King spoke to a huge crowd at Victory Baptist Church, centering his remarks on the theme of death. Medgar Evers, the four young girls of Sixteenth Street church, John Kennedy, the three Mississippi movement workers, and now Malcolm X had all suffered violent death in less than two years time. Included in his comments was an offer to mediate the split within the Muslims before further violence occurred.[36]

King arrived in Atlanta in the predawn hours of Monday, March 1, and after hardly any sleep, headed to Selma for a strategy meeting and a visit to the Dallas County courthouse, where dozens of prospective registrants stood waiting outside in the rain. King told the group, "We are going to bring a voting bill into being in the streets of Selma." Then he was off to give similar encouragement to voter applicants in rural Wilcox and Lowndes counties. Tuesday morning he traveled to Washington to speak at Howard University, where more than forty policemen stood guard because of the numerous threats that had been made against King's life. He spoke on a standard theme—the three evils of racism, poverty, and violence—but expanded the latter point to include a call for a negotiated settlement to the widening war in Vietnam. Both Stanley Levison and Clarence Jones had spoken with King about their opposition to Lyndon Johnson's escalation of that struggle, but this was the first occasion King had expressed that sentiment in public. "The war in Vietnam," he told his Howard audience, "is accomplishing nothing."

King returned to Alabama on Wednesday to attend Jimmie Lee Jackson's funeral. He preached at the memorial service and led a procession of some one thousand mourners through the rain to Jackson's grave site. The constant death threats and the reminders of Malcolm's and Jackson's violent ends, had put King in a morbid state of mind. As the march started out for the cemetery, King beckoned SCLC board member Joseph Lowery to come with him. "Come on, walk with me, Joe, this may be my last walk," King remarked in a bantering tone that did not conceal the serious concern underlying it.

After Jackson's funeral, King flew to New York to confer with his advisors prior to meeting Friday with Lyndon Johnson. Jim Bevel told newsmen that King would return to Selma on Sunday, March 7, to lead a fifty-four-mile march from Selma to Montgomery. The idea of walking, rather than driving, had been suggested by a Marion activist, Mrs. Lucy Foster, in the wake of Jackson's death.[37]

In New York intramural tensions had emerged among King's volunteer counselors. Just like SNCC and SCLC in Selma, or with Young, Bevel, and Williams in Atlanta, rivalries had developed between the New Yorkers. In particular, Jones and Levison, plus Chicago's Chauncey Eskridge, had grown to resent Harry Wachtel, particularly because Wachtel's name had appeared prominently in the press in connection with the White House contacts. King's other advisors avoided such publicity for themselves. Some of the animosity also was due to the fact that Wachtel was white and had an "assertive and take-charge attitude," Jones told King. Levison was displeased that Wachtel, who had more time to devote to King's affairs than Jones, consulted only with Bayard Rustin before taking action. Jones warned both King and Andrew Young of the growing tensions, and King acknowledged the complaints, saying he was aware that Wachtel's outspoken style antagonized some people.

Jones and Levison knew that the constant barrage of death threats was taking an increasing mental toll on King. Depressed, King told Jones that he and other friends should contact the White House and the Justice Department to demand protection for him. Also, he knew he had to return to Selma on Sunday to lead the march to Montgomery that SCLC's staff increasingly expected state authorities to block. Late Friday afternoon King flew to Washington for a meeting with Lyndon Johnson that lasted seventy-five minutes. The president had several items of good news for him. First, the administration had decided to propose statutory changes to ease voter registration rather than pursuing a constitutional amendment, as some Justice Department attorneys had initially thought necessary. Further, he told King, he had a firm commitment of support for a voting rights measure from Senate Republican leader Everett M. Dirksen. Johnson made no promises of success, but the legislative prospects for a second major civil rights bill in less than twelve months seemed brighter than ever before. King told newsmen that the president had advised him to speak with Katzenbach about the details of the bill, and he mused that perhaps he should ask the attorney general to provide federal marshals to ensure the safety of Sunday's march. The following morning King returned to Atlanta to prepare for the trek to Montgomery.[38]

While King was in New York and Washington, both sides in the Alabama struggle had been laying plans for Sunday's demonstration. Governor Wallace and his advisors, including state Public Safety Director Al Lingo, commander of the troopers and a close friend of Sheriff Clark's, discussed how to respond to SCLC's plans. Several aides recommended that the marchers be allowed to head east from Selma along U.S. Highway 80 without any hindrance, for there was no chance that the ill-prepared participants, who expected to be stopped, could complete the fifty-four-mile walk. This approach, gubernatorial press secretary Bill Jones argued, would make King and his compatriots "the laughing stock of the nation," especially if state authorities led the unsuspecting protesters to think they would be halted on the outskirts of Selma. Wallace agreed, and while Alabama newspapers reported that the march would be blocked, word went out to state officials that the column would be allowed to proceed. On Friday, however, a hitch developed in the Wallace strategy. Lowndes County State Representative Bill Edwards, learning of the real plan, warned Wallace that it was likely the marchers would encounter shootings or explosives if state lawmen allowed them to proceed eastward through his county on the often desolate road to Montgomery. Gubernatorial aides Bill Jones and Cecil Jackson confirmed the danger, and with some reluctance Wallace met with trooper commanders Lingo, John Cloud, and William R. Jones to tell them to halt the marchers and turn them back to Selma. Jackson relayed the word to Selma Mayor Smitherman, who tried to convince Public Safety Director Baker that Lingo's troopers would halt the column without reenacting the Marion bloodbath of two weeks earlier.

SCLC's staffers knew nothing of the segregationists' strategic shifts while they were planning a march they were certain would be halted before it left Selma. Young explained to King on Friday that the protesters faced two choices. "One," as he related it to a newsman, "is to go back and get a court order permitting us to march. And the other is to sit down wherever they stop us." "We don't intend to be pushed around or intimidated," he explained to a questioner. "If they are reasonable, we'll probably turn around and go back to [the] church. If they try to bully us, we'll have to stand our ground and refuse to cooperate."

While SCLC considered its choices, SNCC's leader held a meeting in Atlanta to discuss their participation in the Selma campaign and whether they should endorse the Sunday march, which some staffers contended was a waste of energy and resources. Selma Project Director Silas Norman detailed the disagreements that had arisen between SNCC and SCLC, especially the way "SCLC pushes the idea that local people need leaders like Martin Luther King . . . while SNCC says that local people build their own leaders, out of their own communities." Former Project Director John Love voiced stronger criticism, but John Lewis contended that opposing the SCLC march would place SNCC in conflict with many local activists. After much discussion, a majority of SNCC's executive committee voted to oppose the march but to allow any SNCC staffers who wanted to participate as individuals to do so. They also agreed to send King a letter criticizing SCLC's actions in Selma and asking for a meeting to discuss improved relations.[39]

Selma's activists were buoyed by a Saturday demonstration of support for their cause by seventy Alabama whites who came from Birmingham and Tuscaloosa to march to the Dallas County courthouse. Nonetheless, the SCLC staff worried about what Sunday's march might bring, especially in light of the death threats against King. Saturday night Hosea Williams and Jim Bevel phoned King in Atlanta, apprised him of Governor Wallace's declaration earlier that day that troopers would "use whatever measures are necessary to prevent a march," and advised him not to lead the Sunday procession. The column would be blocked, and it was likely that all the participants would be jailed. King wondered whether the march should be postponed a day, but Bevel and Williams said no. Local enthusiasm for the march was substantial, and postponing it would harm morale. Finally, King consented that they would proceed without him. As he explained it the next day, "It was agreed that I not lead the march because of the revelation of the fact that State Troopers would block our move forward. It was suggested that I remain in Atlanta for my Sunday church responsibilities and mobilize national support for a larger thrust forward."

If SCLC was worried about possible injury to King, Selma Public Safety Director Wilson Baker believed that Al Lingo and his state troopers would turn the Sunday confrontation into a violent bloodbath. Saturday night Baker angrily told Mayor Smitherman that he would not allow his men to take part, and announced he was resigning. Sunday morning, after several city council members interceded, an agreement was reached between Baker and Smitherman that city officers would neither arrest the marchers before they reached the troopers' blockade just east of town, as Baker preferred, nor give aid to Lingo's men and Sheriff Clark's volunteer posse when the confrontation came, as state authorities had requested. Baker reluctantly accepted the compromise after being reminded that the hot-tempered Clark, in Washington for a Sunday morning television interview, would not return until after the climax, and that the duplicitous Lingo would be away from the scene, waiting to meet Clark at Montgomery's airfield.

Late Sunday morning, as some six hundred movement supporters gathered at Brown Chapel, SCLC's field commanders were still uncertain about whether to proceed. They knew the troopers were deployed just across the Edmund Pettus Bridge, which spanned the Alabama River on Selma's east flank. Some were hesitant about going ahead, and the suggestion was made that they consider outflanking the lawmen by marching out of town in a northeasterly direction along State Highway 14. Rev. Reese objected to that tactic, and Perry County leader Albert Turner, who had brought a large number of Marion activists to Selma for the march, argued that they had to proceed. As they talked, an impatient Hosea Williams got on the phone and reached Ralph Abernathy at his Atlanta church. Did Abernathy and King agree that the march should go forward? Williams asked. Abernathy said he would phone King, who was busy at his own services at Ebenezer, and call Williams back. Abernathy reached King, explained that Williams had more than five hundred people ready to march, and described how Williams and Bevel insisted on proceeding. King reluctantly gave his approval, and Abernathy relayed the word to Williams.[40]

Several hours behind schedule, SCLC's staffers drew lots to see who would lead the column, and Williams won the nod. SNCC Chairman John Lewis, who had driven back from Atlanta in order to take part, walked with him in the front rank as Williams led the double file down Sylvan Street away from Brown Chapel. The quiet column of marchers turned right on Water Street, and within several blocks they were at Selma's main drag, Broad Street. There they turned left and headed up the steeply arched west side of the Pettus Bridge as several dozen of Clark's possemen eyed them from the shadows of the *Selma Times-*

Journal building. When Lewis and Williams reached the crest of the bridge, they could see the blue-uniformed state troopers deployed across the four-lane width of U.S. 80 about three hundred yards ahead of them. On the troopers' flanks waited more of Clark's possemen, some on horses. One hundred or so white spectators looked on from the car dealerships and hamburger stands that lined the road, and a modest group of newsmen were sequestered off to the side near one of the auto emporiums. Unbeknownst to the marchers, as they descended the east flank of the Pettus Bridge, a car carrying Colonel Lingo and Sheriff Clark pulled up behind the troopers' lines. Some witnesses later recalled an itchy Clark, wearing a business suit and fingering a tear-gas canister, pacing near the front lines as the marchers' column drew up to within fifty feet of uniformed troop commander Major John Cloud.

Williams and Lewis came to a quiet stop upon Cloud's order that they halt. Speaking through a bullhorn, the major told them, "This is an unlawful assembly. Your march is not conducive to the public safety. You are ordered to disperse and go back to your church or to your homes." As they listened to Cloud's words, the beefy troopers gripped their billyclubs and recalled their instructions that tear gas would be used if the marchers refused to disperse.

Hosea Williams responded to Cloud's declaration by asking, "May we have a word with the major?" Cloud replied, "There is no word to be had." They repeated this exchange twice. Then Cloud announced, "You have two minutes to turn around and go back to your church." As they had agreed previously, the column's leaders silently held their ground. Approximately sixty seconds passed. Then Cloud ordered, "Troopers, advance." One eyewitness account recorded the ensuing scene in graphic detail:

> The troopers rushed forward, their blue uniforms and white helmets blurring into a flying wedge as they moved.
> The wedge moved with such force that it seemed almost to pass over the waiting column instead of through it.
> The first 10 or 20 Negroes were swept to the ground screaming, arms and legs flying, and packs and bags went skittering across the grassy divider strip and on to the pavement on both sides.
> Those still on their feet retreated.
> The troopers continued pushing, using both the force of their bodies and the prodding of their nightsticks.
> A cheer went up from the white spectators lining the south side of the highway.
> The mounted possemen spurred their horses and rode at a run into the retreating mass. The Negroes cried out as they crowded together for protection, and the whites on the sidelines whooped and cheered.
> The Negroes paused in their retreat for perhaps a minute, still screaming and huddling together.

Suddenly there was a report like a gunshot and a grey cloud spewed over the troopers and the Negroes.
"Tear gas!" someone yelled.

Marchers reeled from the gas while the troopers, protected by gas masks, continued their assault. Some witnesses reported that Jim Clark heaved the first canister. Reporters and cameramen could observe the assault through the cloud of gas as the marchers turned to flee toward Selma. "Fifteen or twenty nightsticks could be seen through the gas, flailing at the heads of the marchers." John Lewis went down from a hard blow to his head, and Mrs. Boynton was rendered unconscious by a combination of blows and tear gas. As troopers and possemen pursued them, the screaming victims fled back across the Pettus Bridge to seek refuge in the black residential neighborhood surrounding Brown Chapel. The mounted possemen chased them the entire way, and other officers attempted to force injured marchers and angry onlookers off the street and into Brown Chapel or nearby homes. Bottles and bricks began to fly as a furious Wilson Baker arrived on the scene, cursing Clark and telling the sheriff to withdraw his men from the area immediately. In time, Clark's and Lingo's forces withdrew to a block's distance from Brown Chapel and cordoned off the area. Movement leaders struggled to restore order and obtain medical treatment for the many who had been injured, and physicians at Good Samaritan Hospital reported that wounds ranged from broken teeth and severe head gashes to fractured ribs and wrists. Seventy to eighty people were treated, and seventeen of the most seriously injured were admitted for further observation.[41]

It was early evening by the time that news reports of the bloody attack on Highway 80 began to spread across the country. Many television viewers were astounded by the graphic film of the troopers' assault on the peaceful marchers as ABC interrupted a movie broadcast, *Judgment at Nuremberg,* to present footage that depicted how racial hatred could generate awful violence in contemporary America, not just Nazi Germany. In Selma, Andrew Young and Hosea Williams called King in Atlanta to pass on the details of the horrifying situation and to discuss what steps should be taken next. A lengthy conference call was arranged between King and Abernathy in Atlanta, Young and others in the Brown Chapel parsonage, and Clarence Jones in New York in which a variety of alternatives was considered. Eventually, King decided upon two initiatives: The movement should deluge the White House and Congress with telegrams denouncing the attack, and a public call should go out urging civil rights supporters to converge on Selma by Tuesday for a second attempt to march to Montgomery. Movement lawyers would seek a federal court order enjoining any interference with a march, and SCLC headquarters would dispatch telegrams to several hundred prominent religious leaders inviting them to take part in the Tuesday march. "In the vicious maltreatment of defenseless citizens of Selma, where old women and young children were gassed and clubbed at random, we have witnessed an eruption of the disease of racism which seeks to destroy all America," King's message said. "No American is without responsibility," and "it is fitting that all Americans help to bear the burden. . . . Clergy of all faiths" should join the Tuesday protest.

Monday morning's headlines announced the Selma violence to millions, and accompanying photos depicted troopers with upraised clubs attacking the helpless marchers. Members of Congress denounced the event as "an exercise in terror" against peaceful citizens who had been seeking their constitutional right to vote. Minnesota Senator Walter Mondale declared that the Selma outrage "makes passage of legislation to guarantee Southern Negroes the right to vote an absolute imperative for Congress this year." President Johnson conferred with Attorney General Katzenbach about Selma, and in Montgomery, an angry George Wallace summoned Sheriff Clark to his office for a private condemnation of Sunday's violent excesses. "The Governor was real upset and mad at Clark," said Mayor Smitherman, who witnessed the scene. State and local authorities braced for more protests in the days ahead as SCLC attorneys petitioned Federal District Judge Frank M. Johnson, Jr., for an order barring state obstruction of Tuesday's march.

Martin King's aides were fearful that there would be attempts on his life when he arrived in Selma from Atlanta. They conveyed those fears to Louis Martin, the influential black deputy chairman of the Democratic National Committee. Martin phoned King to ask about his plans and to inquire about what the administration could do to ease the crisis. As Martin described their conversation in a subsequent memo, King responded:

> The President might publicly announce the appointment of a top governmental figure to mediate the situation . . . "someone like Attorney General Katzenbach."
> Such action would give him some reason for calling off the march which is scheduled for 10:00AM Tuesday, March 9. He said he was "too deeply committed" to call it off unless some such action was taken by Washington.

King also told Martin that SCLC was calling on national figures to join the Tuesday protest, and suggested that federal marshals be assigned to protect the demonstrators.

Louis Martin immediately passed King's comments on to top Johnson aide Marvin Watson, and recommended that the president, the vice-president, or the attorney general make contact with Governor Wallace to press for concessions that would obviate the movement's need for a Tuesday march. Martin had understood that King would give up his Tuesday plans in exchange for meaningful federal intervention, and Watson mulled whether CRS Director LeRoy Collins could be assigned to mediate the situation before the new march got under way.[42]

While the Johnson administration was considering how to preclude a second march, the movement leadership had its own questions to discuss when King returned to Selma on Monday evening. Montgomery attorney Fred Gray, King's old bus boycott colleague, told the group gathered at Jean and Sullivan Jackson's home, where King always stayed in Selma, that Judge Johnson was unwilling to issue a restraining order against state authorities until a full hearing could be convened later in the week. The judge wanted SCLC to postpone the march, and would issue an order barring it if the movement did not accede. Hosea Williams argued that they had an obligation to their followers to go ahead with the march whether the Johnson in Washington or the Johnson in Montgomery wanted them to or not. CORE's James Farmer, a new arrival in town, said that he understood Williams's attitude, but that the rational choice was to wait. SNCC's representatives, led by James Forman, contended that the Tuesday march must go ahead. Just as the discussion broke up so that everyone could attend that evening's mass meeting at Brown Chapel, King indicated he was inclined to postpone the march and go along with Judge Johnson's request.

It was almost midnight by the time King addressed the hundreds of people crammed into Brown Chapel. Some listeners thought him unusually "subdued," and found his remarks "strangely personal." He implied there was no doubt the movement would attempt to march to Montgomery the next day, but one witness noted his tone and demeanor "gave the distinct impression that he was involved in some profound struggle with his conscience." By the time he returned to the Jacksons' home in the wee hours of the morning, King had painfully reconsidered his earlier decision. Movement lawyers, who already had informed Judge Johnson of SCLC's acceptance of his plan, were exasperated with King's change of heart, as was Assistant Attorney General John Doar, the Johnson administration's highest-ranking representative on the scene, who had informed the president and the attorney general earlier that the deal was set. Doar went to the Jacksons' home to confer with King across the kitchen table; Doar's subtle assurances that both the administration and Judge Johnson would endorse a subsequent march to Montgomery if Tuesday's effort was called off were not enough to shake King from his conviction that it would be wrong to betray the expectations of thousands that the Tuesday procession would take place. The pressure to march exerted by SNCC's adherents, local leaders, and even some of his staff at least counterbalanced the administration's pleas. Indications were strong that Judge Johnson would issue a Tuesday morning order barring the march if King did not announce a cancellation, and that would place SCLC in the position of defying a federal judge, something King had never done before. Attorney General Katzenbach pleaded with King by phone to endorse a postponement, reminding him of the agreement reached earlier that evening. "The Attorney General kept repeating, 'Dr. King, you promised you would not,'" recalled Legal Defense Fund Director Jack Greenberg, who joined the conference call from New York. "This conversation went back and forth repetitively several times," and then "Dr. King stated the overwhelming fact controlling the event: 'But Mr. Attorney General, you have not been a black man in America for three hundred years.' That ended the exchange." Katzenbach hung up thinking that King still was looking for a way out of a tight fix, but the word was passed among the tired group of movement leaders clustered at the Jackson house that the march would go forward later that morning—the movement was honor-bound to attempt the long trek eastward.[43]

While King and his colleagues were getting a few hours of sleep, Lyndon Johnson had roused CRS Director LeRoy Collins and ordered him and CRS mediator A. M. Secrest to fly immediately to Craig Air Force Base outside Selma to see if a solution could be reached before the marchers got under way. Collins and Secrest landed in Alabama shortly after breakfast, conferred with John Doar at Selma's small federal building, and then drove to the Jacksons' to see King and two other CRS representatives, James Laue and Fred Miller, who also had been striving to win a postponement. Collins and Doar found King in his pajamas and pleaded with him to postpone the march. King responded that his conscience commanded that he go forward, and that many movement supporters—especially the SNCC people—would go ahead with a march even if he told them it should be called off. Fred Shuttlesworth interjected that the government officials ought to be talking to Lingo and Clark, urging them not to use violence, rather than trying to persuade civil rights advocates not to pursue peaceful protests. Collins responded that repetition of Sunday's brutality would be a tragedy not just for the victims, but for the entire country. King replied that he had to stay the course. Collins then made a new suggestion to King, drawing on an idea the other CRS men and Doar had kicked around. If King would not call off the march, what about marching out to where the troopers would be waiting, make a symbolic witness, then turning around and walking back into Selma? King doubted the Alabama lawmen would allow such an action. "I don't believe you can get those people not to charge into us even if we do stop." Collins pressed the point, asking if King would accept the proposal if CRS could get Lingo and Clark to promise a peaceful reception if King turned the marchers around. King replied, "I cannot agree to do anything because I don't know what I can get my people to do, but if you will get Sheriff Clark and Lingo to agree to something like that, I will try." That was good enough for Collins, who told King he would seek to get such an assurance from the lawmen, and then would get back to him. While Collins set out in search of Lingo and Clark, King and his colleagues pondered what they might do in the few minutes remaining before the march was scheduled to leave from Brown Chapel.

Soon after Collins departed, King and Young were informed that Judge Johnson had issued an order banning any attempted march to Montgomery before a full hearing, set to begin Thursday, could be held on the movement's petition for a restraining order against any further official obstruction. Depressed by that development, King arranged a conference call with Greenberg, Clarence Jones, Harry Wachtel, and Bayard Rustin in New York to discuss whether he would be in contempt of federal court if he went ahead with a march that now appeared inescapable. Wachtel and Rustin advised King that he had no choice but to proceed, and Wachtel remarked that King had to face the fact that he had to violate the injunction. Greenberg recommended against any march, and told King that Johnson's order would probably not be upheld if they appealed it. Wachtel suggested King announce that his counsel had told him the injunction was improper. A dispirited King thanked his advisors and told them he would proceed.

Collins found Lingo and Clark at the Lehman Pontiac dealership on Highway 80, where the troopers and possemen were preparing to block the road just as they had on Sunday. Initially the lawmen were antagonistic to Collins's proposal, but the former Florida governor explained that allowing the protesters to march across the bridge and then turn back in the face of the blockade would be a face-saving compromise for both sides. Slowly Clark and Lingo became more interested in the idea, and then Lingo left for a few moments to speak with someone by phone, whom Collins presumed to be George Wallace. When Lingo returned, he conferred with Clark and then informed Collins that they would try his arrangement on one condition: that the marchers follow a precise route from Brown Chapel to the Pettus Bridge and back, a route that Sheriff Clark drew on a piece of paper. Collins could not fathom why the map, which traced the same streets the marchers had used on Sunday, was so important to the lawmen, but he saw no point in asking.[44]

King had already told the hundreds of eager marchers waiting at the church to "put on their walking shoes" and follow him toward Pettus Bridge by the time that Collins concluded his conference with Clark and Lingo. The CRS director, with Clark's map in hand, caught up with King as the column made its way from Brown Chapel toward downtown Selma. He pulled King aside, told him of his conversation, and handed him the hand-drawn map. King said he would try to turn the column around as it approached the troopers' line, but that he was not certain all the people would follow his lead. If Collins could promise that the lawmen would remain in place and take no action, "I'll do my best," he said, to turn the procession around. Collins assured him that he would stand beside the troopers and do everything possible to ensure that the scenario went properly. King nodded and gestured toward the column. "I'll do my best to turn them back. I won't promise you, but I'll do my best."

As Collins hurried back across Pettus Bridge in advance of King and the two thousand marchers, U.S. Marshal H. Stanley Fountain approached King to read him the text of Judge Johnson's order barring any march to Montgomery. King listened without comment, and when Fountain stepped aside, the long line made its way across the bridge toward the troopers. King led the procession to within fifty yards of the blockade, while Lingo described the scene over an open phone line to Wallace in Montgomery and John Doar did the same to Attorney General Katzenbach in Washington. King brought the marchers to a halt. He informed the lawmen that his followers would conduct prayers, and different notables came forward to recite homilies as a tense LeRoy Collins watched from the roadside. Then after singing "We Shall Overcome," King and those immediately behind him turned and began to lead the column in a narrow loop back toward Pettus Bridge. Just as they turned, however, the line of troopers that had been blocking the highway suddenly withdrew to the side of the road, leaving it wide open. As newsmen and nervous federal officials looked on, however, each successive rank of marchers followed those in front and turned back across the bridge. "I have never before or since felt the relief I did when that great mass of people turned and retraced their steps over the bridge," LeRoy Collins remembered. "Both sides had kept their word to the letter."[45]

If newsmen were bemused over whether the troopers' withdrawal, reportedly ordered by Wallace, had been an attempt to embarrass King, SCLC's president found himself in an extremely unpleasant situation when the marchers returned to Brown Chapel. SNCC's staff members, who had not been privy to King's late-breaking conversations with Collins, were outraged that a deal to terminate the march had been cut without their knowledge. Strong words were directed at King and other SCLC leaders, and King was caught in a strange crossfire between movement workers seeking his assurance that he had not made a secret deal and newsmen asking if he had agreed to the turnaround so as not to violate the court order. It was extremely awkward. If King admitted he had agreed not to march to Montgomery, it might save him a contempt-of-court citation, but at the cost of confirming SNCC's worst fears about him. If he denied there had been an understanding, it might reassure his in-house critics, but evince to Judge Johnson that King had given no heed to his injunction. Torn between two unattractive choices, King waffled and dissembled. "We knew we would not get to Montgomery," he told newsmen. "We knew we would not get past the troopers," and "we agreed that we would not break through the lines." Two days later he conceded under Johnson's questioning that there had been a "tacit agreement," but at weaker moments he asserted inaccurately that "no prearranged agreement existed." No matter how he phrased it, King's contradictory explanations served neither himself nor SCLC well.

In the aftermath of the "Tuesday turnaround," King sought to assuage his critics on both sides. He phoned the Justice Department to tell Ramsey Clark, Katzenbach's new deputy, that he had not wanted to violate the court order, but that his leadership would have been badly weakened had he not gone ahead. He voiced similar opinions to Collins and Secrest at a meeting at the Jacksons, but King's most serious problems were with his movement allies. A livid James Forman denounced King's behavior as "a classic example of trickery against the people," and the atmosphere around Brown Chapel turned chilly. Just twenty-four hours earlier, as hundreds of supporters poured into Selma from all over the country, the black community had experienced what Rev. Reese termed "one of the most exhilarating moments" of their long struggle. Now, as SNCC and SCLC staffers sniped at each other in front of local onlookers who could not understand the reasons for the heated exchanges, the movement's spirit weakened despite the growing influx of supporters.[46]

Tuesday evening a band of white toughs attacked three newly arrived Massachusetts ministers in downtown Selma. One of the three victims, Rev. James J. Reeb of Boston, suffered a serious blow to the head. Several hours passed before Reeb was transported to Birmingham's University Hospital, and word spread in Selma that his prognosis was not good. That attack led to stepped-up law enforcement efforts to protect civil rights sympathizers from violence, and by early Wednesday state and local lawmen had cordoned off the neighborhood around Brown Chapel. While movement supporters held vigils and sang freedom songs, everyone waited for word on when another march to Montgomery would take place.

Tuesday brought further expressions of outrage over Sunday's violence from all around the country. Sympathy marches were organized in Chicago, New York, Detroit, and Boston, among other cities, and six hundred pickets appeared at the White House to call for federal intervention. Fifty members of Congress denounced the attack, and a group of prominent movement supporters, led by SCLC's Walter Fauntroy and Michigan Congressman John Conyers, met with Vice-President Humphrey. Late in the day, presidential press secretary George Reedy issued Lyndon Johnson's first public comment on Sunday's events. The administration, he said,

has been in close touch with the situation and has made every effort to prevent a repetition. I am certain Americans everywhere join me in deploring the brutality with which a number of Negro citizens of Alabama were treated when they sought to dramatize their deep and sincere interest in attaining the precious right to vote.

The best legal talent in the federal government is engaged in preparing legislation which will secure that right for every American. I expect to complete work on my recommendations by this weekend and shall dispatch a special message to Congress as soon as the drafting of the legislation is finished.

Justice Department attorneys had been instructed to take an *amicus curiae* role in Judge Johnson's upcoming hearing on the movement petition seeking an unhindered march to Montgomery, and the president said he looked forward to a peaceful resolution of the issues.[47]

Wednesday was a painful day for Martin King as SNCC's anger became increasingly vocal. Angry exchanges occurred as movement staffers organized a march from Brown Chapel to the courthouse, but the procession was blocked less than one hundred yards from the church by city officials worried that any forays into downtown might produce more violence. King remained in seclusion throughout the day, and Wednesday evening he retreated to the Montgomery home of an old friend from Dexter days, Richmond Smiley, for more peace and quiet than could be found in Selma. SNCC's workers, fed up with their SCLC colleagues, also decided that they wanted a respite from Selma, and announced they were shifting their base of operations to Montgomery, where James Forman organized black students from Tuskegee Institute to stage protests at the state capitol.

In Washington efforts to finalize the administration's voting rights bill continued apace. As lawyers from the Civil Rights Division and the solicitor general's office worked on the draft, administration officials met with Senate Majority and Minority Leaders Mike Mansfield and Everett Dirksen to ensure that they would be amenable to the bill's provisions calling for the suspension of literacy tests and assignment of federal registrars in difficult counties. In response to congressional criticism that the administration was moving too slowly, Johnson and Attorney General Katzenbach briefed sixty legislators at the White House. They emphasized that a comprehensive bill would be ready within days.

Thursday morning Judge Johnson's hearing on SCLC's petition for an unobstructed march opened in Montgomery. A nervous Martin King was one of the first witnesses, and he conceded to the frowning jurist that he had termed the restraining order "unjust," but he did not believe he had violated it. "We never anticipated getting to Montgomery," King said, but he had seen no alternative to leading the procession out to where the troopers waited.

"I did it to give them an outlet," King explained, saying that his supporters' energies had to be channeled in a constructive direction. "I felt that if I had not done it, the pent up emotions, the inner tensions . . . would have exploded into retaliatory violence." No one in the courtroom challenged King on those assertions, but the judge did press him on his conversations with LeRoy Collins. Reluctantly King conceded there had been "a tacit agreement" between them. The hearing continued on Friday with testimony about the Sunday assault, and Johnson set a third day of proceedings for Saturday.[48]

Thursday was a quiet and rainy day in Selma, and movement supporters conducted a nonstop vigil outside Brown Chapel as scores of lawmen kept the civil rights advocates confined to that safe neighborhood. Late that evening word came from Birmingham that James Reeb had become the second fatality of the Alabama campaign. His death generated far more response than had Jimmie Lee Jackson's, including phone calls of condolence to Reeb's widow and father from President Johnson and Vice-President Humphrey. The death of the Boston minister also led to further outcry from the nation's clergy, and two groups of religious leaders called on President Johnson on Friday to demand stronger federal action in Alabama.

Friday afternoon Governor Wallace wired Johnson to request a meeting. The president granted the request, so Saturday morning the Alabama governor flew to Washington. Wallace told the president that King's demonstrators, not their grievances about the right to vote, were the real problem in Alabama, but Lyndon Johnson would have none of it. Looking directly at the nervous governor, Johnson told him he was wrong, that the protesters were being denied one of America's most fundamental rights, and that Wallace and his state troopers should protect, not attack, peaceful demonstrators seeking to draw attention to their plight. With Wallace somewhat cowed, Lyndon Johnson escorted him into the Rose Garden to watch the president conduct his first press conference since Alabama's "Bloody Sunday." As over one thousand civil rights enthusiasts marched outside the White House fence, Johnson explained to reporters and a national television audience how heartfelt his reaction had been to the events of the past week. The nation had witnessed, he said, "a very deep and painful challenge to the unending search for American freedom." The original march had "attempted peacefully to protest the denial of the most basic political right of all—the right to vote." In return, the demonstrators "were attacked and some were brutally beaten." Those events highlighted "a deep and very unjust flaw in American democracy. . . . Ninety-five years ago our Constitution was amended to require that no American be denied the right to vote because of race or color. Almost a century later, many Americans are kept from voting simply because they are Negroes." On Monday Johnson's voting rights proposal would go to Congress, where he hoped it would win speedy passage. The president emphasized the importance of Selma:

What happened in Selma was an American tragedy. The blows that were received, the blood that was shed, the life of the good man that was lost, must strengthen the determination of each of us to bring full and equal and exact justice to all of our people.

This is not just the policy of your government or your President. It is in the heart and the purpose and the meaning of America itself.

We all know how complex and how difficult it is to bring about basic social change in a democracy, but this complexity must not obscure the clear and simple moral issues.

It is wrong to do violence to peaceful citizens in the streets of their town. It is wrong to deny Americans the right to vote. It is wrong to deny any person full equality because of the color of his skin.

Johnson concluded by saying he had advised Governor Wallace to do three things: declare his support for universal suffrage; assure the right of peaceful assembly in Alabama; and hold biracial meetings with his state's citizens. Wallace had no comments, and after Johnson was finished, Attorney General Katzenbach briefed the reporters on the final draft of the voting rights bill, which had been completed only hours earlier.[49]

Martin King, buoyed by Johnson's remarks but depressed by the movement's internal tensions, returned to Atlanta Saturday before flying to Chicago for a speech. On Sunday evening Lyndon Johnson phoned King to invite him to the voting rights address that he, Johnson, and the congressional leadership had agreed he would deliver to a nationally televised joint session of Congress on Monday night. King thanked him for the courtesy but declined, since he had to be back in Selma Monday to preach at a memorial service for James Reeb. The service was held on the steps of the Dallas County courthouse. It was the first time in six days that movement supporters had been allowed to protest outside the Brown Chapel neighborhood, or that Martin King had appeared publicly in Selma. More than two thousand marchers made their way to the pale green building, where King, flanked by church leaders, union presidents, and U.S. congressmen, presided over a twenty-minute service. King spoke to the crowd about "the agonizing loneliness that characterizes the life of the pioneer," the same theme he had sounded in Chicago, where he had told an audience that "you can never know the agonies and the lonely moments of leadership."

Monday evening a nationwide television audience of seventy million people watched Lyndon Johnson give his address. The memorable speech marked the first time in nineteen years that an American president had personally presented a special message to Congress on a domestic issue. Johnson reviewed the events in Selma, noting that the protests and their violent reception sprang from the long history of black disfranchisement in the South. "It is wrong—deadly wrong," he said, "to deny any of your fellow Americans the right to vote in this country." The Congress should approve the administration's new bill with no delay and no hesitation because "outside this chamber is the outraged conscience of a nation." Johnson endorsed the Selma demonstrations, saying that the black American's "actions and protests, his courage to risk safety and even to risk his life, have awakened the conscience of this nation." Selma, he said, was a milestone in the nation's development comparable to Lexington, Concord, and Appomattox, one of those events where "history and fate meet at a single time in a single place to shape a turning point in man's unending search for freedom." Then, Lyndon Johnson uttered the movement's slogan, vowing that "we shall overcome" America's "crippling legacy of bigotry and injustice." Listening to the president's repeated invocation of that hallowed phrase as he watched in the Jacksons' living room, Martin King was overcome by emotion. His colleagues and friends had never seen him cry before. "Tears actually came to Dr. King's eyes when President Johnson said, 'We shall overcome,'" John Lewis remembered. Never before, in nine years time, had the movement received the breadth of national support, and the strength of federal endorsement, that this week had witnessed. It was an emotional peak unmatched by anything that had come before, nor by anything that would come later.[50]

On Tuesday Judge Johnson's hearing concluded with the SCLC attorneys submitting a detailed plan outlining the proposed march to Montgomery. The day's quiet was shattered, however, when a group of Montgomery County sheriff's deputies suddenly attacked a group of SNCC protesters near the Alabama state capitol. Most of the attackers were on horseback and armed with nightsticks, canes, or whips, and the assault was brutal, as one newsman described it:

> A posseman dressed in green clothes and a white 10-gallon hat stepped up on foot and, while the horses partly hid him from view, began clubbing the demonstrators. Several still refused to move, and the man's nightstick began falling with great force on their heads.
>
> There was a moment of freakish near-quiet, when the yells all seemed to subside at once, and in that instant the man in green struck hard on the head of a young man. The sound of the nightstick carried up and down the block.

It seemed like Selma's "Bloody Sunday" all over again, and some of the protesters called out hysterically to the press contingent witnessing the scene. "'They're killing them. They're killing them,' a voice kept crying. 'There, you photographers, get pictures of them killing them.'"

In time the demonstrators retreated to the safety of black churches, but the response to the violence, locally and nationally, was outrage. Denunciations were issued from Washington, and in Montgomery the attack sent SNCC's leader into new paroxysms of anger. The days since their departure from Selma had been marked by repeated shouting matches with SCLC's Jim Bevel, and prior to Tuesday's assault, "We were perhaps more furious with Bevel than with the police," James Forman remembered. SNCC was also angry at the lay leaders of King's former church, Dexter Avenue Baptist, who had vetoed SNCC's use of their building as a headquarters. King tried unsuccessfully to mediate, but the lawmen's attack drove James Forman to a heightened fury. That night, at a mass meeting at Beulah Baptist Church, Forman told the crowd that if the powers that be were unwilling to let his people sit at the table of government, then SNCC stood ready to knock the "fucking legs" right off the table. A chagrined Martin King, fully aware that a decade's worth of community church rallies offered no precedent for Forman's language, sat silently through the choleric remarks before rising to make a long address that ignored Forman's outburst. The next day King led a march to the Montgomery County courthouse, where Sheriff Mac Sim Butler publicly apologized for the violence, but this did not alleviate King's concern about SNCC. He expressed his fears by phone to Bayard Rustin and Harry Wachtel, telling them he was worried that SNCC was growing violent and might stage objectionable disruptions in the Alabama capital. Forman was advocating "violent overthrow of the government," and King said he feared SNCC was seeking a martyr in Montgomery. Rustin said that sooner or later King and SCLC would have to divorce themselves from SNCC.[51]

Wednesday afternoon Judge Johnson handed down his decision on SCLC's proposal to march from Selma to Montgomery. He reviewed the tawdry record of both state and Dallas County law enforcement authorities over the preceding two months. Citing the gripping testimony that had been offered by numerous movement witnesses, Johnson concluded that "the evidence in this case reflects that . . . an almost continuous pattern of conduct has existed on the part of defendant Sheriff Clark, his deputies, and his auxiliary deputies known as 'possemen' of harassment, intimidation, coercion, threatening conduct, and, sometimes, brutal mistreatment toward these plaintiffs." The lawmen had acted not to enforce valid laws, but simply to prevent Alabama blacks "from exercising their rights of citizenship, particularly the right to register to vote and the right to demonstrate peaceably for the purpose of protesting discriminatory practices." Then, Johnson made his central finding:

It seems basic to our constitutional principles that the extent of the right to assemble, demonstrate and march peaceably along the highways and streets in an orderly manner should be commensurate with the enormity of the wrongs that are being protested and petitioned against. In this case, the wrongs are enormous. The extent of the right to demonstrate against these wrongs should be determined accordingly.

Hence, Johnson approved SCLC's proposal. It called for a maximum of three hundred marchers on the two-lane segments of Highway 80 and an unlimited number on the four-lane sections closer to Selma and Montgomery. Although state authorities claimed that any march would obstruct traffic, Judge Johnson termed the plan "reasonable" in light of "the wrongs and injustices inflicted upon these plaintiffs" in the past. SCLC spelled out how support services for the trek, and evening camp grounds for the five-day affair, were already lined up, and Johnson enjoined Alabama officials from failing to assist the procession. The federal government would provide whatever aid Governor Wallace might request to protect the marchers.

SCLC, pleased by Judge Johnson's decision, announced that the march would begin on Sunday, March 21, and began dealing with a myriad of details. Food, toilets, sleeping bags, and other camping equipment had to be provided. Movement leaders also faced the sensitive task of selecting the three hundred marchers who would walk the entire route. George Wallace greeted the judge's decision by going on statewide television to denounce Judge Johnson's "mock court" and to claim that Alabama had insufficient personnel to protect the marchers. He telegraphed the president to request that "federal civil authorities" guard the procession, but Lyndon Johnson responded that too few U.S. marshals were available and suggested that Wallace call up the Alabama National Guard. On Friday, after appeals to postpone the march were rejected by both Judge Johnson and the Fifth Circuit Court of Appeals, Wallace informed the president that Alabama could not afford to call the Guard into state service. Early the next morning President Johnson signed an executive order placing 1,800 Alabama guardsmen in federal service and named Deputy Attorney General Ramsey Clark to coordinate the march.[52]

Fast-paced congressional hearings on the administration's voting rights bill had gotten under way Thursday in the House of Representatives. Attorney General Katzenbach presented the proposal to Emanuel Celler's judiciary committee, explaining that the key element was a "trigger formula" that would suspend all literacy tests and similar registration devices in all areas in which less than 50 percent of the adult population had turned out to vote in the 1964 presidential election. Those jurisdictions would also be barred from instituting any new voter qualifications, and the executive branch could assign federal registrars to those counties without having to obtain prior judicial authorization. Although several Republicans complained that the "trigger formula" would not allow for direct federal action in areas where discrimination persisted despite a voter turnout greater than 50 percent, Democratic spokesmen pointed out that those locales could be tackled under the county-by-county court suits authorized by the 1957, 1960, and 1964 Civil Rights Acts. Some civil rights supporters were troubled by the bill's failure to include a statutory ban on state poll taxes or a provision penalizing intimidation of prospective voters, but discussions about pushing for such amendments were not aired publicly.[53]

Early Sunday afternoon King and a host of national dignitaries took the lead as more than three thousand marchers set out from Brown Chapel and filed across the Pettus Bridge. Scores of cameramen and hundreds of uniformed National Guardsmen looked on. Freedom songs rang out as the procession passed the site of Bloody Sunday and the Tuesday turnaround. By nightfall the marchers had covered seven miles and arrived at their first campsite, where the core group of three hundred bedded down while the remainder were bused back to Selma. After spending the night under two large tents and being treated to meals that were cooked in Selma and trucked out to the campsite, the marchers resumed the trek the next morning. Tight security protected the participants while they slept and as they marched, with teams of guardsmen ensuring that no armed segregationists lay in wait as they made their way toward Montgomery on the narrow, two-lane segment of Highway 80 that ran through rural Lowndes County. Large trees heavy with Spanish moss hugged the roadside, lending an air of foreboding to the procession and causing the marchers to hurry along the sixteen miles they had to cover to reach Monday night's campsite. On Tuesday they walked eleven miles in heavy rain that made their next campground a muddy resting place.

Martin King walked most of those miles on the first three days of the march, joining in the songs and chatting with fellow marchers while federal officials and SCLC aides saw to the procession's administrative needs. A mobile home furnished King somewhat fancier resting quarters than the other participants. King appeared "terribly tired" to some of his compatriots, one of whom was struck by how King had "a kind of detachment." "He seemed to kind of have his mind on something else all the time." He "wasn't anything like a leader in the sense of communicating with people with any freedom," a surprised Pittsburgh theologian remembered. "He seemed to be a kind of a symbol, and an inspiring figure, but all the actual organizing and leadership was done by other people in his entourage." King would not have quarreled with that judgment, and by the end of Tuesday's hike his major concern was his badly blistered feet, a condition other marchers were also suffering. Wednesday morning King rested as the others set out on a sixteen-mile walk that would bring them to the western outskirts of Montgomery. At midday he flew to Cleveland for a fund-raising rally. Reporters noted that he "looked tired," and King told his audience he would be returning to Alabama late that night for Thursday's final march into Montgomery.[54]

Wednesday night the marchers were treated to an outdoor stage show by visiting entertainers at the procession's final campground. Then, on Thursday morning, with an exhausted Martin King in the front rank, the huge column, its numbers swelled by thousands of local supporters and thousands of newly arrived out-of-state sympathizers, marched through Montgomery's westside residential neighborhoods into the center of the city and up the gentle slope of Dexter Avenue to the Alabama state capitol. Coretta, Ralph and Juanita Abernathy, and a host of dignitaries joined King in leading the column up the avenue, past the red brick church he had once pastored, and into the plaza that lay between that little church and Alabama's pure white capitol building. Only five years had passed since King had left Montgomery, but this magnificently triumphant homecoming seemed to suggest that most of a lifetime, and perhaps most of an age, had swept past in a small handful of years.

Thousands of people—25,000, the best estimate said—most of them black, crowded into every available space within sight of the platform on the state capitol steps. The scene suggested that perhaps Alabama and America had changed in some very basic way since King had seen his vision in the kitchen nine years earlier. The old parsonage on South Jackson Street was two blocks away, and the crowd was filled with faces of old friends. This remarkable homecoming filled King with a profound sense of how much had happened in so brief a time and at a speed that, upon reflection, seemed breathtaking.

As the back of the crowd moved up Dexter Avenue toward the platform, guest speakers told the marchers that they had reached their long-sought goal, the Alabama state capitol, despite all of George Wallace's, Al Lingo's, and Jim Clark's efforts to stop them. Then, at the rally's climax, King delivered one of his most memorable speeches. The response to Selma's "Bloody Sunday," he said, had been "a shining moment in the conscience of man" and heralded the fact that "we are on the move now" to "the land of freedom." A "season of suffering" still lay ahead, but eventually "a society at peace with itself, a society that can live with its conscience," would be won. "How long will it take?" King asked. "However difficult the moment, however frustrating the hour, it will not be long." He repeated the question "How long?" and his answer, "Not long," building to a rousing climax that drew a thundering ovation from the thousands of listeners. Nervous Justice Department officials, fearful of an attempt on King's life, looked on with a sense of relief as the rally concluded.[55]

King was tired but in a good mood as he and Coretta flew home to Atlanta early that evening. His happiness was short-lived, as he learned that tragedy had again struck in Alabama. A white housewife from Detroit, Viola Gregg Liuzzo, who had come to Selma in support of the movement, had been shot and killed by a carload of Klan night riders as she and a young black SCLC volunteer were driving through Lowndes County on their way to Montgomery to help ferry the marchers back to Selma. Her colleague survived uninjured, and word of her death spread quickly, bringing fear to movement activists. The shooting was a brutal reminder that the true reality of Alabama was not King's melodious phrases but racist violence delivered without warning. It was a chilling confirmation that King had been right about a "season of suffering" that still lay ahead, that successful completion of the trek to Montgomery did not mean the larger struggle had been won or that triumph was close at hand.

At midday Friday President Johnson, flanked by Attorney General Katzenbach and FBI Director Hoover, went on national television to announce that four suspects in the Liuzzo murder had been taken into custody. Though no mention was made of the fact, one of the four Klansmen in the car that had overtaken Liuzzo on that deserted stretch of Highway 80 was an FBI informant, Gary Thomas Rowe. Rowe had notified his control agent of the shooting incident hours after it occurred, and the Bureau took him and his three Klan companions into custody without revealing his special status. President Johnson promised that the defendants would be vigorously prosecuted and vowed that the Ku Klux Klan would be eliminated from American society. Martin King was impressed by the fast action, and sent a congratulatory telegram to Director Hoover.[56]

Resting in Atlanta, King felt angry at Alabama over the Liuzzo murder. The Alabama campaign was not intended to end with the Selma-to-Montgomery march, and King discussed a further expansion with his aides. Andrew Young had announced that SCLC would pursue voter registration in the rural counties surrounding Selma. King recommended that SCLC also press ahead with an idea that had been discussed for application to Mississippi rather than Alabama: a nationwide economic boycott of all the state's products. Eric and Ann Kindberg had done enough research on Alabama's economy to suggest that a boycott would hit the state's segregationist leaders where it could hurt them the most, in their wallets, and might be the most realistic way to force Alabama's business leaders to insist upon substantial changes in their state government's racial stance. King had focused on the idea the night of Liuzzo's murder, and now he proposed to announce this new plan during an appearance on Sunday's *Meet the Press* in San Francisco. The SCLC staffers and New York advisors Wachtel and Rustin agreed. King expected tough questions about the increasingly visible differences between SNCC and SCLC, but this prominent national news show would be perfect for proclaiming that SCLC's nonviolent assault on Alabama had not peaked and that now it would be intensified.

On Saturday an exhausted King flew to San Francisco for a long-scheduled Sunday preaching engagement. During the flight, he mulled over how to handle the questions that would likely confront him at the *Meet the Press* appearance following his sermon. On Sunday morning King spoke to several thousand worshipers at Grace Cathedral before sitting down with the television panel. Voting rights demonstrations in Alabama would continue, he proclaimed, because "we have a moral obligation to keep these issues before the public, before the American conscience . . . so that somebody will do something about it." All obstacles to the right to vote had to be eliminated, and police brutality had to end, before SCLC's campaign was complete, King said. Then he announced SCLC's Alabama boycott. This effort, King asserted, would force businessmen and people of good conscience in Alabama to demand that Governor Wallace halt the state's "reign of terror." SCLC would ask unions to refuse to transport any Alabama goods, would request the U.S. Treasury to withdraw all federal funds from Alabama banks, and would try to halt the flow of all federal program monies into the state. "It is necessary for the nation to rise up and engage in a massive economic withdrawal program" and "an economic boycott of Alabama products" if the movement's goals were to be attained, King insisted. After the show he said the boycott would be discussed at SCLC's upcoming board meeting in Baltimore.[57]

King's proposal received a hostile reception from national news commentators and some civil rights leaders. *The New York Times* attacked it in an editorial, and Johnson administration spokesmen declared it would receive no support from them. New York Republican Senator Jacob Javits decried it, and the National Urban League's Whitney Young publicly stated his opposition. On March 30, King met in New York with his research committee advisors, who strongly counseled him that SCLC should back off from a plan that many observers thought would harm all

Alabamians, black and white, and not just economic power brokers. Bayard Rustin termed the idea "stupid," but King stuck to his guns. He told newsmen that SCLC's board would consider the details, and that the boycott might be selective and implemented in stages rather than all at once.

Although the boycott controversy was the hottest topic of conversation as SCLC leaders gathered at the Lord Baltimore Hotel on March 31, King also had other plans he wanted to put before his colleagues. Harry Boyte and Randolph Blackwell had prepared a new program, "Operation Dialogue," which Boyte believed could produce racial progress by establishing small interracial discussion groups in communities across the South. Hosea Williams proposed launching an expanded version of Mississippi's 1964 Freedom Summer all across the South, a "Summer Community Organization and Political Education" program, or SCOPE, which would bring hundreds of northern volunteers south to work with the SCLC field staff. Most important, King wanted board approval to make exploratory soundings in northern cities about extending the organization's activities nationwide. Ever since receiving the Nobel Prize, King had thought "more and more about what I consider as mankind's second great evil" besides racism, poverty. "I realize I must more and more extend my work beyond the borders of the South," King said, and "become involved to a much greater extent with the problems of the urban North."[58]

While King addressed a thousand-person banquet his first night in town, Jim Bevel created more controversy over the boycott. Asked by newsmen to comment on Whitney Young's opposition, Bevel called the Urban League director a "Mickey Mouse Negro" with "a $50 hat on a $2 head." The board meetings began on April 1, and King directed the members' attention to the staff proposals. Andrew Young spoke about how the movement had to offer hope to black citizens trapped in northern ghettos, and recommended that SCLC adopt a "new direction" that would take it into cities such as New York, Philadelphia, Baltimore, Chicago, Los Angeles, and Detroit. After several objections, the board grudgingly approved a resolution declaring that while "SCLC will continue to devote most of its energies to the fight against injustice in the South . . . many so-called Southern problems are national and require a national solution. Therefore, . . . SCLC will respond in an ever-increasing way to demands from Northern communities to provide assistance." Then Bayard Rustin asked the board to endorse an increase in the federal minimum wage to $2, a public-works jobs program, and national health insurance. They approved those declarations in language that underlined SCLC's increased interest in "the fundamental economic, political and social problems of full employment, decent housing and quality education."

Then Boyte presented "Operation Dialogue," an approach to "group conversation" which he believed should concentrate on "the poorer white communities" in racially polarized towns. Dialogue appealed to King's belief that racial fears were rooted in human ignorance. If individuals of different races could get to know each other as real human beings, through Dialogue's small discussion groups, much racial hostility might be eliminated. Two social activists with experience in the technique, Rachel Davis DuBois and Mew Soong Li, had joined SCLC's staff to assist Boyte, and several noted academicians—Margaret Mead and Gordon Allport, plus writer Ralph Ellison—met with King in early February to evaluate Dialogue's usefulness. Some SCLC insiders were perplexed as to the program's value, but everyone saw it as a constructive venture for Boyte, who seemed increasingly out of place as the SCLC office manager. Although his efforts to lend administrative efficiency and a businesslike decorum to the Atlanta headquarters were well-intentioned, "it just wasn't SCLC," one sympathetic staff member later explained, and "it didn't work." Boyte had "retreated into the woodwork," exuding a painful sense of white racial guilt. Dialogue was a potentially useful way to use his energies.

Hosea Williams's SCOPE proposal was a larger and bolder endeavor. It envisioned sending teams of SCLC staff workers—mainly northern white summer volunteers—into as many as 120 rural southern counties and ten major southeastern cities. Williams proposed recruiting five hundred volunteers and assigning them to locales where black voter registration stood far short of its potential. If the voting rights bill became law by midsummer, as some observers predicted, SCLC's troops would be in a position to take advantage of the federal registrars authorized by the legislation. Aside from registration, Williams said, the workers could also help local citizens with community organizing, which would be a valuable expansion of the long-standing citizenship education program that Dorothy Cotton and Septima Clark were still overseeing. Letters seeking summer applicants from leading colleges had already been dispatched, and both King and Rustin enthusiastically endorsed the proposal after Williams outlined it. Privately some staff members noted that the plan would transfer control of SCLC's Deep South field staff from the mercurial Bevel to the explosive Williams, but no board members raised any objections and the program won easy approval.

That night King addressed a heavily guarded rally at Baltimore's Cornerstone Baptist Church. A large crowd turned out, and King told them that SCLC would no longer be an exclusively southern organization. "I know that we will have to take the nonviolent movement all over the United States."[59]

When SCLC's board resumed its discussions on Friday, King brought up an awkward subject. SCLC, he said, needed to prepare for an orderly presidential succession should he be killed. The bylaws should be amended to provide for the automatic installation of a designated successor, Ralph Abernathy. His declaration struck some as morbid, and a few gentle remonstrances were offered, but no one quarreled openly with his desire to designate Abernathy as his heir. In private, however, many colleagues were deeply displeased. "It was a lot of emotions in that meeting," longtime Vice-President C. K. Steele later indicated. Steele was upset because King had said nothing to him ahead of time about Abernathy's designation. "I went to his room afterwards and jumped on him about it. He apologized and said that he should have said something to me about it. He said some other things that I would not dare go into and haven't."

Also unhappy was Daddy King, who spread the word that Abernathy had pressured M.L. to announce the designation. Ever since the Nobel Prize, Abernathy had continued to lobby for more perquisites akin to King's. "I think Martin, out of his love for Ralph, that Ralph almost forced him into putting him in this position," Coretta subsequently told Levison. He agreed. "Martin found himself unable to give Ralph a piece of the Nobel Prize which Ralph was demanding, so therefore he had to promise him he could be his heir. Otherwise Ralph would have gone berserk with envy." Levison and others regretted "what a burden Ralph was to Martin," but Coretta understood why her husband valued Abernathy's companionship so highly. "Martin . . . realized there were few people he could rely on." Coretta and Levison were not alone in believing that Abernathy subtly but successfully took advantage of King's feeling that only happenstance ten years earlier had put King rather than Abernathy in the top role. Nonetheless, the private unhappiness did not stop the board from endorsing Abernathy's designation.

Daddy King, always an active board member, then took up a related issue, his son's lack of life insurance, and "made an impassioned plea for some type of security for his four grandchildren." His son received only a modest salary and few benefits from his co-pastorship at Ebenezer, and the least SCLC could do, Daddy King said, was to pay the premium on M.L.'s church-sanctioned life insurance policy. Eager to put the entire subject behind them, the board quickly approved the senior King's request.

Then King raised the subject that had been on everyone's mind: the Alabama boycott. Despite the many condemnations of it, King said, an economic boycott was necessary to force Alabama's white moderates to take constructive action. He explained that he appreciated hearing the objections but said the boycott proposal was more refined than critics believed. It would be implemented in three stages. First, SCLC would ask that no companies locate new plants in Alabama and that the Johnson administration vigorously enforce the provisions of the 1964 Civil Rights Act that called for no federal financial support of discriminatory enterprises. That call would be issued immediately, and if Alabama did not make improvements, SCLC would follow up with two more intense stages: First, a request that private organizations and federal authorities withdraw all funds and investments from the state; and, second, a nationwide call for civil rights supporters to boycott all Alabama products. SCLC's administrative committee would determine if and when those further steps were necessary. The board approved this format and the meeting concluded. Newsmen greeted King's announcement of the refined plan with suggestions that he had "watered down" the boycott, but he vigorously contested that interpretation. "If there's any softening it's only to give Alabama a chance for the decent people and moderates to rise up," King asserted. "The whole purpose is to arouse a sense of concern within what I call the people of good will so that they will rise up and bring an end to the reign of terror" by toppling the "racist oligarchy" that held Alabama in a tight grip of "poverty, ignorance, race hatred and sadism." As King's strong rhetoric since the Liuzzo murder clearly indicated, and as one newsman noted after the Baltimore meetings, "The movement seems to have taken on a new militancy that was not apparent in previous campaigns led by Dr. King."[60]

In the days after the Baltimore gathering King's advisors pressed him to get more rest, to back off from the boycott, and to think critically about his vague program for moving SCLC into northern cities. Rustin had contended at the board meeting that the boycott could cost King much of the active white middle-class support that Selma had produced, and in a subsequent discussion in New York, Stanley Levison voiced the same concern. King nodded as he listened to his friend's advice, and to warnings that SCOPE would spread SCLC's resources too thinly across the South, but, tired as he was, he would not retract the boycott plan. "This boycott is no different from other boycotts—the bus boycott in Montgomery, the boycott in Birmingham," he told one reporter. Perhaps some timid supporters would be offended by the plan, but "I don't think in a social revolution you can always retain support of the moderates." Such a depletion was probably both inevitable and necessary, King mused, because "I don't think that a person who is truly committed is ever alienated completely by tactics." The movement's ranks had swollen greatly after Selma, but that did not mean that strategy and tactics should change to accommodate these newcomers.

Despite King's insistence on the boycott, Stanley Levison was convinced that his old friend did not appreciate how great a sea change Selma had wrought in the movement's world. Criticism of the boycott, he explained in a long letter, was only one by-product of a substantially altered situation to which King had to give careful thought. "Selma was bigger than Birmingham, though it was smaller in scope, because for the first time whites and Negroes from all over the nation physically joined the struggle in a pilgrimage to the deep south. This was a new level of commitment because it entailed danger and continuity. But more important, the elements who responded were for the first time a true cross-section of America," a much broader coalition of support for the movement than ever before. Such a development presented King with both opportunities and dangers, Levison counseled. "*Selma and Montgomery made you one of the most powerful figures in the country—a leader now not merely of Negroes, but of millions of whites.*" The civil rights movement was "one of the rare *independent* movements" America had seen, "and you are one of the exceptional figures who attained the heights of popular confidence and trust without having obligations to any political party or other dominant interests. Seldom has anyone in American history come up by this path, fully retaining his independence and freedom of action." That position was all the more influential, Levison told King, because "the movement you lead is the single movement in the nation at this time which arouses the finer democratic instincts of the nation." While "there is a sense of shame people feel over the rampant greed and materialism surrounding us," and while "doubt and concern trouble millions about our actions in Viet Nam," King and the movement are "the great moral force in the country today. . . . You symbolize courage, effectiveness, singleness of will, honesty and idealism. You are free of the taint of political ambition, wealth, power or the pursuit of vanity. Your image has more purity than any American has attained in decades."

Several factors complicated the situation, Levison warned. One was the dynamics of the Selma protests:

> Nonviolent direct action was proven by Selma to have even greater power than anyone had fully realized. We would be at fault if we believed our own propaganda that Selma was a terrible expression of brutality and terrorism. Considerable restraint was exercised by the authorities. The degree of violence was shocking and startling, but not excessive. Few were injured seriously in the "bloody events of Sunday." The murders of Jackson and Reeb were not the direct work of the authorities but of the extremist fringe of hoodlums [sic]. The bombings in Birmingham and the deliberate and continuous violence of Connor there were far worse. Yet Selma provoked a far greater indignation and resolution to halt the injustice. How is this explained?

Levison was not certain, for he had not studied the crucial differences between how the Birmingham and Selma protests had been presented to the nation by the news media. A more pressing puzzle, however, was why this "far greater indignation" had been followed by such a negative response to the boycott. The answer, Levison told King, is that "whenever one attains a commanding position of power he also evokes fear." Additionally, "There are some who fear you are hitting at sacred structures of economic interests when you embrace the weapon of boycott." Those negative reactions had been reinforced by King's "casual manner" in announcing the plan and by his failure to state a clear rationale for the boycott. "It was not the best selection of alternatives for action, and it was not logical to emerge from a struggle for voting rights." The SCOPE effort, if SCLC could organize it properly, would be a far more attractive venture.

Additionally, King had to appreciate the limits of the popular support generated by Selma. "The coalition of Selma and Montgomery, with its supporting millions," Levison warned, is not a coalition with an unrestricted program. It is a coalition around a fairly narrow objective. . . . It is basically a coalition for moderate change, for gradual improvements which are to be attained without excessive upheavals as it gently alters old patterns. *It is militant only against shocking violence and gross injustice.* It is not for deep radical change,

as the response to the boycott showed. "When you sought to use a weapon of swift and crushing power, some elements of the coalition would inevitably split away." That lesson was especially important in light of Rustin's insistence that a "majority liberal consensus" that would support far-reaching economic reforms was already at hand if only the movement would "expand its vision beyond race relations to economic relations" and join forces with other liberal interests, such as organized labor, to pursue that broader agenda. Rustin's belief that a March on Washington-style coalition would support "a radical program" to "alter the social structure of America" was hopelessly naïve, Levison told King. "America today is not ready for a radical restructuring of its economy and social order. Not even the appeal of equality will weld all into one fighting unit around a program that disturbs their essentially moderate tendencies." Civil rights forces had to appreciate those clear limits on achievable goals, for "the movement can head into a cul-de-sac if it can see no real progress without radical alteration of the nation." The challenge, Levison said, would be to achieve those "great changes" that "may well be possible within the limits of the basic system we now have." King might think the movement was "revolutionary" within the southern context, but "in the north this movement is not revolutionary. It is a reform movement not unlike the essentially reform movement of the trade unions in the thirties," and would have to be seen as such by potential supporters in the North, Levison emphasized. Only if King and the movement did not overreach their grasp could the opportunities that lay ahead be exploited fully:

It is certainly poor tactics to present to the nation a prospect of choosing between equality and freedom for Negroes with the revolutionary alteration of our society, or to maintain the status quo with discrimination. The American people are not inclined to change their society in order to free the Negro. They are ready to undertake some, and perhaps major, reforms, but not to make a revolution.

King would do well to keep that in mind when considering initiatives such as the Alabama boycott plan.[61]

As King pondered Levison's message, a new series of SCLC problems confronted him. James Bevel, displeased with the emphasis being given Hosea Williams's SCOPE plans, turned his attention to SCLC's northern possibilities. He told a fund-raising rally at Northwestern University in Illinois that SCLC would launch a campaign to "break up ghetto life" in nearby Chicago as soon as the Alabama voting rights effort was complete, and that race discrimination in housing would be a major focus. Back in Alabama, SCLC's field staff's endeavors were undersupervised and unfocused, and the new generation of Montgomery Improvement Association (MIA) leaders notified King that they did not want any relationship with the SCLC workers headquartered in their city. Two stolen MIA checks had been found in the possession of an SCLC staff member, and interorganizational relations were "at an all time low," MIA President Rev. Jesse Douglas told King. "The morale is extremely bad and conduct of the clientele drawn in is beneath that of decency." If SCLC wanted to continue operating in King's old hometown, more responsible staffers should be sent in.

By the second week of April, King was still exhausted and depressed. A number of public engagements were canceled as he took to bed to rest. Several days later Bernard Lee accompanied him on a trip to Miami and Nassau, to seek greater privacy and seclusion. His closest friends were deeply worried about this new bout of mental and physical fatigue. They spoke with concern about a medical diagnosis that his intense depression stemmed from exhaustion. Rest and relaxation were the best cure, and they knew that it was not the first time he had been caught in the throes of such an illness and suffered a breakdown. A respite from his demanding schedule had helped King recover before, and the quiet days in Miami and Nassau were exactly what he needed. On April 17 he returned to Atlanta in far better condition.[62]

Upon his return, King had to confront another problem that had long weighed on his mind. For years Coretta had suggested that they leave their aging rented home on Johnson Avenue and buy a larger house better suited for raising four young children, but King had resisted. For one, as Coretta later explained it, "he was reluctant in the first place to own a house. He didn't want to own a house because he felt that this would set him apart," and "felt it was inconsistent with his philosophy" and his strong doubts about America's celebration of private property. He had "strong feelings about owning a lot of property or acquiring a lot of wealth," and brushed off his wife's frequent reminders that the family deserved a better abode. "Martin always had a revulsion for the idea of owning a fine house in an exclusive neighborhood," Coretta said, and "for a long time he made no move to improve our housing situation." Eventually, early in 1965, she was able to convince him to purchase, for the modest sum of $10,000, a brick home on Sunset Avenue in southwest Atlanta and to authorize some renovations. Still hesitant, King agreed to go ahead. After all, it was not a fancy structure, and the neighborhood in which it was located was certainly a "common folks" area. The renovations, however, seemed to entail more than King had envisioned. "When it was completed," Coretta recalled, "my husband said he did not realize the house was going to be quite that nice. He wasn't sure that he needed such a nice house." King spoke to several of his friends about the new home. "The house troubled him greatly," Stanley Levison remembered. "When he moved from a very small house to one that was large enough to give the growing family some room, he was troubled by it and would ask all of his close friends when they came to the house whether they didn't think it was too big and it wasn't right for him to have. And though everyone tried to tell him that this big house wasn't as big as he thought it was—it was a very modest little house—to him it loomed as a mansion and he searched in his own mind for ways of making it smaller." By the time he returned from the Bahamas, the family's move was complete, and King began to accept his new home. Unbeknownst to him, moving to the Sunset Avenue house brought an end to the wiretap that the FBI had placed on his home phone eighteen months earlier, a wiretap the Bureau did not bother reinstalling at the new abode.[63]

Back at SCLC, King had to deal with the uncertainty about the Alabama boycott. Federal Community Relations Service (CRS) officials approached Andrew Young to ask that SCLC meet privately with several Alabama business leaders before implementing the boycott plans, but Young told the CRS people at an April 16 session that the businessmen would have "to use their power to speak out for equal opportunity in every area of life" before SCLC would change its plans. King visited Selma and two outlying towns to check recent developments, and found that an atmosphere of fear and intimidation was still palpable despite weekly meetings between Mayor Smitherman and local black leaders. Young worried that further acts of racist terrorism were likely, and King returned to Atlanta to tell both SCLC and SNCC staffers that the boycott plans would remain on track.

King's first exploration of a test site for SCLC's northern aspirations occurred during a mid-April tour of Boston. He stopped in New York to consult with his advisors and to attend a small fund-raiser that Marian Logan, a new and influential member of SCLC's board, had put together. He also spoke to the New York City Bar Association, telling the audience of 1,500 lawyers that discrimination in employment, housing, and education was pervasive in the North despite the absence of explicitly racist laws. Nonviolent civil disobedience would be an appropriate tactic for combating those practices, King said, as long as activists remembered that their "goals must be clearly stated." The following morning he expressed similar sentiments in a meeting with Massachusetts Governor John Volpe and an address to the state legislature, in which he stressed that "strong legislation to end discrimination in housing" was a pressing national need. He toured Boston's Roxbury ghetto, where he denounced the city's segregated schools and warned city politicians that Boston was a likely target for a voter registration campaign that summer. Reporters listening to King's comments, which included a statement that the United States ought to end the Vietnam War, asked if he had any special memories of the city where he had attended graduate school. Yes, he did, King said, bringing their attention back to housing discrimination. "I remember very well trying to find a place to live" upon arrival in the fall of 1951. "I went into place after place where there were signs that rooms were for rent. They were for rent until they found out I was a Negro and suddenly they had just been rented." Like the incident in the New Jersey restaurant during his time at Crozer, the search for an apartment had been a painful lesson that being black in the North was oftentimes no different from being black in the South.[64]

From Boston, King flew west for speaking engagements in Los Angeles and Iowa. The California visit allowed him to rendezvous with a lady friend from Chicago, and also offered an opportunity to spend some time with a young magazine writer. In Iowa, one reporter asked King if he was getting pudgy, and King nodded yes. "Too many banquets" were the bane of his existence. "Eating's my big sin," King told the newsman.

While King was traveling, the Johnson voting rights bill moved through the Senate Judiciary Committee and onto the floor. Both in the Senate and in the House Judiciary Subcommittee markup, a statutory poll tax ban had been added to the legislation, a provision that Justice Department officials contended was of dubious constitutionality. Attorney General Katzenbach sought unsuccessfully by phone to convince King that the movement's insistence upon the poll tax provision might make the act vulnerable to southern challenges in the courts, but King replied that a greater problem was an amendment being pushed by Senate Republican leader Dirksen that would provide an escape hatch from federal coverage for certain southern counties. That threat was eliminated by the end of April, but Senate debate on the bill bogged down as supporters of the legislation sought to resolve the poll tax issue without recourse to a divisive floor vote.

More painful for King were the tensions with SNCC. After Selma many SNCC workers' distaste for King and SCLC had become more pronounced, and a number of news stories aired the complaints. One reporter wrote that part of the problem lay in SNCC's "contempt for bourgeois values," which some staffers thought King exemplified. Another said more accurately that "SNCC despises the 'cult of personality' which has surrounded King, and the leader-worship" that prevailed within SCLC. Some simpletons thought the division was simply a question of militancy, but one acute observer pointed out that in reality, "King's SCLC is no less militant than SNCC. It is, however, less radical in its approach to the problems of society. SCLC is a strategic command; SNCC is an ideological army." Much of the tension was rooted in a basic disagreement about leadership and the best role for movement staffers. "We don't believe in leadership," SNCC's Jim Forman explained to one newsman. "We think the people should lead, but SCLC thinks there should be one leader." SCLC aides contemptuously dismissed many of the SNCC assertions, saying that rhetorical excess did no one any good. Bernard Lee, in an uncharacteristically harsh public comment that reflected SCLC's internal tensions as well as those with SNCC, griped that "both Bevel and Forman don't know the difference between militancy and arrogance." Nonetheless, growing substantive differences did separate the two organizations. "King is concerned with arousing the 'national conscience'; SNCC wants to organize the rural Negroes in the South," one commentator pointed out accurately, and SNCC was concerned about the real impact that SCLC's media-oriented campaigns had upon the black citizens of those chosen towns. Some leaders, a SNCC worker explained, had gotten so caught up in being leaders that they had lost touch with their grass-roots followers and failed to appreciate how campaigns that were national successes could be local failures for the black citizens who had to bear the brunt of the effort. "Many times they are [left] worse off than before the leaders came in. . . . That's Birmingham and St. Augustine and soon, probably Selma." "No one," he declared, "has the right to go into an area to lead people and not allow them to decide in which direction they want to go." People must be encouraged to make their own decisions and generate their own indigenous leadership. No matter what the national payoff, "using people as a means to an end cannot continue."[65]

King and his SCLC colleagues knew they were vulnerable to such criticisms. On Friday, April 30, with Harry Belafonte acting as intermediary, SCLC and SNCC staffers met in Atlanta to thrash out their differences and try to agree upon a joint unity statement that might quell the media's fixation on the movement's incipient split. The lengthy sessions were surprisingly cordial and productive. SNCC's representatives would not agree to SCLC's request that the statement include a declaration that Communists were not welcome in the movement, but they reached a general accord on all other points of discussion. King told newsmen after the meeting that the much-reported split was "not serious" and that the discussions had been arranged in order "to keep a cleavage from developing and getting serious." Press accusations that one or both groups were becoming too extreme were neatly dismissed in the formal statement that King and Forman issued jointly. "The civil rights movement is by its very nature a radical movement which seeks to eliminate an established order of racism and segregation."[66]

Throughout the first half of May, King's schedule was more relaxed than usual. A three-day visit to Philadelphia for several speaking engagements allowed him to evaluate that city as a site for northern SCLC efforts. Most of the questions he faced upon return to Atlanta concerned the muddled Alabama operation. James Bevel insisted that the boycott be pursued at full tilt and that a new round of demonstrations be mounted in the Black Belt. Many staffers were losing interest in the boycott plan, and local black leaders reported bluntly that their troops had little enthusiasm for new protests. Selma's activists were angry about what they regarded as SCLC's withdrawal from their community. Locally, divisions had arisen over both the unproductive discussions with city officials and the poorly administered distribution of essential supplies that SCLC had sent to Selma to aid the scores of black citizens fired from their jobs for participating in the demonstrations. Many local people who had sacrificed greatly for the movement could see no improvements resulting from the protests, and Randolph Blackwell, dispatched from Atlanta to see if black Selma's morale could be improved, reported to King that his offer to send a new SCLC staffer into town to assist the leaders there was met with "something less than enthusiasm."[67]

Alabama matters took a bleaker turn on May 7 when a Lowndes County jury deadlocked and refused to convict Klansman Collie Leroy Wilkins of the Liuzzo murder despite the testimony of eyewitness FBI informer Gary Thomas Rowe. King said that indicated how civil rights murders ought to be made a federal crime, and he undertook a two-day swing through seven rural west Alabama counties to inject new life into SCLC's relatively moribund Black Belt voting rights effort. Speaking to church rallies in small towns such as Eutaw, Greensboro, and Demopolis, he said that when Alabama's all-white legislature convened in Montgomery on May 18, SCLC would have representatives from each of their counties present to demand that the state's black citizens receive their due. "It will start as a good-faith attempt to talk to the people who represent us in the legislature. But if they won't sit down and talk, and negotiate, then we're going to be on the legislative agenda. If it takes presenting our bodies and filling up jails all over Alabama, we are ready to do that." SCLC aides asserted that two thousand demonstrators a day would flood Montgomery if the legislature were not responsive, just as Bevel had outlined in his original blueprint.

Two relatively quiet weeks passed before King returned to Alabama to pursue that declaration. He flew to New York, where an FBI bug in his hotel room overheard Levison telling King, as Rustin had earlier, that he had a responsibility to speak out on issues of war and peace, such as the growing conflagration in Vietnam. King knew the FBI still had an active interest in his personal life, and he worried greatly about a public revelation of the Bureau's embarrassing tapes. He asked a longtime family friend, Chicago's Rev. Archibald J. Carey, Jr., to speak with his friends in the FBI hierarchy. Carey did so, reporting back to King that it would be wise to keep up his public commendations of FBI accomplishments.[68]

In mid-May King traveled with Coretta and Daddy King to Louisville for the formal installation of A.D. King as pastor of the city's largest black church, Zion Baptist. It was his younger brother's third new pulpit in less than four years, and though the visit afforded a pleasant opportunity to see A.D.'s five growing children, King was deeply troubled by the serious problems his brother faced. A.D., unlike M.L., had never devised a strategy for escaping the debilitating struggles with their father that had been a constant fact of life since childhood. M.L. had learned to disagree and go his own way without having to best his father in direct verbal argument, but A.D. had never been able to walk away from the challenges that Daddy King constantly posed. Over the years those struggles had taken an increasing toll on A.D., an energetic but stubborn man who seemed unable to find internal peace because of those deep familial tensions. More and more he had turned to alcohol for escape, and by the time he came to Louisville a pattern had developed. "His problem was too much," a Birmingham colleague who was a longtime family friend recalled. "It was getting worse. He would get in difficulty from one church to another," and "had to move on." Zion Baptist offered him a chance to start over, but only if he could force some basic changes upon himself. M.L. hoped for the best, but knew there were few grounds for optimism.

From Louisville King flew to New York for more public appearances. At one dinner Vice-President Humphrey greeted him with the news that the voting rights bill and its crucial machinery for providing federal registrars ought to become law before the end of June. Certain Senate passage was less than a week away, and easy approval was assured in the House. That would be perfect timing for the SCOPE registration project SCLC would launch during the third week of June. Even though Program Director Randolph Blackwell had serious doubts about Hosea Williams's ability to administer so large a project, Williams's burgeoning staff was predicting great achievements. Humphrey's projection was invigorating news, and despite his fatigue King decided to tackle a difficult issue he had been thinking about for several months. Although Stanley Levison and King remained in touch regularly, Levison was not invited to the research committee meetings because of the repeated federal warnings about his Communist connections. King's grudging tolerance for the supposed exclusion of Levison from his and SCLC's affairs had weakened with the passage of time, and now he told Jones, Wachtel, and Rustin that there was no reason for Levison's continued banishment. Wachtel, whose sense of competition with Levison for King's ear was the subject of open talk among King's friends, recommended caution, but King was insistent. He wanted to schedule a staff and research committee retreat for early June to discuss SCOPE and SCLC's northern options, and he wanted Levison to attend. The edict was accepted, and planning got under way.[69]

On May 24, King returned to Montgomery for SCLC's somewhat delayed "descent" upon the Alabama state legislature. In the weeks that had passed, Jim Bevel had realized that there was little enthusiasm for renewed protests. What initially had been envisioned as the first day of a large-scale sit-in at the state capitol turned out to be a cordial one-time visit to some willing legislators by a modest number of well-attired black constituents. King remained in town for little more than twenty-four hours. His schedule was packed with speaking engagements, including one at the annual convention of A. Philip Randolph's Negro American Labor Council. A week earlier he had alluded to how "the profit system" would become one target of the movement, but before this sympathetic audience, King let down his rhetorical guard much more than usual. "Call it what you may, call it democracy, or call it democratic socialism, but there must be a better distribution of wealth within this country for all of God's children."

The two-day retreat for SCLC staff and advisors at northern Virginia's Airlie House included a comprehensive review of all the organization's programs, but much of the discussion centered on King's and Young's desire that SCLC move into one or more northern cities. Some in attendance, such as Clarence Jones, were opposed to the idea, but a consensus emerged that SCLC explore New York and Chicago. No matter which city was selected, the group agreed, racism in education, in employment, and in housing would be attacked with nonviolent methods.

When the discussions turned to SCLC's other endeavors, Program Director Randolph Blackwell took an active role in criticizing a number of undertakings. His doubts about the SCOPE project were known to all, but with the opening of the Atlanta training sessions for white northern volunteers less than a week away, Blackwell concentrated his warnings on one specific matter: a request from some Wisconsin sociologists that they be allowed to study the project and its youthful recruits. Given the many unknowns and potential problems that the program and its young, inexperienced volunteers might encounter, "we should discourage . . . those who would want to make in-depth inquiries," Blackwell said. "It might just be to our advantage if this information was never collected and recorded." Others sympathized with his concerns, but King said no. The researchers were well intentioned, and good friends in Atlanta vouched for their reliability.

Blackwell also had other serious issues to raise. Affiliates Director C. T. Vivian was promoting a summer tutorial program, "Vision," that would take St. Louis college students to ten Alabama cities to help prepare black high school youngsters for college, but, Blackwell complained, Vivian's interest in the program meant that he was neglecting his duty of maintaining liaison with SCLC's many local affiliates. In places, he said, "there are some cases that are at an explosive stage, and threatening to embarrass us and rupture our relations with the community irreparably." Selma's troubles with distributing foodstuffs was only one case. Alabama's Greene County Civic Organization, a band of local activists in an important black-majority county, had told SCLC its staffers were not welcome there. The other Airlie House discussants tried to alleviate Blackwell's worries, but he told them that SCLC's entire salary structure and personnel policies needed an overhaul. One blatant example, he said, was a young black accountant in the finance office who had been with the organization hardly eight months, but whose $6,000 annual salary placed him high up on a scale that was topped by Blackwell's modest $8,750. "How do we justify paying James Harrison $500 [per month] with his limited experience and total lack of commitment to what the Conference is doing?" Once more, his colleagues soothed Blackwell's feelings, and King promised to authorize the review he wanted.[70]

Hard on the heels of the Airlie House retreat came the SCOPE orientation sessions in Atlanta. Bayard Rustin coordinated several days of addresses to the assembled volunteers, with Ralph Abernathy and Andrew Young discussing the movement's history, and SCOPE staffers Williams, Ben Clarke, and Stoney Cooks describing the summer plans. Williams explained that teams of four to seven volunteers would be sent to fifty rural counties to work on voter registration, community organizing, and political education under the direct supervision of local leaders. Teams would be made up of volunteers from a single college and would be subject to oversight by traveling SCLC field staffers and SCOPE's central administrators. Local details would vary from county to county, and the volunteers would have to remember that they were there to assist, not direct, local citizens. King spoke to them about the importance of their work, stressing that the registration of hundreds of thousands of new black voters across the South would alter fundamentally not just the politics of that region, but those of the entire nation as the South began to send more moderate senators and representatives to Congress. He ranged widely in his remarks, calling for a negotiated settlement and end of U.S. escalation of hostilities in 'Vietnam and warning that America was a "nation suffocating with material corruption." Later King informed newsmen that this program, and not the Alabama boycott, would be SCLC's summer focus. One reporter asked about King's northern intentions; he replied by expressing strong support for the demonstrations that a group of Chicago activists had launched a week earlier against their city's segregated schools and insensitive superintendent. King said he had been invited to participate in those protests, but that it would be sometime later in the summer before he could do so.[71]

In mid-June King flew to Jamaica for a weeklong vacation. He felt drained almost constantly now, and although he had not experienced a profound exhaustion since those extremely dark days in April, he mused to Young and Wachtel about taking a year's leave from SCLC for some rest and reflection. The World Council of Churches had a retreat in Switzerland where a house would be available, but King was hesitant to leave the movement, even temporarily, for such a comfortable setting. He knew that he needed the respite and time for thought that a sabbatical would provide, but such a move would leave SCLC without a leader. His hectic schedule of constant plane trips and speeches brought him little joy, but "if I have to go through this to give the people a symbol, I am resigned to it," King wearily admitted.

In Jamaica he took time out from his vacation to lay a wreath and address a crowd at a Kingston shrine to native son Marcus Garvey, who had had a major impact on American blacks in the 1920s. "Garvey was the first man of color in the history of the United States to lead and develop a mass movement. He was the first man on a mass scale and level to give millions of Negroes a sense of dignity and destiny and make the Negro feel he was somebody," King told a crowd of two thousand.

He pondered the idea of a sabbatical during his Jamaica sojourn, but realized that an entire year's leave would raise serious questions for SCLC, not the least of them financial. The organization had taken in more than $1.5 million in the preceding ten months, thanks in large part to the public support garnered by Selma, but SCLC's leaders appreciated how unpredictable their finances were. In 1964 they briefly had to borrow funds to meet the payroll, and before Selma, SCLC had been nearly $100,000 in debt. A huge influx of spring contributions, greater than in the wake of Birmingham, had remedied that deficit, and a small number of extremely wealthy individuals, such as New York heiress Ann Farnsworth, could be counted on to make annual five-figure donations. Nonetheless, aside from the well-run direct-mail appeals administered by Adele Kanter and Stanley Levison, SCLC possessed no systematic source of funding beyond the substantial sums produced by King's speaking appearances. If that income were to disappear for a year, SCLC would have to make it up. Levison had long urged "the necessity for a full scale commitment to fund-raising," and now he sharpened his warnings. In light of the possibility of King's taking a sabbatical, Levison told Andrew Young, "the question of an organized structure not dependent on him becomes critically urgent." Additionally, in view of the organization's desire to confront discriminatory housing, employment, and schooling in northern cities, "we may find some sources of funds," such as direct mail, "diminishing as SCLC bites deeper below the skin of more people, north as well as south." Both considerations suggested that SCLC ought to exploit an appropriate source of funds that it had never focused upon: the black church. It was imperative, Levison said, to "build a structure of fund-raising among the churches" and to hire a new staff member to coordinate the program. With a large-scale southern program such as SCOPE, which was consuming more than $100,000 per month, and the plan to move north, "you are going to need big money," Levison told Young and King. Although no immediate action was taken to pursue the black church idea, King returned from his Jamaican holiday talking less about taking a sabbatical and more about the need for SCLC to select a northern city as a launching pad for a nonviolent assault on urban discrimination.[72]

He also returned from Jamaica talking more about a subject to which he had been making consistent but low-key reference for several months: America's growing involvement in Vietnam. On July 2, King addressed an SCLC rally in Petersburg, Virginia. Speaking more forcefully than he had in prior public appearances, King declared that "the war in Vietnam must be stopped. There must be a negotiated settlement," and the United States should spare no effort in pursuing one. "We must even negotiate with the Vietcong." Americans should speak out in favor of a quick settlement, and could hold "peace rallies just like we have freedom rallies," King suggested. His remarks received prominent play in papers across the country, and in the ensuing days reporters pressed him to explain his interest in a subject not tied to civil rights. "I'm much more than a civil rights leader," King told one interviewer while explaining that the Vietnamese conflict was not outside his purview. "I feel that it is necessary for me to continue to speak on it," to point out the "need for a negotiated settlement." He had not called for a "unilateral withdrawal" by the U.S., King noted, and "I never said anything about organizing demonstrations around the Vietnam situation," as some had interpreted his Virginia remarks. "I merely said that I will have to speak out on this issue." His principal focus, King reiterated, was America's nationwide oppression of blacks, not American foreign policy. That was why SCLC was looking for a northern city in which to become active; "the poverty issue is now the pressing one." Housing, schools, and jobs were all areas in which most black Americans suffered pervasive discrimination, North as well as South. The movement owed it to all citizens to confront those problems without regard to regional boundaries, and if that obligation brought with it new risks, then he was willing to take them. Four days after King's ground-breaking speech in Petersburg, he flew north for discussions with civil rights leaders in Chicago, where local activists were eager to host the northern protests that SCLC wanted to develop. In so doing, King took the first step down a path that would fundamentally alter the nature of the movement and hasten the expansion of his own critical perspective on American society.[73]

8

Chicago and the "War on Slums," 1965–1966

Civil rights activism in Chicago had traveled a fitful path in the years preceding Martin King's exploration of the city in July, 1965. Chicago's main racial issue was the extensive segregation of the city's schools, and the grossly inferior facilities to which black children were assigned. A biracial group, Teachers for Integrated Schools, was formed in 1961 to combat these conditions, and in April, 1962, two of its most active members, Al Raby and Meyer Weinberg, joined with other Chicago civil rights leaders to organize a new association of activist groups, the Coordinating Council of Community Organizations (CCCO). This caucus limited its activities to monthly meetings until the fall of 1963, when Chicago's hard-line school superintendent, Benjamin C. Willis, tendered his resignation after local CORE chapter members picketed the Board of Education for several weeks to protest how school assignment boundaries maintained segregation. A ten-to-one vote of the school board, whose members were appointed by Chicago Mayor Richard J. Daley, rebuffed Willis's attempt to resign, and on October 16 the controversial superintendent returned to his job with a strong endorsement of his policies. Civil rights activists were outraged, and on October 22, CCCO called a student boycott to protest the maneuver. More than 200,000 youngsters, almost 50 percent of those enrolled in the city system, stayed home from classes that day, but neither CCCO nor other civil rights forces followed up on that success.

By January, 1964, Raby had become CCCO's chairman or "convener," and in late February a second school boycott took place. Participation fell short of October's, and CCCO, lacking both an office and regular staff, drifted quietly into the summer months despite a report issued by University of Chicago Professor Philip Hauser that rigorously documented CCCO's charges against the segregationist policies of Superintendent Willis. King's appearance at a massive June rally at Soldier Field gave

Chicago civil rights activists a moment of celebration, but no notable efforts were undertaken during the balance of the year. In early 1965, CCCO was "in disarray," with one Chicago newspaper columnist proclaiming that "for all effective purposes it has expired." Public calls for Willis's removal continued, and two spring demonstrations were mounted in the hope of influencing the Board of Education not to renew the sixty-three-year-old superintendent's contract. On May 27 the board reappointed Willis until his sixty-fifth birthday in December, 1966, a decision that "brought life back to the moribund civil rights movement in Chicago."[1]

Two days later, CCCO met to consider new protests, and many recommended that a new school boycott of longer duration be mounted. Among those present was SCLC's Jim Bevel, who had taken an interest in Chicago's civil rights situation since April, when former SNCC activist Bernard Lafayette, now urban affairs director for the local office of the American Friends Service Committee, invited him to give a series of workshops on the southern movement. Those visits had led Bevel to agree with Lafayette's suggestion that Chicago was an ideal target for SCLC's expansion into the North. Bevel went on leave from SCLC to become program director at Chicago's West Side Christian Parish, and enthusiastically endorsed efforts by Lafayette and his AFSC colleagues to make discriminatory housing practices a top item on Chicago's civil rights agenda. "The real estate dealers in Chicago are the equivalent to Wallace and Jim Clark in the South," Bevel told one group. "These are the cats who are most vulnerable to an attack because this is one thing that everybody can see and understand—that is, you don't even need to philosophize about housing in Chicago, you can show that on television."

The renewed turmoil over Willis and school conditions, however, offered an excellent opportunity for reviving mass action in the city. Looking toward longer-range possibilities, Bevel told the May 27 CCCO meeting that a protest should not be rushed into without adequate planning. "You want to declare war without counting your troops," he warned, but a two-day boycott on June 10 and 11 was approved nonetheless.

During the following week, CCCO wavered in its commitment to the protest as some members argued that another mass rally or march, perhaps one featuring Dr. King, should be called instead. On June 6 the boycott plan was reaffirmed, but two days later a state court injunction barring the protest was handed down at the city's behest. CCCO responded with a June 10 march to City Hall by several hundred supporters, and repeated the procession the following day. City police arrested all 250 demonstrators the second day, and took more into custody when CCCO marched again on June 12. The federal Community Relations Service (CRS) tried to arrange negotiations between the protesters and the mayor, but the daily marches continued without interruption for more than two weeks. Finally, on June 28 Mayor Daley granted an audience to

Raby and other CCCO representatives. Daley rejected their demand that he use his appointive power over the school board to oust Willis, and CCCO decided to appeal to other allies in order to break the impasse. Raby wrote to U.S. Education Commissioner Francis Keppel asking that federal school aid to the city be cut off until segregationist policies were ended, and a decision was made to follow up on the contacts with Jim Bevel by asking King for assistance in future protests against the school system.[2]

King arrived in Chicago on July 6 for a speech to a church convention. He met with Raby, who requested that he return later that month for protests against Willis and Chicago's segregated schools. King agreed to come back for a three-day visit, and the next morning joined Raby to announce those plans to Chicago newsmen. King said that a dozen SCLC staffers would accompany him, and that his visit would be part of SCLC's explorations in a number of cities. "We've begun some work in Boston and we'll also be quite active in Chicago and four or five other major northern cities," he explained. "Our voter rights drive is doing well in the South and we are anxious to work hard in the North as well." Asked if he would meet with Mayor Daley to discuss the problems, King said that was "a real possibility," but only if he accompanied local black leaders.

As the Chicago activists discussed how to draw King into their future efforts, SCLC's staff arranged for King to visit other cities that were candidates for a northern initiative. Plans were made for a midsummer swing that would take King and his assistants to four northern cities besides Chicago: Cleveland, New York, Philadelphia, and Washington. Although SCLC had not yet selected a city for its northern focus, King thought more and more about Chicago in the wake of his conversations with Raby. He told an audience at Syracuse University that problems in public education, especially school segregation in the North, were among the most important issues for the movement to deal with, and he cited the case of Chicago's Willis as an example of what was wrong.[3]

In Chicago heavy advance publicity announced that King would address fourteen neighborhood rallies on Saturday and Sunday July 24 and 25, with the climax of his trip being a Monday march to City Hall. Several newsmen reported that CCCO planned to target future protests against Willis's boss, Mayor Daley, rather than the school superintendent. The astute mayor telegrammed King a week before his arrival to offer a personal appointment. The city's civil rights situation, Daley suggested, was far better than King might think. CCCO responded that such a meeting would not be possible because of King's tight schedule.

King and his aides flew into Chicago on Friday, July 23, where they received a surprise greeting at the airport from Edward Marciniak, director of Mayor Daley's Chicago Commission on Human Relations. That evening King met with fifty Chicago activists, and the next morning he set out on a series of neighborhood rallies that kept him speaking literally from dawn to dusk. On Sunday he preached at two different churches before resuming the neighborhood appearances, and that evening he spoke to a crowd of fifteen thousand in suburban Winnetka. That made approximately twenty speeches in barely forty-eight hours. A Monday morning breakfast address was canceled so that an "ailing and exhausted" King could undergo an emergency checkup prior to that afternoon's mass rally and march to City Hall. Emerging from the doctor's office, King told newsmen he had a "slight case of bronchitis, and I need to rest." The "extreme fatigue," he explained, was due to the fact that "I think I've talked more in the last three days in Chicago than I have at any time in my life," and that he had not been getting much rest. "The doctors tell me I can't get by on two or three hours of sleep a night. I try to do it, and I learn I just can't."

Exhausted, King resumed his schedule, barely missing a beat. He met with the Catholic Interracial Council in midmorning, with a businessmen's group at lunch, and then delivered a lengthy address at Buckingham Fountain to a crowd estimated at between fifteen thousand and thirty thousand people. His weariness showed as he spoke about how "so often in these past two years I have had to watch my dream transformed into a nightmare." His March on Washington optimism, he suggested, counted for little in the face of problems like those plaguing Chicago's schools. "It is criminal," he declared, "to allow the education of our children to be entrusted to the kind of insensitive, unimaginative, mediocre leadership which is now being provided." After leading the crowd to the doors of City Hall, King voiced his increasing appreciation of the challenges that lay ahead. "We stand at the gate of a new understanding of the dimensions and depth of our struggle with racial injustice in this country; dimensions not limited by geographic boundaries or adequately addressed by civil rights laws." Those dimensions were symbolized by the problems of schools, housing, and employment that existed in Chicago, problems that SCLC would help the local movement tackle. Asked by newsmen why Chicago had drawn his interest, King reminded them it was the nation's second largest city. More important, he said, was CCCO's energy. "Since there is a vibrant, active movement alive here, we felt that this was the first community in which we should work and start our visits in the north."[4]

King and his aides felt the Chicago whirlwind had been a great success despite the profusion of threatening phone calls received at his hotel and his physical exhaustion. King arrived late in Cleveland, the tour's second stop, and Andrew Young told reporters that King's bronchitis had left him completely worn out. King nonetheless addressed a mass meeting and tried valiantly to keep up with a hectic Wednesday schedule. He arrived at 9:00 A.M. for a breakfast that had been scheduled at 7:30, and made a number of daytime appearances to encourage voter registration efforts. Then, despite a fever of 102 degrees, he spoke at a poorly attended rally at the city arena. He was eighty minutes late, and was "noticeably precarious" in delivering his remarks, one writer observed. He spoke favorably of black mayoral candidate Carl Stokes, and then returned to his hotel. Even there he found no rest, for Attorney General Katzenbach was on the phone to press him about an urgent legislative problem. The House had approved the Voting Rights Act on July 9, but had included a statutory poll tax ban that the Senate version of the bill lacked. The different versions had been sent to a conference committee, but no agreement had been reached because of the House conferees' insistence upon retaining the poll tax provision. Since that stalemate threatened to delay the bill's final enactment into law, Katzenbach wondered if King would be willing to endorse a poll tax compromise in order to attain speedier approval. King was dead tired when Katzenbach phoned, but he listened patiently as the attorney general explained how King's opinion might prove influential with two House conferees—Peter Rodino of New Jersey and Harold Donohue of Massachusetts—whose commitment to the poll tax ban was blocking final enactment. King agreed that speedy action was an overriding consideration, and authorized Katzenbach to tell the House conferees that the more modest Senate and administration-backed poll tax language was acceptable to him. The next day the attorney general passed the word to Capitol Hill. King's message had the desired effect, and that afternoon the House conferees accepted the Senate language. Final floor votes in both houses were scheduled for the following week, with approval and a speedy presidential signature assured.[5]

King and his aides were far less happy with their Cleveland visit than with the one to Chicago, but more serious problems arose concerning their next two stops, New York and Philadelphia. Harlem Congressman Adam Clayton Powell, whose behavior toward King had been erratic for years, let it be known that King should avoid Powell's turf during his northern tour. SCLC reluctantly consented not to go. Then a similar objection threatened to scratch King's Philadelphia visit. Local NAACP leader Cecil B. Moore, angry that he had not been consulted, informed the SCLC leaders they would not be welcome. Moore expressed his views to King by phone on Saturday, July 31, and SCLC announced cancellation of the visit, which had been scheduled to begin Sunday evening. Philadelphia supporters of the King pilgrimage were outraged by Moore's action, and met throughout the day Saturday before persuading SCLC to go forward with the visit despite the NAACP complaint. Late Saturday night SCLC reversed itself, and on Sunday evening King arrived to an airport greeting of three hundred enthusiastic supporters. Newsmen thought King "seemed bewildered" by the cheering in light of the local controversy. He went out of his way to stress that no one should feel threatened by his visit. "We are here not to establish a movement, but to support the one that is already here." Andrew Young told reporters that King was still "very tired," and the next morning he was an hour late for a twelve-hundred-person breakfast banquet at Friendship House. His northern visits, King told the crowd, were the first step toward confronting the serious domestic problems that plagued the entire country. "We need massive programs that will change the structure of American society so there will be a better distribution of the wealth."

Despite his exhaustion, King's Philadelphia schedule was hectic. An SCLC promise that the funds generated by his appearances would go into local coffers convinced Cecil Moore to support the tour, and he joined King for a friendly press conference before King set out on a string of appearances that did not end until after midnight. On Tuesday King met for lunch with the Philadelphia Chamber of Commerce before joining Moore for a series of street rallies that climaxed with a five-thousand person protest at Girard College, a segregated institution that Moore's followers had been picketing for three months. That evening he spoke to a larger crowd at a Baptist church and reiterated his call for a "negotiated settlement" in Vietnam. Early the next morning King left for Washington, the final stop on his tour.[6]

King's three-day visit to the nation's capital had been planned to combine a series of community appearances along with a White House visit so that he could brief President Johnson on the impressions garnered during his northern swing. His first day's schedule, delayed slightly by bomb threats that forced him to take a different flight from Philadelphia, featured eight appearances throughout the Washington area. King voiced his support of Washington residents' demands that Congress grant their city home rule. On the second day of his visit he interrupted his string of neighborhood appearances to have lunch at the Capitol with those members of the House and Senate who served on the committees that exercised jurisdiction over Washington's local government. Late that afternoon, he, Abernathy, and Walter Fauntroy met with President Johnson and White House aide Lee White and listened as the chief executive described his plans for holding a White House Conference on Civil Rights in 1966. King told Johnson he feared segregation was on the increase in the North, that federal school aid should be cut off to de facto segregated systems, that new housing and job-training initiatives were required, and that legislation should be drafted making ownership of decrepit slum housing unprofitable. Johnson encouraged King to submit a report detailing his recommendations, and King told newsmen that the session had been "fruitful and meaningful." Later that evening he addressed a "home rule" rally and walked at the head of a procession that marched to Lafayette Park across from the White House to express thanks for the support Johnson had given home rule. King told the five thousand demonstrators that he would call for protests if Congress failed to take speedy action on their demand. The next morning he went to the Capitol for the signing of the Voting Rights Act of 1965. A few hours later, a tired King headed home to Atlanta, his first round of northern explorations complete.

King and his SCLC colleagues discussed their reactions to the cities they had visited. Cleveland and Philadelphia had clear shortcomings, and

New York was unattractive since Adam Powell had now publicly warned that King would be "unwise" to visit Harlem. Chicago seemed promising, however; the local movement leadership had been pleased with the visit. At a CCCO meeting on August 4, Raby said that SCLC's Walter Fauntroy already had indicated that Chicago looked especially attractive. "He thought maybe they would come back and dig in, not just for three days," and had been amenable to Raby's warning that SCLC work in conjunction with CCCO, not just "come in and take over." CCCO agreed with Raby's evaluation that "King did a good job stirring the people we may be able to organize," and authorized Raby to work out with King the details of a second trip during which King could confront Mayor Daley and help CCCO mobilize its forces for another mass boycott of Chicago's schools.[7]

While King was receptive to the Chicago activists' entreaties, his immediate concern was the SCLC annual convention, which opened on Monday, August 9, in Birmingham. Levison, Jones, Wachtel, and Rustin had discussed the value of an SCLC resolution defending King's comments about Vietnam. Rustin suggested that King issue a public letter to President Johnson calling for the inclusion of the Viet Cong and the North Vietnamese president, Ho Chi Minh, in negotiations to end the conflict. Wachtel prepared a forceful declaration of support for King in the name of SCLC's board. "We shall not hesitate to challenge the policies and actions of our government," Wachtel's draft declared, "whenever we believe that they may lead our world closer to war and annihilation." By the time King flew to Birmingham on Monday to open the meeting, he had agreed with his advisors that he should dispatch personal letters to the leaders of all the countries involved in Vietnam, urging a speedy negotiated settlement.

King and Young described SCLC's prospects in the North to the board. Young spoke positively about the recently completed tour, but confessed that "we don't have a program yet for the North." Sometime during the coming fall, he explained, "we will have a retreat to get away for a day or two and plan for building a movement over the next year or two." Although Chicago seemed likely to be the first city where staffers would be deployed, Washington also offered a good locus for action that could be centered around home rule, King said. Young emphasized that SCLC would not start its urban effort from scratch, but would coordinate with local groups ready to accept such assistance. "Our role in the North is not to organize our own unit but to pull together everything else." That might prove more difficult than during protest campaigns in the South, in part because the movement's opponents would be "more sophisticated and subtle. In the past we could count on a Bull Connor or Jim Clark to create such a savage and brutal image that our own weaknesses were ignored amid the blatant horror and injustice which surrounded all our demonstrations," Young said, but in future challenges the movement's shortcomings might be more visible.

The board's second day of meetings began with a discussion of SCOPE and the new voter registration possibilities offered by the Voting Rights Act. King expressed concern that the Justice Department would not send federal registrars into all the southern counties eligible for them under the bill's provisions. Then the discussion turned to a Vietnam resolution. Board member Benjamin Hooks challenged the entire idea. "I question whether it is wise for us to go too far in the international arena." King responded that "I think we have an obligation as individuals to express our concern about the peace question. There is a need to call for a negotiated settlement." Considerable discussion ensued, and the final resolution was far different from what King's advisors had envisioned. Indeed, the language stopped just short of an implied dissent against King's public remarks. Board members "recognize that [King's] conscience compels him to express his concern" about Vietnam, and "commend him for courageously expressing these concerns," the statement conceded. "We must still, however, affirm that the primary function of our organization is to secure full citizenship rights for the Negro citizens of this country." SCLC's "resources are not sufficient to assume the burden of two major issues," and the organization would not pursue questions of peace or foreign affairs.[8]

That implicit rebuke to King's outspokenness was overshadowed by the heavy coverage given his own comments. King made no complaint about the wording of the resolution, and faced no probing questions when he explained to newsmen that it was simply based on the fact that SCLC had "neither the resources nor the energy to organize demonstrations on the peace question." He had never advocated such an attempt because "it's physically impossible to go all out on the peace question and all out on the civil rights question." SCLC's priorities were clear to all, but this did not mean that King should not voice his individual views. His annual report as SCLC's president focused upon ongoing programs such as SCOPE, citizenship education, Operation Breadbasket, and Vivian's Project Vision, which was now being supported by a federal grant. King's personal focus remained the Vietnam initiative that he and the New York advisors had discussed. King announced his intention to send letters to Lyndon Johnson and the leaders of the U.S.S.R., China, North and South Vietnam, and the Viet Cong, and explained that his goal was not to "argue the military or political issues involved," but simply to "make an urgent plea for all sides to bring their grievances to the conference table." Asked by reporters why he was undertaking this initiative, King responded that "I held back until it got to the point that I felt I had to speak out." It was imperative that the United States "seriously consider halting the bombing" of North Vietnam and that President Johnson "make an unequivocal and unambiguous statement that we're willing to negotiate with the Viet Cong." Although his letter-writing initiative was front-page news across the country, and although Jim Bevel told reporters that an "international peace army" would take the place of a civil rights movement made obsolete by the Voting Rights Act, King said he sought no role in any Vietnam negotiations or in antiwar protests. "I don't see the development of a peace army right now" he informed reporters at the conclusion of the convention.[9]

From Birmingham, King and Bernard Lee flew toward what they hoped would be a restful vacation in San Juan. In Miami, however, King learned that the violent disturbances that had begun in Los Angeles's Watts ghetto two nights earlier were intensifying. On Friday the thirteenth, unrestrained mobs roaming the streets had set fire to block after block of stores with Molotov cocktails. King was uncertain about whether to continue on to Puerto Rico or heed requests from black Los Angeles churchmen to aid them in restoring peace to the ravaged area. King consulted with Bayard Rustin, who urged him to deplore both the rioting and the underlying economic brutalities of ghetto life which produced it. Both men agreed that there seemed little use in King's entering a situation that even the National Guard was having difficulty quelling. King went on to San Juan and addressed a Disciples of Christ convention, but by noontime Sunday he decided to return to Miami to prepare for a Los Angeles trip that he could not in good conscience avoid. Several SCLC colleagues joined Rustin in warning King that an appearance in Los Angeles would be as politically risky as his ill-fated involvement in the New York disturbances a year earlier, but King replied that he could not say no. Rustin agreed to rendezvous with King and Lee in Los Angeles, and on Tuesday afternoon King arrived, telling waiting newsmen that he had come to help local black leaders in their negotiations with Los Angeles Mayor Sam Yorty and hard-nosed Police Chief William H. Parker. The next morning he met with *Los Angeles Times* publisher Otis Chandler, then headed to Watts to address several hundred ghetto residents at the Westminster Community Center. King was awed by the physical devastation of the area, and was nonplussed when a hostile Black Muslim heckled him as he spoke to the crowd. Then he met with California Governor Edmund G. Brown for a conversation that King termed "very fruitful and amicable." Later that evening, reflecting on the day's events, King expressed to Rustin and Lee how his visit to Watts had brought home to him more than ever the material and spiritual desolation that shattered the lives of the millions of black citizens trapped in America's ghettos. "I'll never forget the discussion we had with King that night," Rustin recalled. "He was absolutely undone, and he looked at me and said, 'You know, Bayard, I worked to get these people the right to eat hamburgers, and now I've got to do something . . . to help them get the money to buy it.'" Rustin had been telling King for nearly two years that the most serious issues facing the movement were economic problems of class rather than race, but on this evening Rustin sensed that the day's experiences had convinced King of the truth of that analysis. "That struck Martin very, very deeply," Rustin explained. "I think it was the first time he really understood."[10]

The following morning King and Rustin met with Mayor Yorty and Police Chief Parker in a heated session that lasted almost three hours. The mayor listened politely as King explained that Los Angeles would benefit from a civilian review panel empowered to investigate allegations of police brutality, which blacks viewed as a serious problem. Then Chief Parker erupted at King's suggestion, telling him in blunt terms that racial prejudice was not a problem in Los Angeles. The angry police chief also refused to let King visit jailed black rioters, and the SCLC contingent left the session shaking their heads over a racial insensitivity that seemed as acute in Los Angeles as in Birmingham or Selma. Mayor Yorty attacked King in comments to local newsmen, and King told reporters that although he appreciated the mayor's meeting with him, Chief Parker ought to be removed as police commander immediately. King met with newsmen again on Friday before departing for Atlanta, and stated that black ghetto dwellers were disillusioned with both white liberals and the black middle class. "It was a class revolt of underprivileged against privileged." They had not benefited from the gains won by the movement in the South and had "been bypassed by the progress of the past decade." For them "the main issue is economic," namely the widespread need for jobs. When King phoned Lyndon Johnson in Washington to repeat that message, Johnson took the opportunity to chide King for his remarks about the war. "The President never asked me not to speak out on Vietnam. He just explained his position." King said later that the president had pledged to improve Los Angeles's slow-footed antipoverty program. Though King praised Johnson as a "sensitive" president "prepared to give us the kind of leadership and vision we need," the size of the problems, King knew after his visit to Watts, was far greater than anyone—the president or he himself—probably yet realized.[11]

Back in Atlanta King tried to steal some rest while catching up on developments that had escaped his attention during a summer in which he had spent little time in the Deep South. Morale in the SCLC Atlanta offices was not good. Much of the grousing was due to tensions that had developed between Hosea Williams's free-spending SCOPE staffers and the remainder of SCLC's troops. Williams's project had put almost five hundred volunteers into some four dozen Deep South counties. SCOPE claimed to have registered thousands of new black voters, but many SCLC leaders were dubious about its real achievements. A contingent of workers in Americus, Georgia, had precipitated a protest campaign that antagonized longtime SNCC workers in the area who resented SCLC's sudden intrusion. "We've been operating in Americus for three years," SNCC's Willie Ricks told a reporter, "and now we've got to figure out how to clean up the mess Dr. King will leave behind." SCLC's token presence in Selma could do little to offset the devastating blows to the black community's morale when one free-lance civil rights preacher was hustled out of town for taking indecent liberties with underage girls, or when Dallas County Voters League President F. D. Reese was arrested for allegedly embezzling movement funds. Although the charges were subsequently dropped, visiting newsmen pronounced the black community "shocked and divided" and disappointed that the protests had produced "no discernible change in the racial climate of the city." Reporters found some local leaders ready to endorse SNCC's longtime complaint that all SCLC ever left behind it was "a string of embittered cities." An arrogant Hosea Williams, asked to respond to those criticisms, dismissed the local leaders' unhappiness brusquely. "They need us more than we need them. We can bring the press in with us and they can't." Some movement observers wondered if SCLC would return to St. Augustine, where the long-planned quadricentennial celebration would soon take place, but local black activists who had welcomed SCLC's first venture there were unenthusiastic. "We were cut off in September of 1964," Robert Hayling lamented to a reporter when asked about a possible return by King. "He and the SCLC put the screws on us real tight." Another St. Augustine activist was more blunt: "I don't want him back here now."

Americus, Selma, and St. Augustine aside, however, the most serious problems concerned SCOPE. Blackwell and Young contended that Williams's effort was sloppily administered and had recruited far more inexperienced volunteers than it could use or supervise, and that events had, if anything, shown that their warnings had been understated. Tens of thousands of dollars had been spent with little to show in return except angry local leaders and frustrated volunteers. Local activists decried SCLC's failure to supervise the young recruits. One Georgia minister wrote Williams to say that SCOPE was "the worst run program I have ever seen." The volunteers, most of whom found demonstrations more enjoyable than tedious voter canvassing, often became exasperated with local leaders and took out their energies in other ways. Blackwell summarized the situation in a confidential memorandum to King and Abernathy, warning that "most of the evidence" to support his summary "need never be written down or remembered.

> The SCOPE project as it presently exists should be brought [to] an end just as soon as it possibly can without inviting public inquiry . . . it has cost freedom contributors ten times what it should have. In my candid opinion, the project has degenerated in the main to an experiment in liquor and sex, compounded by criminal conduct, no less than a series of reported rapes.

Blackwell also noted his "suspicion of financial dishonesty" on the part of some involved in SCOPE's administration.[12]

One week after King's return to Atlanta from his Watts trip, he assembled SCLC's staff for a three-day meeting at a downtown hotel. Those present included young field-workers as well as longtime associates like Young, Bevel, Cotton, Williams, and Stanley Levison, who came down from New York. King explained that the purpose of the gathering was "to discuss and think through anew our programmatic thrust in the light of recent developments in the North" and the Chicago request that SCLC make a major commitment to that city. First, however, there was a lengthy discussion of SCOPE. Williams delivered a glowing report, but Young and Levison asserted that a complete evaluation would require more information. King emphasized that everyone had to avoid actions or statements that could injure the organization, and Blackwell expressed his concern about rumors of misconduct in SCOPE. There was general agreement that Williams's project had become too separate from the rest of the organization, and that "there is a need to unify SCLC."

King focused the discussion back on the North. His summer visits had convinced him that urban blacks needed leadership. The widespread talk about violence was a challenge that the nonviolent movement had to meet. The Chicago activists wanted SCLC to begin work there in September, and "we must not ignore their call. We must find the real issues and examine our structure to determine what we can do." King opened the floor for comments and heard general agreement that "the problem in the North is a bankruptcy of leadership." Bevel was especially eager to undertake a Chicago campaign, but others insisted that SCLC had to define its purpose for going into Chicago. Some wondered if Chicago should be taken on without SCLC first developing a tangible program or recruiting the prior support of likely white allies. King challenged that concern, arguing that "the movement pulls people out, helps them regain their souls and that we make a mistake to wait. We have brought about growth in the press and white people as the movement grew and developed power. We cannot expect such allies in the beginning. The present mood dictates that we cannot wait. We must . . . commit ourselves to the whole long-range program."

Several participants suggested that the northern campaign involve more than one city, but Levison cautioned that southern staff members might not appreciate how different and complex running a campaign in even a single large city would be. Young agreed, saying that SCLC could work in tandem with Chicago's CCCO while offering assistance to local leaders in other cities such as Cleveland. Many disagreed, however, and argued that while Chicago would be a first step, in time SCLC's effort would have to be expanded further. "The final consensus," Dorothy Cotton noted, was that "we move beyond one city or one issue and attempt to get at the heart of the problem (distribution of wealth). We must, however, use a concrete, live issue within a community in order to do this."

On the final day of the discussions King focused on the immediate questions concerning Chicago. Some were worried that CCCO "is not in touch with the masses," and that many black Chicagoans believed violence was a more effective tool than nonviolence. "It was the consensus that we must deal with this feeling and accept the challenge to prove that nonviolence is *the way*," Cotton wrote. "Mr. Levison suggested that we must move into . . . Chicago with a nonviolent movement immediately with a set of demands that would improve the lot of people living in [ghetto] areas." The final decision, she noted, was expressed in two points:

1. Because of the condition of oppression that Negroes are facing in the North, it is absolutely necessary for SCLC to move in on a supportive basis.
2. We will do intensified work in the North, using Chicago as a pilot project.

Young would meet with Al Raby to brief him on SCLC's decision, and arrangements would be made for the SCLC staff and CCCO leadership to meet jointly for intensive discussions within six weeks. In mid-September SCLC's executive and field staffs would have separate retreats at the Penn Center in Frogmore, South Carolina, to prepare for the campaign, and a task force of a dozen workers would be dispatched to Chicago immediately.[13]

King's thoughts continued to center on urban blacks' problems during the days following the Atlanta discussions. In New York for a national television appearance, a research committee meeting, and a presidentially instigated discussion of Vietnam with Johnson's U.N. ambassador, Arthur Goldberg, King told both newsmen and his advisors of his growing concern about America's ghettos. The problems in the North were "not out in the open" like the simpler ones in the South, and most whites in positions of power "still fail to grasp the depths and dimensions of racial injustice" all across America, he said. Antipoverty efforts needed to be "greatly expanded," and the Watts riots had left the black movement in an unhappy state where "something is needed today to give it a lift." The perfect initiative, King suggested, would be a presidential tour of the country's ghettos, a tour that ought to convince Lyndon Johnson that "vast sums of money" and "major economic reforms" were needed to meet the crises facing America's largest cities. "The tour by the President—seeing poverty conditions for himself—should be followed by a massive economic program, a program to give the people in the ghetto a stake in society."

Although King's meeting with Goldberg was postponed by the ambassador, reporters questioned King about his Vietnam letter-writing initiative. He explained that he had not yet sent the appeals, but that it was "very urgent to work passionately and unrelentingly for a negotiated settlement of this very dangerous and tragic conflict." Although he had no desire to become a negotiator, and no intention of making SCLC active in any peace effort, his ministerial role placed upon him prophetic as well as priestly responsibilities, King said. One of those prophetic obligations was to declare that "war is obsolete," and opponents of that view should not confuse his "creative dissent" with disloyalty to the nation.[14]

Back in Atlanta on September 1, King and Young announced publicly

SCLC's new commitment to Chicago. Raby would be flying in for discussions the next day, and Young explained that one of Chicago's most attractive features was CCCO, which he termed "probably one of the best coalitions of civil rights forces existing anywhere in the country." Pressed by reporters to elaborate the reasons behind SCLC's choice, Young ticked off three additional features that were attractive to SCLC. First, Chicago was the nation's second largest city and an especially challenging target. Employing the same rationale for Chicago that SCLC had used two years earlier in selecting Birmingham meant that "if northern problems can be solved there, they can be solved anywhere." Second, Mayor Daley's powerful Democratic machine made for a potentially more effective city response to the movement's efforts. Unlike in some other cities, such as New York, Chicago's bosses "can make changes in behalf of the people if their conscience is sharpened and the issues clearly raised before them." Third, Young said, was the strong support for civil rights offered by Chicago's influential religious community.

King's and Young's announcement stressed that the initial focus would be on "the school issue—a fight for quality integrated education." The drive might later expand to issues of jobs and housing and might last upward of a year, but the crux of SCLC's commitment was to make Chicago the same sort of symbolic city as Birmingham and Selma. "I have faith," King declared, "that Chicago . . . could well become the metropolis where a meaningful nonviolent movement could arouse the conscience of this nation to deal realistically with the northern ghetto."

Chicago's politicians, already furious at the CCCO marches that black entertainer Dick Gregory had been leading through Mayor Daley's own segregated neighborhood, greeted King's announcement with coolness. Black alderman Ralph H. Metcalfe, a devoted Daley supporter, accused King of having "ulterior motives" and announced formation of a new "community action" group of his own. "We have adequate leadership here," Metcalfe huffed. Jim Bevel and nine other SCLC staffers arrived in town and attended a CCCO executive committee meeting where Bevel detailed his vision of creating a "nonviolent army" of 100,000 to 150,000 Chicagoans. Young and Fauntroy arrived shortly after, and examined how best to tackle Chicago's segregated schools. Some activists recommended that King chair a series of hearings on educational shortcomings, while others favored an indefinite boycott of selected Chicago schools. The immediate goal was Willis's ouster as superintendent, but no decisions had been made by the time SCLC's staffers departed for the mid-September retreat at Frogmore.[15]

While the Chicago task force was getting oriented, King was in New York for his postponed meeting with U.N. Ambassador Arthur Goldberg. Their conversation lasted over an hour, after which King told reporters he had recommended to Goldberg that the United States halt its bombing of North Vietnam and announce that it would negotiate with the Viet Cong. King said he was "deeply distressed" about Vietnam, and had found the conversation "very fruitful and amicable." King also volunteered that the United States should end its opposition to the admission of the People's Republic of China to the United Nations.

Although Goldberg's comments about the meeting were friendly, the next day a close Senate ally of the Johnson administration, Connecticut Democrat Thomas Dodd, blasted King for his comments on Vietnam and "Red China" and pointed out that an obscure federal criminal statute barred private citizens from free-lance foreign policy ventures. King was very upset by Dodd's attack and became distraught as he worried about the additional public criticism that might follow. He arranged a conference call with Levison, Wachtel, Jones, Cleveland Robinson, and Young, and explained that he felt Lyndon Johnson had put Dodd up to the speech, just as the president had instructed Goldberg to meet with him in the hope of muting his criticisms of the war. King feared attacks that would go beyond the merits of the issues. "The press is being stacked against me." Commentators would charge that "I am power drunk and that I feel that I can do anything because I got the Nobel Prize and it went to my head," King said. "I really don't have the strength to fight this issue *and* keep my civil rights fight going," he told his friends. "They have all the news media and TV and I just don't have the strength to fight all these things. . . . This would take too much of my time to fight this," and other civil rights leaders like Wilkins would not support him. "The deeper you get involved the deeper you have to go . . . and I'm already overloaded and almost emotionally fatigued."

Three issues had to be dealt with immediately, King told his colleagues. First, they had to show people that King was not alone in his Vietnam position. Second, how should he deal with the Dodd attack? Third, what ought to be done about his letter-writing idea, which he now wanted to drop. "We have to face the fact that sometimes the public is not ready to digest the truth," King warned. "The average mind is not sophisticated enough to analyze a statement and what it means. If they did they would know who Dodd is and that he is the strongest supporter of the FBI and its invasion of privacy and the Un-American Activities Committee." The bottom line, King told his friends, was that he ought to back away from the peace issue and return to an emphasis on civil rights. "I have to find out how I can gracefully pull out so that I can get on with the civil rights issue because I have come to the conclusion that I can't battle these forces who are out to defeat my influence," forces that "are going to try to cut me down." If he fought back, "they will take the Communist China thing and what Dodd said and use it to say that I am under the influence of Communists." King felt that as a citizen and as "a moral leader" he had a right to speak out on "a question that deals with the survival of mankind," but the adverse reactions indicated he should "withdraw temporarily." None of his advisors disagreed with him on dropping the Vietnam issue. Levison and Wachtel recommended that King respond to any press queries by saying that he had spoken his piece on the war and on China, and now would be getting back to his regular work. During another conference-call discussion the following evening, everyone agreed that King would not pursue the letter-writing idea. King's advisors would urge liberal spokesmen and publications to defend his right to voice such criticisms, and King reiterated his belief that he ought to change course. He said he knew that his "star is waning" because of the public controversy, that he had to put Vietnam behind him temporarily, but that he would still speak out when necessary.[16]

With that painful decision made, King joined SCLC's staff retreat on the South Carolina coast. Other questions besides Chicago faced the organization. A decision had been made to set up a new department of economic affairs, which C. T. Vivian would head, with Virginia staffer Herbert Coulton taking Vivian's place as director of affiliates. Three other new people would be joining the top staff: Michigan State Professor Robert L. Green as education director, former Connecticut activist John Barber as an executive assistant in King's office, and white consultant Bill Stein as the black church fund-raiser Levison had recommended. Harry Boyte's Dialogue project was now concentrating most of its efforts in Miami, and Diane Nash Bevel had joined the staff to develop an educational program on nonviolence for use throughout Alabama. SCLC's Alabama presence had dwindled to a small Selma office headed by Harold Middlebrook and a network of field staffers in rural counties overseen by Marion's Albert Turner. Hosea Williams was hoping to strengthen those remnants now that SCOPE's summer effort had ended.

One pressing issue discussed at the retreat was a burgeoning local protest movement in Natchez, Mississippi. Andrew Young had visited the town at the invitation of Mississippi NAACP activist Charles Evers. Young announced he would recommend a protest campaign aimed at obtaining legislation that would make violence against civil rights activists a federal crime. Natchez, he said, had "some bad white folks," and "Dr. King will be glad to hear that. It was bad white folks in Birmingham that gave us the Civil Rights Bill. It was bad white folks like Jim Clark and Al Lingo in Alabama that gave us the right to vote." Similar Mississippians might be just what was needed to reinvigorate civil rights protests in the South. One local NAACP leader had been seriously injured when his car was bombed, and five SCLC staffers were sent to explore the Natchez situation. They concluded that Natchez was an oppressive locale where the black population suffered from brutal police, rigid segregation, and an employment situation that was bad even for the small-town South. Evers and the local NAACP chapter were eager for help, and by the third week of September the SCLC contingent had organized mass meetings and a downtown protest march that drew close to one thousand demonstrators. The SCLC workers hoped that King might visit, but by their second week in Natchez, debilitating tensions had developed between the younger SCLC staffers and the local NAACPers. The campaign weakened as internal conflict grew, and by the end of the month, Natchez was no longer as attractive for a major effort as Young had initially hoped.[17]

Several days after the Frogmore retreat King traveled to Washington for an unpublicized meeting with other movement leaders and Vice-President Humphrey. The setting was an evening dinner cruise down the Potomac on the presidential yacht; both the atmosphere and the guest list were designed to generate positive sentiments toward the Johnson administration. Accompanying King from SCLC were Andrew Young and Walter Fauntroy. Jack Greenberg, Clarence Mitchell, and John Morsell represented the NAACP, while Floyd McKissick was present from CORE and Whitney Young from the National Urban League. CUCRL sponsor Stephen Currier and former CUCRL Director Wiley Branton, now a Humphrey aide, were also along, but no SNCC representative was present. Although the vice-president wanted to convey the administration's continuing commitment to civil rights, he was confronted with strong expressions of dissatisfaction from King and others about the Justice Department's limited use of federal registrars in the six weeks since the Voting Rights Act had taken effect. Although the law's provisions covered almost the entire Deep South, Attorney General Katzenbach had sent federal representatives into barely a dozen locales. While Justice officials argued that national intervention would do little good in counties where local authorities were complying with the act's suspension of literacy tests, the movement leaders argued that fearful black applicants would feel more comfortable registering with a federal official than with a local white, and that assignment of U.S. registrars would spur registration drives in many areas. Branton defended the administration's strategy, but Mitchell "exploded" at him, calling him a "traitor" to the movement, and "a very bitter confrontation" ensued. Humphrey tried to placate his guests' concerns, but with minimal success.

King had become disturbed about the low morale of SCLC's staff. Several important staffers, including Blackwell and Vivian, were talking about leaving. Many workers were unhappy about the low wages and the absence of raises, but King explained that SCLC's income had fallen off so greatly since the spring that salary increases were out of the question. Bernard Lee, who spent more time with King than anyone, told his boss that he should not expect the same degree of self-sacrifice from others that King imposed upon himself. Lee knew "that God called you to do a job," but King ought to appreciate the staff's complaints. "I have seen the Cross that you must bear and I know deep down within, that you have denied yourself to follow Him."[18]

Although King was temporarily slowed after he fell backward in a chair and cut his arm on a glass, preparations for the Chicago campaign went ahead. Bevel's staffers met regularly with the CCCO, and drafted plans for a three-day joint retreat at a camp at Williams Bay, Wisconsin. Al Raby told a questioner, "We don't have specifics yet" for the campaign, but "we're laying the groundwork for a massive push in this city to bring the issue of northern ghettos to national attention. We're going to

broaden our interest—not just schools but housing, political emascula-
tion, poverty, welfare, jobs." The local activists received an unexpected
boost on October 1 when the federal Office of Education, responding to
CCCO's summer complaint, froze U.S. funding for Chicago's schools.
Movement leaders were ecstatic, and King sent a congratulatory telegram
to the White House. The city's Democratic power brokers demonstrated
the reach of their influence, however, when five days later the funding
freeze was overriden by higher-ranking Johnson administration decision-
makers.

On October 6, King flew to Chicago for the first time since July to join
the other activists for the retreat. "We want to be sure we have a strongly
mobilized and well organized community before we take action," King
told newsmen. The target would be Chicago's civil rights problems, not
the city administration. "I don't consider Mayor Daley as an enemy," and
"eventually" King hoped to meet with him. At the Williams Bay camp,
Raby and other local figures made the initial presentations, with Raby
stressing how CCCO and SCLC viewed the upcoming campaign as a cooperative partnership. "SCLC needs us to help set a pattern for the entire
nation; we need them for their experience and inspiration." Saturday afternoon King addressed the group and moderated an informal discussion
led by Young and Bevel. King reiterated that SCLC was in Chicago for
several reasons: CCCO's attractiveness, the past support city activists had
given the southern movement, and the innate challenge it offered.
"Chicago represents all the problems that you can find in the major urban
areas of our country," King said. "If we can break the system in Chicago,
it can be broken anywhere in the country." SCLC knew it was entering a
new environment. "The movement in Chicago will be different from that
in the South. There will be fewer overt acts to aid us here . . . naive
targets such as the Jim Clarks and George Wallaces will be harder to find
and use as symbols." Several people interjected that development of electoral power would be essential, and King agreed. "Reforms will require
political power. Direct action in and of itself will not get what we want—
but it will point out the need."

Jim Bevel sounded a different note, saying that electoral participation
would not attain the types of changes the Chicago campaign ought to
seek in American society:

> You fight a machine by making people grow so that they don't fit into
> the machine any more. We ought to be realistic enough to say that if
> we do in the next two years what we have done in the last two, we
> won't be any further along then than we are now. We've got to go for
> broke. But a crucifixion is necessary first. If Negroes can't break up a
> ghetto in fifteen months, they will never get out. Let us be more inter-
> ested in doing something about the ghetto than in securing candi-
> dates. . . . We are going to create a new city. Nobody will stop us—not
> Daley, not the syndicate. We need laborers . . . an army.

Only through mass action could they "get the whole community to see the real issues," Bevel added. "Problems must be on the front page every day."

King opened the floor to questions, and was asked about the usefulness of civil disobedience in Chicago. "Constitutional rights was the subject of the fight in the South. In the North, human rights is more the question. So here, the concept of civil disobedience is different. There are fewer unjust laws. Also, nonviolence falls on more sympathetic ears in the North." Young agreed that "here the problems are greater," and more difficult to expose, "but the resources are greater also" in Chicago than in a Selma. Dramatizing Chicago's ills would be a challenge compared to what was done in the South, for "there the issues were very clear cut" and easily covered by the news media. Bevel interjected that here they would have more white church support than they had had anywhere in the South. King nodded in agreement, asking him if he had detected much black nationalist sentiment in Chicago. No, Bevel said, "I don't think this is a problem here." In contrast to the South, "here people are more angry than afraid," and the Chicago campaign would have to channel that emotion constructively. "We build people. People build organizations. Organizations move." That should be the campaign's course of development.

Young stressed that SCLC would "work through existing organizations" and not "try to take over anything. We will be here for the duration until problems are effectively confronted. This means we expect to be here full time for at least a year and then be on call indefinitely." At the retreat's final session, Young again cautioned that SCLC's primary role in Chicago would be to "raise the issues. . . . Raising issues smokes out politicians—forces them to respond, then people can see what they want. By raising issues, we educate the whole nation."[19]

Although the SCLC leadership felt the weekend had been useful in exposing the CCCO activists to SCLC's ideas, it had not generated detailed plans for a campaign that King knew would meet "sophisticated and subtle opposition." Young had warned the group that "nothing you do is secret," that "infiltrators are everywhere," and that "movements can be betrayed," but neither he nor King had had a chance to concentrate on the detailed planning they knew was necessary if the Chicago initiative were to succeed. Both men were due in the small central Georgia town of Crawfordville on Monday to assist a newly formed local protest movement. King, however, was preoccupied with Vietnam. Although he had not commented on the subject in almost a month, in private conversations he expressed continued anguish. When Clarence Jones told him that Senators Ernest Gruening and Wayne Morse had voiced new opposition to the Southeast Asian conflict, King remarked that "as I have said all along, there is much more support for my position than the press is willing to admit." While privately licking his wounds from September's public lambasting, King's antiwar sentiments grew stronger. "There is no doubt about it," he told Jones, "the position of our government is wrong and it is getting wronger every day."[20]

When King and Young arrived in Crawfordville on Monday, October 11, they found the black community ready for sustained protests against local whites' efforts to avoid school integration. Every white pupil had transferred to schools in neighboring counties rather than accept desegregation, and Taliaferro County officials, citing the lack of students, had closed the building scheduled for integration. Demonstrations had been under way for two weeks, and black students had begun a mass boycott rather than return to their segregated facility. Hosea Williams had stepped in to lend a hand, and local protesters spoke of marching to Atlanta, 110 miles away, to present their grievances to Georgia Governor Carl Sanders. SCLC's appearance in town made local whites reconsider their course, and King told the seven hundred people at a Monday night rally that SCLC was willing to make Crawfordville the Birmingham and Selma of integrated education if authorities did not remedy the situation. After the rally Young led the crowd on a one-and-a-half-mile march to the Taliaferro County courthouse, and further protests were discussed. Three days later, however, a court placed the county school system in receivership under the direction of state education authorities, and King announced that demonstrations would be halted.[21]

Although King was looking forward to a late October European trip that would take him and Coretta to London, Amsterdam, and Paris, several SCLC problems worried him. In Natchez the local NAACP branch had asked that he withdraw all SCLC workers from their town. The branch alleged that the staffers had "engaged in acts calculated to cause divisions, dissensions, confusions and suspicion among members and officers of our local and national organizations and Colored residents of this city," and had demonstrated an "unwillingness to cooperate with our local branch in a constructive manner." The breach had become irreparable when SCLC's Al Sampson had "denounce[d] the local leadership in general, and the NAACP by name, as unreliable, untrustworthy, and incapable" at an October 18 mass meeting. Mississippi NAACP leader Charles Evers was also furious, and phoned Atlanta. King dispatched Robert Green to conduct an investigation, but that incident brought the Natchez project to an unpleasant end.

Word of SCLC's troubles began to spread. Longtime board member Joseph Lowery warned King about "rumors of sharp dissension and threats of resignation among the executive staff," and complained that board members felt "entirely ignorant of what's going on" because "all policy and decisions . . . are made by just a few in the office." Most worrisome to King was SCLC's rapidly deteriorating financial situation. Matters had been confused since an August burglary of the office safe by a young field staffer had resulted in the loss of a $190,000 check. The real problem, though, was that SCLC was spending $3,000 a day and taking in only $800. Either SCLC would have to substantially reduce its now siz-

able staff, or big money would have to be obtained. Some large contributors—such as New York Governor Nelson Rockefeller, who donated
$25,000 in mid-October—could be attracted by SCLC's tax-exempt ad-
junct, now named the American Foundation on Nonviolence, but other
new sources had to be found. King discussed his worries with Jones,
Levison, and Wachtel, who were puzzled that neither King nor SCLC
Treasurer Ralph Abernathy could institute meaningful controls to limit
SCLC's profligate spending.[22]

King and Coretta had been in Europe for only four days when word
reached them in Paris that Collie Leroy Wilkins, accused killer of Mrs.
Liuzzo, had been acquitted of the murder in his Lowndes County retrial.
King announced that this loathsome decision underscored the need for
new legislation making civil rights killings a federal crime. He cut short
his European trip and announced a new round of Alabama protests. Back
in Atlanta, he met with SCLC's executive staff and found strong agreement that demonstrations should be organized. Hayneville, site of the
two Wilkins trials, would be a good focal point, and the protesters could
demand both a federal criminal statute plus legislation designed to eliminate the widespread racial discrimination that made all-white juries commonplace in most southern courtrooms. A "dramatic action program"
would put new life into a southern movement that seemed moribund; it
might also draw renewed public attention to SCLC at a time when contributions were badly needed.

SCLC announced early in November that protests would get under way
in Birmingham, Selma, Anniston, and Gadsden before the end of the
month. "Our main goal," Young said, "is to dramatize the tremendous
injustice in the jury system of this country," and to show the nation, as
King put it, that "the whole structure of southern justice is contaminated
with racism and corrupted by color consciousness." Hosea Williams
would oversee the effort, and the protests would be coupled with a considerable expansion of SCLC's Alabama staff so that dramatic gains in
black voter registration could be achieved prior to the Alabama Democratic primary in May, 1966. Five days after that initial announcement,
King told the Atlanta Press Club that his commitment to this new project
was serious indeed:

> We in SCLC have decided that we have no alternative but to mobilize
> massive demonstrations around the issue of segregated justice. In order
> to arouse the conscience of the nation on this issue we will probably
> have to develop a Selma-Montgomery type march.[23]

King's declaration aside, however, SCLC's southern staff was moving
with no more effectiveness in organizing the Alabama protests than the
Chicago contingent was exhibiting in developing a tangible program
there. While King was preoccupied with SCLC's financial troubles, Bevel
was making slow progress in fashioning a Chicago project. As he had said

at Williams Bay, Bevel was "thinking big," and Chicago's problem, in his definition, was "getting rid of slums." SCLC's task, he wrote in his first outline of the Chicago Project, "is not to patch up the ghetto, but to abolish it." To do that, the movement would have to contend with the "four major forces which keep the ghetto in place: a. lack of economic power, b. political disenfranchisement, c. lack of knowledge and information, [and] d. lack of self-respect and self-dignity among the people of the ghetto." The last of these should be the first target, for it was "something that would be reachable, given the resources we have available," Bevel stated. The project had "to create enough self-dignity and self-respect in the people of the ghetto so that they will not tolerate the inhumane system under which they are now forced to live" and will replace it with "a community of love."

More practically, the Chicago staffers set up a headquarters at the Warren Avenue Congregational Church and began helping local neighborhood organizations canvass their communities in preparation for initial mass meetings. Between October 20 and November 4, kick-off rallies were held in the Near West, Near North, Oakland, and East Garfield Park areas. Volunteers recruited at the meetings began attending weekly workshops on the nonviolent movement run by SCLC staffers. James Orange, Jimmy Collier, and Jimmy Wilson started working with west side youth-gang members, some of whom seemed ripe for a "real transformation," while divinity student Jesse Jackson and former Birmingham activist Rev. Charles Billups built support for the movement among black ministers. The overall goal, Andrew Young told reporters, was "to mobilize the masses in Chicago so that they will be ready to act" when the campaign began.[24]

The kickoff seemed unlikely to occur until early 1966, since King was not pushing for quick action. A busy travel schedule took him back and forth across the country—to New York for his first meeting as a member of the Morehouse College Board of Trustees and for a Sunday appearance at Adam Clayton Powell's church, then to Detroit and Milwaukee for speaking engagements. While SCLC's intended focus was on demonstrations concerning southern justice, little was developing on that front, and King all but ignored it in his speeches. Instead, his remarks reflected a desire to broaden the movement's purview. First and foremost, King said, the movement had to transform itself from a southern to a countrywide effort. Until now it had been "essentially regional, not national. . . . The issues and their solution were similarly regional and the changes affected only the areas of combat," and did nothing to help northern blacks, whose lives were changing "not for the better but for the worse." Movement leaders "had long thought that the North would benefit derivatively from the Southern struggle. . . . This was a miscalculation. It was founded on the belief that opposition in the North was not intransigent; that it was flexible and was, if not fully, at least partially hospitable to corrective influence." CCCO's Chicago school campaign had shown that belief to be false and that "hope of voluntary understanding was chimerical; there was blindness, obtuseness, and rigidity that would only be altered by a dynamic movement." Such an effort offered the country its best chance of avoiding large-scale urban violence, and would show blacks as well as whites that nonviolence was the most effective tactic. "If 100,000 Negroes march in a major city to a strategic location, they will make municipal operations difficult to conduct . . . and they will repeat this action daily, if necessary," until tangible gains were won.

King also spoke of how the movement could not ignore violence and racism when they appeared in the international arena. "Violence is as wrong in Hanoi as it is in Harlem," and the Vietnam conflict was a vivid reminder that "war is wrong." In the long run, "we must disarm the whole world," because "total disarmament is the only answer" for eliminating mass violence from international relations. King emphasized that "I speak as an individual and as a minister, and not as president of the Southern Christian Leadership Conference." The responsibility of speaking out was brought home to him on a late November airline flight when noted pediatrician and antiwar activist Benjamin Spock approached him to say that the burgeoning domestic peace movement needed a symbolic leader. King gently parried Spock's request that he take that role, but the encounter further strengthened his growing anger at official attempts to shame opponents of the Vietnam conflict into silence. "We're at a terrible stage when we confuse dissent with disloyalty and we view every protester as a traitor." He warned a New York audience that "an ugly repressive sentiment to silence peace-seekers is assuming shape," one that "depicts advocates of immediate negotiation . . . as quasi-traitors, fools, or venal enemies of our soldiers and institutions." He would not look on in silence, King declared. "I cannot stand idly by and see war continually escalated without speaking out against it. I don't think our nation has done enough to indicate it wants a settlement." As a minister, he said, "I am mandated by this calling above every other duty to seek peace among men and to do it even in the face of hysteria and scorn."[25]

Those late fall antiwar comments attracted little of the publicity and abuse that King's earlier statements had received. At the same time, King also voiced increased concern over U.S. policy toward Africa. Black Americans had a special responsibility to keep a close eye on their country's relations with racist states such as Rhodesia and South Africa, and to urge that U.S. condemnations of apartheid be backed up with real action. All contact with Ian Smith's renegade Rhodesian regime should be cut off, and a massive economic boycott of South Africa could show how nonviolent action could be effective in the international as well as domestic arena. Verbal castigation of South Africa's policies counted for little when "we give them massive support through American investments," which ought to be terminated immediately.

After a month's delay, SCLC took its first step toward mounting new Alabama protests when King made a two-day tour through the Black Belt counties of Butler, Sumter, Clarke, and Greene on December 6 and 7. He repeatedly called for federal legislation to protect civil rights workers and ensure justice in southern courts. King's call was muted by administration promises to seek such a bill, plus the December 3 federal court convictions of Mrs. Liuzzo's assailants on charges of violating her civil rights. Those verdicts, and the maximum ten-year sentences meted out, "have made it more difficult for us to dramatize the need for changes in the structure of courts and law enforcement agencies in the South," King admitted to reporters.

Five days later he spoke at the MIA's tenth anniversary and told the ACMHR's weekly mass meeting that SCLC had selected Birmingham as the site for its Alabama plans. Although King spoke of the need for integrated juries and for Birmingham to hire black police officers, he indicated that Hosea Williams's staffers would focus on voter registration. Jefferson County was only one of many Alabama locales where disappointing registration gains were being blamed on the absence of federal registrars. An intensive organizing effort to turn out prospective registrants was necessary to show the Justice Department how badly those officials were needed. Williams was eager to get the effort going, and told Andrew Young he was "very upset" that SCLC's top echelon intended to monitor his expenditures. SCLC's southern program "is on trial" in Alabama, he told Young, and too many accounting requirements could impede the project. "I am sure I've not come up to standards in handling the conference's funds many times in the past, but haven't we all," Williams said. Young responded that the new supervision was for Williams's own good in light of the concerns generated by SCOPE and by a two-month-old FBI inquiry into whether Williams and other staffers had purchased stolen rent-a-cars for SCLC's use. Funds for the Alabama effort were being channeled to SCLC from the newly organized American Foundation on Nonviolence (AFON), and that connection heightened the "need for great caution," Young warned. "Any question whatsoever might jeopardize our future tax exemption and thereby jeopardize the whole movement. . . . The questions which are now being raised by our auditors, board members and the FBI concerning your past administration of funds make it necessary for someone else to participate in the administration of funds *in order to protect you.*" Williams grudgingly went along, and by New Year's the Birmingham effort was under way. Even Young conceded he was "impressed with the way things are going in Alabama."[26]

Although King's aides sought to shield him from the unpleasant news about the FBI queries, King had not forgotten Archibald Carey's pragmatic advice about praising the Bureau. When a promotion was announced for Hoover aide Cartha "Deke" DeLoach, the FBI's liaison to Lyndon Johnson and the press, King dispatched a congratulatory telegram. Otherwise, he spent much of December wrestling with the upcoming Chicago campaign, whose kickoff was set for January 6 and 7. Bayard

Rustin and two of his close movement allies, Tom Kahn and Norm Hill, recommended that King reconsider making a major commitment to Chicago, but he rejected their arguments. Rustin insisted King realize that a campaign there would inevitably bring him nose-to-nose with the city's powerful mayor, Richard Daley. King replied that Rustin was wrong, that a Chicago campaign need not mean mortal combat with Daley. He conceded that organizing the urban ghettos would be different from the South, but he insisted that SCLC could succeed. At one Atlanta meeting, Rustin and Kahn pressed their concerns upon Andrew Young and an unreceptive King. As Kahn remembered:

> King had this naive faith that he could do in Chicago what he had done in the South, that he could reach down and inspire them, mobilize them, and so forth. And Bayard kept saying, 'You don't know what you are talking about. You don't know what Chicago is like. . . . You're going to be wiped out.'

However, King's patience with Rustin's insistent argument had run out. He ended the discussion, Kahn recalled, by "saying, 'I have to pray now. I have to consult with the Lord and see what he wants me to do.'" Rustin, long familiar with King's proclivity for invoking God's name to avoid disagreements he did not care to hear, was furious. Seeking refuge in prayer—"This business of King talking to God and God talking to King"—would not resolve serious strategic questions. When they left, Kahn recalled, "Bayard was very distressed and very worried about what would happen to King in Chicago."

King's impatience with Rustin's cautionary arguments was based on a feeling that Rustin did not adequately appreciate the movement's responsibility to tackle the basic issues of wealth and class underlying the evils of American society. In earlier years Rustin had done more than anyone to heighten King's appreciation of those issues, but now the two men's strategic instincts were diverging. A sharp edge was increasingly apparent in King's public rhetoric as he decried "our vicious class systems" and explained that "we are now embarked upon a radical refurbishing of the former racist caste order of America." "Compensatory fairness" and significant economic reforms were needed in U.S. society, even if Lyndon Johnson's Vietnam venture meant that domestic social programs would be trimmed back more and more. Such a reduction "comes as no surprise. I expected it all along," a pessimistic King remarked just before Christmas. It was one more reminder that peace abroad and racial justice at home were "inextricably bound together," and of how in the two years since 1963, "I have constantly watched my dream turn into a nightmare. I have constantly watched my dream shattered." Some men and their ideas, he mused to his Ebenezer congregation on the second day of 1966, were destined to be ahead of their times, just like Jesus Christ. Ideas like racial equality and "a better distribution of wealth" eventually would triumph, aided by leaders who realized they must do what is right, and not only what is popular. "If our economic system is to survive," he told his parishioners, "there has to be a better distribution of wealth . . . we can't have a system where some people live in superfluous, inordinate wealth, while others live in abject, deadening poverty."[27]

On Wednesday, January 5, King arrived in Chicago for three days of meetings that would mark the beginning of SCLC's campaign. Accompanied by Young, Abernathy, and Bevel, he met with Raby and other local activists for two days, and refined a thirteen-page proposal outlining the movement's plans. That detailed document, designed for distribution to CCCO's membership and the press, discussed at length the primary question that local and SCLC strategists had taken up at the two-day conclave: whether the Chicago Freedom Movement, as the CCCO-SCLC effort would be called, should focus upon one issue or several. For several years King and his lieutenants had appreciated the invaluable lesson of Albany, that the movement's goals were best conveyed and attained when articulated in specific terms. Such an approach had paid off in Selma and Birmingham, where "the issue was simplified deliberately" by concentrating on a particular goal, such as integrating lunch counters. In a southern battleground like Birmingham, "it was the simplification of the issue to the point where every citizen of good will, black and white, north and south, could respond and identify that ultimately made . . . [for a] watershed movement." SCLC's advance team had "given a great deal of thought to the crystalization and definition of the problem in Chicago in terms which can be communicated to the man on the street," however, and had concluded that the standard strategy should be altered. As Bevel had argued all fall, and as King now agreed, the issue had to be defined broadly rather than narrowly. "The Chicago problem," the final draft stated, "is simply a matter of economic exploitation. Every condition exists simply because someone profits by its existence. This economic exploitation is crystalized in the SLUM," which was "a system of internal colonialism." Each specific ill—inferior education, discriminatory housing practices, and racial exclusion from skilled trades—stemmed from that common cause. Although Young had articulated a different approach, and some Chicago activists were uncomfortable with Bevel's vague rhetoric about a "war on slums," it was Bevel's definition of the issue that went into the document King presented to the CCCO at a Thursday evening meeting:

There are two possible ways to concentrate on the problems of the slum: one would be to focus on a single issue, but another is to concentrate all of our forces and move in concert with a nonviolent army on each and every issue.

In the South concentration on one issue proved feasible because of a general pattern of state and local resistance. However, in Chicago we are faced with the probability of a ready accommodation to many of the issues in some token manner, merely to curtail the massing of forces and public opinion around those issues. Therefore, we must be prepared to concentrate all of our forces around any and all issues.

In the discussions SCLC's staff emphasized the need to draw many different constituencies—black ministers, college students, high school students, unemployed youths, and slum dwellers—into active participation in the movement. Bevel was especially vocal about organizing slum dwellers into neighborhood "unions to end slums." A "three phase battle plan" was drawn up for the gradual expansion of the movement. Phase one would involve organization and education, "a campaign to awaken the people" and recruit troops for the "nonviolent army" through block-by-block tenant organizing. Phase two, beginning about March 1, would consist of demonstrations to "reveal the agents of exploitation and paint a portrait of the evils which beset us in such a manner that it is clear the world over what makes up a slum and what it is that destroys the people who are forced to live in a slum." In a revealing statement, the document added that "by the first of March, community response and live issues should have evolved to the point where some consensus has been reached about specific targets." Then, around May 1, the third and climactic phase would begin, featuring some form of "massive action" that would "create the kind of coalition of conscience which is necessary to produce change in this country" and achieve "a direct confrontation" between "the power of the existing social order and the newly acquired power of the combined forces of good-will and the under-privileged."

After presenting that vague outline to Thursday night's CCCO session, King released the same text at a press conference on Friday morning. The verbosity of the document left reporters grasping for exactly what the movement had in mind, but King was vague even in his answers to direct questions about the purpose of the drive. "Our primary objective will be to bring about the unconditional surrender of forces dedicated to the creation and maintenance of slums and ultimately to make slums a moral and financial liability upon the whole community." Pressed on specific aims, King said that programmatic responses would be sought from city, state, and federal authorities. "On the federal level we would hope to get the kind of comprehensive legislation which would meet the problems of slum life across this nation." Asked if his local goals, or his targeting of "forces" which upheld slums would put him at odds with Chicago's mayor, King insisted that "we're not interested in a campaign against Mayor Daley. We're fighting the system," not a single man. Questioned about SCLC's immediate plans, he said that the Chicago staff would be increased to several dozen, that he would be staying in a rented west side apartment during the three days each week he expected to be in Chicago, and that rent strikes and school and economic boycotts might be tactics the movement would employ in its second phase.[28]

The three days of intensive discussions did little to advance the CCCO-

SCLC coalition toward precise goals and a tangible action program. The lack of a specific program was partially obscured by Jim Bevel's powerful rhetoric and by the efforts of SCLC's expanding staff to canvass ghetto neighborhoods, but the campaign was getting under way without well-defined issues or targeted goals. Bevel's contention that slums were "domestic colonies" and King's belief that the profit system and America's distribution of wealth were the real issues had not been translated into specific programs the movement could undertake. As King left Chicago with Young and Lee for a respite in Los Angeles, he knew that the northern campaign needed more time and effort before its merits could be weighed.

King's vacation was interrupted on the second day by news from Atlanta that the Georgia state legislature was threatening to bar one of its newly elected members, SNCC press aide Julian Bond, from taking his seat because of SNCC's advocacy that young men take up civil rights work rather than submit to the military draft. "We are in a dangerous period when we seek to silence dissent," King told newsmen while warning that massive protests would follow if Bond was not seated. Julian Bond's right to oppose the draft must be protected, King said, and while he himself would not take part in actions such as draft-card burning, "in my current role as a pacifist I would be a conscientious objector."

King returned to Atlanta on Tuesday, January 11, as the Bond controversy grew. He spoke with the young legislator-elect and announced the next day that a protest march to the Georgia state capitol would take place Friday. King told reporters the controversy would also lead to another movement initiative. "This whole situation has caused us to see the urgency of going throughout the state of Georgia in a massive voter registration campaign designed to purge the state of political leaders with myopic vision. We will immediately embark on this campaign." Newsmen paid little attention to King's bold assertion, but pressed him on his views about SNCC's opposition to the draft. He said he endorsed it "in principle," but refused to comment on specific details; then he carefully straddled the fence by adding that he had "never encouraged evading the draft, and I am certainly not prepared at this point to encourage evading the draft." Civil rights work should qualify as an alternative to military service, King said, but he conceded that few people would agree with his or SNCC's position on that or Vietnam. "I would imagine that the vast majority of people in the United States support the policy of the administration."

Friday's protest at the state capitol drew hardly 1,500 people to listen in cold, raw weather as King attacked the legislature's exclusion of Bond. After King left, a group of SNCC protesters tried to force their way through police lines and into the capitol building. A brief clash ensued, an encounter the hostile Atlanta press played to the hilt. King, already displeased with SNCC's increasing loss of direction, had SCLC press spokesman Junius Griffin say that he was "hurt and shocked" by the violence. In his Sunday sermon to the Ebenezer congregation, King talked of how dissent and nonconformity were the essence of true Christianity. It might not be popular to say so, King noted, but "we aren't doing enough to end the war in Vietnam. . . . Our hands are dirty," and most Americans were ignorant of the facts. That was the real reason, he suggested, that there was not more disagreement with Lyndon Johnson's war policy: "Most people really aren't educated about what's happening in Vietnam."[29]

While King was preoccupied with Bond and Vietnam, his Chicago assistants continued to prepare for his January 19 return. Bernard Lee was assigned to find an apartment for King, and after a week of looking at rundown flats, settled on a four-room, $90-per-month apartment on the third floor of an aging building at 1550 South Hamlin Avenue in the heart of the Lawndale ghetto. Lee signed the lease before the management firm realized who the occupant would be. Both neighborhood residents and the Chicago press looked on with cynical glee as a small army of repairmen descended upon the building to improve its condition before its world-famous tenant moved in. While field-workers such as Jimmy Collier and Jesse Jackson organized block meetings of slum tenants in both west side and south side neighborhoods, press wags suggested King's best bet for improving ghetto housing would be to move from building to building. Lack of heat in the Hamlin flat kept King in a downtown hotel for his two-day visit, and he spent most of his time in private meetings with CCCO leaders and other interested groups. SCLC staffers were pleased with how "phase one" of the campaign was progressing, and tentatively planned a large rally for March 12 to mark the transition to the direct action of "phase two." Until that time, the movement leadership agreed,

> Dr. King's chief role will be the detailed selling of ideas. In mass meetings, his role should be one of teaching, not preaching. He would give a short period of instruction at mass meetings, with someone else as the chief speaker. Only on major occasions will he make a major address.

King had no quarrel with that approach, and agreed that grass-roots organizing would have to precede the sorts of demonstrations that could create "a movement so dramatic that it will bring about state and federal legislation that will rectify conditions not only in Chicago but in every urban slum."[30]

After a weekend stay in New York to preach at the Riverside Church, King flew to Birmingham to lend support to the voter canvassing and protest marches that had succeeded in pressuring the Justice Department to send federal registrars into Jefferson County. King told a series of mass meetings that registering tens of thousands of eligible black citizens could "make the Negro voter a real balance of power" in Alabama's upcoming May Democratic primary. In private, King supported his aides against SNCC criticism that SCLC's encouragement of such mainline electoral participation was undercutting SNCC's effort to create a series of all-black political organizations modeled on the successful "Black Panther" party that was being created in Lowndes County. A joint meeting of SCLC's and SNCC's Alabama staffers dissipated some of the tensions, but Randolph Blackwell told King that the best way to avoid interorganizational conflict was for the two groups to work separately and for SCLC staffers "to avoid discussion of the SNCC program whenever possible."[31]

On January 26, King returned to Chicago, with Coretta at his side, to move into his rehabilitated slum flat. He told reporters that SCLC's tenant organizing would lead to rent strikes against landlords of bad buildings, and that evening at a neighborhood church, King listened as a dozen slum dwellers testified at a movement "hearing" about housing problems they had encountered. The next day King toured the area on foot despite the zero-degree temperature, and took Coretta, Al Raby, and several others to a next-door eatery, Belinda's Pit, for the ninety-six-cent lunch special of beef stew, black-eyed peas, turnip greens, and peach cobbler. He also met at police headquarters with Superintendent Orlando W. Wilson to promise that the movement would keep the lawmen informed of their plans, and conceded that as the campaign developed, "civil disobedience probably will take place." On Friday he headed south for another one-day trip to Birmingham to spur SCLC's voter registration drive.[32]

SCLC's financial situation had deteriorated during the winter as contributions dropped further and efforts to reduce expenditures failed. King worried increasingly about the problem, and after a long Atlanta meeting with Stanley Levison, he told the staff that spending would be sharply curtailed. Unmet bills exceeded $50,000, and Randolph Blackwell informed him that the problem resulted from profligate spending. King, however, was more interested in developing new sources of funding than in controlling expenditures. Before returning to Chicago, he stopped in New York to confer with his advisors and to urge a group of clergymen assembled by fund-raiser Bill Stein to pledge regular contributions from their churches to SCLC. The pastors were surprisingly unreceptive, but their coolness did not dampen King's excitement about the Chicago campaign. Although some Chicago activists were concerned about Bevel's free-wheeling style and his inclination to focus the campaign on Mayor Daley, King was not worried. He told Levison that Daley, who had cautiously welcomed SCLC to Chicago with a defensive declaration that "all of us are for the elimination of slums," seemed intimidated by the movement's potential. Bayard Rustin, who was unenthusiastic about SCLC's northern venture, nonetheless fortified King's optimism by telling him that Roy Wilkins was saying Daley was already prepared to make major concessions to the movement.

Back in Chicago on February 2, King met for an hour with Catholic

Archbishop John Cody to explain the movement's goals. He then presided at a rally marking the founding of the Kenwood-Oakland Community Organization (KOCO), a neighborhood group put together by young staffer Jesse Jackson. Two days later, with a bad case of bronchitis, King spoke to another new movement-inspired group, the East Garfield Park "Union to End Slums." Then he headed home to Atlanta.[33]

King continued to be troubled by Vietnam, worrying that he was shirking a moral responsibility to speak out more strongly about the war. He told his Ebenezer congregation that "it's just as evil to kill Vietnamese as it is to kill Americans," and explained that it was morally wrong and emotionally painful to avoid issues one ought to face up to. "God's unbroken hold on us is something that will never permit us to feel right when we do wrong, or to feel natural when we do the unnatural. God has planted within us certain eternal principles, and the more we try to get away from them the more frustrated we will be." Although the moral also applied to other aspects of King's life, his remarks reflected the worry he had felt about Vietnam for many months.

On Monday the SCLC executive staff wrestled with the financial difficulties and a growing dissatisfaction with Hosea Williams's conduct of the Birmingham campaign. Williams was reprimanded for his personal behavior and for his failure to abide by the financial guidelines. However, a crackdown on wasteful spending could do little to solve the basic problem. Contributions had fallen below $300 per day, and as that was only a fraction of what SCLC was spending daily, the organization was accumulating a substantial debt. King was upset because the problem was distracting his attention from the Chicago campaign, but he agreed to an emergency meeting of his staff and advisors on February 12 to discuss the subject once again.

Returning to Chicago on February 9 for his weekly Wednesday-to-Friday stay, King heard Mayor Daley announce a new city program to clean up all of Chicago's slums by the end of 1967. Daley made no reference to King's incipient drive. However, one hundred civic leaders gathered at a hotel luncheon where King announced a March 12 "Chicago Freedom Festival" to raise an initial $100,000 for the CCCO-SCLC campaign. Then King and Ralph Abernathy, reporters in tow, toured a slum building at 1321 South Homan near King's apartment where tenants were suffering from a lack of heat and hot water and an infestation of rats. King told the newsmen that those conditions exemplified the need slum dwellers had for neighborhood "unions," organizations that could stage widespread rent strikes against landlords and city housing officials who were unwilling to eliminate such inhumane situations. That challenge, King said, was far tougher than SCLC's past work in the South, in part because Chicago was "so much larger than anything we've ever touched. . . . Here," he explained, "we've got to do more in terms of organizing people into permanent units, rather than on a temporary basis just for demonstrations." Such short-term organizing had been productive in the South, but "it did not lead to a permanent structure through which they could continue to work," King pointed out. If the SCLC-CCCO effort were to succeed in Chicago, long-term organizations of thousands of exploited tenants would have to be built in dozens of neighborhoods on the west and south sides. That might mean remaining in Chicago for as long as a year and a half, King volunteered, for "it will take about that time to see real improvements" in those areas.[34]

In addition to Bevel's organizing work, a second movement initiative was taking shape in Chicago: a local chapter of SCLC's four-year-old Operation Breadbasket program. Although the Atlanta ministers who comprised the initial unit had won an impressive series of black employment gains from local industries, Director Fred Bennette had been slow to pursue the coast-to-coast expansion of the program King envisioned. The Breadbasket plan particularly appealed to Jesse Jackson, a ministerial student and Chicago staffer who had had his first exposure to SCLC as one of the thousands who made the spring pilgrimage to Selma. Jackson had talked throughout the fall with Rev. Clay Evans, president of the Chicago Baptist Ministers Conference, about how the city's hundreds of black pastors could be drawn into the Freedom Movement. Aided by advice from Al Pitcher, one of his divinity school professors, Jackson pursued the Breadbasket idea when he found many black clergy unreceptive to the protest campaign Jim Bevel was promoting. "It was clear that the ministers preferred a separate, but related program to the movement," Jackson explained. He arranged for King to describe Breadbasket at a mid-November meeting of city pastors, where King found considerable interest and authorized Jackson to proceed. "The introduction of Breadbasket into Chicago," Jackson's closest colleague, Gary Massoni, later said, "was at first something of a concession to several ministers who agreed with the overall goals of the movement, but who wanted to pursue a program under their own supervision rather than merge into the mass actions being projected." Efforts went forward, and King addressed a February 11 gathering of over two hundred black ministers that marked the kickoff of Breadbasket in Chicago. In subsequent days a group of forty clergymen set up committees to gather racial employment statistics from four industries—bakeries, milk companies, soft drink bottlers, and soup companies—suspected of employing too few blacks relative to the heavy minority patronage of their products.[35]

King felt better about SCLC's financial troubles after the February 12 emergency meeting in Atlanta. Clarence Jones expressed hope that unions such as the Teamsters, which had given SCLC $25,000 a year earlier, would be willing to contribute more, and Harry Belafonte was ready to give a series of benefit concerts in Europe. Levison recommended that SCLC not touch its secret reserve of a $100,000 mutual fund account in order to pay current outstanding bills of $30,000. A forthcoming mass mail appeal was expected to produce some steady contributions within a month or two. Chicago attorney Chauncey Eskridge suggested that a syndicated radio program using tapes of King's sermons could be a regular source of income, and King's advisors persuaded him that SCLC should borrow $35,000 from Atlanta's Citizens Trust Company to tide the organization over until the new income became available.

Internal tensions at SCLC's headquarters continued to cause problems. Program Director Blackwell gave King a lengthy memo listing twenty serious issues that had to be dealt with. Most urgent were the constant arguments with Hosea Williams about his inadequate supervision of SCLC's southern field staff. "The conflict between myself and Mr. Williams," Blackwell told King, "has now reached beyond the two of us and now reaches into the core of all that we are concerned about as an organization." It "is not a personality conflict," but

> a conflict that goes to the bottom of the philosophy of the organization. It raises in a very serious way the question of whether we can at this point develop the internal structural discipline needed and whether we as a body can examine and seek out program economies.

Unless financial accountability, field staff behavior, and relations with southern affiliates were improved dramatically, Blackwell said, SCLC would continue to fritter away its resources and opportunities. A painful example of the affiliates' problem was Selma, where a split had developed between middle-class black leaders, such as Rev. Reese, and poorer citizens allied with SCLC's sole remaining staffer, Shirley Mesher, whose antipoverty work had produced a new grass-roots political organization deeply resented by the established Dallas County Voters League leadership. Blackwell also noted that "general morale within the ranks of the office clerical staff continues to leave much to be desired." No one was happy about the pay, and some were offended by the attitudes and conduct of several higher-ranking executives. Four secretaries had resigned in less than two months, and one departing worker was threatening to spread negative information about SCLC and its leaders unless her complaints were settled. Rumor had it that a sum of money had been paid to ensure the woman's silence, a report that outraged other staffers into submitting, and then withdrawing, angry letters of resignation. King found the entire business unpleasant, and he was relieved to return to Chicago, leaving SCLC's administrative problems behind.

Although King was relentlessly and harshly self-critical, his tolerance for his aides' shortcomings and internal staff disputes was almost infinite. A succession of personality conflicts between top staffers—Bevel and Walker, Bevel and Williams, Williams and Blackwell, and particularly Williams and Young—had generated almost constant turmoil for several years. Outsiders often thought those principals "arrogant beyond belief" and found the level of internal conflict amazing. "The staff . . . was totally impossible," one collaborator remembered. King "seemed to assemble every egocentric character in America." Indeed, ego was seen by most SCLCers as the primary factor in their regular battling. "I was almost immediately stunned by the egos not only at the top but all the way down," one new executive staff member recalled. "You had to have ego to stay in the movement," Williams observed. "Ain't no money out there, ain't no nothing—you've got to have an ego to stay in that movement." "Egos had much more to do with what happened" than substantive differences over program, another staffer explained. "Everybody in SCLC had those same ego troubles. Everybody wanted to be like Martin," or to be closer to him than were their colleagues. "Not only did everybody want to be next to Dr. King, but they also wanted the other guys not to be." "Ego needs," one Chicago aide complained, "often get in the way of important decisions."

The tensions were expressed in everything from teasing to fistfights. Andrew Young's calmness and moderation made him a particular target. "We used to tease Andy more than anybody else—'you're the CIA,'" recalled Joe Lowery. Even King occasionally joined in. "'How ya doing, Tom,'" one startled onlooker heard King greet Young one morning in Selma. At times it would get out of hand, however. "Andy jumped on me physically one day and fought me and whopped me all up side the head," Williams remembered. "I [had] called him a white Uncle Tom."

King often missed the worst of it, however. "Nobody wanted to act crazy around Dr. King, you just didn't do that," one staffer recalled. "I've seen them going after each other, and when Dr. King walked in, everybody just kind of cooled it." In some staff meetings, however, King would purposely tolerate all sorts of exchanges in the hope of stimulating substantive dialogue. "I've seen the staff damn near crawl across the table and slit each other's throats, and King would just sit there until it would come to an end," one aide remembered. King appreciated that some staffers, Williams in particular, were excessively combative, but some colleagues were unhappy at his reluctance to crack down on his subordinates. "He hated to even speak harshly to anybody. That was just a part of his nature," Fred Shuttlesworth recalled. "It really pained him to have to speak harshly or deal harshly with somebody."

Though some viewed King's passivity and gentleness as faults, others saw both value and skill in his stance. "One of his greatnesses," Williams observed, "was his ability to master, to orchestrate a group of individuals that probably pretty much approached egomania." Another aide agreed. "He had a remarkable facility for sitting through long, contentious meetings and then summarizing what everybody had said and synthesizing that" into a conclusion that appealed to all. That skill was not happenstance, but a repeated, practical application of the Hegelian method of thesis-antithesis-synthesis that King had been fascinated with and attached to ever since graduate school. Andrew Young understood the format. "He would want somebody to express as radical a view as possible and somebody to express as conservative a view as possible. We kind of did this sort of like a game and it almost always fell to my lot to express the conservative view. . . . . He figured . . . the wider variety of opinions you got, the better chance you had of extracting the truth from that."

King's appreciation of the positive values of SCLC's staff dynamics was also reflected in the thoroughgoing calmness with which he responded to staff blowups. "I never saw him get angry, I really didn't, and we worked together for years," one personal secretary remembered. "He had unusual and unique patience," another aide noted. "King would never get excited in a meeting. King just never would," one colleague recalled. That basic demeanor also contributed heavily to King's increasing reliance on and respect for Andrew Young. "Dr. King hardly moved without Andy's counsel," Dorothy Cotton stressed. Education Director Robert Green agreed. "There were two people that Martin talked to and listened to before he made a firm decision: Andy and Stanley [Levison]." In earlier years Levison and Rustin had been the principal substantive influences on King, but Young had increasingly moved to the fore. "Andrew Young was Dr. King's true alter ego," another executive staff member declared. "Without Andrew Young SCLC would have failed and Martin would have faltered."[36]

When King returned to Chicago, SCLC's tenant organizers reported enthusiastic local responses to their efforts. King met with a sizable group of union officials assembled by Charles Hayes of the United Packinghouse Workers to urge greater labor support of the Chicago movement. Though King often stayed at Chauncey Eskridge's comfortable home rather than in his drafty ghetto apartment, this Wednesday evening found him in the Hamlin Avenue flat when a priest brought to his door five families from the still unheated building at 1321 South Homan that King had visited a week earlier. King commiserated with them, agreed to visit them the next day, and told his staffers that the movement could not just stand by and await official rectification of these families' plight while they suffered through Chicago's frigid winter. Accompanied by Raby, he kept his promise the following day and also visited other decrepit buildings.

The following Wednesday, King and his aides undertook a dramatic initiative by seizing the South Homan apartment building in order to repair it. Dressed in work clothes and accompanied by Coretta and Al Raby, similarly attired, King told newsmen that SCLC would collect the tenants' rent and use the money to improve the building. Asked by reporters how the movement could legally just seize the structure and bypass its landlord, King answered that "the moral question is far more important than the legal one." Then he and his companions started shoveling up the mounds of decayed trash while arrangements were made to install new wiring and heating. As the media scurried to locate the building's ailing eighty-one-year-old owner, King kept a late-night appointment with Elijah Muhammad, head of the Black Muslims. It was the first time King had met the founder of the Nation of Islam, and though he had often condemned Elijah's harsh antiwhite rhetoric, their one-hour conversation was cordial. King said later that they had discussed topics upon which they could agree, and that Elijah Muhammad had expressed support for the movement's efforts to eradicate slums.

Chicago's press largely ignored King's visit to the Black Muslim leader, but harshly denounced SCLC's slum seizure. The *Tribune* asserted that King's disregard of the law could lead to anarchy, and each of the city's papers took pleasure in reporting the denunciations of King voiced by black U.S. District Judge James B. Parsons, who called the action "theft" and "a revolutionary tactic." King repeated his assertion that the morality of the tenants' plight was more important than the legality of SCLC's initiative. City officials charged building owner John Bender with twenty-three housing code violations, and the Cook County welfare department announced that it would withhold its rent-subsidy payments to the five tenants rather than have the money passed on to SCLC. King headed to New York for a CUCRL meeting, and then went on to Atlanta, feeling extremely pleased with this newest tactical venture.[37]

The Chicago movement worked hard the first two weeks of March selling the twelve thousand tickets for the entertainment festival scheduled for March 12. Mayor Daley criticized unnamed persons who did not appreciate the city's antislum efforts. King reiterated that the movement was not an anti-Daley effort. In his address to the festival's capacity crowd, King denounced the economic system underlying the slum rather than Chicago's political establishment. "The purpose of the slum," he declared, "is to confine those who have no power and perpetuate their powerlessness. . . . The slum is little more than a domestic colony which leaves its inhabitants dominated politically, exploited economically, [and] segregated and humiliated at every turn." At its root "the problem is economic," and the solution was to "organize this total community into units of political and economic power."

The festival rally was a grand success, netting the Chicago Freedom Movement over $80,000. The following day, still suffering from a long bout with the flu, King set out for a series of additional fund-raising events that took him to Hartford, Bridgeport, Detroit, and Dallas. He talked about the economic issues facing the movement, remarking in one forum that "a stage has been reached in which the reality of equality will require extensive adjustments in the way of life of some of the white majority." "Slums with hundreds of thousands of living units are not eradicated as easily as lunch counters or buses are integrated," and although past years had seen "a wholesome national consensus develop against *extremist* conduct toward nonwhite Americans," most members of the majority race did not yet appreciate that "depressed living standards for Negroes are a structural part of the economy. . . . Many white people of even reasonably good will simply know too little of the agony of ghetto existence," and could not be relied upon to respond positively when it was brought to their attention. "A hardening of opposition to the satisfaction of Negro needs must be anticipated as the movement presses against financial privilege," King warned, but the quest for "economic security" would go forward. "Whether the solution be in a guaranteed annual wage, negative income tax or any other economic device, the direction of Negro demands has to be toward substantive security. This alone will revolutionize Negro life."[38]

King's travels kept him from attending, at Mayor Daley's invitation, a March 18 parley designed to inform Chicago clergy of what the city administration was doing to combat slums. When the White House called to say that Lyndon Johnson wanted to meet with the major civil rights leaders at 1:00 P.M. on the eighteenth, however, King adjusted his schedule. The president's primary purpose was to alert the leaders to his plans for introducing a new civil rights bill. It would include provisions aimed at racial discrimination on juries and violence against civil rights workers, plus a title banning discrimination in the sale or rental of housing. Attorney General Katzenbach warned that prospects for passage would not be bright, and that any housing provision would be "particularly difficult," though "not impossible," because of the possible opposition of Republican Senate leader Everett Dirksen of Illinois. Johnson nonetheless would press ahead.[39]

After a weekend in New York, King returned to Chicago in time for a movement "hearing" on deteriorated housing that included an appearance by the owners of a notorious west side realty firm. He also attended Mayor Daley's second meeting with city clergy and listened silently as Chicago officials detailed Daley's antislum efforts. Longtime Chicago friend Archibald Carey asked King to share his thoughts with the group. King said that "Chicago has a long way to go," and engaged Daley in a dialogue that continued for more than thirty minutes. "It was as if there was no one else in the room," one observer commented, but the exchange was a calm one that King described to newsmen as "very friendly." Following two more days of meetings and speeches to Chicago organizations, King flew to New York to join Coretta for a trip to Europe to appear at Harry Belafonte's series of SCLC benefit concerts.

While King was away in Paris and Stockholm, some Chicago activists expressed their concern that the Freedom Movement still had not defined its goals and how to pursue them. Several CCCO members were troubled by Bevel's free-wheeling style and by SCLC staffers' assumption that the Chicago activists were very much the junior partners in the CCCO-SCLC coalition. Relations between Bevel and Al Raby were particularly strained, and the movement was floundering without any unifying focus. Bevel, SCLC's Al Sampson, and AFSC staffer Bernard Lafayette concentrated upon East Garfield Park's Union to End Slums, but the pace of tenant organizing was slowing and there was little focus on tangible goals that the tenant groups might pursue. "Ending slums" was a fine slogan, but it was not a program, and as one CCCO delegate remarked, "The movement must further articulate and clarify its goals for the city as a whole," or the CCCO-SCLC coalition would lose steam. Asked about such criticisms, Andrew Young admitted their validity. "We haven't gotten things under control. The strategy hasn't emerged yet, but now we know what we're dealing with and eventually we'll come up with the answers."[40]

Richard Daley was not pained by the movement's lack of direction, and his city police department kept watch on the activists' meetings and plans. Although FBI Director J. Edgar Hoover, fearful of a congressional inquiry into electronic surveillance, had ordered a halt to the bugging of King's hotel rooms early in 1966, the federal snoopers continued to keep track of King's and SCLC's daily activities. All of the phone lines at the Atlanta headquarters were still monitored by the FBI, and the New York wiretaps on Stanley Levison remained in place despite the Bureau's failure to develop information tying him to Communist activities. Additionally, in the fall of 1965 the FBI began receiving reports on SCLC's inner workings from a paid informant, accountant James A. Harrison, who had joined the organization in October, 1964. Harrison had little personal exposure to King, and less to do with SCLC's Chicago activities, but he knew and reported everything happening at SCLC's Atlanta headquarters. Early in 1966, with FBI headquarters pressing for better information on King's Chicago activities, the Bureau field office there began developing as a "probationary racial informant" a young black staff member at an allied organization who worked closely with SCLC's top local organizers. He was able to brief Chicago agents about movement discussions and gossip, including the fact that "it is a common belief among civil rights workers that Andrew Young is furnishing information concerning SCLC to the FBI." Bureau executives may have gotten a good chuckle out of that tale, but they certainly wished it were true, for to their chagrin they had no informant closer to King than the accountant, Harrison.[41]

King returned from Europe early in April to meet in New York with his research committee advisors before returning to Chicago, where he spent two days catching up on developments before heading to the semi-annual SCLC board meeting in Miami. One subject on the agenda was SCLC's finances, which still were in disarray. Fund-raiser Bill Stein asked King to approve a special appeal letter to clergymen, explaining that "the drama of the peace movement and the absence of a civil rights crisis has dulled their concern for the movement." Some also "haven't realized that SCLC could be short of funds," and unable to maintain project staffs in towns such as Selma, given the hundreds of thousands of dollars that had flowed in after the crisis a year earlier. That combination of events, plus the fact that only a small percentage of SCLC's funds went to support field staff volunteers, who subsisted on $25 per week, infuriated many movement allies. One was legal activist Henry Schwarzschild, who expressed his anger in a letter to Andrew Young:

SCLC's exploitation of local crisis situations in the interest of its larger, national objectives has been a scandal for years. Everyone in the

Movement has, by and large, covered up for SCLC in public, and I have defended your procedures publicly on many occasions, with a very ambivalent heart. . . .

I don't know anything about SCLC's financial condition, but I do know that you *raise* a lot of money and that none of you on the inner, national staff would for one day live, to say nothing of work, under the conditions that you impose upon the people who are doing the real work for you in the field. I cannot and will not be a silent witness to this sort of thing any longer, absent a showing that the SCLC national staff cannot afford to stay at the Americana when it comes to New York.

Publicly King brushed off criticism of SCLC's leaders' high living by declaring, "I don't pay any attention to it," but on reflection he found the accusations painfully accurate.

The most difficult topic slated for discussion was Vietnam. King had made public references to the war during the preceding months, telling one audience it was "unwinnable" and confiding to another that certain unnamed leaders had told him they shared his views but not his willingness to voice them. He wrote to New York Senator Robert Kennedy, praising his public dissent from Johnson's war policy, but he reassured another prominent public figure that the board's August, 1965, resolution "proscribes SCLC taking any stands or spending any monies, directly or indirectly, on matters of international affairs," including "my personal feelings" about Vietnam. An article in the *Christian Century* observed that King's "statements on the war seem curiously circumspect, almost tame," as if "King seems to be trying to walk a tortuous middle path: opposing the war as a matter of form but doing so as quietly as possible." Author Charles Fager, a former SCLC staffer and King jailmate, noted that "it seems unlikely that he can continue to be quiet in the face of continuing escalation of the fighting without seriously compromising his acknowledged role as a man of principle." King knew that was true, and he went to Miami committed to persuading the board to agree to a stronger condemnation of America's military policy than it had endorsed the preceding August.[42]

King's first day in Miami was taken up with preliminary topics, such as Harry Boyte's desire to expand his Miami office into a large-scale affiliate that could pursue a Breadbasket program. King also met with movie producer Abby Mann, whom Harry Belafonte had recommended to film King's life story. Mann was impressed by how King "seemed to be such an ordinary man," and he asked King facetiously, "'How does the movie end?'" King responded, "'It ends with me getting killed.'" Mann was taken aback. "I looked at him. He was smiling but he wasn't joking."

The next day King succeeded in winning approval of a strongly worded declaration of SCLC's opposition to America's Vietnam policy. Some board members, such as Rev. Roland Smith, were uncomfortable with the resolution, for it pulled no punches. It spoke of the "immorality and tragic absurdity" of U.S. sustenance of South Vietnam's undemocratic military junta, "a bankrupt government we have blindly supported and even exalted." Not only had America's foreign policy "become imprisoned in the destiny of the military oligarchy" in Saigon, but Lyndon Johnson's domestic "promises of the Great Society top the casualty list of the conflict" because huge war expenditures had wreaked havoc with antipoverty efforts at home. The United States should not help the South Vietnamese military repress antiwar dissent, and the administration ought to "seriously examine the wisdom of prompt withdrawal" and free elections for a democratic government. "SCLC as an organization committed to nonviolence must condemn this war on the grounds that war is not the way to solve social problems" abroad or to ensure America's most important interests. "The intense expectations and hopes of the neglected poor in the United States must be regarded as a priority more urgent than pursuit of a conflict so rapidly degenerating into a sordid military adventure."

SCLC's board also approved a sheaf of resolutions on other topics, but when King released the texts at a press conference, journalists focused almost exclusively on the Vietnam statement. Reporters challenged the wisdom of the SCLC declaration, and a front-page story in *The New York Times* noted that a recent national public opinion poll had found that 41 percent of respondents felt increased black criticism of the war made them less interested in supporting civil rights. King shook off the rebukes and returned to Chicago for another round of meetings and community rallies. Operation Breadbasket had launched its first "selective buying campaign," or boycott, against Country's Delight Dairy, and after less than a week of picketing, the company announced it would hire forty-four black workers within thirty days. On the west side, however, increased staff grousing hampered SCLC's tenant-organizing work. Unhappiness with the slow pace and lack of direction was growing, and one member of the CCCO-SCLC agenda committee warned that "no coordinated movement has emerged." More than four months of effort had produced no clear sense of direction, and the movement's future prospects were now seriously threatened by an "inability to focus on a major issue where some victories may be achieved."[43]

King recognized the danger and spent much of late April commuting back and forth to Chicago for an endless round of meetings. One small Chicago victory was the ongoing boycott of the Jenner School, where concerned parents had forced the removal of an unpopular principal. On April 28, King returned to Washington for another White House meeting marking the public announcement of Johnson's civil rights bill. From there, King went on to Alabama for a whirlwind tour aimed at encouraging black voter turnout for the May 3 Democratic primary. Throughout the Black Belt, King sought support for black candidates running in local races as well as for racially liberal State Attorney General Richmond Flowers, who had challenged George Wallace's designated gubernatorial successor, his wife, Lurleen. Civil rights workers feared whites would harass black voters in many locales and were distressed that the Justice Department had dispatched few federal observers to watch over potentially troublesome polling places. Attorney General Katzenbach informed President Johnson that "observers are not going into any but the most difficult counties" and that "I am attempting to do the least that I can safely do without upsetting civil rights groups." King and others felt they had good cause for anger when Election Day brought numerous reports of harassment and disappointing primary results. Dallas County voters replaced Sheriff Clark with black-supported Selma Public Safety Director Wilson Baker, but none of the fifty-four black candidates in other races won an outright victory. In public, King expressed mild disappointment; in private, his thoughts echoed a written observation he had made two months earlier: "The missing ingredient is no longer the will of governments to enact legislation; what is absent is the will to make it operative." Had he known of Katzenbach's intention "to take as limited action in connection with these elections as possible," his displeasure would have been far more vocal.[44]

King shuttled back and forth between Chicago and Atlanta as complaints about SCLC staffers increased on both fronts. UAW leaders were furious about anti-labor remarks reportedly uttered by Hosea Williams. Former NAACP staffer Vernon Jordan, now head of a revived Voter Education Project, complained to King about Williams's "screaming and cursing" whenever a VEP decision was not to his liking. The Chicago activists' dissatisfaction with Jim Bevel grew more acute, and the director of one organization working with SCLC complained about the "uncertainty and frustration" that plagued the project. The situation was exacerbated when Bevel showed a one-hour film of the Watts rioting to 150 Blackstone Rangers gang members. His intent was to draw Chicago's street youth into the movement and illustrate that violence did little more than leave a ruined community in its wake. More moderate leaders and Chicago city officials feared that the Rangers might choose to emulate the Watts example rather than reject it. King arrived back in town just as the discord was peaking, and found he had to spend more time mediating the movement's internal disagreements than addressing the usual spate of evening church rallies. King met with one hundred gang members on the night of May 11, and reiterated Bevel's advocacy of the tactical advantages of nonviolence. He defended Bevel's actions and lent his voice to a series of CCCO rallies to encourage black voter registration in advance of the June 14 city primary. With the movement's troubles on the rise, several activists left shaking their heads when one staff session ended in a heated dispute between Andrew Young and Al Sampson after the suggestion was made that SCLC's Chicago effort might be more effective if Bevel and Sampson were assigned elsewhere.[45]

Accompanied by Bernard Lee, King took a five-day break in Miami, and then enjoyed a more complete escape to Bimini. He returned to

Chicago on May 25 to confront the movement's problems. In his absence, some staff members had pressed for a shift into more visible action. The movement's "introductory phases . . . must come to an end, and we must get about the nonviolent action which we hope will dramatize the problems and call for a solution." A mass march of tens of thousands from Soldier Field to City Hall should be scheduled for June 12, because "the time for action has come." Others, however, such as Chicago Urban League Executive Director Edwin C. "Bill" Berry, recommended that the march be postponed because of the danger that an impressive crowd—fifty thousand to one hundred thousand people—could not be generated on such short notice. A rush to make up for the slow pace of action over the preceding few months, Berry warned, might do more harm than good. "Anything less than spectacular success in turning people out for any rally will be a severe blow to the entire movement and its leaders."

King agreed with Berry's counsel, and on May 26 announced plans for a hundred-thousand-person Soldier Field rally and march to City Hall to take place one month later to kick off the campaign's "action phase." That June 26 pilgrimage to City Hall would culminate with the marchers presenting detailed demands concerning jobs, education, welfare, health, and housing. King did not know if Mayor Daley would receive them, but the movement would make the presentation, even "if I have to tack them on the door." Reporters pressed him for details, but King commented only that sit-ins or "tent-ins" might be tactics the movement would use at realty offices or in Chicago's suburban neighborhoods in the wake of June 26. Reporters asked his reaction to the declaration by new SNCC Chairman Stokely Carmichael, who had recently replaced John Lewis, that SNCC would boycott the upcoming White House Conference on Civil Rights. King avoided criticizing his fellow activists, decrying instead the "tragic gulf between promise and fulfillment" created by the Johnson administration's passive enforcement of the 1964 and 1965 acts. Only a renewed federal commitment to black advancement could blunt the increasing radicalism of SNCC that the white press was bemoaning. "We need a massive outpouring of money," some $100 billion spread over ten years, "including a guaranteed annual income" for the poor, to combat the basic problems facing black people. No matter how sincere Lyndon Johnson might be about his Great Society promises, the soaring costs of the Vietnam War would prevent their implementation.

King also renewed his public call for an immediate halt in the U.S. bombing of North Vietnam and "an unequivocal statement that we will negotiate with the Viet Cong." America "must do more to seek to develop the climate for a negotiated settlement of this conflict," and should be more attentive to the pleas of South Vietnam's antiwar dissenters, such as Buddhist monk Thich Nhat Hahn, who joined King at a Chicago news conference. King also repeated his demand that the United States recognize "Red China" and stop blocking that country's admission to the U.N.[46]

While the civil rights leadership gathered in Washington for the long-planned White House Conference on Civil Rights, James Meredith, who had become a national celebrity as the University of Mississippi's first black student, announced that he would undertake a sixteen-day, 220-mile "walk against fear," beginning in Memphis on June 5 and concluding at the Mississippi state capitol in Jackson. He said he hoped to encourage black voter turnout in the state's June 7 primary election, but his principal purpose was to demonstrate that he and other Mississippi blacks could overcome the fear of white violence that had so long inhibited them.

The two-day White House conference, despite SNCC's absence, generated more internecine tensions to plague the movement. CORE's Floyd McKissick charged that the outcomes of certain deliberations had been fixed in advance, and expressed anger that an anti-Vietnam resolution was brushed aside. King was out of favor with Johnson loyalists and so was relegated to an onlooker's role. Although he spoke at one conference session, press accounts barely mentioned him. SCLC aides were infuriated by this treatment, but King returned home to Atlanta without public complaint.

He was in his SCLC office on Monday afternoon, June 6, when word arrived that James Meredith had been shot from ambush on the second day of his walk through Mississippi. Initial information suggested that Meredith was seriously injured, but later reports indicated that his multiple pellet wounds from shotgun blasts were superficial. Meredith was being treated in a Memphis hospital, and his assailant, Aubrey James Norvell, an eccentric Memphian, had been taken into custody. King told Atlanta reporters that the "dastardly" shooting indicated that "a reign of terror still exists in the South," and CORE Director McKissick, also in Atlanta, announced that his organization would take up Meredith's trek from the spot of the ambush. McKissick spoke with King, who endorsed the idea and called longtime acquaintance Rev. James M. Lawson, now pastor of Centenary Methodist Church in Memphis. King told Lawson of their plans and asked him to take the news to Meredith and inform him that King and other leaders would be arriving the next morning. Mississippi NAACP leader Charles Evers and SNCC Chairman Stokely Carmichael both indicated that they supported a continuation of Meredith's walk. Calls went out to Roy Wilkins and Whitney Young to join the others in Memphis the next day. In the space of several hours, the entire civil rights movement mobilized for the first major protest crisis since Selma's climax fifteen months earlier.

King, like Carmichael and McKissick, was pleased at the opportunity to revive the movement in the Deep South. Taking up Meredith's march would distract King's attention from Chicago, and perhaps force a delay in SCLC's plans there, but the opportunity to launch a southern crusade in a state that needed it more than any other was something the movement could not ignore. It might relieve some of the tension between SCLC, CORE, and SNCC that had increased since McKissick's accession in January and Carmichael's election in May. It might also succeed in bringing tangible change to Mississippi. There were dangers—chiefly the possibility that a cooperative venture would bring the movement's internal differences into more public view—but King decided that the risk was worth it. On Tuesday morning, after a brief stop in Chicago to apprise local leaders of what was developing, King and his aides flew to Memphis to take up the walk that James Meredith had begun.[47]

9

The Meredith March, "Black Power," and the Chicago Open-Housing Protests, 1966

Floyd McKissick, Martin King, and several SCLC aides arrived almost simultaneously at the Memphis airport on Tuesday morning. James Lawson met the group and escorted them to James Meredith's room at Bowld Hospital. "During our drive," Lawson recalled, "it became very clear that they were in complete agreement that the march had to continue." The one possible obstacle, however, was whether Meredith would object to its continuation. The leaders agreed that if Meredith did not consent, "they would be quite reluctant to take up the demonstration," Lawson remembered. Meredith was glad to see his visitors, and talked with King, McKissick, Lawson, and Memphis attorney A. W. Willis. They were surprised to learn that Chicago comedian Dick Gregory already had visited and voiced his own plans to take up the trek, and King and McKissick immediately volunteered that they wanted to resume Meredith's march that very afternoon. His shooting, and a continuation of the march, King explained, could focus renewed attention on the need for change in Mississippi and the importance of the civil rights protection provision in Lyndon Johnson's new civil rights bill. Meredith said he very much wanted his "walk against fear" to continue, and responded warmly when SNCC Chairman Stokely Carmichael and Program Secretary Cleveland Sellers arrived to join the discussion. The leaders promised to return later that day, then headed for Lawson's church to make arrangements for the march and to draw more movement activists to Memphis.

That afternoon twenty-one people set out by car for the spot where Meredith had been ambushed on U.S. Highway 51 near Hernando. They held a brief prayer service and headed south. Fifty yards up ahead, at the crest of a modest hill, stood several Mississippi highway patrolmen. As the group approached, an officer, L. Y. Griffin, shouted, "Stay off the pavement." Reporters watched quietly. "Dr. King stopped, almost as though he were surprised and then said, 'It's your duty to give us protection.' 'Off the pavement,' Griffin shouted," and several patrolmen moved toward King and the others at the head of the column: Carmichael, Sellers, McKissick, and SCLC Education Director Robert L. Green. The officers began shoving them toward the shoulder. "'We walked from Selma to Montgomery in the middle of the road,' Dr. King said in his steady baritone. The policeman answered in an angry voice, 'You had a permit to do that.' In the next instant there was more police shoving, this time more violently," and several activists were pushed to the ground. Sellers fell into the mud at the side of the road, and Green and McKissick, both shoved aside, stepped back onto the pavement and were pushed off once again. One patrolman was visibly agitated, and Carmichael began to lunge toward him, only to find one of his own arms still linked elbow-to-elbow with King. "Carmichael wanted to charge him with his bare hands," Lawson recalled, but King's firm grasp held him back. King gathered his colleagues in a huddle and told them forcefully that it would be better to march on the shoulder than not to march at all. Tempers cooled and the column set off southward with the patrolmen in close escort. As time and miles slowly passed, the mood picked up and a lively banter broke out, with much of the teasing aimed at Carmichael, who insisted he was nonviolent despite his brief loss of temper. "'Stokely,' Dr. King twitted, 'if you'd been in my position, you'd have let someone get shot.' 'I couldn't fight,' Carmichael answered. 'I had my arms locked in your arms.'" In time the humorous exchanges turned to some slightly bitter joshing about how and where one could find a white moderate, and King nodded in agreement at some of his companions' cynical observations. Too many whites, he assented, were "interested more in order than in justice."[1]

The marchers covered six miles before halting in late afternoon near the small town of Coldwater. The leaders returned to Memphis and an evening rally at Lawson's Centenary Methodist Church, where King told the crowd that the nonviolent movement was still the best course, that even Meredith's shooting was not adequate reason to strike back, and that this near-tragedy would allow them to press for further initiatives. "We are going to put President Johnson on the spot. We are demanding immediate action by the federal government. We need help and we need it now." His tone seemed to betray an inner tension, as if he feared that some who heard him might dismiss his advocacy of nonviolence, but the evening's real business began after the rally, when the movement's leaders huddled to discuss the strategy and goals of the "Meredith March" for the first time. Roy Wilkins and Whitney Young had arrived from New York and stood ready to endorse a March that would focus national attention on achieving congressional passage of the Johnson administration's new civil rights bill. Carmichael, however, was unwilling to accept such an emphasis. Any statement of the marchers' purpose, Carmichael argued, ought to focus on the importance of eliminating black fear, not on legislation. It also should make clear that those who advocated armed self-defense, such as the Louisiana-based Deacons for Defense and Justice, were welcome to join the March. Any statement on national issues, Carmichael said, had to point out that Lyndon Johnson's policies left much to be desired. Neither Wilkins nor Young had ever dealt face-to-face with SNCC's new chairman, and both were angered at how Carmichael wanted to put "the blame for everything, personally, on the President," as Wilkins later characterized it. Carmichael also insisted that the marchers demand improvements in Johnson's civil rights bill rather than endorse it, and he presented his fellow leaders with a draft "manifesto" calling upon the president to make good on his promises. Carmichael later asserted that he purposely wanted to maneuver Wilkins and Young into refusing to go along with the March, and his actions that night certainly encouraged that result. He steadfastly refused Wilkins's request that the March push for passage of the Johnson bill, and used colorful language to tell Wilkins and Young that they were out of date. "I started acting crazy . . . I just started cursing real bad," Carmichael recalled. "Some very terrible things were said about them to their faces in some awful language." Concerning Wilkins, "What we wanted to let him know was that it would be impossible to work with" SNCC, Carmichael said. "King knew us, so King knew that he could work with us," but Wilkins and Young "didn't know us; all they knew about us was what newspapers said about us, so we played out the image" in order to drive them away.

King remained largely silent throughout the long and contentious discussion. He spoke up at one point, during the debate about the Deacons, to insist that the March had to be committed to nonviolence, but said nothing during the heated exchanges over Lyndon Johnson. King's silence gave assistance to Carmichael's goal of dissuading the NAACP and the National Urban League from taking part. "We weren't concerned with Young and Wilkins, we were concerned with King." If the two moderate leaders remained in the March, they would dilute its militance, and "King could take a middle position among the organizations and appear to be the real arbitrator," as he had for years. "We wanted to pull him to the left," and put SNCC's imprint on the March. "Once we got rid of the right wing completely, King would have to come to the left," Carmichael asserted, and by remaining silent King allowed SNCC's divisive desires to run their course. Carmichael interpreted King's silence as either intentional or unintentional support for SNCC. "When we were acting really impolite . . . King made no move at all. He kept quiet."

Wilkins and Young became increasingly angry at Carmichael and at the others' refusal to support them. The NAACP would not endorse a statement that disparaged the administration's bill or attacked the president. When Carmichael responded by condemning "that cat the president," Wilkins had had enough. "Don't give me any of 'that cat the president' crap, Stokely," he replied, deciding it was useless to continue. "Finally, in disgust, I left," Wilkins recalled, and with Young headed back to New York.[2]

While Carmichael was pleased with how "Young and Wilkins fell completely into the trap and stormed out of there," many others were not. The national press reported that Meredith's shooting had drawn new congressional attention to the protection provisions of the Johnson bill, and administration spokesmen were declaring that the incident should give fresh impetus to the legislation. The open-housing provisions might face "a rough road," *The Washington Post* reported, but "Meredith's sacrifice ought to spur congressional concern and move this bill to swift enactment," a *Post* editorial declared. "It ought also to spur federal authorities to the most vigorous implementation of federal power. The Department of Justice has even clearer reason to use every device at its command to protect civil rights."

By early Wednesday, June 8, SNCC's manifesto had been tempered to include implicit support for the civil rights bill, and calls went out to New York to ask Young and Wilkins to reconsider their withdrawal and endorse the March. Wilkins listened as the document was read to him, but it "had NOT been changed in any essential respect, although they said it had been. MOREOVER," he later asserted, he was told that Whitney Young had accepted this new version, "*which was untrue,* as Mr. Young advised later that day." Fortunately for all involved, these disagreements remained private, but the tensions and disunity meant that the March got off to a slow and disorganized start. On Wednesday morning King and Floyd McKissick met at Bowld Hospital for three hours with Meredith, who had become agitated the previous evening over the leaders' failure to return to his bedside, and by a phone call from Lawson that Meredith had interpreted as suggesting that actions would be taken in his name but without his prior approval. King and McKissick apologized for their failure to reappear on Tuesday evening. They briefed him on the problems of the late-night meeting, but Meredith had no interest in the disputes over the manifesto and was prepared to leave the hospital and complete his recuperation in New York. Indeed, he felt so well that he accompanied King and McKissick downstairs to a press conference. The two leaders released the revised manifesto, which declared forthrightly that "this march will be a massive public indictment and protest of the failure of American society, the Government of the United States and the state of Mississippi to 'Fulfill These Rights,'" the axiom of Johnson's recent White House Conference on Civil Rights. It called upon the president to implement the Voting Rights Act more fully, to strengthen his proposed civil rights bill, and to provide an "adequate budget" for antipoverty and social welfare programs.[3]

King resumed the March Wednesday afternoon at the point where it had halted on Tuesday. The second day's column, numbering some two hundred marchers, moved southward at a good pace with King in the first rank and Mississippi highway patrolmen looking on. Thirty minutes into the walk two armed white men placed their pickup truck in the marchers' path, and lawmen intervened to allow the column to proceed. The marchers covered six miles before stopping for the evening, nine miles short of their goal. King returned to Memphis for another rally and a Thursday morning leadership discussion that delayed resumption of the March until noon, when King told reporters the leaders had agreed on a new goal. "We have decided to restructure the March to stress voter registration. Volunteers will go into surrounding communities after each day's march and urge voter registration and local civil rights activity." Then the column, now numbering three hundred, headed south in the ninety-degree heat. One elderly participant collapsed and died of a heart attack, and at 4:00 P.M. the column halted for the day in the small town of Como so that King could return to Memphis and catch a flight to Chicago.

King returned to Chicago knowing that neither the Freedom Movement there nor the Meredith March in Mississippi were developing promisingly. In Mississippi the divisions among the March's constituent organizations became more apparent each day. In Chicago there was continuing disagreement about whether the June 26 date of the Soldier Field rally was realistic enough to allow time to attract a large crowd. There was also grumbling about the lengthy laundry list entitled "Chicago Freedom Movement Demands for Creating an Open City" that staffers had begun distributing; some activists complained that the document was so inclusive as to give the movement no focus whatsoever. Final approval of the demands was not scheduled until shortly before the mass rally, and after consulting with the CCCO-SCLC agenda committee, King announced that the Meredith March would force the Chicago Freedom Movement to postpone the Soldier Field rally until July 10. Then, after meeting with members of several Chicago youth gangs, King returned to Memphis to spend Saturday night at his usual resting place, the Lorraine Motel.

During King's two-day absence, the Meredith March covered twenty-three miles. Local whites seemed "surprised and possibly shocked" by the four hundred marchers, but displayed little hostility. Black residents welcomed the participants to their small towns, but newsmen emphasized that the March's spirit was different from that of the Selma trek: less intense, less emotional, less purposive. SCLC staffers wished they had had more time to arrange logistics, and worried about SNCC comments that white participation was unnecessary if the purpose was to convince Mississippi blacks to take control of their state.[4]

Sunday morning King rejoined the marchers in the small town of Pope before heading back to West Marks to preach at the funeral of Armistead Phipps, the elderly participant who had died three days earlier. King explained to reporters later that the marchers had decided to undertake voter registration canvassing in each of the towns and counties they passed through. "This demonstration will build up the kind of pressure we need on the federal government to get federal registrars into more counties and bring about passage of the new civil rights bill." Such canvassing was the grass-roots emphasis that SNCC wanted, but other activists, like white Unitarian leader Homer Jack, worried that "there won't be a national impact" if the marchers "get bogged down in voter registration." On Monday, however, teams of canvassers spread out through Tallahatchie, Sunflower, Bolivar, and Quitman counties before the March resumed at midday with CORE's Floyd McKissick in the lead.

King spent Sunday evening and Monday in Atlanta worrying about SCLC's financial plight. Stanley Levison had advised several weeks earlier that "emergency action" was needed because of a continuing decline in contributions. Part of the problem, Levison said, was that the Vietnam War was supplanting civil rights as the foremost concern of American liberals. If SCLC's income did not pick up, the $100,000 reserve fund would last hardly a month at the rate the organization was spending money. Jones, Wachtel, and Levison all joined King in Atlanta to discuss the situation. King gave them an upbeat report on the Meredith March. The voter registration efforts were going well, and a climactic rally in Jackson on June 26 could draw a crowd of 25,000. He wanted Bayard Rustin and Walter Fauntroy to organize the rally, but Rustin was reluctant to do so, fearful that Carmichael, with an assist from McKissick, might turn to "black nationalist" themes. King agreed that Carmichael would likely cause trouble, but said it was fortunate he did not have a large following. These concerns led King's advisors to agree that SCLC should send out its own Meredith March fund-raising appeals rather than join the other organizations in a combined effort. Levison reminded King that the best way to contain SNCC's and Carmichael's proclivities would be to encourage moderates and whites to take part. King returned to Mississippi on Tuesday morning, intent on keeping the March's internal differences as private as possible.[5]

The marchers entered the town of Grenada several hours before King's return, and a crowd of six hundred gathered in the central square as McKissick and other leaders exhorted local blacks to register and vote. SCLC's Robert Green took an American flag and placed it atop the statue of Confederate President Jefferson Davis standing in the middle of the square, a symbolic action that infuriated white onlookers. March spokesmen demanded that local officials appoint black registrars to process the scores of applicants that movement canvassers were recruiting, and white leaders realized then that their town might become a civil rights focal point. City attorney Bradford Dye met with McKissick and King and promised that blacks would be assigned to conduct registration at multiple sites throughout the county. King announced that breakthrough to a nighttime crowd at the courthouse, and then led the group to a rally at a nearby church. The next morning, while some of the marchers headed off down Route 7 to the key Delta city of Greenwood, other participants pursued intensive canvassing in and around Grenada.

King's hopes to the contrary, the tone of the March threatened to deteriorate. Expressions of resentment toward white participants were on the rise among SNCC's constituency, and King used one Grenada mass meeting to stress that he was "so happy to see white people in this March." Trouble also developed when a dozen male marchers got boisterously drunk in one of the movement's tents on Tuesday evening. Staffers' demands that they quiet down were physically rebuffed, and national reporters gave the incident prominent play in their stories. On Wednesday King participated in several small-town voter registration rallies, and then left for a two-day trip to Chicago, where CCCO and SCLC staffers were trying to get some visible activity under way as soon as possible.[6]

King's first day away, Thursday, June 16, was the tensest the marchers had experienced. A white onlooker drew a pistol when a movement supply truck pulled up beside his property. Highway patrolmen intervened but declined to arrest the man. The marchers' anger intensified when state officials reduced the number of patrol guards from twenty to four officers, and when Greenwood's city council announced it would not allow the marchers to camp on public property. The column was still five miles from town as nightfall approached, and the participants boarded trucks to ride into Greenwood. When the convoy arrived at the Stone Street Negro Elementary School to set up camp, Greenwood Public Safety Commissioner B. A. Hammond confronted SNCC's Stokely Carmichael and told him he was trespassing. Carmichael and two colleagues, Robert Smith and Bruce Baines, refused Hammond's demand to leave and were promptly arrested. While the SNCC leader was held for several hours before being released on bond, the March convoy moved on to Broad Street Park, where it erected tents after receiving grudging permission from the city. An angry Carmichael returned to the park just as a late-evening rally was getting started. Greenwood had long been a center of SNCC activity, and many people knew Carmichael from when he had worked there in 1964. When he mounted the speakers platform, he gave free vent to his emotions, telling the audience that black people had to take charge and that "every courthouse in Mississippi should be burnt down tomorrow so we can get rid of the dirt." Black sheriffs ought to preside over the Delta counties, and black citizens ought to demand "black power." SNCC activists had used the phrase previously in private conversations, and earlier generations of leaders had occasionally employed it, but on this Thursday night in Greenwood, Carmichael's words struck a chord among his listeners. "We want black power," he shouted, and the crowd took up the chant: "We want black power. We want black power." Although Friday's news accounts paid the new phrase little heed, the marchers knew that the divisions that had plagued them since the outset of the March had now been given a name.

King arrived in Greenwood in time to lead a midday column of one thousand marchers to the Leflore County courthouse. A white gas station attendant attempted to disrupt the procession by spraying the marchers with a hose and threatening them with a gun. When the column reached the courthouse, deputies ordered King, Carmichael, and Hosea Williams to keep their people off the lawn. Williams started to walk forward, but King restrained him and then walked up the steps to confront Leflore County Sheriff George Smith. "You can't hold a meeting here," Smith told King. "We're going to meet here," King replied. "You can't hold a meeting here," Smith repeated. "But we have to hold a meeting here. We have to tell these people to come in and register," King asserted. "No meeting," Smith responded, as the courthouse square filled with more and more marchers. The face-off continued for several moments, and then Smith relented. "All right, go ahead," he barked at King. The March leaders conducted a twenty-minute program, then the column headed out of Greenwood toward Itta Bena. After King left the March to speak in nearby Winona, the procession headed south under the eerie gaze of Byron de la Beckwith, known by thousands as the unconvicted assassin of Medgar Evers. Beckwith, whose threatening presence had been noted back in Grenada, drove his truck back and forth past the marchers three times as participants and lawmen watched closely. At nightfall, with portable sleeping accommodations still poorly organized, the marchers were trucked back into Greenwood to spend the night.[7]

Friday evening's rally was Martin King's first exposure to the "black power" slogan Carmichael had introduced the night before. Longtime SNCC worker Willie Ricks, an even more ardent proponent of black separatist ideology than Carmichael, had been overjoyed at the response to the new rallying cry. Ricks used Carmichael's fiery speech at the Friday rally to lead the enthusiastic crowd in repeated chants of SNCC's new watchword: "We want black power. We want black power." SCLC's Hosea Williams responded by leading the audience in similarly strong chants of "freedom now, freedom now." Even if many in the crowd did not realize the conflict between the two cries and their organizational sponsors, those on the speakers platform certainly did. "Immediately," King later wrote, "I had reservations" about "black power" and how it might widen internal divisions while also conveying hostile connotations to white onlookers both near and far. King avoided any direct response to the SNCC slogan that evening, but as he led the column south through Itta Bena on Saturday, his worries about the phrase nagged at him.

When King left for a Sunday speaking engagement in Detroit, he considered whether he and SCLC should pull out of the March and dissociate themselves from the black separatist rhetoric that increasingly dominated the procession. White newsmen spoke of the "mounting tension" in the March, and on Sunday SNCC's staffers started a "black power" chant as the marchers entered the town of Belzoni. A troubled King arrived in Atlanta on Monday, discussed his options with SCLC aides, and released a brief public statement declaring that "the term 'black power' is unfortunate because it tends to give the impression of black nationalism." Back in Mississippi, SNCC and SCLC workers argued openly about use of the slogan, and SCLC Education Director Bob Green declared that King was so unhappy with it that SCLC would leave the March if there were a way to do so without public embarrassment.[8]

On Tuesday some March participants took a sharp detour to join a rally in Philadelphia, Mississippi, commemorating the deaths of the three kidnapped COFO workers—James Chaney, Michael Schwerner, and Andrew Goodman—exactly two years earlier. King arrived in Philadelphia in time to lead 250 marchers from the Mount Nebo Baptist Church into downtown Philadelphia. Hostile white onlookers taunted the demonstrators, and two cars sped past the column, missing the protesters by inches. No state highway patrolmen were on the scene, and a truck made a pass at the marchers as a man with a club repeatedly tried to strike the protesters from the passenger-side window. King and Ralph Abernathy led a prayer service when the head of the column reached the county jail, and then the marchers moved one block to the Neshoba County courthouse. When King tried to lead the group on to the lawn, Chief Deputy Sheriff Cecil Ray Price stepped forward to block his path. "You're the one who had Schwerner and those fellows in jail?" King asked quietly. "Yes, sir," Price responded in a tone of sarcastic pride. With the courthouse lawn blocked, and an angry white mob of three hundred growing more aggressive by the minute, King led the marchers in a short memorial service out in the street. Heckling from the whites almost drowned out King's words, and newsmen looked on nervously as he spoke prayerfully about the three young men's sacrifice. "King appeared to be shaken" as the whites' shouts grew more vociferous, and his voice quavered when he declared that "I believe in my heart that the murderers are somewhere around me at this moment" while Cecil Price smirked only a few steps behind him. "You're damn right, they're right behind you right now," Price muttered. King later recalled that at that moment, "I had yielded to the real possibility of the inevitability of death." King then headed the column back toward the black section of town. Halfway there several dozen whites attacked the rear of the column. The demonstrators struggled to avoid the blows, but as the assaults continued, several marchers began to return the blows. Only then did the onlooking lawmen intervene, and while the protesters hurried back to the church, the white rowdies turned their violence against two camera crews that had been filming the attack. Safe at the church, a visibly upset King told reporters that Philadelphia "is a terrible town, the worst city I have ever seen. There is a complete reign of terror here." King's schedule required that he leave almost immediately by private plane for a Meredith March rally in Indianola, but King vowed that he and a larger band of protesters would return to Philadelphia before the week was out.[9]

In Indianola King conferred with CORE's McKissick, who agreed that the movement should devote further attention to Philadelphia. After a rally at the Sunflower County courthouse, the March headed to Yazoo

City, the Tuesday night stopping point. Word arrived that a dozen marchers had been injured by the beatings in Philadelphia, and later that night further news filtered in that white snipers had attacked Philadelphia's black community. Yazoo City's evening mass meeting featured the competing chants of "black power" and "freedom now" as SNCC's Willie Ricks and SCLC's Hosea Williams struggled for superiority in a contest that was becoming less friendly each day. King arrived late, missing some of the contentious shouting, and delivered what many observers agreed was "his most impassioned speech" of the March. The internecine turmoil and the violence in Philadelphia had brought him to a point where he now was ready to express the growing frustration he had felt for more than a week. He noted how "in Mississippi murder is a popular pastime," but that meeting violence with violence was no solution, that the power of violence was not the sort of power to which anyone in the black freedom struggle should aspire. "I'm not interested in power for power's sake, but I'm interested in power that is moral, that is right and that is good. This is what we are trying to do in America." Nothing would please blacks' opponents more, he emphasized, than for the movement to respond to their violence in kind. Some earlier speaker, King noted, had said that blacks were in the majority in that part of Mississippi, perhaps wanting to suggest that blacks would benefit from using violence. King came down hard against any such implication. "We are ten percent of the population of this nation," and it would be foolish for anyone to think that black people could "get our freedom by ourselves. There's going to have to be a coalition of conscience, and we aren't going to be free here in Mississippi and anywhere in the United States until there is a committed empathy on the part of the white man." Blacks would win nothing through violence. "The minute we started, we will end up getting many people killed unnecessarily. . . . We can't win violently. We have neither the instruments nor the techniques at our disposal, and it would be totally absurd for us to believe we could do it." The movement could triumph in Mississippi without violence, just as it had over Bull Connor in Birmingham. "We can't be stopped," King declared. "We are going to win right here in Mississippi."[10]

On Wednesday morning King and the other leaders met for five hours to discuss plans for Sunday's arrival in Jackson. All three of the major organizations were almost out of funds because of March expenses, and King pledged to raise $10,000 by the weekend to tide them over. The leaders also agreed to return to Philadelphia on Friday. Most of the discussion, however, centered upon SNCC's new battle cry, which had received extensive negative coverage in the national press. "I pleaded with the group to abandon the Black Power slogan," King recounted. "It was my contention that a leader has to be concerned about the problem of semantics," and not simply ignore the harmful connotations of his words. Carmichael and McKissick both contended that the March needed a slogan, and that the enthusiastic response of Mississippi's common people showed that "black power" expressed their desires. King complained that whites would read intimations of black separatism and violence into the phrase, and suggested his colleagues use "black consciousness" or "black equality" instead. Neither Carmichael nor McKissick would budge, however, and the SCLC contingent was equally adamant that it would not surrender "freedom now." Finally, after interminable argument, both sides agreed on a compromise: Neither would give up its slogan, but the competitive chanting would stop. As the session was breaking up, Carmichael went up to King, saying, "Martin, I deliberately decided to raise this issue on the march in order to give it a national forum and force you to take a stand for Black Power." King, sensing that Stokely's assertion was part truth and part arrogant self-justification, smiled easily. "I have been used before. One more time won't hurt."

In spite of King's calm response to Carmichael, he was depressed by the new SNCC rhetoric and the changes it was making in the tenor of the movement. He had been unhappy from the beginning about the presence of several members of the Louisiana Deacons for Defense and Justice, CORE and SNCC allies who preached—and claimed to practice—armed self-defense and "defensive" violence. He had tolerated their participation, just as he had tolerated Carmichael's antics in Memphis and SNCC's thinly veiled anti-white attitudes throughout the March, but his patience was waning. "I'm sick and tired of violence," he told a Yazoo City audience. "I'm tired of the war in Vietnam. I'm tired of war and conflict in the world. I'm tired of shooting. I'm tired of hatred. I'm tired of selfishness. I'm tired of evil. I'm not going to use violence, no matter who says it."[11]

On Thursday morning an advance party from the March tried to raise its tents on the grounds of a black elementary school in Canton. The Madison County sheriff arrested the group for trespassing. When the main body of marchers arrived at the county courthouse late in the afternoon, King told them that they would try again. "It's an all-Negro school—our school—and we won't be denied." The demonstrators moved to the nearby school, and King began another rally as everyone warily eyed the contingent of highway patrolmen that looked on. King, Carmichael, and McKissick stood on a flatbed truck, with the marchers gathered around, while the troopers shifted to the windward side of the field. Despite the urgings of Justice Department civil rights chief John Doar, city and school officials insisted the marchers could not spend the night, and movement leaders likewise refused to retreat. Finally, highway patrol commanders ordered the protesters to vacate the grounds immediately. Tension gripped the crowd. King shouted to them, "I don't know what they plan for us, but we aren't going to fight any state troopers." Everyone waited for the lawmen's first move. King cried out for a nonviolent response. "There's no point in fighting back. Don't do it." Suddenly, there was a loud noise and clouds billowed from a canister that had landed near the flatbed truck. "It's tear gas. Everybody put a handkerchief over your face," King bellowed. "Nobody leave. Nobody fight back. We're going to stand our ground." More canisters began to land, and as the tear gas welled up, King's effort to lead the group in singing "We Shall Overcome" failed. Choking and gagging, scores of marchers fled. The patrolmen advanced across the fields, swinging their billyclubs at those who had not yet left.

In less than five minutes the school grounds were clear of all marchers. Enraged, the leaders gathered at the parsonage of the Asbury Methodist Church. Carmichael was "hysterical" and "near collapse," two different reporters said, and CORE's McKissick was "almost incoherent with rage." Conspicuous for his calm, however, was King, who seemed completely "unruffled" by it all. The attack, he said, "was one of the best expressions of a police state I have ever seen." He had wired President Johnson just twenty-four hours earlier to ask for federal protection when the protesters returned to Philadelphia on Friday, and had been told by presidential emissary Doar that the state patrol would take care of the task. Now, King said, he felt differently about that offer. This evening's attackers were "the very same state patrol that President Johnson said today would protect us." After calming his colleagues, King went to the Asbury church sanctuary, where the marchers had gathered, and spoke about the necessity of meeting violence with nonviolence. As arrangements were made for the marchers to sleep in the gym of a Catholic mission, SNCC and CORE staffers vowed that they would return to the school grounds the next day.[12]

On Friday morning King led a heavily guarded and uneventful march through downtown Philadelphia before returning to Canton to wrestle with the questions left unanswered from the previous evening's brutal assault. Local white officials informed newsmen that Thursday's clash had been precipitated by the movement's refusal to accept any of three alternative campsites offered by officials. Local black leaders announced that they would boycott Canton businesses as retribution for the assault, while Stokely Carmichael insisted that they again attempt to take possession of the schoolyard. As the day passed, city officials feared that the marchers might indeed launch a second encampment at the school, so late in the afternoon, they made an offer: If the marchers foreswore any attempt to camp at the school, lawmen would allow them to hold an evening rally on the grounds. The national leaders were undecided, and King recommended that the decision be made by local leaders, who promptly said yes. The marchers walked back to the school, where most participants expected that another attempt would be made to raise the tents. Only after the schoolyard rally was under way did Ralph Abernathy announce that the tents had been sent ahead to the next stopping place, and that everyone would spend the night in the gym. Many booed as Abernathy explained the accord that the leaders had reached with Canton's white officials.

Saturday morning brought a more visible dispute involving James Meredith. March leaders were already at Tougaloo College on the outskirts of Jackson when Meredith, angered by an apparent slight, decided to set out on his own course to Tougaloo from the Madison County courthouse in Canton. Newsmen were perplexed by this action, and several movement representatives, including SCLC's Bob Green and Andrew Young, joined Meredith in order to hide the appearance of discord within the movement's ranks. Matters got worse when a hostile Meredith shoved Young and Green aside as they attempted to join his column. Only later in the day, when Meredith was approaching Tougaloo, were the differences resolved as King arrived to apologize for any oversight and joined Meredith for the final mile hike to the Tougaloo campus.

Saturday evening was filled with more internal contention as March leaders argued over who would speak at Sunday's climactic rally at the Mississippi state capitol in Jackson. Whitney Young of the National Urban League, who had declined to sign the March manifesto two weeks earlier, was now on the scene and ready to endorse it. Young's participation was accepted, but SNCC and CORE leaders were unwilling to extend similar treatment to the NAACP. Mississippi State Director Charles Evers—who had first joined the March, then denied signing the manifesto, and finally reappeared on June 16 as the March began generating good voter registration gains in the Delta—wanted a place on Sunday's program even though the national NAACP would not allow him to endorse the manifesto. King argued that Evers should be allowed to speak whether or not the NAACP joined in the manifesto, but CORE, SNCC, and state MFDP leaders insisted that participation be limited to those who would endorse the March's basic document. In the end, SCLC lost out in its effort to win Evers a place on the program in the city where his brother had been murdered three years earlier.[13]

On Sunday morning, after only a few hours of sleep, King and the other leaders led a column the eight miles from Tougaloo to the Mississippi state capitol. While SNCC loyalists mischievously affixed "Black Power" bumper stickers to Jackson police cars, SCLC's Jim Orange encouraged the marchers to take up the chant of "freedom now." SNCC supporters responded with rounds of "black power," and when Orange returned to "freedom now," the mercurial Meredith angrily waved his walking stick at Orange and ordered him to shut up. Estimates of the crowd size when the marchers reached the capitol ranged from twelve thousand to sixteen thousand, but the tone of the rally struck many onlookers as oddly dispirited. Hundreds of whites jeered the speakers from nearby street corners, and even sympathetic observers could not avoid concluding that the rally was distinctly anticlimactic.

One listener described King's speech as "despondent," an accurate characterization of his state of mind. The attack in Canton and the movement's increasing internal divisions had heightened the pronounced unhappiness King had felt since the advent of "black power." A reporter who had followed King for over two years recalled that those days were "the only time I can remember, from a memory encompassing dozens of times I saw him hard-pressed, that he seemed physically and emotionally shaken. 'I don't know what I'm going to do,'" King remarked. "The government has got to give me some victories if I'm going to keep people nonviolent. I know *I'm* going to stay nonviolent no matter what happens, but a lot of people are getting hurt and bitter, and they can't see it that way any more." Interviewer after interviewer pressed him for evaluations of the March and "black power," and King struggled to put a good face on things. "This March symbolizes the spirit of our total movement, and it is a movement that works for brotherhood, for true intergroup, interpersonal living, and black and white together, we must solve this problem, so that the term 'Black Power' does not represent racism. . . . If we are to solve our problems," King said, "we've got to transform our powerlessness into positive and creative power." King was asked again and again if he and Carmichael had the same thing in mind when they talked about "power." "Well, I'm not sure about that," King parried.

> When I talk about power and the need for power, I'm talking in terms of the need for power to bring about the political and economic change necessary to make the good life a reality. I do not think of political power as an end. Neither do I think of economic power as an end. They are ingredients in the objective that we seek in life. And I think that end or that objective is a truly brotherly society, the creation of the beloved community.

Furthermore, King emphasized, "we must never forget that there are some white people in the United States just as determined to see us free as we are to be free ourselves."[14]

While King tried to reassure sympathetic whites, a vociferous argument broke out Sunday evening among movement staffers. Neither SNCC nor CORE had raised any funds to help cover the costs of the March's final days, and it appeared that SCLC would be left with the bills. SCLC aides were bitter and spoke to newsmen in the same words that had once been directed at SCLC by NAACP loyalists. "We felt we were doing all the work and paying all the bills," Andrew Young complained, "but somebody else was getting all the credit." Various ideas were proposed for continuing the voter registration efforts that the March had stimulated in the Delta, but it was unlikely that the major organizations would be willing to work with one another. SNCC's grass-roots projects in the state had been weakening for more than a year, and both SCLC and the NAACP realized the opportunities that that presented. SCLC announced that Hosea Williams and a team of field-workers would be assigned to Mississippi full time. A day later the NAACP declared that Charles Evers would head up a major expansion of their work in Mississippi.

King and his aides returned to Atlanta on Monday morning as angry exchanges between different movement groups continued. King admitted to a friend that "in my own mind, I just feel I can't cooperate with SNCC" any longer. SCLC's anger at SNCC and CORE was at least equaled by the NAACP's anger toward them all, an anger that had not abated since the disastrous session in Memphis. Roy Wilkins was still furious that the March had failed to focus on national legislative goals. "The refusal of the 'March' organizations to join in a strong nationwide effort to pass the civil rights bill was a civil rights tragedy," Wilkins wrote in a letter to many NAACP loyalists a few days after Charles Evers's exclusion from the Jackson rally. "The whole business," Wilkins said, "showed the NAACP again how difficult it is to have genuine cooperation, on an equal responsibility basis, with groups that do not have the same commitments and which may very well be pursuing certain goals that have nothing to do with civil rights at all."

In response to complaints like those, King admitted that serious shortcomings had damaged the March. "Because Stokely Carmichael chose the March as an arena for a debate over black power, we didn't get to emphasize the evils of Mississippi and the need for the 1966 Civil Rights Act," King told one newsman in uncharacteristically harsh words. "Internal dissension along the March helped Mississippi get off the hook somewhat," and reduced the gains the movement might have realized from the renewed attention Meredith's shooting had drawn to the southern struggle. No one could tell yet what the full impact of "black power" would be, but King made no secret of how troubled he was by the anti-white hostility that had spawned "black power" and that was now so visible in SNCC. His real fear, King admitted, was whether Carmichael and his SNCC colleagues would remain committed to nonviolence despite their new rhetoric. "I am confused by it all," King told one questioner. The outcome would probably have more to do with the strength of whites' commitment to racial justice than with Carmichael's proclivities. "I'm trying desperately to keep the movement nonviolent, but I can't keep it nonviolent by myself. Much of the responsibility is on the white power structure to give meaningful concessions to Negroes."[15]

King was home in Atlanta for only twenty-four hours before heading to Chicago, where the northern initiative had been all but ignored—by King and his aides, as well as by the press—for three weeks. Few important events had occurred. The ministers of Operation Breadbasket had won seventy-five new jobs from two dairy firms they had targeted, Borden and Hawthorn-Mellody, and were on the verge of a forty-four-job settlement with a third, Wanzer Dairy. Several meetings of local activists had produced minor revisions in the list of demands drawn up for presentation to the city on July 10, but preparations for the July 10 rally had been lagging. Organizers had set a goal of one hundred thousand people for the Soldier Field event, and wanted to recruit James Meredith and Catholic Archbishop John Cody as drawing cards. Jimmy Collier, an SCLC staffer assigned to the East Garfield Park Union to End Slums, had begun "amicable" negotiations with the owners of an important neighborhood realty firm, Condor and Costalis, over repair and grievance policies, and several other staffers had begun working with Chester Robinson, leader of an influential grass-roots group of slum dwellers, the West Side Organization (WSO).

Much of King's time was spent in public appearances aimed at boosting attendance at the July 10 rally, which SCLC staffers were heralding as the formal kickoff of the Chicago movement's "action" phase. King made a one-day trip to New York to accept a $100,000 check from the Swedish consul general, the proceeds of the Stockholm fund-raising rally. King canceled plans to speak to CORE's annual convention in Baltimore because of the "black power" tone of the gathering. The "implications of Black Nationalism" were simply unacceptable to him, King declared. In a long phone call to Stanley Levison, King talked of how they had to reiterate the importance of nonviolence, perhaps by means of a prominent national magazine article. Levison counseled that civil rights was not as popular an issue as it once was, that major publications would be interested only if King had something new to say, and that perhaps it was time for King to write another book.[16]

During his Chicago appearances, King made little secret of his unhappiness with the state of the national movement. Asked whether the major civil rights groups were on the verge of a public split, he answered that "we're very, very close to one." The controversy over "black power" had accelerated the diverging tendencies that had existed for five years or more, and to a disheartened King it appeared that both ends of the spectrum, the NAACP as well as SNCC, were encouraging a public break. Given Roy Wilkins's sentiments, King said, "I get the impression that the NAACP wouldn't mind a split because they think they are the only civil rights organization." Clearly the times called for increased militancy, King acknowledged, but that militancy had to be free of the connotations of violence that many associated with "black power." Three things, King explained, pointed toward that conclusion: the popularity of the phrase, which King interpreted as "an attempt to develop pride," a growing black restlessness, which "black power" also reflected, and the difficulty of winning meaningful commitments from white officialdom. For example, white officials in Grenada had reneged on the voter registration agreement reached when the Meredith March passed through, and in Chicago the movement had experienced six months of official double-talk. Mayor Daley, King said, seemed to have decided "to play tricks with us—to say he's going to end slums but not doing any concrete things." Daley's most dangerous mistake, King added, is that "he fails to understand that if gains are not made, and made in a hurry through responsible civil rights organizations, it will open the door to militant groups to gain a foothold." To encourage the mayor in the proper direction, King said, the movement would step up its tactics:

We'll use something that avoids violence, but becomes militant and extreme enough to disrupt the flow of a city. I know it will be rough on them when they have to get 200 people off the Dan Ryan [Expressway], but the only thing I can tell them is, which do you prefer, this or a riot?

As SCLC and CCCO workers spread the word for the July 10 Soldier Field rally, one obstacle was the outspoken opposition of the Reverend Joseph H. Jackson, an influential black Chicagoan and a nemesis of King's ever since the 1961 turmoil that had marked the breakaway of hundreds of progressive black ministers from Jackson's still-powerful National Baptist Convention. Jackson was no fan of civil rights activism even when King was not involved, but his animus toward King remained strong. Civil disobedience as advocated by King was "not far removed from open crime," Jackson claimed, and he asserted that Chicago needed no help from King when such true-hearted friends of black people as Richard J. Daley and Benjamin C. Willis held important public posts. King rightfully responded that "I don't think Dr. Jackson speaks for one per cent of the Negroes in this country."[17]

Two days before the rally, Daley's office announced that King had requested an appointment with the mayor on Monday to discuss the movement's demands that King planned to tape on the door of City Hall at the conclusion of a downtown march following the Soldier Field program. The demands, which had been revised at innumerable agenda committee meetings, acknowledged that some points were "long-range" targets, but that others could be implemented right away. At the top of the list were "Immediate Action Demands" aimed at ten target institutions. Real estate brokers would be asked to support the nondiscriminatory listing and showing of properties, banks to halt discriminatory loan practices, city government to establish a civilian review board for the police department, and the Chicago Housing Authority to improve the supply of low-cost public housing. Other "immediate" points called for meaningful desegregation of the city's schools, tenant protection legislation from the Illinois state legislature, better federal housing policies, and "a federal guarantee of income for every man." The "primary target," however, was housing discrimination in Chicago. SCLC announced its commitment to "organize a series of direct actions which will make the injustice so clear that the whole community will respond to the need to change."[18]

At the Sunday rally, movement leaders were disappointed when the turnout fell visibly short of their announced goal of one hundred thousand. However, a surprisingly strong message of support from Archbishop Cody and a pleasingly moderate speech by CORE Director Floyd McKissick contributed to a positive atmosphere and seemed to lessen the importance of the poor turnout. The centerpiece of the program was King's address, in which he articulated the new themes that had begun appearing in his public remarks since the advent of "black power." Although most listeners were not aware of it, King's language reflected the changes that were taking place in the movement and his hope that the beneficial aspects of "black power" could be combined with a new tactical militancy and a renewed emphasis on the importance of white support. Such a course might not please either the Wilkinses or the Carmichaels, but it appeared to be the best strategy for reestablishing the movement's sense of direction after the disconcerting events of June.

King mixed his appeals well. Indicating his desire to find some good in the "black power" hubbub, he told his listeners that "we must appreciate our great heritage. We must be proud of our race. We must not be ashamed of being black. We must believe with all of our hearts that black is as beautiful as any other color." King also declared that "freedom is never voluntarily granted by the oppressor; it must be demanded by the oppressed," but he coupled that challenge with a reminder that

> I do not see the answer to our problems in violence. Our movement's adherence to nonviolence has been a major factor in the creation of a moral climate that has made progress possible. This climate may well be dissipated not only by acts of violence but by the threats of it verbalized by those who equate it with militancy.

He expanded on his implied rebuke of Carmichael by declaring that black activists "must avoid the error of building a distrust for all white people. In seeking the profound changes full integration will involve, Negroes will need the continued support of the white majority," and ought not to forget that "there exists a substantial group of white Americans who cherish democratic principles above privilege."

Following the rally, some five thousand participants marched to City Hall and watched King tape a copy of the movement's demands on the outside door. News coverage of the rally focused as much on the wildly divergent estimates of attendance—SCLC claiming 60,000, official spokesmen 23,000, and press observers 30,000 or 35,000—as on the content of the speeches and demands. The next morning King and eleven movement colleagues met at City Hall to go over the demands with Daley and his lieutenants. King began the session by telling the mayor that the movement sought real action, not just verbal commitments. Then he turned to Raby for a detailed exposition of the demands. When the subject of a civilian review board for police conduct was broached, a heated discussion ensued as a defensive mayor took umbrage at the activists' distrust of city government. Daley refused to respond specifically to any of the movement's points, even when King asked him to endorse Lyndon Johnson's still-pending civil rights bill. Daley's evasiveness angered the movement representatives. At one point Raby looked the mayor in the eye and said, "I want you to know we're going to begin direct action, immediately." The meeting turned into a combative confrontation, and when the session ended and the two principals spoke to waiting reporters, neither sought to camouflage his feelings. King decried Daley's lack of substantive response and complained that "we had hoped the enormity of the problem, rather than the surface phases, would be met." The movement's bill of particulars, he said, required immediate action; "we are demanding these things, not requesting them." Daley, looking "visibly angry," responded that King and his companions did not have ready answers to the problems they were complaining about. Chicago was doing its best to alleviate slum conditions, and would continue to, Daley declared.[19]

That night at the movement's regular mass meeting, AFSC staffer Bernard Lafayette told the crowd that the first focus of the new "action" phase would be exclusionary real estate practices in Gage Park, one of Chicago's many all-white neighborhoods. Lafayette and his AFSC colleague William Moyer had suggested for months that the movement highlight how such discriminatory practices were a crucial link in the network of exploitation that kept poor blacks trapped in inferior ghetto housing—dwellings that often cost more than what residents of all-white enclaves paid for superior quarters. "At the beginning of the year," Moyer said later, "most of the staff saw little relationship between slums and the closed housing market, but by spring most recognized the fact that slums cannot be ended unless there is an open housing market." Bevel's tenant-organizing efforts had been pursued for six months with only modest results, and SCLC to date had no tangible gains to show for its costly investment in Chicago. The movement would have to mount a powerful and visible offensive before the close of the summer or be ridiculed as ineffective. Daley greeted word of SCLC's and CCCO's Gage Park plans with a condescending dismissal of King's efforts. "Dr. King is very sincere in what he is trying to do," but "maybe, at times, he doesn't have all the facts on the local situation. After all, he is a resident of another city."[20]

Tuesday evening King and Coretta had dinner at the home of singer Mahalia Jackson before heading to that night's mass meeting. On the way, King saw a group of people running wildly down a street. "Those people—I wonder if there's a riot starting," he remarked as they passed through the heart of the west side ghetto. He instructed the car to pull up at a local church, Shiloah Baptist, to learn what was happening. The word was that police had shut off a fire hydrant that young people had been using to cool themselves—the temperature had been in the mid-nineties all week. Some youths had resisted, and six had been arrested and taken to a local police station. News of their arrests had spread through the neighborhood, transforming latent hatred of the police into spontaneous street protests. The disruptions so far could not be called a "riot," but the potential was high. With Coretta, Andy Young, and Al Raby in tow, King headed for the Racine Avenue police station. He asked the startled officers to release the youngsters from custody, and as he waited for a command-level response, he paced the foyer nervously. One surprised onlooker watched as King "kept saying over and over again, to no one in particular, 'I told Mayor Daley, I told Mayor Daley something like this would happen if something wasn't done.'" His laments were interrupted when officers reported that approval had been given to release the youngsters. King and his colleagues took them back to Shiloah church, where a crowd of several hundred people had gathered as word spread of King's success in winning the youths' release. Many in the crowd, however, were in no mood to listen to King's soothing words. He told them of his efforts to avoid violence, introduced two of the released young men, and called for members of the audience to share their thoughts with him and their neighbors. Several people denounced the Chicago police, and King endorsed their denunciations, but he was unable to hold the crowd's attention. Some youths scoffed at his statements and walked out, and gradually people drifted away. An apprehensive King huddled with his aides as the churning crowd outside the church became larger and more hostile. The situation was deteriorating rapidly, so King and his aides, along with West Side Organization Director Chester Robinson, retreated to the WSO office "feeling that not much could be done at that moment on the streets." Distressed, King stayed at the office until 2:00 A.M. as turmoil continued in the surrounding area. Distraught at the violence and embarrassed by the crowd's disdain, King finally left to meet Coretta at Mahalia Jackson's home.[21]

The next morning King canceled his plans to fly home to Atlanta and returned to the scene of the west side disturbances. He met with Chester Robinson, told reporters that police conduct the night before had left much to be desired, and repeated the movement's demand that Chicago set up a civilian review board to hear citizen complaints. At noon he met with a group of community residents, ranging from businessmen to gang leaders, at the Community Presbyterian Church. Along with Robinson and Andrew Young, King listened to their reports that the neighborhood was extremely tense in the stifling midsummer heat. Early that evening he convened another session at the WSO office, where the local police commander, summoned at King's behest, listened uncomfortably to black youths state their grievances against his men with a surfeit of hostility. Unbeknownst to the commander, King, or the WSO hierarchy, other youths were at the same time making Molotov cocktails in the alley behind the building. As darkness fell, a second night of disturbances began. Two teams of WSO men went out on the streets to dissuade youngsters from rioting, and by the early morning hours quiet had returned to the area.

Many observers were relieved that Wednesday night's disorders had been more limited than Tuesday's, but they were still concerned that the crisis had not passed. On Thursday afternoon King called on black and white clergymen from across the city to meet that evening at Shiloah Baptist Church. About 150 appeared, and both Robinson and King addressed the group, with King almost pleading that the ministers do all in their power to prevent further violence. "A lot of people have lost faith in the establishment," he conceded. "They've lost faith in the democratic process. They've lost faith in nonviolence." The only way to regenerate that faith would be for the nonviolent movement to win substantial concessions from the power structure. "We've got to have progress that will make certain structural changes," changes that would end the hopelessness of the ghetto and give real opportunity to those who were trapped in neighborhoods like Roosevelt Road. He urged the clergymen to work for those changes, and to join that evening in walking tours aimed at preventing west side violence. While those teams headed out, King went to New Friendship Baptist Church for a previously scheduled speaking engagement. In mid-evening word came that serious violence had broken out in another neighborhood, Lawndale, some three miles from the site of the previous disturbances. King conferred with Young and other aides, and then ordered SCLC's available staffers into that area to help restore peace. He, Young, and activist comedian Dick Gregory set off by car for the area, and spent the next five hours driving from corner to corner urging people to return to their homes and to forsake violence. King did not alight from the car, but spoke to people and allowed Young to take a more visible role. Finally, at about 4:00 A.M., the area became quiet and King and his colleagues stopped for an early-morning breakfast.[22]

Later that day King met with other civil rights leaders at a downtown hotel. The group agreed that immediate city action was necessary if tensions on the west side were to be lessened, and they decided to make an impromptu appearance at Mayor Daley's office to request that hydrant sprinklers and portable swimming pools be deployed without delay, and that new consideration be given to setting up a police civilian review board. Within moments of King's arrival, Daley and a number of other notables, including Archbishop Cody and Rev. Joseph H. Jackson, appeared at the office. Recent city administration charges that King's activism had encouraged the rioting initially created a tense atmosphere, but Daley graciously invited everyone to discuss the last few days' events. King and other movement spokesmen presented their pleas for the sprinklers and pools, and King in particular asserted that he and his staff had done nothing to encourage rioting, and everything possible to discourage it. The mayor was less hostile to the movement's demands than he had been prior to the west side turmoil and promised immediate efforts to make hydrant sprinklers and swimming pools available. He and his aides were less enthused with King's recommendation that city officials join with movement activists to work more closely with Chicago's youth gangs, but King gave a positive report to newsmen when the ninety-minute session concluded. "We've had a very fine meeting," and the mayor's receptivity was clearly "a move in the right direction."

King felt burdened by what he believed was a personal responsibility to do all he could both to end the violence and eliminate the wretched conditions that produced it. To some acquaintances he seemed discouraged at the realization that so much would have to be done to change the conditions that trapped tens of thousands of people in the ghetto, but he allowed neither his emotional commitment nor his physical strength to lag. Even though he had had little sleep over the preceding nights, late Friday King had his SCLC aides call the leaders of Chicago's major gangs—the Cobras, the Vice Lords, and the Roman Saints—to his own west side slum apartment. For several hours he listened as the young men talked about the conditions in which they lived, especially the absence of jobs for youths of their age, race, and education. King argued that non-violent protest offered the only possible course for substantially changing those conditions. The gang leaders, who had been impressed by King's forays through the streets, listened respectfully to his tactical argument. After a lengthy dialogue, King convinced Richard "Peanut" Tidwell, the twenty-year-old leader of the Roman Saints, to accept his point. Tidwell joined him in telling the other gang chieftains to give King's proposal a try, and the discussion went back and forth into the early-morning hours in the sweltering apartment. Two Justice Department officials, John Doar and Roger Wilkins, arrived at King's door in the middle of the session, and listened with quiet respect from a corner as King's arguments won over more and more of the gang leaders. Finally, at 3:00 or 4:00 A.M., the entire group agreed to tell their members to avoid further violence.[23]

Despite his positive comments at the conclusion of Friday's meeting with Daley, King resolved that the movement would have to keep the mayor's feet to the fire and point out that the west side disorders were evidence that Chicago's problems were more serious than its elected leadership would admit. Andy Young dismissed Daley's Friday commitments as "only a few minor concessions and no real response to basic needs." King canceled a trip to a Geneva World Council of Churches convention in order to give more thought to Chicago and to pressing questions confronting the movement. The urban violence, like the tensions in the southern movement, led King to consider how an increased militance concerning goals could be combined with a renewed commitment to non-violence and biracial cooperation. One interviewer found him "peculiarly relaxed" as he mulled over how to bring the movement's disparate groups together. "'Somewhere,' he said over and over again, 'there has to be a synthesis. I have to be militant enough to satisfy the militant yet I have to keep enough discipline in the movement to satisfy white supporters and moderate Negroes.'" He was encouraged by the headway being made with the black youth gangs, and he was infuriated by the City Hall rumors that SCLC's contacts with the gangs were the cause of the riots.[24]

No rioting took place over the weekend, and on Monday King flew home to Atlanta for three days of rest. SCLC's financial situation remained shaky, and prospects for increased contributions were hurt by news articles declaring that "black power" and the urban disorders marked the end of the civil rights movement. Even liberal journals such as *The Nation* declared that the movement was "nearing the end," and editorial writers in several publications were critical of King's efforts. "What Dr. King lacks—and it is surely only to a minor degree his fault," *The Nation* declared, "is (1) a program; (2) a political strategy; [and] (3) a political vehicle to carry out the program and the strategy." More and more commentators articulated the "political coalition" argument that Bayard Rustin had been putting forward for over a year. King believed that Rustin's strategizing discounted the real value of direct-action protests, and that Rustin's plans were more attuned to white supporters than to poor blacks in America's slums. The controversy over "black power" indicated the growing division within the movement, and King hoped desperately that he could secure the "synthesis" he had talked about in Chicago. Stanley Levison convinced King it was imperative that SCLC's dissent from "black power" be registered prominently with a broad national audience as soon as possible, and King approved a Levison draft of a statement run under King's name as a paid advertisement in *The New York Times*. "Black power," the statement declared, was "an unwise choice" of words that had "caused substantial confusion and alarm" and had proven "dangerous and injurious" to the movement. Its popularity in the black community came "not from a sense of strength but from a feeling of weakness and desperation" and from some activists' desperate search for a "method to shock and pressure the white majority to come to terms with an evil of staggering proportions." Much of its appeal was due to blacks' perception that the federal commitment to civil rights was lessening and that "extravagant promises made less than a year ago are a shattered mockery today." King professed to *Times* readers that "I confidently believe that the call for 'Black Power' will rapidly diminish," but his true feelings were different. "You just can't communicate with the ghetto dweller and at the same time not frighten many whites to death," he admitted to one questioner. "I don't know what the answer to that is. My role perhaps is to interpret to the white world. There must be somebody to communicate to two worlds."[25]

King returned to Chicago on July 21 and was greeted by the news that a prominent black Daley ally, Ernest E. Rather, was publicly inviting him to go back South, by a national newspaper declaring that not since Montgomery had "his position been so insecure," and by continued sniping from Daley loyalists, who said SCLC had no real program for Chicago and was to blame for the west side riots. He told newsmen that he categorically rejected those "phony accusations" of riot involvement, and declared that "the key issue with us today is the powerlessness of the oppressed people who inhabit our slums and ghettos." King identified a more immediate obstacle in how Chicago's "power structure is treating the Chicago Freedom Movement as though it were an invisible man." Recent events suggested that city leaders responded more positively to rioting than to nonviolent appeals, and unless Daley pursued the "fundamental structural changes required to right our racial wrongs," more rioting would be inevitable. "A nonviolent movement cannot maintain its following," King warned, "unless it brings about change."

Although King was defensive about why the Chicago effort had been slow to flower, aides such as Andrew Young were more frank. "The trouble here is that there has been no confrontation," Young told one interviewer, nothing of "the kind where they interrupted the network TV programs to say that Negroes in such-and-such a white area are doing something." SCLC had been too painstaking in Chicago, "when we should have waded right in." That vacillation explained why "we haven't found the Achilles heel of the Daley machine yet." They hoped to find it soon, however. While King headed east for a one-day visit home and a two-day stop in New York, Al Raby, Jim Bevel, and Jesse Jackson made plans to follow through with the Gage Park realty firm protests that Bernard Lafayette had announced two weeks earlier. Lafayette's and Moyer's suggestion that racist brokers be targeted for nonviolent demonstrations fit perfectly with the desire of Young and others that the movement precipitate an open confrontation with white Chicago.

On Thursday evening, July 28, King announced to a mass meeting at New Friendship Baptist Church that the movement would stage a Friday night vigil outside the Gage Park office of the Halvorsen Realty Company, a firm whose record of discriminating against black clients was firmly established. Fifty movement protesters arrived on the scene Friday afternoon, intending to remain until Saturday morning, but as darkness fell a crowd of hostile whites began taunting the demonstrators. Several dozen policemen were on hand, but by mid-evening the angry whites numbered almost one thousand and had begun throwing debris at the protesters. Police commanders encouraged the demonstrators to terminate the vigil for their own safety, and at 9:00 P.M. the protest leaders took their group back to New Friendship church. Once there, a debate broke out on whether the movement had erred in retreating from the violence. Al Raby was angry that the protesters had not stood their ground, and asserted that the movement would have to return to the Halvorsen office the next day to show that open-housing demonstrations could not be halted by violence.[26]

Saturday afternoon five hundred marchers set out from New Friendship church to walk to the Halvorsen office in Gage Park. When they entered the white neighborhood, hostile onlookers unleashed a barrage of rocks and bottles, and both Raby and Jesse Jackson were hit. Policemen did little to halt the attack, and only half a dozen arrests were made as the column made its way through another all-white neighborhood, Marquette Park, and headed back to New Friendship church. Indignant movement leaders vowed that the demonstrators would repeat their pilgrimage the next day, and on Sunday afternoon Raby led a lengthy caravan of cars to Marquette Park. Angry white residents were waiting, and even the presence of several hundred policemen did not dissuade the hecklers from heaving stones and bottles at the demonstrators as they walked from their cars to a Methodist church. Police efforts to halt the violence were far from energetic, and AFSC executive Kale Williams noted that "it was obvious that some officers were torn between their duty and their identity with their friends and neighbors in the crowd." The onslaught forced the marchers to retreat on foot toward New Friendship church. Several dozen participants were injured by the bottles and bricks, and as the column marched away, the white hoodlums attacked the cars that the protesters had parked in Marquette Park. Automobiles were overturned and set afire, and fifteen vehicles were destroyed before police brought the area under control.

Movement leaders were outraged by both the violence and the lack of police response. Officers who had promised to guard the cars in Marquette Park had not done so, and had also done little to stop the attack. AFSC Director Williams complained to Police Superintendent Orlando W. Wilson about the many "friendly interchanges" between officers and "obvious breakers of the law," and Community Relations Service observer Sam Dennis agreed that the marchers had been given "very little protection." King was out of town over the weekend, giving a speech in North Carolina and attending to SCLC's affairs in Atlanta, and would not return until Tuesday, but he issued a statement decrying the police laxity. The Chicago protesters took a break on Monday, but announced plans for a Tuesday afternoon march into another all-white area, Belmont-Cragin. Police Superintendent Wilson blamed the weekend violence on the fact that commanders had not had advance notice of the movement's plans, but Mayor Daley, worried by the national media attention accorded the turmoil in neighborhoods constituting his own political base, summoned white community leaders to City Hall. "Ignore the marchers and they'll go away," Daley told the group while stressing that "law and order is necessary" no matter how distasteful their neighbors found the protests.[27]

Tuesday's march through Belmont-Cragin was peaceful, and a similar Wednesday procession also was free of violence. King remained in the background of these events, although he participated on Thursday in a highly-publicized meeting between CCCO activists and the city's black elected officials. Movement leaders trumpeted the resulting endorsement of their demands by the politicians, and on Thursday night King told a 1,700-person audience at New Friendship that he would join a Friday march to four realty firms in the Gage Park and Chicago Lawn neighborhoods. Despite "black power" and the violent turmoil in Chicago, "I still have faith in the future," King declared to his listeners.

Friday's pilgrimage began with a caravan of more than one hundred cars heading from New Friendship church to a heavily guarded Marquette Park. The plan was for the six hundred participants to march from the park to the realty firm offices that lined nearby Sixty-third Street, while more than one thousand Chicago policemen kept the white mobs at a safe distance. The hostile whites, however, were already in position and armed with stones when the lead cars of the procession pulled into the center of Marquette Park. Police officers surrounded King as he stepped from the first car, but seconds later he was knocked to one knee by a rock that struck him on his right temple. Aides rushed to his side as photographers snapped pictures, and King knelt with his head bent for several moments before being helped to his feet. The blow had dazed him, though not drawn blood, and he appeared "visibly shaken" as more stones rained down and aides shielded him. After a pause, King steadied himself and the procession got under way as bottles and bricks continued to fly despite police efforts to control the crowd. "I had expected some hostility, but not of this enormity," King told reporters. The angry mob trailed the marchers as they walked, and at the end of the protest, the final tolls showed forty-one arrests and thirty injuries. King declared that he had "never seen anything so hostile and so hateful as I've seen here today," but said he would march again, stones or no stones. "I have to do this—to expose myself—to bring this hate into the open."[28]

Saturday morning, while news headlines across the country reported the Chicago violence, King flew to Atlanta for a two-day rest before heading to Jackson, Mississippi, for SCLC's annual convention. CCCO organized a Sunday afternoon march of one thousand people through Belmont-Cragin, and once again hundreds of policemen strained to hold back large crowds of angry hecklers. SCLC aides Bevel and Jackson complimented the more aggressive police action, and on Monday announced plans for future marches in the all-white communities of Bogan and Cicero. "We expect violence," Jackson admitted. Local white leaders complained that officers were becoming too physical in restraining march opponents, and demanded that city officials halt the civil rights processions. The *Chicago Tribune* denounced the open-housing marches in a vituperative editorial and called for the black populace to throw out "paid professional agitators" such as King, Raby, and Bevel. The message being articulated to Chicago whites by the protesters, the *Trib* claimed, was "give up your homes and get out so that we can take over."[29]

In Jackson, King told reporters that Chicago would remain SCLC's main focus. He said he was even considering a name change to make SCLC appear more national in scope. "We still need to be a southern-based organization," but the board would be expanded to include more northerners and the first white members in SCLC's history, civil liberties lawyer Charles Morgan and Democratic party activist Allard Lowenstein. King said more attention would be given to economic issues such as a federally guaranteed annual income, but SCLC would have to deal with several staff departures before new initiatives could be launched. White administrator Harry Boyte had resigned, C. T. Vivian had left to take a position with Chicago's Urban Training Center, and Education Director Robert Green was about to return to his position at Michigan State University. More important, Program Director Randolph Blackwell had finally had enough and begun a year's leave of absence to work with the Citizen's Crusade Against Poverty. King was heartsick to lose him, and feared that Blackwell would not return. He pleaded with him to appreciate how crucial he was to SCLC, and apologized for not having given Blackwell's complaints and recommendations more heed. "I cannot begin to explain the great burden of my schedule, the impossible day-to-day demands that confront my life, and the endless travel that keeps me wondering whether I am going or coming," King confessed in a long letter.

King escorted Massachusetts Senator Edward M. Kennedy, the convention's keynote speaker, through the first night's activities, but King's participation was ended by a virus and high fever that kept him in bed. Andrew Young stood in for King at convention functions, but King was not too ill to keep posted by phone on developments in Chicago, where movement leaders were angry that SCLC's Jesse Jackson had not gotten their approval before announcing more marches into additional all-white communities. On Tuesday night thirty CCCO and SCLC activists met at the Chicago Theological Seminary for four hours to review Jackson's plan to march through Bogan on Wednesday. After consulting with King by phone, the group substituted picketing of the downtown offices of the Chicago Real Estate Board for the Bogan march. The cancellation of the neighborhood protest was ascribed to press coverage of white violence obscuring the movement's focus on open housing, and city officials were angered when without any advance warning several hundred demonstrators appeared outside the realtors' association offices for a twenty-minute vigil. Al Raby announced that a march into Bogan would take place the following afternoon, and that additional protests, including one in the infamous all-white town of Cicero, would follow soon after. If city officials wanted the demonstrations ended, they should appeal not to the movement, but to the real estate brokers to halt discriminatory practices and abide by Chicago's open-housing ordinance.[30]

By Wednesday it was clear that Chicago authorities wanted the protests stopped before additional mob violence occurred. The dangers of continued demonstrations were discussed at a lengthy Tuesday meeting of Mayor Daley's Chicago Commission on Human Relations, and "the commissioners unanimously agreed that some effort should be made to set up a meeting with the Mayor, the civil rights leaders, the Chicago Real Estate Board and other interested organizations and citizens." Later that day the suggestion was presented to Daley, who agreed and recommended that the convening authority be an independent body. Daley passed on his sentiments to Real Estate Board President Ross Beatty, and two members of the Human Relations Commission, Hale Nelson and Inland Steel executive William Caples, called upon a good friend who was an influential board member of the Chicago Conference on Religion and Race (CCRR), Paul Lund of Illinois Bell. They persuaded Lund of the wisdom of such a summit meeting, and the next morning Caples and Lund went to visit Eugene Callahan, the executive director of the business-backed CCRR. Callahan and the Conference chairman, Episcopal Bishop James Montgomery, both agreed to their proposal that the Conference sponsor high-level negotiations. Other business and religious leaders were asked to support the initiative, which Callahan and Montgomery would announce as soon as possible.

At the same time that the CCRR was moving into action, Catholic Archbishop John Cody, a strong supporter of the movement only a month earlier, issued a call for a temporary halt in the open-housing demonstrations. It was his hope, Cody declared, that officials "will immediately convene meetings between realtors and civil rights advocates in order to achieve a just and lasting resolution of the present crisis." Simultaneously, Cook County Sheriff Richard B. Ogilvie, Illinois State Police Commander William Morris, and State Human Relations Commission Director Roger Nathan warned Al Raby that unless the movement gave law enforcement officials advance notice of its protests, such as the planned trek through Cicero, authorities would seek a court injunction against the demonstrations. Raby promised them seven days' notice of any Cicero march, and then headed south to the SCLC convention.[31]

In Jackson, SCLC's board approved resolutions that called for a guaranteed annual family income of at least $4,000, decried the Johnson administration's "inadequate enforcement" of the 1964 and 1965 civil rights acts, and denounced a recent House vote striking the open-housing provision from Johnson's 1966 legislative package. Another resolution, prepared for King by Stanley Levison, denounced Johnson's "relentless escalation" of the Vietnam War, a conflict that "is corrupting American society from within and degrading it from without." It demanded an immediate and unilateral de-escalation, and warned that "never in American history have we been so isolated and so explicitly rebuked by the world community."

King was sick in bed with a fever and laryngitis as the convention ended on August 11. Andrew Young read King's address and annual report to the group, including several strongly worded declarations that SCLC would pursue an increasingly broad agenda of issues. "The majority of the people in our society are now powerless, and in no way able to participate in the decision-making," one passage avowed. "I am afraid that the cries of warning and the shouts of desperation of our ghettos now fall on deaf ears. . . . Self-determination for an oppressed people requires power." SCLC would seek those goals in Chicago and elsewhere, and "we believe that the many unmet demands will be realized through intensified application of nonviolent direct action." Propped up on pillows in his bed, King whispered to a visiting reporter his firm commitment to the Chicago protests. "If some of us have to die, then we will die."[32]

Late Thursday SCLC's Chicago staff announced a Friday march through Bogan. The next day, as eight hundred policemen protected seven hundred marchers in what turned out to be the most peaceful neighborhood march to date, the Conference on Religion and Race announced its call for a summit-level discussion of Chicago's racial situation and the Freedom Movement's demands on Wednesday, August 17. Local movement leaders quickly accepted the invitation, and Urban League director "Bill" Berry told newsmen that King was elated that Real Estate Board President Ross Beatty had also accepted. At a Saturday afternoon strategy session, movement leaders resolved to keep up the pressure in the face of these signals that Chicago's power structure was eager to negotiate. On Sunday the movement undertook its most extensive protest effort yet by scheduling three simultaneous marches through different all-white neighborhoods. Al Raby led five hundred demonstrators through Gage Park and Chicago Lawn, Jesse Jackson three hundred through Bogan, and Jim Bevel four hundred through Jefferson Park as scores of policemen held back angry white onlookers. The movement rested on Monday, but announced plans to picket City Hall, the Real Estate Board, and several realty firms the following day.

Various maneuvering went forward as Wednesday's summit meeting approached. The Conference on Religion and Race, after consulting with city officials, endorsed the mayor's recommendation that well-known industrialist Ben W. Heineman moderate the session. The Conference's board met on Tuesday to define their organization's position for the Wednesday talks. They agreed that while the movement might be ready to suspend its protests in exchange for meaningful progress on open housing, the Real Estate Board would likely not make any concessions. No one should expect a breakthrough at the first meeting, and every effort should be made to ensure that further discussions were agreed to. Rabbi Robert J. Marx of the Union of American Hebrew Congregations recommended that a "smaller committee to work out" an agreement should be suggested, and influential black Rev. Arthur Brazier voiced a similar opinion. Callahan agreed and said he would speak with moderator Heineman about a course of action if Wednesday's session should deadlock.

Movement spokesmen expressed cautious expectations for the Wednesday talks. "We're not too hopeful," Andrew Young said. "We haven't been able to put on enough pressure yet. In Birmingham and Selma we almost needed martial law before we got anywhere." The movement's agenda committee quickly ratified a set of demands that paralleled the laundry list released at the July 10 rally. Some participants worried that greater care should be taken in specifying the demands, but Jim Bevel stressed to newsmen that the focus of the talks ought to be on "the methods of implementing open housing" throughout Chicago. "It will not be a negotiating session," he declared, "because we cannot compromise."[33]

King arrived in Chicago Wednesday morning, just a few hours before the "summit meeting" convened at the Episcopal diocese offices. The several dozen participants sat around a long conference table, and Chairman Heineman asked Richard Daley if he had any opening remarks. "We have to do something to resolve the problems of the past few weeks," the mayor declared. Heineman offered King a similar opportunity, and King expressed thanks to the Conference for this chance to begin a dialogue. In Chicago, he explained, "we have a dual school system, a dual economy, a dual housing market," and other segregated conditions, and the movement's goal was "to transform this duality into a oneness. We cannot solve this alone; we need the help of the people with real power." Then he turned to Al Raby, who sounded a distinctly different note. "I am very pessimistic about the negotiations today," he declared bluntly, "because my experience with negotiating has indicated that our success has always been very limited." Fifteen years ago, when a black family tried to move into Cicero, serious violence erupted, just as would happen today if the movement marched there:

> So there has not been any significant change . . . The Movement has exposed by its marches how we all have failed. We must admit that this dialogue that's beginning today would not have occurred without the marches. But there will be no resolution of this situation until we have a factual change in the circumstances of Negroes. We will not end our marches with a verbal commitment.

Heineman then asked the chairman of the Chicago Commission on Human Relations, Ely M. Aaron, to present his group's proposals. Aaron read eleven recommendations, which included calls for the Real Estate Board to instruct its members to abide by the city's pro-forma antidiscrimination ordinance and for the movement to institute "an immediate moratorium on marches." A black businessman, A. L. Foster, representing the Cosmopolitan Chamber of Commerce, broke in to say that the key point was for the Real Estate Board to declare its support for open occupancy without regard to race. Board President Ross Beatty responded immediately. "The most important thing for us to understand is what the situation really is as it exists, not what we'd like it to be or want it to be, but what it really is. . . . We are not here to negotiate because the problem can't be solved between us and the civil rights people." Realtors were nothing more than agents for others, and "we cannot persuade property owners to change their attitudes about whom they want to sell their property to. . . . We are the ones that are easy to blame, . . . but the problem is not ours. The realtor is an agent; we must represent our clients. And therefore, because our clients are opposed to the open occupancy law, we must oppose the law if we are to honestly represent our clients." Change could take place only if public attitudes shifted, and "realtors cannot take the lead in this."

Then Raby read the Chicago Freedom Movement's nine demands. They called for the city to begin vigorous enforcement of the existing fairhousing ordinance, for the mayor to consider a tougher provision that would apply to owners as well as brokers, for the realtors' association to withdraw its ongoing court challenge to the existing ordinance and to end its opposition to a state fair-housing bill pending in the Illinois legislature. They also specified that the Chicago Housing Authority end the practice of concentrating high-rise public-housing projects in the ghettos, and that the Public Aid Department stop referring its recipients to available housing on the basis of race. They further demanded that lending authorities, business and labor leaders, and urban-renewal planners all pledge to end discriminatory practices.

A representative of city mortage bankers volunteered that his group could accept that demand in full, and Mayor Daley broke in to ask if demonstrations would halt if all the movement's demands were met. King responded, "Yes, the demonstrations in the neighborhoods might stop, but we have demands also in the areas of education and employment and you are hearing here only our demands in the area of housing." Somewhat miffed, Daley replied, "If we do all we can as a city, then why can't the marches stop?" Heineman tried to clarify the situation, and King asked Daley directly if he was ready to grant each of the movement's demands. The mayor took the sheet, read each of the points out loud, and agreed that he and the city would meet each one. A clearly suspicious Al Raby questioned Daley in detail about some of the items, and then Heineman asked King what he meant with regard to halting the neighborhood marches. King said that open-occupancy protests aimed at realty firms would end, but that neighborhood marches aimed at educational or employment issues would not be ruled out. John Baird, an influential businessman, interjected a more basic concern. "The Mayor can't really do all of the things that he has said here immediately, with all due respect. Will the marches stop before the Mayor has been able to accomplish the specifics?" Al Raby, worried that things were moving too fast, pointed out that a number of the movement's demands had not yet been addressed. Housing Authority chief Charles Swibel conceded he could not promise an immediate halt in the construction of high-rise ghetto projects, and a lengthy exchange about high-rise public housing ensued.

The discussion was brought back into focus by Arthur Mohl, a Real Estate Board member, who declared that the board would abide by the city ordinance, but that discrimination was not a realtors' problem because "we are not the creators, we are the mirror." King responded immediately:

All over the South I heard the same thing we've just heard from Mr. Mohl—from restaurant owners and hotel owners. They said that they were just the agents, that they were just responding to the people's unwillingness to eat with Negroes in the same restaurant or stay with Negroes in the same hotel. But we got a comprehensive civil rights bill and the so-called agents then provided service to everybody and nothing happened and the same thing can happen here.

After a pause, Heineman declared that "I don't intend to recess this day until we have resolved these issues." Thomas G. Ayers, president of Consolidated Electric and Chicago's most powerful business leader, voiced agreement with King's remarks. "I think we support all the points in the proposals of the Chicago Freedom Movement," he added significantly. A labor representative expressed a similar commitment, and then Jim Bevel returned to the question of the Real Estate Board. "The core problem is that realtors refuse to serve Negroes in their offices, and that must change. That is insulting and it is humiliating. And the burden is to change service to Negroes."

Board President Beatty responded that he, Mohl, and a third representative, Gordon Groebe, did not have the authority to accept any specific demands. He added there would have to be further discussion after a regularly scheduled meeting of the Real Estate Board that afternoon. Heineman recognized the opening Beatty had provided. "Were you saying that there should be a subcommittee of the Conference on Religion and Race, the Freedom Movement and the Chicago Real Estate Board to talk about this further?" he asked. "We can't sit across the table and bargain with the civil righters for something that we don't have the power to give," Beatty parried. Gordon Groebe, sensing the trap, objected:

> If King would come out against the fair housing ordinance, then he would lose his supporters and he would lose his position and he would not be a leader. And you've got to realize that you're asking us to do the same thing. When we ask our realtors to abrogate their position as agents, then you're asking us to do what you'd be asking Dr. King to do if you told him he had to come out against the fair housing ordinance.

King responded immediately:

> I must appeal to the decency of the people on the Chicago Real Estate Board. You're not negotiating this question with us. You are men confronted with a moral issue. I decide on the basis of conscience. A genuine leader doesn't reflect consensus, he molds consensus. Look at myself. There are lots of Negroes these days who are for violence, but I know that I am dealing with a moral issue, and I am going to oppose violence if I am the last Negro in this country speaking for nonviolence. Now the real estate people must act on principle in that same manner, or they're not leaders. The real estate industry has not only reflected discriminatory attitudes, it has played a significant part in creating them. In fact, in California the real estate people spent five million dollars to kill the open occupancy law there. Now don't tell me that you're neutral.

Just the previous day, King went on, Attorney General Katzenbach had remarked to him on the phone that if the federal government had all the funds that the real estate industry had employed in opposing the fair-housing provisions in the administration's civil rights bill, it could eliminate all the slums in one major city. "I appeal to the rightness of our position and to your decency," King declared.

> I see nothing in this world more dangerous than Negro cities ringed with white suburbs. Look at it in terms of grappling with righteousness. People will adjust to changes, but the leadership has got to say that the time for change has come. The problem is not the people in Gage Park, the problem is that their leaders and institutions have taught them to be what they are.

In the face of that appeal, Ross Beatty retreated a bit. "Well, we will recommend to our board that we sit down with you and discuss this further. But we have got to be clear on what the Chicago open occupancy ordinance really requires." A Presbyterian churchman, betraying some exasperation, pointed out that the Freedom Movement's demands were straightforward and that "I think the Chicago Real Estate Board can act on these." Rabbi Marx added his voice even more bluntly. "We have heard this same thing from the Real Estate Board over and over. They must understand that we must have a change now." United Auto Workers representative Robert Johnson expressed the same feeling: "I agree we must have change. This is an urgent situation. The Real Estate Board must realize that there must be change now." Bishop Montgomery voiced his agreement, and then Al Raby suggested that they adjourn. Mayor Daley immediately disagreed. "No, let's not adjourn the meeting. The Chicago Real Estate Board should get on the phone to their members and do something about these demands now." Daley's blunt declaration surprised many. By indicating his support for the stance taken by the religious leaders and by businessmen such as Ayers, Daley "placed a terrific burden" on the realtors, Civil Rights Commission observer John McKnight noted. All eyes turned toward Beatty, and he again tried to duck responsibility. "We cannot possibly deal on the phone; we cannot possibly work out a resolution to these things today."

Chairman Heineman added his voice to the consensus:

> Gentlemen, the big stumbling block here is the Chicago Real Estate Board and what it's going to do about the demands on it. And the representatives of the Real Estate Board must realize that they are the key to this thing. The monkey, gentlemen, is right on your back, and whether you deem it as fair or not, everyone sees that the monkey is there. And the question is how are you going to deal with the demands placed on you?

Then Heineman and Eugene Callahan whispered to each other about breaking for lunch and recessing until Beatty and his colleagues had an opportunity to meet with their board. Heineman announced that suggestion and everyone agreed to break until 4:00 P.M. to allow the realtors to reassess their position.[34]

During the three-hour recess, King spoke privately with Heineman and Archbishop Cody while also caucusing with the other Freedom Movement representatives to discuss under what terms they would be willing to grant a moratorium on neighborhood marches. With urging from Bevel and Raby, the movement delegation agreed that it would be a mistake to halt protests simply in exchange for promises, and not actual, concrete results. Meanwhile, Mayor Daley was pressuring the Real Estate Board to adopt a more flexible position. Daley put it bluntly to Beatty in a midafternoon phone call: "In the interest of the city of Chicago, you cannot come back here this afternoon with a negative answer." Beatty briefed his board on Daley's sentiments and those of the other influential Chicagoans who had spoken up at the morning meeting, and with great reluctance and some anger, the realtors approved a new statement for Beatty to take back to the afternoon session.

Heineman reconvened the gathering by asking Beatty to report on the Real Estate Board's discussions. Text in hand, Beatty read the new statement to the hushed room. It declared that "freedom of choice in housing is the right of every citizen," but warned that "street demonstrations will harden bigotry and slow down the progress." It added that "if demonstrations do not terminate promptly, we may lose control of our membership and be unable to fulfill the commitments we have here undertaken." Those commitments, the statement went on, were two: first, a pledge to "withdraw all opposition to the philosophy of open occupancy legislation at the state level—provided it is applicable to owners as well as to brokers"; and second, a promise to remind all members to obey the city's fair-housing ordinance. When Beatty concluded by denouncing the movement's testing of brokers' racial practices as "unwarranted harassment," King whispered, "This is nothing." Then King asked Beatty to clarify his remarks. Beatty reread his text, and an exasperated Raby declared that "we've heard your statement; we're not sure what you're saying." Raby said he wanted precise responses to each of the movement's demands, and Jim Bevel added that the crucial question was whether blacks would actually be served at white realty company offices. Human Relations Commission attorney William Robert Ming, who had helped defend King against the Alabama tax charges six years earlier, pointed out that the ordinance required that, but Andrew Young reiterated Bevel's point: "We need a plan to do right and not a law to stop wrong." Beatty chimed in, "I couldn't agree with you more. We should take the monkey off our back and put it on the back of all the people."

Discussion bogged down on the question of whether a Real Estate Board commitment to instruct its members to obey the ordinance would result in blacks being served. "We're still not clear on some points of the ordinance," Beatty asserted while avoiding any direct answer. Al Raby asked the mayor whether brokers could be forced to post a nondiscrimination statement in their windows. Daley was flustered. "I said already this morning that I would do that, and I keep my word."

After several other exchanges, Jesse Jackson interrupted to assert that the basic questions were not legal but theological. Raby sought to get the discussion back on track, and Bill Berry declared that the realtors' new statement was "totally unacceptable." If the board could do nothing about the movement's demands, then what about the mayor? he asked. Daley responded forcefully:

I think they've done a lot. It shows a real change that they've come in here indicating that they will no longer oppose open occupancy. . . . We have agreed to virtually all the points here and everyone says that they are going to move ahead. Now let's not quibble over words; the intent is the important thing. We're here in good faith and the city is asking for your help.

Heineman joined in and pressed Berry to admit that the realtors' promise to end their opposition to a state open-housing law was a significant concession. Berry conceded the point, and then King spoke up:

I hope that people here don't feel that we are just being recalcitrant, but we do have a little history of disappointment and broken promises. . . . We see a gulf between the promise and the fulfillment. We don't want to fool people any longer; they feel they have been fooled; so we are saying today that Negroes, so we are asking today that Negroes can buy anywhere. When will that be? Tell us, so that we won't fool the people. We need a timetable, something very concrete. We want to know what your implementation is.

Heineman responded immediately. "We don't see you as recalcitrant. Anyone here can understand why you want to nail down the terms of this agreement." Looking at the Freedom Movement representatives, the chairman summarized the situation:

The Mayor has accepted your demands on him. The Real Estate Board has stated that it will withdraw its opposition to a state open occupancy law. And this is a great victory, a major victory, and probably ensures passage of that legislation. The other demands have been mainly accepted.

Then Heineman stated the bottom line. "The Chair feels that we are well on our way to realization and that the demonstrations could now cease until we see if these agreements are working out."

Jim Bevel was the first to respond. Laws alone were not the heart of the matter. Actual, tangible changes were. "I can't suggest anything to the Negro people of this town until I can say to them, 'You can buy land from the people who sell land.' Nothing less." Then Robert Spike, a theology professor close to the movement, surprised almost everyone by agreeing with Heineman and badly undercutting Bevel:

> I consider the change by the Chicago Real Estate Board as profound, and I don't think, on the other hand, that we should take Bevel's frustration lightly. But we've got to make clear here that the Chicago Freedom Movement didn't say, in its three demands to the Real Estate Board, what Bevel is saying, and that is that Negroes would be served in all the offices. I think we need some terms here for a moratorium.

While some listeners tried to conceal their astonishment, Raby tried to put on the brakes. "I don't think we're nearly so clear on all these things as Mr. Heineman thinks." He drew the group into a detailed colloquy on the items pertaining to the Department of Public Aid that was interrupted only when Andrew Young broke in to try to redirect the discussion to the larger issues involved. "Who is going to bear responsibility for desegregating the city? The society must change. . . . We must take responsibility here for implementing a plan for an open city. We need a plan to aggressively desegregate this city." Young then launched into a commentary on the establishment's eagerness to halt the open-housing protests and the attendant white violence:

> As to your fears of violence, let me say that it is more dangerous in Lawndale with those jammed up, neurotic, psychotic Negroes than it is in Gage Park. To white people who don't face the violence which is created by the degradation of the ghetto, this violence that you see in Gage Park may seem like a terrible thing, but I live in Lawndale and it is safer for me in Gage Park than it is in Lawndale. For the Negro in the ghetto, violence is the rule. So when you say, "cease these demonstrations," you're saying to us, "go back to a place where there is more violence than where you see violence taking place outside the ghetto."

Intentionally or not, Mayor Daley asked if he had understood Young correctly. "Did I hear you say that we are going to have more violence in this city?" Young responded:

> No, I'm saying that Negroes who are jammed into ghettos are people who are forced into violent ways of life. I'm saying that the Blackstone Rangers are the product of what happens to people when you live in a ghetto. I'm saying that the ghetto has to be dispersed, that this city must be opened up, and this high concentration ended, or we will have violence whether there is a movement or not.

Daley insisted that "the city didn't create this frustration or this situation. We want to try to do what you say." Young moved to exploit the opening:

Well, we need a program. We need to know how much is going to be accomplished in thirty days, and how much in sixty days. We will find [black] families to move into twenty [white] communities in the next thirty days. . . . We've got to have a plan for an open city to take to the people.

Skillfully, Chairman Heineman returned to Robert Spike's point that the movement's demands were nowhere near as far-reaching as Young's and Bevel's disquisitions. "Now, I think we've got to understand what we're talking about here. We understood that your proposals were on these two pages, and it sounds now like you're changing things." Young disagreed. "No. What I'm talking about is a plan to implement what is on those two pages." He gave several examples, and Housing Authority Chairman Charles Swibel piped up to say that his unit and others were committed to following through. "I want to see these marches ended to-day. If we are dealing on the top of the table, then call off the marches for twelve months." The movement representatives groaned audibly at Swibel's mention of twelve months, and Raby asked for a fifteen-minute adjournment so that the movement representatives could caucus privately. Before the meeting broke up, however, black Packinghouse Workers executive Charles Hayes uttered a powerful warning.

We've got to see that we're in changing times and we can't go out after these negotiations and tell the guy on the street that what we got was an agreement from the Chicago Real Estate Board that they philosoph-ically agree with open occupancy. The people want to hear what we're going to do for them now. If I as a union negotiator ever came back to my men and said to them, "I got the company to agree that philosophi-cally they were in support of seniority," I'd be laughed out of court.

Hayes's sentiments were endorsed unanimously in the movement's brief caucus. No one believed that the promises uttered so far by the city and the Real Estate Board were meaningful enough to halt the neigh-borhood protests, and when the session reconvened, Raby reported the movement's decision to a hushed room:

We view this meeting as very important and significant. For the first time there are verbalizations at least that show that we have some op-portunities for change. But I would remind you that the important thing, that we stressed at the beginning of the meeting, was the actu-ality, the implementation. That's the key. We can see the need for further discussions. In your mind the question may be a moratorium, but we would have to say that we would have a moratorium on demon-strations if we had a moratorium on housing segregation. We would like to see a meeting one week from now to see what you're doing in terms of implementation. In the meantime we would meet in a subcom-mittee on specifics. . . . During this week we will have to continue our present plans.

Heineman asked if that meant ongoing protests. Raby said yes. "Demonstrations will continue for the next week." Then Daley spoke up in a tone of irritation:

I thought we were meeting to see if . . . there couldn't be a halt to what is happening in our neighborhoods. . . . I repeat, as far as the city is concerned, we are prepared to do what is asked for. I appeal to you as citizens to try to understand that we are trying. I asked why you picked Chicago? I make no apologies for our city. In the name of all our citizens, I ask for a moratorium and that we set up a committee. We're men of good faith and we can work out an agreement. . . . What's the difference between today and a week from today with men of good faith? We're defending your rights, and also there's no question about the law. Can't you do today what you would do in a week?

Thomas Ayers, who had not spoken since the morning, asked that everyone persevere. "We started on this document, this two page document; I don't think we should leave it now. We've gotten substantial agreement; we ought to make sure at least that we know what the outstanding areas are."

Raby quickly spoke up: "Well, let me give you an example. Is the Mayor going to ask for the legislation to require brokers to post the ordinance in their windows; will he ask [the City Council] for that legislation next Tuesday and will he get it? Will that actually be implemented?" Daley's response was immediate and blunt. "We've got to show the City Council that you'll do something. We'll pass what we said we'd pass if we get a moratorium." That statement of a quid pro quo infuriated Raby. "If I come before the Mayor of Chicago some day, I hope I can come before the Mayor of Chicago with what is just and that he will implement it because it is right rather than trading it politically for a moratorium." Heineman tried to calm the situation. "In a cooler moment, I think you'll realize that the Mayor cannot help but want fewer demonstrations. He's concerned about the safety of the people. And the Mayor is accustomed to having his word taken." Raby refused to back down, and in a "very angry and tense" voice told Heineman, "I won't reply to what you've said for the sake of harmony." He took the two-page statement of demands in hand, and went down the points one by one, indicating that the verbal commitments offered so far fell short of what the movement wanted.

The air was tense when Raby stopped. It seemed possible that the entire day's effort would collapse. Then, with what one onlooker termed a "grand and quiet and careful and calming eloquence," King spoke up:

This has been a constructive and creative beginning. This represents progress and a sign of change. I've gone through this whole problem in my mind a thousand times about demonstrations, and let me say that if you are tired of demonstrations, I am tired of demonstrating. I am tired of the threat of death. I want to live. I don't want to be a martyr.

And there are moments when I doubt if I am going to make it through. I am tired of getting hit, tired of being beaten, tired of going to jail. But the important thing is not how tired I am; the important thing is to get rid of the conditions that lead us to march.

I hope we are here to discuss how to make Chicago a great open city and not how to end marches. We've got to have massive changes. Now, gentlemen, you know we don't have much. We don't have much money. We don't really have much education, and we don't have political power. We have only our bodies and you are asking us to give up the one thing that we have when you say, "Don't march."

We want to be visible. We are not trying to overthrow you; we're trying to get in. We're trying to make justice a reality. Now the basic thing is justice. We want peace, but peace is the presence of justice. We haven't seen enough for the massive changes that are going to be needed. To the Chicago Real Estate Board, I want to say particularly that your second point about the demonstrations being the wrong approach bothers me, because the problem is not created by the marches. A doctor doesn't cause cancer when he finds it. In fact, we thank him for finding it, and we are doing the same thing.

Our humble marches have revealed a cancer. We have not used rocks. We have not used bottles. And no one today, no one who has spoken has condemned those that have used violence. Maybe there should be a moratorium in Gage Park. Maybe we should begin condemning the robber and not the robbed. We haven't even practiced civil disobedience as a movement. We are being asked to stop one of our most precious rights, the right to assemble, the right to petition. We asked Chicago to bring justice in housing, and we are starting on that road today.

We are trying to keep the issue so alive that it will be acted on. Our marching feet have brought us a long way, and if we hadn't marched I don't think we'd be here today. No one here has talked about the beauty of our marches, the love of our marches, the hatred we're absorbing. Let's hear more about the people who perpetrate the violence.

We appreciate the meeting. We don't want to end the dialogue. We don't see enough to stop the marches, but we are going with love and nonviolence. This is a great city and it can be a greater city.

When King finished, his remarks had "changed the mood completely."

After several brief comments, Andrew Young declared that "we need a working committee. The Real Estate Board did a good job, they moved along in the hour and a half they had, and tomorrow by noon we could start working out a program. As soon as concrete proposals are worked out we can get back together." Robert Johnson of the UAW seconded Young's suggestion and Heineman moved quickly:

The Chair will appoint a committee, under the chairmanship of Bishop Montgomery, that will be composed of no more than five representatives of the Freedom Movement, two representatives of the Real Estate Board, the president of the Association of Commerce and Industry

[Thomas Ayers], an officer of the Commercial Club of Chicago, a representative of labor, and the Mayor of Chicago or his representative. And they will meet at the call of Bishop Montgomery. We'll reconvene this group to have a report from them. I propose that we reconvene this group a week from this Friday.

Some were surprised at the nine-day time frame, and one person asked Heineman what the subcommittee's purpose would be. "The purpose of the subcommittee," he answered, "is to come back with proposals designed to provide an open city."

Montgomery stated that the first subcommittee meeting would take place Friday, and discussion turned to what the different parties ought to say to the press. Heineman asked if he might issue a statement for all, including an explanation that there would be no moratorium, but that the movement would proceed with restraint. King voiced a dissent. "Can't you say that if there are demonstrations, you want to call on the violent people to be restrained?"

Heineman tried a different formulation, still using the word "restraint." King objected. "I think we've been restrained." Bevel and Bob Ming offered suggestions, and then Raby interrupted in a tone of disgust. "I can stand anything you say about me; I really don't care. The important thing is what is the substance of what we're willing to do to open up this city." With tempers starting to fray, Daley cut the discussion off. "I think everybody should be allowed to say anything they want to and that it be made clear that this is a continuing meeting, and that this has been a beginning." No one objected, and the lengthy session ended as the clock neared 9:00 P.M., King spoke briefly to waiting newsmen and then headed off to a church rally.[35]

Thursday afternoon King and a dozen other activists met at the Urban League office to review Wednesday's session, make plans for the Friday subcommittee meeting, and pick the five representatives who would attend. News reports said that the mayor was "disappointed and frustrated" that Wednesday's negotiations had not produced a moratorium. Key movement leaders were also unhappy. The two principal concerns were that they had started negotiating before the neighborhood protests had reached peak intensity, and that they might be held to the hurriedly prepared demands that Wednesday's discussions had focused on. Concern about the latter problem was especially serious. A number of CCCO leaders had realized in advance that the list of items was incomplete and vaguely worded, but no one had expected Daley to be so eager to reach a settlement or that the city would focus so precisely on the movement's demands. Movement leaders hoped the subcommittee's agenda could be expanded to include a broad discussion of all the issues raised by the initial demands, and they selected four Chicagoans—Raby, AFSC executive Kale Williams, Catholic Interracial Council Director John McDermott, and Berry of the Urban League—plus one SCLC staffer,

Jim Bevel, as their subcommittee representatives. They also agreed to announce multiple neighborhood protests for Sunday despite suggestions that the city might move for a court injunction if the movement persisted with its demonstrations. King and his aides mused that an attempt by Daley to block ongoing protests would be a strategic error that would play into the movement's hands, and King talked about that possibility at a Thursday night mass meeting:

I want to tell you a secret and I hope the press won't hear and I hope the mayor won't hear. We've had movements all across the nation and all across the South and do you know, our movement won not only because of our ingenuity and because of our ability to mobilize—that was just one side of it—but it won as much because of the mistakes of our opponents. Now we will welcome any mistake our opponents are willing to make in Chicago.

Blocking either the Sunday marches or a Friday house-hunting expedition into Gage Park that he would lead would be just such a mistake, King declared. Although those remarks seemed to indicate an almost playful eagerness to see the Chicago protests through, King was deeply drained by the events of the summer. The tensions of the Meredith March, the turmoil over "black power," and the Chicago demonstrations had all combined to make him weary. Now, at the conclusion of his Thursday night mass-meeting speech, he spoke to that theme, a theme that rarely emerged in his public comments. "I'm tired of marching," he told the crowd,

tired of marching for something that should have been mine at first. . . . I'm tired of the tensions surrounding our days . . . I'm tired of living every day under the threat of death. I have no martyr complex, I want to live as long as anybody in this building tonight, and sometimes I begin to doubt whether I'm going to make it through. I must confess I'm tired. . . . I don't march because I like it, I march because I must.

It was unusual for King to confess his deep weariness to anyone other than his closest aides, but the words, just like his Wednesday comments to the negotiators, revealed his state of mind most clearly. The pace of his life was brutal in its relentless demands, and the events of the summer had offered little solace and much sorrow. Perhaps the Chicago Freedom Movement would soon reach a productive climax.[36]

Friday morning, as King rested, the movement's five representatives gathered for breakfast before the subcommittee's first meeting. When they joined the other members at the Episcopal parish house, they found both a surprisingly large number of delegates—nineteen people, all told—as well as a newly designated chairman, Commonwealth Edison President Ayers, whom Montgomery had asked to take over his duties.

The subcommittee began its discussions with a lengthy consideration of what the city's fair-housing ordinance required and how its enforcement might be improved. They had been assembled for several hours when Housing Authority Chairman Charles Swibel passed a note to Al Raby indicating that a court injunction had been handed down against the movement just minutes earlier. Raby stepped out to a phone, confirmed the report, and returned to break the news to the full group. At the request of Mayor Daley, Police Superintendent Wilson, and city attorney Raymond Simon, Cook County Circuit Court Judge Cornelius J. Harrington had issued an order drastically limiting the allowable scope of the neighborhood protests. Marches would be restricted to one area of the city per day, could involve no more than five hundred participants, and would have to be held during daylight and not at rush hours. Additionally, police would have to be informed in writing, at least twenty-four hours in advance, of the route, leaders, and size of any column.

The subcommittee members were stunned by the news. Professor Spike was infuriated by the city's double-dealing, and Eugene Callahan of the Conference on Religion and Race lashed out angrily at city Human Relations attorney Bob Ming, who denied knowing anything about the injunction. The movement representatives demanded an immediate recess in order to discuss whether negotiations should be broken off because of Daley's bad-faith behavior. Although both Raby and Bevel had voiced strong emotions on Wednesday, at this crucial juncture both men reacted calmly after the initial anger had passed. They and their fellow negotiators decided that a walkout would be counterproductive, and the subcommittee reconvened for an afternoon session that went surprisingly well. When the group adjourned after agreeing to continue deliberations on Monday, representatives from both sides expressed optimism to newsmen.

King learned of the injunction in a phone call from city attorney Simon, and reacted more strongly than the movement's negotiators. He told reporters he might have to defy the order, and met with attorneys before watching Mayor Daley appear live on television to explain this new action. Although the mayor coupled his defense of the legal initiative with calls for an end to discrimination and harassment of the marchers, King denounced Daley in harsh terms. The injunction was "unjust, illegal, and unconstitutional," and the mayor was "more of a politician than a statesman and not good at either." Daley should have moved to control the white hecklers and provide greater protection for the marchers rather than restrict the movement's right to protest. "I deem it a very bad act of faith on the part of the city in view of the fact we're negotiating," King complained. "This just stands in the way of everything we're trying to do."[37]

Saturday morning King huddled with attorneys and other movement leaders to discuss the injunction. The lawyers advised that the movement should not defy an order that was not all that unreasonable, and after extensive discussion King agreed. The injunction would not hinder the ongoing negotiations, and Sunday's protest plans would be altered to conform to the court's requirements. One march would take place in the South Deering neighborhood, and two others would occur in suburbs that were not part of Chicago and hence not covered by the order—Chicago Heights and Evergreen Park. However, King told newsmen, if the city did not meet the movement's demands at the next summit session on Friday, the marches would be intensified. Not only would they defy the court order, there would also be a Sunday procession into Cicero, where American Nazis were recruiting new supporters. "White power" sentiments were drawing an enthusiastic response in many all-white neighborhoods, and city officials worried that any movement trek into Cicero might result in a literal slaughter.

King decided to lead the Sunday march through South Deering, but first took time out to appear on an edition of *Meet the Press* that featured all the major civil rights leaders. He explained that the Chicago protesters would abide by the injunction even though it was unjust, and left the broadcast early to address a church rally prior to the march. A seventy-car caravan took King and five hundred other participants to South Deering; four policemen flanked King at all times as the protesters marched through the area and held a prayer vigil at one realty office. A steady rain soaked the marchers but also kept down the number of hostile whites. Some hoodlums tossed debris at the column as it moved along Ewing Avenue, but King told reporters that he believed most Chicago whites supported the movement's efforts. "The people out here throwing rocks and tossing bottles at us represent only a minority. They are only a minority."[38]

Monday morning King flew to Atlanta for a one-day visit while the subcommittee negotiators resumed their discussions. The city representatives and Chairman Ayers were insistent that the movement not expand its demands beyond the initial two-page statement presented at the Wednesday summit conference, and the civil rights negotiators felt trapped. McDermott and Williams, the two white movement representatives, pressed for a comprehensive "open city" and open-housing package that would provide "clear timetables and targets for changes in population in every neighborhood and every suburb over a measured period of time," but they ran into strong resistance. The city people, McDermott explained, were "not happy about our introducing new ideas in the course of the negotiations," ideas that had not been spelled out in the initial demands. Bevel began to wonder whether a walkout might not be better, and at the conclusion of Monday's session, an equally displeased Raby told the press that "whether something meaningful" would emerge "remains to be seen."

Official concern about the movement's plan to march into Cicero on Sunday increased as more reports came in about the likely white response. Cook County Sheriff Richard Ogilvie sent telegrams to movement leaders on Monday, asking that they cancel such a "suicidal act," but King told newsmen in Atlanta that the movement would not be dissuaded. "We fully intend to have the march. We have talked with Ogilvie about this and announced our plans last Saturday. We gave more than the seven days notice." Tuesday evening Ogilvie and Cicero town attorney Christy Berkos announced plans to ask Illinois Governor Otto Kerner for National Guard troops should the movement go forward. King returned to Chicago and reiterated the protesters' intent. One column of marchers headed into the tough South Deering neighborhood that evening under heavy police protection. A similar safeguard would have to be provided in Cicero, King declared, even if it did require mobilizing the National Guard.[39]

Wednesday morning Governor Kerner announced that the Guard would be called up on Friday if the movement proceeded with the Sunday march. At the same time, the subcommittee reassembled for its third meeting, and movement negotiators renewed their effort to win acceptance of more far-reaching demands. McDermott and Williams pressed for specific goals and timetables as part of the open-housing provisions, but found no receptivity. When Bevel also attempted to expand the list of demands, Chairman Ayers told him bluntly that the subcommittee's task was limited to the movement's initial proposal. "We tried to get more," McDermott said, but they were unable to increase the demands in the face of the city's insistence. "We got stuck with them," Williams explained, and "eventually we felt that we had to take what we could get." Bevel suggested that a break in negotiations and resumption of intensified protests might be better, but the CCCO representatives felt that would be futile. Any serious expansion of demonstrations would violate the injunction and would shift the issue from nondiscrimination in housing to "law and order," a shift that would not be in the movement's favor. Although Bevel was reluctant to accept that analysis, by midday Wednesday the movement's negotiators were committed to getting the best and most specific agreement they could within the scope of the initial demands.

With only twenty-four hours to go before the second scheduled summit session, the Ayers subcommittee met on Thursday for the fourth and final time to hammer out a written agreement, working from a draft that Ayers had prepared. A hue and cry about the threatened Cicero march and the scheduled National Guard call-up dominated the Chicago press, and the drafting session took place amid an air of growing tension. Accord had been reached on the Real Estate Board's responsibility to tell realtors to obey the city ordinance, on expanded enforcement of the ordinance by the Human Relations Commission, on nondiscriminatory mortgage practices by Chicago lending institutions, and on the establishment of some ongoing forum for discussion of implementation.

By the end of Thursday's meeting a final draft had been agreed upon for submission to the full summit conference. Some movement activists believed it was a mistake to agree to an accord until the city withdrew the court injunction, and several "back channel" conversations took place about possibly trading a cancellation of the Cicero march for a withdrawal of the injunction. King vowed at a Thursday night mass meeting that the Sunday march would take place, but Raby told newsmen that no final decision would be made until after the Friday summit session. Subcommittee Chairman Ayers, speaking carefully to the press, said there was "a high degree of consensus" on the draft agreement, but sentiments within the movement were divided despite the positive indications that SCLC aides voiced to reporters. Overall, the situation was muddled, with many signals suggesting that the Friday meeting might bring the entire campaign to a peaceful end, but with other signals indicating that the dangerous trek into Cicero would indeed take place.[40]

On Friday morning movement leaders met at the AFSC office to discuss the draft agreement before heading to the summit session at the Palmer House. Almost all of the major CCCO activists, including negotiators Raby, Berry, McDermott, and Williams, were committed to accepting the accord, but a significant minority, including Bevel and others who had served on the protest-oriented "action committee," argued that the agreement did not go far enough and that demonstrations should continue. King listened patiently as both sides stated their points, and indicated he was still concerned about the injunction. The debate swung back and forth, with some stressing the city's concessions and others arguing that the agreement did not give the movement anything of substance in exchange for halting the marches. The differences had not been resolved as the hour of the meeting approached, and King's decision remained unstated as the movement representatives made the short trip to the Palmer House.

The different parties sat around a huge U-shaped table that placed the city establishment on the left, the Freedom Movement representatives on the right, and the leaders of the Conference on Religion and Race at the base. Bishop Montgomery and Chairman Heineman began by asking Thomas Ayers to report on the subcommittee's work, and Ayers distributed and read out loud the draft agreement. Numbering ten points in all, the document amounted to a codification of the verbal commitments that had been offered at the initial Wednesday summit meeting. The four most important items provided for intensified enforcement of the city housing ordinance, public endorsement of open occupancy by the Real Estate Board, a change from construction of high-rise public housing to scatter-site projects by the Chicago Housing Authority, and nondiscriminatory housing assignments for welfare recipients from the Cook County Department of Public Aid.

When Ayers finished reading the eleven-page document, he announced that all subcommittee members had approved it and formally moved its acceptance by the full summit conference. Chairman Heineman asked Richard Daley for his comments, and the mayor spoke briefly before calling for an immediate vote. Al Raby interrupted at once:

Well, just a minute here. We are all concerned in the Freedom Movement about the personal commitments of the individuals who are here. For instance, we want to know whether or not the churches will take responsibility for a specific number of families in each all-white community—of Negro families. Will we be able to have one per cent Negro occupancy in every community in the city of Chicago by 1967? Will there be a concrete date when the city and the Chicago Real Estate Board can guarantee us that the communities are opened to all? And the ultimate question is still the question raised by Jim Bevel, "when do we foresee the time when a Negro can go into a real estate office in Chicago"—

"and the suburbs," Mayor Daley interjected—"and be served?"

Bishop Montgomery quickly stood up and said he believed he could speak for all of Chicago's faiths in saying that the religious community's affirmative obligations were understood across the board. Archbishop Cody, Rabbi Marx, and other churchmen expressed their commitment to the accord, and Ross Beatty described how the Real Estate Board had had "a very, very difficult meeting" with its members the previous day. The task ahead would be extremely difficult, Beatty said. Then King spoke up, directing his remarks at Beatty:

Now I think that it would be very bad to have any wrong statements made by anybody that would hurt the acceptance of this agreement by our people. I am wondering about a statement that you made yesterday on the radio, Mr. Beatty. It went to the effect that if realtors are forced to sell and rent to Negroes, the real estate industry will go out of business.

Obviously agitated, Beatty fumbled for a response, and voiced several equivocations:

Frankly, I am confused. The last two weeks have been the most confusing of all my life. I think that there are a lot of specifics that we just aren't going to be able to work out here. But I hope that everyone will understand that we are all not bums. Real estate dealers are people and we need commitment from all people in this community, but on the other hand we are not hedging on anything.

Beatty's muddled remarks, civil rights observer John McKnight noted, "made everybody very nervous, even Mayor Daley. I could see that Daley was afraid that he was going to blow the deal, because it sounded after his statement like nothing was firm." Bishop Montgomery volunteered that everyone knew how difficult things would be, and would support the board's efforts. UAW representative Robert Johnson, whom the movement team viewed as a fence-straddling Daley sympathizer, also offered some upbeat comments.

Then Al Raby muddied the waters further. "Before we vote, I think we should understand that this vote is indicative of an intent to facilitate the agreement. We can't accept a vote that is binding. It should only be an indication of sentiment." Chairman Heineman took issue with Raby's declaration. "I would think that the Chicago Freedom Movement would want a unanimous and a binding vote and on the other hand I am sure that those who are committing themselves to the Movement's demands want also to see the Movement's commitment." Raby backed off and suggested a different step. "Well, before we take a vote I think we may need to caucus on the details. We want to be sure of some things. It is unfair for any of us to make commitments unless we are perfectly clear, so I ask for a fifteen minute recess." Neither Heineman nor Daley were happy about the request, but they had little choice but to grant it. As the other participants waited, the movement's representatives caucused privately. Jim Bevel and Jesse Jackson, citing Beatty's noncommittal utterings, renewed their contention that it would be a mistake to accept the agreement as it stood. Others argued that they needed more specific details about the future role of the ongoing summit group called for by the subcommittee document. Concern about the injunction remained, but a majority favored acceptance, and King agreed.[41]

When the movement leaders rejoined the other conferees, King explained their position:

We have decided that we are prepared to vote on the issue before us and we want to agree that this is a most significant document. However, we have one or two questions that still remain.

First, while we recognize that this is not a matter involved in these negotiations, we are much concerned about the injunction we face. We feel that injunction is unjust and unconstitutional. . . . If we want to have a great march, only five hundred people can march and thousands of people will be denied their freedom of assembly. We are acting in good faith and since we are, we will agree to limit the demonstrations. And therefore, we want to know if the city will withdraw the injunction. We make the request of the city, "What will you do?"

Second, we are very concerned still about implementation. Maybe we are over-sensitive, but there have been so many promises that haven't materialized, that this is a great thing in our minds. We want to know if the continuing body that will be established to hammer out the specifics will be an action body or whether it will be just a forum. We want to know how soon it will be underway, because ultimately we want to know how soon a Negro can go to a real estate office and feel reasonably sure that he will get fair treatment, that he will be served. And we also want to know how we can deal with the Negro that is not served.

Bishop Montgomery spoke up: "On Monday we hope to have the organizing body set up as an action group and ready to roll." A Presbyterian representative, Dr. Donald Zimmerman, volunteered that the injunction ought to be tested all the way to the Supreme Court, a comment that left many in the room stunned. King responded: "I'm sure you're aware that this will take at least three years and $200,000 of the movement's resources to get an answer to." Zimmerman backed off, saying "perhaps it could be at least a continuing item to be discussed on the agenda," but Al Raby was not about to let it drop:

> I am forced to respond here. I don't see that the judicial process has really helped the Negro. I think it is very gratuitous of anyone to suggest that we suffer this injunction for three years just to get a legal opinion, because legal opinions haven't done us much good. The same process, the process of legal opinion, got us twelve years ago a decision of the United States Supreme Court that we would have integrated schools, that segregation would be done away with. And the result of that legal opinion twelve years later is largely insignificant.
>
> We want from the city an answer and not a debate. I felt it was bad faith for the city on Wednesday to say that they would negotiate with us and then go out on Friday and seek an injunction against us.

Richard Daley broke in heatedly: "People can make all the statements that they care to about bad faith," but he had had no choice. "It was with heavy heart, yet firmness, that I sought that injunction. There was no other course for me." A long silence followed, and some wondered if a breach was at hand. Then King calmly spoke again:

> I appreciate what Mayor Daley has said, and I know he made the decision with heavy heart. I don't want to stress bad faith. I hope we are operating here by the law of life which is that reconciliation is always possible. But I think I've got to say that if that injunction stands, somewhere along the way we are going to have to break it. We are going to have to break it tomorrow, or in a week, or a month, or sometime as the movement proceeds.

Heineman tried to resolve the problem by asking if the injunction would limit a downtown rally or just the neighborhood marches, and might the city discuss this with the movement? "The city will sit down and talk over anything with anybody," Daley volunteered. Movement representatives pressed the question, however. Would Daley withdraw the injunction? Heineman answered for him: "I think that the Mayor is saying he will not at this time withdraw the injunction but he will discuss its amendment." Daley nodded vigorously and declared, "I call for a vote."

Once again, Al Raby objected. "No, let's wait. We want to discuss this more." Hurriedly, a number of movement representatives huddled around King and whispered to each other. After a few seconds, King ended the informal caucus and spoke up: "I don't think that we can accept a conference to modify the injunction because we are opposed to the injunction totally, but we would accept a separate negotiation through the continuing body on this issue." Raby remained silent, and the last obstacle to ratification of the agreement had been disposed of. Chairman Heineman called for the formal vote, and the result was unanimous. Heineman and then Daley expressed their thanks to those present, and the chairman asked King for his parting words:

I do want to express my appreciation for everybody's work and the appreciation of the Chicago Freedom Movement. I want to thank the subcommittee. We read in the scripture, "Come, let us sit down and reason together," and everyone here has met that spiritual mandate. There comes a time when we move from protest to reconciliation and we have been misinterpreted by the press and by the political leaders of this town as to our motives and our goals, but let me say once again that it is our purpose, our single purpose to create the beloved community. We seek only to make possible a city where men can live together as brothers.

I know this has been said many times today, but I want to reiterate again that we must make this agreement work. Our people's hopes have been shattered too many times, and an additional disillusionment will only spell catastrophe. Our summers of riots have been caused by our winters of delay. I want to stress the need for implementation and I want to recognize that we have a big job. Because I marched through Gage Park, I saw hatred in the faces of so many, a hatred born of fear, and that fear came because people didn't know each other, and they don't know each other because they are separate from one another. So, we must attack that separation and those myths. There is a tremendous educational job ahead of us.

Now, we don't want to threaten any additional marches, but if this agreement does not work, marches would be a reality. We must now measure our words by our deeds, and it will be heard. I speak to everyone on my side of the table now, and I say that this must be interpreted, this agreement, as a victory for justice and not a victory over the Chicago Real Estate Board or the city of Chicago. I am as grateful to Mayor Daley as to anyone else here for his work. I think now we can go on to make Chicago a beautiful city, a city of brotherhood.

Spontaneous applause rang out from all sides of the table. Heineman closed the meeting by declaring that the agreement was a tribute to the democratic process. As the group filed out, one CCCO activist turned to a friend. "Democratic process, shit. It was forced out of them."[42]

Soon after the meeting broke up, King went before the press to describe the accord and to announce that Sunday's march through Cicero was being deferred indefinitely. He praised the "far-reaching and creative commitments" in the agreement and labeled the fair-housing provisions "the most significant program ever conceived" for the pursuit of open occupancy. "The only ultimate justification of nonviolent conflict is the achievement of a higher integration of harmony," and this agreement promised to do that. "The total eradication of housing discrimination has been made possible," and in exchange the movement would "halt neighborhood marches and demonstrations in Chicago on the issue of open housing, so long as these pledged programs are being carried out." King's positive portrayal of the settlement was so strong that some wondered whether his rhetoric was overblown. One indication came when a reporter asked James Bevel if he was happy with the pact. "I don't know. I'll have to think about it."

A number of local black activists had no doubts about their opinions of the settlement. Chester Robinson of the West Side Organization told newsmen that "we feel the poor Negro has been sold out by this agreement." Robinson, as well as CORE Chapter President Robert Lucas, declared that the Sunday march into Cicero ought to go forward because poor black Chicagoans "reject the terms of the agreement." Intensive private lobbying convinced Robinson and Lucas by midday Saturday to postpone their march one week, but angry expressions of dissatisfaction with King's settlement percolated throughout the black community. King spoke to a discordant Friday night mass meeting at Stone Temple Baptist Church on the west side before leaving the next day for Atlanta, but the local situation remained troubled. One Community Relations Service observer noted that the "general feeling" was that the movement had "'sold out' to the city administration. There is much animosity in the Negro community."[43]

To his Atlanta congregation, King repeated his characterizations of the Chicago accord and talked about how discouraging the events of the summer had been. The settlement was only "a first step in a thousand mile journey," but it was also the "most significant and far reaching victory that has ever come about in a northern community on the whole question of open housing. . . . The whole power structure was forced by the power of the nonviolent movement to sit down and negotiate and capitulate and make concessions that have never been made before." Although the negotiations had left him exhausted, King said, and even though the summer as a whole had been depressing, he would still struggle on:

I choose to identify with the underprivileged. I choose to identify with the poor. I choose to give my life for the hungry. I choose to give my life for those who have been left out of the sunlight of opportunity. I choose to live for and with those who find themselves seeing life as a long and desolate corridor with no exit sign. This is the way I'm going. If it means suffering a little bit, I'm going that way. If it means sacrificing, I'm going that way. If it means dying for them, I'm going that way, because I heard a voice saying, "Do something for others."

It was the voice he had heard in the kitchen in Montgomery ten years earlier, the voice that gave him the stamina to carry on when others were calling the Meredith March a failure, falling victim to the angry sentiments of "black power," or castigating the Chicago settlement as a "sellout." Even when times were bad—and it was hard to remember when events had been more frustrating and debilitating than over the past three months—that voice sustained him. He was profoundly uncertain of what would come next, terribly vulnerable to doubts about where he and the movement were headed, but still he had the strength to go forward.[44]

10

Economic Justice and Vietnam, 1966–1967

Martin King reacted strongly to the angry criticisms of the Chicago settlement and his descriptions of it. He vowed that SCLC would do all it could to ensure success, and he even contemplated closing down SCLC's Atlanta headquarters in order to give complete attention to implementing the new accord.

Many people in the movement disagreed with King's evaluation of the agreement. CORE and the West Side Organization had vowed to go ahead with a march into Cicero, and on Wednesday, August 31, King encountered heckling at a mass rally at Chicago's Liberty Baptist Church unlike anything he had ever experienced before. Scurrilous handbills had been circulated by local SNCC sympathizers in advance of the meeting, and when King was introduced to the audience, a large contingent of SNCC loyalists booed him. Once King began to speak, catcalls of "black power" constantly interrupted his remarks. Finally, his patience wearing thin, King stopped and asked if there was someone who wanted to speak. When SNCC Chicago Chapter President Monroe Sharp appeared from the rear of the church, King offered him four minutes to state his position. Sharp took that and more to attack the settlement and King personally, but received only polite applause when he finished. Then King, "still apparently shaken" and "possibly angered," returned to the pulpit and delivered his most impassioned speech of the year. He reminded the audience of the central role SCLC had played in SNCC's birth, criticized "black power" and racial separatism in strong terms, and called Sharp badly misguided. "Whenever Pharaoh wanted to keep the slaves in slavery, he kept them fighting among themselves," King declared in dismissing Sharp's remarks. The crowd responded warmly, and King emerged clearly as the rhetorical victor.

As Sunday's threatened march into Cicero by movement renegades came closer, King tried to head it off. Chester Robinson's West Side Organization had been debating whether to go forward with the plan. At a Wednesday night meeting a large WSO crowd ratified a Robinson proposal that they withdraw from the march so long as King promised to pursue with Chicago's power structure a list of twenty-five specific complaints that WSO had drawn up in response to the summit agreement. "They determined to make no public announcement of the decision," one observer noted, "but to allow Dr. King to make an advertised intervention in the dispute and take public credit for resolving the difficulty. The further implication would be that Dr. King and his leadership were acceding to WSO demands for better representation and attention to the grievances of the poor."[1]

On Thursday morning, September 1, King, Andrew Young, and Jesse Jackson arrived at the WSO office to discuss the demands with Robinson and his staff. King perused the list and

> said that he realized now that some mistakes had been made in the negotiating procedures, that more specifics should have been included in what was agreed to, and that Chester should have been in on the negotiating. However, he felt bothered by the charge that there had been a sell-out by him. He said he was willing to acknowledge mistakes he had made, but not that he had ever sold out.

King said he was committed to pursuing a Chicago movement and that he had not and would not give in to any under-the-table offers from the opposing side. Robinson declared that he did not distrust King's motives, and King spoke about the future, saying

> that he felt unsure, at present, exactly what major attack to launch, now that the first round of the fifteen round battle had been won. Perhaps it ought to be the employment problem. . . . But, he said, he was about to conclude that the welfare issue was the most critical one for the movement to tackle at once, on a wide scale.

Both Robinson and another WSO activist, Bill Darden, told King he would have to move beyond the middle-class leadership of CCCO to create a true mass movement in Chicago. They also questioned him about whether Cicero's virulent racism eventually would be confronted. "King responded affirmatively, saying they would *have* to go to Cicero. The real question was *when* to go to effect the greatest good." The session ended on that cordial note, and King announced to newsmen that the WSO would not march into Cicero on Sunday, whether or not the CORE group went ahead.

King reiterated that the Cicero option was only being deferred, not canceled. "Cicero in the North," he told CBS's Mike Wallace, "symbolizes the same kind of hard core resistance to change as Selma in the South. And I think it will in fact eventually be the Selma of the North in the sense that we've got to have a confrontation in that community." But any plan was far down the movement's agenda, as other issues demanded immediate attention. SCLC's Chicago field staff was leading a growing rent strike by the tenants of one large apartment complex. At the same time, Operation Breadbasket was moving forward from its victories in the dairy industry to successful boycotts against Pepsi and Coca-Cola and an ongoing campaign aimed at Seven-Up. More important, the group that would monitor implementation of the summit agreement was being formed. The idea was to constitute the nucleus of the nineteen-person Ayers subcommittee as a "Metropolitan Leadership Council for Fair Housing" that would ensure that all parties to the accord fulfilled their promises. A first meeting was set for September 6, but before it took place, King again had to confront continuing dissent within the black community.[2]

CORE leader Robert Lucas was adamant about marching into Cicero. Although Lucas had long been a member of the CCCO leadership, the events of August had widened the differences that had always existed between him and the CCCO majority. Lucas had supported the open-housing marches as an excellent way "to dramatize racism in the north," but he had been particularly outspoken in criticizing his colleagues' approach to the summit negotiations. While others like John McDermott and Kale Williams had concluded that the movement should settle for what it could get, Lucas had argued that the movement's demands were too modest and that the negotiators had not been forceful enough. "Nobody really knew what to ask for, nobody really made any demands of any significance," Lucas said later. "These white men were afraid to death of blacks and they could have gotten almost anything that was reasonable." Instead, the movement negotiators "had really agreed to nothing. . . . The agreement really wasn't worth the paper it was written on." Lucas had voiced his objections, but "I was known as a renegade anyway, and I was ignored." He did not blame King for the failure—"Martin was ill-advised; he just had the wrong cats around him"—but numerous admonitions that Lucas's Cicero venture would embarrass King did not dissuade him. Plans went ahead for the Sunday march, and officials readied the National Guard to protect Lucas and his small band of followers. Late Saturday or early Sunday, King phoned Lucas to voice a gentle and almost certainly futile request. As Lucas later related it, "Martin said, 'Bob, I understand that you're going to Cicero,' and I said, 'Yeah, Doc, we're going.' He said, 'Well, I'd like to talk you out of it, but I know I can't, but since you're going, you have my blessing.'" Lucas may have condensed the exchange, but he portrayed King's attitude accurately. "There wasn't any bitterness at all," he recalled. "I know the guy really meant it . . . I could tell the way it came over the wire." In the end, the controversy concluded undramatically. Sunday afternoon Lucas led 250 followers through Cicero and aside from heckling, no disruptions occurred. Lucas's march irritated CCCO colleagues, who later termed it "a pathetic little show of petulance."[3]

After the Cicero issue had passed, Chicago activists began to turn their attention to implementing the accord. The subcommittee group met for three hours on Tuesday, September 6, and agreed to constitute itself as an interim board for the Metropolitan Leadership Council for Fair Housing. A tentative plan called for two delegates from each supporting organization, and a chairman who would appoint a fifteen-person executive board, but a second confab on September 9 failed to produce agreement on a chairman. Al Raby laconically declared that he was "neither dismayed nor heartened" by this development, but Andrew Young told a mass meeting that new protests over school segregation, job discrimination, and slum housing would soon begin.

The slow start toward implementation gave credence to the negative evaluations of the settlement. The locally edited *Christian Century* termed the agreement "the beginning of the beginning," but a *Chicago Daily News* reporter who had covered the story since SCLC arrived termed it "only a paper victory" and said that "to many Chicagoans . . . the achievement has been nil." Many commentators looked askance at King's contributions to the Chicago black community, contending that "only the threat of the Cicero march eventually brought realistic bargaining and the final agreement." The *New Republic* stated that "so far, King has been pretty much of a failure at organizing" and called the agreement "obviously no major victory." It also declared that "King has hardly begun to do the work which could force the necessary basic changes." Even longtime King loyalists like Bayard Rustin observed that the entire Chicago venture looked like "a fiasco" or "a disaster."[4]

King was "greatly disturbed" by the crescendo of criticism, and his distress was intensified by other troubling events. First, SNCC's descent from nonviolence into the least attractive aspects of "black power" reached a new low point with the arrest of Stokely Carmichael on charges of inciting a September 6 riot in the Summerhill section of Atlanta. Conflicting accounts of the incident made King reluctant to comment, but he was extremely perturbed. Five days later, as community unrest continued, SCLC's Hosea Williams was taken into custody. Williams announced that SCLC would mount major protests, but SCLC board member Samuel Williams countermanded that call, labeling Hosea "a hired hand" who "does not set SCLC policy." King returned from a speaking trip to find the city's traditional black leaders, the Atlanta Summit Leadership Conference, meeting with Mayor Ivan Allen to head off further disruptions. The next day, SCLC announced that there would be no protests and that ten staffers had been assigned to help calm the Summerhill area. Samuel Williams told newsmen that King would observe his policy of holding demonstrations only where local leaders invited him to, and that no invitation would be issued in Atlanta.[5]

That same day serious violence erupted in Grenada, Mississippi, as a white mob tried to block the desegregation of local schools by attacking young black children. One month earlier, SCLC staffers had begun demonstrations after local officials had reneged on the voter registration agreement reached when the Meredith March passed through Grenada. Hosea Williams ordered provocative protests so as to attract national news coverage, but SCLC's field staff rejected his instructions, arguing that the danger of deadly force from lawmen outweighed the publicity value. One worker, Mike Bibler, told Williams that "I realize that there are many times . . . that our goals can be advanced by violence inflicted upon us, . . . that news cameras by covering the event can produce a great deal of public sympathy and support for our cause. However, I feel that we should carry out our program risking violence, rather than structuring our program to induce violence."

SCLC responded to the school desegregation turmoil by dispatching additional staffers to lead new protests, and state authorities sent in a large contingent of highway patrolmen to monitor the demonstrations and protect the 160 black children attending previously all-white schools. The SCLC team worked to keep up the black community's courage as tensions mounted, and on September 19, King made a one-day visit to fortify the Grenada activists. Walking hand in hand with a young child, King led an early-morning march that escorted the black students to their schools. Town officials refused King's request for a meeting, but leading whites issued a public statement pledging support for law and order and deploring the previous violence.

Another depressing event was the announcement in Washington that Lyndon Johnson's 1966 civil rights bill was officially dead. Attorney General Katzenbach had told the president ten days earlier that the proposal had no chance of passing the Senate, and that Republican Minority Leader Everett Dirksen had sealed the bill's fate by deciding not to support the powerful open-housing title. "I don't believe there is any advantage to seeking a civil rights bill without the housing provision," Katzenbach advised. "Civil rights groups are adamantly opposed and I think it better to let Dirksen take the total responsibility." King had been pessimistic about the bill's prospects, but when that final word came, he, like other critics, pinned the blame on Senate Republicans. Illinois's Dirksen, King declared, had practiced "sheer hypocrisy" by professing to support equal rights while torpedoing Johnson's bill.[6]

This series of disheartening events deeply demoralized King. Although in Chicago he talked of how the local movement planned protests to get more and better jobs for black workers, there was no follow-through on his announcement that picketing of downtown stores and mass "try-ons" of clothes would soon take place. Chicago activists were tired, and King was depressed about the problems that beset him on every side. SCLC's financial troubles remained a daily concern, as did the need to restructure the staff in order to surmount the organizational shortcomings that had become more pronounced since Randolph Blackwell's departure. Speaking trips kept him constantly on the go, and expressions of disillusionment crept into his public addresses. "Large segments of white society are more concerned about tranquility and the status quo than about justice and humanity," King complained in one sermon. Two weeks later he told his Ebenezer congregation that American society and Western civilization were "lost" on the basic questions of justice and morality that confronted the world. "There are few things more thoroughly sinful than economic injustice," he told a church convention in Texas. "Negroes are impoverished aliens in an affluent society," and the road ahead would be difficult. In a particularly revealing passage, King indicated how troubled he had become:

> We are gravely mistaken to think that religion protects us from the pain and agony of mortal existence. Life is not a euphoria of unalloyed comfort and untroubled ease. Christianity has always insisted that the cross we bear precedes the crown we wear. To be a Christian one must take up his cross, with all its difficulties and agonizing and tension-packed content, and carry it until that very cross leaves its mark upon us and redeems us to that more excellent way which comes only through suffering. . . .
>
> Will we continue to march to the drum beat of conformity and respectability, or will we, listening to the beat of a more distant drum, move to its echoing sounds? Will we march only to the music of time, or will we, risking criticism and abuse, march only to the soul-saving music of eternity?[7]

Although King struggled to keep up his spirits in the face of adversity, the victory of racist Atlanta restaurateur Lester Maddox in Georgia's September 27 Democratic gubernatorial primary sent him into a tailspin. He told newsmen that the election results left him "ashamed to be a Georgian" and showed that Georgia was "a sick state." King talked of little else for several days. The success of someone whose racial views were as extreme as Maddox's boded ill for America's future, he said. "I am afraid of what lies ahead of us. We could end up with a full scale race war in this country. It is very frightening." His friends knew how dispirited King had become, and discussed what they might do to ease his pain. Stanley Levison phoned to comfort him, and King told him that Urban League Director Whitney Young had called to say something had to be done to shock white America. Young was considering quitting his position in order to send such a message, King said, and he was thinking about doing the same thing. Levison replied that neither step would sufficiently shock whites. King said SCLC was confused about what to do in a situation where both white racism and "black power" were on the rise. King told Levison they ought to hold a meeting to discuss their next steps. Levison agreed, and King made plans for a mid-October gathering in Atlanta.

King continued to sound pessimistic in his public remarks. The last few months had witnessed "some very depressing developments all across our nation," and "we confront very desolate days ahead." He worried that he

had made a serious strategic mistake by not taking a more negative position on "black power." Some advisors, such as Bayard Rustin, strongly
recommended that King join Roy Wilkins and Whitney Young in an explicit denunciation of the slogan; others, like Levison, argued that such a
step would only worsen an already bad situation. King pondered how
greatly "black power" had contributed to the negative turn of events, or
whether whites simply were using the phrase to blame blacks for a re-
trenchment of white sympathy that would have taken place in any event.
Although King joined his father and other local black ministers in mediating an Atlanta firemen's strike, he had more time than usual for reflection in the ten days preceding SCLC's mid-October conference.[8]

On Wednesday night, October 12, SCLC's top staffers and King's principal advisors—Levison, Rustin, Jones, and Wachtel—gathered in Atlanta for what Andrew Young termed "a total analysis of the whole
situation." One immediate question was whether King would lend his
name to a statement that Rustin, Randolph, Wilkins, and Whitney Young
had already prepared for Friday's *New York Times* implicitly condemning
"black power" and explicitly denouncing "strategies of violence." It was
decided that King would not sign it, and that the movement's most pressing need was to rise above the "black power" controversy and address
more significant questions of goals and strategies. It would be wrong,
King decided, to jump on the anti-"black power" bandwagon and encourage the perception that the decline in white support was due to a backlash
against "black power." Instead, King and his advisors prepared a lengthy
statement explaining his views and detailing where the movement should
turn next. The document, issued to the press at a Friday news conference, rejected the advocacy of violence and separatism associated with
"black power" and decried "extremism within the civil rights movement."
It highlighted the issues King considered most important. "America's
greatest problem and contradiction is that it harbors 35 million poor at a
time when its resources are so vast that the existence of poverty is an
anachronism." That was the chief grievance that the black freedom movement had to pursue. Turning a popular phrase around, King bluntly
noted that "the Negro is not moving too fast, he is barely moving." The
"black power" controversy "has been exploited by the decision-makers to
justify resistance to change." Faced with these obstacles, SCLC would
undertake three urgent programs: the "political reformation of the
South," "a reconstruction of youth through meaningful training and education," and, most important, the organizing of "the poor in a crusade to
reform society in order to realize economic and social justice." That last
effort, King explained, would entail mass protests for a guaranteed annual income program like the one recently put forward in Rustin and A.
Philip Randolph's "Freedom Budget," a comprehensive proposal for how
social welfare dollars could be allocated productively.

Questioned by reporters, King said he expected SCLC's economic justice protests to begin in Mississippi, perhaps in mid-November, before

expanding to other locales, including northern cities such as Washington. The journalists tried to draw King out on "black power" beyond the carefully worded statement. "We are not interested in furthering any divisions in the civil rights movement." It was most important to keep channels of communication open between contending organizations. King reiterated his criticisms of "black power," and then indicated that he had no differences with, and could endorse, the Rustin-Randolph-Wilkins-Young statement that had appeared in that morning's *New York Times*.[9]

That incidental endorsement of the anti-"black power" declaration was a serious misstep. Many newspapers treated it as King's most important pronouncement and relegated his comments about economic justice protests and a guaranteed annual income to secondary attention. More important, much of the coverage suggested that King had abandoned his middle-of-the-road position to side with those who wanted to read "black power" and its adherents out of the civil rights movement. Saturday morning, after a *Times* headline announced KING ENDORSES RACIAL STATEMENT, Stanley Levison recommended that a clarification be issued. If King were serious about preventing the civil rights movement from splitting into two separate wings, he needed to correct the impression that he had signed up with the Wilkins-Young contingent. Bayard Rustin, who had argued all along that King ought to endorse the anti-"black power" statement, contended that there was no need for a clarification. An embarrassed King agreed with Levison's advice. An explanation might make it seem that he was either indecisive or confused, but King felt he had no choice but to correct his mistake. "It makes me look as if I don't have any integrity," as if "I'm playing a game of duplicity," he told Levison. "What bothers me is when I make these tactical errors it's usually when I'm trying to deal with Bayard." Before the weekend was over, King sent a telegram to the *Times* stating his position in careful detail. He was of course committed to each of the four major principles expressed in the leadership statement—nonviolence, integration, democracy, and Negro-white cooperation—but he could not formally endorse the statement because it "fostered an impression that one wing of the civil rights movement sought to destroy another wing." Monday morning, under a headline of KING CLARIFIES HIS RACIAL STAND, the *Times* ran a story emphasizing King's belief that no one should be excommunicated from the movement.[10]

Neither the Atlanta conference nor its portrayal in the press did much to lift King's spirits or clarify SCLC's plans. Although King's press statement had declared an upcoming focus on Mississippi, there was no follow-through. SCLC's financial troubles prevented that, since more attention was being paid to meeting the payroll than to expanding programs. The United Church of Christ was perturbed that the Citizenship Education Project's funds and staff were being used to support SCLC's other endeavors, and sought to exert more control over the program. Consultant Bill Stein envisioned a moneymaking syndicated radio program using tapes of King's sermons, and got his approval to launch *Martin Luther King Speaks*. Clarence Jones hoped that new funds could be secured from unions such as the Teamsters, and King went to New York to seek Ford Foundation money for voter registration. It was a difficult time, and when King spoke in Birmingham at the Alabama Christian Movement's tenth anniversary dinner, some of his words reflected a greater bitterness than ever before. "White America never did intend to integrate housing, integrate schools, or be fair with Negroes about jobs," King told the crowd. The very next day he spoke to Atlanta's newly integrated Junior Chamber of Commerce, advocating a guaranteed annual income of $4,000 for every American adult. When his first questioner, however, asked if the time had not come for blacks to start helping themselves and stop asking government for assistance, King's weariness and exasperation showed clearly. Afterward, King talked to several aides about the difficulty of getting people to see problems that were right before their eyes:

> He said he'd been thinking that possibly the only way to get the country to look at poverty was to get a large number of very poor people in the country to go to Washington, and possibly to some other large cities. . . . He said, "We ought to come in mule carts, in old trucks, any kind of transportation people can get their hands on. People ought to come to Washington, sit down if necessary in the middle of the street and say, 'We are here; we are poor; we don't have any money; you have made us this way; you keep us down this way; and we've come to stay until you do something about it.' "[11]

At the end of October, King turned his attention to Chicago for the first time in more than a month. Some local activists had been drawn into a boycott of Englewood area stores to protest a planned urban-renewal project that would level much of the neighborhood, and some CCCO leaders had again turned their attention to the issue of school desegregation. There were few signs of any implementation of the summit agreement, and AFSC's William Moyer prepared a biting report on how the major parties had failed to keep their promises. Realtors were no less discriminatory, the Human Relations Commission had not intensified its enforcement efforts, and the Housing Authority, Public Aid Department, and urban-renewal program had not altered their policies. Word of the statement was leaked to reporters, and when King arrived in Chicago on October 28, reporters pressed him for comment. "It is time to have some tangible results," King declared. Twenty-four hours later, after hearing CCCO's well-documented complaints, King sounded a harsher note. "If the agreement is not being implemented, we will have no alternative but to resume demonstrations."

Richard Daley wasted no time in assailing King for that declaration. Congressional and state elections were hardly a week away. Daley emphasized, and King's comment might stimulate a "white backlash" against liberal Democratic candidates such as Illinois Senator Paul Douglas, who was in danger of losing his seat to Republican challenger Charles Percy. Local civil rights spokesmen dismissed Daley's broadside as an attempt to blame King for the state Democratic party's problems, and King emphasized that the idea that blacks were responsible for the increase in perceptible white racism was nonsense. "It is not a backlash, but a surfacing of basic hostilities already present."

Although Percy did defeat Douglas, and although many liberal Democratic congressmen elected in the 1964 Johnson landslide lost their seats to Republicans, King's response was measured. Results such as Massachusetts's election of black U.S. Senator Edward Brooke allowed for "a mixture of encouragement and discouragement," but King emphasized that "large segments of America still suffer from a repulsive moral disease." The day after the election, King told a Washington audience that "we must face the fact that we are now in the most difficult phase of the civil rights struggle." "We need civil rights legislation," like Johnson's fair-housing proposal, "but that isn't enough." From now on the movement would tackle "basic class issues between the privileged and underprivileged."[12]

SCLC's search for new funding sources led King to agree reluctantly to Clarence Jones's suggestion that he ask Teamsters Union President James Hoffa for support. King was hesitant to approach someone with Hoffa's unsavory reputation, and his disquiet increased when newsmen inquired about possible ties between the Teamsters and SCLC. Alerted to King's plans by FBI officials hoping to embarrass him and derail any Teamster contributions, reporters asked King why he was considering an alliance with Hoffa. A flustered King admitted he planned to see Hoffa, but denied seeking Teamster financial support. Upset by the negative publicity, King postponed his appointment with Hoffa until November 10. With Jones and Teamsters Vice-President Harold Gibbons sitting in, King said he would support a union effort to organize Chicago hospital workers, and Hoffa in return pledged a $50,000 contribution to SCLC.

King's most pressing concern was how he and the movement could pursue the economic justice issues which increasingly preoccupied him. By early November he had decided to hold a retreat for SCLC's seventy-five-person staff to consider the organization's future. On Sunday, November 13, the group assembled at the conference center in Frogmore for three days of discussion. The first day was given over to reports on each staff department and project. Some aides suggested that SCLC close down all its activities for two months so that funds could be conserved and all workers brought to Atlanta for intensive training. The second day King spoke to the staff and admitted that he was uncertain about what should come next. "I am still searching myself. I don't have all the answers," he explained. The last six months, he said, had brought home in a painful fashion the limitations of the gains the movement had won between 1954 and 1965. "This period did not accomplish everything," King emphasized. "Even though we gained legislative and judicial victories . . . these legislative and judicial victories did very little to improve the lot of millions of Negroes in the teeming ghettos of the North." In fact, "the changes that came about during this period were at best surface changes; they were not really substantive changes." More recent events had shown that "the roots of racism are very deep in America," and that "our society is still structured on the basis of racism." That realization, however, should lead not to despair, but to an understanding of the cycles that all movements encounter. "We have to face the fact that we may be in one of those periods when we do have a dip, which is only inevitable in any social revolution . . . a period of recession. . . . What we see now, in a sense, is the counter-revolution taking place." The catcalls of one-time supporters must also be understood in context, for "what happens in the revolution is when the hopes are blasted, those who built up the hope are often the targets of the most bitter criticism precisely because they could not deliver."

Now the movement would have to pursue "substantive" rather than "surface" changes, and would be "making demands that will cost the nation something" because they would raise "class issues"—"issues that relate to the privileged as over against the underprivileged." At the heart of the matter, King stressed, was the fact that "something is wrong with the economic system of our nation . . . something is wrong with capitalism." It was a belief he had long held but rarely stated in public because of the obvious political dangers. "I am not going to allow anybody to put me in the bind of making me say, every time I said there must be a better distribution of wealth, and maybe America must move toward a democratic socialism, [that] I am saying that we must be Communist or Marxist." Actually, he went on, there was much to admire about Karl Marx, who had "a great passion for social justice" but had fallen afoul of the theoretical errors of materialism. Marxism ought not to be mistaken for the economic goals that the movement sought, King stressed.[13]

By the third day of the retreat, a consensus had emerged that SCLC should not alter course but should focus its available resources better. The Grenada and Chicago projects would continue, and an intensive, two-month-long voter registration effort would be launched in Chicago in early December to maximize black voting strength for the city council elections at the end of February. Most of the southern field staff would go to Chicago to work on that drive, even though many of them would loathe going north in the dead of winter to work on unfamiliar turf. Field staff morale had been sagging for over a year, with a building resentment toward the higher-salaried executive staff who rarely worked the streets or canvassed door-to-door. Some of that resentment was expressed on the final afternoon of the retreat, but workers who were upset about the Chicago assignment were mollified by the reminder that it would last only a few months. Once the registration drive was complete, the staff would reassemble in Atlanta to prepare for a mass-action campaign focused upon an annual guaranteed income and other economic justice goals.

In the wake of the Frogmore retreat, King seemed more relaxed and accepting of the slow, tough struggle ahead. "There's a realistic feeling that it's harder now," King remarked to one questioner. Also, he admitted, "there's a readjustment of the time schedule: we know we're not going to accomplish all these things overnight or in a matter of a few months." Serious money problems remained, so King convened a two-day executive staff meeting in Atlanta to discuss possible fund-raising strategies. New responsibilities for searching out money had been delegated to Jesse Jackson, whose Chicago Operation Breadbasket program had won sizable job gains from soft drink firms and grocery store chains. Jackson had hopes of branching out in new directions, and Breadbasket's most recent agreement—with High-Low Foods, a string of fifty supermarkets—reflected the possibilities. Beyond a commitment to hire 183 black workers, High-Low also promised to open accounts at two black banks and to stock the products of six black manufacturing firms. In this way, Jackson argued, Breadbasket's goals could be expanded into a far-reaching program for economic development of black communities. Additionally, he suggested, by bringing together progressive private investors and government-supported housing-improvement programs, SCLC could pursue redevelopment of black communities' housing stock. An impressed King—who several weeks earlier had doubled Jackson's SCLC salary from $3,000 to $6,000—voiced praise for his creative proposals.[14]

On December 2, King returned to Chicago to announce the voter registration drive. Hosea Williams and fifteen other southern workers would staff the effort, which King emphasized would be nonpartisan and not an anti-Daley crusade. "We do not endorse candidates. We feel the people will be intelligent enough to vote for the right candidate when they know the issues." In private, King focused on the guaranteed annual income issue. He already had asked Levison to prepare a briefing paper on the subject, and he planned to spend much of December and some of January resting and reflecting—perhaps one week in California, one in Miami, and then some time on Bimini after the Christmas holiday. The more King thought about the subject, and the more he saw press reports of how the Johnson administration planned to reduce its antipoverty spending because of increasing Vietnam War costs, the more he concluded that the guaranteed income could be the centerpiece of a new economic agenda. Instead of piecemeal efforts aimed at education, jobs, and housing, this would offer a comprehensive approach. "Many of us who have led movements for these reforms," King told one New York audience, "have proposed larger and broader programs in the same general direction. . . . However, we may now have reached a point at which a change of direction toward a new concept holds a surer promise of solution." In pursuing that new direction, "our emphasis should shift from exclusive attention to putting people to work over enabling people to consume," for "if we directly abolish poverty by guaranteeing an income, we will have dealt with our primary problem."[15]

King hoped to use his vacation to think about these ideas, and perhaps to begin work on a book incorporating them. Stanley Levison encouraged that plan and began preparing for King a lengthy statement on America's domestic needs that King had been invited to deliver at a December 15 hearing of Senator Abraham Ribicoff's Government Operations Committee. King was enthusiastic about the opportunity to address the congressional session, and emphasized in repeated phone calls to Levison that the text had to identify the Vietnam War as the major obstacle to adequate funding for the social welfare programs that America desperately needed. "Everything we're talking about really boils down to the fact that we have this war on our hands." Levison acceded, and when King appeared before Senators Ribicoff and Robert Kennedy that Thursday morning, his forty-four-page statement was a powerful declaration of the problems facing both the movement and the United States.

"We aim too low," he told the crowd in the Senate hearing room. "Our goal is not to bring the discriminated up to a limited, particular level, but to reduce the gap between them and the rest of American society. As standards of life rise for affluent Americans, we cannot peg the poor at the old levels of 'subsistence.' . . . We are dealing with issues of inequality, of relative standing," issues that would require sizable expenditures. The problem was not that money was unavailable, but that it was being squandered on the Vietnam War and the "striking absurdity" of a manned space program. "With the resources accruing from termination of the war, arms race, and excessive space races, the elimination of all poverty could become an immediate national reality," King declared. "At present the war on poverty is not even a battle, it is scarcely a skirmish."

Antipoverty efforts, he emphasized, should not be divided into separate programs targeted at education, employment, and housing, but ought to be one coordinated project aimed at "assuring jobs and income for all" and "equitable income distribution." To date, all antipoverty programs had tried "to solve poverty by first solving another condition," and such "fragmentary and spasmodic reforms have failed to reach the needs of the poor.

> I am now convinced that the simplest approach will prove to be the most revolutionary—the solution to poverty is to abolish it directly by a now rather widely discussed measure—the guaranteed annual income. . . . Our emphasis should shift from exclusive attention to putting people to work over to enabling people to consume.

Explaining why there was not yet a national consensus behind such an approach, King exhibited both his new bitterness and his increasing radicalism. "The attainment of security and equality for Negroes has not yet become a serious and irrevocable national purpose. I doubt that there ever was a sincere and unshakable commitment to this end." Although white America had been outraged at the excesses of Bull Connor and Jim Clark, "large segments of white society are more concerned about the tranquility and the status quo than about justice and humanity." White support for the movement was unlikely to grow because now "the issues which we confront are the hard-core economic issues." This would be a "much harder" struggle, for it would call "for something of a restructuring of the architecture of American society,"

Despite the edge in his voice, King told the senators he was neither impatient nor pessimistic. "We know that in spite of a marvelous open housing agreement on paper that we reached in Chicago, open housing is not going to be a reality in Chicago in the next year or two." Nonetheless, "I am quite optimistic about the future. . . . We are just in one of those periods that is somewhat inevitable," when hostile reaction sets in on one side and anger at the halt in rapid progress springs forth on the other. "We raised the hopes tremendously but . . . we were not able to really produce the dreams and the results inherent in that hope," King explained. "We as leaders lifted the hope. We had to do it. It was a fine thing to do. But we were not able to produce," and America's ghetto dwellers had responded by expressing in violence "the deep despair and the deep frustration and the deep sense of alienation" that characterized their lives.

Summing up, King emphasized three points. First, to date, "the civil rights movement has too often been middle-class oriented, and . . . has not moved to the grassroots levels of our communities. . . . The great challenge facing the civil rights movement is to move into these areas to organize and gain identity with ghetto dwellers. . . . All of the civil rights organizations must work more to organize the grassroots levels of our communities." Second, the nation had to realize that over the past eighteen months, "the leaders who try to preach nonviolence and work through the democratic process have not been given enough victories." And third, "the point that I would like to bring out today more than anything else," King said, "is that America as a nation has never yet committed itself to solving the problem of its Negro citizens," and for its own good had better do so quickly.[16]

Two days prior to King's congressional appearance, SCLC had announced that he would be taking a two-month leave to work on a book and reflect upon the current situation. Some acquaintances recommended that he step up his criticism of the Johnson administration and especially its Southeast Asia policy. He was sympathetic to their views, but hesitated, as Andrew Young explained to a friend just before Christmas:

for many reasons, we are not ready for the categorical break with the federal government which you call for. I don't think we have any illusions about Johnson or either of the parties. We have long since realized the political control of the FBI and the Justice Department, and while we try never to depend on their help, neither do we refuse it when it is offered. . . .

Certainly our opposition to the war in Vietnam is clear. The question that stymies us is the question of effective tactical opposition along with specific alternatives around which we can begin to rally public opinion. Martin has felt that an occasional well placed and well timed opposition is more valuable than a continued "again and again" denunciation of war, Vietnam, or the draft.

Eventually, however, there was a good possibility that SCLC would expand its purview:

We could not have moved North prior to Selma, but Selma brought us an additional corps of trained people and money, so that we could continue our attempts at political reform and economic development in the South and send some of our more experienced staff to Chicago. Before we can develop an international movement we must establish some kind of base in 10 or 12 Northern cities. I would say this is 2 to 4 years off.

In the meantime, Martin is considering some personal tours to Latin America, Africa,

and Europe. Looking back at his own five years with SCLC, Young noted in another letter that "what started out as a simple matter of political reform has now emerged as a total fight for economic justice and world peace." Although Young's vision might have sounded grandiose, his statements accurately reflected the fundamental questions King was pondering.

Before beginning his period of reflection, King made one more trip to Chicago to unveil an SCLC-sponsored slum housing rehabilitation program funded by a $4 million insured loan from the Federal Housing Administration. Little was happening with Hosea Williams's voter registration effort, and the southern field-workers were deeply frustrated by the Chicago activists' lack of enthusiasm. SCLC's Fred Bennette told King of the problems, but many of the grievances were those that had been aired at Frogmore a month earlier. Unless King implemented a different approach to staff discipline, such tensions would remain a daily fact of SCLC's life.[17]

King spent the holiday season at home with his family. He and Coretta called Stanley and Beatrice Levison to wish them a Merry Christmas, and viewed a performance of *Sleeping Beauty* put on by the King and Abernathy children. On January 3, King flew to Los Angeles with Bernard Lee for a week of rest at the Hyatt House Hotel. There, King tried to start on an outline for his book, but twice was interrupted by calls from Levison relaying messages from important friends and supporters. First was an appeal King had heard several times before: Liberal activists such as Al-

lard Lowenstein, *Nation* editor Carey McWilliams, Yale chaplain William
Sloane Coffin, and socialist leader Norman Thomas wanted King to take
a stronger antiwar stand. McWilliams hoped he would deliver a Vietnam
speech at an important *Nation* forum in Los Angeles in late February,
and Coffin, Thomas, and Lowenstein wanted to talk to King about his
possible availability as a third-party presidential candidate in 1968. The
FBI's ubiquitous wiretappers summarized the discussion succinctly:

> King remarked that this would admittedly be not with the idea of win-
> ning, . . . that it would be to give an alternative. King opined that such
> a meeting would be for the purpose of discussing politics, adding that
> he thought running would be an interesting idea. Levison commented
> that as things are going, with the prospect that 1968 could be one of
> those fantastically frustrating situations for people, he thought it had to
> be given some more sober thought. King agreed with Levison.

Several days later, Levison called again to say that black leaders were
puzzled that King had not spoken up in support of Congressman Adam
Clayton Powell, whose controversial ways had precipitated a congressional vote depriving him of his right to take the House seat to which his
constituents had reelected him in November. King agreed his silence
seemed odd, especially in light of Roy Wilkins's support of Powell, but
Wilkins and other black leaders did not know Powell as well as he did,
King said. In light of Powell's threats about Bayard Rustin years earlier,
his public criticisms of other civil rights leaders, and his basic lack of
personal integrity, King frankly did not care what became of him.

King made a one-day visit to New York to attend a board meeting of
the American Foundation on Nonviolence, the tax-exempt SCLC adjunct
that had succeeded the Gandhi Society as a channel for large contributors
seeking to aid King. Despite a $50,000 gift from wealthy heiress Ann
Farnsworth, SCLC's finances remained troubled. Unfortunately, the session did nothing to resolve the problems. Old Montgomery colleague L.
D. Reddick told King it had been "a waste of time. Nothing appeared to
be planned. All discussions were impromptu. No policy proposals were
presented. No guidance was offered for the civil rights crises." SCLC had
better do "some purposeful thinking," and consider three particular topics: finances and fund-raising, organization and staff changes, and, most
important, program content. "Obviously, the civil rights movement is in
disarray," Reddick told King. "What should SCLC do in attempting to
heal the breach? The mood of the nation has changed. Are there new
denominators around which we can mobilize a coalition? Should we take
leadership in the merging movement of 'poor' people to protest the cuts
in the poverty program?" He suggested no answers, but the questions
were ones that King already was wrestling with.[18]

On Saturday, January 14, King and Bernard Lee flew to Jamaica for
four weeks of solitude at a secluded house in Ocho Rios that had every-

thing except a telephone. Dora McDonald followed several days later, and Coretta would join them for one week of the stay, but King wanted to work full time on his book. He packed several suitcases of research materials, and at the airport newsstand he bought a handful of magazines before joining Lee in the restaurant. As he ate, King flipped through the magazines until he came upon an illustrated story, "The Children of Vietnam," in the January *Ramparts*. Many of the photos showed the burn wounds suffered by youngsters who had been struck by American napalm. Bernard Lee never forgot King's reaction.

> When he came to *Ramparts* magazine he stopped. He froze as he looked at the pictures from Vietnam. He saw a picture of a Vietnamese mother holding her dead baby, a baby killed by our military. Then Martin just pushed the plate of food away from him. I looked up and said, "Doesn't it taste any good?," and he answered, "Nothing will ever taste any good for me until I do everything I can to end that war."

Looking back, Lee explained, "That's when the decision was made. Martin had known about the war before then, of course, and had spoken out against it. But it was then that he decided to commit himself to oppose it."

The days in Jamaica were the first time in his adult life that Martin King was free of the telephone and its demands for any stretch of time. As he wrote page after page of longhand manuscript in his large, sloping stroke, McDonald dispatched chapter upon chapter to Levison in New York. At peaceful evening dinners, he talked with Lee, McDonald, and eventually Coretta about his growing resolve to take a stronger stand against the Vietnam War when he returned home. "I spent a lot of time there in prayerful meditation. I came to the conclusion that I could no longer remain silent about an issue that was destroying the soul of our nation."

Few interruptions disturbed King's repose, but one day James Bevel showed up on King's doorstep. Bevel had come to discuss the Vietnam War, which he had long been pushing King to oppose more outspokenly. One week earlier the Spring Mobilization Committee, an antiwar group planning a massive April 15 demonstration in New York, had asked Bevel to become their national director, in the hope that Bevel could enlist King. Bevel asked King for a leave of absence to take the "Spring Mobe" position, and also requested that King speak at the April demonstration. "We can't afford to be silent. That's like betrayal," he told King. Advocating nonviolence to American blacks at home morally required insisting that the United States practice it internationally, Bevel asserted. King thought Jim Bevel was becoming mentally unbalanced, but agreed with his argument and endorsed Bevel's accepting the Spring Mobe post. King reserved decision on speaking at the New York protest, but said he would give it serious consideration.[19]

Another interruption was an emergency message from King's stateside colleagues concerning remarks Hosea Williams had made to *The New York Times* about SCLC's troubled Chicago voter registration drive. Williams had called the effort "a nightmare. Our schedule is way off base, largely because of division in the Negro leadership," some of whom wanted to oppose Daley's city council supporters and others of whom did not. "I'm having a lot of problems," Williams said, partially because Chicago blacks seemed disinterested in SCLC's efforts. "I have never seen such hopelessness." Field-worker Lester Hankerson chimed in, saying "A lot of people won't even talk to us."

Stanley Levison and Andrew Young reacted with outrage. Young and Ralph Abernathy headed to Chicago to repair the situation and get the registration effort back on track, and Levison arranged a three-way conference call between himself, Young and Abernathy, and King in Jamaica. King also was furious, and Levison recommended they fire Williams. King said that would be too drastic an action, but he instructed Young to tell Williams how extremely angry he was. Several days later a meeting was held in Chicago to revamp the drive before the registration books closed at the end of January. A heavy blizzard derailed those last-minute efforts, and local observers caustically pointed out that the entire two months of work had produced only a few hundred newly registered black voters.

On February 13, King returned to Miami from Jamaica and holed up for five days at the Dupont Plaza Hotel, working on his book and spending hours in the health spa. He asked Dora McDonald to alert Levison that he wanted to use the February 25 *Nation* forum in Los Angeles to make a speech on Vietnam, but Levison's attention was focused upon serious shortcomings in King's manuscript. Along with Joan Daves, King's literary agent, and free-lance editor Hermine Popper, who had done yeoman work on *Why We Can't Wait,* Levison was troubled by the lack of original material in King's writing. A chapter on "black power" was promising, and Levison prepared extensive revisions of two others, but in at least one section, King had repeated almost verbatim large chunks from his last book. Levison pointed out the problem, and an embarrassed King wrote to Popper apologizing for his error. "I made a definite literary mistake which I am aware of. I lifted a great deal of what I had said in the last chapter of *Why We Can't Wait* because I felt it was so relevant at this point." Popper was worried that some of King's and Levison's passages were incompatible with each other, but in a conference call both men said no. "There is practically nothing you can come up with where I say anything that Martin disagrees with because I work too closely with him not to know what his thinking is," Levison insisted. "I am expressing his thinking. . . . There couldn't be an area anywhere in which the thinking is not Martin's thinking. I am much too careful about that." King agreed, saying, "I haven't seen any serious inconsistencies."

Several days later King, Levison, Popper, and Daves rendezvoused at a New York airport to hash out their differences.[20]

As King resumed an active schedule, the uppermost subject in his mind was not the book but Vietnam. On February 18 he called Levison and Cleveland Robinson to say he wanted to take a more active role in opposing the war. King referred to how the *Ramparts* article had affected him, and said he was ready to make an explicit break with the Johnson administration, even if it cost SCLC some financial support. Levison warned King that it would be better to join forces with political heavyweights like Robert Kennedy and Walter Reuther rather than antiwar activists such as Norman Thomas and Dr. Spock, but King emphasized that the time had come for mass action against the war. "I see it as tying the peace movement to the civil rights movement or vice-versa. I don't see getting out of civil rights, but we could be much more successful if we could get the peace people . . . to cooperate, to have a march on Washington around the cutbacks in the poverty programs." The Los Angeles speech would be one step, but addressing the April 15 Spring Mobe demonstration would be a more dramatic move. Robinson was supportive and Levison skeptical of King's desire to become a peace movement leader, but all agreed that the Spring Mobe question could be decided at a March 6 research committee meeting.

King's February 25 speech in Los Angeles was his first public appearance in more than two months. Designated the main speaker on a program that also featured four antiwar senators—Ernest Gruening, Mark Hatfield, Eugene McCarthy, and George McGovern—King said that the physical injuries of the war were not the only casualties of Vietnam. Among others were America's "declining moral status in the world," self-determination for third world countries, and the domestic programs of the Great Society. Johnson's war policy had placed the nation "in the position of being morally and politically isolated," and America's support for the dictatorial South Vietnamese military regime represented both "a new form of colonialism" and "an ominous expression of our lack of sympathy for the oppressed" of the world. "Our nation, which initiated so much of the revolutionary spirit of the modern world, is now cast in the mold of being an arch anti-revolutionary. We are engaged in a war that seeks to turn the clock of history back and perpetuate white colonialism." America's forces were "committing atrocities equal to any perpetrated by the Vietcong," and Johnson's policies exposed both "our paranoid anti-Communism" and "the deadly western arrogance that has poisoned the international atmosphere for so long." America was now "isolated in our false values in a world demanding social and economic justice. We must undergo a vigorous reordering of our national priorities," and could start by halting the bombing of North Vietnam and declaring a willingness to negotiate with the Viet Cong. American society simply had to alter its entire course, King emphasized. "I am disappointed with our failure to deal positively and forthrightly with the triple evils of racism, extreme materialism and militarism."[21]

King was pleased at the wide national coverage accorded his remarks, but feared that his new stance might harm SCLC's already weak financial condition. Andrew Young had told *The New York Times* that SCLC's contributions were 40 percent lower than a year earlier, and King worried that an SCLC proposal seeking Ford Foundation support might be jeopardized. SCLC was hoping that Ford would begin funding the Citizenship Education Program, and bankroll a northern expansion that would pay staffers such as Bevel, Jackson, and Al Raby to provide leadership training for activists from Chicago and other cities. The request had not yet been acted on, and King feared that such funding might be lost because of his antiwar declarations.

Vietnam remained King's major concern, and he returned to New York to discuss his possible participation in the Spring Mobe demonstration with his advisors. The night before that meeting, King had an angry argument about Vietnam with National Urban League Director Whitney Young at a private Long Island reception. As witnesses described it, Young told King that his Los Angeles speech had been most unwise because of how it might alienate Lyndon Johnson from the civil rights leadership. "Whitney, what you're saying may get you a foundation grant, but it won't get you into the kingdom of truth," King responded forcefully. Young's eyes flashed, and he gestured toward King's pudgy midsection. "You're eating well." King started to reply in kind, but Harry Wachtel stepped in and pulled King aside. Gradually his anger at Young subsided, and after several hours had passed, he began to feel guilty about losing his temper. "I never saw Martin so disgusted at himself," Wachtel remembered. Sometime after midnight King phoned Young to apologize for the outburst but also to renew the argument. The two men talked for more than an hour, but neither succeeded in changing the other's mind on Vietnam or on Lyndon Johnson. Later, after King's death and just before his own, Young admitted he had been wrong. "I must confess I have changed somewhat in my own thinking now and feel maybe Dr. King was more right than probably I was."[22]

The March 6 research committee meeting found King's advisors unsympathetic to his desire to take part in the April 15 protest. Many old friends were present—Levison, Jones, Wachtel, Rustin, Robinson, Andrew Young, Bevel, and Robert Green—but only Bevel supported King's participation in the protest. Rustin warned that such a move would forever close Lyndon Johnson's White House door to King, but Bevel's emotional remarks carried the day. "Bevel had a very uncanny way of making an impact on Martin," Bob Green remembered. Several participants warned that since the protest was an open event, King could end up associated with any number of colorful fringe elements. This was why many opponents of the war, including liberal Democrats and socialist leader Norman Thomas, were lukewarm toward the Spring Mobe. King replied that he would be a coward not to join a protest that expressed his own sentiments. Opposition to the war and to Lyndon Johnson's presidency was gaining a large constituency, King said, and many white liberals who had once been active in civil rights now saw Vietnam as America's most pressing issue. King agreed he should insist that Spring Mobe concentrate on attracting mainstream opposition to the war, and choose its policies and speakers accordingly. King told his advisors he would think about his decision for several more days, and headed off to a fund-raising dinner hosted by wealthy New York liberals who were close friends of Senator Robert Kennedy. There King found support for his outspoken opposition to Lyndon Johnson's policies, both foreign and domestic. Along with Andy Young, he spoke with influential Democrats like Bill and Jean Stein vanden Heuvel and found agreement that the movement and political progressives such as Kennedy should work hand in hand. Together they might form a powerful "pincer movement," Young suggested in a follow-up letter. "It seems to me that with you working from within the structure of politics and economics and us working on the outside we can move the country along much more quickly." He told them to "feel free to give me a call anytime you see a complimentary role for Dr. King and/or SCLC," since "there are many things that Senator Kennedy cannot say or do that present no problem for Dr. King. Our problem quite frankly is that we are struggling with such a limited staff that it is impossible for us to keep abreast of all issues."[23]

Staff problems remained a serious concern for SCLC, and three days after the research committee meeting in New York, King convened SCLC's top staff in Atlanta to discuss their internal troubles. The southern field staff's disastrous experience in Chicago had dampened morale and aggravated old tensions, difficulties that Hosea Williams discussed in a memo to King just prior to the discussions. In the South, he pointed out, SCLC suffered from a reputation for abandoning local communities once the drama of direct action had passed. Because of that, no true mass movement had emerged in the South. "My main concern and frustration about SCLC," Williams wrote, "is the fact that we have a very few more volunteers and followers in our nonviolent army than we had after you left Montgomery." All across the South the belief had grown up that

> people are secondary to our primary objectives—building images, getting publicity and raising funds. The leadership of many of our past battlefronts and campaign grounds, like Albany, Savannah, St. Augustine, Selma, Americus and others, question in depth our strategy and techniques as they relate to our dedication to bringing about meaningful change. Many seriously question whether or not their communities were bettered or worsened by our presence. To me, this means we failed to define or to bring about identifiable change. . . . Many community leaders will divulge the true sentiment of their community to others, when at the same time they will tell you or someone that is very close to you . . . something entirely different.

Moreover, that was not the only serious problem, nor the only one of which King might be largely ignorant, Williams said. "Dr. King, I just do not believe you have been apprised of the psychological, moral and physical status of your staff. Personally, I have been at a loss finding a way to communicate my feelings to you." People were exhausted and needed a lengthy retreat. "Our staff problems are unbelievable." Two of the greatest obstacles to solving them, Williams asserted, were his two chief rivals, Jim Bevel and Andy Young. Most staff members had "lost complete respect" for Bevel, and Young "has allowed the staff to question his authority and his position on staff independence to the point that he is unable to require many staff members to function to the degree which is necessary if SCLC is going to bring about meaningful change." The difficulties encountered in the Chicago registration drive were largely the result of how SCLC's Chicago staff had refused to cooperate with their southern colleagues and had disregarded Williams's orders. "Many of SCLC's regular Chicago staff members were doing little more than laying around their rooms all day, playing cards, drinking and smoking pot." The solution, Williams advised, was to transfer a number of higher-ranking people to less demanding posts, and fire some two dozen lower-ranking staffers who were not producing.

King wanted to avoid a bloody postmortem on the winter debacle in Chicago, but he agreed with Williams that SCLC needed a full-time administrator to ride herd on the staff. He told his colleagues during the two days of discussions on March 9 and 10 that he wanted either Walter Fauntroy or Joseph Lowery to become executive director, and that a young Tuscaloosa minister, T. Y. Rogers, who had served as his assistant at Dexter Avenue church years earlier, should become director of affiliates. Andrew Young would function solely as King's executive assistant, and three new departments would be created: a youth department, proposed by Stoney Cooks, to fill the void created by SNCC's transformation, a labor and economic affairs department to be headed by Jesse Jackson that would expand Operation Breadbasket into a national program, and a housing department to pursue rehabilitation projects.[24]

King and his aides also agreed to revive the Chicago protests in late spring. Additionally, they decided to consider a campaign in Louisville, Kentucky, where black leaders had been struggling to win city council approval of an open-housing ordinance. Ralph Abernathy had visited there the previous August, and young field staffer Eddie Osburn was recommending expanded involvement. SCLC's spring board meeting had been scheduled for Louisville, and King instructed Young to explore the local situation.

After the Atlanta meeting, King went to Washington to lead a protest march in the Shaw community, but canceled a scheduled White House meeting with Lyndon Johnson, which left Johnson perplexed. He and King had had one long phone conversation during the winter months, in which King had preached to the president about the immorality of America's involvement in Vietnam. The two men had not met in almost a year despite two White House invitations to King. Press commentators opined that the lack of contact was by Johnson's design, but in fact the absence of communication was largely King's doing, based upon a reluctance to confront a man whom he personally mistrusted and whose policies he regarded with ever-increasing distaste. Three days after the scheduled meeting failed to take place, King authorized Bevel to announce that he would indeed speak at the April 15 anti-Vietnam protest in New York.[25]

On March 23 and 24, in both Atlanta and Chicago, King announced his and SCLC's upcoming plans for the first time since his return from Jamaica. First, he would take "a much stronger stand" against the Vietnam War. Second, SCLC would renew its slum organizing efforts, particularly in Chicago, with an eye toward mobilizing mass support for a guaranteed annual income. "We have got to go all out to grapple with this economic problem," and there was no better focus than Chicago, where "nothing much" had been done to implement "a marvelous agreement on paper." Breadbasket would expand as part of this economic thrust, but the principal emphasis would be on renewed mass demonstrations. Citing the conclusions that had been reached by Chicago activists, King pointed out that "city agencies have been inert in upholding their commitment to the open housing pact. . . . If this kind of foot-dragging continues, we will have no alternative but to resume demonstrations . . . on a much more massive scale" than the previous summer. "I think it's going to be absolutely necessary for us to march into Cicero this summer," King declared. "Just as we confronted the colossus of Selma in the South, we're going to confront the colossus of Cicero in the North."

In addition to housing, the Chicago movement would target the city's schools. "In order to grapple with the problem of de facto segregation, we are going to have to bring the issue to the streets," perhaps in the form of black school children marching on white schools. Asked by reporters if these interests were not quite different from his professed focus upon Vietnam, King said no, that civil rights and opposition to the war were "very compatible" concerns. "I do plan to intensify my personal activities in taking a stand against this war. And I do that . . . because the war is hurting us in all of our programs to end slums and to end segregation in schools and to make quality education a reality, to end the long night of poverty." In short, "we need a radical reordering of our national priorities."[26]

Saturday morning King and noted pediatrician Benjamin Spock led five thousand demonstrators through downtown Chicago, the first antiwar march of King's career. Afterward, King spoke about Vietnam to a sizable crowd at the Chicago Coliseum, repeating many of the remarks he had made in Los Angeles a month earlier but adding several sentences that caught journalists' attention. The U.S. government's conduct left America "standing before the world glutted by our own barbarity," and required that people strongly dissent. "We must combine the fervor of the civil rights movement with the peace movement." Editorial reaction to the speech was modest but negative. A Chicago television station saw a contradiction between King's Vietnam stand and his promise of more urban protests. "He marches for peace on one day, and then the very next day threatens actions we think are coldly calculated to bring violent response from otherwise peaceful neighborhoods," namely "nonviolent marches which have a consistent history of provoking violence."

King's feelings about Vietnam grew stronger despite his concern that SCLC would suffer for his outspokenness. "At times you do things to satisfy your conscience and they may be altogether unrealistic or wrong tactically, but you feel better," he explained to Levison. "I know . . . I will get a lot of criticism and I know it can hurt SCLC, but I feel better, and I think that is the most important thing." The war was so evil that "I can no longer be cautious about this matter. I feel so deep in my heart that we are so wrong in this country and the time has come for a real prophecy and I'm willing to go that road." There had been no decline in SCLC's direct-mail contributions, Levison reported, but he and other advisors feared the effects of King's Spring Mobe appearance. They lobbied for an earlier, comprehensive presentation of King's Vietnam views in a more respectable setting, and arranged for him to give an April 4 address to a prominent antiwar group, Clergy and Laymen Concerned About Vietnam, at New York's Riverside Church.[27]

On March 29, King arrived in Louisville for SCLC's board meeting in a serious but good-natured frame of mind. He met privately with boxing champion Muhammad Ali, a Louisville native, and joshed with friends as the board assembled for its first session. Ralph Abernathy asked one Atlanta minister how his assignment as convenor or "call-man" for the local Operation Breadbasket was going, and King broke in with a joke. "I was in one city where they asked me if we couldn't change the name. They said that the 'call-man' idea gives the impression of the 'call-girl' idea, and they weren't sure of the responsibility."

King's remark was a good reflection of his witty and often bawdy sense of humor, a side of him that only close friends and FBI sound men were privy to. Mother King remembered that M.L.'s proclivity as a joke teller went back to childhood, and longtime intimates knew him as a relentless teaser and "a perfect mimic." "If he felt close to you, he would tease you," one personal secretary remembered, and ghostwriter Al Duckett never forgot King's "fantastically funny impersonations of other people." King particularly enjoyed jokes or stories that poked fun at overly pompous clergymen. Additionally, "Martin could tell everyday happenings in ways that would just make you roar with laughter because he had such a fantastic sense of humor."

Andrew Young reflected that King "never had the time to be the fun-loving man that he really was." Coretta remembered that "my husband used to say I was too serious-minded. . . . Martin was so much fun when he relaxed; he'd just tell jokes for hours. . . . But he'd say to me, 'You don't laugh enough.'" For Dorothy Cotton, "he really was a lot of fun to be with. He could be the life of the party, and more often than not he was." In particular, "he was a big teaser," Coretta recalled. "This was part of his technique for really sort of getting back at me when I would say something that he didn't like." As Bernard Lee put it, "a lot of times when he was teasing, he was also making a point. . . . This was his fashion of saying in a jocular fashion what he wanted to say. . . . He did it teasingly."

The joking aside, SCLC's board listened patiently as various administrators delivered their reports, with Jesse Jackson and Fred Bennette detailing the accomplishments of Breadbasket and Public Relations Director Tom Offenburger explaining that a monthly staff newsletter, *North & South*, had been started. Stoney Cooks presented the Chicago report, and noted that the 1966 efforts had fallen short because of the failure "to relate the masses of people mobilized" for the open-housing marches to either SCLC's grass-roots organizing or "the reinforcement of existing community organizations." Andrew Young spoke about how SCLC needed to take a stronger organizational stand on Vietnam, and confront domestic economic questions head on. "Any movement that calls itself a civil rights movement has got to begin to put up or shut up for poor people." King agreed and told the group, "We must see two things during this period of transition that are absolutely necessary—one is that we keep our vision centered on the ultimate goal of integrated schools, integrated housing, and what have you; secondly, we in the process [have to] improve the quality of the ghetto."

On Thursday King granted an interview to a *New York Times* reporter. The movement, King said, faced two major challenges. First, it was no longer simply an effort to eliminate segregation and expose southern brutality. "What we are faced with now is the fact that the struggle must be and actually is at this point a struggle for genuine equality," a struggle "to organize the Negro community for the amassing of real political and economic power." The first ten years of the movement had produced "a new sense of dignity, a new sense of destiny, a new sense of self-respect" among black Americans, but despite the importance of the 1964 and 1965 acts, they "did very little to rectify conditions facing millions of Negroes in the teeming ghettos of the North."

Second, King told *Times* correspondent John Herbers, "we are merely marking time in the civil rights movement if we do not take a stand against the war." King had come to "more of a realization of the interrelatedness of racism and militarism," and to a belief that civil disobedience might be necessary to oppose the war. Unfortunately, "the heart of the administration is in that war in Vietnam," and America had to realize that international violence was just as immoral for humanity as racial segregation. "It is out of this moral commitment to dignity and the worth of human personality," King said, "that I feel it is necessary to stand up against the war in Vietnam."[28]

Later that day, at the final session of SCLC's board, King and Andrew Young asked for a strong declaration that would commit SCLC to active opposition to Johnson's war policies. Since the Vietnam conflict might lead to war with China or the Soviet Union, King said, "the survival of the world" was at stake. Opposition had its costs, he noted. In 1965, "I went through a lot of bitter and certainly vicious criticism by the press for taking that stand." Even though "it's a little more popular now to do it," popularity was not a consideration. King reminded the board about "those little Vietnamese children who have been burned with napalm," and told about a conversation at the New York fund-raiser he had attended three weeks earlier in which Bill vanden Heuvel had expressed surprise about how limited black opposition to the war was, especially since blacks were paying the heaviest price, both at home and in battlefield casualties, for America's Vietnam policy. Underlying it all, King told his colleagues, was the fact that "the evils of capitalism are as real as the evils of militarism and the evils of racism."

Many board members, however, would not accept King's and Young's point of view. "It appeared to me," Mississippi's Aaron Henry explained later, "that we were taking a position here that we had really no knowledge of exactly what we were doing." Henry's position was shared by others, such as outspoken Little Rock minister Roland Smith. "The argument went," Henry recalled, that "if this is what Martin wants to do, it's all right for Martin to do it if he understands what he's doing. I don't understand it, and I'm not going out there with them." After some rancorous discussion, the proposed resolution was tabled.

King did not take the rebuff hard, and that evening he led a five-hundred-person march from a black church to Louisville's Municipal Auditorium, where open-housing *opponents* were meeting. Speaking from the auditorium steps, King told the marchers that SCLC would aid their antidiscrimination drive, and that he would return to help them. The next day he headed to Atlanta before going to New York for his speech to the Clergy and Laymen Concerned group.[29]

On Tuesday, April 4, King met with Levison and Wachtel, then held a press conference before going to Riverside Church. King's address to the three-thousand-person crowd was the fullest statement he had made on the war, and the setting ensured that his words would receive more coverage than had his speeches in Los Angeles and Chicago. There were, King said, many reasons why he could no longer remain silent about Vietnam. For one, the war was "an enemy of the poor" that exploited them both in the service and on the streets of America's slums. Also, with regard to urban riots, "I knew that I could never again raise my voice against the violence of the oppressed in the ghettos without having first spoken clearly to the greatest purveyor of violence in the world today—my own government." Additionally, his ministerial role and Christian convictions gave him "allegiances and loyalties which are broader and deeper than nationalism," and required him to adopt a world perspective rather than a narrowly American one. Furthermore, "another burden of responsibility" which increased his moral obligation "was placed upon me in 1964" by the Nobel Peace Prize.

King denounced America's conduct in harsh terms. The U.S.'s first South Vietnamese puppet, Ngo Dinh Diem, had been "one of the most vicious modern dictators," and recent American actions had created "the concentration camps we call fortified hamlets." America was siding with "the wealthy and the secure while we create a hell for the poor" of Vietnam, and if U.S. policy was not altered, King said, "there will be no doubt in my mind . . . that we have no honorable intentions" in the war. "It will become clear that our minimal expectation is to occupy it as an American colony."

King called for the Johnson administration to take five specific actions to end the war: halt all bombing, north and south; declare a unilateral cease-fire; curtail military activities in Thailand and Laos; accept a Viet Cong presence in peace negotiations; and set a date by which all foreign troops would be out of Vietnam. He also called for all young men to declare themselves conscientious objectors when drafted, and for ministers who were of draft age to give up their ministerial deferments. "The war in Vietnam is but a symptom of a far deeper malady within the American spirit." America's reactionary stance, King said, was rooted in the country's refusal to give up the exploitative profits derived from overseas investments. "If we are to get on the right side of the world revolution, we as a nation must undergo a radical revolution of values. We must rapidly begin the shift from a 'thing-oriented' society to a 'person-oriented' society."[30]

King was in a buoyant mood after his speech, pleased that he had finally made the moral declaration he had felt obligated to deliver ever since that January day when he saw the photos in *Ramparts*. In most other quarters, however, reaction to King's remarks was far from enthusiastic. Old friends such as Phil Randolph and Bayard Rustin refused to comment for publication, and Roy Wilkins and Whitney Young disassociated themselves from him. A barrage of negative newspaper editorials began on April 6 with a biting statement by *The Washington Post* condemning King's speech as "not a sober and responsible comment on the war but a reflection of his disappointment at the slow progress of civil rights and the war on poverty." Some of his statements had been "sheer inventions of unsupported fantasy," the *Post* said; others had conveyed "bitter and damaging allegations and inferences that he did not and could not document." All in all, the *Post* declared, King

has done a grave injury to those who are his natural allies . . . and . . . an even graver injury to himself. Many who have listened to him with respect will never again accord him the same confidence. He has diminished his usefulness to his cause, to his country and to his people. And that is a great tragedy.

Other denunciations followed. *The New York Times* decried any combining of the civil rights and peace movements, and rebuked King for "recklessly comparing American military methods to those of the Nazis." The black *Pittsburgh Courier* complained that King was "tragically misleading" American Negroes on issues that were "too complex for simple debate." New York Senator Jacob Javits branded the speech "harmful," and *Life* magazine called it "a demagogic slander that sounded like a script for Radio Hanoi." King "goes beyond his personal right to dissent," *Life* said, "when he connects progress in civil rights here with a proposal that amounts to abject surrender in Vietnam," and by so doing "King comes close to betraying the cause for which he has worked so long."

Even among King's closest advisors, reaction to the speech was not positive. Levison told him that the text had been unbalanced and poorly thought out. King reacted defensively, saying that while he had not prepared a full advance text, he had outlined it carefully. "I spent a whole afternoon thinking about this speech and I thought I had to say something." Levison told King that was not enough. "I don't know if careful thinking would have caused me to revise the speech," King replied. "I was politically unwise but morally wise. I think I have a role to play which may be unpopular." "I really feel that someone of influence has to say that the United States is wrong, and everybody is afraid to say it," King explained. "What I did was go beyond the point that anyone has done who is of influence. I have just become so disgusted with the way people of America are being brainwashed . . . by the administration." Levison warned that "I am afraid that you will become identified as a leader of a fringe movement when you are much more," and won King's agreement that the text of his Spring Mobe speech would be prepared by Levison and Wachtel.[31]

A few newspapers and magazines commended King for the April 4 speech. The *Detroit Free Press* endorsed his stand, and the *Christian Century* called his remarks "a magnificent blend of eloquence and raw fact, of searing denunciation and tender wooing, of political sagacity and Christian insight, of tough realism and infinite compassion." In other quarters, however, such as the Johnson White House and J. Edgar Hoover's FBI, the evaluation was far more negative. Presidential advisor John P. Roche told Johnson that King, "who is inordinately ambitious and quite stupid," had "thrown in with the commies" because he was "in desperate search of a constituency." The "Communist-oriented 'peace' types," Roche alleged, "have played him (and his driving wife) like trout. . . . There will always be a crowd to applaud, money to keep up his standard of living, etc." Presidential press secretary George Christian informed his boss that he had contacted black columnist Carl Rowan, who was "exploring the Martin Luther King matter. He said everyone in the Civil Rights movement has known that King has been getting advice from a Communist, and he (Rowan) is trying to firm up in his own mind whether King is still doing this. He wants to take out after King, because he thinks he has hurt the Civil Rights movement with his statements." Several days later Rowan made good on his vow with a column that mourned "the transformation of King from the . . . boycott leader with an uncanny knack for saying the right things into the King of today who has very little sense of, or concern for, public relations, and no tactical skill." The problem, Rowan wrote, without naming Levison, was "that King is listening most to one man who is clearly more interested in embarrassing the United States than in the plight of either the Negro or the war-weary people of Vietnam." The FBI interpreted the latest turn of events even more seriously, as Hoover explained in a private communication to Lyndon Johnson. "Based on King's recent activities and public utterances, it is clear that he is an instrument in the hands of subversive forces seeking to undermine our nation."

Pained but not shocked at the public excoriations, King pledged not to be daunted by the unpopularity of his stand. "It was a heavy cross," James Lawson noted, but one King knew he had to bear. He accepted an offer to become co-chairman of Clergy and Laymen Concerned About Vietnam, and the following Sunday, at the Chicago church of Rev. John Thurston, King broke away from his standard sermon text to utter a personal message in front of his host and Bernard Lee, his regular companion:

> And John, if you and Bernard happen to be around when I come to the latter day and that moment to cross the Jordan, I want you to tell them that I made a request. I don't want a long funeral. In fact, I don't even need a eulogy of more than one or two minutes.
>
> I hope that I will live so well the rest of the days. I don't know how long I'll live, and I'm not concerned about that. But I hope I can live so well that the preacher can get up and say he was faithful. That's all, that's enough. That's the sermon I'd like to hear. "Well done thy good and faithful servant. You've been faithful; you've been concerned about others."
>
> That's where I want to go from this point on, the rest of my days. "He who is greatest among you shall be your servant." I want to be a servant. I want to be a witness for my Lord, do something for others.[32]

The controversy over King's antiwar remarks increased on April 10 when the NAACP Board of Directors adopted a resolution labeling any attempt to merge the civil rights and peace movements "a serious tactical mistake." Although the text did not mention King by name, there was no doubt about the target. *The New York Times* reported the declaration with a page one headline reading NAACP DECRIES STAND OF DR. KING ON VIETNAM, and two days later U.N. Undersecretary-General Ralph Bunche announced that he had been one NAACP director who had pushed for the strong statement. King, Bunche declared, ought not to be both a civil rights leader and an antiwar spokesman and should "give up one role or the other."

King denied any desire to "merge" the civil rights and peace movements and said he was "saddened" that the NAACP would assail him publicly. The truth was, he told the press, that "there is deep and widespread disenchantment with the war in Vietnam" among American blacks. "I have held these views myself for a long time," King explained, "but I have spoken out more frequently in the recent period because Negroes in so many circles have explicitly urged me to articulate their concern and frustration." Speaking out might not be easy in a nation suffering from "a kind of paranoid or morbid fear of communism," but his motive for doing so was neither that alleged by Rowan nor the frustration cited by the *Post*. "I do it not out of anger, I do it out of great anxiety and agony and anguish."

The growing criticism made King worry that a concerted campaign was under way to undermine his public influence. He talked about his concerns in lengthy phone calls with Levison, Wachtel, Robinson, and Harry Belafonte, and acknowledged Wachtel's fear that perhaps "J. Edgar Hoover's old stuff" might be dragged out to lend credence to those assaults. He was exasperated when Ralph Bunche phoned him to apologize privately for his public remarks and to profess complete agreement with King's views on the war, if not his mode of opposition. It was too bad, King lamented, that Bunche did not have the courage to state his honest opinion in public. Experiences such as that only helped transform "the buoyancy of hope into the fatigue of despair," as King described the movement's situation to one audience. "The struggle," he said, "is much more difficult today than it was five or ten years ago" because popular support had declined substantially and many past backers could not understand how civil rights and Vietnam "are inextricably bound together." People had "to see that there is a mutual problem involved. Racism and militarism are very closely tied together," especially in what was "basically a war of colonialism."[33]

King attached great importance to his upcoming appearance at the April 15 Spring Mobe demonstration, and was concerned about some of the other speakers who would share the platform, particularly SNCC's Stokely Carmichael. King assigned Andrew Young to represent him in the contentious negotiations about who would speak and what banners and slogans would be highlighted. Stanley Levison repeatedly cautioned King to align himself with people of power in the antiwar coalition and not with fringe elements, so as to avoid becoming isolated. When the Saturday protest got under way, with 125,000 marchers assembling in Central Park for the twenty-block procession to United Nations Plaza, King joined Bevel, Benjamin Spock, and Harry Belafonte in the front line. SNCC Chairman Carmichael headed a contingent carrying Viet Cong flags, and other groups carried banners indicating similarly radical sentiments. Carmichael and CORE's Floyd McKissick were among the featured speakers at the U.N. Plaza rally, but the real centerpiece, King's address, was a more moderate speech than the one he had delivered at Riverside Church. "Everyone has a duty to be in both the civil rights and peace movements," King said, but he stated carefully that "I have not urged a mechanical fusion" of the two. It was not a memorable oration, but his concluding refrain—"stop the bombing, stop the bombing"—did generate some enthusiasm in the crowd. Other speakers followed with angrier statements. One of them, William F. Pepper of the newly founded National Conference for New Politics, recommended a 1968 King presidential candidacy as an ideal way to coalesce opposition to the war. After the rally, King, Spock, and several others met briefly with U.N. official Bunche before adjourning for private discussions.[34]

Little-known NCNP organizer Pepper was far from the only antiwar activist who wanted King to take up a 1968 presidential crusade. Spock wanted him to head up a King-Spock ticket, and Norman Thomas was also pressing the idea of his candidacy, but King did not lean toward any candidacy of his own. That evening Harry Belafonte hosted a meeting that brought together many of King's advisors and some SNCC representatives. King indicated little interest in a presidential race while agreeing with a surprisingly cooperative Stokely Carmichael that they ought to avoid public criticism of each other and concentrate on shared objectives. Later, Stanley Levison accompanied King back to his hotel room to prepare for questions that might be asked the following morning when King appeared on CBS's *Face the Nation*.

King used the national television appearance to reiterate his opposition to the war while disowning such controversial actions as the carrying of Viet Cong flags or the burning of draft cards and American flags. He also pointed out that he had advocated draft resistance, not draft evasion, and that "I myself would be a conscientious objector if I had to face it." Concerning the Vietnam War, "something must be done on a much more massive scale to oppose it. I do not at this point advocate civil disobedience. I think we have to do a lot of groundwork in massive education before that," groundwork that would include pointing out how the war "has strengthened the forces of reaction in our country." Pressed to explain his position on the relationship between the war and civil rights, King explained that "the two are tied together from a content point of view, although the two are not tied together from an organizational point of view."

After the show, other journalists asked King if the country should expect another summer of urban riots. "I'll still preach nonviolence with all my might, but I'm afraid it will fall on deaf ears," King warned, especially in such "powder keg" cities as Cleveland, Chicago, Los Angeles, Oakland, Washington, Newark, and New York. Then King headed off to a luncheon meeting of the major civil rights leaders sponsored by the Field Foundation. Some of those present renewed their criticisms of

King's antiwar efforts. King responded that he would be devoting only a small percentage of his time to those concerns. Afterward, Roy Wilkins needled King further. "I saw your picture in the paper, Martin," the publicity-conscious NAACP chief remarked, alluding to coverage of the Saturday antiwar protest. "Yes, Roy," King replied. "Why weren't you there with me?"[35]

Tired but not depressed, King returned to Atlanta and entered a hospital for a routine checkup. The previous two weeks had been stressful, but "I'm not despairing over the long run," he told one interviewer. "I live out of a suitcase most of the time," and rest was a luxury. "Four hours sleep is enough for me," King told anyone who questioned his habits, but on occasion the exhaustion caught up with him. King's schedule was clear until an April 23 trip to meet Dr. Spock in Massachusetts to plan a summer antiwar mobilization, but his Atlanta repose was interrupted by a series of events concerning his possible presidential candidacy. Johnson confidant Louis Martin called Andrew Young to ask if King was interested in seeing the president. Two days later, *The New York Times* quoted NCNP activist Pepper as saying, "We are negotiating with Dr. King" about a potential candidacy. King and Young were furious that the antiwar enthusiasts would try to force King's hand. "I was going to make it clear that I had no such intentions," King told Levison, who recommended that King disavow any candidacy. Norman Thomas and Allard Lowenstein pleaded with Young to ask King not to bar the door to running, but King told Levison he would issue a disavowal statement. "I need to be in the position of being my own man."

King joined Spock in Cambridge on April 23 to announce plans for "Vietnam Summer," a project that would mobilize grass-roots opposition to the war by developing a nationwide network of volunteers. King and Spock kicked off the recruiting effort by knocking on the doors of two preselected sympathizers' homes. In talking with reporters, King avoided questions about his own political plans. He listened to candidacy pleas from Spock and others in a private meeting, then shook his head and said, "My people would not understand." That evening, after speaking to a Boston crowd, King betrayed a touch of ambivalence when he responded to a question from the floor. "I have never had any political ambitions, and it is strange territory for me to consider. I have never thought of myself moving into the presidential arena."[36]

The next day King joined Americans for Democratic Action Vice-Chairman Joseph L. Rauh at a New York press conference to announce formation of yet another antiwar group, "Negotiation Now," which would try to obtain one million petition signatures calling for immediate Vietnam peace talks. He skirted questions about his political plans, and promised to issue a statement in Atlanta the following day that would respond to those queries. Accompanied by Young, Lee, and Levison, he flew home that night pondering how strong a denial of interest he ought to issue. The truth of the matter, King told Levison, was that he had no interest in being president. Levison agreed it would not be a wise course to pursue at present, and when King met with reporters at Ebenezer church on Tuesday morning, the statement he read had a clear ring of finality. "I have come to think of my role as one which operates outside the realm of partisan politics," raising issues for the entire nation to confront. Thus, "I have no interest in any political candidacy and I am issuing this statement to remove doubts of my position on this subject."[37]

That night King left Atlanta for a two-day visit to Cleveland, where the city's black ministers, the United Pastors Association (UPA), wanted his help in organizing a civil rights effort that might ensure a more peaceful summer than that of 1966, when the Hough ghetto had been wracked by rioting. SCLC staffer Eddie Osburn had been lobbying both King and the UPA to consider an SCLC campaign in Cleveland. King stayed up late talking with UPA leaders, including Rev. O. M. Hoover, a family friend whose daughter Carole was on SCLC's staff. The next day King spoke at three schools and criticized conservative Cleveland Mayor Ralph S. Locher, who had narrowly beaten black challenger Carl Stokes in 1965 and would face Stokes again that coming fall. Reporters were as interested in King's national ambitions as in his view of the local situation, and King repeated his Atlanta declaration. "Being a peace candidate is not my role. I feel I should serve as a conscience of all the parties and all of the people, rather than be a candidate myself." From a civil rights perspective, the two best presidential candidates would be Democrat Robert Kennedy and Republican Charles Percy, King said. His own purview, he emphasized, was not a narrow one. "I'm interested in rights for Negroes, but I'm just as interested in Appalachian whites and Mexican-Americans and other minorities." At an evening rally King announced that Cleveland would become a base for SCLC's future efforts. "I plan to be back real soon." An expanded movement had to be mounted there and in other cities because "things are worse for the mass of Negroes than they were twenty years ago."

From Cleveland, King went to Minnesota and Wisconsin for speaking engagements before stopping in Chicago to announce Operation Breadbasket's biggest pact so far, an agreement with the Jewel food store chain that provided for 512 new jobs, shelf space for black manufacturers' products, and expanded company patronage of black business firms. King made no mention of his late March threat to resume demonstrations in Chicago over the coming summer, and professed to see "some steps forward" in implementing the summit agreement of August, 1966. Among local activists, however, the evaluation of city compliance remained strongly negative, and morale was at a low point, as black trade-union leader and CCCO delegate Timuel D. Black explained in a long letter to King. "Bewilderment and confusion has increased among Negroes and their white liberal friends all over the city," Black wrote. "They feel betrayed and in many ways hopeless and helpless." The movement's participation in the summit conference had been marked by "no real democratic planning and action," and the accord had been a "shattering event" in which "the back of the civil rights thrust was broken" and CCCO left "helpless and all but destroyed." Black warned King to "take a long, hard look at the Chicago scene. . . . Whatever your future ventures are, I hope they will be better planned and more successful than those of last year" in Chicago. "We need no more empty promises. We need no more betrayals." With such angry backbiting rending the Chicago movement, Cleveland seemed a more attractive locale for whatever summer effort SCLC would mount in the urban North.[38]

Back home in Atlanta, King talked to his Ebenezer congregation about his antiwar views, telling them that "the calling to speak is often a vocation of agony." He explained that the Nobel Peace Prize had been "a commission to work harder than I had ever worked before for the brotherhood of man," and he repeated to them some portions of his April 4 address, including his description of the U.S. government as "the greatest purveyor of violence in the world today." He added that "it is a dark day in our nation when high level authorities will seek to use every method to silence dissent," and said that although he would have fought against Hitler, "I happen to be a pacifist." He praised Muhammad Ali's conscientious resistance to military service, and when King concluded, his congregation—SNCC's Stokely Carmichael among them—gave him a standing ovation.

On May 3, King flew to Louisville for his first substantive involvement in the open-housing protests, which had gathered new momentum following the city council's April 11 rejection of a fair-housing ordinance. Local civil rights leaders, including King's brother, A.D., had met several times with city officials, but had received no commitments. In response, the movement had threatened further protests for the May 6 Kentucky Derby horse race, Louisville's major annual event. Five hundred people greeted King at the Louisville airport, and he addressed a sizable crowd at St. James AME Church, after which two hundred marchers walked several miles to hold a late-night prayer vigil at city police headquarters. Privately, movement activists were divided on holding protests that would disrupt the Derby, and King argued for a moderate course, declaring that "we don't believe in disruption for the sake of disruption." At a strategy meeting the night of May 4, the leaders decided that a downtown march on May 6 would be better than a demonstration at the racetrack, but some who had gone along with that decision reluctantly, including A. D. King, threatened to carry out a Derby protest when news of the decision was leaked. After much wrangling, King affirmed the downtown march plans. Then he left town on Derby morning, just hours before a small column of 150 protesters marched through the deserted business district at the same time the race was being run.[39]

At home in Atlanta, King told a black luncheon club how fearful he was about both foreign and domestic developments. Only a few days earlier a young soldier back from Vietnam had approached him on a plane,

King said, to tell how low the morale of U.S. troops was. On the home front the picture also seemed bleak. "There has never been any single, solid, determined commitment on the part of the vast majority of white Americans to genuine equality for Negroes," he asserted. The country needed "a radical reordering of priorities," whether people wanted to admit it or not. "Too often when you're called a responsible leader, it means you're an Uncle Tom leader," King sighed.

On May 10, King returned to Louisville, where protests continued despite the movement's internal dissension. "There is no way to get open housing in Louisville but by creating a crisis so great that the community will have to act and will have to respond," King told an audience at his brother's Zion Baptist Church. In the early evening seventy protesters held a peaceful march, and King, Abernathy, A.D., and another local minister accompanied the column by car. Hostile white youths heckled the marchers, and belligerent teen-agers swarmed around the car as King tried to talk to them. "We've got to learn to live together as brothers," he called out through the open window. One youngster spat back that he was not King's brother. "I love you as I love my four children," King replied. "You're going to grow up in a world that we're going to live together in." Suddenly a rock struck the car and bounced in through the window, grazing King on the neck. He and the others ducked, and the driver, Rev. Leo Lesser, sped away. Later that night King held the rock in his hand as he addressed a movement rally.

From Louisville King went on to Chicago and several speaking engagements in Wisconsin, but his principal concern was a North Vietnamese invitation to join other American antiwar activists and meet with them in Paris. He decided it would be unwise to accept, and told both Young and Levison that the Johnson administration would probably revoke his passport if he undertook such a venture. In time, if he could rally enough domestic opposition to stop America's bombing of North Vietnam, King mused, then he could go to Hanoi to meet with Ho Chi Minh and call for immediate peace negotiations.[40]

In mid-May King confirmed earlier reports that he would lead a November pilgrimage of up to two thousand Americans to holy sites in Israel and Jordan. "I am first a minister of the gospel," he declared at a New York press briefing, but later that day he flew to Cleveland to announce that SCLC would begin a major summer program there on June 1. Voter registration, tenant organizing, and the formation of a Breadbasket project would all be parts of the effort, King said, and he would spend at least two days every other week in Cleveland. Local black leaders, ranging from the NAACP and Democratic city councilmen to militant spokesman Fred Ahmed Evans, all welcomed King's entry, and press observers speculated that the SCLC effort would represent a crucial initiative in a city whose mayor was so racially insensitive that even white business leaders had condemned his behavior.

After his Cleveland stopover, King flew west for speaking engagements

in San Francisco and Denver, accompanied by Lee and free-lance journalist David Halberstam. "For years I labored with the idea of reforming
the existing institutions of the society, a little change here, a little change
there," King told Halberstam. "Now I feel quite differently. I think
you've got to have a reconstruction of the entire society, a revolution of
values," and perhaps the nationalization of some major industries. King
expressed similar views to a crowd of seven thousand at Berkeley's
Sproul Plaza, telling them the movement's new phase would be "a struggle for *genuine* equality," involving "issues that will demand a radical
redistribution of economic and political power." Support for such changes
would be difficult to muster, he warned, because "many Americans
would like to have a nation which is a democracy for white Americans
but simultaneously a dictatorship over black Americans." Scores of signs
calling for a "King-Spock" ticket bobbed in the crowd, and King declared
that "the clouds of a third world war are hovering mighty low." If such a
cataclysm occurred, "our government will have to take the chief responsibility for making this a reality."

When he finished his remarks, student representatives presented him
with petitions asking that he become a candidate, and one questioner
from the audience asked why King was hesitant to declare himself. "I do
not feel that I'm presidential timber," King replied. "I would rather think
of myself as one trying desperately to be the conscience of all the political
parties, rather than being a political candidate. . . . I've just never
thought of myself and I can't now think of myself as a politician. Of
course, I do have sense enough to know I couldn't win, either."[41]

Returning home to Atlanta, King lamented that congressional votes
cutting back federal housing funds were turning "the war on poverty into
a war against the poor." Asked to respond to allegations that Communist
sympathies underlay antiwar protests, King said, "I feel we are in a new
McCarthy-like era. It is not this time one man but a conspiracy of silenc-
ing dissenters from high places." His morale also was challenged by Harris Poll results showing that 73 percent of Americans disagreed with his
opposition to the war, and that 60 percent believed King's Vietnam
stance would hurt the civil rights movement. Additionally, the poll
showed that 48 percent of black respondents thought King was wrong,
and only 25 percent agreed with his comments.

At the same time, SCLC continued to generate problems of its own.
Although Ann Farnsworth had donated another $25,000, the Ford Foun-
dation had not made a decision on SCLC's grant application, and contributions were lagging. King told one questioner that the organization was
in "fairly good shape," largely because field-staff attrition had reduced
the payroll to under one hundred people, but Andrew Young conceded
that financially it was "a rather difficult period right now." More important, SCLC had hardly any program efforts still going forward in the
Deep South. *New York Times* southern correspondent Gene Roberts, observing that the movement had collapsed in all but a few locales, asked

Hosea Williams if SCLC had written off the Deep South. "I wouldn't put it quite that way, because we're still interested in the South, but I guess that is what it amounts to," Williams responded.

SCLC's one ongoing southern project was the eleven-month-old effort in Grenada, Mississippi, which had "rapidly deteriorated" during the spring. The SCLC project leader, according to one Jackson civil rights attorney, was "indolent, unimaginative, and possesses neither the capacity for, nor the interest in, being a community leader. More important," he went on, "the Grenada community does not respect and trust" the man. In short, the attorney declared,

> I do not think that SCLC has lived up to its commitment to Grenada. SCLC is responsible for the lack of leadership of its own project. . . . By and large SCLC has used the local people as conduits for implementing its decisions, without really involving them in the decision-making process, and without training them to take over

when SCLC departed. Unknown to him, SCLC's three-man staff was asking for transfer unless headquarters was willing to commit a modicum of resources to support the Grenada office during the coming summer.[42]

All of these troubles were on King's mind when SCLC's staff gathered at Frogmore for a retreat on May 21 and 22. The discussions produced agreement that the major summer focus ought to be on Cleveland and the problems of northern cities rather than on an antiwar push. King told the staff that the last few months of wrestling with the war issue had made him realize that the movement must undergo a significant transformation. "We have moved from the era of civil rights to the era of human rights," he said, "an era where we are called upon to raise certain basic questions about the whole society." For the past twelve years, "we have been in a reform movement. . . . But after Selma and the voting rights bill we moved into a new era, which must be an era of revolution. I think we must see the great distinction here between a reform movement and a revolutionary movement," and how the former had been directed at making America live up to its professed values. "I'm convinced," he told his colleagues, "that a lot of the people that supported us when we were in those glowing, epic-making days in Alabama and in Mississippi, when we were in Birmingham and Selma, many of the people who supported us supported us because they were against Jim Clark, because they were against Bull Connor, but they were not for genuine equality for Negroes."

Basic changes in perspective would have to take place, King explained. "More and more we have got to come to see that integration must be seen not merely in aesthetic or romantic terms; it must be seen in political terms. Integration in its true dimensions is shared power." One past shortcoming, he said, was that "all too many people have seen power and love as polar opposites," when in fact "the two fulfill each other . . .

power without love is reckless, and love without power is sentimental."
Previous misconceptions had to be put aside; "we must recognize that we
can't solve our problem now until there is a radical redistribution of economic and political power," King declared, repeating the phrase for further emphasis—"a radical redistribution of economic and political
power." In order to do that, America's rules would have to be changed.
"This means a revolution of values and of other things. . . . We must see
now that the evils of racism, economic exploitation, and militarism are all
tied together, and you really can't get rid of one without getting rid of the
others." In short, "the whole structure of American life must be
changed," a difficult challenge in light of the fact that "America's problem in restructuring is that she is a conservative nation." Hence it is imperative that "we in the civil rights movement must come all out now and
make it clear that America is a hypocritical nation and that America must
set her own house in order."

Indicative of the problems to be confronted was U.S. involvement in
Vietnam, which was "symptomatic of a deeper malaise of the American
spirit." With great frankness, King spoke of his own private struggles
over speaking out about the war. "I had my own vacillations and I asked
questions whether on the one hand I should do it or whether I shouldn't,"
and related the crucial event. "I picked up an article entitled 'The Children of Vietnam,' and I read it, and after reading that article I said to
myself, 'Never again will I be silent on an issue that is destroying the soul
of our nation and destroying thousands and thousands of little children in
Vietnam.'" He spoke about the burden that the war issue represented:

> When I took up the cross, I recognized its meaning. . . . The cross is
> something that you bear and ultimately that you die on. The cross may
> mean the death of your popularity. It may mean the death of a founda-
> tion grant. It may cut down your budget a little, but take up your cross,
> and just bear it. And that's the way I have decided to go.

He preached on, indicating just how far he had come over the previous
year and a half:

> I want you to know that my mind is made up. I backed up a little when
> I came out in 1965. My name then wouldn't have been written in any
> book called "Profiles of Courage." But now I have decided that I will
> not be intimidated. I will not be harassed. I will not be silent, and I will
> be heard.[43]

King emphasized SCLC's intention to concentrate on the urban North
when he visited Chicago three days after the Frogmore retreat. "I do plan
to stir up trouble in some of the big cities this summer," he declared
while emphasizing that "there has never been a solid commitment on the
part of the vast majority of whites for genuine equality." He downplayed
the likelihood of protests in Chicago, saying, "I am more encouraged

today than I was two months ago" about implementation of the accord. He also pointed to the success of the local Breadbasket program, which had just won an agreement with the A & P Company that provided for 770 new black jobs before the end of the year.

He repeated his intention of concentrating on northern cities, and not Vietnam, at a meeting of the principal black leaders on May 27 at Kenneth Clark's home just north of New York City. Clark had set up the session to repair the breach that had developed over King's Vietnam speeches, but King reacted hotly when Roy Wilkins repeated his prior criticisms. "He really confronted Roy with a statement that Roy had made about the motives of his opposition and Roy denied it," Clark remembered. "Martin pushed him on it," and became "very upset" as Wilkins repeated his denials. It was "the first time I'd ever seen Martin angry," Clark said, and more conflict was avoided only when Whitney Young interceded. The heated discussion ended with an agreement to hold a second meeting in mid-June, and King headed off to Europe to fulfill a speaking engagement in Geneva.

King returned from Switzerland tired and depressed over the new war that had broken out in the Middle East. He kept an engagement in Virginia, preached at Ebenezer, and made preparations for a visit to Cleveland to kick off the summer campaign, but his aides were worried about his state of mind. After long reflection, one of SCLC's wisest senior staff members, Septima Clark, gave King a note expressing concern about his condition. "I have never seen you in the kind of mood that I witnessed on Monday, June 5," she wrote.

> It has challenged me to talk with people in the organization who I feel have the insight to see what is happening and to tell you that you need to surround yourself with men or a man immediately who will have the foresight and power to counteract the irresponsibility that is facing the organization today.

The absence of a dependable administrative chief at SCLC had not only resulted in turmoil and confusion within the organization, she explained, but had also contributed to a personal burden for King that was becoming more and more dangerous. "Dr. King, if we are to keep a world renowned leader healthy, wholesome and efficient, some of the burdens must be shared." Persuading Blackwell to return would not only ease the demands on King, but would also resolve other problems. "As I travel over the country there are many questions asked and here in the office there are many smouldering grievances," Mrs. Clark warned. Most important of all, though, was King's personal survival, she told him bluntly. "You are certainly more valuable healthy than sick and God help us all if you become exhausted to the point of a non-active person. May God help you to help yourself."[44]

Despite King's physical weariness and emotional depletion, nonetheless he traveled to Cleveland for intensive meetings with black community leaders. SCLC staffers were already on the scene, and influential whites such as the city bar association president were publicly condemning Mayor Locher's refusal to meet with King and volunteering to open a dialogue with him in the mayor's stead. Cleveland's black newspaper, the *Call and Post,* gave King a less than warm welcome in an editorial, asserting that the black community there was blessed with better leadership than Atlanta, Chicago, or Louisville. In private, black mayoral candidate Carl Stokes, worried about a possible white backlash, begged King to rethink or at least reduce his campaign. King rejected the request, but emphasized to the local leaders that SCLC would work within the bounds of the United Pastors Association invitation and would pursue a long-term campaign, not just a brief blitz. King vowed to seek a meeting with Locher, and declared that better police conduct would be one prerequisite for avoiding a second summer of riots in the Hough ghetto.

On Monday, June 12, King was stung by news that the U.S. Supreme Court, in a five-to-four vote, had upheld the 1963 criminal contempt convictions meted out to him, Abernathy, Walker, and five other ministers for leading the April 12 Good Friday march despite a state court injunction against it. Although serving the five-day jail sentences could be postponed by petitioning the Court to reconsider its decision, King was disappointed, telling reporters the ruling was an unfortunate setback for nonviolence at a time when urban blacks were doubting its effectiveness. "Nonviolence," he stressed, "is the most potent weapon available to the Negro in his struggle for freedom and justice. . . . There is a masculinity and strength in nonviolence." He groused more about the case that evening when he, Kenneth Clark, and some eighteen other civil rights leaders assembled for the second session devoted to healing the splits in the movement. In marked contrast to the first session, there was no angry sniping. Bayard Rustin spoke about the importance of not splitting with the Johnson administration, and National Urban League Director Whitney Young chided King by remarking that "I wish you could give more attention to civil rights." Defensively and with some exasperation, King responded that "I am giving most of my attention to civil rights. The press gives all the publicity to what I say on Vietnam." King spoke about SCLC's desire to make Cleveland into a major focal point, and the other leaders agreed that their organizations would assist the SCLC effort. The following day Clark held a Manhattan press conference to issue a unity statement, and he placed particular emphasis upon the Cleveland plans. That city's papers gave the announcement prominent headlines, and when King arrived in town the next morning to meet with Cleveland ministers about Breadbasket, he also stressed that interorganizational cooperation would make the Cleveland civil rights drive an especially potent program.[45]

King returned to Atlanta tired, and he would have little time for rest in the weeks ahead. "The last ten years haven't been easy years, and there have been times that I didn't think I was going to come this far," he told his Ebenezer congregation. That same day he began a media "blitz" to promote his newly published book, *Where Do We Go from Here: Chaos or Community?* One chapter had already been featured in *The New York Times Magazine,* and a tour of personal appearances took him from a national news show to a Sardi's luncheon to taping sessions for syndicated television programs such as *The Merv Griffin Show.* King did not shy away from voicing some of the strong sentiments he had expressed to his staff at the May retreat; on the *Arlene Francis Show* he noted how the past two years had forced him to watch "my dream turn into a nightmare."

King voiced similar opinions in the book's text. The volume related King's experiences on the Meredith March, reiterated his views of black power and advocated an expanded attack upon poverty. "At the root of the difficulty in Negro life today is pervasive and persistent economic want." Remedying that plight was "a problem of power," but the solution was not "black power," which King termed "a slogan without a program" and "a nihilistic philosophy." Instead, the movement would have to supplement demonstrations by "organizing people into permanent groups to protect their own interests and produce change in their behalf." Blacks' problems would not be solved until "the whole of American society takes a new turn toward greater economic justice," and until economic relations were made "more person-centered than property- and profit-centered." Achieving such changes would be difficult. "We deceive ourselves if we envision the same combination backing structural changes in society" as had supported racial reform legislation; it also "is necessary to refute the idea that the dominant ideology in our country even today is freedom and equality while racism is just an occasional departure from the norm." Nonetheless, the movement had to seek "a radical restructuring of the architecture of American society. . . . Let us," King emphasized, "not think of our movement as one that seeks to integrate the Negro into all the existing values of American society. Let us . . . call our beloved nation to a higher destiny, to a new plateau of compassion, to a more noble expression of humaneness."[46]

Although some reviewers welcomed the volume as a "moderate, judicious, constructive [and] pragmatic" statement, others zeroed in on how "his rejection of black power seems more rhetorical than real" and on how King's and Stokely Carmichael's "positions are not as far apart as might be supposed." The predominant reaction, however, was that King, "faced with abuse on all sides," from black militants and from Vietnam loyalists, had been thrown "into great confusion and doubt" and had produced a work that reflected "a certain weariness and bewilderment." King's book "seems to be groping for something it never finds," one reviewer concluded, and another pointed out his "tendency when speaking of the future to substitute rhetoric for specificity" and to cite only "stock generalities" when suggesting programs. A far harsher evaluation appeared in *The New York Review of Books* and asserted that King neither knew what he meant by "structural change" nor did he articulate any clear strategy for pursuing it. "He has been outstripped by his times, overtaken by the events which he may have obliquely helped to produce," journalist Andrew Kopkind decreed. The Chicago campaign, he said, had been King's last stand as America's foremost civil rights figure, and "he is not likely to regain command. Both his philosophy and his techniques of leadership were products of a different world, of relationships which no longer obtain and expectations which are no longer valid." In short, Kopkind alleged, King "had simply, and disastrously, arrived at the wrong conclusions about the world."[47]

While many of the reviewers' criticisms of the book accurately pegged the problems King was wrestling with, they had little effect upon him. He made two more visits to Cleveland, where he was pleased with Andrew Young's evaluation that the project was off to "a very successful beginning." Breadbasket had focused upon local milk companies, and James Orange was working with several tenant unions in Hough. Other workers were pondering how to construct a program that would focus on police brutality, Young told King, because "the main problem in the mind of the man on the street is a problem of the police." King was optimistic but cautious. "We don't want to make the mistakes we made in Chicago by promising to solve all their problems in one summer," he told Levison. Despite Cleveland's prospects, King was emotionally and physically exhausted. A late June trip took him to Los Angeles for two days. There he talked to one church audience about how it was "midnight in our world today. We are experiencing a darkness so deep . . . that we can hardly see which way to turn." "Sometimes I feel discouraged," but his faith gave him the strength to go on. He spent most of the first week of July resting in Atlanta, and took time out on the fourth to attend an SCLC holiday picnic at Stone Mountain Park.[48]

On July 9, King headed to Chicago for a two-day conference aimed at turning Operation Breadbasket into a nationwide program. More than one hundred black ministers from a score of major cities attended the sessions at the Chicago Theological Seminary, and Breadbasket leaders such as Jesse Jackson spoke about how an expanded effort could win thousands of jobs for blacks by targeting companies like General Motors, Kellogg, Kraft, and Del Monte at locations all across the country. King's statements reflected his increasingly harsh view of America's shortcomings, and a rare wistfulness about the past. "Most whites are not committed to equal opportunities for Negroes," he told one interviewer, while informing the Breadbasket conference that "America has been, and she continues to be, largely a racist society. . . . Maybe something is wrong with our economic system the way it's presently going," King suggested, noting that in democratic socialist societies such as Sweden there was no poverty, no unemployment, and no slums. "There comes a time when any system must be reevaluated," and America's time was at hand.

"The movement must address itself to restructuring the whole of American society. The problems that we are dealing with . . . are not going to be solved until there is a radical redistribution of economic and political power." For example, "there's going to have to be more sharing," and "a radical redefinition of work," of how people ought to be paid for housework or going to school, for which they were presently not compensated. Most important of all, though, was the need to reconsider past strategies and the gains they had produced. "We really thought we were making great progress," King said wistfully. "We somehow felt that we were going to win the total victory, before we analyzed the depths and dimensions of the problem." In its heyday, the movement had believed in its slogans, such as winning freedom "all, here, and now." "We had to have slogans," King said. "But the problem is that we couldn't produce what the slogan said. . . . Now I guess I knew all the time we weren't going to get all of our rights, here, and get them now," he added melancholically. "You've got to have these slogans to fire people up, to get them going, to give them a sense of dignity. But if progress isn't on a continual basis, the very slogans backfire on you," as they had been for over a year now. "We still have a long, long way to go," in Chicago and elsewhere. "The awesome predicament confronting the Negro in our slums is directly related to economic exploitation. . . . American industry and business, as part of the broader power structure, is in a large part responsible for the economic malady which grips and crushes down people in the ghetto." Breadbasket would demand proper recompense from American society. "The only way it can rectify sins of the past," King told one interviewer, "is through some form of compensatory action."

Before leaving Chicago, King announced that implementation of the open-housing accord had improved so substantially that there would be no summer protests. Instead, SCLC would conduct a two-month adult education program in Lawndale that the federal Office of Education had granted $109,000 to support. King also told newsmen that although he would be the keynote speaker at the late August convention of the National Conference for a New Politics, he would not be their third-party presidential candidate.[49]

Aside from two brief trips to Cleveland, King spent most of mid-July taking it easy in Atlanta. During the second week of July, however, rioting erupted in Newark, New Jersey. National Guard units were called in, and after several days the death toll mounted to more than twenty as the troops repeatedly exchanged gunfire with snipers. Stanley Levison advised King to issue a statement on the disorders, and when even heavier rioting broke out in Detroit several days later, Levison took the initiative and drafted a press release that he dictated over his wiretapped phone to King's office in Atlanta. "There were dark days before, but this is the darkest," a pessimistic King told Levison. The next morning King discussed the situation with his advisors in a conference call and agreed to respond to the riots, and to President Johnson's condemnation of the disorders, by issuing a telegram to the chief executive calling for immediate, large-scale federal efforts to alleviate the underlying economic causes of the uprisings. King told his colleagues that the worst had not yet happened, that private reports he had received indicated worse violence to come in cities such as Cleveland, Oakland, and Philadelphia. Then, as the FBI's wiretap recorded it, King told Levison and Wachtel what he had heard from sources in Chicago. "They gave me the plan, though, today in Chicago. They don't plan to just burn down the west side, they are planning to get the Loop in Chicago." While King made plans to issue the telegram to Johnson at an Ebenezer press conference, the FBI sprang into action.

Thinking the worst about King's comment concerning Chicago, the Bureau's New York office immediately relayed word of the conversation to headquarters. In Washington, the news was passed to J. Edgar Hoover, and at 10:30—barely an hour after the wiretapped conversation—Hoover called Lyndon Johnson to inform him that Martin Luther King "possessed information indicating there was a plan to riot and burn the Loop District in Chicago," as a subsequent written message to the president phrased it. Johnson had had a particular interest in King's activities ever since his April speeches concerning Vietnam, and only two weeks prior to Hoover's call he had queried FBI liaison Cartha D. DeLoach about whether King's relationship with the subversive Levison could be revealed publicly. "The President," DeLoach said, "asked how such information could get out. I told him that handling such matters with newspapers was perhaps the best way," but that Attorney General Ramsey Clark opposed leaking any negative information about King. Given that history, Hoover correctly assumed he would have an appreciative listener when he called the Oval Office to relay this new alarming tidbit.[50]

While Johnson was learning of King's conversation from Hoover, King was meeting with reporters to release his telegram to the president. "Only drastic changes in the life of the poor will provide the kind of order and stability you desire," King said. Noting that Congress had cut back on urban poverty programs and had refused to pass other measures aimed at ghetto ills, King declared that "the suicidal and irrational acts which plague our streets daily are being sowed and watered by the irrational, irrelevant and equally suicidal debate and delay in Congress." The most important problem was the lack of jobs for tens of thousands of slum residents. "Let us do one simple, direct thing—let us end unemployment totally and immediately," he told Johnson. "I propose specifically the creation of a national agency that shall provide a job to every person who needs work." While "I regret that my expression may be sharp . . . I believe literally that the life of our nation is at stake here at home," King stated. "I urge you to use the power of your office to establish justice in our land by enacting and implementing legislation of reason and vision in the Congress."

The journalists queried King as to whether he would go to Detroit or other riot locations to lend a hand, and he said no, "My only plans are to continue work in Cleveland and Chicago this summer." More questions about the disorders were put to him the next day when he arrived in Chicago for the kickoff of the Lawndale adult education program, and he reiterated that "Congress has created the atmosphere for these riots." At the same time, A. Philip Randolph and Roy Wilkins were readying a joint statement by all the major black leaders condemning the riots. King's name was attached to the announcement despite the fact that he had no opportunity to review it. In his comments to reporters, he emphasized that blame for the uprisings lay not with the rioters, but with the larger white society, which had consigned thousands of black people to hopeless lives in America's urban ghettos. During a Cleveland stop, King proclaimed that rent strikes would be one of SCLC's northern tactics, but when he toured the city's east side neighborhoods on Friday and Saturday, accompanying newsmen noticed that some residents did not take King seriously. "There were times during his most impassioned moments when teenagers in the audience laughed or simply ignored him and began talking among themselves."[51]

King returned to Atlanta on July 30 after making a joint appearance with Roy Wilkins at a Washington convention. King was dispirited over the violent disruptions that had spread from city to city all across the country, and upset at Wilkins's one-sided response. "Roy is hopeless," King complained to Levison. "He has no integrity or philosophy and he is just a hopeless case." Coretta was disturbed by her husband's state of mind. "He got very depressed," she remembered, "a state of depression" that "was greater than I had ever seen it before. . . . He said, 'People expect me to have answers and I don't have any answers.' He said, 'I don't feel like speaking to people. I don't have anything to tell them.'" He was supposed to fly to Louisville on Wednesday, to speak at a voter registration rally, but could not summon the strength to make his scheduled flight. Coretta recalled her husband's phone call from the airport. "'I've missed my flight,'" he told her. "'I know why I missed my flight; I really don't want to go. I get tired of going and not having any answers.' He had begun to take this very personally . . . he would take on all these problems," Coretta explained. "'People feel that nonviolence is failing,'" he had told her. "I said, 'But this is not so. You mustn't believe that people are losing faith in you; there are millions of people who have faith in you and believe in you and feel that you are our best hope.' Then I said to him, 'I believe in you, if that means anything.' He said, 'Yes, that means a great deal.' I said, 'Somehow you've just got to pull yourself out of this and go on. Too many people believe in you and you're going to have to believe that you're right.' He said, 'I don't have any answers.' I said, 'Well, somehow the answers will come. I'm sure they will.'" Seven hours behind schedule, Martin Luther King arrived in Louisville.[52]

A motorcade through the city's black neighborhoods preceded a church rally. King spoke to the crowd about how increased black population in major cities, if coupled with serious voter registration work, would lead to significant minority political influence. However, he emphasized, "our beloved nation is still a racist country" and "the vast majority of white Americans are racist." Local reporters who had heard King's speeches earlier that spring were struck by his new harshness, by how he "had departed from the rhetoric of hope and had taken up the rhetoric of power." "The Dr. King of August was far more militant," more pessimistic, and more dispirited. The following day he and his brother, A.D., flew to Boston to visit their hospitalized father. The family contact lifted his spirits.

When he returned to Atlanta to preach that Sunday at Ebenezer, however, his tone was still dispirited. "These are evil times," King told the congregation, repeating his comment of four months earlier that "the United States of America is the greatest actual purveyor of violence in the world today." He was not certain how society's course could be corrected. Just a few days earlier, King said, a young man had approached him to say that he, King, needed to take a trip. No, King had replied, he was taking too many trips already. "I'm tired of all this traveling I have to do," he told the congregation. "I'm killing myself and killing my health." The young man, however, had responded that King misunderstood him. He did not mean King had to travel more, but that he should try LSD.

King's pessimism continued as he journeyed to Cleveland, where he announced a Breadbasket agreement with Sealtest, then went on to San Francisco to address a convention of black realtors. "Riots are caused by nice, gentle, timid white moderates who are more concerned about order than justice," and "by a national administration more concerned about winning the war in Vietnam than the war against poverty right here at home," King told the realtors. He spoke again about "little children being burned with napalm," and about how "the roots of racism are very deep in our country." Nonetheless, he declared, "I'm not going to despair, even on the race question. . . . Somehow I still believe that we're going to get there."[53]

The next morning King flew to Atlanta to deliver the same speech to a broadcasters convention. In the audience was Atlanta's top-ranking black policeman, Howard Baugh, a friend of King's since childhood and a marine veteran who found King's harsh antiwar statements difficult to take. The next day, a Saturday, as King sat in his study at Ebenezer preparing for a Sunday appearance on *Meet the Press,* Baugh appeared at his door.

"M.L., I'd like to speak to you."

"Yeah, Howard, come on in. You caught me at a good time. Nobody's here but me."

He said, "What's on your mind?" I said, "You know, last night I listened to your speech, and I think you know how I feel. You know where my sincerity is." He said, "Listen, if there's anybody I trust, it's you."

"Well, I'm not so sure whether I deserve that or not."

He said, "What are you talking about?" I said, "M.L., I listened to you last night tell this multitude of people that you cannot condone the war in Vietnam, and our people are over there dying."

He said, "Well, Howard, has that got you to this point?" I said, "Yes." He said, "Let me tell you something," and we sat down.

He said, "You've never really given this organization full credit for what it really stands for. . . . It's a *nonviolent* organization, and when I say *nonviolent* I mean *nonviolent* all the way. . . . Never could I advocate nonviolence in this country and not advocate nonviolence for the whole world. . . . That's my philosophy . . . I don't believe in the death and killing on any side, no matter who's heading it up—whether it be America or any other country, or whether it be for black folks. . . . Nonviolence is my stand, and I'll die for that stand."

And at that time I understood for the first time in my life what was meant by nonviolence,

Baugh subsequently explained.

Later that evening King conferred by phone with his advisors concerning the tough questions about black militancy he would likely encounter on *Meet the Press*. "I think that the time has come to aggressively take Stokely and Rap Brown on," King declared. New SNCC Chairman Brown's violent rhetoric had gone several steps beyond Carmichael's. "Many people who would otherwise be ashamed of their anti-Negro feeling now have an excuse." Nonetheless, "these men do not constitute the basic problem," King stressed. "Stokely is not the problem. The problem is white people and their attitude," and SCLC needed a strategy for confronting it. "I think nonviolence has to be stepped up on a larger scale, to be escalated so its impact would be greater than violence."

The Sunday telecast focused on King's plans rather than black violence. King parried questions about possible future tactics in the anti-Vietnam effort by saying that SCLC's upcoming annual convention would consider the subject, but he reiterated his past criticisms—"we are today engaged in two wars and we are losing both"—while also repeating that under no circumstances would he be a presidential candidate. His own focus would be to expand the movement in the North. "What we must do now is to escalate nonviolence in our large areas of the north, because I think a powerful nonviolent movement can be just as effective in the north as in the south, and I think we can do it, we can disrupt things if necessary, militantly and nonviolently, without destroying life and property."[54]

King enlarged on that theme when he addressed the SCLC convention on Tuesday evening at Ebenezer church. "Our real problem is that there is no disposition by the Administration or Congress to seek fundamental remedies beyond police measures" in responding to America's domestic problems. "The tragic truth is that Congress, more than the American people, is now running wild with racism." Given that, "we must devise the tactics not to beg Congress for favors, but to create a situation in which they deem it wise and prudent to act with responsibility and decency." More precisely, the movement needed tactics that would "cripple the operations of an oppressive society," tactics that might include school boycotts, sit-ins by the unemployed at factory gates, and a march on Washington and a prolonged "camp-in" by jobless teenagers. Civil disobedience was the only alternative, given the electoral facts of life in America and the tactical insights the movement had acquired. With regard to the first factor, King explained, "Negroes are not in a mood to wait for change by the slower, tedious, often frustrating role of political action." Concerning the second, experience indicated that disruptive tactics would be necessary:

> Nonviolent action in the south was effective because any form of social movement by Negroes upset the status quo. When Negroes merely marched in southern streets it was close to rebellion. In the urban communities, marches are less disquieting because they are not considered rebellions, and secondly because the normal turbulence of cities absorbs them as merely transitory drama which is ordinary in life. To raise protest to an appropriate level for cities, to invest it with aggressive but nonviolent qualities, it is necessary to adopt civil disobedience. To dislocate the functioning of a city, without destroying it, can be more effective than a riot because it can be longer lasting, costly to the society, but not wantonly destructive, Moreover, it is difficult for government to quell it by superior force.

This approach, he told reporters, was what SCLC would put into practice. Within several weeks, King said, he would select target cities and plan actions that would commence prior to Congress's late-fall adjournment. Newspapers all across the country accorded his declaration page one headlines, and the message was clear that SCLC and the movement would be moving into a different phase of action. The disruptive tactics of urban "dislocation," tactics that King had dismissed with a laugh four years earlier in the wake of the deaths at Birmingham's Sixteenth Street church, he now advocated. Although the details were fuzzy, the course had been set, as one headline made clear: KING CALLS FOR A NEW DRIVE OF MASSIVE CIVIL DISOBEDIENCE.[55]

11

The Poor People's Campaign and Memphis, 1967–1968

King's proclamation that SCLC would "dislocate" day-to-day life in America's major cities was the foremost event at SCLC's convention, but it was not the only noteworthy development. A resolution was adopted opposing all electoral candidates who supported the Vietnam War, and King announced he would go "all out" to defeat Lyndon Johnson in the 1968 presidential election. King spoke positively about the possible candidacies of Republicans George Romney, Charles Percy, and Nelson Rockefeller. He also stressed the need for greater Afro-American unity, including reaching out to segments of the black community that were not committed to nonviolence. Some activists argued that SCLC should revive its efforts in the South, where its past achievements were substantial. King responded that SCLC still had workers in the region, but one observer noted that delegates "could not escape the impression that Southern activity will be deemphasized." The director of SCLC's one ongoing Deep South project, in Grenada, reported that it was "at present in a state of confusion," and some convention onlookers concluded that the entire organization was "dispirited." Former Montgomery colleague L. D. Reddick admonished King for the "disorganization and confusion" that marked the convention and that left Reddick "exhausted and frustrated." King was correct in asserting that SCLC should concentrate upon the problems of the urban North, but no one had devised a plan for how to do so. "Massive, organized civil disobedience is probably the best *negative* alternative to the burning and looting," but "of greater importance is the question of what is our positive program—our constructive program . . . for our urban ghettos and slums," Reddick asked. "We must demand and secure tremendous resources for rebuilding our cities," and

King needed a tangible program, not simply rhetoric. Stanley Levison gave him similar advice when they discussed staging in Washington some dramatization of America's poverty problem. King had had a thought-provoking discussion of such an initiative several days earlier with Mississippi activist Marian Wright, and had called a mid-September SCLC staff retreat to discuss the subject. King acknowledged such a project would require him to cancel his fall trip to the Holy Land, but promised to take a vacation to rest up. The convention, Levison thought, had left King "all worn out"; one prominent guest had been drunk all week and King had "spent more time trying to counsel her than anything else."[1]

After a brief rest, King visited Cleveland and Chicago. Although SCLC's Cleveland effort had achieved sizable black voter registration gains, and was about to kick off a rent strike in the Hough ghetto, local movement leaders were distressed over the conduct of SCLC's staff. In Chicago, meanwhile, one successful SCLC program, the Lawndale Union to End Slums, had acquired foundation support for its slum-housing-rehabilitation program, and King was called in to make the formal announcement. King also remarked that Robert Kennedy would make a "great president" but would not win the Democratic nomination from the incumbent. Lyndon Johnson, however, would certainly lose the election unless the Republicans nominated someone as bad as Richard Nixon. A progressive Republican ticket, King said, such as Rockefeller-Percy, could sweep the country.

King also reiterated that he would not run as a third-party candidate. As he explained in one emotional sermon, "I have no ambitions in life but to achieve excellence in the Christian ministry . . . I don't plan to do anything but remain a preacher." He spoke about the transforming experience he had had at the kitchen table in the Montgomery parsonage eleven years earlier, and how God had promised never to leave him alone. "I believe firmly in immortality. . . . I'm not worried about tomorrow. I get weary every now and then, the future looks difficult and dim, but I'm not worried about it ultimately because I have faith in God. . . . Sometimes I feel discouraged, and feel my work's in vain, but then the Holy Spirit revives my soul again."[2]

King's struggle with his self-doubts intensified when black columnist Carl T. Rowan, who had attacked King's antiwar stand four months earlier, mounted an even harsher assault on him in *Reader's Digest*. Although right-wing columnists with close ties to the FBI had kept up a steady string of little-noticed attacks upon King's Vietnam stance and "subversive" ties, the *Reader's Digest* thrashing reached several million people and was treated as a news story by *The New York Times*. King, Rowan alleged, had developed "an exaggerated appraisal" of his contributions to racial progress and was no longer "the selfless leader" he had been in the late 1950s. Terming King's anti-Vietnam activism a "tragic decision," Rowan said that the two reasons for his transformation were self-importance and Communist influence. Because of his disastrous change of course, King "has become *persona non grata* to Lyndon Johnson" and "has alienated many of the Negro's friends and armed the Negro's foes," Rowan asserted.

King's response to Rowan was stern but accurate. Not only had the columnist confused dissent with disloyalty, but his allegations of Communist influence were a red-baiting smear, a "McCarthy-like response" that tarnished Rowan. "He engaged in what Mr. McCarthy put us through," King told one interviewer, and had committed a serious mistake. "I think Mr. Rowan made the tragic error," King said, alluding to Rowan's phraseology.[3]

Also weighing on King was his upcoming appearance at the New Politics convention in Chicago, a commitment he wished he had not taken on. Originally designed to promote a King-Spock ticket, the New Politics convention was plagued by splits, including some black militants and white radicals who viewed King as too moderate and bourgeois. King was warned that he might be heckled during his speech, but that was not all that occurred. Hundreds in the 3,500-person audience were so bored by King's address that they walked out or turned to other concerns. Tired and gloomy, King left Chicago for Washington to speak to a group of psychologists. Again, he sounded dispirited and spoke about how trying the present circumstances were. "These have been very difficult days for me personally," he confessed, "days of frustration." Then he headed to New York for Labor Day fund-raising parties at wealthy homes on Fire Island before returning to Atlanta in low spirits.[4]

King encountered new trouble in Atlanta during his brief time at home. Several local ministers had asked SCLC to launch demonstrations there for the first time in SCLC's history. His hometown, King said, had "a false image" of racial justice, an image belied by the double-session arrangements at black schools that the ministers were protesting. Direct action was "very highly probable," King told reporters, and spoke also of demonstrations when he later addressed a local mass meeting. Once more, however, he confessed how weary he was. "I'm tired now. I've been in this thing thirteen years now and I'm really tired." As weeks passed, no demonstrations took place in Atlanta.

More and more, in public and in private, King spoke of the inner turmoil that plagued him. "We often develop inferiority complexes and we stumble through life with a feeling of insecurity, a lack of self-confidence, and a sense of impending failure," he told his Ebenezer congregation one Sunday. "A fear of what life may bring," he went on, "encourages some persons to wander aimlessly along the frittering road of excessive drink and sexual promiscuity," a more personal revelation than his listeners realized. Even at the darkest moments, faith in God gave him the inner equilibrium to face life's problems and "conquer fear." "I know this. I know it from my own personal experience."[5]

At the mid-September SCLC retreat, held at Airlie House in Warrenton, Virginia, King was still depressed. Many of the discussions concerned the northern urban demonstrations SCLC might hold later that fall. Mississippi's Marian Wright described her idea of a fast and sit-in at the office of U.S. Labor Secretary W. Willard Wirtz. "What she proposed," Andrew Young remembered, "was that a group of religious and labor leaders with Dr. King and a half-a-dozen poor folks would go to Wirtz's office and sit-in and just say they were going to stay there and fast or be jailed or whatever it was until they provided jobs." King envisioned successive waves of protesters descending on Washington demanding "jobs or income" for all, staying there, and pursuing civil disobedience until the government responded. James Bevel pressed for a greater focus on antiwar activities, but King said the entire staff would concentrate on the Washington project, with perhaps simultaneous demonstrations in other cities. SCLC's executive staff pondered how to raise the funds necessary for that campaign as well as for electoral challenges to prowar southern segregationists such as South Carolina Congressman Mendel Rivers and Mississippi Senator John Stennis. King suggested scheduling a nationwide series of fund-raising concerts featuring Harry Belafonte and Joan Baez for October and November, while SCLC's staff would draft a "go for broke" Washington action program that could be discussed and ratified at a midfall retreat.

King was despondent during part of the five-days retreat at Airlie House. Baez, a participant, recalled one evening, as everyone relaxed, "I heard him . . . saying that he wanted to just be a preacher, and he was sick of it all. And that the Lord called him to be a preacher, and not to do all this stuff, and he wanted to leave it and he was tired. And he had a couple whiskies in him," and perhaps "he was really just saying it."

After the retreat, King thought more about massive urban civil disobedience and Marian Wright's suggestion that SCLC take some of Mississippi's poorest citizens to Washington for direct confrontation with the federal government. When in late September he lunched in New York with the editors of *Time* magazine, he was surprised by the journalists' pessimistic view of America's domestic problems. He was further struck by a young city activist telling him that the problem with nonviolence was that it had not yet been used on a massive scale to create enough disruption. "To find confirmation both in the South and the North of thoughts and sentiments we were already feeling encouraged us to move ahead," Andrew Young recalled.[6]

While King pondered that topic, other obligations called for his attention. He had to visit some half-dozen cities to publicize the Belafonte-Baez fund-raising concerts. He also had to deal with a Geneva-based initiative calling for King and other Nobel Peace Prize winners to visit Moscow to meet representatives of North Vietnam and South Vietnam's National Liberation Front, the Viet Cong. After considering the idea, King decided not to participate because the unclear sponsorship made it too risky.

On October 3, King returned to Cleveland to encourage voters to support black candidate Carl Stokes in the Democratic mayoral primary. Stokes won a solid victory, and King boasted to friends that SCLC deserved the credit because it had significantly increased black registration. Stokes faced a general election in November, and gave no public acknowledgment to King's and SCLC's role. Within SCLC, however, the Stokes victory was celebrated as the most notable achievement since the Chicago summit accord a year earlier.[7]

Six days after the Cleveland primary, the U.S. Supreme Court issued its final order denying King and his fellow defendants a rehearing on their 1963 Birmingham contempt convictions. Arrangements were made for King to begin serving his five-day jail term on October 30; in the meantime King kept to his schedule of concert appearances. The first of the fund-raisers, featuring Belafonte, Baez, Sammy Davis, Jr., and King at the Oakland Coliseum on October 15, filled only one third of the house. A bomb threat interrupted a King appearance the following day in Los Angeles, and the next evening a rally in Houston drew a respectable crowd, but was disrupted twice by smoke bombs. The third rally, in Chicago, drew a small crowd to hear Belafonte and Aretha Franklin. All in all, neither the rallies nor King's speeches generated much press coverage, even in local newspapers, and King grew increasingly disappointed. "Dr. King has been so despondent over how badly the concerts have been going that he can't bring himself to do a thing," Dora McDonald told Levison.

The same day as SCLC's Washington concert, King testified before the National Advisory Commission on Civil Disorders, a presidentially appointed group examining the summer urban riots. The real cause of the uprisings, King said, was "the greater crimes of white society"—the white backlash, heavy black unemployment, racial discrimination, and the effects of the Vietnam War. After his testimony, reporters asked King about his protest plans. SCLC planned on "escalating nonviolence to the level of civil disobedience" by bringing thousands of needy citizens to Washington to "just camp here and stay" to await meaningful federal action. "The city will not function," he warned, until Congress approved "a massive program on the part of the federal government that will make jobs or income a reality for every American citizen."

While King participated in SCLC concerts in Philadelphia and Boston, Washington's newspapers criticized his plans. He ought to know better, one said, than to think Congress could be coerced into action, and the liberal *Washington Post* decried any project of intentional disruption as "an appeal to anarchy."[8]

King was deeply depressed as he prepared to begin his Birmingham jail term. Fifty Ebenezer parishioners offered a dungaree-clad King and three colleagues—his brother, A.D., Ralph Abernathy, and Wyatt Walker—a warm send-off at the Atlanta airport. King read a statement condemning the Supreme Court's decision as an example of America's "escalating disregard for constitutional freedom," and boarded the plane carrying three

books—the Bible, John Kenneth Galbraith's *The New Industrial State,*
and William Styron's *The Confessions of Nat Turner.* Upon arrival in
Alabama, the group was arrested by Birmingham detectives and jailed in
suburban Bessemer rather than in Birmingham. Although this action disrupted the Alabama Christian Movement's plans to hold protests outside
King's place of imprisonment, the city scheme went awry when King contracted a virus and had to be moved to the Birmingham jail for medical
care. Meanwhile, local leaders planned a demonstration and all-night
vigil at the jail for Friday, November 3, King's last night in custody. Once
again, however, Birmingham officials upset the movement's plans by re-
leasing King and his colleagues twenty-four hours ahead of schedule. Friday evening a mass rally was held to celebrate the early release. King told
the subdued audience that SCLC would apply the 1963 lessons of Birmingham to its upcoming economic justice campaign in Washington.
"We've got to find a method that will disrupt our cities if necessary,
create the crisis that will force the nation to look at the situation, dramatize it, and yet at the same time not destroy life or property. . . . I see
that as massive civil disobedience." "We've got to camp in—put our tents
in front of the White House," and remain until Congress acted. "We've
got to make it known that until our problem is solved, America may have
many, many days, but they will be full of trouble. There will be no rest,
there will be no tranquility in this country until the nation comes to terms
with our problem."

King flew home to preach at Ebenezer, then went to Cleveland to encourage voter turnout for Carl Stokes in the general election. He spent
Election Day visiting bars and shopping areas, urging people to go to the
polls. Once again Stokes prevailed, and King waited in his hotel room for
a call inviting him to join the new mayor on the platform at the victory
party. The call never came, and SCLC's dismay over Stokes's failure to
acknowledge their contributions was voiced in bitter complaints. Neither
King nor his aides ever determined whether the rebuff was intentional or
accidental. The next day, when King spoke with reporters, he focused on
SCLC's desire to finalize its plans for "massive nonviolence," plans that
might include a "nationwide city-paralyzing demonstration" centered in
Washington and featuring simultaneous protests in other major urban
areas.[9]

On November 11, King flew to Chicago to address an antiwar labor
group. He was still depressed, as he made clear to longtime family friend
and SCLC board member Rev. D. E. King. "He said to me privately,"
Reverend King recalled, "'D.E., I haven't discussed this with the board,
but I have found out that all that I have been doing in trying to correct
this system in America has been in vain.' He said, 'I am trying to get at
the roots of it to see just what ought to be done.'" Reverend King, surprised by his old friend's remarks, listened silently as King went on. "He
said, 'The whole thing will have to be done away with,'" Reverend King
remembered. He had not pressed Martin about just what he meant.

From Chicago King went to England to accept an honorary degree from the University of Newcastle-on-Tyne. Then it was back to Atlanta to record some radio speeches for the Canadian Broadcasting Company and to make plans for the upcoming staff retreat to be held at Frogmore from November 27 through December 1. The Ford Foundation had approved a $230,000 grant to SCLC for sessions to train ten black ministers from each of fifteen cities in community organizing and nonviolent tactics. King met in New York with the program's advisory committee, and told them that the project would generate a nationwide cadre of activists whom SCLC could call upon in future protests. "We must develop their psyche," King said. "Something is wrong with capitalism as it now stands in the United States. We are not interested in being integrated into *this* value structure. Power must be relocated, a radical redistribution of power must take place. We must do something to these men to change them."[10]

King expressed similar sentiments to SCLC's staff at the Frogmore retreat. "The decade of 1955 to 1965, with its constructive elements, misled us," King said. "Everyone underestimated the amount of rage Negroes were suppressing, and the amount of bigotry the white majority was disguising." True, the movement had won some battles, "but we must admit that there was a limitation to our achievement," King emphasized. "The white power structure is still seeking to keep the walls of segregation and inequality substantially intact," and was beating back the movement's assaults. "I'm not totally optimistic," King remarked, "but I am not ready to accept defeat. . . . We must formulate a program, and we must fashion the new tactics which do not count on government good will, but instead serve to compel unwilling authorities to yield to the mandates of justice." Among the goals must be a guaranteed annual income and the elimination of slums. "Nonviolence must be adapted to urban conditions and urban moods. Nonviolent protest must now mature to a new level . . . mass civil disobedience. . . . There must be more than a statement to the larger society, there must be a force that interrupts its functioning at some key point. . . . The Negro will be saying . . . 'I am willing to endure all your punishment, because your society will not be able to endure the stigma of violently and publicly oppressing its minority to preserve injustice.'"

Mass civil disobedience was the only option. "The limitation of riots, moral questions aside, is that they cannot win. . . . Hence, riots are not revolutionary," and are inferior to other tactics that are more radical in their possible effects. "The movement for social change has entered a time of temptation to despair, because it is clear now how deep and how systematic are the evils it confronts." Thus, "we in SCLC must work out programs to bring the social change movements through from their early and now inadequate protest phase to a stage of massive, active, nonviolent resistance to the evils of the modern system. . . . Our economy must become more person-centered than property-centered and profit-centered. . . . Let us therefore not think of our movement as one that seeks to integrate the Negro into all the existing values of American society," but as one that would alter those basic values. As Andrew Young noted, "Even if you're a winner in a rat race, you're still a rat."[11]

The following day King and his aides discussed their plans further. Andrew Young talked about such tactics as lying on highways, blocking doors at government offices, and mass school boycotts, all actions likely to provide "enough confrontation to dramatize the situation." King reiterated that their goal was definite economic improvements for the black masses, and that SCLC's protests ought to be "as dramatic, as dislocative, as disruptive, as attention-getting as the riots without destroying life or property." He suggested that a core group of well-trained activists— perhaps two hundred people from each of ten or twelve different locales—be recruited, and that movement leaders start by presenting their demands to an administration official and refusing to leave until tangible actions were taken. Then local contingents from around the country would converge on Washington, with perhaps the southern groups walking "a considerable portion of it through the most tense areas." In the capital those groups would camp in public parks and take over government buildings. Finally, the movement would call for a second "March on Washington" very different from the first. This time the purpose would not be "to have a beautiful day," King said, but literally to occupy the city until the Johnson administration altered both its domestic and foreign policies. "This is a kind of last, desperate demand for the nation to respond to nonviolence. Now, they may not respond. I can't promise that. But I do think we've got to go for broke this time. We've gone for broke before, but not in the way we're going this time, because if necessary I'm going to stay in jail six months—they aren't going to run me out of Washington."

Other ideas were tossed around, including having people in need of health care descend upon hospitals, staging a "call-in" to tie up the White House switchboard, and holding local protests to increase pressure upon federal leaders. A tentative springtime schedule was suggested, with the penultimate mass occupation timed for when college students would be free at Easter recess. An informal designation was made of cities and southern locales where participants could be recruited, and staff assignments were handed out on the retreat's final day. "We must make it clear," King reminded his aides, "that we are coming to stay in Washington until something is done about this extremely serious problem facing our nation."[12]

Two days after the retreat, King held a press conference to announce SCLC's plans. "Waves of the nation's poor and disinherited" would descend upon Washington around April 1, and "will stay until America responds" with "specific reforms, . . . until some definite and positive action is taken to provide jobs and income for the poor." He warned of simultaneous protests in other cities, and asserted that "a clear majority" of Americans would back SCLC's demands. Reporters tried to elicit details about the campaign's goals and tactics. "This will be a move that will be consciously designed to develop massive dislocation," King responded. "We have a very recalcitrant Congress that's behind the times," and that must be forced to act. "These tactics have done it before and they're all we have to go on," King told the journalists, who thought his mood "seemed deeply pessimistic." "I would be the first one to admit that to act at this time is risky," King said, "but not to act represents moral irresponsibility." "We were told when we went into Birmingham that Congress wouldn't move," King reminded one interviewer. "We were told the same thing when we went to Selma." "We have found throughout our experience that timid supplication for justice will not solve the problem. . . . We have got to confront the power structure massively. . . . Our power will be in numbers and in keeping at this until we succeed."[13]

Although King would not speculate about the campaign, Andrew Young spoke freely of what SCLC might do. "We have waited around for almost a year looking for a sign of hope" without seeing one, and had now decided "that we had better go ahead and dramatize these problems," even "if it means tying up the country." SCLC's demonstrators would be the "underclass that is locked out of the economy, people for whom a spring in jail in Washington is heaven compared to a spring of hunger and unemployment in Mississippi or Chicago." Using people who have "nothing to lose," SCLC might close down the nation's capital.

> The way Washington is, a few hundred people on each of those bridges would make it impossible to get in or out—or at least extremely difficult. It would mean that every day, going back and forth, you are thinking about three or four hours each way.

"I would tend against that," Young added,

> because it's not directly pointed to the problem. It would probably be much better to have a thousand people in need of health and medical care sitting in around Bethesda Naval Hospital, so that nobody could get in or out until they get treated. It would dramatize the fact there are thousands of people in our nation in need of medical services.

It also would obstruct the wealthy from receiving their accustomed care. "I mean you've got patients here; treat the ones you've got. Our society now treats patients with money but doesn't treat you if you're poor and if you're colored."

Young admitted "we really haven't spelled out the goals," but emphasized SCLC would employ drastic nonviolent action:

> Right now the "old style" kind of March on Washington isn't sufficiently crisis-packed . . . people don't respond until their own self-

interest is threatened. People don't give up power and money voluntarily.

We have accepted the challenge to so threaten nonviolently the self-interest of the powers that be that they will be able to change, that they will see that a change is necessary. Our threat will be so pointed and well-defined that they will know that a change is possible and will change in the right direction.

Undergirding SCLC's challenge, Young stressed, was the realization that the country's problems were rooted in the basic moral infirmity of American society. "The economic crisis and the political crisis are just symptoms of this far deeper moral crisis: an America of racism, materialism and economic exploitation versus an America where decisions are made on the basis of values."[14]

At Frogmore King also announced some staff changes aimed at bringing order out of SCLC's internal chaos. During the past summer, a black Chicago native and European businessman, William A. Rutherford, had volunteered his skills to SCLC on an interim basis. With Randolph Blackwell refusing King's entreaties to return to SCLC, King asked Rutherford, a talented public relations executive, to become executive director. Rutherford was reluctant to give up his pleasant life in Geneva, but agreed to a one-year commitment. King also hired Bernard Lafayette, who had worked for SNCC in Selma and for the American Friends Service Committee (AFSC) in Chicago, as program administrator, SCLC's fifth-ranked post, and Rutherford's chief assistant. Rutherford arrived in time for the Frogmore retreat and was introduced to SCLC's staff, many of whom were suspicious and resentful of this outsider. King was intent upon having Rutherford clear up the serious internal problems plaguing the organization. King outlined the problems to Rutherford in the presence of only King's most intimate confidants—Abernathy, Young, and Dorothy Cotton. "Martin said to me," Rutherford recalled, " 'Bill, there are two things I want you to do at the outset.' " The first concerned two SCLC staffers whose spending habits King found questionable. " 'Jim Harrison and Hosea Williams have an apartment at the University Plaza apartment complex,' " King told Rutherford. " 'How the hell can they on their salaries maintain a separate apartment,' " in addition to their homes? Neither King nor his colleagues suspected Harrison's mercenary involvement as a paid FBI informant, but King did wonder about his behavior as comptroller and why he could carry on an expensive lifestyle. " 'I want you to find out,' " King instructed Rutherford, " 'find out what's happening in the finance office.' "

King's other mission for Rutherford involved a third staff member about whom King was concerned. "He said, 'The second thing I want you to do is, Jesse Jackson's so independent, I either want him in SCLC or out—you go whichever way you want to, but one way or the other, he's a part of SCLC or he's not a part of SCLC.' " Operation Breadbasket was achieving success in Chicago and Cleveland, but Jackson was viewed as an outsider and an undependable, egotistical self-promoter by many SCLC staffers. Initially, Ralph Abernathy had been much impressed with the youthful divinity student who had turned up in Selma, eager to be helpful, during the crisis there. Later that year, in Chicago, Jim Bevel had taken Jackson under his wing and put him on SCLC's staff. "Bevel was the real creative genius of that period," Jackson remembered, "one of the most creative thinkers I've ever been exposed to." Just as Bevel's eccentricities and single-mindedness rubbed many colleagues the wrong way, Jackson's aggressive efforts to expand Breadbasket into a nation-wide program for fostering black capitalism also troubled many SCLC activists. Although part of the tension was rooted in the Atlanta staffers' desire to keep a tight rein on Chicago-based programs, much of the trouble stemmed from a distrust of Jackson's personal motives. "Jesse was really an outsider in a way, striving very hard to get in, to be accepted, to be respected," recalled Calvin Morris, who became associate director of Breadbasket during that winter. "The doubt about Jesse is what is it for, is it for Jesse or for the movement?" Stanley Levison said to Coretta King six months later. "I know on this Martin had many deep doubts." Bevel often defended Jackson, telling King, "He's just crude 'cause he's young." King disagreed, saying, "No, he's ambitious," and voiced his un-ease to close friends. "Jesse had irritating ways," King's Chicago confidant Chauncey Eskridge explained. "I don't think we cared much for him." Those sympathetic to Jackson saw the dynamics differently. "Martin had problems with Jesse because Jesse would ask questions," but others perceived a fundamental spiritual difference between the two men. "Martin saw it in Jesse," one former SCLC executive recalled. "He used to tell Jesse, 'Jesse, you have no love.'"

Another serious question was the implicit conflict between Bread-basket's black capitalism focus and King's increasingly socialist economic views. "We were very aware of some of the contradictions, and am-bivalent about it," Morris remembered, but other staffers could see that King had "grave doubts" about Breadbasket's goals. Rutherford raised the issue with King early on. "'Martin, I really am very disturbed. You know what you're trying to do? It's to replace white bastards with black bastards.' I said, 'If the whole thrust of assuring oneself profit is to exploit whoever's there, what the hell are we doing with black people, trying to put them in the same odious position where you have to exploit someone else to turn your profit?' He said, 'Bill, there's so much to be done that people are not ready to do right now.'" Rutherford understood King's point. "Obviously we've got to have some form of socialism, but Amer-ica's not ready to hear it yet."

Rutherford appreciated that King's unhappiness with Jackson went beyond spirit and ideology. "He didn't trust Jesse, he didn't even like Jesse. . . . If you ask me if there was any suspicion about Jesse's motives and even devotion to the movement, I would say categorically yes, there was—considerable. And we talked about it." One immediate bone of contention was that Jackson was not fulfilling all his administrative responsibilities, such as attending SCLC's bimonthly executive staff meetings.

Rutherford immediately laid down the rules for Jackson, Hosea Williams, and others. He warned the staff about "expenditures incurred in a completely incoherent manner," and sent Jackson a memo rebuking him for his consistent absences, and announced that personal fines of $25 and $50 would be levied against staff members who were tardy or absent from meetings. "This may appear a bit juvenile," Rutherford admitted, but "the importance of a close-knit and coordinated working relationship" among SCLC's fractious members could not be overstated. Years later, reflecting back upon his attendance rule, Rutherford laughingly recalled how "the first one we caught was Dr. King." Seriously, however, "there was really such gross inefficiency," and "I really was playing the role of dictator." His efforts "didn't sit too well with the other people who'd been there longer." Williams reacted angrily to Rutherford's attempts to enforce organizational discipline. Within two weeks Williams submitted, and then withdrew, a letter of resignation protesting the new regime. As Christmas approached, the tempest passed and the SCLC staff began adjusting to Rutherford's new rules. King was extremely pleased, telling Levison that Rutherford has "really got things moving around here. I see for the first time real administration developing. He's done in a week what hasn't been done in two or three years."[15]

Rutherford received some jolts of his own as he was drawn into SCLC's milieu. "I was really rather surprised and shocked at what I saw. . . . SCLC was a very rowdy place," and "the movement altogether was a very raunchy exercise." Rutherford's first shock stemmed from reports of an Atlanta group party that had featured both a hired prostitute as well as the unsuccessful ravishing of a seventeen-year-old SCLC secretary. Rutherford raised the subject at an executive staff session, "and the meeting cracked up in laughter. . . . The only one who wasn't laughing was Bernard Lafayette," the other newcomer. King was laughing too, a further reflection of SCLC's "very relaxed attitude toward sex" and the "genuine ribald humor" that predominated.

Rutherford received another eye-opener when he finally took King up on his repeated invitation to drop by the house sometime. One night Rutherford and Chauncey Eskridge went by, with Eskridge in the lead. "'Hi Coretta . . . where's Martin?' She said, 'Oh, he's in a meeting at Bill Rutherford's.' And I gulped, and I said, 'Oh yeah, sure, sure, that's right, but it wasn't a meeting I had to be in.' She looked with a very penetrating glance—looking right through me—and we changed the subject, and walked out. I could have died." Other King colleagues encountered similar situations in which Coretta avoided acknowledging unpleasant facts, but that experience made Rutherford face up to the side of King's life that most of his closest colleagues rarely if ever discussed.

"All of his intimates were aware of one very inhibiting fact that none of us has been able to deal with—that was Dr. King's sexuality, and you cannot deal with a saint with clay feet."

Rutherford had quickly become aware of King's extremely close, long-standing relationship with one female colleague, and he also learned about King's similar but less intense liaison with another Atlanta-based woman. Beyond that, however, there were also "a number of instances, quite aside from the sort of formal liaisons . . . other instances where he really was just interested in *women*, period. . . . That's why I don't know how to deal with that." Rutherford empathized with King's situation. "He was far from perfect, and he knew he was far from perfect. He was vain, he was a very brave man, but he knew fear, he had lusts, . . . some of which he was able to exhaust." But "when any of us come to 'what made Martin Luther King tick,' where he really found comfort and solace, you freeze, because I don't know how to deal with that." What inhibited a full and frank answer was known to many. "There was this absolutely duplicitous role or posture Dr. King had to stand—when he represented black America, he had to stand up like the man of iron, the man of perfection, which he certainly wasn't and didn't even pretend to be otherwise. He was a very modest man, a very humble man . . ." Dorothy Cotton understood King's discomfort too. "I sensed in him sometimes a little pain that he really couldn't live up to the old saintly image that people required of him."

King realized the contradiction in which he was trapped even better than his aides. "When I delve into the inner chambers of my own being," he confessed to his Ebenezer congregation, "I end up saying, 'Lord, be merciful unto me, a sinner.'" "I make mistakes tactically. I make mistakes morally, and get down on my knees and confess it and ask God to forgive me." In the sexual realm, King viewed himself as a sinner, a theme he sometimes touched upon in his sermons, such as one where he emphasized that "man is great, but he is a sinner." "We are unfaithful to those we ought to be faithful to," a circumstance that exemplified the more basic duality King saw in human nature. "There is a schizophrenia . . . within all of us. There are times that all of us know somehow that there is a Mr. Hyde and a Dr. Jekyll in us." Nonetheless, "God does not judge us by the separate incidents or the separate mistakes that we make, but by the total bent of our lives," King stressed. "You don't need to go out this morning saying that Martin Luther King is a saint," he told his Ebenezer congregation one Sunday. "I want you to know this morning that I am a sinner like all of God's children, but I want to be a good man, and I want to hear a voice saying to me one day, 'I take you in and I bless you because you tried. It was well that it was within thy heart.'"

King's intensely self-critical nature encompassed all aspects of his life, not just sex, and was often painfully visible to his family and closest friends. "He criticized himself more severely than anyone else ever did," Coretta remembered. "He was always the first one to say, 'Maybe I was wrong, maybe I made a mistake. . . . He would go through this agonizing process of self-analysis many times." Coretta and other longtime colleagues like Stanley Levison came to realize that a good part of King's self-torment stemmed from feelings of guilt, from believing that he was undeserving of much of the praise and public acclaim that had come his way. Many aides were impressed by the depth of King's humility, but Dorothy, Coretta, and Stanley understood that King's profoundly humble nature had more complicated and painful roots. "He never felt that he deserved all the accolades," Cotton recalled. "He almost felt guilty that he got all of that praise and publicity and honor. He was guilty because— for whatever reason one feels that one doesn't deserve some praise. . . . If I had to, I could document it, but I wouldn't want to." Coretta felt similarly, calling her husband "a guilt-ridden man" who "never felt he was adequate to his positions." Levison once expounded the same theme in greater detail: "Martin could be described as an intensely guilt-ridden man. The most essential element in the feelings of guilt that he had was that he didn't feel he deserved the kind of tribute that he got." King believed, Levison stressed, that he simply

was an actor in history at a particular moment that called for a personality, and he had simply been selected as that personality . . . but he had not done enough to deserve it. He felt keenly that people who had done as much as he had or *more* got no such tribute. This troubled him deeply, and he could find no way of dealing with it because there's no way of sharing that kind of tribute with anyone else: you can't give it away; you have to accept it. But when you don't feel you're worthy of it and you're an honest, principled man, it tortures you. And it could be said that he was tortured by the great appreciation that the public showed for him. If he had been less humble, he could have lived with this kind of acclaim, but because he was genuinely a man of humility, he really couldn't live with it. He always thought of ways in which he could somehow live up to it, and he often talked about taking a vow of poverty: getting rid of everything he owned—including his house—so that he could at least feel that nothing material came to him from his efforts.

Underlying it all was a sense of having to live up to the opportunities he had been given:

Martin was always very aware that he was privileged . . . and this troubled him. He felt he didn't deserve this. One of the reasons that he was so determined to be of service was to justify the privileged position he'd been born into . . . [he felt] he had never deserved and earned what he had, and now he didn't deserve nor had he earned in his own mind the acclaim that he was receiving. It was a continual series of blows to his conscience, and this kept him a very restive man all his life.

King continued to wrestle with his personal and emotional tensions as SCLC turned its attention toward the upcoming Poor People's Campaign. After the early December announcement of SCLC's spring plans, King left for a Caribbean vacation, including a visit with Adam Clayton Powell at his Bimini retreat. In the meantime, Andrew Young, who had taken a new title as executive vice-president of SCLC, and Stanley Levison began efforts to raise funds for the spring project from the organization's wealthiest supporters. A crucial consideration was the tax status of such monies, and a special solution was devised. Young explained it in a letter to staunch contributors Martin Peretz and Ann Farnsworth, enclosing a list of churches "pastored by some of our most reliable board members. We have contacted each of them and informed them that they would be receiving a contribution from you which should be forwarded directly to SCLC. This means that all of the contributions would be tax exempt as far as you are concerned and will not place restrictions on our use of the funds." Although the laundering of contributions through religious institutions was of questionable legality, it served the interests of wealthy supporters as well as the financially strapped SCLC.

King took up a busy schedule upon his return from the Caribbean, preaching a ninetieth-anniversary sermon at Montgomery's Dexter Avenue Baptist Church on December 10, and then flying to Chicago to deliver another address that evening. King sounded despondent as he explained to the Dexter congregation that hope was different from optimism, and that while he still possessed the former, he did not hold to the latter. He told Chicago journalists that the newly announced Democratic presidential candidacy of Minnesota Senator Eugene McCarthy was "a healthy thing for American politics," but explained to another interviewer that the election outlook was not promising. King believed that McCarthy could not successfully challenge Lyndon Johnson, and the only Republican candidate who stood a chance of defeating the Democratic incumbent was Nelson Rockefeller, who seemed unlikely to beat out Richard Nixon for his party's nomination.[16]

In mid-December King went to New York to talk with young activist Harry Edwards, CORE's Floyd McKissick, and others about a black boycott of the upcoming 1968 Olympics. Then he flew to Cleveland to meet with SCLC's resident staffers. Community complaints about the workers were vociferous, and King summoned Rutherford to look into the situation. Rutherford bluntly instructed the staffers to improve their performance, then told King, "They have been put clearly on notice that if they are unable to carry out their assignments in a responsible manner they will be replaced."

Similar problems had developed in Philadelphia, where the SCLC team led by James Orange "seem to have spent much of their time with extremists—left-of-left variety," as a prominent Quaker complained to King. "Orange set up one public meeting, and spoke at one of ours. His presentations were unbelievably confusing," and devoid of details about SCLC's Washington project. "Depending on the audience, he gave widely differing pictures of his mission and SCLC plans for coming here. The total effect has been one of unusual irresponsibility," Fellowship House Director Marjorie Penney warned. She told King that unless improvements were made, Fellowship House would not "continue to share an effort which puts you and SCLC in such a light."

King knew that much of the problem was that field staffers had been sent to their recruiting assignments largely unprepared to explain the goals and strategy of the upcoming campaign. James Bevel and Bernard Lafayette complained that better planning and greater clarification were needed for the grass-roots recruitment efforts to succeed. Improvements were particularly necessary, Lafayette told one staff meeting, if SCLC were to obtain financial and staff assistance from other organizations, such as the American Friends Service Committee. King disagreed, saying that the general goals as already articulated for the Poor People's Campaign were sufficient for recruiting volunteers. "You can get persons to respond to anything if they are stimulated, and what is more basic an issue than jobs and income? We have something simple enough to rally most people around," and SCLC's field staff simply needed to get to work. Lafayette responded that a more specific game plan was essential. "We must put down in very clear terms what we want, and our demands must be widely circulated. We must go in not expecting to get everything but there must be some minimal things that we will not negotiate," he pointed out. "Ultimately we will either get our demands or escalate," perhaps to "a day-long, nationwide strike." Bevel demurred, remarking that "I do not know whether Johnson would give enough opposition for us to build up steam and momentum" for such a mobilization. Jesse Jackson seconded Bevel's doubts, reiterating that "there is a problem with the staff not really being clear on this project."

King spoke up again, saying, "The thing that concerns me now more than anything is whether we are convinced that this program is necessary. If we are not convinced I would rather not go into it. I am looking at it as much more than just obtaining jobs, but rather that this country needs a nonviolent movement in order to reassert its present power." Jackson agreed. "If we are sincere on Washington, then everything we do will have to be geared to Washington." Jim Bevel, however, contended it would be a mistake to focus solely on jobs or income and slight the Vietnam War. He recommended a broader, more aggressive campaign. "We need a movement . . . to get the war machine to attack us rather than us attacking the war machine." King disagreed, saying that although the nonviolent movement should expand to its broadest possible reach, it would have to do so gradually. "The thing you are talking about is much harder to mobilize around and takes much longer," he told Bevel. "You have a lot of people agreeing with you but they are not willing to spend five years in jail over it. In addition, you have the national press against

and "clothe those who were naked," "to visit those who were in prison," and, more than anything else, "tried to love and serve humanity."[21]

While King worked to get SCLC's campaign under way, Justice Department officials and Washington police commanders prepared for the April protests. Reports to the White House asserted that SCLC intended to "tie up" the nation's capital completely by blocking traffic and engaging in other forms of civil disobedience. President Johnson used a February 2 press conference to state his hope that civil rights energies would be used in more productive ways. King promptly responded that SCLC would not be deterred from its Washington project. In Chicago to meet with officials of the National Welfare Rights Organization (NWRO), King warned that there would be protests at the summer political conventions—particularly at the Democratic one in Chicago—if Congress had not acted upon the movement's demands. Eager to win NWRO's participation in the Washington project, King was shocked by the tough questions aggressively posed to him by the organization's female board members. Unable to respond to their detailed policy queries, King finally confessed his ignorance and invited the women to educate him. "They jumped on Martin," Andrew Young remembered. "I don't think he had ever been that insulted before in a meeting." King left the session promising NWRO Executive Director George Wiley that he would immediately recommend that SCLC's board endorse NWRO's four top policy demands, including a federal legal-aid program, a stronger welfare bill, and more grass-roots participation in antipoverty efforts.[22]

King had called an SCLC board meeting to discuss the spring campaign, and scheduled it to coincide with both a Washington antiwar protest he had pledged to attend and a meeting of local black leaders SCLC staffers had arranged. The Vietnam demonstration, sponsored by Clergy and Laymen Concerned, featured King leading a procession of 2,500 silent marchers through Arlington National Cemetery to the Tomb of the Unknown Soldier, where the group observed six minutes of solemn prayer. In contrast, SCLC's board sessions did not begin so peacefully. Local black radicals, some allied with former SNCC Chairman Stokely Carmichael, harassed board members as they arrived for the meeting. This incident increased fears that hostile black elements might be one of the campaign's most serious problems. That evening, King spoke to a group of local activists, including Carmichael, who offered a vague commitment not to interfere with SCLC efforts. Some of Carmichael's supporters, however, were not so moderate. One young woman accused King of having sold out the movement at Selma and of being ready to do the same thing again. "Shaking and livid with anger, King denied this in the strongest possible language."

The next morning King met with reporters to announce the demands of the Poor People's Campaign. An overall goal would be a $30 billion annual appropriation for a comprehensive antipoverty effort, but an "absolute minimum" would be congressional passage of (1) a full-employment commitment, (2) a guaranteed annual income measure, and (3) construction funds for at least 500,000 units of low-cost housing per year. King emphasized that opinion polls showed that a majority of Americans supported those initiatives, and said, "We are counting on a response from the people of the nation." SCLC hoped that a positive response from Congress would obviate any need for civil disobedience by the waves of protesters. "Our aim is not to tie up the city of Washington. Our protests will center on the government, Congress, and not the city at large."[23]

Later that day King, Rutherford, and other aides met with Carmichael, Courtland Cox, and SNCC Chairman Rap Brown. Carmichael repeated his assurances of the previous evening, and Cox explained that although the local nationalists would not support the Poor People's Campaign, they would not oppose it or obstruct any black person's efforts to help other black people. Rutherford said he thought that was an admirable position, but King interrupted him to disagree. "You're wrong, you're absolutely wrong." A true commitment to nonviolence meant that one could not tolerate any destructive forms of action, no matter what their purpose. Rutherford let the matter drop, and the meeting concluded with an agreement that the local activists would not publicly criticize SCLC's efforts. As the session broke up, however, King "exploded" at Rutherford. "I would have been humiliated if I hadn't been so shocked," Rutherford remembered, "for Dr. King never ever humiliated anyone in public in front of anyone else. But he was *shaking*. 'Bill, you're wrong, you're wrong.' He went on for about ten minutes, and then I very quickly realized he wasn't talking to me anymore, he was talking to himself or he was speaking for history. 'Violence begets violence, that's what it's all about, and they're wrong and you're wrong.'" In part, Rutherford thought, the eruption was a reflection of how "really exhausted" King was, physically and emotionally. It also "was a measure of his level of frustration" over how slowly the Poor People's Campaign was developing and over his colleagues' doubts that nonviolent demonstrations would be productive. "I think he was beginning to have self-doubts as well—would this really work," Rutherford recalled. That evening, addressing a rally, King expressed his despair more plaintively: "I can't lose hope. I can't lose hope because when you lose hope, you die."

The next day King spoke to the largely black D.C. Chamber of Commerce, telling the businessmen that the Poor People's Campaign ought to be welcomed, not shunned, in that it represented the best alternative to more urban rioting. Another summer of disorders, King warned, would produce not only widespread destruction, but the likelihood of drastic repressive measures and a right-wing takeover. "I don't have any faith in the whites in power responding in the right way," King stated. "They'll treat us like they did our Japanese brothers and sisters in World War II. They'll throw us into concentration camps. The Wallaces and the Birchites will take over. The sick people and the fascists will be strengthened. They'll cordon off the ghetto and issue passes for us to get in and out."

That might be the end result if SCLC's spring project did not succeed. "We're going to be militant," King declared. "We're going to plague Congress."[24]

After a visit to Philadelphia, King returned to Atlanta as press commentators asserted that his Washington protests might turn into riots. One sensible black newsman pointed out that "a greater peril to King's plans is that nothing will happen." Inside Lyndon Johnson's White House, expectations were grim and sentiments were harsh. "We have permitted the Stokely Carmichaels, the Rap Browns, and the Martin Luther Kings to cloak themselves in an aura of respectability to which they are not entitled," assistant Larry Temple said in a memo to the president. "When Martin Luther King talks about violating the law by obstructing the flow of traffic in Washington or stopping the operations of this government, he is talking about criminal disobedience. . . . 'Civil disobedience' is a complete misnomer. There is no such thing. . . . As the time nears for Dr. King's April activities, I hope the President will publicly unmask this type of conduct for what it really is."

Unbeknownst to Temple, King worried that the "April activities" might have to be delayed or canceled. He voiced those worries at a meeting of SCLC's top staff, including Comptroller, and FBI informant, Jim Harrison. "We are not doing our homework," King told his aides. "We have not gotten off the ground as far as engaging in the enormous job ahead." So far,

> we have not recruited twenty folks that are people who will go and stay with us. I am disturbed about the fact that our staff has not gotten to the people we are talking about . . . the hard-core poor people. . . . If we cannot do it, I would rather pull out now—the embarrassment and criticism would be much less now than if we went to Washington with about three hundred people. I am not worried about failing to get what we are trying to get, but I am worried about failing to get the people to go out and get what we want. . . .

Several assistants argued that the situation was not as serious as King believed. "I do not think at this point we need to call off the campaign," Bernard Lee contended. The discussion ranged back and forth until Bernard Lafayette framed an option that everyone found acceptable: If recruitment of enough volunteers had not taken place by April 1, the timetable for Washington action would be pushed back, but the project would not be called off.[25]

Several days later King set out on a swing through Mississippi and Alabama to stimulate interest in SCLC's recruiting efforts. Traveling in a small chartered plane, King, two aides, and two newsmen stopped in Edwards, Mississippi, to meet with black leaders from across the state, most of whom responded favorably. In Birmingham, King told a church rally that he envisioned a mule-cart procession of poor people beginning the Washington trek in Mississippi and picking up additional recruits as they headed north to a shantytown "tent-in" in the nation's capital. In Selma, King told another rally that "we're dealing in a sense with class issues . . . with the problem of the gulf between the haves and the have-nots." He sounded both optimistic and sentimental, observing that "I think we've probably made more progress in Selma, Alabama, than almost any city that I can point to in the South." King told how in December, 1964, just before SCLC went into Selma, Lyndon Johnson had informed him that there would be no push for civil rights legislation in 1965. " 'Martin, we can't go for a voting rights bill in this session of Congress.' " The Alabama protests had changed that, just like the Poor People's Campaign could alter Washington's current assertions that no massive antipoverty effort was possible. "We can change this nation. We can bring it up to the point that it will live up to its creeds," King declared. Jean White of *The Washington Post* was struck by King's pensiveness. "There was almost a tone of wistfulness in Dr. King's speeches," she wrote, "a kind of nostalgia for the past."[26]

King seemed melancholy in his Sunday sermon at Ebenezer. He talked about how several years earlier he had driven past a hitchhiker one evening on a desolate stretch of road in west Atlanta. "I really haven't gotten over it to this day. . . . I didn't stop to help the man because I was afraid." It was wrong to allow selfish concerns to triumph over one's Samaritan duties, even if the risk was substantial. After the service, King flew to Miami for the first of the Ford-funded Ministers Leadership Training Programs. He welcomed the several hundred participants with a somewhat despondent speech. "A kind of genocide has been perpetrated against the black people," he declared. "Not physical genocide, but psychological and spiritual genocide," an onslaught that had not been comprehended in earlier years when "we had not evaluated the depth of resistance in the white community" to real equality. "When hope diminishes the hate element is often turned toward those who originally built up the hope," King observed. "The bitterness is often greater toward that person who built up the hope, who could say 'I have a dream,' but couldn't produce the dream because of the failure and the sickness of the nation to respond to the dream."

King spent much of the conference holed up in his hotel room, which Young and Fred Bennette had searched carefully for bugs. The most heated session featured Daniel Patrick Moynihan, author of a controversial analysis of black family life that King largely endorsed. Moynihan spoke in "an atmosphere of total hostility," one Ford Foundation observer reported, and Moynihan later wrote to Ford President McGeorge Bundy to protest SCLC's venture. The session was "the first time I have ever found myself in an atmosphere so suffused with near madness. . . . The leadership of the meeting was in the hands of near demented Black militants who consistently stated one untruth after another (about me, about the United States, about the President, about history, etc., etc.) without a single voice being raised in objection. King, Abernathy and Young sat there throughout, utterly unwilling (at least with me present) to say a word in support of non-violence, integration, or peaceableness." Ford's observer noted that it was an accomplishment that Moynihan "got out alive."

King emerged from seclusion to address the final session, and called upon the pastors to support the Poor People's Campaign when they returned home. He also met with Roger Wilkins, head of the Justice Department's Community Relations Service. Wilkins found him "very tired and drained," "very discouraged and not very clear about the aims of the campaign." Since 1966, it seemed that King had become "a profoundly weary and wounded spirit," that "a profound sadness" had descended upon him. Others sensed the same thing. Ralph Abernathy was shocked by the changes that had occurred in him over the few weeks that Abernathy had been in Asia. "He was just a different person. He was sad and depressed. And I did everything I could to help him, but I couldn't do much." King's close friends became more and more concerned about his emotional condition, and three days after the Miami conference, he left for a weeklong vacation in Jamaica, accompanied by Coretta and Andrew Young.[27]

Although King was hoping for a complete rest, he was upset by a new and stunning blow. Bayard Rustin publicly criticized him for refusing his advice to reconsider pursuing the Poor People's Campaign. "I seriously question the efficacy of Dr. King's plans for the April project," Rustin told newsmen. Demonstrations would not win congressional support for massive policy changes, or even for the current civil rights bill, which included the open-housing title rejected in 1966. The movement's energies, Rustin said, ought to be directed toward electing Democratic candidates in the fall elections, not street protests. True, King would lose face if he canceled the campaign, "but he'll lose a lot more face if he conducts the demonstrations and fails," Rustin declared.

While King tried to regain his emotional vitality, SCLC's staff moved its recruitment efforts into high gear, and Washington officialdom waited with distinct unease. Justice Department and military officials coordinated their plans with Washington police commanders, but intelligence reports accurately described SCLC's efforts as in disarray. "The word we get," one law enforcement officer admitted, "is that they are in such a muddle that it is quite possible they are not coming at all."

King's vacation was less than peaceful. "The tourists wouldn't let us alone and the phone was our enemy," Young complained to Levison. The final day was brightened by news that the National Advisory Commission on Civil Disorders, appointed by Lyndon Johnson to examine the causes of the summer riots, had concluded in its final report that white racism bore much of the blame and that America's urban ills could be cured only by a massive government effort. Nonetheless, King was in a plaintive mood when he returned home, telling his Ebenezer congregation that "life is a continual story of shattered dreams."[28]

The following day King answered reporters' questions about the riot commission's conclusions. "The Commission's finding that America is a racist society and that white racism is the root cause of today's urban disorders is an important confession of a harsh truth," King stated. It indicated how "the lives, the incomes, the well-being of poor people everywhere in America are plundered by our economic system," and revealed "the absolute necessity of our spring campaign in Washington," the first phase of which would be "a lobby-in against Congress" when it reconvened on April 22. Simultaneously, King said, three caravans of initial recruits would begin converging on the capital from Milwaukee, Boston, and Mississippi. Moving by car, foot, and mule carts, those contingents would arrive in Washington early in May. Although he did not lay out the specifics to the press, the game plan that King and Andrew Young had drawn up called for a march around Capitol Hill on May 5, a Mother's Day demonstration on May 12, and a school desegregation event on May 17, the fourteenth anniversary of *Brown* v. *Topeka*. Throughout those weeks, campaign participants would personally lobby congressmen for approval of the protesters' legislative demands. Then, at the end of May, SCLC would take stock. "May 30," Young wrote, would be a "possible demonstration date with a 'March on Washington' type gathering if congressional response has been favorable. If congressional response has not been favorable," SCLC would pursue "an escalation of civil disobedience." Protests at the political conventions could follow, and King might call for a nationwide economic boycott.

The same day that King announced the April 22 kickoff, the Senate, by a razor-thin 65–32 margin, cut off a filibuster against the pending civil rights bill. Two earlier attempts had failed because of Republican Senate leader Dirksen's opposition to the open-housing provision, but after a weakening amendment was added, Dirksen's objections were assuaged and the necessary votes obtained. King was pleased by the breakthrough, but it did not free him from a deepening depression. A planned trip to Africa to mediate the Biafran conflict was postponed, and he slipped off to Acapulco for a three-day vacation with Ralph Abernathy. "We were in Acapulco for rest and relaxation," Abernathy later recalled, "and there was no rest or relaxation." King "was troubled and worried," had difficulty sleeping, and seemed "frightened" about what the Poor People's Campaign would bring.[29]

When King returned to the States his anxieties about the campaign were heightened by a detailed memo from Marian Logan, one of the SCLC board's most respected members, opposing the protests. "I doubt very seriously," Logan wrote, that the Washington actions would have any positive effect on Congress. "If anything, the demonstrations may well harden congressional resistance and create an atmosphere conducive not only to the victory of reactionary candidates in the coming elections, but also to the defeat of those candidates who are, or would be, friendly to the social and economic objectives of our struggle." Logan was also concerned that King and SCLC would not "be able to preserve the non-violent image and integrity of our organization" once the protests got under way. Given the "explosive potential of the situation," serious violence would be inevitable. "You say, Martin, that you 'will use disruptive tactics only as a last resort.'. . . But you understand, of course," Logan asserted, "that in view of the likely police response to these disruptive tactics, you are in effect saying that you are prepared to court violence as a last resort." Logan was also "troubled and unhappy at how inadequately" the planning had been handled so far. "It does not appear to me, or to anyone with whom I have talked, that an adequate job has been done." And "there is the question of objectives. Have they been clarified? Have you worked out what you will accept, short of your total objectives . . .?"

In response to Logan's admonitions, King phoned her almost daily for more than a week in an unsuccessful effort to persuade her to withdraw the complaints, which she had sent to the entire SCLC board. Andrew Young joined in the attempt, writing Logan and her husband, Arthur, that "we are too far gone to turn around" on the campaign. "This is very much a faith venture. . . . We certainly have nothing to lose."[30]

The following day, March 11, at the same time that the Senate was voting final passage of the 1968 civil rights bill and sending it off to an uncertain future in the House, King met with his research committee to discuss the campaign's demands. Michael Harrington had prepared two previous drafts, and the group asked him, Barbara Moffett of AFSC, and Stanley Levison to work on revised versions. Then King headed back to Atlanta for two important meetings. Over lunch with his executive staff, King said the campaign "ought to be a continuing, massive lobby-in" aimed at the Congress. "I think we've got to pit the President against the Congress. I don't think we ought to make this an anti-Lyndon Johnson battle. . . . I really think we ought to leave Lyndon alone and go on and throw attention on the Congress and have Lyndon in a position where he'll almost be forced to support us." Two days later King addressed several dozen representatives of non-black minority groups whom SCLC wanted to recruit, and announced he would begin a People-to-People tour of SCLC's recruitment spots to spur grass-roots interest.

That night in Grosse Point, Michigan, the first stop on a trip west, King spoke to an audience of three thousand. Outside the auditorium, three hundred right-wing picketers protested his appearance; inside, King was repeatedly interrupted by hecklers shouting, "Commie" and "Traitor." Afterward, a shaken King said, "I have never received a reception on this level." It was "the worst heckling I have ever encountered in all my travels." From Michigan he headed to Los Angeles, where former SCOPE staffer Gwendolyn Green, who helped arrange King's appearances, saw a visible change in him. "He was very unhappy," she recalled. "He was depressed, because he was . . . very tired. He was dark, gaunt, and tired. He felt that his time was up. . . . He said that he knew that they were going to get him."[31]

Other close friends were concerned about King's despondent state and morbid comments about his death. "In the later years he was given to a kind of depression that he had not had earlier," Andrew Young recalled. "He talked about death all the time. . . ." "He couldn't relax, he couldn't sleep. . . . Even when we were away on trips, he'd want to talk all night long. . . . And just physically, I was afraid," Young said, of how worn down King was. "He was spiritually exhausted." Longtime Birmingham friend Deenie Drew noticed the same changes. "In his last year or so, I had a feeling that Mike had a death wish. . . . I had a feeling that he didn't know which way to turn." Bayard Rustin, despite his public break with King, had a similar worry, and discussed it with Levison. "Both Stanley and I had some very serious talks because we thought Martin was becoming a little too concerned about the possibility of death." On one occasion, Rustin suggested that misgiving to King, only to be brushed off. "'You think I'm paranoid, don't you?' Sometimes I do, Martin," Rustin responded. Young had tried to counsel King, but had met the same reception. "If you said anything, he'd brush you off." Once, however, Young pressed the subject, telling King it was unwise "that he was pushing himself so hard." "You ought to go have a good physical examination," and "start taking a little better care of yourself." Young, Bill Rutherford, and other close associates thought that much of King's despondency stemmed from profound physical exhaustion, but underlying it was a deeper spiritual depression. "Fatigue was not so much physical with him as it was emotional," Young explained. "He had the constitution of a bull. He could go on and on and on when things were going well. It was when he didn't have a clear sense of direction that he got very tired." Bill Rutherford held a similar view. "I think he was exhausted, physically and probably more so spiritually. . . . I think he was worn out," and "really asking himself, 'Can it really work, will we really succeed, is nonviolence the real way?' I think he was in very serious self-doubt, self-questioning." Dorothy Cotton believed the change in King went back to the Vietnam controversy of April, 1967, "which might have been the beginning of what some of us perceived. I certainly saw the exhaustion," how King "was just really *emotionally* weary, as well as physically tired." "That whole last year I felt his weariness, just weariness of the struggle, that he had done all that he could do."

Once, after his return from Acapulco, King suggested that "maybe I ought to just take a sabbatical" and get away from SCLC and the movement for a year, Cotton remembered. Coretta King heard similar comments. "There were moments when he would feel depressed . . . even to the point where he would say, 'You know, I think I need to take a year off from everything and reflect on all the problems and just see where

we're going, what do I do from here. I should just take a year off.'" Jesse
Jackson later understood King's feelings quite well. "In our low moments, when the pressures build, you look for a graceful way out, you
have periods when you feel overwhelmed and want to retreat. . . . You
are restless unless you are operating at your highest and your best; when
you feel that you're doing less than your best, there's always the hound of
guilt and anxiety biting away at you."

King raised the subject of getting away with Andrew Young. Young
knew that King had toyed with taking a prominent pulpit and had considered taking a year off to teach at New York's Union Theological Seminary or move to Switzerland or Africa and live quietly. However, both
Young and Coretta thought he had realized he could do none of those
things, that the role in which he was caught would not allow him to jettison the responsibilities that lay on his shoulders. "He knew that it was
unrealistic, but he would think in those terms," Coretta recalled. "It was
just totally impossible and unrealistic to think that he could." "He really
began thinking about doing something else, and it was impossible . . . his
options were very limited," Young explained. "He just got burdened
down."[32]

King had always been a formal, reserved man in public, but some
friends now saw a more profound somberness in him, a melancholy that
seemed to reflect a basic loneliness. In earlier years Dorothy Cotton and
other close colleagues had recognized a certain basic shyness in King, a
shyness that in public situations often manifested itself in stiffness and
decorum. His intimates knew that that was only one part of King, though
it was the part that most casual acquaintances saw. Deenie Drew came to
think of him as "very, very lonely . . . despite the fact that he was surrounded by people all the time. He was still alone—he was apart. . . . He
had very few friends."

Part of the problem stemmed from the fact that there were very, very
few people with whom King could let down his guard and completely
relax. "He liked to bend his elbow a little bit, and he could do that in
very few places," Drew remembered. King's weight problem—"he got
fat"—stemmed from that basic loneliness, she thought. "He ate a lot, for
comfort."

Despite his reserve and his underlying loneliness, King was justly famous among his colleagues for his willingness to talk as an equal with
anyone who approached him. "In personal relations, he was a democratic
man," Michael Harrington recalled. "He was relaxed, easy. There are
people who are number one who don't let you forget it for one second;
he would let you forget it as long as you wanted to." Staffers would watch
with amazement when King left SCLC's headquarters to go a few doors
down Auburn Avenue to a favorite lunch spot, Beamon's restaurant. "It
would literally take him forty-five minutes to an hour to walk one and a
half blocks. . . . If you wanted to talk to him, he was going to take time
to talk to you. That's just the way he was, that was his nature."

Bill Rutherford remembered an occasion when King arrived thirty minutes late for a crucial SCLC meeting at Ebenezer church. "We walked in, and there was the janitor of the church, pushing his broom, and Martin said, 'How's your wife?' He said, 'Well, she ain't doing too well. Her back's bothering her . . .' Martin said, 'Really? It didn't get any better from the medicine?' Anyway, I stood there; there are three hundred people sitting in that church, waiting on the leader, and he's inquiring about the janitor's wife's back. . . . I was so impressed."

King's consideration for others, however, could not help alleviate his own burdens. Young, Cotton, and Levison offered him support, solace, and counsel; Ralph Abernathy's presence was similarly invaluable—"it's hard to find a brother in the spirit like that," Jesse Jackson noted later. Nonetheless, King wished he had more true friends, "somebody you can sit with and discuss your inner weaknesses and confess your agonies and your inner shortcomings, and they don't exploit it, they listen to you and help you bear your burdens in the midst of the storms of life."

His deepening depression notwithstanding, King made it through his Los Angeles schedule without flagging. That Saturday, March 16, Senator Robert F. Kennedy announced his entry into the Democratic presidential race. Asked about this by newsmen, King spoke warmly of both Kennedy and Eugene McCarthy and stressed that a new chief executive was "absolutely necessary. We must end the war in Vietnam. President Johnson is too emotionally involved, and face-saving is more important to him than peace." In other remarks, King sounded a bitter note, telling one audience that "there aren't enough white persons in our country who are willing to cherish democratic principles over privilege."[33]

From Los Angeles King and Young flew back east. Several weeks earlier James Lawson, still pastor of Centenary Methodist Church in Memphis, had asked King to visit that city to support a strike by black sanitation workers that had begun on February 12. Angered by an incident that had sent twenty-two black sewer workers home without pay because of bad weather, while white employees had been kept on and paid, and by city officials' refusal to enter into negotiations concerning a union dues "check-off" system, the 1,300 men of AFSCME Local 1733 had walked out and vowed not to return until Memphis Mayor Henry Loeb recognized their union. The next day they marched to City Hall, and national AFSCME representatives met with the hostile mayor. Angry exchanges ensued, and on February 15, Loeb denounced the strikers for "flaunting the law" and said the city would not negotiate until the men returned to work. Loeb's declaration that he would not recognize the virtually all-black local transformed the labor dispute into a racial conflict. Local white union leaders, the Memphis Ministers Association, and national AFSCME President Jerry Wurf all tried to resolve the impasse, but Loeb refused to budge. A black city councilman, Fred Davis, urged his colleagues to intervene, but the council refused to act and adjourned a special meeting without giving any response to the strikers' demands. The outraged sanitation men milled around the auditorium and then set out on a mass march to a black church. City policemen forced the column to one side of the street, and a police car brushed one marcher. Angry onlookers rocked the car, then the police responded with Mace. As marchers fled, officers used their billyclubs and additional gas on the stragglers. Conservative black ministers and federal observers were gassed, and when black community leaders met that evening, it was clear that the police conduct had created new support for the sanitation workers. A strike support group called COME, or Community on the Move for Equality, was established, and a boycott of downtown stores and white newspapers was announced. Daily marches and evening rallies commenced, and a Community Relations Service observer told Washington that the Memphis situation was "potentially explosive with no solution in sight."

As the strike's racial dimension came to the fore, the COME strategy committee solicited national assistance and outside speakers. Roy Wilkins and Bayard Rustin were contacted in New York, and Lawson phoned King in Atlanta to request a visit. King put him off, pleading a heavy schedule and medical advice that he get more rest. King acknowledged an appearance might be possible during his mid-March Poor People's Campaign recruiting tour in Mississippi, and on Sunday, March 17, Lawson called King at his Los Angeles hotel to ask if his March 18–20 Mississippi schedule had room for a Memphis rally speech. King said his flight arrangements could be changed to put him in Memphis Monday night. The next evening Lawson and AFSCME official Jesse Epps met King and Young at the Memphis airport and whisked them to Mason Temple, where a crowd of fifteen thousand waited.

The previous weeks had witnessed little change in the Memphis situation, King was told. The boycott of downtown stores was having some impact, with sales off 35 percent, but city officials still refused to negotiate. Roy Wilkins and Rustin had visited four days earlier, and a handful of strike supporters had been arrested for obstructing sanitation trucks, but the mayor had not budged. King was impressed by the size and enthusiasm of the crowd, and he mixed some special comments about Memphis into his exhortations concerning the Poor People's Campaign. He spoke of how the pilgrimage would take some dilapidated Mississippi shacks to Washington on flatbed trucks to show the entire nation the conditions in which thousands of people were forced to live, and of how "week after week we're going to stay there" until something was done. "Sometimes I feel discouraged," King admitted, "having to live under the threat of death every day. Sometimes I feel discouraged, having to take so much abuse and criticism, sometimes from my own people. Sometimes I feel discouraged," but eventually the Holy Spirit would revive his soul. The crowd responded enthusiastically. King told them they ought to stage a one-day general work stoppage to put real muscle behind the strike. On the podium behind him, Lawson, Young, and AFSCME President Wurf whispered about scheduling just such an effort. When the sweat-drenched King stepped back from speaking, the crowd's applause thundered throughout the sanctuary. Lawson and his colleagues asked if King would return within a few days to lead a mass march. After some quick deliberations, King said yes, he could be back in Memphis on Friday morning, March 22, after his Mississippi and Alabama appearances. The lively rally left King in an unusually good mood. "I've never seen a community as together as Memphis," he remarked. He chatted with two old friends, Memphis ministers Ben Hooks and Samuel "Billy" Kyles, at the Lorraine Motel, where King had stayed since his earliest visits to Memphis in the 1950s. A girls' choir also staying there insisted upon giving King a midnight serenade.[34]

On Tuesday King addressed rallies in Batesville, Marks, Clarksdale, Greenwood, Grenada, Laurel, and Hattiesburg, Mississippi. Hundreds of people turned out to see him at each stop, and SCLC aides Ralph Abernathy and Hosea Williams asked for volunteers and contributions for the Washington project. Even though the SCLC contingent flew from stop to stop on a chartered plane, by mid-afternoon they were running several hours late. The final rally in Hattiesburg had been planned for 8:30 P.M., but it was after midnight before King arrived at the church, where a crowd of 750 still waited. King and his colleagues delivered their standard remarks and then set out for Jackson, arriving at their motel at 4:00 A.M. after an exhausting twenty-one-hour day.

Late Wednesday morning the SCLC leaders met with their Mississippi staffers and decided that the southern caravan to Washington would set out from Jackson on April 27. A hoarse King addressed a small midday rally at Jackson's Masonic Temple. Afterward, he complained about how few volunteers and dollars the Mississippi tour had produced. A late start put his Wednesday evening Alabama appearances far behind schedule, and stops in Camden and Linden were canceled. In Eutaw King told a crowd that the Washington protests "will so tie that town up that it won't be able to function." He, Abernathy, and Williams went on to Greensboro, Marion, and then by plane to Bessemer. The next morning bad weather forced the cancellation of several rallies in south Alabama, so King and his companions headed home to Atlanta for some rest before Friday's return trip to Memphis.[35]

At 7:00 A.M. Friday Jim Lawson called King to say that their march would have to be canceled on account of a freak twelve-inch snowfall that Memphis had received overnight. They agreed to reschedule King's return for the following week. On Saturday King resumed his Poor People's Campaign recruiting efforts with a Georgia flying tour that took him to Waycross, Albany, Macon, and Augusta. He decided to take his two young sons, Marty and Dexter, along for the trip, a rare treat for the boys. King felt guilty about how little time he spent with his children, and regretted that they were growing up with him usually absent. Seeing so little of Bernice, or "Bunny," who was now five, was particularly painful, for King adored children her age. "He would say, 'Oh, I wish that we could just freeze her and keep her where she is,'" Coretta remembered. "He said, 'You know, there is nothing like the innocence of childhood.'" In the first few years after Bernice's birth, King had told Coretta, "'I think we ought to have another baby,' but he didn't persist in saying this," she recalled in mid-1968. "In recent years he stopped [talking] about having another baby."

At each stop of his Georgia tour, King proudly introduced Marty and Dexter to the waiting crowds. In Albany, *Southwest Georgian* editor A. C. Searles chided King for traveling without bodyguards. "'I can't lead that kind of life,'" King responded. "'I'd feel like a bird in a cage. . . . There's no way in the world you can keep somebody from killing you if they really want to kill you.'" The chartered airplane had engine problems at both Waycross and Macon, putting King hours behind schedule, and he apologized to his Macon audience, saying, "I would much rather be Martin Luther King late than the late Martin Luther King." More plane difficulties made him even later for the Augusta rally. Obviously tired, King offered a maudlin apology. "I came into the airport rather embarrassed and feeling such a sense of humiliation for being so late that I didn't want to face you," he told the 450-person crowd. Finally, after a late dinner in Augusta, a tired King and his two sleepy sons flew back to Atlanta.[36]

The hectic week of Deep South traveling had increased King's fears that the Poor People's Campaign was in trouble. The anticipated number of volunteers had not been recruited, and the financial situation was so bad that not only was SCLC taking in less than it was spending, but funds were not available to meet the most minimal field staff expenses. Additionally, some workers were openly hostile to King's emphasis on drawing other economically deprived groups into the campaign. "I do not think I am at the point where a Mexican can sit in and call strategy on a Steering Committee," one aide told a staff meeting; another remarked that Hispanic leader Reies Lopez Tijerina "didn't understand that we were the parents and he was the child."

In some cities, such as Chicago, Detroit, and Washington, undercover FBI operatives were interfering with the campaign's progress by staging dirty tricks or fanning internal dissension. FBI executives were expanding surveillance and penetration programs aimed at the black community. Since "valuable intelligence data is obtained from legitimate civil rights organizations," the Bureau would "expand contact" with those groups. To supplement the existing "racial informant" program, the FBI was recruiting collaborators for a similar "ghetto informant" undertaking. One mid-1968 summary reported the recruitment of "3,248 ghetto-type racial informants," and one field office boasted to headquarters that "a Chicago source on the SCLC payroll here" was "responsible for developing the degree of promised participation" so far evident there.

Most of the Poor People's Campaign's problems were being generated without any assistance from the FBI, however. In many areas, staff members reported, people were not enthusiastic about traveling to Washington for an indefinite stay and a hostile, and perhaps dangerous, official welcome. "If this is to be a progress report," Virginia worker James Gibson began one memo to Hosea Williams, "I can stop now; there has been none!" Atlanta had not provided him funds to pay the office rent, and out of 120 black ministers invited to a key organizational meeting, not one had shown up.[37]

Somewhat better progress was being made in refining the campaign's policy demands. Michael Harrington, Levison, and three AFSC staffers—Barbara Moffett, Eleanor Eaton, and Phil Buskirk—had prepared different drafts, with the AFSC document being the most detailed of the three. It "names no specific legislation," Moffett explained to King and Levison, and "is not set in a 'demand' framework on the theory that at this stage SCLC does *not* want a *bargaining* stance. We have avoided this and have stated 'challenges' and 'goals' instead of demands." King had little time to examine the details, however, because of the demands of his schedule. Less than twelve hours after returning home from his Georgia tour, King flew to New York to attend the installation ceremony for Wyatt T. Walker at his new pastorate, Harlem's Canaan Baptist Church. King ended his sermon with a melancholy refrain that was appearing more and more in his public addresses, that referred back to the transforming vision he had had twelve years earlier in Montgomery. "He promised never to leave me, never to leave me alone, no, never alone, no, never alone. He promised never to leave me, never to leave me alone."

On Monday King met with SCLC's top staffers at a New York hotel to review the campaign's timetable for the April 22 Washington kickoff. Then King flew upstate to speak at the annual convention of the Rabbinical Assembly. The rabbis peppered him with questions, and King volunteered that SCLC would drop its policy of no political endorsements in advance of the fall election in the hope that either Robert Kennedy or Eugene McCarthy could unify the anti-Johnson forces and wrest the Democratic nomination from the president. In response to a query about the future of black-white relations, King stressed that "it is absolutely necessary to see integration in political terms.

> Integration is more than something to be dealt with in esthetic or romantic terms. I think in the past all too often we did it that way . . . and it ended up as merely adding color to a still predominantly white power structure.
>   What is necessary now is to see integration in political terms where there is a sharing of power.

and real movement toward "that ultimate goal, which is a truly integrated society where there *is* shared power."

The Poor People's Campaign, King emphasized, was designed to seek that end, to bring the full range of domestic issues "out in the open enough so that the congressmen, who are in no mood at the present time to do anything about this problem, will be forced to do something about it." The movement had to confront America's domestic crisis, to make everyone "face the fact that America is a racist country," to discover some method "as attention-getting as a riot" to make the nation deal with its problems. "The leader has the responsibility of trying to find an answer," King said. "I have been searching for that answer a long time, over the last eighteen months," and he hoped the Poor People's Campaign would be it.[38]

That evening King returned to New York City and went to the home of Marian and Arthur Logan, where he argued with Marian into the early-morning hours about the memo she had distributed to SCLC's board. King was depressed and exhausted, and downed drink after drink as he pressed her to withdraw her objections to the Washington protests. The Logans had spent many similar evenings with King when he had wanted to talk and drink until dawn, seemingly unable to find any rest in sleep, but this night was different and worse. King was unwilling to accept Logan's position and talk about something else. His mood changed repeatedly as the hours passed, from tension to calm, and then back to barely restrained anger, and throughout it all he betrayed unusual anxiety, with one hand tightly holding his frequently refilled glass and the other clenched into a fist with his thumb ceaselessly rubbing against the other fingers. It seemed that King was "losing hold," Marian Logan recalled. The long, strange night finally ended when Arthur Logan told King that he was not going to change Marian's mind and should persist no longer.

Several of King's Tuesday morning appearances in New York were canceled because King was too tired to go through with them. "I've been getting two hours sleep a night for the last ten days," King told reporters when he arrived at a tenement on West 147th Street in Harlem for a noontime lunch with a welfare mother, Mrs. Bessie Fowler, whom SCLC staffers had selected for the media-oriented event. Later he spoke to a group of Harlem community activists, to an assembly of Queens clergymen, and at a Long Island public school before ending the day with an address to a small crowd at Convent Avenue Baptist Church. The next day, still "very tired" and one and a half hours behind schedule, he made a series of appearances in Newark, meeting with a group of ministers, lunching with twenty-five businessmen at New Jersey Bell Telephone headquarters, visiting briefly with black playwright LeRoi Jones, and speaking at church rallies in Paterson, Orange, and Jersey City as well as Newark.[39]

After a late-night flight to Atlanta, King returned to the airport early Thursday morning for a flight to Memphis and the rescheduled mass march. Since his first visit ten days earlier, negotiations between city officials and AFSCME representatives had resumed, but had ended after four lengthy sessions produced no progress. Meanwhile, internecine tensions had developed within COME, the strike-support organization, over Chairman Lawson's unreceptive stance toward a group of self-styled college-age radicals, the "Invaders," who wanted a central role in the protest movement. Even though some Invaders—John Smith, Charles Cabbage, Coby Smith, and Calvin Taylor—often attended strategy committee meetings, "Lawson wouldn't recognize them," one observer recalled. Although King had heard nothing of these tensions during his first visit, by the time of his return trip, relations between the Invaders and the adult strategy committee were so strained that the youths no longer regularly attended its meetings.

King was scheduled to arrive in Memphis well before the 10:00 A.M. start of the march, but his flight was late, and it was nearly 11:00 A.M. before King got to Clayborn Temple AME Church. Lawson delayed the start of the procession to await King, but had a difficult time keeping the impatient crowd calm, partially because of rumors that Memphis police had injured and perhaps killed a black high school student while attempting to keep youngsters from joining the march. Rev. "Billy" Kyles attempted to persuade Lawson to start the march and let King join the column en route, but by the time King arrived and the procession got under way at 11:05, he, Abernathy, and others in the front rank could sense the angry mood of the younger participants. The local leaders had appointed marshals to supervise the column, but most gathered near the front, and the rear ranks were composed largely of ill-disciplined youths.

King's face exhibited his exhaustion and discomfort as the march moved up Hernando and made a left on Beale, heading toward City Hall. Just as the head of the column turned right onto Main Street, turmoil erupted at the rear of the march, several blocks back, where some long wooden sticks that had originally held placards were thrown through the plate-glass windows of two Beale Street businesses. Within seconds, the disruption spread, with more sticks being used to break store windows. Some of the youngsters, plus a handful of street people, started looting goods from the shattered storefronts, and onlooking policemen called for more officers. At the front of the column, King and Lawson heard the tumult, and police commanders instructed them to halt. Lawson borrowed a bullhorn and asked the marchers to head back the way they had come, but police reinforcements were arriving on the scene with orders to disperse the crowd. Officers attacked peaceful marchers along with looters as the participants made their way back toward the church.

At the first sounds of the violence, those around King—Abernathy, Lee, Lawson, and Bishop B. Julian Smith—agreed that King ought to leave the area immediately. King appeared confused and frightened as the turmoil mounted, and remarked, "I've got to get out of here." King's group moved west on McCall Street, and Bernard Lee flagged down a white Pontiac to ask if King could use the car. The driver consented, and King and Abernathy hopped in, with Lee getting behind the wheel. A motorcycle policeman, Lieutenant M. E. Nichols, pulled alongside and led them to the Holiday Inn Rivermont, where King and his aides secured rooms. Plans to return to Atlanta and fly to Washington the next day were canceled, and a distraught King tried to make sense of why a peaceful march had turned into a violent conflict.[40]

At Clayborn Temple angry youths stoned police who tried to drive the marchers into the church, and officers responded with a tear-gas barrage aimed at both the church and the neighboring AME offices. COME leaders struggled to halt the violence, but police shot and killed a young black man who they believed was looting. Slowly the situation cooled down, and as word spread that King had retreated to the Rivermont, many COME activists gathered in his hotel room. They found him sitting in bed under the covers with his clothes on, and intent upon finding out what had gone wrong. Billy Kyles, one of the first to arrive, recalled that King "really didn't have any idea of what had happened. . . . He was very disturbed, [but] he wasn't angry . . . just upset." The local leaders apologized, and explained that they believed that the Invaders had intentionally caused the violence. Lawson underlined that point, and King declared that an accord would have to be reached with the youngsters and another march scheduled to counteract the negative publicity certain to ensue from this one. Lawson recommended they announce a march for the next day, but Lee and Abernathy, angry at local leaders for allowing King to be caught in a public relations disaster, insisted that he not participate in another protest until SCLC's staff had checked the plans.

After the local leaders departed, King's discouragement became more visible. Along with Lee and Abernathy, he spoke dejectedly with Hosea Williams at the SCLC Atlanta headquarters about the day's events. Williams passed on the details of the conversation to his colleague, secret FBI informant Jim Harrison, who in turn called his Bureau control agent, Al Sentinella, to relate the Memphis news. Harrison's story was transmitted to Bureau headquarters, where top-ranking FBI executives ordered that special efforts be made to develop full information on King's involvement in the riot-torn march. Such information might be leaked to cooperative reporters as part of the FBI program to disrupt the Poor People's Campaign.[41]

In his Rivermont room, King grew more despondent as he thought about how critics of his spring campaign would use the Memphis turmoil to argue that he could not keep his Poor People's legions peaceful once they reached Washington. "I had never seen him so depressed," Ralph Abernathy remembered. "Dr. King was greatly, greatly disturbed." Bitter and exhausted, King told Abernathy, "Maybe we just have to admit that the day of violence is here, and maybe we have to just give up and let violence take its course. The nation won't listen to our voice—maybe it'll heed the voice of violence." Abernathy tried to reassure King and lift his spirits, but made little headway. "Ralph, we live in a sick nation. . . . Maybe we will just have to let violence run its course."

Unable to fall asleep, King called Coretta in Atlanta to commiserate about the disastrous march. "He was very depressed about it and I kept trying to tell him, 'You mustn't hold yourself responsible, because you know you aren't,'" but she could not raise his spirits. Despite his exhaustion, King was agitated and disturbed. "It was the most restless night," Abernathy recalled. "It was a terrible and horrible experience for him. I had never seen him in all my life so upset and so troubled." Thinking of who might soothe King's worries, Abernathy suggested they telephone Levison. King told Stanley he was so distressed about the day's events that he was thinking of calling off the Poor People's Campaign. Levison advised him that his gloom was the product of exhaustion, and that he should not be so self-critical about the Memphis disorder. King spoke of how worried he was about the negative press coverage the event would receive, and Levison recommended that he emphasize that the majority of the marchers had been peaceful, and that the Washington protests would not be subject to turmoil because SCLC's experienced staff would select and organize the participants. King agreed, and Levison concluded by telling King to get some rest. King lay down, but he did not fall asleep until dawn. "He was worried, worried. He didn't know what to do, and he didn't know what the press was going to say," Abernathy remembered.[42]

King was in better spirits when he arose at 10:00 A.M. the next morning. While he was dressing for a press conference, three young men knocked at the door and told a hostile Abernathy that they—Charles Cabbage, Calvin Taylor, and Charles Harrington—were leaders of the Invaders. They wanted to explain to King that the reports that they had organized the disruption of Thursday's march were false. Abernathy told them that King was busy, but if they would wait in the hall for a few moments, King would speak to them briefly. When the three youths were allowed in, King greeted them and indicated he knew Cabbage, who had worked with Hosea Williams in Atlanta the previous summer and whom Williams had proposed adding to SCLC's staff as a field organizer. Abernathy bluntly demanded that they explain why they had disrupted the march. Cabbage, angered by the accusation, replied that the Invaders had not been responsible for the violence. Indeed, he said, none of the group's leaders had been at the scene, and while some of their supporters might have been involved, both that tumult and the leaders' absence was the result of Lawson and the other adults excluding them from the movement. "It was not our intention that the march erupt into anything," Taylor explained later. "We represented the element that really did break it, but . . . these people were not controlled by us. None of our people started it."

Abernathy and King asked why the youths had not tried to warn King before the march. Indeed they had, but with no success, Cabbage responded. "We explained," Taylor recounted, "that we had tried to see Dr. King," during his first visit on March 18, to complain about their exclusion, "but that Lawson and them wouldn't let us see Dr. King." Cabbage's strained relations with Lawson went back almost a year, to a Memphis antipoverty effort that had put them at loggerheads, and he told King that it was Lawson's fault that their tensions had boiled over into violence on Thursday. Cabbage's statements changed the atmosphere in the hotel suite. "Jim didn't tell me about the black power elements in the city. He led me to believe that there were none," King said. "We have been trying to talk to Lawson—he won't hear us," Cabbage went on. Even to the youths, it was apparent that King was dispirited, and that Cabbage's clarifications made him even more downcast. "It was unbelievable, . . . the depressed mood that he was in over the fact that there had been a riot," Calvin Taylor said later. "Dr. King was very depressed when he heard" Cabbage's explanation, and told his visitors that he had sensed from the outset on Thursday that "'the atmosphere was just wrong.'"

King was not totally accepting of Cabbage's claims that the Invaders were not to blame for Thursday's disorder, but he did tell the threesome that he would see to it that the COME leadership included them in future deliberations. The most crucial question, however, was "what must be done to have a peaceful march, because you know I have got to lead one. There is no other way." SCLC and its Memphis allies simply *had* to demonstrate that a nonviolent protest could be staged and that Thursday's turmoil was a onetime occurrence. Cabbage replied that the Invaders wanted some financial help for their community organizing plans, and would be happy to cooperate with SCLC in staging a second march, but that King had to understand that their leadership was not monolithic and could not *absolutely* guarantee that there would be no problems the second time around. That mixed message did not sit well with King, but he told Cabbage that SCLC staffers would be in touch with him and that King would inquire about possible funds for the Invaders. "'We should have sat down and talked before the march,'" King concluded wistfully, and the youths departed.[43]

Half an hour later, King met with reporters and apologized for his tardiness, explaining that a conversation with the Invaders had delayed him. Questioned about the previous day's riot, King emphasized that SCLC had "had no part in the planning of the march. Our intelligence was totally nil." He announced that there would be a second major march, organized by SCLC. The Memphis strike, with its clear portrayal of how issues of race and economics overlapped, and with the city's refusal to recognize its black workers and negotiate with them, was powerful evidence of just how important the Poor People's Campaign was for

America's future. The spring protests, King stressed, would not be called off. "We are fully determined to go to Washington. We feel it is an absolute necessity."

Although King performed impressively at the news conference his mood was low and he was deeply pessimistic about the future. "Ralph, I want to get out of Memphis," he said to Abernathy after the press conference. "Get me out of Memphis as soon as possible." The hostile, disparaging tone of many of the reporters' questions had induced more self-doubt in King about his future and the prospects of the Poor People's Campaign. A deeply concerned Abernathy made reservations for them to fly to Atlanta that afternoon. King spoke again with Stanley Levison, lamenting the situation. "I think that we have to face the fact that from a public relations point of view and every other way we are in serious trouble. I think as far as the Washington campaign is concerned it is in trouble. It is going to be much harder to recruit people now, because most people we are recruiting are not violent people. And if they feel they are going to be in a campaign that is going to be taken over by violent elements, you know, they will hold back, and I think we will have some holding back just out of fear . . . you'll begin to see it in the newspapers. This is not a failure for SCLC; we have enough of a program to affirm its own position, but it is a personal setback for me. Let's face it."

Levison responded forcefully, "No, Martin, I couldn't disagree more completely with you." King demurred. "All I'm saying is that Roy Wilkins, that Bayard Rustin and that stripe, and there are many of them, and the Negroes that are influenced by what they read in newspapers, Adam Clayton Powell, for another reason . . . their point is, 'I'm right. Martin Luther King is dead. He's finished. His nonviolence is nothing, no one is listening to it.' Let's face it, we do have a great public relations setback where my image and my leadership are concerned." Levison objected again. "That is only if you accept their definition, and this, I think, is a profound error you are making." "I don't accept it myself," King replied. "What I'm saying is that many people will accept it." Levison emphasized that only a tiny percentage of Thursday's marchers had engaged in violence. King agreed. "We all know it was just a few people, and frankly, it was a failure of the leadership here." He described the Invaders' visit. "They came up here, they love me. They were fighting the leadership of Memphis. They were fighting Jim Lawson and the men who ignored them, who neglected them, who would not hear them, wouldn't give them any attention. . . . I had no knowledge of all this. I know the fellows, and they really do, they love me. They were too sick to see that what they were doing yesterday was hurting me much more than it could hurt the local preachers."

King explained his next step. "I was so upset about this thing and so shocked that I was just going to announce that I was going on a fast, and through this fast to appeal to the leadership of Memphis as well as those who participated in the violence to come to me in a united front and let's take up the cudgel and move on in this movement. I think that that kind of powerful spiritual move would be the kind of thing that would pull all the forces, and make all the students come to me. I think it will make my staff work harder everywhere along the way. It will force them . . . to come in here and get with these students and say that we can't allow this to happen. It would be a way of unifying the movement and transforming a minus into a plus." SCLC should concentrate on staging a second, completely nonviolent march in Memphis, since "this was a riot that broke out right in the ranks of our march." Levison argued that King should not accept the press's logic that he was a failure if 99 percent of the protesters followed his nonviolent lead, and 1 percent did not, but King disagreed. "I think our Washington campaign is doomed." He emphasized that he was "a symbol of nonviolence," and that in Thursday's wake "everything will come out weakening the symbol. It will put many Negroes in doubt. It will put many Negroes in the position of saying, 'Well, that's true, Martin Luther King is at the end of his rope.' So I've got to do something that becomes a kind of powerful act . . . of unifying forces, of refuting the claims that would be made by the press." Levison reiterated that King was setting a trap for himself if he accepted the media assumption, but King was insistent. "You can't keep them from imposing it. . . . You watch your newspapers. . . . I think it will be the most negative thing about Martin Luther King that you have ever seen."[44]

King was still upset when he arrived in Atlanta. Abernathy dropped him off at the Butler Street YMCA, where King often went for a workout and a rubdown by a blind masseur whose skill and dexterity always impressed him. He called Abernathy from the Y to say that he was too tired to go ahead with their tentative plans to take their wives out to a movie; instead, King and Coretta went to Ralph and Juanita Abernathy's for a quiet dinner. An SCLC executive staff meeting had been scheduled for Saturday morning at Ebenezer to discuss Memphis and how further activity there could be combined with the Poor People's Campaign. "He was experiencing a great deal of anxiety," Coretta recalled. King was worried both about the progress of the campaign and about staff sentiment that any serious commitment of resources to Memphis would put the Poor People's effort even further behind schedule.

Press response to the Memphis march was at least as bad as King had anticipated. The hostile *Memphis Commercial Appeal* declared that "King's pose as leader of a nonviolent movement has been shattered" and criticized him for having "fled the melee." "He wrecked his reputation" when "he took off at high speed when violence occurred, instead of trying to use his persuasive prestige to stop it." *The New York Times,* which in one piece termed Thursday's riot "a powerful embarrassment to Dr. King," warned in an editorial that King ought to call off the Poor People's Campaign. "None of the precautions he and his aides are taking to keep the capital demonstration peaceful can provide any dependable insurance against another eruption of the kind that rocked Memphis." Indeed, the *Times* said, SCLC's descent upon Washington "is likely to prove even more counterproductive," seriously harming the chances for the policy initiatives the campaign hoped to win.[45]

At Saturday's meeting of the SCLC executive staff, King's weariness and despair was obvious to his colleagues. He talked about the necessity of holding a second, peaceful march in Memphis, about his possible fast, and about how a team of SCLC staffers should go into Memphis to prepare for that second protest. If that was successful, it would give a major boost to the entire Poor People's Campaign. King's recommendations received a cool response from his top aides, many of whom opposed returning to Memphis and felt that if SCLC went there, the Washington project ought to be canceled or postponed. The underlying problem, as Bill Rutherford saw it, was that "no one was really enthusiastic about the Poor People's Campaign" except King, and a few staffers—Jim Bevel and Jesse Jackson in particular—remained openly opposed. Public criticism distressed King, but more disappointing was the lack of support from aides and board members. Especially painful, Andrew Young said later, "was the flak we were getting from friends. They kept telling him he was failing." At the Saturday meeting, King was "really demoralized," Walter Fauntroy recalled. It was not so much the question of Memphis or even the Poor People's Campaign that weighed so heavily upon him, but his feeling that his closest friends and assistants were failing to stand by him in his hour of greatest need. After the meeting had gone on for several hours without any consensus being reached on King's suggestions, he erupted. "'Look,'" Young recalled King saying, "'You guys come up with your projects, and you always pull me in, and a lot of times I had other things I was interested in, but if I sensed that this was important to the movement and to you, it always had my full support, no question about it.'" His aides squirmed as King went on. "'Now, I'm not just getting *your* full support.'" His anger and despair flowed out forcefully.

"I had never seen him under such a spiritual cloud before," Jackson said later. King railed at the staff's disunity and finally announced he was going to leave to see if they could sort out their problems better without him. As King headed to the door, Jackson started to follow, but King turned and delivered a personal blast: "If you are so interested in doing your own thing that you can't do what the organization is structured to do, go ahead. If you want to carve out your own niche in society, go ahead, but for God's sake don't bother me!" King headed out the door, and Abernathy went after him, asking him where he was going and what was wrong. "Tell me what is bugging you," Abernathy pleaded. "'All I'll say is, Ralph, I'll—I'll snap out of it. Didn't I snap out of it yesterday? You said I did yesterday at the press conference, I'll pull through it.'" Abernathy returned to the meeting, and discussion resumed among the thoroughly abashed staffers. As one aide later admitted, King left for the one place he knew he could find solace. "He got so depressed by the opposition he could still feel within all of us that he got up and went off to see his girlfriend" at their hideaway apartment.

King's departure and choice of refuge reflected the emotional stress he was experiencing. Some aides thought that that stress stemmed from both his personal life as well as the movement's political difficulties. Bill Rutherford was one who saw Coretta's and King's marital tensions as a significant cause. "That poor man was so harassed at home," Rutherford remembered while emphasizing that "you cannot write about Dr. King without dealing with the reality." "She was as much a part of his depression as his staff. . . . Coretta was a part of the problem, but . . . also in many ways she probably was a much put-upon person." Rutherford and other aides recognized what different conceptions of the wife's role King and Coretta held, and how her unhappiness with the constraints King successfully imposed on her made King's home life so tense. "Had the man lived, the marriage wouldn't have survived, and everybody feels that way," one staffer observed. Coretta was "completely and totally out of her depth in this milieu in which Martin moved and functioned," Rutherford thought, but she "saw for herself a role," a public role as a substantive figure, "that Dr. King didn't accept or agree with at all." Some aides saw Coretta's acceptance of all the home and child-rearing tasks as a blessing for King—"Coretta was the ideal wife for Martin"—but those same aides had no illusions about the marriage. "Coretta King was most certainly a widow long before Dr. King died." Her resentment of that made for unpleasantness all around. As Rutherford noted, "That again was why he couldn't go home."

Many top staffers nonetheless realized that King's depression had less to do with his private life than with the state of the movement. "Dr. King's lack of solace, his discomfort and malaise at the end of his life, was based much more . . . on intellectual considerations and spiritual considerations than on personal, physical" ones, Rutherford emphasized. "I know he found a great deal of comfort and solace with these extramarital relationships . . . but they never would have been adequate to respond to his spiritual needs. He was uneasy and unhappy about his own philosophy."

While King was off with his lady friend that afternoon, his chagrined aides agreed that they had to overcome their differences, forge ahead with the Poor People's Campaign, and repair the damage of Thursday's violence in Memphis. A second march would be organized, and a team of staffers—Jackson, James Orange, Jim Bevel, and Hosea Williams—would be sent in to talk with the Invaders and be certain that all segments of the black community were included.

The staff also agreed that the public focus ought not to be on whether SCLC could guarantee nonviolence from each protester, but on the greater evils of poverty and racism. Everyone vowed to redouble their commitment to the campaign, and pledged there would be no further dissent about going ahead with it. By the time King returned to the meeting from his midday dalliance, the staff agreement was complete. Both Memphis and the Washington project would be pursued with full energy. Pleased and relieved, King endorsed the decision to send the advance team to Memphis, and said that he would return there at midweek.[46]

On Sunday morning King flew to Washington to keep a long-scheduled preaching engagement at National Cathedral. After his sermon he met with reporters and emphasized that "there will be a Poor People's Campaign" and it would move forward on schedule. He had canceled his mediation trip to Nigeria to devote more time to the campaign, which had to succeed if more riots and white backlash were to be avoided. "We cannot stand two more summers like last summer without leading inevitably to a rightwing takeover and a fascist state," King warned. One questioner asked if there were any chance that an accord could be reached before the Washington protests, and under what conditions King would call off the campaign. The only possibility would be if Lyndon Johnson and the Congress quickly implemented the policy recommendations of the riot commission. "I would be glad to talk to President Johnson or anyone else," King said. "We're always willing to negotiate." However, there would have to be a specific government offer—"a commitment with a positive timetable for this summer—for us to call off the march. And I don't see that forthcoming."

Later that day King and Andrew Young met with Michigan Congressman John Conyers and Mayor Richard Hatcher of Gary, Indiana, to discuss creating a national "commission of inquiry" to examine the positions of all 1968 presidential candidates with respect to blacks' needs. King had reiterated to the press that "I cannot support President Johnson for re-election," and while his strong private preference was for Robert Kennedy, he believed that he no longer could avoid an active role in electoral politics. King was still downcast—"I don't know when I have ever seen him as discouraged and depressed," Young recalled—but that evening his spirit was buoyed by the most surprising political event in several years: Lyndon Johnson's dramatic declaration on national television that he would not be a candidate for reelection.[47]

While King returned to Atlanta for a Monday Poor People's Campaign meeting, Williams, Bevel, Jackson, and Orange flew to Memphis to organize the second march, tentatively scheduled for Friday, April 5. Sunday evening they met with the COME strategy committee, and the following night they held a lengthy session with the Invaders to ensure their cooperation. Orange promised that SCLC would attempt to secure funds for their organizing program. Jackson assured them that SCLC understood their distrust of the local adult leadership and pledged that changes would be made. Tuesday night Orange presented the Invaders' requests to the strategy committee, and although their demand that Lawson be replaced as chairman was rejected, agreement was reached that two Invaders could join the panel. The committee also decided to reschedule the second march for Monday, April 8. Later that night the SCLC staffers and the strategy committee vice-chairman, H. Ralph Jackson, met with the Invaders to cement the accord.[48]

King was scheduled to attend that Tuesday night confab, but at midday Tuesday, still dispirited, he had phoned Abernathy to suggest they delay their flight to Memphis until Wednesday morning. Abernathy agreed, and at 7:00 A.M. he drove to King's home to pick him up and head to the airport. Coretta offered Ralph breakfast and coffee, but Abernathy declined, for the plane would leave in less than an hour. Coretta bid her husband good-bye—"It was just an ordinary good-bye," she said later—and the two men drove off. King was in a better mood, Abernathy thought, actually "in good spirits" for a change, and at the airport Bernard Lee, Andrew Young, and Dorothy Cotton joined them for the flight to Memphis. After they boarded the plane, it remained at the gate for an uncommonly long time before the pilot announced that a bomb threat had caused the delay and that they would soon be on their way. Upon arriving in Memphis, King and his colleagues were driven to their usual lodging place, the Lorraine Motel, and then to a meeting of black clergy at Lawson's church, where King, Young, and Jesse Jackson addressed the group. Word arrived that city lawyers had gone into federal court seeking to ban a second march, and that District Judge Bailey Brown had signed a temporary restraining order prohibiting King and his allies from staging a mass protest within the next ten days. King joked to Billy Kyles that once again the movement's opponents were playing into his hands. After the church meeting, King returned to the Lorraine, where federal marshals served him with a copy of Brown's order.

As news of the court order spread, movement lawyers in Atlanta and New York phoned colleagues in Memphis to ask that they assist King in fighting the ban. Six different Memphis attorneys agreed to join forces, and in midafternoon they went to the Lorraine to meet their new client. King told the lawyers it was essential that the second march be completely peaceful. The most senior attorney, Lucius Burch, asked King what his feelings were about the restraining order, and he responded that he intended to proceed with the Monday march whether or not the ban was rescinded. The lawyers suggested seeking a modification of Brown's ban to allow a limited and tightly disciplined march. That way King could avoid violating the edict and maximize his chances of keeping the protest totally nonviolent. King endorsed the recommendation, and they agreed to go into Brown's court the next morning to seek changes in the order. King was impressed with Burch, and hopeful that the strategy would ensure a successful Monday protest, but he told one newsman he would go ahead with the march whether or not the court order was modified.[49]

After supper in the Lorraine dining room, King joined his SCLC colleagues to hear the Invaders' case for why SCLC should give them funds in exchange for their assistance with Monday's march. Several of King's aides had little tolerance for a proposal that amounted to little more than blackmail, but King accorded the youths a respectful hearing. James Orange spoke in support of the Invaders' community-organizing plans, and King responded positively to their proposals. He explained that although SCLC did not have funds to finance their project, he would make some phone calls to organizations that might. King also promised to have Andrew Young sit down with Cabbage and prepare a proposal describing their ideas. He emphasized how important their peaceful cooperation in Monday's march would be. He spoke of how he appreciated their past difficulties with the adult leadership, and asked that they trust his commitment that that treatment would not reoccur and that SCLC would work with them on their plans. The youths understood the terms, and accepted the exchange. "I think what he was trying to do," one Invader explained later, "was to eliminate the possibility of our disrupting the march."

After the meeting King phoned Coretta to say that it had been a good day, then called New York to chat with Marian Logan. In the meantime, Ralph Abernathy left to speak at a mass meeting at the huge Mason Temple. The rainy weather would make for a modest crowd, and there was no need for King to leave himself open to unflattering press comments about his popularity when he could just as well get some rest. Abernathy found hardly two thousand people waiting in the sanctuary which two weeks earlier had held seven times that number to hear King. However, Abernathy sensed that the crowd was disappointed to see him appear without King, and he phoned King at the Lorraine to ask him to come over. When King arrived, Abernathy stepped to the podium and launched into a lengthy introduction of his old friend. Then King stepped forward and, as the angry weather rattled the windows, told his listeners that the Memphis movement would go forward, federal court or no federal court. "We aren't going to let any injunction turn us around." He talked about how everyone ought to boycott the products of firms with unsatisfactory black employment records, and then related the parable of the Good Samaritan. He recounted his stabbing in the Harlem department store ten years earlier, how the letter-opener's blade had come so close to killing him that the doctors had said even a sneeze might have been fatal, and how he had never forgotten that one get-well letter from a schoolchild in suburban New York saying she was glad King had not sneezed.

> And I want to say tonight, I want to say tonight that I too am happy that I didn't sneeze. Because if I had sneezed, I wouldn't have been around here in 1960, when students all over the South started sitting-in at lunch counters. And I knew as they were sitting in, they were really standing up for the best in the American dream, and taking the whole nation back to those great wells of democracy which were dug deep by the founding fathers in the Declaration of Independence and the Constitution.

If I had sneezed, I wouldn't have been around here in 1961, when we decided to take a ride for freedom, and ended segregation in interstate travel.

If I had sneezed, I wouldn't have been around in 1962, when Negroes in Albany, Georgia, decided to straighten their backs up. And whenever men and women straighten their backs up, they are going somewhere, because a man can't ride your back unless it is bent.

If I had sneezed, I wouldn't have been around here in 1963, when the black people of Birmingham, Alabama, aroused the conscience of this nation and brought into being the civil rights bill.

If I had sneezed, I wouldn't have had the chance later that year, in August, to try to tell America about a dream that I had had.

If I had sneezed, I wouldn't have been down in Selma, Alabama, to see the great movement there.

If I had sneezed, I wouldn't have been in Memphis to see a great community rally around those brothers and sisters who are suffering.

I'm so happy that I didn't sneeze. . . .

Now it doesn't matter now. It really doesn't matter what happens now.

He told about the bomb threat on his plane that morning, and alluded to the rumors that some in Memphis were threatening him too.

Well, I don't know what will happen now. We've got some difficult days ahead. But it really doesn't matter with me now, because I've been to the mountaintop. And I don't mind. Like anybody, I would like to live a long life. Longevity has its place. But I'm not concerned about that now. I just want to do God's will. And He's allowed me to go up to the mountain, and I've looked over, and I've seen the promised land. I may .not get there with you. But I want you to know tonight, that we, as a people will get to the promised land. And so I'm happy tonight. I'm not worried about anything. I'm not fearing any man. Mine eyes have seen the glory of the coming of the Lord.[50]

Sweat streaming from his brow, and his eyes watering heavily, King moved to his seat. Some thought him so overcome by emotion that he was crying, and even Abernathy and Andrew Young, who had heard King deliver essentially the same peroration on other occasions, mused that tonight he had gone beyond the maudlin to the morbid. Young knew from experience that King would relate the stabbing story whenever he was preoccupied with death, but this evening, after the rally concluded, he seemed refreshed rather than gloomy. "He was very happy and relaxed," Abernathy said in recalling King's mood as they had gone off to a late dinner at Benjamin Hooks's home before returning to the Lorraine in the wee hours of the morning. There King discovered that his brother, A.D., and several friends had arrived from Louisville. He chatted and joked with them until dawn before finally going to bed and sleeping until almost noon.

Amid rumors that SCLC was looking for a way out of the Monday march, and other reports that the Memphis effort would force a postponement of the Washington campaign's April 22 kickoff, the COME strategy committee met late Wednesday night to discuss both the legal challenge to the court order and SCLC's negotiations with the Invaders. The lawyers were up late preparing for what would be an all-day court session, and back at the Lorraine several Invaders got into a heated exchange with some SCLC staff members about their demands for money. A number of Invaders had been hanging out in rooms at the motel, rooms they could not afford, in order to avoid police harassment. The late-night wrangling finally ended when SCLC agreed to pick up some of the Invaders' motel bills.[51]

Thursday morning Andrew Young and Jim Lawson headed to federal court long before King awoke. Longtime SCLC attorney Chauncey Eskridge had flown in and joined Burch's team, and both Lawson and Young took the stand to testify in support of SCLC's motion that Judge Brown approve a tightly disciplined Monday march. Back at the Lorraine, King convened a meeting of other SCLC staffers where the talk turned to whether the Invaders could really be trusted not to disrupt Monday's protest. King's attitude was "grim and businesslike," Abernathy said later in recalling how weary he had appeared. "He was still terribly depressed," Bernard Lee explained. "He had a great deal of anxiety" about how the Memphis march would come out, but insisted that fear could not deter them. "I'd rather be dead than afraid. You've got to get over being afraid of death," he stressed to his aides.

When the discussion came back to the Invaders, Hosea Williams mentioned his previous recommendation that Charles Cabbage be hired as a field-worker. King, who knew that Cabbage had no commitment to nonviolence, erupted at Williams much as he had at Rutherford two months earlier. "Hosea, no one should be on our payroll that accepts violence as a means of social change. The only way to have a world at peace is through nonviolence." Williams backed off, and the meeting broke up. King phoned Atlanta to let Ebenezer know the title of his Sunday sermon—"Why America May Go to Hell"—and made several other calls before joining his brother in A.D.'s first-floor room. Together they telephoned Mama King and talked for almost an hour. Then Abernathy joined the two brothers as they watched the early local news on television and waited for word from Young about what had transpired in court.[52]

King was irritated that the entire day had passed without any news from Young, but the hearing ran late and afterward Judge Brown summoned the attorneys to a private session in his chambers. Brown told Burch and Eskridge that he would approve a circumscribed Monday march, with details to be worked out Friday, but Young had little chance to relate those developments when he got back to the Lorraine and located King:

He immediately started fussing in a kind of joking way about "why don't you call and let me know what's going on? We're sitting here all day long waiting to hear from you and you didn't call"—and he picked up a pillow and threw it at me. And I threw it back, and we ended up with five or six of us in a pillow fight.

"Occasionally he would get in those kinds of hilarious moods," Young remembered.

Then Young briefed King on the day's developments. A few minutes later Eskridge returned from the courthouse to report on the private conference with Judge Brown, and King, nodding at the TV set, said, "Now we can get the straight news; we don't have to look at television." Eskridge described the judge's commitment to modify his order and allow the Monday march, and King was pleased. Then, with the hour fast approaching six, King told his friends it was time to get dressed for dinner, for Billy Kyles had invited them all to a soul food supper.

King and Abernathy walked upstairs to their second-story room. King shaved, an awkward and time-consuming process for a man whose sensitive skin forced him to use a distasteful smelling depilatory powder called "Magic Shave" rather than a razor. Abernathy talked about the difficulty he was having in scheduling a revival-week speaker for his Atlanta church at a time that would not conflict with the Poor People's Campaign. King offered to telephone a New Orleans pastor to ask him to help Abernathy out. Billy Kyles knocked at the door, encouraging them to hurry along, and King struggled to button the collar of a tight shirt as Kyles teased him about how he was getting fat. They bantered on as King found a larger shirt and started searching for his tie. Kyles urged them along, and King, finished with his tie, stepped out onto the second-floor balcony as Abernathy applied some cologne. Down in the courtyard, some eight feet below, waited the white Cadillac that a Memphis funeral home always loaned King when he was in town. Its driver, Solomon Jones, Jr., stood beside it, with Young, Eskridge, Bevel, Jackson, and Williams all waiting to leave. Kyles stood beside King on the balcony, extending greetings to Eskridge. Jackson called up to King to introduce a Chicago band member, and Jones interjected that King ought to get a topcoat, for the air was getting chill. "O.K.," King replied, and Kyles turned to head downstairs. He had gone only a few steps when the loud report—a car backfire, some thought—echoed through the courtyard. Young and some others instinctively took cover near the limousine. Simultaneously, Kyles on the balcony and Abernathy inside the motel room realized that the sound was not a backfire but a rifle shot. Kyles turned. He could see King's body prone on the balcony floor, his feet extending to the lower rail. Abernathy could see King from the motel room door. He stepped out, bent over, and saw the gaping wound in King's right jaw. He patted King on the left cheek, and saw his eyes move toward him. "Martin, Martin, this is Ralph. Do you hear me? This is Ralph." It seemed as if King could hear him, as if his lips moved in a futile attempt to respond. Andrew Young rushed up and felt King's wrist for a pulse. He thought he could detect a faint one, but a glance at King's shattered jaw showed blood pulsing from the ugly wound. Someone placed a towel under King's head, with part of it reaching up to cover the injury. Kyles tried to summon an ambulance from the phone in King's room, but the motel switchboard did not respond. A policeman appeared in the courtyard and said one was on its way. Kyles took one of the orange bedspreads from the room and draped it over King's body. Abernathy knelt beside him, asking his old friend if he could hear him. Kyles looked down and thought he could see the color of King's complexion change right before his eyes. He turned away and sobbed.[53]

Epilogue

"By idolizing those whom we honor," writes black educator Charles Willie, one of King's Morehouse classmates, "we do a disservice both to them and to ourselves. By exalting the accomplishments of Martin Luther King, Jr., into a legendary tale that is annually told, we fail to recognize his humanity—his personal and public struggles—that are similar to yours and mine. By idolizing those whom we honor, we fail to realize that we could go and do likewise."

"You have a tendency to romanticize," Yolanda King notes, "when you're looking back on it." Andrew Young states that "I think it's time to tell it all now," and Christine Farris, King's sister, says she wants to "help to demythologize one of our heroes." "My brother," she emphasizes, "was no saint," but "an average and ordinary man." Indeed, many of King's colleagues worry, as Vincent Harding puts it, that people today are turning King into a "rather smoothed-off, respectable national hero" whose comfortable, present-day image bears little resemblance to the human King or to the political King of 1965–1968. Hosea Williams says it bluntly: "There is a definite effort on the part of America to change Martin Luther King, Jr., from what he really was all about—to make him the Uncle Tom of the century. In my mind, he was the militant of the century."

Ella Baker aptly articulates the most crucial point, the central fact of his life which Martin King realized from December 5 in Montgomery until April 4 in Memphis: "The movement made Martin rather than Martin making the movement." As Diane Nash says, "If people think that it was Martin Luther King's movement, then today they—young people—are more likely to say, 'gosh, I wish we had a Martin Luther King here today to lead us.' . . . If people knew how that movement started, then the question they would ask themselves is, 'What can I do?'"[1]

Acknowledgments

Researching and writing this book has been the most deeply satisfying and emotionally enjoyable experience of my life. My greatest debt is to the several hundred individuals who have taken the time to speak with me, often at considerable length, about their own involvement in the movement and their relationships with Dr. King. Their names, along with those of other oral history interviewees whose recollections have greatly aided me, are listed alphabetically in the Bibliography.

My second greatest debt is to the more than two dozen friends or colleagues who have been kind and generous enough to share with me the tapes or transcripts of their own oral history interviews with King friends and movement veterans: Arvil V. Adams, Lee Bains, Jim Bishop, Richard Brasch, Mary Brown, Clay Carson, David Colburn, Dennis Dickerson, Fred Downing, Chuck Fager, Vincent Fort, Henry Hampton and the other good people at Blackside, Inc., in Boston, Steve Hill, Jack Ice, Peter Joseph, Nick and Mary Lynn Kotz, John LaCrosse, David Levering Lewis, Steve Longenecker, Keith Miller, Vic Navasky, Steve Oates, Scott Rafferty, John Ricks, Arthur Schlesinger, Jr., Feay Shellman, Jean Stein, Sue Thrasher, Milton Viorst, and Rob Weisbrot. Much of the strength of this book comes from the more than seven hundred interviews that contributed to it.

I owe a special thanks to the many individuals who have labored long and hard in retrieving and processing the tens of thousands of pages of federal government documents released to me pursuant to Freedom of Information Act requests, particularly to Bill Smith, Kirk Cromer, and Shirley Wiles at the FBI; Terry Stewart, Renee Holmes, and Janet Blizard at the Justice Department's Civil Rights Division; and Gail Padgett at the Community Relations Service. I also owe special thanks to Marvin Whiting at the Birmingham, Alabama, Public Library's Archives division, and to John and Michael Moscato, as well as August Meier and the late Elliott Rudwick, at University Publications of America (UPA), for the financial support their programs have given to my FOIA requests. This book has been greatly strengthened by thousands of previously unavailable documents, particularly hundreds of transcripts of Dr. King's wiretapped phone conversations, that have been released to me by the FBI, thanks to FOIA. In this regard I also owe very deep thanks to two of Dr. King's closest advisors, Clarence B. Jones and Bayard Rustin, both of whom were wiretapped by the FBI and who have allowed me unrestricted access to the resulting FBI documents, documents that otherwise would not have been available, pursuant to the Privacy Act, during their lifetimes.

I owe particular thanks to a number of other friends whose assistance has been invaluable. Jackie White and Stoney Cooks have repeatedly provided the kindest help, and made available three extremely valuable sets of documentary materials. Lucy Keele and Joan Daves several years ago both gave me the only surviving transcript copies of several score of Dr. King's taped but unpublished sermons and speeches; these are now available at the King Center in Atlanta to everyone, and all King scholars, now and in the future, will be eternally grateful to them. As soon as copies are made, all of my taped interviews will also be deposited at the King Center, as well as at Howard University's Moorland Spingarn Research Center and the New York Public Library's Schomburg Center.

A variety of institutions have helped to support my research in numerous ways, and I extend my thanks to them. At the Ford Foundation, Robert B. Goldmann and Carol Arnold oversaw a personal grant that assisted me for over eighteen months; at the American Association for State and Local History, Dr. James B. Gardner oversaw a National Endowment for the Humanities grant that aided my research with regard to Albany, Georgia. Both the Lyndon Baines Johnson Foundation and L. Arthur Minnich at the Eisenhower World Affairs Institute have supported my research at the Johnson and Eisenhower presidential libraries.

There are many archivists, librarians, and other staff members at institutions across the country to whom I also owe thanks. They include: Jerry Roden and Alberta Fears Harris at the Alabama Council for Human Relations in Auburn; Joseph D. Caver at the Alabama State Archives; Marcia Martin Miller and Mary Chames at the Alabama State University Library; Susan M. Eltscher at the American Baptist Historical Society in Rochester, N.Y.; Florence E. Borders and Clifton H. Johnson at New Orleans's Amistad Research Center; Joyce E. Jelks at the Atlanta Public Library; Lee C. Alexander and Minnie H. Clayton at Atlanta University's Woodruff Library; Marvin Whiting, Bob Corley, Teresa Ceravolo, and Tom Haslett at the Birmingham Public Library Archives; Howard Gotlieb, Margaret Goostray, Charles Niles, and Doug McDonald at Boston University's Mugar Library; Archie Motley and Linda Evans at the Chicago Historical Society; Emerson Ford and Bob Byrd at Duke University's Perkins Library; Martin Teasley, Karen Rohr, and David Haight at the Eisenhower Library in Abilene, Kansas; Linda Matthews at Emory University's Woodruff Library; Charles Reeves at the Federal Records Center in East Point, Ga.; Ann Shockley at the Fisk University Library; Nathaniel Bunker and Martha Richardson at Harvard University; Elinor DesVerney Sinnette, Esme Bhan, Charlynn Spencer Pyne, Karen Jefferson, Denise Harbin, and Thomas Battle at Howard University's Moorland Spingarn Research Center; Tina Lawson, Martin Elzy, Gary Gallagher, Linda Hanson, Claudia Anderson, and Nancy Smith at the Johnson Library in Austin; Carol Sylvester and Auriel Pilgrim at the Joint Center for Political Studies; Henry Gwiazda, Deborah Greene, Will Johnson, and William Moss at the Kennedy Library in Boston; Cynthia Lewis, Steve Klein, Paula Williams, Diane Ware, Heather Gray, Lloyd Davis, David Levine, and Les and Brenda Carter at the King Center in Atlanta; Tom Shick, James Hutson, and Sylvia Render at the Library of Congress in Washington; Chuck Elston, Phil Runkel, and Tracy Muench at the Marquette University Library Archives; John E. Harkins at the Memphis/Shelby County Public Library Archives; Eleanor McKay, Marcy Kinkennon, and Louisa Bowen at Memphis State University's Brister Library; Montgomery County, Alabama, District Attorney Johnny Evans; Nancy Breschler at Princeton University's Mudd Library; Eva Mosely, Kathy Kraft, and Jane Knowles at Radcliffe College's Schlesinger Library; Walter Naegle and Harriet Siani at the A. Philip Randolph Institute; Father Irenaeus Herscher at the St. Bonaventure University Library; Howard Dodson and Robert Morris at the Schomburg Center of the New York Public Library; Harold Miller, Josephine Harper, George Talbot, and Keene Tomsyck at the State Historical Society in Madison, Wisconsin; Bernice Nichols, Jean Soderland, Wilma Moshelder, Mary Ellen Clark, Eleanor Barr, and Barbara Addison at the Swarthmore College Peace Collection; Feay Shellman, Sheri Sterling, (and Fred Baldwin) at the Telfair Academy in Savannah; Sara Harwell at the Tennessee State Library and Archives; Elizabeth Alexander and Stephen Kerber at the University of Florida Library in Gainesville; Mary Ann Bamberger and Terry Littman at the University of Illinois at Chicago Library; Luke Swindler, Mitch Ducey, Richard Shrader, Randy Wall, and Faye Phillips of the University of North Carolina Library; Paul E. Camp of the University of South Florida Library in Tampa; Warner Pflug at Wayne State University's Reuther Library; Arthur Charpentier at the Yale University Law School Library; Jane Gordon, Clerk of the U.S. District Court for the Middle District of Alabama in Montgomery; and Gladys Dimmick in the Durham office of U.S. Circuit Judge J. Dickson Phillips, Jr.

Although I first began research for this volume in the winter of 1978–1979 while still in graduate school at Duke University, much of the early reading and research was carried out during 1979–1980 at the Institute for Advanced Study in Princeton, N.J., where I owe special thanks to Clifford Geertz, Peggy Clarke, and Catherine Rhubart. During my four years on the faculty of the University of North Carolina, Charles Phillips, Catherine Hawes, Thad and Pat Beyle, Colin Palmer, and Lou Lipsitz were especially helpful and supportive friends; Betsy Taylor, Debbie Crowder, and Doris Atwater also gave repeated assistance.

My time as a Visiting Fellow at the Joint Center for Political Studies in Washington was especially pleasant, and I recall with special fondness Eleanor Farrah, Milton Morris, Ed Dorn, Armand Derfner, Cathy Iino, Debbie Rivers, Mary Nathan, Tom Cavanagh, and Lorn Foster. Here in New York at City College, Gardenia Hobbs, Barbara Blair, and Marilyn

Santomauro have been repeatedly helpful. At JCA Literary Agency, the late John Cushman, whom I mourn greatly, plus Jane Cushman, Jane Wilson, and Kris Dahl have given substantial assistance. At William Morrow & Company, Elizabeth Terhune, Tom Dolgenos, and my editor, Bruce Lee, have assisted this book on its way. Sonia Greenbaum did a thorough and excellent job of copyediting the manuscript.

There are also many, many friends and acquaintances who have provided assistance or sounding boards over these past five years. They include Irwin Abrams, Bro Adams, Renata Adler, Alan Anderson, John Ansbro, Ray Arsenault, Marian Ash, Judy Baer, Lewis Baldwin, Bill Banks, Bill and Holly Barnard, Jack Bass, Fred Battle, Joan Beifuss, Roy Bennett, Marshall Berman, Merle Black, Rhoda Blumberg, Jean Claude Boffard, Harry Boyte, Carl Brauer, Jacquelyn Braveboy-Wagner, David Brothers, Bernard O. Brown, Mavis Bryant, Paul Burstein, Jim Button, Tony Cappadona, Lawrence E. Carter, Doug Cassel, Bill Chafe, David Chalmers, Julius Chambers, Alex Charns, David Colby, Walt Conser, Greg Craig, Mary Cronquist, Julius Debro, Pam DeLargy and Craig Calhoun, Bogdan Denitch, Tom Dent, John Dittmer, Kelly Dowe, Charles Eagles, Adam Fairclough, Susan R. Falb, George Felkenes, Alex Field, Alan Fiellin, Leon Fink, Peter and Barbara Fish, Ben Franklin, Robert Brank Fulton, Jim Gallagher, Joyce Gelb, Tom Gentile, Hugh Gloster, Bea Gomez, Armando Gutierrez, Sheldon Hackney, Mary Hahn, John Hallowell, Rick Halpern, Virginia Hamilton, Henry Hampton, James Hanigan, Larry and Diane Hanks, John Herbers, Joe Herzenberg, Robert Hill, Sam Hill, Paul Hoch, Gerry Horwitz, Robert Hoyt, Jack Jacobson, Marie Stokes Jemison, Craig Jenkins, Charles Kaiser, Craig Kaplan, Alecia Kaplow, Tom Karis, Harvey Klehr, Ethel Klein, Ted Kornweibel, Neil Kotler, Randall Kryn, Steve Lawson, Harry Lazer, Chiquita Lee, Dallas Lee, Richard Lentz, Bill Leuchtenburg, Ralph Levering, Betty Levinson, Andrew and Bea Levison, Leonard Levy, John Lewis, Walter Lippincott, Worth Long, Steve Longenecker, Andrea Low, Townsend Ludington, Mark Lynch, Pat Lynch, Arline McCord, Juliette McGinnis-Nelson, George McKenna, George and Cecily Deegan McMillan, Neil McMillan, Linda McMurry, Ray MacNair, Jim and Nancy MacRae, Diane McWhorter, Steve Mastrofski, Cynthia Maude-Gembler, Judy Miller (and Bill Bartlett), Serge Molla, J. Kenneth Morland, Walter Naegle, Barry Nakell, Syd Nathans, Jim and Selaine Neidel, Jeff Norrell, Jack Novik, Tony Oberschall, David and Jane Hoyt Oliver, Ken O'Reilly, Gary Orfield, Nell Painter, David Paletz, Les Payne, Wayne Pond, J. Stanley Pottinger, Fred Powledge, Bill Preston, David and Lisa Price, George and Stuart Rabinowitz, John Reed, Judy Richardson, Linda Rocawich, Bob and Pat Madden Roth, Hank Sanders, Ned Schneier, Joe Schott, Tony Scott, Reva Seybolt, Susan Shaffer, Quinlan Shea, Bob Shepler, Ken Sherrill, Tom Shick, David Sobel, Leon Spencer, Barbara Stearns, Judith Stein, Paul Stekler, Mark Stern, Ed Still, Steve Suitts, Catherine Taylor and Rob Dean, Allen Tullos, Jack Walker, Lee Walker,

Jim Washington, Frank Watkins, Denton Watson, Pat Watters, Paul Wehr, Harold Weisberg, Nancy Weiss, Randall Williams, Charles R. Wilson, Kathryn T. Windham, Lawrence Wofford, Peter Wood, Virgil Wood, Linda Young, and Ira Zepp. I am certain there must be others whom I should include as well.

J. Mills and Brenda Thornton have several times been gracious hosts in Montgomery, and Mills's painstaking reading of the first three chapters of this book has given me the benefit of counsel and correction from our most knowledgeable scholar of Montgomery politics and the bus boycott.

Finally, five people in particular deserve special citation for their help and counsel, for without any one of them this would not be as good a book as it is. James David Barber has been a supportive and loyal advisor and sponsor since I first embarked on the idea of this book in late 1978. Deborah Louise Cook, director of the King Center's Library and Archives since 1980, has done as much over the past six years as anyone ever likely will to ensure that the full historical record of Dr. King and the movement is preserved and made available to all. Without her help, this book would be a far less rich account; without her invaluable contributions to the King Center, the long-term course of King scholarship would be distinctly different from the historical blossoming that now lies ahead.

Martha Moutré Kinney has put more time into this manuscript than anyone besides me; her line-by-line pruning has strengthened its clarity and flow and kept its length within manageable bounds. James H. Cone, at Union Theological Seminary in New York, has done more to strengthen and reinforce my commitment to and understanding of Martin King than any other person; our proximity these past two years has afforded me a tremendously valuable and stimulating opportunity for collegial discussions of Martin King's spiritual strength, political message, and prophetic role. Lastly, Susan Foster Newcomer has given more aid than anyone in seeing this book through to completion. To everyone noted above, and to these five people in particular, I am deeply thankful. It has been the most pleasant and fulfilling endeavor one could ever hope for.

Notes

Chapter One

1. Parks Interviews (Horton; Britton; Greenlee; Blackside; Wigginton & Thrasher); Parks interviews in Schulke, *King*, p. 25, Selby, *Odyssey*, pp. 54–57, Raines, *My Soul*, pp. 40–42, Thomas, *Like It Is*, pp. 46–53; Parks et al., "Montgomery Story," 8/21/56, HTSA; *MA* 12/2/55, p. A9; *A1aJ* 12/2/55, p. C6; Hackney, "Montgomery," pp. 3–4; Montgomery Police Department arrest reports, 12/1/55, in *Browder* v. *Gayle* file; *Parks* v. *City of Montgomery*, A1a. Ct. Appeals Vol. 1188, Case #4459; *AA* 3/3/56, p. 1; Parks, *Southern Courier*, 12/11–12/65, p. 1; *CT* 11/30/75; *LAS* 4/11/68, p. C6; *USA Today* 2/11/85, p. D3; Thornton, "Challenge," p. 163; Yeakey, "Montgomery," pp. 249–62. Also see Greenfield, "Parks"; Brown, "Parks"; Stevenson, "Parks"; & Sterne, *Dream*, pp. 94–115, the last two of which are undependable.

2. Nixon Interviews (Smith; Lewis; Joseph; Barton; Lumpkin; Viorst; Garrow; Long; Adams; Wigginton); Clifford & Virginia Durr Interview (Lumpkin); Clifford Durr Interviews (Smith; Sargent); Virginia Durr to Myles & Zilphia Horton, 1/30/56 & 2/24/56, HLW 11; Virginia Durr Interviews (Smith; Porter; Long; Blackside; Barnard; Brown); Rosa Parks to Myles Horton, 2/22/56, HLW 22; Parks Interviews (Britton; Greenlee; Blackside; Wigginton & Thrasher); Parks in Thomas, *Like It Is*, pp. 46–53; Parks et al., "Montgomery Story," n. 1 above; Septima Clark Interviews (Wood; Roth); Barnard, *Outside*, pp. 278–81; Gilliam, "Montgomery," pp. 3–7; Mohr, "Journey," p. 51; Parks Papers; Austin, "Behind the Boycott"; Hartstein, "Montgomery," pp. 43–46; Selby, *Odyssey*, pp. 56–59; Hackney, "Montgomery," pp. 7–8; Yeakey, "Montgomery," p. 263; Gardner, "Montgomery Interviews"; Raines, *My Soul*, pp. 38–45; *CT* 12/1/75, p. 5. Just before attending the workshop, Mrs. Parks wrote Highlander's Henry F. Shipherd that she was "hoping to make a contribution to the fulfillment of complete freedom for all people." 7/6/55, HLW 22. In 1900, when segregation was first imposed on Montgomery streetcars, blacks mounted a summer boycott until the ordinance was clarified to specify that no person had to give up one seat unless another was available. See Thornton, "Challenge," p. 188; Barnes, *Journey*, pp. 11–12; and Meier & Rudwick, "The Boycott Movement."

3. Robinson Interviews (Garrow; Blackside); Robinson, "Montgomery Story," pp. 2–7, 24; Robinson to Gayle, 5/21/54, in "Complaint File," MCDA; Hartstein, "Montgomery," pp. 18–20, 31–35, 47; Burks Interview (Garrow); Millner, "Montgomery," pp. 108–109; Giddings, *When and Where,* p. 264, which is undependable. Throughout the early 1950s the black leadership also often discussed how to improve upon Montgomery's segregated parks and recreation facilities. See Yeakey, "Montgomery," pp. 158–67; *BW* 7/22/55, p. 1; & Thornton, "Challenge," pp. 175–76.

4. Nixon Interviews (Smith; Lumpkin; Viorst; Garrow); Robinson Interviews (Garrow; Blackside); Robinson, "Montgomery Story," pp. 16–26; Burks Interview (Garrow); Fred Gray Interviews (Garrow; Lumpkin); Hartstein, "Montgomery," pp. 36–42, 47–50; Montgomery Police Department arrest reports, 3/2/55, in *Browder* v. *Gayle* file; *MA* 3/19/55, p. A7; *A1aJ* 3/19/55, p. B5; Virginia Durr to Curtiss MacDougall, 4/11/55, VFD 4-56, Durr to Clark Foreman, 4/25/55, & to Clark & Mairi Foreman, 5/10/55, VFD 2-27; Virginia Durr

Interviews (Barnard; Garrow); Durr to Garrow, 1/5/80; Colvin's 5/11/56 testimony in *Browder*, transcript pp. 17–26; Durr to Clark Foreman, 12/7/55, VFD 2-30; Valien, "Montgomery," pp. 125–26; Yeakey, "Montgomery," pp. 231–45; Millner, "Montgomery," pp. 110–16; Parks et al., "Montgomery Story," n. 1 above; Irene West Interview (Barton); J. H. Bagley, "Complaints," 5/4/55, & "This is for Monday, December 5, 1955" leaflet, both in "Complaint File," n. 3 above. King later stressed how crucial this leafletting was. "I'm sure that if we had had discussions a week earlier about setting up a bus boycott, we never would have had a boycott." *CSM* 1/16/62, p. 4.

   5. Nixon Interviews (Smith; Lewis; Joseph; Barton; Lumpkin; Viorst; Garrow; Wigginton); Nixon, "How It All Started"; *Southern Courier* 12/11–12/65, p. 5; *Militant* 12/20/65, p. 8; Raines, *My Soul*, pp. 45–46; *Marietta Daily Journal* 4/26/82; Selby, *Odyssey*, pp. 59–62; Abernathy, "Natural History," pp. 10–12, 19–20; Abernathy Interview (Smith); Abernathy in Cotton, "Conversation," & in Conconi, "Interview"; King, *Stride*, pp. 44–49; Smith, "King," pp. 89–90; Hartstein, "Montgomery," pp. 52–58; Coretta King, *My Life*, pp. 113–14; Pierce Interview (Lumpkin); Pierce in Parks et al., "Montgomery Story," n. 1 above. On Nixon also see Maxine Streety, *Profile of Dr. E. D. Nixon* (Montgomery: n.p., n.d. [ca. 1979]), & Joe Azbell, "The Man Who Made M. L. King," *Montgomery Independent* 1/30/75. Also note Thornton's telling comments in *Alabama Review* 32 (7/79): 232–34, and Reddick's observations in *Crusader*, pp. 125–26.

   6. "This is for Monday" leaflet, n. 4 above; Nixon Interviews (Smith; Lewis; Barton; Garrow; Adams); Azbell Interviews (Brown; Blackside); Henry F. Bedford, *Trouble Downtown* (New York: Harcourt Brace, 1978), pp. 141–42; *A1aJ* 12/3/55, p. 1; *MA* 12/4/55, p. A1, 12/5/55, p. A1; Gilliam, "Montgomery," p. 26; Abernathy, "Natural History," pp. 19–20; Abernathy Interview (Smith); Abernathy in Cotton, "Conversation"; King, *Stride*, pp. 46–49; Pierce Interview (Lumpkin); Lewis Interviews (Barton; Lumpkin; Smith; Garrow); Millner, "Montgomery," p. 150; *PC Magazine* 11/9/57, p. 1; Gray Interviews (Garrow; Lumpkin); Hartstein, "Montgomery," pp. 23–25, 55, 59; Stevenson, *Montgomery*, pp. 17–18.

   7. King, *Stride*, pp. 53–55; *A1aJ* 12/5/55, p. A1; Nixon Interviews (Lewis; Barton; Garrow); Selby, *Odyssey*, pp. 60–61; Raines, *My Soul*, pp. 46–48; Abernathy, "Natural History," pp. 20, 29; Abernathy Interviews (Smith; Blackside); Abernathy in Cotton, "Conversation"; French, "Beginnings," pp. 37–39; Hartstein, "Montgomery," pp. 67–69.

   8. Abernathy, "Natural History," pp. 29–32, 40; Abernathy Interview (Smith); Abernathy in Cotton, "Conversation"; King, *Stride*, pp. 55–58; Nixon Interviews (Barton; Garrow; Wigginton); U. J. Fields, MIA Minutes, 12/5/55, exhibit #44 in *State* v. *King*, Montgomery Co. Circuit Ct. #7399, transcript p. 334; Lewis Interviews (Lumpkin; Barton; Garrow; Brown; Blackside); Gray Interviews (Lewis; Lumpkin); Mohr, "Journey," pp. 52–54; Selby, *Odyssey*, pp. 61–62; Smith, "King," pp. 93–94, & Smith, "King: In the Beginning," pp. 9–11; Peters, *Southern Temper*, p. 180; Hartstein, "Montgomery," pp. 63–64; Millner, "Montgomery," p. 151; Yeakey, "Montgomery," pp. 313–22; *AC* 1/19/86, p. S2. In a 1/1/58 interview King told Mohr "I was surprised to be elected . . . both from the standpoint of my age, but more from the fact that I was a newcomer to Montgomery." "Journey," p. 54. Early MIA notes usually refer to King as "chairman" rather than "president."

   9. King, "Address," 12/5/55, in Keele, "Burkeian Analysis," pp. 299–303; King's eight-item, handwritten program outline on the back of a half-page mimeographed boycott leaflet, King's annotated three-page copy of the "Resolutions," and a two-page carbon to the "Honorable Commissioners" entitled "The Negro Protest Against the Montgomery City Lines," all in MLK 1-38; *BW* 12/13/55, p. 1; *AT* 12/16/55 p. 1; Abernathy, "Natural History," pp. 23–25, 32–33; King, *Stride*, pp. 58–64; Hartstein, "Montgomery," pp. 79–80; Smith, "King," pp. 102–107, and Smith, "King: In the Beginning," p. 12; Yeakey, "Montgomery," pp. 332–34.

10. *MA* 12/6/55, p. A1, 12/7/55, pp. A1, A4; *AIaJ* 12/6/55, p. A1, 12/7/55, p. A13; Mohr, "Journey," pp. ii–iv; FBI Mobile to Director, 12/7/55, & Director to Asst. Attorney General William Tompkins, 12/14/55, both 100-135-61-3; SAC Mobile to Director, 12/9/55, & Director to Tompkins, 12/16/55, both 100-135-61-4.

11. King, *Stride,* pp. 71–75, 108; Robinson, "Montgomery Story," p. 62; Thrasher, "Meeting of the Board . . .," 12/7/55, SRC 1-67-13; Thrasher, "Alabama's Bus Boycott"; Gilliam, "Montgomery," p. 71; Hughes letter in *MA* 12/13/55, p. A4; *ACHR Newsletter* 12/55, p. 3; Hughes Interview (Garrow); Thompson, "History," pp. 36–38, 76–81.

12. King, *Stride,* pp. 109–13; *AIaJ* 12/8/55, p. A1; *MA* 12/9/55, p. A1; Thrasher, "Alabama's Bus Boycott"; MIA Minutes, 12/8/55, in *State* v. *King,* transcript pp. 335–36, n. 8 above; Gray Interviews (Garrow; Lumpkin); Robinson Interview (Garrow); King, "Statement of Negro Citizens on Bus Situation," n.d., MLK 1; Robert Johnson Interview (Britton); Crenshaw Interview (Garrow); Abernathy, "Natural History," p. 33; "Negroes Map Plans . . .," 12/12/55, CAB 387-1; Thornton, "Challenge," pp. 204–205; Hartstein, "Montgomery," pp. 108–109, 134. A year later King wrote that "the intolerable behavior of a prominent member of the white group was largely responsible for prolonging the protest. In fact, considerable tension arose from his initial intransigence. At the beginning we felt that this gentleman treated us rather rudely." *Liberation* 12/56, pp. 6–9.

13. Cotton, "A Conversation," p. 26; Abernathy Interview (Blackside); King, *Stride,* pp. 75–80; MIA to National City Lines, n.d. [12/8/55], MLK 1; Robinson, "Montgomery Story," p. 86; Robinson Interview (Garrow); *MA* 12/8/55, pp. A1, A4; *BW* 12/13/55, p. 1; T. J. Jemison Interview (Barton); *NYT* 6/16/53, p. 15, 6/21/53, p. 65; Morris, *Origins,* pp. 17–25; Barnes, *Journey,* p. 117; King's program outline, handwritten on pink paper, MLK 1-38.

14. *AIaJ* 12/9/55, p. A1, 12/10/55, p. A1, 12/12/55, p. A7, 12/14/55. p. C4; *MA* 12/10/55, p. A1, 12/11/55, p. A1; 12/13/55, p. A2; Walton, "Walking City, I."

15. Robinson Interview (Garrow); *MA* 12/9/55, p. A4, 12/12/55, p. A4, 12/15/55, p. A4; *AA* 12/17/55, p. 1; and King's annotated 12/15/55 mass meeting program ("The papers reveal that we have many whites with us"), MLK 1-38. Less than two years later Morgan committed suicide. Virginia Durr to Clark Foreman, 7/22/57, VFD 2-29.

16. Patton to Wilkins et al., "Montgomery . . .," 12/19/55, NAACP III-B-192; King, *Stride,* pp. 113–14; *MA* 12/14/55, p. B2, 12/15/55, p. E4, 12/16/55, p. A8; *AIaJ* 12/15/55, p. D2, 12/16/55, p. A2; *BW* 12/16/55, p. 1, 12/20/55, p. 1; *PC* 12/17/55, p. 3; *AA* 12/24/55, p. 1.

17. *MA* 12/17/55, p. A1, 12/18/55, p. A1, 12/19/55, p. A1, 12/20/55, p. A1; *AIaJ* 12/17/55, p. A1, 12/19/55, p. A1; Thrasher, "Alabama's Bus Boycott"; *BW* 12/20/55, p. 1, 12/23/55, pp. 1, 6; *AA* 12/24/55, p. 1; *ACHR Newsletter* 12/55, p. 3; Yeakey, "Montgomery," pp. 445–49; Gilliam, "Montgomery," pp. 72–87; King, *Stride,* pp. 114–21; Robinson, "Montgomery Story," pp. 72–78; Crenshaw Interview (Garrow).

18. *AIaJ* 12/19/55, p. A1, 12/22/55, p. A1; *BW* 12/23/55, p. 1, 12/27/55, p.1, 12/30/55, p. 1; *MA* 12/21/55, p. A1, 12/23/55, p. A1, 12/25/55; Negro Ministers of Montgomery et al., "To the Montgomery Public," n.d., MLK 1; *AA* 12/31/55, p. 1; SAC Mobile to Director, 12/21/55, & Director to Tompkins, 1/4/56, both 100-135-61-5. Jackson's stories are an invaluable and never-before-tapped source. On Jackson, see Suggs, *Black Press,* pp. 44–46; on Montgomery's white newspapers, see Daniel W. Hollis III, *An Alabama Newspaper Tradition* (University: University of Alabama Press, 1983), pp. 102–110.

19. *BW* 12/23/55, p. 6; Reddick, *Crusader,* p. 133, & "Boycott," p. 109; King, *Stride,* pp. 84–85; "To the Montgomery Public," n. 18 above. As King explained it in 1958, "The spirit of passive resistance came to me from the Bible and the teaching of Jesus. The technique of execution came from Gandhi. . . . After all . . . the Negroes of Montgomery had known about Christian love long before they even heard of Gandhi." Mohr, "Journey," p. 81.

20. King, Sr., *Daddy King,* pp. 13–22, 58–139; Mrs. King's taped remarks, 1/18/73, KC; Esther M. Smith, "A History of Ebenezer Baptist Church . . . ," 3/56, MLK 1; Farris, "Young Martin," p. 56; Reddick, *Crusader,* pp. 5, 24–54; Peters, "Our Weapon," p. 71; King, "An Autobiography of Religious Development," n.d. [ca. 1949], MLK, in Warren, "Rhetorical Study," pp. 269–84; King, *Stride,* pp. 18–19; Christine King Farris Interview (Brown); *NYP* 4/8/57, pp. 4, 42; *CST* 1/21/63, pp. 16, 29; Bennett, *What Manner,* pp. 7–8, 19; Baugh Interviews (Garrow; Joseph); Joseph, *Good Times,* pp. 297–300; Thomas Kilgore Interview (Garrow); Lewis, *King,* pp. 7–8. On the question of King's name, the most dependable account is one given Ted Poston (*NYP* 4/8/57, p. 4) by King, Sr.:

> I had been known as Michael Luther King or "Mike" up until I was 22 . . . when one day my father, James Albert King, told me: 'You aren't named Mike or Michael either. Your name is Martin Luther King. Your mother just called you Mike for short.' I was elated to know that I had really been named for the great leader of the Protestant Reformation, but there was no way of knowing if papa had made a mistake after all. Neither of my parents could read or write and they kept no record of Negro births in our backwoods county. . . . I gladly accepted Martin Luther King as my real name and when M.L. was born, I proudly named him Martin Luther King, Jr. But it was not until 1934, when I was seeking my first passport . . . that I found out that Dr. Johnson, who delivered M.L., had listed him in the city records as Michael Luther King, Jr., because he still thought that was my real name.

Presently available records do not verify any formal name change for either King. On black Atlanta and the Auburn community of King's youth, see Alexander, "Negro Business in Atlanta"; Meier & Lewis, "Negro Upper Class"; & Vowels, "Atlanta Negro Business."

21. Williams Interview (Garrow); King, "Autobiography," & Mrs. King Tape, n. 20 above; Reddick, *Crusader,* pp. 53–60; Farris, "Young Martin," pp. 56–57; Downing, *To See,* chs. 3 & 6; Peters, "Our Weapon," p. 72; Bennett, *What Manner,* pp. 18–19; *NYP* 4/8/57, pp. 4, 42, 4/10/57, pp. 4, 65; Garrow interviews with Baugh, James R. Jones & John Gibson; Ella Mae Gaines Sydnor, "Martin Luther King, the Boy, as I Knew Him," 2/17/65, SCLC 5; King, Sr., *Daddy King,* p. 109; King, *Playboy* 1/65, p. 66; Lewis, *King,* pp. 12–16. Speaking of the bus trip years later, King said, "That was the beginning of my determination to lead a bus boycott." *BS* 6/20/65, p. D3, & *WES* 6/20/65, p. C2.

22. King, Sr., *Daddy King,* pp. 107–109; King, *Stride,* pp. 20–22, 90; Farris, "Young Martin," p. 57; Reddick, *Crusader,* pp. 55–60; King, "Autobiography" & Mrs. King Tape, n. 20 above; King, "Face to Face Interview," 10/29/61, KP; Farris Interview (Brown); Bennett, *What Manner,* p. 20; *NYP* 4/8/57, pp. 4, 42, 4/9/57, pp. 4, 36; *PC* 6/29/57, p. 7; *AA* 10/24/64, p. 2; Proctor Interview (Brown); Oliver "Sack" Jones Interview (Holmes); *Time* 2/18/57, p. 18; Lewis interviews with Carrie Harper, India Amos & Beulah Lewis. Although some accounts of King's teenage years portray him as a nonviolent youngster, neighborhood friends reject that portrait. "That's bullshit. He was not a nonviolent teenager." John Gibson Interview (Garrow).

23. Reddick, *Crusader,* pp. 61–74; Mays, *Born,* p. 265; Charles V. Willie, "A Journey in Faith . . ."; Garrow interviews with Willie, Robert Williams, Larry

Williams, Elliott Finley & James Jones; Holmes interviews with McCall, Kennedy & Herman F. Bostick; Proctor Interview (Brown); Smith interviews with Chandler & N. P. Tillman; *NYP* 4/10/57, pp. 4, 65; King, *AN* 5/22/65, p. 14; Peters, "Our Weapon," p. 72; *PC* 4/14/56, p. 6; *NJG* 4/21/56, p. 1; Garrow conversation with Kelsey; Bennett, *What Manner,* p. 27; Samuel Williams Interview (Lewis) & Williams in CBS, "Some Friends . . .," 4/7/68; Mays Interviews (Lewis; Newton; Britton); Beifuss et al. interviews with Russell Sugarmon & Maxine Smith; B. R. Brazeal Interview (Barton); Smith, "King," pp. 22–24; Lewis, *King,* pp. 22–24; King "Autobiography," n. 20 above. "I had doubts that religion was intellectually respectable," King later told an interviewer. "I revolted against the emotionalism of Negro religion, the shouting and the stomping. I didn't understand it and it embarrassed me." Peters, "The Man," p. 94, & "Our Weapon," p. 72. On King's favorite sociology professor, Walter Chivers, see Charles Willie's profile in *Phylon* 9/82, pp. 242–48.

24. The principal interracial group was the Intercollegiate Council and Forum, a "tea and discussion" group which alternated its monthly meetings between Emory University and the Atlanta University colleges. It featured rather formal interactions. Emory Via Interview (Garrow); King's Morehouse transcript, KC; King, "Autobiography" & Mrs. King Tape, n. 20 above; Reddick, *Crusader,* pp. 73–76; *NYP* 4/10/57, pp. 4, 65; King, Sr., in Schulke, *King,* pp. 114–15; King Interview (Smith); King, Sr., to Charles E. Batten, 3/5/48, King to Crozer Theological Seminary, 10/27/47, & Batten to King, 10/29/47, KP. Regarding his "feeling of resentment," King later said that "I don't think it ever went to the point of being an extreme bitterness, but it was certainly a resentment where I for a period just felt like all white people were bad." Calling it "a temporary experience," King added that "it was never something that took its toll in terms of damaging my whole personality and giving me an eternal bitterness and hate." Wallace, "Self-Portrait of a Symbol, III," *NYP* 2/15/61, p. 42. Emmett Proctor recalls going to Connecticut with King for the summer of 1944 (Brown Interview), but the best present evidence indicates that King spent both that summer and the 1947 one, between his junior and senior years, at a Simsbury tobacco farm. Farris, "Young Martin," p. 58.

25. King, Sr., to Batten, 3/5/48, Mays to Batten, 2/28/48, Brazeal to Batten, 3/23/48, Kelsey to Batten, 3/12/48, King, "Application . . .," n.d. [ca. early 2/48], Lucius Tobin to Batten, 2/25/48, & Mrs. John W. Burney to Batten, 3/9/48, all in KP; King, "Autobiography," n. 20 above. Ten years later, King's memory was remarkably consistent: "My call to the ministry was neither dramatic nor spectacular. It came neither by some miraculous vision nor by some blinding light experience on the road of life. Moreover, it did not come as a sudden realization. Rather, it was a response to an inner urge that gradually came upon me. This urge expressed itself in a desire to serve God and humanity, and the feeling that my talent and my commitment could best be expressed through the ministry." That urge had remained while he considered first medicine and then the law. "During my senior year in college I finally decided to accept the challenge to enter the ministry. I came to see that God had placed a responsibility upon my shoulders and the more I tried to escape it the more frustrated I would become. A few months after preaching my first sermon, I entered theological seminary." King, "Statement . . .," 8/7/59, MLK 3.

26. Batten to King, 4/27/48, King's Crozer transcript, KP; Smith & Zepp, *Search,* pp. 13–21; Crozer *Bulletin* 41 (1/49) & 42 (1/50); Garrow interviews with Jordan, Stewart, Whitaker, Wood, Pyle, Walter Stark, Jack Bullard & Kenneth Smith; McCall Interview (Holmes); Barbour Interview (Lewis); Barbour, "Meditations"; *NYP* 4/9/57, pp. 4, 36, 4/10/57, pp. 4, 65; Reddick, *Crusader,* pp. 77–83; King, *Stride,* p. 95; Lewis, *King,* pp. 26–33; Hanigan, "Shaping" & *King,* pp. 116–18; Witherspoon, *King,* p. 9; Robinson, *Abraham,* pp. 277–78; King's

University of Pennsylvania Graduate School transcript, KP. King's girl friend was Betty Moitz, whose mother Hannah was the seminary's cook.

27. Smith, "Reflections"; Crozer *Bulletin* 43 (1/51) & 44 (1/52); Zepp, "Intellectual Sources," pp. 11–17; Smith & Zepp, *Search,* pp. 21–45, 71–97 & "King's Vision," p. 361; Barbour Interview (Lewis); Smith Interviews (Lewis; Garrow); Lewis, *King,* p. 354; Whitaker Interview (Garrow); Crozer Placement Committee evaluations, 8/23/50, 11/15/50 & 2/4/51, plus "Fieldwork Questionnaire" & Gardner rating sheet, KP; Garrow conversations with Mrs. Matilda Sims, Mrs. Bessie Gardner & Rev. Richard Gay; *NYT* 6/8/74, p. 34; Barbour, "Meditations"; King, "Autobiography," n. 20 above; King in *Christian Century* 4/13/60, pp. 439–41; King, *Stride,* pp. 91–92, 97–100; Reddick, *Crusader,* p. 79; Niebuhr, *Moral Man,* pp. 163, 210; Niebuhr, "Walter Rauschenbusch," p. 533. Rauschenbusch's major books were *Christianity and the Social Crisis* (New York: Macmillan, 1907), *Christianizing the Social Order* (New York: Macmillan, 1912) & *A Theology for the Social Gospel* (New York: Macmillan, 1917).

28. King, *Stride,* pp. 95–97; Stewart Interview (Garrow); Smith & Zepp, *Search,* pp. 47–69; King, "War and Pacifism," n.d. [ca. spring 1951], MLK 15; King in *Peace News* 1/31/58, p. 2, & *Hindustan Times* 1/30/58; Placement Committee evaluations, n. 27 above, including those by Batten & Raymond J. Bean; Enslin to Chester M. Alter, 12/14/50, KP; Reddick, *Crusader,* pp. 75–76, 80–81, 86–87; O. S. Rankin to King, 12/15/50, MLK 15; Warren, "Rhetorical Study," p. 85; Mrs. King, Sr., to Batten, 5/10/51, KP; *ADW* 5/20/51, p. 2, 6/30/51, p. 4; King to Batten, 6/1/51, Batten to King, 6/4/51, & Batten to Chester Alter, 6/4/51, all KP. Regarding the Johnson lecture, King recalled in 1958 that "my interest was purely academic . . . Gandhi had taken the ethic of love to the level of social strategy, but I never thought I would be involved in a social movement where this would be used." Mohr, "Journey," pp. 80–81.

29. King, *Stride,* pp. 100–101; *NYP* 4/11/57, pp. 4, 46; Reddick, *Crusader,* pp. 87–90, 104–106; Bennett, "The King Plan," p. 68; Smith & Zepp, *Search,* pp. 99–118, 123–25; King, "How Modern Christians Should Think of Man," n.d., MLK 15; Sandon, "Boston University Personalism"; Steinkraus, "King's Personalism," p. 103; Cornish Rogers Interview (Garrow); Coretta Scott, "Why I Came to College"; Coretta King, *My Life,* pp. 51–57; Coretta King Interview (Mayerson III, pp. 32–34, 41–47, 51–55); King, Sr., *Daddy King,* p. 147.

30. Reddick, *Crusader,* pp. 106–107; Coretta King, *My Life,* pp. 60–67; Coretta King Interview (Mayerson III, pp. 46, 64); Zepp, "Intellectual Sources," pp. 272–78; Smith & Zepp, *Search,* pp. 114–18; DeWolf, "King as Theologian," p. 8; King to Batten, 7/29/52, and King's BU transcript, KP; King, "Reinhold Niebuhr's Ethical Dualism," 5/9/52, MLK 15, pp. 4, 6, 11, 14. King added that "the more aggressively one relates the gospel to life, the more sensitively he realizes that the social unit can accommodate only justice, not agape" (p. 5). More than a dozen of King's graduate papers, including those named earlier plus another simply titled "Reinhold Niebuhr," can be found in MLK 15.

31. Coretta King, *My Life,* pp. 67–75, 89; Coretta King Interviews (Smith; Mayerson III, pp. 52–54, 57, 60); *ADW* 6/20/53, p. 3, 6/27/53, p. 3, 7/4/53, p. 3; King, Sr., *Daddy King,* pp. 148–51; Reddick, *Crusader,* pp. 106–108; DeWolf, "King," pp. 19–21; DeWolf, "In Memoriam," pp. 1–2; DeWolf Interviews (Britton; Lewis); Carberg, "The Story"; *Montreal Gazette* 2/25/67; Rogers, Dialectical Society Minutes, n.d. [ca. early 4/54]; Garrow interviews with Rogers & Major Jones; Rogers, "Foundation"; Walter Muelder, *Boston University Currents* 4/1/70, pp. 1, 8. Also see Muelder, "Philosophical"; Muelder in Paul Deats, Jr., ed., *Toward a Discipline of Social Ethics* (Boston: Boston University Press, 1972), pp. 295–320; and Muelder's "Martin Luther King's Ethics of Nonviolent Action," unpublished paper, 1985, all of which fail to grasp the evolution of King's views concerning Niebuhr. Rogers notes that King "became more monogamous" after meeting Coretta and that following their marriage "he did appear to be monogamous." (Garrow Interview) Rogers also points out that King "was eager to learn systems of thought about God which he could connect with to rationalize and fill out his own inclinations—inclinations shaped by his experiences." As King wrote his former Crozer professor, George W. Davis, "When Schleiermacher stressed the primacy of experience over any external authority he was sounding a note that continues to ring in my own experience." Rogers, "Foundation"; King to Davis, 12/1/53, author's files.

32. King, *Stride,* pp. 16–17; Coretta King, *My Life,* pp. 94–97; Mays, *Born,* p. 266; Mays Interviews (Lewis; Newton); B. R. Brazeal Interview (Barton); King Interview (Smith); Nesbitt Interviews (Garrow; Barton; Long); Bennett, *What Manner,* p. 49; Reddick, *Crusader,* pp. 108–109; G. A. Key to King, 1/12/54, J. T. Brooks to King, 1/16/54, & R. D. Crockett to King, 2/8/54, MLK 15-50; John Thomas Porter Interview (Garrow); *CT* 12/2/75; Yeakey, "Montgomery," pp. 100–11; "Ralph David Abernathy," in *Current Biography Yearbook 1968,* ed., Charles Moritz (New York: H. W. Wilson Co., 1968), pp. 1–4; Abernathy, "My Last Letter" and "The Nonviolent Movement"; *AC* 1/14/78, p. B1; Cotton, "Conversation"; Abernathy in U.S. Congress, House Assassinations Committee, *Hearings,* vol. 1, p. 11 (8/14/78); Lumpkin interviews with Thelma Rice & Fred Gray. The intermediary between King, Sr., and Nesbitt was W. C. Peden, who like Nesbitt worked for the Pilgrim Life & Health Insurance Company. Recalling his first meeting with King, Nesbitt said, "He was a very unassuming young man, very humble, and he had a very easy flow of expression." King's Chattanooga sermon was 1/17/54, and his first Dexter one apparently 1/24/54. Also see Walton, "A Short History," Johns's obituary in *Jet* 7/22/65, and Samuel L. Gandy, ed., *Human Possibilities: A Vernon Johns Reader* (Washington: Hoffman Press, 1977).

33. Reddick, *Crusader,* pp. 109–112; King's BU transcript, KP; King, *Stride,* pp. 17–18, 21–27; Bennett, *What Manner,* p. 49; King Interview (Smith); Coretta King, *My Life,* pp. 97–101; Coretta King Interviews (Mayerson III, p. 65; Blackside); *NYP* 4/11/57, pp. 4, 46; Cotton, "Conversation"; A. A. Banks to King, 2/19/54, R. D. Nesbitt & T. H. Randall to King, 3/7/54, J. C. Parker to King, 3/10/54, Nesbitt to King, 3/15/54, J. T. Brooks to King, 4/15/54, Nesbitt to King 4/19/54 & 5/13/54, all MLK 15-50; Oates, *Trumpet,* p. 49; Garrow interviews with Thomas Kilgore, John Porter & Mary Fair Burks; Robert Nesbitt Interviews (Garrow; Long); King to Benjamin E. Mays, n.d. (ca.10/21/54), BEM I-15; *MA* 10/28/54, and Dexter 10/31/54 installation program, MLK 10-17; King, "Recommendations . . .," 9/54, MLK 10; Social & Political Action Committee Reports #2 (10/17/54) & #3 (10/31/54), and Digests, 1/55 & 6/55, MLK 10; Dexter programs for 6/19/55, 6/26/55 & 7/24/55, MLK 10; King, "A Comparison of the Conceptions of God . . ."; Paul Tillich to King, 9/22/53 & 11/3/54, MLK 15. Several years later King said, "I went back South mainly because I felt that there were great opportunities to transform a section of the country into something rich . . . in spirit and beautiful. . . . I went back mainly because I saw the vast potentials there." Wallace, "Self-Portrait III," n. 24 above.

34. King Interview (Smith); King, *Stride,* pp. 30–42, 120–23; King, "Report . . .," 10/55, in Evans, *Dexter,* pp. 80–94; John Porter Interview (Garrow); Coretta King, *My Life,* pp. 102–107, 110–11; *NYP* 4/12/57, pp. 4, 43; Robert Hughes Interview (Garrow); *ACHR Newsletter* #2, 8/55; Reddick, *Crusader,* pp. 111–12, 133; Hartstein, "Montgomery," pp. 38, 61–62; Nixon Interviews (Lewis; Joseph; Barton; Lumpkin; Garrow); *MA* 7/13/79; Johnnie Carr Interviews (Long; Barton); Millner, "Montgomery," pp. 153, 156; Parks to King, 8/26/55, MLK 15; *BW* 8/19/55, p. 3, 8/23/55, p. 3, 8/26/55, p. 3, 12/27/55, p. 6; Garrow interviews with Ralph & Juanita Abernathy; Ralph Abernathy in Cotton, "Conversation." In mid-October King made a six-day trip to Fort Valley State College in Georgia, where his old friend Walter McCall was dean of men, to speak for religious emphasis week. On 12/30 one Montgomery policeman told a local FBI agent that he had been instructed "to find out all he could about Reverend Martin L. King," and that "he had been requested especially . . . to uncover all the derogatory information he could about King." SAC Mobile to Director, 1/4/56, 100-135-61-7. Two Montgomery officers, Jack Shows and K. W. Jones, even traveled to Atlanta to search for possible dirt, but concluded "he was clean as a hound's tooth." Shows Interview (Garrow).

35. Wilkins to Patton, 12/27/55, & Patton to Gloster Current, "Supplementary Report, Montgomery . . .," n.d. [received 1/3/56], NAACP III-B-192; Wilkins Interviews (Wright; Lewis); Wilkins, *Standing Fast*, p. 228; *MA* 12/29/55, p. A2, 12/30/55, p. B8, 12/31/55, p. A4, 1/4/56, pp. A1, A4, 1/5/56, pp. A1, A4, 1/7/56, pp. A1, A4, 1/8/56, p. B2, 1/9/56, p. A4, 1/10/56, p. A6; *BW* 1/3/56, p. 1, 1/6/56, p. 1, 1/10/56, pp. 1, 6, 1/13/56, p. 1; MIA Finance Committee Report, 1/5/56, MLK 1-38; *AIaJ* 1/7/56, p. A5, 1/9/56, p. A1, 1/10/56, p. A8; Thornton, "Challenge," pp. 210–13, 222–23.

36. *AA* 1/14/56, p. 1; *PC* 1/14/56, p. 2; *MA* 1/10/56, p. A4, 1/11/56, pp. A2, A4, B9, 1/12/56, p. A4, 1/17/56, pp. A4, B5, 1/18/56, p. A1, 1/19/56, p. A2, 1/20/56, p. A7, 1/21/56, p. A1; *BW* 1/17/56, p. 1; *MT* 1/22/56, p. A1, 1/23/56, p. A1; *Lutheran Standard* 2/18/56, pp. 14–15; Graetz Interview (Garrow) & Graetz in Parks et al., "Montgomery Story," n. 1 above; Yeakey, "Montgomery," p. 470; Thornton, "Challenge," pp. 223–24.

37. *MA* 1/19/56, p. A4; *AA* 1/21/56, p. 1; Reddick, *Crusader*, pp. 131, 134; Mohr, "Journey," p. 56; MIA "Strategy Committee Meeting," [1/21/56], MLK 1-38; *BW* 2/7/56, p. 6; Garrow interviews with Graetz, Gray & Robinson; *Ebony* 6/65, p. 166; Abernathy, "Natural History," pp. 13, 18.

38. *MA* 1/22/56, p. A1, 1/24/56, p. A1, 1/25/56, p. A1, 1/26/56, p. A1; *NYT* 1/22/56, p. 68; *ACHR Newsletter* 1/56; Reddick, "Boycott," pp. 113–15; King, *Stride*, pp. 124–27; Rowan, *Go South*, pp. 130–31; *AT* 1/27/56, p. 1; *BW* 1/20/56, p. 1; 1/24/56, p. 1, 1/27/56, p. 1; Robinson, "Montgomery Story," pp. 14–44; Hartstein, "Montgomery," pp. 116–19; Thornton, "Challenge," pp. 213–14. As Mrs. Robinson recalled, "They feared that anything they gave us would be viewed by us as just a start. And you know, they were probably right." Millner, "Montgomery," p. 199.

39. King, *Stride*, pp. 127–35; Coretta King, *My Life*, pp. 123–26; Coretta King Interview (Brown); *AIaJ* 1/27/56, p. B7; *AA* 2/4/56, p. 1; *BW* 1/31/56, p. 1; *PC* 2/4/56, p. 3; *NYT* 1/28/56, p. 36; Abernathy, "Natural History," pp. 16–17; Bishop, *Days*, p. 156; Valien, "Montgomery," p. 119; King, "Thou Fool," 8/27/67, & *Strength*, pp. 106–107; Garrow interviews with Williams, Hunter, Elliott Finley, Robert Graetz, Glenn Smiley, Thomas Kilgore & Gardner Taylor; Kilgore in *LAS* 4/2/70, p. C8; Taylor, *How Shall*, pp. 88–89; Arthur Schweitzer, *The Age of Charisma* (Chicago: Nelson-Hall, 1984), p. 212; *AIaJ* 1/28/56, p. A1; *MA* 1/29/56, p. A2; Mohr, "Journey," p. 72. King later said that "when I was first arrested in Montgomery, I thought I was going to be lynched." Peters, "The Man," p. 96.

40. *MA* 1/27/56, p. A1; *AA* 1/28/56, p. 1; *BW* 1/31/56, p. 1; Reddick, "Boycott," p. 116; Gray Interviews (Garrow; Lumpkin); Nixon Interviews (Joseph; Barton; Adams); Clifford Durr Interview (Sargent); Yeakey, "Montgomery," pp. 497–502; Selby, *Odyssey*, pp. 63–64; Viorst, *Fire*, pp. 46–47; Gray & Langford, *Browder*, "Complaint," n.d.

41. Roscoe and Mary Lucy Williams Interview (Barton); King, *Stride*, pp. 135–40; Abernathy, "Natural History," pp. 59–61; Coretta King, "The World," pp. 36–37; Coretta King, *My Life*, pp. 127–32; Coretta King Interviews (Mayerson I, p. 9; Brown); *MA* 1/31/56, p. A1; Garrow interviews with Robert Williams & Jack Shows; Joe Azbell Interviews (Brown; Blackside); Barnard, *Outside*,

p. 286; Current to Wilkins et al. "Bombing . . .," 1/31/56, NAACP III-B-185; Hurley to Current, "Report . . .," 3/1/56, NAACP III-H-214; *NYT* 2/1/56, p. 64; *PC* 2/11/56, p. 3; *AA* 2/11/56, p. 1; Reddick, *Crusader,* pp. 134–36, 176–77; *NT* 6/18/63, p. 8. Also see Levison Interview (Stein); Kenneth Clark Interview (Leventhal); John Maguire Interview (Garrow); & Davis, *Leadership,* p. 206.

42. *MA* 2/1/56, p. A1, 2/2/56, p. A1, 2/3/56, p. A1, 2/4/56, p. B3, 2/8/56, p. A1, 2/9/56, p. A1; Abernathy, "Natural History," pp. 60–61; King, *Stride,* pp. 140–41; *AA* 2/11/56, p. 1; Roscoe & Mary Lucy Williams Interview (Barton); Richmond Smiley Interview (Barton); Coretta King, "The World," p. 29; Garrow interviews with Coretta King, Robert Williams, Elliott Finley & Fred Gray; Robinson, "Montgomery Story," p. 124; Reddick, "Boycott," p. 116, & *Crusader,* p. 133; *Sepia* 11/67, pp. 48–49; *BW* 2/3/56, p. 1: Nixon Interview (Viorst). Folsom's later assertions that he pressed Gayle to settle the dispute are of uncertain accuracy. See, e.g., Benjamin Muse, "Visit to North Alabama . . . 6/18–28/61," 7/13/61, SRC; *Southern Courier* 4/27–28/68, p. 5; and especially Gilliam, "Montgomery," pp. 96–99. Also see *AIaJ* 3/13/56, p. A1; *BW* 3/1/6/56, p. 1; *PC* 3/24/56, p. 2. As Robert Graetz later described how the MIA leaders coped with the death threats, "All of us on the board regularly discussed the fact that we knew that some of us were going to die, we just didn't know who and when." (Garrow Interview)

43. *MA* 2/9/56, p. A1, 2/14/56, p. A1, 2/15/56, p. A1, 2/19/56, p. A1, 2/20/56, p. A1, 2/21/56, p. A1; Frances Jett, "Proceedings . . .," 2/13/56, UPW 373-6; Eugene Cotton to Ralph Helstein, 2/14/56, Helstein to Cotton, 2/15/56, Richard Durham to Helstein, 2/29/56, & Helstein to Emil Mazey, 3/16/56, UPW 129-6; Bear to William Thetford, 2/15/56, & attachment dated 2/13, MCDA; *AA* 2/18/56, p. 1, 2/25/56, p. 1; *PC* 2/18/56, p. 4, 3/3/56, p. 3; *NYHT* 2/13/56, p. 1; Major Jones to King, 2/28/56, MLK 15; *Jet* 2/16/56, pp. 8–12; *AIaJ* 2/15/56; *CT* 2/15/56, p. 6; Crenshaw Interview (Garrow); King, *Stride,* pp. 121–22; *BW* 2/21/56, p. 1, 2/24/56, p. 1; Abernathy to Men of Montgomery, 2/20/56, MCDA; Reddick, "Boycott," p. 116; Hackney, "Montgomery," p. 34; Robinson, "Montgomery Story," pp. 150, 160–62; Thornton, "Challenge," pp. 219, 224.

44. *MA* 2/22/56, p. A1, 2/23/56, p. A1, 2/24/56, p. A1; *NYHT* 2/22/56, p. 1, 2/23/56, p. 1, 2/24/56, p. 1; *NYT* 2/22/56, p. 1, 2/23/56, p. 1, 2/24/56, p. 1, 2/25/56, p. 1; King, *Stride,* pp. 142–46; King, Sr., *Daddy King,* pp. 170–71; Coretta King, *My Life,* pp. 133–36; Coretta King Interviews (Mayerson I, p. 9; Garrow); Coretta King, "The World," pp. 36–37; Lewis interviews with Mays & Yates; C. A. Scott Interview (Barton); Reddick, *Crusader,* pp. 136–41; Raines, *My Soul,* pp. 64–65; Mays, *Born,* pp. 267–68; *WP* 11/28/75, p. C1; Nixon Interview (Viorst); Millner, "Montgomery," pp. 136–37; S. S. Seay, Sr., Interviews (Garrow; Long); *BW* 2/24/56, p. 7, 2/28/56, p. 2; *PC* 3/3/56, pp. 3–4; *AA* 3/3/56, pp. 1, 6–7; Edward P. Morgan (ABC 2/24/56) in *New Republic* 3/12/56, p. 7. Also see Reinhold Niebuhr, *Christianity and Society* Spring 1956, p. 3, who termed the boycott "the most obviously effective way of bringing pressure for the sake of justice" and "a long overdue application of economic pressure for the achievement of justice." He added that "one cannot help but question the definition of the boycott as the 'way of love,'" since it was principally a method for achieving justice. Other commentaries include *Nation* 3/3/56, pp. 169–70; *Christian Century* 3/7/56, pp. 294–95; *Newsweek* 3/5/56, pp. 24–26; *Jet* 3/8/56, pp. 8–11; *Hue* 6/56, pp. 4–9; *American Negro* 4/56, pp. 17–22; and *Crisis* 3/56, pp. 136–38 & 189.

45. Rustin Interviews (Mosby; Leventhal; Garrow; Baker; Viorst I & II; Dickerson); Rustin, "Montgomery Diary"; Rustin, *Report on Montgomery*; Abernathy in SCOPE Tape 0079-3, 6/14/65, Project South; Raines, *My Soul,* pp. 52–54; Viorst, *Fire,* pp. 210–13; Coretta King, *My Life,* p. 137; Robinson, *Abraham,* p. 117; Farmer, *Lay Bare,* pp. 186–87; Abernathy Interview (Dickerson); Garrow interviews with Glenn Smiley, Graetz & Robert Hughes; Graetz to

Alfred Hassler, 5/15/57, & John Swomley to Wilson Riles, 2/21/56, FOR; *NYT* 2/26/56, p. 52, 2/27/56, p. 17; *BW* 2/28/56, p. 1, 3/2/56, pp. 1, 2, 5, 8; *SLA* 3/2/56, pp. 1, 8, 11, 13; King to Roy Wilkins, 1/28/56, & NAACP press releases, 2/3 & 2/23/56, NAACP III-B-191 & 192; *AA* 3/3/56, pp. 1, 7, 9, 3/10/56, p. 6; *MA* 2/25/56, p. A1, 2/26/56, p. A1, 2/27/56, p. A1, 2, 8, 2/28/56, p. B5; E. Frederic Morrow to Sherman Adams, 2/27/56, OF 142-A, Box 731, DDEL; *National Guardian* 3/5/56, p. 1. As Smiley later described Jackson's stance toward Rustin, "Emory gave him an ultimatum . . . if he would leave town, he would not break it, but that if he didn't leave town, he was gonna bust it wide open." Smiley believed Jackson "really didn't have anything against Bayard . . . he really loved the movement, and he thought that this was the way to save it . . . he thought he had the good of the movement at heart."

46. Smiley Interviews (Garrow; Shannon); Swomley to Riles, 2/21/56, Smiley, "Report from the South," n.d., Smiley to Neil Bolinger et al., 2/29/56, FOR; Smiley to King, 2/28/56, MLK 10; Swomley to Smiley (3), 2/29/56, Smiley to Swomley, n.d. [ca. 2/29/56], Swomley to Smiley, 3/1/56, FOR; Smiley, "A Man Remembered"; Worthy to Norman Thomas, 3/3/56, & Thomas to Worthy, 3/6/56, NT 62; Graetz Interview (Garrow); & the Inez Adams materials, UCC. Also see Smiley, "An Interview with . . . King," n.d., FOR, which appears in less complete form as King, "Walk for Freedom, *Fellowship* 5/56, pp. 5–7. In later years Smiley sometimes misremembered his arrival in Montgomery as 2/14 rather than 2/27. See, e.g., Smiley to Shannon, 6/21/67, RBOHC, MSRC. Norman Thomas shared Swomley's worries about Rustin's presence, remarking that "he is entirely too vulnerable on his record—and I do not mean his record as a c.o.—if any trouble should arise and would, therefore, greatly handicap Southern Negroes who would use him in a critical situation." Thomas to Homer Jack, 3/12/56, NT 62. Jack responded that Rustin "did a necessary job which nobody else apparently had the foresight to do: to help indoctrinate the Negro leadership into some of the techniques of Gandhism." Jack to Thomas, 3/15/56, NT 62. Thomas also wrote King that "the intrusion of Northerners in Montgomery will do more harm than good." Thomas to King, 3/23/56, & King to Thomas, 4/27/56, NT 62 & 63.

47. *NYHT* 3/8/56, p. 1, 3/9/56, p. 1; *NYT* 3/4/56, p. E6; Garrow interviews with Graetz, Robinson & Mary Fair Burks; Durr to Clark Foreman et al., 2/24/56, VFD 2-27; *Militant* 3/19/56, p. 1, 3/26/56, p. 3; *LCJ* 3/8/56, p. 1, 3/9/56, p. 1, 3/10/56, p. 1; *PC* 3/10/56, p. 4, 3/17/56, p. 2; *AA* 3/10/56, pp. 1, 6, 8, 3/17/56, p. 1; King to Wilkins, 3/3/56, Wilkins to King, 3/8/56 & 4/12/56, King to Wilkins, 5/7/56, NAACP III-B-191 & 192; Wilkins, *Standing Fast*, pp. 237–38. Also see Homer Jack to "Those Interested in . . . Montgomery," 3/9/56, HJ; H. L. Mitchell, "The White Citizens Councils . . .," 3/12/56, SRC.

48. Smiley, "Report . . .," n. 46 above; Rustin, "Notes of a Conference . . .," 3/7/56, BR; Rustin, *Report*, pp. 2–3; Smiley Interview (Garrow); Rustin Interviews (Baker; Garrow; Mosby; Leventhal); *MA* 3/7/56, p. A1; Rustin to King, 3/8/56, MLK 10; King, "Our Struggle," *Liberation* 4/56, pp. 3–6. Years later Smiley corrected those "who talk about Martin's lifelong interest in nonviolence. It's not true." In 1963 King recalled how "one time I did have a gun in Montgomery. I don't know why I got it in the first place. I sat down with Coretta one night and we talked about it. I pointed out that as a leader of a nonviolent movement, I had no right to have a gun, so I got rid of it." *Time* 1/3/64, p. 27. Part of the attraction of nonviolence for King lay in how easily it fit into his favorite analytical typology. "Like the synthesis in Hegelian philosophy, the principle of nonviolent resistance seeks to reconcile the truths of two opposites—acquiescence and violence—while avoiding the extremes and immoralities of both." *Stride,* p. 213. Also see *Where,* p. 129.

49. *MA* 3/1/56, p. E4, 3/3/56, p. A1, 3/16/56, p. A9, 3/18/56, p. A1, 3/19/56, p. A1, 3/20/56, p. A1, 3/21/56, p. A1, 3/22/56, p. A1, 3/23/56, p. A1; *AlaJ* 3/13/56,

p. 1; *BW* 3/13/56, p. 1, 3/16/56, pp. 1, 7, 8, 3/23/56, p. 1, 3/27/56, p. 1; *LD* 3/29/56, p. 7; *NYT* 3/20/56, p. 1, 3/21/56, p. 28, 3/22/56, p. 20, 3/23/56, p. 1, 3/24/56, p. 15; Jack Shows Interview (Garrow); *State of Alabama* v. *M. L. King, Jr.*, 3/19–22/56, Montgomery Co. Circuit Ct. #7399; King, *Stride*, pp. 147–50; Reddick, *Crusader*, pp. 141–46; *PC* 3/24/56, p. 2, 3/31/56, pp. 2, II-1; *AA* 3/24/56, p. 1, 3/31/56, pp. 1, 2, 7, 4/6/56, p. 6; King, "Excerpts from Address . . .," 3/22/56, MLK 10. Other trial accounts include *National Guardian* 4/2/56, p. 1; *Militant* 4/2/56, p. 1; *Reporter* 4/5/56, pp. 18–21; *Hat Worker* 4/15/56, p. 6; & *Universalist Leader* 5/56, pp. 110–12; sketches of King include *Jet* 4/12/56, pp. 22–26; *NJG* 4/21/56, p. 1; & a three-part profile in *PC* 4/7/56, p. 15, 4/14/56, p. 6, & 4/21/56, p. 6.

   50. *NYT* 3/26/56, p. 27, 4/3/56, p. 21, 4/24/56, p. 1, 4/25/56, p. 1, 4/26/56, p. 27, 4/27/56, p. 15; *NYHT* 3/26/56, p. 6; *MA* 3/26/56, p. A6, 4/2/56, pp. A1, 6, 4/3/56, p. A1, 4/24/56, p. A1, 5/10/56, p. A1; *AA* 4/7/56, pp. 1, 3, 8, 4/14/56, p. 1, 4/21/56, p. 3, 4/28/56, p. 1, 5/5/56, p. 1, 5/12/56, p. 8; *AlaJ* 4/16/56, p. A5, 4/24/56, p. A1, 4/25/56, p. A1, 5/1/56, p. A1, 5/3/56, p. A1; *American Negro* 6/56, pp. 13–15; Barnes, *Journey*, pp. 118–20; Yeakey, "Montgomery," pp. 528–29; Barbour in *National Baptist Voice* 5/56, pp. 4–5, & 9/56, p. 7; *BW* 4/27/56, p. 8; J. E. Pierce to C. H. Parrish, 4/27/56, SRC I-67-18; Crenshaw to O. D. Street, 5/1/56, Browder; Crenshaw Interview (Garrow); King, *Stride*, pp. 151–52; Durr to Foreman, 5/7/56, VFD 2-27; Gilliam, "Montgomery," pp. 127–28; *City of Montgomery* v. *Montgomery City Lines*, 1 *RRLR* 534; Yarbrough, *Johnson*, pp. 54–55. During King's New York trip he met with several members of A. J. Muste's newly formed "Committee for Nonviolent Integration" to discuss northern assistance possibilities like those Rustin had advanced in early March. Muste to Norman Thomas, & to Benjamin Mays, 4/13/56, NT 63 & BEM I-16. The day after the 5/11 federal hearing, King and Abernathy attended an Atlanta meeting of south-wide activists organized by Smiley. No concrete plans emerged. See Smiley to Swomley, 4/7/56, 4/10/56 (3), 4/26/56, Smiley, "Memo to Staff," 4/7/56, Smiley to King, 4/13/56, Smiley to Regional Secretaries, 5/2/56, & Smiley, "Minutes of the Atlanta Conference," 5/12/56, FOR. On two other King speaking trips to New York, see *NYP* 5/13/56, p. M2; *NYT* 5/18/56, p. 15, 5/25/56, p. 8; *NYHT* 5/18/56, p. 8, plus the texts of King's two major 5/17 addresses in MLK 1 & 10.

   51. Yeakey, "Montgomery," pp. 541–49; Millner, "Montgomery," pp. 168–70, 187; MIA Meeting Notes, 2/8/56 & 3/14[56], MLK 1-38 & 1-11; *CT* 12/3/75, 12/4/75, p. 1; Nixon Interviews (Lewis; Viorst); *NYP* 6/15/56, p. 4, 6/20/56, pp. 4, 56, 6/22/56, pp. 4, 52; *AA* 5/12/56, p. 8; King, "Recommendations . . .," 5/24/56, MLK 1. Those three *NYP* stories were part of a twelve-part series written by Ted Poston and published between 6/11/ and 6/24/56. Also see the first issue of the *MIA Newsletter* 6/7/56; Patton to Wilkins et al., 5/14/56, NAACP III-B-192; & *Christian Century* 6/20/56, pp. 744–46.

   52. Coretta King Interview (Mayerson XXXIII, p. 20); King, *Stride*, pp. 153–57; Nixon Interviews (Lewis; Garrow); *AlaJ* 6/5/56, p. A1; *NYT* 6/6/56, p. 1; *MIA Newsletter* #2, 6/23/56; Moses Jones Interview (Barton); Graetz Interview (Garrow); Fields, *Montgomery*, p. 40; *PC Magazine* 11/23/57, p. 1; Millner, "Montgomery," p. 166; Yeakey, "Montgomery," pp. 550–67.

   53. *SFC* 6/27/56, p. 10, 6/28/56, p. 7; King, "The Montgomery Story," 6/27/56, MLK 11 (& *U.S. News* 8/3/56, pp. 82, 87–89); *New Republic* 7/16/56, pp. 9–11; Bennett, "The King Plan."

   54. *MIA Newsletter* #3, 7/26/56; *Socialist Call* 8/56, pp. 6–8; King to Smiley, 7/5/56, FOR; King, "Sworn Deposition," 12/10/56, MLK 8; Smiley, "A Man Remembered," pp. 5–6; *NT* 7/13/56; Whitaker Interview (Garrow); *MA* 8/26/56, p. A1; King et al. to Eisenhower, 8/27/56, GF 124-A, Box 909, DDEL; *National Baptist Voice* 9/56, p. 7; MIA Executive Board Minutes, 9/18/56, MLK 1; *MIA Newsletter* #4, 9/21/56; King, *Stride*, pp. 157–58; Addine Drew Interview (Garrow); *MA* 9/19/56; MIA Finance Report, 10/10/56, MLK 14–16; *NYT* 9/22/56, p. 38; King to Rustin, 9/20/56, MLK 8. King's summer appearances included a funeral directors' convention, a national fraternity gathering, and the Democratic National Convention's platform committee. See *BW* 8/18/56, p. 1; *CT* 8/12/56, p. 3; *NYT* 8/13/56, p. 42; *LAT* 8/28/56; King's 8/11 platform statement in MLK 11; plus Smiley, "Report from the South #2," 8/15/56, King to Smiley, 8/21/56, FOR.

55. King to S. S. Robinson, 10/3/56, MLK 8; King report in Evans, *Dexter,* pp. 94–107; *NYT* 10/14/56, p. 51; *AIaJ* 10/26/56, p. A1, 10/27/56, p. A1, 10/29/56, p. A1, 11/2/56, p. A1; *MA* 10/28/56, p. A1, 11/14/56, p. A1, 11/16/56, p. A1; *AT* 11/2/56, p. 1; *RTD* 11/3/56; Walton, "Walking City, III," pp. 102–104; King, *Stride,* pp. 158–63; *MIA Newsletter* #5, 11/26/56; *NYT* 11/14/56, p. 1, 11/15/56, p. 38; King, "Statement," 11/14/56, MLK 1; Graetz Interview (Garrow); *AIaJ* 11/15/56, p. A1, 11/20/56, p. A1; *Newsweek* 11/26/56, p. 49; *Time* 11/26/56, p. 20; Gilliam, "Montgomery," pp. 140–42. MIA leaders wondered why the city had not made this move earlier. Gray Interviews (Lumpkin; Garrow).

56. *MIA Newsletter* #5, 11/26/56; *AIaJ* 12/3/56, p. B5, 12/4/56, p. A1, 12/18/56, p. B1, 12/21/56, p. C2; King, "Annual Address . . .," 12/3/56, MLK 10; King, *Stride,* pp. 163–64, 169–73; Reddick, *Crusader,* pp. 154–55; *MA* 12/4/56, 12/22/56, p. A1; *NJG* 12/15/56, p. 11; Emory Via & Fred Routh "Memorandum," 12/17/56, SRC IV-7-8; Walton, "Walking City, IV," pp. 147–48; MIA, "Integrated Bus Suggestions," 12/19/56, & King, "Statement . . .," 12/20/56, MLK 15; *NYT* 12/21/56, p. 1, 12/22/56, p. 1; *Nation* 1/5/57, pp. 11–14; *NYT Magazine* 12/16/56, pp. 8–9, 48–50; *AA* 12/8/56, p. 1; *WP* 12/7/56, p. C15. On Tallahassee, see Smith & Killian, *The Tallahassee Bus Protest;* Killian, "Organization"; Padgett, "C. K. Steele," pp. 25–77; Rabby, "Out of the Past," pp. 10–62; Professor Jack Ice's fine interviews with participants, FSU Library; & the police-informant reports in LC 33; on Birmingham, see Shuttlesworth, "An Account of the Alabama Christian Movement for Human Rights," 5/59, in Clarke, "Goals and Techniques," pp. 133–53, & *BW* 8/1/56.

Chapter Two

1. *MA* 12/24/56, p. A12, 12/25/56, p. E4, 12/27/56, p. A1, 1/3/57, p. A1, 1/4/57, p. A5; *AIaJ* 12/24/56, p. A2, 1/3/57, p. A1; *NYT* 12/23/56, p. 14, 12/24/56, p. 6, 12/29/56, p. 1, 12/30/56, p. 1, 1/1/57, p. 15; Will Campbell to Oscar Lee, 1/9/57, NCC 6-47-17; *MIA Newsletter* #6, 3/8/57; Reddick, *Crusader,* pp. 171–74. King discussed the first shooting with the FBI and U.S. Attorney Hartwell Davis. See SAC Mobile to Director, 12/26/56, & Director to Attorney General, 12/28/56, both 100-135-61-286.

2. *AA* 1/5/57, pp. 2, 16; Wofford, *Kennedys,* p. 12; Wofford Interviews (Garrow; Bernhard); Wofford, "Gandhi the Civil Rights Lawyer," 11/10/55; *BW* 11/25/55, p. 2; Levison Interview (Mosby); Coretta King, *My Life,* pp. 163–64; Baker Interviews (Britton; Walker; Hogan); Rustin Interviews (Baker; Viorst; Garrow); Rustin to King, 12/23/56, & two attachments, "The Negroes Struggle for Freedom" & "Memo," BR; Levison to A. Philip Randolph, 1/2/57, Randolph to John Neustadt, 1/4/57, Randolph to Levison, 1/4/57, Neustadt to Randolph, 1/5/57, Jack Clareman to Randolph, 2/5/57, Randolph to George Cannon, 6/21/56, & Levison to Randolph, 7/16/56, APR; Kinoy, *Rights,* pp. 152–55. In the Levison-Rustin memo, they told King:

> Regional groups of leaders should be brought together and encouraged to develop forms of local organization leading to an alliance of groups capable of creating a Congress of organizations. Such a Congress would create both

the alert leadership capable of reacting promptly and effectively to situations and possessing ties to masses of people so that their action projects are backed by broad participation of people who gain experience and knowledge in the course of the struggles. We will be sending a prospectus on this later. The final stage may be the conference of leaders on transportation but its broader perspectives must be implicit in the deliberations.

Baker's interview with Britton underlines an important point: "Q. What you're saying then is that the genesis of the idea for SCLC started in the minds of people in the North, not in Montgomery? A. That's correct." As Levison remarked to Rustin years later, "You were there with me when it was designed, in my kitchen." FBI NY 100-111180-9-1738A, 7/21/68, p. 5. Thomas Kilgore puts it even more strongly: "The strategies for the whole nonviolent movement were largely the product of Baker, Bayard and Levison." (Garrow Interview) On Wofford, also see his articles "Nonviolence and the Law" in *Journal of Religious Thought* 15 (Autumn-Winter 1957–58): 25–36, and *Fellowship* 5/1/58, pp. 5–11. For a similar pre-Montgomery articulation of the efficacy of nonviolent mass action, see an 11/19/55 speech by Kenneth B. Clark, published as *The Crisis of American Democracy and the Negro* (New York: National Committee for Rural Schools, 1956). On the creation and activities of In Friendship, see James H. Robinson et al. to Channing Tobias, 12/19/55, Walter Petersen, "Proceedings of Conference on Aid to Race Terror Victims," 1/5/56, "Memorandum to Mr. Wilkins from Miss Black," 1/20/56, "Memo on In Friendship," n.d. [ca. 2/17/56], Baker to "Dear Co-Worker," 7/11/56, & Baker to Wilkins, 11/10/56, NAACP III-B-186; Norman Thomas to Wilkins et al., 1/12/56, Randolph to Baker, 3/7/56, & Baker "Minutes . . . 7/19/56," 8/3/56, APR; In Friendship to Cooperating Organizations . . ., 3/27/56, ACLU; *AA* 10/6/56, p. 3; King to Mrs. Bunche & Mrs. Wilkins, 11/23/56, FOR; & SAC New York to Director, 11/28/56, 100-424895-1.

 3. *ADW* 1/2/57, p. 1; *BW* 1/5/57, p. 1; Lt. C. C. Hamby & C. J. Strickland to Chief H. T. Jenkins, 1/1/57, HTJ 5; Rustin, *Strategies*, p. 38; MIA press release, 1/7/57, MLK 4; & Rustin's seven working papers, all in MLK 14. The invitations went out 1/5/57 signed by King, Shuttlesworth & Steele. Also see Reddick, "The History of SCLC," in Clayton, *SCLC*, pp. 12–14; Steele Interview (Ice); and Morris, "Rise," p. 198, quoting Steele & Baker.

 4. *AlaJ* 1/10/57, p. A1; *MA* 1/11/57, p. A1; *ADW* 1/9/57, p. 1, 1/11/57, p. 1, 1/12/57, p. 1; *NYT* 1/11/57, p. 1, 1/12/57, p. 38; Abernathy, "Nonviolent," pp. 24–26; King, *Stride*, pp. 175–77; Reddick, *Crusader*, pp. 183–85; Campbell to Alfred Kramer, 1/16/57, & "Report" to Oscar Lee, 6/7/57, NCC 6-47-3; Campbell Interviews (Caudill, pp. 56–57; MSRC, pp. 89–92); Baker Interview (Walker); Steele Interview (Ice); Coretta King Interview (Smith); Garrow interviews with Juanita Abernathy, Shuttlesworth & Lowery; *Time* 1/21/57, p. 15; SAC Mobile to Director, 1/10/57, & Director to Attorney General, 1/11/57, both 100-135-61-312; Southern Leaders Conference, "A Statement . . .," 1/11/57; Rustin, "Even in the Face"; Russell Lasley, "Report on the Southern Leaders Conference . . .," 1/10–11/57, & Lasley & Charles Hayes, "Report of the Southern Negro Leaders Conference . . .," 1/14/57, UPW 381-5; *AC* 1/12/57; King et al. to Eisenhower, 1/9 & 1/11/57, & Maxwell Rabb to King, 1/11/57, GF 124-A-1, Box 912, DDEL. Also see A. L. Davis Interview (Barton); Kelly Miller Smith Interview (Hill); and "That You Might Know—A Brief Digest of the Activities of In Friendship," 3/6/57, APR.

 5. *MA* 1/11/57, p. A1; Rosen to Boardman, 1/11/57, SAC Mobile to Director, 1/11/57, Nichols to Tolson, 1/12/57, Rosen to Boardman, 1/14/57, Nichols to Tolson, 1/14/57, & Hoover to Tolson, 1/15/57, 100-135-61-317, 327, 324, 318, 325 & 315; King, *Stride*, pp. 175–78; Reddick, *Crusader*, p. 166; *NYT* 1/14/57, p. 14;

MA 1/15/57, p. A6, 1/16/57, p. B1; *DDT* 1/15/57; Graetz Interview (Garrow). Also see *NB* 1/14/57 regarding a bomb threat that disrupted a King speech in Nashville.

   6. Reddick, *Crusader,* pp. 178–79; Lewis, *King,* p. 89; *National Baptist Voice* 1/57, p. 13; Durr to Clark & Mairi Foreman, 12/17/56, Durr to Clark Foreman, 1/7/57, 1/22/57, 2/1 or 2/57, 2/15/57 & 2/28/57, VFD 2-28; Durr to Myles Horton, 11/5 & 11/15/56, HLW 11-1; Fields to Roy Wilkins, 4/22/57, RW 4; Graetz Interview (Garrow). On Mrs. Parks's difficulties and financial hardships throughout 1956–1957, see Durr to Mairi & Clark Foreman, 3/15/56, 5/15/56, Durr to Clark Foreman, 11/5/56, 3/20/57, 3/25/57 & 5/5/57, VFD 2-27, 28.

   7. *NYT* 1/17/57, p. 25, 1/18/57, p. 13, 1/24/57, p. 12, 1/28/57, p. 25, 2/2/57, p. 17, 2/7/57, p. 15; Sherman Adams to King, 1/18/57, GF 124-A-1, Box 912, DDEL; *MT* 1/22/57, p. 1; *MA* 1/28/57, p. A1, 1/29/57, p. A3; *AlaJ* 1/28/57, p. A1; *AT* 2/8/57, p. 5; *PC* 2/9/57, p. 2; King, *Stride,* pp. 178–79; Reddick, *Crusader,* pp. 166, 185; Parmet, *Eisenhower,* pp. 504–505; Burk, *Eisenhower,* pp. 219–20.

   8. *MA* 2/2/57, p. A1; *NOTP* 2/2/57; Jack Shows Interview (Garrow); Lawson Interview (Yellin & Beifuss); *NYT* 2/15/57, p. 15, 2/16/57, p. 6; *AC* 2/15/57; *NT* 2/15/57; *NOTP* 2/15/57; Davis Interview (Barton); Russell Lasley, "Southern Negro Leaders Conference," 2/14/57, UPW 381-5; Garrow interviews with Ralph Helstein & Charles Hayes; King et al. to Eisenhower & to Herbert Brownell, 2/14/57, GF 124-A-1, Box 912, DDEL; *PC* 2/23/57, p. 3, 3/2/57, p. 4; *MW* 2/20/57, p. 1; *AA* 2/23/57, p. 1; *Time* 2/18/57, pp. 17–20; *NYP* 4/12/57, pp. 4, 43; Reddick, *Crusader,* pp. 157–58, 185–86; *MA* 2/17/57, p. A1, 2/21/57, p. A1, 2/24/57, p. A1; Durr to Clark Foreman, 2/21/57, & "Wednesday" [3/6/57], Durr to Clark & Mairi Foreman, 2/27/57, VFD 2-28; *AlaJ* 2/19/57, p. A1; Walton, "Walking City, IV," pp. 151–52, 166; *MIA Newsletter* #6, 3/8/57; *NYT Magazine* 3/3/57, pp. 11, 67–69, 74.

   9. King to Rustin, 2/23/57, BR; Reddick, *Crusader,* pp. 180–84; *Christian Century* 4/10/57, pp. 446–48; *PC* 3/16/57, p. 2; Morrow, *Black Man,* p. 133; King, "The Birth of a New Nation," Dexter sermon, 4/7 or 14/57; C.L.R. James to Dear Friends, 3/25/57, James Papers; Coretta King, *My Life,* p. 154. According to Reddick (p. 2), King was so concerned about his Ghana illness that he "wondered if he could pull through." As James recounted his conversation with King in that letter, "He had had no idea whatsoever of being a leader for the struggles of his people. . . . He had had someone else in mind to propose" as MIA president.

   10. "Memo Regarding Prayer Pilgrimage" & "Telegram of Call," n.d. [ca. 3/57], "That You Might Know . . . ," n. 4 above, APR; Wilkins to Evers, 4/2/57, & Evers to King, 8/20/57, NAACP III-B-204; Myrlie Evers Interviews (Leventhal; Blackside); Wilkins, *Standing Fast,* p. 237; Bennett, "The South"; *NYT* 4/6/57, p. 11, 4/25/57, p. 19; *PC* 4/27/57, p. 2, 5/4/57, p. 2; King, "A Realistic Look . . . ," 4/19/57, in *MW* 4/24/57, p. 4; *NYHT* 4/25/57, p. 14. Also see Sam Williams's remarks at p. 6 of "Workshop Notes," n.d. [ca. 9–10/57], HTSA 7-3; *MW* 3/27/57, p. 1, 5/1/57, p. 1; *SLPD* 4/11/57. On the NAACP, see John Dittmer's excellent paper "The Ordeal of Medgar Evers . . . ," 12/83. On Powell's dealings with the White House, see Powell to Sherman Adams & Eisenhower, 3/28/57, "Janet" to Adams, 4/2/57, Maxwell Rabb to Adams, 4/2/57 & 4/3/57, Warren Olney to Rabb, 4/15/57, & Rabb to Adams, 4/17/57, all in OF 142-A, Box 731, DDEL, & Parmet, *Eisenhower,* pp. 505–508.

   11. "Memorandum on Opening Remarks—by A. Philip Randolph, 4/18/57," APR; *NB* 4/26/57; Reddick, *Crusader,* pp. 187–97; *NYT* 5/4/57, p. 15, 5/12/57, p. 50, 5/18/57, p. 1; Rustin to King, 5/10/57, MLK 12; *PC* 5/11/57, p. 18, 5/18/57, p. 3, 5/25/57, pp. 2, 3; *NT* 5/12/57; Sherman Adams to King, 3/13/57, & Max Rabb to [Jack] Toner, 5/16/57, GF 124-A-1, Box 912, DDEL; King to Bernard Shanley, 5/16/57, MLK 9; *Nation* 6/1/57, pp. 477–79; King, "Address . . . ," 5/17/57, in U.S. Congress, Senate, *Congressional Record* 103 (pt. 6, 5/28/57): 7822–24; Rabb to Files, 5/23/57, & to Shanley, 5/23/57, & "Memorandum," 6/25/57, GF 124-A-1, Box 912, DDEL; Morrow to Adams, 6/4/57, & Rabb, "Memorandum," 6/20/57, Morrow 10, DDEL; Rabb to Adams, 6/5/57, OF 142-A, Box 731, DDEL; *Ebony* 8/57, pp. 16–22; Nixon to King, 5/23/57, MLK 1; *AN* 6/1/57; *AlaJ* 5/28/57, p. A2; *PC* 6/1/57, p. 3. Also see Thomas Kilgore et al. to Hicks, 6/4/57, APR, and two FBI serials detailing Bureau fears of Communist participation in the Pilgrimage and a private warning conveyed to NAACP counsel Thurgood Marshall: Hoover to Tolson et al., 5/10/57, & Hoover to Attorney General, 5/10/57, 62-101087-246 & 244.

12. *AlaJ* 5/27/57, p. Al, 5/28/57, p. A1; *WP* 5/30/57, p. B6; Walton, "Walking City, V," pp. 75–76, 81; King, *Stride,* pp. 179–80; Stevenson, *Montgomery,* p. 58; *MA* 5/31/57, p. A1; Jack Shows Interview (Garrow); Graetz to Alfred Hassler, 5/15/57, FOR; William R. Miller to King, 2/25/57, & King to Miller, 4/23/57, MLK 2; Garrow interviews with Graetz & Smiley; Nixon to King, 6/3/57, MLK 4.

13. Rustin to King, 6/13/57, MLK 1; Lewis, *King,* pp. 94–95; Brooks, *Walls,* pp. 134–35; *NYT* 6/14/57, p. 1; *WP* 6/14/57, p. A10; *PC* 6/22/57, pp. 1–2; Reddick, *Crusader,* pp. 198–202; *SC* 6/14/57; *AA* 6/22/57, pp. 1–2; Max Rabb to Sherman Adams, 6/24/57, OF 142-A, Box 731, DDEL; Adam Clayton Powell to Eisenhower, 1/28/58, Alpha Box 2486, DDEL. On King's speeches and appearances in June and early July, see *LCJ* 6/3/57; *Intercollegian* 5/58, pp. 8–9; *WP* 6/8/57, p. D12; *SFC* 6/24/57, p. 6; *NYT* 6/29/57, p. 36; *PC* 7/13/57, p. II-1; King, "Remarks in Acceptance of 42nd Spingarn Medal," 6/28/57, Boyte; *MA* 7/3/57.

14. *PC* 3/23/57, p. 7; *NYP* 4/14/57, p. M5; *PC* 4/27/57, p. 7; King to Johnson, 7/5/57, MLK 1; King to Dwight Loder, 8/5/58, & Loder to King, 8/11/58, author's files; *PC* 6/29/57, p. 5; Nixon to King, 11/4/57, MLK 4; Garrow interviews with Robinson, Smiley & Graetz; Nixon Interviews (Lewis; Viorst). As King told Garrett President Loder, "There has been something of a pendulum swinging in my mind between an affirmative answer on the one hand and a negative answer on the other. There have been moments that I found myself saying, 'This is just the thing for me.' I came out of the seminary with a strong desire to enter the teaching profession and even though I have fallen in love with the pastorate I am sure that this desire still lingers somewhere in my subconscious mind." Even though he was saying no, "I am not absolutely convinced that I am doing the right thing." King expressed similarly mixed feelings in a 1/4/57 letter to Boston University Professor DeWolf. "At this point I am not sure of what area of the ministry I would like to settle down in. I have had a great deal of satisfaction in the pastorate, and have almost come to the point of feeling that I can best render my service in this area, however, I can never quite get the idea out of my mind that I should do some teaching." MLK 2.

15. Reddick, *Crusader,* pp. 202, 204; Pleasure Interview (Garrow); Moore, "Billy Graham," p. 454; *MW* 8/28/57, p. 1; press release, "Dr. King Calls Meeting . . .," 7/25/57, KP; *MA* 8/7/57, p. A1, 8/9/57, p. A1; press release on 8/8/57 meeting, MLK 4; untitled 3pp. memo, n.d. [ca. early 8/57], BR; Rustin Interview (Garrow); *MW* 8/10/57, p. 1, 8/14/57, p. 1; *PC* 8/17/57, p. 2; Will Campbell to Oscar Lee, 8/12/57, NCC 6-47-3; Pleasure to Lasley, n.d., UPW 379-24; 9/30–10/4/57 transcript, pp. 208–34, UPW 526; Charles Hayes Interview (Garrow); Ralph Helstein Interviews (Wigginton; Garrow); Wilkins to Current, 8/21/57, & Current, "Memorandum . . .," 8/23/57, NAACP III-B-204.

16. *NYHT* 8/28/57, p. 1; *NB* 8/30/57; Adams, *Unearthing,* pp. 122–27; King, "The Look to the Future," 9/2/57, Highlander, KP; Braden Interviews (Garrow; Thrasher, pp. 343–46); Reddick, *Crusader,* pp. 202–204; Lawson, *Black Ballots,* pp. 149–202; Garrow, *Protest,* pp. 12, 246–47; William E. Leuchtenburg, "The White House and Black America . . .," in Namorato, ed., *Have We,* pp. 121–26; Parmet, *Eisenhower,* pp. 509–12; Tony Freyer, *The Little Rock Crisis* (Westport, Conn.: Greenwood Press, 1984); Burk, *Eisenhower,* pp. 174–203; Max Rabb to

Fred Morrow, 7/13/57, Morrow 10, DDEL; Morrow to Sherman Adams, 9/12/57, & Rabb to Adams, 9/27/57, OF 142-A, Box 731, DDEL: *CSM* 9/10/57; *Ebony* 9/57, p. 74, 10/57, p. 53, 12/57, p. 120.

17. Pleasure Interview (Garrow); Hazel Gregory Interview (Brown); *PC Magazine* 8/31/57, p. 7, 11/16/57, p. 1; Inez Baskin to Claude Barnett, 9/2/57, CAB 135-6; Virginia Durr to Myles Horton, 8/14/57, HLW 11-1; Virginia Durr to Clark Foreman, 10/14/57, 10/24 or 25/57, & n.d., VFD 2-29; MIA, *Looking Forward* (n.d.); SCLC Minutes, 10/18/57, Atlanta, MLK 4; Graetz Interview (Garrow); *MIA Newsletter* #7, 11/18/57; King's report in Evans, *Dexter*, pp. 107–23; Coretta King Interview (Mayerson XVIII, p. 48); *MA* 10/28/57, p. A1; Reddick, *Crusader*, pp. 207–208. On King's other appearances, see *CT* 10/3/57, p. 14, 10/11/57, p. 21; *CST* 10/3/57, p. 5; King to Smiley, 10/24/57, & King to Alfred Hassler, 10/28/57, FOR.

18. *MW* 10/26/57, p. 1, 11/2/57, p. 1, 11/9/57, p. 1; *MCA* 11/1/57, 11/6/57, p. 30; King press statement & King to Eisenhower, 11/5/57, MLK 4. Also see the untitled, undated 3pp. memo cited in n. 15 above, "Proposed Plans for Kick-Off . . . ," n.d., "Crusade . . . Project #1," "Work in Washington," n.d., & an untitled, undated 4pp. memo, all ca. 10/57, BR; King to Nixon, 8/30/57, Rogers 50, & King to Eisenhower, 9/25/57, OF 142-A-5-A, Box 773, DDEL; Henry C. Bunton, *A Dreamer of Dreams: An Autobiography* (n.p., n.d.), pp. 108–109. In private, some participants were "fantastically vehement" that King not use Bayard Rustin as SCLC's press person. "Martin tried to smooth it over," since Rustin's sexuality "didn't bother him," but the others "were insistent, and Martin was a master of compromise," so Rustin did not attend. Pleasure Interview (Garrow). Some accounts erroneously date the Memphis meeting as 10/5 or 10/18.

19. *AC* 11/18/57, p. 1; *MW* 11/20/57, p. 1; *PC* 11/30/57, p. II-1; *MA* 11/28/57, p. A4; King, "Loving Your Enemies," 11/[17]/57; King, "Love Your Enemies" (11/10/57), *Journal of Religious Thought* 27 (Summer Supplement 1970): 31–41; *WP* 11/11/57, p. B2; *PC* 11/23/57, p. 16; *PC Magazine* 12/21/57, p. 6; *NYT Magazine* 12/29/57, p. 11; *NYT* 2/2/58, p. 65; *AlaJ* 11/26/57, p. A1; *WP* 11/25/57, p. A25; *King v. Alabama*, 3 *RRLR* 54 (4/30/57); Reddick, *Crusader*, pp. 208–12; Nixon to King, 11/4/57, MLK 4; Durr to Clark Foreman, n.d. [late 1957], VFD 2-29; Mohr, "Journey," pp. 50, 55, 123; King, "Some Things We Must Do," 12/5/57; *MA* 12/6/57, p. A1, 12/7/57, p. A5, 12/9/57, p. A5; Brooks, *Walls*, p. 140; MIA Finance Report, 12/57, and Pleasure to Fred Gray, 12/27/57, MLK 1-38; MIA Executive Board Minutes, 1/20/58, MLK 4-16; *Christian Century* 1/22/58, pp. 104–105; *AlaJ* 1/8/58, p. Al.

20. King to Randolph, Wilkins et al., 12/16/57, MLK 6; "Minutes of the Ministers' Meeting at Talladega College," 12/16–17/57, ACHR; C. O. Simpkins, "Meeting of Administration Committee," 12/19/57, SCLC 32; Reddick, *Crusader*, p. 211; *AC* 1/9/58, 1/31/58; *TDT* 1/9/58; Rustin Interview (Garrow); Levison Interview (Mosby); Baker Interviews (Britton; Hogan; Thrasher & Hayden; Walker); *ADW* 1/19/58, p. 1, 1/30/58, p. 1; Evers to Ruby Hurley, 1/24/58, & Wilkins to Benjamin Mays, 1/31/58, NAACP III-B-204 & 154; Abernathy, Treasurer's Report . . . , 1/31/58, BR; undated SCLC press release, MLK 9; "Crusade for Citizenship Meetings, 2/12/58," n.d., King, "Follow Through . . . ," 2/4/58, King to Speakers, "Crusade . . . ," n.d., & King to SCLC Representatives, 2/8/58, all BR; *PC* 2/1/58, p. 5; *N&O* 2/11/58; *GDN* 2/12/58; King, "Section of Speech . . . ," 2/12/58, MLK 11, and *Liberation* 3/58, pp. 13–14; *Newsweek* 2/24/58, p. 32; Baker, "Report of Activities . . . ," 4/3/58, MLK 6; *WP* 3/13/58, p. A16. The treasurer's report listed total income to date as some $13,000 ($11,000 from the Packinghouse Workers and $2,000 from the MIA) and expenses of less than $1,500. Baker went on salary 1/9/58 at $125 per week.

21. Baker to Tilley, 3/20/58, Tilley 5-4; Baker Interviews (Britton; Walker); Baker in Lerner, *Black Women*, p. 349; Reddick, *Crusader*, pp. 212–16; Levison to Randolph, 4/22/58, APR; *PC* 2/15/58, p. 2; Hermine Popper to King, 3/27/58, MLK 4; King, "Statement," 4/6/58, MLK 1-11; *WP* 4/7/58, p. A7; Director to Attorney General, 4/14/58, 62-101087-5-38; Garrow interviews with Julianna Jacobs (a newly hired SCLC secretary), Elliott Finley & Graetz; *Ebony* 12/57, p. 120, 1/58, p. 34, 2/58, p. 84, 3/58, p. 92, 4/58, p. 104, 5/58, p. 112, 7/58, p. 86, 8/58, p. 78, 9/58, p. 68, 10/58, p. 138, 11/58, p. 138, 12/58, p. 154; King to Rustin, 2/20/58 & 3/22/58, MLK 1, Levison to King, 4/1/58 (2), MLK 4; Levison in *WP* 2/14/78, p. B5. One year later, King wrote that "I sincerely believe that capital punishment is wrong." King to G. W. Sanders, 6/15/59, MLK 9. On the FBI's interest, also see Director to SAC, Mobile, 9/5/58, 100-135-61-500, denying permission to develop a new source in the MIA after Reverend Graetz left Montgomery in 9/58. On King's travels, see *SFC* 2/21/58, p. 4; *N&O* 4/10/58; *CST* 4/27/58; *HP* 5/19/58, p. II-6; *AG* 5/28/58. On the growing closeness between King and Levison, see their extensive correspondence in MLK 1, 5 & 16. Ten years later, in a 7/21/68 phone conversation transcribed by the FBI, Rustin and Levison discussed their early writing for King:

> BR: In the very early days, we by speech writing for Martin created the direction for him.
> SDL: That's right. No, I don't want to take too much on it because the man was very independent always. But I do think we helped to direct the mode in which he was going. Remember when we used to sit up in your place late at night writing those things?
> BR: Basically . . . we were analyzing Martin and saying 'how did he view these kinds of problems, what would be the way for him to tackle them?' It was not we directing him so much as we working with him and giving expression to ideals we knew he had or would quickly accept.

Rustin added:

> I don't like to write something for somebody where I know he is acting like a puppet. I want to be a real ghost and write what the person wants to say. And that is what I always knew was true in the case of Martin. I would never write anything that wasn't what he wanted to say. I understood him well enough.

FBI NY 100-111180-9-1738A, p. 6.

22. *PC* 5/31/58, p. II-1, 6/7/58, p. II-1, 6/21/58, p. 6; Reddick, *Crusader,* pp. 216–19; Brooks, "Report of SCLC Meeting," 6/1/58, Evers to Wilkins, "Report on SCLC . . .," 6/2/58, NAACP III-B-204; Brooks to Wilkins, 6/2/58, RW 4; SCLC, "Statement . . .," 5/29/58, & King to Eisenhower, 5/29/58, MLK 6; Siciliano, "Memorandum for the Files," 6/9/58, Siciliano to Sherman Adams, "Report and Recommendation . . .," 6/10/58, Blanche Lavery, "Memorandum for the Files," 6/13/58, & Siciliano to James Hagerty, 6/16/58, all OSAPM Box 42, DDEL; Morrow Interview (Wright); *NYT* 6/20/58, p. 21.

23. Reddick, *Crusader,* pp. 217–25; Wilkins to Morrow, 9/4/58, Morrow 10; Granger to NUL Board et al., "June 23rd Conference . . .," n.d., King et al., "A Statement to President Eisenhower," 6/23/58, & Siciliano to Files, "Meeting of Negro Leaders with President . . .," 6/24/58, OSAPM Box 42, DDEL; Siciliano to Hagerty, 5/18/59, & Hagerty to Reddick, 5/29/59, OF 142-A, Box 731, DDEL; Parmet, *Eisenhower,* p. 553; Morrow, *Black Man,* pp. 226–27; Morrow Interviews (Wright; Edwin); Wilkins, *Standing Fast,* p. 256; *NYT* 6/24/58, p. 1; *WP* 6/24/58, p. A12; *PC* 6/28/58, p. 2, 7/5/58, p. 2.

24. *MA* 8/26/58, p. A1, 8/27/58, p. A1; Graetz Interview (Garrow); Abernathy, "Natural History," p. 67; *AlaJ* 9/17/58, p. A1; S. S. Seay to MIA Executive

Board, "Report of the Executive Secretary," 6/5/58, & Seay to Board, 6/30/58, KC; Fred Gray to Board, 7/10/58, MLK 4; Baker to King, "SCLC Meeting in Norfolk . . .," 7/16/58, & Baker to Rustin and Levison, 7/16/58, BR; Coretta King Interview (Mayerson XXVII, p. 36); Dexter Echo II-18, 7/9/58; Granger to Randolph et al., 7/7/58, RW 4; Randolph to King, 7/9/58, MLK 4; King to Randolph, 7/18/58, & Randolph to King, 8/19/58, APR; Randolph to Eisenhower, 8/1/58, & Siciliano to Randolph, 9/4/58, OSAPM Box 42, DDEL; Levison to King, 8/14/58 & 8/15/58, MLK 1. On King's engagements see MA 7/2/58; NYP 7/11/58, p. 27; King (6/27) in Friends Journal 7/26/58, pp. 442–44; and King, Measure, two sermons he delivered 8/21–22/58 at Purdue University. Baker told Rustin and Levison that "it is obvious that more spirit needs to be injected in the Civil Rights struggle in the South. It seems to me also obvious that SCLC should not become so involved with routine procedures for promoting registration and voting that it fails to develop and use our major weapon—mass resistance."

25. Reddick, Crusader, pp. 225–29; MIA Newsletter #10, 9/27/58; NYT 9/4/58, p. 14; "Statement by Rev. Martin Luther King while on Trial . . .," n.d., APR; King, "Statement Presented to Judge Eugene Loe," 9/5/58, Boyte; MA 9/6/58, p. A1; PC 9/13/58, p. 2; Will Campbell to Oscar Lee, 9/8/58, NCC 6-47-4; King to E. D. Nixon, 9/16/58, MLK 4; & Henderson to King, 9/17/58, RW 4. The undated "Statement" may have been a draft that King did not use.

26. PC 9/13/58, p. 2, 9/27/58, p. 4; "Mass Rally, Hotel Theresa . . . 9/19/58," APR; NYHT 9/21/58, p. 1, 9/22/58, p. 1; NYT 9/21/58, p. 1. 9/22/58, p. 23, 9/23/58, p. 68, 9/24/58, p. 14, 9/25/58, p. 67, 9/27/58, p. 19, 9/28/58, p. 45, 10/1/58, p. 23, 10/4/58, p. 12; Ebony 1/59, pp. 33–38; Coretta King, My Life, pp. 166–71; Coretta King Interview (Smith); Reddick, Crusader, pp. 229–32; King, "How to Deal With Grief and Disappointment," Ebenezer, 5/23/65, KP; NYP 9/24/58, p. 4, 9/30/58, p. 8; King, "Statement . . .," 9/30/58, MLK 15; NJG 10/4/58, pp. 1, 2, 18; Jackie Robinson, Never, p. 176. On Mrs. Curry see PC 10/4/58, p. 4, & Jet 10/9/58, pp. 14–18.

27. Youth March press release, 9/23/58, APR; PC 10/4/58, p. 3, 10/18/58, p. 4; NVP 10/1/58, p. 9, 10/2/58, p. 56; NJG 10/4/58, p. 1; "Pattern for work . . .," n.d., Tilley 2-6; Baker Interview (Garrow).

28. King, Stride, pp. 34, 84, 90–107, esp. 98–99; Zepp, "Intellectual Sources," esp. pp. 143–46 & 183–84. Many of Levison's passages made their way word for word into the text, particularly in the final chapter. Compare the texts of two memos, one entitled "A Wind is Rising" (originally given to King several weeks before the Prayer Pilgrimage; see Rustin to King, 5/10/57, n. 11 above), and the other beginning "What are the tasks ahead?," in MLK 11 and 16, with the text of Stride at pp. 203–204 & 214–15. Zepp also points out "a remarkable similarity in wording" between pp. 192–93 & 196 of Stride and Wofford's article, "Nonviolence and the Law" (n. 2 above). Wofford mused to Zepp (in a 5/13/70 letter quoted in "Intellectual Sources," pp. 339–40) that "King may have had the 1957 talk in hand while doing the first draft of Stride. It is even possible that I personally added a few of the lines because I worked with him directly on the manuscript, editing some of the sections on civil disobedience." Also see Smith & Zepp, Search, pp. 62, 93; Wofford, Kennedys, p. 117; Smylie, "On Jesus," p. 79; Reddick, Crusader, p. 12; Hanigan, King, pp. 67, 150–51, 160; & Niebuhr, Moral Man, pp. 242–44. Reviews of Stride are listed in Fisher, Free, pp. 155–56.

29. Barbour to King, 11/19/58, MLK 3; King to MIA, 10/6/58, KC; NYT 10/18/58, p. 8, 11/18/58, p. 40; J. Edgar Hoover to Gordon Gray, 10/1 & 10/27/58, OSANSA-FBI Box 2, DDEL; Randolph to Eisenhower, 10/10/58, & George Butler to Jacob Seidenberg, 10/25/58, OSAPM Box 43, DDEL; King, "Statement," 10/24/58, MLK 13; WP 10/26/58, p. A17; PC 11/1/58, pp. 2–3, 11/8/58, p. 3; Levison & Rustin, "Financial Report," 10/31/58, BR; Siciliano to Randolph, 10/29/58, &

Randolph to Siciliano, 11/19/58, OSAPM Box 42, DDEL; King, "Address . . .,"
10/25/58, APR. Despite Randolph's 10/10 declaration that the Youth March rejected communism and Hoover's 10/27 report that the Communist party "had no
official connection with" it, White House aide L. Arthur Minnich nonetheless
recorded that the 11/6/58 Cabinet meeting included discussion that the March had
been "completely organized by known Commies." Minnich Notes, p. 35, DDEL.
   30. Levison to King, 11/3/58, 11/28/58, & King to Rustin, 11/5/58, MLK 1;
Evans, *Dexter,* pp. 124–30; Durr to Clark Foreman, 11/19/58, Durr to Clark &
Mairi Foreman, 2/9/59, & Durr to Clark Foreman, n.d. [early 5/59], VFD 2-29,
31; Nixon to Conrad Lynn, 12/16/58, & Nixon to G. L. Weissman, 12/20/58,
CCRI; *NYT* 12/7/58, p. 59; *MA* 12/23/58, 12/31/58, p. A1; S. S. Seay, "Executive
Secretary's Report," 1/7/59, KC; *AC* 12/11/58, p. 6; *ADW* 12/14/58. The recreation initiative had its roots in a new city ordinance forbidding interracial games
and in unsuccessful discussions between the MIA and the local YMCA about the
construction of a large, new Y toward which the MIA would contribute $20,000.
Suddenly the YMCA board asked that the MIA acknowledge that the new building would be segregated. King responded in a controlled fury, calling for the
integration of all recreational facilities. See King to Royce Kershaw, 12/17/58,
MLK 1.
   31. King, "My Trip to the Land of Gandhi," *Ebony* 7/59, pp. 84–92; Corinne
Johnson to R. E. Nelson, 1/13/59, Stewart Meacham to King, 1/20/59, & Johnson
to King, 1/29/59, BR; Jon Bradshaw, *Dreams That Money Can Buy* (New York:
William Morrow & Co., 1985), pp. 309–10; *AIaJ* 1/27/59; Swami Vishwananda,
"I Go Round with the Kings," pp. 3–7, and Bristol, "Notes from My Tour Di-
ary," pp. 8, 17–24, both in *With the Kings in India* (New Delhi: Gandhi National
Memorial Fund, 1959); Bristol, "Memories"; Bristol Interview (Garrow); *NYT*
2/1/59, p. 5; King, "Farewell Statement . . .," 3/9/59, & "Statement Upon Land-
ing . . .," 3/18/59, MLK 1; *NYT* 3/19/59, p. 6; *MA* 3/25/59; King, "A Walk
Through the Holy Land," Dexter, 3/29/59, "The Dimensions of a Complete Life,"
Chicago, 4/19/59, KP; Durr to Mairi & Clark Foreman, n.d., VFD 2-31; King,
"On Gandhi," Dexter, 3/22/59, KP.
   32. Coretta King Interviews (Mayerson III, pp. 55–56, XXIV, p. 39; Garrow);
Coretta King, *My Life,* pp. 160–61, 178–79; Peters, "The Man," p. 91; *BS*
6/20/65, p. D3; *Crusader* #1, 2/59; SCLC, "Plans of Action . . .," 2/59, MLK 6;
Baker to Tilley, 3/4/59, SCLC 32; Abernathy to Tilley, 3/17/59, Tilley 1-7; King to
Harry Belafonte, 3/24/59, King to Tilley, 4/3/59, & Shuttlesworth to King,
4/24/59, MLK 3, 9 & 9; King to Clay Maxwell, 4/25/59, MLK 4; Garrow interviews with Shuttlesworth & Lowery; Levison to Randolph, 5/20/59, APR.
   33. King to Rustin, 11/10/58, Levison to King, 12/11/58, King to Levison,
12/15/58, Levison to King, 12/16/58, 1/8/59, 1/12/59, King to Levison, 1/12/59,
1/26/59, 4/11/59, 5/8/59, 5/18/59, 6/24/59, all MLK 1; Levison Interviews (Mosby;
Schlesinger).
   34. *NYT* 4/4/59, p. 19; Randolph & Rustin, "Youth March . . . Interim Report," 12/30/58, APR; Randolph to Eisenhower, 2/17/59, and E. Frederic Morrow
to James Hagerty, 4/10/59, OF 142-A-5, Box 732, DDEL; *WP* 4/19/59, p. B3; *PC*
4/25/59, p. 3; King, "Statement . . .," 4/18/59, APR; Baumgardner to Belmont,
"Youth March . . .," & Director to SAC New York, "Youth March . . .," both
4/22/59, 100-392452-NR; Morrow Interview (Wright). Levison had been a subject
of FBI scrutiny from 1952 until mid-1956. Informed initially in 1952 by two newly
recruited, high-ranking party informants, Jack and Morris Childs, that Levison
was a key financial supporter of American communism, the FBI had monitored
Levison's involvement in the party's secret financial affairs. According to the
Childses, Levison was one of very few Communists who were directly involved in
administering the financial subsidies that the American party secretly received

from the Soviet Union. Then, in mid-1955, Levison's active involvement ended, and the Childs brothers had little to report about him. The FBI had known of Levison's involvement with In Friendship, and that group's aid to the MIA, but in 3/57, just after Levison met King, the FBI removed him from its list of "key" Communists. Throughout the remainder of 1957–1958, Levison received little attention from the FBI. In the spring of 1959 the FBI began an inquiry into whether the MIA had received any "subversive" funds, but the brief, unproductive probe was closed on 7/21/59. (HQ file 100-429326) Neither that MIA investigation, nor the Youth Marches, led the FBI to pay any special attention to whether Levison was close to King. The FBI had yet to develop any curiosity about King, and its interest in Levison's role in the marches passed without any answer being obtained.

35. *NYT* 5/12/59, p. 19; *WP* 5/12/59, p. A13; King, "Address . . .," 5/11/59, MLK 11; King to Mboya, 7/8/59, MLK 1; *PC* 5/9/59, p. II-4, 11/21/59, p. 7; Baker, "Report of the Director . . .," 5/15/59, & SCLC, "Full Text of Open Statement . . .," 5/15/59, MLK 6 & 1.

36. Shuttlesworth to King, 6/15/59, & Baker to King, "Recent Efforts," 7/2/59, MLK 9; Mary Fair Burks Interview (Garrow); Seay, "Report of Executive Secretary," 7/8/59, MIA, KC; Durr to Clark & Mairi Foreman, n.d. [6/12/59], Durr 2-31; King to Earl Mazo, 9/2/58, MLK 4. On King's appearances, see *PC* 5/2/59, p. 2; *NYT* 5/2/59, p. 26; *MA* 6/3/59.

37. King, "Address . . .," 8/20/59, MLK 6; *MJ* 8/21/59, p. II-1. Also see *NYT* 7/5/59, p. 40, & King, "Address . . .," 9/23/59, KP; *JDN* 9/23 & 24/59; *Jet* 10/15/59, p. 8.

38. MIA Executive Board to Montgomery County Board of Education, 8/28/59, MLK 1-38; *MA* 8/30/59; *NYT* 8/31/59, p. 13; *NYHT* 8/31/59, p. 5; *WES* 9/3/59; *PC* 10/3/59, p. 4; *MIA Newsletter* II-1, 10/7/59; Baker, "Report of Executive Director . . .," 9/29/59, & King, "Recommendations to the Board," 9/29–30/59, MLK 9 & 6; "Recommendations" & "Resolutions," 10/1/59, SCLC 32; Baker Interviews (Britton; Garrow); Richberg, "Highlander," p. 22; Tjerandsen, *Education,* pp. 139–73; *CNC* 9/22/59; *SC* 9/30/59, 10/1/59. Between 9/13 and 9/23, King traveled to Honolulu, Los Angeles, Tucson, Dallas & New Orleans; also see *MT* 10/17/59, p. 1; *Jet* 10/1/59, p. 4.

39. *Jet* 10/22/59, pp. 10–11; *PC* 11/21/59, pp. 7, II-3; King to Booker, 10/20/59, & King to Brown, 10/19/59, MLK 3; Baker, "SCLC as a Crusade," 10/23/59, & King, "Recommendations to Committee on Future Program," 10/27/59, MLK 6; *Crusader* #2, 11/59.

40. Barbour, "Dr. King Returns 'Home,'" *Dexter Echo* 12/9/59, FOR; King et al., "Dear Friend" letter, 11/5/59, KP; Garrow interviews with Shuttlesworth, John Porter, Thomas Kilgore, Mary Fair Burks, Lillie Hunter & Robert Williams; Coretta King Interviews (Mayerson XXIV, pp. 14–15, 34–35; Garrow); Robert Nesbitt Interviews (Barton; Long; Garrow); Hazel Gregory Interview (Brown); King, Sr., *Daddy King,* p. 172; P. O. Watson et al. to King, 11/17/59, & King to Watson, 11/19/59, MLK 3-27; King to Levison, 11/19/59 & 11/25/59, MLK 1; Levison to Rustin, n.d. [ca. 11/59], BR; Rustin to Randolph, 11/5/59, BSCP 25; *MA* 11/30/59, p. A1; *NYT* 12/1/59, p. 23; *Southern School News* 1/60, p. 9.

41. King, "Annual Address . . .," 12/3/59, MLK 15; *MA* 12/4/59; *PC Magazine* 12/19/59, p. 7; *PC* 12/26/59, p. 2, 1/2/60, p. 20, 1/9/60, p. 3; Farmer, *Lay Bare,* pp. 190–91; *BN* 12/9/59; *NB* 12/9/59; *CT* 12/16/59, p. III-19; *ADW* 12/29/59, p. 1; *NYT* 12/29/59, p. 15; Klibaner, "SCEF," pp. 318–19; Also see *AM* 12/30/59, p. 1, 12/31/59, p. 2; *CP* 12/31/59, p. 20.

42. *WP* 1/2/60, p. A9; *AA* 1/9/60, p. 20; Walker Interviews (Britton; Garrow); Levison to King, 12/27/59, & King to Levison, 1/5/60, MLK 7 & 4; *NYT* 1/15/60, p. 16, 1/25/60, p. 18; *WP* 1/15/60, p. A9; *CG* 1/25/60, p. 3; Harrington Interview

(Garrow); Evans, *Dexter,* p. 131; *MA* 2/2/60, p. A3; *PC* 2/13/60, p. 3; *Jet* 12/17/59, pp. 12–17.

Chapter Three

1. Chafe, *Civilities,* pp. 99–130, and "Greensboro Sit-Ins"; Miles Wolff, *Lunch at the Five and Ten* (New York: Stein & Day, 1970); SRC, *Student Protest Movement;* Taylor, "Nashville Sit-In Movement"; *Dissent* 7–8/67, pp. 461–66; Moore Interview (Wright); John Lewis Interviews (Viorst; Carson); Lawson Interview (Viorst); Garrow interviews with Carey & Floyd McKissick; Carey in *CORE-lator* 3/60, p. 1; Morris, *Origins,* pp. 192–93, 197–201. On the Oklahoma and Kansas sit-ins, see Oppenheimer, "Genesis," pp. 51–53; Saxe, "Protest"; and Carl R. Graves, "The Right to be Served," *Chronicles of Oklahoma* 59 (Summer 1981): 152–66. As Lewis stressed to Carson, "The sit-in movement was not a coordinated effort . . . it was a spontaneous effort with very little organization."

2. *AJ* 2/3/60; *AC* 2/4/60, p. 16, 2/8/60, p. 5, 2/17/60, p. 7; Ballou Interview (Garrow); *CO* 2/12/78, p. C1; King, Sr., *Daddy King,* p. 172; Harold Fleming Interview (Leventhal); Garrow interviews with Coretta King & Donald Hollowell; *PC* 2/20/60, p. II-3; King to P. J. Ellis, 2/6/60, MLK 6; Moore Interview (Wright); Wehr, "Field Report," pp. 11, 21–25, and "The Sit-Down Protests," pp. 28, 54; King, "A Creative Protest," Durham, 2/16/60, KP; *DMH* 2/17/60, p. A1; DS 2/17/60, p. A1; *Newsweek* 2/29/60, pp. 24–25; Allan Sindler, *Negro Protest and Local Politics* (New York: McGraw-Hill, 1965), pp. 6–9.

3. *AC* 2/18/60, p. 1, 2/19/60, p. 9; *MA* 2/18/60, p. A1, 2/25/60, 2/28/60, p. B8, 3/1/60, 3/4/60; *PC* 2/27/60, p. 2, 3/12/60, pp. 5, II-4; *NYT* 2/18/60, p. 14, 2/25/60, p. 14, 2/26/60, p. 8, 3/1/60, p. 20, 3/10/60, p. 25; *AA* 2/20/60, p. 1; *BN* 2/24/60; Coretta King, *My Life,* pp. 185–86; Levison & Rustin to King, 2/26/60, MLK 7; *CT* 2/22/60, p. III-15; *A1aJ* 2/23/60; King to Eisenhower, 3/17/60, OF 124-A, Box 913, DDEL; *U.S. News* 3/21/60, pp. 72–78; Bernard Lee Interview (Garrow); McMillan, "Racial Violence," pp. 18–23; Reddick, "The State"; Dan Wakefield, *Revolt in the South* (New York: Grove Press, 1960), pp. 20–31, 86–95; Levison, "Minutes of Board Meeting," 3/7/60, APR. Montgomery white liberal Aubrey Williams, a close acquaintance of E. D. Nixon's, wrote another friend that "Nixon isn't so sure there isn't a lot of truth in what they are saying" about King's finances. John Salmond, *A Southern Rebel* (Chapel Hill: University of North Carolina Press, 1983), p. 253.

4. Walker, *Sit-Ins* & "Protest"; Mays, *Born,* pp. 287–99; Roslyn Pope Walker Interview (Lewis); Julian Bond Interviews (Viorst; Thrasher & Hall); Lonnie King Interview (Britton); Samuel Williams Interview (Lewis); Otis Moss Interview (Garrow); Baker Interviews (Britton; Walker; Hogan; Carson); Baker to King & Abernathy, "Student Conference . . . ," 3/23/60, SCLC 32; FBI 100-135-61-541, 3/22/60; "Minutes of Board Meeting," 3/21, 3/28 & 4/4/60, APR; *NYT* 3/29/60, p. 25, 4/8/60, p. 34, 4/9/60, p. 12; *MA* 4/7/60, p. A4; Farmer to Wilkins, 4/8/60, NAACP III-B-337. The 3/28 minutes, taken by "J. H. O'Dell, Acting Recorder," mark O'Dell's first appearance as a staff member of the defense committee. One reason for calling the Shaw conference, Baker told Carson, was that "there didn't even seem to be any communication, real communication between one city and the others," though there was some.

5. SCLC news release, 4/5/60, KC; *AC* 4/11/60, p. 9, 4/12/60, p. 13; King, "Statement . . . ," 4/15/60, MLK 4; *N&O* 4/16/60; *NYT* 4/16/60, p. 15, 4/17/60, p. 32, 4/18/60, p. 21; Baker Interviews (Walker; Britton; Hogan; Carson; Garrow); Baker in Cantarow & O'Malley, "Ella Baker," p. 84, and "NAACP . . . ," pp. 79–80; Walker Interview (Britton); Garrow interviews with Bernard Lee, James

Bevel & Diane Nash; Lawson Interviews (Viorst; Beifuss & Thomas); John Lewis Interview (Viorst); Marion Barry Interview (Shannon); Benjamin Brown Interview (Britton); Charles McDew Interview (Shannon); Charles Jones Interviews (Garrow; Shannon; Ricks); John Gibson Interviews (Garrow; Britton); Julian Bond Interviews (Viorst; Gillon; Thrasher & Hall); Carson, *In Struggle,* pp. 19–24; Morris, *Origins,* p. 217; Forman, *Making,* p. 216; Sellers, *River,* pp. 35–37; *Commentary* 6/60, pp. 524–28; Southwide Youth Leadership Conference ("eb"), "Recommendations of the Findings and Recommendations Committee," 4/15–17/60, KC.

6. "Meet the Press," 4/17/60, KP; King to Truman, 4/19/60, MLK 9; *NYT* 4/17/60, p. 32, 4/18/60, p. 21; Wilkins to King, 4/27/60, KP; Wilkins to Lawson, 5/13/60, BEM I-22; Wilkins, *Standing Fast,* pp. 269–70; Benjamin Mays to Wilkins, 5/18/60, RW 5; Wilkins to Mays, 5/19/60, BEM I-22; Lawson Interviews (Viorst; Leventhal); Robinson, *Abraham,* p. 121; King to Allan K. Chalmers, 4/18/60, MLK 3; King, untitled, undated 6pp. handwritten text, MLK 15, some of which appears in *Christian Century* 4/27/60, p. 510. Also see *New Republic* 4/25/60, pp. 13–16, 5/2/60, pp. 14–16.

7. *NT* 4/21/60; *WP* 4/25/60, p. A14, 4/26/60, p. A3; McKee, *King,* p. 39; Oppenheimer, "Genesis," p. 203; Louis Lautier, *AA* 4/30/60, p. 6; *AA* 5/7/60, p. 4; *NYHT* 5/4/60, p. 1; *NYT* 4/20/60, p. 25, 5/16/60, p. 22, 5/31/60, p. 20, 5/12/60, p. 28, 5/18/60, p. 23; Peters, "The Man," p. 91; *AJ* 10/24/60; Coretta King Interview (Mayerson XIII, p. 38); Lewis, *King,* p. 121; SCLC, "Conference on General Organization," 5/10–11/60, MLK 1-31; Walker Interviews (Garrow; Britton); Carson, *In Struggle,* p. 25; *AC* 5/18/60, p. 1. On King's other appearances see *AC* 4/30/60, p. 3; *CHW* 5/9/60, p. 1, 5/12/60; *DMH* 5/9/60, p. A3; *DS* 5/9/60, p. A3.

8. *NYT* 5/17/60, p. 19, 5/21/60, p. 23, 5/26/60, p. 67, 5/28/60, pp. 11, 13, 5/29/60, p. 1, 5/30/60, p. 20, 7/19/60, p. 21; *MA* 5/29/60, p. A1; *AC* 5/30/60, p. 20, 5/31/60, p. 11; *PC* 6/4/60, p. 2, 6/18/60, p. 3; Eskridge Interview (Garrow); *RNL* 5/31/60, 6/2/60; Cotton Interviews (Garrow; Wigginton & Thrasher); *Sepia* 1/62, p. 15. King's defense committee raised and spent $86,000. See Levison to Randolph, 9/2/60, & committee press release, 10/7/60, APR; King, "Dear Friend" letter, 10/6/60, MLK 1; & *AA* 10/22/60, p. 20.

9. Lomax, "Negro Revolt"; Nat Hentoff, *Commonweal* 6/10/60, pp. 275–78; Phillip Thompson, *Contemporary Review* 11/60, pp. 613–16; James Farmer to Roy Wilkins et al., "Report . . .," 6/10/60, NAACP III-B-337; King to Robinson, 6/19/60, MLK 9; King & Randolph, "Statement," 6/9/60, APR; *NYT* 6/10/60, p. 18; *NYHT* 6/10/60, p. 5; *NYC* 6/18/60, p. 2; Rustin to King, 6/15/60, MLK 1; Clarence Jones to Rustin, 6/21/60, BR; *PC* 6/25/60, p. 3; King to Powell, 6/24/60, MLK 3. King later wrote that "while I privately agreed with many of the things that Mr. Lomax said in the article, I feel a moral obligation to preserve a public image of unity in our organizational work." King to Marie Rodell, 11/30/60, MLK 1.

10. King to Chester Bowles, 6/24/60, MLK 3; King Interview (Bernhard); *NYT* 6/25/60, p. 13; *Look* 11/17/64, pp. 61, 64; Rustin Interviews (Garrow; Baker; Viorst II); Levison Interview (Lewis); King to Rustin, 7/1/60, BR; Garrow interviews with Tom Kahn & Rochelle Horowitz; Robinson, *Abraham,* p. 122; *NYCC* 7/2/60, p. 4; *NYC* 7/9/60, p. 3; *PC* 7/9/60, p. 2; Baldwin, "Dangerous Road," p. 42; Wofford, *Kennedys,* p. 115. Also see *Saturday Evening Post* 7/11–18/64, pp. 76–78; *NYT Magazine* 2/16/69, pp. 24–25, 104–12.

11. King, "Remarks . . .," 7/10/60, KP; *LAHE* 7/12/60; Garrow interviews with Harrington, Clarence Jones & Norman Hill; Harrington, *Fragments,* pp. 108–15; *CT* 7/26/60, p. 1; Wilkins, *Standing Fast,* pp. 274–75.

12. Walker Interviews (Britton; Garrow); Cotton Interview (Garrow); Moses Interview (Carson); Carson, *In Struggle,* pp. 26, 46; *AC* 8/5/60, p. 9, 8/6/60, p. 14; *AJ* 8/5/60; *ADW* 8/6/60, p. 1; "Report of the August Meeting," 8/5–7/60, SNCC 1; Baker Interviews (Britton; Hogan; Carson; Garrow); Lawson Interview (Viorst);

King, Sr., *Daddy King*, p. 181; John Porter Interview (Garrow). Moses shared Walker's reaction. "There wasn't much of anything to be done in the SCLC operation. They were putting out a fundraising letter," and "it looked like they were going to take most of the summer to get this fundraising letter out." In one brief conversation with King, "I guess what struck me was that he wasn't as interested in me as a person as Ella was." (Carson Interview) On King and Baker, Andrew Young asserted that "we had a hard job with domineering women in SCLC because Martin's mother, quiet as she was, was really a strong, domineering force in that family. She was never publicly saying anything, but she ran Daddy King and she ran the church and she ran Martin, and so Martin's problems with Ella Baker, for instance, in the early days of the movement were directly related to his need to be free of that strong matriarchal influence." (Kotz Interview)

13. Walker, *Sit-Ins* & "Functions"; Rich to COAHR, 8/10/60, Hill to Rich, 8/30/60, & Rich to Hill, 9/1/60, Rich 53; King, "Address . . .," Louisville, 8/23/60; *LT* 8/24/60; *LCJ* 8/24/60, p. II-1; King, "Address . . .," 9/6/60, MLK 11; *NYT* 9/7/60, p. 34, 9/15/60, p. 28; King, "Address . . .," Charlotte, N.C., 9/25/60, KP; *CO* 9/26/60, p. B1. Also see Wyatt Walker to Wilkins, 8/24/60, 9/21/60, RW 6.

14. King Interview (Bernhard); Wofford Interview (Bernhard); Wofford, *Kennedys*, p. 12; *Look* 11/17/64, pp. 61, 64; *AJ* 10/24/60; Peters, "The Man," p. 91; 9/23/60 sentence form in *Georgia* v. *King*, DeKalb Co. #10443.

15. *AC* 10/4/60, p. 6, 10/6/60, p. 15; *NYT* 10/4/60, p. 38; *NYHT* 10/9/60, p. 14; "Minutes of Annual Board Meeting," 10/11/60, SCLC, KC; Walker, "Report of the Director," 10/11/60, MLK 16; *PC* 10/22/60, p. 2; SAC New Orleans to Director, 10/20/60, 100-438794-X3; *New America* 11/1/60, p. 1; Michael Harrington Interview (Garrow); Oppenheimer, "Genesis," pp. 92–97; Laue, "Direct Action," pp. 45, 129–30; Carson, *In Struggle*, pp. 27–30.

16. Otis Moss Interview (Garrow); Walker, *Sit-Ins*; Lincoln, "Strategy"; Julian Bond Interviews (Viorst; Burrell); Lonnie King Interviews (Harriford; Britton); M. D. Jackson to Roy Wilkins, 10/19/60, RW 6; Raines, *My Soul*, pp. 88–90; Glenn Smiley Interview (Garrow); *AC* 10/20/60, p. 1, 10/21/60, pp. 1, 10, 12, 10/22/60, p. 1, 10/24/60, p. 1, 10/25/60, pp. 1, 11, 16; *NYT* 10/20/60, p. 39, 10/21/60, p. 27, 10/23/60, p. 77, 10/25/60, p. 31, 12/15/60, p. 30; *AJ* 10/20/60; *PC* 10/29/60, p. 2; *AA* 10/22/60, p. 1; *New America* 11/1/60, p. 1, 11/15/60, p. 6; *Guardian* 10/31/60, p. 1, 11/21/60, p. 16; *Negro Digest* 11/61, pp. 45–49; Wofford, *Kennedys*, pp. 13–16; Wofford Interviews (Bernhard; Blackside; Garrow); Abram, *Day*, pp. 125–30; Hartsfield to Paul Tillet, 4/7/64, Hartsfield 30-1; Coretta King Interviews (Mayerson XIII, p. 38; Blackside); Stein, *American Journey*, pp. 90–91; Garrow interviews with Harold Fleming & Bernard Lee.

17. Hollowell Interviews (Lewis; Garrow; Britton); *AC* 10/26/60, p. 1; *NYT* 10/26/60, p. 1, 12/15/60, p. 30; *Georgia* v. *King*, DeKalb Co. #10443, 10/25/60; Coretta King Interview (Mayerson XIII, pp. 44–45); "Suggested Statement Dictated by Judge Walsh—10/31/60," OF 142-A-4, Box 731, DDEL; Morrow, *Black Man*, p. 296; Morrow Interviews (Wright; Soapes); Nixon, *Six Crises*, pp. 362–63; Burk, *Eisenhower*, pp. 86, 259–60; Wofford, *Kennedys*, pp. 11, 16–18; Wofford Interviews (Bernhard; Garrow); Louis Martin Interviews (Garrow; Wright); Bass, *Unlikely Heroes*, p. 162. Also see Bowles, *Saturday Evening Post* 3/1/58, pp. 19–21, 87–89.

18. *PC* 11/5/60, p. 2; King Interview (Bernhard); Hollowell Interviews (Lewis; Garrow); Coretta King Interview (Mayerson XIII, p. 49); Wofford, *Kennedys*, pp. 18–22; Wofford Interview (Bernhard); Stein, *American Journey*, pp. 91–93; Martin in Thompson, *Kennedy*, p. 87; Schlesinger, *Robert Kennedy*, pp. 216–18; *AC* 10/27/60, p. 1; *NYT* 10/27/60, p. 22; *AA* 10/29/60, p. 1; King, Sr., *Daddy King*, pp. 174–75; Abram, *Day*, pp. 131–32; Robert Kennedy Interview (Lewis).

19. *PC* 11/5/60, p. 2; Coretta King Interview (Mayerson XIII, p. 59); King, Sr., *Daddy King*, pp. 174–75; King to Coretta King, 10/26/60, KP.

20. Hollowell Interviews (Lewis; Garrow; Britton); *AC* 10/28/60, p. 1, 11/2/60, p. 6, 11/5/60, p. 1; *AJ* 10/28/60, 11/7/60; *NYT* 10/28/60, p. 1, 12/15/60, p. 30, 11/7/60, p. 24; Abram, *Day,* pp. 131–32; Brauer, *Kennedy,* pp. 49–50; Wofford, *Kennedys,* pp. 22–26; Wofford Interview (Bernhard); King, "Statement . . .," 11/1/60, MLK 4; King Interview (Bernhard); "Special Meeting with Doctor M. L. King . . .," 11/2/60, MLK 4; *Time* 11/7/60, p. 30; *PC* 11/12/60, p. 3, 12/31/60, p. 3; King to DeWolf, 11/2/60, MLK 3. Also see Lee, "Apocalyptic," p. 8.

21. Wood to Horton, 11/18/60, Anne Lockwood to Wood, 12/8/60, & Lockwood & Clark, "Report on Discussions . . .," 1/30/61, HLW 38-3; Wood, "Report . . .," 11/23/60, SCLC 120; *RNL* 11/5 & 11/19/60; SCLC press release 11/23/60, KC; Reid Interview (Garrow); Walker, *Sit-Ins,* "Protest," and "Functions"; Otis Moss Interview (Garrow); *Jet* 11/10/60, pp. 3–6; SNCC "Minutes," 11/25–27/60, SNCC; King & Kilpatrick, "The Nation's Future," 11/26/60, MLK 4; Kilpatrick Interview (Leventhal); Laue, "Direct Action," p. 169, quoting a 3/19/62 interview with Baker. "We are not seeking to upset the social structure of the nation," King added in a 1/1/61 address in Savannah. KP, p. 16.

22. Walker, *Sit-Ins; AC* 12/20/60, p. 14; *AJ* 12/20/60; *CHT* 12/31/60; *MA* 12/31/60; *AIaJ* 12/31/60; *PC* 12/24/60, p. 7, 1/14/61, p. 4; King Interview (Bernhard); Gordon Carey Interview (Garrow); Farmer, *Lay Bare,* p. 194; Meier & Rudwick, *CORE,* p. 131; Wood to King, "Proposed . . . Training Program," 1/20/61, SCLC 136; SCLC, "Leadership Training . . .," 1/27/61, UCC 21-4; SCLC press release, 2/14/61, KC; *NYT* 2/23/61, p. 28; *SLPD* 11/28/60, p. A3.

23. Levison to King, 10/13/60, & Angelou to Walker, 11/10/60, MLK 1; Levison to Randolph, 1/10/61, APR; Angelou, *Heart,* pp. 53, 58–60, 68–69, 86, 92, 97, 104, 127; *Sepia* 4/61, pp. 42–47; King, "The Man Who Was a Fool," *Pulpit* 6/61, pp. 4–6 (Chicago, 1/29/61); Walker, *Sit-Ins,* "Protest," and "Functions"; *Look* 4/25/61, pp. 31–40; *AC* 2/16/61, p. 10, 3/11/61, p. 3; *ADW* 2/16/61, p. 1; King to J. R. Butts, 2/8/61, KP; Fort, "Atlanta," pp. 40–43; Ivan Allen Interviews (Viorst; Leventhal); Allen, *Mayor,* pp. 36–42; Lonnie King Interview (Britton); Herschelle Sullivan to Howard Zinn, 4/13/61, Zinn 3–7; John Calhoun Interview (Britton); Garrow interviews with Otis Moss, John Gibson & Bernard Lee; Julian Bond Interview (Hall & Thrasher); "For Release 9:30 A.M. 3/7/61," Rich 53; Newsom & Gorden, "Stormy Rally"; Carl Holman Interview (Britton); Mays, *Born,* p. 293; Raines, *My Soul,* pp. 91–92; *NYT* 3/11/61, p. 21; *PC* 3/18/61, p. II-2; Alton Hornsby, "A City That Was Too Busy to Hate," in Jacoway & Colburn, *Southern Businessmen,* pp. 120–36; *SFC* 3/26/61, p. 12.

24. SCLC, "Minutes of . . . Administrative Committee," 3/8–9/61, MLK 7; *Life* 11/7/60, pp. 123–34; Ballou Interview (Garrow); McDonald Interviews (Garrow; Smith); Coretta King Interview (Mayerson XXIII, p. 1); *PC* 4/15/61, p. 7; King to Thomas Kilgore, 12/30/63, KP; Fauntroy Interviews (Garrow; Leventhal); Young Interviews (Garrow; Wigginton); Young to King, 3/24/61, King to Levison, 4/25/61, King to Young, 4/25/61, King to Myles Horton, 4/25/61, MLK 7; Young to Robert Spike, 4/25/61, UCC 27-14; Dorothy Cotton to Septima Clark, 4/18/61, & Young to Horton, 5/11/61, HLW 38-3. On King's travels, see *WP* 2/18/61, p. A5; *CA* 2/27/61, p. 4; *KCT* 3/16/61, p. 3; *PC* 4/1/61, p. 2; *SC* 3/27/61; *SFC* 3/25/61, p. 5, 3/26/61, p. 12, 3/27/61, p. 2; *LCJ* 4/20/61, p. II-1. On 3/22/61, King wrote A. J. Muste that "over the last year my responsibilities have more than tripled. The demands on my time are unbelievable." He declined a post on the NAACP's board because "it would probably be too much added to my schedule," and told Muste, "I know that I am doing a grave injustice to the southern struggle by being away from the scene of action so often." King to Muste, MLK 4-19, and King to Kivie Kaplan, 3/6/61, MLK 1. The first Young-King meeting was 3/31/57, when both took part in a program at Talladega College. Young and his wife, Jean (who, like Coretta, was from Marion County), offered the Kings a ride home. "We drove from Talladega back to Montgomery and had dinner with them. . . . And we sat around talking, and I knew he had written his . . . dissertation on Paul Tillich. I had read a lot of Paul Tillich and I had been fortunate enough to meet Dr. Tillich . . . in New York, and I wanted to talk theology. And he wasn't interested . . . we ended up having a nice little chat about family and children; we made no comments about the social situation, nothing profound." Young Interview (Moyers); also Young in Gloria Steinem's "A Conversation With," PBS, 4/12/84.

25. King, "Equality Now," *Nation* 2/4/61, pp. 91–95; King to Reeves, 2/28/61, WHCF 1478 JFKL; King to Kennedy, 3/16/61, Wofford to O'Donnell, 3/20/61, Reeves to O'Donnell, 3/22/61, O'Donnell to King, 3/25/61, & Reeves to Kennedy, 5/5/61, WHCF 358 JFKL; *AA* 5/13/61, p. 9; King Interview (Bernhard); *Look* 11/17/64, pp. 61, 64.

26. Farmer to John Kennedy & to Robert Kennedy, 4/26/61, CORE SHSW Reel 25-117; Schlesinger, *Robert Kennedy,* p. 295; Barnes, *Journey,* pp. 157–75; Marshall Interview (Viorst); Farmer, *Lay Bare,* pp. 196–200; Viorst, *Fire,* pp. 133–44; Farmer Interview (Britton); Navasky, *Kennedy Justice,* p. 205; SRC, *The Freedom Ride;* Peck, *Freedom Ride; AJC* 2/20/83, p. A1; Braden Interview (Garrow); Klibaner, "SCEF," p. 347; *AJ* 5/2/61; Walker, "Semi-Annual Report . . .," 4/30/61, KC; Lee Interview (Garrow); James Wood to Board, "Report of Public Relations Program," 5/10/61, KC; *MIA Newsletter* II-4, 3/15/61; *PC* 5/13/61, p. 3, 5/20/61, p. 3.

27. Walker Interview (Britton); Farmer Interviews (Britton; Blackside); Farmer, *Lay Bare,* pp. 200–204; Viorst, *Fire,* pp. 128, 144–45, 148–53; Farmer on "ABC Close-Up," 11/11/83; Gordon Carey Interview (Garrow); Meier & Rudwick, *CORE,* pp. 136–37; John Lewis Interviews (Viorst; Shannon; Porter); *New Republic* 6/5/61, pp. 21–23; Schlesinger, *Robert Kennedy,* pp. 296–97; Carson, *In Struggle,* pp. 33–37; Nash, "Inside"; Nash Interview (Garrow); Helen Fuller, *Year of Trial* (New York: Harcourt Brace & World, 1962), pp. 134–39; John Seigenthaler Interviews (Garrow; Blackside); Navasky, *Kennedy Justice,* pp. 20–23, 124; Thornton, "The Montgomery Freedom Rider Riots"; Justin Finger to Arnold Forster, "Montgomery, Ala.—Race Riots . . .," 5/24/61, ADL.

28. Schlesinger, *Robert Kennedy,* pp. 297–98; Viorst, *Fire,* pp. 146–48, 153–55; SRC, *The Freedom Ride;* King, "Address . . .," 5/21/61, KP; *NYT* 5/22/61, p. 1; *NYHT* 5/22/61, p. 1; *AC* 5/22/61, pp. 1, 8, 11; Mitford, *Poison Penmanship* (New York: Alfred A. Knopf, 1979), pp. 73–76; Marshall Telephone Logs, BM 9-12; Marshall Interview (Oberdorfer); Robert Kennedy (& Marshall) Interview (Lewis); Guthman, *We Band,* pp. 172–73, 177–78; Blackside interviews with John Patterson, Floyd Mann & Wyatt Walker. After one of those late-night calls, James Farmer writes, King informed him that "the attorney general asks that you halt the Freedom Rides and have a cooling-off period to give him time to try to work things out," a request King thought wise. Farmer and Diane Nash said no, and King acquiesced. *Lay Bare,* pp. 204–206.

29. John Lewis Interviews (Shannon; Viorst); James Bevel Interview (Shannon); Garrow interviews with Diane Nash & John Maguire; Laue, "Direct Action," pp. 169–70; Stein, *American Journey,* pp. 96–103; *LAT* 1/16/84; Schlesinger, *Robert Kennedy,* p. 298; Viorst, *Fire,* pp. 156–58; Coffin, *Once,* pp. 151–56; SRC, *The Freedom Ride;* Meier & Rudwick, *CORE,* pp. 138–41; *NYHT* 5/23/61, p. 3, 5/24/61, p. 1; *AC* 5/23/61, p. 1, 5/24/61, p. 1, 5/25/61, p. 1; *NYT* 5/24/61, p. 1; *NYP* 5/23/61, p. 3; *Ebony* 8/61, pp. 212–18; *Spectator* 4/19/68, pp. 516–17; Baker Interview (Britton); Raines, *My Soul,* pp. 123–24; Farmer, *Lay Bare,* pp. 206–207. King's refusal, Farmer says, elicited "loud laughter and derisive comments."

30. SRC, *The Freedom Ride*; Marshall Telephone Logs, n. 28 above; Guthman, *We Band,* pp. 154–55; Marshall in Thompson, *Kennedy,* pp. 79–80; Schlesinger, *Robert Kennedy,* pp. 299–300; *NYT* 5/26/51, p. 1; *AC* 5/26/61, p. 1;

Coffin, *Once*, pp. 151–56; Wofford, *Kennedys*, pp. 125, 153–57; John Maguire Interview (Garrow).

31. Wood, "Report of Meeting . . .," 5/26/51, SCLC; *NYT* 5/27/61, p. 9; *AC* 5/27/61, p. 1, 5/31/60, p. 10; *AJ* 5/27/61; Gordon Carey Interview (Garrow); Walker Interview (Britton); SRC, *The Freedom Ride*; Laue, "Direct Action," p. 338; Meier & Rudwick, *CORE,* pp. 139–41; Robert F. Williams to King, 5/31/61, MLK 7; Walker & Henry Schwarzschild to Robert Kennedy et al., "Interstate Travel . . .," 7/3/61, KC. Walker was arrested in Jackson on 6/21 as part of the ongoing rides.

32. *NYT* 6/6/61, p. 29; *NYHT* 6/6/61, p. 1; *AA* 6/17/61, p. 1; Wofford, *Kennedys,* p. 124; "Citizenship School Committee Meeting," 6/8/61, UCC 21-5; Horton to Hahn, 6/19/61, & Young to Horton, 6/20/61, HLW 38-2 & 3; "Memorandum on Citizenship Program," 6/26/61, & Horton to Executive Council, "Citizenship School Committee," n.d. [ca. 7/1/61], HTSA; Horton, "Report to Citizenship School Committee," 6/30/61, HLW 38-2; Young to Wood et al., 6/27/61, UCC 27-14; "Citizenship School Committee Meeting," 7/12/61, UCC 21-5; "Minutes of Executive Council . : .," 7/28–29/61, HTSA 5-10; Horton, "Highlander," pp. 267–96; Richberg, "Highlander," p. 27; Adams, *Unearthing,* p. 133.

33. Robert Kennedy Interview (Lewis II, p. 2); Burke Marshall Interviews (Viorst; Wright; Garrow); Garrow interviews with Harold Fleming, Jane Lee Eddy, Louis Martin, Wiley Branton, Diane Nash & Charles Jones; Meier & Rudwick, *CORE,* pp. 172–75; Raines, *My Soul,* pp. 227–31; Fleming in Stern, "Contemporary Black Suffrage," pp. 26–27; Tim Jenkins Interview ("JM"-Zinn). Martin confessed that "its origins were pure Democratic politics with the White House and Justice Department fully knowledgeable of where we were going." With regard to the protection issue, Marshall told Wright that "what we always said was we could do much more if they were doing something in voting rights." At a mid-July Baltimore meeting that King and Walker attended, SNCC debated a proposal by Charles Jones and Tim Jenkins that SNCC commit itself to the Marshall-Fleming-Currier registration program by hiring up to ten staff members (only one field-worker, Charles Sherrod, was then on the payroll). A decision was deferred until August.

34. Walker Interviews (Garrow; Smith); *NYT* 6/17/61, p. 10; *NYHT* 6/17/61, p. 5; *MA* 6/18/61, p. A8; *NVP* 7/1/61; *NJG* 7/8/61, pp. 1–2; *JDN* 7/7/61; *AA* 7/29/61, p. 16, 8/26/61, p. 2; *HC* 7/16/61, p. 1; *BS* 7/16/61, pp. 22, 14; *SFC* 7/24/61, p. 4; Coretta King Interview (Mayerson XXVII, pp. 32–33); *NYT* 8/14/61, p. 12, 8/17/61, p. 1; *MH* 8/17/61; *PC* 8/26/61, p. II-3.

35. SCLC, "Leadership Training Program & Citizenship Schools," n.d., & "Citizenship Education Program," n.d., MLK 14; SNCC Minutes, 7/14–16/61, Baltimore, HLW 71-16; Charles Jones, "Report of Harry Belafonte Committee," 8/11/61, and "SNCC Office Report," [8/11/61], Braden 62-3; "Minutes for Meeting of Co-Committee," 8/11/61, HLW 71-16; Charles Jones Interviews (Garrow; Ricks; Shannon); Garrow interviews with Diane Nash & Bernard Lafayette; McDew Interview (Shannon); Marion Barry Interviews (Wigginton; "JM"-Zinn); Tim Jenkins Interview ("JM"-Zinn); Baker in Cantarow, "Baker," pp. 80–81; Carson, *In Struggle,* pp. 39–42; Moses to Walker, 8/3/61, MFDP; Moses, "Mississippi"; Moses Interview (Carson); Dittmer, "The Movement in McComb"; Harold Fleming Interview (Garrow); Walker, "Southwide Voter Registration Prospectus," n.d. [ca. 9/61], MLK 14; Young, "A Proposed Strategy for the Citizenship School Program," n.d. [6/20/61], SCLC 136; Horton to Walker, 8/22/61, HLW 30-3; Bruce Galphin, *Nation* 9/23/61, pp. 177–80.

36. *Sepia* 12/61, pp. 15–19; Bond Interviews (Viorst; Hall & Thrasher); *AC* 1/14/78, p. B1; Peters, "The Man," pp. 91–94; FBI NY 100-111180-7-17A, 4/5/62;

Coffin, *Once*, p. 170; Walker Interview (Smith); Harold Fleming Interview (Garrow); Coretta King Interview (Mayerson XVII, p. 19).

37. Walker Interview (Garrow); Wood to King, n.d. ["Monday night"], & 3/18/62, KC; Garrow interviews with Maude Ballou & Dorothy Cotton; Booth, *Progressive Story*, pp. 14–40; *NYT* 6/16/60, p. 16; *CD* 6/26/61; Garrow interviews with Taylor & D. E. King; *Sepia* 1/61, pp. 66–71; Charles King, "Untold Story"; *PC* 9/16/61, p. II-3, 9/23/61, pp. II-2, 3; *AA* 9/23/61, p. 7; *Jet* 9/28/61, pp. 18–19; King to Charles Butler, 9/20/61, MLK 1; King to Erma Hughes, 9/19/61, CAB 386-10; Edward Wheeler, "Beyond One Man," *Review and Expositor* 70 (Summer 1973): 309–19; Thomas Kilgore Interview (Garrow); Jackie Robinson, *Never*, pp. 143–44; Peeks, *Long Struggle*, pp. 311–14; Paris, *Black Leaders*, p. 24; *WP* 9/11/82, p. C12. Jackson wrote King (9/12/61, CAB) that "I did not say that you had masterminded the invasion of the convention hall that resulted in a delegate's death." King friend and writer Al Duckett later commented that Wilkins was "almost as psychotic about Martin as J. H. Jackson." (Oates Interview)

38. Carson, *In Struggle*, pp. 44–55; Bond Interviews (Viorst; Britton; Hall & Thrasher); McDew Interview (Shannon); Forman, "What is SNCC . . .," 11/64, pp. 7, 14, 14A, 17, UCLA 8-A13; Forman, *Making*, pp. 244–45. In a summer 1962 interview, Bond said that King "is a very simple man . . . he is blind to the faults of others close to him. He lets himself be used by them. And this is not a fault, this is not being naive, this is being simple. He has let his name be bandied about. He has used his prestige to smother others who do the same thing. His organization has taken credit for other things. I can't say I don't have respect for him, because I do. I'm just very disappointed in him. And I think Negro students are, more so than anyone else." Rose & Greenya, *Black Leaders*, p. 34.

39. Young Interview (Garrow); Young to Walker 8/8/61, Young to King & Walker, 9/11/61, MLK 7; *NYT* 9/24/61, p. 75, 9/26/61, p. 22; Walker, "Report of the Director," 9/28/61, KC; Levison & O'Dell, "Report on New York Office—10/15/60 to 8/31/61," KC; "Minutes of Annual Board Meeting, 9/27/61, KC; *NB* 9/29/61; *CT* 9/29/61; *NT* 9/29/61, 9/30/61; Lomax, *Negro Revolt*, p. 88, & *To Kill*, p. 120; Kunstler, *Deep*, pp. 75–79, and *Trials*, p. 50; SCLC press release, 11/16/61, MLK 7. On CEP's start, see Young to Wesley Hotchkiss, 10/3/61, SCLC 136; Young to Myles & Aimee Horton, 10/3/61, HLW 30-5; Clark, *Echo*, pp. 213–23; *Southern Exposure*, Summer 1979, pp. 74–76; Bernice Robinson Interview (Thrasher & Wigginton III, pp. 13–14).

40. *WJ* 10/16/61, p. 8; *PI* 10/22/61, p. 9, 10/24/61, p. 23, 10/25/61, p. 43; *AA* 10/28/61, p. 1, 11/4/61, p. 8; *Presbyterian Life* 12/1/61, p. 29; "Minutes of Administrative Committee," 10/19/61, KC; *NYT* 10/17/61, p. 1, 10/21/61, p. 23; Wofford to O'Donnell, 6/12/61 & 10/4/61, WHCF 358; *WP* 10/17/61, p. A2; *PC* 10/28/61, p. 6, 11/4/61, p. II-2; King's 2/12/62 description of the visit in a Birmingham speech, as set down in R. R. Long to Jamie Moore, 2/20/62, Connor; Wofford, *Kennedys*, pp. 128–29, 164–66; Wofford Interviews (Bernhard; Garrow). As Wofford wrote one researcher (3/25/64), he saw the president on an average of only "once a month." Sullivan, "Civil Rights," p. 206.

41. *Reporter* 9/23/61, pp. 39–40; *MA* 10/18/61; *PC* 11/18/61, p. 6; Young to Hotchkiss, 11/17/61, SCLC 136; Young to Myles Horton, 11/29 & 12/13/61, HLW 30-5; Levison to King, 11/1/61, MLK 7; King Interview (Smith); King, "Face to Face Interview," 10/29/61, KP. King told another questioner, "My religion has come to mean more to me than ever before. I have come to believe more and more in a personal God—not a process, but a person, a creative power with infinite love who answers prayers." Peters, "The Man," p. 91. Comparisons to Christ or Gandhi were "quite embarrassing," King said. "When I compare myself with all these great persons . . . I can see such a great difference. I am sure that the commitment of all proved to be much greater than my commitment. Their ideas were greater." He added that "when you are aware that you are a symbol, it causes you to search your soul constantly, to go through this job of self-analysis, to see if you live up to all of the high and noble principles that people surround you with." Wallace, "Self-Portrait," *NYP* 2/15/61, p. 42.

42. O'Dell, "Climbin' Jacob's Ladder," pp. 13–14; Lerone Bennett, *Confrontation: Black and White* (Baltimore: Penguin Books, 1965), p. 225; King to Harold Courlander, 10/30/61, MLK 7. "I'm not worried about the future and my own career" as he had been in the late 1950s, King noted. "There was a time when I worried about reaching the zenith of my career too early, when I felt I might be on the decline at a fairly early age." Wallace, n. 41 above; Peters, "The Man," p. 92.

Chapter Four

1. Sherrod interviews (Garrow; Ricks); untitled Sherrod essay, n.d., SNCC 95; Sherrod, "Report on Terrell County," n.d. [8/11/61], Braden 62-3; untitled Reagon report, n.d., SNCC 19; Carson, *In Struggle,* pp. 56–58; Bolster, "Civil Rights," pp. 259–61; E. D. Hamilton Interviews (Garrow; Ricks; Barton; 7/67, KC); Anderson Interview (Garrow; KC); C. B. King Interviews (Barton; Ricks; Lewis); Marion Page Interview (Smith); Ricks interviews with E. James Grant & Benjamin Gay; "Origins of the Albany Movement," in *Albany Movement 1st Anniversary Celebration Booklet,* 11/12–16/62, KC, & in *SWG* 1/27/62; C. B. King in Christine P. Clark, ed., *Minority Opportunities in Law* (New York: Law Journal Press, 1974), pp. 29–40; *New America* 12/22/61, p. 4; Hamilton et al. to Asa Kelley et al., 12/15/60, & Kelley to Hamilton, 12/22/60, ALB; Anderson et al. to Dougherty Co. Board of Registrars, 1/27/61, SK-F; *PC* 12/30/61, p. II-3, 2/17/62, p. 11; Franklin, "Comparison," pp. 24–25; *The Albany—S.W. Georgia Movement 20th Anniversary Celebration,* 8/5–8/81.

2. Sherrod essay & Reagon report, n. 1 above; Sherrod Interview (Garrow); Watters, *Down to Now,* pp. 152–55; Bernice Reagon in Cluster, *They Should,* pp. 11–30; Eliza "Goldie" Jackson Interviews (Garrow; Ricks); Pfister, "Twenty Years," p. 26; H. C. Boyd Interview (Ricks).

3. Kelley to Dennis, 9/13/61, Dennis to Kelley, 9/15/61, Kelley to Anderson, 9/23/61, & Stephen Roos to Kelley, "Lincoln Heights Improvement Association," 10/24/61, ALB; City Commission Minutes, 10/24/61, p. 464; Garrow interviews with Roos & Kelley.

4. Sherrod essay, n. 1 above; Salynn McCollum, "Bus Terminal Survey," 11/1/61, SNCC 111; Anderson Interviews (Garrow; Blackside); Garrow interviews with Pritchett, Sherrod & "Goldie" Jackson; "Minutes of Special Meeting of City Commission," 10/30/61, ALB; Samuel Bigbie (terminal manager) to F. W. Mills, 11/1/61, DOJ Micro 111; Hamilton Interviews (Garrow; Barton); Bernice Reagon Interview (Blackside); Slater King Interviews (Smith; Lewis); Samuel B. Wells Interviews (Garrow; Ricks); C. B. King Interview (Lewis); Ricks interviews with H. C. Boyd, E. James Grant, Benjamin Gay, Thomas Chatmon & Anderson.

5. "Albany Handbill," 11/9/61, in Lynd, *Nonviolence,* pp. 442–43; Sherrod essay, pp. 10–11, n. 1 above; Slater King Interview (Lewis); Garrow interviews with Anderson & Jordan; "The Albany Movement, Minutes," 11/17/61, SNCC KC; Page, "Minutes of the Albany Movement," 11/17/61, ALB; Chatmon Interview (Ricks); Hamilton Interviews (Garrow; Ricks; Barton); "Transcript of Telephone Conversation Between Vernon Jordan & Gloster B. Current," 12/14/61, NAACP III-B-408; Sherrod Interview (Blackside); "Statement of Blanton Hall," 11/22/61, & C. B. King to Charles Minor, 11/28/61, SNCC 95; Reagon report, n. 1 above; Zinn, *Albany,* 1/8/62.

6. Reagon report & Sherrod essay, n. 1 above; "Transcript," n. 5 above; *Student Voice,* Albany, 11/26 & 12/1/61; *AH* 11/27/61, p. 1, 11/28/61, p. 1, 11/29/61, p. 1; Tom Hayden & Herb Mills, ". . . Report on Albany," 11/29/61, SNCC 117; City Commission Minutes 11/28/61, p. 470; Anderson Interviews (Garrow; Blackside).

7. "Transcript," n. 5 above; *AH* 12/1/61, p. 1, 12/2/61, p. 4; "Meeting: Dean Minor . . .," 12/2/61, SNCC 95; Jones to James Forman, 12/7/61, SNCC 15; Tom Hayden, *New America* 1/5/62, p. 1; Zinn, *Albany,* 1/8/62; Watters, *Down,* p. 157; Garrow interviews with Jones & Jordan & Bernard Lee; Burke Marshall to J. Edgar Hoover, 12/14/61, 157-492-X; Pritchett Interviews (Garrow; Ricks; Reston); *AH* 12/11/61, p. 1; *PC* 12/30/61, p. II-3; Bolster, "Civil Rights," p. 266. As Asa Kelley later commented, "That was our biggest mistake. We never should have arrested those Freedom Riders." *NYT* 8/13/62, p. 1; *WP* 8/5/62, p. A1.

8. *AH* 12/12/61, p. 1, 12/13/61, p. 1; *AC* 12/13/61, p. 1, 12/14/61, p. 1; *NYT* 12/13/61, p. 51, 12/14/61, p. 47; Slater King Interview (Smith); Garrow interviews with Jones & Sherrod; Anderson Interviews (Garrow; Ricks); Anderson to King, 12/14/61, KP; Sherrod essay, n. 1 above; C. B. King Interviews (Lewis; Barton); Reagon in Morris, *Origins,* pp. 243–45; Edward P. Morgan, ABC, 12/13/61, KC; SNCC press release, 12/13/61, NCCIJ 20-17; *PC* 12/23/61, p. II-3. Anderson had attended school in Atlanta in the 1940s and had met King several times. He finished his undergraduate studies at Alabama State in Montgomery, where he attended Dexter under King's predecessor, Vernon Johns, before going to medical school in Iowa. Anderson had tried unsuccessfully to reach King to invite him to the 11/16 rally. Anderson Interviews (Garrow; Ricks); *PC* 3/3/62, p. 5; King's 8/8/62 testimony in *Kelley* v. *Page,* vol. 4, pp. 1139, 1149. On King's November and early December appearances, see *PO* 11/9/61, p. 1; *CP* 11/27/61, p. C10; *NYT* 12/2/61, p. 25, 12/12/61, p. 49; *PC* 12/9/61, p. II-3, 12/16/61, p. II-4; *NOTP* 12/15/61.

9. *AH* 12/14/61, p. 1, 12/15/61, p. 1; *AC* 12/15/61, p. 1, 12/16/61, p. 1; *NYT* 12/15/61, p. 29, 12/16/61, p. 18; Garrow interviews with Kelley, Pritchett, Roos & Sherrod; Burke Marshall to Robert Kennedy, 12/14/61, 12/18/61, BM; *AJ* 12/15/61, p. 1; *SWG* 12/16/61; *PC* 12/30/61, p. 2; S. W. Walker to Mayor et al., 12/15/61, Kelley to J. F. Wilson, 12/15/61, & to M. S. Page, 12/16/61, & Grady Rawls, "Complaint," 12/15/61, ALB.

10. Watters, *Down,* pp. 11–15, 358, 365; Garrow interviews with Anderson & Jones; *AH* 12/16/61, p. 1, 12/17/61, p. 1; *AJ* 12/16/61, p. 20; Kelley to Anderson & Page, 12/16/61, ALB; *NYT* 12/17/61, p. 1; *AJC* 12/17/61, p. 1; Laue, "Direct Action," p. 178; Zinn, *Albany,* 1/8/62, pp. 15–17; *AA* 12/23/61, p. 1; *Newsweek* 12/25/61, pp. 17–18; SAC Atlanta to Director, 12/17/61, McGowan to Rosen, 12/17/61, & Rosen to Belmont, 12/18/61, 157-6-2-225, 229 & 231.

11. *AJC* 12/17/61, p. 1; *AC* 12/18/61, p. 1; SCLC press release, "Abernathy Issues Call . . . , 12/17/61, KC; Watters, *Down,* p. 147; *NYT* 12/18/61, p. 1, 12/24/61, p. E5; *AH* 12/18/61, p. 1; *NYHT* 12/18/61, p. 1; *Newsweek* 1/1/62, pp. 13–14; Walker Interviews (Britton; Garrow); C. B. King Interview (Lewis); Lewis, *King,* pp. 152–54.

12. Untitled 2pp. handwritten chronology, untitled six-point memo signed "M. S. Page," & "10:30 A.M., 12/18/61" draft, ALB; "Report of Telephone Conversation Between Ruby Hurley, Vernon Jordan & Gloster Current," [noon] 12/18/61, & "Transcript . . . ," 3:30 P.M., 12/18/61, NAACP III-B-408 & H-215; Garrow interviews with Hollowell & Jones; Sherrod Interviews (Lewis; Garrow); Walker Interviews (Britton; Garrow); Smith interviews with Slater King & Page; SAC Atlanta to Director, 12/19/61, 157-6-2-232X1.

13. *AA* 12/30/61, p. 8; Hollowell Interview (Garrow); Anderson Interviews (Garrow; Ricks; Blackside); Anderson in Morris, *Origins,* p. 249; M. L. King

Interview (Smith); *AJ* 12/18/61, p. 1, 12/19/61, p. 10; SAC Atlanta to Director, 12/18/61 (2), 157-6-2-219, 223; *AC* 12/19/61, p. 1; *NYT* 12/19/61, p. 1; *NYHT* 12/19/61, p. 1; Sherrod essay, pp. 36–37, n. 1 above; *AJC* 12/24/61, p. A10. "I didn't understand at the time what was happening," King later said. "We thought that the victory had been won. When we got out, we discovered it was all a hoax." *Time* 1/3/64, p. 15. Anderson blamed "naivete, inexperience, and . . . misplaced trust." (Garrow Interview) An erroneous explanation appears in Lomax, *Negro Revolt,* p. 99, and *To Kill,* p. 118; and Walker Interview (Britton, p. 33).

14. *AC* 12/18/61, p. 1, 12/19/61, p. 1, 12/20/61, p. 6, 12/21/61, p. 10, 12/22/61, p. 15; *AH* 12/19/61, p. 1; *NYHT* 12/19/61, p. 1; *AJ* 12/20/61, p. 26, 12/22/61, p. 2; SAC Atlanta to Director, 12/19/61, 157-6-2-227; Garrow interviews with Pritchett & Roos; Marshall to Kennedy, 12/21/61, BM; *AA* 12/30/61, p. 7; *ADW* 12/19/61, p. 6, 12/21/61, p. 6; *NYT* 12/24/61, p. E5; Walker Interviews (Garrow; Britton); Marshall to Leslie Dunbar, 3/30/62, SRC I-71-3.

15. Young Interviews (Garrow; Blackside); Walker Interviews (Garrow; Britton; Blackside); Margaret Long, *Progressive* 5/68, pp. 20–24; "SCLC Board—Staff Consultation," 1/4–5/62," KC; King, "Statement to Time Magazine," 1/12/62, KP. Walker nonetheless termed Robert Kennedy the "American of the Year" for his civil rights efforts. Walker to Arthur Carter, 12/26/61, KC; *AA* 1/6/62, p. 20.

16. Watters, *Down,* p. 149; Anderson Interviews (Garrow; Ricks); Vernon Jordan, "Monthly Report . . .," 1/31/62, NAACP III-B-408; Current to Hurley, 12/20/61, NAACP III-H-213; Paul Rilling to Pauley, 12/29/61, SRC IV-19-32; *SWG* 1/6/62; *PC* 1/6/62, p. 2, 1/13/62, pp. 4, 7, 1/20/62, pp. 3, 8, 1/27/62, p. 5, 2/3/62, pp. 4, 5; *BW* 1/10/62, p. 1; Charles Jones notes, 1/8–10/62, SNCC 15; *Student Voice,* Albany, 1/20/62; Zinn, *Albany—A Study;* Jones to James Forman, 1/18/62, & "Statement of Joseph Charles Jones," 1/18/62, SNCC 15 & 95; Harold McCoy (ICC) to Burke Marshall, 2/1/62, DOJ Micro 111.

17. City Commission Minutes, 1/23/62, p. 15; Albany Movement to City Commission, n.d. [1/23/62], SCLC 34 & *SWG* 1/27/62; SNCC press release, 1/23/62, KC; Kelley Interviews (Garrow; Ricks); Garrow interviews with Roos & Pritchett.

18. *NYT* 1/28/62, p. 65; "Special Meeting . . . City Commissioners," 1/27/62, Albany Movement, "Meeting with Bus Officials," 1/29/62, "Minutes of Special Meeting of the City Commission," 1/29/62, Carter to Mayor et al., 1/30/62, "Special Meeting of . . . City Commissioners," [10:00 A.M.] 1/31/62, City Commission, "To the Leaders of the Albany Movement" [1/31/62], & "Special Meeting of the City Commission" [11:45 A.M.] 1/31/62, ALB; *AH* 1/31/62, p. 1.

19. "Statement of the Albany Movement," 2/1/62, ALB; *NYT* 2/2/62, p. 20, 2/3/62, p. 9, 2/4/62, p. 74; *AH* 2/2/62, p. 1; *PC* 2/10/62, p. 7; *AA* 2/10/62, p. 1, 2/17/62, p. 1; *Student Voice,* Albany, 2/4/62; SAC Atlanta to Director, 2/4/62, 2/5/62 & 2/7/62 (2), 157-6-2-249, 256, 270 & 272; Burke Marshall to Robert Kennedy, 2/5/62, BM.

20. "President's Meeting, 2/2/62," 2/3/62, KC; Andrew Young to Maxwell Hahn, 1/5/62, King to Hahn, 2/6/62, & Hahn to Wesley Hotchkiss, 2/8/62, SCLC 136; Jack O'Dell to King, 1/26/62, KC; *JDN* 2/2/62; SCLC press release, 2/21/62, KC; King, *AN* 3/3/62, pp. 9, 23; *PC* 3/24/62, p. II-4; Fulton, "With Dr. King," pp. 23–24; McDonald to King, 2/15/62, KC; Walker Interviews (Smith; Garrow); King, *AN* 2/17/62, p. 9; also see King, *Nation* 3/3/62, pp. 190–93. On King's other appearances see *HC* 1/15/62, p. 13; *CSM* 1/15/62, p. 3; *BW* 2/17/62, p. 1.

21. Garrow, *FBI,* pp. 26–46; Garrow interviews with Wofford, Marshall, Seigenthaler, Louis Martin, Edwin Guthman & Courtney Evans; Wofford Interview (Bernhard); Wofford, *Kennedys,* pp. 213–16; Marshall Interviews

(Hackman; Blackside); Robert Kennedy (& Marshall) Interview (Lewis); Seigenthaler Interview (Campbell); Seigenthaler in Thompson, *Kennedy*, pp. 106–14. The two informants were brothers Jack & Morris Childs. On O'Dell see n. 4, ch. 3 above & Garrow, *FBI*, pp. 237, 244.

22. *PC* 2/17/62, p. II-6, 2/24/62, p. 6, 3/3/62, p. 2, 3/10/62, p. 2; Frances Pauley to Paul Rilling, "Quarterly Report," 3/9/62, Pauley to Herbert Haley & to R. W. Smith, 3/1/62, GCHR; Burke Marshall to Robert Kennedy, 2/27/62, BM; *AC* 2/27/62, p. 3, 2/28/62, p. 1; *AA* 3/3/62, p. 1, 3/10/62, p. 1; *New Republic* 3/19/62, pp. 6–7; SNCC, "Minutes of Staff Meeting," 3/6/62, SNCC 7; *BW* 3/7/62, p. 3; SNCC press release 3/8/62; *Student Voice*, Albany, 3/12/62, Cordell Reagon & Blanton Hall, "Field Report" [ca. 3/10/62], & Albany Movement "To the Merchants of Albany," 3/62, all SNCC 19.

23. "Minutes of SNCC Regional Meeting," 3/24/62, SNCC 7; *NJG* 3/24/62; *AA* 4/7/62, p. 9; *PC* 3/31/62, p. 2, 4/14/62, p. 3; King, *AN* 4/14/62, pp. 9, 12; Curtis Harris Interview (Garrow); Hahn to Hotchkiss, 3/28/62, & King to Hahn, 4/3/62, KC; King, "Statement . . . ," 4/5/62, KP; Young to Myles Horton, 4/24/62, HLW 30-5; Garrow interviews with Bevel, Coulton, Branton & Dunbar; O'Dell to Branton, 4/18/62, KC; Calhoun, "Report . . . ," 5/15/62, SRC VI-5-21; Dunbar & Branton, *First Annual Report of the VEP*, 3/31/63. On other King appearances see *BW* 3/14/62, p. 1; *HT* 3/20/62; *WISJ* 3/31/62; *AC* 4/3/62.

24. *WP* 4/9/62, p. B1, 4/10/62, p. A13; *AA* 4/21/62, p. 8; *PC* 4/21/62, p. II-7, 5/5/62, p. 2; SCLC press release 4/25/62, KC; Marshall Interview (Garrow); SAC New York to Director, 3/30/62, 100-106670-33.

25. *CNC* 4/13/62; *PC* 4/28/62, p. 4; King, *AN* 5/12/62, pp. 11, 16; *AC* 4/3/62, 4/7/62; *SWG* 4/14/62; Anderson & Page to Pritchett, 4/16/62, & Pritchett to Albany Movement, 4/16/62, ALB; Slater King to Preston King, 4/19/62, SK-F; *BW* 5/5/62, p. 8; Frances Pauley to J. Fred Wilson, 4/23/62, 5/9/62, GCHR; Franklin, "Comparison," pp. 49–50.

26. SCLC Board Minutes, 5/15–16/62, KC; King to Wachtel, 11/7/61, 2/12/62, Wachtel to King, 12/5/61, 2/16/62, Jones, "Progress Report," 4/10/62, & Jones to King et al., 4/10/62, KP; *CT* 5/16/62; *PC* 5/5/62, p. II-8, 5/26/62, p. 1; *NT* 5/12/62; King, "Address . . . ," 5/17/62, MLK 11; *WP* 5/18/62, p. A2; Kunstler, *Deep*, pp. 89–92; *NYT* 5/21/62, p. 33; *WES* 5/21/62, p. B5; King, *AN* 5/26/62, pp. 11, 14. Jones had first met King while assisting Hubert Delaney with King's 1960 tax case, and in turn had introduced Wachtel to King. On 3/14/62, King declared that "a great number of white southerners are ready to do what is right and lawful." "The White South . . . ," Montreal, KP.

27. *Nation* 5/4/62, pp. 397–401; Dick Shapiro to Alex Miller, "Boycott in Birmingham," 3/30/62, ADL; Norman Jimerson to Nat Welch, 11/29/61, & to Per Laursen, 3/2/62, ACHR; Jimerson, "Birmingham," 4/5/62, SRC IV-7-45; *Christian Century* 5/30/62, pp. 689–90; McNair, "Social Distance," pp. 97–99, 107; *AA* 3/10/62, p. 9; *PC* 4/14/62, p. 2, 6/16/62, p. II-14; SAC Atlanta to Director, 5/17/62, 100-427079-12; King, *AN* 6/9/62, p. 11, & 6/23/62, pp. 11, 16; Walker & O'Dell to Branton, 6/22/62, KC; SAC Atlanta to Director, 6/6/62, & Rosen to Belmont, 6/6/62 (2), 100-438794-X20, X17, X18; *AC* 6/8/62, p. 14; King to Massell, 6/9/62, KP.

28. *Christian Century* 6/13/62, pp. 735–36, 8/1/62, pp. 929–30; King to Harold Fey, 6/23/62, KP; FBI NY 100-111180-5-NR, 6/20/62; Director to Attorney General, 6/25/62 (2), 100-106670-79, 80; King, "Address . . . ," 7/5/62, MLK 11; *NYT* 7/6/62, p. 23; *AC* 7/6/62, p. 12; *BW* 7/11/62, p. 6; *AA* 7/7/62, p. 13; *PC* 7/14/62, p. II-14. King also became embroiled in a public controversy concerning an 11/61 phone call he had made to a federal banking official on behalf of two Miami friends, Henry H. Arrington and Rev. Edward Graham, who wanted to charter a black savings and loan association. A competing group alleged that was unfair lobbying, but the tempest passed. *WP* 6/21/62, p. A8; *AC* 6/29/62, p. 12, 7/6/62, p. 9; *PC* 2/14/59, p. II-6, 6/30/62, p. 1, 7/7/62, p. 1, 7/14/62, p. 1, 7/21/62, p. 1; King, "Affidavit," 7/16/62, KP.

29. *AJC* 7/8/62; Frances Pauley to Paul Rilling, 6/8/62, GCHR; Anderson et al. to Pritchett, 6/14/62, ALB; *AC* 6/26/62, 6/29/62, p. 21, 7/11/62, p. 1; *SWG* 6/30/62; Anderson to John Kennedy, 6/30/62, WHCF 368 JFKL; Samuel B. Wells Interview (Garrow); *AJC* 7/1/62, *AA* 7/14/62, p. 6; Doar to Marshall, 6/25/62, BM; Coretta King Interview (Mayerson XIII, p. 48); Bond in Rose & Greenya, *Black Leaders*, p. 34; Diane Nash Bevel, "A Message," 4/30/62, KC; Nash Interview (Garrow); "Statement of Dr. King . . .," 7/10/62, KC; *AH* 7/10/62, p. 1; SCLC press release, 7/11/62, KC; *NYT* 7/11/62, p. 1; SAC Atlanta to Director, 7/10/62 (2), 157-6-2-406, 417. Six months pregnant, Nash ended up serving only ten days.

30. *AH* 7/11/62, p. 1, 7/12/62, p. 1, 7/13/62, p. 1; *AC* 7/12/62, p. 1, 7/13/62, p. 1; *NYT* 7/12/62, p. 1, 7/13/62, p. 10; King's 8/8/62 testimony in *Kelley* v. *Page*, vol. 4, p. 1144; *AA* 7/21/62, p. 1; Brauer, *Kennedy*, p. 169; Kelley Interviews (Garrow; Ricks); Pritchett Interviews (Garrow; Ricks); Roos Interview (Garrow); Ricks interviews with James Gray & C. B. Pritchett; Ricks, "De Lawd," p. 8; Raines, *My Soul*, pp. 362–63. Laurie Pritchett later acknowledged that "I know what happened . . . frankly, you know, it was a matter of strategy. I knew that if he stayed in jail, we'd continue to have problems, so I talked to some people. I said, 'We've got to get him out, and once we do, I think he'll leave here.' An arrangement was made. . . . It accomplished what we wanted to do." (Blackside Interview)

31. *AC* 7/13/62, p. 1, 7/14/62, p. 1, 7/16/62, p. 1; *AH* 7/13/62,, p. 1, 7/14/62, p. 1; *NYT* 7/14/62, p. 8, 7/16/62, p. 1; *AJC* 7/15/62, p. 1; "Albany Manifesto," 7/15/62, SCLC 34-4; "Position Paper, Albany Movement," 7/17/62, ALB; *AA* 7/21/62, p. 1; *PC* 7/21/62, p. 1. A minor weekend controversy erupted over the presence in Albany of a Justice Department lawyer. See Nicholas Katzenbach to Kelley, 7/14/62, ALB; *NYT* 7/15/62, p. 28; *AH* 7/15/62, p. 1; SAC Atlanta to Director, 7/15/62, 157-6-2-423; Marshall to Kennedy, 7/17/62, BM.

32. "Albany Manifesto," n. 31 above; "Statement from City Commission," 7/16/62, ALB; *AH* 7/16/62, p. 1, 7/17/62, p. 1, 7/19/62, p. 1, 7/20/62, p. 1; *NYT* 7/17/62, p. 16, 7/18/62, p. 30, 7/19/62, p. 24, 7/20/62, p. 23, 7/21/62, p. 11; *AC* 7/17/62, p. 1, 7/18/62, p. 1, 7/19/62, p. 1, 7/20/62, p. 1, 7/21/62, p. 1; Anderson et al. to City Commission, 7/17/62, Anderson to Roos, 7/19/62, ALB; Director to Attorney General, 7/17/62, SAC Atlanta to Director, 7/20/62 (2), 157-6-2-419, 503, 565; King, "Address . . .," 7/19/62, KC; *WP* 7/20/62, p. B2, 7/22/62, p. A4; *CSM* 7/20/62, p. C13; Anderson, "Television Address," 7/19/62, KC; "Police Committee," 7/20/62, Albany City Commission Minute Book.

33. *AH* 7/21/62, p. 1, 7/22/62, p. 1; Kunstler, *Deep*, pp. 101–105, *Trials*, pp. 51–52; Young Interviews (Baker; Brown); & Young in 11/12–13/73 MSU videotape, KC; Vernon Jordan Interview (Garrow); Pritchett et al., "Activities of Dr. King . . . 7/21–22/62," 7/23/62, ALB; King statement to FBI, 7/24/62, 157-6-2-504, pp. 4–5; *NYT* 7/22/62, p. 1, 7/23/62, p. 1; *AC* 7/23/62, p. 1; *AA* 7/28/62, p. 1; King Interview (Bernhard); Marshall to Kennedy, 7/24/62, BM.

34. Penny Patch, "Lee County . . .," 8/2/62, SNCC 19; Jones Interview (Garrow); Slater King Interviews (Lewis; Smith); Kunstler, *Deep*, pp. 105–11; *Progressive Labor* 10/62, pp. 6–8; *AH* 7/23/62, p. 1; *NYT* 7/24/62, p. 32; SAC Atlanta to Director, 7/23/62, 7/24/62, & Rosen to Belmont, 7/24/62, 157-6-2-453, 515, 494; Marion King, *New South* 2/63, pp. 9–10; *AC* 7/24/62, p. 1; Pritchett et al., "Surveillance on Dr. W. G. Anderson Home," 7/23/62, ALB; Vincent & Rosemarie Harding, "Dear Friends" letter, 10/62, & "Albany: The Search for Reconciliation," 10/23/62, KC.

35. Kunstler, *Deep*, pp. 111–114; *AH* 7/24/62, p. 1, 7/25/62, p. 1, 7/26/62, p. 1;

AC 7/25/62, pp. 1, 10, 13, 7/26/62, p. 1; *NYT* 7/25/62, p. 1, 7/26/62, p. 1; Harding & Lynd, "Albany," pp. 74–75; Anderson et al. to City Commission, 7/24/62, Pritchett et al., "Activities of the Albany Movement," 7/24/62, & 7/25/62, ALB; SAC Atlanta to Director, 7/25/62, 7/26/62, 157-6-2-490, 495; King & Anderson, "Statement," 7/25/62, n.a., "A New Thrust for Albany, Ga.," SCLC, KC; Leonard Gilberg to Pritchett, 7/23/62, & J. E. Lloyd to Pritchett, 7/25/62, ALB.

36. *NYHT* 12/18/61, p. 1; *AC* 12/18/61, p. 1; *NYT* 7/23/62, p. 13; *AJC* 7/29/62, p. 1; *LAT* 8/6/62, p. 3; *Time* 8/10/62, p. 14; Pritchett Interviews (Garrow; Ricks; Reston); Jones Interview (Garrow); Pritchett to S. A. Roos, "Informant Fee," 10/30/62, "Albany Movement," 11/10/62, & "Geechie Marks," 3/5/63, ALB; Ricks, "De Lawd," p. 13, based upon interviews with Hamilton & Page's widow; "Goldie" Jackson Interview (Garrow). Pritchett stated in the 10/30 memo about the stock clerk that "we have used this informant for the last twelve months in order to keep up with the activities of the Albany Movement. We have used him extensively, sometimes three to four times per week." Concerning the adults, Pritchett later acknowledged that "some of the leaders in the Albany Movement cooperated with me as far as information is concerned . . . I didn't classify them as informers; they were people who I respected, who respected me, and they cooperated with us." (Blackside Interview) Page was "kind of all things to all people," Vernon Jordan recalled when asked about the collaboration. "It was naivete; it was the omnipresence of the hand of the law; it was fear; it was a kind of modus operanda." (Garrow Interview) Pritchett's success was not a complete secret to Albany Movement leaders; as Slater King told Martin King in one phone call, "He has a pretty close working relationship with Marion Page." FBI NY 100-73250-1C-11, p. 3, 8/15/63. During the 1964 protests in St. Augustine, Fla., St. Johns County Sheriff L. O. Davis found newsmen just as useful as Pritchett had. "The newspapermen were invaluable. They would be right down there in the meetings and they'd tell us when they were going to march and what time and so forth." (Kallal Interview)

37. *Newsweek* 8/6/62, p. 19; Watters, *Down*, p. 214; *AC* 7/26/62, p. 1, 7/27/62, p. 1, 7/28/62, p. 1; *NYT* 7/27/62, p. 9; *AH* 7/27/62, p. 1; SAC Atlanta to Director, 7/27/62, & Director to Attorney General, 7/28/62, 157-6-2-514, 513; Pritchett et al., "Activities of . . . the Albany Movement," 7/27/62, & Roos, "Memorandum for the File," 7/27/62, ALB; *PC* 8/4/62, p. 1; *AA* 8/4/62, p. 1; Albany Movement, "Why a Prayer Vigil?," & Walker to "Dear Friend of Freedom," 7/27/62, KC. Pritchett's later assertions that he had a quite friendly relationship with King were not without foundation; King gave him an autographed copy of *Strength to Love,* inscribed "With best wishes and deep hopes that the system of segregation will soon pass away so that we can be brothers indeed."

38. *NYT* 7/28/62, p. 1, 7/29/62, p. 1, 7/30/62, p. 1; King jail diary, MLK (an edited version appears in *Jet* 8/23/62, pp. 14–21); *AH* 7/28/62, p. 1, 7/29/62, p. 1; Pritchett et al., "Rev. Martin Luther King, Jr. . . . ," 7/28/62, ALB; Anderson Interview (Garrow); Anderson "Meet the Press" interview, 7/29/62; Director to Attorney General, 7/30/62, 157-6-2-518; *AC* 7/30/62, p. 1.

39. *AH* 7/30/62, p. 1, 7/31/62, p. 1, 8/1/62, p. 1, 8/2/62, p. 1; *NYT* 7/31/62, pp. 1, 12, 17, 8/1/62, p. 63, 8/2/62, p. 1, 8/3/62, p. 21; *AC* 7/31/62, p. 1, 8/1/62, p. 1, 8/2/62, p. 1, 8/3/62, p. 1; King jail diary, n. 38 above; *Time* 8/10/62, p. 14; Marshall Interview (Lewis, pp. 69–70); Marshall remarks, 7/30/85, Boston; King statement, 8/1/62, KC; King to Kennedy, 8/2/62, WHCF 1478 JFKL; Kelley Interviews (Garrow; Ricks); Anderson to City Commission, 8/2/62, ALB. Tuesday night King was visited in jail by New York Congressman William F. Ryan. *Congressional Record* 108 (8/1/62); 15320–23; Director to Attorney General, 8/2/62, 157-6-2-554.

40. *NYT* 8/4/62, p. 11, 8/5/62, pp. 56, E5, 8/6/62, p. 22; *AA* 8/11/62, pp. 1, 2, 13; Kunstler, *Deep*, pp. 118–19; Wulf to Kennedy, "Suggestions on Albany . . . ,"

8/2/62, & Wulf to Kennedy, 8/3/62, ACLU 35; *AC* 8/4/62, p. 1, 8/6/62, p. 3; *AJC* 8/5/62, pp. 1, 15, 20; *PC* 8/11/62, pp. 1, 2, 4; *AH* 8/5/62, p. 1; King jail diary, n. 38 above; McKee, *King,* p. 49. C. B. Pritchett had met privately with black leaders in June, but the new demonstrations ended those conversations.

41. King jail diary, n. 38 above; *NYT* 8/7/62, pp. 18, 19, 8/9/62, p. 1; King to Slater King, 8/7/62, SK-F; "Brief for the United States . . .," 8/8/62, ACLU 35; *AC* 8/9/62, p. 1, 8/10/62, p. 1; *Kelley* v. *Page,* vol. 4, pp. 1138–71; *AH* 8/8/62, p. 1, 8/9/62, p. 1; *PC* 8/18/62, pp. 1, 2, 4, 7; *Newsweek* 8/20/62, pp. 78–79.

42. *NYT* 8/10/62, p. 6, 8/11/62, p. 1, 8/12/62, p. 1, 8/13/62, p. 1; *AH* 8/10/62, p. 1, 8/11/62, p. 1, 8/12/62, p. 1; King jail diary, n. 38 above; Director to Attorney General, 8/11/62, 157-6-2-617; *AC* 8/11/62, p. 1, 8/13/62, p. 3; Anderson et al. to City Commission, 8/10/62, ALB.

43. *AA* 8/18/62, pp. 1, 2, 14; *AC* 8/14/62, p. 10, 8/16/62, p. 1; *NYT* 8/14/62, p. 16, 8/15/62, p. 34, 8/16/62, p. 18, 8/18/62, p. 44; *AH* 8/14/62, p. 1, 8/15/62, p. 1, 8/16/62, p. 1; Anderson et al. to City Commission, 8/15/62, ALB; City Commission Minutes, 8/15/62, p. 108; *Newsweek* 8/27/62, pp. 25–26; *PC* 8/25/62, pp. 1, 2, 4, 7; Marion King to Slater King, 8/15/62, SK-F; SAC Atlanta to Director, 8/15/62, 157-6-2-631. On Wednesday King twice visited the ruins of a burned Lee County church where SNCC had held meetings.

44. *AC* 8/17/62, p. 11, 8/20/62, p. 1, 8/27/62, p. 1, 8/28/62, p. 10, 8/29/62, p. 1; "Minutes of SCLC Staff Meeting," 8/17/62, KC; Albany Movement press release, 8/15/62, & Anderson to Branton, 8/16/62, SRC VI-6-15; *AA* 8/25/62, p. 1, 9/8/62, p. 1; Walker to Lee White, 8/24/62, White 21 JFKL; *PC* 9/1/62, p. 1, 9/8/62, p. 6; *Newsweek* 9/10/62, p. 47; *AH* 8/26/62, p. 1, 8/27/62, p. 1, 8/28/62, p. 1, 8/29/62, p. 1, 8/30/62, p. 1, 8/31/62, p. 1; SAC Atlanta to Director, 8/31/62, 157-6-2-736; *NYT* 8/29/62, p. 14; King to Kennedy, 8/31/62, WHCF 368 & 1478 JFKL; Marshall to Robert Kennedy, 9/4/62, BM. Accounts of the ministerial pilgrimages include Stephen C. Rose, *Albany Report* (Chicago City Missionary Society, 9/6/62); *United Church Herald* 9/20/62, pp. 4–5; *New America* 9/28/62, p. 7; *AN* 10/20/62, p. 11; *Christian Century* 9/26/62, pp. 1155–56; George Murphy, "Report on Interview . . . with Mr. Burke Marshall," 9/13/62, CFGC 36-4.

45. *U.S. News* 9/3/62, pp. 43–46; *Newsweek* 8/13/62, pp. 17–18; Zinn, *Albany—A Study,* p. 21; Walker, *SCLC Newsletter* 9/62, p. 1; Walker, "Albany," pp. 3–8; Coretta King, *My Life,* p. 206; Young Interview (Baker); Watters, *Down,* pt. 3, esp. p. 175; Slater King, "Bloody Battleground," pp. 96–99; Slater King Interviews (Smith; Lewis); C. B. King Interview (Lewis); Jones Interview (Garrow); Walker Interviews (Garrow; Smith); M. L. King Interview (Smith). Also see *PC* 9/15/62, p. 5, 9/22/62, p. 3; *AA Magazine* 9/15/62, p. 1, 9/22/62, p. 4, 10/6/62, p. 5.

46. Walker Interviews (Garrow; Britton); Wells in Watters, *Down,* pp. 150–52; Harding & Lynd, "Albany," pp. 69–78; Young Interview (Garrow). Young later added that "when Martin left Albany he was very depressed." (Blackside Interview) In late 1965 Harding wrote that "many a strategic battle has surely been won, but no one seriously speaks any longer of 'redeeming the soul of the South' or of America. . . . Power has become the theme," but "new institutions and control over them . . . do not produce either humanity nor dignity." "Where Have," pp. 32, 34.

47. King to Mays, 9/6/62, KP; King to Glenn Smiley, 9/7/62, FOR; King to Kennedy, 9/12/62, WHCF 1478 JFKL; King, "Address . . .," 9/12/62, KP; *NYT* 9/13/62, p. 38, 9/15/62, p. 12; SAC Atlanta to Director, 9/14/62, 157-6-2-826.

48. Shuttlesworth Interviews (Garrow; Mosby; Ladner); Walker Interview (Britton); David Vann Interview (Garrow); King, *AN* 8/17/63, p. 10; Paul Rilling to Leslie Dunbar, "Field Report, Birmingham . . .," 9/18/62, SRC IV-7-18; Thad Holt, "Memorandum . . .," 5/10/63, BPLA; ACHR to USCCR, "Birmingham," 8/31/62, & USCCR Alabama Advisory Committee, "Special Memorandum . . .,"

9/62, DOJ Micro 2; Bains, "Birmingham," p. 10; Shuttlesworth, "Birmingham Revisited," p. 117; Corley, "The Quest," ch. 6, & "In Search," pp. 185–86; McNair, "Social Distance," p. 144; *NYT* 9/16/62, p. 1, 9/26/62, p. 23, 9/27/62, p. 29, 9/28/62, p. 23; *AJ* 9/20/62, p. 58; *MA* 9/21/62, p. A6, 9/25/62, p. A5, 9/26/62, p. A1, 9/28/62, p. E4; SAC Atlanta to Director & Rosen to Belmont, 9/25/62, 100-438794-7X, 7X1; Walker, "Report of the Director," 9/26/62, O'Dell, "Report on Voter Registration Work," 9/28/62, & "Resolutions Adopted . . .," KC; *BW* 10/3/62, p. 3; *PC* 10/6/62, p. 2.

49. *BN* 9/28/62, p. 1, 9/29/62, p. 1; *NYT* 9/29/62, p. 6; Robert B. Fulton, "To Whom it May Concern," 9/29/62, FOR, & "With Dr. King," p. 24; Garrow interviews with Otis Moss, Septima Clark, Herbert Coulton & Edward Gardner; C. K. Steele, "Nonviolent Resistance," p. 7; Hendricks Interview (Brown).

50. King's 10/62 schedule, KP; *WJ* 10/12/62, p. 10; *WSS* 10/12/62, p. 7; *NYT* 10/14/62, p. 20, 10/21/62, p. 65; *CO* 10/21/62, p. E2; King, *AN* 10/27/62, p. 13; *SLPD* 11/20/62, p. C2; *DMR* 10/16/62, p. 11, 10/17/62, p. 7; *WDN* 10/20/62; *BN* 10/21/62, p. B5; *PC* 11/3/62, p. 3; Garrow interviews with Shuttlesworth & David Vann; Nat Welch to Harold Fleming, 10/3/62, & Norman Jimerson to Paul Rilling, 10/25/62, SRC IV-7-22 & 44; Jimerson to Burke Marshall, 10/19/62, ACHR; Bains, "Birmingham," pp. 11–14; Corley, "The Quest," ch. 6.

51. King, "Address . . . ," 10/23/62, KP; Gandhi Society Board of Directors "Minutes," 12/12/62, KC; *AUC* 10/25/62, p. A4; *SLGD* 10/26/62, p. A1; *NOTP* 10/26/62, 11/2/62; *LISJ* 10/26/62, p. 1, 11/2/62, p. 1; Garrow, *FBI,* pp. 53–54; FBI NY 100-111180-8-7, p. 2A; *BN* 11/2/62; O'Dell to King, 12/4/62, & Walker to O'Dell, 2/1/63, KC; & Henry Cabirac to Mathew Ahmann, 1/18/63, NCCIJ 31-4, which notes O'Dell's presence in New York despite how "Walker agreed to fire him when Les Dunbar became upset."

52. [Jack Minnis], untitled 5pp. memo, n.d. [ca. late 11/62], "Report on Voter Registration for SCLC . . . 9/10–10/10/62" & "Report . . . 10/10/62–11/10/62," SRC VI-6-19; Branton Interview (Garrow); SCLC press releases, 10/23/62, 10/31/62, KC; *AC* 11/17/62, p. 5; *PC* 11/10/62, p. 2; *NYT* 11/25/62, p. 1; Sullivan Interview (Britton, pp. 11–12); Leon Sullivan, *Build Brother Build* (Philadelphia: Macrae Smith Co., 1969), p. 77. Calhoun and Bennette did registration work in Albany through 10/1, and Bernard Lee assisted a drive in Gadsden, Ala.

53. *CDN* 11/1/62, p. 8; *KCT* 11/5/62, p. 1; *PC* 10/6/62, p. 7, 12/1/62, p. 5; Pritchett to Roos, "Dr. W. G. Anderson," 10/31/62, ALB; "Police Committee Meeting," 10/31/62, City Commission Minute Book; Frances Pauley, "Confidential Report . . . ," 9–11/62, GCHR. The anniversary also witnessed release of a special SRC study of Albany by Howard Zinn, who strongly criticized the federal government. Local FBI agents were nothing more than "vaguely-interested observers of injustice, who diffidently write down complaints and do no more." Questioned by a reporter, King endorsed Zinn's criticisms of the Kennedy administration and the FBI. "One of the great problems," King said, "is that the agents are white southerners who have been influenced by the mores of the community. To maintain their status, they have to be friendly with the local police and people who are promoting segregation. Every time I saw FBI men in Albany, they were with the local police force." Zinn, *Albany—A Study,* p. 31; *Nation* 12/1/62, pp. 373–76; *NYT* 11/19/62, p. 21. FBI executives reacted to King's comments by ordering two officials to contact King to tell him his statements were erroneous, but King failed to return their calls. That failure, FBI executive Cartha "Deke" De-Loach wrote in one memo, indicated King "obviously does not desire to be given the truth" and was "a vicious liar." Garrow, *FBI,* pp. 54–59, 246–47; Director to Attorney General, 1/18/63, 157-6-2-950. In Albany savvy black newsman T. W. Anderson, a Macon-based correspondent for the *Pittsburgh Courier,* launched his own effort to persuade three influential whites, Richard Tift, E. E. Weatherly, and banker Herbert B. Haley, Jr., to press the commission to open talks with the black community. The men demurred. Black businessman Thomas Chatmon ran a strong second for one commission seat in the early November city elections, but lost in a runoff four days after King's visit. *PC* 9/29/62, p. 2, 11/10/62, p. 1, 11/24/62, p. 4; Slater King Interviews (Lewis; Smith).

54. King to Kennedy, 11/20/62, WHCF 1478 JFKL; King, *AN* 12/22/62, p. 13; King Interview (Bernhard); King, "Statement . . . ," 11/24/62, & *AN* 12/8/62, p. 13; *U.S. News* 1/11/65, pp. 60–61.

55. *MA* 12/4/62; *AA* 1/5/63, p. 17; SAC Mobile to Director, 12/8/62, 100-438794-13X1; Coretta King, *My Life,* p. 219; Bishop, *Days,* pp. 278–79; *SCLC Newsletter* 3/63; *BW* 12/12/62, p. 2; King, *AN* 8/17/63, p. 10; Garrow interviews with Porter, Shuttlesworth & Addine Drew; Walker Interview (Britton); *SFC* 12/14/62, p. 12; *HP* 12/17/62, p. 1; King to Kennedy, 12/15/62, WHCF 1478; *WP* 12/18/62, p. A4; *AA* 12/22/62, p. 1; King Interview (Bernhard); Dunbar, "Visit," pp. 92–96.

56. Gandhi Society Board "Minutes," 12/12/62, O'Dell to King, 12/18/62, KC; Young, "Report to the President . . . ," n.d. [ca. mid-12/62], SCLC 138, Bernard Lee, "Fieldwork . . . ," 1/22/63, SCLC 139; "Minutes of the SCLC Field Secretaries Meeting . . . ," 12/19–21/62, SCLC 138; *NVP* 12/21/62, p. 31; *PC* 1/5/63, p. 1, 1/19/63, p. 16, 1/26/63, p. 16; *SFE* 1/2/63, p. 1, 1/3/63, p. 9; Director to Attorney General, 1/10/63, 100-106670-107.

57. King Interview (Smith); Walker Interviews (Garrow; Britton); Shuttlesworth Interviews (Mosby; Colburn); Shuttlesworth in Raines, *My Soul,* p. 155; Young, "And Birmingham," pp. 21–23. Also see King, *Why,* pp. 54–55, King in *Time* 1/3/64, p. 15, *Playboy* 1/65, p. 66, & *AN* 6/8/63, p. 10 (also in *SCLC Newsletter* 7/63, p. 1).

58. Walker in *BPH* 4/16/81; Walker Interviews (Britton; Blackside); King in *Playboy* 1/65, p. 68, & *Progressive* 12/62, p. 37; Levison Interviews (Stein I; Lewis); Young Interviews (Viorst; Blackside); SAC Savannah to Director, 1/16/63, 100-358916-228; King, "Address . . . ," 1/1/61, Savannah, KC. Also see Young in L. H. Whittemore, *Together* (New York: William Morrow & Co., 1971), p. 56; in Gloria Steinem's "A Conversation With . . . ," PBS, 4/12/84, & a 1/22/85 address, Nashville.

Chapter Five

1. "Executive Staff Meeting," 1/23/63, "Tentative Schedule for Project X— Birmingham, Ala.," n.d., KC; "Memorandum re Birmingham," n.d. [ca. mid-1/63], SRC IV-7-8; Paul Anthony to Leslie Dunbar, "Alabama Visit, 1/17–18/63," ACHR, BPLA; King, *Why,* pp. 55–56; Joe D. Brown, *Saturday Evening Post* 3/2/63, pp. 11–19; Bains, "Birmingham," pp. 15–22; David Vann Interviews (Garrow; Blackside).

2. *CST* 1/28/63, p. 12; Smith, "King," pp. 331–32; Coretta King, "The World," pp. 29–30; Coretta King Interview (Mayerson XXX, p. 11); Ted Brown to King, 3/14/63, KP; Garrow interviews with Septima Clark & Bernard Lee. Also see *CDN* 1/16/63, p. 1; *NYT* 1/17/63, p. 7; *CT* 1/17/63, p. 3, 1/18/63, p. 3; *MT* 1/29/63, p. 17.

3. Bennett, *Negro Mood,* p. 4; CEP, "Semi Annual Report," 1/31/63, KC; Maxwell Hahn to Wesley Hotchkiss, 4/9/63, SCLC 136; Negro Ministers of Atlanta, "Atlanta Employment . . . ," ca. 2/8–9/63, KC; *PC* 2/16/63, p. 1, 3/9/63, p. 2; Minnis to Branton, 2/12/63, SCLC 138; Branton, "Memorandum re Talk with . . . King," 2/20/63, SRC VI-6-20; Garrow interviews with Branton & Dunbar; Young to Minnis, 2/26/63, SCLC 138; "Conference Memo re Meeting with SCLC,

2/28/63," 3/5/63, & Branton to King, 2/28/63, SRC VI-6-20; Dunbar & Branton, *First Annual Report of the VEP,* 3/31/63.

4. Brauer, *Kennedy,* pp. 221–22; Robert Kennedy (& Marshall) Interview (Lewis II, pp. 2–4); King, *Nation* 3/30/63, pp. 259–62; SAC New York to Director, 3/7/63, 100-106670-118; FBI NY 100-111180-9-98A, 3/6/63; *NYHT* 5/2/63; Carson, *In Struggle,* p. 81; Walker Interviews (Garrow; Smith); Drew Interview (Garrow); Norman Jimerson to Paul Rilling, 3/11/63, SRC I-67-19; King, *Why,* pp. 55–57; SAC New York to Director, 3/13/63, 100-392452-194; Shuttlesworth, "Special Memo," 3/19/63, & SCLC press release, 3/19/63, KC. Two of King's closest Birmingham friends, businessman John Drew and his wife, Deenie, lobbied hard. "I remember saying to Mike—Dr. King—'For our sake, please wait,'" Mrs. Drew recalled. "And he said, 'Deenie, do you think it's going to make a difference, whether it's Bull Connor or Boutwell or whomever?' I said, 'It will make a difference to us psychologically. I don't think Boutwell will have any kind of feelings toward us, but we have been mistreated so badly by Bull Connor all these years that black people will feel better with him out of office. I will.'" King "never felt that that was too important, but if we wanted it so much, he waited," Mrs. Drew added. (Garrow Interview)

5. *PC* 3/9/63, p. 3; *AIaJ* 3/16/63; King to James Forman, 3/14/63, SNCC; FBI NY 100-111180-9-102A, 124A, 3/10/63, 4/1/63; King, *Why,* pp. 57–58; Kunstler, *Deep,* pp. 173–75; Young Interview (Moyers); Shuttlesworth to Walker & King, 3/15/63, KP. The Belafonte meeting was Sunday night, 3/31/63.

6. Jones to King, 2/20/63, King to O'Dell, 1/18/63, O'Dell to King, 1/29/63, KP; Garrow interviews with Jones & Leslie Dunbar; O'Dell to Young, 4/17/63, SCLC 135; FBI NY 100-111180-9-112, p. 2, 3/20/63; SAC New York to Director, 4/3/63, 8/15/66, 100-392452-196, NR; author's conversations with Roy Bennett. Levison told him, Harris said, that "a series of business reverses affecting all of them makes impossible the continuation of [their] former support."

7. Coretta King Interview (Mayerson XXIV, p. 38, XVIII, pp. 38–40); Coretta King, *My Life,* pp. 60, 220; Coretta King Interviews (Smith; Garrow); Walker, "Growing Strength," pp. 150–51; Yolanda King Interview (LaCrosse); SCLC press release, 3/25/63, KC; *WP* 3/27/63, p. B7. "It was with great difficulty that he kept her in the house," Andrew Young recalled. "He insisted both of them couldn't be gone all the time." *AJC Magazine* 2/1/76.

8. *BN* 4/3/63, p. 1; J. H. Calhoun, "Activities of Chairman . . .," 4/2/63, SRC VI-10-13; *WP* 4/4/63, p. A2, 4/5/63, p. A2; *BN* 4/4/63, p. 7, 4/5/63, p. 2, 4/6/63, p. 2, 4/7/63, p. 2; Walker Interview (Smith); King, *Why,* pp. 59–64; *MA* 4/4/63, p. 1; Whitehouse et al. to Moore, 4/5/63 (2), Connor; ACMHR press release, 4/4/63, BPLA; Shuttlesworth & Nelson Smith, "The Birmingham Manifesto," *SCLC Newsletter* 7/63, p. 2 [also *Freedomways,* Winter 1964, pp. 20–21]; Young, "And Birmingham," pp. 21–22; *NYT* 4/5/63, p. 16, 4/7/63, p. 55; Shuttlesworth to Connor, & Connor to Shuttlesworth, 4/5/63, Connor; Whitehouse et al. to Moore, 4/10/63 (re 4/5), Connor; *New Republic* 4/20/63, p. 9.

9. Walker Interviews (Garrow; Britton); Lewis Jones, "Fred Shuttlesworth," pp. 31–32; John Porter Interviews (Garrow; Brown); C. Herbert Oliver Interview (Garrow). On Shuttlesworth and ACMHR's earlier history, see Shuttlesworth, "An Account of the Alabama Christian Movement . . .," 5/59, in Clarke, "Goals and Techniques," pp. 133–53; ACMHR, *They Challenge Segregation at Its Core!,* n.d. [ca. late 1959]; Nichols, "Cities," pp. 92–93, 102, 253; ACMHR, *Birmingham—People in Motion* (1966), which also appears in Grant, *Black Protest,* pp. 284–89; Shuttlesworth, "Birmingham," pp. 16–19, and "Birmingham Revisited"; Braden, "History"; and Sterne, *I Have a Dream,* pp. 167–92, which contains some errors. One earlier controversy had involved a Glenn Smiley letter describing Shuttlesworth as "headstrong and wild for publicity, almost to the point of neurosis, undemocratic and willing to do almost anything to keep [the] spotlight on himself" that Birmingham police had seized and made public. See Smiley to "Bob," 11/10/58, Smiley, "Birmingham," 11/18/58, & Shuttlesworth to Smiley, 12/23/58, FOR; Smiley Interview (Garrow).

10. Drew Interview (Garrow); King, *Why*, pp. 65–67; Robert Kennedy in 5/21/63 Kennedy White House Tape #88-6, JFKL; *Time* 4/19/63, pp. 30–31; Marshall to Robert Kennedy, 4/9/63, Navasky; *BN* 4/5/63, p. 2; *NYT* 4/6/63, p. 20, 5/26/63, p. 58; *WP* 4/6/63, p. A4; *AlaJ* 5/4/63; Bass, *Unlikely Heroes*, pp. 202–203; Marshall Interviews (Lewis, pp. 95–96; Leventhal); ACMHR press release, 4/4/63.

11. King, *Why*, pp. 65–69; Young, "And Birmingham," pp. 22–24; Young Interview (Kotz); Whitehouse et al. to Moore, 4/10/63 (re 4/6), Connor; *BN* 4/8/63, p. 2, 4/9/63, p. 2; *NYT* 4/8/63, p. 31, 4/9/63, p. 53, 4/10/63, p. 29; Walker Interviews (Britton; Garrow; Blackside); Walker in Warren, *Who Speaks*, p. 226; Nichols, "Cities," pp. 280–92; Forman, *Making*, p. 312.

12. King, *Why*, pp. 66–68; *BN* 4/10/63, p. 6; *BW* 4/13/63, p. 1; C. Herbert Oliver Interview (Garrow); John Cross Interview (Barton); Kunstler, *Deep*, pp. 179–84; Allison et al. to Moore, 4/10/63 (re 4/8) & Whitehouse et al. to Moore, 4/11/63 (re 4/9), Connor; *NYT* 4/11/63, p. 21; Jimerson, ACHR "Quarterly Report," 7/15/63 draft, ACHR, & 7/16/63 final, SRC BPLA; Jimerson to Robert & Dorothy Hughes, 6/24/63, ACHR; "Outline of Negotiations," n.d., Vann, BPLA.

13. *BW* 4/10/63, p. 6; Walker Interview (Britton); Whitehouse et al. to Moore 4/12/63 (2, re 4/10, 4/11), Connor; *BN* 4/11/63, p. 8, 4/12/63, p. 3; *NYT* 4/12/63, p. 1; Westin & Mahoney, *Trial*, pp. 59–60, 68–80; FBI NY 100-111180-9-124A, 4/1/63; King, *Why*, p. 70; *ADW* 4/12/63, p. 1; *PC* 9/28/63, p. 1; Fulton, "With Dr. King"; Orange Interview (Garrow); Orange, "With the People"; *AJC* 2/19/84, p. F1.

14. Westin & Mahoney, *Trial*, pp. 80–84; King, *Why*, pp. 71–74; Walker Interview (Britton); Abraham Woods Interview (Garrow); Young, "And Birmingham," p. 27, "Dynamics of a Movement," pp. 10–12; Young Interviews (Moyers; Blackside); Young in *Playboy* 7/77, pp. 72–73; Young in *AJC* 7/17/83, p. C1; Cotton Interviews (Garrow; Wigginton & Thrasher); Cotton in *Southern Exposure* 9–10/82, p. 29; Gardner in Raines, *My Soul*, pp. 143–44; *NYT* 4/13/63, p. 1.

15. Whitehouse et al. to Moore, 4/18/63 (re 4/12), Connor; *BN* 4/12/63, p. 16, 4/13/63, p. 2; C.C.J. Carpenter et al. in *New Leader* 6/24/63, p. 5; King, *Why*, pp. 74–75; Westin & Mahoney, *Trial*, pp. 84–86. King told one questioner: "This is the most uncomfortable jail experience I have ever had. The jailers are very unfriendly and unbelievably abusive in their language." *Jet* 5/2/63, pp. 14–19. As Levison later explained, "Solitary was the hardest thing for him. When he was cut off from people, he really went into a depression. . . . He got his strength from people. When he was cut off from them he worried . . . he brooded, he felt bewildered. As a matter of fact, he told me one time that he broke down completely in solitary." (Stein Interview)

16. Westin & Mahoney, *Trial*, pp. 84–92; *BN* 4/14/63, p. 2, 4/15/63, p. 2; Walker to Kennedy, 4/13/63, 4/14/63, WHCF 1478 JFKL; *NYT* 4/14/63, p. 1, 4/15/63, p. 1; Coretta King, "My Dream," p. 146, *My Life*, pp. 224–26; Coretta King Interview (Blackside); Watkins to Moore, 4/15/63 (re 4/13), Connor; King, *Why*, p. 75.

17. Coretta King, *My Life*, pp. 226–27; Coretta King Interview (Smith); *WP* 1/15/78, p. N1; transcript of King's conversation, 4/15/63, BPLA; Allison et al. to Moore, 4/17/63 (re 4/15), Connor; *NYT* 4/16/63, p. 1, 4/17/63, p. 22, 4/18/63, p. 21; *BN* 4/16/63, p. 2, 4/17/63, p. 5, 4/18/63, p. 4; *BPH* 4/18/63, p. 18; *AJ* 4/16/63, p. 5; King to Kennedy, 4/16/63, WHCF 1478 JFKL; Walker to Marshall, 4/16/63, BM; & police memos, 4/18/63, re 4/16 & 17 mass rallies, Connor.

18. *Jet* 5/2/63, pp. 14–19; Coretta King, *My Life*, p. 229; Watkins et al. to Moore, 4/19/63 (re 4/18) & Whitehouse et al. to Moore, 4/23/63 (re 4/19), Connor; *NYT* 4/19/63, p. 9, 4/20/63, p. 12, 4/21/63, p. 70; *BN* 4/19/63, p. 2, 4/20/63, p. 2, 4/21/63, p. 4; Walker Interviews (Britton; Garrow); Walker in Selby, *Odyssey*, p. 285; Anne Peterson Interview (Brown); Walker to King & Abernathy, "Project 'C' Progress Report," n.d. [4/19/63], KC; Marshall Phone Logs, JFKL; Marshall to Robert Kennedy, 4/23/63, BM 8. Worried that the letter was too long, King discarded two thirds of his first draft. As he told Levison, "When I was writing the letter, it was getting so long that I cut out a lot that I feel may be said—15,000 additional words that I could put in the letter . . . whole sections that I took out. For instance, I had a section—strong—[that the] whole idea [of the] struggle was not just something for the Negro but how it also frees the white man. . . . And it's to save the soul of America and goes into what this thing is doing to the image of the U.S. The fact that we are seeking to gain the respect— here you have [a] neutralist sector composed of about a billion people and they are looking at both Russia and [the] west—I had a long section on that. I was appealing to them on the basis of understanding this. There's more I could put in on this." FBI NY 100-111180-9-174, p. 6, 5/21/63. "He had no conception that he had written something that was going to be so lasting," Levison said later. (Stein Interview) Excerpts from King's Birmingham jail letter first appeared, unbeknownst to King, in *NYP Magazine* 5/19/63, p. 4 (see FBI NY 100-111180-7-431A, 5/24/63), before fuller versions appeared in other periodicals. The *New Leader* version cited in n. 19 below is the most dependable. Important commentaries on the letter are Mott, "Rhetoric"; and Fulkerson, "Public Letter"; less valuable are Bosmajian, "Rhetoric"; Colaiaco, "American Dream"; and William E. Coleman, *Foundations* 16 (1–3/73): 41–56.

19. *NYT* 4/23/63, p. 20, 4/24/63, p. 19, 4/25/63, p. 20; *WP* 4/23/63, p. A6; *BN* 4/23/63, p. 5, 4/24/63, p. 2, 4/25/63, p. 2; Watkins et al. to Moore, 4/23/63 (2, re 4/22), Allison et al. to Moore, 4/25/63, & Whitehouse et al. to Moore, 4/24 (both re 4/23), Allison to Moore, 4/24/63, & Watkins et al. to Moore, 4/26/63 (both re 4/24), Allison to Moore, 4/29/63, & Watkins et al. to Moore, 4/26/63 (both re 4/25), Connor; Reynolds to James Farmer, n.d. [ca. 4/24/63], & Reynolds to Gordon Carey, 4/26 & 28/63, CORE Reel 37-263; Dorman, *We Shall*, p. 48; Harding, "A Beginning"; Justin Finger to Arnold Forster, "Birmingham," 4/26/63, ADL; King, "Letter from Birmingham City Jail," *New Leader* 6/24/63, pp. 3–11. King regularly chided himself for being too hopeful, especially about the white church. "I'm such an optimist about everything," he later remarked to Levison. "Maybe again I have been too optimistic," he noted in his Birmingham letter. FBI NY 100-111180-9-1375A, 7/24/67; "Letter," p. 9.

20. *BN* 4/26/63, p. 5; *NYT* 4/27/63, p. 9, 4/29/63, p. 15; Whitehouse to Moore, 4/26/63, & Allison et al. to Moore, 4/30/63 (both re 4/26), Whitehouse et al. to Moore, 4/29/63, 4/30/63 (both re 4/27), Whitehouse et al. to Moore, 4/29/63, 4/30/63 (both re 4/28), Allison to Moore, 4/30/63 (re 4/29), Connor; *AG* 4/29/63, p. 1; *AIaJ* 4/29/63, p. B9; *HP* 4/30/63, p. I-11; Garrow interviews with Porter & Bevel; Nichols, "Cities," p. 282; Frye Gaillard, *LCJ Magazine* 2/5/78, p. 10; Walker Interview (Britton).

21. House to Moore, 4/30/63, Allison et al. to Moore, 5/2/63 (re 4/30), Allison to Moore, 5/2/63 (re 5/1), Connor; *MCA* 5/1/63, p. 34; Young, "The Day"; *United Church Herald* 6/13/63, pp. 6–8, 25; *BN* 5/2/63, p. 2; Garrow interviews with James Orange & Bevel; Anne Peterson Interview (Brown); *NYT* 5/2/63, p. 1; Bevel Interviews (Shannon; Blackside); Shuttlesworth Interview (Ladner); Kunstler & Myles Horton in Terrell, "Discarding," p. 75; Meier, "New Currents," p. 19, & Meier & Rudwick, *CORE*, p. 219; Walker Interviews (Garrow; Britton); Walker in Cleghorn, "King," p. 16. Kunstler asserted that "Martin was about the most indecisive man I've ever seen. He really had trouble being decisive." Also see Belafonte in CBS, "Some Friends"; & Steele, "Nonviolent Resistance."

22. Watkins et al. to Moore, 5/3/63 (re 5/2), blind memo, 5/3/63, Connor;

NYT 5/4/63, p. 1, 5/5/63, p. 1; *WP* 5/4/63, p. 1; *Time* 5/10/63, p. 19; Marshall Phone Logs, JFKL; Marshall Interview (Baker); Robert Kennedy (& Marshall) Interview (Lewis); *NYP* 5/12/63; King's 5/3/63 speech, in Charles V. Hamilton, *The Black Experience in American Politics* (New York: G. P. Putnam's Sons, 1973), pp. 159–64; Whitehouse et al. to Moore, 5/7/63 (re 5/3), Connor; Schlesinger, *Thousand Days,* p. 959; Garrow, *Protest,* pp. 140–41. As Robert Kennedy put it, "Many in the Negro leadership didn't know what they were demonstrating about, they didn't know whether they were demonstrating to get rid of Bull Connor, or whether they were demonstrating about the stores, or whether they're demonstrating against the city government. Ninety percent of the people who were demonstrating certainly didn't know what they were demonstrating about, and none of the white community knew what they were demonstrating about, and none of the white community would get near the Negro community at that juncture because they felt that they were being disorderly and so nobody was talking to anybody." Kennedy White House Tape #88-6, 5/21/63.

23. King, *Why,* p. 103; "Outline of Negotiations," n.d., Vann; Kennedy White House Tape #88-6, 5/21/63; *BN* 5/4/63, p. 2, 5/5/63, p. 8; *NYT* 5/5/63, p. 1; *WP* 5/5/63, p. 1; Lewis, *Portrait,* pp. 159–61; *Reporter* 5/23/63, pp. 12–14; *Commonweal* 5/24/63, pp. 238–39; Marshall in Thompson, *Kennedy,* pp. 76–78.

24. Nichols, "Cities," pp. 275–76, 282–84, quoting an 8/73 interview with Walker; Garrow interviews with Moore & Maurice House.

25. *AC* 5/6/63, p. 6; *BN* 5/6/63, p. 2: *NYT* 5/6/63, p. 1; Young in *AJC* 7/17/83, p. C1; Nichols, "Cities," p. 289; Whitehouse et al. to Moore, 5/7/63 (re 5/5), Connor; "Outline . . .," n. 23 above; Jimerson, ACHR "Quarterly Report," n. 12 above; "Points for Progress," n.d., & [Young] "Prospective Negotiation Procedure . . .," n.d., KC.

26. *NYT* 5/7/63, p. 1; Len Holt, *National Guardian* 5/16/63 [also in Grant, *Black Protest,* pp. 344–49]; *Nation* 5/25/63, pp. 436–37; *New America* 5/31/63, p. 1; Forman, *Making,* pp. 312–14; "Outline . . .," n. 23 above; Allison to Moore, 5/7/63 (re 5/6), Connor.

27. "Outline . . .," n. 23 above; Corley, "The Quest," ch. 6; Kennedy White House Tape #88-6, 5/21/63; *BN* 5/7/63, p. 1; Holt, n. 26 above; Marshall Interview (Lewis); Vann Interview (Garrow); *NYT* 5/8/63, pp. 1, 28, 29; Dorman, *We Shall,* p. 157; *CD* 5/29–31/63, p. 19; *Newsweek* 5/13/63, pp. 27–28; *U.S. News* 5/20/63, pp. 37–39. As Robert Kennedy put it, "We felt that if we could get the substantial white citizens who owned the—ran the financial life of Birmingham behind the department store heads, that perhaps we could get the department store heads to move." Kennedy White House Tape #88-6, 5/21/63.

28. Kennedy White House Tape #88-6, 5/21/63; Forman, *Making,* pp. 314–15; *NYT* 5/8/63, pp. 1, 28, 29, 5/11/63, p. 9; *WP* 5/8/63, p. 1, 5/12/63, p. E1; "Outline . . .," n. 23 above; Thad Holt, "Memorandum . . .," 5/10/63, BPLA; Shuttlesworth, "Birmingham Revisited," p. 118; Dorman, *We Shall,* pp. 157–58; Harding, "A Beginning," p. 17; Allison et al. to Moore, 5/8/63, 5/9/63 (both re 5/7), Connor; Vann Interview (Blackside).

29. Harding, "A Beginning"; Porter Interview (Garrow); [L.H. Pitts], untitled memo beginning "My personal opinion . . .," n.d., BPLA; Gutwillig, "Six Days"; *BN* 5/8/63, p. 1; *NYT* 5/9/63, p. 1; Kennedy, *Public Papers,* 1963, pp. 372–79.

30. Shuttlesworth Interviews (Garrow; Ladner; Mosby); Raines, *My Soul,* pp. 157–61; Ella Baker Interview (Britton); C. Herbert Oliver Interview (Garrow).

31. *NYT* 5/9/63, p. 1, 5/10/63, p. 1, 8/3/63, p. 18; *BN* 5/9/63, p. 2; Shuttlesworth Interview (Garrow); *NYP* 5/10/63, p. 1; *CDN* 5/10/63, p. 1; Navasky, *Kennedy,* pp. 218–19; FBI NY 100-111180-9-163, pp. 4–5, 172A, 5/10 & 19/63; Gaston, *Green Power,* pp. 123–24; Brooks, *Walls,* p. 208; Blackside interviews with Gaston & Vann; Dorman, *We Shall,* pp. 161–62; Young notes, n.d. [5/9/63], SCLC 49-29.

32. "The Birmingham Truce Agreement," n.d., BM 17; "Statement . . .," 5/10/63, KC; King statement, 5/10/63 (reprinted in *AN* 5/25/63, p. 10); *BN* 5/10/63, p. 2, 5/11/63, pp. 2, 5; *NYT* 5/11/63, pp. 1, 8, 9; Gutwillig, "Six Days"; Dan Rather, *The Camera Never Blinks* (New York: Ballantine, 1977), pp. 97–98; Shuttlesworth Interview (Garrow). On King and "CPT," see Morris, *Origins,* p. 113.

33. Watkins to Moore, 5/15/63 (re 5/10), Whitehouse to Moore, 5/13/63 (re 5/11), Connor; Stephen Rose, *Christian Century* 5/29/63, pp. 714–16, and *Christianity & Crisis* 6/10/63, pp. 103–10; Len Holt, "The Birmingham Fix," *Liberator* 7/63, pp. 3–5, 18; Garrow interviews with Lowery, House & Ben Allen; Bains, "Birmingham," p. 44; *BN* 5/12/63, p. 1, 5/15/63, p. 1; *NYT* 5/12/63, p. 1. FBI interviews disclosed that while King and Abernathy were both registered in room 30, one of them slept alternately in room 29, for which King had registered under the pseudonym "Marion L. Lewis." SAC Birmingham to Director, "Unsubs, Bombing of Gaston Motel . . .," 5/24/63, 157-881-NR, pp. 40–41, 55.

34. King, "What a Mother Should Tell Her Child," Ebenezer, 5/12/63; *NYT* 5/13/63, pp. 1, 24, 25, 5/14/63, pp. 1, 26, 27; Kennedy White House Tape #86-2, 5/12/63; [Jack Rosenthal], "Some Sketchy Notes on Birmingham," 5/12/63, Navasky; Kennedy television appearance, 5/12/63, *Public Papers,* pp. 397–98; Donald R. Coppock, "Birmingham Detail," 5/29/63, DOJ Micro 120; *WSJ* 5/14/63, p. 16, 5/23/63, p. 18; *BN* 5/14/63, p. 1; Dorman, *We Shall,* pp. 175–76; *New Republic* 5/18/63, pp. 1–5.

35. Allison et al. to Moore, 5/14/63 (re 5/13), 5/16/63 (re 5/15), Connor; *NYT* 5/15/63, p. 1, 5/16/63, p. 1, 5/17/63, p. 1, 5/18/63, p. 12; "Notes," 5/14/63, & "Background Briefing," 5/14/63, Navasky; *BN* 5/16/63, p. 1, 5/17/63, p. 1; *CP* 5/16/63, p. A4; *Time* 5/24/63, p. 22; Shuttlesworth et al. to Smyer, 5/17/63, BM 17; *CST* 5/20/63, p. 22.

36. *NYT* 5/19/63, p. 64, 5/21/63, p. 1, 5/22/63, p. 27, 5/23/63, p. 1, 5/24/63, p. 1; *BN* 5/21/63, p. 1; FBI NY 100-111180-9-174, 176, 5/21 & 23/63; SAC New York to Director, 5/21/63, 157-6-4-1067; Whitehouse to Moore, 5/21/63 (re 5/20), Connor; *Newsweek* 6/3/63, pp. 19–20. As King told Levison in a 1:00 A.M. Tuesday phone conversation, "If all these kids are out of school they [the state troopers] are going to beat some, and I do not feel right now that we have the violent elements of the Negro community in hand enough to keep a riot from emerging."

37. Walker Interviews (Garrow; Britton); Young, "And Birmingham," p. 25, & "New World"; Young Interviews (Shellman; Brown).

38. King, "Address . . .," 5/26/63, KP; *LAT* 5/27/63, p. I-2; *CST* 5/28/63; *SLPD* 5/29/63, p. A3; *LCJ* 5/30/63, p. 1; *NYT* 5/30/63, p. 10; *Time* 6/7/63, pp. 17–19; *U.S. News* 6/10/63, p. 21; *Jet* 6/13/63, pp. 54–63; FBI NY 100-111180-7-435A, 5/28/63; Director to Robert Kennedy & to Kenneth O'Donnell, 5/31/63, 100-106670-127, 129. In Chicago King said, "The president of the United States must be ready to take a stand even if it means assassination." Kennedy did not want to meet King in the absence of other black leaders; as he put it, "The trouble with King is everybody thinks he's our boy anyway, so everything he does, everybody says we stuck him in there." Kennedy White House Tape #88-4, 5/20/63.

39. King to Kennedy, 5/30/63, WHCF 363 JFKL; Director to Robert Kennedy & to Kenneth O'Donnell, 5/31/63, 100-106670-127, 129; White to King, 6/1/63, WHCF 363 JFKL; SAC New York to Director, 6/4/63, 100-106670-132X2 (re 6/1 & 6/2); FBI NY 100-111180-9-185A, 6/1/63. The FBI also reported to Robert Kennedy that "our liaison program with the responsible leadership of some of the principal groups favoring integration . . . has enabled this Bureau to obtain and pass on to the Department and local law enforcement authorities . . . a constant flow of intelligence type information pertaining to pending and proposed action which these various groups have planned. . . . This information has also enabled us to alert local law enforcement agencies in advance in order that these agencies may take appropriate action to maintain peace and order and to prevent unwarranted situations from developing. The furnishing of such information has enabled us to maintain effective liaison during the critical period with the local authorities." Director to Attorney General, 5/23/63, 157-00-54. Five months later one FBI official informed another that "the Bureau has excellent contacts through James Farmer in CORE and Roy Wilkins in the NAACP." Baumgardner to Sullivan, 10/16/63, 100-3-104-3883.

40. FBI NY 100-111180-7-441, 442A, 6/3 & 6/4/63; FBI NY 100-111180-9-188A, 190, 6/4 & 6/6/63; SAC New York to Director, 6/7/63, 100-106670-141; Garrow interviews with Bevel, Rustin, Kahn, Hill & Cleveland Robinson; Baker interviews with Young & Rustin; *New America* 5/31/63, p. 1; Harding, "So Much," pp. 60–61, and *Other American,* pp. 165, 170–72; untitled 3pp. 1/28/63 memo, & Kahn to "Donnie" [Slaiman], 2/6/63, Kahn; *NYT* 2/25/63, p. 4; Randolph to Young, 3/26/63, n.a., "Meeting with Brother A. Philip Randolph," 4/4/63, & Young to Randolph, 4/30/63, NUL II-I-25, 26; FBI NY 100-111180-9-166, 5/13/63; [Randolph], "A Call to Black America . . .," 5/7/63, & Randolph, "Why the Emancipation March on Washington for Jobs?," 5/15/63, BR; Viorst interviews with Rustin & Kahn; Hill Interview (Mosby); Robinson remarks, 8/26/83, Smithsonian; Newman, "Black Labor," pp. 87–89; Anderson, *Randolph,* pp. 323–24; Viorst, *Fire,* pp. 216–17; Gentile, *March,* pp. 14–15. Less dependable are Anna A. Hedgeman, *The Trumpet Sounds* (New York: Holt, Rinehart & Winston, 1964), pp. 168–70, & *The Gift of Chaos* (New York: Oxford University Press, 1977), p. 63; & Hedgeman Interview (Martin).

41. *NYT* 6/10/63, p. 1, 6/12/63, p. 25; FBI NY 100-111180-9-194, 6/10/63; SAC New York to Director, 6/10/63, 100-106670-143; *WP* 6/12/63, p. A7. Also see King in Clark, *Negro Protest,* p. 45.

42. Robert Kennedy (& Marshall) Interview (Lewis); Marshall Interview (Hackman); Ramsey Clark Interview (Baker); Berl Bernhard to Theodore Sorensen & Lee White, 5/15/63, DOJ Micro 6; *New Yorker* 6/1/63, pp. 100–108; Dorman, *We Shall,* p. 201; FBI NY 100-111180-9-179A, 5/26/63; Jones to James Reston, 6/7/63, KP; Kenneth Clark, *King,* pp. 14–15; John Doar Interview (Lewis); Marshall & Lewis Martin in Thompson, *Kennedy,* pp. 71, 92–94; Whalen, *Longest Debate,* p. 16. Also see Alsop, *WP* 6/7/63; Michael Riccards, *Presidential Studies Quarterly,* Summer 1981, pp. 395–98; & *Dissent,* Summer 1963, pp. 205–14.

43. *NYT* 6/12/63, p. 1, 6/15/63, 6/16/63, 6/23/63, p. 56; *WP* 6/12/63, p. 1; FBI NY 100-111180-9-196, 6/12/63; SAC New York to Director, 6/12/63, 100-106670-146; King to Kennedy, 6/12/63, WHCF 1478 JFKL; Rather, *Camera,* pp. 106–107; *New Republic* 7/6/63, p. 17; Salter, *Jackson,* pp. 199–203; Roger Wilkins Interview (Garrow); Wilkins, *Man's Life,* p. 123; *Newsweek* 7/1/63, pp. 19–21; *NYJA* 7/16/63, p. 8. As Robert Kennedy told his brother, "Roy Wilkins hates Martin Luther King." Kennedy White House Tape #88-4, 5/20/63.

44. Garrow interviews with Jane Lee Eddy, Harold Fleming & Wiley Branton; *Taconic Foundation Report,* 12/65; Cleghorn, "Angels"; James Farmer Interview (Lewis); Dorothy Height Interview (Cowan, pp. 130–32, 159–60); Forman, *Making,* pp. 365–67; "March Committee on Jobs Meeting," 6/18/63, SNCC 133; *NYJA* 7/17/63, p. 8.

45. Whitehouse et al. to Moore, 6/24/63 (re 6/20), WH; *U.S. News* 6/17/63, p. 46; *NYT* 6/23/63, p. E3; *WSJ* 7/10/63, p. 1; Jack Minnis, "Birmingham Field Trip," 6/20/63, SRC BPLA; Kenneth J. Lenihan, "Birmingham: A Sociological Perspective," 6/63, ADL; *SCLC Newsletter* 7/63, p. 1; Shuttlesworth to Shortridge, 6/1/63, Shortridge to Abernathy, 7/10/63, KC; Edward Gardner & Shuttlesworth in *SCLC* v. *Ryles,* C. A. #70-351-S (N. D. Ala.), transcript pp. 64–65, 111–12; *DR* 6/22/63, p. 1.

46. Schlesinger, *Thousand Days,* pp. 968–71, & *Robert Kennedy,* pp. 357–58;

Lewis Interviews (Shannon; Carson); Joseph Rauh Interview (Shannon); Young Interview (Moyers); Young in *NYT* 1/15/74, p. 37; Levison Interview (Schlesinger); Garrow, *FBI*, pp. 61, 248.

47. *NYT* 6/23/63, p. 1; *WP* 6/23/63, p. A7, 6/24/63, pp. A1, B3; Wilkins, *Standing*, pp. 291–92; Young Interviews (Garrow; Moyers); Raines, *My Soul*, pp. 430–36; Howell, "Interview with Young," p. 17; Garrow, *FBI*, p. 61; *Newsweek* 5/6/63, pp. 27–28; King, "Address . . . .," 6/21/63, Gadsden, Ala., KP; Walker on "The American Experience—Race Relations in Crisis," 6/12/63, WNEW-TV, KC; King, "Interview on 'Press Conference USA,'" 7/5/63, KP.

48. *NYT* 6/24/63, p. 20, 6/26/63, p. 22; "The Great March to Freedom," Detroit, 6/23/60, Gordy/Motown record #906; Mahoney notes, 6/24/63, SNCC 133; Cleveland Robinson Interview (Garrow); Diggs to King, 6/27/63, KP.

49. *BN* 6/30/63, p. 1; O'Dell to King, 5/14/63, MLK 5; Marshall Interview (Garrow); King to O'Dell, 7/3/63, Marshall 8; Dora McDonald to Robert Kennedy, 7/3/63, 100-106670-3656; O'Dell to King, 7/12/63, KP; Young Interview (Garrow); Levison Interview (Schlesinger); *AC* 12/21/75, p. A1.

50. *CDN* 6/19/63, p. 7; "The American Experience," n. 47 above; Farmer, *Lay Bare*, pp. 226–27; SAC New York to Director, 6/19/63, 100-106670-152; *NYT* 7/1/63, p. 1; King in Warren, *Who Speaks*, p. 220. On that TV appearance, Walker said that "granting the Negro full emancipation means a readjustment of the entire economy of the United States. . . . I think it's an inevitable move toward some kind of socialism." 6/12 transcript, p. 12.

51. *NYT* 7/2/63, p. 14, 7/3/63, p. 10, 8/16/63, p. 9; Rustin to Farmer et al., "Proposed Plans . . . .," 7/2/63, BR; Wilkins, *Standing*, p. 292; CUCRL finance sheets, SNCC 23 & 111; Klibaner, "SCEF," p. 290; John Lewis Interview (Viorst); Whitney Young Interview (Wright); Cleveland Robinson Interview (Garrow); Rustin Interviews (Viorst; Garrow); American Friends Service Committee, Community Relations Executive Committee Minutes, 7/3/63, AFSC. Wiley Branton of SRC and VEP became CUCRL's director.

52. Sources on Danville include Powell, "Black Cloud"; Ely, "Negro Demonstrations"; Len Holt, *An Act of Conscience* (Boston: Beacon Press, 1965); Charity et al., "Danville"; Kunstler, *Deep*, pp. 211–32; Forman, *Making*, pp. 326–31; Arthur Kinoy, *Rights on Trial* (Cambridge, Mass.: Harvard University Press, 1983), p. 181; *Progressive* 11/63, pp. 27–31. Regarding SCLC's involvement, see Neil Cohen to King, 6/8/63, KP; *NYT* 6/13/63, p. 16, 6/23/63, p. E3, 7/12/63, p. 8, 8/11/63, p. 71; *DR* 6/18/63, p. 3, 6/29/63, p. 3, 6/30/63, p. B1, 7/2/63, p. B1, 7/3/63, p. B1, 7/7/63, p. B1, 7/9/63, p. B1, 7/10/63, p. B1, 7/12/63, p. B1, 7/13/63, p. 3, 7/14/63, p. B1, 7/31/63, p. 3; *WES* 6/29/63, p. A9; *NVP* 6/29/63; Coulton, "Voter Registration in Danville," n.d. [7/16/63], & "Voter's Registration . . ." n.d. [ca. 8/21/63], SCLC 142; SCLC press release, 7/17/63, KC; Ivanhoe Donaldson, "Danville Report," 9/63, SNCC 105; *Newsweek* 3/1/65, pp. 34–37.

53. Allison et al. to Moore, 7/10/63 (re 7/8), BM 31; *NYT* 7/14/63, p. 44, 7/17/63, p. 14, 7/22/63, p. 1; Watkins et al. to Moore, 7/19/63 (re 7/15) & Allison et al. to Moore, 8/1/63 (re 7/29), WH; SCLC press release, 7/17/63, KC; Norman Jimerson to George Murray, 6/24/63, ACHR; [Red Holland], "Memo," n.d. [ca. 7/63], DOJ Micro 10; Minnis to Branton, "Memorandum," 8/23/63, SRC VI-6-31.

54. King, "Remembering Who You Are," Ebenezer, 7/7/63, KP; "1st Plan of Operation . . . .," 7/8/63, BR; *WES* 7/11/63; transcript of 7/11/63 conference, Reedy 8; Rodney Clurman to Charles Horsky, 7/11/63, WHCF 365 JFKL; Arthur Caldwell to Marshall, 7/11/63, BM 31; *NYT* 7/12/63, p. 10, 7/24/63, p. 15, 7/25/63, p. 11; Bill Mahoney, "Report . . . .," 7/19/63, SNCC 16, 177.

55. *NYT* 7/18/63, pp. 1, 10, 8/4/63, p. 61; King to Diggs, 7/17/63, KP; "For Freedom Now" transcript, WGBH-TV, 7/22/63, KC; *Newsweek* 7/29/63, pp. 30–32; Brink & Harris, *Negro Revolution*, pp. 116–24; Cleghorn, "Angels"; Wiley Branton Interview (Garrow); Lewis Interview (Viorst).

56. *NYT* 7/13/63, p. 1, 7/26/63, p. 1, 7/27/63, p. 8, 7/30/63, p. 13; *WP* 7/13/63, p. A1; *AC* 7/25/63, p. 1, 7/26/63, p. 1, 7/27/63, pp. 4, 9, 7/30/63, p. 5, 8/16/63, p. 3, 8/17/63, p. 3; *AJ* 7/25/63, p. 2, 7/26/63, p. 4; King, "Statement . . .," 7/25/63; *ADW* 7/26/63, p. 1; *JDN* 7/29/63, p. 9; Garrow, *FBI,* pp. 65–67.

57. *NYT* 8/10/63, p. 1; *New America* 8/31/63, p. 7; National Committee for the Albany Defendants, *The Albany Cases* (1963); Slater King, "Bloody Battleground," pp. 99–100; *PC* 12/22/62, p. 1, 1/12/63, p. 10, 2/16/63, p. 8, 2/23/63, p. 8, 3/9/63, pp. 1, 4, 8, 3/16/63, p. 1, 3/23/63, p. 1; Anderson et al. to City Commission, 2/8/63, & Commission to Anderson et al., 2/22/63, ALB; *AH* 2/27/63; King in *SCLC Newsletter* 3/63, p. 1 [also *AN* 4/13/63, p. 10]; John Doar to Robert Kennedy, "Albany," 5/9/63, BM 8; *AC* 5/11/63, p. 5; Walker, "Albany"; *NYT* 6/23/63, p. 61, 7/5/63, p. 44; Hoover to Lee White, 6/27/63, White 21 JFKL; Roos, "Memorandum for File," 7/3/63, & Slater King et al. to Asa Kelley, 7/5/63, ALB; Reese Cleghorn, *New Republic* 6/20/63, pp. 15–18; Ralph Allen field report, summer 1963, SNCC 96; King, *AN* 1/18/64, p. 8; *Liberator* 5/64, pp. 14–16; Kunstler, *Deep,* pp. 128–29; Zinn, *SNCC,* pp. 211–12 & *Southern Mystique,* p. 212; Donald Hollowell Interviews (Britton; Garrow).

58. "Agenda—August 3," BR; *NYT* 8/4/63, p. 57, 8/12/63, p. 12, 8/13/63, p. 22, 8/14/63, p. 21; Prinz Interview (Leventhal); Randolph Interview (Baker); "Organizing Manual #1" [7/24/63], Rustin to Chairmen et al. "Agenda for . . . 8/16," 8/12/63, Rustin & Kahn to Randolph, "Memorandum," 8/16/63, & "Proposed Program . . .," n.d., all BR; Anderson, *Randolph,* p. 327; Victor Reuther, *The Brothers Reuther* (Boston: Houghton Mifflin, 1976), p. 371; Robert Kennedy (& Marshall) Interview (Lewis); Robert Kennedy Interview (Lewis II, pp. 73–75); Schlesinger, *Robert Kennedy,* pp. 350–51; Gentile, *March,* pp. 62–66; Duckett Interview (Oates); FBI NY 100-73250-144; SAC New York to Director, 8/11/63, Bland to Sullivan, 8/12/63, & Director to Robert Kennedy, 8/12/63, 100-106670-184, 190, 178; SAC New York to Director, 8/13/63, 157-970-364; Coretta King Interview (Mayerson XXVII, p. 34); Coretta King, *My Life,* p. 236; Garrow, *FBI,* pp. 67, 250. Taps on Jones's two offices began 7/29 & 7/30/63, the one at home began 8/5/63. FBI HQ File 100-407018. When South Carolina Senator Strom Thurmond did make a personal attack on Rustin, it did "us more good than harm," Tom Kahn wrote Jane Stembridge. "All kinds of people who formerly were a little shaky have rallied to Bayard's defense. The top leadership is absolutely solid, surprisingly enough." 8/19/63, BR. The best account of the march organization is Harvey Swados, *Nation* 9/7/63, pp. 104–107.

59. "Organizing Manual No. 2" [8/20/63]; *NYT* 8/21/63, p. 24, 8/27/63, p. 23, 8/28/63, p. 1; *CST* 8/19/63, p. 3, 8/22/63, p. 12; Rustin to Chairmen, "Agenda . . .," 8/23/63, BR; King & Wilkins "Meet the Press" interview, 8/25/63, KP; *NYT Magazine* 8/25/63, pp. 7–9, 57–61; King in *SLPD* 8/25/63, p. C1; King, *AN* 8/24/63, p. 10; King Interview (Smith); King, "Advance Text . . .," 8/28/63, Boyte; *CDN* 8/29/63, p. 12; *Time* 8/30/63, pp. 9–14; *Newsweek* 9/2/63, pp. 17–21. One problem concerned the absence of any woman from the speakers' list; after an objection by staffer Anna Hedgeman brief tributes to several female activists were added to the program. Hedgeman, *Trumpet,* pp. 178–79; Gentile, *March,* p. 141. King discussed the upcoming speech in an 8/24 phone conversation with Al Duckett, telling him he wanted it to be brief, "sort of a Gettysburg address." (FBI NY 100-73250-144 & 100-73250-1C-20A, p.5) Duckett later asserted that "on the final preparation of the speech, I did a great deal of the writing and developing of ideas. . . . I gave him ideas and I gave him language." (Oates Interview)

60. Garrow interviews with Rochelle Horowitz & Mathew Ahmann; Lewis, "A Serious Revolution," *Liberation* 9/63, p. 8; Lewis Interviews (Viorst; Carson; Blackside I & II; Brasch); Lewis, "Six Month Report," 12/27/63, SNCC 1; Lewis remarks, 8/26/83, Smithsonian; King Interview (Smith); Kahn Interviews (Viorst;

Garrow); Kennedy (& Marshall) Interview (Lewis, p. 76); Marshall Interviews (Viorst; Blackside); O'Boyle Interview (Shannon); Forman Interview (Blackside); Rustin Interviews (Garrow; Viorst; Leventhal); *NYT* 8/29/63, p. 20; *Jet* 9/12/63, pp. 28–29; *Liberation* 9/63, pp. 6–7; Rustin remarks in Syracuse, N.Y., 1/4/64, SHSW Tape 544; Forman, *Making,* pp. 333–36; Viorst, *Fire,* p. 229; Gentile, *March,* pp. 147, 171–76. As Ahmann recalled the cardinal's unhappiness with Lewis's text, "It was the administration that called it to O'Boyle's attention," who told Ahmann. "The Kennedys were very concerned about the rhetoric." On the podium the revised text "was given to O'Boyle, and he gave it to me and asked me to read it. He said, 'Is it OK?,' and I said, 'It's fine.'" (Garrow Interview)

61. King, "Advance Text . . .," n. 59 above; King Interview (Smith); Whitehouse et al. to Moore, 4/11/63 (re 4/9—"I had a dream tonight"), Connor; "The Great March to Freedom," 6/23/63, Detroit, Gordy/Motown record #906; Albert Cleage Interview (Harriford); King, "I Have a Dream," 8/28/63, on "The Great March on Washington," Gordy/Motown record #908; Saunders, *The Day,* esp. pp. 3–14, 79; *NYT* 8/29/63, p. 1; *New South* 9/63, pp. 3–19. In a 3/68 interview King also recalled using the dream motif once in Albany. Cannon, "King," p. 220. Also see Bosmajian's extremely valuable "Inaccuracies" essay; Erwin G. Krasnow, *Georgetown Law Journal* 53 (Winter 1965): 403–29, at 403–405; *King* v. *Mister Maestro,* 224 F. Supp. 101 (1963); *AN* 2/16/63, p. 38; *PC* 2/16/63, p. 2; *AA* 2/23/63, p. 12; *NYT* 10/5/63, p. 10; *WP* 10/5/63, p. A4. Undependable are Ralph Abernathy's recollections in Lynda Obst, ed., *The Sixties* (New York: Random House, 1977), p. 94. General accounts of the March include *Time* 9/6/63, pp. 13–15; *Newsweek* 9/9/63, pp. 19–22; *Christian Century* 9/11/63, pp. 1094–95; *New Republic* 9/14/63, pp. 19–20; *New Yorker* 9/14/63, pp. 159–66; *Commonweal* 9/20/63, pp. 551–54; *Gandhi Marg* 10/63, pp. 299–303; *Ebony* 11/63, pp. 35–46, 119–24; *Midwest Quarterly* Winter 1964; *Journal of Human Relations* 12 (1st Quarter 1964): 73–87.

62. Coretta King Interview (Mayerson XVI, p. 47); *NYT Magazine* 11/26/72, p. 48; Wilkins Interview (Baker); Young Interview (Wright); Ahmann Interview (Garrow); "Notes for Meeting . . .," 8/28/63, White 4 LBJL; Kennedy White House Tape #108-2, 8/28/63; *NYT* 8/29/63, p. 1; Jay Kennedy Interview (Garrow); Garrow, *FBI,* pp. 139–44; Jay Kennedy to King, 10/28/63, KP; "March on Washington—Report by the Leaders," WTTG-TV, 8/28/63, KC; Jay Kennedy to Farmer, 11/5/63, CORE 25 KC; King, "I Have a Dream." Presidential aide Lee White remembers John Kennedy observing that "that guy is really good" while watching King's speech on TV. Whalen, *Longest Debate,* p. 26, and White Interview (Garrow). Throughout the White House meeting, Kennedy referred to King as "Reverend."

Chapter Six

1. *NYT* 8/30/63, p. 1, 9/1/63, p. 44; Rustin to Chairmen, "Follow-Up to the March . . .," 9/5/63, BR; Haley to Carey et al., ". . . Administrative Meeting, 9/5," 9/10/63, CORE 34 KC; Rustin, "Meaning of the March," p. 11; Kahn, *New America* 9/24/63, p. 1; Rustin, "Prospectus . . .," pp. 6–7. Also see Lynd, "New Radicalism"; Zinn, "Double Job"; & *New Politics* Fall 1963, pp. 43–52.

2. Young Interviews (Viorst; Baker; Garrow); Young in Raines, *My Soul,* pp. 425–27; Garrow interviews with Abernathy, Cotton, Anderson, Smiley, Fauntroy, Jesse Jackson, Gardner Taylor, Joseph Lowery, Donald Hollowell & John Gibson; King, "Interview . . . for ABC's Good Company," 9/67, KP; King, *Playboy* 1/65, p. 78; Bevel 4/21/65 remarks, UICC JLB; King, "Address . . .," 5/21/61, Montgomery, & King briefcase notes, n.d., KP; King, "Three Dimensions of the

Complete Life," 3/14/65, Chicago, CSEC 7; Annell Ponder, "Minutes . . .,"
9/5–7/63, SCLC 153; Vivian Interviews (Garrow; Braden); Minnis to Branton,
"SCLC . . .," 9/16/63, SRC VI-10-12. Apropos of Young's remarks, James Cone
has emphasized that "the most important source for King's thought was unques-
tionably the black church tradition from which his faith was derived and to which he
returned for strength and courage in the context of crisis during his ministry."
Fellowship 1–2/84, pp. 32–33. Also see King's "Foreword" in Daniel C.
Thompson, *The Negro Leadership Class* (Englewood Cliffs, N.J.: Prentice-Hall,
1963), pp. ix–x, where he quotes Gandhi's statement "There go my people, I must
catch them, for I am their leader," and Coretta King, "We're Sharing Him," who
states that "from those first meetings in December 1955 through the call for help
that brought him to Memphis, he always preferred that somehow others could lead
the marches, or make the speeches, or be the inspirational force." Andrew Young
had visited Savannah in midsummer and decided that despite the achievements of
talented local activist Hosea Williams, Savannah's divisions militated against SCLC
involvement. See Shellman interviews with Young & Williams; Baldwin, *Ain't We;*
Clark, "Siege."

   3. Flynt, "Ethics"; King et al. to Kennedy, 9/5/63, WHCF 1478; *RNL* 9/8/63,
p. A2; C. Herbert Oliver Interview (Garrow); SAC NY to Director, 9/11/63,
100-438794-NR; Director to Attorney General, 9/13/63, 100-106670-208; Garrow,
FBI, pp. 69, 251.

   4. *NYT* 9/16/63, p. 1, 9/17/63, p. 25; SAC NY to Director, 9/16/63,
100-106670-214; King to Kennedy, 9/15 & 16/63, WHCF 367, 1478; Kennedy,
"Statement," 9/16/63, *Public Papers,* pp. 681–82; Joseph Dolan to Nicholas
Katzenbach, "Birmingham Possibilities II," 9/18/63, DOJ Micro 120; Garrow
interviews with Diane Nash, James Bevel & John Gibson; Diane Bevel, "Proposal . . ." & "Report, 9/17–20/63," SCLC 141; Braden, "Southern Freedom,"
p. 56; *Liberator* 3/69, p. 5; Young remarks, SCOPE Orientation, 6/15/65, Project
South Tape 0432, pp. 7–8.

   5. Diane Bevel, "Report . . .," n. 4 above; King, "Farewell . . .," 9/18/63, in
Cain, *King Treasury,* pp. 139–40; *NYT* 9/19/63, p. 1; John Cross Interview (Bar-
ton); Diane Nash Interview (Garrow); John Porter Interviews (Garrow; Brown);
Shuttlesworth Interview (Ladner); SAC NY to Director, 9/17/63, 100-106670-219;
Whitehouse et al. to Moore, 9/20/63 (re 9/16), Hamilton; Douthard to Carey,
n.d., CORE 83 KC.

   6. Lee White to King, 9/18/63, WHCF 1478; *NYT* 9/19/63, p. 1, 9/20/63, p. 1;
Kennedy White House Tapes 111-7, 112-1, 6, 9/19 & 23/63; Kennedy, "Further
Statement . . .," 9/19/63, *Public Papers,* pp. 692–93; *PC* 9/28/63, p. 2; Shuttlesworth Interview (Ladner); Gaston, *Green Power,* p. 135; Henderson to
Marshall, "Proposed Plan . . .," 9/23/63, BM 8; Henderson Interview (Wright);
Marshall, "Protest," p. 792; Theodore White, *Life* 11/29/63, p. 86. President Kennedy's comments about SNCC to the white Birmingham delegation were repeated
by at least one participant, Catholic Bishop Joseph Durick, to other associates,
stimulating worries about SNCC that were already present in liberal religious circles. The National Catholic Council for Interracial Justice executive director,
Mathew Ahmann, co-leader of the March on Washington, asked a well-connected
official of the Atlanta archdiocese, Gerard Sherry, for his information, noting the
"revolutionary imagery" of John Lewis's original speech plus the fear expressed
by other Catholics that SNCC "is a Communist front of some sort." Sherry promised to speak with the FBI, and a southern NCCIJ staffer, Henry Cabirac,
checked with Justin Finger of the Anti-Defamation League, "who maintains regular contact with the FBI," Cabirac told Ahmann. Sherry finally reported back
that there were "no known Communists" in the SNCC leadership and "nothing
concrete to go on." Ahmann to Sherry, 9/25/63, NCCIJ 20-44, Sherry to Ahmann,
9/27/63, 20-13, Cabirac to Ahmann, 3/8, 9/30 & 10/17/63, 31-4 & 20-13, Cabirac to

Sherry, 10/17/63, 20-13, Sherry to Cabirac, 10/24/63, & Sherry to Ahmann, 11/5/63, NCCIJ 20-13.

7. *WP* 9/23/63, p. A7, 9/24/63, p. A7, 9/25/63, p. A6, 9/26/63, p. E24, 9/27/63, p. A7, 9/28/63, p. C2; *NYT* 9/25/63, p. 32, 9/26/63, p. 29, 9/27/63, p. 30, 9/28/63, p. 22, 9/29/63, p. 77; "Minutes of the Board . . .," 9/24-27/63, KC; Walker, "Techniques," p. 8; *RNL* 9/26/63, p. 4; King, "Address . . .," 9/27/63, KP; *CSM* 9/28/63, p. 5, 9/30/63, p. 3; SCLC *Annual Report 1962-1963*, KC; Curtis Harris Interview (Garrow); *RTD* 9/29/63, p. 1; Young to King et al., "SCLC Program . . .," 9/63, KC; *PC* 10/5/63, p. 1; *AA* 10/5/63, p. 1; *CP* 9/30/63, p. B5.

8. *NYT* 9/29/63, p. 79, 10/5/63, p. 10; *PC* 10/12/63, p. 1; Rustin to Chairmen, "The Future of the March on Washington Movement," 9/27/63, NAACP III-B-373; Reddick to Rustin, 9/27/63, KC; Walker Interviews (Garrow; Britton); Garrow interviews with Bevel, Dora McDonald, Curtis Harris, Joseph Lowery, Milton Reid & Thomas Kilgore; Walker to King, 10/4/63, KP. Also see FBI NY 100-111180-7-316A, 1/29/63; *AC* 4/2/63, p. 6; *ADW* 4/3/63, p. 1. Antipathy toward Walker, Harris said, "was not strong as such among the Board. But one person, the right person, having a difference of opinion with you . . . could make the difference." As Lowery emphasized, "Somebody might officially have tried to put it off on the Board, as people often do," but that all personnel decisions were King's.

9. SAC NY to Director, 10/1/63, 100-106670-242, 10/2, 10/5, 10/7 & 10/9/63, 100-3-116-375, 365, 440, 402; FBI NY 100-111180-9-297A, 9/21/63, 100-111180-7-567A & 568A, 10/7 & 8/63; Garrow, *FBI*, pp. 72-74, 252; King, "Confidential Memorandum, Re Direct Action . . .," n.d. [ca. early 10/63], KP. Duckett later recalled that "I did just about all the finished writing and contributed some of the important ideas" for the book. (Oates Interview) Also see Robinson, *Never*, p. 225.

10. *NYT* 10/9/63, p. 28, 10/10/63, p. 26; Whitehouse et al. to Moore, 10/21/63 (re 10/14), WH; C. Herbert Oliver Interview (Garrow); King, "Excerpt from Address," 10/14/63, CBS, KP; FBI NY 100-73250-1A-70a, 10/16/63; Boynton to King, 10/8/63, KP; Watkins et al. to Moore, 4/23/63 (re 4/20 comments by Andrew Young about Selma), Connor. On SNCC's previous involvement in Selma, see Reggie Robinson, "Field Report . . .," 9/25/62, SNCC 19; Frank Holloway, "Partial Report . . .," 2/8-15/63, SNCC; *STJ* 5/15/63; Bernard Lafayette in Carawan, *Freedom*, pp. 146-47; Lafayette Interviews (Garrow; Weisbrot); Boynton Interviews (Fager; Blackside; Garrow); C. C. Brown Interview (Fager); L. L. Anderson Interviews (Fager; Garrow); Reese Interviews (Smith; Vasser); Garrow interviews with Marie Foster & E. L. Doyle; *Presbyterian Life* 1/15/64, pp. 12-22, 38; and especially Boynton, *Bridge*. On events in early fall, 1963, see Wilson Brown to Worth Long, "Selma . . .," ca. 8/22/63, SNCC 11 & 42; Boynton to James Forman, 9/4 & 9/10/63, SNCC 10; B. L. Tucker, "Report . . .," 9/16-24/63, SNCC 22; *NYT* 10/6/63, p. 79, 10/13/63, p. 77; Justin Finger to Milton Ellerin, "Selma . . .," 10/7/63, & Finger to Monroe Schlactus, "Selma . . .," 10/14/63, ADL, BPLA; John Pratt, "Report . . .," 10/1/63, & Pratt to Robert Spike et al., "Report . . .," 11/14/63, RES; *New Republic* 10/26/63, pp. 11-12, 11/16/63, pp. 29-30; Zinn, *SNCC*, pp. 147-66; Bruce Gordon, "Field Report . . .," 11/9/63, SNCC 13; *Correspondent* 11-12/63, pp. 43-53; *Community* 12/63, pp. 4-5; Forman, *Making*, pp. 316-26, 345-54; Henderson, "The Law"; Alan Gropman, *The Air Force Integrates* (Washington: Office of Air Force History, 1978), pp. 197, 205-206; Garrow, *Protest*, pp. 31-33, 262; & Maurice Ouellet to Henry Cabirac, 2/6/64, NCCIJ 33-1.

11. *WES* 9/9/63; King, *NYT Magazine* 9/29/63, pp. 91-92; *NYT* 10/18/63, p. 18, 10/23/63, p. 28; *SBT* 10/19/63, p. 1; *HC* 10/21/63, p. 3, 10/22/63, p. 23; King, "Excerpt . . .," 10/21/63, ABC, KP; Watkins et al. to Moore, 10/21/63, WH; Norman Jimerson to Hamilton, 10/23/63, ACHR; *WSJ* 10/28/63, p. 1; King,

"Address . . .," 10/23/63, MLK 11; FBI 100-3-116-462, 10/29/63; Young to King, "Voter Registration . . .," 10/21/63, SCLC 135; "SCLC Voter Registration Report," n.d. [ca. 11/6/63], SRC VI-10-24. Also see Robert Kennedy to John Kennedy, 10/23/63, Navasky.

12. SAC NY to Director, 11/4 & 8/63, 100-3-116-491, 509; Garrow, *FBI*, pp. 72–74, 91–96; Robert Kennedy (& Marshall) Interview (Lewis); Marshall Interview (Hackman); Hoover to Kennedy, 10/28/63, 100-3-116-illegible; Rustin to King, 11/5/63, KP; Shuttlesworth Interview (Garrow). As Levison once reminded Wachtel, "The great decisions were made on the phone." FBI NY 100-111180-9-2073A, 6/21/69. Concerning the FBI's wiretap accounts, Rustin later said that "I must give them credit . . . almost every conversation was what I said, and what King said. They didn't distort." (Garrow Interview)

13. Sartain et al. to Moore, 11/5/63 (re 11/4), WH; King, *AN* 11/9/63, p. 10; *AC* 11/9/63, p. 4; *NYT* 11/7/63, p. 30; Shuttlesworth to King, 11/7/63, KP.

14. SCLC press release, 11/5/63, SCLC 121; *New Republic* 11/2/63, pp. 11–12; *NYT* 11/10/63, pp. 80, 81; *PC* 11/23/63, p. 3; *WP* 11/13/63, p. A14, 11/16/63, p. C2; FBI NY 100-73250-246, 11/16/63; Walker Interview (Smith); Meier, "Dynamics"; Young to King et al., "Danville . . .," 11/18/63, KC.

15. *WP* 11/7/63, p. 1; Henderson Interview (Wright); Nick Flannery Interview (Rafferty); Garrow interviews with Bernard Reynolds, McLean Pitts, James G. Clark, John Gibson, Septima Clark & Bernard Lee; Walker Interview (Smith); *AC* 9/25/63, 11/12/63, p. 20; SCLC press release, 11/6/63, KC; *SWG* 11/16/63; FBI 157-6-2-1434; Eliza Jackson to Rustin, 9/28/63, BR; Slater King to Clancy Sigal, 11/10/63, King SHSW; Charles Sherrod, "Southwest Georgia . . .," 12/27/63, SNCC 21; FBI NY 100-111180-7-592A, 11/1/63; *NYP* 11/20/63, p. 3; SAC NY to Director, 11/21/63, & Director to Attorney General, 11/26/63, 100-3-116-562, 536.

16. Coretta King Interview (Mayerson XVI, p. 60); Coretta King, *My Life,* p. 244; Pierce, "Legacy," p. 164; FBI 100-3-116-625; King, *NYHT* 11/24/63, p. 13, 11/22/64, p. 16; King, *AN* 12/21/63, p. 12; King Interviews (Bernhard; Smith); Bernard Lee Interview (Burrell); Wiley Branton Interview (Garrow); King, "Remarks . . .," 11/26/63, KP; *NYT* 11/27/63, pp. 20, 24; King to Executive Staff, 10/30/63, KC; Smith interviews with Walker & Boyte; *WP* 11/4/63, p. B3.

17. *LIP* 11/25/63, p. 9; SAC NY to Director, 12/4/63, 100-3-116-662; Jones to King, 11/26/63, KP; White to Johnson, 12/3/63, Ex HU2 Box 2; *NYT* 12/4/63, p. 1; *AC* 12/4/63, p. 1; *WP* 12/4/63, p. A2; *U.S. News* 12/16/63, pp. 48–49; King, *AN* 2/1/64, p. 10.

18. *BS* 12/20/63, p. 40; SAC NY to Director, 12/17 & 18/63, 100-438794-NR; Clark to King, 12/12/63, SCLC 154; Young to Clark et al., 12/17/63, KP; Clark Interview (Garrow); *United Church Herald* 2/1/64, pp. 18–21; Clark in Clayton, *SCLC,* p. 53; Clark, "Literacy"; Cotton, "CEP"; Tjerandsen, *Education,* pp. 180–81, 191–93.

19. King, "Address . . .," 12/15/63, MLK 1; *AC* 12/16/63, p. 1; *NYT* 12/16/63, p. 17; King, *AN* 2/15/64, p. 10; Coretta King Interview (Mayerson XVIII, pp. 48–50); Coretta King, "My Dream," p. 77; *Time* 1/3/64, pp. 13–16, 25–27; FBI NY 100-111180-9-401, 1/3/64; SAC NY to Director 1/6 & 7/64, 1/10/64 (2), all 100-438794-NR; Jones to King, 1/31/64, KP; Garrow, *FBI,* pp. 102–107; Sullivan to Belmont, 12/24/63, 100-3-116-684; FBI 100-106670-1024, 12/2/64; Director to Attorney General, 1/17/64, 100-3-116-illegible.

20. Whalen, *Longest Debate,* pp. 94–95; *NYT* 1/19/64, p. 1; *WP* 1/19/64, p. A2; *CNC* 1/24/64, p. B8; King in *AN* 1/4/64, p. 6, *DFP* 1/5/64, p. B1, & *SCLC Newsletter* 1/64, p. 7. Also see *NYT* 7/1/63, p. 1 ("There must be some concrete, practical preferential program") & *SLPD* 9/21/63, p. A3 ("a crash program of special treatment").

21. Jones to King, 1/29/64, & Reddick to King, 1/29/64, KP; *CNC* 1/24/64, p. B8; Garrow interviews with Walker, Bevel, Jones, C. T. Vivian & John Gibson;

Walker Interview (Britton); Pat Watters, *Nation* 2/3/64, pp. 117–20, & 2/17/64, pp. 162–65; Margaret Long, *Progressive* 2/64, pp. 10–14; FBI 100-3-116-857, 1/30/64; Coretta King Interview (Mayerson XXII, pp. 37–38); Cotton Interview (Garrow); *Jet* 2/6/64, pp. 14–18.

22. *DP* 1/25/64, p. 1, 1/26/64, p. A3, 1/27/64, p. 2; Garrow, *FBI*, p. 107; *MJ* 1/28/64, p. II-1; Sullivan to Belmont, 1/27 & 28/64, 100-3-116-792, 801; King to Kivie Kaplan, 1/30/64, KP; SAC NY to Director, 2/1/64, 100-3-116-893; FBI NY 100-111180-7-689A, 2/6/64; Jones to King, 1/29/64, KP; various Levison notes in Popper 17 & 22; King to Popper, 2/3/64, Popper 17.

23. SAC NY to Director, 2/10/64, 100-3-116-889; King, "Interview with Ladies of the Press" [2/6/64], KP; *U.S. News* 2/24/64, pp. 59–61; SCLC press release, 2/5/64, KC; FBI 100-3-116-869, 896, 908; *SFC* 2/15/64, p. 3; *LAT* 2/17/64; *LAS* 2/20/64, p. 2; Garrow, *FBI*, pp. 107–10; *HA* 2/19/64, p. A1, 2/20/64, p. A1; SAC NY to Director, 2/26, 2/27 & 3/4/64, 100-3-116-illegible, 1016, 1072; *NYT* 3/1/64, p. 80.

24. [Bevel], "Program for Action in Alabama," n.d. [ca. 2/64], SCLC 148; Garrow interviews with Bevel & Diane Nash.

25. John Doar to Burke Marshall, "Conference with Dr. Lucius Pitts . . .," 1/15/64, BPLA; *NYT* 3/5/64, p. 26, 3/16/64, p. 25; Norman Jimerson to Lyndon Johnson, 3/9/64, ACHR; Shuttlesworth, "Why We Must Demonstrate," 3/19/64, KC; SCLC press release, 3/4/64, KC; *SCLC Newsletter* 3/64, pp. 1–2; *MA* 3/5/64, p. 30; FBI 157-6-61-558.

26. *NYT* 3/6/64, p. 27; *LCJ* 3/6/64, p. 1; *OES* 3/6/64; FBI 100-3-116-1043 & 100-106670-331; Hayling Interviews (Britton; Garrow); Vivian Interview (Garrow); Twine Interviews (Colburn; Harvey); Hartley, "Long, Hot Summer," pp. 1–41; Colburn, "St. Augustine Business," pp. 214–21, & *Racial Change*, pp. 27–60; *CSM* 7/13/64; R. W. Puryear Interview (Colburn); *Ebony* 8/64, pp. 92–98; *Harper's* 1/65, pp. 74–81; Robert Saunders to Gloster Current, "St. Augustine . . .," 3/19/63, Saunders; *SAR* 6/18/63, 6/19/63; SAC Jacksonville to Director serials from 6/19 to 9/19/63 in FBI HQ File 157-6-63, esp. #s 449, 450, 457, 460, 464, 645 & 888; Director to Attorney General 6/29/63, 157-6-63-469; King phone message books, 7/1/63, 7/9/63, 8/12/63 & 10/25/63, MLK & KP; King to Johnson, 7/8/63, LBJ VP 5; Hobart Taylor to Walker, 8/8/63, KC; Kallal interviews with L. O. Davis & Holstead Manucy; Director to SAC Jacksonville, 9/19/63, 157-6-63-903X; Rosen to Belmont, 10/30 & 12/19/63, 157-6-63-1008, 1147; John Murphy to Marshall, & Marshall to Kennedy, 11/5/63, DOJ-CRD 144-17M-86; Saunders to Current, 11/15/63, NAACP III-H-200; Saunders Interview (Garrow); Shelley Interview (Heinsohn); Fannie Fullerwood et al. to Charles Barrier, 1/14/64, Mal Ogden to Bryant, 2/10/64, & Randolph Tucker to Bryant, 2/20/64, Bryant 130, 131. Other substantive documents concerning St. Augustine can be found in NAACP-III-H-14 & 200; Saunders; Bryant 130 & 131; LBJ VP 5; & Lee White JFKL 22.

27. "Florida Spring Project" brochure [3/11/64], KC; Virgil Wood & Harvey Cox, "Dear Pastor" letter, 3/18/64, NCCIJ 30-4; Ann Orlov to Jack [Sisson], [3/30/64], NCCIJ 33-4; Colburn, *Racial Change*, pp. 60–74; *FS* 3/21/64, p. 1, 4/4/64, p. 1; SAC Jacksonville to Director, 3/20, 27, 29 & 31/64, 157-6-63-1228, 1242, 1252, 1256; "Demands of the St. Augustine Chapter . . .," 3/31/64, KC; Hayling Interview (Garrow); King to Hayling, 4/1/64, KP 20-40; *FTU*, 4/2/64, p. 24; *NYT* 4/9/64, p. 30; *SCLC Newsletter* 6/64, p. 12; Hartley, "Long, Hot Summer," pp. 42–52; Kunstler, *Deep*, pp. 272–84, & *Trials*, pp. 90–91; *Saturday Evening Post* 5/16/64, pp. 74–76; Tom Brown, "Report on St. Augustine . . .," n.d. [ca. 4/3/64], SNCC 22; Florida Committee, *Racial and Civil Disorders*, pp. 2–9, 28–36; Shelley Interview (Heinsohn).

28. Garrow interviews with Bevel, Walker, Curtis Harris, Dora McDonald & Joseph Lowery; Walker Interview (Britton); *Jet* 3/12/64; FBI NY

100-111180-9-469A, 3/11/64; FBI 100-3-116-1118, 1120, 1136, 3/14, 16 & 24/64; SAC Atlanta to Director, 3/10/64, 100-3-116-1067; Director to SAC Atlanta, 3/19/64, 100-438794-NR; *TN* 3/9/64, p. 11; *HC* 3/12/64, p. 1; FBI 100-3-116-1070, 1103; *NYT* 3/15/64, p. 46; *DFP* 3/20/64, p. A3; FBI NY 100-111180-7-710A, 2/27/64; FBI 100-106670-338, 340, 343, 4/14/64; FBI 100-106670-1024, 11/27/64; *NB* 3/19/64, p. 1; *SLPD* 3/23/64, p. A3; King, *AN* 3/14/64, p. 12 (& *SCLC Newsletter* 3/64, p. 7); *WES* 3/26/64, p. A5; *WP* 3/27/64, p. A6; King, *Playboy* 1/65, p. 74.

29. Bevel to King, "Nonviolent vs. Brinkmanship," 4/13/64, SCLC 148; Garrow interviews with Bevel, Diane Nash, Orange & John Gibson; SCLC [Diane Nash] *Handbook for Freedom Army Recruits,* n.d.; *BW* 4/11/64, p. 1, 4/22/64, p. 1; Gwen Patton Interview (Long); SAC NY to Director, 4/2/64, 100-3-116-1190; Jones to King, 4/15/64, KP; *AA* 4/4/64, p. 16; Noles et al. to Moore, 3/30/64, WH. Also see *WSJ* 4/14/64, p. 1; King, *AN* 4/25/64, p. 10.

30. Minutes, 4/16–17/64 (2 different sets), KC; *WP* 4/17/64, p. B10.

31. Alsop, *WP* 4/15/64, p. A23; *NYHT* 4/15/64, p. 28; SAC NY to Director, 4/21 & 22/64, 100-3-116-1294; 1285; SAC Atlanta to Director, 4/22/64, 100-3-116-1322; Fauntroy Interview (Garrow); *NYT* 4/22/64, p. 30; King, "Statement . . .," 4/23/64, KP; *SFE* 4/24/64, p. 1; *SFC* 4/24/64, p. 1; *NB* 4/24/64, p. 1; SAC NY to Director, 4/27/64, 100-106670-NR.

32. *AJ* 4/23/64, p. 37; Young to Branton, 3/10/64, Branton to Young, 3/21/64, & Weldon Rougeau to Branton, 4/24/64, SRC VI-18-21, 22; King to Dorothy Height et al., "World's Fair Stall-In," 4/21/64, KP. Also see King, *AN* 5/9/64, p. 8.

33. Garrow, *FBI,* pp. 115–16, 265; SAC Las Vegas to Director, 5/15/64, 100-3-116-1425; [deleted] to Hoover, 5/20/64, O&C File Item 141; *LVRJ* 4/27/64, p. 1.

34. Norman Jimerson to Leslie Dunbar, 4/23/64, SRC I-67-1; "Confidential Report from Alabama Legislative Commission . . .," 4/30/64, 100-438794-91; Gibson, "St. Augustine . . .," 5/2/64, & untitled memo to King et al., 5/4/64, KC; Gibson Interviews (Britton; Garrow); C. T. Vivian Interviews (Garrow; Browne); Young Interview (Shellman); Colburn, *Racial Change,* pp. 74–75; *FTU* 4/20/64; *FS* 4/25/64, p. 1, 5/2/64, p. 7; *MH* 4/22/64; p. A7; White to King, 4/24/64, Gen FG 740 LBJL; FBI 100-3-116-1386, 5/2/64; SCLC Executive Staff Minutes, 5/4/64, KC; Walker to Roy Wilkins, 5/11/64, & Walker to "Dear SCLC Supporter," 5/28/64, KC; Blackwell Interview (Fager).

35. King Interview, "Face the Nation," 5/10/64; *BS* 5/12/64, p. 6; *WES* 5/17/64, p. A5; *HP* 5/18/64, p. 1; Bill Moyers to Johnson, 5/15/64, WHCF FG 135-6; Kennedy to Johnson, 5/21/64, WHCF Ex HU2 Box 2.

36. *MH* 5/19/64, p. A12; *FS* 5/23/64 p. 1, 5/30/64, p. 1; Mrs. Rether Shank Johnson Interview (Shellman); FBI serials from SAC Jacksonville to Director, 5/25–29/64, HQ File 157-6-63; Stoner Interview (Kallal); Kunstler, *Deep,* pp. 286–89; Walker to King, "Suggested Approach and Chronology for St. Augustine," n.d. [ca. 5/26/64], KC; Colburn, *Racial Change,* pp. 75–79. SCLC staffer Dana Swan later emphasized that "young people were the backbone of the civil rights movement everywhere," and Juanita Abernathy added that "men ran the movement, but the women and the young people *were* the movement." (Garrow Interviews)

37. King, "Remarks . . .," 5/28/64, MLK 11; King, "WINS News Conference," 5/31/64, KP; *NYT* 5/29/64, p. 10; *BS* 5/29/64, p. 6; King, *AN* 5/23/64, p. 1.

38. *SFC* 5/30/64, p. 2, 5/31/64, p. 1; *LAT* 6/1/64, p. 5; SAC Los Angeles to Director, 6/1/64, 100-438794-NR; SAC San Diego to Director, 6/6/64, 100-3-116-1501; SAC Phoenix to Director, 6/11/64, 100-3-116-1561; *NYT* 5/30/64, p. 14, 5/31/64, p. 50; Hartley, "Long, Hot Summer," pp. 55-63; Boyte's 6/1/64 testimony in *Young* v. *Davis;* King to Johnson, 5/29/64, LBJL Name File; SAC Jacksonville to Director, 5/28/64 (2), 6/1/64 (2) & 6/8/64, 157-6-63-1344, 1353, 1360, 1366, 1382; Kallal interviews with Davis & Manucy; Rosen to Belmont,

6/2/64, 157-6-63-1364; White "Memorandum . . .," 6/1/64, WHCF HU2/ST9; Colburn, *Racial Change,* pp. 79–89.

39. Director to SAC Atlanta, 6/8/64, 100-3-116-illegible; FBI 62-108052-8, p. 10, citing Director to SAC Atlanta, 2/10/64, and SAC Atlanta to Director, 2/14/64 ("On 2/5/64 she argued with King for not spending enough time at home with her"); Dan R. Warren Interview (Garrow). As Coretta once put it, "Every now and then he gets peeved and I get peeved. He can shout. Every now and then he'll blow up." *BS* 6/20/65, p. A3. "When we get in an argument, usually he just stops talking." *AG* 6/20/65, p. A14.

40. *NYT* 6/3/64, p. 19, 6/4/64, p. 18, 6/6/64, p. 10, 6/7/64, p. 48; *MH* 6/4/64, p. D1, 6/5/64, p. A1, 6/6/64, p. A1; Simpson Interview (Colburn); Colburn, *Racial Change,* pp. 121–23; Shelley Interview (Heinsohn); Dolan to Marshall, 6/5/64, CRS FOIA; Kunstler, *Deep,* pp. 289–95; Watters, *Down,* p. 287; E. F. Emrich to Bryant, "Racial Situation . . .," 6/5/64, Bryant 130; *FS* 6/6/64, p. 1; *JJ* 6/5/64, p. 8; Hartley, "Long, Hot Summer," pp. 68–69.

41. *PJ* 6/8/64, p. 17; *HC* 6/8/64, p. 4; Director to Attorney General & to Walter Jenkins, 6/10/64, 100-106670-373, 377; Lee White, "Memorandum . . .," 6/10/64, White LBJL 5; Garrow interviews with Hayling & John Gibson; *Young* v. *Davis,* 9 *RRLR* 590; FBI 157-6-63-1387, 1388; *NYT* 6/10/64, p. 1, 6/11/64, p. 23, 6/12/64, p. 17; *MH* 6/10/64, p. A1, 6/11/64, p. A1, 6/12/64, p. A1; King & Hayling to Johnson, 6/10/64, White "Memorandum . . .," 6/10/64, White to King & Hayling, 6/11/64, & White to Walker, 6/10/64, all Ex HU2/ST9; Garrow interviews with White & Dana Swan; Frady, "Prophet"; *WP* 6/12/64, p. A8; *FS* 6/13/64, p. 1; Colburn, *Racial Change,* pp. 89–92, 123.

42. Douglass Cater to Lyndon Johnson, 6/11/64, & Carl Holman to William Taylor, 6/11/64, Ex HU2/ST9; Simpson to Dolan & to Elbert Tuttle, 6/11/64, Simpson 3; *DBEN* 6/12/64, p. 1; *NYT* 6/13/64, p. 21; *MH* 6/13/64, p. A1; Warren Interviews (Garrow; Colburn); "Detail to Jacksonville (King Transportation)," 6/12/64, Bryant 130; Colburn, *Racial Change,* pp. 93–97; King's brief 6/13 A.M. testimony in *Young* v. *Davis,* pp. 276–73, at 270; Pat Watters, *New Republic* 6/27/64, p. 6, *Progressive* 9/64, pp. 37–39, & *New South* 9/64, pp. 3–20; *Life* 6/26/64, p. 21; *Saturday Evening Post* 8/22/64, pp. 80–82; Stoner Interview (Garrow).

43. *MH* 6/14/64, p. A1, 6/15/64, p. A5; Hosea Williams Interview (Garrow); *NYT* 6/14/64, p. 59, 6/16/64, p. 34; *WP* 6/16/64, p. A4; White, "Memorandum . . .," 6/13/64, White LBJL 5; *Nation* 6/29/64, pp. 648–51; *NYT Magazine* 7/5/64, pp. 5, 30–31; *SU* 6/15/64, p. 1; Colburn, *Racial Change,* p. 97; *BS* 6/15/64, p. 5; Reddick to King, 6/19/64, KP; Young to Douglas & Hotchkiss, 6/10/64, SCLC 136; *Newsweek* 6/22/64, pp. 26–27; Young to Branton, 6/23/64, SRC VI-20-14; SAC NY to Director, 6/9, 11 & 16/64, 100-3-116-1563, 1564, 1631; Hill & Rustin to Baker et al., n.d. [post 6/15/64], BSCP 25. On prior MFDP developments, see "Minutes of Meeting on the Challenge . . .," 5/5/64, SNCC 136; "Meeting Following Atlanta CUCRL . . .," 5/15/64, SNCC 7; Haley to Farmer, "Meeting of CUCRL," 5/16/64, CORE 79 KC; & esp. Rauh Interview (Romaine) & Romaine, "MFDP," pp. 2–5.

44. *NYT* 6/15/64, p. 23; *MH* 6/15/64, p. A1, 6/16/64, p. A2, 6/17/64, p. A1; Davis Interview (Kallal); SAC Jacksonville to Director, 6/15/64, 157-6-63-1408; "Governor's Proclamation," 9 *RRLR* 1516 (6/15/64); *DBEN* 6/16/64, p. 1; *WSJ* 6/19/64, p. 1; *FS* 6/20/64, p. 1; Colburn, *Racial Change,* pp. 97–98; Director to Walter Jenkins, 6/18/64, 157-6-63-1428; Leon Friedman, ed., *Southern Justice* (New York: Random House, 1965), pp. 187–213; Albert Vorspan, *Midstream* 9/64, pp. 15–21, & "Why We Went," 6/19/64.

45. Corp. Marrs to Maj. Jourdan, "Incident at Monson Motel . . .," 6/18/64, Lt. Norris to Maj. Jourdan, "Information" 6/18/64, & Lt. Randell to Col. Kirkman, "Monson Motel Pool Wade In," 6/19/64, Bryant 130, 131; *MH* 6/19/64, p. A1; *NYT* 6/19/64, p. 1; *Newsweek* 6/29/64, pp. 26–27; SAC Jacksonville to

Director, 6/18/64, 157-6-63-1427; Hartley, "Long, Hot Summer," p. 87; Twine Interview (Harvey); Colburn, *Racial Change,* pp. 99–102; *FTU* 6/21/64, p. 22; "Presentment of Grand Jury," 6/18/64, KC; Warren Interviews (Garrow; Colburn).

46. *MH* 6/19/64, p. A1, 6/20/64, p. A1, 6/21/64, p. A2, 6/22/64, p. A1; King, "Answer to Presentment . . .," 6/19/64, KC; Jack [Sisson] to Matt [Ahmann], "St. Augustine," 6/9/64, & "Report on St. Augustine," 6/17/64, NCCIJ 33-4 & 30-4; Young to Simpson, 6/19/64, Simpson 1; *NYT* 6/20/64, p. 12, 6/21/64, pp. 68, 69, 6/22/64, p. 16, 6/23/64, p. 1, 6/24/64, p. 19; *Christianity Today* 7/17/64, pp. 37–38; Colburn, "St. Augustine Business," p. 227, and *Racial Change,* pp. 103–105; Director to Walter Jenkins, 6/22/64, 157-6-63-1434; Bryant Executive Order #2, 9 *RRLR* 1516 (6/20/64); Warren Interviews (Garrow; Colburn); *CST* 6/22/64, p. 1; McGowan to Rosen, 6/21/64, 100-438794-NR; Capt. Cesson to Maj. Jourdan, "St. Augustine Beach Violence," 6/22/64, Bryant 130; Dorothy Cotton, "St. Augustine," in Carawan, *Freedom,* pp. 24–28; Elizabeth J. Miller, "Report on St. Augustine . . .," 10/64, KC.

47. *NYT* 6/25/64, p. 19, 6/26/64, p. 1; DeWolf, *Hard Rain,* pp. 195–98; De-Wolf Interview (Britton); Richardson, "Pilgrimage," pp. 31–34; Simpson to Wolfe, 6/24/64, Simpson 3; SAC Jacksonville to Director, 6/26/64, 157-6-63-NR; SAC NY to Director, 6/25 & 26/64, 100-3-116-1676, 1648; Colburn, *Racial Change,* pp. 105–108.

48. *Young* v. *Davis,* 9 *RRLR* 1515 (6/22/64); Simpson Interview (Colburn); Bryant Interview (Frantz); *NYT* 6/27/64, p. 1, 6/28/64, p. 48, 6/29/64, p. 1, 6/30/64, p. 20; *MH* 6/27/64, p. A12, 6/28/64, p. A1, 6/29/64, p. A1, 6/30/64, p. A2; *FS* 6/27/64, p. 1; DeWolf Interview (Britton); Richardson, "Pilgrimage," pp. 33–34; Warren Interviews (Garrow; Colburn); Shelley Interviews (Heinsohn; Colburn); Colburn, "St. Augustine Business," p. 228, & *Racial Change,* pp. 11, 109, 123–26; FBI 100-3-116-1729, 6/29/64; *Newsweek* 7/6/64, pp. 16–17; Tobias Simon to Simpson, 6/29/64, Simpson 3; Colburn interviews with Hamilton Up-church & Michael Gannon; Florida Committee, *Racial and Civil Disorders,* p. 44. For a far-right perspective, see A. G. Heinsohn, *American Opinion* 10/64, pp. 1–10.

49. *MH* 7/1/64, p. A1, 7/2/64, p. A2; *NYT* 7/1/64, p. 1, 7/2/64, p. 1; *FS* 7/4/64, p. 1; Warren Interviews (Garrow; Colburn); Shelley Interviews (Heinsohn; Colburn); Colburn, "St. Augustine Business," p. 228, & *Racial Change,* pp. 109–11, 148; Florida Committee, *Racial and Civil Disorders,* p. 22; Miami FBI memo, 7/1/64, DOJ-CRD 144-17M-181-NR; Tobias Simon to Simpson, 7/1/64, Simpson 3; DeWolf to the Kings, 7/3/64, KP; Brock to Simpson, 6/29/64, & Simpson to Brock, 7/1/64, Simpson 3; "Lucille" to Bryant, 7/1/64, Bryant 131.

50. *NYT* 6/24/64, p. 14; FBI 100-3-116-1729, 6/29/64; Garrow interviews with Young & John Gibson; Walker Interviews (Garrow; Britton); *AJ* 11/8/65, p. 4; Young to Clark, 7/9/64 & 7/20/64, SCLC 154; Young to Slater King, 7/21/64, King-SHSW; M. L. King to A. J. Muste, 6/29/64, Slater King-Fisk; King to James Tanner, 6/30/64, KP.

51. Lee White to Files, 7/6/64, Ex LE HU2 Box 2; *WP* 7/3/64, p. 1; Coretta King Interview (Mayerson XXI, p. 29); DeWolf to the Kings, 7/3/64, KP. On the act, see Young, "Presidential Leadership"; Whalen, *Longest Debate;* Joseph Rauh's untitled, unpublished 33pp. essay (author's files); Alexander Bickel, *Commentary* 8/64, pp. 33–39; Carl Rachlin, *Law in Transition Quarterly,* Spring 1965, pp. 67–86; Clifford Lytle, *Journal of Negro History* 51 (10/66): 275–96; James L. Sundquist, *Politics and Policy* (Washington: Brookings Institution, 1968), pp. 259–71; Hubert H. Humphrey, *Beyond Civil Rights* (New York: Random House, 1968), pp. 80–97; *Contemporary Review* 1/65, pp. 10–13; and *Political Quarterly* 4–6/65, pp. 142–53.

52. *BN* 7/7/64, p. 2; King to Tanner, n. 50 above; *New Republic* 8/8/64, pp.

17–18; Robert Fulton, *Christian Century* 8/12/64, pp. 1012–13; blind memo, "A. D. King, Shuttlesworth, and M. L. King," 7/6/64, WH; Young at 6/16/65 SCOPE Orientation, Project South Tape 0432, pp. 8–9; Bevel to "Dear Fellow Co-workers," 7/15/64, KC.

53. *MH* 6/8/64, p. A8; King, *AN* 7/18/64, p. 20; FBI 100-3-116-1973, 7/5/64; King, "Statement . . .," 7/7/64, MLK 1; Katzenbach to Johnson, 7/1/64, Ex HU2/ST24 Box 26; Garrow, *FBI*, pp. 117–18, 266; "Minutes, COFO Executive Committee . . .," 7/10/64, SCLC 141; Young to Clark, 7/20/64, SCLC 154; SAC Mobile to Director, 7/17/64, 100-3-116-1798; *Commonweal* 8/7/64, pp. 536–39; John Love, "Selma . . .," 8/13/64, SNCC 47.

54. King, "Statement . . .," 7/16/64, KP; *ADW* 7/17/64, p. 1; Lee White to Johnson, "St. Augustine," 7/15/64, & White to Files, 7/20/64, Ex HU2/ST9 Box 25; Jay Janis to LeRoy Collins, "The Crisis at St. Augustine," 7/21/64, & Janis to Harold Fleming, "St. Augustine . . .," 7/23/64, CRS FOIA; Colburn, *Racial Change*, pp. 111–12, 128; John Gibson Interviews (Britton; Garrow). "It was that night that he gave himself to the movement like he had never before done," Gibson thought.

55. DeWolf Interview (Britton); *BG* 9/27/64, p. A1; FBI 100-106670-400, 401, 402, 410, 7/21/64; Hoover to Tolson, 7/21/64 (3), 157-6-54-4, 173-1-54-2, 100-106670-396, & 7/22/64, 157-6-34-917; Hoover to All SACs, 7/22/64, 157-00-74; King, "Statement . . .," 7/22/64, KP; *WP* 7/22/64, p. A3, 7/23/64, p. A4, 7/25/64, p. A4; *NYT* 7/22/64, p. 20, 7/23/64, p. 15, 7/25/64, p. 9, 7/27/64, p. 17; *DDT* 7/23/64, p. 7; Rosen to Belmont, 7/24/64, 100-106670-416; FBI 100-3-116-1978, 1998, 7/26/64; *JDN* 7/25/64, p. 1; *MS* 7/25/64, p. 1; *New Republic* 8/22/64, pp. 17–21.

56. FBI 100-3-116-1979, 7/25/64, 100-3-116-1978, 1998, 7/26/64; King, "Statement . . .," 7/27/64, KP; *NYT* 7/28/64, p. 15, 7/29/64, p. 1; FBI 100-3-116-1941, 1969, 1999, 7/28/64; Rustin Interview (Baker); Cleveland Robinson Interview (Garrow); King, "Statement . . .," 7/29/64, KP. As Ruby Dee and Ossie Davis wrote King on 7/28, "We were amazed and disappointed to see you . . . fall for the oldest, and surely one of the most vicious, 'white man tricks.' It appears you permitted the Mayor to call you in in an attempt to invalidate, downgrade and undercut the efforts of others who are much closer to the scene, and who have been working hard to construct some kind of racial peace in Harlem." BR.

57. Farmer, *Freedom*, p. 43, and *Lay Bare*, pp. 215–19, 298–99; Farmer Interview (Mulhollan); Rustin Interviews (Garrow; Viorst II); Ralph Helstein Interview (Garrow); *NYT* 7/30/64, p. 1; Wilkins, *NYT Magazine* 8/16/64, pp. 11, 15–18, and *Standing*, p. 304.

58. *NYT* 7/30/64, p. 1; FBI 100-3-116-1994, 2027, 7/30 & 31/64; King, "Statement," 7/30/64, KP; *JDN* 8/1/64.

59. *SAR* 7/24/64, p. 1; *NYT* 7/25/64, p. 9, 8/6/64, p. 16; Brock to Simpson, 7/25/64, Simpson 2; Colburn, *Racial Change*, pp. 111–12; "Further Presentment of Grand Jury," 8/5/64, LCDC 1; *ADW* 8/7/64, p. 1; Boyte, "Progress Report . . .," 8/3/64, SCLC 139; Al Bronstein to Henry Schwarzschild, 8/13/64, LCDC 1; Fred Martin to SCLC, 9/23/64, and Hayling et al. to "Dear Fellow Citizens . . .," 9/22/64, SCLC 139; Garrow interviews with Hayling, John Gibson & Dana Swan. "Hayling was bitter. He felt we'd dumped him," Gibson remembered. "St. Augustine should never have been left in the shape it was left in," young field staffer Swan added.

60. Director to SACs, NY & Atlanta, 7/31/64, 100-3-116-1937; Coretta King Interview (Mayerson XXVII, p. 35); Coretta King, *My Life*, p. 247; SAC NY to Director, 8/6/64, 100-3-116-2101; King to Johnson, 8/7/64, King Name File LBJL; FBI 100-3-116-2100, 2158, 2142, 8/7, 12 & 13/64. Also see *PI* 8/6/64, p. 5, 8/11/64, p. 2; *BG* 8/11/64, p. 2; *NYT* 8/11/64, p. 23.

61. *NYT* 8/17/64, p. 21; FBI 100-3-116-2203, 2215, 2230, 2167, 8/14, 18, 19 &

20/64; Garrow interviews with Blackwell, Bevel, James Orange, Willie Bolden & Lee White; "Report by Bernard Lafayette" [on Rochester], 8/7–13/64, AFSC; Rauh Interview (Romaine); [White], "Note," 8/19/64, DeLoach Name File LBJL; Director to Walter Jenkins, 7/30, 8/8 & 19/64, 100-3-116-2070, 2108, 2224; King to Johnson, 8/19/64, King Name File LBJL; *WP* 8/20/64, p. A1.

62. *NYT* 8/23/64, p. 1; King, "Statement . . .," 8/22/64, KP; Arthur Waskow, "Notes on the Democratic National Convention," 8/64, SHSW; Garrow, *Protest,* p. 253; Carson, *In Struggle,* pp. 124–26; Zinn, *SNCC,* pp. 252–57; Rauh Interviews (Romaine; Mulhollan; Garrow); Garrow, *FBI,* pp. 118–19; Romaine interviews with Ella Baker & Walter Tillow; Edith Green Interview (Viorst).

63. Rauh Interviews (Romaine; Shannon); Waskow, "Notes," n. 62 above; Garrow, *FBI,* pp. 118–19; DeLoach to Mohr, 8/25/64, 100-106670-NR; DeLoach to Walter Jenkins, 8/25/64, & DeLoach to Mohr, 8/29/64, in U.S. Senate, Select Committee to Study Governmental Operations, *Intelligence Activities Hearings—FBI,* 94th Cong., 1st sess., 1976, pp. 714–17, 495–502; Bassett to Callahan, "Special Squad at Democratic National Convention . . .," 1/29/75, in *Hearings,* pp. 503–509; Charles Sherrod, *Union Seminary Bi-Weekly* 10/12/64, pp. 6–7; McLemore, "MFDP," pp. 148–49; Walter Tillow Interview (Romaine); Rustin Interview (Baker); Young Interview (Viorst).

64. Aaron Henry Interviews (McMillen & Burson; Wright; Long; Baker); Hamer Interview (McMillen); Rauh Interviews (Romaine; Shannon; Blackside; Mulhollan); Allard Lowenstein Interview (Viorst); Waskow, "Notes," n. 62 above; Richard Cummings, *The Pied Piper* (New York: Grove Press, 1985), pp. 265–68; Rustin Interviews (Baker; Viorst I & II); Rustin, *Strategies,* pp. 52–53; Edwin King Interview (Romaine); Edwin King, *Sojourners* 12/82, pp. 18–21; Walter Tillow Interview (Romaine); Forman, *Making,* pp. 391–93; Young Interview (Viorst).

65. Hamer Interview (Romaine); Edwin King, *Sojourners* 12/82, pp. 18–21; Lewis Interview (Viorst); Smith, "A Lesson in Democracy," *Liberator* 10/64, pp. 12–13; Edward Brown Interview (Lewis); Dittmer, "Freedom." As McLemore observes in "MFDP," p. 153, "Moses and company, for all practical purposes, refused to listen to the counsel they had sought before the Atlantic City convention. Martin Luther King, Bayard Rustin, James Farmer, and Joseph Rauh were dealt with by the 'purists' in the caucus as if they were arch-enemies of the Freedom Democrats." King viewed such settlements pragmatically: "You tell the people that you won't settle for anything less than total victory in order to get them all worked up, even though you know all along you'll only get part of your demands. . . . Then when it's all over, you tell them you won a great victory." *WP* 2/1/65, p. E1. As Andrew Young put it, "Martin felt you couldn't sustain people . . . in a continuous struggle, that they get disillusioned, they get tired; that you push them as far as they'll go, or lead them as far as they'll go, and then you take what you can get, and you let them rest and you wait for the next battle." (Viorst Interview)

66. *NYT* 5/22/64, p. 3, 9/14/64, p. 36, 9/19/64, p. 3; *CSM* 9/11/64, p. 2; *BG* 9/12/64, p. 3; *LAT* 9/13/64, p. A4; *WES* 9/13/64, p. A23; King, "Comments . . .," 9/13/64, KP; *NYHT* 9/14/64, p. 2, 9/19/64, p. 6, 9/22/64, p. 16; *RDA* 9/18/64, p. 1, 9/19/64, p. 1; *BS* 9/19/64, p. 2; *Sun* (London) 9/22/64; *Ebony* 11/64, pp. 41–46. Also see SAC Detroit to Director, 8/31/64, 100-438794-NR, & Gale to DeLoach, 5/21/69, King O&C.

67. "Rough Minutes . . .," 9/18/64, SNCC 108; Curtis Gans to Leon Shull, "Atlanta Trip . . .," 11/20/64, ADA; SCLC Annual Financial Report, 9/29/64, KC; Minutes of SCLC Board Meeting, 9/30/64, KC; King, "President's Annual Report," 10/1/64, APR; *Jet* 10/15/64, pp. 5–7; *NYT* 9/30/64, p. 22, 10/2/64, p. 27, 10/3/64, p. 25; *SMN* 10/2/64, p. B10; SCLC press release, 10/3/64, KC; *SCLC*

Newsletter 10–11/64, pp. 10, 12. Also see FBI 100-438794-181, 9/27/64, & *Commonweal* 2/19/65, pp. 661–63.

68. *NYT* 10/12/64, p. 25, 1/31/64, p. 3, 7/19/64, p. 38, 10/15/64, p. 1; SAC NY to Director, 10/13/64, 100-442529-190; *SLPD* 10/13/64, p. A5; *Jet* 10/29/64, pp. 14–27; Coretta King, *My Life,* pp. 1–4; *WP* 1/31/64, p. A12, 10/7/64, p. A1, 10/15/64, p. A1; *U.S. News* 2/8/65, pp. 76–77; *AJ* 10/14/64, p. 1; *AC* 10/15/64, p. 1; SAC NY to Director, 1/10/64, 100-3-116-758; King, *Negro Digest* 12/64, p. 31; King, *AN* 11/7/64, p. 10, 11/28/64, p. 1; Garrow interviews with Lee & McDonald; Lee Interview (Burrell).

Chapter Seven

1. *AA* 10/24/64, p. 10; *AJ* 10/14/64, p. 1; *Ebony* 12/64, p. 126; Rustin Interview (Garrow); Coretta King Interview (Mayerson XX, pp. 29–30); Hoover to William Moyers, 10/20/64, 100-442529-203; *CST* 10/22/64, p. 98, 10/30/64, p. 8; *CP* 10/23/64, p. A4; *CDN* 10/29/64, p. 6; *BS* 11/1/64, p. 26; *NYT* 11/3/64, p. 1; *AC* 11/3/64, p. 12; Fauntroy Interview (Lewis). A research committee discussion of the travel costs ended when King angrily walked out after his advisors insisted that his friends would have to pay their own bills. Ralph (& Nina) Helstein Interview (Garrow).

2. Hoover to Moyers & to Katzenbach, 11/6/64, 100-442529-NR, 355; *NYT* 11/5/64, p. 1, 11/7/64, p. 56; King in *Playboy* 1/65, pp. 70–74.

3. SCLC Executive Staff Retreat, 11/10–12/64, KC; Fauntroy Interview (Lewis); Blackwell Interview (Fager); Young remarks at 6/16/65 SCOPE Orientation, Project South Tape 0432, pp. 8–9; Garrow interviews with Boynton, Bevel & Young. As Joseph Lowery put it, "We chose Selma because they were being repressive in Selma." (Wright Interview, p. 22) That 11/64 choice was the fruition of the game plan Jim and Diane Nash Bevel had devised after the bombing of Sixteenth Street church; as John Gibson put it, "Selma was a direct outgrowth of the killing of those four kids." (Garrow Interview)

4. King, *Saturday Evening Post* 11/7/64, pp. 8–10; *DMH* 11/14/64, p. B1; *WJ* 11/14/64, p. 1; *DS* 11/14/64, p. 2; *PC* 11/28/64, p. 5; SAC Miami to Director, 11/17/64, 100-438794-203X1; Garrow interviews with Vivian & E. L. Doyle; Reese Interviews (Vasser; Garrow; Blackside).

5. *NYT* 11/19/64, p. 1, 11/20/64, p. 1; *WP* 11/19/64, p. A1, 11/20/64, p. A2, 11/26/64, p. A2, 12/1/64, p. A3; *Newsweek* 11/30/64, pp. 29–30; DeLoach to Mohr, 11/18/64, 62-109811-3513; King to Hoover, 11/19/64, 100-106670-584; *SCLC Newsletter* 10–11/64, p. 9; Bernard Lee Interview (Burrell); Jones to De-Loach, 12/1/64, 100-106670-647, p. 10; SAC Atlanta to Director, 11/20/64, 100-442529-445; *NYHT* 11/20/64, p. 1; *MCA* 11/26/64, p. 7; *U.S. News* 11/30/64, pp. 56–58, 12/7/64, pp. 44–48; *AN* 11/28/64, p. 1. King had opted for his vacation over the meeting, explaining that "the pressures of public life leave one very little time for study and meditation." King to Johnson, 11/17/64, & Valenti to Johnson, 11/13/64, King Name File LBJL.

6. Garrow interviews with Jones, Clark, Rustin, Wachtel, Ralph Helstein & Dorothy Cotton; Baumgardner to Sullivan, 11/19/64, 100-106670-537; Schlesinger, *Robert Kennedy,* p. 364; Garrow interviews with Katzenbach & Marshall; De-Loach to Mohr, "Roy Wilkins . . .," 11/27/64, 62-78270-16; Murphy Report, pp. 38–39; Wilkins, *AN* 11/28/64, p. 8; Hoover to Lyndon Johnson, 11/30/64, 62-78270-15; Farmer Interviews (Garrow; Mulhollan); Farmer, *Lay Bare,* pp. 268–70; FBI 100-442529-484, 11/24/64; SAC NY to Director, 12/1/64, 100-442529-475. DeLoach's memo about his conversation with Wilkins asserts that "I told him that the Director, of course, did not have in mind the destruction of the civil rights movement as a whole. . . . I told him my point was that he was attempting to prevent the FBI from exposing King, yet certain highly-placed informants of ours [the wiretaps] had tipped us off to absolutely reliable information that King had organized a bitter crusade against the Director and the FBI. . . . I asked Wilkins how in the hell could he expect the FBI to believe his offers of friendship and request for peace when King was at this time attempting to ruin us. Wilkins merely hung his head and stated he had no idea that King was carrying on such a campaign. He stated that this upset him greatly and made him all the more determined to initiate action to remove King as soon as possible." Also see *WP* 5/29/78, p. A1, 5/31/78, p. A6, 6/2/78, p. A2.

7. DeLoach to Mohr, 12/1 & 2/64, 100-106670-570, 634; Murphy Report, p. 39; Hoover to Johnson, 12/2/64, 100-106670-607; Garrow interviews with Young & Abernathy; Fauntroy Interviews (Lewis; Garrow); *NYT* 12/2/64, p. 1; *WP* 12/2/64, p. A1, 12/5/64, p. E15; *Newsweek* 12/14/64, pp. 22–24; *AC* 12/6/75, p. A2; Howell, "Interview with Young," p. 16; Young, *Playboy* 7/77, p. 75; Young Interviews (Baker; Moyers); *Quill* 2/76, pp. 14–15; Garrow, *FBI,* pp. 129–31; Rather, *Camera,* pp. 101–102.

8. FBI 100-442529-514 & 100-106670-600, 12/2/64; *AJ* 12/3/64, p. 33; *NYT* 12/5/64, p. 18, 12/6/64, p. 2, 12/7/64, p. 1, 12/8/64, p. 53, 12/24/64, p. 17; King, "Statement . . .," 12/4/64, KP; Oates, *Trumpet,* p. 318; Wachtel Interview (Garrow); *AJC* 12/6/64, p. 46; *WP* 12/7/64, p. A1; *AC* 12/7/64, p. 20, 12/24/64, p. 9; London *Daily Mail* 12/7/64, p. 2; *Daily Telegraph* 12/7/64, p. 13; *Daily Mirror* 12/7/64, p. 6, 12/8/64, p. 11; *NYJA* 12/7/64, p. 1; *ADW* 12/11/64, p. 5.

9. *NYT* 12/9/64, p. 3; Coretta King Interview (Mayerson XX, p. 35); Coretta King, *My Life,* pp. 9–11; Logan Interview (Garrow); King, "Press Conference . . .," 12/9/64, KP; *NYT* 12/10/64, p. 58, 12/11/64, p. 1; King, *Liberation* 1/65, pp. 28–29; *AJ* 12/10/64, p. 6; King, "The Quest for Peace and Justice," in Frederick W. Haberman, ed., *Nobel Lectures—Peace, 1951–1970,* vol. 3 (Amsterdam: Elsevier, 1972), pp. 333–46.

10. *AJ* 12/11/64, p. 11; Coretta King Interview (Mayerson XX, p. 35, XXI, pp. 8–9); Coretta King in Sanders, "Finally," p. 175; Garrow interviews with Maude Ballou, Elliott Finley, Juanita Abernathy, Lillie Hunter, Fred Gray, Dora McDonald, Glenn Smiley, Septima Clark, Michael Harrington, James Orange, John Gibson, Hosea Williams, Junius Griffin, Marian Logan & Bill Rutherford; Rustin Interviews (Baker; Garrow); Walker Interview (Britton, p. 80); Septima Clark Interviews (Hall; Barton; Walker); Abernathy to Eric Kindberg, 5/20/64, KC; *NYT Magazine* 5/20/68, pp. 28–29, 91–97; Baumgardner to Sullivan, 12/17/65, 100-106670-635; Williams, *King,* p. 198; *NYT* 12/12/64, p. 1, 12/13/64, p. 56, 12/14/64, p. 3, 12/15/64, p. 48; Sanders, *Ebony* 3/65, p. 36.

11. King, "Address . . .," 12/17/64, & "Statement . . .," 12/17/64, KP; King to Wiley Branton, 1/13/65, KP; Coretta King Interview (Mayerson XXI, p. 8); Hoover to Bill Moyers, 12/17/64, 100-106670-622; *NYT* 12/18/64, p. 37; *NYHT* 12/18/64, p. 18; *WP* 12/10/64, p. A31, 12/11/64, p. A18; Lee White to Johnson, 12/18/64, Diary Backup LBJL; King, "Address . . .," 2/23/68, KP.

12. *NYT* 12/19/64, p. 32; *WP* 12/19/64, p. A2; *AC* 12/19/64, p. 3; *ADW* 12/20/64, p. 1; Baugh Interview (Garrow).

13. Boyte to Blackwell, "Report on Selma . . .," 12/14/64, SCLC 146; John Love, "Selma . . .," 9/14/64, SNCC 47; Ralph Smeltzer to Arthur Lewis, 10/9/64, RES; Dennis to Gordon Carey, 12/22/64, CORE 81 KC; Garrow interviews with Smitherman, Capell, Reese & Muriel Lewis; Smitherman on "David Susskind's Open End," 4/25/65, KC; Muriel & Art Lewis's letters on "The Selma Situation," 3/19/65 & 4/13/65; Muriel Lewis in *Southern Exposure,* Fall 1974, p. 215; Smitherman Interview (Blackside).

14. SAC Birmingham to Director, 1/6/65, 100-438794-223, 224; Smeltzer notes on conversations with James Bevel (1/2/65), John Doar (12/30/64), C. C. Brown (1/1/65), John Love (12/29/64) & Frank Soracco (12/30/64), RES; *BN* 1/31/65, p. 1, 2/1/65, p. 6, 2/2/65, p. 26; Robert Mikell, *Selma* (Charlotte, N.C.: Citadel Press, 1965), pp. 28–38.

15. *OWH* 12/31/64, p. 1; *LEJ* 12/31/64, p. 8; SAC Atlanta to Director, 12/29 & 30/64, 100-106670-701, 702; Murphy Report, p. 43; DeLoach to Mohr, 12/31/64, 100-106670-NR; Young in Sonnenschein, "Penthouse Interview," p. 144; James Orange Interview (Garrow); Bevel to Blackwell, 1/12/65, SCLC 146; *NYT* 1/2/65, p. 16, 1/3/65, p. 1, 1/4/65, p. 58; *WP* 1/2/65, p. A2, 1/3/65, p. A9; *STJ* 1/3/65, p. 1, 1/5/65, p. 2; Fager, *Selma,* pp. 8–11.

16. Smeltzer, "SCLC/SNCC Joint Staff Meeting," 1/3/65, & "Notes of Steering Committee Meeting," 12/11/64, RES; "Staff Meeting," 1/7/65, SNCC 7; Ward Reports dated 1/7 & 12/65, SNCC 45 & 199.

17. *Ebony* 1/70, pp. 40–50; Oates, *Trumpet,* p. 329; Garrow, *FBI,* pp. 125–26, 133–34; SAC Atlanta to Director, 1/5 & 6/65, 100-106670-715, 716; Murphy Report, pp. 44–45; Young in Raines, *My Soul,* pp. 427–28; Howell, "Interview with Young," pp. 17–18.

18. Murphy Report, pp. 44–46; *People* 2/20/78, pp. 72–83; Coretta King in Sanders, "Finally," p. 176; King, *Playboy* 1/65, p. 77; Garrow, *FBI,* pp. 134–35; Young Interview (Baker); Garrow interviews with Eskridge, Branton, John Maguire, Thomas Kilgore, Cornish Rogers, Harrington, Rochelle Horowitz & John Porter; *LCJ Magazine* 3/31/67, p. A18; *AJC Magazine* 2/1/76; Lee Interview (Burrell); Cotton in Raines, *My Soul,* pp. 432–34; Cotton Interview (Garrow); King, "Today Show Interview . . .," 4/18/66, "Sunday With . . . King," 4/16/66, "The Prodigal Son," 9/4/66, & "Three Evils," 1/7/65, KP; *AC* 1/8/65, p. 6; SAC NY to Director, 1/8, 9 & 10/65, 100-106670-686, 719, 721; DeLoach to Mohr, 1/8/65, 100-106670-713; *BG* 1/11/65, p. 1; *BH* 1/11/65, p. 1; *NYT* 1/11/65, p. 27; *BS* 1/12/65, p. 10. As Eskridge later described the tape, "I had to laugh because I didn't believe it . . . I didn't believe that I was listening to an actual conversation because it was so bizarre." The FBI also considered some harassment regarding "a woman with whom King was involved and a child born to her in 1965, reportedly fathered by King." Peelman to Gallagher, 2/2/77, 100-106670-4619. King noted regretfully in one sermon that he had to have his secretary remind him of his wife's birthday and their anniversary. "Is the Universe Friendly?," 12/12/65, Ebenezer, KP.

19. DeLoach to Mohr, 1/11/65, 100-106670-730; Murphy Report, pp. 46–47; Young Interview (Baker); Young in Raines, *My Soul,* pp. 368–70, 429–30; Garrow, *FBI,* pp. 134–35, 273–74; Hoover to Katzenbach, 1/8/65, 100-106670-673.

20. Bevel to Blackwell, 1/12/65, SCLC 146; "Staff Meeting Notes," 1/15 & 16/65, SNCC 7; *NYT* 1/15/65, p. 14, 1/19/65, p. 1; *WP* 1/15/65, p. A7, 1/18/65, p. A3, 1/19/65, p. A1; *STJ* 1/6/65, p. 4, 1/7/65, p. 4, 1/15/65, p. 1, 1/18/65, p. 1; "Notes from Meeting with Rev. King . . .," 1/14/65, SNCC 7; Garrow interviews with Clark, Pitts, Smitherman, Bernard Reynolds & Louise Clark; "Agreement," 1/12/65, Pitts; Smeltzer notes on conversations with Baker & Capell, RES; Secrest to John Griffin, "Selma . . .," 1/26/65, Collins 7-B-1; Morland, "A Report to the CRS . . .," 2/6/65, Morland; *Time* 1/29/65, pp. 20–21.

21. Fager, *Selma,* pp. 30–34, 226; Boynton Interview (Fager); Boynton, *Bridge,* p. 162; FBI 100-438794-393, p. 35; Garrow interviews with Fager & Robert "Cotton" Nichols; *STJ* 1/19/65, p. 1, 1/20/65, p. 1, 1/21/65, p. 1, *NYT* 1/20/65, p. 1, 1/21/65, p. 1; *WP* 1/20/65, p. 1, 1/21/65, p. B8; *PB* 1/21/65, p. 44.

22. Secrest to Griffin, & Morland, "Report," n. 20 above; Wilkins, *Man's Life,* pp. 146–47; *WP* 1/22/65, p. A10; Rosen to Belmont, 1/18/65, 44-27969-3; Garrow interviews with Reese, Foster, Doyle, L. L. Anderson, Bevel & Young; King, *AN* 1/30/65, p. 8; *NYT* 1/22/65, p. 16; Garrow, *Protest,* pp. 41–42; Clarence

Mitchell to Roy Wilkins, 2/1/65, Wilkins 7; *Newsweek* 2/1/65, pp. 21–22. As Bevel put it, "When we go to the courthouse, Jim Clark I know will be there acting the fool—he has never let us down." 4/3/65, Chicago, Bevel Fld., UICC.

23. *STJ* 1/22/65, p. 1, 1/24/65, p. 1, 1/25/65, p. 1, 1/27/65, p. 1; *NYT* 1/23/65, p. 18, 1/24/65, p. 40, 1/26/65, p. 1, 1/29/65, p. 9, 1/30/65, p. 10, 1/31/65, pp. 49, 55; Reese Interviews (Garrow; Blackside); *WP* 1/23/65, p. A7, 1/26/65, p. A2; *Boynton* v. *Clark,* 10 *RRLR* 215; *Time* 2/5/65, p. 24; *Newsweek* 2/8/65, p. 24.

24. *STJ* 1/27/65, p. 1; *NYT* 1/27/65, p. 16, 12/29/64, p. 1, 12/30/64, p. 28, 12/31/64, p. 11, 1/24/65, p. 39, 1/28/65, p. 15; *WP* 1/27/65, p. A2, 1/28/65, pp. A4, 15; Baumgardner to Sullivan, 1/28/65, 100-106670-780; Jenkins Interview (Garrow); Raines, *My Soul,* pp. 353–54; Valenti to Johnson, 1/12/65, Ex PE2 Box 8; White to Johnson, 1/13/65, Diary Backup 1/15 LBJL; FBI 100-106670-747, 1/15/65; Garrow, *FBI,* pp. 135–36; *AC* 1/13/65, p. 14, 1/28/65, p. 9; Mathew Ahmann note, ca. 2/65, NCCIJ 20-16; King, "Address . . .," 1/27/65, KP; *AJ* 1/28/65, p. 12; *Time* 2/5/65, p. 24; Mays, *Born,* pp. 271–73; Allen, *Mayor,* pp. 97–99; SAC NY to Director, 1/29 & 31/65, 100-106670-779, 778.

25. Fager, *Selma,* p. 47; FBI 44-27969-64; *NYT* 2/1/65, p. 16, 2/2/65, p. 1; *STJ* 2/1/65, p. 1, 2/2/65, p. 1; *WP* 2/2/65, p. A1; Fager, *In These Times* 2/9–15/83, pp. 23–24; King to Young, Selma jail notes, 2/1–5/65, KP 22-6.

26. *WP* 2/3/65, p. A3, 2/4/65, p. A1; *NYT* 2/3/65, p. 1, 2/4/65, p. 1; FBI 100-106670-790; Hoover to Moyers, 2/3 & 4/65, 44-12831-298, 100-106670-804; White to Johnson, 2/3/65, Ex HU/ST1 Box 24; King to Young notes, n. 25 above.

27. *NYT* 2/5/65, pp. 1, 15, 17; 10 *RRLR* 210; Johnson, *Public Papers,* pp. 130–31; King to Young notes, n. 25 above; *STJ* 2/5/65, p. 1. As Coretta King wrote, "Brutal treatment of anyone, especially the symbol of a movement, helps the movement—it brings people together. The more they persecute you, the more sympathy is created for the individual and the movement." "The World," p. 36.

28. *NYT* 2/6/65, pp. 1, 10, 2/7/65, p. 1, 2/8/65, p. 17; *STJ* 2/7/65, p. 1; "Staff Meeting" notes, 2/4 & 6/65, SNCC 7; White to Johnson, 2/5/65, Diary Backup LBJL; Garrow interviews with Wachtel & White; Westin & Mahoney, *Trial,* pp. 167–68; SAC NY to Director, 2/6 & 7/65, 100-106670-827, 822; *WP* 2/7/65, p. A1; King, "Statement . . .," 2/7/65, KP; White to Johnson, "Notes . . .," 2/8/65, King Name File LBJL. As White put it, "No President, especially a very proud and vain one, wants to have some son of a bitch telling him who he's going to see. It took a little kind of skillful working with him to make sure that he, the President, didn't say anything and kept his own temper in check." (Garrow Interview)

29. *STJ* 2/8/65, p. 1, 2/9/65, p. 1; *NYT* 2/9/65, p. 17, 2/10/65, pp. 1, 18; Shuttlesworth Interviews (Garrow; Mosby; Ladner); *NYHT* 2/10/65, p. 4; Garrow interviews with Wachtel & White; *WP* 2/10/65, p. A8; *WES* 2/10/65, p. 1.

30. *STJ* 2/10/65, p. 1; *NYT* 2/11/65, p. 1; "2/10/65, Wednesday Night at the Torch Motel," SNCC 7.

31. *DN* 2/12/65, p. B8; FBI 100-106670-829, 841; *STJ* 2/11/65, p. 1, 2/14/65, p. 1; *NYT* 2/12/65, p. 58, 2/13/65, p. 1, 2/14/65, p. 70, 2/15/65. p. 15; Garrow, *Protest,* pp. 58–59; Secrest to Calvin Kytle, 2/3/65, Collins 7-B-1; Nat Welch to Collins, 2/8/65, Gen HU2/ST1, LBJL; Morland, "A Report to the CRS . . .," 2/22/65, Morland; FBI 100-442529-769, 2/14/65; Welch to Smitherman & to Seymour Palmer, 2/15/65, & Ed Stanfield to Welch, 2/21/65, ACHR.

32. Garrow interviews with Doyle, Foster, Reese & Anderson; *NYT* 2/14/65, p. E5, 2/16/65, p. 18, 2/17/65, p. 35; Morland, "Report," n. 31 above; SAC Mobile to Director, 2/19/65 (2), 44-17669-159, 56-2295-133; *STJ* 2/15/65, p. 1, 2/16/65, p. 1; Smeltzer notes on 2/16 conversation with Secrest, RES; Fager, *Selma,* p. 70; Clark, *Story,* pp. 105–106; Garrow interviews with Clark, L. C. Crocker, Louise Clark, L. L. Anderson & Vivian; Clark Interview (Blackside); *Time* 2/12/65, pp. 16–17, 2/19/65, p. 23; *Newsweek* 3/1/65, p. 39.

33. *NYT* 2/18/65, p. 26, 2/19/65, p. 1, 2/20/65, pp. 1, 12, 2/21/65, p. 22, 2/22/65,

p. 12; FBI 100-106670-881, 2/17/65; SAC Mobile to Director, 2/18/65, 44-12831-illegible; *STJ* 2/18/65, p. 1; *WP* 2/19/65, p. A1; *Jet* 3/18/65, pp. 14–19; Raines, *My Soul*, pp. 190–93, 371–72; Garrow, *Protest*, p. 62; Albert Turner Interviews (Garrow; Blackside); Valeriani Interview (Blackside).

34. *STJ* 2/22/65, p. 1, 2/23/65, p. 1, 2/24/65, p. 1, 2/25/65, p. 1; *NYT* 2/23/65, p. 16, 2/24/65, p. 1, 2/26/65, pp. 14, 15, 2/27/65, p. 1; *WP* 2/24/65, p. A3; *NYJA* 2/24/65, p. 1; King, "Press Conference," 2/24/65, KP; Hosea Williams in Schulke, *King*, pp. 130–31; Katzenbach Interview (Garrow); Louw & Wicklein, "King"; Fager, *Selma*, pp. 78–81.

35. *WP* 3/27/64, p. A6; *Now* 10/31/64, pp. 5–10; FBI 100-442529-769, 2/14/65; *STJ* 2/4/65, p. 1; *Jet* 3/11/65, pp. 28–30; Goldman, *Death*, pp. 95, 230–31; *The Autobiography of Malcolm X* (New York: Grove Press, 1965), p. 427; Coretta King Interviews (Mayerson XXII, p. 43; Blackside); Coretta King, *My Life*, pp. 256–58; King, "Press Conference," 2/24/65, KP. Also see King, *AN* 3/13/65, p. 10; Halberstam, "Second Coming," p. 51; and Lewis V. Baldwin, "Malcolm X and Martin Luther King, Jr.," unpublished paper, 1985, author's files.

36. *LAT* 2/25/65, p. I-1, 2/26/65, p. I-2, 2/27/65, p. I-12, 3/1/65, p. I-5; *WES* 2/26/65, p. A13; *NYT* 2/27/65, p. 8; *LAHE* 3/1/65, p. A12; *NYHT* 3/1/65, p. 4; *NYP* 3/1/65, p. 5.

37. *NYT* 2/28/65, p. 55, 3/1/65, p. 17, 3/2/65, p. 1, 3/3/65, p. 24; *STJ* 3/1/65, p. 1, 3/4/65, p. 1; *WP* 3/3/65, p. D2; Levison to Lyndon Johnson, 2/14/65, & Jones to Johnson, 3/4/65, Name Files LBJL; *BS* 3/3/65; *BW* 3/6/65, p. 1; *NYT* 3/4/65, p. 23, 3/5/65, p. 29; Coretta King Interview (Mayerson XXII, pp. 35–36); Raines, *My Soul*, pp. 194–95; Young at 6/16/65 SCOPE Orientation, Project South Tape 0432, pp. 2–3; James Orange Interviews (Garrow; Brown); Albert Turner Interview (Garrow).

38. Garrow, *FBI*, pp. 137, 275; FBI 100-442529-782, 2/20/65; Garrow interviews with Jones, Wachtel, Rustin & Young; SAC NY to Director, 3/5/65, 100-442529-812; Hoover to Katzenbach & Marvin Watson, 3/5/65, 100-106670-929, 931; Lee White to Johnson, 3/4/65, Ex HU2 Box 3; *WP* 3/6/65, p. A4; *NYT* 3/6/65, pp. 9, 10; FBI 100-106670-964, 967, 3/6/65. On 10/3/65, Jones, just back from an Atlanta meeting, told Levison, "Harry is sort of a big joke, and Martin is very open about it. At the meeting they were kidding about the officers and someone said, kidding, that we ought to make Harry Wachtel the president of SCLC and Martin said, 'Oh no. He already is. He kicked me me out of it.'" FBI NY 100-111180-9-716A.

39. *STJ* 3/7/65, p. 1; *NYT* 3/7/65, p. 1; Jones, *Wallace*, pp. 355–56; Wallace Interview (Blackside); Smitherman Interview (Blackside); Webb, *Selma*, p. 86; Cloud testimony in *Williams* v. *Wallace*, p. 4, 3/16/65; *NYHT* 3/7/65, p. 7; Silas Norman & John Love, "Selma . . .," [ca. 3/6/65], "Executive Committee Meeting" Minutes & "A Short Summary . . .," 3/5–6/65, Long; Forman, *Sammy Younge*, p. 75; Sellers, *River*, pp. 118–21; Lewis & Norman to King, 3/7/65, KP; Julian Bond Interview (Britton); Lewis Interviews (Shannon; Brasch; Bass & DeVries); Raines, *My Soul*, pp. 206–207.

40. *NYT* 3/7/65, p. 1; *NYHT* 3/7/65, p. 7; Joseph Ellwanger Interview (Blackside); Helen Baer et al. Interview (Baer); King, "Statement . . .," 3/7/65, KP; King, *Saturday Review* 4/3/65, pp. 16–17, 57; Garrow interviews with Bevel, Williams, Turner, Young, Abernathy & James Orange; Blackside interviews with Turner, Young & Abernathy; Kryn, "Bevel"; Coretta King, "The World," pp. 30–31; Coretta King Interview (Mayerson XXI, p. 45, XXII, pp. 8–9); Coretta King, *My Life*, p. 259; Fager, *Selma*, pp. 86–93; Raines, *My Soul*, pp. 201–203, 385–86; Eugene Walker, "SCLC," pp. 173–74; *STJ* 3/8/65, p. 1, 2/25/79, p. B1, 7/29/79, pp. A4, B1; Garrow interviews with Smitherman, Clark, Robert Nichols & L. C. Crocker; Clark, "Issues and Answers," 3/7/65; Webb, *Selma*, pp. 86–92, 98; Reese Interviews (Smith; Vasser; Garrow); Lewis Interview (Shannon);

Selby, *Odyssey*, p. 79; L. L. Anderson Interview (Garrow); Boynton Interview (Fager); Abernathy remarks at SCOPE Orientation, 6/14/65, Project South Tape 79-5; Jones to Lyndon Johnson, 3/7/65, Name File LBJL; Ed Strickland to George Wallace, 3/8/65, Wallace 406.

41. *NYT* 3/8/65, p. 1; *WP* 3/8/65, p. A1; Cloud testimony in *Williams* v. *Wallace*, p. 18, 3/16/65; Lewis Interviews (Brasch; Bass & DeVries); Raines, *My Soul*, pp. 207–12; Boynton Interview (Blackside); John Crear Interview (Fager).

42. Garrow, *Protest*, pp. 78–83; *Lutheran* 4/7/65, pp. 8–11; *Nation* 5/10/65, pp. 502–505; FBI 100-442529-813, 3/7/65; Fager, *Selma*, p. 97; Garrow interviews with Reese, Mathew Ahmann, Smitherman, Clark, Gray & Louis Martin; Reese Interview (Blackside); Martin to Watson, 3/8/65, Ex HU/ST1 Box 24; *NYT* 3/9/65, p. 1; *WP* 3/9/65, p. A1.

43. Forman, *Sammy Younge*, pp. 76–78; Forman Interview (Blackside); Sellers, *River*, pp. 124–25; Garrow interviews with Sellers, Gray & Jean Jackson; Shuttlesworth Interview (Ladner); Solomon Seay, Jr. Interview (Wright); Blackside interviews with Doar & Katzenbach; *NYHT* 3/10/65, p. 1; Yarbrough, *Johnson*, p. 241; *New Republic* 3/20/65, pp. 7–9; *Time* 3/19/65, pp. 23–28; Boynton Interview (Fager); Greenberg, "King and the Law."

44. Wagy, "Collins" and "A South to Save," unpublished Ph.D. dissertation, Florida State Univ., 1980, pp. 335–41; Collins, *Society* 11–12/79, pp. 80–83; Collins Interview (Bass & DeVries); Chapman, "Southern Moderate," pp. 54–55; William "Fred" Miller Interview (Lewis); Lewis, *King*, pp. 278–82; FBI 44-12831-520, 3/9/65; Clark Interview (Garrow); Lingo testimony in *Williams* v. *Wallace*, pp. 96–100, 3/13/65; Bishop, *Days*, pp. 386–88.

45. *NYT* 3/10/65, pp. 1, 22; Wagy, "Collins"; Collins Interview (Bass & DeVries); William "Fred" Miller Interview (Lewis); King testimony in *Williams* v. *Wallace*, pp. 50–52, 67–70, 98, 3/11/65; *WP* 3/10/65, p. A1; Smeltzer notes on 3/9 conversation with Secrest, RES; *Christianity & Crisis* 4/5/65, pp. 67–69; *Newsweek* 3/22/65, pp. 18–21; *New South* 3/65, pp. 11–13; *NYT Magazine* 3/21/65, pp. 29–30, 118–20; *Community* 4/65, pp. 4, 14; *Christian Century* 3/24/65, pp. 358–60; *Congress Bi-Weekly* 3/29/65, pp. 5–6; Fager, *Selma*, pp. 101–105; Wofford, *Kennedys*, pp. 181–83; Collins, *Society*, n. 44 above; Blackside interviews with Young & Katzenbach.

46. Garrow, *Protest*, pp. 87, 273–74; *NYT* 3/10/65, p. 22; King testimony in *Williams* v. *Wallace*, pp. 25–110, at 67, 3/11/65; King, *Saturday Review* 4/3/65, pp. 16–17, 57; Clark Interview (Baker); Garrow interviews with Cleveland Sellers, James Orange & Reese; Willie Ricks Interview (Carson); Forman, *Making*, p. 441; *Commonweal* 4/9/65, pp. 75–77. King in *Saturday Review* also listed four conditions for successful protests, one being that "racists resist by unleashing violence." Queried on this by a reader, an SCLC-prepared response answered that "I did state that racial violence against peaceful demonstrators was an essential prerequisite to securing racial justice. . . . We learned this in Albany, Georgia, where we marched but were never met with violence. Our demonstrators were arrested and placed in jail in a rather orderly fashion, but because there was no true confrontation the movement gradually died and none of our demands were met." Draft for King to Marion R. Hart, 6/25/65, KP; also see *National Review* 4/20/65, p. 327, & Garrow, *Protest*, pp. 228–30, 325–36, plus Coretta King, "'We're Sharing Him,'" who writes that "when the majority of white Americans saw on television the brutality of segregation in action . . . they reacted as Martin knew they would—with revulsion and sympathy and with demands that somehow this . . . must stop. . . . Little would have been accomplished without television." As Ralph Abernathy put it, "The southern white segregationists always make the mistakes necessary to create and sustain the movement." *WP* 6/7/65, p. A11.

47. Fager, *Selma*, pp. 108–109; Mendelsohn, *Martyrs*, pp. 153–75; *NYT*

3/10/65, p. 23, 3/11/65, p. 1; Garrow, *Protest*, pp. 87–91; Humphrey to Johnson, 3/10/65, MW 31.

48. *NYT* 3/11/65, p. 1, 3/12/65, p. 1, 3/13/65, p. 1; Hinckle & Welsh, "Five Battles," pp. 32–33; Smiley Interview (Barton); Howard Glickstein Interviews (Wright; Rafferty); Forman, *Sammy Younge*, pp. 79–80; Garrow, *Protest*, pp. 91–97; King testimony in *Williams* v. *Wallace*, pp. 62, 67, 105, 109, 3/11/65.

49. *NYT* 3/13/65, p. 1, 3/14/65, p. 1; *New Republic* 4/3/65, pp. 8–9; Garrow, *Protest*, pp. 97–102; Wilkins, *Man's Life*, pp. 149–50; Wallace to Johnson, 3/12/65, Ex HU/ST1; Jones, *Wallace*, pp. 375–78; Lyndon B. Johnson, *The Vantage Point* (New York: Holt, Rinehart & Winston, 1971), p. 162; Johnson, *Public Papers*, pp. 274–81.

50. *CST* 3/15/65, p. 3; *CDN* 3/15/65, p. 4; *CA* 3/15/65, p. 4; King, "A Knock at Midnight," 3/14/65, KP; Garrow, *Protest*, pp. 105–108; Chapman, "Southern Moderate," p. 59; *Register-Leader* 5/65, pp. 6–9; *Commonweal* 4/9/65, pp. 71–75; *Peace*, Spring 1965, pp. 1–22; *NYT* 3/15/65, p. 1, 3/16/65, p. 1; Lewis in Beardslee, *The Way*, p. 27; Jean Jackson Interview (Garrow); C. T. Vivian Interview (Blackside).

51. *NYT* 3/17/65, p. 1, 3/18/65, p. 1; Garrow, *Protest*, pp. 108–11; Forman, *Sammy Younge*, pp. 91–101; Gwen Patton Interview (Long); *National Observer* 3/22/65; Kunstler, *Deep*, pp. 354–55; Benjamin Epstein, "Notes . . .," 3/16–21/65, Smeltzer; FBI 100-106670-NR, 3/18/65; *Forman* v. *City of Montgomery*, and *Johnson* v. *City of Montgomery*, 245 F. Supp. 17, 25 (1965).

52. *Williams* v. *Wallace*, 240 F. Supp. 100 (1965); Garrow, *Protest*, pp. 111–12, 278–79; *NYT* 3/19/65, pp. 1, 20, 3/20/65, p. 1, 3/21/65, p. 1.

53. Garrow, *Protest*, pp. 113–16; *WP* 3/28/65, p. E7.

54. *NYT* 3/22/65, p. 1, 3/23/65, p. 1, 3/24/65, p. 1; Elwyn Smith Interview (Fager); *CP* 3/24/65, p. B4; *CPD* 3/24/65, p. 11; *U.S. News* 4/5/65, pp. 37–38. Accounts of the march include *Jet* 4/8/65, pp. 6–17, 52–55; *New Republic* 4/3/65, pp. 7–8; *New Yorker* 4/10/65, 121ff; *New South* 3/65, pp. 2, 13–16; *National Observer* 3/29/65; *Ebony* 5/65, 46ff; *America* 5/8/65, pp. 660–64; *Look* 5/18/65, pp. 32–37; *Saturday Evening Post* 5/22/65, pp. 30–31, 89–95; *American Journal of Orthopsychiatry* 10/65, pp. 972–80; *International Journal of Social Psychiatry*, Spring 1968, pp. 119–24; Fager, *Selma*, pp. 150–59.

55. *NYT* 3/25/65, p. 1, 3/26/65, p. 1; *Peace News* 4/16/65, p. 3; King, "Address . . .," 3/25/65, KP; Ramsey Clark Interview (Baker).

56. Coretta King Interview (Mayerson XXII, pp. 31–32); *NYT* 3/27/65, p. 1; Rochelle Horowitz Interview (Garrow); Mendelsohn, *Martyrs*, pp. 176–95; Don Whitehead, *Attack on Terror* (New York: Funk & Wagnalls, 1970), pp. 305–10; King to Hoover, 3/27/65, and Hoover to King, 3/29/65, 100-106670-1164. Undependable are Rowe, *My Undercover Years with the Ku Klux Klan* (New York: Bantam, 1976); and J. A. Gordon, *Nightriders: The Inside Story of the Liuzzo Killing* (Birmingham: Bralgo Publications, 1966).

57. *NYT* 3/28/65, p. 1, 3/29/65; *Jet* 3/18/65, pp. 20–22; *WDN* 3/24/65, p. 29; SCLC Staff Meeting Tape, 3/28/65, KC; Jay Janis to Calvin Kytle, "Suggested Alabama Plan," 3/30/65, CRS FOIA; King's handwritten notes on Bernard Lee stationery, ca. 3/27/65, KP; FBI 100-106670-NR, 3/28/65; *SFC* 3/28/65, p. 9, 3/29/65, p. 1; King, "Meet the Press," 3/28/65, KP; *WP* 3/29/65, p. A1. King later wrote that "Southerners are making the Marxist analysis of history more accurate than the Christian hope that men can be persuaded through teaching and preaching to live a new and better life. In the South, businessmen act much more quickly from economic considerations than do churchmen from moral considerations." *Ebony* 8/65, pp. 77–80, at 79.

58. *NYT* 3/30/65, pp. 1, 28, 46, 3/31/65, pp. 17, 22; *WP* 3/31/65, p. A22; FBI 100-106670-1148, 1153, 3/30/65; SAC NY to Director, 4/1/65, 100-438794-NR;

Newsweek 4/12/65, pp. 28–29; Boyte, "Dialogue—An Interpretation," 11/12/64, & Blackwell to King, "A New Department . . .," n.d., SCLC 145; *AI* 2/13/65; *PC* 2/13/65, p. 5; King, "Dear Friend" letter, 2/3/65, 100-438794-266; King, *Ebony* 3/65, p. 35; Stoney Cooks Interviews (Leventhal; Garrow).

59. *WP* 4/1/65, p. A1, 4/2/65, p. A1; *BS* 4/1/65, p. 54, 4/2/65, p. 44; SCLC Board Meeting Minutes, 4/1–2/65, KC; *NYT* 4/2/65, p. 24; Fred Shuttlesworth Interview (Garrow); SCLC Board Resolutions, 4/2/65, KC; Boyte, "Dialogue," n. 58 above; DuBois, *Fellowship* 7/65, pp. 10–12; Garrow interviews with Dorothy Cotton & Lillie Hunter; SCOPE Proposed Budget & Program, n.d., KC; Williams Interview (Project South); Stoney Cooks Interviews (Garrow; Leventhal); Ben Clark Interview (Garrow); King, "Dear Friend," n. 58 above; Coretta King, *My Life,* pp. 270–71.

60. SCLC Board Minutes, n. 59 above; *Ebony* 6/65, pp. 164–73, 1/70, pp. 40–50; Garrow interviews with D. E. King, Hosea Williams & Otis Moss; Steele Interview (Ice); Coretta King & Levison in FBI NY 100-111180-9-1671, 1676A, 1738, 5/15, 5/20 & 7/21/68; Raines, *My Soul,* p. 464; King, "Statement . . .," 4/2/65, KP; *WP* 4/3/65, p. A1, 4/4/65, p. A6; *BS* 4/3/65, p. 32; *NYT* 4/3/65, p. 14, 4/4/65, pp. 76, E7; King, *AN* 4/10/65, p. 16; *AA* 4/17/65, p. 4; King, "An Open Letter . . ." in Carawan, *Freedom,* p. 171.

61. FBI 100-106670-1245, 4/6/65; *BN* 4/6/65; *AC* 4/7/65, p. 2; Levison to King, 4/7/65, KP; Garrow, *Protest,* pp. 135–36, 144–60; Rustin, "From Protest"; Rustin & Kahn, "Johnson So Far."

62. Garrow interviews with Bevel, Bernard Lafayette, Bernard Lee, Andrew Young & Coretta King; Bevel Interview (Blackside); *Chicago Reader* 7/20/84, p. 1; *CA* 4/1/65, p. 8; *CT* 4/4/65, p. 5; *CST* 4/5/65, p. 3; *CDN* 4/5/65, p. 10; Notes on "James Bevel," 4/2, 4/3 & 4/21/65, UICC-JLB; Douglas to King, 4/7/65, SCLC 144; FBI 100-106670-1269, 4/17/65; SAC NY to Director, 4/23/65, 100-106670-1275.

63. Coretta King Interviews (Mayerson XXVI, p. 37, XVIII, p. 27; Garrow); Coretta King, "The World," p. 30; *AA* 4/10/65, p. 8; McKee, *King,* p. 123; Levison Interview (Stein I); Garrow, *FBI,* pp. 138, 276. In 9/67, King said that "one of the reasons we chose this neighborhood was because I wanted to be at the heart of the Negro ghetto." ABC's "Good Company," KC.

64. FBI 100-106670-NR, 4/15 & 16/65; James Laue to LeRoy Collins et al., "Summary of Meeting . . .," 4/19/65, CRS FOIA; *National Observer* 4/12/65; *AC* 4/20/65, p. 16; *NYT* 4/20/65, p. 25, 4/21/65, p. 29, 4/22/65, p. 21, 4/23/65, p. 15, 4/24/65, p. 1; Laue to Kytle et al., "SCLC . . .," 4/27/65, CRS FOIA; *BN* 5/2/65, p. 1; King, New York City Bar Association *Record* 5/65 Supplement, pp. 3–24; *New Yorker* 5/1/65, pp. 35–37; King, Massachusetts House of Representatives, *Special Reports,* No. 4155 (4/22/65), pp. 7–14; *BG* 4/23/65, p. 1, 4/24/65, p. 1; *NYHT* 4/23/65, p. 1; *WP* 4/23/65, p. A23; *Time* 4/30/65, pp. 32–33. Commentaries on King's bar association speech include Louis Waldman, *New York State Bar Journal* 37 (8/65): 331–37; & Ansbro, "King's Civil Disobedience."

65. FBI 100-106670-1306, 1367, 4/23 & 27/65; *LAT* 4/28/65, p. 3; *DMR* 4/29/65, p. 1; *DTD* 4/29/65, p. 1; Garrow, *Protest,* pp. 120–24; Harrington, *Fragments,* pp. 122–23; Harrington Interview (Garrow); Paul Good, *Reporter* 4/8/65, pp. 23–26; Andrew Kopkind, *New Republic* 4/10/65, pp. 13–16; *Jet* 4/1/65, pp. 50–52; Jimmy Garrett, *Movement* 4/65, pp. 1–2. Also see *Newsweek* 4/12/65, pp. 30–31; Vincent Harding, *Christian Century* 5/5/65, pp. 580–81, 5/12/65, pp. 614–16; *Ebony* 7/65, pp. 146–53; *Nation* 7/19/65, pp. 38–40; Bruce Payne, "SNCC . . .," in Mitchell Cohen & Dennis Hale, eds., *The New Student Left* (Boston: Beacon Press, 1966), pp. 86–103; & Norm Fruchter, *Studies on the Left* 5 (Winter 1965): 74–80.

66. FBI 100-442529-1030, 5/2/65; *AC* 5/1/65, p. 9; *NYT* 5/1/65, p. 9; SCLC *Newsletter* 4–5/65, p. 16.

67. *PB* 5/2/65, p. 1, 5/3/65, p. 2, 5/4/65, p. 3; *PI* 5/2/65, p. 1; *PDN* 5/4/65, p. 4; Laue to Janis et al., "SCLC's . . . Plans," 5/3/65, CRS FOIA; Blackwell, "A Report on . . . Selma," 5/10/65, KC; FBI 100-438794-325, 326; E. L. Doyle Interview (Garrow); David Smith, "Report from Selma," 5/13/65, & "The Pulse of Selma," 5/18/65, Gould; *BN* 5/2/65, p. 7; *NYT Magazine* 5/30/65, 8ff.

68. *NYT* 5/8/65, p. 1, 5/11/65, p. 25, 5/12/65, p. 27, 5/13/65, p. 7, 5/14/65, p. 23, 5/16/65, p. 72; *BN* 5/11/65, p. 6; Wright interviews with James & John Haskins; *WES* 5/13/65, p. A7; FBI 100-106670-1373, 5/13/65; Hoover to Watson, 5/15/65, 100-442529-1073; *PC* 4/30/60, p. 9; Carey to King, 12/11/64, KP; De-Loach to Mohr, 5/19/65, 161-2040-30.

69. *LT* 2/27/65, p. 2; *LCJ* 5/17/65, p. II-1; John Porter Interview (Garrow); Warren Cochrane Interview (Downing); FBI NY 100-111180-9-2103A, 7/21/69; *NYT* 5/21/65, p. 36; King, *AN* 6/19/65, p. 16; Blackwell to King, 5/19/65, KP; FBI 100-106670-NR, 5/21 & 24/65; Garrow interviews with Jones, Wachtel & Rustin.

70. *NYT* 5/24/65, p. 19, 5/25/65, p. 23, 5/26/65, p. 1, 5/29/65, p. 11, 6/1/65, pp. 26, 28; *CST* 5/25/65, p. 20; *MA* 6/1/65, p. 14; *CDN* 6/5/65, p. 4; *WSJ* 6/7/65, p. 1; *AC* 6/19/65, p. 10; *DDT* 6/23/65, p. 9; FBI 100-442529-1130, 1140, 6/11 & 12/65; FBI 100-106670-NR, 6/13/65; Blackwell to King, 6/10/65 (2), KC; *Progressive* 5/68, p. 24; SCLC "Vision" brochure, KC; Blackwell, "Summary Report . . .," 6/10/65, KC; Blackwell to King, "Employees and Payroll," 6/10/65, SCLC 64, plus Francis Covington to Young, 12/3/64, KC.

71. *SC* 6/3/65, p. 5; Project South Tapes 0092, 93, 95, 6/15 & 16/65; *NYT* 6/15/65, p. 26, 6/20/65, p. 61; "SCOPE Project" brochure, KC; Leventhal, "Odyssey"; Gwendolyn Green Interview (Leventhal); King, *New America* 6/30/65, p. 6, & *AN* 7/3/65, p. 16; *SCLC Newsletter* 4–5/65, p. 2; Junius Griffin to Blackwell, 6/28/65, SCLC 145.

72. FBI 100-106670-1510, NR, 6/18 & 25/65; *DDN* 6/20/65, p. A10; *AG* 6/20/65, p. A14; King, "Address . . .," 6/20/65, KP; *Daily Gleaner* 6/23/65; SCLC Financial Report, 6/30/65, KC; *NYT* 6/6/65, p. 52; FBI 100-442529-1111, 5/29/65, & 100-438794-435, 501, 7/23 & 8/6/65; Farnsworth to King, 6/29/65, King to Farnsworth, 7/16/65, Levison to Young & to King, 6/27/65, KP.

73. *MH* 6/27/65, p. A30; *MN* 6/27/65; *RTD* 7/2/65; *WP* 7/3/65, p. A2; *NYT* 7/3/65, p. 6, 7/5/65, p. 4; *AJ* 7/8/65; *Time* 7/16/65, p. 20; Garrow interviews with Curtis Harris, Herbert Coulton & Milton Reid; King, "KNXT Newsmakers," 7/10/65, KP; King, "Modern Man's Crucial Problems," Ebenezer, 6/6/65, KP; *CDN* 7/7/65, p. 1.

Chapter Eight

1. Anderson & Pickering, "Chicago," pp. 163–487; "Chicago Background . . .," n.d. [ca. 6/65], SCLC 149; *New America* 10/21/63, p. 5; Raby Interviews (Viorst; Garrow); Edwin "Bill" Berry Interviews (Britton; Garrow); Don Rose Interview (Garrow); Garrow conversation with Weinberg; *CDN* 2/20/65, 6/14/65; *Renewal* 3/65, pp. 3–6; Mary J. Herrick, *The Chicago Schools* (Beverly Hills, Calif.: Sage Publications, 1971), pp. 312–38; Selby, *Odyssey*, pp. 341–44; *CT Magazine* 4/17/83, pp. 26–39.

2. Anderson & Pickering, "Chicago," pp. 487–629; Garrow interviews with Bevel & Lafayette; AFSC, "Housing Opportunities Program . . .," 10/65–10/66, GM; *CA* 4/1/65, p. 8; *CT* 4/4/65, p. 5; *CST* 4/5/65, p. 3; *CDN* 4/5/65, p. 10, 8/29/66, p. 3; Notes on "James Bevel," 4/2, 3 & 21/65, UICC-JLB; George Culberson, "Chicago," 6/16/65, George Roberts to File, 6/30 & 7/5/65, Culberson to Jean Preston, 7/7/65, CRS FOIA; Raby, "Statement . . .," 6/28/65; *Renewal* 7/4/65, pp. 2–6; Raby to Keppel, 7/4/65, Weinberg & Faith Rich, "A Report on

Official Segregation . . .," 7/27/65, Chicago CORE 3-19; *Reporter* 11/4/65, pp. 30–31.

3. King, "Address . . .," 7/6/65, KP; *CDN* 7/7/65, p. 1; *WP* 7/8/65, p. A5, 7/15/65, p. G1; *NYT* 7/8/65, p. 36, 7/12/65, p. 20; SCLC "People to People Northern City Tour," KC; King, "Address . . .," 7/15/65, KP. Also see *LAS* 6/24/65, p. A9; *LAT* 6/20/65, p. 15, 7/10/65, p. 4, 7/12/65, p. 20. On 7/21, King, Young, and Abernathy met with several major businessmen at a Washington luncheon hosted by CRS Director Collins and Commerce Secretary John Connor. Laue to Kytle, 5/19/65, Collins to Connor, 5/21/65, CRS FOIA; Connor to Lyndon Johnson, 7/23/65, LC 7-B-2; Connor to King, 7/27/65, KP; Wilkins, *Man's Life,* p. 174.

4. *CDN* 7/16/65, p. 19, 7/17/65, p. 9, 7/20/65, p. 7, 7/24/65, p. 1, 7/26/65, p. 1, 7/27/65, p. 1, 7/28/65, p. 12; *CA* 7/18/65; *WSJ* 7/22/65; "Schedule . . .," 7/23–26/65, SCLC 150; Marciniak Interview (Garrow); *NYT* 7/25/65, p. 39, 7/26/65, p. 12, 7/27/65, p. 18, 8/1/65, p. 59; *CT* 7/26/65, p. 1; King, "Address . . .," 7/26/65, KP; *CD* 4/16–22/66, p. 10; *New America* 8/9/65, p. 1; *Christian Century* 8/11/65, pp. 979–80; *Community* 9/65, pp. 4–6; *Negro Digest* 3/66, pp. 54–58; Anderson & Pickering, "Chicago," pp. 637–38.

5. *CP* 7/27/65, p. B9, 7/28/65, p. A4, 7/29/65, p. D7; D. J. Burns, "Itinerary . . .," 7/27–28/65, KC; *CCP* 7/31/65; SCLC press release, 7/31/65, KC; Garrow, *Protest,* pp. 131–32; Clarence Mitchell to Roy Wilkins, 7/22/65, RW 7; FBI 100-106670-1662, 7/28/65.

6. *NYT* 8/1/65, p. 59, 8/3/65, p. 17, 8/4/65, p. 19; SAC Philadelphia to Director, 8/2/65, 100-438794-NR; *PI* 7/30/65, p. 10, 8/1/65, p. 1, 8/2/65, p. 1, 8/3/65, p. 1, 8/4/65, p. 1, 8/5/65, p. 1; *ADW* 8/4/65, p. 1.

7. Lee White to Johnson, 7/23/65, King Name File LBJL; *NYT* 8/5/65, p. 12, 8/6/65, p. 12, 8/7/65, p. 8, 8/9/65, p. 11, 8/11/65, p. 21; *WP* 8/5/65, p. C1, 8/6/65, p. A4, 8/7/65, p. A1; White to Johnson, 8/5/65, Diary Backup LBJL; Raby letter, 8/1/65, "Minutes of CCCO . . .," 8/4/65, and Glanze & Glanze, "Civil Rights Events . . .," 8/1–8/65, all Chicago CORE 3-20; Anderson & Pickering, "Chicago," pp. 651–72; Garrow interviews with Raby & Edwin "Bill" Berry; Robert Lucas Interview (Britton).

8. FBI 100-106670-1609, 1693, 1712, 7/14 & 8/3/65; Wachtel draft, 7/26/65, KP 14; Dowdy, "Nonviolence," pp. 72–88; Fairclough, "Vietnam," pp. 25–26; SAC NY to Director, 8/10/65, 100-438794-505; SCLC Board Minutes, 8/9–13/65, KC; Young, "An Experiment in Power," 8/11/65, KC; *NYT* 8/10/65; *BN* 8/11/65, p. 2, 8/12/65, p. 36; *WP* 8/12/65, p. A17; Fauntroy Interview (Lewis); Hosea Williams Interviews (Garrow; Leventhal); Garrow interviews with Otis Moss & Curtis Harris; Fred Shuttlesworth Interviews (Garrow; Mosby); Pendergrast, "Interview with Lowery," pp. 10–12; SCLC "Summary of 9th Annual Convention" booklet, esp. p. 16; FBI NY 100-111180-9-665A, 8/13/65; FBI 100-106670-1727, 8/14/65.

9. *NYT* 8/12/65, p. 12, 8/13/65, p. 1, 8/14/65, p. 3, 8/15/65, p. 73; King, "Annual Report," 8/11/65, "Statement," 8/12/65, & press interview, 8/13/65, KP; *BN* 8/13/65, p. 5, 8/15/65, p. C18; *WP* 8/13/65, p. A7, 8/14/65, p. A8; *NYJA* 8/15/65, p. A3; *Southern Courier* 8/20/65, p. 1.

10. FBI 100-106670-1720, 100-442529-1375 & 100-438794-536, 8/14/65; *MH* 8/15/65, p. 1, 8/16/65, p. 1; *SJS* 8/16/65, p. 1, 8/22/65; FBI 100-106670-1717, NR, 8/16 & 17/65; *NYT* 8/16/65, p. 17, 8/17/65, p. 16, 8/19/65, p. 1; King, "Statement . . .," 8/17/65, KP; *LAHE* 8/17/65, p. 3; *LAT* 8/18/65, p. 3; Rustin Interviews (Viorst I & II).

11. *LAT* 8/20/65, p. 1, 8/21/65, p. 4; *NYT* 8/20/65, p. 16, 8/21/65, p. 1; *HT* 8/22/65; *Newsweek* 8/30/65, pp. 19–20; Rustin, "Watts," p. 32; King, *AN* 8/28/65, p. 14; FBI 100-106670-1783, 8/20/65; *U.S. News* 8/30/65, p. 16; *National Review* 9/7/65, pp. 769–70.

12. Director to SAC Atlanta, 7/27 & 8/18/65, 100-438794-443, 526; SCLC press release, 7/22/65, KC; Williams Interview (Project South); *NYT* 8/1/65, p. 1; *WSJ* 8/5/65, p. 1; *Southern Courier* 7/23/65, p. 4; *WES* 7/26/65; Fager, *Selma*, pp. 172–78, 188–203; *MN* 6/27/65; Hal Hunton to File, "St. Augustine," 7/23 & 29/65, CRS FOIA; Hayling Interviews (Britton; Garrow); Garrow interviews with John Gibson, Dana Swan, Blackwell & Young; Williams Interviews (Garrow; Leventhal); Stoney Cooks Interviews (Garrow; Leventhal; LaCrosse); Rev. F. R. Rowe of Fitzgerald to Williams, 8/19/65, in Bolster, "Civil Rights," pp. 222–24; N. J. Demerath et al., *Journal of Social Issues* 27 (1971): 63–80; Blackwell to King & Abernathy, 8/25/65, KC.

   13. FBI NY 100-111180-9-677, 100-111180-1631, 8/25/65; SAC NY to Director, 8/27/65, 100-442529-illegible; "Minutes of SCLC Executive Staff . . .," 8/26–28/65, KC; *CST* 9/25/66, p. 52; Fauntroy Interview (Lewis); Lowery Interview (Garrow).

   14. *NYT* 8/25/65, p. 3; *NYWJT* 4/17/67, p. 1; King, "Face the Nation," 8/29/65; *NYWT* 8/28/65, p. 3, 8/31/65, p. 1; *NYT* 9/1/65, p. 12.

   15. *CST* 9/2/65, p. 1, 9/11/65, p. 39, 9/12/65; *CT* 9/2/65, p. 1; *CDN* 9/2/65, p. 22, 9/7/65, p. 6, 9/21/65, p. 10; *NYT* 9/2/65, p. 20, 9/8/65, p. 24; King, *AN* 9/11/65, p. 16; *Nation* 8/30/65, pp. 92–95; Anderson, "Year," p. 25; Raby to Jack Greenberg, 9/18/65, & SCLC, "Programmatic Action Proposal for Chicago," 9/65, SCLC 149.

   16. *CDN* 9/10/65, p. 3; *NYT* 9/11/65, p. 9; *NYHT* 9/11/65, p. 4; *WP* 9/11/65, p. A7; King press conference, 9/10/65, KP; Marvin Watson to Johnson, 9/14/65, King Name File LBJL; *Christian Century* 9/29/65, pp. 1180–81; Coretta King, *My Life*, p. 291; Young Interview (Garrow); FBI NY 100-111180-9-695A & FBI 100-442529-1446, 9/12/65; FBI 100-106670-NR, 9/13/65.

   17. *CDN* 9/14/65, p. 13; *SEP* 9/15/65, p. 18; *WP* 9/15/65, p. A4; Garrow interviews with Vivian, Coulton, Green & Stein; Harold Middlebrook Interview (Beifuss & Thomas III); [Vivian], "The Department of Economic Affairs," [11/8/65], & CEP "Quarterly Report," 11/8/65, SCLC 145; FBI 100-438794-666, 9/27/65; *AJ* 7/8/65, p. 6; *MH* 7/8/65, p. A22; Diane Bevel, "Job Description," 9/23/65, & Middlebrook, "Proposal for Alabama Staff," [ca. 9/65], SCLC 146; *NYT* 9/4/65, p. 22; FBI 100-438794-626, 9/10/65; King, *AN* 9/25/65, p. 16; Junius Griffin et al. to King, "On-Sight Visitation to Natchez . . .," 9/27/65, "Telephone Report from Stoney Cooks . . .," 9/27/65, & "Telephone Report from Al Sampson . . .," 9/30/65, SCLC 146. As Stein explained, "SCLC being what it was, I said, 'You're kidding. You want *me* to call on black churches?'" (Garrow interview)

   18. FBI 100-106670-1861, 9/7/65, & 100-438794-687, 10/4/65; *WES* 9/23/65, p. A4; *Jet* 10/7/65; Whitney Young et al. to John Johnson, 10/4/65, KP; Garrow, *Protest*, pp. 183–84; Lawson, "Preserving," p. 62; McGraw, "Interview with Young," p. 325; Young Interview (Baker); Chapman, "Southern Moderate," pp. 85–86; Branton Interview (Garrow); *New Leader* 10/11/65, pp. 3–6; Director to SAC Atlanta, 9/27/65, 100-438794-657; Lee to King, 10/1/65, KP.

   19. FBI 100-438794-717 & NY 100-111180-9-714A, 10/1/65; *CA* 9/26/65, p. 3; FBI 100-438794-705X1, 9/30/65; King to Johnson, 10/2/65, King Name File LBJL; *CDN* 10/6/65, p. 1, 10/7/65, p. 1, 10/8/65, p. 3, 10/9/65, p. 1; *CT* 10/8/65, p. 14; *MJ* 10/9/65, p. 3, 10/10/65, p. 22; "Notes from the Conference," 10/8–10/65; [John McDermott], "CCCO-SCLC Conference . . .," 10/8–10/65, NCCIJ 11-9; Anderson, "Year."

   20. *NYT* 10/11/65, p. 44; "Notes," p. 29, n. 19 above; FBI 100-442529-1482 & NY 100-111180-9-711A, 9/28/65; King, "Statement," 10/5/65, KP; FBI 100-106670-1948, 10/10/65. In the 9/28 discussion, King queried his advisors about a text: "Should I say in this speech how wrong we are in Vietnam . . . how immoral this is? I think someone should outline how wrong we are—uh, I don't know if I'm the person to do this." Levison, referring to the previous discussions, immediately responded, "Martin, we've just gone over this and decided that you're not the person to do this." King: "O.K. I'll go along with this. O.K."

21. *AC* 10/6/65, p. 1, 10/7/65, p. 1, 10/9/65, p. 1, 10/11/65, p. 1; untitled Crawfordville memo [10/7/65], SCLC 165; Dana Swan Interview (Garrow); King, "Address," 10/11/65, KP; *CDN* 10/12/65, p. 10; *Southern Courier* 10/16–17/65, p. 2; *NYT* 10/12/65, p. 34, 10/15/65, p. 1; *AC* 10/12 through 10/16/65, all p. 1; *PEB* 10/16/65, p. 3.

22. Archie Jones to King, 10/19/65, & Blackwell to Jones, 10/21/65, SCLC 143; Lowery to King, 10/29/65, Young; FBI 100-438794-476, 592, 8/5 & 9/2/65; FBI 100-106670-NR & NY 100-111180-9-689A, 9/6/65; FBI 100-106670-1948, 10/10/65; Rockefeller to King, 10/15/65, & King to Rockefeller, 11/1/65, KP; *AC* 10/18/65, p. 1; FBI 100-438794-NR, 888, 11/5 & 13/65. Rockefeller also donated $5,000 in 1962, Rockefeller to King, 8/15/62, KP.

23. *NYT* 10/24/65, p. 1, 10/26/65, p. 21, 11/4/65, p. 36, 11/11/65, p. 30; *WP* 10/24/65, p. A2, 10/30/65, p. A2; *CDN* 10/25/65, p. 3; *ADW* 10/26/65, p. 1, 11/6/65, p. 1; *AC* 10/27/65, p. 3, 10/29/65, p. 61, 11/6/65, p. 11, 11/11/65, p. 3; *MCA* 10/27/65; Courtland Cox to Williams, 11/3/65, SNCC 45; King, "Address . . .," 11/10/65, KP; King, *AN* 11/20/65, p. 16, 12/4/65, p. 33.

24. Bernard Lee to Williams, "Montgomery Report," 11/8/65, Williams to King, "Quarterly Report," 11/6/65, Bevel, "SCLC—Chicago Project," 10/26/65, KP; Bevel, "SCLC—Chicago Project," 11/8/65, SCLC 150; AFSC, "Housing Opportunities . . . ," n. 2 above; Jackson to C. T. Vivian, 12/10/65, Jackson, "From October to May: A Report to Rev. C. T. Vivian," 5/17/66, & "Interview with Rev. Jesse Jackson," 12/17/68, GM; Garrow interviews with Jackson, Clay Evans, Al Pitcher, David Wallace & Gary Massoni; *CT* 10/29/65, p. 1A-3. As Jackson described it in the 5/66 report, "Last summer with an anticipation of a movement developing in Chicago and a deep appreciation for the potential power of the church, I started working with one minister [Evans] as the first step of bringing the clergy of Chicago into full understanding and participation in the freeing of people in the slum. . . . Our relationship led to expansion to include other pastors," and to an 11/19/65 clergy meeting that King addressed.

25. SAC Chicago to Director, 11/22/65, 100-438794-921; *NYT* 11/11/65, p. 30, 11/15/65, p. 1, 12/6/65, p. 73; *WP* 11/15/65, p. A6, 12/2/65, p. A5; King to James Phelan, 12/6/65, KP; *CDN* 11/19/65, p. 10; *DN* 11/19/65, p. A3; *DFP* 11/19/65, p. C10; *MJ* 11/24/65, p. II-I; King, *Saturday Review* 11/13/65, pp. 33–35, 105; King, *CD* 1/1–7/66, p. 10; Coretta King Interview (Mayerson XXVII, p. 3); Garrow interviews with Spock & Andrew Young; *NYHT* 12/2/65, p. 9, 12/6/65, p. 16; FBI 100-106670-2137, 12/4/65; King, "Address . . .," 12/5/65, KP; *AC* 12/6/65, p. 40. King's 4/65 election to the Morehouse board had been delayed more than two years because of conservative opposition. Benjamin E. Mays to Hughes Spaulding et al., 3/19/63, KP; Clayton Yates Interview (Lewis); Charles Willie Interview (Garrow); Mays, *Born*, pp. 273–74.

26. *NYT* 11/4/65, 12/7/65, p. 33, 12/8/65, p. 33, 12/13/65, p. 33; *AC* 12/4/65, p. 9; King, "Address to . . . the American Committee on Africa," 12/10/65, KP; King, *Southern Courier* 12/11–12/65, p. 1; *Newsweek* 12/20/65, pp. 29–30; Williams, "Voter Registration . . .," in SCLC *Report to the Board*, 4/12–13/66, KC; *Reporter* 12/2/65, pp. 21–27; Waites et al. to Moore, 12/14/65, & blind memo, "Notes" [12/13/65], WH; *BN* 12/14/65, p. 34; *BPH* 12/14/65, p. 17; Fauntroy to King, 12/9/65, & to John Doar, 12/15/65, KP; Williams to Young, 12/30/65, & Young to Williams, 12/31/65, SCLC 167; Williams Interview (Garrow). On the car case, see Garrow, *FBI*, pp. 178, 288. AFON was a direct successor to SCLC's previous tax-exempt adjunct, the Gandhi Society, and received $25,000 of King's $54,000 Nobel award.

27. FBI NY 100-111180-9-750, 11/6/65; King to DeLoach, 12/6/65, KP; *CT* 12/25/65, p. 8; Rustin Interviews (Garrow; Viorst); Kahn Interviews (Viorst; Garrow); Garrow interviews with Hill, Rochelle Horowitz & Ralph Helstein; Young Interview (Baker); *WP* 12/15/65, p. A25, 2/10/66, p. A25; King, "No Room at the Inn," Ebenezer, 12/19/65, KP; King, *Southern Courier* 12/11–12/65, p. 1; King, "Address . . .," 12/15/65, KP; *AC* 12/16/65, p. 26; *WP* 12/17/65, p. A1; *LCJ* 12/17/65, p. II-1; *LT* 12/17/65, p. A1; King, "New Wine," Ebenezer, 1/2/66, KP. Even three years earlier King had remarked that "God never meant for some to be wealthy while others lived in abject, deadening poverty . . . If you are to be a Christian you must make economic equality a reality." *KCT* 11/5/65, p. 1.

28. *CT* 1/6/66, p. 14, 1/12/66, p. 1A-1, 1/18/66, p. 5; *CST* 1/6/66, p. 18, 1/7/66, p. 20, 1/8/66, p. 5; *CA* 1/6/66, p. 3, 1/7/66, p. 8, 1/8/66, p. 5; *CDN* 1/6/66, p. 1, 1/7/66, p. 3; Robert Lucas to Raby, 1/2/66, Chicago CORE 4-26; SCLC, "A Proposal for the Development of a Nonviolent Action Movement . . .," [1/7/66], "Proposed Plan of Organization & Action for the Chicago Freedom Movement," n.d., KC; King, "The Chicago Plan," 1/7/66, KP; King, *AN* 1/15/66, p. 10, 2/5/66, p. 21; *NYT* 1/8/66, p. 22; *WP* 1/8/66, p. A6; *CCCO Newsletter* vol. 1, #1, 1/66; *CD* 1/8–14/66, p. 1.

29. *CST* 1/9/66, p. 41; *AJC* 1/9/66, p. 1; FBI 100-106670-2189, 1/11/66; *NYT* 1/10/66, pp. 1, 10, 1/11/66, p. 7, 1/12/66, p. 18, 1/13/66, p. 18, 1/15/66, p. 1; Clifford Alexander to Johnson, 1/7/66, & King to Johnson, 1/13/66, King Name File LBJL; *WES* 1/12/66, p. A14; *AC* 1/12 through 1/15/66, all p. 1; King, "Statement . . .," 1/12/66, & "Address . . .," 1/14/66, KP; Carson, *In Struggle*, pp. 188–90; King, "Non-Conformist," Ebenezer, 1/16/66.

30. *NYHT* 1/16/66, p. 16; *CA* 1/16/66, p. 3, 1/23/66, p. 4; *CDN* 1/19/66, p. 6, 1/20/66, p. 4; *CST* 1/20/66, p. 26, 1/23/66, p. 5; *National Observer* 1/24/66, p. 1; *CD* 1/22–28/66, p. 1; *Newsweek* 1/31/66, pp. 24–25; *NYT* 1/21/66, p. 27; *CT* 1/23/66, p. 3; *SCLC Newsletter* 1–2/66, p. 1; *Ebony* 4/66, pp. 94–102; "Phase 1: Orientation & Indoctrination," n.d., KC.

31. *BN* 1/4/66, p. 7, 1/14/66, p. 1; Schulman to Alex Miller, 1/12/66, ADL; *NYT* 1/13/66, p. 18, 1/14/66, p. 1, 1/20/66, p. 22, 1/24/66, p. 19, 1/25/66, p. 35; Rosen to DeLoach, 1/14/66, 100-106670-NR; *NYHT* 1/20/66, p. 11; King, "Address . . .," (2), 1/24/66, & "Statements Made by . . . King," 1/24/66, WH; Stokely Carmichael Interview (Garrow); *BPH* 1/25/66, p. 8; *WP* 1/27/66, p. A7; Blackwell to Young, "SNCC-SCLC Alabama Staff Meeting," 1/28/66, KC.

32. *CDN* 1/25/66, p. 6, 1/27/66, p. 3, 1/28/66, p. 3; *CT* 1/26/66, p. 8, 1/27/66, p. 5, 1/28/66, p. 3; *CST* 1/26/66, p. 3, 1/27/66, pp. 3, 32, 1/28/66, p. 18; *CA* 1/27/66, p. 6, 1/28/66, p. 6; *NYT* 1/27/66, p. 37, 1/28/66, p. 13; *CD* 1/29–2/4/66, p. 1; King, "Address . . .," 1/27/66, KP; King, "Address . . .," 1/31/66, & Montgomery et al. to Moore, 2/1/66, WH; Lawson, *Pursuit*, pp. 32–33.

33. Blackwell to King, 1/27/66, SCLC 145; FBI 100-438794-1058, 1/14/66; Abernathy to King, 1/21/66, SCLC 62; FBI 100-438794-1130, 2/3/66, 100-106670-2259, 2266, 2269, 2/1/66; *NYT* 2/1/66, p. 24; Stein Interview (Garrow); *CST* 2/2/66, p. 14, 2/4/66, p. 32, 2/6/66, p. 68; *CT* 2/3/66, p. 4, 2/4/66, p. 1A, 2/6/66, p. 14; *CDN* 2/4/66, p. 5; *CA* 2/4/66, p. 6; *CD* 2/5–11/66, p. 2; *Community* 2/67, p. 5; *Renewal* 3/67, pp. 21–22. On Jackson's work with KOCO, see Jackson to Vivian, 12/10/65 & 2/1/66, Jackson, "Report . . .," 5/17/66, & Jackson "Interview," n. 24 above, GM.

34. King, "Who Are We?," 2/6/66; DeWolf Interview (Lewis); FBI 100-438794-1162 & 100-106670-2279, 2/8/66, 100-438794-1151, 2/11/66; CCCO press release, 2/10/66, KC; FBI 100-106670-2300, 2/10/66; *CT* 2/11/66, pp. 3, 10; *CST* 2/11/66, p. 2, 2/12/66, p. 3; *CDN* 2/11/66, p. 10, 2/12/66, p. 1; *CD* 2/12–18/66, p. 1. Also see King, *Where*, p. 158.

35. Massoni, "Perspectives," pp. 1–10; Jackson, "Report . . .," 5/17/66, n. 24

above; Garrow interviews with Jackson, Evans, Pitcher, David Wallace & Massoni; Jackson, "King—A Recollection"; David Wallace, "Fullness"; Pitcher & Wallace, *Breadbasket News* 10/67, p. 2; *CT* 2/12/66, p. 5; *CDN* 2/12/66, p. 5; *CA* 2/13/66, p. 5; "Minutes of Operation Breadbasket Steering Committee," 2/28/66, GM.

36. FBI 100-438794-1171, 1180, 2/12 & 14/66; FBI NY 100-111180-9-850A, 2/14/66; Levison to Abernathy, 2/18/66, KC; Abernathy to Executive Staff, 2/21/66, SCLC 62; Blackwell to King, "A General Overview . . .," 2/14/66, KP; "SCLC's Southern Field Staff . . .," 2/21/66, KC; Mesher, "Selma—One Year Later . . .," in SCLC *Report to the Board*, 4/12–13/66, KC; Junius Griffin to King, n.d., & Debra Frankle to King, n.d. [both ca. 2/28/66], KP; Septima Clark Interviews (Garrow; Barton; Hall; Walker); Garrow interviews with Junius Griffin, Lillie Hunter, Tom Offenburger, Hosea Williams, Thomas Kilgore, James Orange, Dana Swan, Willie Bolden, Michael Harrington, Calvin Morris, Al Pitcher, Joseph Lowery, Maude Ballou, Stokely Carmichael, Al Raby & Robert Green; Jerry Wurf Interview (Yellins); Pitcher, "Chicago," p. 23; Bob Fitch in Spruill, "Southern Exposure," p. 305; James Laue Interview (Lewis); Cotton Interviews (Garrow; Wigginton & Thrasher); Shuttlesworth Interviews (Garrow; Mosby); Young Interviews (Garrow; Shannon); Dora McDonald Interviews (Smith; Garrow); Green, *King*; Willie Barrow in *Ebony* 4/84, pp. 33–40. For indications of King's latter-day Hegelian approach, see *Where*, pp. 53, 129.

37. "Progress Report . . .," 2/21/66, KC; *CT* 2/17/66, p. 20, 2/19/66, p. 4, 2/22/66, p. IA-9, 2/24/66, p. 3, 2/25/66, pp. 1, 18, 2/26/66, p. 3; *CA* 2/17/66, p. 12, 2/24/66, p. 4; *NYT* 2/17/66, p. 18, 2/24/66, p. 75, 2/25/66, p. 18, 2/26/66, p. 11; Eskridge Interview (Garrow); *CST* 2/18/66, p. 22, 2/19/66, p. 4, 2/22/66, p. 34, 2/24/66, p. 38; *CDN* 2/18/66, p. 17, 2/24/66, p. 4, 2/25/66, p. 3, 2/26/66, p. 2, 2/28/66, p. 8, 3/3/66, p. 13; *CD* 2/19–25/66, p. 1, 1/26–3/4/66, p. 1; *CCCO Newsletter* vol. 1, #2, 2/66; *Southern Courier* 3/5–6/66, p. 4; *Time* 3/25/66, pp. 18–19. As Eskridge explained, "He didn't like it on the west side . . . That was PR hype that he was living on the west side." At the CUCRL session, Whitney Young pressed King to support the administration on Vietnam. Forman, *Making*, pp. 369–70.

38. *CT* 3/5/66, p. 3, 3/8/66, p. 8, 3/13/66, p. 22; *NYT* 3/5/66, p. 10; *CD* 3/12–18/66, p. 1; King, "Address . . .," 3/12/66, KP; Levison to King, 3/17/66, KP; *CCCO Newsletter* vol. 1, #3, 3/66; *HC* 3/14/66, p. 1; *DFP* 3/16/66, p. C6; *DN* 3/16/66, p. A12; FBI 100-106670-2393, 3/17/66; King, *Nation* 3/14/66, pp. 288–92.

39. *CT* 3/15/66, p. 1, 3/19/66, p. 3, 3/20/66, p. 7; *CST* 3/15/66, p. 4, 3/19/66, p. 3; *CDN* 3/15/66, p. 3; *CD* 3/19–25/66, p. 1; Ramsey Clark Interview (Baker); Katzenbach to Johnson, 3/17/66, Diary Backup 3/18 LBJL; *WP* 3/19/66, p. A2; *NYT* 3/19/66, p. 17, 3/24/66, p. 33. Immediately after meeting with Johnson, King was summoned to an emergency phone call from Young and Blackwell warning that the *Atlanta Journal* had just "broken" the six-month-old federal investigation into Hosea Williams's alleged involvement with the stolen rent-a-car ring. King decided not to make a public comment. Although the next day's *Atlanta Constitution* reported that two "hot" cars had been recovered, one from Daddy King, the embarrassing story was not picked up by the national press. *AJ* 3/18/66, p. 1; FBI 100-438794-1266, 3/18/66; *AC* 3/19/66, p. 1.

40. *CDN* 3/22/66, p. 13, 3/24/66, p. 15, 3/25/66, p. 7, 3/26/66, p. 24; *NYT* 3/24/66, p. 33, 3/25/66, p. 37, 3/29/66, p. 15; *CT* 3/25/66, p. 6, 3/26/66, p. 6, 3/28/66, p. 1, 4/1/66, p. 22; *CST* 3/25/66, p. 4; *Look* 6/14/66, pp. 70–80; *WP* 3/31/66, p. A24; King, "Address . . .," 3/31/66, KP; "Notes of Meeting . . .," 2/16/66, KC; *Christianity & Crisis* 2/21/66, pp. 18–21; *WP* 4/10/66, p. A2, 4/11/66, p. A6; *CD* 4/16–22/66, p. 1; *Commonweal* 4/29/66, pp. 175–77, CRS, "City Profile—Chicago," n.d., CRS FOIA; *Community* 7–8/66, pp. 6–8; Ed Riddick,

Notes & Comment, 4/66; Pitcher, "Chicago Freedom Movement"; Raby Interviews (Garrow; Viorst); Garrow interviews with Bevel, Jackson, Pitcher, Bill Berry, Kale Williams, John McDermott & Don Rose.

41. Lynwood Harris to Sgt. Edward J. McClellan, "Mass Rally, Friendship Baptist Church," 2/25/66, BPI; Garrow, *FBI,* pp. 149–50, 173–77, 286; SAC Atlanta to Director, 4/22/65, 100-438794-305; Abernathy to "Presiding Judge," 6/17/65, KC; SA Thomas E. Burns to SAC, Chicago, "[name deleted]," 3/24/66, 157-953-9; Director to SAC Chicago, 5/4/66, 100-438794-1369. The idea of wiretapping SCLC's Chicago office was rejected. SAC Chicago to Director, 6/8/66, & Director to SAC Chicago, 6/21/66, 100-438794-1484, NR.

42. *CDN* 4/5/66, p. 1, 4/6/66, p. 8, 1/19/66, p. 6; *CA* 4/6/66, p. 16; *CST* 4/6/66, p. 3, 4/8/66, p. 12; *CT* 4/6/66, p. 1, 4/7/66, p. 8, 4/8/66, p. 16; *NYT* 4/6/66, p. 28; *WES* 4/17/66, p. 1; FBI 100-438794-1309, 4/7/66; Stein to King, 3/25/66, KP; Schwarzschild to Young, 3/28/66, LCDC 3; Jack Sisson to Mathew Ahmann, 5/24/66, NCCIJ 20-43; *DN* 3/16/66, p. A12; King, *AN* 2/26/66, p. 1; King to Kennedy, 3/2/66, & King to Jonathan Bingham, 2/28/66, KP; Fager, *Christian Century* 3/16/66, pp. 331–32.

43. Boyte to Blackwell, 3/21/66, & Bennette to Blackwell, 4/3/66, KC; *MN* 4/11/66, p. 1, 4/14/66, p. 13; *MH* 4/12/66, p. B2, 4/13/66, p. A16, 4/14/66, p. A22, 4/15/66, p. B1; SCLC Board Resolutions, 4/13/66, KC; Garrow interviews with Curtis Harris, Milton Reid, D. E. King & Chauncey Eskridge; Mann, *LAT* 4/21/68, p. C9; *CT* 4/14/66, p. 1D-2, 4/18/66, p. 1; *NYT* 4/14/66, p. 1; *WP* 4/14/66, p. A8; King, "Statement," 4/14/66, KP; *CDN* 4/15/66, p. 1; Massoni, "Perspectives"; *CCCO Newsletter* I-4, 4–5/66; Donald Benedict, *Renewal* 5–6/66, p. 22.

44. King, "Statement . . .," 4/20/66, KP; *CT* 4/20/66, p. 1, 4/21/66, p. 1, 4/22/66, p. 5, 4/24/66, p. 1A-8, 4/29/66, p. 1; *CA* 4/21/66, p. 10; *BS* 4/23/66, p. B20; *CST* 4/24/66, p. 3, 4/25/66, p. 30, 4/28/66, p. 4; *NEN* 4/25/66, p. 1; *WP* 4/29/66, p. A1, 5/19/66, p. H3; *NYT* 4/30/66, p. 1, 5/1/66, p. 72, 5/5/66, p. 1; Katzenbach to Johnson, 4/26/66, Ex PL/ST1 Box 31; Garrow, *Protest,* pp. 187–88; Lawson, *Pursuit,* pp. 34–35, 69–77, 106; King, "Statement . . .," 5/4/66, KP; King, *AN* 5/14/66, p. 14; blind memo, "Notes," 5/4/66, WH; *CD* 5/7/66, p. 1; King, *Nation* 3/14/66, p. 290.

45. Horace Sheffield to King, 5/6/66, & Jordan to Williams, 4/28/66, KP; *CT* 5/6/66, p. 1; *SC* 5/9/66, p. B1; Robert F. Jemilo to Young, 4/28/66, KC; Bevel, "Speech," 5/9/66, GM; John H. Fish, *Black Power/White Control* (Princeton, N.J.: Princeton University Press, 1973), p. 120; CRS, "History of Ranger Activity," ca. 10/15/66, CRS FOIA; *CST* 5/9/66, p. 3; *CA* 5/9/66, p. 5; *CDN* 5/10/66, p. 6, 5/12/66, p. 58; *Reporter* 8/11/66, pp. 21–23; Bill Berry Interview (Garrow); Arthur Brazier Interview (Lewis); FBI 100-106670-NR, 5/11/66; Dowdy, "Nonviolence," pp. 119–20; *NYT* 5/16/66, p. 5; *CD* 5/21–27/66, p. 1; *U.S. News* 5/23/66, pp. 34–38; FBI 100-438794-2541, 5/19/66.

46. King, "Ware Lecture," 5/18/66, KP; *MH* 5/19/66, p. A10; Garrow, *FBI,* pp. 177–78; "Outline for Discussion . . .," 5/24/66, KP; Jesse Jackson, "A Strategy to End Slums . . .," 5/31/66, GM; Berry to King & Raby, 5/23/66, KP; Finley, "Open Housing," pp. 6–7; *CT* 5/27/66, p. 1, 6/1/66, p. 1B-3; King, "Statement," 5/27/66, KP; *CDN* 5/27/66, p. 4, 5/28/66, p. 3; Carson, *In Struggle,* pp. 204–205; *NYT* 5/28/66, p. 1; King, "Face the Nation," 5/29/66; *WP* 5/30/66, p. A8; *PI* 5/30/66, p. 3; *CST* 6/1/66, p. 8.

47. Garrow interviews with Meredith, McKissick, Stoney Cooks, Jesse Jackson & Robert Green; Peeks, *Long,* pp. 366–67; Lawson, *Pursuit,* pp. 24–29, 43–49; *Life* 6/3/66, pp. 88–101; Fauntroy Interview (Lewis); *New Republic* 6/18/66, pp. 15–16; *Nation* 6/20/66, pp. 734–37; *NYT* 6/6/66, p. 1, 6/7/66, pp. 1, 28, 6/8/66, p. 1; James Draper to George Culberson, "James Meredith March," 6/6/66, & Paul Jones, "Report . . .," 6/13/66, CRS FOIA; King, *Where,* pp.

23–24; *AC* 6/7/66, p. 1; *MCA* 6/7/66, p. 1; *CT* 6/7/66, p. 1; *CDN* 6/7/66, p. 1; Green, *King*; Lawson, "Meredith March"; Lawson Interview (Beifuss & Thomas II); *New Statesman* 7/1/66, pp. 4–5.

Chapter Nine

1. Lawson, "Meredith"; Lawson Interview (Beifuss & Thomas II); King, *Where*, pp. 24–26; Meredith, "Big Changes"; *Newsweek* 6/20/66, pp. 27–31; *Jet* 6/23/66, pp. 14–27; Carmichael Interviews (Garrow; Viorst); Garrow interviews with Meredith, McKissick, Cleveland Sellers, Hosea Williams & Robert Green; Sellers, *River*, p. 161; *MCA* 6/8/66, p. 1; *WP* 6/8/66, p. A1; *NYT* 6/8/66, p. 1; *CT* 6/8/66, p. 1; *CDN* 6/8/66, pp. 1, 6.

2. King, "Address . . .," 6/7/66, KP; King, *Where*, pp. 26–29; *WP* 6/8/66, p. A1; *Newsweek* 6/20/66, pp. 27–31; *Jet* 6/23/66, pp. 14–27; Carmichael Interviews (Garrow; Viorst); Garrow interviews with Sellers, McKissick, Green, Charles Morgan & Hosea Williams; Sellers, *River*, p. 162; Viorst, *Fire*, pp. 371–72; Wilkins, *Standing*, pp. 315–16; Wilkins to Convention Delegates, 7/5/66, NAACP III-B-374; Morgan, *One Man*, pp. 73–74; Homer Jack, "Black Power." "My definition of nonviolence precludes defensive violence as well as aggressive violence," King had remarked earlier. *CT* 4/7/66, p. 8; also see *Redbook* 1/65, p. 81, & C. Herbert Oliver Interview (Garrow), recounting a 10/15/63 conversation. On the Deacons, see *NYT Magazine* 8/15/65, pp. 10–11, 20–24, *Sepia* 10/67, pp. 10–17, & Raines, *My Soul*, pp. 416–23. SCLC's Bob Green finds Carmichael's and Sellers's explanation of their purposeful strategy quite believable. "They're probably correct," and "probably did deliberately try to offend Roy." They were "very polite to Martin, but awfully offensive" to Wilkins. (Garrow Interview)

3. Carmichael Interview (Viorst); Viorst, *Fire*, p. 372; *WP* 6/8/66, pp. A1, 12; Meredith March "Manifesto," 6/8/66, KP; Wilkins to Delegates, n. 2 above; *MCA* 6/9/66, p. 1; *NYT* 6/9/66, pp. 1, 32; Meredith, "Big Changes"; Meredith Interview (Britton); James Draper to Roger Wilkins et al., "Memphis," 6/8/66, CRS FOIA; Jack Sisson to Mathew Ahmann, "Meredith Mississippi Freedom March," 6/30/66, NCCIJ 20-28.

4. *MCA* 6/9/66, p. 24, 6/10/66, p. 3, 6/11/66, p. 4, 6/12/66, p. 7; *CT* 6/9/66, p. 1; *CDN* 6/8/66, p. 1, 6/9/66, pp. 3, 7, 6/10/66, p. 37, 6/11/66, pp. 1, 4; "Summary of Attainable Goals," n.d., KP; *CD* 6/11–17/66, p. 1; *CA* 6/12/66, p. 5; *NYT* 6/10/66, pp. 1, 34, 6/11/66, p. 1, 6/12/66, p. 1; *CCCO Newsletter* I-5, n.d. [ca. 6/8/66]; Jerome Heilbron, "James Meredith March," 6/13/66, CRS FOIA.

5. *MCA* 6/13/66, p. 10, 6/14/66, p. 16; *NYT* 6/13/66, p. 32, 6/14/66, p. 19; *CT* 6/13/66, p. 17; *CDN* 6/13/66, pp. 1, 5, 6/14/66, p. 42; King, "Remarks at Funeral . . .," 6/12/66, KP; *WP* 6/14/66, p. A1; Levison to King, 5/20/66, KP; FBI NY 100-111180-9-968, 971, 998A, 6/12, 6/15 & 7/12/66.

6. *WP* 6/15/66, p. A1, 6/16/66; *NYT* 6/15/66, p. 1, 6/16/66, p. 35; *CT* 6/15/66, p. 1B-5; *CDN* 6/15/66, p. 37, 6/16/66, p. 5; Jaffe, "Grenada"; King, "Address . . .," 6/14/66, KP; Heilbron, ". . . Meredith March," 6/15 & 6/16/66, CRS FOIA; "Urban Affairs Weekly Report," 6/19/66, AFSC Chicago.

7. Jerome Heilbron, ". . . Meredith March," 6/17/66, CRS FOIA; *NYT* 6/17/66, p. 1, 6/18/66, p. 28; *WP* 6/17/66, p. A1; Garrow interviews with Carmichael, Cleveland Sellers & Stoney Cooks; *WES* 6/17/66, p. 1; *CDN* 6/17/66, p. 1, 6/18/66, p. 1; Carson, *In Struggle*, p. 209; *MCA* 6/18/66, p. 4. A Grenada gas station attendant, seeing King in the passenger seat of a nearby car, also pulled a gun. "'Nigger, I'm gonna blow your god damn brains out.' . . . Martin didn't flinch," Bob Green recalled. Hardly six feet away, "Doc looked at him and said, 'Thank you, thank you,'" until King's driver sped away. Green Interview (Garrow); Green to Marion Eply, Jr., 11/1/66, SCLC KC.

8. *MCA* 6/18/66, p. 14, 6/19/66, p. 18; Garrow interviews with Carmichael, Sellers, McKissick & Green; King, *Where,* pp. 29–30; Forman, *Making,* p. 456; *NYT* 6/18/66, p. 28, 6/19/66, p. 60, 6/20/66, p. 20, 6/21/66, p. 30; *CT* 6/19/66, p. 5; *CDN* 6/20/66, p. 1; Lawrence, "Mississippi Spies," p. 86; FBI NY 100-111180-9-978A, 6/22/66.

9. *CDN* 6/21/66, p. 1; *NYT* 6/22/66, p. 1; Heilbron, ". . . Meredith March," 6/21/66 (3), CRS FOIA; *CT* 6/22/66, p. 1; *MCA* 6/22/66, p. 1; *Time* 7/1/66, pp. 11–13; King in Louw & Wicklein, "King."

10. *NYT* 6/22/66, pp. 1, 25; *MCA* 6/22/66, p. 1; *CDN* 6/22/66, p. 1; *WP* 6/22/66; *WSJ* 6/22/66, p. 1; King, "Address," 6/21/66, Yazoo City, KP.

11. FBI NY 100-111180-9-978A, 6/22/66; King, *Where,* pp. 30–32; Stoney Cooks Interview (Garrow); *NYT* 6/23/66, p. 23; *CT* 6/23/66, p. 8; *CDN* 6/23/66, p. 1; King, "Address," 6/21/66, Yazoo City, KP; CBS, "The March in Mississippi," 6/26/66.

12. *NYT* 6/24/66, p. 1; *MCA* 6/24/66, p. 1; *CT* 6/24/66, p. 1; *CDN* 6/24/66, p. 1; *Newsweek* 7/4/66, pp. 14–16; *New Yorker* 7/16/66, pp. 21–25; *National Catholic Reporter* 7/6/66, p. 12; Henry Schwarzschild Interview (Garrow); McKissick Interviews (Wright; Garrow); King to Johnson, 6/22/66, & Harry McPherson to Johnson, 6/23/66, Ex HU2-7, Box 57. King also reprimanded news photographer Flip Schulke, who had covered the movement for several years, for getting involved in the melee rather than taking pictures of it. "'I can understand you losing your temper and acting that way but we have plenty of people who were doing that anyway. Unless you record the injustice, the world won't know that the child got beaten.' He said, 'We have been beaten all the way along and those children have been beaten and they probably will be beaten again or be hurt in other ways. . . . There were plenty of other people around to jump in but if you would have only stayed and took pictures of what was happening—' . . . King said, 'I'm not being cold blooded about it, but it is so much more important for you to take a picture of us getting beaten up than for you to be another person joining in the fray. . . . Next time do it with your camera, because people will see the pictures.'" Schulke in Spruill, "Southern Exposure," pp. 271–73.

13. *NYT* 6/25/66, p. 1, 6/26/66, p. 1; *CT* 6/25/66, p. 1, 6/26/66, p. 14; *CDN* 6/25/66, p. 1; Young to NUL Board et al., "The Meredith March . . .," 7/5/66, KP; Jim McGuire to Mathew Ahmann, "Group Dynamics . . .," 6/24/66, & ". . . the Meredith Freedom March," 6/29/66, NCCIJ 20-28; A. I. Botnick to Ted Freedman, 6/28/66, ADL; Gloster Current to Charles Evers, 6/29/66, NAACP III-A-256; Good, "Meredith March"; Garrow interviews with Meredith & Cleveland Sellers.

14. *NYT* 6/27/66, p. 1, 6/28/66, p. 23; *CT* 6/27/66, p. 1; *CDN* 6/27/66, p. 1; *Economist* 7/2/66, p. 39; *Christian Century* 7/13/66, pp. 880–81, 7/20/66, pp. 903–904; *Ramparts* 7/66, pp. 51–54; Good, *Troubles,* p. 261; Garrow interviews with Stoney Cooks, Al Raby & Fred Shuttlesworth; CBS, "The March in Mississippi," 6/26/66.

15. *AC* 6/29/66, p. 1; *WP* 6/29/66, p. A10; *NYT* 6/29/66, p. 29; Cleveland Sellers Interview (Garrow); *Reporter* 7/14/66, pp. 12–13; *New Statesman* 7/15/66, p. 75; *U.S. News* 7/18/66, pp. 31–34; *Nation* 8/8/66, pp. 112–17; *Ramparts* 10/66, pp. 4–8; McKee, *King,* p. 144; Wilkins to Delegates, n. 2 above; *NYT* 7/2/66, p. 24.

16. Massoni, "Perspectives"; *Christian Century* 6/22/66, pp. 792–93; *CDN* 6/22/66, p. 19, 6/30/66, pp. 3, 20, 30, 8/8/66, p. 5; *New Republic* 7/2/66, pp. 15–19; Junius Griffin, "Progress Report . . .," 6/28/66, SCLC 149; *CST* 6/30/66, p. 88; *CT* 7/1/66, 7/5/66, p. 1A-12; *NYT* 7/6/66, p. 15; FBI 100-438794-1493 & NY 100-111180-9-987, 7/1/66.

17. *NYT* 7/7/66, p. 22, 7/9/66, p. 1, 7/10/66, p. 54; *CDN* 7/7/66, p. 5, 7/9/66, p. 6; *CT* 7/8/66, p. 4, 7/9/66, p. 7, 7/10/66, p. 3; *CD* 7/9–15/66, p. 1; *WP* 7/10/66, p. A5; Jackson, *Unholy Shadows,* esp. pp. 106–15, 144–69, 254–63; *CD*

10/15–21/66, p. 1. On Grenada, see Jaffe, "Grenada"; *NYT* 7/10/66, p. 35, 7/11/66, p. 1; *JDN* 7/12/66, p. 1; *WP* 7/22/66, p. A13; also see *AC* 7/2/66, p. 9.

18. *CDN* 7/8/66, p. 5; "Chicago Freedom Movement Demands," n.d., Chicago March news release, "Demands . . .," 7/10/66, & "Program of the Chicago Freedom Movement," 7/66, SCLC 150.

19. *WP* 7/11/66, p. A1, 7/12/66, p. Al; *CT* 7/11/66, p. 1, 7/12/66, p. 1; *NYT* 7/11/66, p. 1, 7/12/66, p. 26; *CDN* 7/11/66, p. 1, 7/12/66, p. 4; Garrow interviews with Junius Griffin & Ed Marciniak; *Commonweal* 8/5/66, pp. 492–93; King, "Address . . .," 7/10/66, KP; Eugene Kennedy, *Himself* (New York: Viking Press, 1978), pp. 195, 205; *CST* 7/12/66, p. 1.

20. *CA* 7/12/66, p. 1; AFSC, "Open Communities: A Prospectus . . .," 3/66, & Moyer, "Housing Opportunities Program . . .," 10/66, GM; Pitcher, "Chicago Freedom Movement"; Anderson, "Year," pp. 13–14; *CT* 7/13/66, p. 16; Moyer Interview (Garrow).

21. Coretta King Interview (Mayerson XXV, p. 31); Brown, *Ideology,* pp. 49–53; *Renewal* 9/66, pp. 6–8; *NYT* 7/13/66, p. 39; *CDN* 7/13/66, p. 3; Raby Interview (Garrow); William W. Ellis, *White Ethics and Black Power* (Chicago: Aldine, 1969), pp. 89–91; *Commonweal* 8/5/66, pp. 492–93.

22. *CDN* 7/13/66, p. 3, 7/15/66, pp. 10, 11; Brown, *Ideology,* pp. 53–59; *NYT* 7/14/66, p. 23, 7/15/66, p. 1; *CST* 7/15/66, p. 3; *CA* 7/15/66, p. 3; King, "Address . . .," 7/14/66, KP; *Commonweal* 8/5/66, pp. 492–93; James Orange Interview (Brown).

23. *CT* 7/16/66, p. 1; *NYT* 7/16/66, p. 1, 7/17/66, p. 1; *CDN* 7/16/66, p. 1; Joseph Califano to Lyndon Johnson, 7/15/66, Ex HU2/ST13, Box 26, LBJL; Wilkins in *WP* 4/4/72, p. A18; Wilkins, *Man's Life,* p. 208; Wilkins Interview (Garrow).

24. *NYT* 7/17/66, pp. 1, E5, 7/18/66, p. 17, 7/19/66, p. 19, 7/20/66, p. 23; King, "Statement . . .," 7/17/66, KP.

25. King to Executive Staff, 7/8/66, KP; *Nation* 7/25/66, p. 68; *Commonweal* 8/5/66, pp. 500–503; Rustin, "Black Power"; Cook, "Tragic Myth"; *Dissent* 9–10/66, pp. 472–77; *Commentary* 9/66, pp. 41–46; *Ebony* 11/66, pp. 27–37; FBI 157-6-9-2892, 7/21/66; *NYT* 7/25/66, p. 1, 7/26/66, pp. 22, 23; FBI NY 100-111180-9-1012, 7/26/66; *WP* 7/25/66, p. A1; King, *Progressive* 11/66, pp. 15–16. In private, King told SNCC leaders Carmichael, Sellers, and Ricks, whom he invited over for dinner one evening in Atlanta, that they should not act in ways that would allow the press to highlight or exaggerate the differences between them. (Garrow interviews with Carmichael & Sellers).

26. *CT* 7/22/66, p. 5; *WP* 7/25/66, p. A1; *CDN* 7/22/66, p. 4, 7/23/66, p. 3; *CST* 7/22/66, p. 3; King, "Statement," 7/21/66, KP; Moyer, "Housing Opportunities . . .," n. 20 above; Don Rose, "Open City Background Memo . . .," 7/25/66, GM; Al Raby Interviews (Garrow; Viorst); Garrow interviews with Jesse Jackson, Al Pitcher, Kale Williams, John McDermott, Rose & Stoney Cooks; *CDN* 7/29/66, p. 3; *NYT* 7/30/66, p. 11; *CT* 7/30/66, p. 7; King, "Address . . .," 7/29/66, KP; Sam Dennis, "Field Report: Chicago . . .," 8/1/66, CRS FOIA. Apropos of Young's comments, Bill Berry later noted that "marches don't do much good unless somebody attacks you." (Garrow Interview) As CCCO staffer Al Pitcher wrote later in reflecting on how poorly the movement implemented the idea of linking the open-housing marches to its existing ghetto-organizing efforts, which Pitcher thought should remain the focus, "the effort to escalate that action fast, because King wanted it escalated in the light of many things, may have destroyed that possibility because there was not enough staff or time to develop these community organizations." As Pitcher recalled the decision, "King came to us and said that August was coming and that it was the month of riots. We had to have an alternative to them. His suggestion for stepped up action also was probably based on other maintenance needs as well as the fear that they [SCLC] would be associated with riots. So the action committee changed its pattern of develop-ment for the open housing action. That was the reason for the proposed all-night vigil in Gage Park, the beginning of the summer tension—a direct result of King's personal interference. SCLC made the decision for the most part to escalate. In the action committee Bevel presented it as if it were an idea that needed to be followed through, not as King's request. As a result, we escalated as over against what we had planned to do." "Chicago Freedom Movement," pp. 16, 27. Finley writes that "the decision to hold the all-night vigil . . . was chiefly Dr. King's; he felt that it was time to escalate. . . . A violent response of some sort was antici-pated." "Open Housing," p. 28.

27. *CT* 7/31/66, p. 8, 8/1/66, p. 1, 8/2/66, p. 1A-3, 8/3/66, p. 1A-2; Dennis, "Field Report," n. 26 above; *CST* 8/1/66, p. 5; *NYT* 8/1/66, p. 1, 8/2/66, p. 12; *Ramparts* 11/66, pp. 13–18; Williams to O. W. Wilson, 8/2/66, Williams; *N&O* 8/1/66, p. 1; Ed Marciniak Interview (Garrow).

28. *CT* 8/3/66, p. 1A-2, 8/4/66, p. 10, 8/5/66, p. 10, 8/6/66, p. 1; *NYT* 8/4/66, p. 15, 8/6/66, p. 1; *CDN* 8/4/66, p. 1, 8/5/66, pp. 3–4, 8/6/66, p. 1; King, "Address . . .," 8/4/66, KP; *CST* 8/5/66, p. 4; *CD* 8/6–12/66, p. 1; Raby Interview (Garrow).

29. *NYT* 8/7/66, p. 47, 8/8/66, p. 1, 8/9/66, p. 25; *CT* 8/7/66, p. 1, 8/8/66, pp. 1, 2, 8/9/66, pp. 3, 14; *CDN* 8/9/66, p. 1; *CD* 8/13–19/66, p. 1.

30. *NYT* 8/9/66, p. 24; McGraw, "Interview with Young," p. 326; *JCL* 8/8/66, p. 1, 8/10/66, p. 1; *JDN* 8/8/66, p. 1, 8/9/66, p. 1, 8/10/66, p. 5; Boyte to King, 5/23/66 & 8/2/66, KC; *WES* 8/11/66, p. A4, 8/12/66, p. A5; Garrow interviews with Vivian, Green & Blackwell; James Laue to George Culberson et al., 7/12/66, CRS FOIA; King to Blackwell, 8/16/66, KC; Jim McGuire to Mathew Ahmann, "SCLC Convention," 8/25/66, NCCIJ 20-43; *Newsweek* 8/22/66, pp. 58–59; *National Guardian* 8/27/66, p. 5; Reynolds, *Jackson*, p. 65; *CDN* 8/10/66, p. 1; *CT* 8/10/66, p. 1, 8/11/66, p. 1; *NYT* 8/10/66, p. 28, 8/11/66, p. 23; *CCCO Newsletter* I-6, n.d. [8/66]; Finley, "Open Housing," p. 30; Maria Pappalardo, "Chicago Logs," 8/12 & 8/13/66, AFSC.

31. Connolly, "Chicago," pp. 17–18, quoting 8/9 Commission minutes; Gar-row interviews with Callahan & Ed Marciniak; *CT* 8/10/66, p. 1, 8/11/66, p. 1; *CDN* 8/10/66, p. 1, 8/11/66, pp. 1, 10; *Commonweal* 11/11/66, pp. 159–63.

32. SCLC Board Resolutions, 8/11/66, KC; Levison, "Draft Resolution on Vietnam," n.d., KC; FBI 100-438794-1559, 8/12/66, NY 100-111180-9-1030A, 8/13/66; King, "President's Annual Report . . ." and "Excerpts from an Ad-dress . . .," 8/11/66, KP; *JCL* 8/11/66, p. 1; *JDN* 8/11/66, p. 1, 8/12/66, p. 2; *WP* 8/11/66, p. A16; *NYT* 8/12/66, p. 16; *CDN* 8/12/66, p. 6.

33. *CT* 8/12/66, p. 1, 8/13/66, pp. 1, 2, 8/14/66, p. 1, 8/15/66, p. 1, 8/16/66, p. 1A-1, 8/17/66, p. 1; *CDN* 8/12/66, p. 1, 8/13/66, p. 1, 8/15/66, p. 1, 8/27/66, p. 1; *NYT* 8/13/66, p. 8, 8/14/66, p. 48, 8/15/66, p. 1, 8/16/66, p. 16, 8/17/66, p. 23; Connolly, "Chicago," pp. 19–20; Chicago Conference on Religion and Race Ex-ecutive Board Minutes, 8/16/66, CCRR; Garrow interviews with Callahan, Ed Marciniak, John McDermott, Kale Williams, Al Raby, Al Pitcher & Don Rose.

34. *CDN* 8/17/66, p. 1, 8/27/66, p. 1; McKnight, "The Summit Negotiations," pp. 1–14; Aaron, "Proposals . . .," 8/17/66; "Statement of the Chicago Real Es-tate Board . . .," 8/17/66; Chicago Freedom Movement, "To Achieve Jus-tice . . .," 8/17/66; Connolly, "Chicago," pp. 26–27; Garrow interviews with John McKnight, Al Raby & Ed Marciniak.

35. *CT* 8/18/66, p. 1; Connolly, "Chicago," pp. 27–28; McKnight, "The Sum-mit Negotiations," pp. 14–29; Real Estate Board "Statement," 8/17/66; Garrow interviews with Marciniak, Ayers, Raby, Bevel, John McKnight & John McDer-mott; *CA* 8/18/66, p. 1; *NYT* 8/18/66, p. 31; *CDN* 8/18/66, p. 1, 8/27/66, p. 1; *CD* 8/20–26/66, p. 1.

36. *CDN* 8/18/66, p. 1; *CT* 8/19/66, p. 1; *NYT* 8/19/66, p. 19; Garrow inter-views with Raby, McDermott, Bill Berry, Bevel, Kale Williams & Don Rose;

Maria Pappalardo, "Chicago Logs," 8/18/66, AFSC; King, "Address . . .," 8/18/66, KP.

37. *CDN* 8/19/66, pp. 1, 11, 8/20/66, p. 1, 8/27/66, p. 1; *Chicago* v. *King,* 11 *RRLR* 1695, 8/19/66; Garrow interviews with Ayers, Raby, Bevel, Berry, McDermott, Williams, Callahan & Marciniak; *CT* 8/20/66, p. 1; *CST* 8/20/66, p. 2; *NYT* 8/20/66, p. 1.

38. *CT* 8/21/66, p. 1, 8/22/66, p. 1; *NYT* 8/21/66, pp. 47, E5, 8/22/66, p. 1; Maria Pappalardo, "Chicago Logs," 8/19 & 8/20/66, AFSC; *CST* 8/21/66, p. 42; King, "Meet the Press," 8/21/66, KP; *CDN* 8/22/66, pp. 1, 3; *Nation* 3/27/67, pp. 398–401.

39. *CT* 8/23/66, p. 1, 8/24/66, pp. 1, 3; *NYT* 8/23/66, p. 1, 8/24/66, p. 34; Garrow interviews with Ayers, McDermott, Williams, Berry, Bevel, Raby & Marciniak; Ayers notes for "Leadership Council Luncheon," 5/14/80, Ayers; *CDN* 8/23/66, p. 1; Maria Pappalardo, "Chicago Logs," 8/22 & 8/23/66, AFSC.

40. *CDN* 8/24/66, p. 1, 8/25/66, pp. 1, 3, 8/27/66. p. 1; *WSJ* 8/24/66, p. 10; *CT* 8/25/66, p. 1, 8/26/66, pp. 1, 20; *NYT* 8/25/66, p. 24, 8/26/66, p. 16; Connolly, "Chicago," pp. 34–35; Garrow interviews with Ayers, McDermott, Williams, Berry, Bevel, Raby & Marciniak; Maria Pappalardo, "Chicago Logs," 8/24 & 8/25/66, AFSC. While Ayers recalls only Commonwealth Edison lawyer Hubert Nexon helping him prepare the draft, Human Relations Commission Director, and Daley deputy, Ed Marciniak recollects that he joined Ayers and Nexon in writing the text, and then obtained Daley's approval. "I took in a draft of the Ayers statement to the Mayor, read it to him. . . . I don't think the Mayor changed one word. . . . The fact that Tom Ayers was willing to say yes to it was very important" for Daley, who "had a lot of confidence in Tom." Ayers's approval "took care of a lot of the mayor's problems." (Garrow Interview)

41. *CDN* 8/26/66, p. 1, 8/27/66, p. 1; Connolly, "Chicago," pp. 36–37; Garrow interviews with Raby, Berry, McDermott, Williams, Bevel, Ayers, Al Pitcher & Marciniak; Ayers, "Report of the Subcommittee . . .," 8/26/66, Massoni; McKnight, "The Summit Negotiations," pp. 30–36.

42. McKnight, "The Summit Negotiations," pp. 36–41; McGraw, "Interview with Young," p. 326; Al Pitcher Interview (Garrow).

43. King, "Statement . . .," 8/26/66, KP; *CDN* 8/26/66, p. 1, 8/27/66, p. 1; *NYT* 8/27/66, p. 1, 8/28/66, pp. 50, 51, 55; *CT* 8/27/66, p. 1, 8/28/66, p. 1; *CD* 8/27–9/2/66, p. 1; Brown, *Ideology*, pp. 63–65; Sam Dennis, "Chicago," 8/29/66, CRS FOIA; Maria Pappalardo, "Chicago Logs," 8/29/66, AFSC.

44. King, "The Good Samaritan," 8/28/66, KP.

Chapter Ten

1. Tom Offenburger Notes, 8/31/66, Young; *CDN* 9/2/66, p. 4; *NYT* 8/29/66, p. 14, 8/30/66, p. 28, 8/31/66, p. 32; King, *Where*, p. 45; Chicago SNCC leaflet, "Who Speaks for the Black Man in Chicago?," Young; *CST* 8/30/66, p. 16, 9/1/66, p. 1; *CT* 9/1/66; *CD* 9/10–16/66, p. 2; Brown, *Ideology*, pp. 64–70; Garrow interviews with Stoney Cooks & Robert Green.

2. Brown, *Ideology*, pp. 71–73; *CDN* 9/2/66, pp. 4, 35, 9/3/66, p. 2; CBS Reports, "Black Power, White Backlash," 9/27/66, p. 20; Massoni, "Perspectives"; "Notes on Follow-Up Action . . .," 8/29/66, & "Report of the Subcommittee on Structure of Follow-Up Body . . .," 9/7/66, CCR&R; Berry, *Open Housing*.

3. *NYT* 9/3/66, p. 48, 9/4/66, p. 54, 9/5/66, p. 18, 9/6/66, p. 27; Lucas Interview (Britton); Lucas in Travis, *Autobiography*, pp. 250–53; McDermott Interview (Garrow).

4. *CDN* 9/6/66, p. 5, 9/8/66, p. 47, 9/9/66, p. 9, 9/10/66, p. 2; *NYT* 9/7/66, p. 38; "Report of the Subcommittee . . .," n. 2 above; *CA* 9/8/66, p. 5; *Time* 9/9/66,

p. 22; *Christian Century* 9/7/66, pp. 1071–72; *Nation* 9/19/66, pp. 237–42; *Christianity & Crisis* 9/19/66, pp. 200–201; *New Republic* 9/17/66, pp. 9–10.

5. Bill Berry Interview (Garrow); *AC* 9/8/66, p. 6; Carson, *In Struggle*, pp. 225–26; FBI 100-438794-1965, NY 100-111180-9-1057A, 9/9/66; Allen Interview (Hatcher); *NYT* 9/12/66, p. 49, 9/13/66, p. 26; *CDN* 9/12/66, p. 9; *AC* 9/13/66, p. 1.

6. *NYT* 8/9/66, p. 1, 8/10/66, p. 1, 8/11/66, p. 21; Bibler to Williams, 8/13/66, Young; Jaffe, "Grenada"; Southern Regional Council, *Justice in Grenada, MS.* (Atlanta: SRC, 10/66); Willie Bolden Interview (Garrow); *NYT* 9/13, p. 1, 9/14, p. 1, 9/15, p. 1, 9/16, p. 34, 9/17, p. 26, 9/18, p. 1, 9/19, p. 1, 9/20, p. 34, 9/21/66, p. 1; *CDN* 9/20/66, p. 18; Katzenbach to Johnson, 9/9/66, Ex LE/HU 2, Box 65; *AC* 9/20/66, p. 8; *NYT* 9/20/66, p. 35.

7. *CT* 9/16/66, p. II-20; *WP* 9/16/66, p. A8; Operation Breadbasket Steering Committee "Minutes," 9/16/66, GM; FBI 100-438794-1571, NY 100-111180-9-1057A, 9/9/66; Levison to King (2), 9/8/66, KP; *CO* 9/22/66, p. C1; *CD* 9/24–30/66, p. 1; King, "The Prodigal Son," 9/4/66, Ebenezer, KP; King, "Beyond Discovery, Love," 9/25/66, Dallas, KP; *NYT* 9/26/66, p. 35; *CST* 9/26/66, p. 5; *PEB* 9/27/66, p. 3. Similar to King's 1/17/63 remarks (see frontispiece), the 9/25 comments also mirrored a 7/6/65 King address to a United Church of Christ convention in Chicago.

8. *AC* 9/29/66, p. 21, 10/1/66, p. 18, 10/6/66, p. 1; *AJ* 10/4/66, p. 7, 10/6/66, p. 2; *CST* 10/1/66, p. 42; *NYT* 10/1/66, p. 15; FBI 100-438794-1583, NY 100-111180-9-1077A, 9/29/66, NY 100-111180-9-1079A, 10/1/66; *NYT* 10/10/66, p. 1; Brink & Harris, *Black and White*, p. 68; *AC* 10/10/66, p. 9; *AJ* 10/10/66, p. 7; *PI* 10/11/66, pp. 6, 9.

9. *AJ* 10/13/66, p. 25, 10/14/66, p. 1; *AC* 10/14/66, p. 1; *NYT* 10/14/66, pp. 27, 35; King, "Statement," 10/14/66, KP. In private, Carmichael and his SNCC colleagues were quite aware of, and happy with, the ambiguous connotations of "black power." "The intent, initially, was not to get it boxed into a particular definition," Cleveland Sellers explained. There was a purposeful "SNCC effort *not* to give it a definition," so that "it meant everything to everybody. . . . There was a deliberate attempt to make it ambiguous." (Garrow interviews with Carmichael & Sellers.) Also see Carmichael, "What We Want," and "Toward Black Liberation"; plus *Newsweek* 8/22/66, pp. 33–35; *Esquire* 1/67, pp. 130–35; *Dissent* 1–2/67, pp. 69–79.

10. *NYT* 10/15/66, p. 14; *AC* 10/15/66, p. 5; *WP* 10/15/66, p. A6; FBI 100-106670-2740, NY 100-111180-9-1093A, 10/15/66; Blackwell to King, 10/14/66, KP; *NYT* 10/17/66, p. 42; *AC* 10/17/66, p. 9; *AJ* 10/17/66, p. 8; *Economist* 10/22/66, pp. 370–73; *DFP* 10/17/66, p. A3.

11. FBI NY 100-111180-9-1096, 1097A, 10/18–19/66; Wesley Hotchkiss to Leslie Dunbar et al., 9/7/66, & Hotchkiss to Andrew Young, 10/6/66, KC; Garrow interviews with Robert Green & Bill Stein; *AC* 10/20/66, p. 14, 10/21/66, p. 15; *BN* 10/20/66, p. 22; *NYT* 10/21/66, p. 28, 10/25/66, p. 32; *Southern Courier* 10/22–23/66, p. 1; Nelson et al. to Moore, 10/26/66, WH; Tom Offenburger Interview (Shannon). Stanley Levison objected to some of Stein's sermon selections. "When he heard some of the tapes that I was going to use, which was Martin preaching in a black church, for instance, he didn't want that to go on for all the public to hear, so I said, 'why?' And he said, 'That's the black idiom,'" which Levison feared would not play well with potential northern contributors. Stein responded, '"Yeah, that's Martin Luther King,'" and got King's support. (Garrow Interview)

12. *CDN* 10/21/66, p. 37; *CCCO Newsletter* I-7, Fall 1966; *CDN* 9/30/66, p. 3; Moyer, "Report of the Follow-Up Committee . . .," 10/23/66; Moyer Interview (Garrow); Paul Mundy et al., "Implementation of 'Summit Accord' . . .," 11/3/66, CCR&R; *CDN* 10/28/66, p. 1, 10/29/66, p. 37, 11/1/66, p. 1; *CST* 10/29/66, p. 3; *WES* 10/29/66, p. A16; *NYT* 10/29/66, p. 17, 11/2/66, p. 25; *CDN*

11/2/66, p. 3, 11/3/66, p. 9; *CT* 11/2/66, p. 1, 11/4/66, p. 13; *CA* 11/3/66, p. 4; *WSJ* 11/16/66, p. 1; *PP* 11/2/66, p. 1; *PPG* 11/3/66, p. 1; *NYT* 11/3/66, p. 29; *CST* 11/4/66, p. 2; *CD* 11/5–11/66, p. 1, 11/12–18/66, p. 1; King, "Statement . . .," 11/9/66, KP; *NYT* 11/10/66, p. 30; *WP* 11/10/66, p. B4; King, ". . . .Lecture," 11/9/66, Howard Univ., KP.

   13. *NYDN* 11/8/66, p. 21; *NYT* 11/8/66, p. 23; *WP* 11/8/66, p. 3; *WES* 11/9/66, p. A1; Garrow, *FBI*, p. 179; FBI 100-438794-1643, 1659, NY 100-111180-9-1117A, 11/8/66, 100-106670-2764, 11/9/66; King, *Ebony* 10/66, pp. 27–34; *BS* 11/12/66, p. B20; *AA* 11/26/66; *New South,* Winter 1966, pp. 93–103; *Ramparts* 12/66, pp. 39–43; FBI 100-438794-1645, 1668, 11/3 & 16/66; King, "Address . . .," 11/14/66, KP. In his handwritten outline for that speech, King wrote "we must honestly face the fact that the movement must address itself to the restructuring of the whole of American society. . . . We must develop programs that will drive the nation to a guaranteed annual income. . . . More and more we must see the movement and the peace issue as one. We must question the very values upon which America thrives. Three evils—racism, materialism + militarism. They are unseparable twins." King notes, AY. King understood a point of Weber's: "The charismatic leader gains and maintains authority solely by proving his strength in life. If he wants to be a prophet, he must perform miracles." H. H. Gerth & C. Wright Mills, eds., *From Max Weber* (New York: Oxford University Press, 1946), pp. 248–49.

   14. FBI 100-438794-1668, 11/16/66; "Frogmore—Wednesday Evaluation Session," [11/16/66], SCLC 49; Garrow interviews with Hosea Williams, Samuel Wells & Dana Swan; *Newsweek* 11/28/66, pp. 30–31; *CST* 11/18/66, p. 32; *CDN* 11/18/66, p. 8; *HC* 11/21/66, p. 8; Jackson to King, "Fund Raising in the Context of Economic Development," 11/2/66, KC; SCLC press releases, 11/23 & 12/16/66; *WES* 11/25/66, p. B6; *NYT* 11/26/66, p. 32; *CST* 11/26/66, p. 5; *WP* 11/27/66, p. A14; Massoni, "Perspectives," esp. pp. 22–24; *Commerce* 4/68, pp. 24–25, 49–50; Operation Breadbasket "Minutes," 12/2 & 12/16/66, GM; *AC* 11/28/66, p. 18; *AJ* 11/28/66, p. 14. At Frogmore, King initially erupted at Hosea Williams's reluctance to go to Chicago. " 'All right, just forget it, forget it. Don't do nothing, let's forget it.' And it really got to me when I saw I had upset him and I said, 'Doc, you know I'll go.' 'No, no, just forget it.' I said, 'I'll go. I'll go.' So finally he cooled down and agreed I would go." Williams Interview (Garrow)

   15. *CDN* 12/2/66, p. 4, 12/3/66, p. 32; *CST* 12/3/66, p. 5; *CD* 12/3–9/66, p. 1; FBI 100-438794-1680, 11/30/66; King, "Address . . .," 12/6/66, KP.

   16. FBI 100-438794-1680, 1692, 11/30 & 12/12/66, NY 100-111180-9-1145, 12/6/66; King, "Statement and Testimony," in U.S. Congress, Senate, Committee on Government Operations, *Federal Role in Urban Affairs—Hearings Before the Subcommittee on Executive Reorganization,* 89th Cong., 2nd Sess., pp. 2969–95; *WES* 12/15/66, 12/16/66, p. 1; *NYT* 12/16/66, p. 33; *WP* 12/16/66, p. A1; *CT* 12/16/66, p. I-8. King also emphasized the war question at a Thanksgiving dinner to which he invited SCLC aides Stoney Cooks and Tom Offenburger plus New York friends Arthur and Marian Logan. "All we discussed . . . was the Vietnam war." King "was obsessed with the war." "The entire Thanksgiving dinner was an argument with Arthur and Marian Logan and why Vietnam had to be a focus of the civil rights movement." Cooks Interviews (Leventhal; Garrow).

   17. *NYT* 12/14/66, p. 42; Young to Ira Sandperl, 12/21/66, KC; Young to Board Members et al., n.d. [ca. late 12/66], Young; Garrow interviews with Young, Dana Swan, Stoney Cooks & Al Raby; King, "Statement," 12/20/66, KP; *CDN* 12/20/66, p. 30; *CT* 12/21/66, p. 9; Katzenbach to Johnson, "Civil Rights Activities in Chicago," 2/21/67, Ex HU2/ST13, Box 26; "Minutes of Steering Committee . . .," 12/28/66, & "Staff Meeting" transcript, 12/14/66, SCLC 171. Young added in that second letter that "we must be able to do in a dozen or more major cities what we did in Birmingham . . ."

18. *North & South* 1/67; FBI NY 100-111180-9-1164A, 12/25/66, FBI 100-106670-2809, 2810, 2811, 1/3–5/67, FBI NY 100-111180-9-1175A, 1/5/67; Arthur Waskow to Lowenstein, 11/17/66, AL; Thomas to King, 12/31/66, NT 108; Garrow conversation with Coffin; Thomas Powers, *The War at Home* (New York: Grossman, 1973), p. 272; FBI NY 100-111180-9-1179, & 100-106670-2814, 1/9/67, FBI NY 100-111180-9-1184, 1161A, 1/14/67 & 12/22/66; Abernathy to Richard Battle, 1/17/67, KC; Reddick to King, et al., 1/16/67, KP. Also see Clifford Alexander to Johnson, 1/11/67, Louis Martin Name File LBJL. King also called Levison on 12/25/67; FBI NY 100-111180-9-1529A. Thomas had had a King candidacy in mind for several months. Assuming no strong antiwar presidential candidate emerged in Democratic or Republican ranks, Thomas wrote Sanford Gottlieb on 7/12/66, "It may be necessary to have some kind of a third party candidate who could be run. . . . Homer Jack once suggested Martin Luther King but I am not sure he could or should try to undertake the job in view of his peculiar obligations to the civil rights movement." On 11/14/66, Thomas raised the third-party option in a letter to SANE Executive Director Donald Keys. "The one man I think of in this connection is the Rev. Martin Luther King, Jr., whose name and deeds will rally such a coalition, and whose stand on civil rights and the war on poverty will speak loudly for us." NT 134.

19. Garrow interviews with Lee, McDonald, Coretta King & Bevel; Levison Interviews (Lewis; Stein); Lee in Mark Lane & Dick Gregory, *Code Name 'Zorro'* (Englewood Cliffs, N.J.: Prentice-Hall, 1977), pp. 53–54; Coretta King Interview (Mayerson XXVII, p. 32); King, *My Life*, p. 303; Pepper, "The Children"; *Ebony* 6/67, pp. 112–19; Spring Mobilization "Working Committee Minutes," 1/3, 1/9 & 1/13/67, NMC 1; Halstead, *Out Now*, pp. 261–62; Zaroulis & Sullivan, *Who Spoke Up*, pp. 96, 110; *NYWJT* 4/17/67, p. 1; *WDN* 4/17/67, pp. 7, 16; FBI NY 100-111180-9-1183, 1189A, 1/13 & 1/19/67; *NYT* 1/28/67, p. 3; *Mobilizer* I-1, 12/19/66, & 1-2, 2/6/67; *Chicago Reader* 7/20/84, p. 1, 22–30. As early as 1/20/67, however, Bevel was telling Spring Mobe colleagues he already had King's agreement to endorse and speak at the demonstration, as well as "to join a pilgrimage to Vietnam" that Bevel envisioned a group of notables undertaking sometime after 4/15. Bevel also "pledged the official full cooperation of the SCLC and promised maximum turnout of its membership and followers" on 4/15. Abner Grunauer to Donald Keys, "Report" on 1/20 Spring Mobilization Committee meeting, & "Minutes," 1/20/67, NT 138 & 137. As Keys wisely noted in a later memo, "There appears to be no present confirmation" of Bevel's claims. Keys to National Board, "SANE Participation in Spring Mobilization," n.d. [ca. 2/5/67], NT 137.

20. *NYT* 1/16/67, p. 22; *CDN* 1/19/67, p. 28; *Newsweek* 2/13/67, pp. 37–38; Williams Interview (Garrow); FBI 100-438794-1753, 1761, 1/19 & 1/24/67, NY 100-111180-9-1204A, 1205A, 2/3 & 2/4/67; FBI 100-438794-1772, 2831 & 2834, 2/8, 13 & 15/67, NY 100-111180-9-1214A, 1216A, 2/13 & 2/15/67; King to Popper, n.d. [ca. 2/13/67], HP; FBI NY 100-111180-9-1221A, 2/20/67, FBI 100-106670-2836, 2835, 2/20 & 24/67. Levison and King also discussed what label to use for King's economic view, with King accepting Levison's recommendation of "socialized democrat." "I was trying to avoid the word 'socialism,'" King explained. "People have so many hangups to it and respond so emotionally and irrationally to it." FBI NY 100-111180-9-1228A, 2/27/67.

21. FBI NY 100-111180-9-1219, 2/18/67; Spring Mobilization "Working Committee Minutes," 2/16 & 3/2/67, NMC 1; King, "The Casualties of the War in Vietnam," 2/25/67, KP. King's phraseology in the 2/18 conversation leaves open the possibility that, contrary to Lee's memory, King encountered the *Ramparts* article upon returning from Jamaica, and not earlier. In King's handwritten outline for the 2/25 speech, he wrote that "we must combine the fervor of the civil rights movement with the peace movement." Young.

22. *NYT* 2/26/67, pp. 1, 3; *LAT* 2/26/67, p. 1; FBI NY 100-111180-9-1228A, 2/27/67; *NYT* 2/7/67, p. 26; Christopher Edley to John Coleman, 2/6/67, Ford Log File 67-82, & Edley to Young, 3/14/67, Ford 67-580; SCLC to Ford, "A Request for Funds to Support a Project in Basic Adult Education and Leadership Training . . .," 3/1/67, KC; *PPG* 3/2/67, p. 9; *MAT* 3/3/67, p. 1; *WP* 4/16/67, p. A1; *CPD* 4/14/67; Halberstam, "Second Coming," p. 49; Harry Wachtel Interview (Garrow); Wachtel in Oates, *Trumpet,* p. 432; Whitney Young Interview (Baker).
23. FBI 100-438794-1796, 1801, 3/1 & 3/6/67, FBI NY 100-111180-9-1235A, 3/6/67; Garrow interviews with Green, Bevel, Jones, Rustin, Robinson, Young & Wachtel; Spring Mobilization Steering Committee & Working Committee Minutes, 3/10/67, NMC 1; Young to Bevel et al., 3/14/67, AL; William vanden Heuvel letter, 2/17/67, King Name File LBJL; Norman Thomas to Benjamin Spock, 3/10/67, R. J. Neuhaus to Spock, 3/16/67, BS 25; Thomas to Dave Dellinger, 3/17/67, & Thomas to Andrew Young, 3/17/67, NT 109; *WP* 4/26/67, p. B15; Young to vanden Heuvels, 3/10/67, KC.
24. Williams to King, "SCLC," 3/8/67, KC; Roosevelt Barnett Interview (Wright); SAC Atlanta to Director, 3/15/67, 100-438794-unknown; King to Edward O. Jones, 4/3/63, KC; FBI 100-438794-1829, & NY 100-111180-9-1254, 3/25/67; Garrow interviews with Dana Swan, Fauntroy, Lowery, Young, Cooks & Jackson; "Proposed Structure of the Department of Special Programs and Economic Development," 3/13/67, GM; Cooks to King, "SCLC and Its Future Structure and Program," n.d., KC; Massoni, "Perspectives," pp. 33–34.
25. Garrow interviews with Osburn, Hosea Williams & Stoney Cooks; FBI 157-6-27-515, 516, 8/25 & 8/26/66; *LCJ* 1/24/67, p. B1; Horton, *Not Without Struggle,* pp. 122–31; *HC* 3/13/67, p. 17; *WP* 3/13/67, p. A1; Marvin Watson to Johnson, 2/24/67 & 3/13/67, & John Criswell to Watson, 3/23/67, King Name File LBJL; Young Interview (Baker); Spring Mobilization "Working Committee Minutes," 3/16/67, NMC 1; *NYT* 3/17/67, p. 4; *Mobilizer* I-3, 3/18/67.
26. *CDN* 3/23/67, p. 1, 3/24/67, p. 1; *NYT* 3/24/67, p. 1; *WP* 3/24/67, p. A8; *AC* 3/24/67, p. 57; Operation Breadbasket Steering Committee Minutes, 3/17/67, GM; King, "Press Conference . . .," 3/24/67, KP; King, *CSM* 3/14/67, p. 9; *CT* 3/25/67, p. I-4; Chicago Freedom Movement Delegates to Leadership Council, "Implementation of Summit Agreement . . .," n.d. [ca. late 2/67], & CFM Statement, 3/28/67, LC 37.
27. King, "Address to Operation Breadbasket . . .," & "Address to Peace Parade . . .," 3/25/67, KP; *WP* 3/26/67, p. A1; *CT* 3/26/67, p. I-3; *CST* 3/26/67, p. 1; *NYT* 3/26/67, p. 44; Spock to R. J. Neuhaus, 3/30/67, BS 25; Paul Miller & Marjorie Rosenberg to SANE National Board, 4/14/67, NT 134; WBBM-TV Editorial, "Dr. King's Usefulness," 3/29/67, KC; *AC* 4/1/67, p. 4; FBI NY 100-111180-9-1254, 1256A, 3/25 & 3/27/67; Richard R. Fernandez to Young, 3/21/67, CALC II-3; Young, *Christian Century* 5/3/71, pp. 80–82; Frank, *American Death,* p. 412. A February mailing to 90,000 SCLC contributors had generated $200,000 by the end of March. "National Direct Mail Fund Raising Program," 3/28/67, SCLC 133.
28. *LCJ* 3/29/67, p. 1, 3/30/67, p. B1; Tape of SCLC Board Meeting, 3/29–30/67, KC; Garrow interviews with Addine Drew, Maude Ballou, Dorothy Cotton, Rochelle Horowitz, Robert Williams, Mose Pleasure, Thomas Kilgore, Cornish Rogers & Milton Reid; Mrs. King Tape (KC); Joseph Lowery, *AC* 1/14/78, p. B1; Duckett, "Five Years," p. 46; Young, "Remembering King"; Coretta King Interview (Mayerson III, pp. 59, 63); Coretta King in *AJC Magazine* 2/1/76; Cotton in *Ebony,* 4/84, pp. 33–40; Lee Interview (Burrell); Jackson, "Annual Report . . . Chicago's Operation Breadbasket . . .," 3/67, Bennette, "Operation Breadbasket," [3/67], Public Relations Department, "Report to the Board," 3/29–30/67, & Cooks, "Annual Report, Chicago Project," 3/67, KC; *NYT* 4/2/67, p. 1.

29. SCLC Board Meeting Tape, 3/30/67, KC; Henry Interview (Baker, pp. 15–16); Garrow interviews with Joseph Lowery, Milton Reid, Dorothy Cotton & Chauncey Eskridge; *LCJ* 3/31/67, p. A1; *AC* 4/1/67, p. 11. Though no document supports it, Hosea Williams recalls a formal vote that went against King. "That's the only argument Martin ever lost with that Board. . . . They beat him by 35 to 15. His own father voted against him." Williams Interview (Leventhal).

30. FBI 100-106670-2874, 4/4/67; *NYT* 4/5/67, p. 1; King, "Beyond Vietnam," 4/4/67, KP. Large segments of the speech were drafted by Vincent Harding, smaller portions by John Maguire and Andrew Young. Garrow interviews with Maguire & Young; "Interview with Vincent Harding," in MARHO, *Visions of History* (New York: Pantheon, 1983), pp. 219–44, at 228–29; Garrow conversation with Harding.

31. FBI 100-106670-2877, 4/5/67; *NYT* 4/6/67, p. 10; *WP* 4/6/67, pp. A10, A20; *NYT* 4/7/67, p. 34; *PC* 4/15/67, p. 6; *NYT* 4/10/67, p. 2; *Life* 4/21/67, p. 4; FBI NY 100-111180-9-1268A, 4/8/67. Also see *AJ* 4/5/67, p. 36; *AC* 4/6/67, p. 4, 4/7/67, p. 4, 4/11/67, p. 4; *Newsweek* 5/1/67, p. 17. As Coretta King later put it, "There were times—especially when the criticisms came against him on his Vietnam position—that he naturally would begin to evaluate . . . his whole image and just what people thought of him in terms of his leadership, whether or not he could continue to be an effective leader." (Mayerson Interview XXVII, p. 24)

32. *DFP* 4/6/67; *Christian Century* 4/19/67, pp. 492–93; *Nation* 4/24/67, pp. 515–16; *Christianity & Crisis* 5/1/67, pp. 89–90; McPherson Interview (Baker); Roche to Johnson, 4/5/67 & 4/18/67, Rustin Name File & Watson 29 LBJL; Charles DeBenedetti, *Peace and Change* 9 (Spring 1983): 31–41; Christian to Johnson, 4/8/67, King Name File LBJL; Rowan, *CPD* 4/14/67; Hoover to Mildred Stegall, 4/19/67, 100-106670-2895; Lawson Interview (Leventhal I, p. 8); *NYT* 4/12/67, p. 3; *NT* 4/8/67; *NB* 4/8/67; King, "Three Dimensions of a Complete Life," 4/9/67, KP. Levison remained shy about any *public* association with King, as he once explained to Jones. "You know with all the attention that is bound to be focused on this now, I don't believe I should go. There will be people that will see me there and they are going to ask, 'What's my role, what's my background,' and some extraneous things can be introduced, and it might not do the movement any good." FBI NY 100-111180-9-1117A, 11/8/66.

33. *NYT* 4/11/67, p. 1; *AC* 4/11/67, p. 2; *WP* 4/11/67, p. A6; *NYT* 4/13/67, p. 1; King, "Press Conference," 4/12/67, KP; *LAT* 4/13/67, p. 28; FBI NY 100-111180-9-1269A, 1271, 1272A, 1273A, 4/9, 11, 12 & 13/67; King, "The Other America," 4/14/67, Stanford Univ., KP; *SFC* 4/15/67, p. 2; *SFE* 4/15/67, p. 4; *NYWJT* 4/14/67, p. 3; Rustin, *AN* 4/22/67, p. 4; *WP* 4/16/67, p. C1. Public hints about "Hoover's stuff" had begun appearing in the press; see James Reston, *NYT* 12/14/66, p. 46, and Marquis Childs, *WP* 7/11/66, p. A24, 5/12/67, p. A24.

34. FBI NY 100-111180-9-1269A, 1272A, 1273A, 4/9, 12 & 13/67; Young, *Christian Century* 5/3/71, pp. 80–82; *NYT Magazine* 2/6/77, pp. 17–19, 56–64; Bevel Interview (Garrow); Donald Keys to SANE National Board, "Accusations at Board Meeting," 5/1/67, NT 134; Lowenstein Interview (Viorst); Dave Dellinger, *More Power Than We Know* (Garden City, N.Y.: Doubleday, 1975), pp. 5–9, 115; Zaroulis & Sullivan, *Who Spoke Up*, pp. 110–12; King, "Speech . . .," 4/15/67, KP; *NYT* 4/16/67, p. 1, 4/22/67, p. 32; *WP* 4/16/67, p. A1; *Nation* 5/1/67, pp. 550–52. Both the peroration and the "fusion" denial were Levison recommendations.

35. NCNP Executive Board Minutes, 3/4 & 3/5/67, New York, BS 53; Norman Thomas to David McReynolds, 3/28/67, NT 109, & to Charles Bloomstein et al., 3/30/67, APR; *NYT* 4/22/67, p. 32; *Ramparts* 5/67, p. 6; Garrow interviews with Spock & Carmichael; FBI NY 100-111180-9-1276A, 1277A, 1279, 4/16, 17 & 19/67; King, "Face the Nation," 4/16/67, KP; *NYT* 4/17/67, p. 1; *WP* 4/17/67, p. A5; *AC* 4/17/67, p. 2; Lynn Z. Bloom, *Doctor Spock* (Indianapolis: Bobbs-Merrill, 1972), pp. 270–74; *Newsweek* 5/15/67, pp. 27–34; Leslie Dunbar Interview (Garrow).

36. *NYWJT* 4/17/67, p. 1; *WDN* 4/17/67, p. 7; FBI NY 100-111180-9-1279, 1281, 4/19 & 21/67; *NYT* 4/22/67, p. 32; FBI NY 100-111180-9-1282A, 4/22/67; Thomas to George Woywod, 5/2/67, & to David McReynolds, 5/16/67, NT 111; *BG* 4/24/67, p. 1; *NYT* 4/24/67, p. 14; *CDN* 4/24/67, p. 2; Walter Fauntroy Interviews (Lewis; Garrow); *U.S. News* 5/8/67, p. 14; Spock Interview (Garrow).

37. "Memorandum for the File," 3/2/67, NT 139; Katz, "Peace Liberals," p. 25; *NYT* 4/25/67, p. 16; *PI* 4/25/67; *NYWJT* 4/25/67, p. 26; Dowdy, "Nonviolence," pp. 150–52; FBI 100-438794-1861, 4/25/67; King, "Statement," 4/25/67, KP; *AC* 4/26/67, p. 11; *NYT* 4/26/67, p. 19.

38. *North & South* 3/67; Osburn Interview (Garrow); *Movement* 6/67, pp. 5, 8; *CP* 4/22/67, p. 1, 4/26/67, p. A1, 4/27/67, p. A5; *NYT* 4/27/67, p. 38; *MT* 4/28/67, p. 1; SCLC press release, 4/28/67; *CDN* 4/28/67, p. 29, 4/29/67, pp. 3, 7; Black to King, n.d., KP; *CT* 4/9/67, p. 22; *NYT* 6/30/67, p. 15.

39. King, "Why I am Opposed to the War . . .," 4/30/67, KP; *NYT* 5/1/67, p. 1; *ADW* 5/2/67, p. 1; Garrow interviews with Carmichael & Cleveland Sellers; *GN* 5/1/67, p. 1; *NYT* 5/4/67, p. 30, 5/5/67, p. 20, 5/6/67, p. 19, 5/7/67, p. 40; *LCJ* 5/4/67, p. B1, 5/5/67, p. B1, 5/6/67, p. 1, 5/7/67, p. 1; *LT* 5/4/67, p. 1; Osburn Interview (Garrow); Horton, *Not Without Struggle*, pp. 145–46; Fairclough, "SCLC," pp. 356–60. King had called Carmichael to invite him to the service.

40. King, "America's Chief Moral Dilemma," 5/10/67, KP; *AC* 5/11/67, p. 68; *LCJ* 5/11/67, p. 1; Horton, *Not Without Struggle*, pp. 148–51; FBI 100-106670-2956, 2959, 5/11 & 12/67; *MJ* 5/13/67, p. 3; FBI 100-442529-2230, NY 100-111180-9-1302, 5/12/67.

41. *NYT* 5/16/67, p. 39; *NYWJT* 4/20/67, p. 20; *WP* 4/21/67, p. A12; *AJC* 4/23/67, p. B4; King "Dear Friend" letter in "Pilgrimage . . ." brochure, 3/1/67, KC; SCLC press release, 5/16/67; *CP* 5/16/67, p. A1, 5/17/67, p. A1; *NYT* 5/17/67, p. 32, 5/21/67, p. 51; *CST* 5/17/67, p. 6; *Reporter* 6/15/67, pp. 38–41; Osburn Interview (Garrow); Halberstam, "Second Coming," pp. 48–50; King, "America's Chief Moral Dilemma," 5/17/67, KP; *SFC* 5/18/67, p. 8, 5/19/67, p. 19; *DP* 5/18/67, p. 15, 5/19/67, p. 17. King described his conversation with Evans in FBI NY 100-111180-9-1452, 10/9/67.

42. *SFC* 5/19/67, p. 19; *NYT* 5/21/67, p. 26, 5/23/67, p. 38; *AJ* 5/23/67, p. A4; *WP* 5/22/67, p. A2; FBI NY 100-111180-9-1307, 5/17/67; *NYT* 5/29/67, p. 15, 5/7/67, p. E6; Williams Interview (Garrow); Paul Brest to Young, 4/27/67, & Robert Johnson et al. to Young, 6/1/67, KC.

43. FBI 100-106670-3526, p. 16, 3/12/68; King, "To Charter Our Course for the Future," 5/22/67, KP. "I'm convinced that many of the very people who supported us in the struggle in the South are not willing to go all the way now," King put it on 4/14/67 at Stanford University. "I came to see this in a very difficult and painful way in Chicago over the last year." "The Other America," KP.

44. *NYT* 5/26/67, p. 29; *CDN* 5/25/67, p. 14, 5/26/67, p. 4; *CST* 5/26/67, p. 3; *CT* 5/26/67, p. 19; Massoni, "Perspectives," pp. 122–23; Clark Interviews (Leventhal; Garrow); Floyd McKissick Interview (Garrow); Clark, *King*, p. 9; Weiss, "Whitney Young," pp. 342–43; *NYT* 5/30/67, p. 6; FBI NY 100-111180-9-1322, 1327A, 6/1 & 6/67, FBI 100-106670-2994, 2996, 6/2 & 6/67; King, "Judging Others," 6/4/67, Ebenezer, & Clark to King, 6/12/67, KP.

45. *CP* 5/23/67, p. A4, 5/24/67, p. B8, 5/29/67, p. A4, 6/2/67, p. A4, 6/8/67, pp. B5, B6, 6/9/67, p. A1; "SCLC Field Staff Assignments," 6/12/67, KC; *C&P* 6/10/67, p. B4; Osburn Interview (Garrow); Stokes, *Promises*, pp. 100–103; *NYT* 6/10/67, p. 19, 6/11/67, p. 61; *CE* 6/12/67, p. 31; *CPTS* 6/2/67, p. 10; *CST* 6/13/67, p. 30; Otis Moss Interviews (Porter; Garrow); FBI 100-442529-2250, 6/12/67; Bernard Schwartz, *Super Chief* (New York: New York University Press, 1983), pp. 632–34; *AJ* 6/13/67, p. A4; *NYT* 6/13/67, p. 1, 7/6/76, p. 20, 6/15/67, p. 31; King,

"America's Chief Moral Dilemma," 5/17/67, Berkeley, KP; *CP* 6/14/67, p. 1, 6/15/67, pp. A2, A12, 6/16/67, p. A10.

46. King, "Ingratitude," 6/18/67, Ebenezer, KP; *NYT Magazine* 6/11/67, pp. 26–27, 93–103; King, "ABC's Issues and Answers," 6/18/67, "Appearance on Merv Griffin Show," 6/19/67 [broadcast 7/6], & "Appearance on Arlene Francis Show," 6/19/67, KP; *NYT* 6/20/67, p. 25; King, *Where,* pp. 108, 18, 36, 44, 131, 50, 133, 151, 69, 133. Also see Zepp, "Intellectual Sources," p. 198. King later cited the Sixteenth Street church bombing on 9/15/63 as a turning point: "Not long after talking about that dream I started seeing it turn into a nightmare." *Trumpet,* p. 76 (12/17/67).

47. *Saturday Review* 7/8/67, pp. 29–30; *Commonweal* 11/17/67, pp. 215–16; *Observer* 3/24/68, p. 28; *WP Book Week* 7/9/67, p. 1; *America* 7/22/67, pp. 88–89; Kopkind, *New York Review* 8/24/67, pp. 3–6. Also see Meier, "Urban Ghetto."

48. *CP* 6/22/67, p. A4; *CST* 6/24/67, p. 46; *CP* 6/27/67, p. A4, 6/28/67, p. A4, 6/29/67, p. A2; Young, "Report on the SCLC Cleveland Project," 6/26/67, KC; Orange Interview (Shannon); MacNair, "Social Distance," pp. 87–88, 131–32; FBI NY 100-111180-9-1345A, 6/24/67; King, "A Knock at Midnight," 6/25/67, KP; *LAT* 6/26/67, p. 2; Coretta King Interview (Mayerson XXIII, p. 19).

49. *CP* 7/4/67, p. A12, 7/8/67, p. A2, 7/13/67, p. 1; SCLC press release, 6/22/67; *CT* 6/25/67, p. 10; *CD* 6/29/67, p. 11; *Jet* 7/27/67, pp. 20–26; *NYT* 7/12/67, p. 23; *CP* 7/12/67, p. B9; *CDN* 7/12/67, p. 3, 7/13/67, p. 14; *Ebony* 8/67, pp. 78–86; *Business Week* 8/19/67, pp. 37–38; Massoni, "Perspectives," pp. 34–35; Jackson to King, "National Operation Breadbasket," 9/7/67, & to King et al., "Report on Operation Breadbasket," 12/27/67, GM; King, "The Crisis in Civil Rights," 7/11/67, KP; SCLC press release, 7/17/67; Garrow interviews with Otis Moss & Robert Green; *NYT* 7/9/67, p. 38, 7/11/67, p. 17; *WP* 7/11/67, p. A7; NCNP Executive Board Minutes, 5/19–20/67, NCNP 1; SANE National Board Minutes, 6/15/67, NT 134, & 7/15/67, SANE A-4; Norman Thomas to David McReynolds, 6/15/67, to Earl Bourdon, 6/20/67, & to Hal Drake, 7/19/67, NT 110-111; King to Sanford Gottlieb, 6/29/67, SANE E-13; National Mobilization Administrative Committee Minutes, 7/8/67, NMC 1. King accepted the NCNP invitation largely because one of the primary initiators was Martin Peretz, husband of SCLC's top contributor, Ann Farnsworth.

50. *CP* 7/19/67, p. A15, 7/20/67, p. A13; Coretta King Interview (Mayerson XXIII, p. 45); FBI 100-438794-1825, NY 100-111180-9-1375A, 7/24/67, 100-106670-3030, 100-438794-1927, NY 100-111180-9-1376A, 7/25/67; Hoover to Mildred Stegall, 7/31/67, 100-106670-3035; DeLoach to Clyde Tolson, 7/10/67, 100-106670-NR (sec. 84).

51. King to Johnson, 7/25/67, King Name File LBJL; King, "Press Conference," 7/25/67, KP; *NYT* 7/26/67, p. 19, 7/27/67, pp. 1, 17, 19; *AC* 7/26/67, p. 7; King, "Statement . . .," 7/26/67, KP; Andrew Young Interview (Baker); *CDN* 7/27/67, p. 6; FBI 100-106670-3067, NY 100-111180-9-1378, 7/27/67; *CP* 7/27/67, p. 1, 7/29/67, p. A1; *NYT* 7/30/67, p. 54; *WP* 7/29/67, p. A8. Also see Willard Wirtz to Johnson, 7/28/67, Ex LA2 Box 8, & George Christian to Johnson, 7/31/67, Ex HU2 Box 6.

52. *NYT* 7/29/67, p. 9; *WP* 7/29/67, p. A1; *Congressional Record* 113, pt. 16, 8/9/67, pp. 22055–59; *CNC* 7/31/67, pp. A1, A8; *SC* 7/31/67, p. B1; *NYT* 7/31/67, p. 17; FBI NY 100-111180-9-1380A, 7/29/67; Coretta King Interview (Mayerson XXVII, pp. 51–52). Also see *AC* 8/1/67, p. 3, 8/2/67, p. 3; *ADW* 8/1/67, p. 1; *NYT* 8/1/67, p. 19, 8/2/67, p. 18.

53. *LCJ* 8/3/67, p. A1; *LT* 8/3/67, p. A31; King, "Which Way Its Soul Shall Go," 8/2/67, KP; *LCJ Magazine* 8/20/67, pp. 7–10; Coretta King Interview (Mayerson XXVII, p. 52); King, "Standing By the Best in an Evil Time," 8/6/67, Ebenezer, KP; *CP* 8/8/67, p. A13, 8/9/67, p. A4; David Wallace to Jesse Jackson,

"Cleveland . . . Visit," 7/23/67, GM; *SFC* 8/11/67, p. 1, 8/12/67, p. 7; King, "Transforming a Neighborhood . . .," 8/10/67. Also see *New Yorker* 4/13/68, pp. 35–37.

54. King, "Transforming . . .," 8/11/67, KP; *AC* 8/12/67, p. 3; *NYT* 8/12/67, p. 28; Baugh Interviews (Garrow; Joseph); FBI NY 100-111180-9-1393A, 8/12/67; Carson, *In Struggle,* pp. 253–57; King, "Meet the Press," 8/13/67, KP.

55. King, "The Crisis in American Cities," 8/15/67, KP; *NYT* 8/16/67, p. 1; *ADW* 8/16/67, p. 1; *WP* 8/16/67, p. A1; *AC* 8/15/67, p. 6, 8/16/67, p. 1; Harding, *Other Revolution,* p. 198, & "So Much History," p. 69.

Chapter Eleven

1. King, "President's Address . . .," 8/16/67, KP; *AC* 8/17/67, p. 5, 8/18/67, p. 1; *NYT* 8/18/67, p. 14, 8/19/67, p. 12, 8/20/67, p. E12; *MT* 8/18/67; *AJ* 8/18/67, p. A8; *CSM* 8/19/67; *Time* 8/25/67, p. 18; *Southern Courier* 8/26–27/67, p. 1; *U.S. News* 8/28/67, p. 10; *Jet* 8/31/67, pp. 6–8; Paul Wahrhaftig to Irwin Schulman, "SCLC 10th Annual Convention . . .," 8/23/67, ADL; Leon Hall, "Project Report," 8/21/67, SCLC; Reddick to King, 8/17/67, KP; Young Interviews (Viorst; Kotz; Garrow); Coretta King, *My Life,* p. 297; Garrow interviews with Walter Fauntroy, Stoney Cooks & Tom Offenburger; Schlesinger, *Robert Kennedy,* p. 873; blind memo, "Rev. M. L. King," 8/23/67, WH; FBI NY 100-111180-9-1398, 1402A, 1404, 8/16, 20 & 22/67.

2. *CP* 8/23/67, p. A11, 8/31/67, p. A4; *NYT* 8/27/67, p. 64, 8/30/67, p. 19; *CDN* 8/29/67, p. 7; *CT* 8/30/67, p. IA-2; *CST* 8/30/67, p. 6; David Wallace to Jesse Jackson, "Cleveland . . . Visit," 7/23/67, GM; SAC Cleveland to Director, 9/21/67, 100-106670-illegible; Devereux Bowly, Jr., *The Poorhouse* (Carbondale: Southern Illinois University Press, 1978), pp. 151–52; King, "Thou Fool," 8/27/67, KP.

3. Rowan, "King's Tragic Decision"; *CA* 8/22/67, p. 11; *Washington Observer Newsletter* #45, 9/15/67; *NYT* 8/28/67, p. 10; Norman Thomas to *NYT,* to *Reader's Digest* & to King, 8/28/67, to Rowan, 9/7/67, & to King, 9/11/67, NT 111; King, "Interview . . . for ABC's 'Good Company,'" 10/11/67, KP.

4. FBI 100-438794-1965, 8/22/67; Zaroulis & Sullivan, *Who Spoke Up,* pp. 128–29; Halstead, *Out Now,* pp. 316–20; King, "The Three Evils . . .," 8/31/67, KP; Septima Clark Interview (Garrow); Al Raby Interviews (Viorst; Garrow); FBI NY 100-111180-9-1414, 8/31/67; *NYT* 9/1/67, p. 15; *CDN* 9/1/67, p. 3; Sanford Gottlieb, "Report on NCNP Convention," 8/29–9/4/67, NT 137; *New Leader* 9/11/67, pp. 6–8; *New Republic* 9/16/67, pp. 9–12; *New Yorker* 9/23/67, pp. 56–88; *Fellowship* 11/67, pp. 6–7; *DMR* 4/5/68, p. 10; Andrew Young to Martin Peretz & Ann Farnsworth, 9/6/67, KC; King, "To Take Possession of Society," 9/1/67, in *Journal of Social Issues* 24 (1/68): 1–12; *NYT* 9/4/67, p. 15; *Daily Tar Heel,* Univ. of North Carolina, 4/5/68, p. 1.

5. *AC* 9/8/67, p. 1; *CP* 9/8/67, p. C6; *NYT* 9/10/67, pp. 5, 40; King, "Address . . .," 9/18/67, KP; *AC* 9/19/67, p. 19; *AJ* 12/19/67, p. A2; King, "Mastering Our Fears," 9/10/67, Ebenezer, KP.

6. Tom Offenburger Notes, Airlie House Retreat, 9/13–17/67, TO; Offenburger Interview (Shannon); Young Interviews (Shannon; Kotz); Young, "Address . . .," 1/15/73, Ebenezer, Young; SAC Atlanta to Director, 9/21/67, CG 157-953-56; *LAT* 9/24/67, p. G1; Baez Interview (Leventhal); FBI NY 100-111180-9-1434, 9/21/67; McGraw, "Interview with Young," p. 327.

7. *SFE* 9/22/67, p. 9; *SFC* 9/22/67, p. 8; FBI 100-106670-3097, NY 100-111180-9-1434, 9/21/67, 100-106670-3108, NY 100-111180-9-1440, 9/27/67; *NYT* 10/4/67, p. 1; *CP* 10/3/67, p. A4, 10/5/67, p. C12; Kenneth Weinberg, *Black*

Victory (Chicago: Quadrangle Books, 1968); Kenneth Clement Interview (Britton); Garrow interviews with Osburn & Orange.

8. *NYT* 10/10/67, p. 40, 10/11/67, p. 59, 10/21/67, p. 18; *AJ* 10/10/67, p. A20; *PI* 10/14/67, p. 1; FBI 100-106670-3121, 10/15/67, NY 100-111180-9-1460, 10/17/67; *HP* 10/18/67, p. 1; *CD* 10/23/67, p. 3; FBI NY 100-111180-9-1466A, 10/23/67; King, "Statement . . .," 10/23/67 (also *NYT* 11/12/67, p. E11), King press conference, 10/23/67, KP; *PEB* 10/26/67, p. 56, 10/27/67, p. 1; *BG* 10/28/67, p. 1; *DMR* 10/30/67, p. 1; *WES* 10/28/67, p. A4; *WP* 10/26/67, p. A20.

9. Mays, *Born*, pp. 269–70; FBI 100-106670-3138, 11/8/67; King, "Statement," 10/30/67, KP; *AC* 10/31/67, p. 17, 11/4/67, p. 2; *ADW* 10/31/67, p. 1, 11/3/67, p. 1, 11/5/67, p. 1; *NYT* 10/31/67, p. 1, 11/4/67, p. 21; *WP* 10/31/67, p. A2; SCLC press release, 11/1/67; *Christian Century* 11/1/67, pp. 1412–14; *Southern Courier* 11/4–5/67, p. 1, 11/11–12/67, p. 1; King, "Address . . .," 11/3/67, KP; blind memo, "Notes," 11/6/67, WH; *BN* 11/4/67, p. 3; *AJC* 11/5/67, p. A2; King, "But, If Not . . .," 11/5/67, Ebenezer, KP; FBI 100-106670-3143, NY 100-111180-9-1481, 11/7/67; Garrow interviews with Young, Osburn, Orange, Fauntroy & Cooks; *CP* 11/9/67, p. A7; *CPD* 4/5/68, p. 6; *Ebony* 11/70, p. 173.

10. *CST* 11/21/67; *CA* 11/12/67; *Nation* 11/27/67, pp. 561–63; D. E. King Interview (Garrow); Wachtel to Lowenstein, 11/8/67, AL; FBI 100-106670-3174, 11/13/67; King, *Trumpet*; Christopher Edley to Andrew Young, 5/4/67, & to John Coleman, 5/9/67, Young to Edley, 5/17/67, Steve McNichols to Edley, 6/7/67, Edley to Files, 8/17/67, & William Nims to Chauncey Eskridge, 10/17/67, Ford 67-580 & Log 67-82; "Minutes of National Advisory Committee," 11/24/67, KC.

11. Tentative Schedule, SCLC Staff Retreat, 11/27–12/1/67, GM; *NYT* 11/27/67, p. 53; *AJ* 11/27/67, p. A5; King, "The State of the Movement" (also known as "A New Sense of Direction"), 11/28/67, KP; Andrew Young Notes, Young; Young Interview (Baker); Gary Massoni Notes, GM.

12. SCLC Staff Workshop transcript, 11/29/67, KC; Andrew Young Notes, Young; FBI CG 157-953-63, 11/29/67; Stoney Cooks Interview (Shannon).

13. King press conference, 12/4/67, KP; *NYT* 12/5/67, p. 1; *AC* 12/5/67, p. 1; *WP* 12/5/67, p. A2; *ADW* 12/7/67, p. 1; *Washingtonian* 2/68, pp. 51–53; Viorst, *Fire*, pp. 433–34.

14. McGraw, "Interview with Young" (12/21/67), pp. 327–30; Young 2/5/68 speech, Washington, in Clergy & Laymen, *In Whose Name?*, pp. 12–13; *NYT* 1/22/68, p. 19. So far, Young said on 2/5/68, "ours has been the mildest and most respectable dissent. When are we going to really stand up and challenge the values of this country?" Young later remarked that "the civil rights movement, up until 1965 anyway, was really a middle-class movement. There were middle-class goals, middle-class aspirations, middle-class membership, and even though a lot of poor people went to jail—say for the Voting Rights Act—it was still essentially a middle-class operation." (Kotz Interview)

15. *North & South* 12/67; King, "SCLC Organizational Structure and Staff," 12/4/67, KP; *AC* 12/14/67, p. 34; *WP* 12/14/67, p. A5; *Ebony* 10/66; FBI 100-438794-1929, 1938, 7/14 & 8/2/67, NY 100-111180-9-1454A, 10/11/67; Garrow interviews with Rutherford, Lafayette, Jackson, Bevel, Gary Massoni, David Wallace, Otis Moss, Morris, Eskridge, Billy Hollins, Junius Griffin & Stoney Cooks; FBI NY 100-111180-9-1671, p. 5, 5/15/68; Ralph Helstein Interviews (Wigginton; Garrow); Austin, "Goodby," VII, p. 20; Reynolds, *Jackson*, p. 55; Rutherford to Jackson, & to All Staff Members, 12/11/67, SCLC; *AJC* 12/24/67, p. A6; Williams to King, 12/13/67, KP; Williams Interview (Garrow); Stoney Cooks Interview (LaCrosse); FBI NY 100-111180-9-1517A, 12/13/67. On Jackson, also see *Penthouse* 4/73, 78–80ff, & Phillip T. Drotning and Wesley W. South, *Up from the Ghetto* (New York: Cowles, 1970), pp. 19–43. On 5/10/68, Rutherford told Levison, "Doc told me to be very careful with Jim. That's the reason we raised Jim's salary last year. You can't put a person like that in a position of trust and pay him starvation wages." Levison replied. "That doesn't help you if a guy is dishonest." FBI NY 100-111180-9-1666A. Also see Garrow interviews with Andrew Young, Joseph Lowery, Robert Green, Hosea Williams, Stoney Cooks, Tom Offenburger, James Orange, Willie Bolden & Dana Swan.

16. Garrow interviews with Rutherford, Marian Logan & Cotton; King, "Great, But," 7/2/67, "Transforming a Neighborhood . . .," 8/11/67, Atlanta, p. 19, "Unfulfilled Dreams," 3/3/68, pp. 4–6, KP; King, *Playboy* 1/65, p. 78; Coretta King, *My Life,* pp. 61–62, 171, 274; Coretta King Interview (Mayerson XXVI, pp. 29–30); Garrow interviews with Bernard Lee, Herbert Coulton, Calvin Morris & Stokely Carmichael; Levison Interview (Stein); Belafonte & Levison, "King"; Young Interview (Viorst); Abernathy in Landess & Quinn, *Jesse Jackson*; FBI NY 100-111180-9-1514A, 12/10/67, NY 100-111180-9-1493, 1519A, 11/19 & 12/15/67; *AA* 2/10/68, p. 1; Young to Peretz & Farnsworth, 12/6/67, KC, & A. A. Peters to King, 1/9/64, KP; King, "The Meaning of Hope" & "Sleeping Through a Revolution," 12/10/67, KP; *CA* 12/11/67, p. 6; *CT* 12/11/67, p. II-17; *CST* 12/11/67, p. 11; *AC* 12/22/67, p. 13; *NYT* 12/22/67, p. 28, 12/23/67, p. 19. On the sexual matters, also see Beulah Lewis Interview (Lewis); FBI NY 100-111180-9-1187A, 1/17/67; and three Drew Pearson-Jack Anderson columns, *AC* 8/21/69, p. A4; *WP* 8/15/70, p. C11, 4/12/71, p. B11, which detail how former baseball pitcher Don Newcombe volunteered various assertions about King to the FBI after first writing two unsolicited letters to Lyndon Johnson, 12/21/67 & 1/23/68, WHCF Gen PL2, LBJL. On King's statement about prayer, also see Addine Drew Interview (Garrow); Drew recalled how once "I had sneaked into my guest room to get a dress out of the closet and found him on his knees alone with the door closed, praying." Concerning humility, in 6/67, King inscribed a copy of *Where Do We Go from Here?* to Union Seminary's John Bennett, an antiwar colleague, "in appreciation for your significant Christian witness during these turbulent days and your support of my humble efforts." On King's sense of guilt, also see Miller, *King,* pp. 98–99; and Vander Zanden, "Nonviolent Resistance," & *Race Relations in Transition* (New York: Random House, 1965), ch. 5, plus Allison Davis, *Leadership,* pp. 239–41, who asserts that "the typical response by King to his own angry and aggressive feelings was to feel guilty, and to *turn his anger against himself as punishment for this guilt.* . . . There was some deep compulsion in King to suffer, to sacrifice himself."

17. *NYT* 12/15/67, p. 65; *CP* 12/16/67, p. A3; Rutherford to Lafayette, "Cleveland . . .," 12/19/67, Penney to King, 12/19/67, & Executive Staff Minutes, 12/27/67, KC; Barbara Moffett to Colin Bell, 12/12/67, AFSC.

18. SCLC, "Washington Guidebook," 1/1/68, "Statement of Purpose . . .," 1/68, "Questions and Answers . . .," n.d., & "Poor People in America," 1/68, SCLC; *WP* 12/15/67, p. C1; *NYT* 12/18/67, p. 26; *Christianity Today* 1/5/68, pp. 364–66; SCLC, "The Poor People's Campaign," n.d., SCLC; Rustin Interview (Garrow); *NYT* 9/25/85, p. A18; Rutherford to Richard Boone, 2/3/68, & aide-mémoire, "Meeting with AFSC, 1/5/68," 1/10/68, SCLC; "AFSC Staff Discussion . . .,with SCLC," 1/5/68, & Barbara Moffett to Rutherford & Lafayette, 1/8 & 1/9/68, AFSC.

19. King press conference, 1/5/68, Chicago, King, "Prelude to Tomorrow," 1/6/68, KP; "SCLC Operation Breadbasket," 1/4–5/68, GM; Garrow interviews with Calvin Morris, Bill Rutherford, Billy Hollins & Tom Offenburger; Stoney Cooks Interviews (Garrow; LaCrosse); King, "The Meaning of Hope," 12/10/67, KP; King, *Trumpet,* p. 76 (12/17/67); King, "What Are Your New Year's Resolutions?," 1/9/68, KP; *NYT* 1/7/68, p. 6; *WP* 1/12/68, p. B5; *NYT* 1/13/68, p. 4; *Lutheran Forum* 5/68, p. 19; *Commonweal* 5/31/68, p. 315; King, "Address at Santa Rita Prison," 1/14/68, KP; FBI 100-106670-3188, 1/14/68. Marxist intellectual C.L.R. James later recalled a conversation with King similar to the Breadbasket remarks. King voiced some economic views and remarked, "'You don't hear that from me in the pulpit, do you? I don't say that there but that is what I believe.'" "King leaned over to me saying, 'I don't say such things from the pulpit, James, but that is what I really believe.'" "King wanted me to know that he understood and accepted, and in fact agreed with, the ideas that I was putting forward—ideas which were fundamentally Marxist-Leninist. . . . I saw him as a man whose ideas were as advanced as any of us on the Left, but who, as he actually said to me, could not say such things from the pulpit. . . . King was a man with clear ideas, but whose position as a churchman, etc. imposed on him the necessity of reserve." James to Garrow, 2/27/85. King had smoked for at least almost a decade, but virtually never did so in public and rarely carried cigarettes, usually relying on Bernard Lee or bumming them from another aide. Garrow interviews with Lee & Willie Bolden; Harold Middlebrook Interview (Beifuss & Thomas).

20. Stoney Cooks, "Dr. King's Last Birthday"; Shannon interviews with Bevel, Andrew Young & Al Sampson; Cooks Interviews (Garrow; Leventhal); Garrow interviews with Jackson, Bevel, Tom Offenburger, James Orange & Albert Turner; Dorothy Cotton Interview (Wigginton & Thrasher); King, "Why We Must Go to Washington," 1/15, "Press Conference . . . ," 1/16, & "See You in Washington," 1/17/68, KP; Louw & Wicklein, "King"; SCLC Staff Workshops Agenda, 1/14–16/68, AFSC; *WP* 1/17/68, p. A1, 1/27/68, p. A1; *ADW* 1/17/68, p. 1; *AC* 1/17/68, p. 7; *NYT* 1/17/68, p. 44.

21. *ADW* 12/30/67, p. 1; *Jet* 2/8/68, p. 41; *AC* 1/19/68, p. 16; *KCT* 1/20/68, p. B1; *NYT* 1/20/68, p. 5; King, "Interruptions," 1/21/68, Ebenezer, KP; FBI 157-8428-109 & NY 100-111180-9-1566A, 1/31/68; Rustin to King, "Strategy and Tactics," 1/29/68, in Rustin, *Down the Line,* pp. 202–205; Rustin Interviews (Garrow; Viorst; Baker); Tom Kahn, *Commentary* 9/68, pp. 50–55; Garrow interviews with Young, Jones, Wachtel, Fauntroy, Hill & Harrington; Barbara Moffett, "Report on AFSC . . . Support of the SCLC Campaign . . . ," 2/15/68, AFSC; Harrington, *Fragments,* p. 128; George Goodman, *Look* 4/15/69, pp. 29–31; King, "The Drum Major Instinct," 2/4/68, KP.

22. "Memorandum for Marvin Watson," 2/2/68, King Name File LBJL; *NYT* 2/3/68, p. 6; *WP* 2/6/68, p. A6; *CT* 2/6/68, p. II-6; Young Interview (Kotz); Kotz & Kotz, *Passion,* pp. 248–52.

23. *NYT* 2/7/68, p. 17; *WP* 2/7/68, p. B1, 2/8/68, p. A1; King, "A Proper Sense of Priorities," 2/6/68, KP; *AA* 2/10/68, p. 1, 2/17/68, p. 1; *Soul Force* I-1, 2/15/68; FBI 157-6-53-1284, 3/11/68; *NYT* 2/8/68, p. 30.

24. Garrow interviews with Rutherford, Tom Offenburger & John Gibson; Carmichael Interviews (Garrow; Viorst); Stoney Cooks Interview (LaCrosse); *WES* 2/8/68, 2/9/68, p. C3; *WP* 2/9/68, p. B5, 2/11/68, pp. C1, D1; *NYT* 2/11/68, p. E4, 2/23/68, p. 67; FBI 157-8428-153, 100-106670-3194, 2/8/68; King, "In Search for a Sense of Direction," 2/7/68, KP. On 2/8, Rutherford told Levison that "Martin got very upset with me and started shouting and cussing me out after they left. . . . He said to me the enemy is violence, violence begets violence, and he went on to one of these preaching things. I didn't react at all." NY 100-111180-9-1579A. King earlier had remarked that "I have my moments of frustration, my moments of doubt, and maybe temporary moments of despair, but I have never faced absolute despair because I think if you face absolute despair, you lose all hope, you have no power to move and act, because you really feel that there is no possibility of winning." BBC Interview, n.d. [ca. early 12/67], KP.

25. *WP* 2/10/68, p. A2, 2/11/68, p. C1; *NYT* 2/11/68, p. 60; *Reader's Digest* 4/68, pp. 65–69; *America* 2/24/68, p. 247; Larry Temple to Johnson, 2/14/68, Ex HU2 Box 7, LBJL; "Action Committee Meeting," 2/11/68, Young. "We look back and we see what is happening and it is almost too difficult to face," Young remarked at the time. 2/5/68 speech, n. 14 above.

26. FBI 100-106670-3199, 3204, 2/15 & 16/68; King, "Address . . .," 2/15/68, Edwards, Miss., KP; Leon Hall to Hosea Williams, "Recruitment . . .," 2/19/68, SCLC 178; Albert Turner to Williams, "February 3–10 in Alabama," 2/10/68, AFSC; King, "Address . . .," 2/15/68, Birmingham, "Address . . .," 2/16/68, Selma, "Address . . .," 2/16/68, Montgomery, KP; Louw & Wicklein, "King"; *WP* 2/17/68, p. A1; *NYT Magazine* 3/31/68, p. 59.

27. King, "Who Is My Neighbor?," 2/18/68, KP; FBI 157-8428-229, 2/18/68; King, "Address . . .," 2/19/68, KP; Bryant George, "Report to the Ford Foundation," 2/25/68, Moynihan to Bundy, 2/27/68, Ford 67-580; Moynihan, *Congressional Record* 10/18/83, pp. S14014–15; King, "Address . . .," 2/23/68, KP; Christopher Edley to Mitchell Sviridoff, 2/28/68, Ford 67-580; Wilkins Interview (Garrow); Wilkins, *WP* 4/4/72, p. A18; Abernathy in U.S. Congress, House Assassinations Committee, *Hearings*, vol. 1, pp. 25–26; FBI NY 100-111180-9-1593A, 2/27/68. King said in a 10/29/65 speech that "the shattering blows on the Negro family have made it fragile, deprived and often psychopathic. This is tragic because nothing is so much needed as a secure family life for a people seeking to pull themselves out of poverty and backwardness." King, "The Dignity of Family Life," in Lee Rainwater & William L. Yancey, *The Moynihan Report and the Politics of Controversy* (Cambridge: MIT Press, 1967), pp. 402–409, at 407.

28. *WP* 2/26/68, p. A3, 3/6/68, p. A22; *AJ* 2/26/68, p. A4; *Jet* 2/29/68, pp. 14–19; Lafayette to Field Staff, 2/21/68, GM; *AA* 2/24/68, p. 1; Arthur Waskow to Tony Henry & Bill Moyer, 3/1/68, SCLC 179; Moyer Interview (Shannon); *NYT* 3/4/68, p. 22; *WP* 3/1/68, p. 26; FBI NY 100-111180-9-1597A, 1602, 3/2 & 7/68; *NYT* 3/2/68, p. 1; King, "Unfulfilled Dreams," 3/3/68, KP. Also see Benjamin Mays's 4/9/68 eulogy of King, where he notes that King was "occasionally deeply hurt because friends betrayed him." "Eulogy," p. 165.

29. King, "Statement . . .," 3/4/68, KP & SCLC 122; *NYT* 3/5/68, p. 28; *AC* 3/5/68, p. 3; *LAT* 3/5/68; *U.S. News* 3/18/68, p. 44; "Report by Andrew Young . . .," 3/5/68, & "Outline of Action Plan," n.d., SCLC 179; Larry Temple to Johnson, 2/23/68, Ex LE/HU2 Box 66, LBJL; Harvey, *Black Civil Rights*, pp. 49–53; *AA* 3/9/68, p. 24; Abernathy in U.S. Congress, House Assassinations Committee, *Hearings*, vol. 1, pp. 25–26, and in Witherspoon, *King*, pp. 212, 214–15.

30. Logan to King, "1968 April Demonstrations in Washington, D.C.," 3/8/68, CRS FOIA; Garrow interviews with Logan & Tom Offenburger; Frank, *American Death*, pp. 39–40; Young to Arthur & Marian Logan, 3/21/68, KC.

31. Barefoot Sanders to Johnson (2), 3/13/68, Ex LE/HU2 Box 66, LBJL; Ramsey Clark Interview (Mosby); FBI NY 100-111180-9-1606A, 1618A, 3/11 & 23/68; Eleanor Eaton to Barbara Moffett, "SCLC's Second Draft . . .," 2/21/68, Moffett to King & Harry Wachtel, "Comments on Second Draft . . .," 2/23/68, Community Relations Division Executive Committee Minutes, 3/19/68, Moffett to Stan Levison, 3/25/68, & Moffett to King, 3/25/68, AFSC; Garrow interviews with Harrington & Moffett; King to Action Committee, 3/11/68, KP; Louw & Wicklein, "King"; "Participants of Minority Group Conference," 3/14/68, TO; Eleanor Eaton to Moffett, "Minority Leaders Conference . . . 3/14/68," 4/2/68, AFSC; Austin, "Goodby," p. 6; Austin to Garrow, 9/30/81; Tom Houck Interview (La-Crosse); Al Sampson Interview (Beifuss et al.); Patricia Blawis, *Tijerina and the Land Grants* (New York: International Publishers, 1971), pp. 98, 107; *AC* 3/14/68, p. 16, 3/15/68, p. 32; *NYT* 3/15/68, p. 30; Religious News Service, "Dr. King Speaks in Detroit . . .," 3/18/68, KC; Thomas Gumbleton, *Maryknoll*, 4/78, pp. 35–38; FBI 100-106670-3235, 3/16/68; Green Interview (Leventhal); *WES* 4/5/68, p. A10. SCLC staffer Ernest Austin later wrote about King that "it was with an almost unbelieving shock that he found out there are more poor white folks in this country than there are poor black folks. I remember the look on his face when I showed him the figures." "Goodby," VII, p. 20.

32. Young Interviews (Moyers; Garrow; Viorst); Young in Raines, *My Soul,* p. 431; Young in Stein, *American Journey,* p. 252–53; Howell, "Interview with Young," p. 19; Range, "Interview with Young," p. 73; Young, "Remembering Dr. King;" Young in *Look* 4/15/69, pp. 29–31; Coretta King Interview (Mayerson XXIII, p. 37, XXVII, pp. 24, 28–29, XXX, pp. 11–12); Coretta King, *My Life,* pp. 304; Garrow interviews with Drew, Rustin, Dora McDonald, Rutherford, Cotton, Jackson, Thomas Kilgore, Bill Berry, John Maguire, Tom Offenburger & John Bennett; *New Yorker* 4/13/68, p. 35; DeWolf, "King," p. 11; Oates, *Trumpet,* p. 473.

33. Garrow interviews with Cornish Rogers, Cotton, Drew, Harrington, Willie Bolden, Rutherford, Jackson, Tom Offenburger, Gardner Taylor, Marian Logan, John Porter & Floyd McKissick; King, "The Levels of Love," 5/21/67, Ebenezer, KP; Wyatt Walker Interview (Smith); Taylor, *How Shall,* pp. 71, 142; *New Yorker* 4/13/68, pp. 35–37; *LAT* 3/17/68, p. 3, 3/18/68, p. 3; King, "The Other America" & "The Sickness of America," 3/16/68, KP; *LAS* 3/21/68, p. A3.

34. Lawson Interviews (Yellin & Thomas; Yellin & Beifuss II, III, IV & V); Frank, *American Death,* pp. 10–18; Stanfield, *In Memphis,* 3/22/68; Harold Middlebrook Interview (Beifuss & Thomas); Beifuss, *River,* passim, esp. pp. 137, 156, 191, 193–96; Marshall & Adams, "Memphis"; Bailey, "Sanitation Strike"; Collins, "Analysis"; Richard Billings & John Greenya, *Power to the Public Worker* (Washington: Robert B. Luce, 1974), pp. 171–79; Lentz, "Sixty-Five Days"; Lewis, "Social Religion"; David M. Tucker, *Black Pastors and Leaders* (Memphis: Memphis State University Press, 1975), and *Memphis Since Crump* (Knoxville: University of Tennessee Press, 1980); Joseph C. Goulden, *Jerry Wurf* (New York: Atheneum, 1982), pp. 142–82; *Village Voice* 1/27/82, p. 8; Ann Trotter, "The Memphis Business Community . . .," in Jacoway & Colburn, *Southern Businessmen,* pp. 282–300; Jackson Baker, "Henry Loeb," *Memphis* 1/80, pp. 25–33, & 2/80, pp. 25–33; Loeb to City Council, 2/15/68, Loeb; *WSJ* 3/8/68, p. 10; *Nation* 4/22/68, pp. 529–31; Cornelia Crenshaw Interview (Mosby); Ezekiel Bell Interview (Viars); H. Ralph Jackson Interviews (Trotter et al.; Mosby; Adams); Henry Starks Interview (Beifuss & Schulz); James Jordan Interview (Beifuss & Hurley); Jesse Turner Interviews (Mosby; Trotter & Yellin); Charles Schneider Interview (Mosby); Ozell Sutton to James Madison, ". . . Memphis Sanitation Worker Strike," 2/29/68, CRS FOIA; *NYT* 3/18/68, p. 28; Malcolm Blackburn Interviews (Trotter & Yellin; Beckner & Thomas); Mose Pleasure Interview (Garrow); King, "Address at Mason Temple," 3/18/68, KP; Wurf Interviews (Mosby; Yellins); *MCA* 3/19/68, p. 1; *MPS* 3/19/68, p. 1; FBI NY 100-111180-9-1621A, 3/26/68; Kyles Interview (Beifuss & Thomas); Louw & Wicklein, "King." Instructive interviews with union activists include T. O. Jones (2), Jesse Baldwin, Tommy Eldridge, L. C. Reed, P. J. Ciampa, and William Lucy. From the city side, see the interviews with Loeb (2), Charles Blackburn, James Manire, Frank Gianotti, and council members Gwen Awsumb (2), Jerred Blanchard (2), Wyeth Chandler, Fred Davis (2), Lewis Donelson (2), Billy Hyman, Robert James, James Netters, J. O. Patterson and Thomas Todd, plus Baker, "Henry Loeb." Valuable white union leader interviews include Taylor Blair, Dan Powell (2), & W. T. "Bill" Ross, plus Blair to Loeb, 2/22/68, Loeb. From the church side, see the interviews with William Dimmick, Frank MacRae, and James Wax, plus the "Ministers' Negotiations" transcripts, 2/16 & 18/68, MVC, MSU. Valuable interviews with intermediaries, negotiators, and well-informed observers include Baxton Bryant (3), David Caywood, E. W. "Ned" Cook, Gerald Fanion, William Ingram, Frank Miles (2), Joe Sweat, Sam Weintraub, and Jacques Wilmore. On the events of 2/23, see particularly the interviews with Fred Davis, Gladys Carpenter, and Henry Lux. Local NAACP secretary Maxine Smith related that "actually, the community wasn't as involved as people have been led to believe. . . . Your demonstrators were made up primarily of your sanitation workers. . . . It's good that everybody thought this was a big, community involvement type of thing, but it actually wasn't." Mosby Interview, p. 15. Also see *Memphis* 5/80, pp. 24–33; Garrow, *FBI*, pp. 189–90, 295–96; & Director to Attorney General, 3/4/76, 100-106670-4356.

   35. Transcripts of King's speeches in Marks, Clarksdale, Grenada, Laurel & Hattiesburg, 3/19/68, KP; Louw & Wicklein, "King"; *NYT* 3/20/68, p. 18; *Jet* 4/4/68, p. 31; Willie Bolden Interview (Garrow); FBI 100-106670-3249, 3/21/68, 157-8428-425, 3/22/68; *JCL* 3/21/68, p. 6; *Southern Courier* 3/30–31/68, p. 1; transcripts of King's speeches in Jackson & Eutaw, 3/20/68, KP; *AC* 3/22/68, p. 24. Also see Willie Williams Interview (Fort), who was King's barber from 1965 on and whom King visited on 3/21/68.

   36. Lawson Interview (Yellin & Beifuss V); Beifuss, *River,* pp. 204–205; Ozell Sutton to George Culberson, "Situation in Memphis," 3/22/68, CRS FOIA; Young in Louw & Wicklein, "King" ("a man with four nice children that he sees very seldom," 3/14/68); Coretta King Interview (Mayerson XVIII, pp. 52–53, XXX, p. 3); Yolanda King Interview (LaCrosse); *Jet* 2/3/72, pp. 18–29; transcripts of King's speeches in Waycross, Albany, Macon & Augusta, 3/23/68, KP; A. C. Searles Interview (Ricks); FBI 100-106670-3275, 3/23/68; also Willie Williams Interview (Fort).

   37. FBI 157-8428-422, 3/23/68; Billy Hollins to Hosea Williams & Herbert Coulton to Williams, 3/20/68, SCLC 178; Hollins Interview (Garrow); "Action Committee Meeting," 3/21/68, TO; Sampson Interview (Shannon); FBI 100-448006-40, 84, & 66, 3/18, 23 & 4/4/68; Hoover SAC letter 68-16, 3/12/68, 157-00-NR; Moore to Sullivan, "Liaison with Groups Sponsoring Integration," 6/4/68, 170-00-102; Moore to Sullivan, "Racial Informants," 9/3/68, 170-00-113; SAC Chicago to Director, 4/22/68, 100-448006-102, p. 3; Gibson to Williams, 3/24/68, SCLC 178.

   38. Moffett to King, 3/25/68, & Levison to Young, n.d., SCLC 177; Moffett Interview (Garrow); King, "A Knock at Midnight," 3/24/68, Canaan, KP; *NYT* 3/25/68, p. 46, 3/26/68, p. 20; Offenburger Notes on 3/25/68 Action Committee Meeting, TO; "Conversation with Martin Luther King," *Conservative Judaism* 22 (Spring 1968): 1–19 (3/25/68). To Levison, King remarked that "I think we have to be realistic enough to see that if there's any possibility of stopping Lyndon, it's going to be Kennedy." FBI NY 100-111180-9-1621A, 3/26/68.

   39. Logan Interview (Garrow); Frank, *American Death,* pp. 39–42; Frady, "Prophet," p. 83; *NYT* 3/27/68, p. 24, 3/28/68, p. 40; *CSM* 3/30/68, p. 11; *NYC* 1/17/70, p. 3.

   40. Stanfield, *In Memphis,* 4/3; Beifuss, *River,* pp. 211–42; John Spence Interview (Thomas & Yellin); Bobby Doctor Interview (Thomas & Yellin); Jacques Wilmore Interview (Britton); Darrel Doughty Interview (Beifuss & Yellin); Mosby interviews with Richard Moon, Charles Cabbage & Charles Ballard; Calvin Taylor Interview (Thomas & Viar); Lawson Interviews (Beifuss & Yellin; Yellin & Beifuss V); Lawson, *Civil Liberties Review* 7–8/78, pp. 30–32; *MCA* 3/29/68, pp. 1, 10, 25, 4/1/68, p. 25; *WP* 3/31/68, p. A1; James Turner to Stephen Pollak, "Memphis Disturbance . . . ," 4/1/68, CRD 144-72-658; Frank, *American Death,* pp. 25–27; Kyles Interview (Beifuss & Thomas); *Time* 4/5/68, p. 25; *PC* 4/6/68, p. 2; *Newsweek* 4/8/68, pp. 33–34; FBI 157-9146-45 & 47, 3/29/68; Paul Barnett Interview (Yellins); *NYT* 3/29/68, p. 1.

   41. Interviews with Lawson (Yellin & Beifuss V); David Caywood (Trotter & Yellin); Kyles (Beifuss & Thomas); Gilbert Patterson (Beifuss & Thompson); Ezekiel Bell (Viar & Thomas); Gerald Fanion (Beifuss & Evans); Baxton Bryant (Beifuss & Beckner III); Malcolm Blackburn (Beckner & Thomas); Beifuss,

River, pp. 252–53; Franks, *American Death,* p. 28; FBI 157-9146-38, 1390, ME 157-1092-167, 168, 3/28/68, 157-1092-173, 3/29/68. SCLC's antipathy about 3/28 was substantial. "Jim Lawson has one of the most unproductive careers in the movement," Andrew Young later told Levison. FBI NY 100-111180-9-1691, 6/4/68.

42. *Ebony* 5/68, p. 180; Abernathy in U.S. Congress, House Assassinations Committee, *Hearings,* vol. 1, p. 16; Abernathy, "Nonviolent Movement," p. 198; Abernathy in Franks, *American Death,* p. 29; Abernathy in Bennett, *What Manner,* p. 237; Coretta King Interview (Mayerson XXVIII, p. 30); FBI 100-106670-3272, 3291, 3292, NY 100-111180-9-1623A, 3/28/68; Levison in 11/12–13/73 videotape, KC; Abernathy in Raines, *My Soul,* p. 465.

43. Franks, *American Death,* pp. 30–33; Abernathy in *Hearings,* n. 42 above, pp. 16–17; Calvin Taylor Interview (Thomas & Viar); Williams to King, 3/13/68, SCLC 48; Williams Interview (Garrow); Lawson Interview (Beifuss & Yellin).

44. *MCA* 3/30/68, p. 1; *NYT* 3/30/68, pp. 1, 31; Abernathy in Raines, *My Soul,* p. 465; FBI 100-106670-3271, 3291, 100-438794-2345, p. 6, 157-8428-431, NY 100-111180-9-1624A, 3/29/68; Levison Interviews (Lewis; Schlesinger). As Young commented later, "The difference that I saw over the years was that he changed from the kind of person who was resisting leadership and trying to avoid the burdens of responsibility for the movement to a person who almost went to the other extreme and felt totally responsible and burdened by the movement." Especially concerning riots and the northern cities, "Martin felt terribly guilty . . . felt like he'd failed, that he hadn't done as much as he could do. And I thought that was ridiculous." Similarly, "one of the big problems Martin had was getting people to disagree with him. Everybody . . . told him what they thought he wanted to hear, and Stanley never would do that . . . Stanley was very bold and blunt" (Garrow Interview); also *NYT* 9/15/85, p. 30.

45. Abernathy in Raines, *My Soul,* p. 466, & in *Hearings,* n. 42 above, pp. 17–18; Coretta King Interview (Mayerson XXVIII, p. 30); *MCA* 3/30/68, p. 6; *NYT* 3/31/68, pp. 46, 66, E2, 3/30/68, p. 32; *CSM* 4/3/68, p. 5.

46. Tom Offenburger Notes, 3/30/68 Action Committee Meeting, TO; Carl Farris Diary Notes, 3/30/68, CF 3; Selby, *Odyssey,* pp. 146–47; Rutherford Interview (Garrow); Young in *Look* 4/15/69, p. 29; Fauntroy in Oates, *Trumpet,* p. 481; Young Interview (Garrow); Jackson in Bennett, *What Manner,* p. 238; Jackson, "Playboy Interview," p. 104; Reynolds, *Jackson,* pp. 85–86; Garrow interviews with Jackson, Offenburger, Hosea Williams, James Orange, Dana Swan & Junius Griffin; Bevel Interviews (Garrow; Shannon); *WSJ* 1/4/84, p. 1; *WP* 1/19/84, p. A1; Abernathy in Raines, *My Soul,* p. 467; FBI NY 100-111180-9-1626A, 1627A, 3/31 & 4/1/68; Offenburger to SCLC Staff, "The Memphis Situation . . .," 4/1/68, SCLC; Beifuss, *River,* pp. 255–56. "'Maybe I should just fast to the point of death,'" Jackson recalls King telling the staff he had considered after the 3/28 turmoil. (Garrow Interview)

47. King, "Remaining Awake . . .," 3/31/68, KP; *WP* 4/1/68, p. A1; *MCA* 4/1/68, p. 35; *NYT* 4/1/68, p. 20; "Meeting on National Negro Politics," 3/31/68, KP; Young Interview (Moyers); Conyers Interview (Leventhal); Hatcher in *CT Magazine* 3/30/69, pp. 40–41; Young in Stein, *American Journey,* p. 253.

48. "Minutes of the Meeting," [4/1/68], NCCIJ 20-43; *MCA* 4/1/68, p. 1; *AC* 4/1/68, p. 2; Bobby Doctor Interview (Thomas & Yellin); Garrow interviews with Jackson, Orange, Williams & Bevel; Ron Ivy Interview (Yellin); Calvin Taylor Interview (Thomas & Viar); Darrel Doughty Interview (Beifuss & Yellin); Ozell Sutton to James Madison, "Memphis Crisis," 4/3/68, CRS FOIA; FBI 157-9146-64, 4/3/68; Massoni Notes, "Call from Jesse," 4/2/68, GM.

49. Abernathy in Raines, *My Soul,* p. 467; Coretta King Interview (Mayerson XXVIII, p. 37); Abernathy in *Hearings,* n. 42 above, p. 37; Franks, *American Death,* pp. 43–45; Lawson Interview (Yellin & Beifuss VI); Kyles Interview

(Bishop); Harold Middlebrook Interview (Beifuss & Thomas); *City of Memphis*
v. *King*, #C-68-80, 4/3/68; Charles Morgan Interview (Garrow); David Caywood
Interview (Trotter & Yellin); Walter Bailey Interview (Beifuss et al.); Lucius
Burch Interview (Beifuss & Yellin); *NT* 4/4/68; *NYT* 4/4/68, p. 30; Beifuss, *River*,
pp. 268–72.

50. Ron Ivy Interview (Yellin); *TSD* 2/28/76, p. 6; Garrow interviews with
Orange & Williams; Kyles Interview (Bishop); Coretta King Interview (Mayerson
XXVIII, p. 37): Frank, *American Death*, p. 42; *Ebony* 5/68, pp. 180–81; Aberna-
thy in Raines, *My Soul*, p. 468; Harold Middlebrook Interview (Beifuss &
Thomas); Beifuss, *River*, pp. 276–81; *MCA* 4/4/68, p. 11; King, "I've Been to the
Mountaintop," 4/3/68, KP. Earlier that evening, King again berated Jackson, who
often "would hang around . . . currying favor," Bill Rutherford recalled. "The
evening prior to his death, Dr. King . . . was so frustrated and annoyed with Jesse
. . . [that] prior to going to the church . . . he said, 'Jesse, just leave me alone.
Go any place you want to, do anything you want to do, but leave me alone.'"
Chauncey Eskridge recalls the scene similarly, saying Jackson responded, "'Don't
send me away, Doc. Don't send me away.'" (Garrow interviews)

51. Young Interview (Moyers); Young in Stein, *American Journey*, p. 253;
NYT 4/5/68, p. 24; Abernathy in Raines, *My Soul*, p. 468; James Laue Interview
(Lewis); Kyles Interview (Beifuss et al.); Franks, *American Death*, pp. 55–57;
FBI 157-9146-9, 4/6/68; David Caywood Interview (Trotter & Yellin); Ron Ivy
Interview (Yellin); Garrow interviews with Orange & Williams. On the settle-
ment rumors, see the interviews with Frank Miles (Adams; Beifuss & Yellin);
Downing Pryor (Mosby; Trotter et al.); Dan Kuykendall (Yellin & Thomas); &
Junius Griffin (Garrow) & Beifuss, "King."

52. Lawson Interview (Yellin & Beifuss VI); Franks, *American Death*, pp.
56–58; *City of Memphis* v. *King* transcript, 4/4/68, MVC, MSU; Bishop interviews
with Abernathy & Lee; Rutherford & Williams in *AC* 4/5/68, pp. 8, 9; Harold
Middlebrook Interview (Beifuss & Thomas); Beifuss, *River*, pp. 283–93; Garrow
interviews with Eskridge, Rutherford, Williams & Offenburger; Coretta King Interview (Mayerson XXIX, p. 3); Coretta King, *My Life*, p. 316; Abernathy in
Hearings, n. 42 above, p. 19; King, Sr., "The Day," p. 36. On 4/7/68, Williams
recalled that King "said the other day, . . . 'Truly America is much, much sicker,
Hosea, than I realized when I first began working in 1955." CBS, "Some
Friends," p. 10.

53. Young Interview (Moyers); Burch Interview (Beifuss & Yellin); Garrow
conversation with Brown; Caywood Interview (Trotter & Yellin); Bailey Interview (Beifuss et al.); Eskridge Interview (Garrow); Frank, *American Death*, pp.
66–76; Abernathy in Cotton, "Conversation" & in Raines, *My Soul*, pp. 468–70;
James Laue Interview (Lewis); Young in *Soul Force*, 4/4/69, p. 5, and *N&O*
4/5/84, p. A14; Kyles in *Ebony* 4/84, pp. 33–40; Kyles Interviews (Beifuss et al.;
Bishop). Young later commented that "I was almost strangely relieved when Martin died. This was the only way he could know peace. He was so tormented by the
violence in this country. He could not understand it." Stein, *American Journey*, p.
253. Chauncey Eskridge agreed. "After Martin was killed, Andy and I said that
maybe this was the best thing because he'd run out of things to do." (Garrow
Interview) Coretta King wrote later that "my husband's martyrdom provided him
that final freedom and peace we all seek." "We Must," p. 7. Also see *Liberation*
4/68, p. 16. Exceptionally harsh assessments of King once were common among
prominent historians—David Lewis ("Martin Luther King failed," *King*, p. 393),
August Meier ("King's career was a tragedy," *Saturday Review* 2/14/70, p. 40),
and Louis Harlan (King an "ultimate failure," *American Historical Review* 10/70,
pp. 1797–98). Similar contemporaneous critiques appear in *Liberator* 5/63, p. 19,
12/64, p. 3, 2/65, pp. 10–13, 3/65, pp. 11–15, & 5/65, pp. 4–6, plus Austin C.

Clarke, *The Confessed Bewilderment of Martin Luther King, Jr.* (Burlington, Ont.: Al Kitab Sudan Publications, 1968).

Epilogue

1. Willie, "King: His World Mission"; Yolanda King Interview (LaCrosse); Farris, "Young Martin," p. 56; Young, "Address at Vanderbilt University," 1/22/85, Nashville; Harding, "The Land Beyond," p. 18; Williams in *AC* 1/14/78, p. B1; Baker Interview (Britton, p. 39); Nash Interview (Garrow). On Willie's point, also see Sibley, "King and the Future"; on Harding's, also see Lentz, "Resurrecting the Prophet," pp. 780, 924; Garrow, *King: Challenging America*; and Robert Weisbrot, *New Republic* 1/30/84, pp. 10–16.

Bibliography

Selected Books and Pamphlets

Abram, Morris B. *The Day is Short.* New York: Harcourt Brace Jovanovich, 1982.

Adams, Frank. *Unearthing Seeds of Fire: The Idea of Highlander.* Winston-Salem, N.C.: John F. Blair, 1975.

Ahmann, Mathew H., ed. *The New Negro.* Notre Dame, Ind.: Fides Publishers, 1961.

Alabama Christian Movement for Human Rights. *They Challenge Segregation at Its Core!* Birmingham, Ala.: Southern Conference Educational Fund, 1959.

Allen, Ivan, Jr. *Mayor: Notes on the Sixties.* New York: Simon & Schuster, 1971.

Anderson, Jervis. *A. Philip Randolph: A Biographical Portrait.* New York: Harcourt Brace Jovanovich, 1973.

Angelou, Maya. *The Heart of a Woman.* New York: Random House, 1981.

Ansbro, John J. *Martin Luther King, Jr.: The Making of a Mind.* Maryknoll, N.Y.: Orbis Books, 1982.

Baldwin, Frederick C. *". . . We ain't what we used to be."* Savannah, Ga.: Telfair Academy of Arts and Sciences, 1983.

Barkan, Steven E. *Protesters on Trial: Criminal Justice in the Southern Civil Rights and Vietnam Antiwar Movements.* New Brunswick, N.J.: Rutgers University Press, 1985.

Barnard, Hollinger F., ed. *Outside the Magic Circle: The Autobiography of Virginia Foster Durr.* University: University of Alabama Press, 1985.

Barnes, Catherine A. *Journey From Jim Crow: The Desegregation of Southern Transportation.* New York: Columbia University Press, 1983.

Bass, Jack. *Unlikely Heroes.* New York: Simon & Schuster, 1981.

Beardslee, William R. *The Way Out Must Lead In: Life Histories in the Civil Rights Movement.* Atlanta, Ga.: Center for Research in Social Change, Emory University, 1977.

Beifuss, Joan T. *At the River I Stand: Memphis, the 1968 Strike, and Martin Luther King.* Memphis, Tenn.: B & W Books, 1985.

Bennett, Lerone, Jr. *The Negro Mood and Other Essays.* Chicago: Johnson Publishing Co., 1964.

Bennett, Lerone, Jr. *What Manner of Man: A Biography of Martin Luther King, Jr.* Chicago: Johnson Publishing Co., 1964, 2nd ed. 1965, 3rd ed. 1968.

Berry, Brian J. L. *The Open Housing Question: Race and Housing in Chicago, 1966–1976.* Cambridge, Mass.: Ballinger Publishing Co., 1979.

Bianchi, Eugene C. *The Religious Experience of Revolutionaries.* Garden City, N.Y.: Doubleday, 1972.

Bishop, Jim. *The Days of Martin Luther King, Jr.* New York: G. P. Putnam's Sons, 1971.

Bleiweiss, Robert M., ed. *Marching to Freedom: The Life of Martin Luther King, Jr.* Middletown, Conn.: American Education Publications, 1968.

Blumberg, Rhoda L. *Civil Rights: The 1960s Freedom Struggle.* Boston: Twayne Publishers, 1984.

Boesak, Allan. *Coming in Out of the Wilderness: A Comparative Interpretation of the Ethics of Martin Luther King, Jr. and Malcolm X.* Kampen, Nederland: Theologische Hogeschool der Gereformeerde Kerken, n.d.

Booth, William D. *The Progressive Story: New Baptist Roots.* St. Paul, Minn.: Braun Press, 1981.

Boynton, Amelia P. *Bridge Across Jordan.* New York: Carlton Press, 1979.

Brauer, Carl M. *John F. Kennedy and the Second Reconstruction.* New York: Columbia University Press, 1977.

Brink, William, & Louis Harris. *The Negro Revolution in America.* New York: Simon & Schuster, 1964.

Brink, William, & Louis Harris. *Black and White.* New York: Simon & Schuster, 1967.

Brisbane, Robert H. *Black Activism.* Valley Forge, Pa.: Judson Press, 1974.

Brooks, Thomas R. *Walls Come Tumbling Down.* Englewood Cliffs, N.J.: Prentice-Hall, 1974.

Brown, Bernard O. *Ideology and Community Action: The West Side Organization of Chicago, 1964–67.* Chicago: Center for the Scientific Study of Religion, 1978.

Burk, Robert F. *The Eisenhower Administration and Black Civil Rights.* Knoxville: University of Tennessee Press, 1984.

Cain, Alfred E., ed. *A Martin Luther King Treasury.* Yonkers, N.Y.: Educational Heritage, 1964.

Carawan, Guy & Candie. *Freedom Is a Constant Struggle.* New York: Oak Publications, 1968.

Carmichael, Stokely, & Charles V. Hamilton. *Black Power: The Politics of Liberation in America.* New York: Random House, 1967.

Carson, Clayborne. *In Struggle: SNCC and the Black Awakening of the 1960s.* Cambridge, Mass.: Harvard University Press, 1981.

Cartwright, John H., ed. *Essays in Honor of Martin Luther King, Jr.* Evanston, Ill.: Garrett Evangelical Theological Seminary, 1977.

Chafe, William H. *Civilities and Civil Rights.* New York: Oxford University Press, 1980.

Clark, James G. *The Jim Clark Story—I Saw Selma Raped.* Birmingham, Ala.: Selma Enterprises, 1966.

Clark, Kenneth B. *King, Malcolm, Baldwin.* Middletown, Conn.: Wesleyan University Press, 1985. [Originally published as *The Negro Protest* (Boston: Beacon Press, 1963).]

Clark, Septima P. *Echo in My Soul.* New York: E. P. Dutton & Co., 1962.

Clayton, Edward T. *Martin Luther King: The Peaceful Warrior,* 3rd ed. Englewood Cliffs, N.J.: Prentice-Hall, 1970.

Clayton, Edward T., ed. *The SCLC Story.* Atlanta, Ga.: SCLC, 1964.

Clemens, Thomas C. *Martin Luther King: Man of Peace.* Washington, D.C.: USIA, 1965.

Cluster, Dick, ed. *They Should Have Served That Cup of Coffee.* Boston: South End Press, 1979.

Coffin, William S., Jr. *Once to Every Man.* New York: Atheneum, 1977.

Colburn, David R. *Racial Change and Community Crisis: St. Augustine, Florida, 1877–1980.* New York: Columbia University Press, 1985.

Cone, James H. *For My People.* Maryknoll, N.Y.: Orbis Books, 1984.

Davis, Allison. *Leadership, Love, and Aggression.* New York: Harcourt Brace Jovanovich, 1983.

Davis, Lenwood G. *I Have a Dream—The Life and Times of Martin Luther King, Jr.* Westport, Conn.: Negro Universities Press, 1969.

DeWolf, L. Harold. *A Hard Rain and a Cross.* Nashville, Tenn.: Abingdon Press, 1966.

Dorman, Michael. *We Shall Overcome.* New York: Delacorte Press, 1964.

Downing, Fred L. *To See the Promised Land: The Faith Pilgrimage of Martin Luther King, Jr.* Macon, Ga.: Mercer University Press, 1986.
Evans, Sara. *Personal Politics.* New York: Alfred A. Knopf, 1979.
Evans, Zelia S., with J. T. Alexander, eds. *Dexter Avenue Baptist Church, 1877–1977.* Montgomery, Ala.: Dexter Avenue Baptist Church, 1977.
Fager, Charles E. *Selma 1965.* New York: Charles Scribner's Sons, 1974.
Fager, Charles E. *Uncertain Resurrection: The Poor People's Washington Campaign.* Grand Rapids, Mich.: William B. Eerdmans, 1969.
Fager, Charles E. *White Reflections on Black Power.* Grand Rapids, Mich.: William B. Eerdmans, 1967.
Farmer, James. *Freedom—When?* New York: Random House, 1965.
Farmer, James. *Lay Bare the Heart.* New York: Arbor House, 1985.
Fields, Uriah J. *The Montgomery Story: The Unhappy Effects of the Montgomery Bus Boycott.* New York: Exposition Press, 1959.
Fisher, William H. *Free at Last: A Bibliography of Martin Luther King, Jr.* Metuchen, N.J.: Scarecrow Press, 1977.
Florida Legislative Investigation Committee. *Racial and Civil Disorders in St. Augustine.* Tallahassee: Florida State Legislature, 1965.
Forman, James. *The Making of Black Revolutionaries.* New York: Macmillan, 1972.
Forman, James. *Sammy Younge, Jr.* New York: Grove Press, 1968.
Frank, Gerold. *An American Death.* Garden City, N.Y.: Doubleday, 1972.
Garrow, David J. *The FBI and Martin Luther King, Jr.: From "Solo" to Memphis.* New York: W. W. Norton, 1981.
Garrow, David J. *Martin Luther King, Jr.: Challenging America at Its Core.* New York: Democratic Socialists of America, 1983.
Garrow, David J. *Protest at Selma: Martin Luther King, Jr., and the Voting Rights Act of 1965.* New Haven, Conn.: Yale University Press, 1978.
Gaston, Arthur G. *Green Power.* Birmingham, Ala.: Birmingham Publishing Co., 1968.
Gentile, Thomas: *March on Washington: August 28, 1963.* Washington, D.C.: New Day Publications, 1983.
Giddings, Paula. *When and Where I Enter.* New York: William Morrow, 1984.
Goldman, Peter. *The Death and Life of Malcolm X.* New York: Harper & Row, 1973.
Goldman, Peter. *Report from Black America.* New York: Simon & Schuster, 1970.
Good, Paul. *The Trouble I've Seen.* Washington, D.C.: Howard University Press, 1975.
Goodwin, Bennie E. *Dr. Martin Luther King, Jr.: God's Messenger of Love, Justice and Hope.* Jersey City, N.J.: Goodpatrick, 1976.
Grant, Joanne, ed. *Black Protest.* Greenwich, Conn.: Fawcett Books, 1968.
Green, Robert L. *The Legacy of Martin Luther King, Jr.* Wichita, Kans.: Wichita State University, 1973.
Green, Robert L. *Martin Luther King, Jr.* n.p., Michigan Conference News, 1972.
Guthman, Edwin. *We Band of Brothers.* New York: Harper & Row, 1971.
Halstead, Fred. *Out Now! A Participant's Account of the American Movement Against the Vietnam War.* New York: Monad Press, 1978.
Hanigan, James P. *Martin Luther King, Jr., and the Foundations of Nonviolence.* Lanham, Md.: University Press of America, 1984.
Harding, Vincent. *The Other American Revolution.* Los Angeles: Center for Afro-American Studies, UCLA, 1980.
Harrington, Michael. *Fragments of the Century: A Social Autobiography.* New York: Saturday Review Press, 1973.
Harvey, James C. *Black Civil Rights During the Johnson Administration.* Jackson:

University and College Press of Mississippi, 1973.

Horton, John B. *Not Without Struggle*. New York: Vantage Press, 1979.

Hoyt, Robert G. *Martin Luther King, Jr.* Waukesha, Wisc.: Country Beautiful Foundation, 1970.

Jackson, Joseph H. *Unholy Shadows and Freedom's Holy Light*. Nashville, Tenn.: Townsend Press, 1967.

Jacoway, Elizabeth, & David R. Colburn, eds. *Southern Businessmen and Desegregation*. Baton Rouge: Louisiana State University Press, 1982.

Jones, Bill. *The Wallace Story*. Northport, Ala.: American Southern Publishing Co., 1966.

Joseph, Peter. *Good Times: An Oral History of America in the Nineteen Sixties*. New York: Charterhouse, 1973.

King, Coretta Scott. *My Life with Martin Luther King, Jr.* New York: Holt, Rinehart & Winston, 1969.

King, Martin Luther, Jr. *The Measure of a Man*. Philadelphia: Christian Education Press, 1959.

King, Martin Luther, Jr. *Strength to Love*. New York: Harper & Row, 1963.

King, Martin Luther, Jr. *Stride Toward Freedom: The Montgomery Story*. New York: Harper & Brothers, 1958.

King, Martin Luther, Jr. *The Trumpet of Conscience*. New York: Harper & Row, 1968.

King, Martin Luther, Jr. *Where Do We Go from Here: Chaos or Community?* New York: Harper & Row, 1967.

King, Martin Luther, Jr. *Why We Can't Wait*. New York: New American Library, 1964.

King, Martin Luther, Sr. *Daddy King: An Autobiography*. New York: William Morrow, 1980.

Kondrashov, Stanislav. *The Life and Death of Martin Luther King*. Moscow: Progress Publishers, 1981.

Kotz, Nick & Mary Lynn. *A Passion for Equality*. New York: W. W. Norton, 1977.

Kunstler, William M. *Deep in My Heart*. New York: William Morrow, 1966.

Kunstler, William M. *Trials and Tribulations*. New York: Grove Press, 1985.

Landess, Thomas, & Richard Quinn. *Jesse Jackson and the Politics of Race*. Ottawa, Ill.: Jameson Books, 1985.

Lawson, Steven F. *Black Ballots: Voting Rights in the South, 1944–1969*. New York: Columbia University Press, 1976.

Lawson, Steven F. *In Pursuit of Power: Southern Blacks and Electoral Politics, 1965–1982*. New York: Columbia University Press, 1985.

Lerner, Gerda, ed. *Black Women in White America*. New York: Pantheon, 1972.

Lewis, Anthony. *Portrait of a Decade*. New York: Random House, 1965.

Lewis, David L. *King: A Critical Biography*. New York: Praeger, 1970.

Lincoln, C. Eric, ed. *Martin Luther King, Jr.: A Profile*, rev. ed. New York: Hill & Wang, 1984.

Lokos, Lionel. *House Divided: The Life and Legacy of Martin Luther King*. New Rochelle, N.Y.: Arlington House, 1968.

Lomax, Louis. *The Negro Revolt*. New York: Harper & Brothers, 1962.

Lomax, Louis. *To Kill a Black Man*. Los Angeles: Holloway House, 1968.

Lynd, Staughton, ed. *Nonviolence in America*. Indianapolis, Ind.: Bobbs-Merrill, 1966.

McClendon, James W., Jr. *Biography as Theology*. Nashville, Tenn.: Abingdon Press, 1974.

McKee, Don. *Martin Luther King, Jr.* New York: G. P. Putnam's Sons, 1969.

Marable, Manning. *From the Grassroots*. Boston: South End Press, 1980.

Marable, Manning. *Race, Reform and Rebellion: The Second Reconstruction in*

Black America, 1945–1982. Jackson: University Press of Mississippi, 1984.

Marshall, Burke. *Federalism and Civil Rights.* New York: Columbia University Press, 1964.

Mays, Benjamin E. *Born to Rebel.* New York: Charles Scribner's Sons, 1971.

Meier, August, & Elliott Rudwick. *CORE: A Study in the Civil Rights Movement.* New York: Oxford University Press, 1973.

Mendelsohn, Jack. *The Martyrs.* New York: Harper & Row, 1966.

Miller, William R. *Martin Luther King, Jr.* New York: Weybright & Talley, 1968.

Mitchell, Glenford E., & William H. Peace III, eds. *The Angry Black South.* New York: Corinth Books, 1962.

Morgan, Charles, Jr. *One Man, One Voice.* New York: Holt, Rinehart & Winston, 1979.

Morris, Aldon D. *The Origins of the Civil Rights Movement.* New York: Free Press, 1984.

Morrow, E. Frederic. *Black Man in the White House.* New York: Coward-McCann, 1963.

Muller, Gerald F. *Martin Luther King, Jr., Civil Rights Leader.* Minneapolis, Minn.: T. S. Denison & Co., 1971.

Muse, Benjamin. *The American Negro Revolution.* Bloomington: Indiana University Press, 1968.

Namorato, Michael V., ed. *Have We Overcome?* Jackson: University Press of Mississippi, 1979.

Navasky, Victor S. *Kennedy Justice.* New York: Atheneum, 1971.

Newfield, Jack. *A Prophetic Minority.* New York: New American Library, 1966.

Niebuhr, Reinhold. *Moral Man and Immoral Society.* New York: Charles Scribner's Sons, 1932.

Nixon, Richard M. *Six Crises.* Garden City, N.Y.: Doubleday, 1962.

Oates, Stephen B. *Let the Trumpet Sound.* New York: Harper & Row, 1982.

Paris, Peter J. *Black Leaders in Conflict.* New York: Pilgrim Press, 1978.

Parmet, Herbert S. *Eisenhower and the American Crusades.* New York: Macmillan, 1972.

Peck, Ira. *The Life and Words of Martin Luther King, Jr.* New York: Scholastic Book Services, 1968.

Peeks, Edward. *The Long Struggle for Black Power.* New York: Charles Scribner's Sons, 1971.

Peters, William. *The Southern Temper.* Garden City, N.Y.: Doubleday, 1959.

Power, Jonathan. *Martin Luther King—A Reassessment.* London: Fellowship of Reconciliation, 1976.

Powledge, Fred. *Black Power—White Resistance.* Cleveland, Ohio: World Publishing, 1967.

Raines, Howell. *My Soul Is Rested: Movement Days in the Deep South Remembered.* New York: G. P. Putnam's Sons, 1977.

Reddick, Lawrence D. *Crusader Without Violence: A Biography of Martin Luther King, Jr.* New York: Harper & Brothers, 1959.

Reynolds, Barbara A. *Jesse Jackson: The Man, The Movement, The Myth.* Chicago: Nelson-Hall, 1975.

Robinson, Jackie. *I Never Had It Made.* New York: G. P. Putnam's Sons, 1972.

Robinson, Jo Ann O. *Abraham Went Out: A Biography of A. J. Muste.* Philadelphia: Temple University Press, 1981.

Rose, Stephen C. *Albany Report.* Chicago: Chicago City Missionary Society, 1962.

Rose, Thomas, & John Greenya. *Black Leaders: Then and Now.* Garrett Park, Md.: Garrett Park Press, 1984.

Rowan, Carl T. *Go South to Sorrow.* New York: Random House, 1957.

Rustin, Bayard. *Down the Line.* Chicago: Quadrangle Books, 1971.

Rustin, Bayard. *Report on Montgomery, Alabama.* New York: War Resisters League, 1956.

Rustin, Bayard. *Strategies for Freedom.* New York: Columbia University Press, 1976.

Salter, John R., Jr. *Jackson, Mississippi: An American Chronicle of Struggle and Schism.* Hicksville, N.Y.: Exposition Press, 1979.

Saunders, Doris E., ed. *The Day They Marched.* Chicago: Johnson Publishing Co., 1963.

Schlesinger, Arthur M., Jr. *A Thousand Days.* Boston: Houghton Mifflin, 1965.

Schlesinger, Arthur M., Jr. *Robert Kennedy and His Times.* Boston: Houghton Mifflin, 1978.

Schulke, Flip, ed. *Martin Luther King, Jr.: A Documentary—Montgomery to Memphis.* New York: W. W. Norton, 1976.

Schulke, Flip, & Penelope McPhee. *King Remembered.* New York: W. W. Norton, 1986.

Selby, Earl & Miriam. *Odyssey: Journey Through Black America.* New York: G. P. Putnam's Sons, 1971.

Sellers, Cleveland. *The River of No Return.* New York: William Morrow, 1973.

Sitkoff, Harvard. *The Struggle for Black Equality.* New York: Hill & Wang, 1981.

Slack, Kenneth. *Martin Luther King.* London: SCM Press, 1970.

Smith, Charles U., & Lewis M. Killian. *The Tallahassee Bus Protest.* New York: Anti-Defamation League of B'nai B'rith, 1958.

Smith, Ervin. *The Ethics of Martin Luther King.* Lewiston, N.Y.: Edwin Mellen Press, 1981.

Smith, Kelly Miller. *Social Crisis Preaching.* Macon, Ga.: Mercer University Press, 1984.

Smith, Kenneth L., & Ira G. Zepp, Jr. *Search for the Beloved Community: The Thinking of Martin Luther King, Jr.* Valley Forge, Pa.: Judson Press, 1974.

Southern Regional Council. *The Freedom Ride.* Atlanta, Ga.: SRC, 1961.

Stanfield, J. Edwin. *In Memphis: Mirror to America.* Atlanta, Ga.: Southern Regional Council, 4/28/68.

Stanfield, J. Edwin. *In Memphis: More Than a Garbage Strike.* Atlanta, Ga.: SRC, 3/22/68.

Stanfield, J. Edwin. *In Memphis: Tragedy Unaverted.* Atlanta, Ga.: SRC, 4/3/68.

Stein, Jean. *American Journey: The Times of Robert Kennedy.* New York: Harcourt Brace Jovanovich, 1970.

Sterne, Emma G. *I Have a Dream.* New York: Alfred A. Knopf, 1965.

Stevenson, Janet. *The Montgomery Bus Boycott.* New York: Franklin Watts, 1971.

Stokes, Carl B. *Promises of Power: A Political Autobiography.* New York: Simon & Schuster, 1973.

Suggs, Henry L., ed. *The Black Press in the South, 1865–1979.* Westport, Conn.: Greenwood Press, 1983.

Taylor, Gardner C. *How Shall They Preach.* Elgin, Ill.: Progressive Baptist Publishing House, 1977.

Thomas, Arthur E. *Like It Is.* New York: E. P. Dutton, 1981.

Thompson, Kenneth W., ed. *The Kennedy Presidency: Seventeen Intimate Perspectives of John F. Kennedy.* Lanham, Md.: University Press of America, 1985.

Tjerandsen, Carl. *Education for Citizenship: A Foundation's Experience.* Santa Cruz, Cal.: Emil Schwarzhaupt Foundation, 1980.

Travis, Dempsey J. *An Autobiography of Black Chicago.* Chicago: Urban Research Institute, 1981.

Tull, James E. *Shapers of Baptist Thought.* Valley Forge, Pa.: Judson Press, 1972.

Tweedle, John. *A Lasting Impression: A Collection of Photographs of Martin*

Luther King, Jr. Columbia: University of South Carolina Press, 1983.

U.S. Congress. House of Representatives, Select Committee on Assassinations. *The Final Assassinations Report.* New York: Bantam Books, 1979.

U.S. Congress. House of Representatives, Select Committee on Assassinations. *Hearings on Investigation of the Assassination of Martin Luther King, Jr.,* vols. 1, 6, 7. 95th Cong., 2nd sess., 1978.

U.S. Congress. Senate, Select Committee to Study Governmental Operations with respect to Intelligence Activities Church Committee. *Final Report,* books II & III. 94th Cong., 2nd sess., 1976.

U.S. Congress. Senate, Select Committee to Study Governmental Operations with respect to Intelligence Activities Church Committee. *Hearings—Federal Bureau of Investigation,* vol. 6. 94th Cong., 1st sess., 1976.

U.S. Department of Justice. *Report of the Department of Justice Task Force to Review the FBI Martin Luther King, Jr., Security and Assassination Investigations,* 1/11/77.

Viorst, Milton. *Fire in the Streets.* New York: Simon & Schuster, 1979.

Vivian, C. T. *Black Power and the American Myth.* Philadelphia: Fortress Press, 1970.

Vivian, Octavia. *Coretta.* Philadelphia: Fortress Press, 1970.

Walker, Jack L. *Sit-Ins in Atlanta.* New York: McGraw-Hill, 1964.

Walker, Wyatt T. *"Somebody's Calling My Name": Black Sacred Music and Social Change.* Valley Forge, Pa.: Judson Press, 1979.

Walker, Wyatt T. *The Soul of Black Worship.* New York: Martin Luther King Fellows Press, 1984.

Walton, Hanes, Jr. *The Political Philosophy of Martin Luther King, Jr.* Westport, Conn.: Greenwood Publishing Co., 1971.

Warren, Robert Penn. *Who Speaks for the Negro?* New York: Random House, 1965.

Washington, James M., ed. *A Testament of Hope.* San Francisco: Harper & Row, 1986.

Watley, William D. *Roots of Resistance: The Nonviolent Ethic of Martin Luther King, Jr.* Valley Forge, Pa.: Judson Press, 1985.

Watters, Pat. *Down to Now: Reflections on the Southern Civil Rights Movement.* New York: Pantheon, 1971.

Watters, Pat, & Reese Cleghorn. *Climbing Jacob's Ladder.* New York: Harcourt, Brace & World, 1967.

Webb, Sheyann, & Rachel West Nelson. *Selma, Lord, Selma.* University: University of Alabama Press, 1980.

Westin, Alan F., & Barry Mahoney. *The Trial of Martin Luther King.* New York: Thomas Y. Crowell, 1974.

Whalen, Charles & Barbara. *The Longest Debate: A Legislative History of the 1964 Civil Rights Act.* Cabin John, Md.: Seven Locks Press, 1985.

Wilkins, Roger. *A Man's Life.* New York: Simon & Schuster, 1982.

Wilkins, Roy. *Standing Fast.* New York: Viking Press, 1982.

Williams, John A. *The King God Didn't Save.* New York: Coward-McCann, 1970.

Witherspoon, William R. *Martin Luther King, Jr.—To the Mountaintop.* Garden City, N.Y.: Doubleday, 1985.

Wofford, Harris. *Of Kennedys and Kings.* New York: Farrar, Straus & Giroux, 1980.

Yarbrough, Tinsley E. *Judge Frank Johnson and Human Rights in Alabama.* University: University of Alabama Press, 1981.

Zaroulis, Nancy, & Gerald Sullivan. *Who Spoke Up?* Garden City, N.Y.: Doubleday, 1984.

Zinn, Howard. *Albany.* Atlanta, Ga.: Southern Regional Council, 1/8/62.

Zinn, Howard. *Albany: A Study in National Responsibility*. Atlanta, Ga.: SRC, 11/62.
Zinn, Howard. *The Southern Mystique*. New York: Alfred A. Knopf, 1964.
Zinn, Howard. *SNCC: The New Abolitionists*, 2nd ed. Boston: Beacon Press, 1965.

Selected Articles

Abernathy, Ralph. "Martin Luther King's Dream," in Lynda R. Obst, ed., *The Sixties* (New York: Random House, 1977), p. 94.
Abernathy, Ralph. "My Last Letter to Martin." *Ebony* 23 (7/68): 58–61.
Abernathy, Ralph. "The Nonviolent Movement: The Past, the Present, and the Future." *Drum Major* 1 (8/71): 18–35, & in Rhoda L. Goldstein, ed., *Black Life and Culture in the United States* (New York: Thomas Y. Crowell, 1971), pp. 180–209.
Alexander, Robert J. "Negro Business in Atlanta." *Southern Economic Journal* 17 (4/51): 451–64.
Anderson, William G. "The Spirit of Albany." *Labor Today* 3 (Winter 1962–63): 11–14.
Ansbro, John J. "Martin Luther King's Civil Disobedience—A Rejoinder." *Gandhi Marg* (II) 3 (3/82): 709–21.
Ansbro, John J. "Martin Luther King's Conception of Agape." *Gandhi Marg* (II) 2 (1/81): 556–71.
Austin, Aleine. "Behind the Montgomery Bus Boycott." *Monthly Review* 8 (9/56): 163–67.
Baldwin, James. "The Dangerous Road Before Martin Luther King." *Harper's* 222 (2/61): 33–42.
Baldwin, Lewis V. "Martin Luther King, Jr., the Black Church, and the Black Messianic Vision." *Journal of the Interdenominational Theological Center* 12 (Fall 1984–Spring 1985): 93–108.
Barbour, J. Pius. "Dr. Martin Luther King Returns 'Home.'" *Dexter Echo* 4 (12/9/59): 4.
Barbour, J. Pius. "Meditations on Rev. M. L. King, Jr." *National Baptist Voice* 28 (3/56): 4–5.
Beifuss, Joan. "The Night Martin Luther King Was Killed." *Memphis* 2 (7/77): 25–31.
Belafonte, Harry, & Stanley Levison. "Martin Luther King, Jr., 1929–1968." *Encyclopedia Yearbook 1968* (New York: Grolier, 1969), p. 160.
Bennett, Lerone, Jr. "The King Plan For Freedom." *Ebony* 11 (7/56): 65–69.
Bennett, Lerone, Jr. "The Martyrdom of Martin Luther King, Jr." *Ebony* 23 (5/68): 174–81.
Bennett, Lerone, Jr. "The South and the Negro." *Ebony* 12 (4/57): 77–81.
Bosmajian, Haig. "The Inaccuracies in the Reprintings of Martin Luther King's 'I Have a Dream' Speech." *Communication Education* 31 (4/82): 107–14.
Bosmajian, Haig. "Rhetoric of Martin Luther King's Letter From Birmingham Jail." *Midwest Quarterly* 8 (1/67): 127–43.
Braden, Anne. "The History That We Made." *Southern Exposure* 7 (Summer 1979): 48–54.
Braden, Anne. "The Southern Freedom Movement in Perspective." *Monthly Review* 17 (7–8/65): 1–93.
Bristol, James E. "Memories of Martin Luther King, Jr." *Studies in Education* 39 (Spring 1980): 13–15.
Brown, Cynthia S. "Rosa Parks." *Southern Exposure* 9 (Spring 1981): 16–17.

Cannon, Poppy. "Martin Luther King, Jr.," in Will Yolen & Kenneth S. Giniger, eds., *Heroes for Our Time* (Harrisburg, Pa.: Stackpole, 1968), pp. 201–21.

Cantarow, Ellen, & Susan G. O'Malley. "Ella Baker: Organizing for Civil Rights," in Cantarow, ed., *Moving the Mountain* (Old Westbury, N.Y.: Feminist Press, 1980), pp. 52–93, & in *Ms.* 8 (6/80): 56ff.

Capeci, Dominic J., Jr. "From Harlem to Montgomery: The Bus Boycotts and Leadership of Adam Clayton Powell, Jr., and Martin Luther King, Jr." *Historian* 41 (8/79): 721–37.

Carberg, Warren. "The Story Behind the Victory." *Bostonia* 30 (Spring 1957): 6ff.

Carmichael, Stokely. "Toward Black Liberation." *Massachusetts Review* 7 (Autumn 1966): 639–51.

Carmichael, Stokely. "What We Want." *New York Review of Books* 7 (9/22/66): 5–8.

Carter, George E. "Martin Luther King: Incipient Transcendentalist." *Phylon* 40 (12/79): 318–24.

Chafe, William. "The Greensboro Sit-Ins." *Southern Exposure* 6 (Fall 1978): 78–87.

Charity, Ruth H., Christina Davis & Arthur Kinoy. "Danville Movement." *Southern Exposure* 10 (7–8/82): 35–45.

Clark, Benjamin Van. "Siege at Savannah." *Freedomways* 4 (Winter 1964): 131–36.

Clark, Kenneth B. "The Civil Rights Movement: Momentum and Organization." *Daedalus* 95 (Winter 1966): 239–67.

Clark, Septima P. "Literacy and Liberation." *Freedomways* 4 (Winter 1964): 113–24.

Cleghorn, Reese. "The Angels Are White." *New Republic* 149 (8/17/63): 12–14.

Cleghorn, Reese. "Martin Luther King, Apostle of Crisis." *Saturday Evening Post* 236 (6/15/63): 15–19.

Colaiaco, James A. "The American Dream Unfulfilled: Martin Luther King, Jr. and the 'Letter From Birmingham Jail.'" *Phylon* 45 (3/84): 1–18.

Colaiaco, James A. "Martin Luther King, Jr. and the Paradox of Nonviolent Direct Action." *Phylon* 47 (Spring 1986): 16–28.

Colburn, David R. "The Saint Augustine Business Community: Desegregation, 1963–1964," in Elizabeth Jacoway & Colburn, eds., *Southern Businessmen and Desegregation* (Baton Rouge: Louisiana State University Press, 1982), pp. 211–35.

Collins, Thomas W. "An Analysis of the Memphis Garbage Strike of 1968." *Public Affairs Forum* 3 (4/74): 1–6.

Conconi, Charles N. "'A Long Way From Canaan'—An Interview With Ralph David Abernathy." *Washington Post*, 8/19/73, pp. C1, C5.

Cone, James H. "Martin Luther King, Jr., Black Theology—Black Church." *Theology Today* 41 (1/84): 409–20.

Cone, James H. "Martin Luther King: The Source for His Courage to Face Death." *Concilium* 183 (3/83): 74–79.

Cone, James H. "The Theology of Martin Luther King, Jr." *Union Seminary Quarterly Review* 40 (1/86): 21–39.

Cook, Samuel D. "Is Martin Luther King, Jr., Irrelevant?" *New South* 26 (Spring 1971): 2–14.

Cook, Samuel D. "Martin Luther King." *Journal of Negro History* 53 (10/68): 348–54.

Cook, Samuel D. "The Tragic Myth of Black Power." *New South* 21 (Summer 1966): 58–68.

Cooks, Stoney. "Dr. King's Last Birthday." *Atlanta* 23 (1/84): 82.

Corley, Robert G. "In Search of Racial Harmony: Birmingham Business Leaders and Desegregation, 1950–1963," in Jacoway & Colburn, eds., *Southern Busi-*

nessmen and Desegregation (Baton Rouge: Louisiana State University Press, 1982), pp. 170–90.

Cotton, Dorothy. "CEP: Challenge to the 'New Education.'" *Freedomways* 9 (1st Quarter 1969): 66–70.

Cotton, Dorothy. "A Conversation with Ralph Abernathy." *Journal* (UCC) 9 (11–12/70): 21–30.

Cotton, Dorothy. "St. Augustine," in Guy & Candie Carawan, *Freedom Is a Constant Struggle* (New York: Oak Publications, 1968), pp. 24–28.

Darby, Henry E., & Margaret N. Rowley. "King on Vietnam and Beyond." *Phylon* 47 (Spring 1986): 43–50.

Dent, Tom. "Interviews with Civil Rights Activists." *Freedomways* 18 (3rd Quarter 1978): 164–69.

DeWolf, L. Harold. "In Memoriam: Martin Luther King, Jr." *Nexus* 12 (Fall 1968): 1–4.

DeWolf, L. Harold. "Martin Luther King, Jr. '55." *Nexus* 8 (2/65): 19–21.

DeWolf, L. Harold. "Martin Luther King, Jr., as Theologian." *Journal of the Interdenominational Theological Center* 4 (Spring 1977): 1–11.

DuBois, Rachel Davis. "Dialogue: Latest Weapon in the South." *Fellowship* 31 (7/65): 10–12.

Duckett, Alfred. "Five Years After: Memories of Martin Luther King." *Sepia* 22 (4/73): 44–53.

Dunbar, Ernest. "A Visit with Martin Luther King." *Look* 27 (2/12/63): 92–96.

Ely, James W. "Negro Demonstrations and the Law: Danville as a Test Case." *Vanderbilt Law Review* 27 (10/74): 927–68.

Fairclough, Adam. "Martin Luther King, Jr. and the Quest for Nonviolent Social Change." *Phylon* 47 (Spring 1986): 1–15.

Fairclough, Adam. "Martin Luther King and the War in Vietnam." *Phylon* 45 (3/84): 19–39.

Fairclough, Adam. "The Southern Christian Leadership Conference and the Second Reconstruction, 1957–1973." *South Atlantic Quarterly* 80 (Spring 1981): 177–94.

Fairclough, Adam. "Was Martin Luther King a Marxist?" *History Workshop* 15 (Spring 1983): 117–25.

Farris, Christine King. "The Young Martin: From Childhood Through College." *Ebony* 41 (1/86): 56–58.

Frady, Marshall. "Prophet With Honor." *New York Review of Books,* 10/27/83, pp. 79–83.

French, Edgar N. "Beginnings of A New Age," in Mitchell & Peace, eds., *The Angry Black South* (New York: Corinth Books, 1962), pp. 30–51.

Fulkerson, Richard P. "The Public Letter as a Rhetorical Form: Structure, Logic, and Style in King's 'Letter From Birmingham Jail.'" *Quarterly Journal of Speech* 65 (4/79): 121–36.

Fulton, Robert B. "With Dr. King in Puerto Rico and Birmingham." *Frontiers* 15 (10/63): 23–29.

Garber, Paul R. "Black Theology: The Latter Day Legacy of Martin Luther King, Jr." *Journal of the Interdenominational Theological Center* 2 (Spring 1975): 100–13.

Garber, Paul R. "King Was a Black Theologian." *Journal of Religious Thought* 31 (Fall–Winter 1974–1975): 16–32.

Gardner, Tom. "Montgomery Bus Boycott Interviews." *Southern Exposure* 9 (Spring 1981): 13–21.

Garrow, David J. "Black Civil Rights During the Eisenhower Administration." *Constitutional Commentary* 3 (Summer 1986): 601–13.

Garrow, David J. "Black Ministerial Protest Leadership, 1955–1970," in Samuel

S. Hill, ed., *Encyclopedia of Religion in the South* (Macon, Ga.: Mercer University Press, 1984), pp. 106–108.

Garrow, David J. "The Helms Attack on King." *Southern Exposure* 12 (4/84): 12–15.

Garrow, David J. "The Intellectual Development of Martin Luther King, Jr.: Influences and Commentaries." *Union Seminary Quarterly Review* 40 (1/86): 5–20.

Garrow, David J. "The King We Should Remember." *Focus* 14 (1/86): 3–7.

Garrow, David J. "Martin Luther King, Jr.: An Honorable Man." *Focus* 12 (1/84): 3–7.

Garrow, David J. "Martin Luther King, Jr.: Bearing the Cross of Leadership." *Peace and Change* 11 (Fall 1986): forthcoming.

Garrow, David J. "The Origins of the Montgomery Bus Boycott," *Southern Changes* 7 (10–12/85): 21–27.

Good, Paul. "The Meredith March." *New South* 21 (Summer 1966): 2–16.

Graetz, Robert. "They're Still Walking in Montgomery." *Economic Justice* 24 (3/56): 1–3.

Greenberg, Jack. "Martin Luther King, Jr., and the Law," 5/17/68, in U.S. Congress, House of Representatives, *Congressional Record* 114 (pt. 13, 6/13/68): 17109.

Greenfield, Eloise. "Rosa Parks." *Ms.* 3 (8/74): 71–74.

Griffin, John Howard. "Martin Luther King," in Melville Harcourt, ed., *Thirteen For Christ* (New York: Sheed & Ward, 1963), pp. 27–45.

Gutwillig, Robert. "Six Days in Alabama." *Mademoiselle* 57 (9/63): 116ff.

Haines, Herbert H. "Black Radicalization and the Funding of Civil Rights: 1957–1970." *Social Problems* 32 (10/84): 31–43.

Halberstam, David. "Martin Luther King, American Preacher." *Esquire*, 12/83, pp. 306–11.

Halberstam, David. "Notes From the Bottom of the Mountain." *Harper's* 236 (6/68): 40–42.

Halberstam, David. "The Second Coming of Martin Luther King." *Harper's* 235 (8/67): 39–51.

Hammer, Richard. "The Life and Death of Martin Luther King." *Midstream* 14 (5/68): 3–16.

Hanigan, James P. "Martin Luther King, Jr.: The Images of a Man." *Journal of Religious Thought* 31 (Spring–Summer 1974): 68–95.

Hanigan, James P. "Martin Luther King, Jr.: The Shaping of a Mind." *Debate & Understanding* 1 (1977): 190–206.

Harding, Vincent. "A Beginning in Birmingham." *Reporter* 28 (6/6/63): 13–19.

Harding, Vincent. "Black Radicalism: The Road from Montgomery," in Alfred F. Young, ed., *Dissent* (DeKalb: Northern Illinois University Press, 1968), pp. 319–54.

Harding, Vincent. "The Land Beyond." *Sojourners* 12 (1/83): 18–22.

Harding, Vincent. "Recalling the Inconvenient Hero: Reflections on the Last Years of Martin Luther King, Jr." *Union Seminary Quarterly Review* 40 (1/86): 53–68.

Harding, Vincent. "The Religion of Black Power," in Donald R. Cutler, ed., *The Religious Situation: 1968* (Boston: Beacon Press, 1968), pp. 3–38.

Harding, Vincent. "So Much History, So Much Future: Martin Luther King, Jr., and the Second Coming of America," in Michael V. Namorato, ed., *Have We Overcome?* (Jackson: University Press of Mississippi, 1979), pp. 31–78.

Harding, Vincent. "Where Have All the Lovers Gone?" *New South* 21 (Winter 1966): 27–38.

Harding, Vincent, & Staughton Lynd. "Albany, Georgia." *Crisis* 70 (2/63): 69–78.

Harper, Fredrick. "Self-Actualization and Three Black Protesters." *Journal of Afro-American Issues* 2 (Fall 1974): 303–19.

Hart, John. "Kennedy, Congress and Civil Rights." *Journal of American Studies* 13 (8/79): 165–78.

Henderson, Thelton. "The Law and Civil Rights: The Justice Department in the South." *New University Thought* 3 (1963): 36–45.

Hinckle, Warren, & David Welsh. "Five Battles of Selma." *Ramparts* 4 (6/65): 19–52.

Hines, Ralph H., & James E. Pierce. "Negro Leadership After the Social Crisis: An Analysis of Leadership Changes in Montgomery, Alabama." *Phylon* 26 (Summer 1965): 162–72.

Howard, Jan. "The Provocation of Violence: A Civil Rights Tactic?" *Dissent* 13 (1–2/66): 94–99.

Howell, Leon. "An Interview With Andrew Young." *Christianity and Crisis* 36 (2/16/76): 14–20.

Hubbard, Howard. "Five Long Hot Summers and How They Grew." *Public Interest* 12 (Summer 1968): 3–24.

Jack, Homer A. "Black Power and the Meredith March." *Gandhi Marg* 10 (10/66): 295–302.

Jackson, Jesse. "Completing the Agenda of Dr. King." *Ebony* 29 (6/74): 116–20.

Jackson, Jesse. "Dr. Martin Luther King—A Recollection," in John Tweedle, *A Lasting Impression* (Columbia: University of South Carolina Press, 1983), n.p.

Jackson, Jesse. "Playboy Interview." *Playboy* 16 (11/68): 85ff.

Jaffe, Andrew. "Grenada, Mississippi." *New South* 21 (Fall 1966): 15–28.

Johnson, Robert E. "How the King Children Remember Their Father." *Ebony* 27 (4/72): 75–82.

Kahn, Tom, & August Meier. "Recent Trends in the Civil Rights Movement." *New Politics* 3 (Spring 1964): 34–53.

Katz, Milton S. "Peace Liberals and Vietnam: SANE and the Politics of 'Responsible' Protest." *Peace and Change* 9 (Summer 1983): 21–39.

Killian, Lewis M. "Organization, Rationality and Spontaneity in the Civil Rights Movement." *American Sociological Review* 49 (12/84): 770–83.

King, Andrew A. "The Rhetorical Legacy of the Black Church." *Central States Speech Journal* 22 (Fall 1971): 179–85.

King, Charles H. "The Untold Story of the Power Struggle Between King and [J.H.] Jackson." *Negro Digest* 16 (5/67): 6–10, 71–79.

King, Coretta Scott. "The Legacy of Martin Luther King, Jr." *Theology Today* 27 (7/70): 129–39.

King, Coretta Scott. "My Dream for My Children." *Good Housekeeping* 158 (6/64): 77, 144–52.

King, Coretta Scott. "We Must Keep Climbing." *Maryknoll* 72 (4/78): 7–11.

King, Coretta Scott. "We're Sharing Him with All Americans . . ." *TV Guide,* 2/11/78, pp. 4–6.

King, Coretta Scott. "The World of Coretta King." *New Lady,* 1/1/66, pp. 24–37.

[King], Coretta Scott. "Why I Came to College." *Opportunity* 26 (Spring 1948): 42 & 70.

King, Martin Luther, Jr. "Playboy Interview." *Playboy* 12 (1/65): 65–78.

King, Martin Luther, Sr. "The Day They Killed My Son." *McCalls* 105 (4/78): 33ff.

King, Slater. "The Bloody Battleground of Albany." *Freedomways* 4 (Winter 1964): 93–101.

King, Slater. "Our Main Battle in Albany." *Freedomways* 5 (Summer 1965): 417–23.

Lafayette, Bernard. "Selma, Alabama," in Guy & Candie Carawan, *Freedom Is a Constant Struggle* (New York: Oak Publications, 1968), pp. 146–47.

Laue, James H. "The Movement, Negro Challenge to the Myth." *New South* 18 (7–8/63): 9–17.

Lawrence, Ken. "Mississippi Spies." *Southern Exposure* 9 (Fall 1981): 82–86.

Lawson, James. "The Meredith March." *Concern* 8 (7/15/66): 4–5, 13.

Lawson, Steven F. "Civil Rights," in Robert A. Divine, ed., *Exploring the Johnson Years* (Austin: University of Texas Press, 1981), pp. 93–125.

Lee, Bernard S. "We Must Continue to March." *Freedomways* 6 (3rd Quarter 1966): 255–61.

Lester, Julius. "The Angry Children of Malcolm X." *Sing Out* 17 (10–11/66): 20–25.

Lester, Julius. "The Martin Luther King I Remember." *Evergreen Review* 74 (1/70): 16ff.

Leventhal, Will. "A Personal Odyssey." *New South* 27 (Fall 1972): 73–80.

Levering, Ralph B. "Martin Luther King, Jr.: A Christian's Quest for Social Transformation," in Charles DeBenedetti, ed., *Peace Heroes in Twentieth Century America* (Bloomington: Indiana University Press, 1986).

Levine, Richard. "Jesse Jackson: Heir to Dr. King?" *Harper's* 238 (3/69): 58–70.

Lewis, David L. "Martin Luther King, Jr., and the Promise of Nonviolent Populism," in John Hope Franklin & August Meier, eds., *Black Leaders of the Twentieth Century* (Urbana: University of Illinois Press, 1982), pp. 277–303.

Lomax, Louis E. "The Negro Revolt Against 'The Negro Leaders.'" *Harper's* 220 (6/60): 41–48.

Lynd, Staughton. "The New Negro Radicalism." *Commentary* 36 (9/63): 252–56.

McAdam, Doug. "The Decline of the Civil Rights Movement," in Jo Freeman, ed., *Social Movements of the Sixties and Seventies* (New York: Longman, 1983), pp. 298–319.

McAdam, Doug. "Tactical Innovation and the Pace of Insurgency." *American Sociological Review* 48 (12/83): 735–54.

McClendon, James W., Jr. "Biography as Theology." *Cross Currents* 21 (Fall 1971): 415–31.

McClendon, James W., Jr. "M. L. King: Politician or American Church Father?" *Journal of Ecumenical Studies* 8 (Winter 1971): 115–21.

McGraw, James R. "An Interview with Andrew J. Young." *Christianity and Crisis* 27 (1/22/68): 324–30.

McKnight, Gerald D. "The 1968 Memphis Sanitation Strike and the FBI: A Case Study in Urban Surveillance." *South Atlantic Quarterly* 83 (Spring 1984): 138–56.

McMillan, George. "Racial Violence and Law Enforcement." *New South* 15 (11/60): 4–32.

McMillen, Neil R. "Black Enfranchisement in Mississippi: Federal Enforcement and Black Protest in the 1960s." *Journal of Southern History* 43 (8/77): 351–72.

Marshall, Burke. "The Protest Movement and the Law." *Virginia Law Review* 51 (6/65): 785–803.

Marshall, F. Ray, & Arvil V. Adams. "The Memphis Public Employees Strike," in W. Ellison Chalmers & Gerald W. Cormick, eds., *Racial Conflict and Negotiations* (Ann Arbor: Institute of Labor & Industrial Relations, University of Michigan, 1971), pp. 71–107.

Matusow, Allen J. "From Civil Rights to Black Power: The Case of SNCC, 1960–1966," in Barton J. Bernstein & Matusow, eds., *Twentieth Century America*, 2nd ed. (New York: Harcourt Brace Jovanovich, 1972), pp. 494–520.

Mays, Benjamin E. "Eulogy on Dr. Martin Luther King, Jr.," 4/9/68, in Lester Thonssen, ed., *Representative American Speeches: 1967–1968* (New York: H. W. Wilson, 1968), pp. 161–68.

Meier, August. "The Dilemmas of Negro Protest Strategy." *New South* 21 (Spring 1966): 1–18.

Meier, August. "Dynamics of Crisis and Unity in Southern Movement." *New America,* 1/10/64, pp. 4–5.

Meier, August. "Negro Protest Movements and Organizations." *Journal of Negro Education* 32 (Fall 1963): 437–50.

Meier, August. "New Currents in the Civil Rights Movement." *New Politics* 2 (Summer 1963): 7–32.

Meier, August. "The Revolution Against the NAACP." *Journal of Negro Education* 32 (Spring 1963): 146–52.

Meier, August. "On the Role of Martin Luther King." *New Politics* 4 (Winter 1965): 52–59.

Meier, August. "The Urban Ghetto and Black Politics." *Social Education* 32 (2/68): 183–87.

Meier, August, & David Lewis. "History of the Negro Upper Class in Atlanta, Georgia, 1890–1958." *Journal of Negro Education* 28 (Spring 1959): 128–39.

Meier, August, & Elliott Rudwick. "The Boycott Movement Against Jim Crow Streetcars in the South." *Journal of American History* 55 (3/69): 756–75.

Meredith, James H. "Big Changes Are Coming." *Saturday Evening Post* 239 (8/13/66): 23–27.

Miller, James A. "Martin Luther King, Jr.: The End of an Era." *Black Academy Review* 1 (Fall 1970): 27–34.

Miller, William R. "Gandhi and King: Trail Blazers in Nonviolence." *Fellowship* 35 (1/69): 5–8.

Morris, Aldon. "Black Southern Student Sit-In Movement: An Analysis of Internal Organization." *American Sociological Review* 46 (12/81): 744–67.

Moses, Bob. "Mississippi: 1961–1962." *Liberation* 14 (1/70): 7–17.

Mott, Wesley T. "The Rhetoric of Martin Luther King, Jr.: Letter From Birmingham Jail." *Phylon* 36 (12/75): 411–21.

Muelder, Walter G. "Philosophical and Theological Influences in the Thought and Action of Martin Luther King, Jr." *Debate & Understanding* 1 (1977): 179–89.

Nash, Diane. "Inside the Sit-Ins and Freedom Rides," in Mathew Ahmann, ed., *The New Negro* (Notre Dame, Ind.: Fides Publishers, 1961), pp. 43–60.

Newsom, Lionel, & William Gorden. "A Stormy Rally in Atlanta." *Today's Speech* 11 (4/63): 18–21.

Niebuhr, Reinhold. "Walter Rauschenbusch in Historical Perspective." *Religion in Life* 27 (Autumn 1958): 527–36.

Niebuhr, Reinhold. "The Way of Nonviolent Resistance." *Christianity and Society* 21 (Spring 1956): 3.

Nixon, E. D. "How It All Started." *Liberation* 1 (12/56): 10.

Oates, Stephen B. "The Intellectual Odyssey of Martin Luther King." *Massachusetts Review* 22 (Summer 1981): 301–20.

Oberschall, Anthony. "The Decline of the 1960s Social Movements," in Louis Kriesberg, ed., *Research in Social Movements, Conflicts and Change,* vol. 1 (Greenwich, Conn.: JAI Press, 1978), pp. 257–89.

O'Dell, J. H. "Climbin' Jacob's Ladder: The Life and Times of the Freedom Movement." *Freedomways* 9 (Winter 1969): 7–23.

Orange, James. "With the People." *Southern Exposure* 9 (Spring 1981): 110–16.

Page, Marion S. "Report from Albany, Georgia." *Liberation* 10 (2/66): 46.

Pendergrast, Nan. "Twenty-Five Years of Love in Action—An Interview with Joseph Lowery." *Fellowship,* 1–2/83, pp. 10–12.

Pepper, William F. "The Children of Vietnam." *Ramparts* 5 (1/67): 44–68.

Peters, William. "The Man Who Fights Hate With Love." *Redbook* 117 (9/61): 36ff.

Peters, William. "'Our Weapon Is Love.'" *Redbook* 107 (8/56): 42ff.

Pfister, Joe. "Twenty Years and Still Marching." *Southern Exposure* 10 (1–2/82): 20–27.

Pierce, Ponchitta. "The Legacy of Martin Luther King." *McCalls* 101 (4/74): 28ff.

Pitre, Mergione. "The Economic Philosophy of Martin L. King, Jr." *Review of Black Political Economy* 9 (Winter 1979): 191–98.

Radosh, Ronald. "From Protest to Black Power: The Failure of Coalition Politics," in Marvin Gettleman & David Mermelstein, eds., *The Great Society Reader* (New York: Random House, 1967), pp. 278–93.

Raines, John C. "Righteous Resistance and Martin Luther King, Jr." *Christian Century* 101 (1/18/84): 52–54.

Range, Peter R. "Interview with Andrew Young." *Playboy* 24 (7/77): 61–83.

Rathbun, John W. "Martin Luther King: The Theology of Social Action." *American Quarterly* 20 (Spring 1968): 38–53.

Reagin, Ewell. "A Study of the Southern Christian Leadership Conference." *Review of Religious Research* 9 (Winter 1968): 88–96.

Reddick, L. D. "The Bus Boycott in Montgomery." *Dissent* 3 (Spring 1956): 107–17.

Reddick, L. D. "The State vs. the Student." *Dissent* 7 (Summer 1960): 219–28.

Richardson, H. Neil. "Pilgrimage of Reconciliation: A Trip to St. Augustine." *Nexus* 8 (11/64): 31–34.

Ricks, John A. "'De Lawd' Descends and is Crucified: Martin Luther King, Jr., in Albany, Georgia." *Journal of Southwest Georgia History* 2 (Fall 1984): 3–14.

Roberts, Adam. "Martin Luther King and Nonviolent Resistance." *World Today* 24 (6/68): 226–36, & *Gandhi Marg* 12 (7/68): 291–301.

Rowan, Carl T. "Martin Luther King's Tragic Decision." *Reader's Digest* 91 (9/67): 37–42.

Rustin, Bayard. "'Black Power' and Coalition Politics." *Commentary* 42 (9/66): 35–40.

Rustin, Bayard. "'Even in the Face of Death.'" *Liberation* 2 (2/57): 12–14.

Rustin, Bayard. "The Meaning of Birmingham." *Liberation* 8 (6/63): 7–9, 31.

Rustin, Bayard. "The Meaning of the March on Washington." *Liberation* 8 (10/63): 11–13.

Rustin, Bayard. "Montgomery Diary." *Liberation* 1 (4/56): 7–10.

Rustin, Bayard. "A Prospectus for Civil Rights: The New Phase." 8/29/63, *New America,* 9/24/63, pp. 6–7.

Rustin, Bayard. "From Protest to Politics: The Future of the Civil Rights Movement." *Commentary* 39 (2/65): 25–31.

Rustin, Bayard. "The Washington March—A Ten-Year Perspective." *Crisis* 80 (8–9/73): 224–27.

Rustin, Bayard. "The Watts 'Manifesto' and the McCone Report." *Commentary* 41 (3/66): 29–35.

Rustin, Bayard, & Tom Kahn. "Johnson So Far: Civil Rights." *Commentary* 39 (6/65): 43–46.

Sanders, Charles L. "'Finally, I've Begun to Live Again.'" *Ebony* 26 (11/70): 172–82.

Sandon, Leo, Jr. "Boston University Personalism and Southern Baptist Theology." *Foundations* 20 (4–6/77): 101–108.

Scott, Robert L. "Black Power Bends Martin Luther King." *Speaker and Gavel* 5 (3/68): 80–86.

Sellers, James E. "Love, Justice, and the Nonviolent Movement." *Theology Today* 18 (1/62): 422–34.

Sessions, Jim, & Sue Thrasher. "A New Day Begun: An Interview with John Lewis." *Southern Exposure* 4 (Fall 1976): 14–24.

Sherry, Paul. "A Sense of Place: A Conversation with Andrew Young." *Journal of Current Social Issues* 13 (Winter 1976): 44–48.

Shuttlesworth, Fred. "Birmingham Revisited." *Ebony* 26 (8/71): 114–18.

Shuttlesworth, Fred. "Birmingham Shall Be Free Some Day." *Freedomways* 4 (Winter 1964): 16–19.

Sibley, Mulford. "Martin Luther King and the Future." *Liberation* 13 (4/68): 7–9.

Sibley, Mulford. "Negro Revolution and Nonviolent Action: Martin Luther King." *Political Science Review* 9 (1–6/70): 173–93.

Smiley, Glenn. "A Man Remembered." *Fellowship* 44 (4–5/78): 5–6.

Smiley, Glenn. "The Voice That Will Not Be Silenced." *Fellowship* 34 (5/68): 5–6.

Smith, Donald H. "Martin Luther King, Jr.: In the Beginning at Montgomery." *Southern Speech Journal* 34 (Fall 1968): 8–17.

Smith, Kenneth L. "Martin Luther King, Jr.: Reflections of a Former Teacher." *Bulletin of Crozer Theological Seminary* 57 (4/65): 2–3.

Smith, Kenneth L., & Ira G. Zepp, Jr. "Martin Luther King's Vision of the Beloved Community." *Christian Century* 91 (4/3/74): 361–63.

Smylie, James H. "On Jesus, Pharaohs, and the Chosen People: Martin Luther King as Biblical Interpreter and Humanist." *Interpretation* 24 (1/70): 74–91.

Sonnenschein, Allan. "Penthouse Interview: Andrew Young." *Penthouse* 14 (2/83): 123–44.

Spillers, Hortense J. "Martin Luther King and the Style of the Black Sermon." *Black Scholar* 3 (9/71): 14–27.

Steinkraus, Warren E. "Martin Luther King's Personalism and Nonviolence." *Journal of the History of Ideas* 34 (1–3/73): 97–111.

Stevenson, Janet. "Rosa Parks Wouldn't Budge." *American Heritage* 23 (2/72): 56ff.

Stoper, Emily. "The Student Nonviolent Coordinating Committee: Rise and Fall of a Redemptive Organization." *Journal of Black Studies* 8 (9/77): 13–34.

Terrell, Robert. "Discarding the Dream." *Evergreen Review* 78 (5/70): 34ff.

Thornton, J. Mills. "Challenge and Response in the Montgomery Bus Boycott of 1955–1956." *Alabama Review* 33 (7/80): 163–235.

Thrasher, Thomas R. "Alabama's Bus Boycott." *Reporter* 14 (3/8/56): 13–16.

Turner, Otis. "Nonviolence and the Politics of Liberation." *Journal of the Interdenominational Theological Center* 4 (Spring 1977): 49–60.

Valien, Preston. "The Montgomery Bus Protest as a Social Movement," in Jitsuichi Masuoka & Valien, eds., *Race Relations* (Chapel Hill: University of North Carolina Press, 1961), pp. 112–27.

Vander Zanden, James W. "The Nonviolent Resistance Movement Against Segregation." *American Journal of Sociology* 68 (3/63): 544–50.

Vowels, Robert C. "Atlanta Negro Business and the New Black Bourgeoisie." *Atlanta Historical Bulletin* 21 (Spring 1977): 48–63.

Wagy, Thomas R. "Governor LeRoy Collins of Florida and the Selma Crisis of 1965." *Florida Historical Quarterly* 57 (4/79): 403–20.

Walker, Alice. "The Growing Strength of Coretta King." *Redbook,* 9/71, & in Walker, *In Search of Our Mothers' Gardens* (San Diego, Cal.: Harcourt Brace Jovanovich, 1983), pp. 146–57.

Walker, Jack L. "The Functions of Disunity: Negro Leadership in a Southern City." *Journal of Negro Education* 32 (Summer 1963): 227–36.

Walker, Jack L. "Protest and Negotiation: A Case Study of Negro Leadership in Atlanta, Georgia." *Midwest Journal of Political Science* 7 (5/63): 99–124.

Walker, Wyatt T. "Albany, Failure or First Step?" *New South* 18 (6/63): 3–8.

Walker, Wyatt T. "The Contemporary Black Church," in Harold A. Carter et al., *The Black Church Looks at the Bicentennial* (Elgin, Ill.: Progressive National Baptist Publishing House, 1976), pp. 43–74.

Walker, Wyatt T. "The Techniques of Winning Freedom Now." *Negro Digest* 13 (3/64): 6–10.

Wallace, David M. "From the Fullness of the Earth: The Story of Chicago's Operation Breadbasket." *Chicago Theological Seminary Register*, 11/66, pp. 16–20.

Wallace, Mike. "Self-Portrait of a Symbol: Martin Luther King." *New York Post*, 2/13/61, p. 24, 2/14/61, p. 62, & 2/15/61, p. 42.

Walton, Hanes, Jr. "The Political Leadership of Martin Luther King, Jr." *Quarterly Review of Higher Education Among Negroes* 36 (7/68): 163–71.

Walton, Norman W. "A Short History of the Dexter Avenue Baptist Church," in *The Eightieth Anniversary of the Dexter Avenue Baptist Church* (Montgomery, Ala.: Dexter Avenue Baptist Church, 1958).

Walton, Norman W. "The Walking City: A History of the Montgomery Boycott." *Negro History Bulletin* 20 (10/56): 17–21, (11/56): 27–33, (2/57): 102–4, (4/57): 147ff., 21 (1/58): 75ff.

Weiss, Nancy J. "Whitney M. Young, Jr.: Committing the Power Structure to the Cause of Civil Rights," in John Hope Franklin & August Meier, eds., *Black Leaders of the Twentieth Century* (Urbana: University of Illinois Press, 1981), pp. 331–58.

Wigginton, Eliot, & Sue Thrasher. "To Make the World We Want: An Interview with Dorothy Cotton." *Southern Exposure* 10 (9–10/82): 25–31.

Willhelm, Sidney M. "Martin Luther King, Jr., and the Black Experience in America." *Journal of Black Studies* 10 (9/79): 3–19.

Wills, Gary. "Martin Luther King Is Still on the Case!" *Esquire* 70 (8/68): 98ff.

Yglesias, Jose. "Dr. King's March on Washington." *New York Times Magazine*, 3/31/68, pp. 30ff.

Young, Andrew. "And Birmingham." *Drum Major* 1 (Winter 1971): 21–27.

Young, Andrew. "The Day We Went to Jail in Birmingham." *Friends* 111 (2/9/64): 3–11.

Young, Andrew. "Dynamics of a Birmingham Movement in the Sixties," in Andrew Levison, ed., *Nonviolence in the 70's* (Atlanta: King Center, 1972), pp. 9–15.

Young, Andrew. "Easter Sunday: Parting of the Red Sea." *Atlanta Journal Constitution*, 7/17/83, pp. C1, C14.

Young, Andrew. "In Memoriam: Martin Luther King, Jr." *Soul Force*, 4/4/69, p. 5.

Young, Andrew. "Remarks." *Christianity and Crisis* 31 (5/3/71): 80–82.

Young, Andrew. "Remembering Dr. King," in Lynda R. Obst, ed., *The Sixties* (New York: Random House, 1977), pp. 232, 236.

Young, Andrew. "There's a New World Coming." *Bulletin of the Peace Studies Institute* (Manchester College, Ind.), 8/71, pp. 5–10, 15–16.

Young, Andrew. "We Will Keep the Dream." *Maryknoll* 72 (4/78): 12–16.

Zinn, Howard. "The Double Job in Civil Rights." *New Politics* 3 (Winter 1964): 29–34.

Theses, Dissertations, and Essays

Abernathy, Ralph. "The Natural History of a Social Movement: The Montgomery Improvement Association." M.A. thesis, Sociology Department, Atlanta University, 8/58. Author's files.

Abernathy, Ralph. "Martin Luther King, Jr.: Pastor, Leader, Prophet." Address at Colgate-Rochester Divinity School, Rochester, N.Y., 11/15/68. Author's files.

Anderson, Alan B. "The Issue of the Color Line: Some Methodological Considerations." Ph.D. dissertation, University of Chicago, 1975.

742   Bibliography

Anderson, Alan B. "A Year of Transition in the Struggle for Racial Justice." Unpublished paper, 1981. Author's files.

Anderson, Alan B., & George W. Pickering. "The Issue of the Color Line: A View from Chicago." Joint appendix to Ph.D. dissertations, University of Chicago, 1975.

Austin, Ernest. "Goodby America—I Loved You." Unpublished manuscript, ca. 1979. Author's files.

Bailey, Robert E. "The 1968 Memphis Sanitation Strike." M.A. thesis, Memphis State University, 1974.

Bains, Lee E. "Birmingham 1963: Confrontation Over Civil Rights." B.A. thesis, Harvard University, 1977. BPLA.

Bennette, Bernita D. "Rev. Adam Daniel Williams." Unpublished paper, n.d. Author's files.

Bolster, Paul D. "Civil Rights Movements in Twentieth-Century Georgia." Ph.D. dissertation, University of Georgia, 1972.

Bradley, Michael R. "Martin Luther King and the Birmingham Movement of 1963." Paper presented at Southern Historical Association Convention, St. Louis, Mo., 11/8–11/78. Author's files.

Brown, Coleman B. "Grounds for American Loyalty in a Prophetic Christian Social Ethic—With Special Attention to Martin Luther King, Jr." Ph.D. dissertation, Union Theological Seminary, 1979.

Brunson, Drexel T. "The Quest for Social Justice: A Study of Walter Rauschenbusch and His Influence on Reinhold Niebuhr and Martin Luther King, Jr." Ph.D. dissertation, Florida State University, 1980.

Burns, Emmett C. "Love, Power, and Justice as Central Elements in a View of Social Change: A Comparison and Evaluation of the Thought of Reinhold Niebuhr and Martin Luther King, Jr." Ph.D. dissertation, University of Pittsburgh, 1974.

Busacca, Richard L. "Social Movements and the Construction of Reality: A Study of the Civil Rights Movement and Its Role in the Transformation of American Politics, 1954–1968." Ph.D. dissertation, University of California, Berkeley, 1976.

Carpenter, Joseph, Jr. "The Leadership Philosophy of Dr. Martin Luther King, Jr.: Its Educational Implications." Ph.D. dissertation, Marquette University, 1970.

Carr, Carol E. "Public Images of Martin Luther King." Ph.D. dissertation, Ohio State University, 1977.

Carson, Clayborne, Jr. "Toward Freedom and Community: The Evolution of Ideas in the Student Nonviolent Coordinating Committee, 1960–1966." Ph.D. dissertation, University of California, Los Angeles, 1975.

Ceynar, Marvin E. "A Thematic Analysis of Twelve Sermons on Race Relations Delivered by Martin Luther King, Jr. Between 1954 and 1963." M.A. thesis, State University of Iowa, 1965.

Chapman, Julia Sullivan. "A Southern Moderate Advocates Compliance: A Study of LeRoy Collins as Director of the Community Relations Service." M.A. thesis, University of South Florida, 1974.

Clarke, Jacquelyn M. J. "Goals and Techniques in Three Negro Civil Rights Organizations in Alabama." Ph.D. dissertation, Ohio State University, 1960.

Coleman, Susie H. "Martin Luther King's Chicago Campaign—An Experiment in Paradox." M.A. paper, Austin Peay State University, 1969.

Connolly, Kathleen. "The Chicago Open-Housing Conference." Unpublished paper, 1/12/67. Author's files.

Corley, Robert G. "The Quest for Racial Harmony: Race Relations in Birmingham, Alabama, 1947–1963." Ph.D. dissertation, University of Virginia, 1979.

Darby, Henry E. "Martin Luther King, Jr.'s Opposition to the War in Vietnam." M.A. thesis, Atlanta University, 1985.

Dittmer, John. "Black and White Together: The Freedom Summer Experience." Paper presented at Southern Historical Association Convention, 11/13/80. Author's files.

Dittmer, John. "The Movement in McComb, 1961–1964." Paper presented at Organization of American Historians Convention, Los Angeles, 4/84. Author's files.

Dittmer, John. "In the Name of Freedom: The Politics of the Mississippi Movement, 1954–1964." Paper presented at University of Mississippi, Oxford, 10/3/85. Author's files.

Dittmer, John. "The Ordeal of Medgar Evers: Politics and Policy in the Mississippi Movement." Paper presented at American Historical Association Convention, 12/83. Author's files.

Dowdy, Russell E. "Nonviolence vs. Nonexistence: The Vietnam War and Martin Luther King, Jr." M.A. thesis, North Carolina State University, 1983.

Fairclough, Adam. "A Study of the Southern Christian Leadership Conference and the Rise and Fall of the Nonviolent Civil Rights Movement." Ph.D. dissertation, University of Keele (U.K.), 1977.

Finley, Mary Lou. "The Open Housing Marches, Chicago, Summer '66." Unpublished paper, Spring 1967. Author's files.

Forman, James. "What is the Student Nonviolent Coordinating Committee—'A Band of Brothers, A Circle of Trust.'" Unpublished paper, 11/64. Author's files.

Fort, Vincent D. "The Atlanta Sit-In Movement, 1960–1961: An Oral Study." M.A. thesis, Atlanta University, 1980.

Franklin, Clyde W., Jr. "A Comparison of Two Social Movements in Two Southern Cities: Montgomery, Alabama, and Albany, Georgia." M.A. thesis, Atlanta University, 1962.

Garber, Paul R. "Martin Luther King, Jr.: Theologian and Precursor of Black Theology." Ph.D. dissertation, Florida State University, 1973.

Gillespie, Paul C. "A Theological Investigation of Civil Disobedience with Special Reference to Henry David Thoreau, M. K. Gandhi, and Martin Luther King, Jr." Ph.D. dissertation, New Orleans Baptist Theological Seminary, 1965.

Gilliam, Thomas J. "The Montgomery Bus Boycott of 1955–1956." M.A. thesis, Auburn University, 1968.

Goodwin, Bennie E. "Martin Luther King, Jr.: American Social Educator." Ph.D. dissertation, University of Pittsburgh, 1974.

Green, Earl, Jr. "Labor in the South: A Case Study of Memphis, the 1968 Sanitation Strike and Its Effect on an Urban Community." Ph.D. dissertation, New York University, 1980.

Grice, Nurline H. "The Influence of Black Power on the Rhetorical Practices of Dr. Martin Luther King, Jr." M.A. thesis, Miami University (Ohio), 1968.

Hackney, Sheldon, & Raymond Arsenault. "The Montgomery Bus Boycott: A Case Book." Unpublished manuscript, n.d. Author's files.

Hanigan, James P. "Martin Luther King, Jr. and the Ethics of Militant Nonviolence." Ph.D. dissertation, Duke University, 1973.

Harper, Frederick D. "Maslow's Concept of Self-Actualization Compared with Personality Characteristics of Selected Black American Protesters: Martin Luther King, Jr., Malcolm X, and Frederick Douglass." Ph.D. dissertation, Florida State University, 1970.

Harris, John C. "The Theology of Martin Luther King, Jr." Ph.D. dissertation, Duke University, 1974.

Hartley, Robert W. "A Long, Hot Summer: The St. Augustine Racial Disorders of 1964." M.A. thesis, Stetson University, 1972.

Hartstein, Gordon L. "The Montgomery Bus Protest 1955–1956: What Precipitated, Sustained, and Prolonged the Boycott." B.A. thesis, Princeton University, 1973.

Horton, A. Romeo. "Tribute to the Late Dr. Martin Luther King, Jr." Unpublished paper, 4/9/68. BEM II-40.

Horton, Aimee I. "The Highlander Folk School: A History of the Development of Its Major Programs Related to Social Movements in the South, 1932–1961." Ph.D. dissertation, University of Chicago, 1971.

House, Secil V. "The Implications of Dr. Martin Luther King's Work and Philosophy for the Field of Adult Education." Ed.D. dissertation, Indiana University, 1975.

Johnson, Michael W. "The Roles of Law and Coercion (or Soul Force and Social Change) According to: M. K. Gandhi and M. L. King Jr." Ph.D. dissertation, University of Minnesota, 1979.

Johnson, Ralph A. "The Influence of the Fellowship of Reconciliation on Martin Luther King, Jr." M.A. thesis, Indiana University, 1974.

Jones, Lewis W. "Fred L. Shuttlesworth, Indigenous Leader." Unpublished paper, 1961, UCC 15-11. Author's files.

Jones, Nancy B. "Nonviolence to Revolution: The Ideological Evolution of Five Black Leaders." M.A. thesis, Texas Christian University, 1970.

Kallal, Edward W., Jr. "St. Augustine and the Ku Klux Klan: 1963 and 1964." B.A. thesis, History Department, University of Florida, 1976.

Kane, Brian M. "The Influence of Boston Personalism on the Thought of Dr. Martin Luther King, Jr." M.Th. Studies thesis, Boston University, 1985.

Keele, Lucy A. M. "A Burkeian Analysis of the Rhetorical Strategies of Dr. Martin Luther King, Jr., 1955–1968." Ph.D. dissertation, University of Oregon, 1972.

King, Martin Luther, Jr. "A Comparison of the Conceptions of God in the Thinking of Paul Tillich and Henry Nelson Wieman." Ph.D. dissertation, Boston University, 1955.

Klibaner, Irwin. "The Southern Conference Educational Fund: A History." Ph.D. dissertation, University of Wisconsin, 1971.

Kryn, Randall L. "James L. Bevel: The Strategist of the 1960s Civil Rights Movement." Unpublished paper, 8/84. Author's files.

Lafayette, Bernard. "The Strategy of Martin Luther King, Jr." Paper presented at University of Southern California, Los Angeles, 4/28/84. Author's files.

Lawson, James M. "Martin Luther King, Jr. and the King Movement." Address at Southwestern College, Memphis, 1978. Author's files.

Lee, Bernard. "The Apocalyptic Implications of Martin Luther King, Jr.'s Moral Authority." Paper presented at University of Southern California, Los Angeles, 4/26/84. Author's files.

Lee, Shin Heng. "The Concept of Human Nature, Justice, and Nonviolence in the Political Thought of Martin Luther King, Jr." Ph.D. dissertation, New York University, 1979.

Lentz, Richard. "Resurrecting the Prophet: Dr. Martin Luther King, Jr., and the News Magazines." Ph.D. dissertation, University of Iowa, 1983.

Lentz, Richard. "Sixty-Five Days in Memphis: The *Commercial Appeal,* The *Press-Scimitar* and the 1968 Garbage Strike." M.A. thesis, Southern Illinois University, 1976.

Lewis, John. "The Continuing Agenda of Martin Luther King, Jr.: Our Challenge for the Eighties." Paper presented at University of Southern California, Los Angeles, 4/27/84. Author's files.

Lewis, Selma S. "Social Religion and the Memphis Sanitation Strike." Ph.D. dissertation, Memphis State University, 1976.

Luellen, David E. "Ministers and Martyrs: Malcolm X and Martin Luther King, Jr." Ph.D. dissertation, Ball State University, 1972.

McGregor, Marjorie. "Martin Luther King, Jr.: An Analysis of His Washington March Speech." M.A. thesis, University of Oklahoma, 1965.

McGriggs, Lee A. "Martin Luther King, Jr.: An Account of His Civil Rights Movement in Alabama, 1953–1965." M.S. thesis, Tennessee State University, 1969.

McKnight, John L. "The Summit Negotiations, Chicago, August 17, 1966–August 26, 1966." Unpublished manuscript, 1966. Author's files.

McLemore, Leslie B. "The Mississippi Freedom Democratic Party: A Case Study of Grass-Roots Politics." Ph.D. dissertation, University of Massachusetts, Amherst, 1971.

MacNair, Ray H. "Social Distance Among Kin Organizations: Civil Rights Networks in Cleveland and Birmingham." Ph.D. dissertation, University of Michigan, 1970.

Marty, William R. "Recent Negro Protest Thought: Theories of Nonviolence and 'Black Power.'" Ph.D. dissertation, Duke University, 1968.

Massoni, Gary. "Perspectives on Operation Breadbasket." M.Div. thesis, Chicago Theological Seminary, 1971.

Mays, Benjamin E. "Tribute to Martin Luther King, Jr." 1/15/70, Ebenezer Baptist Church, Atlanta. BEM II-49.

Millner, Steven M. "The Montgomery Bus Boycott: A Case Study in the Emergence and Career of a Social Movement." Ph.D. dissertation, University of California, Berkeley, 1981.

Mohr, Peter C. "Journey Out of Egypt: The Development of Negro Leadership in Alabama from Booker T. Washington to Martin Luther King." B.A. thesis, Princeton University, 1958. Author's files.

Moore, Edward L. "Billy Graham and Martin Luther King, Jr.: An Inquiry Into White and Black Revivalistic Traditions." Ph.D. dissertation, Vanderbilt University, 1979.

Morris, Aldon D. "The Rise of the Civil Rights Movement and Its Movement Black Power Structure, 1953–1963." Ph.D. dissertation, State University of New York, Stony Brook, 1980.

Morris, William W. "Strategies for Liberation: A Critical Comparison of Martin Luther King, Jr. and Albert B. Cleage, Jr." D.Min. dissertation, Vanderbilt University, 1973.

Muelder, Walter G. "Martin Luther King, Jr.'s Ethics of Nonviolent Action." Paper presented at King Center, Atlanta, 1985. Author's files.

Murphy, Robert G. "Martin Luther King, Jr." 3/31/76 Report to J. Stanley Pottinger, Civil Rights Division, U.S. Justice Department. CRD FOIA.

Neal, Velma. "An Analysis of the Issue and Representative Speeches by Martin Luther King, Jr., on Nonviolence." M.A. thesis, Baylor University, 1970.

Newman, Mark J. "Black Labor in the 1960s: The Negro American Labor Council." B.A. thesis, Princeton University, 1976.

Niccolls, S. Thomas. "The Nature and Function of Rhetorical Imagery: A Descriptive Study of Three Speeches by Martin Luther King, Jr." M.A. thesis, Ohio University, 1966.

Nichols, Michael C. "'Cities Are What Men Make Them': Birmingham, Alabama, Faces the Civil Rights Movement, 1963." B.A. thesis, Brown University, 1974.

Oglesby, Enoch H. "Ethical Implications of the Works of Selected Black Theologians: A Critical Analysis." Ph.D. dissertation, Boston University, 1974.

Oppenheimer, Martin. "The Genesis of the Southern Negro Student Movement (Sit-In Movement): A Case Study in Contemporary Negro Protest." Ph.D. dissertation, University of Pennsylvania, 1963.

746   Bibliography

Padgett, Gregory B. "C. K. Steele and the Tallahassee Bus Protest." M.A. thesis, Florida State University, 1977.

Payne, James C. "A Content Analysis of Speeches and Written Documents of Six Black Spokesmen." Ph.D. dissertation, Florida State University, 1973.

Pickering, George W. "The Issue of the Color Line: Some Interpretive Considerations." Ph.D. dissertation, University of Chicago, 1975.

Pitcher, Al. "The Chicago Freedom Movement—What Is It?" Unpublished paper, 11/66, GM. Author's files.

Powell, Gordon B., Jr. "Black Cloud Over Danville: The Negro Movement in Danville, Virginia, in 1963." M.A. thesis, University of Richmond, 1968.

Rabby, Glenda A. "Out of the Past: The Civil Rights Movement in Tallahassee, Florida." Ph.D. dissertation, Florida State University, 1984.

Rae, Keith D. "The Theology and Ethics of Dr. Martin Luther King, Jr., with Special Reference to the Thought of Paul Tillich and Reinhold Niebuhr." Th.M. thesis, Boston University School of Theology, 1971.

Rafferty, Scott J. "Building the Consensus: Civil Rights and the Department of Justice 1961–1963." B.A. thesis, Princeton University, 1976.

Rahming, Philip A. "The Church and the Civil Rights Movement in the Thought of Martin Luther King, Jr." Th.M. thesis, Southern Baptist Theological Seminary, 1971.

Reagon, Bernice J. "Songs of the Civil Rights Movement 1955–1965: A Study in Culture History." Ph.D. dissertation, Howard University, 1975.

Reddick, L. D. "The Montgomery Movement—An Historian's View." Paper presented at MIA Institute on Nonviolence, 12/4/56, Montgomery. Author's files.

Richberg, Velma D. "The Highlander Folk School Involvement in the Civil Rights Movement from 1957 to 1961." M.A. thesis, Fisk University, 1973.

Ridley-Thomas, Mark. "Martin Luther King's Theology of Hope: Eschatological Ethics in Praxis." Unpublished paper, 8/82. Author's files.

Robinson, JoAnn G. "The Montgomery Story: Reflections on the Inside Story of the Bus Boycott that Set a People Free, 1955–1957." Unpublished manuscript, 1984.

Rogers, Cornish R. "The Foundations of Martin Luther King's Theology." Paper presented at University of Southern California, Los Angeles, 4/28/84. Author's files.

Romaine, Anne. "The Mississippi Freedom Democratic Party Through August, 1964." M.A. thesis, University of Virginia, 1969.

Ross, Edmund B., Jr. "The Montgomery Bus Boycott of 1955–1956." B.A. thesis, Princeton University, 1973.

Rudzka-Ostyn, Brygida I. "The Oratory of Martin Luther King and Malcolm X: A Study in Linguistic Stylistics." Ph.D. dissertation, University of Rochester, 1972.

Sackler, Seymour S. "Nonviolent Resistance as an Instrument of Change in Society: A Study of the Southern Christian Leadership Conference and Negro Protest, 1960–1963." M.A. thesis, Ohio University, 1965.

Saunders, Richard L. "Dr. Martin Luther King's Intellectual Resources as Studied in Two Selected Speeches." M.A. thesis, San Diego State College, 1967.

Saxe, Alan. "Protest and Reform: The Desegregation of Oklahoma City." Ph.D. dissertation, University of Oklahoma, 1969.

Schmeidler, Emilie. "Shaping Ideas and Actions: CORE, SCLC, and SNCC in the Struggle for Equality, 1960–1966." Ph.D. dissertation, University of Michigan, 1980.

Seastrom, Jayne E. "A Critical Study of the Nonviolent Civil Rights Rhetoric of Martin Luther King, Jr." M.A. thesis, San Jose State College, 1968.

Shapiro, Herbert. "The Albany Movement: A Turning Point in the Civil Rights Struggle." Unpublished paper, 1980. Author's files.

Shelton, Robert L. "Black Revolution: The Definition and Meaning of 'Revolution' in the Writings and Speeches of Selected Nationally Prominent Negro Americans, 1963–1968." Ph.D. dissertation, Boston University, 1970.

Sloan, Rose Mary. "'Then My Living Will Not Be In Vain:' A Rhetorical Study of Dr. Martin Luther King, Jr., and the Southern Christian Leadership Conference in the Mobilization for Collective Action Toward Nonviolent Means to Integration, 1954–1964." Ph.D. dissertation, Ohio State University, 1977.

Smith, Donald H. "Martin Luther King, Jr.: Rhetorician of Revolt." Ph.D. dissertation, University of Wisconsin, 1964.

Smith, Ervin. "The Role of Personalism in the Development of the Social Ethics of Martin Luther King, Jr.," Ph.D. dissertation, Northwestern University, 1976.

Spruill, Larry H. "Southern Exposure: Photography and the Civil Rights Movement, 1955–1968." Ph.D. dissertation, State University of New York, Stony Brook, 1983.

Steele, C. K. "Nonviolent Resistance: The Pain and the Promise." Address at Florida State University, Tallahassee, 9/27/78. FSU.

Stennett, Janeda G. "An Analysis of the Rhetorical Techniques of Dr. Martin Luther King, Jr., as Observed in Selected Sermons and Speeches." M.A. thesis, Texas Technological College, 1965.

Stern, Mark. "The Contemporary Black Suffrage Movement and the Public Policy Agenda." Paper presented at American Political Science Association Convention, New Orleans, 8/85. Author's files.

Stoper, Emily S. "The Student Nonviolent Coordinating Committee: The Growth of Radicalism in a Civil Rights Organization." Ph.D. dissertation, Harvard University, 1968.

Sullivan, Donald F. "The Civil Rights Programs of the Kennedy Administration: A Political Analysis." Ph.D. dissertation, University of Oklahoma, 1965.

Taylor, Sandra A. "The Nashville Sit-In Movement, 1960." M.A. thesis, Fisk University, 1972.

Thompson, Jan G. "A History of the Alabama Council on Human Relations, from Roots to Redirection, 1920–1968." Ph.D. dissertation, Auburn University, 1983.

Thompson, Joseph M. "Martin Luther King, Jr. and Christian Witness: An Interpretation of King Based on a Theological Model of Prophetic Witness." Ph.D. dissertation, Fordham University, 1981.

Thornton, J. Mills. "The Montgomery Freedom Rider Riots of 1961." Paper presented to Alabama Historical Association Convention, Florence, 4/83. Author's files.

Turner, Otis. "Toward an Ethic of Black Liberation Based on the Philosophy of Martin Luther King, Jr., and Stokely Carmichael's Concept of Black Power." Ph.D. dissertation, Emory University, 1974.

Walker, Douglas A. "The Thoreauvian Legacy of Martin Luther King." M.A. thesis, Texas Christian University, 1970.

Walker, Eugene P. "A History of the Southern Christian Leadership Conference, 1955–1965: The Evolution of a Southern Strategy for Social Change." Ph.D. dissertation, Duke University, 1978.

Warren, Mervyn A. "A Rhetorical Study of the Preaching of Dr. Martin Luther King, Jr., Pastor and Pulpit Orator." Ph.D. dissertation, Michigan State University, 1966.

Wasserman, Lois D. "Martin Luther King, Jr.: The Molding of Nonviolence as a Philosophy and Strategy, 1955–1963." Ph.D. dissertation, Boston University, 1972.

Watley, William D. "Against Principalities: An Examination of Martin Luther King, Jr.'s Nonviolent Ethic." Ph.D. dissertation, Columbia University, 1980.

Wehr, Paul E. "Field Report on the Sit-In Protests Occurring in North Carolina, Winter and Spring 1960." Unpublished paper, 1960. Author's files.

Wehr, Paul E. "The Sit-Down Protests—A Study of a Passive Resistance Movement in North Carolina." M.A. thesis, University of North Carolina, 1960.

White, Clarence, Jr. "Dr. Martin Luther King, Jr.'s Contributions to Education as a Black Leader." Ed.D. dissertation, Loyola University, 1974.

White, Robert M. "The Tallahassee Sit-Ins and CORE: A Nonviolent Revolutionary Submovement." Ph.D. dissertation, Florida State University, 1964.

Williams, Juanita T. "The Impact of Education, Socio-Economic Status, and Self-Concept on Out-of-State Participants in Selma, Alabama, Movement Dissent, March, 1965." M.A. thesis, Atlanta University School of Education, 1967.

Willie, Charles V. "A Journey in Faith with Martin Luther King, Jr." Address delivered in Syracuse, N.Y., 1/20/74. Author's files.

Willie, Charles V. "Martin Luther King, Jr.: His World Mission for Peace." Address delivered 1/17/82. Author's files.

Willingham, Alex W. "The Religious Basis for Action in the Political Philosophy of Martin Luther King, Jr." M.A. thesis, State University of Iowa, 1965.

Wilson, Emile L. "The King of Peace: An Analysis and Interpretation of the Life, Writings and Philosophy of Martin Luther King, Jr." D.Phil. thesis, Queen's College, Oxford University (U.K.), 1981.

Wofford, Harris. "The Status of the Negro in Dallas County, Alabama." Unpublished paper, 1953. Author's files.

Yeakey, Lamont H. "The Montgomery, Alabama Bus Boycott, 1955–1956." Ph.D. dissertation, Columbia University, 1979.

Young, Andrew. "Dynamics of a Movement: Birmingham in the Sixties." Transcript of an address, ca. 1970. Author's files.

Young, Andrew. Address at Ebenezer Baptist Church, Atlanta, Ga., 1/15/73. Author's files.

Young, Andrew. Address at Vanderbilt University, Nashville, Tenn., 1/22/85. Audiotape.

Young, Roy. "Presidential Leadership and Civil Rights Legislation, 1963–1964." Ph.D. dissertation, University of Texas at Austin, 1969.

Zepp, Ira G., Jr. "The Intellectual Sources of the Ethical Thought of Martin Luther King, Jr., As Traced in His Writings with Special Reference to the Beloved Community." Ph.D. dissertation, St. Mary's Seminary & University, 1971.

Court Cases

Anderson v. *City of Albany,* Civil Action #731, M. D. Ga., 1962; 8 RRLR 1114, 9 RRLR 1124, 321 F. 2d 649 (1963, 1964).

Anderson v. *Kelley,* 8 RRLR 192, 9 RRLR 1382 (1963).

Billingsley v. *Eskridge,* Civil Action #74-H-242-S, N. D. Ala., 1974.

Bolden v. *Allen,* C. A. #64-184, M. D. Fla., 1964.

Boynton v. *Clark,* 10 RRLR 215 (1965).

Browder v. *Gayle,* C. A. #1147-N, M. D. Ala., 1956; 1 RRLR 678, 202 F. Supp. 707, 352 U. S. 903 (1956).

City of Chicago v. *King,* 11 RRLR 1695 (1966).

City of Memphis v. *King,* C. A. #C-68-80, W. D. Tenn., 1968.

City of Montgomery v. *Montgomery Improvement Association,* 2 RRLR 123 (1956).

City of Montgomery v. *Montgomery City Lines,* 1 RRLR 534 (1956).

City of Montgomery v. *Parks,* Montgomery Co. Circuit Ct. #4459, 1956.

Forman v. *City of Montgomery,* 245 F. Supp. 17 (1965).

Georgia v. *King,* DeKalb Co. Circuit Ct. #10443, 1960.

Johnson v. *City of Montgomery,* 245 F. Supp. 25 (1965).

Johnson v. *Davis,* C. A. #64-141, M. D. Fla., 1964.

Kelley v. *Page,* C. A. #727, M. D. Ga., 1962; 9 RRLR 1115, 335 F. 2d 114 (1964).

King v. *Alabama,* 3 RRLR 54 (1957).

King v. *Mathis,* C. A. #64-186, M. D. Fla., 1964.

King v. *Mister Maestro,* 224 F. Supp. 101 (S. D. N. Y., 1963).

Lee v. *Kelley,* C. A. #76-1185, D. D. C., 1977.

Parks v. *City of Montgomery,* Montgomery Co. Circuit Ct. #4459, Alabama Court of Appeals Vol. 1188, 1956; 38 Ala. App. 681, 92 So. 2d 683 (1957).

Plummer v. *Brock,* #64-187, M. D. Fla., 1964.

Southern Christian Leadership Conference v. *Ryles,* C. A. #70-351-S, N. D. Ala., 1976.

State of Alabama v. *King,* Montgomery Co. Circuit Ct. #7399, 1956.

U.S. v. *Clark,* C. A. #3438-64, S. D. Ala., 1964; 249 F. Supp. 720, 10 RRLR 568 (1965).

Walker v. *City of Birmingham,* #249 October Term, 1966; 388 U. S. 307 (1967).

Williams v. *Connell,* C. A. #64-183, M. D. Fla., 1964.

Williams v. *Wallace,* C. A. #2181-N, M. D. Ala., 1965; 240 F. Supp. 100 (1965).

Young v. *Bryant,* C. A. #64-152, M. D. Fla., 1964.

Young v. *Davis,* #64-133, M. D. Fla., 1964; 9 RRLR 590, 1515 (1964).

Interviews

Abernathy, Juanita. Garrow, 8/26/85, Atlanta, Ga.

Abernathy, Ralph. Donald H. Smith, 12/3/63, Atlanta, Ga., SHSW.

Abernathy, Ralph. Jim Bishop, 9/3/70, Atlanta, Ga., SBU.

Abernathy, Ralph. Garrow, 9/14/79, Atlanta, Ga.

Abernathy, Ralph. Dennis C. Dickerson, 10/26/83, Atlanta, Ga.

Abernathy, Ralph. Blackside, 11/6/85, Atlanta, Ga.

Ahmann, Mathew. Garrow, 3/9/84, Washington, D.C.

Alexander, Clifford. Robert Wright, 2/5/69, Washington, D.C., MSRC.

Alexander, J. T. Judy Barton, 1/25/72, Montgomery, Ala., KC.

Allen, Ben. Garrow, 9/17/79, Montgomery, Ala.

Allen, Ivan. John Britton, 1/23/68, Atlanta, Ga., MSRC.

Allen, Ivan. Milton Viorst, Fall 1974, Atlanta, Ga., MSRC.

Allen, Ivan. Carolyn Hatcher, 4/10/75, Atlanta, Ga., APL.

Allen, Ivan. Will Leventhal, n.d., Atlanta, Ga., KC.

Amos, Mrs. India. David Lewis, 8/68, Atlanta, Ga.

Anderson, L. L. Charles Fager, 1/11 & 15/71, Selma, Ala., HU.

Anderson, L. L. Garrow, 3/14/79, Selma, Ala.

Anderson, William G. John Ricks, 8/81, Detroit, Mich.

Anderson, William G. Garrow, 1/6/82, Detroit, Mich.

Anderson, William G. Blackside, 11/7/85, Atlanta, Ga.

Armstrong, James. Lee Bains, 8/23/76, Birmingham, Ala. BPLA.

Austin, Ernest. Katherine Shannon, 7/9/68, Washington, D.C. MSRC.

Awsumb, Gwen. Anne Trotter & David & Carol Lynn Yellin, 4/26 & 5/8/68, Memphis, Tenn., MSU.

Ayers, Thomas G. Garrow, 12/10/84, Chicago, Ill.

Azbell, Joe. Mary Brown, 10/22/85, Montgomery, Ala.

Azbell, Joe. Blackside, 10/31/85, Montgomery, Ala.

Baer, Helen, et al. Maurice Baer, 10/27/75, Birmingham, Ala., UAB.

Baez, Joan. Will Leventhal, n.d., n.p., KC.

Bailey, Mel. Blackside, 11/2/85, Birmingham, Ala.
Bailey, Walter. Joan Beifuss, Bill Thomas & David Yellin, 6/26/68, Memphis, Tenn., MSU.
Baker, Ella. Anne Romaine, 3/25/67, New York, N.Y., SHSW.
Baker, Ella. John Britton, 6/19/68, Washington, D.C., MSRC.
Baker, Ella. Clayborne Carson, 5/5/72, New York, N.Y.
Baker, Ella. Eugene Walker, 9/4/74, Durham, N.C., UNC.
Baker, Ella. Sue Thrasher & Casey Hayden, 4/19/77, New York, N.Y., UNC.
Baker, Ella. Lenore Hogan, 3/4/79, New York, N.Y., HC.
Baker, Ella. Garrow, 9/27/84, New York, N.Y.
Baldwin, Jesse. James Mosby, 7/13/68, Memphis, Tenn., MSRC.
Ballard, Charles. James Mosby, 7/13/68, Memphis, Tenn., MSRC.
Ballou, Maude. Garrow, 8/4/84, Charlotte, N.C.
Barbour, J. Pius. David Lewis, 9/68, Chester, Pa.
Barnet, Roosevelt. Robert Wright, 8/13/69, Montgomery, Ala., MSRC.
Barnett, Paul. David & Carol Lynn Yellin, 8/8/72, Memphis, Tenn., MSU.
Barry, Marion. "JM"—Zinn, 12/18/65, n.p., SHSW.
Barry, Marion. Katherine Shannon, 10/3/67, Washington, D.C., MSRC.
Barry, Marion. Eliot Wigginton, 12/4/81, Washington, D.C., HC.
Baugh, Howard. John Britton, 1/22/68, Atlanta, Ga., MSRC.
Baugh, Howard. Peter Joseph, 8/71, Atlanta, Ga., CU.
Baugh, Howard. Garrow, 9/9/79, Atlanta, Ga.
Bell, Ezekiel. Wilson & Jerry Viar, 5/28/68, Memphis, Tenn., MSU.
Bell, Ezekiel. Jerry Viar & Bill Thomas, 6/14/68, Memphis, Tenn., MSU.
Bennett, John C. Garrow, 4/8/84, Claremont, Cal.
Bennett, Roy. Garrow, 12/12/79 & 1/3/80, New York, N.Y.
Berry, Edwin C. "Bill." John Britton, 2/22/68, Chicago, Ill., MSRC.
Berry, Edwin C. "Bill." David Lewis, 9/68, Chicago, Ill.
Berry, Edwin C. "Bill." Garrow, 2/22/84, Chicago, Ill.
Bevel, James. Katherine Shannon, 7/6/68, Washington, D.C., MSRC.
Bevel, James. Garrow, 12/12/84, Chicago, Ill.
Bevel, James. Blackside, 11/13/85, Chicago, Ill.
Blackburn, Charles. Selma Lewis, Bill Thomas & David Yellin, 5/29/68, Memphis, Tenn., MSU.
Blackburn, Malcolm. Anne Trotter & David Yellin, 5/24/68, Memphis, Tenn., MSU.
Blackburn, Malcolm. Tom Beckner & Bill Thomas, 8/2/68, Memphis, Tenn., MSU.
Blackwell, Randolph. Charles Fager, 2/3 & 5/71, Atlanta, Ga., HU.
Blackwell, Randolph. Garrow, 9/15/79, Atlanta, Ga.
Blair, Taylor. Tom Beckner & David Yellin, 9/13/68, Memphis, Tenn., MSU.
Blanchard, Jerred. Anne Trotter, Tom Beckner & Carol Lynn Yellin, 5/27/68, Memphis, Tenn., MSU.
Blanchard, Jerred. Craig Leake, 3/71, Memphis, Tenn., MSU.
Bolden, Willie. Garrow, 1/13/84, Atlanta, Ga.
Bond, Julian. Gwen Gillon, 7/6/67, Atlanta, Ga., SHSW.
Bond, Julian. John Britton, 1/22/68, Atlanta, Ga., MSRC.
Bond, Julian. Norman Apter, 1/72, Atlanta, Ga., CU.
Bond, Julian. Milton Viorst, Fall 1974, Atlanta, Ga., MSRC.
Bond, Julian. Bob Hall & Sue Thrasher, Winter 1975–1976, Atlanta, Ga., UNC.
Bond, Julian. Walter Burrell, 6/15/77, Atlanta, Ga., KC.
Bond, Julian. Sue Thrasher, 11/8/81, Atlanta, Ga., HC.
Booker, Simeon. John Stewart, 4/27/67, Washington, D.C., JFKL.
Borders, William H. Marcy Dalton, 3/5/76, Atlanta, Ga., APL.
Bostick, Herman. Herbert Holmes, 3/30/70, Atlanta, Ga., KC.

Boyd, H. C. John Ricks, 6/16/81, Albany, Ga.
Boynton, Amelia. Charles Fager, 1/7 & 14/71, Selma, Ala., HU.
Boynton, Amelia (Robinson). Garrow, 8/19/85, Tuskegee, Ala.
Boynton, Amelia (Robinson). Blackside, 12/6/85, Selma, Ala.
Boyte, Harry. Donald Smith, 12/2/63, Atlanta, Ga., SHSW.
Braden, Anne. Sue Thrasher, 4/18/81, Louisville, Ky., HC.
Braden, Anne. Garrow, 3/24/82, Louisville, Ky.
Braden, Carl & Anne. James Mosby, 9/18/68, Louisville, Ky., MSRC.
Branton, Wiley. Garrow, 3/8/84, Washington, D.C.
Brazeal, Brailsford R. Judy Barton, 2/16/72, Atlanta, Ga., KC.
Brazier, Arthur. David Lewis, 9/68, Chicago, Ill.
Bristol, James E. Garrow, 1/29/86, Philadelphia, Pa.
Brown, Bailey. Garrow, 10/24/85, Memphis, Tenn. (phone)
Brown, Benjamin D. John Britton, 8/16/67, Atlanta, Ga., MSRC.
Brown, Claude C. Charles Fager, 1/9/71, Selma, Ala., HU.
Brown, Edward. Harold Lewis, 6/30/67, Washington, D.C., MSRC.
Brown, Fairro. Charles Fager, 1/14/71, Selma, Ala., HU.
Brownell, Herbert. Blackside, 11/15/85, New York, N.Y.
Brownlee, Henry. Feay Shellman & Fred Baldwin, 1/8/83, Savannah, Ga., TA.
Bryant, Baxton. Joan Beifuss & Tom Beckner, 6/25 & 8/3/68, Memphis, Tenn.,
  MSU.
Bryant, Baxton. Robert Campbell, 7/9/68, Nashville, Tenn., MSRC.
Bryant, Baxton. Arvil Adams, 4/28/69, Memphis, Tenn.
Bryant, C. Farris. Joe Frantz, 3/5/71, Jacksonville, Fla., LBJL.
Bullard, Jack. Garrow, 1/25/86, Charlotte, N.C.
Burch, Lucius. Joan Beifuss & David Yellin, 9/3/68, Memphis, Tenn., MSU.
Burks, Mary Fair. Garrow, 7/29/84, Salisbury, Md.
Cabbage, Charles. James Mosby, 7/68, Memphis, Tenn., MSRC.
Calhoun, John H. John Britton, 5/23/68, Atlanta, Ga., MSRC.
Callahan, Eugene. Garrow, 7/27/83, Chicago, Ill.
Campbell, Will. n.i., n.d., n.p., MSRC.
Campbell, Will. Orley Caudill, 6/8/76, Mount Juliet, Tenn., USM.
Capell, Arthur. Garrow, 3/14/79, Mt. Vernon, Ala.
Carey, Archibald. Robert Wright, 3/24/70, Chicago, Ill., MSRC.
Carey, Gordon. Garrow, 1/29/85, Raleigh, N.C.
Carey, Gordon. Blackside, 11/6/85, Washington, D.C.
Carmichael, Stokely. Milton Viorst, n.d., n.p., MSRC.
Carmichael, Stokely (Kwame Toure). Garrow, 11/7/84, New York, N.Y.
Carpenter, Gladys. Joan Beifuss & David Yellin, 9/11/68, Memphis, Tenn., MSU.
Carr, Johnnie R. Judy Barton, 1/27/72, Montgomery, Ala., KC.
Carr, Johnnie R. Worth Long, 8/18/83, Montgomery, Ala.
Carter, Harold A. Garrow, 1/27/86, Baltimore, Md.
Caywood, David. Anne Trotter & David Yellin, 5/20/68, Memphis, Tenn., MSU.
Chandler, Gladstone Lewis. Donald Smith, 12/4/63, Atlanta, Ga., SHSW.
Chandler, Wyeth. Joan Beifuss & Carol Lynn Yellin, 6/20/68, Memphis, Tenn.,
  MSU.
Chatmon, Thomas. John Ricks, 10/27/83, Albany, Ga.
Ciampa, P. J. David & Carol Lynn Yellin, 2/3/72, Washington, D.C., MSU.
Clark, Benjamin Van. Fred Baldwin, 8/16/81, Savannah, Ga., TA.
Clark, Benjamin Van. Garrow, 12/27/83, Savannah, Ga.
Clark, James G. Garrow, 1/25/85, Scottsboro, Ala.
Clark, James G. Blackside, 2/19/86, Alexandria, Ala.
Clark, Kenneth B. Will Leventhal, 9/5/75, New York, N.Y., KC.
Clark, Kenneth B. Garrow, 12/3/84, New York, N.Y.

Clark, Louise. Garrow, 5/12/79, Selma, Ala.
Clark, Ramsey. T. H. Baker, 10/30/68, 2/11, 3/21, 4/16 & 6/3/69, Washington, D.C., LBJL.
Clark, Ramsey. James Mosby, 12/17/68, & 4/21/69, Washington, D.C., MSRC.
Clark, Septima. Judy Barton, 11/9/71, Charleston, S.C., KC.
Clark, Septima. Jane Roth, 5/23/73, Charleston, S.C., SHSW.
Clark, Septima. Jacquelyn Hall, 7/25/76, Charleston, S.C., UNC.
Clark, Septima. Eugene Walker, 7/30/76, Atlanta, Ga., UNC.
Clark, Septima. Peter Wood, 2/3 & 4/81, Charleston, S.C., HC.
Clark, Septima. Eliot Wigginton, 6/20/81, Charleston, S.C., HC.
Clark, Septima. Garrow, 12/28/83, Charleston, S.C.
Clayton, Xernona. David Lewis, 8/68, Atlanta, Ga.
Cleage, Albert. Willie Harriford, 3/5/70, Atlanta, Ga., KC.
Clement, Kenneth. John Britton, 6/6/68, Washington, D.C., MSRC.
Cochrane, Warren R. Fred Downing, 7/3/85, Atlanta, Ga.
Coffin, William S. Garrow, 11/8/85, New York, N.Y. (phone)
Collins, LeRoy. Jack Bass & Walter DeVries, 5/19/74, Tallahassee, Fla., UNC.
Conyers, John. Will Leventhal, 6/20/75, Washington, D.C., KC.
Cook, Edward W. "Ned." Joan Beifuss & David Yellin, 2/11/69, Memphis, Tenn., MSU.
Cooks, Stoney. Katherine Shannon, 7/12/68, Washington, D.C., MSRC.
Cooks, Stoney. Will Leventhal, 6/16/75, Washington, D.C., KC.
Cooks, Stoney. Garrow, 8/23/84, Washington, D.C.
Cooks, Stoney. John LaCrosse, 2/26/85, Atlanta, Ga.
Cotton, Dorothy. Garrow, 9/8/79, Atlanta, Ga.
Cotton, Dorothy. Eliot Wigginton & Sue Thrasher, 6/20/81, New Market, Tenn., HC.
Coulton, Herbert. Garrow, 8/7/84, Petersburg, Va.
Crear, John. Charles Fager, 1/17/71, Selma, Ala., HU.
Crenshaw, Cornelia. James Mosby, 7/68, Memphis, Tenn., MSRC.
Crenshaw, Jack. Garrow, 4/1/82, Montgomery, Ala.
Crocker, L. C. Garrow, 3/13/79, Selma, Ala.
Cross, John. Judy Barton, 3/23/72, Atlanta, Ga., KC.
Crowley, John. Charles Fager, 1/5 & 8/71, Selma, Ala., HU.
Davis, A. L. Judy Barton, 4/13/72, New Orleans, La., KC.
Davis, Fred. Joan Beifuss & Jack Hurley, 5/22/68, Memphis, Tenn., MSU.
Davis, Fred. James Mosby, 7/68, Memphis, Tenn., MSRC.
Davis, L. O. Edward Kallal, 2/6/76, St. Augustine, Fla., UF.
Dennis, David. Blackside, 11/10/85, Jackson, Miss.
DeWolf, L. Harold. John Britton, 4/23/68, Washington, D.C., MSRC.
DeWolf, L. Harold. David Lewis, 9/68, Washington, D.C.
Diggs, Charles C. Blackside, 11/6/85, Washington, D.C.
Dimmick, William A. Joan Beifuss & Judy Schulz, 7/16/68, Memphis, Tenn., MSU.
Doar, John. Anthony Lewis, 11/13/64, Washington, D.C., JFKL-Navasky.
Doar, John. Garrow, 1/2/80, New York, N.Y. (phone)
Doar, John. Blackside, 11/15/85, New York, N.Y.
Doctor, Bobby. Bill Thomas & David Yellin, 6/17/68, Memphis, Tenn., MSU.
Donaldson, Ivanhoe. Blackside, 5/15/79, Washington, D.C.
Donelson, Lewis. Anne Trotter, Tom Beckner & Carol Lynn Yellin, 6/29/68, Memphis, Tenn., MSU.
Donelson, Lewis. Arvil Adams, 6/10/69, Memphis, Tenn.
Doughty, Darrell. Joan Beifuss & David Yellin, 6/26/68, Memphis, Tenn., MSU.
Doyle, Ernest L. Garrow, 3/13/79, Selma, Ala.
Drew, Addine. Garrow, 9/12/79, Birmingham, Ala.

Duckett, Al. Stephen Oates, 9/19/78, New York, N.Y.
Dunbar, Leslie. Garrow, 7/6/83, New York, N.Y.
Dupont, K. S. Jack Ice, 7/21/78, Tallahassee, Fla., FSU.
Durick, Joseph. Joan Beifuss & Judy Schulz, 5/21/68, Memphis, Tenn., MSU.
Durr, Clifford. Stanley Smith, n.d., n.p., MSRC.
Durr, Clifford. James Sargent, 4/17–19/74, Wetumpka, Ala., CU.
Durr, Clifford & Virginia. Norman Lumpkin, 4/15/73, Wetumpka, Ala., ACHE.
Durr, Virginia. Stanley Smith, n.d., n.p., MSRC.
Durr, Virginia, Johnnie Carr, & Irene West. William Porter, 1970, Montgomery,
    Ala., KC.
Durr, Virginia. William Barnard, 10/8 & 24/74, Wetumpka, Ala., CU.
Durr, Virginia. Garrow, 3/31/82, Wetumpka, Ala.
Durr, Virginia. Worth Long, 8/18/83, Montgomery, Ala.
Durr, Virginia. Mary Brown, 11/13/85, Montgomery, Ala.
Durr, Virginia. Blackside, 2/21/86, Boston, Mass.
Eddy, Jane Lee. Garrow, 4/23/80, New York, N.Y.
Eldridge, Tommy. James Mosby, 7/68, Memphis, Tenn., MSRC.
Ellwanger, Joseph. Blackside, 11/13/85, Chicago, Ill.
Epps, Jesse. Tom Beckner & Joan Beifuss, 7/31/68, Memphis, Tenn., MSU.
Epps, Jesse. Arvil Adams, 7/8/69, Memphis, Tenn.
Epps, Jesse. Joan Beifuss, 11/69, Memphis, Tenn., MSU.
Eskridge, Chauncey. Garrow, 7/25/83, Chicago, Ill.
Evans, Clay. Garrow, 2/12/85, Chicago, Ill.
Evans, Courtney. Victor Navasky, 2/13 & 11/6/68, Washington, D.C., JFKL.
Evans, Courtney. T. H. Baker, 3/27/69, Washington, D.C., LBJL.
Evers, Charles. Joe Frantz, 4/3/74, Fayette, Miss., LBJL.
Evers, Myrlie. Will Leventhal, 3/5/75, New York, N.Y., KC.
Evers, Myrlie. Blackside, 11/27/85, Los Angeles, Cal.
Fager, Charles. Project South, Summer 1965, Selma, Ala., SU.
Fager, Charles. Garrow, 4/24/79, Arlington, Va.
Fanion, Gerald. Joan Beifuss & Walter Evans, 6/10/68, Memphis, Tenn., MSU.
Fanion, Gerald. James Mosby, 7/12/68, Memphis, Tenn., MSRC.
Farmer, James. John Britton, 9/28/68, New York, N.Y., MSRC.
Farmer, James. David Lewis, 12/68, New York, N.Y.
Farmer, James. T. H. Baker, 10/69, Washington, D.C., LBJL.
Farmer, James. Paige Mulhollan, 7/20/71, Washington, D.C., LBJL.
Farmer, James. Milton Viorst, 5/20/74, Washington, D.C., MSRC.
Farmer, James. Garrow, 5/15/81, Washington, D.C.
Farmer, James. Dennis Dickerson, 3/8/84, Washington, D.C.
Farmer, James. Blackside, 11/1/85, New York, N.Y.
Farris, Christine King. Mary Brown, 11/18/85, Atlanta, Ga.
Fauntroy, Walter. David Lewis, 9/68, Washington, D.C.
Fauntroy, Walter. Edward Thompson, 2/23 & 3/5/73, Washington, D.C., MSRC.
Fauntroy, Walter. Will Leventhal, 7/3/75, Washington, D.C., KC.
Fauntroy, Walter. Garrow, 8/9/84, Washington, D.C.
Finley, Elliott. Garrow, 8/22/85, Montgomery, Ala.
Finney, Leon. Milton Viorst, 10/12/74, Chicago, Ill.
Flannery, Harold "Nick." Scott Rafferty, 7/3/75, Washington, D.C., JFKL.
Fleming, Harold. Will Leventhal, 7/2/75, Washington, D.C., KC.
Fleming, Harold. Garrow, 1/10/83, Washington, D.C.
Forman, James. "JM"—Zinn, 11/12/65, n.p., SHSW.
Forman, James. Blackside, 12/11/85, New York, N.Y.
Foster, Marie. Garrow, 3/15/79, Selma, Ala.
Gannon, Michael. David Colburn, 5/3/71, St. Augustine, Fla.
Gardner, Edward. Garrow, 9/11/79, Birmingham, Ala.

Gaston, A. G. Blackside, 11/1/85, Birmingham, Ala.
Gay, Benjamin. John Ricks, 10/28/83, Albany, Ga.
Gianotti, Frank. Joan Beifuss & Carol Lynn Yellin, 5/10/72, Memphis, Tenn., MSU.
Gibson, John. John Britton, 4/26/68, Washington, D.C., MSRC.
Gibson, John. Garrow, 3/4/85, Washington, D.C.
Gilmore, Georgia. Blackside, 2/17/86, Montgomery, Ala.
Gilmore, Thomas. Robert Wright, 8/3/68, Forkland, Ala., MSRC.
Glickstein, Howard. Robert Wright, 11/10/69, Washington, D.C., MSRC.
Glickstein, Howard. Scott Rafferty, 11/18/75, Washington, D.C., JFKL.
Graetz, Robert. Garrow, 2/23/84, McArthur, Ohio.
Granger, Lester. John Britton, 5/22/68, Atlanta, Ga., MSRC.
Grant, E. James. John Ricks, 6/16/81, Albany, Ga.
Gray, Fred. Stanley Smith, 12/14/67, Tuskegee, Ala., MSRC.
Gray, Fred. David Lewis, 8/68, Tuskegee, Ala.
Gray, Fred. Norman Lumpkin, 9/1/73, Tuskegee, Ala., ACHE.
Gray, Fred. Garrow, 8/20/85, Tuskegee, Ala.
Gray, James. John Ricks, 6/81, Albany, Ga.
Green, Edith. Milton Viorst, 6/12/74, Washington, D.C., MSRC.
Green, Gwendolyn. Will Leventhal, n.d., Los Angeles, Cal., KC.
Green, Robert L. Garrow, 6/21/85, Washington, D.C.
Greenberg, Jack. Milton Viorst, 5/28/74, New York, N.Y., MSRC.
Greenberg, Jack. Will Leventhal, 1975, New York, N.Y., KC.
Gregory, Hazel, & Georgia Gilmore. Mary Brown, 10/23/85, Montgomery, Ala.
Griffin, Junius. Garrow, 1/21/85, Johnson City, Tenn.
Grigg, Charles. Jack Ice, 7/78, Tallahassee, Fla., FSU.
Grimes, Joe. Garrow, 5/10/79, Selma, Ala.
Griswold, Erwin. Scott Rafferty, 10/29/75, Washington, D.C., JFKL.
Guthman, Edwin. Garrow, 11/14/79, Philadelphia, Pa.
Hall, Peter. Garrow, 9/12/79, Birmingham, Ala.
Hamer, Fannie Lou. Anne Romaine, 11/22/66, Ruleville, Miss., SHSW.
Hamer, Fannie Lou. Neil McMillen, 4/14/72 & 1/25/73, Ruleville, Miss., USM.
Hamilton, E. D. Judy Barton, 3/16/72, Albany, Ga., KC.
Hamilton, E. D. John Ricks, 6/16/81, Albany, Ga.
Hamilton, E. D. Garrow, 5/13/82, Albany, Ga.
Hamilton, Grace T. David Lewis, 8/68, Atlanta, Ga.
Hankerson, Lester. Feay Shellman & Fred Baldwin, 3/13/83, Savannah, Ga., TA.
Hannah, John. Paige Mulhollan, n.d., Washington, D.C., LBJL.
Harding, Vincent. Vincent Browne, 8/16/68, Washington, D.C., MSRC.
Harper, Carrie. David Lewis, 8/68, Atlanta, Ga.
Harrington, Michael. Garrow, 2/18/84, New York, N.Y.
Harris, Curtis. Garrow, 8/3/84, Hopewell, Va.
Harris, McCree. John Ricks, 6/16/81, Albany, Ga.
Haskins, James. Robert Wright, 8/15/69, Demopolis, Ala., MSRC.
Haskins, John. Robert Wright, 8/15/69, Demopolis, Ala., MSRC.
Hayes, Charles. Garrow, 12/11/84, Chicago, Ill.
Hayling, Robert B. John Britton, 8/16/67, Atlanta, Ga., MSRC.
Hayling, Robert B. Garrow, 1/11/84, Ft. Lauderdale, Fla.
Hedgeman, Anna A. Robert Martin, 8/27 & 29/68, New York, N.Y., MSRC.
Height, Dorothy. James Mosby, 2/13/70, New York, N.Y., MSRC.
Height, Dorothy. Polly Cowan, 2/11/74–11/6/76, New York, N.Y., & Washington,
    D.C., BWOHP.
Heinz, Chris. Garrow, 5/10/79, Selma, Ala.
Helstein, Ralph. Eliot Wigginton, 5/4/81, Chicago, Ill., HC.
Helstein, Ralph, & Nina Helstein. Garrow, 2/11/85, Chicago, Ill.
Henderson, Thelton. Robert Wright, 11/16/68, San Francisco, Cal., MSRC.

Hendricks, Lola. Mary Brown, 10/21 & 11/15/85, Birmingham, Ala.
Henry, Aaron. Robert Wright, 9/25/68, Clarksdale, Miss., MSRC.
Henry, Aaron. T. H. Baker, 9/12/70, Clarksdale, Miss., LBJL.
Henry, Aaron. Neil McMillen & George Burson, 5/1/72, Clarksdale, Miss., USM.
Henry, Aaron. Worth Long, 5/22/83, Clarksdale, Miss.
Hesburgh, Theodore. Paige Mulhollan, 2/1/71, South Bend, Ind., LBJL.
Hill, Norman. James Mosby, 3/12/70, New York, N.Y., MSRC.
Hill, Norman. Garrow, 11/9/84, New York, N.Y.
Hollins, Billy. Garrow, 1/27/85, Atlanta, Ga.
Hollowell, Donald. John Britton, 5/23/68, Atlanta, Ga., MSRC.
Hollowell, Donald. David Lewis, 8/68, Atlanta, Ga.
Hollowell, Donald. Garrow, 5/27/82, Atlanta, Ga.
Holman, M. Carl. John Britton, 10/3/67, Washington, D.C., MSRC.
Hooks, Benjamin. Bill Thomas & David Yellin, 6/25/68, Memphis, Tenn., MSU.
Hooks, Benjamin. Craig Leake, 3/71, Memphis, Tenn., MSU.
Horowitz, Rochelle. Garrow, 8/10/84, Washington, D.C.
Horton, Myles. Frank Adams, n.d., Knoxville, Tenn., SHSW-HLW 17.
Houck, Tom. John LaCrosse, 3/6/85, Atlanta, Ga.
House, Maurice. Garrow, 9/11/79, Birmingham, Ala.
Hudson, James. Jack Ice, 8/2/78, Tallahassee, Fla., FSU.
Hughes, Robert E. Garrow, 8/24/85, Gadsden, Ala.
Hulett, John. Charles Fager, 1/14/71, Trickem, Ala., HU.
Humphrey, Hubert H. Michael Gillette, 6/21/77, Washington, D.C., LBJL.
Hunter, Lillie Armstrong Thomas (Brown). Garrow, 8/31/85, Tuskegee, Ala.
Hurley, Ruby. John Britton, 1/26/68, Atlanta, Ga., MSRC.
Hyman, Billy. Carol Lynn Yellin & Wilson Viar, 7/8/68, Memphis, Tenn., MSU.
Ingram, William B. Tom Beckner & Bill Thomas, 9/7/68, Memphis, Tenn., MSU.
Ivy, Ron. David Yellin, 5/7 & 9/68, Memphis, Tenn., MSU.
Jackson, Eliza "Goldie." Garrow, 5/13/82, Albany, Ga.
Jackson, Eliza "Goldie." John Ricks, 10/83, Albany, Ga.
Jackson, Emory O. Stanley Smith, 2/68, Birmingham, Ala., MSRC.
Jackson, H. Ralph. Anne Trotter, Bill Thomas & David Yellin, 5/24/68, Memphis, Tenn., MSU.
Jackson, H. Ralph. James Mosby, 7/10/68, Memphis, Tenn., MSRC.
Jackson, H. Ralph. Arvil Adams, 7/21/69, Memphis, Tenn.
Jackson, Jean. Garrow, 5/12/79, Selma, Ala.
Jackson, Jesse. n.i., 12/17/68, n.p., GM.
Jackson, Jesse. Garrow, 3/3/85, Atlanta, Ga., & Montgomery & Selma, Ala..
Jacobs, Julianna. Garrow, 9/6/85, Atlanta, Ga.
James, Robert. David Yellin & Churchill Roberts, 5/9/68, Memphis, Tenn., MSU.
Jelinek, Donald. Robert Wright, 8/1/68, Selma, Ala., MSRC.
Jemison, Theodore, & Johnnie Jones. Judy Barton, 4/12/72, Baton Rouge, La., KC.
Jenkins, Herbert. T. H. Baker, 5/14/69, Atlanta, Ga., LBJL.
Jenkins, Herbert. Garrow, 9/6/79, Atlanta, Ga.
Jenkins, Tim. "JM"—Zinn, 12/18/65, n.p., SHSW.
Johnson, Frank M. Garrow, 4/30/76, Montgomery, Ala.
Johnson, Rether Shank. Feay Shellman, 5/5/83, Savannah, Ga., TA.
Johnson, Robert E. John Britton, 9/6/67, Chicago, Ill., MSRC.
Jones, Clarence B. Garrow, 1/25 & 3/18/80, New York, N.Y.
Jones, James R. Garrow, 5/15/82, Fort Valley, Ga.
Jones, J. Charles. Katherine Shannon, 8/10/67, Washington, D.C., MSRC.
Jones, J. Charles. John Ricks, 6/81, Charlotte, N.C.
Jones, J. Charles. Garrow, 3/31/84, Charlotte, N.C.
Jones, Major. Garrow, 9/13/79, Atlanta, Ga.
Jones, Moses. Judy Barton, 1/26/72, Montgomery, Ala., KC.

Jones, Oliver "Sack." Herbert Holmes, 4/8/70, Atlanta, Ga., KC.
Jones, T. O. Anne Trotter & Jack Hurley, 5/9/68, Memphis, Tenn., MSU.
Jones, T. O. Joan Beifuss & David Yellin, 1/30/70, Memphis, Tenn., MSU.
Jordan, DuPree & Margaret. Garrow, 1/14/84, Atlanta, Ga.
Jordan, James. Joan Beifuss & Jack Hurley, 7/19/68, Memphis, Tenn., MSU.
Jordan, Vernon. John Britton, 1/26/68, Atlanta, Ga., MSRC.
Jordan, Vernon. Stanley Smith, 8/68, Atlanta, Ga., MSRC.
Jordan, Vernon. Garrow, 3/7/84, Washington, D.C.
Kahn, Tom. Milton Viorst, 6/74, Washington, D.C., MSRC.
Kahn, Tom. Garrow, 8/14/84, Washington, D.C.
Katzenbach, Nicholas. Paige Mulhollan, 11/12 & 23, & 12/11/68, Washington, D.C., LBJL.
Katzenbach, Nicholas. Garrow, 10/27/79, Princeton, N.J.
Katzenbach, Nicholas. Blackside, 12/10/85, New York, N.Y.
Kelley, Asa. Garrow, 5/13/82, Albany, Ga.
Kelley, Asa. John Ricks, 7/19/85, Albany, Ga.
Kennedy, Jay Richard. Garrow, 2/23 & 3/2/80, Tarzana, Cal.
Kennedy, Melvin. Herbert Holmes, 4/22/70, Atlanta, Ga., KC.
Kennedy, Robert F. John B. Martin, 4/13/64, New York, N.Y., JFKL.
Kennedy, Robert F., & Burke Marshall. Anthony Lewis, 12/4, 6 & 22/64, New York, N.Y., & McLean, Va., JFKL.
Kilgore, Thomas. Garrow, 1/21/85, Richmond, Va.
Kilpatrick, James J. Will Leventhal, 7/10/75, Washington, D.C., KC.
King, Alberta W. n.i., 1/18/73, Atlanta, Ga., KC.
King, C. B. David Lewis, 8/68, Albany, Ga.
King, C. B. Stanley Smith, 8/68, Albany, Ga., MSRC.
King, C. B. Judy Barton, 3/15/72, Albany, Ga., KC.
King, C. B. John Ricks, 6/81, Albany, Ga.
King, Coretta Scott. Donald Smith, 12/7/63, Atlanta, Ga., SHSW.
King, Coretta Scott. Charlotte Mayerson, 7/15–8/5/68, Manchester, N.H.
King, Coretta Scott. Garrow, 12/10/83, Atlanta, Ga.
King, Coretta Scott. Mary Brown, 11/19/85, Atlanta, Ga.
King, Coretta Scott. Blackside, 12/23/85, Atlanta, Ga.
King, Dearing E. Garrow, 7/29/83, Chicago, Ill.
King, Lonnie. John Britton, 8/29/67, Washington, D.C., MSRC.
King, Lonnie. Willie Harriford, 3/1/70, Atlanta, Ga., KC.
King, Martin Luther, Jr. Donald Smith, 11/29/63, Atlanta, Ga., SHSW.
King, Martin Luther, Jr. Berl Bernhard, 3/9/64, Atlanta, Ga., JFKL.
King, Martin Luther, Sr. Bernita Bennette, 12/13/67, Atlanta, Ga. BEM I-37-16, #76.
King, R. Edwin. Anne Romaine, 9/5/66, Knoxville, Tenn., SHSW.
King, Slater. David Lewis, 8/68, Albany, Ga.
King, Slater. Stanley Smith, 8/68, Albany, Ga., MSRC.
King, Yolanda. John LaCrosse, 1/18/85, Atlanta, Ga.
Kuykendall, Dan. David Yellin & Bill Thomas, 8/30/68, Memphis, Tenn., MSU.
Kyles, Gwen. Joan Beifuss, Jerry Viar & Carol Lynn Yellin, 5/28/68, Memphis, Tenn., MSU.
Kyles, Samuel "Billy." Joan Beifuss, Bill Thomas & David Yellin, 6/12/68, Memphis, Tenn., MSU.
Kyles, Samuel "Billy." Joan Beifuss & Bill Thomas, 7/30/68, Memphis, Tenn., MSU.
Kyles, Samuel "Billy." Jim Bishop, n.d., Memphis, Tenn., SBU.
Kyles, Samuel "Billy." Craig Leake, 3/71, Memphis, Tenn., MSU.
Lafayette, Bernard. Robert Weisbrot, 7/25/84, Atlanta, Ga.
Lafayette, Bernard. Garrow, 8/19/85, Tuskegee, Ala.
Laue, James. David Lewis, 2/69, Washington, D.C.

Lawson, James M. David Yellin & Bill Thomas, 7/1/68, Memphis, Tenn., MSU.
Lawson, James M. David Yellin, Bill Thomas & Joan Beifuss, 9/10 & 18/68, Memphis, Tenn., MSU.
Lawson, James M. David Yellin & Joan Beifuss, 1/21, 5/27, 9/23 & 24/69, 7/8/70 & 5/25/72, Memphis, Tenn., MSU.
Lawson, James M. Joan Beifuss & Bill Thomas, 7/21 & 8/21/69, Memphis, Tenn., MSU.
Lawson, James M. Will Leventhal, 5/15/75, Los Angeles, Cal., KC.
Lawson, James M. Milton Viorst, 1/78, Los Angeles, Cal., MSRC.
Lawson, James M. Blackside, 12/2/85, Los Angeles, Cal.
Lee, Bernard. Jim Bishop, 9/5/70, Atlanta, Ga., SBU.
Lee, Bernard. Walter Burrell, 6/23/77, Atlanta, Ga., KC.
Lee, Bernard. Garrow, 8/21/82, Washington, D.C.
Levison, Stanley. David Lewis, 11/68, New York, N.Y.
Levison, Stanley. Jean Stein, 11/21/69 & 2/23/70, New York, N.Y.
Levison, Stanley. James Mosby, 2/14/70, New York, N.Y., MSRC.
Levison, Stanley. Arthur Schlesinger, 8/3/76, New York, N.Y.
Lewis, Anthony. Larry Hackman, 7/23/70, New York, N.Y., JFKL.
Lewis, Beulah. David Lewis, 8/68, Atlanta, Ga.
Lewis, John. Katherine Shannon, 8/22/67, New York, N.Y., MSRC.
Lewis, John. William Porter, 6/19/70, Atlanta, Ga., KC.
Lewis, John. Clayborne Carson, 4/17/72, Atlanta, Ga.
Lewis, John. Jack Bass & Walter DeVries, 11/20/73, Raleigh, N.C., UNC.
Lewis, John. Milton Viorst, 6/78, Washington, D.C., MSRC.
Lewis, John. Blackside, 5/79 & 11/6/85, Atlanta, Ga.
Lewis, John. Richard Brasch, 4/5–6/82, Atlanta, Ga., KC.
Lewis, Muriel. Garrow, 5/10/79, Selma, Ala.
Lewis, Rufus. Stanley Smith, 1/68, Montgomery, Ala., MSRC.
Lewis, Rufus. Judy Barton, 1/24/72, Montgomery, Ala., KC.
Lewis, Rufus, & Eugene Ligon. Norman Lumpkin, 6/25/73, Montgomery, Ala., ACHE.
Lewis, Rufus. Garrow, 9/16/79, Montgomery, Ala.
Lewis, Rufus. Mary Brown, 11/13/85, Montgomery, Ala.
Lewis, Rufus. Blackside, 10/31/85, Montgomery, Ala.
Loeb, Henry. David & Carol Lynn Yellin, 7/1/68, Memphis, Tenn., MSU.
Loeb, Henry. Henry Mitchell & David Yellin, 9/19/68, Memphis, Tenn., MSU.
Loeb, Henry. Craig Leake, 3/71, Memphis, Tenn., MSU.
Logan, Marian. Garrow, 8/6/80, New York, N.Y.
Lowenstein, Allard. "JM"—Zinn, 11/7/65, n.p., SHSW.
Lowenstein, Allard. Anne Romaine, 3/7/67, Charlottesville, Va., SHSW.
Lowenstein, Allard. Milton Viorst, 5/28/74, New York, N.Y., MSRC.
Lowenstein, Allard. Clayborne Carson, 5/16/77, New York, N.Y.
Lowery, Joseph. Robert Wright, 10/19/70, Atlanta, Ga., MSRC.
Lowery, Joseph. Garrow, 12/9/82, Atlanta, Ga.
Lucas, Robert. John Britton, 2/20/68, Chicago, Ill., MSRC.
Lucy, William. Joan Beifuss & David Yellin, 11/1/68, Memphis, Tenn., MSU.
Lux, Henry. Joan Beifuss & Carol Lynn Yellin, 5/9/72, Memphis, Tenn., MSU.
McCall, Walter. Herbert Holmes, 3/31/70, Atlanta, Ga., KC.
McDermott, John. Garrow, 7/26/83, Chicago, Ill.
McDew, Charles. Katherine Shannon, 8/24/67, Washington, D.C., MSRC.
McDonald, Dora. Donald Smith, 12/2/63, Atlanta, Ga., SHSW.
McDonald, Dora. Garrow, 1/28/85, Atlanta, Ga.
Mack, Benjamin. Blake McNulty, 12/29/66, Columbia, S.C., SHSW.
Mack, John. Helen Hall, 7/17/69, Washington, D.C., MSRC.
McKissick, Floyd. Robert Wright, 10/16/68, New York, N.Y., MSRC.

McKissick, Floyd. Garrow, 8/3/84, Oxford, N.C.
McKnight, John. Garrow, 8/5/83 & 2/20/84, Evanston, Ill.
McPherson, Harry. T. H. Baker, 4/9/69, Washington, D.C., LBJL.
McRae, Frank. Joan Beifuss & Carol Lynn Yellin, 8/6/68, Memphis, Tenn.,
    MSU.
Maguire, John D. Garrow, 4/9/84, Claremont, Cal.
Manire, James. Anne Trotter & David Yellin, 8/7/68, Memphis, Tenn., MSU.
Mann, Floyd. Blackside, 2/18/86, Montgomery, Ala.
Manucy, Holstead "Hoss." Edward Kallal, 2/21/76, St. Augustine, Fla., UF.
Marciniak, Edward. Garrow, 12/10/84, Chicago, Ill.
Marshall, Burke. Louis Oberdorfer, 5/29/64, Washington, D.C., JFKL.
Marshall, Burke. Anthony Lewis, 6/13 & 20/64, Washington, D.C., JFKL.
Marshall, Burke. T.H. Baker, 10/28/68, n.p., LBJL.
Marshall, Burke. Larry Hackman, 1/19–20/70, Bedford, N.Y., JFKL.
Marshall, Burke. Robert Wright, 2/27/70, New York, N.Y., MSRC.
Marshall, Burke. Milton Viorst, Fall 1974, New York, N.Y., MSRC.
Marshall, Burke. Will Leventhal, 9/4/75, n.p., KC.
Marshall, Burke. Scott Rafferty, 1/27/76, New Haven, Conn., JFKL.
Marshall, Burke. Garrow, 10/23/79, New Haven, Conn.
Marshall, Burke. Blackside, 11/30/85, New York, N.Y.
Martin, Louis. Robert Wright, 3/25 & 27/70, Chicago, Ill., MSRC.
Martin, Louis. Garrow, 10/8/82, Washington, D.C.
Massoni, Gary. Garrow, 4/4/84, Pasadena, Cal.
Mays, Benjamin E. John Britton, 1/26/68, Atlanta, Ga., MSRC.
Mays, Benjamin E. David Lewis, 8/68, Atlanta, Ga.
Mays, Benjamin E. Bill Newton, 5/12/76, Atlanta, Ga., APL.
Mays, Benjamin E. Keith Miller, 8/83, Atlanta, Ga., KC.
Meredith, James. John Britton, 10/12/67, New York, N.Y., MSRC.
Meredith, James. Garrow, 3/30/85, Hempstead, N.Y.
Middlebrook, Gwendolyn. Judy Barton, 2/23/72, Atlanta, Ga., KC.
Middlebrook, Harold. Joan Beifuss & Bill Thomas, 7/18 & 21/68, Memphis,
    Tenn., MSU.
Miles, Frank. Joan Beifuss & David Yellin, 9/14/68, Memphis, Tenn., MSU.
Miles, Frank. Arvil Adams, 4/21/69, Memphis, Tenn.
Miller, William "Fred." David Lewis, 8/68, Atlanta, Ga.
Milton, L.D. Nicki Vaughan, 3/25/75, Atlanta, Ga., APL.
Mitchell, Clarence. Robert Martin, 12/6, 11 & 13/68, Washington, D.C., MSRC.
Mitchell, Clarence. T. H. Baker, 4/30/69, Washington, D.C., LBJL.
Moffett, Barbara W. Garrow, 1/29/86, Philadelphia, Pa.
Moon, Richard. Joan Beifuss, Judy Schulz & Jerry Viar, 5/29/68, Memphis,
    Tenn., MSU.
Moon, Richard. James Mosby, 7/10/68, Memphis, Tenn., MSRC.
Moore, Douglas. Robert Wright, 12/12/68, Washington, D.C., MSRC.
Moore, Jamie. Garrow, 9/11/79, Birmingham, Ala.
Morgan, Charles. Garrow, 8/24/84, Washington, D.C.
Morris, Calvin. Garrow, 8/17/84, Washington, D.C.
Morrow, E. Frederic. Ed Edwin, 1/31/68, New York, N.Y., CU.
Morrow, E. Frederic. Robert Wright, 11/17/70, Washington, D.C., MSRC.
Morrow, E. Frederic. Thomas Soapes, 2/23/77, New York, N.Y., DDEL.
Moses, Robert P. Anne Romaine, 9/3/66, Knoxville, Tenn., SHSW.
Moses, Robert P. Clayborne Carson, 3/29/82, Cambridge, Mass.
Moss, Edwin. Steve Longenecker, 6/84, Selma, Ala.
Moss, Otis. William Porter, 8/69, n.p., KC.
Moss, Otis. Garrow, 2/24/84, Cleveland, Ohio.

Motley, Constance B. Kitty Gellhorn, 12/4/76–3/11/78, New York, N.Y., CU.
Moyer, William H. Katherine Shannon, 7/7/68, Washington, D.C., MSRC.
Moyer, William H. Garrow, 3/25/86, San Francisco, Cal. (phone)
Moyers, Bill. Garrow, 6/24/80, New York, N.Y.
Nash, Diane. Garrow, 7/27/83, Chicago, Ill.
Nash, Diane. Blackside, 11/12/85, Chicago, Ill.
Nesbitt, Robert D. Judy Barton, 1/25/72, Montgomery, Ala.
Nesbitt, Robert D. Worth Long, 8/18/83, Montgomery, Ala.
Nesbitt, Robert D. Garrow, 9/1/85, Montgomery, Ala.
Netters, James L. Joan Beifuss & Carol Lynn Yellin, 6/5/68, Memphis, Tenn., MSU.
Nichols, Robert "Cotton." Garrow, 5/7/79, Selma, Ala.
Nixon, E. D. Stanley Smith, 2/68, Montgomery, Ala., MSRC.
Nixon, E. D. David Lewis, 8/68, Montgomery, Ala.
Nixon, E. D. Peter Joseph, 8/71, Montgomery, Ala., CU.
Nixon, E. D. Judy Barton, 1/25/72, Montgomery, Ala., KC.
Nixon, E. D. Norman Lumpkin, 4/11/73, Montgomery, Ala., ACHE.
Nixon, E. D. Milton Viorst, Fall 1974, Montgomery, Ala., MSRC.
Nixon, E. D. Garrow, 9/15/79, Montgomery, Ala.
Nixon, E. D. Frank Adams, 2/25/81, Montgomery, Ala., HC.
Nixon, E. D. Eliot Wigginton, 7/9/81, Montgomery, Ala., HC.
Nixon, E. D. Worth Long, 8/20/83, Montgomery, Ala.
Norman, David. Scott Rafferty, 11/19/75, Washington, D.C., JFKL.
O'Boyle, Patrick. Katherine Shannon, 10/30/67, Washington, D.C., MSRC.
Offenburger, Thomas. Katherine Shannon, 7/2/68, Washington, D.C., MSRC.
Offenburger, Thomas. Charles Fager, 2/4/71, Atlanta, Ga., HU.
Offenburger, Thomas. Garrow, 12/9/83, Atlanta, Ga.
Offenburger, Thomas. John LaCrosse, 2/20/85, Atlanta, Ga.
Oliver, C. Herbert. Garrow, 3/28/80, Brooklyn, N.Y.
Orange, James. Katherine Shannon, 7/17/68, Washington, D.C., MSRC.
Orange, James. Garrow, 12/8/83, Atlanta, Ga.
Orange, James. Mary Brown, 11/18/85, Atlanta, Ga.
Osburn, E. Randel T. "Eddie." Garrow, 3/30/84, Atlanta, Ga.
Page, Marion, E. D. Hamilton, C. W. King & B. F. Cochran. n.i., 7/13/67, Albany, Ga., KC.
Page, Marion. Stanley Smith, 8/68, Albany, Ga., MSRC.
Parks, Rosa. Myles Horton, 3/3–4/56, Monteagle, Tenn., HJ, SCPC.
Parks, Rosa. John Britton, 9/28/67, Detroit, Mich., MSRC.
Parks, Rosa. Marcia Greenlee, 8/22–23/78, Detroit, Mich., BWOHP.
Parks, Rosa. Eliot Wigginton & Sue Thrasher, 6/19/81, New Market, Tenn., HC.
Parks, Rosa. Blackside, 11/14/85, Detroit, Mich.
Patterson, Gilbert. Joan Beifuss & Modeane Thompson, 6/4/68, Memphis, Tenn., MSU.
Patterson, J. O., Jr. Joan Beifuss & David Yellin, 9/11/68, Memphis, Tenn., MSU.
Patterson, John. Blackside, 2/17/86, Montgomery, Ala.
Patton, Gwen. Worth Long, 8/83, Montgomery, Ala.
Peterson, Anne. Mary Brown, 11/16–17/85, Birmingham, Ala.
Pierce, James E. Norman Lumpkin, 4/23/73, Montgomery, Ala., ACHE.
Pitcher, Al. Garrow, 2/22/84, Chicago, Ill.
Pitts, W. McLean. Garrow, 5/9/79, Selma, Ala.
Pleasure, Mose. Garrow, 10/2/85, Memphis, Tenn.
Pope, Roslyn (Walker). David Lewis, 8/68, Atlanta, Ga.
Porter, John Thomas. Garrow, 9/9/79, Birmingham, Ala.
Porter, John Thomas. Mary Brown, 10/21/85, Birmingham, Ala.

Powell, Dan. Arvil Adams, 6/11/69, Memphis, Tenn.
Powell, Dan. Joan Beifuss & Carol Lynn Yellin, 11/19/71, Memphis, Tenn., MSU.
Prinz, Joachim. Will Leventhal, 7/12/75, n.p., KC.
Pritchett, C. B. John Ricks, 7/21/85, Albany, Ga.
Pritchett, Laurie. James Reston, Jr., 4/23/76, Southmont, N.C., UNC.
Pritchett, Laurie. John Ricks, 8/81, Southmont, N.C.
Pritchett, Laurie. Garrow, 5/10/82, Southmont, N.C.
Pritchett, Laurie. Blackside, 11/7/85, Atlanta, Ga.
Proctor, Emmett. Mary Brown, 11/7/85, Atlanta, Ga.
Pryor, Downing. Anne Trotter, Carol Lynn Yellin & Ed Angus, 5/8/68, Memphis, Tenn., MSU.
Pryor, Downing. James Mosby, 7/11/68, Memphis, Tenn., MSRC.
Puryear, R. W. David Colburn, 8/1/80, Winston-Salem, N.C., UF.
Pyle, Cyril. Garrow, 1/28/86, Philadelphia, Pa.
Raby, Al. Milton Viorst, 10/11/74, Chicago, Ill., MSRC.
Raby, Al. Garrow, 3/8/84, Washington, D.C.
Ramsey, Brooks. Joan Beifuss & Judy Schulz, 7/8/68, Memphis, Tenn., MSU.
Randolph, A. Philip. T. H. Baker, 10/29/68, New York, N.Y., LBJL.
Randolph, A. Philip. Robert Martin, 1/14/69, New York, N.Y., MSRC.
Rauh, Joseph L. Anne Romaine, 6/16/67, Washington, D.C., SHSW.
Rauh, Joseph L. Katherine Shannon, 8/28/67, Washington, D.C., MSRC.
Rauh, Joseph L. Paige Mulhollan, 7/30, 8/1 & 8/69, Washington, D.C., LBJL.
Rauh, Joseph L. Garrow, 6/6/84, Washington, D.C.
Rauh, Joseph L. Blackside, 10/30/85, Washington, D.C.
Reagon, Bernice. Blackside, 1/23/86, Washington, D.C.
Redden, Idessa Williams. Worth Long, 8/19/83, Montgomery, Ala.
Redden, Idessa Williams. Mary Brown, 11/14/85, Montgomery, Ala.
Reed, L. C. Bill Thomas, 7/15/68, Memphis, Tenn., MSU.
Reese, Frederick D. Stanley Smith, 8/68, Selma, Ala., MSRC.
Reese, Frederick D. Larry Vasser, 3/13/78, Selma, Ala., AHC-BPLA.
Reese, Frederick D. Garrow, 5/11/79, Selma, Ala.
Reese, Frederick D. Blackside, 12/5/85, Selma, Ala.
Reid, McCann L. James Mosby, 7/13/68, Memphis, Tenn., MSRC.
Reid, Milton. Garrow, 8/6/84, Norfolk, Va.
Reynolds, Bernard. Garrow, 5/10/79, Selma, Ala.
Reynolds, James. Arvil Adams, 6/9/69, Washington, D.C.
Reynolds, James. Joe Frantz, 10/1/70, Washington, D.C., LBJL.
Reynolds, James. David & Carol Lynn Yellin, 2/4/72, Washington, D.C., MSU.
Rice, Thelma. Norman Lumpkin, 8/22/73, Montgomery, Ala., ACHE.
Ricks, Willie. Clayborne Carson, 5/10/76, Stanford, Cal.
Robinson, Bernice. Sue Thrasher & Eliot Wigginton, 11/9/80, Charleston, S.C., HC.
Robinson, Cleveland. Garrow, 7/6/83, New York, N.Y.
Robinson, Jo Ann G. Blackside, 8/27/79, Montgomery, Ala.
Robinson, Jo Ann G. Garrow, 4/5/84, Los Angeles, Cal.
Rogers, Cornish. Garrow, 12/11/84, Chicago, Ill.
Roos, Stephen A. Garrow, 5/14/82, Albany, Ga.
Rose, Don. Garrow, 7/29/83, Chicago, Ill.
Ross, W. T. "Bill." Joan Beifuss & Bill Thomas, 6/4/68, Memphis, Tenn., MSU.
Ross, W. T. "Bill." Arvil Adams, 6/10/69, Memphis, Tenn.
Rustin, Bayard. T. H. Baker, 6/17 & 30/69, New York, N.Y., LBJL.
Rustin, Bayard. James Mosby, 2/13/70, New York, N.Y., MSRC.
Rustin, Bayard. Peter Joseph, 5/28/71, New York, N.Y., CU.
Rustin, Bayard. Milton Viorst, 5/30 & 6/4/74 & 4/19/76, New York, N.Y., MSRC.
Rustin, Bayard. Will Leventhal, 7/17/75, New York, N.Y., KC.

Rustin, Bayard. Garrow, 4/22/82, New York, N.Y.
Rustin, Bayard. Dennis Dickerson, 1/11/84, New York, N.Y.
Rutherford, William A. Garrow, 2/25/82, Washington, D.C.
Rutledge, James C. Garrow, 3/15/79, Selma, Ala.
Sampson, Albert R. Katherine Shannon, 7/8/68, Washington, D.C., MSRC.
Sampson, Albert R. Joan Beifuss, Tom Beckner & Bill Thomas, 8/15/68, Memphis, Tenn., MSU.
Saunders, Robert W. Garrow, 1/12/84, Tampa, Fla.
Schneider, Charles. James Mosby, 7/12/68, Memphis, Tenn., MSRC.
Schwarzschild, Henry. Garrow, 11/19/85, New York, N.Y.
Scott, C. A. David Lewis, 8/68, Atlanta, Ga.
Scott, C. A. Judy Barton, 3/1/72, Atlanta, Ga., KC.
Scott, C. A. Mary Ellen Slaughter, 5/6/76, Atlanta, Ga., APL.
Searles, A. C. John Ricks, 6/15/81, Albany, Ga.
Searles, A. C. Garrow, 5/14/82, Albany, Ga.
Seay, Solomon S., Sr. Judy Barton, 1/26/72, Montgomery, Ala., KC.
Seay, Solomon S., Sr. Worth Long, 8/19/83, Montgomery, Ala.
Seay, Solomon S., Sr. Garrow, 8/21/85, Montgomery, Ala.
Seay, Solomon, Jr. Robert Wright, 8/2/68, Montgomery, Ala., MSRC.
Seigenthaler, John. Robert Campbell, 7/10/68, Nashville, Tenn., MSRC.
Seigenthaler, John. Garrow, 12/29/79, Nashville, Tenn., (phone)
Seigenthaler, John. Blackside, 11/3/85, Nashville, Tenn.
Sellers, Cleveland. Garrow, 8/5/84, Greensboro, N.C.
Shelley, Joseph A. A. G. Heinsohn, 8/64, St. Augustine, Fla., UF.
Shelley, Joseph A. David Colburn, 9/6/77, St. Augustine, Fla., UF.
Sherrod, Charles. David Lewis, 8/68, Albany, Ga.
Sherrod, Charles. John Ricks, 5/81, Albany, Ga.
Sherrod, Charles. Garrow, 4/7/82, Albany, Ga.
Sherrod, Charles. Blackside, 12/20/85, Atlanta, Ga.
Shores, Arthur D. Garrow, 9/10/79, Birmingham, Ala.
Shores, Arthur D. Blackside, 11/1/85, Birmingham, Ala.
Shows, Jack. Garrow, 8/22/85, Montgomery, Ala.
Shuttlesworth, Fred. James Mosby, 9/68, Cincinnati, Ohio, MSRC.
Shuttlesworth, Fred. Dorie Ladner, 11/19/69 & 3/19/70, Cincinnati, Ohio, KC.
Shuttlesworth, Fred. David Colburn, 9/13/78, Atlanta, Ga., UF.
Shuttlesworth, Fred. Garrow, 2/23/84, Cincinnati, Ohio.
Shuttlesworth, Fred. Blackside, 11/7/85, Atlanta, Ga.
Shuttlesworth, Fred. Mary Brown, 11/17/85, Birmingham, Ala.
Simpson, Bryan. David Colburn, 5/24/77, Jacksonville, Fla., UF.
Smiley, Glenn. Katherine Shannon, 9/12/67, Nyack, N.Y., MSRC.
Smiley, Glenn. Garrow, 4/6/84, North Hollywood, Cal.
Smiley, Richmond. Judy Barton, 1/27/72, Montgomery, Ala., KC.
Smith, Elwyn. Charles Fager, n.d., n.p., HU.
Smith, Kelly Miller. John Britton, 12/22/67, Nashville, Tenn., MSRC.
Smith, Kelly Miller. Judy Barton, 4/21/72, Nashville, Tenn., KC.
Smith, Kelly Miller. Steve Hill, 2/10/84, Nashville, Tenn.
Smith, Kenneth. David Lewis, 9/68, Chester, Pa.
Smith, Kenneth. Garrow, 1/31/86, Rochester, N.Y.
Smith, Maxine. Joan Beifuss & Bill Thomas, 6/13/68, Memphis, Tenn., MSU.
Smith, Maxine. James Mosby, 7/11/68, Memphis, Tenn., MSRC.
Smith, Maxine. Craig Leake, 3/71, Memphis, Tenn., MSU.
Smith, Nelson H. Mary Brown, 10/27/85, Birmingham, Ala.
Smitherman, Joseph T. Garrow, 3/13 & 15/79, Selma, Ala.
Smitherman, Joseph T. Blackside, 12/5/85, Selma, Ala.
Speed, Daniel B. Jack Ice, 7/7/78, Tallahassee, Fla., FSU.

Spence, John. Bill Thomas & David Yellin, 6/16/68, Memphis, Tenn., MSU.
Spock, Benjamin. Garrow, 12/2/84, New York, N.Y.
Stark, Walter. Garrow, 1/28/86, Philadelphia, Pa.
Starks, Henry. Joan Beifuss & Judy Schulz, 7/31/68, Memphis, Tenn., MSU.
Steele, C. K. Jack Ice, 1/26 & 2/16/78, Tallahassee, Fla., FSU.
Stein, William S. Garrow, 4/7/84, Santa Monica, Cal.
Stewart, Francis E. Garrow, 3/29/84, Atlanta, Ga.
Stoner, J. B. Edward Kallal, 4/6/76, Jacksonville, Fla., UF.
Stoner, J. B. Garrow, 9/7/79, Marietta, Ga.
Sugarmon, Russell. Clayton Braddock, 5/25/68, Memphis, Tenn., MSRC.
Sugarmon, Russell. Joan Beifuss & David & Carol Lynn Yellin, 4/22/69,
    Memphis, Tenn., MSU.
Sullivan, Leon. John Britton, 9/25/67, Philadelphia, Pa., MSRC.
Sullivan, William C. Arthur Schlesinger, 7/26/76, Sugar Hill, N.H.
Swan, Dana. Garrow, 1/14/84, Atlanta, Ga.
Sweat, Joe. Joan Beifuss & David Yellin, 3/21/70, Memphis, Tenn., MSU.
Taylor, Calvin. Bill Thomas & Jerry Viar, 8/17/68, Memphis, Tenn., MSU.
Taylor, Gardner C. Garrow, 11/2/84, Brooklyn, N.Y.
Thomas, Alfreda Dean. Judy Barton, 1/27/72, Montgomery, Ala., KC.
Tillman, N. P. Donald Smith, 12/4/63, Atlanta, Ga., SHSW.
Tillow, Walter. Anne Romaine, 9/4/66, Knoxville, Tenn. SHSW.
Todd, Thomas. David Yellin & William Sater, 6/5/68, Memphis, Tenn., MSU.
Turner, Albert. Blackside, 5/79, Marion, Ala.
Turner, Albert. Garrow, 8/20/85, Selma, Ala.
Turner, Jesse. Anne Trotter & David Yellin, 5/29/68, Memphis, Tenn., MSU.
Turner, Jesse. James Mosby, 7/11/68, Memphis, Tenn., MSRC.
Turner, Jesse. Craig Leake, 3/71, Memphis, Tenn., MSU.
Twine, Henry. David Colburn, 9/19/77, St. Augustine, Fla., UF.
Twine, Henry. Karen Harvey, 5/13/81, St. Augustine, Fla., UF.
Upchurch, Hamilton. David Colburn, 1/25/78, St. Augustine, Fla., UF.
Valenti, Jack. Joe Frantz, 10/18/69, Washington, D.C., LBJL.
Valeriani, Richard. Blackside, 12/10/85, New York, N.Y.
Vann, David. Garrow, 8/16/85, Birmingham, Ala.
Vann, David. Blackside, 11/1/85, Birmingham, Ala.
Via, Emory. Garrow, 4/5/85, Eugene, Oreg. (phone).
Vivian, C. T. Vincent Browne, 2/20/68, Chicago, Ill., MSRC.
Vivian, C. T. Garrow, 9/5/79, Atlanta, Ga.
Vivian, C. T. Anne Braden, 2/25 & 3/10–11/81, Atlanta, Ga., HC.
Vivian, C. T. Blackside, 1/23/86, Boston, Mass.
Vorspan, Albert. Katherine Shannon, 12/19/67, New York, N.Y., MSRC.
Wachtel, Harry. Garrow, 12/19/78, & 1/24 & 2/26/80, New York, N.Y.
Walker, Wyatt T. Donald Smith, 12/63, Atlanta, Ga., SHSW.
Walker, Wyatt T. John Britton, 10/11/67, New York, N.Y., MSRC.
Walker, Wyatt T. Nick & Mary Lynn Kotz, n.d., New York, N.Y., SHSW.
Walker, Wyatt T. Garrow, 4/18/80, New York, N.Y.
Walker, Wyatt T. Blackside, n.d., New York, N.Y.
Wallace, David. Garrow, 3/26/86, Memphis, Tenn. (phone)
Wallace, George C. Blackside, 3/10/86, Montgomery, Ala.
Warren, Dan R. David Colburn, 12/19/78, Daytona Beach, Fla., UF.
Warren, Dan R. Garrow, 9/4/85, Daytona Beach, Fla.
Wax, James. Selma Lewis & William Sater, 5/68, Memphis, Tenn., MSU
Weber, Chuck. Garrow, 5/10/79, Selma, Ala.
Weintraub, Sam. Bill Thomas & David Yellin, 9/1/68, Memphis, Tenn., MSU.
Wells, Samuel B. John Ricks, 9/8/83, Atlanta, Ga.
Wells, Samuel B. Garrow, 9/6/85, Atlanta, Ga.

West, Irene. Judy Barton, 1/26/72, Montgomery, Ala., KC.
Whitaker, Horace. Garrow, 12/3/85, Boston, Mass.
White, Lee C. Joe Frantz, 9/28/70, 2/18, 3/2–3 & 11/2/71, Washington, D.C., LBJL.
White, Lee C. Garrow, 3/10/84, Washington, D.C.
Wilkins, Roger. Katherine Shannon, 8/14/67, Washington, D.C., MSRC.
Wilkins, Roger. Garrow, 3/9/84, Washington, D.C.
Wilkins, Roy. David Lewis, 11/68, New York, N.Y.
Wilkins, Roy. T. H. Baker, 4/1/69, New York, N.Y., LBJL.
Wilkins, Roy. Robert Wright, 4/29 & 5/5/70, New York, N.Y., MSRC.
Wilkins, Roy. Joan Beifuss, David & Carol Lynn Yellin, 4/18/73, Memphis, Tenn., MSU.
Wilkins, Roy. Milton Viorst, 5/29/74, New York, N.Y., MSRC.
Williams, Clarence. Charles Fager, 1/13/71, Selma, Ala., HU.
Williams, Hosea. Project South, Summer 1965, Atlanta, Ga., SU.
Williams, Hosea. Will Leventhal, 10/21/74 & 7/23/75, Atlanta, Ga., KC.
Williams, Hosea. Feay Shellman & Fred Baldwin, 3/13/83, Savannah, Ga., TA.
Williams, Hosea. Feay Shellman, 6/10/83, Atlanta, Ga., TA.
Williams, Hosea. Garrow, 12/9/83, Atlanta, Ga.
Williams, Kale. Garrow, 7/29/83, Chicago, Ill.
Williams, Larry H. Garrow, 1/24/86, Atlanta, Ga.
Williams, Robert. Garrow, 8/22/85, Montgomery, Ala.
Williams, Roscoe & Mary Lucy. Judy Barton, 1/26/72, Montgomery, Ala., KC.
Williams, Samuel W. David Lewis, 8/68, Atlanta, Ga.
Williams, Willie A. Vincent Fort, 5/83, Atlanta, Ga.
Willie, Charles V. Garrow, 7/30/85, Cambridge, Mass.
Wilmore, Jacques. Bill Thomas, David & Carol Lynn Yellin, 6/12/68, Memphis, Tenn., MSU.
Wilmore, Jacques. John Britton, 9/26/68, New York, N.Y., MSRC.
Windham, Katherine T. Garrow, 5/10/79, Selma, Ala.
Wise, Stanley. Richard Brasch, 4/10/82, Atlanta, Ga., KC.
Wofford, Harris. Berl Bernhard, 11/29/65, Washington, D.C., JFKL.
Wofford, Harris. Garrow, 10/25 & 11/19/79, Philadelphia, Pa.
Wofford, Harris. Blackside 10/31/85, Washington, D.C.
Wood, Marcus G. Garrow, 1/27/86, Baltimore, Md.
Woods, Abraham. Addie Pugh, 10/28/75, Birmingham, Ala., UAB.
Woods, Abraham. Garrow, 9/11/79, Birmingham, Ala.
Wurf, Jerry. James Mosby, 10/21/68, Washington, D.C., MSRC.
Wurf, Jerry. David & Carol Lynn Yellin, 2/3/72, Washington, D.C., MSU.
Yates, Clayton R. David Lewis, 8/68, Atlanta, Ga.
Young, Andrew. Katherine Shannon, 7/16/68, Washington, D.C., MSRC.
Young, Andrew. T. H. Baker, 6/18/70, Atlanta, Ga., LBJL.
Young, Andrew. Nick Kotz, ca. 1973, Washington, D.C., SHSW.
Young, Andrew. Nick & Mary Lynn Kotz, n.d., Washington, D.C., SHSW.
Young, Andrew. Milton Viorst, 5/1/75, Washington, D.C., MSRC.
Young, Andrew. Eliot Wigginton, 7/8/81, Atlanta, Ga., HC.
Young, Andrew. Garrow, 7/27/82, Atlanta, Ga.
Young, Andrew. Feay Shellman, 6/10/83, Atlanta, Ga., TA.
Young, Andrew. Blackside, 10/11/85, New York, N.Y.
Young, Andrew. Mary Brown, 11/19/85, Atlanta, Ga.
Young, Whitney M. T. H. Baker, 6/18/69, New Rochelle, N.Y., LBJL.
Young, Whitney M. Robert Wright, 5/5 & 6/22/70, New York, N.Y., MSRC.

Television Transcripts/Videotape Interviews

"A Conversation With—Andrew Young." Gloria Steinem, Public Broadcasting Service, 4/12/84.
"Andrew Young Remembers Martin Luther King." *Bill Moyers' Journal,* #409, Public Broadcasting Service, 4/2/79.
"Black Power, White Backlash." *CBS Reports,* with Mike Wallace; Leslie Midgley, executive producer; 9/27/66. MSRC.
"Martin Luther King: The Man and the March." Public Broadcasting Laboratory documentary; Joseph Louw & John Wicklein; 1968.
"Selma—The City and the Symbol." CBS documentary, with Alexander Kendrick; Leslie Midgley, executive producer; 3/21/65. MSRC.
"Showdown in Alabama." David Susskind's *Open End;* 4/25/65. KC.
"Some Friends of Martin Luther King." CBS News, with Charles Kuralt; Burton Benjamin, executive producer; 4/7/68. MSRC.
"The March in Mississippi." CBS documentary, with John Hart & Harry Reasoner; Leslie Midgley, executive producer; 6/26/66. MSRC.

SCOPE Orientation Transcripts, 6/14–6/18/65, Project South Collection, Stanford University Archives.
King Center Oral History Videotapes, 11/12–13/73, Michigan State University, East Lansing, Mich., KC.

Newspapers

AA   Afro-American
AC   Atlanta Constitution
ADW   Atlanta Daily World
AG   Arkansas Gazette (Little Rock)
AH   Albany Herald (Georgia)
AI   Atlanta Inquirer
AJ   Atlanta Journal
AJC   Atlanta Journal-Constitution (Sunday)
AlaJ   Alabama Journal (Montgomery)
AM   Athens Messenger (Ohio)
AN   Amsterdam News (New York)
AT   Alabama Tribune (Montgomery)
AUC   Augusta Chronicle (Georgia)
BG   Boston Globe
BH   Boston Herald
BN   Birmingham News
BPH   Birmingham Post-Herald

BS   Baltimore Sun
BW   Birmingham World
CA   Chicago American
CCP   Cleveland Call & Post
CD   Chicago Defender
CDN   Chicago Daily News
CE   Cincinnati Enquirer
CG   Charleston Gazette (West Virginia)
CHT   Chattanooga Times
CHW   Chapel Hill Weekly
CNC   Charleston News & Courier (South Carolina)
CO   Charlotte Observer
CP   Cleveland Press
CPD   Cleveland Plain Dealer
CPTS   Cincinnati Post & Times-Star
CSM   Christian Science Monitor
CST   Chicago Sun-Times
CT   Chicago Tribune
DBEN   Daytona Beach Evening News

DDN   Dayton Daily News
DDT   Delta Democrat Times
  (Greenville)
DFP   Detroit Free Press
DMH   Durham Morning Herald
DMR   Des Moines Register
DN   Detroit News
DP   Denver Post
DR   Danville Register (Virginia)
DS   Durham Sun
DTD   Davenport Times-
  Democrat (Iowa)
FS   Florida Star (Jacksonville)
FTU   Florida Times-Union
  (Jacksonville)
GDN   Greensboro Daily News
  (North Carolina)
GN   Greenville News (South
  Carolina)
HA   Honolulu Advertiser
HC   Hartford Courant
HP   Houston Post
HT   Huntsville Times (Alabama)
JCL   Jackson Clarion-Ledger
JDN   Jackson Daily News
JJ   Jacksonville Journal
KCT   Kansas City Times
LAHE   Los Angeles Herald
  Examiner
LAS   Los Angeles Sentinel
LAT   Los Angeles Times
LCJ   Louisville Courier-Journal
LD   Louisville Defender
LEJ   Lincoln Evening Journal
  (Nebraska)
LIP   Long Island Press
LISJ   Long Island Star Journal
LT   Louisville Times
LVRJ   Las Vegas Review Journal
MA   Montgomery Advertiser
MAT   Marietta Times (Ohio)
MCA   Memphis Commercial
  Appeal
MH   Miami Herald
MJ   Milwaukee Journal
MN   Miami News

MS   Meridian Star (Mississippi)
MT   Minneapolis Tribune
MW   Memphis World
NB   Nashville Banner
NEN   Newark Evening News
NJG   Norfolk Journal & Guide
N&O   News and Observer
  (Raleigh)
NOTP   New Orleans Times-
  Picayune
NT   Nashville Tennessean
NVP   Norfolk Virginian-Pilot
NYC   New York Courier
NYCC   New York Citizen Call
NYDN   New York Daily News
NYHT   New York Herald
  Tribune
NYJA   New York Journal-
  American
NYP   New York Post
NYT   New York Times
NYWJT   New York World
  Journal Tribune
NYWT   New York World
  Telegram
OES   Orlando Evening Star
OWH   Omaha World-Herald
PC   Pittsburgh Courier
PDN   Philadelphia Daily News
PEB   Philadelphia Evening
  Bulletin
PI   Philadelphia Inquirer
PJ   Providence Journal
PO   Portland Oregonian
PP   Pittsburgh Press
PPG   Pittsburgh Post-Gazette
RDA   Rome Daily American
  (Italy)
RNL   Richmond News Leader
RTD   Richmond Times-Dispatch
SAR   St. Augustine Record
  (Florida)
SBT   South Bend Tribune
  (Indiana)
SC   The State (Columbia, S.C.)
SEP   Savannah Evening Press

SFC   San Francisco Chronicle
SFE   San Francisco Examiner
SJS   San Juan Star
SLA   St. Louis Argus
SLGD   St. Louis Globe-Democrat
STPD   St. Louis Post-Dispatch
SMN   Savannah Morning News
STJ   Selma Times-Journal
SU   Springfield Union
    (Massachusetts)
SWG   Southwest Georgian
    (Albany)
TDT   Tampa Daily Times
TN   Tuscaloosa News (Alabama)
TSD   Tri-State Defender
    (Memphis)
WDN   Washington Daily News
WES   Washington Evening Star
WISJ   Wisconsin State Journal
    (Madison)
WJ   Winston-Salem Journal
WP   Washington Post
WSJ   Wall Street Journal
WSS   Winston-Salem Sentinel

Periodicals

ACHR   [Alabama Council on
    Human Relations] *Newsletter*
America
Atlantic
CCCO   [Coordinating Council of
    Community Organizations]
    Newsletter
Christian Century
Christianity & Crisis
Christianity Today
Commentary
Commonweal
Community
CORElator
Correspondent
Crisis
Crusader
Dexter Echo
Dissent

Ebony
Economist
Fellowship
Freedomways
Gandhi Marg
Harper's
Integrated Education
Jet
Liberation
Liberator
Life
Look
MIA   [Montgomery Improvement
    Association] *Newsletter*
Militant
Mobilizer
Movement
Nation
National Guardian
National Review
Negro Digest
New America
New Leader
New Republic
New South
New Yorker
New York Review of Books
Newsweek
North & South
Presbyterian Life
Progressive
Ramparts
Renewal
Reporter
Saturday Evening Post
Saturday Review
SCLC   [Southern Christian
    Leadership Conference]
    Newsletter
Sepia
Soul Force
Southern Courier
*Southern Education Reporting
    Service*
Southern Patriot
Southern School News

Student Voice   U.S. News & World Report
Time   United Church Herald

Papers and Archival Collections

Inez Adams Files, Amistad Research Center, New Orleans, La.
Alabama Council on Human Relations Files, Birmingham Public Library Archives, Birmingham, Ala. (ACHR-BPLA)
Alabama Council on Human Relations Papers, Auburn, Ala. (ACHR)
Albany City Files, Albany, Ga. (ALB)
American Civil Liberties Union Papers, Mudd Library, Princeton University, Princeton, N.J. (ACLU)
American Friends Service Committee Papers, Philadelphia, Pa. (AFSC)
American Friends Service Committee (Chicago) Papers, University of Illinois at Chicago Library, Chicago, Ill.
Americans for Democratic Action Papers, State Historical Society, Madison, Wis. (ADA)
Anti-Defamation League of B'nai B'rith Papers, Amistad Research Center, New Orleans, La. (ADL)
Claude A. Barnett Papers, Chicago Historical Society, Chicago, Ill. (CAB)
Berl Bernhard Papers, Kennedy Library, Boston, Mass.
James Bevel Files, University of Illinois at Chicago Library, Chicago, Ill.
Harry Boyte Papers, Perkins Library, Duke University, Durham, N.C.
Carl & Anne Braden Papers, State Historical Society, Madison, Wis.
Brotherhood of Sleeping Car Porters Papers, Library of Congress, Washington, D.C. (BSCP)
Farris Bryant Papers, Florida State Archives, Tallahassee, Fla.
Chicago/CCCO Files, Horace Mann Bond Center, University of Massachusetts, Amherst.
Chicago Conference on Religion & Race Papers, Chicago Historical Society, Chicago, Ill. (CCRR)
Chicago Sunday Evening Club Papers, Chicago Historical Society, Chicago, Ill. (CSEC)
Church Federation of Greater Chicago Papers, Chicago Historical Society, Chicago, Ill. (CFGC)
Civil Rights Struggle Collection, University of California at Los Angeles Library.
Clergy and Laity Concerned Papers, Swarthmore College Peace Collection, Swarthmore, Pa. (CALC)
LeRoy Collins Papers, Florida State Archives, Tallahassee, Fla.
LeRoy Collins Papers, University of South Florida Library, Tampa, Fla.
Committee to Combat Racial Injustice Papers, State Historical Society, Madison, Wis. (CCRI)
Congress of Racial Equality Papers, King Center, Atlanta, Ga. (CORE KC)
Congress of Racial Equality Papers, State Historical Society, Madison, Wis. (CORE)
Congress of Racial Equality (Chicago) Papers, Chicago Historical Society, Chicago, Ill. (CORE-C)
Eugene T. "Bull" Connor Papers, Birmingham Public Library Archives, Birmingham, Ala.
Stoney Cooks Files, Washington, D.C.
Coordinating Council of Community Organizations Papers, King Center, Atlanta, Ga. (CCCO)
Council of Federated Organizations Papers, State Historical Society, Madison, Wis. (COFO)

Dexter Avenue Baptist Church Papers, King Center, Atlanta, Ga.

Clifford J. Durr Papers, Alabama State Archives, Montgomery, Ala.

Virginia Foster Durr Papers, Schlesinger Library, Radcliffe College, Cambridge, Mass. (VFD)

Episcopal Society for Cultural and Racial Unity Papers, King Center, Atlanta, Ga. (ESCRU)

Carl Farris Papers, King Center, Atlanta, Ga.

Fellowship of Reconciliation Papers, Swarthmore College Peace Collection, Swarthmore, Pa. (FOR)

Fifth Avenue Vietnam Parade Committee Papers, State Historical Society, Madison, Wis.

Ford Foundation Archives, New York, N.Y.

Georgia Council on Human Relations Papers, Woodruff Library, Atlanta University, Atlanta, Ga. (GCHR)

Richard Gould Papers, State Historical Society, Madison, Wis.

Fred D. Gray Papers, King Center, Atlanta, Ga.

William Hamilton Papers, Birmingham Public Library Archives, Birmingham, Ala. (WH)

Bryce Harlow Papers, Eisenhower Library, Abilene, Kans.

William B. Hartsfield Papers, Woodruff Library, Emory University, Atlanta, Ga.

Ralph Helstein Papers, Chicago, Ill.

Aaron Henry Papers, Reuther Library, Wayne State University, Detroit, Mich.

Highlander Folk School Papers, State Historical Society, Madison, Wis. (HLW)

Highlander Folk School Papers, Tennessee State Archives, Nashville, Tenn. (HTSA)

Homer Jack Papers, Swarthmore College Peace Collection, Swarthmore, Pa. (HJ)

C.L.R. James Papers, London, England.

Herbert T. Jenkins Papers, Atlanta Historical Society, Atlanta, Ga. (HTJ)

Lyndon B. Johnson Vice-Presidential Papers, Johnson Library, Austin, Tex. (LBJ VP)

Lyndon B. Johnson Presidential Papers, White House Central Files, Johnson Library, Austin, Tex. (WHCF LBJL)

John F. Kennedy Presidential Papers, White House Central Files, Kennedy Library, Boston, Mass. (WHCF JFKL)

Robert F. Kennedy Papers, Kennedy Library, Boston, Mass.

Howard Kester Papers, Southern Historical Collection, University of North Carolina, Chapel Hill, N.C.

C. B. King Papers, King Center, Atlanta, Ga.

Martin Luther King, Jr., Papers, Special Collections Department, Mugar Library, Boston University, Boston, Mass. (MLK)

Martin Luther King, Jr., Papers, King Center, Atlanta, Ga. (KP, KC)

Slater H. King Papers, Fisk University Library, Nashville, Tenn. (SK-F)

Slater H. King Papers, King Center, Atlanta, Ga.

Slater H. King Papers, State Historical Society, Madison, Wis. (SK-W)

Lawyers Committee for Defense of the Constitution Papers, Mudd Library, Princeton University, Princeton, N.J. (LCDC)

Leadership Council for Metropolitan Open Communities Papers, Chicago Historical Society, Chicago, Ill. (LC)

Henry Loeb Papers, Memphis-Shelby County Public Library Archives, Memphis, Tenn.

Worth Long Papers, King Center, Atlanta, Ga.

Allard Lowenstein Papers, Southern Historical Collection, University of North Carolina, Chapel Hill, N.C. (AL)

John McKnight Files, Evanston, Ill.

Burke Marshall Papers, Kennedy Library, Boston, Mass. (BM)

Gary Massoni Papers, Pasadena, Cai. (GM)
Benjamin E. Mays Papers, Moorland Spingarn Research Center, Howard University, Washington, D.C. (BEM)
Memphis Sanitation Strike Archives, Brister Library, Memphis State University, Memphis, Tenn.
William Robert Miller Papers, King Center, Atlanta, Ga.
Mississippi Freedom Democratic Party Papers, King Center, Atlanta, Ga. (MFDP)
Montgomery County District Attorney's Files, Montgomery Co. Courthouse, Montgomery, Ala. (MCDA)
Montgomery Improvement Association Files, King Center, Atlanta, Ga.
Lucy Montgomery Papers, State Historical Society, Madison, Wis.
Gerald Morgan Papers, Eisenhower Library, Abilene, Kans.
E. Frederic Morrow Papers, Eisenhower Library, Abilene, Kans. (Morrow)
E. Frederic Morrow Papers, Special Collections Department, Mugar Library, Boston University, Boston, Mass.
A. J. Muste Papers, Swarthmore College Peace Collection, Swarthmore, Pa.
National Association for the Advancement of Colored People Papers, Library of Congress, Washington, D.C. (NAACP)
National Catholic Conference for Interracial Justice Papers, Marquette University Library Archives, Milwaukee, Wis. (NCCIJ)
National Committee for a Sane Nuclear Policy Papers, Swarthmore College Peace Collection, Swarthmore, Pa. (SANE)
National Conference for New Politics Papers, State Historical Society, Madison, Wis. (NCNP)
National Council of Churches Papers, Presbyterian Historical Society, Philadelphia, Pa. (NCC)
National Mobilization Committee to End the War in Vietnam Papers, Swarthmore College Peace Collection, Swarthmore, Pa. (NMC)
National Urban League Papers, Library of Congress, Washington, D.C. (NUL)
Victor Navasky Papers, Kennedy Library, Boston, Mass.
Thomas Offenburger Files, Washington, D.C. (TO)
Office of the Special Assistant for Personnel Management Papers, Eisenhower Library, Abilene, Kans. (OSAPM)
Office of the Special Assistant for National Security Affairs Papers, Eisenhower Library, Abilene, Kans. (OSANSA)
Maurice Ouellet Papers, Amistad Research Center, New Orlean, La.
Rosa Parks Papers, Reuther Library, Wayne State University, Detroit, Mich.
W. McLean Pitts Papers, Selma, Ala.
Hermine Popper Papers, Schlesinger Library, Radcliffe College, Cambridge, Mass.
Project South Collection, Green Library, Stanford University, Stanford, Cal.
A. Philip Randolph Papers, Library of Congress, Washington, D.C. (APR)
George Reedy Papers, Johnson Library, Austin, Tex.
Richard Rich Papers, Woodruff Library, Emory University, Atlanta, Ga.
William P. Rogers Papers, Eisenhower Library, Abilene, Kans.
Bayard Rustin Papers, New York, N.Y. (BR)
Robert W. Saunders Papers, University of South Florida Library, Tampa, Fla.
Charles Sherrod Papers, State Historical Society, Madison, Wis.
Fred Shuttlesworth Files, King Center, Atlanta, Ga.
Bryan Simpson Papers, University of Florida Library, Gainesville, Fla.
Ralph E. Smeltzer Papers, Harvard University Library, Cambridge, Mass. (RES)
Glenn E. Smiley Files, Fellowship of Reconciliation Collection, Swarthmore College Peace Collection, Swarthmore, Pa.
Theodore Sorenson Papers, Kennedy Library, Boston, Mass.

Southern Christian Leadership Conference Papers, King Center, Atlanta, Ga. (SCLC)
Southern Regional Council Papers, Woodruff Library, Atlanta University, Atlanta, Ga. (SRC)
Benjamin Spock Papers, Syracuse University Library, Syracuse, N.Y. (BS)
Spring Mobilization Committee to End the War in Vietnam Papers, State Historical Society, Madison, Wis.
Student Nonviolent Coordinating Committee Papers, King Center, Atlanta, Ga. (SNCC)
Norman Thomas Papers, New York Public Library Manuscripts Department, New York, N.Y. (NT)
John L. Tilley Papers, Amistad Research Center, New Orleans, La.
United Church of Christ, Board for Homeland Ministries, Race Relations Department Papers, Amistad Research Center, New Orleans, La. (UCC)
United Packinghouse Workers of America Papers, State Historical Society, Madison, Wis. (UPW)
David Vann Papers, Birmingham Public Library Archives, Birmingham, Ala.
George C. Wallace Papers, Alabama State Archives, Montgomery, Ala.
Marvin Watson Papers, Johnson Library, Austin, Tex. (MW)
White House Conference on Civil Rights Papers, Johnson Library, Austin, Tex. (WHCCR)
Lee C. White Papers, Johnson Library, Austin, Tex. (LCW-J)
Lee C. White Papers, Kennedy Library, Boston, Mass. (LCW-K)
Roy Wilkins Papers, Library of Congress, Washington, D.C. (RW)
Kale Williams Files, Chicago, Ill.
Harris Wofford Papers, Kennedy Library, Boston, Mass.
Andrew Young Files, Washington, D.C. (AY)
Howard Zinn Papers, State Historical Society, Madison, Wis.

Federal Government Freedom of Information Act Releases

Central Intelligence Agency

Martin Luther King, Jr.
Stanley D. Levison

Civil Rights Division, U.S. Department of Justice

Kennedy Administration Microfilm Files ("DOJ Micro") comprising:
   —Burke Marshall Correspondence (Reels 1–4)
   —Burke Marshall Memoranda (Reel 5)
   —Commission on Civil Rights (Reel 6)
   —Individuals and Organizations (Reels 7 & 126)
   —Demonstrations (Reels 9–11)
   —*U.S.* v. *Dallas County* (Reel 57)
   —*U.S.* v. *McLeod* (Reel 58)
   —Bombing of Gaston Motel, Birmingham (Reel 103)
   —Bombing of Arthur Shores's Home, Birmingham (Reel 104)
   —Danville, Virginia (Reel 106)
   —Albany, Georgia (Reel 111)
   —March on Washington (Reel 113)
   —Birmingham, Alabama (Reels 119–120)

Martin Luther King, Jr.
St. Augustine, Florida

Community Relations Service, U.S Department of Justice

Albany, Georgia Memphis, Tennessee
Birmingham, Alabama Meredith March
Chicago, Illinois St. Augustine, Florida
Martin Luther King, Jr. Selma, Alabama
Southern Christian Leadership Conference

Federal Bureau of Investigation, U.S. Department of Justice

(Listed by FBI numerical file number; not all have been processed in full; only major releases are included in this list.)

44-00 Civil Rights Policy File
44-12831 Election Laws, Selma/Dallas County, Alabama
44-14106 Election Laws, Alabama
44-25760 Voter Registration, Selma, Alabama
44-28544 Selma to Montgomery March, 1965
62-78270 Roy Wilkins
62-101087 Prayer Pilgrimage; Southern Segregation
62-101087-5 Racial Situation, Montgomery, Alabama
62-105187 Youth Marches for Integrated Schools
62-108052 Coretta Scott King
77-59135 Archibald J. Carey, Jr.
100-3-116 Communist Party USA, Negro Question (plus Atlanta 100-6520)
100-135-61 Racial Situation, Alabama
100-106670 Martin Luther King, Jr. (plus Atlanta 100-5586, Mobile 100-1472, Newark 100-47520, New York 100-136585, and various smaller headquarters files)
100-158790 Bayard Rustin (plus New York 100-46729)
100-392452 Stanley D. Levison (plus New York 100-111180 and its attendant alpha and numeric subfiles, designated as, e.g., 100-111180-9, etc., as well as *all* other field office files)
100-407018 Clarence B. Jones (plus New York 100-73250 and its attendant alpha and numeric subfiles)
100-424895 In Friendship
100-429326 Montgomery Improvement Association
100-433520 March on the Conventions Movement, 1960
100-438794 Southern Christian Leadership Conference
100-439190 Student Nonviolent Coordinating Committee (plus Atlanta 100-6488)
100-442529 Communist Influence in Racial Matters ("CIRM") (plus Atlanta 100-6670)
100-448006 COINTELPRO "Black Nationalist Hate Group"
157-00 Racial Matters Policy File
157-6-2 Racial Matters, Georgia (Albany) (plus headquarters Albany files 157-4-2 and 157-492)
157-6-61 Racial Situation, Selma, Alabama
157-6-63 Racial Situation, St. Augustine, Florida
157-970 March on Washington, 1963
157-8428 "Washington Spring Project" 1968 (Poor People's Campaign)
157-8460 The Invaders, Memphis, Tennessee
157-9146 Sanitation Workers Strike, Memphis, Tennessee (plus Memphis 157-1092)
161-2040 Archibald J. Carey, Jr.
170-00 Racial/Extremist Informants Policy File

U.S. Department of the Army, U.S. Department of Defense
Martin Luther King, Jr.

U.S Information Agency, U.S. Department of State
Martin Luther King, Jr.

Index

Aaron, Ely M., 504
Abernathy, Juanita, 51, 86, 203, 245,
366, 412, 615, 682n36
Abernathy, Ralph, 98, 128, 135, 167,
321, 342, 428, 436; and birth of
MIA, 17–19, 20, 21–24; and
Montgomery negotiations, 25–26,
30–31; and friendship with King, 49,
51, 77–78, 110, 122, 289; and
Montgomery boycott, 54, 56, 60, 62,
64, 67, 82; and early SCLC, 86, 95,
111, 120, 124; as SCLC treasurer,
90, 115, 270, 271, 451; and MIA, 96,
125, 130; *1958* assault on, 108, 109;
and SNCC, 131, 132, 133, 141;
moves to Atlanta, 151, 171; and
Freedom Ride, 157, 159, 160; in
Albany, 180, 183–84, 195, 198,
201–7 *passim,* 211, 213–14; and
Breadbasket, 223, 232, 550; and
Birmingham, 225, 236, 240, 241,
243, 246, 257–62 *passim;* and
Alabama Project, 294, 295, 296–97,
314; in St. Augustine, 324, 330; and
9/64 Europe trip, 351–52; and
Selma, 359, 379, 382, 397, 399, 412;
and FBI, 362, 373, 377; and Nobel
trip, 364, 366; as King's successor,
372, 393, 416–17; and Chicago, 456,
461, 544; and Meredith March, 483,
486; and Louisville, 548, 561; and
Birmingham *1967,* 567, 579; and
SCLC staff troubles, 584, 585; and
early *1968,* 594, 599, 600, 604, 606;
and Memphis, 610–15, 616, 619,
620–24
Abram, Morris B., 144–45, 147, 148,
150

Adair, Euretta, 60
Adams, Sherman, 106
Advise and Consent (Drury), 169
AFL-CIO, 194, 280
Africa. *See* King, Martin Luther, Jr.
Relationships: Organizations/Topics,
and Africa.
AFSCME, 604, 605, 610
Agronsky, Martin, 99–100
Ahmann, Mathew, 280, 677n60, 678n6
Alabama boycott. *See* Southern
Christian Leadership Conference,
and Alabama boycott.
Alabama Christian Movement for
Human Rights (ACMHR), 81, 199,
314, 535, 580; and Birmingham *1963,*
224–25, 227, 234, 238, 256, 264, 271,
277, 302
Alabama Council on Human Relations
(ACHR), 25, 28, 51, 67, 220, 231
Alabama Journal, 19
Alabama Project (SCLC), origins of,
292–95, 296–97, 301, 302, 314–16,
319–25 *passim,* 332, 337; postponing
of, 338, 339; becomes Selma
campaign, 358–59, 370–71, 372
Alabama State College, 14, 18, 20
Albany, Ga., origins of movement,
173–77; *12/61* protests, 173–88; early
1962 events, 189–93, 195–96, 198;
summer *1962* events, 201–16; lessons
of for King, 217–19, 225–29, 235,
290, 326, 456; fall *1962,* 223–24;
1963 events, 279–80, 281, 306
Albany Herald, 174, 178, 179, 182,
191, 205
Albany Ministerial Association, 181
Albany Movement, birth of, 176–77,

773

Robinson, Jo Ann, 68; and origins of
Montgomery boycott, 14–16, 18–19,
21; and Montgomery negotiations,
25, 28, 30
Roche, John P., 554
Rochester, N. Y., 345, 353
Rockefeller, Nelson, 162, 368, 383;
contributes to SCLC, 219–20, 451;
and *1968* election, 575, 576, 589, 592
Rockwell, George Lincoln, 378
Rodino, Peter, 435
Rogers, Cornish, 48
Rogers, T. Y., 548
Rogers, William, 87
Romney, George, 575
Roos, Stephen, 204, 205
Rosenberg, Joe, 181, 204
Rowan, Carl T., and Montgomery
boycott, 54–55; and Vietnam,
554–55, 556, 576–77
Rowe, Gary Thomas, 413, 425
Royall, Kenneth, 296
Ruppenthal, G. J., 26
Rustin, Bayard, and Montgomery
boycott, 66–69, 72–73, 79,
642nn45–46; and creation of SCLC,
66, 73, 83–84, 85–86, 93, 97, 102,
103, 120, 644–45n2; negative
attitudes toward, 67, 69, 94, 648n18;
and King's writings, 73, 105, 111,
649n21; and *1957* Pilgrimage, 91,
92–93; and King, 95, 113, 116, 121,
123, 125, 136, 465, 602; and *1960*
conventions, 128; and *1960*
Committee to Defend King, 130;
and Adam Powell, 138, 139–40, 542;
and origins of *1963* March, 265–67,
270, 276–77, 277–78; and *1963*
March, 280, 282–83, 284, 287–88,
299, 676n58; and coalition politics
argument, 288, 348, 349, 352, 353,
420, 497; considers SCLC New York
job, 291, 310, 312, 313, 318; and
winter *1963–64* civil rights options,
303–4, 305; and FBI, 304, 361, 368;
and Research Committee, 332, 426;
and MFDP/*1964* Democratic
convention, 332, 341, 344–45,
345–46, 347, 348–51, 686n65; and
1964 New York riots, 342–44; and

Nobel Prize trip, 357, 363–64,
366–67; and Wachtel, 395; and
Selma, 403, 410; and Alabama
boycott, 414, 415, 418; and SCOPE,
416, 428; and Vietnam, 425, 437,
546, 553, 566; and *1965* Watts riots,
439–40; opposes Chicago campaign,
454–55, 460, 530; and Meredith
March, 480; and Black Power,
533–34; opposes Poor People's
Campaign, 591, 594, 599, 614; and
Memphis, 605
Rutherford, William A., joins SCLC,
584–86, 589; and King, 586–87, 596,
602, 604, 617, 622; and Poor
People's Campaign, 591, 616
Rutledge, Mrs. I. B., 28
Ryan, William F., 665n39

St. Augustine, Fla., beginnings of
SCLC involvement, 316–18, 323–34;
1964 protests, 325–38, 339, 340–41,
344, 685n59; later events, 441
St. Augustine Record, 316
St. Joseph's Infirmary (Atlanta), 354,
355, 357
Salinger, Pierre, 243
Sampson, Al, 450, 467, 471
Sanders, Carl, 204, 207, 450
Sanders, Charles, 364
Savannah, Ga., 290, 678n2
Schulke, Flip, 703n12
Schwarzschild, Henry, 468
Schwerner, Michael, 342, 361, 483
Scott, C. A., 65
Scott, Coretta. *See* King, Coretta
Scott.
Scott, John B., 21
Scott, Obie, 61
Scripto strike, 368, 369
Searles, A. C., 607
Seay, Solomon S., Jr., 130
Seay, Solomon S., Sr., 81, 135
Secrest, Andrew M., 378, 380, 402, 405
Seeger, Pete, 98
Seigenthaler, John, 157, 195, 273
Sellers, Cleveland, 475, 476, 707n9
Sellers, Clyde, 83, 109; and
Montgomery boycott, 19–20, 52, 53,

For the ROMA, *a who**ple*

For NINA whose book this is also

For BARRY who shed light on the mysteries

KU-592-366

Acknowledgements

I shall be for ever grateful to Mai Ghoussoub who forged dream into reality; to Paula Rego who graces this work with her prodigious art; to Dr Donald Kenrick, the Roma's best *phral*, who guided me with tireless dedication and encyclopaedic knowledge; and to Peter Day who so generously bestowed his impeccable critical eye.

And for nourishing me always with their presence, friendship, faith, encouragement, counsel and support, I am indebted to: Prof. Thomas Acton; Tom Aitken; Prof. Tamar Alexander; Duncan Barford; Tricia Barnett; David, Erol and Etty Baruh; Selim Baruh and Nadia Friedman; Dennis Binns; Ayşem Çelikiz; Ian and Anthea Davidson; Tony Dinner; Dr Rajko Djuriċ; Ahmad Ebrahimi; Bensiyon Eskenazi; Dr Lenny Fagin; Ceki, Deborah, Vivian and Yaël Farhi; Palomba Farhi; Isabel Fonseca; André Gaspard; Maggie Gee, Nick Rankin and Rosa Rankin-Gee; Marius Ghenea; Nicolae Gheorghe; Jana Gough; Danièle, Eric, Sara and Nathaniel Gould; Joshua, Kezia, Phil, Samuel and Rachel Gould; Emmanuel Gould and Yaël Hadari; Rebecca Gould and Guy Granot; Andrew Graham-Yooll; Brigitte and Prof. Hagop Hacikyan; the late Dr Yossi Hadar; Prof. Ian Hancock; Jennifer Kavanagh; Zbigniew Kotowicz; Diana and Michael Lazarus; Julian Lewis; Roy Harley Lewis; Ziv Lewis; Robin Lloyd-Jones; Dr Elena Marushiakova and Dr Vassilen Popov; Anthony and Robina Masters; Naomi and Dr David Mayall; Asher and Elizabeth Mayer; Faith Miles; Julita and Tomasz Mirkowicz; Ceinwen and Richard Morgan; Wojciech Oberc; Maureen O'Farrell; Ljumnje Osmani; Ursula Owen; Adem and Pinar Öner; Dr Saliha Paker; Roger Parkes; Bariş Pirhasan; Gabrièle and Prof. Paul Preston; Prof.

Donné Raffat; Maureen Rissik; Hazel Robinson; Manoush Romanov; Anthony Rudolf; Hazim Saghie; Andrew Samuels; Isabella, Janine and Dr Nicholas Sawyer; Rachel Sievers; Diane Tong; Prof. Martin Tucker; Vedat Türkali; Diana Tyler; Dr Enis Üser; Judith Vidal-Hall; Irene Way; the late Edward Whittemore; Kevser and Šaip Yusuf.

PROLOGUE
MAY 1944

Todor searched for a star for his son. The trick was to keep the eyes hovering and wait for the one that moved sturdily, then swoop. Once a star was chosen, it was for life; its possessor lived as long as the star did. A hardy star never died young.

He spotted a stretch of sky that had not been ravaged by the smoke and scrutinized the stars there. New ones, born suddenly, toddled uncertainly. Others perished in dark eddies, just as suddenly.

Nearby, the partridge grated dolefully: *krrr-ik, krrr-ik*. It had stopped struggling with its tether; it knew it would be slaughtered at dawn.

The children, assigned to transform the partridge into a lamb, bleated in counterpoint, remarkably energetically: *me-eh-eh, me-eh-eh*.

The children's mummery failed to hearten Todor. It was difficult to believe, nowadays, that animals could be transformed from one kind into another. Those tales of Gypsies outwitting enemies by turning into wily foxes belonged to a time when everything about creation, including evil, could be explained. Today, nothing had reason. Today, no one – except perhaps the seer, Branko – could make sense of this wasteland with its watch-towers, electrified barbed-wire fence and crematoria that never ceased belching smoke.

He continued scanning the sky. Exhaustion seeped further into his bones.

He wondered whether the partridge had a star of its own. All creatures with souls have stars, his mother had once told him. He didn't know about many creatures – only about bears. Bears had souls, for sure.

'Todor – you got good eyes . . .' Zara proffered a length of string and a piece of wire that had been twisted into a crude sewing-needle. '. . . Thread this for me . . .'

She held the baby pressed against her bosom.

Todor responded robustly, trying to conceal his debility. 'What's this for?'

Zara showed him the rubbish she had collected in her apron: pieces of rag, paper, rubber, leather. 'I'll make a quilt – for the boy . . .'

Todor shook his head. Zara would always amaze him. Here they were, half-dead and all Romany tents laid waste, and she was behaving as if they'd snugly camped for the winter. She was like the bleating children, rubbing rainbows into her eyes, determined to live by another reality. 'Woman . . .'

She tugged his sleeve forcefully. 'Do it!'

Todor threaded the string. Maybe she wasn't rubbing rainbows into her eyes; maybe she could see further than most. Nothing different about this place, she'd said, when they'd got here after that earthless, airless, waterless journey in a cattle-truck; nothing different, our life's always been a slaughter-house.

He prodded her towards their block. 'Go – rest.'

She'd have the place to herself tonight. Tomorrow was St George's Day. Some gold had been organized and the *Rapportführer* had been bribed. Tonight the Gypsies could sit outside, even stroll up and down the compound. Tonight, only the dying would be in bed – not the usual eight packed on a bunk. There would be room for her to stretch out. 'Go on!'

Zara spat. The block was a long, lightless, wooden barrack. Modified from SS stables, according to Jano. Which only proved what pea-brains the SS were because no horse with any sense would set foot in a coop that had water pouring in from its roof and where the boggy clay floor sucked in all those who stepped on it.

Block 31. One of a line of nineteen. Across the way: another line of nineteen. Except for the latrine barracks, all numbered like houses in a street – odd numbers this side, even ones, the other. And this was just Sector B-IIe, the Gypsy camp.

Going towards the main gate: more sectors. Every sector surrounded by its own barbed-wire fence. Camps within the camp. Close to three hundred blocks Birkenau had, Jano had told her, as opposed to forty or so in Auschwitz, the base camp.

Droves of people with shrunken, simian faces and unhinged eyes. Carrying the stench of burnt flesh; breathing air singed with cinders. Most of them still sociable, still trying to revive dying spirits with civil words and gestures.

'Wouldn't put rats in such a place.' Zara spat again, this time at the ditch that drained the marshy soil.

She had said the same after they had been tattooed and herded into this compound. Jano, the chief of the Slovene Gypsies who was also the block senior and who had taken them under his wing because they had been rounded up in Yugoslavia, had applauded her for that. To survive in this place, he'd urged, don't change, keep to our ways, then you won't lose your soul, death can't be forever.

Todor sniggered. Zara was not one to change.

Maybe he should follow her example. Because if he let go, if he surrendered to exhaustion, he'd end up like the zombies the inmates called *mussulman*. Besides, as Jano constantly reminded them, there were some blessings. The Gypsies had been allowed to stay together as families and given a whole sector for themselves. They could also thank God for not being Jews – Jews were being incinerated in their thousands. 'Woman, go – rest.'

Zara shook her head. 'The *Urme* visit the child tonight. I must catch them.'

Todor felt a surge of anger. Did she think he had forgotten? The baby was seven days old. That's when the *Urme*, the Angels of Destiny, visit the newborn. That's why the mother had to stay awake: to pounce on Breath, who was the queen of the *Urme*, and beg Her to bless the boy.

Couldn't Zara see he, too, bled with worry for the boy? Look how desperately he searched for a good star. Maybe he should remind her, it had been he who had insisted the baby should be unmarked because that way they'd have a better chance of catching Breath's eye; he who had concealed the birth from the *Rapportführer* with suicidal sleight of hand so that they wouldn't tattoo the boy like they'd tattooed him and her, Z-10821 and Z-10822, Z for *Zigeuner*, Gypsy.

Why did she always behave as if she knew everything and he nothing? 'Keep awake – but rest also!'

'I'll make the quilt.' Wistfully, she stroked the baby's forehead. 'When he leaves here, he'll have something to keep him warm.'

The roughness of her hand chafed the infant; he opened his eyes and immediately started crying.

Zara rocked him, then pointed angrily at the nearest crematorium. 'It's them Jews going up in smoke. They keep screaming, keep waking him up!'

Todor turned and stared at the spurts of flame bursting out of the chimney. That was Crematorium III. A squat, nondescript brick building where death was made commonplace.

There was another crematorium on the other side of the railway siding. And two more in the woods. Gas chambers and incinerators snorting all hours.

They were burning Hungarian Jews, Yerko had told him. Those who had arrived on yesterday's transport from Budapest. Yerko worked in *Kanada*, the depot where all the arrivals' belongings were sorted out; he knew everything that went on in the camp.

All very well for Jano to say hang on to your soul and survive. Surely the Jews, too, were hanging on to their souls; but they weren't surviving.

What would happen when the SS turned their mortuary eyes from the unloading ramp to the Gypsy camp? Had Jano thought of that?

There were some political prisoners who argued that the camp was a vast place, that a foxy inmate could blend with the landscape, evade the SS and death. Wishful thinking! Birkenau was no bigger than a potter's field; it would take a couple of hours to walk round it. And ask any Ursari: potters' fields had insatiable hunger. This potter's field, they would agree, was determined to bury the whole world. The Ursari knew because they were one tribe who grieved over the abuse of the earth, which was why they preferred animals to mankind and never stayed in one place.

No wonder, then, much of the time his guts went across to the Jews and screamed with them as if all the Romanies' names, too, had been scored in the soot of those chimneys.

Miserably, Todor watched his son cry. 'Maybe he's hungry.'

Zara protested. 'I fed him.'

He wished she'd go and sleep. Even amidst the stench and slime and diseases like evil spells – typhus, scurvy, diarrhoea, water cancer – she looked untroubled when she slept. She also looked beautiful. Whereas awake, she was a vixen who shunned a woman's soft ways. 'Feed him again! What you got paps for?'

Zara ignored him and turned towards the Slovene Gypsies who had gathered in the yard.

The *Rapportführer* had also given permission to light a fire. In its glow the Gypsies' shadows looked hefty, like dancing bears. So different from those interminable roll-calls when the SS shouted 'sport' and made them jump hours on end and the weak shadows shrank and collapsed and either died where they fell or were beaten to death.

The Slovene Gypsies were getting restive. The festivities would start at dawn. Some of the men were discussing the partridge as if it were a well-fattened lamb. Others reminisced about the times when they used to buy their offerings in Macedonia where the flocks were the best.

The women, appointed to honour their men with signs of wealth, were fashioning jewellery – earrings, necklaces, belts – out of grass, twigs and mud.

Amazingly resourceful these Slovenes were; there was no way this pig-arsed place was going to stop them celebrating their festival.

Zara moved in their direction. 'I'll sit with them.'

Todor was shocked. 'There are men there. You just gave birth. You're still unclean.'

'God burn your tongue! How can we be clean here?'

'We're not of their tribe!'

'They took us in – made room in their bunks.'

'Even so. There are prohibitions . . .'

Zara, shaking her head in exasperation, strode over to the Slovene Gypsies.

Todor clenched his fists. He should teach her to obey. Beat her; pummel her into a proper woman! But he couldn't. Never had done. Neither his bears, nor his wife. This had puzzled friends and relatives. It was said wife-beating was proof of the husband's love and the women were reassured by it. Maybe. But he couldn't – he didn't know why; that's how it was; not everything had a reason.

All the same, it hadn't stopped people respecting him. Or Zara from loving him. And it was because she loved him, needed him, that he hadn't tried escaping from this shit-hole. Not that escape was easy. Many had tried. Some Gypsies, too. Most had been caught and shot.

He watched Zara sit with the Slovene Gypsies. The men ignored her as if she was one of their own. The women obviously liked her; they included her in their conversation. When women got together, they became a pack. Daughters of the moon talking of earthy matters in ancient whispers.

The two young mothers who had also just given birth were suckling their babies. Hadn't they heard breast-feeding had to be done out of sight?

Zara followed their example. Headstrong woman – she'd defy anything, she would! And why couldn't she have suckled when he'd asked her? She knew he liked watching her; she knew he relished the stoutness of her breasts.

That her breasts were still full was a miracle. What they ate here wouldn't feed a midge. See how the breasts of the other mothers had shrunk to pursed nipples; their babies could only sup death.

Maybe he should stop carping about Zara. True, she wasn't what a female should be: a child-bearer who also mothered the husband; nor was she the best in looks or gait or obedience or in boiling up a man's blood like those who could scent musk on every wind. But so what? Those women, in any case, belonged to a time of clear skies, peaceful roads, serene forests and encampments on lush riversides.

Truth be known, Zara was good enough. Back when they used to wend their way through the Balkans, even whilst on the run from the Hitlerites, she never lost the tenderness that was just below her hide. And whenever he had mounted her, she'd always been nicely wet. What's more, she never forgot her first duty was to be fruitful. Five miscarriages, she'd had, but wouldn't give up. Tried everything: herbs; magic; prayers to Holy Mary and Her countless saints; visits to the tombs of Turkish sages; candles in every church; and once, in Sofia, despite her distrust of the *gadje*, a doctor. In the end it had been her dream telling them to do it differently that had made her conceive. Not sparing his blushes, she'd mounted him; and straightaway the foetus had held. Make sense of that. God must have wondered who was the man and who the woman.

Zara stopped feeding the baby. As she covered up, she turned towards Todor and allowed him a brief glimpse of her breast. Teasing him – in front of all those people! Then she started helping the women clean the tin bowls.

Poor Romanies – gone the copper utensils that shone like the sun's sweat. Everything gone from everybody.

Gone also his caravan: a grand splash of colour which animated every landscape. Gone, too, the wedding presents, the bedding embroidered by the aunts, the icons handed down from forefathers. Gone, above all, the bears, the horses, the dogs – brave creatures treacherously killed and eaten.

One of the Slovene Gypsies strummed a lute. Another squeezed his accordion. A third trilled with a clarinet. Men and women began to sing – a haunting song about a brave Rom abducting, as his bride, on St George's Day, the daughter of a despotic chieftain.

Todor resisted the temptation to join in with his pan-pipe.

That was another scrap of blessing in this God-forsaken place: they had been allowed to keep their instruments – for the time being, anyway. Moreover, providing they displayed on their clothes the black triangle which indicated they were *asocials*, whatever that meant, they had been spared from wearing the camp's striped rags. They could also let their hair grow – which was a mercy: in some tribes, cropped hair was the mark of adultery and some of the women who'd been shaved and deloused on arrival had felt so humiliated that they'd wanted to kill themselves.

The women finished polishing the tin bowls.

Zara, holding the baby close to her chest, started sorting out the patches for the quilt. Another thing about her: she never stood idle. She had the grit of a horse. She had had a difficult delivery – she'd been frightened, hungry, sapped – yet, within hours, she had been up and doing things.

The singing stopped.

Jano began to narrate the *Hegira* of the Romanies. This was an account from the long-lost Gypsy Bible which had recently emerged in the camp.

The story of this Bible's discovery was like a fable itself. The Holy Book had perished during one of man's dark times. But, before its dissolution, O Del had carved its contents on the silence that stands between death and rebirth. It had been His will that one day, when the tribes would be peopled with right-minded folk, He would send a seer to reclaim it.

The right-minded folk and the seer had been born into this age. But, given the *gadje*'s hatred of good people, they had ended up in this knacker's yard. Which is something O Del had not foreseen. Which only goes to show He must be as unworldly as his people. Anyway, having realized His error and, desperate to save His children, O Del had promptly brought down the Book and engraved it on the ash that had come to blanket Birkenau. And sure enough, no sooner had the seer, Branko, arrived in the camp than he had beheld the Sacred Writing.

The seer was now in the infirmary, dying. And though he was feverishly transcribing the Bible so that he could provide the Romanies with the complete text, he had also advised that as many people as could should memorize it. 'The Word must outlive death', he had said.

Hence Jano, the exemplary just man, had become one of the memorizers. Surprisingly, so had Yerko.

Todor turned a deaf ear to Jano's recitation. He still felt in two minds about the Slovene Gypsies. Often they showed the reserve – even the hardness – of the *gadje*. Maybe they had dealt a lot with them and learned not to give much away. The Bible, for example. They kept saying it would change history for the Romanies. But they never said how, not even to offer false hope to the thousands here.

On the other hand, they had not hesitated, even for a moment, to help him and his wife. True, helping brothers was one law no Romany, whatever the tribe, would dare break. But in this place laws from the outside died quicker than people.

Against that, they had completely ignored Zara's state of uncleanness – and not because of the conditions in the camp, but because, in their effort to inhabit the *gadje*'s world, they had chosen to abandon the custom that segregated a new mother from the men. Which also explained their disregard of the code whereby breast-feeding women were expected to keep out of sight.

Then again, they would trick the sun and the zodiac in order to celebrate

St George's Day. They had paid solid gold *napoleons* to smuggle in this partridge, thin as a goat's prick, which a work party had caught near the woods.

Todor reprimanded himself: what right had he to cast stones? Whilst on the run from the Hitlerites, he and Zara had ended up eating all their animals – even the bears. That made them untouchable. The Slovene Gypsies should have let them rot. The fact that they didn't proved there was a core in his people that would never disintegrate! That in order to survive when all the horizons were breaking up, it was wise to embrace any serpent, even damnation!

'You decided?'

Todor, startled by the voice, turned round sharply. The *drabarni*, grim as an empty well, was scrutinizing him darkly.

'Not yet.'

'Nights are impatient. The *Urme* more so.'

Todor nodded, agitated. Few, even among the *drabarni*, could commune with the *Urme*. This old witch did it all the time; the Slovene Gypsies swore to that. But he was in two minds.

For a start, he didn't want to interfere with Zara's supplication. Zara had done everything to sweeten Breath's heart: suckled the boy from the right breast first; baptized him in running water – in the latrines and with Todor officiating because they couldn't find a priest – and baptized him not once, but every day, in order to multiply the magic; baptized him also with pebbles of unusual shape which they had been carrying as talismans ever since Zara had begun to show and which, since the birth, she had sewn into the baby's clothes; and despite lacking the traditional herbs and millet, had found a way to baptize him with earthly produce, with the grains she had saved from their soups.

Nor did he want his worst fears confirmed. The *drabarni* had told some Polish prisoners that the only Romanies who would survive Birkenau would be those who escaped or were sent elsewhere; all who remained would die before the end of summer.

In which case the boy's only hope was the German engineer who worked in the *I. G. Farben Buna-Werke* at Auschwitz-Monowitz and who came to Birkenau regularly to select a new batch of workers and each time took a Gypsy child – according to rumours, to sell for adoption. This engineer, Yerko had heard, would be coming again next week. Zara had already decided that Breath would save the boy that way – hence the quilt.

Todor couldn't bring himself to tell her that there were many children in the compound, that it would need a miracle to have their son chosen by all the Romanies in preference to another infant and a second miracle to have him accepted by the engineer. Yet, secretly, he clung to Zara's faith. What if the *drabarni* killed that slim hope?

'I'm still looking for the boy's star. Then I'll decide.'

The *drabarni* waved her stick at him. 'I'll have a smoke. That's as long as I'll wait.'

Todor watched her shuffle next door to Block 29 where Yerko was sitting on the front step and making cigarettes by filling pieces of paper with shreds of tobacco. She filched one of the youngster's roll-ups, then blended into the night.

Yerko, amused by the *drabarni's* behaviour, winked at Todor.

Todor reciprocated with a warm smile.

He liked Yerko – and not because he was his nephew. Though only fourteen, the lad was tougher than most men. He could have been the best forager in the Balkans – faster than bad news, he was. When they had been on the run, it had been Yerko who had kept them alive much of the time. Here, too, inside a few days, Yerko had become an old hand at pilfering tobacco, alcohol and food from the stores and bartering them for gold, silver, even diamonds with the *Sonderkommando* who sifted the clothes of those who were gassed on arrival.

You had to be special to deal with the *Sonderkommando*; manning the crematoria maddened them: they knew their souls would never heal.

Needless to say, it had been Yerko who had procured the *napoleons* that had enabled the Slovene Gypsies to have their St George's Day.

Maybe if he asked Yerko to bribe the engineer . . .

Todor resumed his search for a star. In desperation, he scanned the bottom corner of the sky where the Morning Star would appear. Once there had been a cluster there – almost a hundred: his father's, his mother's, his brothers' and sisters' and uncles' and aunts' and cousins' and grandparents'. Plentiful like an olive tree. Plus that rebellious one, Zara's, which had moved right across the Heavens to stand next to Todor's on the night of her twelfth birthday when Todor's father had bought her as Todor's bride.

All those stars scrawled like claw-scars on a bear-wrestler's shoulders. Good to look at, his father used to say, because that was how the Ursari had always been: united, tempered by the elements, a vision of strength wherever they walked.

But against every strength there was one that was superior; and one strength that crushed all: war.

19

INSTITIÚID TEICNEOLAÍOCHTA AN LEABHARLANN LEITIR CEANAINN

500 40 684

Now, from that kingly band of stars only three remained: his, Zara's and Yerko's. His and Zara's were fading fast, warning them, as surely as owls flying past their pillows, that death was giving them the eye.

Suddenly he spotted a glint. He watched it gather light.

A new star. Increasingly bright. Solid and heavy. Instantly planting itself into the celestial field. Taking root forcefully like ancestral feats. A good star. Proud and doughty. Not to be intimidated. Radiating a sparkle that promised passion. Of greatest importance was its position – far away from Todor's and Zara's, therefore, with a good chance of escaping the fading sickness.

Todor seized it with that ancient whisper of the Romanies that can be heard everywhere in the Universe. 'I claim you for my son.'

Now, full of confidence, he shouted at the sorceress. '*Drabarni*! Come and do your business!'

The old witch appeared immediately. Formidable. A night-wolf. She cackled and shrieked and shouted words that flew like spittle but were incomprehensible.

The Slovene Gypsies fell silent; the women stopped their work.

The *drabarni* gesticulated at Zara. 'The baby! Bring the baby!'

Zara sat, transfixed, the baby pressed against her bosom as if it were part of her body. She looked at Todor, dark eyes censuring.

Todor beckoned her. 'Bring him! It's all right!'

Zara jumped up, scattering her quilt patches, and ran off with the baby.

The *drabarni* yelled and shrieked. 'Bring the baby! Bring the baby!'

Todor chased after Zara.

He caught up with her near the barbed-wire fence that separated them from Sector B-IId.

She spat at him. 'No!'

He raised his hand to hit her.

She stood defiantly.

Bellowing, directing his fury upon himself, he started punching his head. Zara stretched out a hand. 'Don't, Todor . . .'

He stopped. He had drawn blood. He wiped his forehead with his sleeve, then pounced to snatch the baby.

She fought him, screaming, biting, kicking. 'No!'

The baby started to cry.

Todor let go of Zara, then began to weep.

Tentatively, Zara placed her hand on his shoulder. 'Why?'

Todor sobbed. 'We'll know his future.'

The baby was screaming now. Zara gave him her breast. 'He'll be safe. I'll sway Breath.'

'And if She ignores you? *Drabarni* knows how to commune with the *Urme*. She'll make Breath see the boy!'

Zara, glimpsing a shadow of truth in Todor's logic, lost her assurance. She caressed the baby anxiously.

Todor seized her hand. 'We need hope, Zara. We can't die without hope.'

'You're sure we'll die?'

'Yes.'

'If she tells us he'll die, too?'

Todor stared at his hands, then shut his eyes. 'I'll kill him myself . . .'

'No!'

He wailed. 'I'll be very gentle . . .'

'No!'

'You want him gassed?'

'No!'

'That's what they do here, woman!'

Zara nodded. Running her fingers over Todor's tears, she calmed down. 'If . . . When . . . If we have to . . . Not you . . . The mother . . . I'll do it . . .' She started walking back.

Todor, astonished by her conversion, followed. He put on a cheerful voice. 'I found his star.' He pointed at it. 'Strong one. There! That one there!'

Zara gazed at the star for a long time, then smiled. 'Looks good.'

He beamed proudly. 'Yes!'

'Well chosen, Todor.' She kissed his hand.

The *drabarni*, having expected their return, had laid out her divination shawl.

The Slovene Gypsies waited solemnly.

Yerko – such an old young man – kissed Todor and Zara on both cheeks, then handed a bunch of cigarettes to the *drabarni*.

The old woman nudged Zara. 'Baby needs to be naked.'

Zara unswathed the boy.

'On his back.'

Zara placed her son on the *drabarni*'s shawl.

The boy had stopped crying. He was staring at the sky, calmly, as if acquainting himself with his star.

The *drabarni* gesticulated at Zara and Todor. 'Mother by his head. Father by his feet.'

Zara and Todor took up their places.

The *drabarni* addressed the others. 'Rest of you, out of the way!'

The Slovene Gypsies and Yerko fell back a few paces, then squatted down.

The *drabarni* whispered to Zara. 'His name?'

'Mujula.'

'Is that his everyday name?'

'Yes.'

'Everyday name's no good. His secret name?'

Zara hesitated. Her son's secret name was the magic that would keep him safe. It was the name she had entrusted to the wind; the name that was already wandering over rivers, mountains and plains in order to acquire permanence on earth. She had to tell it to the sorceress, she knew. But what if the Hitlerites had ears in the air and heard it and . . .

The *drabarni* hissed. 'The *Urme* must be told. His secret name?'

Todor answered. 'Branko.'

'Like the seer?'

'Yes.'

'Well chosen!'

Todor smiled at Zara. He had wanted to name the boy Jano, in gratitude to the Slovene chief. But Zara, captivated by the history of the Gypsy Bible, had insisted on the name of the seer who had reclaimed it.

The *drabarni* screeched. 'His star?'

Todor pointed at it.

The *drabarni* studied the star at length. Then she sank onto her knees and intoned primeval sounds.

She crawled around the infant seven times; at every turn, she paused first by the baby's face, then by his chest, then by his penis. She sniffed each part seven times. At each sniff she drank seven mouthfuls from her gourd; after each gulp, she counted to seventy-seven.

She produced a crust of bread. She took seven bites from it and, after each bite, examined the baby's palms whilst counting again to seventy-seven.

She lay down next to the baby. As if she, too, were newly born, she kicked her arms and legs – seven times. After each movement, she counted again to seventy-seven.

Eventually she rose and stared at the chimneys for a long time. Occasionally, she shook her head as if disbelieving her own clairvoyance.

Finally, she spoke; and her voice was suffused with that melodious tone which people everywhere recognize as the voice of one of God's companions. 'The *Urme* are with me.'

Zara began to shake.

The *drabarni* had divided herself into nine selves and assumed the features of the *Urme* sisters. Each sister, Zara could clearly see, possessed an essence for life: breath, luck, wisdom, health, ability, strength, fertility, courage, love. Each of these blessings would be purveyed by the particular *Urme* according to her whim, or, if She was directly approached, according to the sincerity of the suppliant.

Zara focused her eyes on Breath. She remembered, in a panic, that the *Urme* expected offerings of food. They would curse the child if none were available. Had the *drabarni* prepared food? Hurriedly, Zara brought out the crust of bread and the turnip she had managed to save. She tore them into pieces and spread them on the ground.

A beautiful woman – or was it the *drabarni* as a young lass? – glided past and gathered the food. Then, drifting away, she looked back.

Zara collapsed, drained. A tearful inner voice questioned her repeatedly. Was that Breath? When She had turned to look, had She looked at the child? Or at Zara? Had She smiled?

Todor watched his son fall asleep. Earlier, as the *drabarni* was receiving the *Urme*, the boy had gazed at Zara and him sadly, as a survivor contemplates the dead. And once, he had waved at them, as if in farewell.

The *drabarni* squatted over the baby's face. '*A new tree will sprout the leaves the donkey ate.*'

She squatted over the baby's chest. '*Hope will run down the mountains and stream to the sea; then it will set sail and become earth.*'

She squatted over the baby's penis. '*The burst pomegranate will be made whole.*'

Then she straightened up, screeching and cackling. 'That's it! That's his destiny!'

Zara crawled towards the baby. 'What does it mean?'

The *drabarni* chortled. 'Plain as anything!'

Todor grabbed her. 'Will he live?'

The *drabarni* cachinnated. 'No less and no more than what's written on his forehead.'

Forlorn, Zara began to swaddle her son.

The boy had woken up again.

Todor stared at him. The eyes were dreamy. Were they eyes that had defeated death? Or eyes ready to close for ever? He bellowed. 'How long is that?'

But the *drabarni* had gone, lost in the echoes of her laughter.

The Slovene Gypsies shuffled uneasily and discussed the prophecy in whispers.

23

INSTITIÚD TEICNEOLAÍOCHTA
AN LEABHARLANN
LEITIR CEANAINN
823
500 40684

Yerko resumed rolling cigarettes.

Zara sat on the ground and cradled her son.

Todor dropped down next to her.

Zara rested her head on his arm. 'I saw her – I think. The *Urme* Breath.'

Todor stared at her. 'Yes? And?'

'I don't know . . . Maybe I imagined it . . .'

Todor shook her by the shoulders. 'Talk sense, woman!'

Zara began to weep. 'Kill the sun, Todor. Stop the new day. Then the boy can live.'

Disconsolately, Todor looked up at the sky. He couldn't see his son's star. It was either hiding behind the glow of the first light or it had been erased by the smoke.

Todor and Zara watched the commencement of St George's Day through their despair.

At dawn, Jano untied the partridge. The children bleated even more shrilly.

Jano thanked God for leading them to another spring. Then, pointing the partridge's head towards the rising sun, he offered some water to the bird and sought its forgiveness for having to kill it. When the partridge finished drinking, he cut its throat and collected its blood in a cup.

He smeared the blood on the foreheads of his people to show God that this was the first time they would be eating meat since the onset of winter, that they had abstained even when their rations had contained slivers of sausage. Had they transgressed this custom, they would have been guilty of eating the flesh of their dead children.

Then Jano went to Todor and Zara. 'You're with us. Do as we do.'

Todor shook his head. 'We took meat. Our animals. We're unclean – *marimé*. If you smear us, you'll all be contaminated.'

Jano hesitated; then, sadly, nodded. 'The boy?'

'Full of Zara's milk.'

'Mother's milk never spoils. Let me smear him.'

Todor nudged Zara, leaving the decision to her.

Zara looked at Jano. 'The boy's destiny – did you understand?'

'Give it time . . .'

Zara shivered. 'Time . . .?'

Jano squatted by her side. 'For some the smear becomes like a shield. Let me . . .'

Zara nodded. 'Why not?'

Jano dipped his finger into the cup and smeared the blood on the baby's forehead. 'May he be a great Rom.'

In the beginning there was O Del. He existed before the Word. He will exist after the final death. He was a hidden treasure. He wanted to be known. So He created Creation. He penetrated the emptiness and implanted it with pure thought. The thought pulsated and grew into a dark light. It fomented, then exploded. Every spark became a substance that carried O Del's image.

Thus He was earth, water, air and fire. Thus He was the soul of all things living and the spirit of all things dead.

In time, O Del took some clay and moulded two kokukli. He called the male Adam, and placed him under an apple tree. The female, he called Lilith, and placed her under a pear tree.

He created them together because O Del is not a god who inflicts solitude. He created them in His image so that they would reflect His love. Thus the male was tempered with the woman's softness and the female fortified by the man's sinew.

After a time, Adam began to consort with demons. He allowed them to breathe upon him.

Thereafter, he repudiated his softness and worshipped his strength. He said to Lilith: 'You are the receptacle to my rod. Therefore, my inferior. Therefore, you must always lie beneath me.'

Lilith protested: 'We were created from the same clay. That makes us equal. We will take turns to lie on top. Thus we will share the pleasure evenly.'

Adam refused to submit to such equality. He abandoned Lilith and stole into the Garden of Eden. There, he ate of the fruit of the Tree of the Knowledge of Good and Evil and learned the secrets of alchemy.

Then he fashioned a new female from his rib. He called her Eve and forced her to lie beneath him. Eve complied because Adam was stronger.

O Del unleashed His wrath. He banished Adam from the Garden. Eve, whom Adam had reduced to a bondwoman, went with the brute.

Then O Del took up with Lilith who was with Adam's child. He made her His consort. And when the child, a boy, was born, He breathed upon him to make him His own son. He called the boy Rom, which means 'God's chosen'.

When Rom grew up, O Del sent him to the world to undo the wicked deeds of Adam.

PART ONE

One

The Matterhorn!

Look, Eloïse! See how it shakes off the Valais' clutter of peaks! How it rises as time's totem!

Look at it now, as the evening sun straddles the summit. Can you see: the fiery embrace brands an image on the last steep. It's the image of our secret selves.

Look at it again. It's God's image. That's how we revert to primary matter. We transmute into mountains.

'Taking a nap, old man?'

Melchior Füssli, still trying to catch his breath, turned toward his son.

Benedict was some seventy metres up the slope, tugging at the rope.

Take him on a climb and he gets cheeky, eh, Eloïse. But do you wonder – look how solidly he is anchored on the ice. Such natural strength so modestly manifested. How strange and extraordinary, Eloïse, that this antithesis of the lofty, elegant Swiss, this compact, chunky man, dark as the sweetest of berries, our son, a gift from Heaven, can tame a mountain like a titan.

Melchior picked up his ice-axe, grabbed the rope and resumed his ascent wearily.

The weight on the rope saddened Benedict. Taking a ride was anathema to Melchior; yet, several times during the day, he had let himself be carried. Was the Olympian feeling his age? 'You should be cantering, old man!'

Melchior paused again. 'Always take time to listen to the ether.' He bent forward to ease the strain on his lungs.

29

Benedict gauged the wind: petulant, unsheathing its sabre. He wondered whether they should proceed to the summit tomorrow. This stretch, a wide couloir gently levelling to the Hornlihütte shoulder, was a romp. But hereafter, they would be on the North-East Ridge proper, exposed to the gale and the cold; there would be traverses and *corniches* to negotiate and the toughest elevation, the Enjambée, to scale.

Melchior, head resolutely forward, resumed his climb. Forty metres more.

Benedict pulled. Almost all of Melchior's weight was on the rope.

Twenty-five metres. Benedict noted the drop in temperature. The sun was withdrawing. The summit, still glistening with the sweat of their coupling, was draping itself with shades. 'Melchior, we should camp here.'

'Right. Grand spot.'

The old man's heartiness failed to conceal his exhaustion. Benedict pulled him the rest of the way.

Melchior slumped on Benedict's shoulder, gasping and wheezing. 'Something ate the air . . .' Then, letting Benedict yank off his rucksack, he sank onto his haunches.

Benedict handed him a thermos of glucose infusion.

Melchior gulped down the steaming tonic, then stretched out on the snow.

Benedict squatted next to him. 'All right?'

'Blissful.'

'Be dark soon.'

Melchior passed the thermos to Benedict. 'Relax a moment.'

'Right.'

'Listen. You can hear the earth spinning. I wouldn't mind dying here.'

'I would.' Benedict took a few sips of the glucose infusion.

Melchior, inhaling more easily now, straightened up. 'See how fast I get my breath back? Still an athlete's heart. A young old man.'

'Sure.'

'Don't humour me! I know what you're thinking. We're not turning back!'

'Let's see the weather tomorrow.'

'Forecast says fine.' Melchior squinted at the summit. 'Look at it – waiting for us!' He snatched the thermos out of Benedict's hand. 'No chickening out!'

Benedict smiled and nodded. 'I'll set up the tent.'

Melchior strained to stand up, then decided against it. 'Yes. Time you contributed something to this climb!'

They had eaten well.

They had talked about Nicaragua and of their hope that the Sandinistas, finally victorious, would fulfil the promise of their revolution, even find a way of recovering the hundreds of millions that Somoza had stolen, piles of which, Melchior suspected, had been laundered through Swiss banks.

And they had discussed Benedict's promotion in the army reserves and agreed that, in a country where advancement in the Forces greatly enhanced a person's career, his preferment to the senior engineer's post in the Lucerne Hydroelectricity Board was now virtually guaranteed. Nettie, his wife, might rage at the longer stretches of duty his new rank would impose. But she would soon see that a young colonel would find the doors to influential quarters wide open. Nettie, lecturer in law and campaigner for a plethora of injustices, regarded influence as an activist's most efficacious weapon. Indeed, it had been her search for influence, for a senior Customs official who would support a policy of favourable tariffs to so-called under-developed countries, that had led her, a few years back, to Melchior and thence to Benedict.

So they sat, ensconced in sleeping bags, hurricane lamps muted, sipping coffee and brandy, smoking *Villigers* and ignoring the wind that sought to hurl them and their tent down the ravine.

Melchior was tipsy; his voice shuttled between ebullience and gravity. 'Incredible. Here we are: two blobs of protoplasm. In the centre of a majesty created, for all we know, just for our appreciation. What say you to that?'

Benedict, still deliberating whether they should proceed to the summit, responded distractedly. 'Whoever's up there – thank you.'

'I love this mountain, Benedict. Loved it the moment I first saw it. Toddler I was – on a hike with my father. Loved it all the more when Eloïse loved it, too. A manly mountain, she used to say.'

Benedict felt a surge of grief. This was their twenty-first ascent of the Matterhorn. They had climbed it once a year since he had been fifteen. And always somewhere around Hornlihütte, Melchior had said the same thing. A manly mountain, Eloïse says, Eloïse says, Eloïse says. But this year: Eloïse *used* to say. Dear God, what terrible pain a mere change of tense produced!

Melchior sighed. 'She always looked awe-struck – as if she was seeing it for the first time. Even after she got ill and had to contend with the photographs you and I took.'

Benedict visualized Eloïse's eyes. That was where the multiple sclerosis could be seen weaving its evil. Always watering – as if lachrymation could heal.

'I never told you why she said that . . .'

'No.' And whenever he had kissed her on her cheekbones, the only part of her face that had not been severely blighted by medication, her eyes had thanked him with a special glitter.

Melchior took another swig. 'I nearly did. Many times. Wanted to boast, you see. Wouldn't have been right – whilst she was alive. I've been the happiest of men . . .'

'Old-timer, we'll end up crying.'

'Nothing wrong with that!'

Benedict put his arms around him. 'No.'

'It reminded her of my erection.'

'Melchior . . .'

'Do I embarrass you?'

'No, but . . .'

Melchior began to weep, softly. 'I never stopped desiring her. To the day she died. She only had to look at me – and I'd be aroused. She never had to doubt me. It wasn't just carnality. Plugged into her, I was alive. Disconnected, I didn't exist. Can you understand?'

Benedict held him tightly. 'I think so . . .'

'Irony was: she saw me as her pillar of strength. A hero tanned by lightning and dunked in magical waters. Great joke, eh – when I couldn't relieve an iota of her suffering . . .'

'You kept her going for years . . .'

Melchior placed his head on Benedict's shoulder. 'I also hate this mountain. It tells me I've failed. Mocks me because I never managed to become what I was born to be: a man like God. That's what we all think we can be – deep down. That we have another self, a glorious self, which can make everything better – cure everybody. What presumption, eh?' Melchior listened to the screaming wind, as if haunted. 'A self we can never find. Which probably doesn't exist. Or exists only in death . . .'

Benedict wiped the sweat off Melchior's forehead. 'You're getting drunk, old man.'

Melchior nodded amiably. 'Just enough to think clearly. You know, maybe there is life after life. Maybe death is the only place where we'll live forever with our loved ones.'

Benedict stubbed out his *Villiger*. 'I'd rather keep faith with life.'

Melchior shifted round to face Benedict. 'Good boy. Absolutely right!

Enough of my nonsense! There's so much to life, so much to achieve! In fact, if I may be a shade critical, much more than you've settled for!'

Benedict stiffened defensively. 'I've got a good life . . .'

'You've got a good job, a good wife, a nice house and enough money to make ends meet comfortably. You thrive in the army because you're in an alpine unit which is capital for someone who loves climbing! But what about the rest?'

'The rest is immaterial. Come on, old man. We've got a hard day ahead. Time to sleep.'

'I'm enjoying talking.'

'We can talk tomorrow.'

'I might not be in the mood tomorrow. Let's have another brandy.'

Benedict yielded and refilled their cups.

Melchior stared at Benedict. He could not pin down the eyes. How sad that this tough, manly man, with swarthy looks that would have made Valentino envious, still had eyes that darted away like deer scenting danger. So much had healed over the years, but not the eyes.

He held Benedict's hand. 'This will sound harsh. But I must say it. I was watching you climb. That's when you're really alive, when you're one with the elements. And, of course, since it's me who taught you, I feel proud, I tell myself I've done a good job. Then I get a nagging thought: has climbing taken the place of something else, something fundamental, something meant to define you? Have you taken a wrong turn somewhere, lost sight of what's essential, what you want to do, what you were born to do?'

Benedict fiddled with the zip of his sleeping bag. 'You make me sound like a wayward prodigy.'

'Wayward, no. Prodigy, definitely. After all, you're my son – flesh of the stalwart spunk I still imagine I have.'

Benedict squeezed Melchior's hands. 'I'm honoured, old man. But I'm likely to disappoint you.'

'Have you never craved immortality? Prayed desperately for more time, say a thousand years?'

Benedict chuckled. 'No.'

'You better start then! That's how you'll begin to fulfil yourself. You'll see time's running out. You'll hit top gear – hoping to achieve whatever needs to be achieved in the little time left. And when you achieve it, which you will, you'll realize that if you hadn't run out of time you could have done much more.'

Benedict extricated his hand. 'You're assuming there's something I want to achieve. There isn't.'

'Why not?'

'Just so.'

'What do you daydream about?'

'I don't.'

'Everybody daydreams.'

'I don't dare.'

'You – what?'

'In case I hear Sirens – and am lured away.'

'But that's the whole point. You must be lured. You must meet life with no clothes on.'

'I prefer an orderly world. Everything well controlled. Toeing the line doggedly. That's what makes me a good officer. If I let myself be seduced, I'd abandon you . . .'

'Sons must abandon their fathers. It's the only way they can become fathers themselves.'

Benedict gulped down his drink. 'This son found his father too late.'

Melchior smiled sadly. 'Sometimes it's fathers who abandon.'

Benedict turned to him sharply. 'What's that supposed to mean?'

Melchior's grin turned ferocious. 'Why haven't you got a child yet?'

The brusqueness of Melchior's reproach startled Benedict. 'In good time.'

'It's been good time for a long time.'

'Nettie doesn't feel ready yet.'

'Fuck Nettie!'

Benedict offered a smile. 'You think that might do the trick?'

Melchior ignored the sarcasm with a growl. 'You are thirty-six – approaching middle age. Man needs children. Must have children. Look at me. I was a hopeless case. Sterile. Testicles like empty tin cans! So what did I do? I went and got you. You can do it the easy way – and pleasurably!'

'I will. Eventually.'

'Unless – it's not right between you and Nettie!'

'We're fine.'

'What's that mean?'

'We get on.'

'Neither tears nor joy?'

'It's not like you and Eloïse were. But it's all right.'

Melchior gazed out into the night. 'Eloïse and I were at odds for years. We found each other only after we adopted you.'

'Oh, come on . . .'

'A man might be able to emulate the Matterhorn, but he's superfluous if his spunk is dead. She was desperate for a child – more than I was. You saved us.'

'You saved me.'

Once again Melchior became tearful. 'Dear God, why did she go and die and leave us? I so miss her . . . I know you do, too . . .'

Benedict lit another *Villiger*. Throughout the evening, two pasts had been seeking to invade the present. The first, the years of childhood, oozed slime. The second, the years of adolescence, contained light and warmth. The first had to be kept at bay; otherwise, like all dank matter, it would blight everything that was good.

'Yes . . . And I hoard her zealously.'

'Hoard her?' Melchior smiled. 'What a nice way to put it.'

Melchior's praise elicited a safe memory from Benedict: Eloïse, pre-MS, buxom, dynamic, teaching him the cithara and, as she had once put it, 'the innermost songs of matter and spirit'; then taking him to the Philharmonic and installing him in the wings where he would have a good view of her on the stage so that he could imagine she was playing the harp not as a member of the orchestra but as a soloist solely for him. 'Her music, particularly.'

Melchior nodded. 'Strange. I seldom think of her music. For me, she's just around – always – like a cocoon. Makes sense, I suppose – the way I wanted to stay inside her forever.'

Benedict retrieved another memory. Aged ten or eleven; disturbed, screaming, threshing about. Eloïse's strong arms haul him up and press him to her bosom. He calms down as he stares, mesmerized, at her cheeks which, crowning high bones, look like aureoles. He kneads them. It tickles her. She laughs and kisses his throat.

Melchior proffered his cup.

Benedict poured him another measure. 'Definitely the nightcap, old man. If we're going for the summit, we should get some sleep.'

Melchior savoured a mouthful. 'It was she who saved you, of course.'

'You both.'

'She who spotted you – straightaway. There you all were – assembled in the refectory. An array of broken boys. And she looked at you and said: that one, he's special.'

The years of dankness invaded. An electric drone, now muffled, now sizzling, rammed the soul. A child's shrill protests echoed along dark, institutional corridors: *you're not hurting me, you can't hurt me*.

Melchior nodded solemnly. 'I just followed her example. You couldn't have survived your childhood – not without a miracle. She was the miracle.'

The electric drone consumed light and warmth.

Melchior leaned back and shut his eyes. 'I should tell you, the more we loved you the more we felt tormented.'

Stubbornly, pitiably: *you're not hurting me, you can't hurt me!*

'We refused to believe – suppressed the very thought that we were collaborating in an iniquity, that we were actually keeping an abducted child.'

The child called for his mother and father: *Dei! Dadoro! Save me!*

'So we accepted the anguish – welcomed it – as our punishment. We even thought, perversely, that it gave us the right to make you our own . . .'

The child continued screaming: *no, please, no!*

'And yet, we were prepared to hand you back. And would have. But only to your parents. Not to Pro Juventute.'

Benedict braced himself as phantasmagorical faces surfaced on to the slime. *You are vermin! Pro Juventute took you in to save you! You have no mother, no father, no people! You have been abandoned! Pro Juventute will redeem you! Today, a scum Gypsy; tomorrow, a human being! All this electricity all these convulsions all these locked doors all these punishments all the pain everything everything everything is for your own good!*

'We never felt sure you'd settle down with us. You had run away from all your previous foster-parents. Maybe you don't remember, you used to be very wild . . .'

Benedict nodded grimly. 'I remember.'

'Well, we decided: if you tried to run away from us, it would mean we'd failed in our love. Then, unbearable as it would have been, we'd do the decent thing: hand you back to your parents.'

You have no mother, no father, no people!

'So I befriended someone at Pro Juventute. Fellow called Leo Leo. Also a Gypsy. One of Pro Juventute's success stories. He disclosed details of your background. Tribe: Sinti . . .'

Today, a scum Gypsy; tomorrow, a human being!

'Your father died some time ago. Your mother is still alive.'

'My mother – did you say?'

'Yes.'

Benedict, incoherent from disbelief, joy and panic, muttered. 'My – my – moth . . .? My mo – ther . . .?'

'Yes.'

The child screamed silently as the electricity surged and his jaws locked. *Dei!*

36

Benedict, trying to contain his confusion, forced a smile. 'My mother – still alive?'

'I'm ashamed to say it, she never stopped searching for you . . .'

But my Dei didn't love me! I was unlovable! That's why she abandoned me! I was scum, vermin! That's why they gave me electricity!

'How do you know?'

Suddenly Melchior sounded very tired. 'Leo Leo told me. Her name is Ariana Croz.'

Benedict bit his lips as the name gently echoed from the past. Ariana Croz . . . Yes . . . How fiercely he had tried to cling to that name.

'Why are you telling me all this, old man?'

'You had to know – sooner or later.'

'Why now?'

Melchior pondered a moment. 'It's night. We're talking as father and son should. And mountains always elicit the truth.' He extinguished his cigar, then put away his cup. 'I never asked Leo Leo where your moth . . . – Ariana Croz – lived. Maybe it's time we did. Maybe, one day, we could visit her . . .'

'Visit her?'

'Why not?'

'After all this time . . .?'

'You'd want to, surely . . . Wouldn't you?'

'Yes . . .On the other hand . . . I don't know . . . I can't say . . .'

'Well, we don't have to decide tonight. Let's think on it . . .'

'Yes . . .'

Melchior slid into his sleeping bag. 'I'm ready for my dreams. You?'

'Soon.'

Melchior nodded and closed his eyes. 'Good night, then.'

'Sleep well, old man.'

Benedict puffed at his cigar and stared into the darkness.

Another self stared back. It was the self who had watched over him in the orphanages; who had gathered his feelings and hidden them beyond his reach so that only his body would hurt which wouldn't matter because physical pain, unlike the mind's, was neither unbearable nor fatal. It was also the self who had forced him to stay with Eloïse and Melchior when all he had wanted to do was escape somewhere; who had cajoled him into loving these strange strangers because they were good people, certainly good parents.

And, in effect, he had loved them easily. He had even pretended they really were his parents – though he had never been able to call them 'mother' and 'father'. And he had grown to love them so deeply that he had been unable to leave them – could not leave them even now. Thus, when he had been called up for the army, he had prevailed on Melchior to pull strings so that he could join the old man's unit and by so doing move into a surrogate home. Equally, he had married Nettie not because he had fallen in love with her, but because Eloïse had judged her worthy of love, which he had taken to mean, in need of protection – protection which he could provide by allotting to her chunks of the boundless love he had received from his foster-parents.

Now there was this intruder, his mother – his real, natural mother – a ghost whom he had banished beyond even the reach of his nightmares. Now, this intruder threatened to take on substance and disturb his safe world.

On the other hand, she was a true mother. The mother who had not abandoned him. That was what Melchior had said. The mother still searching for him . . . For him, for her son.

Could he be reckless and abandon vigilance? Could he convince himself – and the other self – that this time there was no danger, that this time there was likely to be joy because it wasn't a child seeking a mother, begging for deliverance, not a despised child whom any mother would have abandoned, but the ever-loving mother welcoming back her son?

Could he be brave? Did he have the spunk? He who always kept away from life's boundaries so that he would never stray to the edges of the world and face the void?

Perhaps Melchior could endow him with the courage as he had endowed him with everything else.

Melchior began to snore.

Benedict stubbed out his cigar, then burrowed into his sleeping bag.

He curled to his side and summoned his oldest friend.

And the naked, mutilated man, who was composed of ashes and whose congealed blood looked like chunks of amber, came and stretched out next to him.

Benedict closed his eyes. He wondered momentarily – because it had become a habit – whether the mutilated man was his ever-watchful other self or his real father or a Samaritan from the dim past or maybe even a spectre from another time or existence. In fact, the man's identity was inconsequential. What was important was that he was his friend; he had appeared – perhaps Benedict himself had conceived him – at Pro Juventute, during the electric shock therapy sessions. And he had never failed to come when called.

The mutilated man stroked Benedict's back and sang an old song about hope that flowed down mountains whilst the burst pomegranate became whole and a donkey ate vital leaves.

Gradually the muffled shrieks and the sizzle of the electricity died down . . .

The summit throbbed. The moon undulated in anticipation. It was the perfect setting for the last consummation in this life and for the first in the next. Melchior laid his head on Eloïse's belly and whispered that she redeemed him daily with the wondrous ways she celebrated her body with him. Eloïse placed his hands on her breasts.

His watch showed midnight. A new day. The perfect time for the new time.

Melchior held his son by the shoulders and asked forgiveness because though Benedict had reached maturity, he was still a child and would be bereft without his father; but please understand, if I wait for death to come, I'll be reduced to a wasteland which is not how I want you to see me die, certainly not how I want to reunite with Eloïse.

Benedict reassured Melchior that he was strong enough to face life alone. And to prove it, he uncurled himself, lay on his back and displayed his face, arms, chest, groin and legs which were bursting with power.

Quickly, Melchior crawled out of the tent, then resealed the flap.

For a moment he gazed at the world dressed in all shades of silver.

Yes, the world said, this is the place, this is the time.

In order not to wake Benedict with the sound of his footsteps on the snow, he rolled down the slope towards the ledge he had chosen. At first, he progressed gently, then, he gathered speed. When the ground levelled and he could roll no further, he pulled himself up and walked to the ledge.

He was barely out of breath. His stride had the power of former times. He was as close to nature as a child in the womb.

He reached the ledge. He could see Zermatt – all lit up. Earth trying to imitate the sky at night.

He stood on the rim of the horizon. The gelid silhouettes of the neighbouring peaks welcomed him with smiles.

He undressed: sweater; second sweater; lumberjack shirt; silk vest; weatherproof trousers; silk long johns; no boots – he had left them in the tent; socks; watch. And here he was. Naked. But for the St Christopher medallion Eloïse had given him, totally naked.

He leaned against the ice-wall and spread out his arms and legs. Eloïse was calling him. He was aroused. The ice was burning him.

When he died, he would slump forward, topple over the ledge, plunge into the snowy expanse, and be entombed like a noble mammoth. He would die, erect for ever.

The cold had the warmth of Eloïse's flesh and invited him to sleep. He shut his eyes. She clasped him.

He told her: this is for us, my love. Because we can't exist without each other. Because I am afraid of death, of the way it degrades the body, the way it robs life of its bravery. This way, I defy death.

Because much as I quarried every vein in my flesh, I have not been fertile, and what is existence without sons and daughters, how can there be survival, continuity, a family stretching forever and forever, without getting rid of dead wood?

And mostly because, though we stole a son who should be making babies and giving us grandsons and granddaughters, he's not doing it and this is the way to make him do it, the ancient way, the time-honoured way, the way of all people, which is the surrendering of one life so that there can be room for another. I die, my Eloïse, so that in death we can make a child for Benedict; so that he, in turn, can give birth to us.

Routed in the battle of the Gobi desert, Adam begged for peace.

Rom obeyed the meditations of his heart and agreed.

Thus ended the first five hundred years of war between Rom and Adam.

The East whirled with great celebrations. Wise men and women, kings and queens, sorceresses and warlocks, minstrels and acrobats, journeyed to Rom's caravan to honour him. They feasted on roasted lamb, warm bread and raw onions. They drank wine and sheep's milk.

The West wilted. In pursuit of hatred, Adam had forgotten matters of husbandry. His people, unloved and solitary, quarrelled with each other. They scrounged for rodents, bark and grass. They drank stagnant water and snake blood.

And Adam, angry with the world and with himself, commanded Ahitofel, his best blade-man, to steal into the East and there slay Rom.

Now it came to pass that Rom's Brahmin disciples, Melchior, the king of light, Gaspar, the magnolia rajah, and Balthazar, the lord of treasures, prevailed on him to take a wife and beget children. And they asked for maidens to come forth as candidates.

40

For forty days, all the single women of the East, escorted by their mothers and matchmakers, converged on Romanestan. They camped on fields strewn with gold, frankincense and myrrh.

On the summer solstice, Rom arrived to choose his bride.

Ahitofel had been waiting for this occasion to execute his foul deed. Disguised in feminine garb, painted face and a wig of long tresses, he emerged stealthily from behind a line of young women and unsheathed his treble-honed misericord.

But on the Summer Solstice the sun is Argos-eyed. It instantly spotted the sheen on Ahitofel's blade and reflected it to the Brahmins.

Melchior, an acrobat in his youth, proved the swiftest of the three Brahmins. At the very moment that Ahitofel threw the dagger, he ran forward and shielded Rom with his body.

Ahitofel fled upon a mule.

Gaspar waved his hand and transformed the assassin's wig of long tresses into tough lianas.

Balthazar exhaled fiercely and raised a hurricane.

The gale caught Ahitofel's wig and wrapped its strands on to the branches of an oak tree. Thus he was hanged.

Melchior expired in Rom's arms. O Del Himself gave him the kiss of quietus. He was the seventh person in all Creation to be honoured thus.

Melchior became the kapparah – which means forgiveness – for all the generations begat by Rom.

Two

Five flasks of brandy had not sufficed to free Melchior's body from the ice-wall. Benedict had had to urinate on him.

PLEASE FORGIVE ME, BENEDICT.

He had started searching at dawn, immediately after waking up and finding the note tucked between the old man's boots. Written in capital letters, an idiosyncrasy Melchior had developed through his passion for calligraphy, it had obviously been composed before they had started the climb; not last night, on an impulse.

He had assumed that the old man had slipped out at about first light – when sleep, according to army manuals, was heaviest – so that Benedict would not hear him go. Since this would have meant only about an hour's exposure to the elements, Benedict had not expected to find Melchior frozen to death. Hypothermic, yes, and possibly injured; but alive.

I WON'T LEAVE MY SHIT BEHIND.

It had not taken him long to find the naked figure on the ledge and to realize that Melchior had set out early in the night and that he had planned the suicide meticulously.

Which had explained last night's drinking – and the painful conversation.

I THOUGHT IT BEST TO RETURN TO ORIGINAL MATTER.

Whatever last rites Melchior had performed, he had expected, as his apotheosis, the fulfilment of a romantic fantasy. Many mountaineers shared it. Death by sudden dislocation, like a rock breaking loose. The roll into the chasm. A brief and interminable free-fall in uncontaminated air. Instant and permanent dematerialization in a snow Elysium. The slow but relentless journey as a glacier. And the emergence in primordial and future Ice Ages as a redoubtable yeti.

PLEASE UNDERSTAND.

However, against naked flesh ice acts like glue. Consequently, the old man had been deprived of his classic demise.

But death would have been painless – like falling asleep.

And Benedict would have to live with the horror of having had to piss on his father in order to peel him off the serac.

THIS IS THE ONLY TIME I HAVE WRONGED YOU KNOWINGLY.

Whilst swaddling him, Benedict had surveyed Melchior's features. Fine skin. Solid muscles. Barrel chest. Lean belly. Uncannily youthful. Eliciting the shocking feeling that the old man was, in fact, his son. A feeling enhanced by Melchior's ebbed, boyish penis and his tiny, shrivelled testicles – as forlorn in death as they must have been in life. And further affirmed by Benedict's relief that his own genitalia were of an acceptable size.

FOR THE REST, ELOÏSE AND I LOVED YOU TOTALLY – THAT YOU KNOW.

Then the guilt. Sudden, yet unsurprising, as if he had had a sense of it all his life: the father who is the son's son is like a fledgling, therefore, vulnerable.

Why hadn't he protected Melchior? Why hadn't he saved him by chasing death off the mountain? Where had he been when the boy Melchior, his son, had gone out to die? What had he been doing?

Gleefully playing with his cocky cock?

FAREWELL, MY SON. MEND THE WORLD. FULFIL YOURSELF.

In a trance after that. Pulling the old man off the ledge, wrapping him up in a blanket, using the tent as a stretcher, roping him and lowering him down the ridge, dragging him to the cable car at Schwartzee and telephoning the emergency services. A text-book exercise in alpine rescue.

Cradling him whilst the cable car descended to Zermatt and the ambulance, dispersing the electric floats and horse-drawn sleighs, sped to hospital. Surrendering the old man to the morgue. Statements to the police, sundry officials, journalists. Failing to answer, or even make sense, of the question: why should Herr Füssli . . .?

Eventually, turning hostile and monosyllabic. Yes, suicide. Yes, planned. Yes, he left a note. And feeling treacherous for divulging the information.

PLEASE FORGIVE ME, BENEDICT.

Finally, late at night. Standing on one of the bridges on the river, staring at the mountain's moonlit silhouette and shouting. No, Melchior. No, old man. I won't forgive you. I loved you, too. I can forgive Eloïse. Illness has no mercy. But you? Choosing her instead of me! How could you? I haven't been with you long enough! We haven't talked, laughed, cried long enough – not nearly enough! Forgive you? Never!

Then breaking down. Why can't the son, too, return to original matter? Why can't the son, too, return to his father?

And it came to pass that O Del put the patriarch to the test. 'Rom!', He called.

And Rom replied: 'Here I am!'

O Del said, 'Take now your son, your only son, Branko, whom you love, and go to the sacred mountain and there offer him as a sacrifice.'

So Rom rose up early in the morning, saddled his donkey, took with him his son and journeyed to the sacred mountain.

On the third day Rom lifted up his sad eyes and O Del showed him the site for the sacrifice. And Rom collected the wood and laid it on his shoulders. And he gave the fire and the knife to his son.

Branko spoke unto Rom. 'Father?'

Rom answered, 'What is it, my son?'

Branko asked, 'Here is the wood, the fire and the knife, but where is the creature for the offering?'

Rom answered, 'O Del himself will provide him, my son.'

And they came to the place of sacrifice. And Rom built the altar and arranged the wood. Then he lifted up his sad eyes again and saw a thicket by some terebinth trees. He said to Branko, 'Go yonder, lad. There you will find the creature.'

Branko went to the thicket. And there he saw Rom, caught by his arms and legs.

Rom said, 'Branko, my son, my only son, whom I love, I am the creature for sacrifice. Put me on the altar.'

Branko obeyed him and laid him upon the wood.

Rom said, 'Now, slay me with a clean cut on the throat. Then set fire to the wood. Let O Del see what He has asked has been given.'

'I will not kill my father,' protested Branko and placed the knife against his own throat.

And O Del called to them out of Heaven. 'Branko! Rom! Rom! Branko!'

'Here we are!' they answered.

O Del said, 'Wait!' And He began to descend from Heaven.

Rom seized the fire and shouted: 'You will not make me slay my son, O Del! But You shall have Your sacrifice!' And swiftly he immolated himself.

And as Branko saw his father burn, all his blood was drained from his hands. And all Rom's blood flooded into Branko's hands to make him whole again. For a father's love lives beyond death.

O Del arrived and wailed. 'Oh, this is a grievous sight!', He said to Branko. 'Verily, you and your father have taught Me how to be God. I must renounce sacrifice. I must mend Creation so that life is always preserved for its full span and never used for appeasement. Verily, you two have taught Me that any God who demands blood must be disobeyed. Behold, I am a God who is able to beg forgiveness – I do so now. And I swear by My Own Self that I will multiply your seed as the stars of the Heaven and as the sand which is upon the seashore. And in your seed shall all the nations of the earth be blessed.'

Branko took Rom's ashes and invested Ganga, the weaver of the thalassic currents, with them. Thus Rom's spirit, sailing the oceans, always washes the land of Romanestan. And the tribes see that patriarchs entrusted to water flow forever in their people's blood.

Three

The funeral reception is an affectation that does not become the Swiss, the old man had said when they had buried Eloïse. It is kitsch inherited from Teutonic death worship. What we should do is withdraw from the living for a time, immure ourselves in a cave or some such place. After all, we are tough mountain people, lusty and mystic, hard-fighting and soft-hearted; when we are touched by the grave, we are inconsolable.

Why didn't you tell me you were dying, old man?

Nettie, slaloming through the salon with a dish of vol-au-vents, caught Benedict's eye and smiled sympathetically. Moving on, she urged the guests to taste the spicy filling, an innovation, she declared, which confirmed the caterers as the best in the canton.

Benedict's gaze lingered on Nettie: glorious frame, wonderful buttocks, athletic legs.

Why haven't you got a child yet?

Why did you abandon me?

He stepped out on to the balcony.

In the distance, Lake Zurich, reflecting the sun, looked like a celestial mirror.

These Swiss gathered here for your send-off, Melchior, are neither lusty nor soft-hearted. They are parasites, gnomes who thrive on dingy pursuits. See, funerals are their natural environment. Look at them guzzling dead-man's fare as if it were their favourite feed.

Why so bitter, Benedict? Bitterness murmurs deep fear.

I am an orphan, old man. Again.

Young Dr Glanz came out on to the balcony, lit a cigarette and inhaled it with relish.

Benedict joined him. 'Why didn't you tell me he was dying, Nicholas?'

Glanz shook his head sheepishly. 'He said he would tell you. He said you two had a lot to sort out . . .'

'He'd settled everything long ago.'

Glanz looked mystified. 'But he had the tests only recently.'

'Could he have known he was dying? Before the tests?'

Glanz nodded sadly. 'It's possible.'

Benedict gazed at the Limmat valley. 'Cancer. Exploding everywhere, you said. Suddenly? Out of the blue? How, Nicholas?'

'It happens. Grief, very likely . . .'

'Surely he could have had some treatment . . .'

'A few months – that's all he had left. A few months of wasting away.'

I won't leave my shit behind.

'He could still climb, for God's sake!'

'On sheer guts. Typical of him.'

Something ate the air . . .

'Now that I know . . . I'm glad he went that way. Proud of him, in fact . . .'

Glanz nodded; tears appeared in his eyes.

Benedict, also lachrymose, turned his attention to the gathering. It comprised the duty brigades from Melchior's department, Benedict's firm and Nettie's faculty. None of the lusty fellows with whom Melchior had skied, climbed, soldiered and drunk. Those old-timers had solemnized the burial, but delicately side-stepped the reception; they would visit Benedict separately.

But, mercifully, Young Glanz was here. Young Dr Glanz – in his early sixties – was a permanent fixture with the family. Lovable and devoted, he was one of those tireless, overweight, chain-smoking, dishevelled doctors marked for a premature coffin who still believed that there was a simple remedy for all the diseases and that, one day, someone, somewhere, would discover it.

Young Glanz had looked after the Füsslis for some twenty-five years. Each time death had come to appraise Eloïse, he had stood shoulder to shoulder with Melchior. He had also risked daily electrocution whilst deactivating, inch by inch, the supercharged worm of the Pro Juventute years that used to scorch Benedict's innards.

'Nicholas – did the old man talk to you about my . . . mother . . .? My real mother – Ariana Croz? The Gypsy . . .'

Glanz hesitated a moment. 'Yes.'

'What did he say?'

'Mostly how guilty he and Eloïse felt. They could love you and keep you, whilst she . . .'

'Did you meet her?'

'What for?'

'Melchior might have asked you. He himself didn't dare . . .'

'Actually, he very nearly did meet her . . .'

'Really?'

'Oh, long ago – some twenty years back . . .'

'Tell me.'

'He found out she – Ariana Croz – was trying to go on pilgrimage to the shrine of Black Sara, the Gypsies' patron saint. That's in the Camargue, in France, a town called Les Saintes Maries de la Mer. She was going to pray for your return. Black Sara is famous for her miracles.'

'I see.'

'Melchior decided he would turn pilgrim, too, and offer the saint a counter prayer. But Ariana Cr – your mother – couldn't go. She couldn't find the money. So he stayed put.'

'He should have offered her the money!' Benedict forced a smile. 'Sorry. Stupid thing to say.'

Glanz lit a fresh cigarette. 'Matter of fact, he considered it. He was not one to believe in miracles, but the thought of Black Sara passing a Solomonic judgement appealed to him. Given his and Eloïse's devotion to you, he argued, the verdict was bound to be in his favour. Basically, he wanted to assuage his guilt.'

'Well, then . . .?'

'Superstition defeated reason. He feared that Black Sara, being Gypsy herself, might intercede on your mother's behalf. Eloïse was most relieved, I can tell you.'

Benedict smiled grimly. 'So privilege triumphed over justice.'

Glanz nodded. 'Doesn't it always?'

Benedict watched Nettie showing Dagmar and Ilse, her colleagues from the university, the photographs which Melchior had put on display everywhere in the house – photographs uninhibitedly proclaiming that the old man and Eloïse had been indissoluble.

'Do you know where she lives – my mother?'

Glanz shook his head. 'I preferred not to know. Melchior respected that – and never told me.'

Dagmar and Ilse were smiling. Patronizingly. Dagmar and Ilse did not believe in indissoluble relationships. Nor in family units as the preferable environment for children. Dagmar and Ilse were today's wise women; they classified husbands and lovers as mere clones of the archetypal brutal father. God only knew what Nettie saw in them. Thank God, she wasn't like them.

All this rage, Benedict. I thought Eloïse and I had drained you of it.

You shouldn't have died, old man!

'That night on the mountain, Melchior said we should visit her. Meaning, I suppose, I should. Should I?'

Glanz looked perturbed. 'I – I don't know . . .'

'Would you, if you were me?'

'No.'

'Why not?'

'It would only multiply your pain.'

Benedict pondered a moment, then squeezing Glanz's shoulder, moved back into the sitting room.

Nettie had now been accosted by Gunther, famous industrialist, Third World specialist, campaigner for ecological awareness, advocate of nuclear power – safe nuclear power – and, according to a media besotted by immaculately coifed, solarium-tanned, arrogant men reeking of *Aramis*, a charismatic personage. Gunther was Dagmar's latest escort, a devout male chauvinist pig whom, she had sworn, she would reduce to a little boy and then break across her knees.

Nettie was telling Gunther about that dire holiday in Bali and her concern for ancient cultures that were systematically being raped by the juggernaut of Western civilization.

Benedict listened. Disregarding the two clichés, 'rape' and 'juggernaut', obviously contracted from Dagmar and Ilse, Nettie was as eloquent as ever. What was happening to ancient cultures was what had always happened to them: greed and expediency destroying refinement and melting down into junk all that was irreplaceable. Except that now it was happening wholesale. Those countries trying to resist were being gelded by economic pressure. Others, the majority, had been bought off. The rest did not care.

Benedict refilled his glass with brandy. He, too, Gypsy and misfit, did not care. Why?

The old man was right, I've taken a wrong turn somewhere, lost sight of what's essential, what to do, what I was born to do. I just sit in my tent and nurse my anger, spit bitter platitudes. Meanwhile people die in their millions, taking with them their wares and jewellery and embroidery, their wisdom and rituals and words, their songs and poems and images. Soon, unless a new Moses comes, there will be nothing left anywhere – only ashes.

Nettie, head thrown back, her muscular thighs almost bursting out of her skirt, waltzed away from Gunther.

Benedict craved for her.

Why haven't you got a child yet?

She doesn't want to, old man.

Nonsense!

Maybe she doesn't love me enough.

Who says?

Have you ever known her to hunger for me? Can you imagine her jumping on me and sitting on my face?

Make her!

How, old-timer? She wants her man to be all things male: husband, lover, brother, father, son. Can I, a caged Gypsy with seared brains, perform such roles?

Yes!

What if she's holding back because I'm a Gypsy?

Don't be a fool!

Not to ask: why should she love me when everybody else – including you – abandons me? When I, too, but for my bloody-mindedness, would abandon myself?

Can't answer, can you, old man?

Nettie kicked off her shoes, slumped on to the settee and stretched her toes. Scrutinizing her muscled calves, she regretted, as she often did, abandoning ballet classes after the *lycée*. The cushions on the armchair need rearranging. Do it later. Sit. Rest a moment.

She checked her watch: past nine. They should go home. She hadn't prepared anything for dinner. Eat out. No, there were leftovers from the reception.

But they ought to go soon. Benedict should lock up Melchior's house now, whilst the adrenaline was still flowing. Later, as he faced the finality of death, he would be drained.

She turned round to call him. He had gone out on to the balcony again. Without a coat. How come he never felt the cold? His Gypsy blood?

She stared at his neck – thick and solid. So incongruous with his sinewy body. A rough-neck, someone had once jested. But she loved his neck, found it erotic. She had often teased herself that she would rather have his neck inside her than his cock. His neck always looked worldly, replete, serene; whereas his cock constantly stalked – foraged not only for all the goodness she could give him, but also for all those she could not, not to mention his countless other needs which she always failed to detect.

She watched him light a cigar. The match briefly illuminated his face. Such a striking man. So masculine – in repose. But, much of the time, so indecipherable.

She still did not know how to cope with his restlessness. There were times when she feared it would steal him away from her. Casually. Like in her early teens when her brother had kept swimming further and further out, until one day, that dot on the lake had disappeared into the horizon.

Does he love me? Does he know how much I love him?

We should go. 'Benedict . . .'

He didn't hear. Let him finish smoking.

Restlessness – at times turning into disquiet – was to be expected from someone who has been institutionalized, Young Glanz had once told her when she had sought his advice. Such a person cannot inhabit himself; all the shelters inside him have been devastated by his years in the orphanages. Thus, he is deprived of an inner sanctum where he can lick his wounds, get strong, get to like himself. He is forced to search, often desperately, for a place where there is an imposed order and, by the same token, safety. Of course, such a place is but another institution. Then, when the person matures and sees more of life, his difficulties compound. Each experience becomes a new threat. He has to neutralize these threats, reduce them into orderly concerns. He does so by dividing his whole existence – job, army, even family – into manageable institutions.

Benedict started singing.

Nettie looked up sharply. One of his own songs. Dedicated to Eloïse who had made him study the cithara, his people's favourite instrument – or so she had claimed. She had made him believe that, as a Gypsy, music was in his blood. All his compositions had been dedicated to her.

Maybe one day he'll dedicate one to me. Maybe another day he'll publish them instead of keeping them to himself. They are beautiful songs: lyrical and sad.

A wife, too, becomes an institution.

Was that why we seldom talk about his roots? Certainly never seriously about his Gypsy origins. I always thought we were letting sleeping dogs lie.

Now, I tend to agree with Young Glanz: he wants to compartmentalize his life; and I collude. Give unto each institution what belongs to it; then lock it up so that, in isolation, it remains intact.

Institutions are interchangeable; wives can be replaced. I think that's what really scares me.

Being scared doesn't help. Benedict needs me more than ever now. Melchior's death devastated him. He's trying not to show it. But it will take him ages to put himself together again. Keep loving him. Mother him.

I've been doing that since we first met. I'm always trying to contain him. I'm forever running around him so that I can smooth him out. But does he let me? He's either immediately amorous or else slips away to do something else. Why can't he see how good it is when I cuddle him, when we don't rush to devour each other, how the slow boat to bed makes me so eager for sex?

Does he love me? Does he know how much I love him?

'Why haven't we got a child yet?' He sat down next to her.

He had startled her by coming in so quietly. She ran her hand over his high cheekbones and flat, oriental nose. He looked so forlorn. 'We have one. You.'

He kissed the tips of her fingers. 'Seriously.'

She stared into his eyes. 'Would it change anything?'

He got up and stubbed out his cigar. 'What do you mean?'

She rose also and put on her shoes. 'Would it lighten your heart? Would it bring us closer? Or would you just take the child and run off into the sunset?'

'What a strange thing to say . . .'

'Is it?'

'What sunset?'

She gave him a wry smile and rearranged the cushions on the armchair. Then she went into the kitchen and came out carrying a plastic bag with the left-over food. 'Let's go.'

He had paused in front of a photograph of Melchior and Eloïse. Tears were gathering in his eyes. 'We must have a child!'

She put her arm into his. 'We will. One day.'

And it came to pass that Tara, a beautiful maiden with seven eyes, became the protector of travellers. Whenever people took to their caravans, she charted a safe course for them.

Eve, hearing of her popularity, became maddened by jealousy. And she changed Tara into a hyena and condemned her to roam the wilderness and attack humankind.

One day, Tara came upon the heath where Branko was shepherding. She prepared to pounce on him.

Then she heard him sing. It was a voice that coaxed water out of rock, turned serpents into rods and healed plagues. It banished the evil spell Eve had cast over her.

And, reunited with her good soul, Tara desired to make her face shine upon Branko, to journey and set up tent with him and to bear him children. But as she went forth, she caught her reflection on the dew; she saw that, though, in spirit, she was herself again, in the flesh, she had retained the hyena's body. So she withdrew and kept herself hidden.

She became Branko's hearth-maker. Without ever letting him see her, she transformed his cave dwelling into a mansion of many rooms. When Branko returned home after his day's work, he walked into light, warmth and humming butterflies. When he sat at his table, he found ambrosia to keep him young and nectar to sharpen his faculties. When he lay down to sleep, pillows like shapely buttocks induced virile dreams.

And all that time he waited for his mysterious hearth-maker to make herself known.

One day, Eve looked to see how Tara was faring. As she observed her happily keeping house for Branko, her jealousy rekindled. This time, she sowed poisoned thorn-bush around Branko's mansion.

When, later, Tara set out for her hide-out, she became entangled in the thorn-bush; and her wounds instantly suppurated.

And Branko, returning home, found her thus. And seeing her not as she was in herself, but as a hyena, he drew his knife.

But the humming butterflies whirled before his eyes and begged him to spare her.

Branko took pity on Tara; he plucked out the thorns from her flesh and healed her of the poison.

That night, Tara fled to the woodlands, resolved that Branko would never see her beast's aspect again.

Branko waited for forty years. But Tara did not return. She had resumed safeguarding Romany camps and river crossings.

So Branko abandoned his hearth.

No one knows where he now roams.

Four

Benedict had entered the administration wing of Pro Juventute's principal orphanage only once before: when Eloïse and Melchior had come to finalize the adoption formalities and take him home.

He had kept, he had thought, a clear memory of the occasion: Eloïse and Melchior looking awkward; the orphanage's faceless director prattling officiously; and he, himself, feeling inconspicuous in the opulent offices whilst desperately trying to figure out how he had attracted this gentle couple's interest that first time they had seen him – in the refectory, Melchior had said; but surely there had been a line-up before that – so that he could repeat the behaviour and make sure they did not change their minds.

That memory, he could now see, had evolved from the imaginings of a traumatized child for whom any room other than a corner in an institution, any furniture other than a stool, had represented the world of the privileged. Nothing in this building had the stamp of an august organization. 'Reception', as this chamber was called, was as perfunctory as the cruelty the foundation had propagated over its Gypsy charges.

'Ariana Croz . . . Yes, this is it . . .' Leo Leo brought out a fading dossier from the filing cabinet.

Benedict, too restless to sit down, moved to the window.

It was here, in the early twenties, that Pro Juventute, at the time one of Switzerland's most respectable charities for children, had evolved its racist policies for Gypsies. From here, guided by one Alfred Siegfried, an advocate of eugenics, it had launched, in 1926, 'Operation Children of the Roads'.

Thereafter, with the declared intention of extirpating nomadism in

Switzerland – and by so doing eradicating all deviant elements in the country – this mission had culled, often by abduction, some 700 Travellers' children, mainly Jenisch and Gypsy, and subjected them to a rehabilitation programme devised to resettle them as acceptable members of society. Much of this programme, conducted in cloistered orphanages, had entailed crude indoctrination until such time as the children could be consigned to foster-parents or offered for adoption.

Invariably, treatment, both in the orphanages and by foster-parents, had been harsh. A few, like Benedict, had had the good fortune to end up with caring families.

Those Gypsies and Travellers who had sought to reclaim their children had foundered in official or legal labyrinths; children who had clamoured for their parents had been told either that they had been abandoned or that their parents had died. Only in 1971, by virtue of one mother's persistent search for her child, had these iniquities come to light.

Initially, the foundation had denied the accusations of abduction; but, in 1973, having failed to assuage public outrage, it had quietly terminated 'Operation Children of the Roads'.

'I remember her well . . .' Leo Leo was riffling through the file. 'Used to besiege us. Twice a month. On the first and the fifteenth.'

'Used to – when?'

'Until we shut our doors – when the hullabaloo started.'

'That was five years ago. She could be dead now.'

Leo Leo shook his head. 'We'd have known. And we'd have closed the file.'

Benedict felt a surge of joy. All these years since his adoption, he had reduced Ariana Croz to a discarnate, astral mother; now, he could reconstitute her into substance.

Simultaneously, he was seized by fear of failure. Was he capable of recreating a relationship with his mother? Could he regenerate the devotion? Did he want to? Would he not have preferred just to claim her remains, as he had fantasized, and reinter them with lavish exequies in the Füssli family plot?

The fear teamed up with that pernicious inner voice which, panic-stricken by the prospect of an endless commitment, had been drumming a vile refrain: stop this crazy search, you don't need your natural mother, you had Eloïse, the perfect mother.

What say you, old man?

Don't weaken!

'She'd sit downstairs – in the waiting room. Until someone agreed to see her.' Leo Leo smoothed his long, silver hair. 'That often meant myself . . .'

Melchior, who had painstakingly befriended Leo Leo, had kept a meticulous dossier on the Pro Juventute executive. According to one of his notes, Leo Leo had been inspired to style his hair like a lion's mane in homage to his Christian name; this affectation had so gratified him that he had proceeded to change his surname, by deed poll, to echo the first.

Strange turn of events that Melchior's Leo Leo should turn out to be Leo Rominger, a warden during the eternities Benedict had been incarcerated in this orphanage.

'I used to tell her. Your son has been adopted. We don't know where he is. She'd weep and nod as if she'd understood. Two weeks later she'd be back.'

'Some people never learn.'

Leo Leo missed the sarcasm. 'Pitiable. I was often tempted to give her your address.'

'You should have.'

'Rules, Benedict. You don't mind me calling you Benedict? Sounds better than Groz . . .'

'I don't mind.'

'As I was saying . . . Rules . . .'

'Are there to be broken.'

Leo Leo stared at him intensely. 'Coming from a Swiss officer, that's heresy. Where rules are broken only chaos reigns.'

Rominger's dramatic change since his days as warden was not restricted to the length and colour of his hair. He had also acquired what could best be described as a hefty atomic weight. He looked immensely assured – even arrogant – and well armoured. Yet he still parroted the old canon.

'Better chaos than bad rules, Leo.'

Leo Leo put Ariana Croz's file back into the cabinet. 'Ah, the old defiance.'

Rominger was a Gypsy. And he was Pro Juventute's pride and joy. Forcibly removed from his parents at the age of ten, he had been the first to acclaim his rehabilitation; it had transformed him from an asocial, deviant barbarian into a good, sedentary Swiss – or so he had told Melchior.

'Some of us don't change.'

Leo Leo moved to his desk, shaking his head vigorously; the gesture sent his mane billowing. 'You're wrong there, Benedict. We all change.'

Benedict had forgotten the man's size. Over two metres. And well built.

Pity that such an imposing figure should be so misguided.

Leo Leo paused before a wall crammed with the yearly group photographs of children and staff. He gazed at them for a moment, then pointed at a few. 'You're in four of these – did you know?'

Benedict nodded. He had made a point of ignoring them.

Leo Leo looked forlorn. 'If you go by these pictures, we look more or less the same. Physically, people don't change all that much. But inside, we change all the time.'

Interpreting Leo Leo's distraction as a troubled spirit, Benedict mellowed. Perhaps, having compromised a great deal, Leo Leo secretly yearned for redemption.

To be fair, Leo Leo had not always been servile. On many occasions he had valiantly defended his charges; sometimes he had contrived to prolong work periods so that they missed the 'treatment' sessions. One year, he had even prevailed on the administrators to explore the possibilities of containing the children's turbulence with outdoor activities instead of the electro-convulsive therapy. In fact, it had been during that interlude, whilst trying to impress Rominger, who had been an excellent cross-country skier, that Benedict had discovered his talents for that sport.

Leo Leo sat at his desk, readjusted his jacket, straightened the creases in his trousers and picked up a card index. 'I file addresses separately.'

Beneath the desk, his shoes shone like windows at sunset. Because he was a bachelor, Melchior had further observed, narcissism might well be Leo Leo's sole source of affection.

Benedict gazed into the garden.

It was one of those early spring days when the trees could be seen painting their blossom. The flower beds promised a perfumed, tender summer; the lawn was already spuming with daisies. Yet he would always view this garden as an occult place where colour and birdsong had been strangled, where the only sound heard had been the tinnitus of alternating current, the only smell that of temples scorched by electrodes.

One Christmas, by the cloister there, four orderlies had pinned him down and made him eat mud to demonstrate how they would punish him if he tried to escape again.

Between those two poplars, he had beaten the shit out of Artur, the bully. His knuckle still bore the scars where Artur's broken teeth had stuck.

By that rosebush, one night, thinking of Mathilde, the cleaner, whose wide thighs, when she scrubbed the floor, were bliss to behold, he had masturbated for the first time. Then, having waited some ten minutes to be struck dead, he had rushed back to the dormitory and masturbated again, this time in front of his mates, to show them that, contrary to dogma, masturbation was not a sin God punished instantly with blindness. Thereafter, every boy, whether he could produce semen or not, had performed the ritual daily.

And near the enclosure wall, by the hives – God, this place has not changed at all – he had once fumigated the bees and collected the honey without wearing any protective clothing, just for a dare.

Leo Leo found the pertinent card. 'Here we are . . . Ariana Croz . . .' He wrote down the address on a sheet of paper. 'Speaking of rules: normally we don't give information about parents to their children. But, in this case, since Croz is one of Melchior's beneficiaries, I must . . .' He placed the paper on Benedict's side of the desk.

Benedict went across, pocketed the paper and turned towards the door. 'Thank you.'

'Before you go . . .Something I ought to tell you, Benedict . . .'

Benedict faced Leo Leo. 'Yes?'

'For many years, your mother – Croz – tried to go on pilgrimage. To Les Saintes Maries de la Mer. She was going to plead for a miracle to get you back.'

'I heard. She couldn't find the money.'

'Fate is invariably wise.'

'Meaning?'

Leo Leo took out a set of gold-plated cigarette case, lighter and holder. 'You're one of my old boys, Benedict. Melchior was a person I held in great esteem. So I'm being forthright. Let the past rest in peace.'

Benedict bridled. 'You're being patronizing!'

'Think of your mother! You, yourself, might cope – conceivably. She'd be totally lost.'

Benedict edged back to the window. 'I am thinking of her! She'll have a better life! She'll be transformed!'

Leo Leo inserted a cigarette into the holder, then lit it. 'You'll unleash countless problems. For her. And her community.'

'What community?'

'She'd be living with other members of her tribe – maybe a group like a *kumpania*. They won't know what to do, how to receive you.'

'Why?'

Leo Leo drew deeply on his cigarette. 'Because you're no longer one of them. You've escaped. To all intents and purposes, you're a *gadjo*! Antiseptic! You can even pass off your dark skin as deep tan!'

Benedict was shocked. Was that what he was: a whitewashed Gypsy? Sterilized of mind and soul and, therefore, acceptable to the world? 'You make me sound a traitor.'

'Not a traitor. A new Gypsy. A modern Gypsy.'

Benedict caught sight of a person in overalls scurrying through the garden. He watched as the man opened a barred door and went into the adjoining wing.

The dormitories were in that wing; and beyond, at the far end, stood the infirmary which a wit had named 'Shangri-La'.

'Shangri-La' was where they had broiled his brains, where he had left the skin of his hands trying to tunnel his way out.

'Leave my mother to rot – is that what you're saying?'

'There are other ways of helping her – and our people.'

'Sure. Change the world!'

Leo Leo, ignoring Benedict's acerbity, smoothed his hair. 'The world will never change. It can't. It belongs to the *gadje*. But we can. All we need do is abandon our ways.'

'Why should we?'

'The world hates us, Benedict. East, west, north, south – wherever you go. They see us, forgive the jargon, as 'the other': the eternal pariahs, dehumanized beings. In fact, we're the 'other' by which all 'others' are judged.'

'We don't have to accept that!'

'No. But what can we do? For almost a thousand years, since we left India – apart from a brief period when we tricked Europe into thinking we had escaped from the clutches of Islam – we've been persecuted. First, we offended with our dark complexion. So they banished us to the countryside. Then they decided they didn't like our ways either: they couldn't believe – understand – that we weren't interested in power, greed, conflict, subjugation, that our gods teach us to worship life not death. Consequently, they forbade us land and forced us into nomadism. So we became children of the rainbow. Which made them hate us all the more. And fear us twice as much. How, unless we were demons, they told themselves, could we live happily on fresh air and two ears of corn, how could we continue to hold wife, children, elders and Nature sacred and, above all, feel free as the wind? So they enslaved us and, when possible – which was most of the time – they hanged us and quartered us and incinerated us. And, finally, under the Nazis, they classified us as asocial and tried to exterminate us. Today, we're still not considered a people. Today, they claim we don't exist – and, to all intents and purposes, we don't. Or rather, we exist without having an existence!'

'As I said: we don't have to accept that.'

'I agree. Yet the question remains. What can we do? We don't have the luxury of options. In fact, we only have one course of action: we must abandon our ways. Then we can have liberty, equality, prosperity and the rest.'

'Integration, that's what you're proposing. What chance – given the *gadje*'s prejudices against us?'

'Not integration. Assimilation. Acculturation.'

'What's the difference?'

'Integration means fusing identity, race, even religion and culture. It means evolving in such a way that you're always a butterfly, never a larva. It means freedom from fear. Nations can't handle that. They're governed by minutiae. To these minutiae they attach untold fears. And these fears make them feel rooted and safe. Integration is a utopian dream.'

'One people, one world – the vision is gaining ground.'

'Only among the flower people – or what's left of them.'

'Don't be so sure!'

'I know what I'm talking about, Benedict. But when it comes to assimilation, we can make a very good case.'

'Such as?'

'Assimilation demands tolerable coexistence. It's pragmatic, not utopian. Therefore, achievable. This country itself provides proof that people of different races, religions and languages can live together without sacrificing their identities.'

There had been references to Leo Leo's activities in the endless campaign for Gypsy rights in Melchior's notes. In fact, initially, during his university years, Leo Leo had been an ardent advocate of integration. His doctoral dissertation, which he had offered as a manifesto for this policy, had posited that integration, particularly the transformation of misfit ethnic communities into decent citizens, would need paternalist policies similar to those of Pro Juventute – a stance that had secured for him permanent employment with the foundation.

The reactions from Gypsies to these views, particularly from traditionalist leaders who maintained that any contact with the *gadje*, let alone coexistence, would inflict upon the Gypsy the condition of *marimé*, defilement, had caused him to suffer a nervous breakdown. Thus, he had been unable to participate in the creation of the Comité International Tsigane, in Paris, in 1965.

But fully fit again by 1971, when that committee had organized the first World Romany Congress in England, he had made his long-awaited international debut.

His views on integration, by then even more heavily shaded with Pro Juventute canon, his cursory dismissal of the *marimé* taboos as 'antediluvian obscurantism' had caused a furore. Forced to slink away – 'like the proverbial prophet scorned by his own people', as he had remarked to Melchior – he had, thereafter, pursued the more practicable solutions of assimilation and acculturation.

A few years back, still refusing to join the various Gypsy organizations that had come into existence after the congress in England, he had finally set up his own association in order to propagate those ends.

Assimilation, when winnowed from Pro Juventute drivel, appeared an attractive, even laudable, objective. But Benedict felt more attuned to the views of the mainstream Gypsy organizations.

'Assimilation is as unattainable as integration. As you said, we live in the *gadje*'s world where the so-called purity of the white man's blood and his immutable supremacy are commandments. Commingling with so-called lesser breeds, particularly Gypsies, is anathema to them.'

'That's because we're not trying hard enough. We must become like the *gadje*, embrace their dreams and, if need be, their prejudices. Now and again we'll have to eat shit. So what? Everybody does – even the Swiss!'

'And hide our lights wherever we can? Live invisibly?'

'When necessary, yes. Getting accepted is the objective!'

'Some objective.'

'Don't mock it! Look at me! That's exactly what I've achieved! And I did it without any of your privileges!'

Benedict was piqued. 'Privileges?'

Leo Leo stubbed out his cigarette. 'No family adopted me. I was either too dark or too big or too good to be true or too something . . . Too old, eventually . . .'

Benedict felt sorry for him. 'I see. Yes . . .'

Jauntily, Leo Leo adjusted his cuffs. 'Don't get me wrong. I consider myself lucky. My parents were monsters. That's what happens to people crushed by poverty and persecution. Pro Juventute offered me salvation and I grabbed it. I worked hard. Made myself strong. I remoulded our inmates – even increased the intake . . .'

'With more abductions?'

'Yes.'

'How could you?'

'We need more Gypsies like you and me.'

'You and I – we're still bleeding!'

Leo Leo smoothed his hair. 'Compared to 99.9 per cent of our people who are on the scrap-heap – we've no cares in the world!'

Benedict moved to the door. 'Speak for yourself!'

Leo Leo rose and went across to him. 'Benedict, listen . . . You're special – you've always been . . . One could say . . . there's an aura about you . . .'

'What . . .?'

'Whatever it is, I spotted it straightaway when they brought you to the orphanage – don't ask me how . . . In fact – this will amaze you – it made me keep an eye on you – do things for you . . .'

'What sort of things?'

'Like moderating the voltage on your ECT.'

Benedict gaped at him. 'You – the ECT . . .?'

'Regularly.'

'I don't believe you!'

'Why do you think you ended up less damaged than most of the others?'

'Did I?'

Leo Leo smiled smugly. 'Look at yourself!'

Benedict looked away towards the garden. A vague memory flashed through his mind: children stretched out on treatment tables and convulsing; but there was one child – he – who convulsed less and sometimes not at all. 'Doesn't make sense! Why should you have spared me . . .?'

'Like I said, you were special. I don't remember what exactly made me think that at the time. I must have had presentiments. Maybe I felt even then that we should team up.'

'Team up?'

'Which is what I think now.'

'And do what?'

'Help our brothers and sisters assimilate.'

'Come on!'

'Role models – that's what our people need. I promise you, a few Gypsies like us and we can transform the tribes in no time at all – lead them out of the wilderness into the twenty-first century!'

'I don't ask any people to change their identity. Nor should we!'

'If we don't, we'll perish.'

'We'll perish anyway. People without countries seldom survive. Now if we had a historic homeland . . .'

Leo Leo snorted. 'We're not Jews.'

And suddenly, Benedict's old friend, the ashen, mutilated man whose blood had hardened like amber, rushed into his mind and proclaimed an ancient yearning: *Romanestan*!

'What about Romanestan . . .?'

Leo Leo laughed. 'There's no Romanestan – never was.'

The mutilated man whispered another ancient yearning.

Again Benedict rapped out. 'We could create it.'

Leo Leo smiled. 'We do. Constantly. In our hearts.'

The mutilated man shook his head sadly, then vanished.

Benedict strode out of the room.

Leo Leo followed him.

They descended the marble staircase – except for the smart squeak of Leo Leo's shoes – in silence.

They reached the main hall. A janitor opened the heavy iron door.

Leo Leo held Benedict by the arm. 'Don't spurn your luck – that's for romantics. Don't return to the fold – that's a sinking ship. Man a lifeboat instead – save our people.'

Benedict walked out. Suddenly, uncomfortably, Leo Leo had looked like Melchior.

The foundation's door closed with a rich metallic thud.

Benedict thought about the mutilated man. There had been a Gypsy chief who had whispered into his ear that the secret of life was breath, children, dignity and death. Was that memory or dream?

Benedict smoked a *Villiger* as his colleagues surveyed the site which he had recommended for the proposed power station. The location was near perfect: a wide plateau where the confluence of two mountain streams caused a small rapid. The only decision to be taken was which of the two freeholds – the farm to the west or the hostel to the east – should be purchased to accommodate the access road.

Tighe, the board's solicitor, wheezing after having dragged his blubber twenty metres up the slope, officiously pointed at the properties. 'Your verdict, gentlemen!'

Kurt, who was always affected by the cold, stamped his feet to boost his circulation. 'What's their market value?'

Benedict growled. 'We'll decide on merit! We're not speculators!'

He would never warm to Kurt: of aristocratic stock, sugar-coated with social graces, wedded to old wealth and endowed with a brain that moved at the speed of light, Kurt was his main rival for the senior engineer's post. But he was unlikely to eclipse Benedict; Kurt's military record was poor; in the promotion stakes, that was a great handicap.

Tighe droned impatiently. 'Neither owner wants to sell. That means compulsory purchase – paying the full market price.'

'Toss a coin. Let Fate decide.' Emile offered them his flask of *krauterschnaps*.

Kurt and Tighe refused the drink; they would not put their mouths where someone else had put his.

Benedict took a hearty swig. The *schnaps*, brewed by Emile himself, was pure fire-water.

Emile was a man after his own heart. A first-class engineer, he could have taken his pick of the multinationals; but, spurning ambition, he had chosen to remain, on a cantonal salary, with the Lucerne Hydroelectricity Board because the company employed disabled people and, in particular, his partner of many years, a gentle soul with a gecko-walk called François. Spiritual joys were Emile's preference; and he could find these, he maintained, as much in François' delight in lovemaking as in the sunsets of Goa where they always went on holiday.

Benedict drew patterns on the mud with his shoe. 'Who'd benefit most from keeping his property? Let's be guided by that.'

Kurt laughed mockingly. 'What – play God?'

Benedict mimicked him. 'Don't we always?'

Tighe handed out a typewritten memorandum.

The farm belonged to Herling, a lively septuagenarian. He had lost interest in agriculture since his marriage – his fifth – to an overblown Sicilian who, local gossip gleefully maintained, was not only capable of matching his ardour, but also seemed determined to copulate him to death.

Anwar and Jehan Ebrahim, who owned the other property, were a young Egyptian couple, not long naturalized, who had borrowed heavily to buy their place and convert it from a modest farm into a popular hostel for immigrant workers.

Benedict drew on his cigar. 'I'd say Herling should stay put.'

Kurt challenged him. 'Why?'

'Too old for an upheaval.'

Kurt was derisive. 'He can retire to the South of France. He and his wife would thank us for it. Let the Ebrahims keep their place. They're idealists.'

Tighe's face creased superciliously. 'Idealists?'

'They cater for *Gastarbeiters* – provide them with decent accommodation and food at a reasonable price.'

Benedict taunted him. 'That's idealism?'

Kurt replied fervently. 'They're our other Gypsies, the immigrant workers! Slogged to death. Paid a pittance. Abused, despised, marginalized. They keep quiet and out of sight in case they put a foot wrong and get kicked out. The Ebrahims give them dignity.'

Benedict tried to sound impassive. 'Emile – the couple who coddle our other Gypsies or the old man?'

Emile waved his hands. 'I'll sit on the fence, if you don't mind.'

Benedict smiled wryly. Emile distrusted decisions; he would commit himself only on technical matters. 'Tighe?'

The solicitor scoffed. 'When I look at a title deed, I'd like to see a Swiss name on it. We're too small a country to dish out land to foreigners.'

Kurt rasped in disgust. 'Xenophobia from a legal luminary – the mind boggles!'

Benedict stared at Tighe, not without hostility. 'I have the decisive vote then.'

Kurt pleaded with him. 'The Ebrahims are good people. We need their sort for a better future.'

'What do they think of real Gypsies?'

'What? I don't know. Why?'

'It's all very well helping surrogate Gypsies. But nobody helps the real ones!'

'I don't follow . . .'

'Maybe that's how it should be. Strong and solitary! Standing on your own feet! Nobody tramples on you then! Anyway, my vote: Herling keeps his place.'

Kurt was outraged. 'No! Why?'

Benedict strode off.

Kurt shouted. 'I'll go to arbitration!'

Tighe tittered apologetically. 'I'm afraid, in such matters, it's invariably me who's appointed arbiter.'

Kurt groaned. 'Jesus!'

Benedict chuckled. Had Prince Charming thought he would get the better of him? Not many people did.

They got into the car.

Benedict took another look at the properties.

65

The Ebrahims' hostel, dwarfed by dense coniferous trees that formed a natural snow-break on the heights above, already looked forlorn. He tried to visualize the *Gastarbeiters* – young men and women – suffering loneliness and exile in order to support their families back home. And maybe a few couples with children trying to root themselves in a land and among a people that did not want them. The other Gypsies.

He had kicked the weak and defended the strong, he knew. And yet. If he were a Gypsy – not a whitewashed Gypsy – but a real Gypsy, he wouldn't take any hand-outs from the *gadje*. That would be the beginning of the end.

What about my mother then?

I could go to her now. And take her with me. Install her in Melchior's house.

Why not?

Nettie came out of her study and stretched.

Benedict repeated a refrain on his cithara, then jotted the notes down on a sheet of music. 'Finished?'

She discarded her slippers. 'For tonight.'

He put away the cithara. 'Wine?'

She curled up on the settee. 'Lovely.'

He served her a glass of white, poured one for himself, then sat next to her.

She burrowed her feet under his buttocks. 'My feet are frozen.'

He rubbed her ankles. 'Isn't the heating on?'

'It's the French windows. The draught-excluders are hopeless.' She sipped her wine. 'Hmmm . . . Warm hands . . . Sexy . . .'

Benedict ran his hands up to her thighs. 'So are you . . .'

She clenched her legs. 'Slowly. Let me get myself together.'

Benedict pulled away. She always had to get herself together. She could never take him spontaneously. Did she need the time to convince herself he was worth loving? Time to decide that it didn't matter he was a Gypsy? Or, if it did matter, never mind, he was, at least, an exotic sex object?

Nettie, upset by the way he had withdrawn, tried to keep cheerful. 'I worked well today. It's professorship, this paper, I promise you.'

He tried to sound enthusiastic. 'Good girl!'

'What about you?'

'Nothing special. Listen . . . I'm thinking of seeing . . . my . . . mother.'

She looked up, perturbed.

'I'd like to bring her here. She can have Melchior's house.'

She pulled her feet from underneath him. 'It wouldn't work, Benedict. She wouldn't fit in.'

Does she really love me?

'Why not?'

'They never do.'

'They? Do you mean Gypsies?'

'You know what I mean!'

'No, I don't! I am a Gypsy! I've fitted in!'

'You fitted in because you were young, adaptable. You couldn't today. People from other backgrounds – they're used to different ways of life.'

And if she does love me, does she think it's perverse? Does she hate herself for it?

'People readjust. She would – in time.'

'No, Benedict! People don't! You know that! It wouldn't be fair! Not to her! Not to us! Come on, can you see her embracing our lifestyle? Mixing with our friends? Finding her bearings in this city? Everything would be so alien!'

'She's not from outer space, for God's sake! She's lived in this country all her life! She's an ordinary person! Like you and me! Sorry, like me!'

Is it because I'm a Gypsy that she doesn't want my child?

Nettie shouted back. 'Who'd look after her?'

'We will. Who else?'

'You mean I will.'

'We will, I said!'

'I'm the one who has a nine-to-five job! You've got fieldwork all over the canton. Sometimes you're away for days. Add to that: the army! Your call-ups mount up to three months in the year. Now that you've got your promotion, you'll probably be doing more. They've already summoned you for some stupid exercise next week! Who'll look after her during those times?'

'I'll resign my commission!'

'Never! The army's Holy Grail to you! It's even more important than me.' Suddenly, realizing the import of her words, she faced him miserably.

He looked away, unable to meet her eyes. 'Nonsense!'

She smiled sadly and drank her wine.

He became defiant. 'She's my mother! I must take care of her! Melchior thought so, too!'

'Benedict, think on it!' She held his hand. 'Darling, I've got nothing against her, believe me. I just want to spare you from yet another heartache! Think on it, please . . .'

He pulled his hand away and left the room.

She managed not to cry. She refilled her glass.

He returned shortly, dressed in his track suit. 'I'm going for a run.'

She nodded. 'Shall I wait up?'

'I'll be some time.' He kissed her brusquely and strode out.

Why haven't you got a child yet?

Nettie lit a cigarette and inhaled deeply. Then she gulped down her wine and, in a sudden rage, hurled the glass at the wall. 'Oh, fuck it!' She yelled at the top of her voice. 'Fuck it! Fuck it!'

She rose from the settee, paced up and down, then started collecting the pieces of broken glass. When she had finished clearing up, a fit of laughter seized her. She poured herself another glass of wine. 'A cold shower for you, my girl.'

O Del created death so that there would be life and resurrection, wholeness and completion.

After Rom's ashes were consigned to the sea, Branko was seized by unabated loneliness.

And he went to the edge of the earth and gazed into the void.

And an image of a vast, variegated landscape confronted him. This was the face and contours of Prithivi, the Earth Mother.

Branko ate holy lichens and sacred roots and acquired godly magic. Thereupon, taking rocks, breeze, molten minerals and marsh water, he sculpted Prithivi's effigy.

And he rubbed this effigy against his penis.

And the effigy came to life.

Thus the son gave birth to his mother and called her Dei.

And Branko took Dei with him and withdrew into the furthest reaches of his mind.

There, son and mother reconstituted each other.

Five

Blue Unit's artillery and machine-guns pounded Red Unit, preventing it from returning fire effectively.

Blue Unit was advancing too fast. Unless it slowed down, it would come within range of its own fire and either risk being hit by it or be forced to call off the support. In the event of the latter, Red Unit would have the chance to rally. Blue Unit would then face the danger of heavy casualties or retreat.

Benedict noted down these points.

'Jesus! What's he think he's doing?'

The outburst had come from General Lenz, the chief of staff. The other brass at the observation post rushed to his side and stared in the direction he was pointing.

Benedict surveyed the terrain with his binoculars and spotted the incident: a Blue Unit soldier had broken ranks and, heedless of the bullets flying past him, was walking – strolling – back towards his lines; to add insult to injury, he was stripping off his uniform.

He recognized the man: Hansi Müller.

General Lenz chafed. 'The fucker will get killed! Did nobody tell him this is a live-ammo exercise?'

Benedict scanned the battlefield. None of Hansi's comrades was near enough to intercept him. The company commander, under orders to secure a salient, would continue pushing forward.

The observers yelled at Hansi through loudspeakers:

'Get down!'

'On your belly!'

Hansi could not hear; or was not taking any notice. Somebody had to go and save him.

Benedict barely held his rage. That somebody was himself. He was Blue Unit's commanding officer. Even if he were not, how could he shun such a challenge? Fuck it!

He'd very likely get a citation. Fuck it!

He streaked away from the observation post. Fuck it!

He ran at a crouch, zigzagging; his nerve ends watching out for the bullet that might be seeking him.

What the fuck had come over Hansi? He was a good soldier. Strong lad, amiable, good skier, good climber, good with weapons. What the fuck then? What the fuck?

Hansi, down to pants and T-shirt, had seen Benedict and was gesticulating wildly.

Benedict put in an extra spurt. A miracle the fucker hadn't been hit yet! Or he himself, for that matter.

Hansi's voice pierced through the noise of battle. 'I'm deserting, Colonel! Can't stop me! I'm deserting!'

'Get down, fuck-face, before life fucking deserts you!'

'You won't stop me, Colonel!'

Benedict caught up with Hansi and dived at his legs. As they hit the ground, he punched the youth hard on the chin; then he dragged him to the nearest trench and bundled him in.

As Hansi shook off his stupor, Benedict tried to light a *Villiger*. He could not. His hands shook. So did his legs.

Hansi found his voice. 'Through with the army, Colonel. Don't care what they do to me, I'm through!'

'You could have got killed, you moron!'

'No way. I was protected. I had magic.'

'Jesus, Hansi . . .'

'Marianne.'

'You're babbling, you crazy arse-hole!'

'Marianne! Her legs around my face. Her cunt on my lips. Who can kill me with that sort of magic?'

Benedict stared at him. 'What . . .?'

Hansi smiled, then took the *Villigers* from Benedict and, with absolutely steady hands, lit two. He passed one to Benedict and began smoking the other.

He spoke in a torrent. 'I'm not mad – but, bet you, you'll pack me off to the loony bin! Don't matter! I'll keep smiling. They'll declare me unhinged, but not dangerous. And invalid me out. I'll get a job – ski instructor or something – and live happily ever after with my Marianne. Worked it all out, see! Not at all mad!'

Benedict humoured him. 'Sure . . .'

'But I was half an hour ago – when we started the assault – truly off my rocker! And stark staring mad when the firing started! Then revelation! I saw Marianne in my mind's eye! Her face upon my face. Her cunt upon my lips. My face, my hands, my cock in and out of her body. She biting me all over! I swilling her tits! Eyes kissing eyes, soul kissing soul. Ever made love like that, Colonel?'

Benedict, suddenly seized with envy, spat angrily. 'Sure. Everybody has.'

'Like hell!'

'Belt up, Hansi!'

Hansi sniggered. 'Bothers you, right? You don't even know what I'm talking about!'

'Fucking juvenile drivel – that's what.'

'What life's all about – that's what I'm talking about! Simple as that.'

'Shut up!'

Hansi shook his head. 'Can't see – none of you! That's the tragedy. If you could, you'd give up all this shit about flag, country, honour, brothers-at-arms! That was my revelation. I saw bullets for what they are. Killers! Who're we shooting at? We're not at war! We're not defending ourselves or someone else or something! We're playing at war! Is that sane, Colonel?'

Benedict tried to bluster. 'Damn right . . .'

'Damn right, it isn't! That's what I said: this isn't where I want to go, what I want to do, what I was born to do. Lock bodies with Marianne; make children with her – that's what I was born to do! Been together two years; not one child yet! Why? What am I waiting for?'

Why haven't you got a child yet?

'So I wrapped my Marianne's legs around my face and off I went! *Adios*, wankers!'

Benedict scanned the battlefield. 'I've got to get back, Hansi. Do I drag you with me – or will you sit tight until the medics come?'

Hansi looked over the parapet. 'I'll sit tight.'

'Right!'

Hansi saluted him. 'Thanks for coming after me, Colonel. I was safe – but you didn't know that.'

Benedict struck him viciously and knocked him unconscious. As he

71

clambered over the trench, he realized he had hit Hansi not because he had wanted to make sure the youth would stay put, but because he did not have Marianne's – Nettie's – legs around his face.

He brought the cocoa and the Grand Marnier. He placed the cups and glasses on the respective bedside tables, then took off his dressing-gown and clambered on to the bed.

He scrutinized his naked body: lithe, muscular, strong. Did it appeal to Nettie? Had it ever? Would she rather he was rounder, softer? His dark skin – was she repelled by it? What did she really think of Gypsies? What did she really feel – deep down?

He was already aroused.

Such urgency would incur Nettie's censure, provoke the old complaint that he always rushed her, was always too keen, too hungry, that he reduced her to an object, and, therefore, did not specifically desire her, but merely wanted a woman, any woman, all women, so that he could devour everything they could give him and still ask for more.

Which wasn't altogether true.

And if it were, what was so terrible? What was wrong with wanting everything? And more? A limitless capacity for love – isn't that what makes us human?

He remembered arguing in the same vein with – was it Dagmar or Ilse or both – at some gathering or another and being told that men like him didn't want wives, they just needed their mothers.

What's wrong with that? Let's see how you'd fare – any of you – without a mother!

He pulled up the duvet to conceal his arousal. If it weren't for the need for sex, the joys of it . . . and the urgency for children . . .

He lit a cigar, sipped his drink and gazed at the painting on the wall: a cubistic rendition of a reclining nude. Much admired by Nettie. Passion-killer, Melchior had once called it.

Remember Hansi. Show Nettie you're not always eager or hungry or angry. Show her you've got another side. Put her head on your chest. Look into her eyes as she purrs. Let her see your eyes – and beyond. Then the babies will come.

All right, old man, I will.

Nettie came in her nightdress, registered the cocoa and the Grand Marnier and smiled. 'Play-time?'

He raised his glass.

She took out her diaphragm from her bedside table. 'I'll just put this in – then I can relax.'

'Do it later. Let's talk a while.'

She gave him a quizzical look, then climbed into bed. She dropped the diaphragm on the duvet, reclined against the headboard and picked up her glass. 'Bottoms up.' She tapped her hand. 'Patience, girl!'

They smiled at her joke. They sipped their drinks. She took a cigarette. He lit it. She inhaled deeply. 'Thanks.' He held her hand.

She put her head on his shoulder. 'I hate it when you go on exercises. I panic and think: this time, he'll get killed.'

'I'm well protected. I've got magic.'

She knocked on the wood of the bedside table. 'Don't tempt the Devil!'

'Your legs around my face.'

She stared at him, then kissed his neck. 'What a nice thing to say.'

He drew on his cigar.

She sipped her cocoa. 'Whilst you were away . . . I took advice on Melchior's house. We should smarten it up a bit, get new furniture, then rent it out. Apparently foreign companies are queuing up for a decent place. Be an excellent income.'

'I'll think about it.'

'And the house will keep appreciating.'

Pensively, he picked up the diaphragm and scrutinized it.

She watched him, amused. 'A Dutch cap -- in case you were wondering.'

He smiled. 'I'm crystal gazing.'

'More magic. What can you see?'

He became solemn. 'I'll tell you what I don't see . . .'

'What?'

'The future.'

Nettie looked at him warily: 'Meaning?'

Benedict stubbed out his cigar. Then, taking a pair of scissors from his drawer, he cut the diaphragm into pieces. 'Time we got rid of this.'

'Benedict, don't be stupid!'

'I hate it!'

'We don't have a choice. I'm not risking side-effects with the pill. The coil makes my periods painful. And as you're not keen on condoms . . .'

'Why use anything?'

Nettie put out her cigarette, all the while staring at him. Then she grinned and wagged a finger. 'The old refrain, eh? Sorry – not on!' She got out of bed. 'But the night's not lost. I have a spare.'

He pulled her down. 'We don't need it!'

'Yes, we do!'

He raised her nightdress and started kissing her belly. 'No!'

She struggled, giggling. 'Benedict! Stop it!'

'I can't. You're irresistible!'

She pushed him away brusquely. 'Stop it, I said!'

He disengaged from her. 'Why?'

'You're being a pain!'

'If you conceive, what better? We'll be blessed!'

'I don't want to conceive!'

'Never ever?'

'In good time.'

'Why not now?'

'I'm not ready yet.'

'No one ever is. But when it happens, they see there's nothing to it – everything comes naturally.'

'Bullshit! And what about my work? I'm still young! Let's enjoy life for a bit.'

Benedict held her hand. 'Nettie, listen. Please, listen. I want a child. Desperately. How can I make it clearer? I want us to have a child!'

'You're in one of your moods. And no wonder! You haven't stopped running since the funeral. Barely had a chance to mourn. Try and let things ease a bit . . .' She placed her hand on his penis. 'Let's just enjoy each other.' Finding him erect, she smiled. 'Raring to go, as ever.' She climbed off the bed. 'I won't be a sec.'

'Not the cap, Nettie! Please!'

She faced him, sternly. 'No cap, no play.'

'No play then.'

'Suit yourself.' She slid back under the duvet, picked up the remote-control and turned the television on.

Benedict, barely controlling his fury, watched the screen. A book programme. A philosopher with a Scandinavian name arguing about the sanctity of books. Without books there would be no civilization. Without books none of the great religions would have survived. You want to save the world? Save the books first! Make people read!

Nettie interjected. 'That's right! You tell them!'

Benedict got out of the bed. 'There are some condolence letters I still haven't replied to . . .'

She nodded without interrupting her viewing.

He put on his slippers. 'Tell me why you don't want a child – the real reason.'

'I told you, I'm not ready yet!'

'Is it me – my Gypsy blood?'

'Don't be so stupid!'

'Makes sense. Getting fucked by a Gypsy leaves no trace. But having his child . . .!'

She threw a pillow at him. 'You shit-hole!'

'Be honest!'

She looked at him at length, then hissed. 'All right. I'll be honest. But you won't understand!'

'Try me!'

'Your being a Gypsy never bothered me! It might have, possibly, if you hadn't been so . . . assimilated.'

'Whitewashed, you mean.'

Nettie snapped. 'Listen to me! My problem is my fears about giving birth. Actually giving birth – the physical act! It's all right for you – all you need do is hold my hand and watch a miracle unfold! I have to go through with the labour! And I'm petrified by that! Always have been! The thought of all that pain – freaks me out . . .'

The book programme ended. Adverts came on.

She changed channels. A war film.

He shook his head, stunned. 'Does that mean . . .? Won't you ever consider . . .?'

'I don't know . . . It's not that I don't want children, I do. Be patient with me . . .'

Benedict moved to the door. 'I'm going to see my . . . mother. Bring her back with me . . .'

She turned round sharply. 'What?'

' . . . Put her in Melchior's house.'

'Benedict, no! Let's discuss it first!'

Benedict walked out. Behind him, on television, a battle raged.

He went into the bathroom.

He sat on the toilet and masturbated.

Sorry, Melchior . . . old man . . . father.

Sorry . . . Mother . . . Not much of a son, alas . . .

Benedict crumpled up the letter he had just written. Rituals of condolence should be abolished. Rage should rule. Words, unless they could open up the thick earth, give new flesh to corpses, wipe out cancer, old age, decomposition, were merely whiplashes for the soul.

He left the desk, sank into an armchair and gazed at the electric coal-fire. Nettie hated the appliance, considering anything mock as kitsch. But he liked it: it had come to symbolize the Gypsy camp-fire that had warmed his childhood.

And there, not unexpectedly, Eloïse appeared, superimposed over the glow. She was sitting by her harp, half-turned towards him with that ramrod posture imposed by the heavy corset which she had been forced to wear after damaging her back, Benedict was convinced, by struggling to hold him tight and contain him every time he had been seized by fear on those early days of his adoption.

She started talking to him. And playing. Barrios, predictably, because she was advising him on a delicate matter and delicate matters always demanded the *Paraguayan Dance* which was the first piece they had played together after he had mastered the cithara.

I'm so glad you've decided to go to your mother. Don't be afraid. A mother is a bosom and most mothers are good enough. Accept her love. Give her yours. That will repair some of the past. But don't ever stop loving Melchior or me.

'Benedict . . . I've been calling you . . .'

Benedict looked up as Nettie edged in front of the fireplace. Naked.

'I didn't hear you . . .'

She was holding a diaphragm as if it were a banner. 'Sorry – about the row . . .'

'Forget it.'

'I told you the truth. It's not that I don't want a baby. I do. Very much.' She placed the diaphragm on the mock coals of the electric fire. 'So goodbye Dutch cap . . .'

Benedict stared at her uncomprehendingly.

Nettie laughed nervously. 'My variation on bra-burning.' She took his hand. 'Come to bed.'

'Nettie, you don't have to . . .'

She pulled him off the armchair. 'I want you. Come on. Before I change my mind.'

He picked up the diaphragm from the electric coal-fire and threw it in the wastepaper basket. 'We don't want a conflagration.'

She smiled. 'Oh, yes, we do!' She pressed herself against him. 'Will you promise me one thing . . .?'

'If it's a promise I can keep . . .'

'You'll let me have a Caesarean.'

'What?'

'I'll be under anaesthetic – no labour pains . . . Promise, please . . .'

'Shouldn't we decide nearer the time . . .?'

'No. Now. Promise me.'

Benedict nodded confusedly.

And it came to pass that Branko, eager for the wellspring which nurtures all things good, became enamoured of Thyatira and took her to wife.

Now Thyatira, brutalized by Adam, like all daughters of Eve, had vowed to avenge her sisters by withholding her waters from all men.

Thus every time Branko went to lie with her, she refused him. 'I will be as wife to you,' she told him, 'when you prove love is constant.'

Branko agreed to be tested.

Thyatira took him to the wilderness and pushed him into a deep pit. 'If you can climb out,' she taunted him, 'you can take me and go in unto me.'

The pit's walls, Branko observed, were of liquid metal; not even a lizard could scale them. So he emulated a baby's odyssey. He pushed his body continuously towards the opening.

And thus, as if giving birth to himself, he emerged out of the pit.

Still Thyatira rebuffed him. 'Constant love lives but a span.'

Patiently, Branko corrected her: 'Even so, it is eternal. The fusion of man and woman creates a new life which contains both of them but is altogether another. And this process goes on forever.'

Thyatira became distraught. Nevertheless, so that her name should not stink among the people, she agreed to lie down with him. However, in order not to raise up issue for him, she decided to disengage at the moment of joy and make him spill his potency.

As the time for consummation approached, Branko served Thyatira sunflower seeds and pomegranates.

And while Thyatira ate of the delicacy, Lilith, who had instructed Branko on this ritual, came down from the Heavens and whispered unto her: 'Refusing conception is against the natural order. Spillage betrays womankind.'

And so, disburdened of Adam's brutality by these words, Thyatira opened her fountainhead eagerly for Branko.

Six

The encampment was a disused car park.

The site, Benedict had discovered from colleagues in the region, had been made available to the Gypsies through the auspices of an international welfare organization and after considerable political pressure on the local council.

The area, tucked in the Bernese Oberland with a glorious view over the lakes of Thun and Brienz, was popular with hikers and tourists. The council, though it had created a much larger car park on the Interlaken road, still retained the right to evict the Gypsies should, as a clause in the agreement stated, 'ecological considerations make it imperative'.

It had not surprised Benedict that no help had been extended to the Gypsies to ameliorate their living conditions. There had been no improvements to such services as water, sewage, electricity and telephone: the old public lavatories, street-lamps and the single pay phone had been deemed adequate as amenities.

Benedict negotiated an entrance still guarded by a ticket kiosk and parked at a discreet distance from the trailers. Vacillating between apprehension and expectation, he stepped out of the car and strode across.

Judging by the number of trailers – and a few caravans worthy of museums – about thirty families appeared to live at this site.

He wondered whether such small groupings were the norm with Sintis. His ignorance of even the most basic facts of Gypsy life induced a sense of defeat. Unless he knew everything about his blood, how could he take the correct turn, how could he push sinew, bone and spirit to discover what it was, if anything, he was born to do?

Most of the men were tinkering with their cars.

The women, clustered by the trailers, chatted as they performed their chores: washing, sewing, cooking.

In the foreground, a bunch of children played hopscotch.

The men peered at him sullenly. One or two took stock of his Citroen GS which, though a few years old, looked, compared to their jalopies, the height of luxury. Some of the others appeared to be discussing his clothes; they probably thought he was a bailiff. But the children and the women, curiosity tempering their hostility, stopped their activities and waited for him to approach.

Benedict addressed the children nearest to him. 'I'm looking for Ariana Croz.'

A boy, barely ten, but evidently forging himself into a toughie – just as Benedict had sought to be at that age – disengaged from his friends. 'Why?'

'To visit.'

'She's sick.'

Benedict was instantly concerned. That bolstered his confidence: it meant he cared, really cared. He was right to have come, right to have dismissed Nettie's objections. 'Take me to her. I'll get her to a doctor.'

The boy had not expected concern and became confused. 'She has oldies' illness.'

'Where is she?'

The boy looked at his friends. They shuffled about, equally uncertain.

The boy pointed at a trailer which, lacking a car, had seemingly rooted itself into the cracked asphalt.

As Benedict hastened towards the trailer, adults yelled questions. The children shouted answers even more loudly. They spoke Romanes. Some of the words sounded familiar, but Benedict was too tense to dredge up their meaning.

He wanted to shout back: I'm one of you! To go up to them and tell them: I lived with you until they abducted me! But that would have been hypocritical. It was not the loss of his people that weighed on his heart, but the sense of abandonment Melchior had inflicted on him by dying. Leo Leo had been right. He had ceased being a Gypsy. He could not even imagine what being a Gypsy entailed. And yes, deep down, he was grateful that he could pass for a *gadjo*.

So why had he come here?

He directed his gaze to Ariana Croz's trailer. Spruce, like all the others: recently painted; all the chrome well polished; surrounded by pots of flowers and herbs. Ariana Croz might have oldies' sickness, but she was obviously keen on orderliness. She would be living alone. Your father died some time ago, Melchior had said.

My father . . . *My* father . . .

The trailer door opened. A woman, obviously intrigued by the commotion, edged out.

Was that her? Would she recognize me?

She might. Judging by the pictures Melchior had taken of him at the time of his adoption – and the Pro Juventute photographs before those – he had not changed a great deal: same features – craggier now; taller and fuller, of course; but same complexion and same straight, black Asian hair.

The woman was heavily dusted with age. Hunchbacked. One hand holding onto the door-case as she shakily descended the trailer's steps, the other beckoning him.

Yes, she had recognized him. She was crying. And shouting: 'Branko! Branko! Branko!'

Other Gypsies began shouting, too. In surprise and disbelief. 'Branko? Your Branko?'

Tears welled up in him. Branko. The old name. Branko. The name with which this woman, his mother, had consigned him to God as they had dragged him away. The name he had desperately clung to when they had hauled him off to punishment. The name the naked, mutilated man had drilled into him every time he had fished him out of the electricity's fumaroles. The name he had eventually discarded because Melchior and Eloïse, proclaiming him their greatest blessing, had preferred calling him Benedict, softly and lovingly, Benedict.

He ran to her. 'Yes! It is! Branko! It's me . . .!'

She seized him by the arms. She was weeping and muttering. Repeatedly kissing his hands.

He stood. Tearful. Not knowing what to do or say.

People loped over excitedly. Brought chairs. Food. Wine. Tuned up guitars and violins. Pumped breath into accordions. Shook tambourines. Beat drums. And pronounced his name. Repeatedly. Like that of a saviour. Branko! Branko! Branko! Branko! Branko!

It was impossible to guess how old she was. Ariana herself did not know. The only clue she had offered, while reminiscing about other reunions, had been

81

the story that her parents, fleeing the First World War, had settled in Switzerland. Where they had come from and when, no one had bothered to specify: all of Europe was a battlefield; the *gadje*, except for the Swiss, were forever fighting.

She still had strands of black hair. But it was difficult to imprint her face on to the mind: a maze of lines, like fissures on parched earth, camouflaged her features. Her eyes, hostage to cataracts, were clouding. She still possessed most of her teeth; and these were dramatically highlighted by the prominent moustache that some women acquire with age.

She was gaunt, with thin, bandy legs. But for her hunched back, she would have been tall. Her hands, gnarled and heavily callused, were scored with dirt-ingrained cracks; the fingers were virtually devoid of nails; but, to compensate for their deformity, they executed their tasks efficiently, even gracefully.

Her everyday clothes, as she had called them, were a denim skirt, a woollen blouse, a cardigan and a sheepskin coat, all of them ill fitting – probably hand-outs from some charity.

Except for her very pleasant smell of fresh mint, Ariana was as plain as Eloïse had been striking. Yet, Benedict imagined, each would have seen a reflection of herself in the other. They both possessed a softness that sought to redeem an otherwise merciless world and give it meaning. A softness that was also indestructible; otherwise how could both women have disregarded, with total insouciance, the outrage of chronic illness – MS in Eloïse's case, severe arthritis in Ariana's?

'Ah, God is great, Branko! He answered my prayers! Brought you back!'

Those words, and her exhortations to eat, drink and honour the event – echoed, in turn, by everybody in the compound – had been the afternoon's refrain.

And, in no time at all, wise men and women had decreed that Benedict's return constituted a true miracle and that since miracles were secretions from the Milky Way, glory be, the whole camp was awash with blessings.

'Something to eat, Branko?'

'No, thank you. I can't take another morsel.'

Ariana shuffled about shyly and anxiously and tried to glean, every time he looked at an object, his judgement on her. Though the trailer's interior was as spotless as its exterior, everything was worn out.

She had been apprehensive about taking him inside and had begged her neighbours to stay on and continue celebrating. But, knowing what a long journey it would be for mother and son to rejoin each other, they had advised her not to delay matters; prevarication, they had reminded her, always attracted the Devil.

How could she begin to touch him – his face as well as his heart? 'Maybe some more tea, coffee, wine?'

Benedict, feeling equally awkward, welcomed the distraction. 'Another coffee perhaps.'

She beamed and swept to the cooker.

He rose from the divan where she had installed him like a potentate. 'Can I help?'

She turned round, horrified. 'No. No.'

He backed away and paused at the small altar bearing an icon of the Madonna and Child. The rug in front of it was threadbare.

He remembered the altar. Next to it had stood a clothes-trunk painted in every imaginable colour and bearing a cornucopia of images: stars, moons, cherubs, trees, fruit, animals . . . He glanced around, but could not see it. Had he imagined it?

Ariana poured the coffee and placed the cup on the table in front of the divan. 'Sit. Sit.'

He sat down again.

She took a step back and stood at attention like a servant.

He sipped his coffee. 'Wonderful.'

She smiled shyly, pleased.

He lit a *Villiger*. 'Won't you sit down?'

'I see you better if I stand.'

He fixed his eyes on the copper pots hanging by the stove. 'Is this where you've always lived – we lived? I'm trying to remember . . .'

She shook her head. 'Near Lausanne, we were. Those days we had a *vardo* – a caravan. Absolute beauty.'

'There was a clothes-trunk – painted . . .'

She chuckled happily. 'You remember.'

'What happened to it?'

'It was Mihal's. We burned it at his funeral – with the *vardo*.'

'And after his death – we came here?'

'To this canton. About a year after – when I met Karl. This is Karl's trailer.'

Benedict nodded. 'I understand.'

Mihal had been her husband. Karl was the fellow she had taken up with later. Like Mihal, Karl was a good man, especially for singing and laughing. But unlike Mihal, God had given him only brawn, no brains. Farm labour was all he could do. When machines took over and he couldn't get any work, he tried thieving. As even a toad would have predicted, he got caught. In jail for eight years and another two to go.

'I wish I could remember Mihal . . .'

She nodded sadly. 'You were four when he died. Seven when they took you. I tell you, if Mihal had been around, he'd have summoned the ancestral giants and saved you. What could I do on my own?'

Mother, Benedict craved to say. To say it, for once, to the right person instead of secretly to the elements. He had been dispossessed of the word for decades – even Eloïse had discouraged him from addressing her in that manner in order not to offend his natural mother's memory. Hence the word had become mythic, defining times of gentlest tenderness where every breach could be repaired promptly and painlessly.

Mother . . . A word that everybody imbibed. Everybody, save himself. The word that said: I gave you life; I love you; I will always take care of you. And which received the response: I'm good, I'm perfect, don't abandon me.

Benedict indicated the place next to him. 'Please sit down . . .'

He was still dispossessed of that word. Ariana was not his mother.

She edged forward. 'All right. To be nearer.'

Ariana was not his mother. Melchior had been mistaken.

She sat down timidly.

Ariana was not his mother. His mother had once again disowned him.

She wiped a tear. 'Imagine, sitting with you . . .'

That ordinary, plain, standard, everyday mother who suckled everybody else with inexhaustible love was unavailable to him – forever.

She shook her head in wonder. ' . . . with my son . . .'

Ariana was not his mother; Mihal had not been his father. They had been yet another set, the very first set, of foster-parents – so she had explained, painfully, in the course of the afternoon, to everybody present.

Your real father and mother came from the Balkans.

'Tell me about Mihal, Ariana . . .'

Members of the Ursari, a small tribe.

Ariana shrugged. 'He was what he was.'

Bear-tamers, the Ursari are; strong people.

'Do I look like him? I'm sure I look like you . . .'

They travelled between Turkey and Europe; danced and wrestled their bears in towns and villages.

Ariana pushed him playfully. 'When does an eagle look like a crow?'

84

Not many Ursari left now; the war . . .

'Children get to look like their parents – even like their foster-parents – like dogs and their owners. I've often been told I look like both Melchior and Eloïse.'

Your parents tried to run away from the Hitlerites.

Ariana stroked his face; all her wrinkles glowed. 'God is great, Branko!'

Extermination of Gypsies was the Hitlerite policy.

'I've never forgotten you, Ariana . . .'

Your Dei was carrying you at the time . . .

'I kept fighting them at the orphanage.'

It was impossible to escape the Hitlerites, hyena packs with countless heads and twice countless eyes.

'Always tried to keep your face, Ariana, in a corner of my heart . . .'

Gypsies, adorning the landscape like rainbows – where could they have hidden?

'Even when I was with Melchior and Eloïse . . .'

They caught your Dei and Dadoro in Yugoslavia.

'*Dadoro*' meant 'little father'. Oh, God! Benedict stubbed out his cigar and lit another. 'Yet I remember very little of my life with you.'

And sent them to Auschwitz.

Ariana ran her sleeve across her eyes to dam the rush of tears. 'Little is better than nothing . . .'

That's where you were born: Auschwitz-Birkenau.

'I remember a pet: a goat.'

Your everyday name: Mujula. Secret name, real name: Branko.

Ariana laughed. 'Tiger – you called him Tiger.'

You possess a good star.

'Used to take him up the slopes. We used to run for hours.'

You were favoured by the Urme, the Angels of Destiny.

'Sometimes you'd disappear so long I had to go looking.'

You're endowed with a prophecy.

'Yes . . .?'

A new tree will sprout the leaves the donkey ate.

'And I'd beat you. For scaring me . . .'

Hope will stream to the sea, set sail and become earth.

'I was always afraid something would happen to you, Branko . . . like I'd known . . .'

The burst pomegranate will be made whole.

'It's not that I didn't want to remember, Ariana . . . But they were broiling my brains – I had to hide you . . .'

On the strength of the prophecy, your Dei and Dadoro prevailed on the Gypsies in Auschwitz to choose you for survival.

'When I was taken . . . I tried to get back – ran away many times . . .'

They entrusted you, barely ten days old, to a German engineer who worked in a factory nearby and who had smuggled a number of children out of the camp.

Ariana bit her knuckles. 'To come back to me?'

The engineer handed you over to a Red Cross official.

'They always caught me. They had shorn my hair, you see. They did that to all the Gypsy boys – that way we could be identified easily . . .'

The Red Cross official brought you to Switzerland.

Ariana stroked his hair tenderly, as if the gesture could erase the past. 'No explaining the *gadje*'s mind.'

And took you to a Sinti chief whose people he used to employ as fruit pickers.

Benedict spoke softly so that she would not be distracted from caressing his hair. 'Once, I almost made it . . . I was with this family – farmers. The worst of a number of brutal foster-parents. They fed me dregs, beat me up if I got tired, locked me in at nights in the outhouse. So I ran away. I got to where you were . . . I even saw you . . .'

The Sinti chief did his duty. He said: the child will be one of us.

Ariana stared at him in dismay. 'When was that? Where?'

Those days Mihal and I travelled with that chief. So we said to him: please, we've not been blessed with a child, let's not die barren, let's be the boy's Dadoro and Dei.

'You were working in a vineyard. I saw you from the top of the hill. I ran, calling you. That's when they grabbed me. They had been waiting. They knew I'd get back to you. I screamed: Dei! You didn't hear me. They laughed. You have no mother, they said. You're a bastard, born out of nothing, worse, born out of shit!'

The chief said: so be it.

'And they took me back. And strapped me down. And gave me the treatment.'

We called you by your secret name, Branko, your real name, the name with which the Angels of Destiny had saved you.

'Same treatment. Every time they caught me.'

Mihal and I asked the Red Cross man: you've given us the boy's name, even the secret name, and you've given us the prophecy on him, now give us the names of his parents so that when he grows up he can place them in his heart because for us Romanies our ancestors are sacred.

Ariana bit her knuckles. 'They hurt you?'

Father's name: Todor.

'They gave me electricity. Beatings I could take. You get used to pain. But electricity . . .'

Mother's name: Zara.

'Even so they couldn't break me . . .'

Family name: Pehlivan; Turkish for 'wrestler'.

Ariana stared at him, confused. 'I don't understand . . .'

Benedict smiled bitterly. Applying electric shock to a child and calling it 'treatment', or more wholesomely, 'therapy' – who could understand that? Attaching electrodes onto a child's temple, holding down his tongue so that he won't choke on it, then zapping him to galvanic firestorm and piously watching as everything inside him burned and melted down – who could understand that? But that's how it had been, here, in dear, sane Switzerland.

'Hard to explain . . . Or maybe not – if you're a Gypsy . . .'

Ariana was crying. 'Why . . .?'

Benedict stubbed out his cigar. Had Leo Leo really moderated the voltage?

Was it the prophecy Ariana keeps talking about that made me look special?

'People always try and destroy those who are different.'

She pulled him to her bosom. 'But they didn't destroy you. They didn't. They couldn't . . .'

He smelled the mint on her time-worn breasts. 'I was lucky, Dei.'

There, I've said it. I've used the word! Mother! No hell has broken loose. I can never own that word, but I can touch it. 'Dei . . .'

I've said it again!

'Yes, Branko . . .'

'Dei . . .'

Maybe if I keep saying it . . .

'Yes, son . . .'

He rested his head on her lap and closed his eyes. 'Mind if I . . .?'

She rocked him gently. 'Yes, my boy. Rest . . .'

As he fell asleep, Ariana thanked God and His golden heart for saving her son. Then fearing, through all her inner senses, that this might be the last time they would be together, she wept. Then she thanked God again: to those who had abandoned hope, even last times promised life. She went on rocking him.

She stood, washed colourless by the car park's halogen lights. Bent double: an ancient tree. Crying. Holding on to a bucket of water.

The whole community stood with her. Many with buckets of water, too.

Benedict slid into his car, wound down the window, switched on the ignition. 'I'll be back . . .'

She nodded. 'Go with God.'

'I'll send you a doctor. You'll see him – you promised.'

'Yes.'

'And I'll bring Nettie.'

'Yes.'

'Bye . . . Dei!'

She smiled through her tears.

He put the car into gear.

As he drove off, Ariana emptied the bucket of water in the direction of the car. Those neighbours similarly equipped did the same.

Benedict watched them in his mirror. They were libating the earth or chasing away the demons or clearing his path, some such thing, maybe all three. She had told him, but he had not been listening; he had been trying to do the decent thing, asking her – unimaginatively, as he now realized – to go with him, to live with Nettie and him.

I'll be back.

She had refused. She had believed his heart; but she had also sensed his misgivings about Nettie.

He had told her Nettie was trying to conceive. For three weeks now, since 'the burning of the Dutch-cap episode' – as she called it – they had tried every night. As she was a few days late with her period, it was conceivable that, soon, she would be nappy-deep in child.

Ariana had offered a deeper reason for not going with him. Nothing, not even the son she had at last regained, would induce her to journey into the *gadje*'s world and be contaminated there. Benedict had to understand that.

I'll be back.

She had told him stories about his real parents. Because, she had said, stories strengthen people and repair the devastation in them; by recounting what was common to all, by showing how everybody loved, felt, laughed, cried, mourned with identical passion, stories prove that mankind is the same everywhere, that, in God's eyes, no one is different. The *gadje*, sadly, had forgotten this; hence their despair and villainy.

And so she had related anecdotes about Todor and Zara which she and Mihal and Karl had collected over the years from Romany tellers of tales.

Dour people, by all accounts. Like mountain boulders – which was how the Ursari had to be because theirs was the hardest of lives. But when it came to music . . . they could make every creature dance, not just the bears. Todor, in particular, might well have been of the Pied Piper's seed. A seed which Benedict, too, seemed to possess – or so the community had declared, after he had borrowed someone's cithara and celebrated his return with one of his songs.

I'll be back.

He drove out of the gate.

Go to Auschwitz, she had told him. Find the souls of your mother and father. They've been waiting all these years to know for sure that you've survived.

I'll be back.

Ask them about the prophecy. We memorized it and passed it on to you. But no one could interpret it so we don't know what it foretells, though we know you're destined to be a great Rom, and you must be well on the way because look at you, you're like a hero from ancient times.

I'll be back.

Listen to what your Dei and Dadoro have to say. If they tell you to come back, come back.

They will.

Go with God, son.

I'll be back, Dei.

When Amulius, shoot of Adam, heard that the Romanies were flowering again, he was maddened. 'Flowering people perfume the air,' he said. 'They must be exterminated.'

Todor, chief of the Romanies, and his wife, Zara, went up to the mountain to beseech the Heavens.

O Del blanketed them with a dream which showed the fox of the night reviving the quail of the day so that the latter could fetch the sun. And Todor and Zara understood that there is a time when all must die and a time when everything will be reborn.

And so when Amulius led forth his armies, the Romanies took their infants into the forest. There, hiding their history beneath the snow, they put their babes, like ripe figs, on the trees and left them to the care of the beasts.

Amulius caught the Romanies on the plains.

He put them to the sword and scattered their corpses east, west, north and south.

In the forest, as night fell, the animals appeared.

Led by a she-wolf who chose Branko, the newborn of Todor and Zara, they picked the infants from the trees and suckled them.

In time, Branko grew as handsome as a mountain.

Gubbio, the goddess of victorious magic, tutored him on all matters occult.

Apollo instructed him on the cithara.

Birds and butterflies taught him to sing and dance.

And bears primed him in wrestling.

And one day, the she-wolf nursed Branko for the last time; and as she rocked him, she recounted the story of the Romanies. Branko understood that the time to return to the plains had come.

He summoned the Romany youths who had survived with him; they bade farewell to their forest families and left for the plains.

In the course of many seasons, they found the remains of their parents. They put these together and lay fresh earth on them so that their spirits would be reconstituted and their blood thicken anew.

Since then, whenever flowers release their fragrance, the forest animals can be heard calling for their foster-children and telling them how lovingly they are remembered.

PART TWO

Seven

Death should have its own particular venue, an inconspicuous sandbank around a secluded corner where people could divert quietly and never be missed again. All other places, wild shores and deserts, mountain ranges and rain forests, urban jungles and picturesque villages should celebrate only life and beauty.

Certainly here, in Oświęcim, by the confluence of the Vistula and the Soła, a haven for birds and insects, here in this lush land where silence and water play intensely like young lovers, where earth smells of grass and grass of mother's milk, here, where God must have often come fishing, here, death should never have been seen or heard.

Four million men, women and children were murdered here. Their last shrieks are still in the air.

Oświęcim – Auschwitz – used to be a small town with a few historic buildings, notably the church and the municipal hall. Then it acquired a railway junction. That brought the SS.

At the eastern end stands Zakłady Chemiczne, an industrial complex that produces a variety of plastic goods. On this same site, during the war, I. G. Farben produced synthetic fuel and rubber, recruiting its workers from the adjacent labour camp, Monowitz, known as Auschwitz-III. The old fence, with those delicately designed concrete stanchions, still circles the perimeter.

Auschwitz-I is to the west. A compound of two-storey brick buildings. Originally built as barracks for the Polish army. Now a museum. With guide-books.

The gate and its infamous legend: *Arbeit Macht Frei.*
An orchestra greeted the arriving deportees.

Exhibits in various buildings.

An Old Testament, its leather binding scratched and stained. Next to it, a copy of Dante's *Divine Comedy*. The first in Hebrew, the other in German.
The *Divine Comedy* lies open: *Inferno, Canto XIV, Seventh circle, Third ring.*
Nettie reads: *fire falls in flakes, like snow in the Alps, on those who committed violence against God and nature.*

A heap of *Zyklon B* canisters.
The pellets were dropped through vents into gas chambers designed as showers.
Death in 10–20 minutes.
Approximately 5 kilograms for 1,500 deaths.

A mound of human hair.
Those discoloured by cyanide gas were shorn after death.

Piles of victims' property.
Shoes.
Spectacles.
Luggage with names, dates and cities of origin hurriedly scrawled in white paint.
Artificial limbs.
Babies' and children's clothes.
Toys.

Procedure for those not selected for immediate gassing.
Undressing.
Haircut.
Showers.
Assembly in the yard – in the nude.
Distribution of blue-and-grey-striped camp uniforms – by some quirk, Gypsies exempted.
Registration.
Tattooing of identification numbers. Z-xxxxx. Z for *Zigeuner.*

Sewing of identification badges – black triangle for '*asocials*', meaning Gypsies.

Documents:

A testimony, hidden in an aluminium canteen and buried. By Zalman Gradowski, member of *Sonderkommando*, the workforce which cleared up the gas chambers and incinerated the corpses. Found near Crematorium II on 5 March 1945.

Another testimony. By Zalman Lewental. Inmate. Stuffed in a jar and buried. Also found near Crematorium II, this one on 17 October 1962.

A register of Gypsies taken by Polish political prisoners, Roman Frankiewicz, number 9430, and Tadeusz Joachimowski, number 3720, working as clerks in the Gypsy Camp, together with fellow inmates, Ireneusz Pietrzyk, number 1761, and Henryk Porębski, number 5805. Wrapped in pieces of clothing, placed in a large bucket and buried, some time in July 1944, near the fence separating the Gypsy Camp from the Male Camp. Dug up: 9 January 1949.

Block 11. Called the Block of Death, as if the rest of the camp had dispensed life.

Torture cells. Dark cells. Cells with barely enough room to stand. Whipping block. Stake. The Wall of Death – site of some 20,000 executions.

A flag of white and grey stripes – same as the victims' uniform – at half-mast.

Block 10. Medical experiments on prisoners. Research into the physiology of twins.

Sterilization. Pigmentation. Decompression. Water cancer. The effects of extreme temperatures.

Gas chamber and crematorium.

Only one in Auschwitz-I. Four in Birkenau.

Manufacturer's recommended capacity: 4,416 cremations every 24 hours.

Four million people from 28 nations – mainly Jews, Poles, Gypsies and Russians – were murdered here. Barely a few thousand survived. Only 700 or so – some Gypsies among them – escaped successfully.

'Benedict, let's leave! I can't bear it . . .' Nettie had turned pale and was shivering.

Benedict shook his head. 'Birkenau – I must go to Birkenau. Most Gypsies ended up there.'

Nettie hesitated, then nodded.

Through Oświęcim's western suburbs. New houses. New industries.

Birkenau. Brzezinka in Polish. Named after the white birch woods surrounding it. The supreme extermination camp. Auschwitz-II.

The entrance.

A tower disgorging a railway line. Moloch and his tapeworm devouring Mother Earth.

The ramp.

Where the cattle-trucks disgorged the parched, the breathless, the starving, the near dead and those who had suffocated during the long journey.

A mouth like a disembowelment . . . A suppurating eye . . .

Where the angels of death conducted *Selektion* to the infernal din of barking dogs, yelling guards and screaming deportees.

Rule of thumb: those for the *Kamine*, the chimneys, to the left; those for future selections, to the right.

Of some 300 barracks, mostly wooden, about 50 have been preserved.

Most of the smokestacks of those demolished are still standing – a devastated orchard of brick trees.

The Monument to the Victims.

Inscription in various languages, including Romanes: Here 4 million suffered misery and murder at the hands of the Hitlerites.

To the left: Crematorium II. To the right: Crematorium III. As the Russian army approached, the SS tried to demolish them. But they could not destroy the ruins.

Sector B-IIe.

The Gypsy Camp. Originally, two rows of nineteen barracks. Hardly anything standing now.

I was born here.

Here I evaded the eye.

But now . . . Since I met Ariana . . . Now that I know who I am . . . Now, my neck chafes, warning me that the eye is still searching for me.

The site of *Kanada*. So nicknamed by inmates for the abundance of its contents.

It stored the victims' belongings. Thirty barracks often stacked to capacity.

Those who stole from here and participated in the camp's commerce stood a better chance of survival.

Sauna, the bath house. Designed like the showpiece of a spa.

Sumps for sewage. With a capacity most towns would envy.

Crematorium IV and Crematorium V. In the woods. Almost next to each other. Also dynamited by the SS before they fled – though the *Sonderkommando* had already sabotaged Crematorium IV in October 1944.

On the night of 2 August 1944, all the Gypsies who had remained in Birkenau and had survived disease, medical experiments and starvation were gassed.

As the ovens of Crematorium V were out of order at the time, they were burned in nearby pits.

A total of 2,897 souls.

Among them, perhaps Todor and Zara.

Maybe making love for the last time. Not my sick imagination, this. Some couples did. It's on record. *Sonderkommando* had to prize apart their bodies. Todor and Zara. Bear-tamers. Offering death the gift of life. Happily. Because they had managed to save their son.

The pond.

Where the ashes were dumped.

Girdled by white birches.

On some photographs it looks like a pool in a forest. Not so. Barely a few metres in diameter.

Originally, purported to be exceptionally deep.

But now, because of all the ash deposited in it, reckoned to be quite shallow.

Benedict wept.

Nettie, also crying, held on to his arm.

Benedict kissed her hand. 'I'd like to stay a while . . .'

'Sure.'

'Alone.'

Nettie became concerned. 'No . . .'

'Please. Go to the hotel. I'll see you later.'

Birkenau, which Benedict had imagined to be at least the size of a battlefield, was surprisingly compact. A person could cover it in a couple of hours.

He went round several times.

He was seeking, he realized, a sign, an object, a sound that might transport him to the past, deliver him to his mother's or father's arms.

But he found nothing that glorified life; no myths.

Only abandonment.

And self-hate.

Not the kind of self-hate that had afflicted the Hitlerites, and which still threatened to infect all mankind; but the equally dangerous self-hate of the uncommitted, of the indifferent bystander.

And he acknowledged what his soul had always known. He was a broken man, broken many times. Without the will – or the courage – to repair himself. Strutting with his smart masks of soldier, engineer, husband. Wallowing, self-righteously, with his list of grievances: motherless, fatherless, unloved, unwanted; bereft of ideals, illusions, expectations; oh, yes, and childless, seedless.

In effect, a man already dead in many of its selves . . .

But give me credit: a man wanting to die completely.

Offering myself – here, at the very place I was born.

Readiness to die requires courage, too!

Where's the eye?

Come! Select me!

Night fell.

Benedict sat in the ruins of Crematorium V and scanned the darkness.

The pond soughed.

His old friend, the naked, mutilated man who was composed of ashes and whose congealed blood looked like chunks of amber, rose to the surface.

This time Benedict identified him: one of those patriarchs who, like a compassionate god, is born with wounds, but never dies.

The mutilated man whispered into the waters: Zara! Todor!

And Zara and Todor, leading a massive bear on a leash, emerged.

Benedict ran to them. Dei! Dadoro!

They greeted him as a lost son should be greeted. Zara kissed him fervently. Todor hugged him. And the bear nudged him playfully.

Then they spoke to him earnestly.

You have found us, my boy.

Yes, Dei.

He who returns is not a deserter.

I never wanted to be a deserter, Dadoro!

We died so that you could live.

Now open your flesh and give us birth.

I am a broken man, Dei! Not what I seem to be, Dadoro!

Pursue your destiny! Be a great Rom!

Become our mother and father! Deliver your people!

How, Dei? How, Dadoro!

Remember us! Remember your people!

Fulfil the prophecy!

Remember! Remember! Remember!

A new tree will sprout the leaves the donkey ate.

Hope will run down the mountains and stream to the sea; then it will set sail and become earth.

The burst pomegranate will be made whole.

What do they mean, Dei? What do they mean, Dadoro!

A mist rose; the waters engulfed Todor, Zara and the bear.

Benedict strode towards the pond, ready to dive into it.

A voice interjected: Not yet! Not yet!

He stared at the waters, expecting to see the mutilated man.

Instead he glimpsed an old woman, veiled by the reflection of the Milky Way.

She spoke again: Later. The time to embrace the water comes later.

Recognizing the denim skirt, the woollen blouse and the fragrance of mint, he spun round.

Ariana . . .?

Her voice intoned: First you must fulfil the prophecy!

Countless other voices echoed her: Fulfil the prophecy! Fulfil the prophecy! Fulfil the prophecy!

And Branko had a vision:

Whilst flying his eagle across a necropolis, he came upon a flame tree. The tree asked him to carry it to the world of the living. Branko agreed and secured it across his shoulders. Journeying on, he came upon a burst pomegranate which begged him to collect its scattered seeds. When he did so, the pomegranate suckled him with its nectar. Still travelling, he crossed mountains and reached a secret sea. The sea opened its legs and took him in. Then it gave birth to an island of milk, wheat and honey.

Branko asked the shaman to interpret the vision.

'The only soothsayer who can unravel such mysteries', the shaman told him, 'is he whom the snakes made wise, even making him live both as man and woman, namely, blind Tiresias, now long in his grave.'

Branko set out for the Underworld to seek out Tiresias.

After forty months, he came to the Earth's end where the ice freezes the sun. After forty days he reached the bottom of the abyss where the dead sit in strengthless shapes.

He donned a necklace of lapis lazuli to ward off evil spirits and waited.

Blind Tiresias soon sensed Branko's presence and appeared. 'Son of Man, O Del's seed, stout heart, you are here to ask me sooth. But where is my gift?'

Branko dug a pit with his strong hands, then mixed a sherbet of mead, tamarind and rose-water. He poured this into the pit and led Tiresias to it. 'Here.'

Tiresias drank heartily whilst cursing Adam and Eve for striking him blind and depriving him of the sight of the swirling sherbet.

For, once upon a time, Adam and Eve, having disputed as to which gender obtained the greater pleasure in coitus, had gone to consult Tiresias, the only human being that had copulated both as a man and as a woman. Thus, when the seer had told them that it was the female, by no less than nine shares out of ten, who experienced more joy, they had scratched out his eyes: Eve, out of anger, because her sex's secret had been revealed; Adam, out of spite, because he could not accept being inferior to women in any way.

And when Tiresias was sated, he spoke unto Branko. 'Son of Man, O Del's seed, stout heart, your vision is spread over my inner eyes. Riding an eagle like a horse indicates you are in pursuit of your destiny. The flame tree is the Romany Holy Book which was written on cabbage leaves and which perished when a donkey ate it. The burst pomegranate is your dispersed people. The island born to you is Romanestan. Finding the Book, reconstituting your people and streaming to the Promised Land will be your labours.'

'How am I to achieve them?'

Tiresias shuffled away. 'Farewell, stout heart, Son of Man, O Del's seed. You have had your offering's worth.'

Eight

The waiter serving the Japanese businessmen had referred to the Gypsy family as typical flotsam that plagued the open-air restaurants of Eastern Europe.

Benedict observed them.

The father and the two sons played, respectively, the violin, the accordion and the guitar. The mother wove her way through the tables and offered to read fortunes; she was seldom refused. The daughter, about eight, sold roses. All were dressed in bright, delicately embroidered – but frayed – traditional clothes.

They were not typical. The typical Gypsies had been driven into rubbish dumps all over Europe where they toiled desperately for food, air and solid earth. This family was lucky: it was allowed to exist on the peripheries of society where they could earn a crust or two.

Benedict's eyes lingered on their clothes. Were they flags of defiance? Or were they, like their music, palmistry and roses, a gimmick, a romantic image seeking to loosen the punters' purses?

Either way, they were badges that had superseded the *asocial*'s black triangle. They proclaimed that the Gypsy fire was inextinguishable. There was pride in such bravery.

Pride, of course, was the only victual available to the persecuted; it generated the pulse to live on unvanquished. Melchior had had pride – despite his stillborn testicles.

Where's mine?

'*The burst pomegranate will be made whole.*'

Nettie, captivated by the music, mumbled. 'Hmmmm?'

'*Hope will run down the mountains and stream to the sea; then it will set sail and become earth.*'

'Is that what they're singing?'

'*A new tree will sprout the leaves the donkey ate.*'

Nettie smiled. 'Very surreal.'

'It's a prophecy.'

'Are you drunk?'

'No.'

'You should be – after the tedium of getting here.'

Benedict stared into his empty glass. Nettie could divest herself of pain so easily. Then she would wonder why impassable distances opened up between them.

The train journey from Poland had been devotional. Krakow. Brno. Vienna. Budapest. Belgrade. For someone of an older generation, Eloïse, for instance, it would have been a journey reminiscent of the twilight days of Middle Europe, one that Kafka or Zweig might have enjoyed. But for him, it was the journey, in reverse, that had ferried his parents to Birkenau. Before Hitler's era, seasoned travellers used to recommend leisurely stopovers on this route. The Nazi cattle-trucks, given the vagaries of wartime schedules, had covered the distance in several days. Now, in 1978, he and Nettie had taken a mere twenty-four hours despite having to wait for connections in stations where, unlike the deportees, they could stretch, sit, eat and drink.

He refilled his glass and sipped pensively. 'Fulfil it, they said . . . Accept your destiny . . .'

'What? Who?'

'My Dei . . . my mother and father . . . How can I? What do I do? I don't know what the prophecy means. Even Ariana didn't know. Where do I start – assuming I believe in prophecies? I mean, is it truly a pronouncement in the biblical mould, full of thunder, substance and truth? Or just mumbo jumbo? If the first, why should I fret? It'll be fulfilled whatever happens.'

'Benedict, what are you talking about?'

'There was a prophecy when I was born. Ariana reminded me. I told you about it . . .'

'I didn't realize you took it seriously . . .'

'Don't be so supercilious!'

'I'm not!'

Benedict nodded, regretting his outburst. 'That was unfair. I'm sorry. Truly. You know how grateful I am you came along. I'm just tense . . .'

Nettie held his hand. 'Understandably. Digging up the past – always very painful . . . Tell me more about the prophecy . . .'

'The Red Cross official who brought me to Switzerland wrote it down for Ariana. She drummed it into my head all my childhood. When Pro Juventute snatched me, they set out to erase my past. I forgot about the prophecy – until I went to Ariana. Then, in Birkenau, they repeated it – my Dei and Dadoro . . . Fulfil it, they said!'

Nettie held on to his hand. 'Benedict, Auschwitz was . . . One can't keep a grip on reality there. I heard voices, too. And felt those exhibits come to life . . . It's probably how we cope with horror: imagination inducing a catharsis . . .'

'Sometimes imagination is the reality. They were exhorting me – that was real! Be a great Rom! Deliver my people! They want me to repair their deaths, provide meaning for their lives . . . They're still shouting – you can hear them, if you listen . . .'

Nettie kept hold of his hand. 'I'm sure I can . . .'

The waiter arrived with the main course.

Nettie seized the moment to lighten the mood. 'Oh-ho!' She smacked her lips at the cheese-filled meatballs. 'Smells great! What are they again?'

Benedict topped up the wine glasses. '*Cevapcici* with *kajmak* . . .'

The waiter served and left.

Nettie applied herself to the food. 'Yummy!'

Benedict, irritated by her appetite, concentrated on his wine.

They were in Skadarlija, the famous street of old Belgrade, which, in the last century, had ranked as a Bohemian quarter equal to those of Vienna, Prague and Budapest. But little of that erstwhile vitality could be seen. The street lights appeared to have been dimmed by a proficient fifth column; another nefarious force had divested the cobblestones of their good cheer; and the haunts of bygone days, which now functioned as fashionable restaurants for party luminaries and tourists, looked like vulgar copies of lost tapestries. To revive the traditional Serbian sparkle, the street had been turned into a pedestrian enclave, but the people's passion appeared to have been cauterized, like the traffic.

All because, Benedict surmised, the war years had not yet turned into scar tissue. Though Yugoslavia was enjoying an economic boom as a reward for its rapprochement with the West, the ancient conflicts between its religions – Catholic, Orthodox, Islam – and peoples – six republics and two autonomous regions – simmered beneath the trappings of unity. Most families were still traumatized by the purges and vendettas that had erupted at the end of the Second World War. And, of course, the fall-out of gloom that Stalin had bequeathed to Eastern Europe still hung in the air.

'This is delicious. Don't let it get cold.'

Listlessly, Benedict picked at his food.

He had chosen to go to Belgrade as opposed to Zagreb or Ljubljana, in the belief that documentation on Gypsy deportations from Yugoslavia were more likely to be found in Serbia than in Croatia or Slovenia. Most of the records in the latter republics had been destroyed by the *Ustaša* – the Croatian nationalists who had allied themselves to the Nazis – in order to escape retribution as war criminals.

In the event, neither the Serbian National Archives nor the Federal War Records Office had yielded a clue.

What he wanted to find was a link. A record of his parents' deportation. Or a last heroic word or deed by a Gypsy which he could attribute, in his fantasies, to his mother or father. Or a survivor who might have known the Ursari, perhaps even Todor and Zara. A link, in effect, that would feel palpable, that would reconnect him to solid ancestors and fill up his hollowness. Failing that, a link that would offer myth and mystery: an occult link, why not, that would empower him to create a past.

Then he could pull himself out of his *gadjo* complacency and return to a new beginning so that he could start again, this time, on a correct course. Towards a real self. A better self. A made-to-measure, heroic self.

A self without a self. But with a cause. Proving, at the very least, that moral superiority always dwelled with the persecuted and, therefore, it was better to be Gypsy than *gadjo*.

The few Gypsy organizations he had approached – mostly new and in need of support – had lacked the resources for such an endeavour. Ariana had mentioned a few Kalderash *kumpanias* in Romania and Bulgaria that had had dealings with the Ursari, but she had not known their whereabouts or how to contact them behind the Iron Curtain.

He could, of course, approach the Jews, as some officials in Auschwitz had advised him. The Jews were well organized. They had neither forgotten nor forgiven the Holocaust. They had amassed mountains of documents. Many of those would have also chronicled the Gypsy's night and fog.

Benedict pushed his plate away.

Nettie looked up, surprised. 'Aren't you eating?'

Benedict gave vent to his irritation. 'How can you gorge yourself . . .?'

'I'm not gorging myself! I'm trying to enjoy life!' She pointed at his plate. 'If you're not eating, I'll have some of yours.'

Benedict handed her his plate. He poured himself more wine and concentrated on the Gypsy family.

The man, the violinist, was about fifty; his wife, in her forties. There had been concentration camps in Yugoslavia, too. In Jasenovac, for instance, the *Ustaša* had butchered hundreds of thousands – a large proportion of them Gypsies – with a brutality that had shocked even their Nazi masters. How had this couple survived? And how had they generated the courage to believe in a future and produce a family?

The little girl, clutching her bunch of roses to her chest, was approaching their table.

Suddenly Melchior pulled up a chair and sat next to Benedict. And with his heart that remembered every anguish, he related, yet again, the story of someone he had once befriended: a Jew from Thessaloniki, Greece, who had settled in Lausanne before the war, leaving behind mother, father and a sister. His mother and father had died, luckily, before the Nazi occupation; but the sister and her family had been rounded up and deported. A last letter from her had recounted life under the swastika: in order to buy scraps for the family, she had been forced to send her daughters, aged five and six, never knowing whether she would ever see them again, to the seafront tavernas, there to sell flowers to German officers. Even after all these years, the Jew couldn't stop weeping, Melchior said, wiping his own tears, the way he had done at each telling.

Open your flesh and give us birth.

Melchior, old man, what should I do? I don't have any balls!

'A rose for the lady?' The little girl was by his side. She had addressed him in German, the language of wealth for East Europeans.

Benedict handed her a few notes. 'Yes. All of them.'

The little girl stared at the money in amazement; then, dumping the roses onto Benedict's lap, bolted off to her mother.

Nettie was touched. 'How gallant, my darling.'

The little girl was pointing him out to her mother, showing off the money.

The mother was contemplating him. Was she wondering whether he was a deserter?

Benedict turned to Nettie and indicated the violinist. 'My father was a busker, too – of sorts . . . Played the pan-pipes.'

'Is that who you take after? Not Eloïse . . .?'

Benedict smiled. 'I'm an amateur. My father was a pro. He played to make his bears dance . . .'

Nettie made a face. 'Yes. You told me.'

'He also wrestled with them – I didn't tell you that.'

'Ugh! What for?'

'That's what the Ursari do. What I'd be doing today if it hadn't been for the war.'

'Well, thank God for . . . I mean, thank God, you were spared all that . . .'

'It would have been an honest life.'

'Honest?'

'I'd be who I am. Not someone I'm pretending to be. I'd know where I was going, what I had to do, what I was born to do.'

He who returns is not a deserter.

'Oh, really, Benedict! Sometimes you talk such nonsense!'

Benedict grinned contentiously; the fortune-teller was still staring at him. 'Time to have our future read.'

Nettie turned back to her plate. 'No, thank you.'

'Come on – we'll see what's in store.' He beckoned the fortune-teller.

Sombrely, the woman came across. She gave a cursory glance at Nettie, then gazed deeply into Benedict's eyes.

Benedict held out his palm. Could he plunge into her heart and emerge reborn? 'Tell me everything . . .'

The fortune-teller smiled mysteriously. 'You already know.' She moved to go.

Benedict protested. 'Wait! Please. Tell me . . .'

The fortune-teller shook her head. 'I told you, *Manush*, you already know what you need to know.' Gently, she folded his palm. 'The rest has no importance.' She walked away.

Nettie was incensed. 'Patronizing bitch! What did she mean? What did she call you?'

'*Manush*. Another word for Rom. She saw I was a Gypsy.'

'Really?'

'It never occurred to me I could still be spotted . . .'

'Amazing.'

'That's why she wouldn't read my hand. Gypsies don't tell each other's fortunes . . .'

Nettie chuckled. 'Honour among rogues?'

'She's not a rogue!' Benedict, controlling his resentment, lit a *Villiger*. 'Finish eating and let's get out of here!'

They had strolled in Kalemegdan, the park that dominated the confluence of the Danube and the Sava.

Kalemegdan, the guide-book had informed them, was a Turkish word meaning 'Castle Square'. There were, indeed, the ruins of a castle – this being Belgrade's highest point – but it had been built by the Serbs. Nevertheless, it had lived its finest hours under Turkish hands when Austria and Catholicism had cowered, across the Danube, before the Ottoman empire.

Benedict enjoyed being in Kalemegdan.

Since his original surname, Pehlivan, 'wrestler', was of Turkish origin, he could entertain the thought that, in an alternative dimension, Kalemegdan's durability stood as a symbol of his own strength.

Moreover, the countless couples who, lacking privacy in their homes, did their courting in the park, intimated for him a hopeful future. Perhaps this generation will truly be revolutionary. Remember Hansi and his Marianne? Maybe these youngsters sitting and hugging, kissing and caressing, whispering and laughing, on the grass, on the benches, in the shadows, will never be converted to ideologies that worshipped persecution, torture and death.

They had walked back through Knez Mihailova, taking time to look at the drab displays in shop windows, to Terazije, where their hotel, the Moskva, stood. Benedict had insisted on staying at the Moskva, an imposing, *belle époque* building which, having served as the Gestapo headquarters, had been blown up by the partisans then rebuilt after the war.

They had not talked. Nettie had held his hand early on at Kalemegdan. He had clung to it, seeking in the contact a safe texture, like on that first time he had placed his head on her belly, when, repeatedly, in emotions both expressed and left unsaid, she had promised him everything, especially a sanctuary, his very own, unassailable and always available haven where he could be reborn in perpetuity.

Often she had reneged on that promise.

But he had forced himself to believe that one day she would keep to it.

That day had arrived. She had agreed to have a child.

The Moskva's pavement café was still crowded. Some locals. Clusters from Eastern bloc countries, a quota of Russians, a sprinkling of Chinese, a few Eurocrats, the odd Anglo-Saxon and the ubiquitous throng of German tourists.

The last were surrounded by a gang of Gypsy children begging money and cigarettes. The tourists obliged, generously, except for cigarettes; smoking was bad for health, they told the children. The latter mockingly repeated their words and pocketed their alms.

Fury swept Benedict. He grabbed the nearest boy. 'You are Rom! Why are you begging?'

The boy stared at him, scared.

One of the Germans interjected. 'Hey, leave him alone!'

Benedict glared at the man: tall, athletic, greying hair, a distinguished sort, like Leo Leo. No, not like Leo Leo. More like Benedict himself. The sort born to wear uniforms. The sort who, packaged in caps, tunics, fatigues, insignia, boots, glowed and made other men envious. The sort before whom children – and some women – melted. Just like himself, damnation!

Further outraged by these thoughts, Benedict ranted at the boy. 'You should be ashamed of yourselves! Gypsies shouldn't beg! That's not for us! You think you're fleecing the *gadje*? You're not – you're debasing yourself! Where's your pride?'

Nettie tried to pull him away. 'Benedict!'

The tall German shouted at him. 'Let the boy be!'

Benedict released the boy, spun towards the German and fulminated. 'You like them to beg, do you? Seeing them grovelling makes you feel good, does it? Well, come and pick someone your size! Here I am! *Manush*! Z for *Zigeuner*! Come and make me grovel! Try and finish what your father started! Come on, shit-face! Show your balls!'

The Germans were staring at him, stunned.

Nettie strove to pull him away. 'Benedict! Stop this! What's come over you? '

The tall German rose from his seat.

Benedict pushed Nettie away and took an unarmed combat stance. 'Come on, *obersturm-totenkopf*! Let's see what you're made of without a *panzer* division behind you! Come on, come to the *Zigeuner*!'

The others at the table and a woman, presumably the man's wife, pleaded with the German. They prevailed. Reluctantly, the man sat down and ignored Benedict.

Benedict turned to the children. 'Go on, all of you! Stop licking their arses! They're *gadje*! And *gadje* love killing Rom! Remember that!'

Passers-by had gathered. People were rising from their tables to see what was going on; waiters were coming across to intervene.

Nettie, in despair, punched Benedict's arm. 'I'm going in!' She hurried towards the hotel.

Benedict, finally registering Nettie's rage, became indecisive. He glared at the Germans, then at the children, then at the people who had gathered. Then he turned back to the Germans and yelled at them. 'Go to Auschwitz! You might understand!' He strode after Nettie.

Benedict stood by the window and gazed at the city. During the day, Belgrade had looked like the harassed mother of young children fallen on hard times. But nocturnal Belgrade, hiding her desperate eyes, exhausted gait and wrinkles of defeat, looked capable of soothing even the most frightened infant.

Nettie came out of the bathroom, naked, except for the towel wrapped round her head. 'If we leave tomorrow, I can take my last two seminars. I've not been happy delegating them to Dagmar.'

Benedict poured some *šlivovica*, the only drink he could get from room service, into two glasses.

Nettie sat on the bed and started drying her hair. 'Impasse everywhere. Not surprising, really. All we had to go on was that your parents were on the run in Yugoslavia.'

Benedict put her drink by her side. 'Picked the right one, didn't I? Big fellow. He'd have hurt me.'

She discarded the towel and started brushing her hair. 'Would have served you right. Crazy!'

He smiled bitterly and raised his glass. 'Crazy, indeed. Maybe born crazy. Maybe that's why they zapped me with all that electricity . . .'

'Oh, don't start, Benedict. Aren't you undressing?'

'I'm forgiven, am I?'

She put away her brush, moved to him and started unbuttoning his shirt. 'Sometimes you're so thick . . . Can't you see I know what you're going through, how much you're suffering . . .?' She took his shirt off. 'It's been a terrible time. First Eloïse. Then Melchior. Then all that business with Ariana. And then Auschwitz. You're on your knees. You're waiting for something else to hit you.'

Benedict muttered cryptically. 'Maybe it already has . . .'

She unzipped his trousers. 'On second thoughts, let's not go back. To hell with my seminars. Let's take a holiday. You've got ten more days off work. Let's go to the sea. The Dalmatian coast . . . You can touch me, you know . . .'

Abstractedly, he began to stroke her back.

She pulled off his shoes. 'A quiet holiday. Drain away the anguish. Pick yourself off the floor. Let things fall into perspective.' She shook him. 'Don't you want to play?'

'Sure.'

'You're not being very co-operative.'

Desultorily, he pecked her neck, cupped her breasts and ran his tongue around the aureoles.

She manoeuvred him onto the bed, pulled down his trousers and pants and took off his socks. She kissed his erection. 'At least he's enthusiastic . . .'

'Yes . . .'

'I'll play with him then. Join us when you feel like it.' She straddled him.

She became a lake, clear, enfolding and flawlessly liquid – the perfect womb. Suddenly, the impassivity he had been trying to attain, dissolved. He squeezed her breasts, lapped at her nipples.

She rocked on his penis. 'Now you're with me . . .'

He bucked vigorously.

She rolled over and pulled him on top of her. She raised her legs and entwined them around his back. 'Deeply . . . All the way . . .'

He thrust with increasing fervour, kissed, bit and sucked her breasts.

She began to moan. 'Deep – that's it . . . This time it'll happen . . . This time . . .'

He thrust relentlessly.

'The time's right. That's it – deep . . . I'll conceive, I know I will.'

He froze.

She quickened lustily. 'Don't stop. I'm coming!'

He disengaged from her.

She tried to hold on to him. 'No! Stay!'

He rolled over.

She hit him playfully, though not without some anger. 'I was about to come . . .'

'Sorry.'

She went on her knees. 'From behind – that's just as good . . .'

'Let's call it a night . . .'

'You haven't come either . . .'

'Doesn't matter.'

'Oh, yes, it does! A lot!'

'You won't conceive.'

She protested angrily. 'I'm trying to! I want to! I really do!'

'I know.' He rose and moved back to the window. 'You won't conceive with me. I'm sterile.'

'What . . .?'

He lit a cigar. 'Like Melchior. Some irony, eh?'

'This is a sick joke!'

He shouted, full of despair. 'I've had tests!'

She sat up, pulled the blanket over her nudity. 'When? Why?'

'We've been trying for weeks. I began to think. I had mumps – in the army. Soon after my call-up. So I went to Young Glanz . . .'

'We'll go to specialists. There have been great advances . . .'

'I've seen the specialists. My sperm count is almost nil. A few live ones, no more. Certainly not enough to fertilize. 'Not even a snowball's chance in hell,' was how one consultant summed up . . .'

She rose from the bed and moved to him. 'Why didn't you tell me?'

'I couldn't. Not easy to say I'm dead, I'm nothing.'

She slapped him. 'You bastard!'

He turned round sharply, held his genitals with his hands and displayed them to her. 'Look! Gypsy's cherry-splitter – groomed into a civilized Swiss cock. But, in the process, it's turned antiseptic and dried up. Poetic justice, eh?'

She punched his chest. 'Bastard! Bastard!'

When she stopped punching him, Benedict turned away and, softly, began to cry.

Nettie sat on the bed dejectedly. 'You should have told me! All this time – knowing how I've been trying . . . What do we do now?'

Benedict mumbled. 'You can take the flight tomorrow. I'll stay on a few days.'

'What for?'

'To search.'

'Search for what?'

'A burst pomegranate. Hope that will become earth. A new tree . . .'

Adam commissioned Gog and Magog to kill Kurma and Krishna, the Great Avatars. 'One is like a tortoise; the other is half-man, half-lion. Both have six formidable tusks with which they guard the Romanies' aspirations. Bring the tusks as proof of their death.'

Gog and Magog set up a trap: they stole Earth's dew and imprisoned it in a fissure in the land of fumaroles.

Earth wailed. The dew impregnated her daily. How could she be Supreme Mother without it?

Kurma and Krishna consoled her: 'We will retrieve the dew. Else all life will end.'

And they went to the land of fumaroles.

But as they scoured the place, the lapilli, headless maggots, the spilled seeds of Beelzebub, sire of Gog and Magog, coiled around them and pinned them down.

And Gog and Magog swooped upon the Great Avatars.

They cut off their tusks and lanced them with spears.

When Kurma and Krishna failed to return, Earth alerted Branko who was like a brother unto them.

Branko sped to the land of fumaroles.

Finding Kurma and Krishna slain, he pierced his vein and poured portions of his blood into them.

And breath returned to them; but they could not move because without tusks the bodies of Great Avatars are like broken chalices: all their ichor seeps away.

Branko comforted them. 'You must grow new tusks. You need the spittle of a sage who judges the dead. I will go to Dharma, in India, who is such a man.'

No sooner did Branko leave than Munkar and Nkir, Angels Who Serve Immortal Souls, came down from Heaven and started digging the ground near Kurma and Krishna.

The Great Avatars became intrigued.

'Are you searching for the dew?' asked Kurma.

'It is incarcerated in a fissure,' said Krishna.

'We are preparing a double grave,' replied Munkar.

'For two of O Del's children,' added Nkir.

When they finished digging, Munkar and Nkir looked uncertain.

'We forgot to ask O Del how tall His children were,' murmured Munkar.

'Sepulchres must be comfortable,' groaned Nkir.

'We are both children of O Del,' shouted Kurma.

'Take your measurements from us,' urged Krishna.

'Would you lie in this tomb?' asked Munkar.

'So we can see if it is wide enough,' added Nkir.

The Great Avatars willingly agreed.

Gently, Munkar and Nkir laid down Kurma and Krishna side by side.

'A perfect fit,' said Kurma.

'Like a womb,' agreed Krishna.

Munkar produced a rose and offered it to Kurma. 'Smell this. It bears our gratitude.'

Nkir produced an orchid and offered it to Krishna. 'Smell this. It carries our prayers.'

113

And, Kurma and Krishna, smelling their flowers, shed their pain and surrendered their souls.

Munkar and Nkir covered them with clay.

They burned incense on the mound and transformed it into a beautiful lingam.

They planted banyan trees to give it shade.

And they created a jade lake to lure gossamer breezes.

Branko, laden with Dharma's spittle, returned.

Awed by the transformed landscape, he asked Munkar and Nkir. 'Am I dreaming, holy guides? Was not this patch a wasteland?'

'It was. Now it is the shrine of Kurma and Krishna,' replied Munkar.

'We modelled it on Romanestan,' added Nkir.

Branko wept. 'Why did you not wait for me? I would have saved them!'

'Even Great Avatars must die,' said Munkar.

'Else they cannot be reborn,' affirmed Nkir.

'How will I bear their loss?' grieved Branko.

'Retrieve the dew,' advised Munkar.

'And return it to Earth,' exhorted Nkir.

And Branko stormed into the land of fumaroles and crushed the headless maggots.

Then, weaving Dharma's spittle into a web, he trawled the fissures and fished out the dew.

And O Del invested him with the feet of the tiger which has the strongest claws in all Creation and with the eyes of the eagle which are so fast that only two of them have ever been seen by man.

Nine

'Under the Nazis' genocidal policies, Gypsies suffered the same fate as Jews. In some aspects, worse: whereas thousands of Jews left Germany after the Nuremberg laws, Gypsies didn't – couldn't.'

'I didn't know it was as bad as that.'

Dr Hajim Kalderon adjusted his skullcap with gnarled hands. 'You didn't know because prejudice against Gypsies is as virulent as ever. They're still pariahs. Most countries either ignore the *Porajmos* – that's what the Gypsies call the Holocaust, meaning something like a relentless devouring – or suppress it.'

Benedict's eyes strayed again to the tattoo on Dr Kalderon's left forearm: the Auschwitz identification number, the mark with which the Nazis had rendered millions nameless. Holocaust experts, he had read somewhere, could tell, by the serial order, the victims' country of origin and their date of arrival at the camp.

A tattoo he, too, should have borne. In Auschwitz, even newborn babies had been branded. But his parents had thwarted the Hitlerites by keeping his birth secret, an achievement which the Gypsy Camp had interpreted as proof of the prophecy's truth – so the Red Cross official had told Ariana.

Today, he resented its absence. The mark would have defined his past.

Dr Kalderon led him to a display of some faded photographs. He pointed out one that showed the cast of a school play. 'Girl at the far left – Esther Nachmias. She let all the boys kiss her.'

Survivors of concentration camps, Benedict had presumed, would be forlorn, taciturn, even hostile. But everything about Dr Kalderon, ex-president of the Federation of Hebraic Communities of Yugoslavia, founder and curator, in his retirement, of Sarajevo's Jewish Museum, appeared to be praising life. The wrinkles that mapped his gamin face gave him a smiling mien even when serious.

'And that's me.' Dr Kalderon was pointing at another photograph: a large group of teenagers on an outing by a lake. 'The boy pulling a face is Mordo Sion. He and I are the only ones to survive from that band.'

I am a survivor, too. Born in Birkenau, in fact. Had I stayed on, I'd probably have ended up as one of Mengele's guinea pigs. Nevertheless, I am damaged. They sizzled me in the orphanages.

'Mordo married an Egyptian Jewess and settled in Alexandria. After the Arab-Israeli war of '67, they fled to France.'

Benedict began to feel claustrophobic. The Jewish Museum, built in the early nineteenth century as a synagogue and, in adherence to Ottoman dictate, modestly designed in order not to stand higher than the nearby Gazi Husref Bey Mosque, looked like a looted burial ground.

The exhibits were limited to some nondescript household items; only the few photographs stood witness to the thriving community that had all but perished.

The Gypsies couldn't even leave photographs behind!

'Exactly how many Gypsies died – is it known?'

Dr Kalderon, legs and arms windmilling, like a child's drawing of a man, led the ascent to the top floor. 'About a quarter of the Romany population of Occupied Europe. Possibly half a million. Many historians claim more. We'll never know for sure. Though Hitler's psychopaths kept meticulous documentation on Jews, they were often cavalier – except in Auschwitz – with Gypsies. They considered them even baser than Jews. Many thousands were massacred on the spot during round-ups or at roadsides and left uncounted.'

Benedict felt a surge of tears. 'All that's forgotten?'

Dr Kalderon paused at the top of the stairs. 'Swept under the carpet. Germany – both Germanies – have been trying to wash their hands. For instance, in 1950, the Württemberg State Ministry of Interior in the Federal Republic declared that the Nazi persecution of the Gypsies had not stemmed from racial policies, but had constituted measures against their asocial and criminal history. Note: *asocial* and *criminal*: the two halves of the Gypsy archetype invented by our so-called civilized world.'

Benedict nodded. 'Outrageous!'

Dr Kalderon grimaced. 'Banal, actually. We create archetypes in our own image. It's our ways that are asocial and criminal.' He paused, trying to regain his breath.

Benedict waited in awe. The man was over seventy and very frail. But he seemed to possess the passion of a prophet.

Dr Kalderon resumed just as intensely. 'Both Germanies contend that Gypsy demands for reparations are unreasonable and slanderous.'

'On what grounds?'

'Grounds are easy to fabricate. What's unforgivable is that nobody challenges them. Not even the Jews. I hate saying this, but my people have monopolized the Holocaust. Made it exclusive – as if it were a special gift from God. I, too, used to indulge in that mania. Our appropriation of the Holocaust eclipsed the *Porajmos*; whilst the Jews pressed for reparations, the Gypsies lost out. The tragedy is: reparations would have transformed the Gypsies – at the very least, rescued most of them from a marginal existence.'

Benedict nodded mournfully.

Dr Kalderon waited until his breath steadied. 'The situation in countries which had a front-seat view of Nazi terror and which lost vast numbers of their Gypsies – Hungary, Czechoslovakia, Poland, Romania, the Soviet Union – is still abysmal. When Gypsies are not being persecuted or jailed, they are condemned to live as untouchables. Or, as in Romania, where until 1864, they were slaves – literally – they get killed, a few at a time, in periodic atrocities. Even in democratic countries, they are deprived of some of their basic human rights. Doesn't that make you rage?'

The question, put suddenly and directly, riled Benedict. 'Oh, yes! And I rage all the more because Gypsies like me – the lucky ones – collude with the persecutors by choosing to be blind!'

Dr Kalderon laid his eyes on Benedict. 'Good. Hold on to your rage.'

Luminous, coal-black eyes. Capable of soothing despair and providing light and warmth in the darkness. Like Melchior's eyes. Should I tell him I was born in Birkenau?

The top floor constituted the loft and contained a single display: a leather-bound book, about a metre long, hanging down from the rafters.

Dr Kalderon sighed. 'Had this been a museum celebrating the past instead of lamenting it, we could have had the *Sarajevo Haggada* here.'

'What's that?'

'The Passover Book. Narrates the Exodus from Egypt. Our ancestors brought it from Spain when they fled the Inquisition. A beautiful illuminated manuscript. It's in the National Museum Library.'

Benedict approached the book hanging from the rafters. 'This looks very impressive . . .'

Dr Kalderon opened it reverently. 'Our Scroll of the Dead. Those of our community who died in the Holocaust.'

Dutifully, Benedict looked through the pages at the columns of names: Asher, Baruh, Casuto, Danon, Ergas, Farchi, Gategno, Hulli, Israel, Jakar, Kalderon.

He turned to the old man. 'Many Kalderons. Relatives?'

Dr Kalderon nodded sadly. 'Some near, some distant.'

Benedict closed the book. Suddenly he wanted to run out of the museum, flee from its guardian who, having come back from the dead, was dragging him back to life, not the rarefied life Melchior and Eloïse had created for him, but the life lived at ground level, life that scourged Gypsies, Jews and all the downtrodden, life that needed reconsecration.

Dr Kalderon appeared to have sensed his distress. 'How about some tea?'

Baščaršija, the old city's Turkish market, was being rebuilt. Its narrow, cobblestone streets and countless tiny shops, virtually razed to the ground in the blood-letting of the early post-war years, were being restored with great attention to detail and, Dr Kalderon had added wryly, to socialist-universalist ideals. It would be completed in time for the 1984 Winter Olympics which Sarajevo was hosting.

The chaos the restoration had unleashed seemed to have increased the city's vitality. Though there were few signs of prosperity in people's attire, the warren of shops, many still skeletal, specializing in jewellery, sweaters, leather, tin, copper and silver ware, teemed with shoppers fervently bargaining or bartering.

Dr Kalderon, who had been waylaid by a fellow townsman, returned to their table. 'The coffee-house is the Turk's greatest invention. But it has a flaw: you always meet someone you know.' He nodded towards his acquaintance. 'He was interested in you. He thought you had something to do with the Olympics. Rich, in other words.'

Benedict smiled and glanced wistfully at one of the posters announcing the construction of new stadia. As it happened, he could have competed in the Olympics – in the one in Sapporo, in 1972 – and might even have been among the medals; the Swiss association had invited him to join the biathlon team, but he had been courting Nettie at the time and had dropped out.

He still regretted the decision. Nettie often remarked that his 'alpine Tarzan's life' – the climbing, the fieldwork for the Hydroelectricity Board and the eagerly awaited stints in the army – was to compensate for that disappointment.

'Do I look rich?'

'All foreigners look rich.'

'As a good socialist, your friend should be above such considerations.'

'He's also an old plutocrat. He remembers what money is like. And he has a daughter to marry.'

'I'm already hitched.'

'I told him that. He doesn't think you're happy with your wife.'

Benedict looked up sadly. 'He can tell that?'

'From your eyes. You're also travelling alone. So I told him you were a Gypsy. He lost interest immediately.' Dr Kalderon chuckled heartily.

Benedict, finding the old man's laughter infectious, chuckled.

The waiter arrived and served tea and plates of cheese and spinach pasties.

Dr Kalderon's hands twirled ecstatically. 'Time to be serious: time for pleasure.'

The savoury pasty, called *börek*, must have been invented by a Turkish saint, the old man had told Benedict on their way to the café, for so magical was its taste that it could render the clenched fist into an open hand and thus transform a punch into a caress.

Benedict ate one. 'Delicious.'

Dr Kalderon proffered the sugar.

'No, thank you.'

Dr Kalderon placed several cubes on his saucer. 'Wise man. Bad for you, sugar is. Alas, it's my passion.' He put one in his mouth and, beaming, sipped his tea. '*Sastimasa*. "Your health" in Romanes.'

Benedict raised his cup. '*Sastimasa*.'

According to the Federation of Hebraic Communities from whom Benedict had sought a source that might provide information on the Gypsy round-ups, Dr Kalderon was not only an important scholar of the Holocaust, but also someone who had dedicated himself to the Romany cause. During his time in Auschwitz, he had become many Gypsies' blood-brother. And he had learned Romanes. These days, even the ultra-traditionalist Gypsies were distinguishing him from the hated *gadje* by referring to him with the almost affectionate, certainly less offensive, appellation, '*biboldo*', meaning 'un-baptized'.

Dr Kalderon popped another cube into his mouth. 'I used to dream about sugar. I think that's what kept me going.'

Benedict nodded solemnly.

Dr Kalderon gazed pensively at the clock tower, across the square, still indicating, for the Faithful, in Arabic script, the hours of prayer. 'Whatever generates defiance deserves praise. What keeps you going?'

'Children.' Benedict had answered without thinking. Strange that his heart should still believe in his testicles.

Dr Kalderon spread his eyes over him. 'Nothing better.'

'Except that I can't have any.'

What would keep him going now?

Nettie?

She had left him to his quest without demur.

Would she forgive him for bullying her for a baby all those years? Was she relieved she didn't have to have any – would not have to? What about all that femininity she had discovered, all the maternal treacle she had so bravely begun to gush out?

Come back soon, she had said, after kissing him goodbye, as if his infertility were of no consequence. As if she could help him carry his cross.

Dr Kalderon readjusted his skullcap. Was he shading his eyes to conceal his pity? 'So you can't have children of your own. Not the end of the world. There are other children to have.'

A womb facing disuse. A man blighted. What can hold Nettie and me together now?

'Other children?'

Dr Kalderon tipped the rest of the tea into his mouth. 'A man can be father to all.' He attacked another *börek*. 'Tell me. Now that you've found your rage, how will you help your people?'

Benedict, caught by the sharp tone and the sudden change of subject, looked at the old man sheepishly. 'What can I do? What do you do – besides running a museum?'

Dr Kalderon shut his eyes and pondered. Without the luminosity of his pupils, his face looked like an eyeless Roman sculpture. His voice became solemn. 'I stand up to be counted. First: as a Jew. Second: as the Gypsy's *phral*, brother. I didn't – before the Nazis. I was a European then – a so-called enlightened man. I know better now. Being Jewish is a blessing. Or being Romany. Or whoever. What we are is what makes us unique. A world of unique peoples, of countless colours and creeds is what paradise is all about.'

Benedict abandoned his food. 'Except that uniqueness spawns hatred, unleashes evil! Your people and mine – they stood up and were counted! In their millions! In the gas chambers!'

'What's more dignified? Living and dying as yourself? Or hiding behind your shadow, wearing the persecutor's face?'

120

'Swatted to death, nameless and faceless – that's not dignified!'

Dr Kalderon, his arms rotating out of control, roared. 'Who says that? Did you witness their passion? Did you watch them line up for the gas? Silently or in shock or defiant or weeping or protesting or screaming or praying, sometimes even smiling and laughing? Did you see them afterwards, in a heap, children at the top because they'd been held high so that they could breathe another second more because the gas rose up from the floor; husbands and wives entwined, some in a last, desperate act of love; all of them pasted with excreta, mouths open, eyes bulging, faces twisted by frozen screams? Did you?'

Benedict squirmed. 'Please . . . Forgive me . . . I . . .'

Dr Kalderon was now standing up, towering over him, one hand trying to keep his skullcap in place. 'I tell you, not one of them believed what was being done to them was the work of man! Their disbelief, their total incomprehension, was their dignity!'

Benedict lowered his head. 'I'm sorry. Forgive me. I've been very insensitive . . .'

Dr Kalderon threw some money on the table, then pulled Benedict by his jacket. 'Let's breathe some air. There's much you must learn and a lot I have to tell you.'

They had made for Vojvode Stepe, the road that ran parallel to the River Miljacka.

Dr Kalderon had pointed out the university library, a pseudo-Moorish palace that had been the town hall in the days when Austria had ruled Bosnia. From that building Archduke Franz Ferdinand, heir to the Habsburg throne, and his wife, Sophie Chotec, had set out to their assassination at the hands of the Bosnian nationalist, Gavrilo Princip.

Taking Benedict down a block, opposite the bridge that had since been named after Princip, Dr Kalderon had shown him the spot, marked by a crude set of footprints traced on the cement, where the young assassin had stood and fired.

And he had deliberated. Defiance: that's the primary rule – the moral of history, assuming history had a moral. Yet look, here you remove a heinous bigot – which is what the archduke had been – and what happens: you unleash the First World War, snuff millions of souls. Where is the logic of

121

that? On the other hand, what can a decent man do but defy the death-peddlers and, if need be, die?

Why do we accept such an unholy equation? Because we know, in our guts, one day the equation will change. And it will change only through defiance.

Then, declaring that he needed to clear his mind, he had dragged Benedict up to the old fortified citadel of Vratnik.

They sat on a bench by the ramparts and imbibed the stunning panorama. The citadel, encircled by curvaceous mountains, looked like a baby surrounded by a bunch of buxom wet nurses.

They had procured tea from a street-seller.

Dr Kalderon indulged in his quota of sugar.

Benedict, drifting with the old man's mood, lit a *Villiger*.

As if the click of the lighter was the cue he had been waiting for, Dr Kalderon took a deep breath and began speaking. 'What I'll tell you will change you. Being a great believer in destiny, I'd even say fate brought you to my door so that you'd hear this story . . .'

Benedict smiled through the cigar's smoke.

Dr Kalderon laid his eyes, deep as time, on Benedict. 'It's about a Gypsy I knew in Auschwitz.'

Benedict's interest was instantly aroused.

'I never found out where he came from. What his tribe was. He arrived in a transport from Yugoslavia. That's where he was caught. I never found out his name either. In a place where they divested people of identity, he chose to discard his name also. Someone called him Branko because he reminded him of a Branko he knew. The name stuck.'

Benedict interjected soulfully. 'My Romany name is Branko!'

Dr Kalderon responded deferentially. 'A good name. Use it well.'

Benedict waited in suspense.

Dr Kalderon's voice became reverential. 'Branko was always writing – everything people told him. God knows where he found pen and paper. Naturally, we took him for a man of letters. He denied that. He said he was unschooled. He claimed it wasn't he who wrote, but the spirit of the sky who wrote through him. He swore he had no knowledge of anything, except bears . . .'

Benedict felt a sharp pain. 'Bears? My father was a bear-leader. Ursari. He was caught in Yugoslavia, too. And deported to Auschwitz!'

Dr Kalderon looked up, disconcerted. 'Really? Why didn't you tell me? What did he look like?'

'I don't know. Like me, maybe – I mean, maybe I look like him . . .'

'Could he read and write?'

'I don't know.'

'When was he caught?'

'1944.'

Dr Kalderon pondered a moment. 'Branko arrived late '43.'

Benedict felt disappointed. 'Oh . . .'

Dr Kalderon dropped sugar cubes into his tea and stirred them. 'Eventually Branko was taken to Block 21, in the main camp – where SS surgeons conducted experiments on castration. Objective: the best method for reducing undesirable races to a robotic workforce. Branko was a very strong man; and had stayed strong, despite the starvation rations – he was thus a perfect candidate.'

Dr Kalderon, checking that the sugar had melted, mumbled something in Romanes and poured some of the tea onto the ground in libation. 'I was appointed Branko's nurse. I was a real doctor in those days – not long qualified – so I'd been assigned to the camp hospital.'

Tearful and distraught, Dr Kalderon took a deep breath. 'The surgeons did their deed. No anaesthetics. Just two intramuscular injections. For forty-eight hours Branko suffered unimaginable pain. The third day, the pain stopped – or so he said . . .'

Benedict stubbed out his cigar and lit another.

'Whenever I attended to him, he'd be cheerful, but impatient. Hurry up, he'd say, I've got lots of begetting to do. He meant his writing. Once the pain had abated, he had started writing again. Non-stop. They think they've unmanned me, he'd say, but they're in for a surprise: I will sire a colossus.' Dr Kalderon paused, biting his lips.

Benedict touched the old man's hand. 'If it's too upsetting . . .'

'On the seventh day, he was to join a labour force. That was part of the experiment: to see how soon a castrate could start work. The night before, he wrote continuously. Then he stopped and said, I've done it. He handed me the whole pile – bits and pieces of every sort of paper you can think of: toilet paper, wrapping paper, newsprint, book pages, sheets torn from notebooks. He told me to give it to a Polish Gypsy for safekeeping – a man called Tomek who was in a forestry workforce. Then he closed his eyes. In death, we are reborn, he said, and died.'

Benedict held his head in his hands and stared at the ground. Silence cocooned him.

Silence that is heavy and rotund and veined and soft and has nipples; in death we are reborn; silence that is gravid; silence that will bear and suckle . . . Bear what? Suckle whom? Bear a child? Bear a bear? A bear-leader? Bear a leader? In death?

He heard his voice resonate from afar. 'Branko's story will change me, you said. Is it because, unconscionable as it is, it offers hope?'

Dr Kalderon faced Benedict. 'The answer lies in another question – which you haven't dared ask.'

'Which is?'

'What had Branko written?'

Benedict shrugged. 'A testimony, I imagine . . .'

Dr Kalderon looked disappointed, as if Benedict was being perversely mindless. 'Actually, a Testament. The Gypsy Bible.'

'What?'

'The Holy Book of the Romany People.'

Benedict felt goose pimples erupt. 'You're not serious!'

Dr Kalderon gave him a withering look, then rose stiffly from the bench, readjusted his skullcap and shuffled away.

Dr Kalderon, Benedict decided, enjoyed testing people's patience. Since leaving Vratnik, he had maintained the sort of stern face that repulsed any approach.

Now, they were on Mount Trebević, where some of the Olympic events would take place.

It had not been the scenery, splendid though it was, that had prompted the old man to come up here, but the sudden appearance of an acquaintance who had happened to be driving in that direction and had gladly agreed to give them a lift.

They walked along a footpath, occasionally stopping to admire the profusion of spring flowers. Below, Sarajevo, straddling the Miljacka river, looked like a saffron butterfly with a blue spine.

The flowers mollified Dr Kalderon. Linking arms with Benedict, he became, once again, the affectionate patriarch. 'Tell me your thoughts . . .'

Benedict spoke in a torrent. 'Branko was teetering on the edge – even before his castration. Imagining the spirit of the sky writing through him.

When they mutilated him, his mind snapped. He took refuge in evangelistic frenzy.'

Dr Kalderon paused to admire the cyclamens. 'In Auschwitz the Heavens were empty. Not a place for evangelistic frenzy.'

Benedict fumbled for a cigar. 'You don't really believe his writings were sacred text?'

'I do.'

'How could that be possible?'

Dr Kalderon shifted his skullcap. 'According to some Gypsies, in every generation, God finds a person who serves as the custodian of the Holy Book.'

Benedict lit his cigar. 'But Gypsies don't have a Holy Book!'

'They have the *Swatura*.'

'What's that?'

'The oral tradition. Legends. Stories. Tales. Fables.'

'Hardly a Holy Book.'

'Some legends are about the Holy Book. Legends always have a historical basis.'

Benedict became derisive. 'Are you saying Branko was made custodian of the Book in compensation for his castration?'

Dr Kalderon turned towards the afternoon sun as if it held the answer. 'My own view is: the Holy Book exists in the Gypsies' collective unconscious. The moment Branko set foot in Auschwitz, he became receptive to revelation, fathomed his people's deepest memories. He read the Book in their bones – and copied it down.'

Benedict turned impatient. 'But no such Book exists!'

Dr Kalderon looked amused. 'It did once. That which existed never perishes.'

'When?'

'According to one tradition, it was written on cabbage leaves. Then a donkey came and ate it all up.'

Benedict froze.

Dr Kalderon bent down stiffly to smell some hyacinths. 'A strange yarn, I grant you. Like the one that says the world has seventy-two and a half religions of which just the one-half belongs to the Gypsies. The sort of puerile drivel the *gadje* disseminate. But an indication, nevertheless, that the Book existed . . .'

Benedict was barely audible. '*A new tree will bear the leaves the donkey ate.*'

Dr Kalderon rose sharply. 'What did you say?'

'Part of a prophecy. *The burst pomegranate will be made whole. Hope will run down the mountains and stream to the sea; then it will set sail and become earth . . .*'

Dr Kalderon's eyes bored into him. 'How do you know this prophecy?'

Benedict took a deep breath. 'In Auschwitz – did you ever hear about a Gypsy baby who'd been smuggled out?'

'I heard of several. A German engineer, Helmut by name, was the smuggler. It was his way of atoning for the atrocities.'

'I am referring to a particular baby. They hid him from the tattooists – so he does not have a number. He was carrying the prophecy . . .'

'Of course, I know of him. He was smuggled out around the time Branko was dying.'

'That baby was me.'

'What?'

'I am – was – that baby.'

Tears swelled in Dr Kalderon's eyes; his arms, totally uncoordinated, trod the air, then fell in a heap on Benedict's shoulder. '*You.* I told you I believe in destiny. *That baby!* I always believed our paths would cross. That baby. You! Named after Branko. I knew – one day – I would meet you.'

Benedict held on to the skeletal body. It felt like homecoming. After a while, he dared ask. 'The new tree – what does it mean? Do you know?'

Dr Kalderon extricated himself from Benedict's shoulders. 'Resurrection of the Gypsy Bible. Branko's Bible!'

'But that's absurd!'

Dr Kalderon resumed walking. 'Why? Gypsies have camped out with God throughout their history – a Bible is the first thing they would produce! Looking at earth, water, fire and sky, explaining the mysteries of creation, recounting dreams, yearnings, loves, defeats, victories, joys, tragedies – that's what a Bible is. The Gypsies must have had one. It was either destroyed by demented hordes or hidden somewhere nobody remembers any more! Nazis weren't the first to burn books!'

'Isn't that conjecture – a romantic wish?'

Dr Kalderon stamped the ground as if drumming a message for posterity. 'There's also the Gypsies' collective unconscious – which, as I said, Branko fully absorbed. Myths, traditions, beliefs, customs, the massive lore of magic, the *Swatura*. A vigorous culture which remained unimpaired despite dispersion, persecution and tribal divisions. That's a strong pointer to a common source like a Holy Book.'

'Even so . . .'

'Above all, there's the Gypsy dream.'

'What dream?'

Dr Kalderon faced Benedict. 'Reparation of history.'

Benedict held his gaze. 'What chance of that?'

Dr Kalderon strode forward again. 'Ask your people. They'll tell you they owe their troubles to three factors: one: splitting up and going in all directions; two: not having a country; three: lacking Holy Writ. The Gypsy Bible will not only provide the last, it will also beget the rest. It will reunite you. Lead you to your land.'

Benedict pursued him. 'We're scattered all over the world! We've converted, forcibly or for expediency, to many religions – religions that are always in conflict. How can we reunite?'

'Under a new religion. Under your Holy Book.'

'Ramblings of a poor castrate – who would subscribe to such fiction?'

Dr Kalderon, stopped, out of breath. Then, smiling and panting, he spoke as if Benedict were a confused child. 'Fiction, inspiration, revelation – aren't they emanations from the same divine source? As for subscribing to it . . . Branko used to say: every *gadjo* religion is like a heavy coat for the Romanies: to be worn in the white man's cold climes; but let's still keep our native shirt underneath so that when we reach the Promised Land, we can throw away the coats.'

'Promised land – another non-starter! We're talking about Gypsies, not Jews!' Benedict faltered, remembering a similar exchange with Leo Leo. But on that occasion, Leo Leo, not he, had been the reactionary. He became more irascible. 'Or do you mean India? Where we come from originally? Surely, even if the Indians welcome us back, we'd still be in a host country! So what Promised Land are we talking about?'

'Romanestan.'

A sudden vision, that of the ashen man, assailed Benedict. He was whispering from the pond in Auschwitz: Romanestan!

Benedict whimpered: 'Is there such place?'

Dr Kalderon replied with the softest of voices. 'The Holy Book says there is.'

'Where is it?'

Dr Kalderon looked sadly into the distance. 'I never found out. The sections I read, I read in snatches. And those days, I wasn't very proficient in Romanes. I didn't understand everything.'

Benedict gaped at him. 'You actually read Branko's book?'

'Parts, as I said.' Dr Kalderon's pupils dilated tenderly, like aureoles. 'Full of Divine Wisdom.'

Benedict was speechless.

Dr Kalderon put his arms around Benedict's shoulders and, slowly, pulling him along, started walking again. 'I remember a variation on Abraham's binding of Isaac. The Abraham character disobeys God and instead of laying down his son, places himself for sacrifice. Then the son disobeys God and prepares to pre-empt his father. But the father proves quicker and immolates himself. God is left heart-broken and admits He had been ungodly to put father and son to such a perverse test.'

Benedict, struck by the boldness of the story, nonetheless felt threatened. As if its subversive vision might destabilize the order that held him together.

Dr Kalderon sighed. 'I've come to look upon that version as more devotional than the canonical one. A God who can admit to being ungodly has the potential to be what God should be. We can expect Him to see His other mistakes.'

'Fantasy – that won't change the world! Not the *gadje* world!'

Dr Kalderon grabbed Benedict's arm. 'Why are you resisting everything I say? Surrender to your instincts! Understand what is screaming to be understood! Branko's Bible is the ultimate Bible! It doesn't preach death! It distils all the sacred books, all the countless myths and legends that map perdition and salvation. It will redeem the Gypsies!'

Benedict shook his head stubbornly. 'Men like Branko can't write Bibles! Such things don't happen!'

'On the contrary. Such things happen all the time. That's how we reclaim desolations like Auschwitz. In the days when the Gypsies were being exterminated, only a Holy Book – their very own Holy Book – written by someone possessed by the spirit of the sky, could ensure their rebirth.'

Suddenly drained, Benedict surrendered to the old man's zeal. 'If – assuming – that's so . . . what's it got to do with me?'

Dr Kalderon, panting now, perched on a rock. 'According to the prophecy, you'll find it . . .'

'Find it? In Auschwitz?'

'Maybe . . .'

'Surely, everything that could be found there has been found. I mean, documents like the Gypsy register, the testimonies from *Sonderkommandos* – they've all been dug up . . .'

'Not Branko's Bible.'

'What did Tomek, the Polish Gypsy, do with it?'

'He got people to memorize it. Then on 2 August 1944 . . .'

'The day all the Gypsies were gassed?'

'Not all. About a third were transferred to Buchenwald that same day.'

'Tomek, too? He took it with him?'

'No. He thought of handing it over to a transferee, but decided against it – wisely, as it happened. Had he done so, it would have been discovered during the delousing in Buchenwald and destroyed.'

'He buried it then?'

'No. He committed it to water.'

'What water?'

'The Vistula. He managed to get into a work party dredging mud by the river. He returned in time to be gassed.'

'Are you saying he cast the book away – like a letter in a bottle?'

'Entrusted it to the current, I'd say. Like the infant Moses.'

'Madness!'

'Water is a noble element – as an engineer of hydroelectricity you must know that. When you entrust it with something, it carries it to safety. Because it knows there are many daughters of many Pharaohs waiting by the bulrushes.'

'Water also decomposes.'

'It was well swaddled.'

'Even so . . .'

'Stop arguing! Understand this! The Bible is waiting to be found. By you. Waiting to fulfil your prophecy.'

The old man's vehemence plunged Benedict into a dreamy silence.

Dr Kalderon, pointing at a bus stop some hundred metres below the track, rose from the rock and leaned on Benedict's arm. 'Time to go back.'

They walked slowly, an aged father lovingly held by his son.

Benedict felt the compulsion to push forward and explode into violent activity.

Did he believe in prophecies?

Didn't everybody – deep down? All that a person wants to do, that he was born to do – aren't those prophecies?

If not, what was beating this new pulse?

What was inducing a vision of mountains streaming with people? With children!

A man can be father to all . . .

People as children . . .

Dr Kalderon, reduced to a wrinkled child by exhaustion, sat slumped on his chair and stared at his glass of *sambucca*. Occasionally, when he closed his eyes for the briefest of catnaps, he appeared to have gathered ancient dust, like a mummy.

He had brought out the *sambucca*, made of elderberries, in celebration. Both Gypsies and Jews, he had told Benedict, revered the elder flower. For the first, it had magical and medicinal qualities; for the second, associations with the *Kabbalah*.

Benedict, disinclined to leave until the old man had regained some strength, stared round the office.

Spacious, but engulfed by books, newspapers and periodicals. Walls and ceiling criss-crossed by cracks and chequered with damp patches. Portrait of Marshal Tito in uniform. Desk heaped with letters. Tattered coat on the door hook. Two wooden chairs. Sofa in need of upholstering. Pre-war typewriter and telephone. Filing cabinet holding the scant records of an extinguished community. A lair of courage.

Dr Kalderon surfaced from his drowse. He stared at Benedict in surprise, as if trying to place him; then he grinned. 'So. When do you start?'

Benedict approached him. 'One last question: do you know what the rest of the prophecy means?'

Dr Kalderon shook his head. 'It will unfold in time. Where to start, that's what you must decide.'

Surrender to your instincts.

'I'll seek out the Ursari. Maybe I have some family left – survivors . . .'

Dr Kalderon beamed the warmest of smiles. 'The journey back is always the best.'

Benedict did not hide his uncertainty. 'Then again, I could end up nowhere. Like a true Gypsy.'

'You can't improve on a true Gypsy.' Dr Kalderon scribbled an address on a piece of paper. 'I have a friend, Ilyas Rahim, in Skopje, Macedonia. Knows every tribe in the Balkans. He'll put you on the right track.'

Benedict took the paper. 'Thanks.'

'There's a big festival coming up in a few days – St George's Day. He never misses that. You'll have no problem finding him.'

Benedict was close to tears. 'Will you be all right?'

Dr Kalderon pulled himself off the chair and shuffled towards the sofa. 'Sure. I'll rest a bit.'

Benedict helped him lie down.

Dr Kalderon readjusted his skullcap. 'I used to think there's nothing worse than a survivor. Someone who, to all intents and purposes, had finished his portion – in effect, someone full of resentment because he has to live overtime. I couldn't see any sense in that. Now, I realize, I've been waiting for you.'

Benedict covered him with the tattered coat.

Dr Kalderon smiled. 'Thank you. Until tomorrow.'

Benedict paused, wondering how to tell him that he was now fully consumed by his quest and that he had decided to leave first thing tomorrow.

Dr Kalderon spared him the trouble by falling asleep instantly.

The growing conviction that Dr Kalderon's friend in Skopje would lead him to the Ursari bolstered Benedict's hopes.

But he also felt apprehensive. Knocking on ancestral doors, asking to be let in was an audacious undertaking. It required a pithy man. And though the prophecy he carried held the promise of such solidity in due course, today, he was still a frail person, almost an infant. Or, as he had once heard Young Glanz tell Nettie: *a house razed to the ground; its many mansions reduced to imaginary spaces in the void.* Meaning: a hollow man desperately trying to find an essence, failing that, a reflection, that would provide him with substance and transform him from non-being into being.

All of which meant he needed a rock – a helpmate who would have absolute faith in him and who would stand resolutely as his witness. Melchior, who had also started as a hollow man, had healed himself by procuring a son who had worshipped him. He, Benedict, infertile – as well as immature – needed a different mainstay. A woman, preferably. For women, as Eloïse consistently demonstrated, had greater insight into devastation. A woman, yes, whose unfailing eyes would bestow upon the infant both body and soul.

Nettie . . .?

Strange – he had not thought about Nettie since she had returned to Switzerland.

No. He was probably being unfair to Nettie, but he could not trust her . . .

Whereas a Gypsy woman . . .

He went on a hard run. Then, after a long shower, he went to the old city to have dinner.

For the first time since Melchior's death, he ate with appetite.

Then he strolled through the narrow streets.

All Sarajevo appeared to be doing the same.

This nocturnal promenade, known as *corso* and typical of Yugoslavia, appealed to him. The receptionist in the hotel in Belgrade had attributed the ritual to the fact that, under communism, cinemas and theatres, though cheap and subsidized, were state-controlled and boring. And since television was equally dull, there was nothing else to do but take the air.

Maybe. But people were also naturally gregarious. Providing unscrupulous politicians, generals and priests didn't exploit ethnic tensions, people wanted to be with other people, to talk and laugh with them rather than fight them.

And as he strolled, his eyes roamed over the women in the crowd. A sign of regeneration? Or lust from a sterile man?

Towards midnight, passing by the Jewish Museum on his way back to the hotel, he saw Dr Kalderon again. The old man was seated by the window, inside the kiosk which served as the museum's ticket-office and which he had converted into a tiny domicile in order to spare himself the tedium of commuting from his flat in the new city. Illuminated by the blue light of a paraffin heater, the ubiquitous glass of tea and plate of sugar at his elbow, wrapped up in a blanket and skullcap askew, he appeared cosily ensconced.

His eyes were half open; it was impossible to tell whether he was awake, asleep, or dead.

But he was still there, ready to be counted.

If an old man could muster such will, surely he, Benedict, Branko . . .

And Branko was captured by the Death's Heads who were the vassals of Adam, the Power of Cataclysms.

And he was chained to the wilderness.

Two armadillos, both endowed with one thousand and one eyes – of which some were always open – were commissioned to guard him.

In forty days, Adam boasted, Branko's heart would drain of blood and crumble to dust.

But Branko's heart, irrigated by his people's tears, was stalwart; it refused to remain captive.

Branko paid homage to the great rocks by rubbing them reverently and painting them with his memories.

To the armadillos, who, he could see, were tired of eternal vigil, he offered to induce the sleep of life which comes only when every eye is closed.

And he recited odysseys of the flesh and the spirit; when the armadillos, enchanted, fell asleep with all their one thousand and one eyes, he turned them into rainbows and placed them in the sky.

Then Branko broke his chains and set out to rejoin his people.

But the Death's Heads had shuffled the landmarks; he wandered for forty years in an unassailable maze.

One night, he encountered a glow-worm whose green light was fading because it had a spikelet in its throat.

He took the spikelet out and the glow-worm shimmered again.

And the Spirit of the Elements, which is that servant of O Del who protects wind, sand, sun-fire and night-ice and who perpetually fights the Power of Cataclysms, came unto Branko.

'The glow-worm is one of my children,' It said. 'You have healed him. Have a wish.'

Branko said: 'Enable me to traverse this wilderness so that I can return to my Romanies.'

The Spirit of the Elements sang of Dreamtime that created the Beginning.

And all the totemic souls came running: mountain-guardians, water-nymphs, tree-women, horse-men, children-who-create-colours and youths-who-mould-voices.

And they rearranged the hills and the shores, the rivers and the forests, the stars and the valleys.

The Spirit of the Elements pointed at each site: 'Here are your fathers and mothers. Your grandfathers and grandmothers. All the patriarchs and matriarchs before them. If you have not forgotten them, they will welcome you.'

Branko bone-turned his ancestors and reassured them that they were as sacred to him as the earth.

The ancestors wept with joy.

They gave him a god-stick, which is an implement that finds people like a dowser's rod finds water.

And they gave him a handful of topsoil which they had taken, as keepsake, from their last home and which they had intended to put back on their return.

Guided by the god-stick, Branko journeyed for forty months.

He came upon the mountain where bears frolicked.

He climbed to the summit.
When he looked at the valley beyond, he saw his people encamped.
They had been waiting for him all that time.
He joined them.
And he replaced the topsoil the ancestors had given him.

Ten

'You are looking better, Dei . . .'

'He gave me pills – the doctor you sent . . .'

'Young Glanz. Good man.'

'Yes. You'd never know he was *gadje*.'

Benedict stroked Ariana's cheek. 'I rang him – on my way here. Your arthritis is not as bad as I'd led him to believe, he said. The medication will help.'

She placed her head on his shoulder. He held her hand.

She smiled. 'Look at us. Not like mother and son. More like father and daughter.'

'Wonderful.'

'You know, in the clouded parts of my heart, I didn't expect to see you again.'

'I said I'd be back.'

'Yes, you did.' She straightened up, apologetically. 'Your coffee. I forgot your coffee . . .'

'Leave it, Dei . . .'

She scrambled up from the divan and moved to the cooker. 'Only takes a minute.'

He shrugged in resignation, then gazed out of the window.

Despite the constant drizzle, most of the people camped in the disused car park had gathered around Ariana's trailer. Look at the concern on their faces. This is what being Gypsy means. One for all and all for one. Though they had greeted him effusively, congratulated him for being a good son, so good, in fact, as to send to his mother a doctor from Zurich, no less, they had sensed that he had not come up just to pay her his respects, that there was a portentous aspect to this visit, an imperative that would affect Ariana's life, maybe change it altogether. And they were waiting to find out.

Ariana, preparing the coffee, spoke with her back to Benedict. 'Your wife – is she all right?'

'Yes. Fine.'

'No difficulties with her condition . . .?'

'Condition?'

'Her pregnancy . . . Didn't you say she was expecting . . . last time . . .?'

'Last time? Oh, yes . . . No. She isn't.'

She turned round, concerned. 'Miscarried, did she? Is that why you didn't bring her with you . . .?

'No. No. It was a false alarm – I mean, false hope. And . . . I didn't bring her because . . . well, I just got back from Yugoslavia . . . and I'll be off again straightaway . . . I didn't think there was any point contacting her . . . explaining things . . .'

She poured out the coffee and placed it on the table in front of him. She remained standing, troubled by his bluster.

'Please sit down . . . Dei . . . Much has happened . . .'

'Looks like it . . .'

'Before I put you in the picture . . . Do you think you can travel? Young Glanz said you should be able to . . .'

'To Zurich? I told you, cities . . .'

'To Macedonia. Skopje.'

She stared at him, astonished. 'Skopje?'

'It's possible I might be able to trace some relatives there . . .'

'Oh . . .'

'I've decided to . . . pursue my destiny . . .'

She sat next to him. 'Oh, Branko . . .'

'And I need you with me . . .'

Tears welled in her eyes. 'You need *me*?'

'Can you come?'

She held his hands. 'If you need me . . . Always. Even if I had no bones . . . I'd go anywhere – if you need me . . .'

Benedict kissed her hands. 'Thanks, Dei . . .'

She smiled and wept at the same time. 'I'm so proud of you, Branko . . .'

'I've done nothing yet.'

'You'll be fulfilling the prophecy – that's what you'll be doing . . .'

'I don't know about that . . .'

'What else? Fate – you can't escape it. You have to accept it.'

Benedict became solemn. 'That's what they want, too – my Dei and Dadoro . . .'

She nodded, accepting the statement, unquestioningly, as fact.

'You were there also – in Birkenau . . . My other Dei . . .'

Ariana stared at him, perplexed. 'Me?'

'Your face on the pond.'

'You're sure it was me?'

Benedict smiled. 'You were repeating their words. And your scent was in the air – mint . . .'

Ariana turned towards her tiny altar and fixed her gaze on the icon of the Madonna and Child. She communed with it briefly then spoke softly. 'Maybe it's my destiny, too . . . To see you achieve yours . . .'

'My witness - that's right. That's what you'll be.'

Ariana muttered, still in awe. 'I was there – with them – your actual parents . . .?'

Benedict smiled. 'That's how visions appear, I suppose . . . The soul so aches for loved ones that it eventually transports itself to another plane . . . And there it finds them – real as real can be . . .'

Ariana sighed. 'No explaining some things . . .'

'Very scary, I don't mind admitting . . . Times when I felt I was lost inside my head . . . Careening on tangled nerves . . . A little push, I felt – a mere gust of air – and I'd go mad . . .'

Ariana looked up apprehensively. 'Mad?'

'I suppose it's always there – madness . . . Lurking between one breath and the other . . .'

Ariana shivered. 'You think that will be the price – madness?'

'Price?' Benedict became anxious. 'Why should there be a price?'

Ariana mumbled sadly. 'There always is . . .'

Benedict pushed the thought aside. 'Well, let's not worry about it, Dei. I've crossed swords with madness many times – at Pro Juventute. Never failed to send it packing.'

Ariana stroked his hands. 'It is said, those endowed with prophecies – gods, prophets, heroes – are born with wounds. If they are not, then they receive them during their ministry.'

Benedict smiled bitterly. 'Dei, sweet Dei, I'm not god, prophet or hero. Basically I'm a charlatan – good at fooling people. There's no one inside me – nothing except rubble.'

'What are wounds, if not rubble?'

'Are you telling me I should give up?'

Ariana felt like a mother who could not save her son from being sent to war. She wiped her tears with her sleeve. 'You can't. The prophecy must be fulfilled. May O Del give you strength.'

Benedict smiled flatly. 'He will. If you stand by me. If you nurse my wounds . . .'

'When do you want to leave?'

'Soon as you've packed. I'd like to reach Interlaken before the offices close. We need to get you a passport . . .'

Ariana rose from the divan and shuffled to a small cupboard. 'I've not got much to take.'

Benedict looked out of the window. It had not stopped raining. Ariana's people were still waiting. 'On second thoughts – don't pack anything . . . Let's go on a shopping spree . . .'

She opened the cupboard and started taking out some underwear. 'What for? I have all the clothes I need.'

Benedict, registering the rebuke, pointed at the people outside. 'Shall I tell them you're coming with me?'

Ariana put her clothes aside. 'I will. Ask them in.'

Here is a tree.
   Her roots cure the ague.
   Her leaves heal wounds.
   Her berries clean blood that has been poisoned.
   Her pith washes the eye of everything that blinds it.
   Here is a tree.
   She stands to witness the desolation.
   She stands to defy blizzards, hurricanes, droughts and sandstorms.
   She stands, a streak of rainbow, in Adam's lightless universe.
   She stands, deathless, even when her children die.
   Here is a tree.
   Her bark records the chronicles of good and evil.
   Her seed plants the next generation.
   Her wood empowers reincarnation by embracing the fire.
   She is the Tree of Life.
   The Wheel of Time.
   Saramama.
   Mother.

Eleven

The previous day, 5 May, they had risen before sunrise, put on their new clothes and travelled down to the Vardar river which abounded with snow-water.

At Šutalo Pani they had washed their faces three times in the flow and visited the church of Kapišteš to lay out gifts, light candles, kiss the holy frescoes and fill their bottles with sanctified water.

They had sung and danced; they had twined threads from their clothes around the rocks and bushes by the riverbank; and they had cut leafing branches from ancient willows.

Then they had travelled back to their homes where they had put the willow twigs on display to express their joy at the return of spring, the womb of all seasons.

After nightfall, they had written down their wishes on stylish paper and planted these notes around rose saplings.

Now, it was 6 May. Dawn.

The desperate bleating of the lambs announced that the Romanies were ready for the ritual sacrifice. The kermis of *Enderlez*, also known as St George's Day, was about to start. Ahead lay four days of festivities.

Ilyas Rahim, the *Vataf*, had delegated the slaughter of his lamb to a butcher. Consequently he was available to stand witness to the dawn with his honoured guests, Benedict and Ariana.

Since outsiders were unlikely to stray into the morning's celebrations, Ilyas did not require the presence of his *false chief*, the trusted stand-in who protected the real chief from enemies, *gadje* mobs and authorities. In any case, these days in Yugoslavia, the observance of this ancient custom was more for the sake of convention than necessity. Thus Ilyas was openly dressed in the *Vataf*'s traditional clothes: a garish, multicoloured shirt, left unbuttoned to display a bare chest; large game bag; flashy purse belt; wide, dark-blue trousers stuffed into high leather boots; short jacket with gold fasteners. He also carried the *bareski rovli rupui*, the chief's sceptre – a tasselled, silver staff with an apple-shaped knob and engraved with the *semno*, the set of Romanies' ancient emblems: axe, sun, moon, star and cross.

In his early fifties, squat and sturdy, with perennially smiling eyes, chiselled nose, black straight Asian hair and sparse moustache, Ilyas was a throwback to the Mongolian steppes: a man who looked like his stallion's twin.

Among the first Gypsies to have been inspired by Tito's promise of an autonomous Romany province within liberated Yugoslavia, Ilyas had joined the people's uprising against the Nazis on his fifteenth birthday. Wounded and taken prisoner in the disastrous battle of Sutjeska gorge, where more than half of the partisans had been killed, he had ended up in the hands of the SS. Left for dead after interrogation, he had managed to escape. Hiding in the mountains, living off the wilderness, he had healed himself and rejoined the partisans.

At the end of the war, disillusioned by Tito's disavowal of Romany autonomy, he had returned to Macedonia, determined to live in a manner that would earn him, as he had put it, 'the respect of his soul'. He had taken three oaths: to forswear all weapons; to raise a large family; and to plant pomegranate trees up and down the land so that the fruit's magical properties – which, according to the Koran, purged a person of hatred – could renew the generation that had perished in the fighting.

He had kept his word. He did not possess a weapon, not even a knife to serve as a regale of manhood. He had seven children and four grandchildren; his wife, Yildiz, a big, fleshy woman in her forties, was pregnant once again. And though, officially, he was an urban dweller, he still travelled; and wherever his caravan took him, there he planted pomegranate trees.

The bleating of the lambs stopped abruptly. Briefly, grass and mountains, sky and water took the hue of the lambs' blood.

Then day broke.

The youngest daughters went to the rose saplings and plucked up the notes carrying their families' petitions and put them away in sunny corners where they might grow as trees.

The Gypsies swirled into motion: if luck stayed with them, the year would prove beautiful.

Benedict watched the people and observed, with fresh interest, those who had already caught his attention:

The sextuplets, all girls, ten years old and always hand in hand, following their mother everywhere, like a brood of ducklings.

The acrobat with the melancholic smile who appeared to have been limned by Picasso.

The ancient, unsmiling Ursari couple from Greece.

The newly weds from France, looking at the world through each other's eyes.

The violin-maker with a bricklayer's hands from Finland.

Hanro, Ilyas' *false chief*, a taciturn, devout man whose kindness, it was said, always produced, like the sound of wagons' wheels, happy feelings; and his wife, the *phuri dai*, 'wise woman', known also as *Bibi*, 'Auntie'.

Lumnia, the otherworldly young woman who materialized wherever Benedict went and who, according to Ilyas, would acquire witch-lore in five years.

And Omar, the youth with the massive frame and cherub's face, forever orbiting around Lumnia.

'Look at this place. You can see we're not just pollen in the wind. We can also take root.'

Ilyas was appraising Šuto Orizari, the new town for the Romanies – once an inconceivable notion for Gypsies and *gadje* alike – which was rising, with solid houses, some even with plumbing, on the outskirts of Skopje, Macedonia's capital.

Benedict indicated the terrain on which they had assembled; this was Ilyas' plot, but it stood bare, save for his caravan, in the middle of a new terrace. 'When will you build *your* house?'

'I'm father to the people here.' With that strange gait which he had developed to hide the limp of a war wound, Ilyas strode about his land and gazed proudly at the township. 'A father eats last.'

Ilyas would not use a crutch in public; a father – a *Baro Manush*, 'great man', as his people affectionately called him – must look undamaged, so Ariana, whom the Rahims had very quickly come to regard as another *phuri dai*, had been informed by Yildiz.

If he could only imbue himself with such primal pride, Benedict thought, then he would have little difficulty in nurturing the will to find a purpose in life; he might even find a way to compensate for the child he would never beget.

Ilyas' hand encompassed the horizon. 'When all Šuto Orizari is built and when we've planted the *Vesh*, then it'll be my turn.'

141

Benedict scanned the area designated as the *Vesh*, Romanes for 'forest'.

It was the heath which served as the hub of the township. The only aspect that might have justified its glorified appellation was the fact that it opened out to the countryside and appeared to stretch all the way to the Korabi mountains in Albania.

Ilyas had kept reassuring Benedict that after they had finished erecting Šuto Orizari and embroidered it with trees and ponds, the birds and the sylvan animals would come; tomorrow, this fallow ground would grow as a living memorial to the woodlands, the Gypsies' old habitat. After all, Ilyas had propounded, cataclysms always brought blessings in their wake; already the earth was awash with the semen of a noble sky, and unseen smiths were repairing the stars; already, Šuto Orizari qualified as the first miracle of this new age.

It was not surprising Ilyas was Dr Kalderon's friend; he spoke with the Jew's passion.

The cataclysm that had sired Šuto Orizari had been the earthquake, one of the worst in modern times, which had struck Skopje on 26 July 1963, killing over 1,000 people, injuring some 3,000 and devastating 80 per cent of the buildings.

Help from the international community had come swiftly and generously. Within months the rubble had been cleared and restoration begun. Now, in a city that still looked like a vast construction site, foundations of buildings capable of withstanding force 10 on the Richter scale were being laid in quick succession.

Šuto Orizari was tapping into this energy discreetly, with traditional Romany caution and some Canadian help.

'There's enough drink?' Ilyas, addressing Yildiz and Ariana, indicated the bottles of beer and *rakia* which he had set up, in buckets adorned with willow twigs, to offer to passers-by.

The women, sitting side by side in front of the caravan, rolled their eyes to indicate that there was plenty.

Ilyas turned to Benedict. 'What do you think, Branko?'

'I'd say enough to sozzle an army.'

Benedict relished his fluent reply; since Ariana had started calling him by his original name and would only call him so – a decision wholeheartedly commended by Ilyas – the mother tongue had started seeping back; the brain that the *gadje* had broiled was, at last, regenerating.

Ilyas chuckled. 'An army is what will come. And a grand army it will be, Branko. Not one that murders for politicians, generals or mad priests. But an army that fires flowers, songs, poems, dances.' He held Benedict by his arms.

'We're such good people, Branko. God's best. We've never marched to seize someone's land; or to enslave people or to kill them. That's what makes the *gadjo* envious. Why he maligns us. Lies are easier to believe than truths. Sure, we could always change and be like the *gadje*. But what's the sense of that? Why be less than the best? Worse still, why be unclean?'

'Why be pariahs for ever?'

Ilyas thundered. 'Who says we are!'

'We behave as if we are.'

'Sometimes, in order to survive, we have to keep a distance. But think of ourselves as pariahs? Never! We know what God thinks of us! In His eyes we are earth, fire, air and water – everything that's good. That's what counts.'

Benedict, embarrassed by the outburst, glanced towards Ariana.

Ilyas, catching the look, addressed Ariana. 'I'm telling him not to judge us hastily, sister.'

Ariana nodded solemnly.

Ilyas clasped Benedict's head and looked deep into his eyes. 'Only the Devil judges hotfoot, Branko. That's why he and his followers always get in a mess. So make sure you take your time. Examine our teeth and haunches like we're horses you might buy. You'll find we're thoroughbreds.'

A child's liquid voice interrupted them. 'Papo!'

Nur, Ilyas' six-year-old granddaughter, dressed in a caftan embroidered with gold thread, was pulling at Ilyas' sleeve. 'Papo, come. It's time to smear us . . .'

Ilyas started jumping up and down like a chimpanzee. 'Time to smear?' He ran back and forth, thumping the ground. 'Is it? Is it?'

Nur squealed with laughter. 'Papo, you're being silly!'

Ilyas froze in his tracks; assuming a formidable mien, he spun round and roared. 'Me, silly? Big Papo, silly?' Then his ferocity disintegrated into mock tears. 'Oh, silly Papo, useless Papo . . .'

Nur, tempering her giggles with rebuke, grabbed Ilyas by the sleeve. 'Stop playing the fool. Come . . .'

'Yes, my lady. Immediately, my lady.' Ilyas, taking exaggerated meek steps, let Nur drag him away.

Benedict followed, laughing at their antics.

Ilyas' wife and children – four sons and three daughters, of whom all the daughters and one son, Ramzi, were married – had assembled, in sparkling new clothes, as if posing for a group picture, around Yildiz and Ariana, by the caravan.

The daughters' husbands lined up proudly behind their children.

Ramzi's wife stood slightly apart; being the youngest spouse and still on probation as a newcomer to the family, it was her duty to serve them all.

The butcher, qualified to slaughter according to Muslim law, lingered, at the far end of the plot, by the lamb he had just slain.

Ilyas picked up the copper vessel where the butcher had collected the lamb's blood. Starting with Nur, he daubed the blood, with his index finger, onto the foreheads of the members of his family.

Then he did the same to Ariana.

He affirmed, on each person's behalf, that they had not eaten any meat throughout the winter. This declaration, Ilyas had explained, was to reassure Indra, the Hindu god of nature, provider of rain and crops, son of Heaven and Earth, and slayer of Ahi, the Devil who wanted to burn up the whole earth, that in the eternal struggle against evil, the Romanies remained steadfast.

Enderlez – a distortion of Indra's name, Ilyas had added – was a spring festival that the Gypsies had brought with them from the Punjab; it became St George's Day after some of the tribes' conversion to Christianity – with Indra transformed into St George, the evergreen hero against evil, and Ahi into the dragon. One reason why the Gypsies so loved *Enderlez* was that its syncretism provided them with the excuse of worshipping in different houses of God, mosques as well as churches.

Ilyas turned to Benedict. 'Branko! God sent you to my tent. So you become family. I don't want Indra to mistake you for a *gadjo*. Let me mark you also.'

Benedict barely hesitated. 'I'd be honoured.'

Solemnly, Ilyas daubed Benedict's forehead. 'May you live as a good Rom.'

Benedict began to shake. The point where Ilyas had smeared the blood, the location of the proverbial third eye, felt icy cold. Simultaneously, he felt – knew – that this was not his first daubing, that at some point in the past, before his life in Pro Juventute's oubliettes, he had been similarly marked and consequently spared from a dark, sulphurous death. He clung to Ilyas' hand. 'Thank you.'

Ilyas hugged him strongly.

Then Ilyas stained his own forehead and put aside the copper vessel.

He went over to the slaughtered lamb, an unblemished animal worthy of a *Baro Manush*, and skinned it.

He placed the fleece before his wife.

He decorated the carcass with willow twigs and hung it on the door of his caravan.

His voice, when he turned to face his family, trembled with emotion. 'May all Romanies have peace and abundance!'

The family responded with jubilant shouts.

Ariana, tears streaming down her face, shuffled over to Benedict and stroked his head. 'May you be a great Rom, my son.'

Benedict, emotional and feeling awkward, embraced her. 'Dei . . . Dear, dear Dei . . .'

Ilyas' sons, summoning the butcher to join them, poured *rakia* for everybody.

Yildiz, Ilyas' wife, regal in a shimmering, sequinned oriental shift, gathered the women in her family and pronounced their tasks for the day. The daughter-in-law would sweep the caravan with the fleece. The oldest daughter would clean the lamb and make soup with the innards. The second daughter would prepare the stuffing by mixing the lamb's lungs with rice. The youngest would take charge of the liver which, on St George's Day, was endowed with good fortune; having seasoned it with paprika, she would boil it and serve it to Benedict who, caught between *gadje* and Gypsy, was the person most in need of magic. Yildiz herself would prepare the lamb for the fire by tying its legs. And the children would take it to be roasted on the communal spits.

All over Šuto Orizari resident and visiting Gypsies began celebrating.

They strolled and exchanged greetings.

Now and again Ilyas and Yildiz pointed out young men bundling young women into cars, then driving off at speed whilst being chased by cursing relatives.

These were youths who were secretly engaged – albeit with their parents' approval. The men were abducting their fiancées so that when the couples were apprehended, the community would 'force' them to marry.

These abductions were the salt and spirit of the festival; getting married on *Enderlez* promised luck, fertility and happiness. Ilyas and Yildiz, who had wed after such an abduction, could vouchsafe all that.

Visitors arrived to toast Ilyas and his family.

Ilyas became expansive. 'Imagine, all our people, wherever they are – if not falsely imprisoned or running for their lives – are celebrating as we are. So keep faith: the burst pomegranate will be made whole.'

It took Benedict, who had surrendered himself to the festive atmosphere, a long, lingering moment – and a sudden shock – to register the significance of the last remark. He turned to Ariana. 'Dei – did you hear . . .?'

'Yes.'

'What did he mean?'

Ariana pulled herself up and seized Ilyas' hand. 'What you just said, Ilyas – the burst pomegranate will be made whole? Is it a saying? What does it mean . . .?'

'Our oldest dream, sister: one day, all Romanies will be reunited.'

Benedict exclaimed. 'Reunited, did you say?'

'Imagine, Branko. How godlike we will then be. Bursting a pomegranate requires little effort. But to put it together – you need divine strength!'

A new tree will bear the leaves the donkey ate. The burst pomegranate will be made whole . . .

Benedict held on to the thought. Given the Gypsies' dispersion and religious divisions, the host nations' entrenched prejudices, Eastern Europe's tyrannies and this century's disposition for wholesale death – it was an impossible quest . . .

Yet, what a vision! What an irresistible challenge . . .

'Ariana! Branko! Here are brothers and sisters wanting to drink to you.' Ilyas, surrounded by visitors, was beckoning them.

Benedict raised his glass and, taking Ariana by the arm, joined them.

Later, the men visited the cemetery.

Benedict went with Ilyas and Ilyas' sons, Kenan, Ramzi, Šaip and Ismat, to be introduced to the ancestors.

On the way, Ilyas recounted the history of the family.

Tribe: Arlije, from the Turkish word '*yerli*', meaning 'native'. Some scholars traced the appellation to the strange theory that the Gypsies were not immigrants from India, but indigenous to the Balkans, that their dark blood had been acquired during Alexander the Great's campaigns in Asia when his men, in compliance with their king's policy of marrying the East to the West, had taken to wife the women of the Hindu Kush. This theory had been distorted into an even stranger one which claimed that Alexander the Great himself was the product of the union between his mother, Olympias, and a Gypsy paramour from the Sintoi tribe, a phratry which, according to Homer, was much loved by Hephaestus, the god of metal-workers.

For the advocates of these theories, the Arlije's conversion to Islam and the adoption of Turkish names had occurred during Ottoman rule. But, in reality, Ilyas had affirmed, the Arlije were descendants of Anatolian Gypsies who had served the Ottoman armies as traders, horse-keepers, weapon-smiths and makers of gunpowder; the fact that, despite the development of Šuto Orizari, many of the older generation still chose to live in the poorer suburb of Topana – a distortion of the Turkish word for 'arsenal' – was a reminder of that.

The cemetery, located on a hillside, offered a panoramic view of the Vardar river which divided Skopje into old and new towns and which, poets claimed, descanted, at full moon, the countless songs the city had inspired in Macedonia's diverse peoples.

An ornate tombstone mounted with a large medallion bearing a picture of the deceased marked almost every grave. The stone borders were covered by fine earth and adorned simply with plants and flowers.

The majority of the epitaphs bore 26 July 1963, the day of the earthquake, as the date of death.

Ilyas' grandfather, mother, two brothers, a sister, three uncles, four aunts and nineteen cousins had all been victims of that disaster. The tombstone of one uncle, a locomotive driver, had the additional picture of the railway station's broken clock – still preserved as a memorial – showing the precise time of the catastrophe, 5:17 a.m.

It took Ilyas and his sons some three hours to visit all the graves. At each grave, they caressed the picture of the interred, gently combed the soil with their hands, watered the plants and recited brief prayers asking God to provide the departed with abundant earth.

On the way back, Ilyas and Benedict paused at the clump of acacia trees in the *Vesh*, which, standing as the symbol of future woodlands, had become a popular focal point. Here, a crowd had gathered.

Lumnia, having rounded up six of the horses which normally grazed on the heath, was addressing the crowd whilst Omar, her faithful companion, picked out tunes on his concertina.

When Ilyas and Benedict joined the crowd, Lumnia fixed her mysterious smile on Benedict.

Benedict, though flattered, felt uneasy. He had noticed Lumnia the moment he and Ariana had arrived the previous day. She had been at the bus terminal, with Omar, measuring up the people turning up for *Enderlez*. He had felt her gaze on his back long after Ilyas, who had come to meet them, had whisked them away. Thereafter, each time he and Lumnia had crossed paths in the townlet – which had been often – she had stared at him at length with her large almond-shaped eyes. Ariana, to whom he had pointed out this disconcerting conduct, had laughed at his unease and quipped that, given his looks, she would have been most surprised if any of the unattached women had not tried to catch his eye. But, beneath that insouciance, Benedict felt, Ariana was equally intrigued by Lumnia's interest.

According to Ilyas, Lumnia had lost both parents in the earthquake. Barely five at the time, she had been cared for by an aunt, a famous *drabarni*. The latter, soon perceiving Lumnia's supernatural powers, had taken her travelling and taught her the secrets of peoples, plants and wild life; after puberty, still guided by this aunt, Lumnia had entered the labyrinths of witchery.

Now, having reached her twenties, she could not turn back; she had to surrender to her powers, let herself be drawn into sorcery's innermost channels and become a *drabarni*. If she failed or chose to spurn her vocation, she would be destroyed by her own powers.

She was still watching him intensely. Why? Had she seen through him? Noted the rubble inside? Was she shocked? Or scornful?

Benedict concentrated on her patter. She was extolling Omar's prodigious strength, recounting some of his incredible feats, comparing him to Obertshi, the Gypsy Samson, exchanging pleasantries with those who agreed with her, haranguing the sceptics and, invariably, provoking them to a bet.

Ilyas was full of admiration. 'She can outmanoeuvre the Devil, that one. Were she a thief, she'd steal the world, no problem.'

When Lumnia had enough bets going, she nodded at Omar.

Discarding his concertina, Omar went up to the horses. He divided them into two teams and, aligning them to his left and right, bound their reins around his hands. Feet firmly planted, arms outstretched, he held the horses steady.

The crowd watched in silence.

Not yet seventeen, Omar was over two metres tall and seemingly just as wide. But unafflicted by the bovine features and muscular discord of gigantism, he looked quite normal. Moreover, his alert demeanour and engaging smile conjured, for Benedict, the heroic, Herculean person that every man dreamed to be.

Lumnia yelled and hit the horses' rumps.

The teams charged in opposite directions.

Omar held his ground.

The horses strained, snorted, whinnied and reared; but they could not budge Omar. After a while, steaming with sweat, they ceased trying.

Omar dropped their reins and retrieved his concertina.

The crowd stood awed and silent. Then they burst into applause. Even those who had lost bets admitted that there was something divine in Omar's strength.

Lumnia addressed them again. 'Strength is boon enough. But Omar has yet another blessing: luck! Luck that, for him, always flows like a waterfall. A very special blessing because it comes only from O Del!'

The crowd, captivated by her solemnity, quietened down.

'You want proof?'

A few people shouted. 'Yes!'

Lumnia pointed at the acacia trees. 'We're under trees. Teeming with birds. Chattering, busy, busy, because it's spring. See them?'

Many people responded. 'Yes!'

'Bird-shit is a true sign of luck – right?'

Everybody agreed. 'Right!'

'Which of you has been shat upon?'

Seven men came forward, jubilantly pointing at the dirt on their hair, shirts or coats.

Lumnia patted them on the shoulder. 'God bless you!' She dragged Omar forward. 'Now, look at him!'

The crowd inspected Omar with increasing astonishment. His hair and clothes, thick with bird droppings, looked like a painter's palette.

Lumnia gloated. 'Looks like every bird crapped on him. Proof enough?'

Most of the onlookers nodded in agreement.

Quickly, Lumnia collected her winnings and skipped away, humming the tune Omar had played on the concertina.

Omar pounded after her.

Benedict caught her eye as she cast him a parting look. The quiver on her lips: was it a seer's contempt for an unfulfilled man?

Ilyas was excited. 'When I see Omar, my hopes turn to eagles. I see benediction for our people. Pray for luck, Branko! It's Nature's greatest blessing – second only to the gift of life.'

Benedict nodded, acknowledging, despite his scepticism, a supernatural dimension to Omar.

The only member of a large family to survive the earthquake, Omar had been exactly a year old on that calamitous day. The last person to be dug out alive, days after the event, he had been found unscathed, clutching a teddy bear as if still celebrating his birthday party. Inevitably, the miraculous escape had been interpreted as the first manifestation of his inexhaustible good fortune.

'Luck, Branko! You can change the world with it. We, Romanies, know that.'

In the afternoon, Ilyas and his family visited Yildiz's parents who had arrived from Kosovo.

Benedict, overwhelmed and rather unsettled by the intense exposure to the

Gypsy way of life, thought of spending some time on his own. He considered visiting either Sveti Nikita or Markov Manastir, the medieval monasteries that were tucked away on the bluffs surrounding Skopje. Throughout the Turkish occupation of the Balkans, these religious outposts – to this day still inaccessible save to seasoned hikers – had zealously clung to the teachings of the Orthodox Church and, by so doing, had not only provided for the Serbs' spiritual needs, but also preserved their ethnic identity. A few hours in such a place, after a hard climb, Benedict had speculated, might help to disperse much of his confusion.

In the event, not wanting to leave Ariana alone, even though she seemed to need some respite, he stayed with her.

And, indulging in numerous coffees, they talked about the past.

Ariana reminisced about Mihal, her husband. A man of fortitude, he had always overcome the endless tribulations that dogged the Gypsy. But for him, she and Branko would have starved ten times over.

Benedict tried to explain, if only to have a clearer view of it himself, the rift that had opened up, seemingly suddenly, between Nettie and him. He did not disclose – could not yet – the facts about his infertility nor how, as a result, he felt inconsolable.

The conversation left him dejected. Ariana, noting his mood – could she have guessed his affliction? – urged him to go and mix with the people. She promised to join him after she had had a brief rest.

Benedict strolled through Šuto Orizari.

He felt insubstantial, as if mind and matter, reason and emotions, had lost their density. How could he juggle the dual identities of Benedict and Branko? Salvation, as Ilyas had suggested, lay in choosing the identity that would provide his body with a shadow – a wholeness that even an ant possessed. Easier said than done.

He could not think clearly; the sudden urgency to choose, its irrational desperation, paralysed him. Were he back in Zurich, he could have sought refuge in the army, taken his men on strenuous climbs and imagined he had a foothold in the world.

Why not surrender to his people unquestioningly, absorb their culture and history and spirit? Cherish their vitality as well as their strangeness? They had a saying: he who touches honey must lick his fingers.

And accept the poverty, so what! They had another saying: a crust is still a piece of bread. Look at our aura, Ilyas had urged him, we haven't faded like other races, we still feed on all four elements, touch us and you will be filled with earth, sky, water and fire.

So he roamed, determined to touch.

At the centre of the *Vesh*, a giant chairoplane, brought all the way from Italy by the largest articulated vehicle ever seen in Macedonia, stood, with its scintillating lights, like a tree of happiness. Its patrons bellowed, screamed, yodelled and ululated as they spun and swung in the air.

Nearby, a mêlée of caravans and entertainment booths formed a vast fairground.

Benedict took a turn in the chairoplane, laughed with the squealing children, drank with their fathers and mothers, hung precariously from the chairs like the young men seeking to impress the girls.

He ambled to the shooting galleries. He scored bull's-eyes every time. When the booth-holders realized he was not interested in the prizes, they cheered him on. Crowds gathered. Men asked him enviously where he had acquired his marksmanship. He told them, boasting happily, that he used to be a champion in a sport which combined cross-country skiing with shooting and that, but for fate, he would have competed in the Sapporo Olympics. This drew sympathy from his listeners; Fate, a concept they had acquired from Islam, was to them as real a dimension as Luck.

He continued ambling. Here and there, he encountered arm-wrestlers sitting at individual tables, challenging passers-by. He took up each challenge; lost a few, won many. A Rom from Montenegro, after beating Benedict with difficulty, gallantly offered him his table for a while. Benedict notched sixty-seven bouts – most of them witnessed by Lumnia and Omar – before losing. At least, she could see he wasn't a weakling.

He stopped at the outdoor café where musicians took turns to perform. Drinking some *rakia*, he listened to the maestri of the *davuli* and *zurna*, the Anatolian drum and flute. These instruments, he was told, were the progenitors of music: observe how ecstatically they conjoined.

He decided to prove – to himself as well as to those who pointed him out as a hardy Rom – that he was also a sensitive man. He borrowed someone's cithara and played Hadjidakis' score for Lorca's *Blood Wedding*. A Greek composition on a Spanish theme, it was a hybrid like the best of Gypsy music. It proved an excellent choice, not least because the Greek sound was ever present in Macedonia.

Men danced; some linked arms; others shuffled alone; children solemnly imitated the adults.

Then Lumnia took the floor.

She whirled, her gaze fixed on Benedict, and did not seem to turn; her long

Indian-ink hair drew arabesques in the air; her outstretched arms appeared to touch far-off places; her stamping legs demanded passion that was capable of matching her own.

Would her eyes never stop stalking him? He was tempted to engage her. But, given the Gypsy's intolerance of flirtatious behaviour, he did not want to start trouble, certainly not with Omar.

As if on cue, Omar came and squatted by him. 'You're good with cithara.'

'Thank you.'

'Never seen Lumnia dance like this. She's dancing for you.'

'For me?'

Omar put a good-natured hand on Benedict's shoulder. 'Every man is bewitched by Lumnia. Only you have turned her head.'

Benedict, surprised – yet pleased – stopped playing. 'She's your girlfriend . . . fiancée . . .'

Omar chuckled. 'Oh, no. We're like brother and sister. Give her more music. The spirit is with her.'

Benedict resumed playing. His fingers became conduits of yearning and lyricism. He dared engage Lumnia's eyes.

She was not particularly beautiful; but handsome and magnetic. She emanated sensuality, yet also carried a spiritual presence that seemed palpable. If he lay down with her, he ventured to think, he might be healed of his seared past, even of his dead seeds. Strange how a woman harboured salvation.

He finished playing.

She stopped dancing. She smiled at him – intimately, as if they had known each other for ever; and confidently, as if they would know each other always.

He wanted to go to her, hold her hand, tell her if she wanted him . . . undress her . . .

But what for? Could she switch off Pro Juventute's electricity? Provide him with family and roots? Could she give him an image – at the very least, a mask – as Nettie had done? Could she make him give up the army and join her as his tribe? More to the point: what was the sense, for a barren man, to seek another doomed love? What could ever grow if rain, even the purest rain, fell on stones?

Besides, she was much too young for him.

He handed the cithara back to its owner, nodded at Omar and strode out of the café.

He walked straight into Ariana. 'Dei . . .'

She smiled. 'You played very well . . .'

'You saw . . .?'

'But can she dance!'

'Who?'

Ariana teased him. 'Were there other people dancing?'

Benedict shrugged. 'Oh, her. She's good. Yes.'

'You should talk to her – compliment her. Instead of rushing away . . .'

'I'm not good at small talk . . .'

'Don't you like her?'

'Do you?'

Ariana became serious. 'Yes. I do. But I'm also unsure. Is she the woman for you? Can she make you happy?'

Benedict forced a laugh. 'She's much too young, Dei! Besides, I'm a married man . . .'

'Maybe the question should be: is there a woman who can make you happy?'

Benedict grabbed her arm with exaggerated bonhomie. 'Yes, Dei! You! Come on!'

As he dragged her away, he felt Lumnia's gaze burning his back.

Dusk unfurled the time for revels.

The men paraded ostentatiously in their best suits. The women, eager to honour their husbands with proof of prosperity, flaunted their sequinned dresses, earrings, bracelets, belts of gold and silver coins, jewellery and precious stones.

The youngest children went to the spits to fetch the family lamb; returning with sizzling trays, they thickened the air with the aroma of roasted meat. The elders nodded contentedly: surely, even O Del's mouth would be watering.

The women laid out the lambs with onions and lettuce, deemed to be the season's most princely produce. Men invited their neighbours to share the fare. Every family ate of its own as well as of its neighbour's. Repeated toasts consumed countless bottles of beer and endless glasses of *rakia*.

Then the people converged on to the *Vesh* to indulge in reveries of a verdant future.

Here, Hanro, dressed as *Vataf*, but with a simpler staff than Ilyas' *bareski rovli rupui*, took up his role as *false chief*. This ancient ruse was no longer essential strategy. Šuto Orizari was a safe Gypsy enclave – some tribes even regarded it as the Romanies' capital city; and relations with Macedonia's other

153

ethnic groups were cordial. But since, on *Enderlez* nights, there were always police patrols, not to mention *gadje* sightseers, the presence of the *false chief* had become a sensible precaution.

So Hanro, escorted by his wife, *Bibi*, the *phuri dai*, strolled regally. But he always remained within Ilyas' line of vision so that, if need be, the latter could instruct him what to do.

Benedict, with Ariana by his side, drifted with the flow, yearning to become earth, sky, water and fire.

Ilyas and his family stayed close to them.

Almost every tribe was represented. They had come from all over Yugoslavia and Europe; those from the Iron Curtain countries had smuggled themselves through sealed borders.

They strolled and met kinsmen and friends; partook, child-like, of the pleasures of the fun fair; drank more beer and more *rakia*.

They danced indefatigably around indefatigable musicians. *Davuli* and *zurna*, lutes and citharas, accordions and violins, tambourines and pan-pipes competed with each other to cast spells.

Those young men who had not abducted their betrothed earlier did so now, taking advantage of the night and the merrymaking.

A crowd had gathered around the Greek Ursari couple's caravan.

Benedict, Ariana, Ilyas and Ilyas' family stopped to look.

Husband and wife, their faces fossilized by age as well as hardship, were working their bear, a massive brown male. Rattling the animal's chain, the man roused it to stand on its hind legs; the woman played the tambourine, cajoling it to dance.

The old man addressed the crowd. 'Lefteris is my name. Bear-leaders, I'm looking for. I'll teach you. Bear is God's Dog, Rom's true friend. Strong as ten men and wise as twelve.' Getting no response, he became gruff. 'Bear has a bone in his penis. He who wrestles with him also grows a bone in his rod. Who wants to please his woman more than ever?'

Several voices taunted him. 'You!'

Lefteris took off his shirt. 'Watch!'

Benedict stared in awe at the claw scars on the man's chest and back. Like a coat of mail. Had Todor carried as many scars?

Lefteris tussled with the bear. They dragged each other back and forth in strange mummery. The old man, straining every muscle, held his footing; then he ran out of breath and disengaged.

The crowd applauded and threw coins.

Benedict noted the fresh scratches on the man's chest.

Lefteris shouted haughtily. 'Nothing to it – if you're a man. Who dares?'

Benedict glanced at Ariana.

She was biting her bony hands. She seemed to be exhorting him in silence. She had obviously read his mind. But her pride was mixed with apprehension.

Benedict stripped off his shirt.

Ilyas held him by the arm. 'You don't have to.'

Benedict retorted hoarsely, dry-mouthed. 'It's what my father did. I may never get another chance.'

Ilyas nodded. 'I understand.'

Three of Ilyas' sons, Ramzi, Šaip and Ismat smiled in approval. The eldest, Kenan, who had been born with a withered arm, squeezed Benedict's shoulder encouragingly with his good, and very strong, hand.

Ariana stroked his hair. 'Make your Dadoro proud.'

Benedict strode forward, apprehensive, yet eager.

People cheered, whistled, applauded.

He spotted Omar, standing at the edge of the crowd, watching him solemnly.

Then he was sucked into Lumnia's eyes.

Lefteris drew him aside. 'Wrestle with joy – like you mount your wife. Then he won't hurt you.'

Brusquely, Benedict took the chain from him.

Shaking the chain, he goaded the bear to stand on its hind legs. Then yelling, he charged and grappled with it.

Look, Dadoro! Look, Dei!

The stench hit him first: a suffocating blend of excrement, urine and decayed dust; then, he was struck by the immovability of a mass that was both rock-hard and flabby; then, once more, he was pounded by the smell, now enriched with the bear's fetid breath.

To conquer his fear, he reminded himself of the Gypsy lore on bears: benign animals; healers who cured diseases with their fur and dug up medicinal roots with their claws; who drove away evil forces and provided potent talismans with their nails, teeth and bones.

The bear growled. Benedict caught sight of its drooling mouth and sharp teeth. Its claws dug into his flesh. Now we're wrestling!

Look, Dadoro! Look, Dei!

The bear's forelegs encircled him. Large, hairy, humanoid arms. Their grip tightened.

Benedict managed to extricate himself. He was covered with the bear's fur. He remembered: bears moulted in the spring. Now he and the bear were one.

And now the bear revealed his true identity. Doughty Gypsy features. Dark eyes like the moon in eclipse. A timeless smile that mocked death. And a strength which spurted from God's own phallus. The bear was Todor.

Now open your flesh and give us birth.

Benedict clasped him. Hold me, Dadoro, hold me . . .

Todor clasped Benedict. *He who returns is not a deserter.*

Benedict became Todor. And Todor's face was the face of Benedict as Branko. Todor and Branko laid Benedict on the earth; they climbed onto Benedict's chest; their tongues licked Benedict's cheeks.

Benedict emerged, reborn. Those whom the bear mounted received the bear's strength; the son whom the father embraced inherited the father's potency.

Todor and Branko blended with the sky.

Lefteris pulled the bear away.

Ilyas hauled Benedict up.

Ilyas' sons congratulated him.

The crowd applauded enthusiastically and threw more money.

Lefteris nudged Benedict. 'You did well.'

The bear raised a paw, in salute.

Ilyas examined Benedict's chest and back. 'Some scratches are bleeding.'

Ariana draped Benedict's shirt around his shoulders. 'I'll dress them.'

Benedict was elated. At last, at last, his Dadoro and his real self had seen the true colour of his blood.

The meeting had been announced as an informal *divàno*, something akin to a general discussion; but, Ilyas had warned Benedict, it was likely to generate the intensity of a *kriss*, the assembly that sits as the Gypsy's court of law. Moreover, whether or not they succeeded in tracing any of his kinsmen, the inquiry would impose a judgement – not from the gathering, but from Branko himself.

It was a large congregation; ample proof, Ilyas had affirmed, that irrespective of dispersion and multitudinous influences, the Romanies remained a single people. Helping their own was still a commandment.

They sat in that serene stillness which Gypsies had evolved through centuries of deliberations on life and death.

There were chieftains from every tribe between the Netherlands and Turkey, the part of Europe which the Ursari had worked before the Second World War; there were elders from Canada and the United States whence some survivors of concentration camps had emigrated; and there were itinerant entertainers, fairground and circus people who operated in Eastern Europe and the Balkans.

Congregated around *Bibi* who, for once, sat apart from Hanro, were many women, among them Yildiz and Ariana. Women, as everybody knew, were wiser in the pathways of consanguinity than men.

There were also numerous children, because it was incumbent on them, even at an early age, to learn the intricacies of justice.

Lumnia and Omar were present, too: according to Ilyas, the one to spread magic, the other to bestow luck.

And, like worthy guests, magic and luck arrived punctually. No sooner had the proceedings started with the announcement that one among them was seeking information on the Pehlivan family than the Ursari woman stepped forward. 'By your leave, Romale. Eleni from Greece.' She pointed at her husband. 'My old man, Lefteris. We know of one Pehlivan: Yerko . . .'

Benedict felt breathless. A name, unknown and plucked from the ether, but a name that lived.

'Settled in Romania . . .' Eleni nudged her husband. 'Old-timer will tell you . . .'

Lefteris, drawing heavily on his cigarette, scrutinized the assembly sullenly.

Eleni shouted at him. 'Wrapped your tongue round nettles, have you?'

Lefteris spoke gruffly. 'Yerko? Went off with Todor and Zara – before the war.'

Benedict began to shake. 'Todor and Zara?'

'To learn bear-leading. Promising he was, too, I was told.'

Eleni sniggered. 'But he gave up!'

Lefteris turned to her querulously. 'He gave up 'cause he went thieving. Thieving is easier! Thanks to the likes of him, we'll have to give up bears, too.' He turned and whined to the gathering. 'That's the new world: fit for magpies and vultures! Nobody wants rare birds any more!' He pointed at the chairoplane, spinning with all its seats occupied. 'That's what they want for thrills – contraptions!'

The assembly, respectful of the old Ursari's complaint and wistful of the lost world he mourned, remained silent.

Lefteris wagged an accusing finger. 'You've forgotten, all of you, bear is

157

sacred, bear has a soul which is the envy of horses and mountains! I told you about Yerko. You owe me. Give me one of you! Let me teach him all I know before I croak and take part of our soul to the grave!'

Eleni snarled. 'Stop begging!'

The assembly laughed.

Some of the men slapped Lefteris on the shoulder; the couple had become popular. Which was unusual, Ilyas had told Benedict. The Ursari were perennial outsiders. Those Gypsies engaged in more sophisticated vocations saw them as backward people, good only for menial work; the rest resented them for their unsociability, for the Ursari, perversely independent, always chose to travel alone as individual families. But latterly, stuck as most of them were in Bulgaria and Romania, they had come to be missed. Thus, this couple, though devoid of a gentle word to offer the world, had become the festival's mascot.

Sharply, Lefteris turned to Benedict. 'You! You wrestled well! Join me!'

Benedict, still shaking, edged forward. 'You actually knew Todor and Zara?'

Lefteris looked affronted. 'Ursari know Ursari.'

'What were they like?'

Eleni screeched with laughter. 'Same as us. Male and female scarecrows – only younger.'

'I am their son. Branko.'

They stared at him in disbelief.

Lefteris muttered. 'They did have a son, but . . .'

'He was born in Auschwitz.'

'Yeah. But . . .'

'He was smuggled out.'

'Yeah . . .'

'Did Yerko tell you about him?'

'Yeah.'

'How did he know?'

'He was with Todor and Zara.'

'In Auschwitz?'

'Yeah.'

'How did he survive?'

'Transferred to another camp.'

'How was he related to Todor and Zara?'

'Nephew. Zara's sister's son.'

A howl of pain and triumph escaped Benedict. He had a family. The family had a face. And eyes that had seen the past. A family who could speak and recount all that needed telling. He was no longer an infant permanently abandoned in an endless landscape.

He squatted on his haunches. 'My cousin . . .'

He had a family. These were his people. He could float, a wizened chunk of mountain ice in a river, water happily returned to water, all the way to the matriarchal sea. You belong to us. That was what they had been telling him with their eyes whenever they had brushed past, rubbed shoulders, shook hands, tested the strength in his grip, fired good-natured jibes, even when they had stared at him curiously, trying to see beyond his smart clothes and shoes, his hygienic smell, his uncertain gaze, his armour-plated posture and, above all, beyond that attitude of *gadjo* superiority which so starkly exposed the erosion of heart and mind. They were ready to accept him, to receive, sheathe, embrace, incorporate, embosom him. In their fold there would be milk in his breasts like those old men suckling their grandchildren.

And belonging would make him fit to love, fit to build and, irrespective of his dead seeds, fit to multiply. Fit to be the progenitor of all those who had swathed him, fit to be the begetter of his people.

The Bible is waiting to be found – by you. Waiting to fulfil the prophecy.
Why not?

He began to weep.

The assembly waited silently.

Some men nodded gravely, approving the natural flow of his emotions; many women, Yildiz and Ariana among them, succumbed to their own tears; the children, undeceivable in matters of sincerity, stopped fidgeting. Ilyas wrapped his arm around him like a wing. Ilyas' sons edged closer.

Benedict wiped his tears with his sleeve. 'Tell me about Yerko.'

Lefteris shrugged. 'Yerko's Yerko. Always thieving.'

'Settled in Romania, you said. Where?'

Eleni pursed her face. 'Transylvania – Apuseni area.'

Lefteris interjected. 'Not now. In jail now. In Tîrgu Jiu. Labour camp for the mines.'

'How long for?'

Eleni sniggered. 'A Gypsy in jail in Romania? Maybe for ever.'

Benedict gauged the assembly: angry, but stoic. Could he rouse them? 'I want to see him.'

Lefteris shook his head. 'There's madness in Romania. Ceauşescu. Prisoners' visitors end up prisoners.'

'In fact, I want to get him out.'

Eleni chuckled. 'You got influence with O Del?'

'Yes. I have a prophecy.'

Benedict settled on the grass. Scanning the faces in the gathering, he lit a *Villiger* and waited.

One by one, starting with Ilyas and his sons, the men sat down, too.

Then the women; and the children.

Then Lumnia, as she gazed sombrely at Benedict.

And, finally, Omar.

Benedict passed round his *Villigers*.

By the end of the festivities, Ilyas had predicted, Branko would decide whether to come home to his people's airy tents or crawl back to the contaminated cages of the *gadje*.

Branko had decided: he would discard all that was artifice, starting with the person that was Benedict.

Once again, when O Del went to repair other Constellations, Janus, Adam's two-headed son, and Albina, Eve's vampire daughter, brought their people, the Hundred-Handed Ghouls, out of the feculence.

Seeing them seek out blood, the Romanies' king and queen, Laius and Jocasta, consulted the oracle.

The drabarni told them to transport their harps to distant willows; but prior to exile they should smother their newborn son, Branko, so that the sounds he made as he dreamed, played and suckled would not betray their flight.

Laius and Jocasta duly dispersed their people.

But they could not kill their child; entrusting him to the Urme, Life, they abandoned him on a hillside.

As it happened, Life had already focused Her eye on Branko; hence, at sunset, She directed a flock of sheep to the hillside.

And the frisky lambs soon discovered the infant.

The shepherd, an old widower, handed the boy to Ariana and Mihal, a couple who were without issue.

Under these foster-parents' loving care, Branko grew into a strong youngster and became a rainmaker.

One day, the drabarni who had prophesied doom for Laius and Jocasta travelled through the fields where Branko was churning a cloudburst; arrested by the youth's countenance, she offered to read his future.

She told him he would cause his parents' death.

Determined to thwart this prophecy, Branko fled to distant lands; his disappearance plunged Ariana and Mihal into grief; pain caused by the child who runs away is infinite.

For forty seasons, Branko girdled the earth.

Zealously nursing the orphan's anger, he dissipated into brutality.

One day, after a vicious brawl which left him battered on a dung-heap, he had the following dream:

He encounters an old man at a crossroad.

Both claim right of way; neither yields passage.

In the ensuing dispute, Branko slays the old man.

Travelling on, he reaches a verdant domain.

He finds it hostage to a colossal Hundred-Handed Ghoul.

The people live without hope: oracles have told them the monster will be destroyed by a young outcast; and the king of the domain, who set out in search of this saviour, has been killed by a brigand.

Branko confronts the Hundred-Handed Ghoul; he raises his ruddled hands and turns the monster into stone.

The people appoint Branko king; to keep him benign, they give him the widowed queen for wife.

Four children are born of this union.

Many years later, a plague strikes the domain.

The oracle pronounces that the plague will abate only when the old king's murderer is found.

Branko launches an investigation.

Chroniclers gather information on travellers who used the crossroad where the old king was slain.

A witness identifies Branko as the murderer.

Another witness recognizes Branko's birthmark and reveals him as the dead king's son.

The queen kills herself for having lain with her offspring; Branko gouges out his eyes.

His sons, fighting for his throne, kill each other; a daughter is executed for trying to bury her brothers; the other daughter takes to the vale of tears to expiate her father's sins.

After this dream, Branko withdrew to a cave; forty days later, he discovered the dream's meaning:

The absent child deprives his parents of a healthy death; hence, his guilt equals that of absent parents; for as parents must spread their wings over the child with their life experience, so must the child screen his parents with his sixth sense which, in the young, is flawless.

Wiser now, Branko went back to Ariana and Mihal.

They received him with great joy.

When he conveyed the reasons for his flight, they told him he need never have run away, for they were not his natural parents.

So Branko went in search of Laius and Jocasta.

He found them in dank burrows, still hiding from the Hundred-Handed Ghouls.

He confessed his love for them; they wept and welcomed him back.

Together they chased out the Hundred-Handed Ghouls from Romanestan's green lands, thus proving that a loving child can set the world right, even reverse murderous prophecies.

Twelve

Benedict's resolve to spring his cousin Yerko out of prison earned him affection and respect from all quarters. Many men volunteered to help.

As Ilyas' eldest son, Kenan argued that the honour of assisting his family's guest was duly his. But after extensive discussions, he sadly accepted the fact that though his strength, courage and acumen qualified him for the task, his withered arm would prove a handicap.

As a result, Ramzi, Ilyas' second oldest son, claimed the right to accompany Benedict.

Omar completed the team. Benedict's initial consideration that he was too young was dismissed by Ilyas and the elders. Determined to groom Omar as a future leader, they insisted the expedition was just the sort of experience that would bring the youth to age. Besides, they maintained, Omar's extraordinary luck was bound to ensure success.

Benedict, Ramzi and Omar spent the next three days planning the operation. Aided by the general euphoria – the *Enderlez* magic, Ilyas called it – they developed a very close friendship. The amiable Omar soon exposed in Benedict that other great pain of orphanhood, the lack of siblings – sisters whom he could protect, brothers whom he could father.

The last night of *Enderlez* arrived.

Families and *kumpanias* paid valedictory visits.

Those couples who had eloped, straggled back. They were met with the swingeing, but procedural, wrath of their relatives. Their fathers negotiated marriages that had to be solemnized within twenty-four hours.

Ilyas, seeking to consolidate the friendship between Benedict, Ramzi and

Omar, suggested that they become blood-brothers. Ramzi and Benedict agreed heartily. Omar, echoing Benedict's earlier reservation on joining the team, declared himself as yet untested in life, hence, unripe for the privilege of blood-brotherhood; he asked to take the bond on their return from Romania when, with God's help, he would have proved himself. However, he asked to be allowed to officiate.

Benedict and Ramzi came out of Ilyas' caravan and entered the ring of people who had gathered for the ceremony. Omar, waiting for them in the middle of the circle, clasped their hands.

Benedict quivered in anticipation. Blood-brotherhood was a sacred rite for the Romanies, a pledge that held arcane and awesome meanings. He had often fantasized, particularly during the Pro Juventute years, to have, at the very least, such a bond, perhaps with the son of some decent foster-parents, with whom he could have painted bright the shadowy horizon which the abandoned child inhabits. Now, surrendering to the ritual, he perceived that his mind and body, which had separated from each other these past few days, had mercifully reunited. And, whirling in the vortex of this union, he did not care if he never again touched reality. This transcendental state, he felt certain, was an improvement on even the most felicitous reality.

As if to applaud his elation, Lumnia materialized in the midst of the crowd and eclipsed every light with her deep, lustrous eyes.

Omar addressed Benedict and Ramzi. 'Do you wish to mix blood?'

Benedict and Ramzi replied in unison. 'We do.'

'Are there circumstances which prohibit brotherhood?'

'None.'

Omar addressed the gathering. 'Does anybody know of a reason that would make this blessing unclean?'

The crowd remained silent.

Omar tied the two men's right hands, at the wrist, with a silk strap.

He went across to Ilyas and Yildiz who were standing at the edge of the circle, doubly proud, as parents and parents-to-be; Ilyas gave Omar a bottle of *rakia*.

Omar moved back to the centre, broke the bottle's seal and poured most of the liquid, as libation, onto the earth.

Then he emptied the remaining *rakia*, in equal portions, into two glasses and gave a glass each to Benedict and Ramzi.

The latter, using their left hands, took a mouthful of the drink and poured the rest upon the earth.

Then Omar went across to Ariana who was also standing at the edge of the circle; feeling as proud as Ilyas and Yildiz, Ariana gave him another bottle of *rakia*.

Omar returned to the centre, broke this bottle's seal also and again poured most of the liquid, as libation, onto the earth.

Then, taking out two newly forged knives from his pocket, he anointed their sharp blades with the remaining *rakia*.

He poured the rest of the liquor on Benedict's and Ramzi's tied hands, then smashed the empty bottle.

Using a different knife on each, he lanced the tips of the index fingers of their bound hands. 'Suck each other's blood.'

Benedict and Ramzi did so.

Omar placed the cuts over one another.

When the blood coagulated and stuck the fingers together, Benedict and Ramzi held up their tied hands.

Simultaneously, Omar drove the bloodied knives into the ground; the brotherhood would thus be inscribed on the earth.

The crowd ululated.

Omar untied Benedict's and Ramzi's hands, then kissed them on the cheeks. 'Congratulations, brothers.'

Benedict and Ramzi embraced.

The crowd cheered. Friends and relatives celebrated with streams of *rakia*.

Aisha and Amina, Ramzi's sisters, drew Benedict aside and sat him down on a stool.

The third sister, Khatija, brought out a large photo-album from Ilyas' caravan and handed it to him. 'Everybody in these pictures is your family now.'

Benedict riffled through the album. It seemed to contain a whole people. His kin – all of them.

And after forty years alone in the wilderness, Branko came to examine the shadings on his bow and discovered that they were his father's fingerprints.

And he remembered the time when his father had given him the bow, appointed him his siblings' guardian and gone to solve death's riddles.

And he remembered that, one day, distracted by the colours of spring in the highlands, he had strayed from his brothers and sisters and never found them again.

Now, as loneliness swiftly withered his life, he craved to be with his flesh and blood; to drink, eat, talk and wrestle with them.

And so he took his father's bow and shot an arrow towards the rising sun.

He travelled forty months and reached the land of the tundra where his arrow had landed.

He did not find his siblings.

But he befriended long-tusked mammoths who fed him their milk, which gave him strength for his next journey as well as thick hair against the cold.

Then he shot an arrow towards the noon sun.

He travelled another forty months and reached the land of the jungles where his arrow had landed.

He did not find his siblings.

But he befriended mighty gorillas who fed him their milk, which gave him strength for his next journey as well as unabating desire for love.

Finally, he shot an arrow towards the setting sun.

He travelled yet another forty months and reached the highlands where his arrow had landed.

He did not find his siblings.

But he befriended the bears who fed him their milk which gave him strength to inhabit the woodlands.

So Branko set up his tent under a sky embroidered by trees and listened to the leaves' lullabies.

Forty days later, alerted by the bears, his siblings emerged from the depths of the woods where they had been living ever since Branko had lost them.

Cautiously, they waited until Branko fell asleep, then approached him.

They examined his bow and recognized their father's fingerprints.

They drew back his blanket and noted the eye-shaped cicatrices on his soles, which is the birthmark of those who girdle the earth.

They woke him up, yelping with joy, throwing their arms around him.

And, forgiving him for losing them, they lit fires for their father and for all patriarchs.

Thenceforth the siblings kept their eyes on each other; not one was abandoned.

This was true even during the dispersion when they were forced to take separate paths.

Thirteen

Benedict and Ariana stood witness to the dawn. The people of Šuto Orizari, loathe to return to everyday life, were delaying their awakening; and the visitors, still ruminating *Enderlez*'s grace, idled as they prepared to depart. Even Ilyas, dawn's most faithful admirer, had stayed away to spend more time with Ramzi.

A sweep of saffron on the eastern peaks announced the dawn's approach.

Benedict shivered. He was not ready for this day, not ready at all to run into the wilderness and grapple with the unknown. His repeated pronouncements that, having pined every day to be reborn, properly born, born with the mark of dignity stamped on his forehead, here he was, at last, favoured by the Fates, fledged and accoutred as a new man, chosen to be transformed and transfigured, now struck him as little more than bravura.

He was still a pathetic, marginal man. He was not ready to shed his *gadjo* skin. Though he had come to understand that the Romany values he had so cursorily thrown away had been, in reality, the very components of his soul, he still clung to his place in the *gadje*'s false paradise.

Nor could he embrace readily, as a true underdog, the banal dogmas of ethnocentrism, racism or nationalism. Not because he knew that such movements, much as they were the only source to provide marginal people with a sense of soul and identity, always led to horrendous destruction, but because the self who desperately aspired to be a Rom, who rose on its hind legs when called Branko, did not yet have substance; it was merely a romantic image gazing narcissistically at its reflection on the surface of a dream.

He turned to Ariana. 'Do you really believe in the prophecy, Dei?'

'With all my being. So does everybody.'

'I wish I could.'

'Sure, you do!'

'I have so many doubts . . .'

'Doubts are natural – even necessary.'

'Branko, the Scribe. He didn't have any doubts – when he was writing the Bible . . .'

'You don't know that.'

'Do you think Yerko will know . . . where it might be – the Bible . . .?'

'I don't know.'

'If he doesn't – how would I find it? Where would I look?'

'Your destiny will lead you to it.'

'Doubts are natural, you said . . .'

'Even necessary . . .'

'I hope you're right. I hope you're right.'

The stars fell; their blood ran over the peaks. Today, dawn, the purveyor of hope, wore the hues of doom.

Fear loomed. And panic.

As a soldier he could keep these terrors at bay. But did he have the same skills as a Gypsy? If he succumbed to fear, how would he start life again as Branko, the Rom?

The sun overran the mountains.

Nearby, an intrepid menhir saluted the day: Omar. The youth's sudden appearance comforted Benedict; he waved at him. On their return from Tîrgu Jiu, he and Omar would commingle blood, become family. The Gypsies pursued wholeness; the *gadje* favoured disconnection. Nothing more to be said.

Omar waved back; then saluted someone behind Benedict.

Lumnia.

These few days, Omar and Lumnia had reversed roles; it had been she who had kept a protective eye over the youth. As Omar had stood shoulder to shoulder with Benedict and Ramzi, her pride had been as boundless as any mother's; but she had also looked melancholic, seemingly acknowledging that Omar had escaped her gravity and would never again orbit her.

Ariana stood up. 'She has come. I was hoping she would.'

'What do you mean, Dei?'

'It's time for tender looks, whispers and promises . . .'

'You don't have to go . . .'

She smiled. 'I have my share of you. She must have hers.'

Ariana shuffled away; Omar ran across to her and gave her a supporting arm.

Benedict stared at Lumnia. He imbibed her. A plenary woman. A woman who had tamed time, who had blended flesh and spirit into a perfect future. A haven where all men would wish to seek refuge, but to which only one man, if such a man did exist, might be granted access. Could he, Benedict, a middle-aged child with adult yearnings, run to her and suckle from her the potency he desperately needed? Could he cling to her and be delivered from his confusion?

She approached him.

He could barely breathe. They had not yet spoken, not once.

She took his hand. 'I am Lumnia.'

Benedict absorbed her warmth. 'Bened . . . Branko!'

She nodded.

In order not to offend her, he withdrew his hand. But his skin memorized her texture.

She reclaimed his hand. 'I have seen the paths you'll tread. I have also seen your wounds. One day flowers will grow from your flesh.'

'Don't mock me.'

She stroked his face. 'No mockery – never – between you and me.'

'You and me? That's what I want – you and me . . .'

God, what was he saying? He had a wife. If he was looking for a romantic diversion, why Lumnia?

Because she is strange and exotic?

What about the consequences? Enamoured of a witch – might end up, who knows, a slave, a zombie, man into pig?

There were many women, including some friends of Nettie, who would be safer and more fun. Besides, if truth be known, he was awkward with women. They were wonderful when they emulated a family. Wonderful also to make love to. But for the rest, he could never find the feelings, his or theirs, which made some men and women come out from behind their barricades.

'You'll be leaving soon.'

And she was so young – almost half his age. 'This morning.'

'It will be a long time before you come back.'

'Not too long.'

Again, she stroked his face. 'The road you take will be the road that will bring you back. But it stretches out. Be patient. Trust me. When you depart, you will have started to return.'

Why was he hesitating? He wanted her. 'Patience is the last thing I'd tolerate, Lumnia. I have an unchallengeable reason for coming back.'

She smiled. 'Many unchallengeable reasons. Today you can see only one.'

'Just so there is no misunderstanding – it will stay that way . . .'

She laughed. 'You're experiencing the first flames. It will be a blaze in forty seasons . . .'

'Forty seasons?'

She intoned with a different voice, an inner voice. 'Love needs time. And great care. It also needs great magic.'

He stared at her, uncomprehendingly. 'When I leave now, I'll be on my way back – that's what you said.' He realized he was pleading with her.

She went on intoning. 'Soon I shall be a *drabarni*. I'll have knowledge of the unknowable. I will provide the magic.'

'Lumnia! I'll be back! Before the month's out!'

She stroked his face yet again. 'Forty seasons, Branko. That's what it will be.'

Her touch was like balm. 'That's ten years!'

'You have to acquire a shepherd's sinew.'

'What's that mean?'

'Much has to happen to you.'

'Such as?'

'You will see.'

'Like finding the Bible?'

'You will see.'

'Do you see – what I'll see?'

'Yes.'

'Tell me.'

'Then they won't happen because you will have been prepared.'

'Lumnia, I am coming back!'

She pressed his hand to her bosom. 'They will pass – the forty seasons. Quick enough!'

'And if I need your help?'

'You will have it.'

'How – if we won't be together?'

'Look into my eyes, Branko.'

He did. And saw her as a gloriole. Like a psalmist's vision of God. At the core of this gloriole was her body, naked, outstretched, her pudenda pulsating. Flesh into mystery and mystery incarnate. 'I want you. I need you.'

'Now, I inhabit you. We will always be together.'

He saw himself carrying this auroral woman. And saw her magic. She became mist and, saving him from the *gadje*, transported him to rivers that rose from mountain-tops; she became starry skies beneath which they camped, built up fires and lay down together; she became a caravan with scythes on its wheels, like Alexander's chariots of war, and cut through hordes of Nazi soldiers, SS doctors, Pro Juventute orderlies; and she became an ocean and hewed him into a leviathan and together they gave birth to earth. 'I want you, Lumnia. Now.'

'Be patient, Branko. Trust my magic.'

And Branko began laying the foundations for Romanestan.

One day whilst felling a tree he accidentally struck a humming-bird and broke the creature's wings.

Anguished, he took the bird to his tent, put her wings in splints and said: 'Please forgive me.'

The humming-bird said, 'I forget,' which is a nobler sentiment than 'I forgive.'

And animals of every species, seeing the harmony that blossomed between Branko and the humming-bird, stopped preying on each other and gathered around Branko's tent.

Wolves, panthers and lions kept watch over the camp; foxes and jackals picked fruit; goats, sheep and cows gave freely of their milk; bears, stags and wild asses provided warmth by making themselves available as bedding; vultures and eagles fashioned canopies with their wings against rain and snow.

The humming-bird's wings regained their vigour.

And one day, as Branko slept, she kissed him on his forehead and flew away to resume her work.

Branko and the animals felt inconsolable.

But that same day, a beautiful woman came unto the encampment in her vardo.

She introduced herself as Lumnia, a sorceress whose name meant 'light of the world'.

And she revealed that O Del had sent her in thanksgiving to Branko for saving the humming-bird who carries children's souls to the Land Without Evil.

Hereafter, she affirmed, she would be Branko's wife and assist him in matters pertinent to Romanestan such as the nature of seas, tides, trade winds and currents.

Then, one day, Robin flew into the encampment.

Now Robin, as it is known, always brings news of persecution; for he is the bird who removed the spikes from Yehoshua's crown of thorns and in so doing pierced his own heart, which is why he is red-breasted.

And he reported that a band of giants who had sprouted from dragon's teeth had taken Branko's blood-brother, Hiawatha, prisoner.

Branko set out to save Hiawatha.

To ensure his safe return from this dangerous mission, Lumnia wove her magic and implanted her duende into his body.

A duende, as it is known, is the soul's soul; once it enters a host, it inhabits it for ever.

PART THREE

Fourteen

Yerko would be freed with a *Balkan caress*.

The gambit, according to Ilyas, was the very resin that made Levantinism such an undying – and silky – civilization. The sanctimonious vilified the *caress* as a disease. Gypsies lauded it as a panacea. Everybody, from presidents down to lavatory attendants, indulged in it regularly. Sometimes the *caress* hurt, but never unbearably. It imposed a strict code, but always applied discretion; and it seldom, if ever, humiliated. Above all, though it considered life worthless, it always held it sacred.

The *caress* was that illicit grace known as 'bribery' which, in an uncompromisingly unequal world, made living possible, sometimes even agreeable.

In the matter of the particular *caress* which would spring Yerko from jail, a person who had influence over Yerko's movements would be found and his palm sprinkled with gold; this person would then allow Yerko to wander off; and, Benedict, wrapped in shadows, would whisk him away.

Initially Benedict had resisted the idea. He was a man of action, not a creature of the penumbra. He worked with calculable risks. The *caress* contained no constants: the bribed person could double-cross, get them arrested, even killed. What was needed, he had argued, was a commando raid: in and out of the prison at speed. He had successfully executed, in numerous war games, countless exercises on targets infinitely better defended. Half a dozen doughty Gypsies and a month's training would suffice.

But his objections had been dismissed. Violent solutions, being the coinage of blood feuds, ethnic conflicts and political struggles, were against Romany mores, Ilyas and the elders had insisted. Besides, in a totalitarian system, subtler ways were needed to push life in the right direction. As for being double-crossed, no fear of that. A *Balkan caress* was like a marriage made in heaven: the right person was hitched to the right bribe. And Ramzi was a master matchmaker.

Benedict returned to Switzerland for a few days.

Though he knew, in his bones, that the long hiatus Lumnia had predicted would occur as pronounced, he clung to the hope that the period of 'forty seasons', echoing the scriptural measure for a long span of time, constituted poetic licence. She could just as easily have said forty *days* or *months* or *years*.

Thus when he took Ariana back to her community in Interlaken, he urged her to maintain contact with Lumnia during the few weeks he would be away and to impress upon her that he would keep to his word and rush back to her.

Ariana promised to do as he asked. But her prayers for his safety, repeatedly countermined by her conviction that she would not live long enough to see him return, made it plain that she had accepted Lumnia's augury as irrevocable. And by the time Benedict took his leave, she was cheerfully stoic: at least, he was back in the fold; she wouldn't have to peer anxiously, from inside her ashes, into the *gadje*'s world to see what was happening to him.

Benedict stayed the weekend with Young Glanz.

And, wondering whether the answers would make any sense to an empiricist, as doctors were supposed to be – or, indeed, to himself – he opened up his heart. Starting with his conversation with Melchior on that last night on the Matterhorn, he told Glanz about his journey into the past: about Auschwitz-Birkenau, a desolation where death's suppurating eye appeared to be still searching for him; about the surreality of the pond and a state of mind so clear – albeit indistinguishable from madness – that it enabled him to commune with his real parents; about Dr Kalderon's revelations on the Gypsy Bible; and about Lumnia and the homecoming that Skopje had represented. Finally, whilst admitting to being tormented by a legion of doubts, he disclosed his resolve to fulfil the prophecy he carried. There would be satisfaction in that, conceivably some reparation to his soul. And perhaps by setting out to correct the wrong turn he had taken, by attempting to achieve what he had been born to achieve, he would also bring a smile to Melchior, wherever the old-timer might be!

Glanz did not challenge Benedict in any way. But he pointed out that, as Benedict had already experienced, life lived at supranatural dimensions could seriously strain the mind. Was his destiny worth such misery?

Benedict could not offer an answer. What could be the difference between a mind that was strained now – presumably, while it was still sane – and a mind strained at some future date when, in all likelihood, it would have plummeted into madness?

Glanz admitted that he, too, could not think of an answer. So he asked about Nettie.

Benedict acknowledged his pain and guilt at abandoning Nettie. But the marriage was one in which both he and Nettie had invested only superficially. Their spirits, wary of conjoining, had merely touched tangentially. A relationship content to subsist – no more. Henceforth, since there would be no children to bind them together, they would, without doubt, drift apart, slowly and tortuously. Therefore, he believed – or maybe it was wishful thinking – parting now would not prove too disastrous.

Glanz, barely able to express how consummately he would miss Benedict, wished him luck. And he begged Benedict to remember that their friendship was for life, that should he need any help, at any time, he would always be there to provide it.

He also promised he would keep watch over Ariana.

On the Monday, Benedict went to his bank. He opened a new deposit account with half of the savings he and Nettie held jointly. He bought an assortment of gold coins to the value of 25,000 Swiss francs and took them with him.

Then he saw a solicitor – someone Young Glanz had recommended; his own would have challenged every directive.

He transferred his share of the marital home to Nettie and signed affidavits acceding to all the conditions her divorce proceedings would impose.

He divided his inheritance from Melchior equally between Nettie and Ariana and stipulated that should the courts, at some future date, instruct Pro

Juventute to pay compensation to the abducted Gypsy children, his allocation should also be given to Ariana or her nominees.

He wrote two letters of resignation: one to the Lucerne Hydroelectricity Board; the other to the commanding officer of his regiment. He painfully acknowledged, in the second, that his decision, so sudden and devoid of any mitigating circumstances, might be construed as dereliction of duty and lead to a dishonourable discharge.

Finally, he drew up a will and bequeathed all that would accrue in his personal account to a Romany educational fund in Skopje.

Then he went to the university library where Nettie did most of her research.

Her delight at seeing him compounded his guilt.

They sat in the gardens overlooking the city.

He informed her of the arrangements he had made.

She listened in silence. Eventually, hoarse with shock, anger, confusion and disbelief, she managed to ask him, 'Why? Why?'

Anguish muffled his words. 'I have to.'

'Is there someone else?'

'I suppose so. But in ten years time.'

'Don't play the fool!'

'That's what she predicted: forty seasons. Sounds crazy, but I believe it.'

'Who is she?'

He mumbled. 'A witch.'

'If that's the level of conversation we're going to have . . .'

'I'm not being flippant. I mean it . . .'

'A witch?'

'A *drabarni* – that's the Romany word.'

She stared at him for a long time, then seized his hand. 'Witches. Prophecies. How can you believe in all that shit?'

Nettie's eyes had turned opaque, like beads. Alien eyes, dense with anger.

Benedict remembered something Dr Kalderon had told him: many Jewish men, tormented by fears of another Holocaust, were marrying, often disastrously, Gentile women in order to produce Gentile children. Had he, unconsciously, married a *gadjo* for the same reason?

And now that they could not have children, they had reverted to what they were originally: strangers. Would they become enemies?

'Benedict, answer me! How can you believe in . . .?'

'I do – and I don't. More to the point, I want to believe in it. And I will – one day.'

'You don't know what you're getting yourself into! You're not a Gypsy – not any more. Come back to earth, for God's sake! There's a whole reality . . .'

'All that shit, as you put it, is the reality I want.'

'And everything you have here? Me? Your work? The army?'

Tears flooded his eyes. 'Searching in the dark.'

'Searching . . .?'

'And failing. If I can escape that past, I can have a future.'

She punched him. 'You bastard!'

He grasped her hand and kissed it. 'Forgive me.' Then, unable to stay with her any longer, he ran off.

That evening, he flew back to Belgrade and caught the night train to Skopje.

Benedict, Ramzi and Omar, flashy in dress and behaviour, like well-heeled Macedonian workers, departed for Romania via Bulgaria in a hired car. They crossed the Yugoslav border at Kriva Palanka and proceeded to Sofia for their first stopover.

The efficacy of the *Balkan caress*, Ramzi had divulged, was determined by the depth of information gained on the candidate. In the ranks of the various authorities which had dealings with Yerko's labour camp – army, police, party and prison personnel and, especially the Securitate, Romania's dreaded internal security bureau – there were, at a rough estimate, some twenty front runners. A great deal of information, particularly intimate details, was needed before the right person could be chosen.

Since smuggling had developed into the Balkans' most lucrative industry, neighbouring countries had become excellent sources for intelligence. Operators had to know, without a shadow of a doubt, who on the other side of the border could be safely bribed. As members of the smugglers' fraternity – the only fraternity which accepted Gypsies – such information would be available to the trio in Bulgaria. Hence, the detour.

For a few days, they stayed in Sofia, in the monolithic Hotel Balkan.

They visited the Vasil Levski Monument, the famous icon collection in Aleksandar Nevski Memorial Church, the National Art Gallery, the Museum of the Revolutionary Movement – all requisite sites for eager tourists – plus, as would be expected of Muslims, the Banya Bashi Mosque.

They also dawdled in hotel bars and market-places and met various people – some who had been recommended to them, others well known to Ramzi.

Then they drove east to the Valley of the Roses, to Kazanlik, a town on the northern foothills of the Sredna Gora mountains, where Fehmi, a distant cousin of Ilyas, worked for a co-operative that produced attar of roses for an Italian perfumery. They arrived in mid-harvest, and, like all visiting relatives, lent a hand.

To prevent the evaporation of their oil under the sun, the roses had to be picked at night. Consequently, they toiled, in eerie shades of darkness, in fields that soon became sweeps of thorn. During the day, they helped transport the petals, on herds of donkeys, to distilleries. Every sundown they attended the traditional ceremonies of communities working in the subsidiary industries of rose-jam and rose-liqueur, flavourings and pharmaceutics.

For Benedict these days when land, water and sky smelled like paradise – all the way to Asia Minor, if Fehmi was to be believed – should have been a time of liberation. Peacefully, he should have shed his *gadjo* spots, indoctrinated himself with Romany ethos and savoured his new life which promised to be bountiful with kith, kin, purpose and meaning.

Yet, to his dismay, a sense of failure dominated his thoughts. Failure that summed up his life hitherto. Failure that threatened to permeate his mind and body and abort his future. Failure for which Nettie stood as a symbol.

Nettie. His life for so many years. Still his wife. Fertile, yet barren. Forsaken. Never to be touched or spoken to again. Would she survive? Find another man – maybe a good *gadjo* like Melchior? Or would she wilt, her womb forever desolate?

In time, he would forget the contours – and the texture – of her athletic body, so perfect for motherhood. Only his grief at the way he had abandoned her would remain. And it would gnaw at him to his dying day.

Perhaps his sense of failure stemmed from his uncertainty, if not foreboding, about the mission. The intelligence they had gathered had failed to produce a good candidate for the *caress*.

The problem lay with Ceauşescu's latest paranoia: to prevent the formation of a cabal that might unleash a coup, the Romanian president – the 'Giant of the Carpathians', as he wished to be known these days – made sure that not a single officer, party member or Securitate agent stayed in one place for any length of time. Thus Ramzi had had to scrap the option of bribing an official. No one had been at his posting long enough to have been assessed as dependable.

They now had to search among smaller fry: a guard, a foreman or a miner. But since Romanians distrusted strangers, thinking they might be undercover agents, a direct approach would be unproductive. They had to find an intermediary.

Ramzi had been prepared for such an eventuality and knew a trustworthy go-between: one Pietru, chief of a *kumpania* of Zlatari Gypsies. Whether this man could be engaged or, indeed, prove useful, was another matter.

So they left the Valley of the Roses. Motoring through the Stara Planina mountains, they reached Vidin, the picturesque town on the Danube which, since its foundation by the Celts, had been occupied by every power that had passed through the region. There they boarded the ferry to the Romanian river-port of Calafat, on the opposite bank.

They took the tourist route along the stretch of the Danube that served as the border between Romania and Yugoslavia. At Drobeta-Turnu Severin they visited the Roman ruins and the remains of Trajan's bridge which had been the longest bridge in antiquity and which Trajan had built specifically to circumvent the Dacian defences. Then they accorded the obligatory admiration to the Iron Gates dam, and then to new Orşova, a drab modern city that was supposed to replace the original Orşova which had been submerged, with its unique history, some twelve metres deep in the river, to accommodate the massive dam. From new Orşova, they took a boat to the Kazan gorge, where the Danube twisted and turned through sheer cliffs of some five hundred metres in height. Around Moldova Nouã, they pursued the river's arabesques, then imbibed the haunting view of the ruined castle of Golubac, on the Yugoslav bank, where St George had reputedly slain the dragon.

They observed the attitudes of Romanian functionaries, civil and military, and particularly of those whom Ramzi identified as Securitate.

Ramzi's acuity, in fact, was consummate. Thus they learned how to read people's faces and bodies; how to smell, in the fettered air, generosity or greed, rivalry or complacency, blood feuds and ethnic hatred; above all, how to perceive in those armoured with uniforms, ambition or doubt, courage or panic, commitment or alienation.

They learned that dark moods and violent outbursts, from individuals or groups, were not necessarily predictable, that though they could be manipulated, they were often sparked by insignificant incidents or simply by the despair and anger that always lurked in the shadows; a crop half a kilo less than last year's could push someone to murder; the way a person dressed, spoke, ate or drank could unleash racial violence; a sudden change in temperature or an unexpected jig by the wind could make a whole company of soldiers turn on the civilian population.

All of which, though engrossing, struck Benedict as nebulous and time consuming: Balkan ellipses all of them – like the detour to Bulgaria. He rued the fact that they had decided against a raid.

This led to arguments with Ramzi. Which distressed Omar because they asked him to arbitrate and he would not because he revered them both and refused to take sides.

Ramzi always ended the disputes amicably. He would praise Benedict's competence and experience as an expert in many fields, but point out that, in ironclad Romania, these qualities were irrelevant – pearls cast before pigs.

A reasoning which Benedict resented. Damn right, pearls cast before pigs. When Ramzi and his ingenuous Gypsies gave up their rustic ways and broadened their minds, they might start getting somewhere. But unable to voice these thoughts – and berating himself for nurturing such prejudice towards his own people, even towards his blood-brother – he devised a training programme. Insisting that they should keep fit in case the *caress* failed and they had to resort to action, he forced Ramzi and Omar to perform daily exercises which showed off his own stamina, agility and skills.

Ramzi and Omar complied, with a fair degree of competence, in order to appease him.

Then, one day, through intermediaries, Ramzi met Pietru, the Zlatari chief. They struck a deal and set off for Tîrgu Jiu.

The Zlatari panned for gold. Fiercely independent in pursuit of their harsh life, they had often been compared with the Ursari. It was said they had never been slaves, not even in Romania. Having perfected the art of concealment, they could blend with mountain mists or masquerade on the plains as shale or rock or turn into bulrushes in the streams they so painstakingly sifted.

But the Zlatari were thinning out. The *gadje*'s technology was polluting the rivers and turning gold into mud; one day, it would eviscerate man from Nature's flesh by destroying Nature herself.

Pietru's *kumpania*, comprising about a dozen families, worked the western and southern Carpathians, a region that had yielded gold since Dacian times.

They lived with the constant threat of being crimped into the coalmines or assailed by the miners. The latter, coerced into accepting reduced wages and working in deteriorating conditions – despite Ceauşescu's promises of pay rises and modernization during last year's strikes – needed the merest pretext to direct their wrath on the Gypsies.

Consequently, Pietru, a thin, dark man with a full set of gold-capped teeth, had been reluctant to get involved in someone else's dirty work. Only Benedict's hefty advance had overcome his reservations.

Pietru proved an excellent element. Within a few days, he familiarized Benedict, Ramzi and Omar with Tîrgu Jiu and its surroundings and, particularly, with a number of escape routes.

Still uneasy about the uncertainties inherent in their plan, Benedict asked Pietru whether he could procure some weapons. Pietru could, but would not: the Securitate summarily executed anyone caught with arms.

But for the four monumental sculptures donated to it by the region's most famous son, Constantin Brancuşi, Tîrgu Jiu was a dreary, pallid industrial town engaged in the production of cigarettes and cement. Its single hotel, popular with some co-operatives as a venue for conventions, and a quasi-festival that took place in February, served as its only other attractions.

The labour camp stood at the town's eastern boundary.

Comprising ten blocks set in a tight perimeter, it had been built during the Second World War, in the wake of Marshal Antonescu's alliance with Germany, as a prison for communists and nationalists. Ceauşescu himself had served time there in 1943–44.

The camp had fallen into disuse after the establishment of the People's Republic, but had been crudely revamped soon after Ceauşescu had become president. This event had been celebrated with the adage that ex-political prisoners were true socialists for they always shared their jail experiences by locking up everybody else. Thus the camp had dedicated itself to rehabilitating members of the opposition, discredited party officials, liberal academics and tricksters of the arts. In the past few years it had been expanded to intern those minorities deemed *delinquent* – a newfangled synonym for that old word, *asocial* – namely, the Gypsies.

The pits where the prisoners worked were located around Petroşani, sixty kilometres to the north of Tîrgu Jiu. Though there were also mines around

Rovinari, to the south, these were open-cast and, for obvious security reasons, did not use forced labour.

To get to Petroşani, the work party had to travel through the Jiu Valley on Highway 66. Almost half of this road, as far as Bumbeşti-Jiu, traversed a dust-bowl pockmarked by quarries; the rest snaked along the Jiu river's narrow and sharply rising gorge.

Transportation was always a headache. Though a railway line tacked the cliffs of the Jiu gorge – a remarkable feat of engineering – prisoners were not allowed on the trains; for the railway had been built by forced labour – most of whom had been worked to death – and the authorities still feared an act of revenge.

This had reduced the options to a motley collection of dilapidated trucks, buses, coaches and pick-ups. The efficiency of this service, however, was always hostage to the state of repair of either the vehicles or the highway. According to Pietru, no one in Tîrgu Jiu could remember a day when a convoy had reached Petroşani or returned to the camp without leaving behind at least one vehicle with mechanical failure.

During this period of reconnaissance, Benedict, Ramzi and Omar also deliberated on the candidates Pietru and Ramzi had finally chosen for the *caress* – to Benedict's surprise, a young couple.

The woman, Ana, drove one of the buses that transported the prisoners to Petroşani; the man, Radu, was a soldier on escort duty.

Ana was a Hungarian from the Banat, a beautiful but melancholic woman who had somehow drifted to these parts. To the disappointment of the region's bachelors she had kept very much to herself until she had met Radu, a conscript from the Dobrugei plains by the Black Sea. Inexplicably – for Radu was a plain, plump man – they had fallen in love; though had anyone asked Pietru, he could have told them that men and women from the Banat and Dobrugei were like spice and honey: irresistible to each other's flesh.

Ana and Radu planned to get married and move to the coast after Radu had finished his military service. Not having a *leu* to fulfil even this modest dream, they had been ripe for the *caress*; the gold coins they had received had already conjured for them the brazier smell of home.

The day was set for the coming Saturday. It would be market-day; the roads would be clogged by carts and lorries; and most of the soldiers serving in the area would be on weekend leave.

At dawn on Saturday, Benedict stopped his car on the side of a road which ran through dusty fields and offered a perfect view of the labour camp.

Day had broken, and though a layer of clouds made the light crepuscular, visibility was adequate.

Benedict and Pietru got out of the car and went behind some shrubs as if to urinate.

Ramzi and Omar stayed in the car and gauged the traffic. It was building up: horse-drawn carts and the odd truck, bringing produce for the market.

Benedict and Pietru surveyed the camp. The vehicles that would transport the work party had assembled outside the main gate.

Ana, they could see, was by the iron door, smoking. Always impatient to see Radu, she never stayed in her bus.

Not far from her, Tuna, Pietru's wife, bantered with those assembled behind the perimeter fence. A fortune-teller, Tuna had made the labour camp one of her regular haunts. Buxom and attractive, she was popular with both the guards and the prisoners; consequently, she had been asked to alert Yerko.

The inmates, escorted by their guards, began filing out. Pietru pointed out Radu as Tuna, flamboyantly, offered to read Radu's hand.

The prisoners started boarding the vehicles.

Benedict and Pietru noted the procedure: one guard to each bus.

They concentrated on Tuna as she moved among the prisoners.

Casually, Tuna lingered by a haggard convict, then started reading his palm.

Pietru identified the man. 'Yerko.'

Benedict felt a surge of blood. At last, Yerko had a face.

Radu directed Yerko to Ana's bus. The latter, formally shaking Tuna's hand, clambered into it.

As Radu and Ana prepared to board, Radu stroked Ana's cheek.

The gesture enraged one of the soldiers detailed to another bus. Shouting and waving his arms, he rushed across to Radu. An intense quarrel developed.

Benedict tensed up. 'What's going on?'

Pietru chuckled. 'Ion Filipescu, local lad – lust's fool. He wants Ana so much, he'll die. When Radu touches her, he goes mad with jealousy.'

The other guards separated Radu and Ion.

Minutes later, the convoy began to move.

The convoy entered Tîrgu Jiu via Strada Narciselor and rounded the gardens encircling Brancuşi's masterpiece, *The Endless Column*, a totem pole of rhomboidal blocks depicting the 'Pillar of Heaven', a folkloric motif that was still etched on many of the old wooden houses of the region. Continuing along Calea Eroilor, the main street, it turned right into the avenue named after the sculptor.

Benedict, who had parked there, lined up his car behind the convoy at a discreet distance.

Ramzi gave a wistful look at the adjoining park. This housed the other works by Brancuşi: the rectangular arch of *The Gate of the Kiss*, standing like a triumphal portal; the thirty stone chairs of *The Avenue of Seats* that emanated from it; and completing the formation, *The Table of Silence*, a composition of extraordinary simplicity comprising a round table and twelve circular stools representing both the months of the year and the Last Supper as a symbiosis of life and death.

Ramzi lit a cigarette. In the last few days, his mind had wandered to that place where the soul debates the mysteries of being and not-being. Nothing portentous about that. His mind did so every time he undertook a delicate task. At first, he had deplored these disputations as uncharacteristic of a devout Muslim who had surrendered all decisions about life and death to Allah's Will. Thereafter, he had come to accept the condition as a requisite ingredient for success, like the shortage of saliva that afflicts a runner before a race. But this time . . . This time he was not on his own; this time there were others whose fate stood in the balance; this time, failure was unthinkable. And that was proving an almost unbearable burden.

Omar sang softly. A melodious love song that caressed the heart.

Pietru listened with moist eyes.

The convoy turned into Bulevardul 1 Mai for Highway 66.

At the northern end of the Jiu river gorge, a few kilometres south of Petroşani, the convoy, minus one vehicle that had broken down, reached Pit 27 of the Nicolae Ceauşescu mines. Outside a shack daubed with the miners' traditional 'good luck' greeting, '*Noroc Bun*', Yerko's bus discharged its passengers.

Benedict, who had followed the convoy from a distance, turned his car round and drove back to the gorge. After some ten kilometres, he branched off, via a rickety shepherd's bridge, into a track in the wooded foothills.

He and his companions got out, stretched and urinated.

Ramzi and Pietru lit cigarettes.

Omar prepared breakfast: bread, cheese, onions, cucumbers, tomatoes, olives. And thermos flasks of herb tea.

Benedict studied the terrain yet again.

This was where Yerko's escape would take place. Whereas almost everywhere else in the gorge the escarpments rose sharply on both sides of the road, sometimes at angles approaching fifty degrees, here they were negotiable. And the density of the trees offered excellent camouflage.

Here also, the snaking river had imposed a series of sharp bends on the road which not only forced the vehicles to slow down, but also concealed them from the traffic ahead or behind.

Nor could the road be seen by travellers in a passing train: the railway had been tucked into an avalanche tunnel.

Moreover, the track they had chosen connected, near Mount Cindet, with a network of trails that extended south to Yugoslavia and west to Hungary – ancient trails that had been hewn in the Middle Ages by the *Descalecat*, those errant highlanders who had come down from the Carpathians to establish farmsteads on the plains.

To Pietru's disgust, the sedentariness of the *Descalecat* – the word meant 'getting off a horse' and connoted 'setting roots' – was becoming a desirable concept for some Gypsies.

Yerko's shift would down tools at 16:00. Allowing time for cleaning up and assembly, the convoy would start its return journey at about 17:30. Barring breakdowns, Yerko's bus would pass through this stretch at about 18:00. The market-day traffic would be heavy and slow: people would be tired and introspective. And there would be the advantage of dusk.

Yet Benedict was apprehensive.

Ramzi brought Benedict a mug of tea. 'The waiting – that's the worst.' He offered a reassuring smile. 'Don't worry. It'll be as smooth as a summer sea.'

'I'd have preferred the harder way. No nonsense: in and out – before they knew what hit them.'

Ramzi sighed wearily. 'My brother who still thinks like a *gadjo*. Who believes in hardness. Yet soft is so good, Branko. Why hit when you can stroke?'

'We're not in control! We're dependent on besotted lovers. Worse, people who sell themselves!'

Ramzi retorted angrily. 'No! People who struggle for happiness. For which they take great risks. Let me tell you: Radu will pay dearly. In Ceauşescu's army, a soldier who loses a prisoner faces heavy punishment! He'll be jailed – maybe Ana, too. But afterwards, with your gold, they will make a home. Everything will be soft for them. There will be light in their eyes.'

Benedict caught sight of Omar who, holding chunks of bread stuffed with cheese, was watching them. Whenever they argued, Omar became anxious. Brothers, he had once cajoled, should never disagree.

Benedict relented. 'I hope you're right.'

Ramzi, having regained his confidence during the outburst, ruffled Benedict's hair. 'I am, my brother. Hard is never good. We Gypsies know.'

'I'm hungry. Are you?'

Omar approached them happily. 'Here. Food!'

At 17:00 Benedict, Ramzi, Omar and Pietru, each sporting a fishing rod, took up position on the shepherd's bridge.

Somewhere here, Ana would stall her bus. She would try to restart it and fail. She would let the prisoners out and get them to push the bus past the bend to a point where the other vehicles could overtake it. During that time, whilst Benedict, Ramzi, Omar and Pietru increased the confusion by pretending to direct the traffic, Yerko, as instructed by Pietru's wife, would cross the bridge and slip into the woods. Then they would all regroup, pick up the car – concealed halfway up the hill – and make for the mountain trails. Driving all night, they would press on for the Yugoslav border near Deta.

They would have a good head start: Ana and Radu would waste about an hour getting the bus going and only then appear to notice Yerko's disappearance. Since the convoy would have continued its journey, and since Ana and Radu would still have to keep the rest of their prisoners under control, they would not be able to search for Yerko. They would, of course, try to recruit passers-by, but to little avail – people here steered clear of prison matters. Thus, the alert would be raised only after Ana and Radu regained the camp around 23:00. In all probability, the authorities would wait for Yerko to give himself up – hunger and exposure, they would assume, would soon break his resolve. If, however, they deemed him worthy of immediate attention, it would still take them the whole night to organize units and vehicles. By then, Benedict, Ramzi and Omar would have crossed into Yugoslavia; Yerko, lacking any documentation, would have followed, under Pietru's wing, via an old smugglers' route.

A few minutes before 18:00, they heard the convoy labouring along the road.

Benedict, Ramzi and Omar gathered their fishing gear and lit cigarettes. They yawned and stretched like weary men. Those passing by in cars or trucks ignored them; those travelling by cart waved tired greetings.

The lead vehicle came into view. If the convoy had kept to the same order as in the morning, Yerko's bus would be seventh from the front – fourth from the back.

Mouths dry, hearts thumping, they counted the vehicles. They heard Ana's bus long before they saw it splutter into view.

After what seemed an eternity, it shuddered to a halt by the bend in front of them.

The vehicles behind screeched to a stop.

Benedict, Ramzi, Omar and Pietru edged forward, like curious onlookers. They watched Ana turn the ignition repeatedly. She was giving a lot of choke and flooding the engine. Clever girl.

Finally, cursing in frustration, she signalled her passengers to get off the bus.

The prisoners piled out.

Radu herded them to the rear of the bus and ordered them to push. As they did so, Yerko hung back.

Benedict winked at him. Yerko responded with a perky smile. For a moment, they stared at each other, then Yerko edged towards the shepherd's bridge.

Ana steered the vehicle clear of the bend. She jumped off the bus, opened the bonnet and started checking the engine.

Ramzi, Omar and Pietru rushed on to the road and started waving on the vehicles that had stopped behind. Radu and some of the prisoners joined them.

Despite the confusion this caused, the tail end of the convoy started moving past Ana's bus.

Yerko crossed the bridge and edged towards the woods.

As the last vehicle passed Ana's bus, it stopped abruptly. A voice shouted: 'Hold on, angel! I'll get it going!' A moment later, Ion, the soldier enamoured of Ana, jumped off his bus and ran to her. 'Leave it to me, I'll fix it!'

Anxiously, Benedict glanced at Yerko.

Yerko hurried on.

Ana and Radu, blocking Ion's path, tried to coax him to go back to his vehicle. Ion, arguing with them, pushed his way to the bus. Radu grappled with him.

As they struggled angrily, Ion spotted Yerko hurrying towards the woods. He extricated himself from Radu and shouted. 'Hey! You! Stop! You! Stop!'

Yerko started to run.

Ion pulled out his revolver. 'Stop! Stop!'

Radu threw himself at him. Ana, in support of Radu, punched and kicked him.

Her rage only inflamed Ion's jealousy. He lashed out with the revolver and, hitting both Ana and Radu across their faces, knocked them down. Shaking in fury, Ion careened after Yerko. 'You! Stop! Or I'll shoot!'

Yerko ran faster.

Ion stumbled.

From their various corners, Benedict, Ramzi, Omar and Pietru hurtled towards him.

Ion steadied himself to a prone position and fired.

Yerko fell.

Ion scrambled to his feet.

Benedict spun round and yelled at Omar who was closer to Yerko. 'See to him!'

Omar rushed over to Yerko.

Ramzi, Pietru and Benedict, shouting obscenities, closed in on Ion.

Ion faced them.

Ramzi charged.

Ion fired again.

Ramzi collapsed.

Benedict launched himself at Ion. Kicking the revolver out of the man's hand, he grabbed him by the hair and, with a sharp twist, broke his neck.

He dropped Ion and rushed over to Ramzi. The latter, bleeding from his chest, was unconscious.

Omar reached Yerko.

Benedict, cradling Ramzi, shouted at Omar. 'How bad is Yerko?'

Omar's voice shook. 'Hit in the head.'

Benedict picked up Ramzi. 'Let's go!'

Omar hauled Yerko.

The prisoners, standing away from Ion's corpse, watched in frozen silence as Omar and Benedict scurried into the woods with their wounded.

Pietru, conquering his shock, pleaded with the prisoners. 'Stay put! Give us time to get away!'

Some of the prisoners nodded assent. Others went to help the battered Ana and Radu.

Passers-by stopped and formed a curious ring.

Ahead, Ion's driver began hooting impatiently.

Ramzi had died without regaining consciousness.

Yerko lay prostrate. The bullet had scraped the side of his head; the wound had stopped bleeding, but the severe swelling suggested that the skull had been fractured.

Benedict applied a herb poultice, an all-purpose Zlatari remedy provided by Pietru.

There had been a time when he would have lauded a brave death like Ramzi's as the fulfilment of the romantic ideal: a good man conquering chaos through sacrifice. Now, he knew better: nothing could bestow meaning on death. He would be bereft of everything that had constituted Ramzi. And bereft of everything that constituted Ramzi's family, particularly Ilyas. Above all, he would be bereft of Ramzi's knowledge of him, of Ramzi's reasons for loving him, for disputing with him, yet still loving him. That Benedict, Ramzi's noble brother, had also died.

So Benedict prayed that Yerko, his only relative, would not abandon him, too. Without Yerko, he would never become the person he had been born to be.

Yerko opened his eyes, tried to focus, then muttered in panic. 'I can't see . . .'

Benedict stroked his face. 'You'll be all right.'

'They'll be looking for you. Leave me. Run . . .'

'Ssshhhh . . .'

The night, discreetly lit by a half moon, had soothed Yerko's face, highlighting the Asiatic cheekbones and concealing the worn-out, pallid skin, the flesh that had melted down. Yerko was only fourteen years older than he – not yet fifty – yet he looked a frail old man.

Benedict checked his watch: past midnight. Pietru had brought help: six men from his *kumpania*; they had spread out and were keeping watch. Pietru himself was preparing a litter for Yerko. Omar had gone to dispose of the car and was expected back soon.

The authorities would have extracted descriptions of Benedict, Ramzi and Omar from the prisoners who had witnessed Ion's death; Ana and Radu would have no other option but to confirm these; the descriptions would be circulated; some of the people who had seen the trio driving around would come forward and provide details. Thus they would be searching for the car; and the longer they were made to search for it, the further Benedict and his companions would be able to run.

The hunt would be massive. The news on the radio, declaring Ion a martyred hero, had branded the incident an act of Gypsy terrorism. All regional army and Securitate units had been summoned. There would be tracker dogs and helicopters. And, not least, local mobs screaming for Gypsy blood.

The Zlatari had taken these developments in their stride. True, they would have to disappear for a while, but, as Romania's perennial scapegoats, that was how they had always lived; the women and children would have already struck camp and would be waiting on the mountain.

Omar, anxious to get Yerko to a doctor – and to hand Ramzi's body to his family – had suggested risking a run to the border with the car.

But Benedict had overruled him. The hunt was now for killers, not for an unimportant prisoner. There would be roadblocks everywhere and round-the-clock surveillance of mountain tracks. He had decided they would part company. Omar, guided by one of Pietru's men, would regain Yugoslavia, trekking at night and using lanes and pathways known only to the Gypsies. Benedict and Pietru would cremate Ramzi's remains when possible. Then Benedict and Yerko would move up to the mountains.

Benedict knew about head injuries from his army training: Yerko's wound was serious. The optic nerve appeared to have been crushed; if so, Yerko would not recover his sight. And there would be problems of muscular co-ordination, even of autonomous functions such as breathing and blood pressure. Since trying to reach Yugoslavia with an injured man on a litter would be courting disaster, and since any attempt to seek medical help would be foolhardy, he would tend to Yerko in the wild. Mountains were his habitat; he knew how to survive there. He would tend to Yerko for as long as necessary.

Omar's mass emerged from the darkness. 'The car's down a ravine. They'll never find it.'

Benedict nodded. 'Time you left.'

Yerko opened his sightless eyes and mumbled. 'Branko, you go, too . . . Leave me . . . I'll be a burden – wherever we go . . . Where can we go?'

Benedict caressed his cheek. 'The mountains.'

Yerko smiled faintly: '*Hope will run down the mountains . . .*'

Benedict began to shake. He managed to mutter: '. . . *and stream to the sea; then it will set sail and become earth.*'

Yerko seized his hands. 'You know it?'

'Yes . . . The prophecy . . .'

Yerko's eyes swelled with tears. 'I was there when . . . the *drabarni* pronounced . . .'

'Do you know what it means?'

'I worked it out . . . Land . . . Our country . . . Romanestan . . .'

'Where?'

'We'll know . . . when we set sail . . .'

'The rest? *The burst pomegranate will be made whole . . .?*'

'We'll reunite.'

'*A new tree will bear the leaves the donkey ate?*'

'Our Bible . . . we'll find it . . .'

'The Auschwitz Bible? The one Branko wrote?'

'Yes . . .'

'Where will we find it?'

'Somewhere . . .'

'How long will it take us?'

'Forty . . .' Yerko grimaced in pain.

'Forty seasons?'

Yerko fell silent.

Benedict, trembling, turned to Omar. 'You heard all that?'

Omar nodded in awe. 'Yes.'

Benedict embraced him. 'Remember it. Kiss Ilyas' hand for me. Tell him, I'll never stop mourning my brother Ramzi. Tell him, I'll bring honour to the Gypsies.'

Omar's voice trembled with emotion. 'Our souls will clamour for you. You will hear them and return.'

Benedict embraced him again. 'Don't weaken. You'll be our rock. Tell Lumnia – the forty seasons have started. Go with God.'

Omar kissed his hand. 'You're my chief – always.'

A Zlatari went with Omar. The two blended into the night.

Benedict, Pietru and the other Zlatari placed Ramzi and Yerko on litters.

Yerko's blind eyes flickered. 'Forty seasons . . .? That's how long it takes to grow a bear's heart.'

Before giving him birth, Branko's mother dreamed that a beautiful elephant, silver as the monsoon rain, had entered her womb through her side.

Thus, when she surrendered her spirit seven days after her labour, she died happy; for the dream had told her that her son would be a great sage.

Branko attained the ten virtues by receiving, each day, the knowledge of his previous existences.

And when he reached manhood, he went to fight Mara, the evil one.

He dispelled prejudice and ignorance by pursuing the eightfold path to light which maintains the right view, thought, speech, action, state of being, endeavour, mindfulness and concentration.

At full maturity, he was blessed with every gnosis save one, the great enlightenment of absolute truth.

To seek it out, he went to the Vesh and sat down at the base of a pipal-tree.

And it came to pass that an ancestor, Yerko by name, a trickster who had girdled the earth countless times, crawled past.

And Branko, seeing that Yerko's eyes had been gouged, wailed. 'Master, what has happened to you?'

Yerko explained. 'My eyes could see every colour of blood, therefore, heal all pain. For each hurt, being of a different blood, can be healed by the perception of its hue. But as I am also a trickster, that is to say, the free spirit who unshackles people's numinosity, I was despised by the false men of God. So they mutilated me.'

Branko kissed Yerko's hands. 'Use my eyes to regain your omniscience.'

Yerko warned him. 'Such an undertaking requires impalement by every emotion. Can you suffer that?'

'I can!' Branko said and hauled Yerko on to his shoulders.

After forty seasons, endowed with Yerko's eyes, Branko attained the great enlightenment.

He perceived Creation's duality.

He saw that death is the pinnacle of health and that the moment of life's expiration is also the moment of its rebirth. He understood Nirvana.

PART FOUR

Fifteen

Here is the descent of Branko, the son of Rom, the son of O Del, who was sent to Earth to undo the wicked deeds of Adam and who engraved his heavenly spoor as a leopard does.

O Del begat Rom, Rom begat Branko, Branko begat Rom, Rom begat Branko; and thereafter every shoot named his son after his father.

From Branko, grandson of O Del, to Branko Manu of the Flood are forty generations; from the Flood to Branko Theophilus of the Crucifixion are another forty generations; from the Crucifixion to Branko Mithras and the Dispersion from India are yet another forty generations; and from the Dispersion from India to Branko, the Bear-Tamer, who rose from the ashes of Porajmos, are a further forty generations.

Now, this is the story of the Flood.

When Adam's brood laid waste the east, west, south and north, Branko Manu asked O Del to divide him into four entities so that he could engage with the quadriform villains.

And O Del said unto him: 'Worry not. I will send a deluge and cleanse the earth. Go, build yourself an ark. Embark into it, you and your household. And take with you one pair, male and female, of every living thing I have made so that Creation can continue.'

Now, Adam, having overheard O Del, sidled up to Branko Manu's wife, Furrina, a vain woman, and seduced her with precious stones.

And Branko Manu built his ark; and the rains came; and the animals began to board.

Adam took the guise of a rat; and Furrina, who had agreed to smuggle him into the ark, mixed a heady ale for Branko Manu.

And when the male and female rats entered the ark, Adam sneaked in behind them.

Beholding three rats, the inebriated Branko Manu laughed and fondled his wife. 'Furrina, my love, you have mixed a mighty brew. I am seeing treble.'

Forty months later, the rains stopped.

Thereafter, each day, Branko Manu walked the receding waters. And whenever he found patches of earth, he released vegetation, male and female, and creatures, male and female, who would thrive there.

And all the animals and plants began to multiply.

And when the globe greened and the ark came aground, Adam gnawed his way out.

Then, stealing the perfumes of this new earth, he enticed Furrina to raise seed with him.

This is how the Romanies acquired their skills.

Lilith sent unto Rom a maiden called Uma who glowed with the splendour of Heaven.

And Uma bore Rom three sons in one go.

Unable to tell them apart, Rom proposed to name them all Branko; but Uma, knowing how each boy took breast differently, kept the name Branko for the first-born and renamed the others Amengo and Singan.

When it was time to appoint tutors, Amengo was entrusted to the shepherd David, mahatma of the sling, the psalm and domestic animals; Singan was consigned to Mulciber, mahatma over fire, metals, wood and cloth; and Branko was sent to the centaur, Chiron, mahatma of ethics, sport, music and medicine, and the magus of tricksters.

Thus Amengo became the wise man of flocks, herds, farmyard animals, and of poets and bards; Singan achieved excellence over cloth, wood, metals and fire; Branko acquired the trickster's innocent mischief and became the scourge of sham, vice and tyranny.

And when the sap rose in the boys' kars, they became betrothed to the Graces, those sisters who dulcify the living, even the scorpion.

Amengo took Euphrosyne; Singan took Aglaia; Branko took Thalia.

And after O Del took Rom and Uma to His bosom, the people gathered around the brothers.

Farmers, shepherds, herdsmen, hunters, poets and bards took their tents to Amengo; wainwrights, smiths, carpenters, weavers and potters aligned their wagons behind Singan; healers, thinkers, dancers, musicians, acrobats and horsemen travelled with Branko.

And they enjoyed many seasons of honest sweat, laughter and happy couplings.

This is the story of Branko, the Fire-Bearer.

When O Del went to create other galaxies, Adam consorted with petty gods and appropriated the fire.

Now, as it is known, fire is sacred to mankind because it is O Del's favourite guise for manifesting His presence.

Moreover, fire wards off the evil eye, protects the living from the dead, and, when lit at gravesides, warms the spirits.

Fire charts existence; no one may blow on it, lest, by putting it out, he extinguishes life also.

Branko undertook to liberate the fire.

He commissioned a Singan brother to make him a large, but hollow, wooden horse.

When this object was carpentered, he hid in its belly and asked an Amengo brother to take it to Adam as a gift; but so that Adam would not be suspicious of the offering, he instructed the brother to ask for a spark in exchange.

Adam accepted the wooden horse as if it were a tribute. He gave nothing in return.

That night, Branko crept out of the wooden horse and broke into the volcano where Adam had locked up the fire.

He took some flames from the bubbling crater and forged them into a rod; then, wielding the rod like a javelin, he hurled it onto the plains below.

Thus the Romanies became custodians of the fire.

They take it wherever they go. And every night when they camp, they converse with it as man with God.

And when it is time for a person to leave this life, he or she wears it as a shroud.

This is the story of Branko Theophilus who was a soldier of Adam–Caesar, yet was transfigured.

After crucifying two thousand people on the Tiberias–Jerusalem road, Branko and his centurions came upon the buddha, Yehoshua, who was ministering to the families of the crucified.

And Yehoshua told them: 'Death is a lie.'

And the words washed away the cataracts in Branko's head; he cast aside his armour and became Yehoshua's disciple.

As they travelled to succour the people, Branko learned how to find water on parched earth and how to blend with the landscape as if he were a brook, a boulder or a tree; he learned how to stay cool under the burning sun and how to keep his blood running in icefields; he learned which plants to eat, which to use for magic and with which to heal wounds, disease, fear, madness, even death.

And he acquired irreducible love, which is the power to cherish a neighbour as oneself and to respond to a blow by offering the other cheek.

And the people, inspired by Yehoshua's vision of a new world with new selves, rose against Adam–Caesar.

Adam–Caesar crushed the rebellion. And he condemned Yehoshua to the crucifix.

Branko set out to save his master.

He instructed the Romanies to stop making nails and to destroy all that they had already forged.

But Adam–Caesar's men found a rakshasa who duly produced four.

Branko went to thieve these, but could only steal one.

Thus Yehoshua was crucified with three nails: one for each hand and the third, like the arrow that daily injures the sun's ankles, affixing both feet.

Still Branko endeavoured to save his master.

When the executioners prepared to give Yehoshua vinegar to increase his thirst, Branko, with sleight of hand, replaced the acid with a sweet narcotic.

When they pierced Yehoshua for the death-blow, Branko diverted the spear from the buddha's organs with his magic.

And, that night, after Yehoshua had been deemed dead and duly buried,

Branko moved the stone from the tomb and brought his master out.

And in an oasis of paradisean trees, he nursed Yehoshua with herbs, poultices and ointments.

And, on the third day, Yehoshua was whole again.

O Del made India divine by visiting her in the form of an elephant and suckling her at His phallus.

There the Romanies, the loving people, took root and enjoyed the firm, round lips of a meaningful life.

Then, once more, war plagued the world.

The sheikh of the west coveted the lands where the sun rises and the khan of the east hungered for the lands where the sun sets.

And the sheikh's chariots crushed Amengo's tribe; and the khan's juggernaut trampled that of Singan.

The slain blotted out the four horizons. Ashes and carrion devoured aureate India.

With their last breaths, the brothers summoned robins and sent them to warn Branko.

And Branko gathered the Romanies and led them to Exile.

The Romanies' Hegira lasted forty years.

They eked out life in a thousand mountain passes and as many plains.

And they reached the borders of Persia.

The chieftain, Rom, asked shelter from the Shahinshah and reminded him of the ancient teaching: 'Love the stranger in thy midst. For that is man's role in the Divine Purpose.'

The Shahinshah stipulated one condition: that the Romanies supply him with seven maidens and seven youths for Geush Urvan, the bull who had hoarded all the animals and plants which were beneficial to man and would barter them only for human flesh.

Branko, Son of Rom, Son of Man, asked: 'Why don't you kill this monster?'

The Shahinshah replied dispiritedly: 'Geush Urvan lives in a Maze. All who venture there lose their way and fall prey to him.'

Branko begged Rom: 'Father, let me deal with this bull!'

Rom, knowing his son's prowess, proudly agreed.

The Shahinshah told Branko: 'If you free us of Geush Urvan, your people can live with us for ever.'

As Branko set out, Rom prevailed on him to take a flag-man. 'Order him to signal your success with a rainbow-banner,' he said.

Branko, immaculate trickster as he was, procured a ball of thread and entered the Maze.

As he progressed through the dark and indistinct passages, he spun out the thread and laid it down – a ruse which, over the centuries, developed into the code of the patrin whereby Romanies convey to each other the hazards and benefits of a particular trail.

Tracking Geush Urvan's stench, Branko approached the beast silently.

The bull was in its den, listening out for the youths and maidens it had demanded.

Branko swooped upon Geush Urvan and killed it with a single stroke; he disembowelled it and released all the animals and plants it had hoarded.

Then, gathering the thread with which he had marked his way, he led the liberated plants and animals out of the Maze.

But, on the way back to his father's encampment, basking in high spirits, he forgot to tell the flag-man to signal his success.

And Rom, standing watch on the cliffs, saw the flag-man flying the traditional blue ensign instead of the rainbow-banner; and thinking that Geush Urvan had killed Branko, he threw himself onto the rocks below.

Rom was given a grand funeral. He was stretched out in the lion position, right side facing south as the Buddha in death. Then he was immolated with all his possessions so that he would not come back searching for what was left behind.

The Shahinshah named Branko 'Mithras', which means 'friend' and is the name of the deity of sunlight and fertility. And he settled the Romanies among his people. Some, he favoured as minstrels and musicians, courtiers and clerks. He sent others to cultivate the marshes of Mesopotamia. And he appointed the Zott, so named after their caste in India, to guard the domain's borders against Byzantium.

Here is the story of Branko, the Pied Piper.

A plague of rodents invaded the city of Hamelin.

And Branko, who happened to be passing through with Honeypaw, his bear, told the townspeople that he could rid them of the pestilence.

The citizens, dubious that Branko could achieve a feat which had defeated an army of cats, hired him. 'If you succeed,' they promised, 'we will give you all you ask.'

Branko, needing only to replace his well-worn breeches with a pair even more colourful, settled on a modest fee.

And he went to the main square and played on his pan-pipes songs that yearned for sky and water, lichen and ancient stone.

And to this music, Honeypaw danced wistfully.

And the town's children, watching them, wept.

And the rodents, captivated by Branko's melodies, came out of their holes in their thousands; and they, too, began dancing.

And Branko, still playing his pan-pipes, marched out of the town.

Honeypaw followed, undulating as if Pundjel was dancing life into his limbs.

And the rodents caracolled after him.

Branko came unto the River Weser and waded in.

So did Honeypaw.

And the rodents emulated them and were drowned; not one survived.

Branko returned to Hamelin and presented himself for payment.

But the townspeople scorned him. Despite the pleas and protestations of their children, they stoned Branko and Honeypaw and threatened to burn them for sorcery.

Branko and Honeypaw took to the road. But they kept thinking of the children; young souls full of love, they needed to be saved from their parents.

And Branko and Honeypaw went back to Hamelin.

Branko played an irresistible tune.

Honeypaw danced ecstatically.

And the children rushed into the streets and sang and leapt with joy.

Branko and Honeypaw whirled out of the town.

The children, jumping and pirouetting, followed.

The citizens chased after them.

But Branko, Honeypaw and the children disappeared into the bowels of a mountain. And taking an underground route, they trekked to Transylvania.

There they still dwell, waiting to set sail for Romanestan.

And the Romanies, travelling from country to country, preached to the nations. 'Love the stranger in thy midst.'

But the nations paid no heed.

And the Byzantines fought the Persians and the Turks fought the Byzantines and Europe fought the Turks and Europe fought Europe.

And after each blood-letting, a Rom or a Branko, even as he searched for a safer place for his people, preached again. 'Love the stranger in thy midst.'

This is the story of Branko Osiris who was born immaculate.

Perturbed by such radiance, the gadje, who are of Adam's brood, sent the afreet, Set, to kill him.

And Set found the infant Branko playing in a field: tuning his lyre, taming wild beasts, enchanting birds and moving stones, trees and clouds.

As Set attacked, Niltshi, the wind who saves many Navajo braves by whispering advice in their ears, rushed to Branko's rescue and told him to scratch Set's leg with the lyre's plectrum.

Branko did so. And the soulless giant burst open like a gourd.

And two snakes wriggled out from his dusty innards and urged Branko to eat them, saying: 'Let us dwell in your stomach and make you strong.'

Branko, knowing that they would make him unclean, strangled them.

And the gadje's hatred grew. And, as war followed war, they changed O Del into their own image and called him the Great White God.

And seeking a scapegoat on whom they could blame their unlovingness, they selected the loving people, the Romanies.

And they put words into the Great White God's mouth which, they claimed, had been written in sacred books.

'Dark skins carry evil spirits; that is why Romanies never wash; they fear water will whiten them by wiping away their wickedness,' they said.

'Romanies are as vermin on an animal's body; so their lives are not worthy of life,' they said.

'Hunting Romanies like foxes, raping their women, abducting their children, are not inhuman acts; they are good sport,' they said.

'Romanies contaminate white man's purity; to protect blood and honour, it is lawful to exterminate them,' they said.

And, as is known, the more a lie is repeated, the more it is believed. Thus these calumnies passed as truth. Eventually, even the Romanies gave credence to them.

And so when Adam went to Branko Osiris and said that the Great White

God wanted Inti, the Sun, Branko gave it to him as his due.

And when Adam, having melted the Sun into ingots, asked for other treasures, Branko gave him silver and butterflies from the east, turquoise and pollen from the west, pearls and spices from the south, rubies and firewood from the north.

And when Branko Osiris had nothing more to give, Adam dismembered him and scattered his flesh to distant territories.

But, one Amengo haruspex, Isis, who had loved Branko Osiris from afar, roamed the world and collected his parts; reconstituting these, even his kar, she resurrected him and hid him in inaccessible caverns.

And there, until death parted them, she raised many seeds for him.

Hell is not a place where O Del imposes judgement, but a barbed-wire enclosure which Adam builds every generation for the worship of Porajmos.

This is the story of Branko, the Bear-Tamer, who was born in Auschwitz-Birkenau, the Hell built by the Moloch, Adam—Hitler.

As it is known, when the Urme declared that Branko, the Bear-Tamer, was the promised Saviour, a way was found to smuggle him out of that place.

After many seasons in the wild, Branko came upon a crossroads where one path led to oblivion and the other to his destiny. Honouring the prophecy he carried, he chose the latter.

Thence, blind Yerko, an Ursari trickster who had survived Hell, took him under his wings.

And like many sightless who have instructed the sighted how to see, Yerko taught Branko his people's lore, even the secrets of Nature, magic, plants and animals.

Above all, he primed him with the Romany Book of Chronicles which he had memorized in Hell and which, like the Sikhs' *Granth Sahib*, is divine.

And, like the eagle, Tani, whom O Del sent into the mind of Adam in order to chart the dimensions of perdition, Branko travelled back to Hell to reclaim the Holy Book.

This journey is known as The Return.

He searched the pools and the pits, the rotting wood and the ashes, even the shadows of ancient smoke.

And he reappeared, rambling and distracted, pierced and disfigured, with this very scroll, the Gypsy Bible.

Now that Adam's brood have unleashed poisons that mushroom for millennia, now that decay consumes wind and water, soil and fire; now that Gaea, custodian of the Earth, holds O Del by His sleeve and asks Him to impose the End of Days, Branko sires his people anew.

For O Del has charged him to build Romanestan as the new ark . . .

PART FIVE

Sixteen

Time to emerge, Branko! The forty seasons are up!

They were crossing the Goşmanului mountains. Most of the area was scarp land, woods gashed by cliffs. Ahead, the trail bifurcated: to the left, it snaked down towards Moineşti and, beyond, to Moldavia; to the right, it penetrated the Camenca valley and the Transylvanian heartland. One of the tracks led to his destiny.

Branko turned to Yerko. 'Which fork?'

'Can't tell yet.' Yerko perched on a boulder, lit a cigarette and inhaled deeply. 'I'll sit here. Listen to my gut.'

Branko, unburdening himself of the rucksack which contained their few belongings, turned to Honeypaw. 'No use asking you – you're sulking!'

Honeypaw, ignoring the remark, stretched out by Yerko's side.

What was the matter with the animal? Honeypaw was his other self. Not a spirit which endowed magical powers to amulets, bridles, reins or muzzles, but a creature of doughty flesh and noble blood. They had twinned immediately.

He had found Honeypaw wandering in a copse and had challenged him to wrestle. The bear, a lively young adult who had left the maternal den for the more exciting world of the mountains, but still cubbish in many ways, had accepted happily. The bout had ended in a draw. That equality had prevailed. Now Honeypaw possessed a Rom's mind just as he, Branko, possessed a bear's heart. So what was going on?

Branko grappled with him. 'What's the matter with you?'

Honeypaw curled up melancholically.

209

Was he troubled by brumal shadows like those bears who surface from hibernation too soon? But bears were not true hibernators; they lacked the physiological mechanism which lowered heartbeat and breathing rates, body temperature and blood pressure; they were just wintertime slumberers.

Besides Honeypaw was indifferent to sleep. He would curl up only when Branko and Yerko took up amorous pursuits – even then, judging by his lively welcome when they returned, he would appear to have frolicked with a mate himself. So what was the matter with him?

Branko vented his irritation on Yerko. 'How do you know it's time to emerge. How do you know I'm ready?'

'How does water know how to run?'

There was solemnity behind Yerko's smile; it had been there for days.

Branko pointed at Honeypaw. 'Why is he troubled then?'

Yerko smiled. 'He'll miss you.'

'We'll be back. He knows that.'

'It will be hard for him – waiting . . .'

Branko threw himself on Honeypaw. 'I've been waiting ten years for Lumnia! You'll only wait a few months!'

Honeypaw, again rebuffing Branko's caper, rested his head sadly on his paws.

Branko disengaged angrily. 'Bonehead!'

For a few moments, he paced about restlessly. Then he squatted by Yerko who was still smoking pensively. 'Why are *you* troubled?'

'I am not!'

'I can tell!'

Yerko laughed, a shade too loudly. 'I am bewildered – that's all!' He held Branko's face with both hands. 'Look – light has risen in my eyes! All these years – darkness. Yesterday you laid hands on me – and I see.'

'Not my doing. You taught me . . .'

'I taught you rudimentary magic. Every Rom learns that. But the ability to heal blindness – that's a miracle. Only Saviours perform miracles – because they are risen from O Del's spunk.' He pushed Branko off his haunches. 'So no doubts! You emerge on *Enderlez*!'

Branko jumped up. 'Right.' He punched Yerko's chest playfully. 'No doubts!' Exuberantly, he swung onto the branch of a tree and yodelled like Tarzan. 'Aaaaaa-aaaaa-aaaa!' He dropped off the branch and prodded Honeypaw. 'I'll race you!'

Honeypaw stirred, obviously tempted, then lay down again.

Angrily, Branko kicked some earth at him, then sprinted up the scarp. 'I'll be an eagle!'

Yerko watched Branko. Fast as a lynx, steady as an ibex, strong as a lion. Fully transformed from the *gadjo* of old.

And a child-man now. Very important that. A Saviour had to be unworldly, reclaim the babe's wisdom, inhabit the lunacy of innocence. Otherwise, he couldn't beat evil into the ground. Nor defeat weakness – his own or those of his followers. Who but a crazed prophet could lead a people to their promised land?

Few mentors could teach such an admixture of purity and madness. He, Yerko, had. Day after day.

Branko reached the summit effortlessly, like thermal air.

Happy, yet sad, Yerko watched him greet the newly risen sun with open arms.

What a blessing sight was. How lucky he was to see his work finished – not refractorily, through his imagination, but visually.

Soon, there would be total darkness. And total silence. That was the pain Branko had detected. The years of tutelage had ended; the teacher had reached the last of his days. The Saviour had to emerge alone.

On the summit, Branko roared.

The peaks echoed him. Unmistakably, the call of new times.

Yerko strode to the tracks.

Honeypaw sauntered after him.

Yerko pointed at the left fork. 'That way. There stands death – as in Birkenau.'

Honeypaw became agitated and shook his head.

Yerko stroked him. 'What must be, must be.'

The sun roared in homage; Creation embraced him. Thus Saviours were greeted.

Branko surveyed his wilderness: north and east: the oriental Carpathians; south: the Fāgāraş range; west: the Apusenis. Within those boundaries, on pyramidal tors washed by hidden lakes, in temperamental woods and wastelands lying in ambush, he had absorbed the elements as the Holy Book had demanded. In the process, he had come to know the Transylvanian hinterland intimately and learned all it could teach him.

For example, he was now a master of the *patrin*, the coded roadside messages which Gypsies leave for other Gypsies about places, people and officials. Thus he could rearrange leaves, branches, bushes, stones, ashes, animal droppings, furs and feathers as inconspicuously as the wind or inscribe invisibly on rocks, fields, woods, hillsides, springs and riverbanks the tenor of any given location.

Remains of a bat: here, you could strike lucky.

Three twigs forming a triangle: beware, here, *gadje* are trigger-happy.

Yet he had not possessed the territory as earth should be possessed: as root and identity; as land that belonged to him and land to whom he belonged. Perhaps that was why the wilderness was letting him go; perhaps absence would sire Romanestan as death sired life.

Then adieu mountains, valleys, rivers and plains. Thank you for polishing my eyes.

Adieu countless villages large and small: Alba, Griviţa, Rogojel, Iza, Pinca, Vaduri, Curciu, Mosna. Thank you for providing me with food and shelter. Above all, thank you for enlightening me with all those ancient books that lay on your dusty shelves or propped up your rickety pieces of furniture. Like tributaries of a great river, they have all nurtured the Gypsy Bible.

Adieu forgotten farms on solitary bluffs like Cincu of the two widows. Thank you for your hearths.

Adieu all you *pasārela*, my lovely squabs – all you widows and spinsters, abandoned wives, sweethearts, mothers, aunts, daughters, sisters, cousins, nieces – my little songbirds grounded by your folk for being plain or lame or cross-eyed or bald or wise or strong-willed, yet forever defying your misfortune and always managing somehow to fly wingless. Adieu and thank you for your brave eyes, ravenous arms, irrepressible breasts, rippling bellies, liana thighs and nectared pudenda. Thank you for suckling Yerko and me whenever we knocked on your doors. I shall never forget the way we steamed the snow when we rolled in it.

Ramzi's wife is a widow . . .

Had she been used similarly by itinerant men?

Will I always be the keeper of Ramzi's death? It has been ten years.

Savage years.

Forty seasons – how did I live through them?

Learning. Thinking. Waiting. Knowing the time would come. *The burst pomegranate will be made whole.*

In the end, abandoning civilization had been effortless. The wilderness had seduced him with its splendour and challenged him with its caprices. Thereafter, as Yerko had moulded him, any residual appeal of the *gadje* world had rapidly vanished. Today, except for a few stubborn memories, the past was indistinct – even the loving features of Melchior and Eloïse, whom he had catechized every night, had been reduced to soft murmurations in the air.

Similarly, he remembered Zurich only as a place lacking a third dimension: a realm where fleshless people jerked disjointedly to the prods of a sparking rod. Unimaginable that he had been one such himself: Benedict Füssli; created by Pro Juventute – with electricity, like Frankenstein.

He had had a wife. Nettie. Silky, shapely, not broad-hipped like the *pasārela*. Nor as generous.

The ten years had also galloped. There had been no time for sloth.

I honed myself; I came through every trial Yerko set for me. Isolation. Weakness. Pain. Hunger. And the most difficult: the constant struggle against my limitations, the unabated war against my doubts.

Frequently, he and Yerko had stolen into Birkenau to search for the Gypsy Bible.

And he had witnessed the terrible hours of 2 August 1944. He still did, daily.

I stand between the Gypsy Camp and the railway ramp and watch as 1,408 Romanies – 490 women and 918 men, among them 15 boys, plus Yerko – chosen for transfer to Buchenwald, bid farewell, through the barbed-wire fence, to family and friends who remain in Camp BII-e. I note Yerko can barely face Todor and Zara because friends in *Kanada* have told him that all those left behind would be gassed that night. I watch the freight train depart, punctually, at 19:00, bulging, for once, with survivors and not the condemned. After the evening roll call, I watch, helplessly, as armed SS drive their trucks up to the Gypsy Camp. They had descended like this once before, on 16 May, but then the Gypsies, numbering about 6,000, had been forewarned and, arming themselves with stones, had repulsed them. Not so tonight: there are fewer Gypsies tonight – and most of them are weak – and the SS are armed to the teeth and ready to shoot. I see them cart away Todor and Zara, together with 2,897 women, children and men to the gas chambers. And, after the gassing, I watch them incinerate the corpses in pits because the crematorium ovens have broken down.

He had journeyed to other places, too. Conferred with many Romany tribes. Surveyed continents. Studied the seas and their tides. Learned about ships and ship-owners. Charted voyages to uncharted destinations in the hope that one of them would lead to Romanestan. *Hope will run down the mountains and stream to the sea; then it will set sail and become earth.*

Now, having absorbed the history and traditions of his people, he was like an impregnated god, waiting to deliver himself as his people's father.

I am forty-four now – a good age for fathers.

Yet still facing doubts, unconquerable doubts. The fact that doubts were natural, even necessary, as Ariana kept reassuring him, was of little comfort. Doubts ate a man's innards without respite.

Did Ariana understand that the mind's pain, albeit impalpable, bled more copiously than physical wounds?

Of course, she did. Ariana, always ready to drag her twisted body to Cluj or Sibiu or Timişoara or Arad or Oradea or anywhere Yerko and Young Dr Glanz could arrange a safe meeting, had made herself a true mother. Even as she spurred him on and called him *The Chosen One*, she bled with him. She was the proof that it was not the womb that made a matriarch, but the heart.

Young Dr Glanz, too, had understood his pain. That most faithful of men, who had never reneged on his promise to help, still waited, despite the ravages of old age, to set foot on Romanestan with Branko.

Even so . . .

Were he able to look at the man inside him, he would see, Branko suspected, a creature that had been irreversibly mutilated. A child who had lost the primary skin that wisely assesses life by its portion of love. A foetus fallen from original softness and condemned, like a dragon in a wheatfield, to scorch the earth even as it kissed it.

Was it surprising that only Lumnia had kept him sane?

Lumnia, soul of my soul. She had not abandoned his flesh for an instant. Every night, wherever he had made his bed – even those nights when he had lain with a *pasărica* – Lumnia's iridescent body, with its myriad ways of coition, had entwined his. Every day she had anointed him with a protective spell. She was in possession of him now. Bathing him inside her pool; putting charms on his throat, cheeks, lips, tongue, loins.

Lumnia was now a *drabarni* – so Yerko, who heard everything, had reported.

Lumnia would transform him into a Saviour. Lumnia would keep the world in equilibrium, the way Nature does.

Time to emerge, Branko!

Yerko was leaning against the rock. The morning's brightness had gathered around him as if he were the tethered sun.

'Decided, cousin?'

Yerko nodded solemnly. 'To the left.'

Honeypaw, who had been prowling unhappily, growled.

Branko pulled up the bear by his fur. 'Listen to me. Time to emerge. I've been telling you for years what that means. I'll be back – you know I will. So let's be manly: a simple goodbye . . .' He embraced him. 'Come on, a big hug!'

Honeypaw hugged him, almost crushing him.

'That's better. Now Yerko.'

Honeypaw hugged Yerko.

Branko stroked Honeypaw's head. 'Don't put your arm into icy water when you go fishing. That's how you bears lost your tail. Stay away from hunters – I'll kill you if you get shot. Off you go!'

Honeypaw licked Branko's arm, then mournfully slouched away.

Branko heaved the rucksack on to his back and moved forward.

Fear gripped Yerko; but he suppressed it and followed Branko.

As he turned into the left track, Branko broke out in a cold sweat. He became nauseous. His legs started to shake. 'This can't be the way!'

'It is!'

'Something's wrong . . .'

Honeypaw, still within earshot, rose on his haunches and started whimpering.

Yerko walked on. 'Nonsense . . .'

Branko faced him. 'I feel it! Never go against your guts – your teaching!'

'When you become chief! Until then you do what I say!' He pushed Branko forward. 'Move!'

Branko hesitated, then proceeded. His legs stopped shaking. The nausea, not so acute now, burrowed into a corner of his body.

Honeypaw's whimpers became more doleful.

Branko tugged at his bonds. The ropes cut further into his wrists and ankles. He looked across at Yerko.

Also trussed up. Staring into the void. Melancholic gaze with shades of a smile. He had not spoken since they had been captured. Occasionally he had moved his lips as if in silent incantation.

Ileana, the other captive, had been tied only by her hands. The men had left her naked, ready for further abuse. Despite her youth – barely eighteen – she had remained defiant.

Branko whispered to her. 'Try to untie me – use your toes!'

Ileana darted a fearful look at the gang. They were standing on the road, by their truck, discussing where to hold the hunt.

'Go on!'

Ileana glanced at her sleeping baby whom Dumitru, the gang's leader, had wedged between her breasts and thighs. She manipulated her toes, making sure the movement did not disturb the child, then nodded.

As Branko shifted to get closer to her, Dumitru's dog, a kuvasz, caught his movement and, barking savagely, spurted towards them. The other dogs, two mongrels, pelted after the first one.

Ileana screamed at Branko. 'Stop! Stop! My baby!'

Branko, unnerved, yelled at the men. 'Hey! The dogs! The dogs!'

Dumitru whistled sharply.

The dogs, about to leap on Branko and Ileana, stopped, then paced about, growling.

Dumitru and his men ambled over, looking like amiable foresters going to work. For the past two days, they had been on the rampage for Gypsies.

Ileana had related the circumstances. The recent *systemization* programme was getting increasingly unpopular. One of Ceauşescu's obsessive undertakings for consolidating his iron rule, this programme was destroying whole villages – mostly ancient – and replacing them with communes of high-rise blocks.

Predictions that, when completed, *systemization* would have ravaged much of the countryside as well as severely damaged agriculture, the nation's most reliable money-earner, were being denounced as treacherous.

The loss of homes that had belonged to families for generations was unleashing deep resentment in the farmers. To exacerbate matters, rents for the tiny and, often unhygienic, flats were exorbitant. Moreover, the Securitate's efficacy in maintaining surveillance in these prison-like habitations now deprived the peasantry of the last vestiges of freedom which had been available to them in the privacy of their farms.

Not surprisingly, these tensions had rekindled the historic conflict between Romanians and Transylvania's large Hungarian minority. Fuelled by reciprocal xenophobia and religious rivalry – Romanian Orthodoxy versus Hungarian Catholicism – both communities felt menaced.

The Hungarians interpreted *systemization* as the first phase of their expulsion from the country, a course of action that the government had repeatedly threatened; the Romanians, whilst clamouring for the immediate execution of such measures, raged at having to be subjected to the same programme – much as they assumed it to be a ploy – so that Ceauşescu could pretend, to the world at large, that his rule was even-handed.

Lately, the likelihood of riots had increased. Since such contentions would be ruthlessly quelled by Ceauşescu – not because he would want to impose peace, but because he would indict any unauthorized disturbance as treason against the 'perfect society' he had created – there had been need for a scapegoat.

And so, inevitably, the Gypsies . . .

Despite the fact that some of the destroyed villages had been inhabited by Gypsies themselves – forcibly settled in the early days of the communist regime – Securitate posters and announcements, exploiting the rabid prejudice both the Romanian and Hungarian peasantry held against the Gypsies, had claimed that the government had been compelled to launch the *systemization* programme as an urgent measure for cleansing the land of 'vagabond vermin'.

Thus, a number of Gypsies who had taken to the roads after the destruction of their own villages had been waylaid and assaulted by vigilante groups.

Beatings had soon led to murders. Dumitru's gang had already killed Ileana's husband and brother. Other mobs were likely to improve on the score.

The men stood before them.

Branko scrutinized Dumitru. Thick black beard. Big hands. Gold wedding ring. Jeans tucked into boots, fashionable rain-jacket, baseball cap. Smart-looking smart guy. But his real self was visible in the opaque scowl and salivating mouth: a hyena who struck from the safety of the pack.

Dumitru, Branko realized, was a manifestation of the vision which had assailed him on his first visit to Birkenau and which since then had become part of his consciousness . . .

A mouth like a disembowelment . . . A suppurating eye . . .

. . . Watch him as he crosses a bridge over a stretch of fire; the eye and mouth are invariably ensconced in the fire; the bridge is no wider than a hair. If the eye looks to the left, the bridge breaks and he falls into the fire; if it looks elsewhere, he crosses the bridge safely.

Dumitru grabbed Ileana's baby, making it wail. Another man, pulling Ileana by the hair, yanked her to her feet. Two others dragged Branko by his ropes. Another two hauled Yerko.

Branko craned his head. They were being taken to the truck. Yerko, he noted, was alert, watching everything. And smiling. Smiling!

Ileana walked, oblivious of the men who prodded her breasts and buttocks. Her eyes shuttled between Dumitru, who was carrying her screaming baby by one foot, and the dogs which followed, growling and salivating, all too ready to pounce should Dumitru drop the infant.

Branko raged: if he could only save the child. Kill a couple of the men. Or all eleven. Dumitru, at least. Then he wouldn't feel so bad about dying so stupidly!

But Fate had turned its back on Ileana's child.

That morning, having witnessed the killings of her husband and brother from the stream where she had gone to fetch water, Ileana had drugged the infant with herbs and strapped it, out of reach of wild animals, on the upper branches of a tree.

Then she had confronted the gang. She had expected to be killed instantly, like her menfolk; after which, she had assumed, the gang would move on, allowing Fate to fetch a good person who would find the baby and take it to safety.

But the gang had decided to have some fun before killing her; they had been deliberating another round of rape when the baby had finally woken up and cried.

Even then, the child could have been saved. For, unexpectedly, its tears had affected the men and quietened them down. Some, admitting to exhaustion or confessing to having had their fill of violence, had talked of going home. But Dumitru, bullying and coaxing, had reanimated them.

Dumitru, if Yerko's observations could be trusted, was part-Hungarian, part-Romanian with a dash of Gypsy at both ends – which perhaps explained the depth of his hatred. More to the point, he was scared. By putting themselves above the law, the gang had insulted Ceauşescu's consummate rule. If discovered, they would be severely punished; therefore, they had to dispose of all the witnesses.

And to make the killings exciting, Dumitru had come up with the idea of staging a Gypsy hunt, a sport that had been favoured, in bygone days, by many European nations as a thrilling way of culling the Gypsies.

They reached the truck. One of the men clambered into the driving seat; another lowered the tailgate. The rest bundled Ileana, Yerko and Branko on to the platform, then piled in themselves.

Dumitru threw the baby at Ileana. She managed to catch it, despite her tied hands. Defying the growling dogs which took up position inches away from her, she pressed the infant hard to her bosom.

Branko, humiliated by his inability to protect this brave girl, yelled obscenities at the men.

One of them kicked him in the ribs. Another stamped on his face. Dumitru intervened. 'Don't cripple him. Not yet.'

The men sniggered, then lit cigarettes.

They set off.

One of the men, pointing at the woods, shouted. 'Hey, look, a bear!'

Branko twisted round. It was Honeypaw, pelting after the truck. He must have sensed their plight and come to help.

Dumitru raised his gun. 'Always wanted to shoot a bear!'

Branko, making himself roll with the movement of the truck, knocked against Dumitru's leg.

Off-balance, Dumitru fired into the air. Furious, he hit Branko with the butt of his rifle. 'Fucking bastard!'

Branko, his mouth bleeding, saw Honeypaw disappear behind the trees.

Yerko was still smiling, but broadly now, seemingly welcoming the ordeal ahead. Somehow he had propped himself up and was scanning the ascending road, nodding occasionally as if the driver was following a route chosen by him. He had cracked up.

Branko reproached himself. He should have been alert to Yerko's condition. He should have known something was wrong as early as last week when Yerko had bartered their guns for some provisions. He had not even challenged Yerko's contention that since Branko was marching towards his destiny they were safe, that they no longer needed to protect themselves.

In fact, he could still have remedied matters this morning by respecting his foreboding and refusing to take the track Yerko had chosen. Instead, barely a few kilometres after parting from Honeypaw, they had walked straight into Dumitru's ambush.

Even then, Yerko had remained unperturbed. Don't worry, he had said, it'll be all right.

Branko muttered at Yerko in Romanes. 'Time to emerge, eh, cousin?'

Yerko smiled. 'No problem. You'll make it. Only remember me. You hear me – remember me!'

Branko trembled as the injunction found an echo from the past.

The truck screeched to a halt.

Branko scanned the area: high hills; small woods invading meadows; here and there basalt ledges jutting out of the verdure; not a soul or dwelling in sight.

Three men lowered the tailgate and jumped off. They pulled Yerko out and cut him loose. One picked up a gun. Another summoned one of the mongrels. The third pointed at the hills. 'You've got ten minutes' start. Then we'll give chase. Get going!'

Yerko staggered away.

Branko shouted in Romanes. 'Make for the trees, cousin – plenty of cover there . . .'

Yerko, scrambling up the slope as fast as his numbed limbs permitted, shouted back. 'Remember me! Rememberremember . . .'

A few kilometres further on, Ileana was let loose. Because she was burdened by her baby, she was given fifteen minutes.

Four men set out to hunt her. They did not take guns – just knives and a dog.

Branko was hauled out yet further on. As the men cut his bonds, he surveyed the terrain. Similar to Yerko's and Ileana's.

Dumitru and the driver armed themselves with guns and ammunition belts – an act which prompted the kuvasz to jump about wildly. The other men strapped on their knives. Dumitru prodded Branko with his rifle. 'For you – five minutes!'

Rubbing his wrists to get his circulation going, Branko lurched forward.

He ran uphill towards the afternoon sun.

He knew the area. Hillocks dipping and rising in folds and strewn with coppices, coverts and fir brakes. Here and there, some volcanic detritus. Occasional flexures on the anticlines.

He had appraised his pursuers. He was fitter and faster; he should be able to run up a good distance and gain some territorial advantage.

After five minutes, he had reached halfway up the hill and was approaching the nearest copse. He glanced back.

His hunters had set out at a half-run. Having to stare into the sun, they were shielding their eyes. Old trick, but it never failed. They would be lucky to aim well once!

He ran faster now, numbness gone, legs pumping freely. He tried not to think about Yerko and Ileana. He could not help them; but he felt as if he had deserted them.

He reached the copse. Barely slowing down, he collected some broken branches: mostly small and thin, one large and thick.

He took bearings. Further up, there were rock ledges, naturally terraced. He bounded in that direction.

When he reached the lower levels, his hopes surged. The ground was strewn with flints. He filled his pockets with several large chunks. He climbed to the highest ledge, took cover and surveyed the ground below.

His pursuers were lagging. They seemed to have lost sight of him; dazzled by the sun, they were scanning the hillside. Ahead of them, the dog was making for the copse.

Branko picked up two flints and began knapping one with the other – a skill he had first learned in the army's survival course, then perfected under Yerko's tutelage. In less than a minute, he produced a sharp arrow-head.

Keeping an eye out for the kuvasz, which had run into the copse and was trying to sniff out his trail, he knapped a few more arrow-heads.

He unbuttoned his trousers and unravelled the thick string with which a young widow had once repaired the waistband of his pants; he buttoned up his trousers.

He took the thick, long branch and cut nocks at both ends; then bending the branch and hooking the string on to the nocks, he fashioned a bow.

He nicked the edges of a couple of sturdy twigs and inserted the arrow-heads into them. He had been lucky. If he had not found the flints, he would have had to use the twigs themselves as darts by sharpening them with his teeth.

He tore a piece of his shirt and cut it into strips. He doubly secured the arrow-heads by tying them at the joints with the strips.

He crawled to the edge of the ledge. He placed an arrow against the bow's string, and waited.

The kuvasz appeared soon enough – rushing out of the copse, sniffing at his trail and barking as it bounded up the hill. When it reached the lower ledge, it spotted Branko. Pacing wildly up and down, it howled to alert its master.

Branko growled like a bear.

The kuvasz faced him, baring its teeth.

Branko, still snarling, drew his bow and, aiming at the kuvasz's mouth, let the arrow fly.

A jet of blood spurted. The kuvasz yelped.

Branko dropped the bow and, armed with a chunky sharp flint, hurtled down.

The kuvasz was rolling, trying to extricate the arrow that had stuck to its palate with its paws. Branko leapt on to the dog, breaking its spine with his weight; in the same movement, he slashed its throat with the flint.

Leaving the kuvasz to its death-throes, he clambered back to the ledge, picked up his flints, bow and arrows and scrambled further up the hill.

From behind a tree, in a small coppice, Branko watched the four men around the kuvasz.

The realization that their quarry was not easy prey had banished their good spirits. And, judging by the way they hopped from foot to foot, the two who did not possess guns were growing wings on their ankles. Those who want to flee, Yerko had taught him, cannot stand still.

Dumitru was in a rage. Squatting tearfully by his dead dog, he kept loading his rifle and firing it into the air. Eventually, he rose and stared at the heights; then, yelling at the top of his voice, he fired a few more rounds.

One of the bullets whistled perilously close to Branko.

Finally, shouting orders, Dumitru spread out his men.

As they crept up, Branko edged to the side of the coppice, directly above Dumitru's line of ascent.

The minutes limped.

The hunters moved increasingly tentatively. Even Dumitru took inordinate pauses behind whatever cover he could find.

Branko picked up an arrow and waited, breathing softly.

Dumitru, panting raucously, approached the coppice.

Less than ten metres.

Branko flung some flints at Dumitru's flank.

Dumitru spun round and fired at the spot where the flints had landed.

Branko sprang forward.

Dumitru, sensing rather than hearing Branko's movement, swung back.

Branko kicked the rifle out of Dumitru's hands; simultaneously, he punched Dumitru's testicles.

Dumitru buckled.

Branko imbedded the arrow into Dumitru's neck. Dumitru's limbs jerked in terminal reflexes.

For a while silence ruled.

One of the men, the driver, yelled from down the slope. 'Dumitru – did you get him?'

Branko picked up Dumitru's rifle and ammunition-belt and shouted gruffly. 'Yeah.'

The driver, firing into the air, broke cover and ran towards Branko. 'Right, let's cut up the fucker!'

The other men, cheering, broke cover also.

Branko straightened up and shot the driver.

The other men stopped abruptly.

One wailed. 'Holy Mother!'

The second started running away; Branko shot him, too.

The wailing man dropped to his knees and howled. 'Don't! Please! Spare me! Please . . .'

Branko aimed at the man's mouth and fired.

When Branko stopped the truck where Ileana had been let out, her hunters were only just returning from the field. They were gesticulating sexual acts, laughing and slapping each other. Two of them, Branko noted, were still wiping their knives clean. Their mongrel, seeing the truck, ran at it.

Branko picked up the rifle and jumped out of the cabin.

He fired in quick succession, killing first the mongrel, then the men. Some of the latter did not even see their executioner.

Branko ran into the field in search of Ileana.

He found her slashed and battered beyond recognition. She was clutching protectively, even in death, the blood-caked ball that had been her baby.

Yerko's hunters were squatting on the road, smoking.

Branko rammed his foot on the accelerator. He hit the men head-on whilst they stared, puzzled, at the truck careering towards them.

He stopped, reversed and observed his victims.

One of the men appeared to be dead; the other two and the dog twitched in their pools of blood. He slammed the truck into gear and drove it over their heads several times.

He found Yerko's body in a cave. They had spiked his eyes, blinding him – a second time – for his journey beneath the earth. They had cut out his ears and wedged them into his hands, making him look like a beggar. And having castrated him for eternity, they had stuffed his testicles into his mouth.

Branko wept for his mentor. Another father lost. Another father who had transfused his blood into him.

Then he wept for his own soul. It had separated itself from his person. It had grown leftward thumbs and suppurating eyes – marks that identified it as a killer's soul. And, he could see, it was surrounded by the ghosts of the men he had slain. Such ghosts, known as *mule*, Yerko had taught him, having personally experienced the evil of violence, petition O Del, through eternity, to disallow the slayer entry into the land of peace, Romanestan.

From a distance, Honeypaw watched the cave woefully. He could not raise the spirit to go over to Branko. He was ashamed of himself. He had been unable to protect his twin. Though he had run to the point of collapse, he had failed to catch up with the truck.

Eventually, he shuffled away, trying to believe that Branko, now that he had proven himself indomitable, would come back, as he had promised.

Luck favoured Adam's brood.

They killed birds, deer, flowers and pumas, brooks, wheat, summer clouds and dunes, bears, eagles, baobabs and whales.

They captured Yerko as he guided these love-creatures to Anansi's invisible realms.

And, using Yerko as bait, they lured Branko, the Bear-Tamer, to the acid forest where his hair, the repository of all his strength, entangled with the putrefying branches.

And they pierced Yerko's left hand which held grace and severed his right hand which held mercy; they impaled his left foot which held comfort and crushed his right foot which held pity; finally they gouged out his heart which held love.

And they prepared for Branko's execution.

But a young lion, Simba by name, pursuing his rites of passage, appeared. True to his brave nature, he gave his mane to Branko as replacement for Branko's hair.

And Branko's strength returned. He heaved and uprooted the trees that had enmeshed him; he heaved again and broke his bonds.

Adam's brood fired missiles, arrows, spears, bullets, but these turned into damselfish as they struck Branko. So Adam's sons took flight.

Branko went in search of Simba and found him in the plains where he had returned to live with his kind. And Branko paid his debt of gratitude by teaching Simba how to grow a claw in the tuft of his tail.

Seventeen

Memory can return. All it needs is a prompt.

The Swiss embassy had provided Branko with three: the highly polished parquet floors; the smell of the *Villigers* Major Hoffmann, the military attaché, chain-smoked and the ambassador's penchant for bow ties.

The first had transported him to the stately offices of the Lucerne Hydroelectricity Board; the second had rekindled the old addiction for small cigars; and the last had brought to mind Melchior whose love of butterflies had extended to preferring *papillons* to neckties. Thus distance and diffusion had evaporated. The past which had shrunk to a pinpoint, like Nettie's memory of her drowning brother – even that fragment had returned – had re-emerged not in the least defaced, as if the layers of time had possessed the preservative qualities of an ice age.

But for his rusted German and the maddening search for conversational words, Branko could have convinced himself that the ten-year process of changing from Swiss to Gypsy had been a delusion.

The ambassador looked past him and stared at the windowpane. Of pedigreed bearing but bland features, he seemed either too patrician or too shy to focus on the person he addressed. 'Sit down, Herr Füssli.'

Too patrician, Branko decided, taking another look at the lines framing the ambassador's mouth. Lines mapped a person. Gypsies could read them. The ambassador's lines had never suffered doubt.

The security officer motioned Branko to a chair.

Branko kept by the window. 'I'm fine here.'

Leo Leo, seeking an air of authority by readjusting his sleeves and cufflinks, smiled discreetly. He must have remembered that, at their first meeting, too, Branko had preferred to stay by the window. In the Gypsies' racial memory windows represented a means of escape from the *gadje*.

Branko contemplated Leo Leo: Pro Juventute's pride and joy; the executive who had risen from the ranks. The perfectly cut dark suit, silken and shiny like an entertainer's, barely encased his height and girth. His hair had acquired the loftier silver of olive leaves; it had also grown longer and now covered his shoulders like an ermine cape. Rom parading as *gadjo*. If Leo Leo could be made to step outside his misconceptions, he would see that nothing, neither *gadje* accoutrements nor charms that could make doves nest in his mouth, would make him any the less a pariah.

The security officer pointed at the chair again.

Branko growled. 'I'm staying here.'

Major Hoffmann waved the security officer away.

Hoffmann, angular face pockmarked like rain on snow, barrel-chest prolapsing to a beer belly, was an old soldier. Like any veteran scenting mothballs, he had immediately recognized an alter ego and put Branko at ease. Comradeship had escalated to mutual esteem; and Hoffmann, discreetly, had kept his interrogation to a minimum. Thus Branko, presenting himself as a drop-out, had provided all the facts about his life as a Swiss citizen, but little about the last ten years.

Unexpectedly, the ambassador's request to Pro Juventute to confirm Branko's residency in that institution had unearthed Leo Leo; the latter, claiming, as Branko's old warden, an obligation for his welfare, had come to Bucharest to identify him personally.

The ambassador produced a cultivated cough. 'I should tell you, I am not satisfied with all the explanations. Do you mind answering a few more questions . . .?'

Branko shrugged. 'If it will speed up my going home.'

Hoffmann, whose esteem for Branko had risen extensively after receiving Branko's army record, had already ironed out all the snags for repatriation. But the ambassador, tending to associate middle-aged ex-officer drop-outs with drug running or arms smuggling, had decided to conduct an exhaustive investigation. This was the fifth day.

'The so-called Gypsy hunt . . .'

Leo Leo offered a perplexed face. 'A thing of the past, I would have thought, Your Excellency . . .'

As in previous sessions, Leo Leo was taking pains to appear equitable. But behind that he was ferreting. Branko had soon perceived that he had not come all this way for altruistic reasons. He expected to find out what Branko had been doing during the past ten years. Leo Leo had that tautness of the eyelids that betrayed fear; only bears and bear-tamers could detect it. He was right to fear, Branko had been tempted to tell him. Soon every Gypsy leader advocating meekness would become redundant.

Branko mimicked Leo Leo's poise. 'Past, present, future – nothing ever changes for the Gypsy.'

The ambassador became animated. 'If such an atrocity did take place, Herr Füssli, I shall advise my government to take issue . . .'

Branko was surprised. Normally the ambassador's breed, burghers with old money and older lineage, were never animated, not even by their own lives, or deaths.

Leo Leo put on the voice of reason. 'If there has been such an atrocity, protestations would only provoke further incidents.' He addressed Branko softly as if humouring a child. 'Your imagination may have got out of hand. Possibly something disturbing did happen, but I suspect you panicked . . .'

Branko glared at him. The giant Rom so yearned for the *gadje*'s embrace that he was prepared to blindfold himself in order not to see the murderous world surrounding him. 'Maybe I'm crazy.'

Leo Leo riposted sharply. 'Are you?'

Branko spat out of the window.

The ambassador, revolted by Branko's coarseness, shifted his gaze to the ceiling. 'How did you get caught up in this Gypsy hunt, Herr Füssli?'

Branko shrugged. 'I was passing by.'

'That's not a satisfactory answer.'

'Would you prefer a lie?'

Leo Leo reverted to his voice of reason. 'We checked the newspapers – no mention of disturbances.'

Major Hoffmann interjected. 'Actually, there have been rumours. Persistent rumours . . . A number of Gypsies are said to have disappeared – very likely killed. We've also heard some Romanian farmers have vanished – probably hiding . . .'

The ambassador nodded, irritably. 'Tell us again how you escaped, Herr Füssli.'

'Jumped out of the truck.'

'Didn't they go after you?'

'I hid in the woods.'

'They had dogs, you said . . .'

'Gypsies know how to put dogs off the scent.'

The ambassador turned in Leo Leo's direction. 'Is that a fact, Herr Leo?'
Leo Leo, not wanting to appear ignorant, muttered. 'Well . . . Yes . . .'
'Then what happened, Herr Füssli?'
'They hunted the others. I bolted.'
The ambassador became derisive. 'With one great leap?'
Branko responded contemptuously. 'How else?'
Major Hoffmann tried to defuse the tension. 'Given the hatred for Gypsies in this country, I would venture to think that the missing Gypsies have been murdered. Consequently, I for one, accept Colonel – Herr – Füssli's word. I think Securitate are covering up. My guess is the murdered Gypsies have been buried secretly; the killers must have been subsequently caught and either thrown into jail or executed to appease Ceauşescu.'
The ambassador, this time deigning to face Branko, reverted to his diplomatic tone. 'I want all the facts. Why won't you tell us the truth?'
'I've given you the facts! Do your duty! Get me home!'
The ambassador unleashed a measure of his seigneurial anger. 'Herr Leo! He might trust you – Gypsy to Gypsy. I need to be reassured he was not involved in anything felonious. Or no repatriation.'
Leo Leo nodded solemnly. 'I'll try my best.'
Branko glanced at Hoffmann. The latter, unable to intervene, grimaced.
Branko smiled resignedly. 'Right, Leo. Gypsy to Gypsy.' He moved across, sat next to him and waited for the others to leave.

Had he mentioned the killings, the ambassador would have assumed he had massacred his victims in pursuit of some criminal activity. Yet he had been consumed by the need to recount his exploits. It had seemed imperative that somebody, anybody – everybody? – should know he carried a prophecy and possessed the prowess to fulfil it. Indeed, would it not be natural to believe that the killings had been his anointment? Was that a madman's logic?

Then I collected the dead. Piled them into Dumitru's truck.

And so he had found himself telling Leo Leo everything. No, not everything. Not about the prophecy. Or Yerko's tutelage. Or his emergence. That would have been too soon, much too soon.

That night, I returned Yerko, Ileana and the baby to the earth. Buried them together. On a mountainside. Mountains are hallowed places. Infants and livestock who graze on them become stronger. Amulets chipped from summits ward off the evil eye. Herbs from escarpments brew the best love potions. On a mountain, you are closer to your soul.

And the mountains had reminded him of distant Romanestan, of its undulating valleys that stretch out, according to the Holy Book, like a woman eager to be ploughed.

I was going to feed Dumitru and his men to the wolves. But if traces of their remains were found, there'd be more tension between Romanians and Hungarians. And, again, to cool matters down, everybody would blame the Gypsies. So I buried them, too. And their dogs. In a cave. I toiled hard. The earth did not want them. She kept resisting the spade. And the bats flew angrily and scratched my face with their wings.

And vampires with grotesque heads had feasted on his blood, reminding him that Transylvania was Dracula's domain. Or had he imagined that? Break reason's hymen and you get superstition, Yerko used to say. You also get madness!

I sent Dumitru's truck down a ravine. With its guns and implements. Then I set out for Bucharest. I decided not to hitch lifts. Well, couldn't trust the Romanians, could I? I thought of trying the foreigners, but decided against. Their cars have special number-plates. The prefix 12 denotes the vehicle belongs to a visitor – student, embassy official, multinational executive. Prefix 14 means it's rented, therefore, driven by a tourist. Securitate always monitor these vehicles. Anybody not looking like a tourist is taken for questioning. One of the *pasārela* told me that. So I footed it. I travelled only at night. It took me forty days.

And he had realized that he had stopped mourning, that he could accommodate his killer's soul, that, at some level of his being, he had even enjoyed the slaying. To hell with that old stereotyped Gypsy – God's best – who had never marched to steal someone's land, or to enslave people or to kill! The *gadje* refuse to let that Gypsy live! So arise the new Gypsy! Arise the fighting Rom! *Upre Roma!*

I was conspicuous. Though I had shaved off my beard, my hair was wild, as you can see. And my clothes – like the fur of a moulting bear. Also I lacked papers. Yerko wouldn't let me get an identity card. Any certificate bearing a person's particulars is like an effigy. A sorcerer can cast spells on it. Even cause the fellow's death. I could have got one any time – for a modest *Balkan caress*. There, too, Yerko was adamant: never trust government property that's available under the counter. Moreover, I still had my Swiss passport – I had found my rucksack in Dumitru's truck, you see. I had kept the passport though it had expired – in case I had to run for safety. I couldn't risk Securitate finding it. The entry stamp – ten years old – would have raised questions. They would have dug into old files. Maybe come up with Tîrgu Jiu.

So I brooded how – where – I could get out of Romania. And I thought: if I flashed the passport at the embassy, they'd have to repatriate me.

And every day, he had smuggled himself into Auschwitz. And he had searched for the Gypsy Bible. Which waited to be found; which waited for him to find it. Starting from the ramp, he had searched the mud, the ditches and the frozen wastes, the barracks, the crematoria and the mass graves, then gone down to the Vistula, retracing the footsteps of the Polish Gypsy, Tomek, to whom Branko, the castrated scribe, had entrusted it and who, in turn, had consigned it to the river. Every day, the Holy Book unfound, he had asked his Dei and Dadoro: 'Where did the river carry it, do you know?' They had said: 'You know about water, find out!'

So he had assumed the identity of Garuda, the king of birds, the bearer of the cosmic tree; and he had surveyed the Vistula from the air. And he had seen a faint trail in the depths.

Mainly, I kept to country lanes. Easy in Transylvania. Everywhere there's a knoll or a woodland to give cover. But the Danube basin – the Wallachian plains – was hard going. Around Ploieşti it's either oil wells or petrochemical installations. Nearer Bucharest, you have stretches of farmland. Not many holes for hiding. Often I made do with a corner in a field or an orchard. Moved out before the farmers turned up. Hard to get food, too. Couldn't hunt, trap or fish in open space. I had some money – I had riffled my victims' pockets. But I wanted to save it for emergencies. I had some meat and fish which I had smoked in Transylvania. When they were all gone, I lived off pickings: fruit and vegetables.

And night after night, to appease his doubts and fears and despair, his soul had memorized the Book. Passages Yerko had memorized. Which he, in turn, had memorized. Passages he had come to love. Passages he might have written. Passages he had written?

Emerging from the darkness of the leviathan's belly, Branko was amazed to see the Punchaô, the Word's golden image, shining in the depths of the pond.

And gathered around the Word were the spirits of his forefathers.

And O Del pointed at Branko and said: 'He is my Chosen. On him my favour rests.'

There was surveillance everywhere. Ploieşti is a strategic area: oilfields. Roadblocks, checkpoints every other step. But never in the same place from one day to the next. Taxed me to the limit.

There had been times when he had despaired, had thought of returning to the wilderness or dropping in on a widow, maybe staying with her.

But each time Lumnia had reproved him. Loss of faith is a sin Fate never forgives.

Then she had placed his head between her legs and outlined how, together, they would fulfil his prophecy.

On the thirty-seventh day – a Friday – I reached Bucharest. I decided to stay on the outskirts until Sunday night. Cities are quiet at weekends. Strangers become all the more conspicuous. I also thought the embassy staff might be away. I hid around Ştefănestii de Jos. Holiday village for bureaucrats. Situated on the Pasārea river where an island monastery contains the tomb of Vlad the Impaler, the historical Dracula. Packed, the place was. The woods crawling with hikers and lovers. I was lucky nobody spotted me.

And Branko recited the Word. And O Del saw that it was good.

Sunday night I set out in the wake of the weekending crowd. Roads were empty. And dark. Bucharest economizing on electricity. Police and Securitate patrols in the doldrums. Romanians plunge into lethargy after the weekend. Prospect of yet another week under Ceauşescu, Yerko used to say. I found the embassy's address in the telephone directory. I had stolen a map at Ştefănestii de Jos. I got here after midnight. No problems with police on guard duty. They had never had trouble, so they weren't expecting any. I scaled the wall. Hid in the garden. And waited. Just before dawn, the embassy began to wake up. Lights came on. When they switched off the burglar alarm, I climbed onto a ledge and broke into a room. Shining parquet. A secretarial office. I sat down. Then a security officer – I knew, from my army days, he'd be Swiss – came on his inspection round. I surrendered and asked to see the ambassador.

Leo Leo had tried to reject Branko's narrative as the yarn of a madman. But he had known that every word had related the truth.

He had been disturbed by Branko's violence. A man who could act so efficiently in the face of death, who possessed such a facility for killing, above all, a man who could show no mercy – could he be a Gypsy? Brutes of that ilk were of *gadje* stock, and then not any more, not since the Nazis had come and gone.

I have to keep nurturing hope. I have to believe, against all odds, despite all the evidence, despite ineluctable doubts – my own included – that sooner or later, my people, who embarrass me and offend me and alienate me – yes, shame me – with their backwardness and asocial ways, my Romanies, whom I have tried to love – do love, in my patronizing way – would cease to be a hated race, would become everyman's equal and earn the right to sit at his table as part of the family.

Why earn the right? Why not be born with it?

Much as Leo Leo had been repelled by the blood on Branko's soul and had not wanted to touch him or be near him so as not to be contaminated by the *mule*, those terrible ghosts of the slain, he had sat a breath away, almost inside Branko's mouth, like a mystic mesmerized before a cobra.

And he had felt roused by Branko's violence. As he had counted the dead, he had clenched and unclenched his fists like a young tribesman listening to the exploits of a heroic leader.

And when Branko had recounted the fates of Yerko, Ileana and Ileana's baby, he had felt ravaged; he, Leo Leo, man-lion, had seen himself reduced to a mother lamenting at burnt farms and on flockless mountains, by riverbanks and roadsides, the slaughter of the generations she had reared.

Often he had held on to Branko's arms, begging him not to say any more, yet asking him, in the same breath, to continue. And pleading, pleading, for something heard or seen or written or foretold that would suggest the existence of another world for Gypsies, a good world, because, otherwise, his people were certain to face another *Porajmos* and, this time, suffer extinction.

When Branko had described Ileana's dead baby, Leo Leo had broken down completely; sliding onto the floor, burying his head in Branko's hands, he had sobbed and whimpered like an infant.

When Branko had recounted his journey to Bucharest, he had sat entranced, as if listening to a storyteller around a camp-fire, very much like the Gypsy he had chosen not to be.

Then, abruptly, he had left.

He came back a day later.

The wide and straight back which gave him the lion's allure now drooped; his clothes, though neat as ever, appeared to hang loosely. 'You will be repatriated. They have my recommendation.'

Branko nodded. Hoffmann had already told him. He would be flying out next day on a courier's passport. Yet he still feared the ambassador might hand him over to the Romanians as a felon – *asocial*, in *gadje* terminology.

As if he had read his mind, Leo Leo reassured him. 'I didn't tell them about the killings.'

'Good Rom.'

'So – what's ahead?'

Branko shrugged. 'The future.'

'Let me suggest something. Put everything behind you. Be a leader.'

Branko smiled. 'I'll think about it.'

'A wise one. Not with gun in hand. Join us.'

'Us? You mean Pro Juventute?'

Leo Leo smiled sadly. 'These days I am peripheral to Pro Juventute.'

'How so?'

'As you know, we wound down 'Operation Children of the Roads' in the early seventies. But the outcry continued. I saw the light – advised we should consider reparations . . .'

'And got fired?'

'Resigned.'

'I understand.'

'Actually, they want me back. They have decided to pay reparations – announced it last year. But . . .'

'You have better options in hand . . .'

'Yes. About the reparations – you should apply . . .'

'You said 'join us'. Who is 'us'?'

'You may remember I broached the subject when we last met. I run an association which has alliances with other Gypsy organizations. We have representation on various international platforms . . .'

'Assimilation – still struggling for that?'

'That's the ultimate aim, yes. Integration as first priority. We must take our place in society.'

'In *gadje* society?'

'There's no other. We must eat, live, work like the next man. What do you say?'

'It's not my dream. I never believed in assimilation. Now, I consider it suicide.'

'Still dreaming of a Gypsy nation?'

'There is a Gypsy nation. Some fifteen million souls. What I dream is a country. Ingathering. Preservation of our culture.'

'Romanestan – that crazy old drivel?'

'No crazier than yours.'

'Mine's practical.'

'Practical? You still refuse to look at what's really out there! The *gadje* don't want us. They won't let us assimilate. They'll tolerate us only if we are invisible. Here, and all over Eastern Europe, they would much rather get rid of us. As for the West – if they're not saying it, they're thinking it . . .'

'We'll change all that . . .'

'Stop fooling yourself!'

'What have you been doing these ten years?'

'Learning to be a Gypsy.'

'And?'

'Searching for a way to cultivate our garden.'

'Have you found it?'

'I will – one day.'

'You've got too much anger, Benedict. And you've tasted blood. Might you ever learn to turn the other cheek?'

'Branko. That's my name, now. Branko.'

'If you start causing problems, I'll fight you. If need be, I'll destroy you! So be sensible – and join us.'

'If I refuse, will you change your recommendation?'

'Did I say that?'

Branko pondered a moment. 'Sure. Why not? I'll join you.'

'Do I have your word – as a Swiss officer?'

'Why not as a Gypsy?'

'Both then.'

'Sure.'

And while still in the womb, Branko became impatient for earthmakers' games and asked his mother, Ileana, to bear him before his time.

Ileana, instructing him that Nature must not be rushed, gave him a hoop with which to play; but she asked him not to hurl it high so as not to hit the walls of her womb and make them fall.

One day, as he tried a new parabola, Branko forgot his mother's warning and threw the hoop high.

And the walls of the womb tumbled down. And they revealed another infant, identical to Branko.

Since every baby is a gift from O Del, Ileana was overjoyed and did not scold Branko.

She repaired her womb and called the newcomer Tammuz, meaning 'a found child'.

And she planted two trees as counterparts for the twins so that by looking at the respective tree each boy would know how his brother fared.

Branko and Tammuz grew to love each other deeply.

But when the time of birth arrived, they jostled for seniority. For passage through the vulva bestows the gnosis of creation; those who trail the first-born are left with a lesser portion of this knowledge.

Branko, tripping up Tammuz, emerged first.

Tammuz felt bitter and went into the wilderness.

Branko chased him and begged him to return. Recounting the gnosis he had acquired, he told Tammuz that when twins stay together they develop powers that make them huaca, 'sacred'; but if they quarrel O Del condemns them to eternal separation.

And Tammuz was much moved. He embraced Branko and said: 'You and I will be inseparable.'

And thereafter the twins served the Romanies.

They separated land from sky, anchored the sun and the moon and created music and dance.

They invented sleep by replicating the lizard's eyelids; and wakefulness by copying the hawk's iris.

When there was no day, they fetched light; when there was no night, they fetched darkness.

They brought birth from the heavens; and death, without which birth cannot be, from the underworld.

And it came to pass that one warm night, Tammuz, taking the air, was ambushed by the Armoured People.

And at dawn, Branko saw that Tammuz's tree had withered.

Realizing what had happened, he set upon the Armoured People and put them to flight.

And he went in search of Tammuz.

And he found him reduced to a pile of bones.

And, using his spittle, which has healing powers, he rendered Tammuz whole again.

Eighteen

'You're pregnant.'

'In my second month. How did you know?'

'Your step's sturdier. Different hue in your eyes. And the way you listen: one ear inside.'

Nettie stared at him. 'You can see all that?'

'I've learned to see many things.'

A flash of anger animated Nettie's face. 'They haven't been wasted then – the ten years . . .'

'No.' Branko turned to watch Rudi and Steffie, Nettie's children, aged seven and five, as they messily – and noisily – marinated pieces of meat for the barbecue. 'Nor for you.'

'Do you like the house?'

'It's big.'

'We're thinking of moving. Outside Zurich. We've run out of book space.'

'The garden's nice.'

'A bit unkempt, I'm afraid.'

Ettore, Nettie's husband, started firing the barbecue. The children, loving his exaggerated dramatics, hooted and screamed.

Branko enjoyed their laughter. They had received him well, treated him as yet another one of their parents' important visitors. But, instead of losing interest in him immediately, which, Nettie had declared, was their way, they had stayed around, intrigued by his awkwardness; and when he had answered Ettore's questions on the severity of Transylvanian winters, they had listened dreamily as only children do, captivated particularly by the fact that snow-sleighs offered the only suitable transportation for months on end.

They could have been his children. He would have given his soul for them. Even now.

'We thought of getting a gardener. But nowadays, that means a *gastarbeiter*.'

Branko was piqued by her prejudice, but chose to ignore it.

'Leave it unkempt – more natural.'

He directed his gaze to Ettore. A jovial, rotund man in his mid-forties. Professor of international law. Author of several books. Recipient of numerous honorary degrees. Darling of United Nations agencies. It had been Ettore who had prevailed on Nettie to invite him to dinner when, on a sudden impulse, he had gone to the university to see how she had fared. But then Ettore was Swiss-Italian, say Mediterranean. Warm person. Good luck to him. Not that he needed it. With another child on the way, he obviously had the sperm count of a ram.

'Are you happy?'

Nettie answered too quickly. 'Very.' Her voice became metallic. 'Happier than when we were together.'

'You haven't forgotten?'

'No.'

'Nor forgiven?'

Nettie ignored the remark and lit a cigarette.

Branko smiled ruefully. 'Still . . . things worked out well for you . . . Should you be smoking – in your condition?'

'The odd one's all right.' Again that metallic sound. 'And for you – did they work out?'

'Oh, yes. Just right.'

Nettie watched her children and husband as they solemnly fanned the coals to get the barbecue going. 'I might not have it.'

'What?'

'The baby.'

Branko gaped at her. 'Why?'

'Too much work. Too many commitments.'

Her career, too, had flourished. She had had her own share of books and honorary degrees. And she had become dean of her department.

'Does Ettore know?'

'Of course. We take decisions together.'

'Give him to me.'

'What?'

'The baby. Have him. Then give him to me. I'll take him somewhere clean. There's only greed, grime and soullessness here. I'll give him – or her – the chance to grow into a human being.'

'That's not funny!'

'I am serious.'

'You're mad!'

'All the same. Give him to me . . .'

'How can you even think . . .?'

Branko offered a defeated smile, then turned round and shouted at Ettore and the children. 'Do you need any help?'

They shouted back in unison. 'No, thank you!'

As the fire got going, Steffie jumped in joy. 'We've done it! Yeeees!'

Ettore and Rudi started grilling the meat.

Nettie glanced at the table, checking that she had laid everything. 'Hope you aren't starving.'

'Glad to catch up.'

'I meant to ask. Your mother – er . . .?'

'Ariana? Still going – though frail as anything . . .'

'Must have been hard for her – all that time you've been away . . .'

'We kept in touch. Saw each other occasionally. Young Glanz brought her over to Romania . . .'

'Young Glanz – the doctor?'

'You remember him?'

'How is he?'

'Not well.'

'How did he manage to contact you?'

'Yerko found a way – arranged the meetings.' Branko's eyes moistened. 'Nothing Yerko couldn't arrange . . .'

Nettie poured some wine. 'So what are your plans?'

'I'll be off – soon as I get a new passport.'

'Back to the wild?'

'Something like that. Then Skopje . . .'

Nettie's tone became harsher. 'To your . . . witch?'

'*Drabarni.*'

'Whatever that is.'

'Very special.'

Nettie drew heavily on her cigarette. 'Pretty, is she? Sexy?'

Branko gazed into the distance. Over three and a half thousand nights without Lumnia . . . Even so he had managed to lie down with her every night.

And each time his body and soul had refracted in her waters as if they were reeds and her body the river which gave them life. 'We haven't been together yet. Except in my mind.'

'Will you marry her?'

'Oh, yes.'

Nettie gulped down her wine. 'Damn, I'm jealous.'

Her reaction confused him. 'I am not – of Ettore.'

She stubbed out her cigarette. 'Does she know you can't have children?'

'Very likely – being a *drabarni*.'

'She doesn't mind?'

'We'll have a child.'

'Adopt?'

'Different kind of child.'

'Made of cloth? A doll? An effigy?' Nettie lit a fresh cigarette. 'Sorry, bitchy of me. What do you mean – different kind?'

'Our people: the Gypsies – they'll be our child.'

'How?'

'They've already been conceived. They're waiting to be born.'

'I see! The prophecy!'

'You remember.'

'You still believe in it!'

'More than ever. It's written in the Holy Book.'

'You mean the book the old man in Sarajevo told you about?'

'The Gypsy Bible, yes.'

'You found it?'

'I will – shortly.'

'Just like that?'

'I know where it is.'

'Where?'

'In a river.'

'You're mocking me.'

'I am not.'

'A Bible – in a river? Come on!'

'Waiting to be delivered – like Moses in his basket.'

'You *are* serious!'

'And what a Bible! Worthy of a great people. Unlike other holy books, a Book that condemns every form of force and violence. A Book that has only one message: sanctity of life.'

'You're talking as if you've seen it . . .'

'I have. And read it. And memorized parts of it.'

'How – if you haven't got it yet . . .?'

'Yerko knew chunks of it by heart. Other sections appeared in our dreams. Yet others surfaced in mysterious ways – as these things do . . .'

She put her hand on his arm. 'Benedict . . .'

'Branko.'

She withdrew her hand and pulled on her cigarette.

He took a sip of wine. 'You were about to say?'

'I forget. No, I will say it. You sound mad.'

'Very likely. But madness is part of parenthood. What sane mind would put a child into this world?'

'You bastard! That's a stone thrown at me!'

'Look around you: it's the sane who are doing all the killing. Hang on to madness. That way you might never kill.'

Rudi and Steffie rushed over to the table. 'We're ready! Start serving the salad, Daddy says!'

Nettie, giving Branko a troubled look, picked up the plate of coleslaw.

Ettore brought a plate of sizzling meat. 'Not quite like deer on a spit on the mountains . . .' He started serving them. 'But smells good, eh?'

Branko nodded. 'Marvellous!'

Ettore sat down, put a hamburger in a roll and started munching. 'Eat! Eat! Masses more!'

For a while, they ate heartily – and silently.

Then Steffie turned to Branko. 'Are there any children on the mountains?'

Rudi interjected mockingly. 'They'd die, silly!'

Branko smiled. 'Not if they had someone to look after them, Rudi. In fact, there are many children: all those who followed the Pied Piper.'

Steffie was surprised. 'Pied Piper? That's a fairy tale!'

Branko nodded. 'But originally it was a real story. Want to hear it?'

The children shouted in delight. 'Yes! Yes!'

Branko cleared his throat dramatically. 'A plague of rodents invaded the city of Hamelin . . .'

Ettore, he noted, was also listening.

Nettie, still unsettled, got up. 'I'll fetch the rest of the meat.'

Branko watched her as she strode to the barbecue. She was as shapely as before. And, being pregnant, earthy. 'And Branko, who happened to be passing through with Honeypaw, his bear . . .'

It was Sunday. Spring was impersonating summer.

Branko sat by the shade of a tree at the ice-cream kiosk.

The park overflowed with picnickers and strollers; out on Lake Zurich, boats and *pedalos* churned up the sun-drenched water. People laughed, embraced, sang to guitars or harmonicas.

This should be man's birthright: hedonism, optimism, freedom from want.

But, beneath the resolve for joy, beneath all the make-believe, Branko knew, the pulse throbbed in despair. Most of the strollers were immigrant workers: brave seeds from the Mediterranean, Balkans, Middle East, India, South-East Asia, Philippines, Africa, South America, searching for hospitable earth. Tolerated as archetypal servants, they had been allowed to come out of their holes to take the air briefly. They ebbed and flowed as groups, seeking respite from solitude. Some, not many, had wives or husbands and children. Even fewer had found partners among the working-class Swiss. All were dressed in Sunday best. Witness the celibates' hunger as they ogled the sprinkling of women sunbathing or tried to chat up the junkies straggling for a fix further up the park. Without these immigrant workers, Zurich would flounder. So would the rest of Switzerland – and much of Western Europe.

'What's up?' Leo Leo sat next to him.

Many in the crowd stared at Leo Leo as a figure of hope: in fashionable white slacks and open-neck shirt which enhanced his tall figure, silver mane and dark features, he looked like a guest worker who had made good.

'You're punctual.'

'I make a point of it.'

Branko smiled ruefully. 'They do, too, I guess.'

'Who?'

Branko nodded at the crowd. 'Our domestic centurions. They take on all the shit jobs, yet they have no rights, no guarantees of employment, no say in what wages they get or what conditions they work under – no redress on any matter, in fact. So, living in constant fear of instant dismissal, they risk heart failure every step they take.'

Leo Leo watched him intently. 'You brought me all the way here to tell me that?'

'I wanted to buy you an ice-cream. What's your favourite flavour?'

'Chocolate.'

'Same as me.' Branko shouted the order at the waiter, then dropped his voice. 'The waiter – another *gastarbeiter*. Work permits can be cancelled any time, did you know that? Up to the discretion of the authorities. Say a street gang beats him up, he could be deported for disturbing the peace.'

The waiter brought them their ice-creams. Branko paid him.

Leo Leo tucked into his. 'Yet, they're lucky – they'll be the first to tell you that. Lucky to be here instead of in their own countries.'

Branko nodded. 'Lucky to be pariahs instead of being persecuted. Lucky to rub two francs together instead of starving. Lucky to lick the *gadjo* arse-hole instead of machine-gunning, for some despot, masses who happen to be of another nationality, race, colour, creed or language. Yes, I know.'

Leo Leo ran his hand over his mane. 'You're trying to say something – in your subtle way . . .'

Branko smiled. 'Don't know what subtle means. Nice – the ice-cream?'

'Very good.'

'Invented by Gypsies.'

'Is that so?'

'On a hot, dusty road.'

'I almost believed you there.'

'That's what the Gypsy Bible says.'

Leo Leo smiled. 'The Gypsy Bible – that's good!'

'There is one, you know. Our very own Sacred Book.'

Leo Leo chuckled. 'Really? Who wrote it – you?'

'As it happens, someone also called Branko. But origins unknown. Compiled it in Auschwitz.'

Leo Leo looked at him warily. 'Milking the joke, aren't you?'

Branko smiled. 'Here come the last drops. They're the best.'

'I'm listening.'

'I am destined to find it – our Bible.'

'Destined?'

'I carry a prophecy.'

Leo Leo bridled. 'This has stopped being funny.'

Branko grinned, then pointed at the crowd. 'We were talking about these people. Actually, *worker* is a misnomer for them. They're escapologists: wise souls who scented bloodlust and ran away. Not like our Gypsies who stayed on in the Third Reich and perished in the camps. They know their fellow men, this lot. They know genocide is the most expedient political solution. They know the white man collaborates in all the slaughters – either by giving the nod or playing blind. Or – as this country of yours did at the time of the Hitlerites – by shutting borders to refugees. They know, these *gastarbeiters*, our soul brothers and sisters, that life has no sanctity, singly or in millions. They know it's every man – every people – for himself. As it has always been.'

'Come to the point, Benedict.'

'Branko! The name's Branko!'

'The point?'

'I'm not joining you, Leo.'

Leo Leo stood up in fury. 'You gave me your word.'

Branko remained sitting. 'The word of an officer – which is worthless. And of a Rom – well, who gives a toss for that!'

'You're betraying me! Worse, you're betraying our people!'

'Watch what you say, Leo!'

'Why the turn-about?'

'I prefer my dream.'

'What dream? What can you do?'

'Find Romanestan!'

'No such place!'

'You can't see it through the *gadje*'s polluted air, but it's there!'

Leo Leo grabbed Branko by his coat lapels and pulled him up from his seat. 'You tricked me!'

Branko seized Leo Leo's hand and held it in a tight grip. 'What did you expect – let you and the ambassador put me in chains?'

'Such distrust . . .'

Branko applied pressure to Leo Leo's hand. 'No blindfolds on me, Leo. Not since all that electricity – remember all that electricity?'

'I spared you from the worst of it. Don't you forget that!'

'Maybe you shouldn't have!'

Leo Leo let go of Branko's coat and extricated his hand from the painful grip. 'Damn right, I shouldn't have!'

'One last point. I did think maybe – maybe – you had a point about assimilation. But the evidence is against it.'

Contemptuously, Leo Leo nodded in the direction of the immigrant workers. 'You call these dregs evidence? The real evidence is right before you! You and I. We've assimilated. But we're not ersatz *gadje*. We've kept our identity! We're both Gypsy and modern man! End of problem!'

'How many like us, Leo? Ten, twenty thousand? A hundred thousand? Half a million? What about the remaining fifteen, sixteen million – hated and unwanted; killed or burned or hunted at the slightest pretext . . . How will they assimilate?'

'When they change their ways . . .'

'Why should they?'

'That's how society evolves. Even you'd agree: vagabondage and the atomic age are not compatible.'

'You've been brainwashed, Leo! Vagabondage is *gadje* propaganda! A romantic word with which they disclaim centuries of expulsions and ostracism! Today, they won't even let us use their roads! Nor settle down anywhere! There's no earth for us, Leo, in *gadje*'s scheme of things! Never has been! Only no-man's-land!'

'A bit of time – that's all we need . . .'

'But time's not on our side, Leo. If we change our ways, we won't be Gypsies any more. If we don't, the *gadje* will find a pretext to vaporize us. Either way, we'll disappear. I'm not going to risk that. We need to move outside time.'

'What's that supposed to mean?'

'Create a different dimension. Start a new existence. Away from the *gadje*. Get to Romanestan. Be our own people – our own keeper.'

'Fantasies! Naive fantasies! They can only lead to disaster.'

Branko put his hand on Leo's shoulder. 'Let me tell you about the prophecy I carry, Leo – Gypsy to Gypsy . . .'

Leo Leo shook as he stood, his mane erupting outwards like the spikes of a hedgehog. 'You're a dangerous man, Benedict. Mad! You must be stopped!'

Branko sighed wearily. 'I'll leave you with this thought, Leo!' He pointed at the immigrant workers. 'Everybody, including these – dregs, as you call them – can turn killer at the drop of a slogan. Killing is easy. It comes naturally. Or if it has to be learned, it's learned quickly, enthusiastically. Think of that before they start quartering your precious assimilated self!' He patted Leo Leo's shoulder. 'Keep well. We won't meet again.'

'We will! I'll stop you! You're a dangerous man! I'll fight you! Don't say I didn't warn you!'

'Fighting serves a purpose only if you're prepared to kill, Leo. But killing means being haunted by the dead. And, in all likelihood, it also means no promised land. I can accept that – or rather, I'm trying to. Can you?'

Branko spoon-fed Young Glanz with some yoghurt whilst, on the other side of the bed, Ariana gently stroked the doctor's translucent skull as if tenderness could revive the Aesculapian intellect it had once contained.

Those who knew Glanz might easily have thought he had chosen to wait until his seventies before agreeing to do justice to his appellation; though, nowadays, with all the furrows on his face having dwindled into thin lines, 'cherubic' seemed a better description than 'young'. Only a streak of pursed brows which appeared to be constantly questioning the emptiness that had filled his being suggested that, only yesterday, within this frame, there had existed a man – a whole, saintly man.

For Branko, Glanz's Alzheimer's disease seemed the lesser outrage; such was the severity of his emphysematous breathing that even a person whose mind had been totally erased must have found it intolerable.

'Do you think he has any idea – of the state he's in . . .?'

Ariana who, since the onset of Glanz's senility, had moved in to take care of him, nodded sadly. 'I think so. His body must have – certainly.'

'Maybe that's why he's galloping towards death.'

'Maybe.'

'It must be such a strain for you, Dei – watching him suffer so . . . Why don't we get a nurse . . .?'

She shook her head. 'No. He is another son to me.'

'I know . . . But sitting here day in, day out . . .'

'I remember him as he was. All that he was. All he did for us. The many times he took me to see you. All the bribes he paid. The way he worried about you and me and Yerko, but never about himself . . .'

Branko stopped feeding Glanz and, tenderly, wiped his mouth. 'I used to fantasize that when we set out for Romanestan, he'd come with us. Our personal physician – our Grand Vizier of Health. Our *gadjo* who is more Rom than Rom.' Branko's eyes moistened. 'Romanestan, Nicholas – I can see it on the horizon. Hang on, can you? Please . . .'

Glanz, staring blankly with his creased brow, raised one hand to his mouth as if it held a cigarette. But he did not simulate the act of smoking. That was another function he had forgotten.

Branko rose from his chair, moved to the window and gazed at the view below. Glanz's apartment, closely surrounded by a phalanx of residential blocks, overlooked a cul-de-sac which, now serving as a delivery area for a supermarket and several fast-food restaurants, had turned into one of the busiest corners in Zurich. Glanz had moved here early in his career on the assumption that a centrally situated surgery would prove convenient both to his patients and himself. Typically, he had neither noticed the creeping claustrophobia of urban development nor the steady rise in pollution and noise levels. He had used the apartment only as a place to work in and sleep, never as a home. He had had a fiancée once – so Melchior had divulged – but, having soon realized that the dedication his profession demanded would soon wither his marriage, he had wisely broken off the engagement.

Thereafter he had been content to satisfy his sexual needs, at least, as best he could, with prostitutes.

Branko, suppressing a surge of tears, rested his head on the window.

Ariana came across and stood beside him. 'It's very hard for you . . .'

'It is, Dei . . . But not only because of his condition . . .'

'I know.'

'I'm scared, Dei . . .'

Ariana stroked his head. 'I know. Still full of doubts . . .'

'*Enderlez* is round the corner . . . That will be the time to emerge . . . Then all that must follow . . . Can I do it?'

'Yes.'

Branko held her hand. 'You'll be with me, won't you? When we set out?'

'Yes.' For a moment, as if reacting to a sudden presentiment, she looked distraught. 'I'll be there – right to the end.'

'You promise?'

She nodded solemnly. 'I won't die until I've seen Romanestan – I promise.'

Branko embraced her and his desperation eased. This ancient woman who had been scourged by life and broken by illness when he had first met her had transformed herself, over the years, into a person of prodigious strength. Under Young Glanz's care, she had shed all her ailments: her eyes were now clear of cataracts; no longer hunchbacked, she stood taller, albeit still gnarled like a shepherd's stick. Yerko had always favoured her, rather than Lumnia, as Branko's principal witness. Yerko might well be proven right. Branko had come to look upon Ariana's wrinkled, leathery skin as the bark of a tree where generations of Romanies had carved their names. Thus she represented the future. If she survived, he would survive, too. And so would his people.

She stroked his hair, then went back to sit with Glanz.

Branko watched her: a wraith in blue and green, the colours of sky and grass which defined the Gypsy and which, for some years now, she had made her own.

Then he turned to the window again and fixed his gaze on a lorry which was backing into an unloading bay. 'Dei – do you think I'm going mad?'

Ariana took a moment to answer by readjusting Glanz's pillows. 'Not yet.'

'Not yet?'

She tried to be light-hearted. 'Ask a stupid question . . .'

'The other day – when I saw Nettie . . . She's pregnant, I told you . . .'

'Yes. Lucky woman . . .'

'She's thinking of terminating. So I said, give the child to me. I meant it.'

'And she thought you were crazy?'

'Yes.'

'What does she know about childlessness?'

'Right! What, indeed? Whereas you and I, Dei . . .'

'Yes . . .'

'Even so . . . Asking her that – does it make me mad?' Branko strode over to her. 'Another thing . . . When I met Leo Leo . . . I mentioned the prophecy . . . He thinks I'm crazy, too . . .'

Ariana made a disgusted face. 'What do you expect – from a *gadje* lackey!'

'On the other hand, Dei, what does sane mean? Who is sane? When sane men took it upon themselves to decide our fate and we sanely accepted their word, how many died in the gas ovens? And how many at roadsides? And in forest clearings? How many?'

Ariana, troubled by Branko's outburst, smoothed Glanz's blanket.

Branko bent over Glanz. 'What do *you* think, Nicholas? Am I going mad?'

Again, in response to being addressed, Glanz raised his smoker's hand to his mouth.

Branko shook Glanz by his shoulders. 'Is that yes or no?'

Ariana pushed him away. 'Let him be.'

'You tell me then.'

'I told you!'

'*Not yet*, you said. Does that mean I'll go mad later?'

Ariana hesitated a moment. 'If it's part of your destiny.'

'Ah . . . So my fate's sealed. I can't escape my destiny . . .'

Ariana faced him, hoping both for a positive and a negative answer. 'Do you want to?'

'Can I?'

'Destiny's like running water – a strong person can channel it the way he wants. Fate is unchangeable.'

'How can you be sure?'

'Yerko told me.'

Branko shook his head. 'The question remains . . .'

'Do you want to? Give up your destiny?'

Branko sighed. 'If I did . . . What would I do . . . where would I go . . . who would I be . . . ?' He took to pacing the room with a new surge of energy. 'All right . . . Destiny wins! Branko, get a move on! One task left, Dei! Shouldn't take me long . . .'

Ariana smiled, trying to conceal her trepidation. 'I'll be here.'

Branko strode over to Glanz. 'Nicholas, hang on! Just hang on! I'm going to bring you the cabbage leaves the donkey ate!'

Glanz raised his smoker's hand to his mouth.

After another odyssey in search of Romanestan, Branko was left hungry and impoverished. And, at harvest time, he came upon a field which belonged to a Manush named Boaz.

The crop was plentiful. In addition to wheat, maize and barley, there were fig trees with fruits bulging like testicles.

And Boaz came unto Branko and pointed out a corner of the field and told him to reap that part for himself; for such was the law of hospitality towards strangers and paupers.

And Branko filled his vardo with all the produce from the corner of the field.

And when he took a final, envious look at the cropped land, he thought he recognized the place.

And he asked Boaz which country he was in and what this region was called.

Boaz told him.

And Branko wept. For this was his old land; here, before burdening himself with yearnings and prophecies, he had lived as an ordinary man and slept soundly.

Had he lost his mind to think he had the strength of a Saviour? Had he allowed himself to be possessed by treacherous spirits to believe that he could find Romanestan?

PART SIX

Nineteen

Branko sat by the road and waited for nightfall.

Immediately south, beyond the scrubland and the river, the Zaklady Chemiczne plant belched its yellow smoke, vivid even in twilight.

To the west, the Vistula could be heard engorging noisily on the Soła, an Iron-Age warrior drinking a rival's blood. Hereafter, winding through Krakow and Warsaw, it would consume many more tributaries and discharge into the Baltic, at Gdansk, as Poland's most virile river.

To the east, north and south, lush fields slumbered along the banks like babes fallen asleep at the breast.

A few kilometres south-west stood Oświęcim.

Farmers and workers, lumbering home, greeted him warmly. He had become a familiar figure in the area; people were always offering him drinks, meals or lodging. Some even saw him as a harbinger of better times: in today's Poland, a man who went around beach-combing rivers and camped in the open without incurring harassment from the authorities was a sure sign that the battle for freedom, launched by Solidarity, was being won.

Daylight expired.

Branko picked up his gear and waded into the scrub.

Like the infant Moses – they entrusted it to the water. That was how the Gypsies in Auschwitz had saved their Bible, so Dr Kalderon had said; and he had affirmed that, somewhere along the bulrushes, there would be a pharaoh's daughter who would spot the Book and save it.

He, Branko, child of the crematoria and namesake of the Book's compiler, was that person. Finding the Gypsy Bible constituted the very core of his destiny. The compulsion that had led his people to commit the Book to the Vistula was proof of that. Had they hidden it anywhere else, he would never have known how to search for it, never would have stood poised, as he was now, to reclaim it. For, in matters of water, he was a Triton. It used to be said in the Lucerne Hydroelectricity Board that he could get to know a flow as intimately as a favourite piece of music. Indeed, he could assess, with accuracy, how a river would behave, why and where it would seek a new bed, whether its destination would be the sea or another river or a wasteland, how spiritedly it would fetch and carry silt, insects, birds, fish, gold, and even whether it would have the resources to survive man's pollution.

All he had had to do was to determine exactly where, along the Vistula, the Book lay. Consequently, by dazzling the regional water authority with old visiting cards, he had obtained all the available data on the river from 1944 to the present.

He had studied the seasonal levels of the water, the amounts of rain and snow and the scale of their drainage, the rates of evaporation, instances of flooding and drought, geophysical factors and obstructions governing its speed of flow, the corresponding vagaries of the undercurrents, the effects of leisure activities such as fishing, boating and swimming, the demands of installations such as the fish-ponds in nearby Zator, and the purchase of the confluences not only with the Przemsza and the Soła but also with the other tributaries in the region.

He had brought into this equation the weight of the Bible – and its container – a vital coefficient in determining the distance the Book would have been dragged by the current. Since Dr Kalderon had not provided this piece of information, he had assessed it by calculating a range of weights, from a conservative minimum of one kilogram to an implausible maximum – on the off-chance that the container might be a lead casket – of thirty.

His findings had shown that, initially – and regardless of its weight – the Bible would have pitched into the Lower Vistula, beyond the confluence with the Soła, in the autumn of 1949. Thenceforth, taking into consideration the powerful surge produced by the rivers' coupling – a surge which only masses above fifty kilograms would be able to resist – he had calculated that a thirty-kilogram object would have been dragged seven kilometres; that of one kilogram would have been carried twelve times that distance.

Dredging such a long stretch of river, particularly one that became fairly busy from Krakow onwards, would have been a daunting task even with modern equipment and full official support. But providence had once again interceded. In the spring of 1950 – just after the Book would have been carried into the Lower Vistula – work on the much-awaited expansion of the Zaklady Chemiczne plant had commenced. The enterprise had entailed not only the renovation of the main installation – originally built by Auschwitz's inmates for the Nazi war effort – but also the construction of a number of buildings for Allied industries as well as of residential estates for the workforce and of a network of roads to serve the complex. To achieve these objectives, the planners had been compelled to alter the course of the Vistula slightly by straightening the bend north of the plant.

Accommodating this factor into his calculations, Branko had discovered, to his immense relief, that the Holy Book could not have been carried beyond that particular bend: the excavations involved in carving the Vistula's new course would almost certainly have trapped the Bible in the old river-bed.

And that was where he was now – on the old river-bed itself: a scrubland, roughly a kilometre wide and seven kilometres long, waiting to be reclaimed for sugar-beet farming. He had plotted thirteen locations as sites where the Book might have been trapped. He had to dig them up one by one . . .

He dug at night.

The soil still possessed the texture of freshly deposited alluvium. He caressed it, seeking to rouse its riverine memory.

At dawn, he disposed of the earth he had displaced by scattering it over the scrubland.

He dug pits of eight metres, the depth of the old course. To conceal the excavations, he wove his dust-stained sweat into camouflage nettings.

When a pit proved to be empty, he fetched back all the earth and filled it up. Then he started on the next one.

When it rained, the pit became like quicksand. He learned how to swim in mire lest he drowned in it.

One by one, the pits turned up barren. He kept faith; but doubt tormented him. Voices, soughing faintly from Birkenau – his mother's and father's – wailed as if he was failing them. His calculations were correct. But sites were strange phenomena: they could fall prey to distortions; they were even known to shift positions.

On the thirteenth pit, reality divested itself of its disguises. Hope began to die. He decided: if this last site, too, came up empty, he would lie down and shroud himself with the earth he had dug up.

He touched the bottom of the thirteenth pit.

The ground caved in. He spun down to the magma core in a cascade of powdery earth. But a naiad, the river's life-force – or was it Lumnia? – saved him. She scooped him up and guided him through the Vistula's labyrinth of veins – some, as delicate as gossamer – and brought him to the pond in Birkenau. She showed him a pillar of fire that was pointing at the depths. 'The Book is there.'

Branko was amazed. 'How did it get there?'

'I brought it. This is where it belongs.'

Branko felt despondent. 'I failed. I misjudged.'

The naiad – or was it Lumnia? – stroked his locks. 'Your calculations were correct. And your labour was necessary. They led you here.'

'You led me here.'

The naiad – or was it Lumnia? – kissed him. 'I was included in your calculations.'

He surveyed the pond: iced over. But it was April-ice, thinner; it had trapped shards of rainbow and was tracing tiny windows on its surface to let in some light.

Of course, the Holy Book is here; this is where it belongs. This is where the Hitlerites had dumped the Gypsies' ashes. Where he had communed with his Dei and Dadoro. Where his ancient friend, the naked, mutilated man, had stood sentinel. Where the suppurating eye had ogled him. Still ogles him.

Here lie untold Gypsies: bear-tamers, labourers, acrobats, shepherds, horse-traders, farm hands, beggars, magicians, snake-charmers, pickpockets, fortune-tellers, barbers, musicians, smiths, tailors, woodcutters . . .

See – the water is indelible with the ancient colour of incineration: grey here, hoar there, stipples of cinders in between.

Water cursed for failing to engulf the Hitlerites. Forbidden to ripple in joy. Reduced to sustaining only albino reeds, hueless flowers and sallow birch trees. Who would ever think of looking for the Gypsy Bible in its viscous depths?

I did. I can see the obvious as clearly as the mysterious.

Dei! Dadoro! I've come for the Word! I am on our Holy Mount, our watery Sinai. To ascend it, I must dive; to reach its summit, I must plummet to the bottom.

He camps under the ruins of Crematorium V where fireflies glow eternally to commemorate the dead.

He does not expect intruders.

True, there are always voices around the trees, but they are Jews, praying for their untold dead. Even when they stray to the pond to commune with relatives or sages, they don't trouble him or get in the way.

They are soot-brothers: their people's ashes have been dumped here also.

Occasionally, he catches glimpses of Ariana and Young Glanz. The latter, seated on his bed, his brow permanently creased, stares into the ether like an eyeless statue.

Ariana stands motionless, shrunken into a stick and as old as time, but still a tree of life.

He loses track of time. Day after day, he purifies himself with mud from the pond's edges.

Whenever he catches his reflection on the smoke-tinted ice, he observes a face wrinkled with doubt and hunchbacked with fear. He tries to reconstruct his reflection. He tells it: 'Saviours must suffer, but never wilt.'

One day, as he watches a swarm of bees make honey for the souls, he glimpses himself on the dew and sees that he has become a merman. Instead of legs, he has powerful flippers; gills sprout from his neck and chest; his face bears the fearlessness he has sought all his life. He is a rock upon whom a nation can be built.

He is ready.

He dives in and pierces the ice like a meteor.

Immediately, a shadow swoops upon him.

It is his old friend, the naked, mutilated man, composed of ashes and ambery blood. But now he is different. He is young and sturdy; and freshly mutilated.

Branko realizes the man is none other than the person after whom he was named: Branko, the Castrated One, the Gypsy Bible's scribe.

Treading water, hair undulating on the surface, arms folded across the chest enhancing huge biceps, the Castrated One greets him. 'He who returns always brings life.'

Branko stares at the gash between the man's legs. He feels the same void, the same pain, the same despair in his crotch.

The Castrated One puts a commiserative arm around him. 'We couldn't be fathers. But we can be mothers.'

Branko sees that the Castrated One's wound has been transformed into a vagina.

He looks at his own genitals and notes an opening: he, too, has evolved female loins.

They set out for the depths. It is hard going.

The ash is like snow. Sometimes it is soft and he sinks into it; other times it is like slush and becomes slippery; occasionally it thunders down in avalanches and carries them away; now and again it swirls as in a storm and blinds; often it is gelid.

On the walls of the pond, where it is like packed ice, he has to hack footholds for his flippers and use his merman's suction pads as crampons.

The Castrated One leads. He is masterly on the rope. Often he sings. Always the same song. Branko recognizes it: a Balkan lullaby. His Dei and Dadoro had sung it to him the day he was born.

Sleep, my husky lad, sleep;
in your cradle and under your quilt;
your mother bore you on the mountain;
angels swaddled you in silk.

One day, Branko asks the Castrated One: 'Did you have children – before Auschwitz?'

'Many. You're one of them.'

'I am Todor's son.'

'Mine also.'

'How?'

'As I am your son.'

Another day, they compare scars. The Castrated One has many, all on the front of his body. He explains: he has never turned his back to the enemy. Branko has several also, but all on the back of his body. He explains:

the enemy has always struck from behind. They laugh: together, they complete the Gypsy.

The going gets harder. Some of the levels are like glaciers and almost impenetrable.

Sometimes Branko loses his footing and falls. He survives only because the Castrated One holds him on the rope.

Now and again, he is paralysed by the bends. The prescribed remedy, as in altitude sickness, is to reduce height. So the Castrated One hauls him back to the shallows.

Yet other times, his gills prove inadequate; he runs out of oxygen and fights asphyxia. The Castrated One shares his breath with him, mouth to mouth.

Nevertheless, each day they traverse a circle or a terrace or a cornice or a sphere.

At each level, Branko is approached by souls whose mouths and hands are question marks.

He tells them: 'I have come. He who returns is not a deserter.'

Nearer the bottom, the ash is thick like alpine snow.

The souls are huddled together: even in death, there is comfort in proximity. Occasionally, they sing. Surprisingly, the songs are contemporary. One is a favourite of his. Yerko had picked it up on the radio and couldn't stop singing it. Composed by a bard from Skopje.

Is dust kind to man?
Are angels sensual odalisques?
And devils drinking companions?
Can death really be discreet, like rust?

Finally they approach the floor of the pond. There remains one declivity, a chute like an arrow-head that reminds him of the Matterhorn's summit.

He feels strong. He has become steady on his feet and confident on the rope. His breathing is much better.

But the Castrated One imposes a pause. Gathering the Holy Book from the pond's viscera will be arduous; Branko must acquire full strength, ancestral strength.

Branko perches on a ledge. The souls come and sit with him and give him their names. Branko touches their eyes, mouths, cheeks, chests, hands, legs. No one bears the stigmata of sin: no shadow has its back bent by greed or avarice, no flesh has been ravaged by envy.

The Castrated One explains: 'Hell is not here. It is on earth: the life of man.'

The souls assume Zara's and Todor's features. Branko places his head on their bosom. They give him suck. All the breasts, male and female, are bursting with potency.

He attains full vigour.

The Castrated One sends him on the final descent.

Immediately, he is caught in a blizzard.

He secures himself on a ledge and adjusts his eyes to the glare of the darkness. He notes the hail is not composed of solid ash, but of slashed wombs and perforated testicles, of scorched vaginas and mutilated penises.

He is mesmerized by the last: proud ones; shy ones; large ones; small ones; lifeless penises that had given life; circumcised penises killed for their capacity to give life.

He spots the severed penis of the Castrated One. It stands erect, at the bottom of the pond, guarding the Holy Book.

At last, the Gypsy Bible.

The ash-mud is like amber. Its chunks have encased the Scriptures, like fossils, within their translucent resin. They swim and float in shades of sorrel.

Branko descends the last stretch. Wielding a net like an amber-gatherer, he fishes the chunks. Each contains a portion of the Book. Branko fishes in forty levels before he retrieves the complete manuscript.

He erects a pulley. Verse by verse, chapter by chapter, he lifts the Holy Book to the surface.

He dives for the last time.

The Castrated One comes to bid farewell. '*A new tree will bear the leaves the donkey ate.*'

Branko kisses his hand. 'Adieu.'

The Castrated One clasps him. 'Death will be meaningless after you've gone.'

Branko places himself between the Castrated One's legs where the gash has turned into a vagina. The mysteries of creation flow over him. He observes his own vagina.

The Castrated One summons his severed penis. It penetrates Branko, ejaculates words and inseminates him.

Joyfully, Branko watches himself being born. He has become a father. He has sired a son. He has given birth to himself.

And O Del pointed at Branko and said: 'He is my Chosen. On him my favour rests.'

And like birds providing for their young, the spirits of the forefathers fed Branko segments of the Word.

And Branko assumed the contours of a woman.

He dug a hole at the bottom of the pond and sprinkled on it the ashes of a noble bear.

He squatted over the hole and, like a leviathan filling its lungs for a journey, breathed deeply.

And the Word re-emerged through his loins.

He swaddled It and gave It to his people.

There has never risen in Romanestan a spirit like Branko, the Bear-Tamer, whom O Del knew face to face.

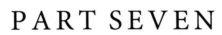

PART SEVEN

Twenty

Belgrade welcomed Branko and Ariana by presenting them with Dr Kalderon's spectre.

As they disembarked from the aeroplane into a sunshine so brilliant as to be portentous, Branko saw the old Jew, gauntly loitering on the tarmac, holding on to his skullcap, the tattooed number on his arm fully visible, smiling with burning eyes as if he knew that the Book had been found.

Ariana was not surprised by the apparition. Naturally Dr Kalderon could hardly wait to see the Gypsy Bible.

That made sense, of course. Branko himself was equally impatient to show him the Book. Only the old Jew could confirm that the ambery sheets he had so painstakingly gathered in the pond constituted the original manuscript.

They flew to Sarajevo immediately.

Dr Kalderon had died seven years ago. The Jewish Museum's new curator, a young man, remembered him only as a name, not for what he had achieved nor for the many ways he had stood up and defied hatred.

Nevertheless, that night, after Ariana had gone to sleep, Branko met the old Jew. He found him, as he knew he would, sitting in the kiosk which served as the museum's ticket-office, sipping tea through a cube of sugar.

By a strange coincidence, Young Glanz was with him.

Or maybe it was not a coincidence. Young Glanz, who had stood witness, with Ariana, to Branko's reclamation of the Holy Book, had died moments

265

after Branko had brought up the last portion, that is to say, after having witnessed, with his eyeless gaze, that the manuscript had been salvaged in its entirety.

So there he was now, seated on his bed, his brow permanently creased, drinking tea with his new companion and chain-smoking.

Branko showed Dr Kalderon the Holy Book, every portion of it.

Dr Kalderon became ecstatic. He cried and embraced Branko. He pointed out the parts he knew and avidly read those he did not. And he said: 'Yes, this is Branko's Book.'

And Branko and Young Glanz cried and drank *sambucca* and danced.

And Dr Kalderon, holding on to his skullcap, joined in the celebrations. 'Yes, this is the Gypsy's Bible. On this O Del's favour rests.'

Branko and Ariana travelled to Skopje by bus. The suggestion had come from Ariana: it would give Branko time to unfold himself slowly, to put away his killer soul and lay bare the orphan who was returning to father a people in order to become their son. Besides, she had added, teasing him, saviours should always utilize humble transportation: Jesus had entered Jerusalem on a donkey.

In the event, the journey was exhilarating. To those travelling by road, Yugoslavia had much to offer: the stark beauty of Bosnia-Herzegovina's highlands and valleys; the mysticism surrounding Serbia's rivers and gorges and the medieval churches on remote hills that stand as their guardians; the mesmerizing roll of the Kosovo plains, still swirling with the dust of ancient blood; and the distant, cloud-hugging ranges of Macedonia, beckoning like bacchantes.

As he basked in such varied enchantment, Branko tried to think how best he could surprise Lumnia. Should he just knock at the door or show up hesitantly, with the sun behind him?

Ariana refused to advise him: let things happen.

Branko barely recognized Skopje. The old town's ramparts and fortifications, beneath which the bus terminal now sprawled, had been dwarfed by the new metropolis across the river. The city, when he had last seen it ten years ago, had still been a massive building site trying to heal the ravages of the 1963 earthquake. Now, stout buildings and skyscrapers – designed, if his memory served him well, to withstand even the strongest tremors – crowded the horizon like a cohort of colossal menhirs.

It was 5 May, the eve of St George's Day.

The mêlée of buses and taxis verged on chaos.

As he tried to guide Ariana through the crowd, a giant shadow fell upon him and kissed his hands. 'Welcome, my chief.'

'Omar . . .' Branko hugged the youth.

Ariana stood back, not wishing to intrude on their meeting.

Branko and Omar embraced and exchanged tears.

The people noticed them. They stopped buffeting each other. They put down their cases, sacks, plastic bags and watched them. Men sighed and wiped their brows with their sleeves. Women chewed their scarves, pressed their children against their bellies and let a few tears run silently. They knew: occasionally life weaves a reunion that is so extraordinary that it realigns the earth to its correct orbit; the lucky few who witness it are sprinkled with stardust.

'How did you know, Omar . . .?'

'Lumnia. She heard your footsteps.'

'Where is she?'

'You'll see her tomorrow.'

People began to disperse. Some of the women patted Branko's and Omar's shoulders. A number of men pressed sweets or chewing-gum into their pockets. Branko could not hide his disappointment. 'Why not today?'

Omar embraced Ariana, then picked up their luggage. 'Tomorrow is *Enderlez*! You'll abduct her as your wife!'

Luck had remained faithful to Omar. He was now a famous bard.

He had started his career, on Lumnia's advice, by playing at births, circumcisions, weddings and deaths. He had soon become popular not only with the Gypsies but also with Skopje's large Turkish and Albanian communities. One day, having to stand in for a vocalist who had been taken ill, he had astonished everybody, not least himself, with the power of his baritone. Thereafter, guided by an astute manager, he had cut discs, established himself on radio and television and toured extensively in the Balkans. Today, his popularity stretched from Italy to Israel. Yerko's favourite song – the song that had haunted Branko in Auschwitz's pond – had been composed by Omar.

Much as he was pleased by Omar's success, Branko felt envious. He, too, used to compose songs; and he had been quite a virtuoso with the cithara. But he had abandoned all that. If a musician became a fugitive, Yerko had advised him, he must renounce his music; for such a man would find no place to hide, not even in the wilderness; it would take just one person to hear him, then the plains and the mountains would broadcast his name to every village and farm – and thence to the ears of the Securitate.

Ilyas Rahim had died – three months after Ramzi's death in Tîrgu Jiu and a month before the birth of his fourth daughter. Ostensibly, of galloping cancer. In reality, that true heart, which had abhorred bloodshed and planted pomegranate trees up and down the country, had simply vacated his body in a desperate bid to transplant itself into his son's bullet-torn chest.

Neither Ilyas, nor any of the family, had ever blamed Branko for leading Ramzi to his death. But Branko knew – and Omar could not deny it – that no matter how lovingly they might welcome him back as Ramzi's blood-brother, their souls would never forgive him.

It was unlikely they would meet again. After the prescribed mourning period, Ramzi's wife had gone to relatives in America. Nothing had been heard of her since. Yildiz, Ilyas' wife, had moved to Kosovo with her youngest daughter and now lived in seclusion with her parents. Her three older daughters and three remaining sons had settled in Germany. They had found good jobs and were still expanding their families; they were also looking after Kenan, the eldest son with the withered arm, who, tormented by the twist of fate that had sent Ramzi to death instead of him, had become an alcoholic.

They had never returned to Skopje, not even for *Enderlez*; nor, knowing that Branko had promised to come back one day, would they ever. Still Branko hoped that when it would be time to set out for Romanestan, they would join the exodus.

Hanro, the coppersmith who had acted as the *false chief* under Ilyas, was the new *vataf*. A quiet man, now in declining health, he had turned out to be a good leader. He was, after all, *Bibi*, the *phuri dai*'s husband, leavened, as Ilyas used to say of him, by his wife's sagacity. Always a devout Muslim, he was now a votary of Sufism, a tradition which further enhanced his sense of justice.

Lumnia had become a *drabarni*, as Yerko – may the earth be plentiful over him – had informed Branko in Romania. Soon after Omar's return from Tîrgu Jiu, she had left Skopje and had wandered the world for years. When she had come back, only recently, she had declared her proficiency publicly and had listed the wisdom she had ingested.

From the east: the knowledge of curative cuts and incisions; the lore of herbs and love philtres.

From the south: the magical properties of images, symbols, numbers, inscriptions and arcane words.

From Europe: the esotericism of taboos, prophecies, curses, the Evil Eye; the detection of omens of life and death; the strategies of the mule and of fairies, devils, werewolves, vampires and the living dead.

From the north: the secrets of the sun, earth, ice, air; of Alako, the divinity of the moon and the vulva; of Kar, the divinity of rain and the phallus.

When she had mastered all this magic, jinn and houris had transported her to the summit of Everest, that most ancient altar. There she had been made to lie on the sun's rays and had been visited by both the spirits of life before life and of life after life; these had duly inseminated her with the mysteries of Creation.

Inevitably, during her long absence from Skopje, she and Omar had become estranged. Yet their concern for one another had never waned. Despite the separation, they had opened up channels – she, with her magic; he, with his music – wherein they had watched over each other. That was how it still was, despite the additional disjunction her status now imposed. She still kept a hundred eyes on him; he still surrounded her like a city's walls. Indeed, when, in the coming days, Ariana would be required to negotiate, on Branko's behalf, Lumnia's price as a wife, she would have to do so with Omar.

And so it was St George's Day. The people flocked to the river.

The musicians, playing in twos or threes or fours, became extensions of their *davulis, zurnas*, violins and accordions. Singers flew from one family to another and drew tears and laughter, often simultaneously. The families honoured them by dancing in abandon. In their best clothes, they created curlicues of new colours.

Here and there groups celebrated their pilgrimage by twining threads from their clothes around stones and bushes. Everyone held up leafing branches and caressed the breeze. From afar, they looked like a camber of weeping willows over ancient Vardar.

Branko stood on the opposite bank.

He wore a florid suit, shiny patent leather shoes and a fedora hat – all purchased, under Omar's guidance, the previous evening. Clothed in such princely manner, Omar had told him, he would impress the people; they would believe he had returned shod with good fortune.

He waited, running his fingers over the moustache he had started growing on the Castrated One's advice, urging it to blossom into one worthy of a chief.

Children paddled by the water; waved at him. Some showed off by swimming against the current.

Ariana, drawn by their antics, had settled on a boulder and watched them.

He waited still more.

Eventually, like a monument on the move, Omar loomed in the distance. He was playing his concertina and singing. Scores of youths, clapping and gyrating, followed him.

Lumnia was not with him.

She'll appear at the river, he had said, and you'll abduct her in broad daylight. She'll take you where no one will find you. You'll consummate your love. When you come back at the end of the festivities, I, her guardian, will challenge you. Then Ariana and I will strike a deal.

Will she recognize me? Will I recognize her? Will she want me?

An orchard rose on the other bank. Earth became a road bedecked with favourable *patrin*.

She materialized. Arrayed in seven skirts, each a different colour of the rainbow. Her luminous, sea-coal hair providing evidence for the beauty of blackness. Her green eyes, reflecting the leaves on the river, speaking of eternal times in hale forests.

'Lumnia! Lumnia! Lumnia . . .'

She beckoned him.

He ran across the waters, seized her by the arms; the texture of her flesh had not changed these ten years. 'Lumnia . . .'

Her breath cupped his ear. 'Take me, Branko!'

He picked her up.

She screamed. 'Help! Save me!'

He put her across his shoulders.

She flailed. 'Help me! Brothers! Sisters! Help me! Omar! Save me!'

Omar ran towards them.

Throngs of Gypsies followed in support.

Branko bounded, instinctively, in the direction of the mountains. 'I'm taking you to the peaks!'

She stroked his forehead. 'Yes, my Rom!' Her screams intensified. 'Help! Save me!'

Branko unfurled his wings and raced the wind.

His pursuers receded as pin-points.

He shouted triumphantly. 'The Bear's son flies like the eagle!'

She placed her face upon his. 'I have kneaded such a great love for us, my Rom . . .'

They alighted on a summit.

Lumnia smoothed the ground and drew a circle which instantly sprouted lush grass. Here they would burgeon seventy thousand heads; each head would sprout seventy thousand mouths; each mouth would bear seventy thousand tongues; each tongue would speak seventy thousand languages and each language would praise their love.

'I have reclaimed the Book, Lumnia.'

'What does it say about love, my Rom?'

'It is the first commandment.'

'Is that wise, my Rom?'

'As wise as I can be.'

'*Drabarnis* are seldom taken to wife. They have received spirits. They are not considered intact.'

'I possessed you every night for forty seasons. Each time we lay down you were a virgin. I will possess you every night until I die and it will always be as the first time.'

'Will you protect my place at our people's hearth?'

'With my life and soul.'

As if laying down the moon, she spread out a white sheet on the grass. 'Undress me.'

Her hair billowed. Warm, bountiful, woven by the winds. Like the tents of a *kumpania*. Velvet skin. Orb-shaped breasts. Aureoles that beamed light. Bread-shaped belly; and a navel like an olive. Wide hips for child-bearing. Sturdy, Doric legs. Sorcerous Asiatic buttocks with footholds for children to climb. Thick, fluffy pubic hair – cushion for gods. And glistening lips at the entrance to her soul. In there he would be born time and time again.

She read his mind. 'One child is not enough, my Rom.'

'Our people will be another, Lumnia.'

'Delivered from our minds. Not from our flesh. I shall forever search for the children that evaded my womb.'

'Discard me, then.'

'I cannot.'

'Is that wise?'

'As wise as I can be.'

'Undress me.'

Truly the Bear's son. Thick hair heavily sprinkled with silver. Grizzled with scars. Chest like a boulder; wide shoulders. Legs tempered by mountains. Every muscle taut and mapped with veins. But desiccated testicles, still raging at the curse of infecundity. Nonetheless, a defiant, eager penis, beating like a heart.

Branko surrendered his head to her bosom. She draped herself around him like holy cloth. Her mouth became the Milky Way. He sucked her nipples and was rewarded with jets of milk; he ate her apricot greedily; the nectar ran down his mouth. They became as Creation had first etched them: skins without blemish, without spoors of age.

They journeyed into each other.

They returned to Šuto Orizari on the last night of *Enderlez*.

Lumnia wore only one skirt. Branko trailed the other six as if they were fragments of a spectrum; the white sheet, smeared with dried blood, billowed on his shoulders.

They proceeded to the *Vesh*. They radiated the bearing of deities, one of the sky, the other of the earth, one carrying water, the other fire.

The people observed their clasped hands in reverend silence. The *Enderlez* fare of lamb, bread, salads, spring onions, beer and *rakia*, so passionately laid out by families, was forgotten.

The funfair stood hushed in its blaze of lights.

Musicians shepherded their *davulis*, *zurnas*, lutes, citharas, accordions, violins, tambourines and pan-pipes into pasture. And the dancers' footsteps sat on the grass and susurrated like crickets out of breath. Even the children stopped their frolicking; sensing an extraordinary dimension, they fixed their eyes on the couple's hips and wished that, one day, their own loins would serve as places of pilgrimage.

'Abductor! Villain!' Omar, wielding a heavy club, confronted them.

Branko faced him. On this very spot, ten years ago, he had wrestled with his first bear. And the Bear had recognized his offspring. 'I am the Bear's son.'

Omar raged. 'Lumnia is my ward! I'll kill you for abducting her! And I'll kill her for submitting to you!'

Branko, pushing Lumnia behind him, picked up several large stones. 'I'll kill you first!'

Omar waved away the gathering crowd. 'Make room!' He beckoned Lumnia. 'You – come here!'

Obediently, Lumnia moved towards Omar.

Branko grabbed her by the arm. 'Stay!'

Lumnia struggled. Branko punched her and knocked her down. Then he tore off the white sheet from his shoulders and threw it at Omar. 'I have her hymen!'

Omar noted the blood on the sheet and burst into tears. He showed the sheet to the crowd.

Angrily, the Gypsies shook their fists. Some spat at Branko; others threw stones.

Branko stood his ground. 'I made her my woman!'

Still weeping, Omar shouted at Lumnia. 'You should have strangled him with your locks. Now, you must wed him!'

Lumnia huddled into herself and mumbled incoherently.

Omar towered over Branko. 'Will you have her as your bride?'

Branko turned to Ariana who having achieved, by virtue of her age, equal status to a man, could negotiate on his behalf. He handed her a large wad of money. 'See to it, Dei.'

Omar thundered. 'She's costly.'

Solemnly, Ariana proffered him some bills. 'Nonsense! She's a *drabarni*.'

'Don't haggle with me!' Omar counted the bills. 'Not enough!'

Ariana gave him more money.

Omar shook his head. 'Still not enough!'

Ariana glared; then, reluctantly, she handed over the rest of the money.

Omar nodded and pocketed the bills. Then he picked up his club and, striking Branko on the head, knocked him to the ground. 'You plunder her maidenhead, yet I can't kill you! Is that justice?' He turned to Lumnia and kicked her. 'You marry in the morning!'

Many pilgrims stayed for the wedding.

Whilst nursing Branko's concussion during the night, Omar shyly admitted that the festivities would be unprecedented. He had organized everything personally.

In the morning, they gathered in the *Vesh*, at the clump of acacia trees which, symbolizing future woodlands, still stood as Šuto Orizari's focal point.

Led by Ariana, still in her role as Branko's parent, and *Bibi*, the *phuri dai*, upon whom it fell to oversee the rituals, the women went in procession to Omar's house where Lumnia had been kept under lock. They bathed and examined her and, declaring their approval, laid out her silver bridal gown. Ariana dyed Lumnia's hands with henna, the mark of piety. Then the women returned to the *Vesh*.

The afternoon brought another procession – also led by Ariana, but this time comprising all those who would attend the wedding.

This time, they found the house barricaded. Omar and his friends, armed with sticks, axes and shovels, were standing guard.

Ariana brought out a bottle of old brandy that was wrapped in a silk handkerchief and wound with velvet strips laden with gold coins. She laid the bottle in front of Omar.

Omar pocketed the gold coins and drank some brandy. Satisfied, he offered the bottle to Ariana. Ariana drank a good mouthful and returned the bottle to Omar.

Omar nodded. 'The union is sealed.'

Ariana replied. 'It is.'

They embraced.

Omar's friends cleared the barricades.

Omar brought out Lumnia who was now dressed in her bridal gown. Screaming and weeping, she tried to regain the house. Forced to hit her occasionally, Omar dragged her to the *Vesh*.

The procession followed.

They returned to the clump of acacia trees where Branko waited in the custody of Hanro, the *Vataf*.

They formed a wide circle around a kilim which had been laid out in the middle of the clearing and on which were placed a jar of water, a single glass, a loaf of bread and an earthenware container filled with salt.

Hanro presided. His wife, *Bibi*, the *phuri dai*, assisted him.

Omar brought Lumnia forward.

Lumnia stopped resisting.

Ariana led Branko and directed him next to Lumnia.

Lumnia and Branko faced Hanro; Omar and Ariana stood on each side.

Branko handed a red handkerchief to Lumnia and addressed the gathering. 'I am here to wed Lumnia.'

Lumnia, tying the handkerchief around her wrist, declared loudly. 'I have consented to be Branko's wife.'

Hanro took up the jug and poured some water into the glass. He handed the glass to Branko.

Branko held the glass to Lumnia. 'I take you as my wife. If I fail as a husband, I'll free you so that you can be happy elsewhere.'

They both drank the water.

Branko handed the glass back to Hanro.

Bibi, the *phuri dai*, took the loaf of bread, tore off two pieces and sprinkled them with salt. She handed a piece each to Branko and Lumnia. 'Bread and salt represent bliss. When you get tired of them, you'll be tired of each other.'

Branko and Lumnia offered the pieces of salted bread to each other. Both ate the other's piece.

Hanro, using a new knife, cut Branko's and Lumnia's right wrists and tied them together so that the blood would mingle. He embraced them. 'You are now wed.'

Omar came forward and hung the gold coins he had received from Ariana around Lumnia's throat. 'May this token gift multiply a thousand times.'

The gathering burst into joyous chants and pelted the couple with rice.

The *patshiv* – banquet – took place in a big tent and went on for a week. The guests, especially the poor and the humble, were treated like royalty.

The day after the wedding, the sheet which contained proof of Lumnia's virginity was displayed. *Bibi*, the *phuri dai*, pouring *rakia* on the dried stains, examined them and confirmed that the blood was Lumnia's. Though, as a *drabarni*, Lumnia had been inseminated by the spirits of life before life and of life after life, as a female she had remained chaste and had not brought disgrace and bad luck on her community.

After the display, Lumnia braided her hair anew and covered it with a *diklo*, the scarf which a married woman must always wear in public.

At the end of the festivities, Hanro, at Branko's request, invited all the chiefs to a special council. Since most of the *kumpanias* had planned to perform the pilgrimage to Les Saintes Maries de la Mer at the end of the month – a devotion as important as *Enderlez* – the date of the meeting was set for mid-June.

And Branko, the Bear-Tamer, built their varda.

He selected an olive tree, long-leafed and of goodly yield and with a trunk so broad that it could contain all the seventy amorous holds.

He wove the branches into a canopy.

He bored the trunk and hewed space for a sizeable bedstead.

He filigreed the surface with precious metals and decked it with soft hides, purple quilts, fine linen and the down of geese.

Around this bed, he wrought the rest of the caravan.

And when he and Lumnia lay down, it was as if man and woman were one.

Whenever they travelled, Branko gathered up the tree's roots and, using them like oars, rowed the air; whenever they camped, he plunged the roots back into the earth.

And Adam swore to destroy the good magic Branko and Lumnia enjoyed. 'The male is born of the eagle and the female of the snake,' he proclaimed. 'Thus north and east is apportioned to the male; south and west to the female. Thus man's head soars and his loins slither. Thus everything above the waist is clean and everything below unclean.'

'No part of the body can be unclean. Above the waist is sky which inseminates; below is earth which bears fruit. Thus harmony is achieved,' retorted Branko and Lumnia and dismissed Adam's bile.

In this they were incautious.

Twenty-One

According to a French wit, the fortress-church of Notre-Dame in Les Saintes Maries de la Mer had not been built to protect its congregation from Moorish invasions, as historians had claimed, but to proselytize for Catholicism those souls foolhardy enough to traverse the Camargue in the summer. For this Romanesque citadel, completed in the fifteenth century, was the only place that offered a taste of a cool Paradise in those steaming months.

The fable, Branko thought, had not taken into account the annual pilgrimage in devotion of Saint Mary Jacobé, Saint Mary Salomé and *Sara-i-Kali*, 'Black Sara'. On this night of 23 May, the eve of the first day of homage, the pilgrims, standing vigil with burning candles and virtually inside each other's skins, had turned the church into a breathless, sweltering cage.

Branko, guiding Ariana and Lumnia, followed in Pablo's wake. The latter, kissing the men and the children in his path, or wiping his sweat with the sleeves of his silk shirt, carved a passage down the stairs to the crypt which was home to *Sara-i-Kali*'s statue.

Though his shipping empire and vast wealth had made him an international personality, Pablo Sanchez would always spurn the *gadje*'s affected convenances. Half-Spanish *Gitano*, half-French Kalderash, he was, he claimed, two Gypsies in one; and he went to great pains to make sure that no one would mistake him for a *gadjo*. Thus, for instance, his perspective on body odours: not for him the purgative redolence of colognes, after-shaves, deodorants, but good old-fashioned Gypsy aroma: the natural smell of sun, breeze and perspiration spiced with the scent of a flower, fruit or herb: lavender, lemon, rosemary.

The people on the stairs, seeing that Pablo and his entourage were bringing a new cloak for *Sara-i-Kali*, tried to make way; being so tightly packed they just managed it. This year, portentously, Pablo had said, there were more Gypsy pilgrims than ever.

At the bottom of the stairs, the crowd thinned. On this night, the crypt was restricted to those who would dress Sara for tomorrow's portage and those given the honour to stand vigil by her side.

They entered the crypt.

Ariana and Lumnia lined up behind the women attending to Sara's robes.

Ariana could barely contain herself. This was the place, she had endlessly told Branko – confirming all that Young Glanz and Leo Leo had told him after Melchior's death – where, after his abduction by Pro Juventute, she had tried to come in search of divine intervention. And her failure to perform the pilgrimage had not deterred her: from her burrows in Switzerland, she had kept praying to *Sara-i-Kali* for the miracle that would return Branko to her. And the miracle had happened. Not only once, by reuniting them, ten years ago, when she had all but surrendered to illness and death; but again, now, by delivering her here so that she could personally thank her benefactor. These wondrous events had not only confirmed the depth of Sara's compassion, but also the totality of her commitment to her people and the indefatigable way she kept her ear to the air in order to hear their complaints and help them out.

And, as if these blessings might prove insufficient, Ariana had also been given the privilege of dressing Sara with the exquisite mantle she and Lumnia were carrying. Pablo, whose offering the mantle was, had asked her to perform the ritual as an act that would seal the friendship between their families.

Pablo, moved to tears, pointed at Sara's statue. 'Look how beautiful she is . . .'

Some chroniclers had attributed the statue's burnished colour to the candle-smoke that had been emitted by pilgrims for centuries. Pablo had dismissed the theory. Sara's face, an autumnal brown, had an innate and eternal luminosity, he had declared; she was like a phosphorescent lagoon that for ever preserved the sun's light.

Branko could see what he meant, particularly as Lumnia, possessing similar lambency, bore a close resemblance to the statue's face. 'Beautiful'.

Pablo growled. 'But the *gadje* can't see it. Instead they go and worship the anaemic ones upstairs!'

'The anaemic ones' were the saints Mary Jacobé and Mary Salomé whose relics were housed in the main part of the church.

There were two versions to the legend that told the story of these three women.

The first related that, soon after the Crucifixion, some of Jesus' prominent disciples – Lazarus; Lazarus' sister, Martha; Mary Magdalene; Mary Jacobé, sister of the Virgin and the mother of the apostles Joses and James; Mary Salomé, the mother of two other apostles, James the Elder and John the Evangelist – had been set adrift, on Herod Agrippa's orders, in a boat that had had no sails, oars or rudder. They had been joined by one other person, Sara, an Egyptian servant girl, who had begged to accompany them and whom Mary Salomé had helped into the boat by laying her cloak over the water. Buffeted by winds and waves, this boat had finally gone aground on these shores. Mary Jacobé and Mary Salomé, attended by the faithful Sara, had stayed in the region and founded Les Saintes Maries de la Mer. The others had dispersed across Gaul to spread the Gospel.

In the second version Sara was neither an Egyptian girl nor a servant; nor had she boarded the boat in the Holy Land. She was a fresh-faced Gypsy maiden from a tribe camped at the Rhone delta. Her involvement with the two Maries had occurred when, whilst mending fishing nets by the seashore, she had spotted their foundering boat. Thenceforth, throwing her dress over the waves, she had run across the water and pulled the boat on to the beach.

The first version, Pablo had passionately argued, was a typical example of the *gadje*'s racial prejudice. It denigrated the Gypsy and stole his goodness. But then what was surprising about that? How could people who had turned Christ's love into a religion of oppression entertain the thought of a Gypsy saviour?

Predictably, the two Maries had been canonized. But not Sara.

Equally predictably, the Gypsies had put matters right by adopting Sara as their own saint.

Pablo and Branko, uncovering their feet and heads, moved to the right of the statue and joined the men keeping vigil – among them, Jeannot, Pablo's burly youngest son.

Branko felt soothed by Pablo's presence.

Pablo had become a devotee of Sara in the early '40s, soon after he had been recruited by the Maquis to smuggle arms and personnel between France and Spain.

It had been one particular communion with the saint, on 6 May 1944, that had begun his transformation from a fisherman with a small boat, registered, with typical audacity, on both sides of the French-Spanish border, to a shipping mogul. On that day – significantly, the first day of *Enderlez* – she had actually spoken to him. And she had told Pablo that he had been chosen for matters of great importance, that there would come a day when his people would need to take to the sea and that he would be asked to provide the boats. Fate would assist him.

Duly, after the war, an American airman – a Jew – whom he had smuggled out to safety, had hired him to run guns and refugees to Palestine. After the creation of Israel, he had found himself owning a tramp steamer. In due course he had built a business that had outstripped that of Onassis.

The story of Pablo's communion with Sara had tallied with the portion in the Holy Book which foretold that arrangements for the exodus to Romanestan would be made in Les Saintes Maries de la Mer. Moreover, 6 May 1944 was also the day when the *Urme* had pronounced their prophecy on Branko in Auschwitz.

As it happened, there had been an echo of the prophecy a few days earlier. Branko, accompanied by Ariana and Lumnia, had been strolling on the promenade when a young girl, barely six, therefore still pure in spirit, who had been hawking talismans etched with the traditional image of the Romany – a man holding a rainbow over his head – had stopped him impulsively. Giving him as a present her most expensive medallion, she had declared, in a sonorous voice that could not have been her own, that he would lead his people into the age of rainbows.

It had not taken long for Branko and Pablo to meet. Having heard of the young hawker's pronouncement which, as with all extraordinary rumours, had swept through the town within minutes, Pablo had contrived a meeting. Friendship had blossomed instantly. Thereafter, they had spent long hours on Pablo's yacht, trying to estimate the number of Gypsies likely to embark for Romanestan and the size of the fleet that would be needed to accommodate them. Pablo, after long discussions with his various companies across the world, had reassured Branko:

'You'll have the boats. Whenever and wherever you want them.'

The women in front, having finished draping Sara with their offering, edged away to the left.

Ariana and Lumnia moved forward and proudly showed the statue the cloak they were carrying.

This year there had been twenty new mantles lavished on Sara – all of them gold-embroidered and each a different colour. Pablo's offering, in lagoon-blue silk and designed by a brilliant young couturière, had earned the right to be her outermost garment, the one with which she would appear to the pilgrims.

Lumnia, spreading the cloak over her arms, yielded the more important task of dressing Sara to Ariana.

Ariana draped the statue with immense care, adjusting the cloak delicately over every contour. Now and again, unable to restrain her rapture, she planted kisses on Sara's arms and hands.

As she finished, Sara turned round and smiled at her.

Ariana froze; then, hesitantly, she looked at Lumnia, wondering whether she, too, had witnessed the wonder.

Lumnia edged forward. 'I saw.'

Joyfully, Ariana began to weep.

Lumnia whispered. 'See if she'll talk to you.'

Ariana, her legs trembling, shuffled closer to the statue.

Sara fixed her gaze on her.

Ariana kneeled before the statue. 'Thank you for everything, my lady.'

Sara stroked her face. 'You have undertaken the worst pain in the world.'

'What is that?'

'A mother's suffering.'

'But what is life for a woman if she cannot be a mother?'

Sara wrapped her arms around Ariana and rocked her like a baby. 'A mother should die before her son, before she witnesses all that will befall him. That is Nature's preference.'

'Will it not be the same for me?'

A tear ran down Sara's face. 'May you always be strong.'

'I will be. With your help.'

Sara nodded.

Lumnia helped with the last touches, then led Ariana to the side. As they, too, started keeping vigil, their eyes spoke.

'Did you hear her, Lumnia?'

'I did.'

'Did you understand?'

'The prophecy is irreversible.'

'Yes.'

'We knew that, Dei.'

'So terrifying – to know for sure.'

'I have not had the chance to open my heart to you, Dei. There was the wedding. Then the rush to get here. I want you to know: I will be a good wife. As good as I am allowed to be.'

'No one can ask for more.'

'And I will be a good daughter. And I will always be *your* daughter. Always. No matter what happens along the way.'

'Do you know what will happen?'
'I have a sense of it. I'd rather not look.'
'I understand. I have a sense of it, too.'
'We must be strong, Dei.'
'When are we not, daughter?'

At three in the afternoon, a winch began to lower the reliquaries of Saint Marie Jacobé and Saint Marie Salomé from the chapel high above the chancel.

The congregation rocked and shouted: '*Vivent les Saintes Maries!*'

Thus the veneration of Saint Marie Jacobé and Saint Marie Salomé began. Though this day, 24 May, was not, in effect, their day, their status had imposed invocatory devotions.

Those near the winch snuffed their long tapers on the base of the reliquaries, a deed that was said to guarantee good luck and good health. Those further away turned towards the shrine at the left of the nave which displayed the wooden, painted statue of the two Maries in their boat. Invalids cast ardent looks at the plaques on the wall which expressed gratitude from those miraculously healed by the saints.

Branko, sweat running down his face, glanced at Lumnia. They had not slept for thirty-six hours; yet she looked as if she had just alighted from a star.

Do my people want me? Can I really save my people?

The congregation became restive. Pablo kept his eyes on the stairs leading to the crypt. Any minute now, the statue of *Sara-i-Kali* would be brought for its procession to the sea.

Ariana, still in a trance, exuded both happiness and sadness.

The winch stopped. The reliquaries were down. Acolytes detached them from their garlanded ropes and placed them on a table in the transept.

Branko peered at the reliquaries: two rectangular cabinets of cypress, shaped like early medieval churches. The one facing him had *Ste Marie Jacobé* written on its pyramidal roof. The painting on its side depicted the two Maries, dressed, respectively, in red and blue flowing robes, grounded on a beach. The red-robed Marie was stepping off the boat; the other had already disembarked and was on her knees, praying.

The painting conjured a memory: he, as a child, standing on a colourful clothes trunk, playing drums on Mihal's bald head while Ariana laughed heartily. Mihal, that tender man, my first foster-father.

Strange how, since Yerko's death, memories surfaced with astounding regularity. But though memories rooted him to life, he felt amnesia might be the better option. Memories, imbued with sadness, as they invariably were, merely confirmed that existence was always punctuated by tragedies.

My people are my children. I'll save them. I'll give meaning to my death.

A gasp resonating like bells escaped the congregation.

Sara-i-Kali, vested in her new cloaks and with Pablo's offering as her outermost clothing, emerged on a pallet carried by Pablo's young son, Jeannot, and three other Gypsies – all four ecstatic at having been chosen as Sara's bearers.

Pablo, a simple man bared open to his very core, began to weep. Jeannot, as he had sorrowfully related, was the only member of his family who had remained a Gypsy. The others, three sons, four daughters and three ex-wives, had all strayed into *gadje* ways: drink, gambling, promiscuity and sloth. Victims of Pablo's indulgence; and of the white man's indifference to spirituality. Sad souls whom he still, periodically, had to bail out.

Sara-i-Kali was carried out of the church.

The congregation – with Pablo once again showing Branko how to shove people aside – followed.

As the statue emerged on to the square outside the church, the crowd burst into fervent shouts of '*Vive Sara! Vive la Sainte des Gitanes!*'

The quaternion bells began to toll. Lodged in the triangular roofs of a belfry that rose like a poop over the church's round, caravel-shaped front, they celebrated the auspicious journey that had brought the saints to these shores.

Hands stretched towards Sara's statue.

Kisses blown at it rested on the dark face like another glow.

The children, raised above their parents' heads to receive her blessing, acquired the paragon's serene smile.

The procession formed. Those who had pilgrimaged regularly took the lead. Some carried a large wooden cross bedecked with flowers and ribbons; others held up a banner embroidered with the image of a Bible protecting a caravan.

Pablo, dragging Branko with him, joined this vanguard group. Other pilgrims aligned behind.

Then the acolytes, bearing candles and the church's processional cross, took their places. They were followed by the parish priest and visiting clergy. Then came *Sara-i-Kali*'s pallet, held shoulder-high by its bearers.

Finally, the women and children, Lumnia and Ariana among them, aligned behind the float. Apart from protecting Sara's sacred purity by creating a safe distance between men and women, they were ready to straighten her mantles should the wind disarrange them.

Now, some dozen *Gardiens*, ranchers of the Camargue who traditionally served as Sara's escort, took charge. Dressed in light trousers and black jackets and hats, carrying tridents, and mounted on white horses that were native to the region, they carved a path for the procession.

The cavalcade eased along the town's narrow streets.

The pilgrims chanted the traditional paean:

'We've come to you, O saints of Provence!

A whole great people to pray at your knees!'

They proceeded to the seafront.

Branko gazed at the tourists and spectators lining the streets. *Gadje* – all of them. Even the weathered ones had pallor beneath their skins. Staring, caught between sympathy and antipathy, as if the Gypsies were freaks. But behind the ambivalence, there was lust. From white men for Gypsy women – sometimes for Gypsy men. And from white women for Gypsy men. A hunger that could not be appeased because it had detached itself from the soul. A hunger Branko still remembered from his time in the *gadje* world.

The procession reached the promenade. The cars and caravans which had made the roads impassable all week had been removed to special sites.

Tourists teemed.

The *Gardiens*' horses, invigorated by the sea breeze, strained to gallop towards the beach.

The pilgrims' exhortations became frenzied.

Branko felt elated. The inexhaustible felicity of Gypsies! A nation of children commissioned to map the boundaries of abandon. Look at them greeting and embracing each other.

'I find you with God.'

'Go with God.'

They had one law: to live! Decently – if at all possible. He remembered Yerko, giving him fatherly advice: 'Always help your brother. Never harm him. Pay your debts – if you have no money, give your labour. Fear no one, not even yourself.'

My people! My destiny!

They reached the beach. The procession fanned out.

The sea, choppy in the distance, but tamed by the breakwaters, gently frothed like a visitation of white flowers. The heat haze undulated over the water.

The *Gardiens*, stirring their horses, cantered out into the sea and formed two parallel lines.

The Gypsies spread out; many of them waded into the water.

Tourists and other pilgrims spilled on to the beach.

First, the garlanded cross, then Sara's pallet were carried to the sea.

Pablo, dragging Branko by the arm, waded after the bearers and approached the statue.

Priests and acolytes led the prayers.

Pablo dipped his hand in the water and sprinkled Sara. Branko, following his example, wondered about the symbolism of immersion. Did it represent birth? And rebirth?

Time passed. A moment and an eternity.

The *Gardiens* spurred their horses out of the water.

The bearers of the garlanded cross and Sara's float followed suit.

Impulsively, Branko slipped away from Pablo and, unconcerned about getting his shirt and trousers wet, swam out.

Treading water at a distance, he watched the pageant. It was leaving the promenade. It would snake back to the church and return Sara to her crypt.

Tomorrow, there would be another portage to the sea. On that occasion, Saint Marie Jacobé and Saint Marie Salomé would be honoured; and the statue showing them in their boat would undergo the symbolical immersion. Though many Gypsies would offer their devotions, the event, in the main, would be a *gadje* celebration.

Branko decided he would not stay for that ritual. Like Pablo, he did not much care for the Maries. They were white man's saints. Whereas the one spurned by the *gadje*, Black Sara, was now part of his being.

The sun was setting. The promenade had emptied of pilgrims. But tourists still milled about.

Branko swam back.

As he clambered on to the beach, Lumnia whispered, 'I'm here.' She was sitting on the sand.

He sat next to her. 'Forgive me, I disappeared into my mind.'

She smiled. 'I know.'

'Where's Dei?'

'She went back to the church. To stay with Sara.'

Branko smiled. 'That's Dei – guardian angel to saints.'

'She spoke to her, you know . . . Sara did . . .'

He stared at her. 'What did she say?'

'The prophecy is immutable.'

Branko nodded, then shivered.

Lumnia guided his head on to her lap.

Somewhere, the Gypsies' refrain rose into the air: '*A whole great people . . .*'

Lumnia stroked his hair. 'Hear that?'

Branko's eyes moistened. 'There's a passage in the Gypsy Bible . . . Those who ate the fruit of the Tree of the Knowledge of Good and Evil sinned not because they disobeyed God, but because by eating the fruit, they destroyed the wholeness of Paradise . . .'

And the Porajmos, which sought to destroy a whole great people, failed.

I, Branko, Bear-Tamer, escaped and delivered myself unto the wilderness where Saviours are forged.

But the wilderness teems with Sacy-Perères, mountebanks who lure souls with ice-eyed bindweed which causes oblivion and decay.

And I became captive of the Sacy-Perères and forgot the purpose of my existence.

But when creating Saviours, O Del also creates saviours of Saviours.

And so I, Branko, Bear-Tamer, Saviour, was sent my own saviour: the Romany people.

They came and sang songs of camp-fires and verdant lands, of births and deaths and rebirths.

And I remembered I carried a prophecy.

I went in search of it.

I came upon Mandorla, the vulva-shaped halo.

She spoke to me, in the manner of an oracle, in two voices, one affirming, the other disclaiming.

She said, 'Take up your Saviour's sceptre!' And she said, 'Indulge in pleasure!'

She said, 'Man cannot live outside his tribe!' And she said: 'Man must abandon his tribe as he must abandon his mother and father!'

She said, 'Sire a great people!' And she said, 'Spill your seed, else you will bury the children you have fathered!'

I seized her by her mystical almond and begged. 'Do not confuse me!'

And I saw she was Parvati, the Black Virgin.

And my confusion dispersed.

Twenty-Two

The special council took place in the *Vesh*.

The turn-out, everybody agreed, would be chronicled even by the *gadje*. There were chieftains from all over the world; and observers from many organizations, both overt and secret; and even a sprinkling of blanched Roms who served the *gadje* as informers. They were all admitted; no Gypsy could be denied admission to a special council.

One came disguised in rough clothes and lurked in the shadows: Leo Leo.

Another, Pablo Sanchez, remained incognito at Branko's request.

A bounteous *patshiv* started the day. Those elders who had recently died or could not come were remembered and toasted.

When everybody had eaten and drunk enough, Hanro sat on the high chair which had served his tribe, for generations, as the throne of justice. He had been invited to judge the proceedings by virtue of his legendary impartiality; and, by accepting this role, he had transformed the meeting into a *kriss*, the Romany judicature.

The person on trial was the *gadjo*.

Since he could not be brought to take the stand and defend himself, and, in any case, had to be counted in millions, the *kriss'* verdict would lack immediate applicability.

But, Branko, as the appointed plaintiff, had declared that the pronouncement would still be momentous. Redemption always started with a judgement; and the judgement of this *kriss* would herald the Romanies' golden age. If there were doubters, he had challenged, they need but touch the air; they would find it urgent with the desire for change and fragrant with the cardamom-taste of hope.

287

The elders assembled to the right of Hanro. Their women gathered behind them. Some lit candles to warm the spirits of ancestors who might be present.

The *drabarnis* and the *phuri dais* – among them Lumnia, Hanro's wife, *Bibi*, and Ariana – stood next to the elders.

The rest of the men and women – every one of whom had the right to testify – and the children – who could give evidence only as eye-witnesses – thronged to Hanro's left.

A large rock draped with a red silk cloth stood at the centre as the altar of justice; figurines of Hindu gods, icons of the Madonna and Child and talismans against the Evil Eye adorned it.

In an ordinary *kriss*, defendants and witnesses would have stopped by this rock and sworn to tell the truth. On this occasion, since the *gadjo* was not present and, in any case, would never be bound by Gypsy oaths, the altar would serve as a totem of Gypsy probity.

Hanro offered the traditional courtesies to the elders and men of consequence. Then he poured wine on the earth in honour of the ancestral spirits and asked death to vacate the deliberations as night vacates the day at dawn.

And the elders exchanged forgiveness for wrongdoings in the past.

Hanro started the disputation: Mikhail Gorbachev's policies of *glasnost* and *perestroika* had galvanized the communist world. But all over Eastern Europe, demands for democracy had impelled the respective governments to sterner measures. Since any move towards repression always threatened the Gypsies, those present had to read the signs for the future.

Branko took the floor. Recounting the 'hunt' which had killed Yerko, Ileana and Ileana's baby, he accused the *gadje* of recommencing genocidal activities against the Gypsies.

Omar reported on Yugoslavia. There were indications that the League of Communists, the Federation's sole authorized party, was losing ground to nationalist elements. The Serbian chief, Slobodan Milošević, was campaigning to integrate the autonomous provinces of Kosovo and Vojvodina with Serbia. In pursuit of this objective, he was prepared to disenfranchise the provinces' ethnic communities – Albanians and Gypsies in Kosovo; and Hungarians, Slovaks, Croats, Gypsies, Romanians and Ruthenians in Vojvodina. Milošević was also eyeing Macedonia, where there were sizeable Gypsy and Albanian communities as well as a large Turkish minority. Moreover, a reciprocal call for a Greater Croatia, to be created by the annexation of Bosnia-Herzegovina – where the Muslims, at 40 per cent, were the largest single group – was being made by Franjo Tudjman, a revisionist historian noted for works which whitewashed the reign of terror of the wartime Nazi puppet state run by the Ustaša. Goaded by these developments, a movement for independence was gaining ground in Slovenia, politically and economically Yugoslavia's most progressive republic. A growing number of voices warned that these rival nationalists could dismantle the Yugoslav Federation and, in the process, unleash brutal wars between its republics as they, in turn, sought independence. The first to suffer in such a situation, Omar concluded, would be the Gypsies; they would either be caught in the crossfire or be crimped as cannon-fodder or simply be rounded up for deportation or execution.

Sasha, the legendary balalaika-maker, a chief from Odessa, spoke next. A frail octogenarian, he was said to have coaxed all the songs of the unjustly slain out of the earth. Declaring that the situation was equally perilous in the USSR, he cited numerous instances where the democratization process was speedily disinterring old enmities between the Soviet Union's bevy of nations. As yet, the Gypsies had not been specifically targeted. At a cursory glance, the 1953 laws which prohibited nomadic life appeared to have improved their status; the famous *Romany Theatre* and numerous publications in Romanes corroborated the official line that Gypsies were accepted as an ethnic minority. In reality, however, they remained outcasts. Moreover, the resurgence of anti-Semitism, particularly in Russia and the Ukraine, was ominous: attacks on Jews always presaged doom for other scapegoats – with Gypsies invariably the next target.

Then Sylwester, a tall, ascetic elder, spoke. He was a wood sculptor from Krakow whose statuettes of the Suffering Jesus had become collectors' pieces. He declared he had forebodings, too. Programmes of forced settlement had fanned the Poles' historic prejudice against Gypsies: whole communities were in conflict; many Gypsies faced loss of citizenship. Most dishearteningly, popular support for Solidarity's struggle for democracy showed scant concern for the Gypsies' plight.

Another elder, Ernst of Zwickau, reported that prejudice had escalated into violence in some parts of East Germany. A red-cheeked, big-framed car mechanic with shoulders reputedly able to carry a thousand crosses, he listed instances where the resurgence of anti-Semitism had fuelled racial hatred and unleashed attacks on Gypsies, causing serious injury and loss of property; some influential voices even bewailed the fact that the Nazis had failed to rid the world of the Gypsy plague.

Ismail, a fisherman with a barnacled face, who had escaped from his native

Albania by swimming to Yugoslavia, spoke next. He reported that the harsh programme for the obligatory assimilation of Albanian Gypsies, decreed by Enver Hoxha, was still the basis for unbridled persecution.

The dapper Sandor, 'King of Smugglers', reputedly wilier than a conference of foxes, hence, despite his youth, already a *vataf*, disclosed that human rights violations against Gypsies were on the increase in Hungary; in some provinces, Romanies were excluded from public places and, often, openly attacked.

Janosh, Sandor's cousin – and partner – from Bratislava, apprised the gathering that, in Czechoslovakia, Gypsy women were being coerced into sterilization. And incidents of teenage gangs terrorizing Gypsies – and sometimes killing them – had taken on epidemic proportions.

From Bulgaria, Yordan, a shepherd seemingly hewn from a slab of granite, revealed that the campaign for the systematic assimilation of the Gypsies, launched in the mid-1950s, had turned into a policy of overt discrimination; the restriction of social, legal and political rights was now prevalent everywhere in the country.

The *vataf*, Marcu, the black-marketeer from Arad, spoke next. Recognizable anywhere in Eastern Europe by his immaculate leather coats and fedora hats, he was revered as a just man. He had saved countless Gypsies from trumped-up charges by bribing officials with his seemingly inexhaustible supply of dollars. As an addendum to Branko's ordeal of the 'hunt', he confirmed that the pursuit of 'ritual purification' – a euphemism for brutal discrimination – was still part of the Romanian communal will. Many Gypsies had already been driven away from their villages and smallholdings.

The patriarchal Andres, an affluent chicken-farmer and a Sinti chief from Bavaria, stated that, though the situation was better in West European democracies, the pariah status was still the norm. In Federal Germany, for instance, immigrant and itinerant Gypsies were being corralled and processed, with total insensitivity, in wartime labour camps or disused toxic waste dumps.

The elders Miguel, Aleko, Ferdinand and Wilfred reported that persecution against Gypsies had dramatically increased in their respective countries.

In southern Spain, there had been a number of killings which had looked very much like lynchings.

In Greece, the authorities dealing with social concerns, such as health, education and housing, were increasingly ignoring their Gypsy charges.

In France and the UK, Gypsies were being subjected to callous and cynical restrictions on matters of travel and camping sites.

In all those countries, demands by high-ranking officials for 'a final solution' – not a malapropism this, but a deliberate reference to the phrase's Hitlerite connotation – had become commonplace.

Even in the distant US, where, after the Balkan wars, and again after the *Porajmos*, large numbers of Gypsies had emigrated, discrimination was rife. Chuck, the owner of a fast-food chain, sadly confirmed that all Romanies, even those prosperous like himself, met harassment at every turn.

The gathering had become restive and dispirited.

To give them – and himself – time to digest the evidence, Hanro adjourned until the afternoon.

When the *kriss* resumed, Hanro pronounced his judgement: 'The *gadjo* hasn't changed since the war. He still considers us creatures who are biologically criminal – in Hitlerite terms, *lives not worthy of life*. He still advocates permanent solutions. This threatens another *Porajmos*.' He directed his gaze at the representatives from the West. 'Some of you, believing there is salvation in integration, have put your faith in the new political climate. Others have discoloured themselves with city hues and turned into counterfeit *gadje*. Yet others, rejecting our culture, eke out a *marimé* existence in chinks and holes and under floorboards. The rest, trapped in wastelands, unseen and unknown, simply wait for death.' Age deserted Hanro; his voice thundered: 'What price survival? – that is the question you must ask! Do we carry on in this manner until the next – the truly final – *Porajmos*? Do we assimilate – assuming the *gadjo* would allow such profanity – and live, at best, in a culture of invisibility, but, in truth, as dust among other dust? Or do we, at long last, strike out for freedom?' He pointed at Branko. 'Here is a man who claims to have the answer.'

Branko took the floor and contemplated the souls of the assembled.

Some heard him say: 'I am you.'

Others thought he said: 'You are me.'

He summoned Lumnia. She came and unlocked the hearts.

The kriss spoke in Branko's voice:

'We can tame bears and horses.'

'We can colour the universe with songs and poems.'

'We can smith every metal.'

'We know Nature's language.'

Then the kriss spoke in the voices of the ancestors:

'For hundreds of years, they hunted us.'

'Bought and sold us.'

'Broke our backs in ships as galley slaves.'

'Transported our women to populate colonies.'

'Forbade us homes, farms, work, literacy, peaceful existence.'

'Finally, they slaughtered us.'

'In villages and fields, forests and roadsides.'

'In Auschwitz-Birkenau, Belzec, Bergen-Belsen, Buchenwald, Chelmno, Dachau, Deutmergen, Flossenberg, Gross-Rosen, Gusen, Jasenovac, Lackenbach, Lety, Łodz, Maidenek, Mauthausen, Mittelbau Dora, Natzweiler, Neuengamme, Niederhagen, Ravensbruck, Rechlin, Sachsenhausen, Sobibor, Stutthof, Theresienstadt, Treblinka, Zemun, Zwodau.'

'Yet we are still here!'

'Still revering life!'

'We can germinate in death.'

'We can be our own mothers and fathers.'

'We have the strength to dream.'

'And the will to abolish divisions, inequality, castes.'

'And the courage to keep faith.'

'Therefore, we can reunite the tribes.'

Omar came forward and stood next to Branko. 'Remember the prophecy!' The kriss shouted. 'The burst pomegranate can be made whole.'

And Branko said: 'It will be so. We will be a people, a nation!'

Now the kriss spoke in the voices of their children: 'To be a nation, we need land.'

'Land that gives us suck!'

'Land that courses in our blood.'

'Land where our music, our rainbow and its colours and our joy of being alive can roam freely!'

Lumnia came forward and made the air verdant. 'Remember the prophecy!'

The kriss shouted: 'Hope will run down the mountains and stream to the sea; then it will set sail and become earth.'

And Branko said: 'Hope has come down the mountains. It is ready to stream to the sea. Before long it will set sail and become Romanestan!'

Ariana came forward and laid the Romany flag upon the winds. 'Remember the prophecy!'

The kriss shouted: 'A new tree will sprout the leaves the donkey ate.'

And Branko said: 'We have a new tree! And it has sprouted those same leaves!'

And the kriss asked in the voices of the unborn: 'Do they contain the Word?'

Branko strode to the altar of justice. 'Yes, and the Word is with me. I have reclaimed the Holy Book. We have our Bible!'

Fathers and mothers came and stood by him: Todor, Zara, Eloïse, Melchior, Mihal, Ramzi, Ilyas, Dr Kalderon, Yerko, Ileana, Ileana's baby.

Branko brought out an ambery stone from his rucksack and placed it on the altar. 'Here is a tablet. Were we prophets ourselves, we would have written this same Bible. It does not carry a single portion that preaches killing, submission or conversion by force.'

He took out some scrolls and laid them also on the altar. 'Here are some pages I have restored.'

An awesome power, palpable, like the pulse of a drift running to avalanche, seized the meeting.

The people stared at the exhibits. And saw scraps of paper, strips of cloth and leather, some no bigger than postage stamps — all of them containing a piece of text — pasted on to the scrolls in the manner of a collage.

And the writing took on life; the letters sprouted, wide and tall as ancestral gods.

A voice, Leo Leo's, shouted: 'The Holy Book doesn't exist! This is a forgery!'

But no one heeded him.

Branko, the Scribe, blood gushing out of his castration, came forward. 'In Auschwitz, O Del came up to me. You will reclaim the Book which contains your people's existence, even their past, present and future, He said. Here, where my children are being exterminated, you will create the matrix for a new generation, He said. And He recited the Book. And I wrote it down.' He pointed at the scrolls. 'Here it is. Every word!'

The kriss wept joyously:

'The Book will be our banner.'

'And our anthem!'

'It will forge us!'

'Lead us to Romanestan!'

Again Leo Leo shouted: 'Romanestan does not exist!'

Again no one heeded him.

Branko, the Scribe resumed. 'A Holy Book always comes with its defender.' He pointed at Branko. 'The Bear-Tamer will keep our enemies at bay.'

Once more, Leo Leo shouted: 'All defenders are false prophets! They cannot die alone. So they force their followers to die with them!'

Still no one heeded him.

Branko held out his arms. 'Renounce the gadje religions. We have our own Bible.'

A light, emanating from Branko's eyes, enveloped the gathering; they became invisible to all but each other.

That night, the gods of wind and electricity raged.

It was natural that there should be a storm, Lumnia declared: the flashes that turned night into silvery day, the heavens which growled and roared like centuries of anger, were simply the echoes of Branko's exhortations earlier that afternoon.

'Will anybody join us?'

Lumnia, brewing mugwort tea, shook her head impatiently. 'You doubt too much, my Rom.'

Branko paced the lounge, gazing at the shelves which were packed with souvenirs from various countries. They were in Omar's house. The bard, insisting that they should have some privacy, had gone to stay with a friend. Ariana had gone with him.

'Who'd want to be a prophet?'

Lumnia stirred the tea. 'No one. That's why they're chosen.'

'Success carries the seed of failure, Yerko used to say.'

'That's true.'

'Why am I bothering, then?'

Lumnia mixed honey into the tea. 'That's how the future is built. Someone forges a season, but fails to create another because that's someone else's work. Same with that someone else. And so on.'

'Building the future with *gadjo* strategy. That's what's galling! Singing the evil song of nationalism! Feeding milk of paranoia! How do I justify the jingoism, the brainwashing?'

Lumnia poured the mugwort tea. 'It's for a short time – that's what you said.'

'But you do see, don't you, without some sort of foundation – a basic notion of national identity – we don't stand a chance. Nationhood elicits respect, guarantees dignity, promises survival. It's the magnet we need to ingather the people. But beyond that . . .'

Lumnia handed him his cup. 'We'll have Romanestan. We won't need notions of national identity. We'll have abandoned them. That's what you've always maintained . . .'

'How do I hold my head high until then? How do I keep spewing such nonsense as "purity of blood", "superiority", "demands of history", without feeling like an everyday Croat or Serb? What of morality?'

'Pray she forgives us.'

'You think she would? And come and break bread with us morning, noon and night?'

'Yes. When we're in Romanestan.'

'If I fail . . .'

'You won't.' She guided him to the table where he had laid out the tablets and scrolls of the Holy Book. 'Work a bit. It will dispel all your doubts.'

He sighed and sat down.

He inspected the fragment he had retouched earlier. The paper was yellow with age. The lower half had been stained by a liquid that had turned brown. Blood?

Carefully, he pasted the paper onto a scroll.

He contemplated the other fragments. The writing in many of them had so faded as to be barely visible. Restoring them would be painstaking; it would also take a long time.

He picked up his old fountain pen, a gift from Yerko, and began tracing the letters of one of the fragments.

He worked feverishly.

When he stopped, Lumnia came and massaged his shoulders. He felt peevish. He had forgotten about her. 'Guess what this bit's about?'

'What?'

'Lumnia, resolved that Branko would return safely from this dangerous mission, wove her magic and implanted her duende into his body. A duende, as it is known, is the soul's soul; once it enters a host, it inhabits it for ever.'

'Imagine – I'm in the Bible . . .'

'Where else, Branko's wife?'

Lumnia kissed him.

Branko cleaned the nib of his pen. 'An easy portion, this was. I wrote it in a trance. But then, I was saturated with you . . .'

She sat on the sofa and made him lie down with his head on her lap. 'How long did it take you to gather the Book?'

'A year. Maybe two. Maybe ten.' He snuggled to her breasts. 'I sometimes fear I might die before I finish it.'

She pressed him against her. 'Stop doubting!'

He closed his eyes.

She lullabied him with the ballad Omar had composed for their wedding. By tradition, it would remain their exclusive property; unless they bequeathed it to the people, it would die with them.

'Before the sun and the moon and the stars
before the earth and the trees and the fire
we bind our flesh.
We are two souls in one body
true water
lies
only
in our well.'

The torrential rain lasted six days. Up and down the countryside, the Vardar burst its banks. Another downpour, an elder was heard saying, and Skopje would become a submerged city, like old Orşova on the Danube, sacrificed to the Iron Gates Dam.

Throughout those days, Branko, Omar, Lumnia and Ariana waited under the acacia trees for volunteers.

Some forty young men and women joined them. So did Hanro, who had abdicated as *vataf*, and his wife, *Bibi*, the *phuri dai*.

Pablo Sanchez, too, asked to join; but Branko dissuaded him. When the time came, he would organize the boats; consequently, he was needed on the sidelines.

The rest of the Gypsies allowed the rains to sweep away their resolve. Or, as rumours went, they had been swayed by visions of assimilation disseminated by a leonine man.

On the seventh day, the skies rested.

It was time to depart for the wilderness.

Branko assembled his followers; they mustered fifty exactly. He felt despondent. 'Hardly a whole people.'

Omar remained cheerful. 'We have you. You count as a whole people.'

Lumnia burned some twigs. Occasionally throwing salt on the embers and causing them to flare, she read the flames. 'We start with fifty. When we reach the sea, we will number a million.'

It was time for the Romanies to extinguish the ageing fires and build new ones.

And so Branko laid his hands over the old hearths and absorbed the flames of times past and the wisdom and miracles they contained.

For seven days, the people ate cold food; and Branko was satisfied that all the old fires had been extinguished.

First he took up the root of a mandrake which is shaped like a man; then he picked up a laurel branch which carries the scent of Heaven.

He rubbed the mandrake root with the laurel branch until the latter ignited.

From the laurel's tongue of flame, he raised the new fires, thus ensuring the health of the people and the wellbeing of their beasts.

PART EIGHT

Twenty-Three

They left Macedonia near Trgoviste and proceeded north through Serbia.

At country lanes all along Leskovac, Niš, Zaječar, Bor and Negotin, they deposited sprinklings of *patrin* so that those who might join them later could find them.

Wishing to prime his modest complement into a core that would be able to deal with any emergency – and, in case of his death, have the capability to continue without him – Branko imposed a schedule that would have tested even seasoned soldiers.

They trekked – mostly at night.

They camped in locations where the spirits of the place, duly honoured by Lumnia's libations and incantations, sheltered them heartily.

Injuries occurred. Lumnia cured most of these with her repertoire of potions, poultices and unguents.

People with serious conditions such as broken bones, deep wounds and infectious diseases were treated by Branko by the laying on of his hands. They, too, recovered swiftly. For, no sooner had Branko returned to the wilderness than he regained the healing powers with which he had restored Yerko's sight.

Five weeks later, they traversed into Romania.

The Zlatari who smuggled them across the Danube joined them.

On the fortieth day, in the Almãjului mountains, Branko's followers crowned him *Vataf*.

First they built a throne of stones.

Briefly, they seated Omar on it. Awed by his readiness to abandon fame and fortune for the Gypsy cause, the company had elected him, unanimously, as the *false chief.*

He would, however, continue composing; he had also been elected the people's bard.

They summoned Branko and stripped him to his underwear.

They pierced his ear and fitted a platinum earring.

They dressed him up in a regalia that reflected the sky's many hues: a cyanic silk shirt, cut open at the front to show his bare chest; wide hyacinthine trousers held by a purse-belt of copper mesh; high boots of ultramarine leather into which the bottoms of the trousers could be stuffed; an azure waistcoat; a thick gold chain bedecked with sapphire talismans against the evil eye; an indigo game-bag; a turquoise jacket with broad brass buttons; and a big cerulean hat that looked like a Stetson and had been specially designed for a chieftain who, by tradition – and, graciously, by the will of Fate – always had a strikingly large head.

Hanro, who had inherited Ilyas' *bareski rovli rupui,* now handed the silver sceptre to the new *Vataf.*

Branko swore to serve his people with devotion.

They sat him on the stone throne.

Ilyas' spirit touched his shoulders in approval.

Omar dishevelled his hair.

Ariana anointed him with orris oil.

Lumnia waxed his chieftain's moustache.

The ensuing days produced extraordinary signs.

In the first instance, O Del appeared to Branko in a dream and instructed him that he must now attain the full stature of a Saviour.

The next morning, Branko withdrew to a mountain lake and, immersing himself in icy waters, acquired an indomitable cortex.

Throughout this process he remained in communion with the Deity.

He returned forty days later, looking as if he had doubled in size. His moustache, as befitted a Saviour, trailed the ground.

In the second instance, Ariana developed a set of stigmata on her palms.

Their appearance did not shock her; having distrusted the temperateness of her additional years as unnatural – years stolen for her by that gentlest of sons, Young Glanz – she had been waiting for adversity to make a furious comeback.

She showed the stigmata to Lumnia.

Lumnia felt perturbed. 'You've been chosen as Fate's chronicler, Dei.'

Ariana was astonished. 'Am I strong enough?'

'You must be.'

'What do they represent – the markings?'

Lumnia studied the stigmata. 'The left palm normally contains the secrets of a person's life. But what you have is Branko's portrait. Look carefully at the discoloration – the shades outline his features.'

Ariana shivered. 'Oh, yes . . .'

'The right palm is showing an hour-glass. The purple stain at its centre is like sand – it indicates the passage of time. Do you see?'

Ariana nodded. 'Can you read them?'

Lumnia, though tempted to espy the future, diligently obeyed the law that forbade a *drabarni* from irresponsible acts. 'I mustn't intrude on Fate's domain.'

That night, Ariana went into a trance and consulted Sara-i-Kali.

The saint pronounced that the stigmata would chronicle the rest of Branko's time on earth. The portrait would manifest the state of his mind and heart; the hour-glass would count down his days.

And she endowed Ariana with the vision to read the stigmata.

In the third instance, Lumnia began to perceive the *Urme*, the Angels of Destiny.

They appeared, all nine of them, whenever the trek became arduous.

Mostly, they hovered around Branko and, in the main, comported themselves like responsible guardians. But a few of them betrayed signs of complacency. Thus, whilst the Sisters of Health, Ability and Courage maintained exemplary concentration, those of Life, Wisdom, Strength and Love strayed their glances like women seeking the tinsels of adultery. And though the Sister of Luck behaved as if she never discriminated between Branko and Omar, Lumnia's unerring eye detected many signs which indicated that, in reality, She continued to dote on Omar.

The Sister of Fertility kept her distance.

Yet there were moments, Lumnia noted, when that most inscrutable *Urme* smiled at her conspiratorially as if to reassure her, behind the others' back, that her breasts would not remain unharvested for ever, that, one day, the disuse of her womb would be commuted. Much as Lumnia considered these observations the fantasies of a woman protesting the forfeiture of motherhood, she came to accept that, despite her vows to Branko, she had not entirely resigned herself to childlessness. Thus when a man crossed her path, she invariably saw him in her mind's eye as the possessor of a scrotum that was bursting with seeds; and she wished – prayed – for a discreet miracle that would enable her to wrest from him a drop of sturdy semen. Indeed, often she was tempted to defy Fate, to rush out and solicit Luck, even boldly force Her hand – perhaps by brazenly rubbing herself against Omar, stealing a measure of his good fortune and, by so doing, giving her eggs the chance to find one of those few live sperm Branko was thought to be carrying.

Naturally, she constantly admonished herself for entertaining such unclean thoughts. But her loins refused to be censured; every reverie opened her up eagerly, unashamedly – even ferociously.

More people joined them.

By the time they reached Transylvania, where they would winter, they numbered over seven hundred.

On the first day of autumn, a bear walked into the encampment.

The people agitated. They could not understand how the animal could have penetrated their defences or skirted round the horses tethered to the outer ring of trees without disturbing them.

Omar and a number of young men closed ranks and tried to send it on its way; since, like all Gypsies, they revered bears, they did not want to harm it.

The bear, unperturbed, ambled forward. Now and again, it stopped and inspected the buckets of water and the heaps of dirt which stood ready to extinguish camp-fires that might turn hazardous.

Branko, who had been restoring a fragment of the Gypsy Bible, heard the commotion and ran out of his tent. When he spotted the bear, he beamed. 'Honeypaw!'

Growling and showing no sign that it knew Branko, the bear proceeded towards him.

Omar and his men blocked its way.

Branko gestured them back. 'Leave him be!'

Omar and his men moved aside, but stood ready to intervene.

Branko approached the bear. 'Honeypaw! It's me! I told you I'd be back!'

The bear scrutinized him impassively.

Branko moved nearer. 'It's me, you dimwit! Branko! Don't you recognize me?'

The bear rose on its haunches threateningly.

For a moment, Branko wondered whether he was deluding himself. But he could not have mistaken Honeypaw's waddle: like someone who had put his right foot into the left shoe and the left foot into the right one. 'Honeypaw, you bonehead! What are you playing at?'

The bear roared, then swiped at Branko and knocked him down.

Omar charged at the bear.

The bear began to dance.

Omar paused uncertainly.

Branko, pulling himself off the ground, burst into laughter.

The bear began laughing, too.

Branko clasped him. 'Honeypaw, you bastard!'

Honeypaw licked Branko's hands and face.

Branko stroked him. 'You took your time finding me! What's the matter – do I smell differently?'

Honeypaw shook his head, almost in tears.

Branko punched him. 'Want to wrestle?'

Honeypaw nodded happily.

They grappled.

The people formed a circle.

Branko and Honeypaw wrestled the whole day.

Late autumn, they set up camp high up in the Fāgāraṣului mountains.

Whilst Omar supervised the storage of provisions, Branko, attended by Lumnia, sat outside his tent so that those who had complaints could come to him and petition their cases.

And the people came and kissed his hands. Instead of airing dissatisfaction, they told him that all was well with them, that they had never in their lives felt so fulfilled, that, at last, they could believe they were truly a free people and, therefore, ready to enter Romanestan.

Their faces, reflecting the tenor of their words, shone like spray from waterfalls. And they wished him and Lumnia all possible joy; above all, many children.

On the night of one such day, Branko and Lumnia lay down for their inexhaustible journey into each other.

As if caressing running water, they ran their hands and lips softly over each other's bodies. They affirmed, as they had every night and morning since their first conjoining on St George's Day, that they had remained indissoluble; surely eternity would acknowledge the wholeness of their love and place it, after their deaths, as a double sun somewhere in the sky.

And yet, on this night, despite their ardour, they could not unite. They felt as if they had taken an oath of chastity at an unremembered time and, having only just remembered it, had put down between themselves an unassailable force – like the Nordic sword that guards virtue – which would ensure they would never transgress again.

And they fought against their dark thoughts.

Eventually, Lumnia whispered. 'Maybe if people stopped wanting us to have children . . .'

Branko muttered. 'Maybe.'

And before dawn, he rose from his wife's arms. He gathered a blanket, some clothing, a few fragments of the Gypsy Bible and moved out of the tent that he and Lumnia had made their home.

Later that morning, Ariana found Lumnia lying by the side of a brook, gazing at the moon, still visible in bright sunshine. She sat next to her and took her hand.

Lumnia averted her eyes from the stigmata. 'How much do you know, Dei?'

'Only what I can see – in my palms.'

'Everything then . . .'

Ariana looked at her miserably. 'Can't I be wrong?'

'Where did he go – Branko?'

'To the mountain.'

'That's where he'll sleep now . . .'

Ariana, staring at her palms, nodded.

'I think – I am sure – we will never make love again. I could see it happening, Dei, but I couldn't believe it . . . If I had . . .'

'What could you have done?'

'I could have killed us both! Defied the prophecy! I'd have failed. But I could have tried . . .'

Ariana stroked Lumnia's forehead. 'Repair one injustice with another? Never works!'

'Maybe I should get someone to inseminate me, Dei . . .'

'What?'

'If I don't have a child, I'll lose him . . .'

'Are you foretelling?'

'I know it. He won't just be going up the mountain. He won't want to be near me – ever. Pride; guilt; anguish! How long can we survive like that?'

'Perhaps forever – if you put your mind to it . . .'

'I'll go on trying. But will he? Can he?'

Ariana contemplated her palms. 'I don't know. I can't tell . . .'

That evening, Branko came down from the mountain, ate supper, then went off again.

As Lumnia sat impassively amidst the remains of their fare, Omar appeared. 'Branko working on the Bible?'

Lumnia pointed. 'He's up on the summit.'

'What for?'

She smiled ruefully. 'He's sleeping with O Del.'

Omar chuckled. 'When he's got you? He's mad.'

'Anything urgent?'

'No. Just that we have a newcomer. Gheorghe's wife has delivered – a girl.'

What about me? What about me?

'That's good. I'll tell him.'

Omar nodded. 'Need anything?'

Give me your luck! Let me have a child!

'I'm fine.'

Omar nodded and left.

Lumnia watched the sway of his hips. He must have streams of sperm. All I need is one. Just one.

She felt aroused. And she felt ashamed. Omar was like a brother.

Winter set in.

One evening, as Branko came down from the mountain for his meal, Ariana waylaid him. 'Omar needs a wife.'

'He asked you?'

'No. But it's time.'

Branko smiled. 'Have you been reading your hands again, Dei?'

Guiltily, Ariana folded her arms and hid her hands. 'Never mind that!'

Branko chuckled. 'Let me see.'

'You can't tell!'

'I can make out some things . . .'

Uneasily, Ariana showed him her palms.

Branko pointed at the outline of his portrait. 'There's a large blemish behind my head? Right?'

'Yes.'

'Trouble?'

'A man. A giant.'

'A giant? You mean Omar . . .?'

'Could be.'

'Are you suggesting . . .? Come on, Dei! Omar would kill himself rather than cause me harm.'

'I know. So let him take a wife. She'll save him from killing himself.'

Next day, Branko spoke to Omar.

Omar agreed enthusiastically.

Ariana spread the word. Listing the miraculous dimensions of Omar's personality and the blessings he infused into everybody, she praised him as a man with whom even angels craved to nest.

Countless women, ranging from those who had just started bleeding to those disclaiming the advent of age, schemed to be considered. Even married women – ready, as they brazenly declared, to sacrifice husband, children and self for the good of the people – put their names forward.

Eventually Omar's gaze turned towards Parno, a dove-like girl whose blonde complexion and blue eyes – the name meant 'white' – indicated that she was the offspring of a *gadje* rape. Having lost her mother at birth, she had been brought up by members of a *kumpania* in the Romanian province of Dolj. Eventually finding herself alienated from her people – like all half-castes, she had been communally loved as a baby for being a child of misfortune but then spurned, in adulthood, for carrying impure blood – she had placed herself in Fate's care and run off to seek work in the locomotive workshops of Craiova. On her way there, she had heard of Branko's flock and, interpreting the news as Fate's intervention, had rushed to join.

Orphanhood had made Parno wise beyond her years. Surmising that to win the favours of a paragon such as Omar, a half-caste like herself would require supernatural help, she decided that only the *drabarni*, Lumnia, could invest her with the right magic. The fact that Lumnia, too, was an orphan, she thought, might prove beneficial to her petition.

Impressed as well as disconcerted by Parno's guile, Lumnia nevertheless agreed to assist. She sent the young girl to the woodlands with instructions to live solely on certain herbs. This diet, she promised, would nurture the principal qualities a man seeks in a woman: the comfort of trees and the naturality of animals.

Before long, Parno's prolonged retreats in the wilderness aroused Omar's interest. Interest developed into obsession. He decided that since Nature welcomed Parno so unreservedly, she must be of pure heart – proof enough that good can triumph over evil even after as vile a transgression as rape.

And so one fine morning, he tracked her to a secluded pool and claimed her.

In less than ten months, Parno brought forth triplets, thus elevating herself above the rest of the women, even above Lumnia, the handmaiden to her happiness.

And more people, trailing the *patrin* Branko had strewn everywhere, came and joined the movement.

One summer day, whilst collecting wood for winter, Lumnia detected a new scent in the air. She alerted Branko.

Branko, summoning Omar and Honeypaw, went to scour the outback.

The three soon picked up the discrepant smell. Tracking it to a mountain path, they spotted Leo Leo, moving along the route mapped out by the *patrin*.

Branko informed them. 'An old opponent.'

They followed Leo Leo.

The latter advanced to within sight of the Gypsy tents, but did not venture further; instead, he picked a vantage point and settled down to spy on the encampment.

Branko explained. 'Wants to know what we're up to.'

Honeypaw, outraged, rose to charge.

Branko held him back. 'Let's see what he intends to do.'

Leo Leo's objective remained a mystery. Though he became a permanent stalker of the Gypsies' trek, he frequently vanished for weeks. Branko suspected that he reported to his associates – or masters. Consequently, on each such occasion, anticipating that Leo Leo might return with a weighty escort – Gypsy assimilationists or *gadje* benefactors or government officials or even soldiers – to disband the Gypsies, Branko restructured his defences.

Lumnia, engaging in divination, shed some light on Leo Leo's disappearances. Lacking the confidence, as yet, to come out into the open and dissuade the members of Branko's flock, he was intercepting them as they set out to join the movement and urging them to refrain from embarking on an adventure destined to end in disaster.

Leo Leo's activities began to perturb Branko.

One day, he stormed into Ariana's tent. 'Let me see the stigmata.'

Ariana showed him her palms.

Branko pointed at a mark. 'This other new blot. Another giant – right? Leo Leo – right?'

'Very likely.'

'Is he a threat?'

'Can't tell yet.'

'I'm letting him hang around. Giving him rope. Am I mad?'

'What do I know about strategy, Branko?'

'I mean, I can kill him easily. But I don't want to!'

'I'm relieved . . .'

'I want to see Romanestan, Dei. I've already killed. In self-defence – mainly. But also in cold blood – though if I hadn't, they might have come after me. Which makes me hope that I'm not really a murderer. Murderers, as the Book says, won't be allowed into Romanestan. So I see myself on probation. That means I mustn't kill again. Makes sense, doesn't it?'

'Branko . . .'

'On the other hand, if I spare Leo Leo and he harms my people . . . That would be unforgivable! So what do I do?'

Ariana caressed his face. 'You'll know, Branko. You're our Saviour.'

Now and again solitary travellers arrived.

One such was Xyris, a striking, voluminous woman, who emerged, like an apparition, out of the folds of a blizzard.

Lumnia, alerted by her powers of premonition, met her and recognized her immediately as a *Suvetar*. Humanoid incarnations of the Divine Journeyman, Suvetars sought out people pulverized by battles, massacres, feuds, famine, persecution and put them together again with honey and the tears of bluebells. She hugged her. 'I wasn't expecting you so soon. But you are welcome.'

Ariana, who had noticed yet another large stain on the stigma that bore Branko's portrait, also found herself at the place of Xyris' arrival. Transfixed by the woman's girth, she noted the deep hues that scored her face like a map of grief. Yerko, the thought came to her mind, would have described her as a woman who had sewn too many shrouds. She greeted Xyris with trepidation. 'Have you come to prepare us for death?'

Xyris reassured them. 'I came to help. I will be sister and daughter to you.'

Lumnia and Ariana never spoke of their first encounter with Xyris, nor revealed any information that she might have imparted to them. Thus no one ever found out about her past or her tribe or her country of origin. Eventually, having noted her ebony complexion and the luminosity that could only have been imbued by the Indian subcontinent, people decided she was a penitent – perhaps a Gypsy swan who, having been sold into concubinage, had elevated herself to a maharanee then escaped.

Enviably self-sufficient, Xyris never became a burden.

Skilled with animals and children, she soon established herself as a shepherdess of the shadows.

And, one day, as she gathered mushrooms in the woods, she spotted Branko and Honeypaw, sitting at a clearing.

Branko, staring disconsolately at some fragments of the Holy Book, was raging at Honeypaw. 'What made me think I could restore the Bible? Why am I still trying? Who do I think I am?'

Honeypaw stroked him reverently.

Branko pushed him away. 'I should give up! Should have – long ago!'

Honeypaw growled in protest.

'A thankless task! And endless! Do you know how long it'll take me to get it all done? Years!'

Honeypaw patted him encouragingly.

'What if I can't finish it? What if I run out of words!'

Honeypaw shook his head, rejecting such a possibility.

'You'd never think it, but I had an easy life – once. Senseless, but easy. Didn't hate my balls then – didn't know they were useless . . . And I had music. Played the cithara. Composed songs. Sang. Great place to escape, music is . . .'

Honeypaw nodded sympathetically.

'And I gave it all up! For what? For Lumnia! For a book! For a people!'

Honeypaw nodded enthusiastically.

'And where did that get me? Lumnia is not only childless, but she, like me, sleeps alone! The Book demands words all the time – as if I, myself, am the scribe! As for the people . . . One day, they'll abandon me – people always do! So what have I got?'

Honeypaw, affected by Branko's mood, kept quiet.

Dusk enveloped them.

Xyris, emerging from the twilight, started playing her pan-pipe.

The strange but melodious sound immediately captivated both Branko and Honeypaw.

Xyris approached and sat next to Branko.

Branko welcomed her into his trance. Her presence melted away his burdens, his own as well as those of his people. Relishing this lightness of spirit, his eyes imbibed Xyris' body, lingered wistfully first on her large breasts then on her ample but shapely thighs. He sighed. 'It'd be so nice to disappear in your folds. Like burial at sea.'

She cradled him. 'You must finish the Book first. Fulfil the prophecy.'

Branko continued with the restoration of the Gypsy Bible.

During a communion, O Del instructed Branko to seek a suitable location where they could tarry for a few seasons so that the people could have the leisure to understand the deeper meanings of freedom and of Romany identity and unity.

The Deity also urged him to build a yurt for the Book in order to provide the people with a hallowed congregational venue where he could reveal unto them the new portions of the Bible; He further advised him to partition a section of this yurt as the Holy of Holies; thus he would not only preserve the scrolls from the elements, but also prevent them losing the power of their words by becoming too familiar.

Branko charged Lumnia to find them a large and secluded site where the spirits of the place would welcome them for an extended stay.

He undertook to build the yurt himself.

And he commissioned Matheas, a master carpenter, to construct the Holy of Holies.

I, Branko, Saviour, write this account:

Whereas to each life there is a measure of light, I have been given total darkness.

So I create my own light; wherever I go, I take tools of combustion and produce sparks; thus I forge myself as the mastodon who survives the ice.

And I give my lights to my people.

Now, Adam's brood speak of the final solution yet again.

They have a new champion, a titan called Goliath, who is taller than ten poplars and wider than five imaginations; who has armour for skin, a single eye that spews flames and deadly maggots inside his mouth.

As my people cower, I take the field against him.

Goliath directs his volcanic eye at me.

Each time he hurls a sheet of flame, I evade it by dancing the steps with which I greet the sun.

Goliath opens his mouth and fires his maggots.

This time I dance like a fisherman; I spin the grass into thick mesh and catch the maggots.

Goliath advances to crush me.

I take out my sling and fire three missiles.

The first hits him in the eye and douses his flames. The second smashes his mouth and spikes his cannon. The third pierces through his armoured skin and drains away his evil.

I, Branko, Saviour, unfurl the rainbow and place it in the sky.

Soon, I shall deliver my people to the coast and put them on the boats for Romanestan.

PART NINE

Twenty-Four

Shards of ice pricked Branko's skin. He woke up. Perspiration had frozen on his body hair.

O Del had summoned him to yet another audience. This time, to a desert. The Deity had glided on the thermals like a vulture and descanted. 'Passion for life is what I gave mankind. The *gadje* alchemized it into passion for death. Now My Romanies, apple of My eyes, will set matters right. Beware of errors, chosen one!'

Same refrain. Dream after dream.

Is O Del warning me about Leo Leo, that *gadje*-coloured Gypsy who has infiltrated my Infant People?

Branko rose, offering the new day a wistful smile. He could see it contained the usual mixture of doubt, fear, inertia, absurdity and, not least, lies that looked like truths and sanity that was indistinguishable from madness.

He watched the dawn penetrate the cave. Hardly a cave. Rather a dent on the escarpment. Accessible only to O Del, in accordance with His wishes.

Branko draped himself with his boar's pelt. Impulsively, he showed off the tusks to the Deity. 'King of the wild, he was. Pulled up by a river. You need my spunk, he said. I took it.'

'You told me – many times.'

Branko moved to the ledge. Below, on the mesa, a jade lagoon of firs and spruces shaded the snowline. Beyond lay the smug horizons of the *gadje*. The morning, blushing like a woman in her first pregnancy, promised clear skies. He opened his arms to receive her.

O Del nudged him. 'I am a master! Admit it!'

Branko snarled. 'You nearly pushed me off!'

The people were waking up. But they stayed concealed, barely disturbing the snow scene. Though they were screened from the *gadje* by Lumnia's magic, he had, nevertheless, imposed his own security measures. Thus he had laid out the tents close to each other, in a semicircle, in dense woodland. A traditional encampment, in effect. The old ways were the best; they had been tested over many centuries.

The snow blinking there – that's Xyris gathering the sheep.

That ripple is Dodo training the *Manush*, our braves. Mao said: guerrillas should move as fish in the sea. I have done better. We are pollen in the wind.

Dodo worships Omar. Avoids me. Thinks I am past it. Worse than a eunuch. For him a man is not a man if he cannot have children.

'Remember people telling me to divorce Lumnia because she wasn't bearing? And that cow, Dodo's mother, bringing figs – remember, O Del? Put these between your woman's legs and her womb will fill up like rain clouds. I told her it wasn't Lumnia that was barren – *drabarnis* never are. So she said: then squeeze them over your nuts; that's just as good. I could have murdered her, remember?'

O Del sounded bored. 'Yes.'

'That's when they started giving me a wide berth. And the slanders: *man who fears the bush; man with the floppy hammer.* Floppy? I used to outfuck them all! Still can.'

'No need to boast!'

'You would, too, if . . .' He broke off the conversation as a kestrel alighted on the ledge. 'What's up?'

The kestrel spoke in Lumnia's voice. 'Did you check the yurt?'

'Not yet. Why?'

'The storm – last night. Didn't you hear it?'

Branko spun round and scanned the heights: the trees on the upper slopes lay strewn like lead soldiers in a child's war game. 'I – I thought it was a dream . . .'

'I cast a protective shield. Just make sure it held.'

Anxiously, Branko clambered to the summit.

The tent, consecrated as the Yurt of the Book, stood secure. Honeypaw, who always guarded it, greeted him joyfully.

'The storm – any damage?'

Honeypaw shook his head.

Branko went in to check for himself.

Since that tedious time when delinquency had ruled the people, the time Lumnia had called 'before we harnessed chaos' . . . How long ago was that? Remember those days, O Del? Madness was natural, you said: all references had changed: no *gadje*, but a harsh wilderness instead; no hunger, but a gelding for a chief – no, you didn't say that last bit . . . Who did? Bet you, it was Leo Leo. That was round about the time he started spreading his heresies . . . Anyway, since then I made a point of erecting the Yurt of the Book on the highest summit, out of harm's way.

And to protect it from the elements I structured it with poles and transoms of oak and weatherproofed it with hides of the local buffalo. And I always camouflaged it against aerial observation – no mean feat when you have to pitch it on a bald, perishing summit.

He edged forward.

The Holy of Holies, which Matheas had carved out of acacia wood and which housed the scrolls, also stood undamaged behind the tapestry that served as the iconostasis.

There were nine scrolls now, all pasted up with relevant portions. After he had compiled the next, the Book would be complete.

The Scriptorium, to the right, was equally undisturbed. The oak desk – another solid piece hewn by Matheas – stood as he had left it the previous day: cluttered with pens and inkpots; the fragments he had been restoring secure under stone paper-weights; and the sheets of vellum, prepared by Miron, the tanner, ready for collage. 'Everything safe. And it's all my work. Solid. Would have stood just as well without Lumnia's shield.'

'But not without mine.'

'Yours?'

O Del snorted. 'Faithless man!'

Branko protested. 'Don't make me laugh! Remember the last time?'

When the north wind had grabbed a clutch of fragments . . .

'I was testing you then.'

Fragments chronicling the *Porajmos* – portions without which no Gypsy Bible could be complete.

'Testing me?'

But for Lumnia's incantations which had wrenched them from the gale's grasp, those fragments would have been lost forever.

'Prophets must be tested regularly.'

Why can't I get along with O Del? It would be wise to have Him on my side. That's what Luck is – God on one's side.

He has made me barren.

Branko moved to the left of the iconostasis and inspected his chief's apparel hanging on an old tailor's dummy which Lalo had salvaged from a scrap-heap. He rubbed the sceptre's silver knob to give it a shine.

The first time he had worn the attire – how many years since we marched into the wilderness? – his followers had numbered fifty. Now they were almost five thousand. Now they were almost a people.

My children. Virile shoots from a dead tree. They'll burgeon, then discard me. Parricides.

There had been a time, after the first flush of euphoria had faded, when the people had asked with their eyes the purpose of their hardship and how long they would have to wander and what would be the tolls they would have to pay. Then he had been able to speak to them as a visionary, like one of those upright chiefs whom tribes of mettle carry in their nosebags as moral authority.

Don't let my anointed brow intimidate you; stand with me on equal footing; if you think I've taken a wrong turn, confront me; challenge me with honest fears and hopes; then we can resolve every problem.

But, much as they had smiled like true brothers, they had kept their disaffection to themselves. As resentment had fermented into venom, they had tallied his shortcomings. Eventually, they had forgotten his sacrifices and ignored his goodness.

And, behind their eyes, they had mocked his desiccated testicles!

Finally – it had been after Hanro and *Bibi* had died one polar night, leaving Ariana and Xyris as the only wise hearts available to him – he had understood: people did not want equality; they did not want to shape their own fate; brief and sanguine pronouncements served them adequately; even as their eyes sniped questions, their hearts and minds evaded the answers. Answers, they well knew, would have jolted them out of their precious indolence. So they had obeyed him unthinkingly – through Omar's intermediacy – and cheered and applauded every patriarchal nod of his head.

Nowadays, he rarely mingled with them.

Besides, he possessed a powerful glow which blinded the onlooker. This emanated from the furrow on his forehead, at the location of the third eye, which O Del had notched as the prophet's mark. Consequently, he had taken to covering his face like a desert-dweller. This had made the people think that he was mad; and they had kept out of his way.

Were they right?

Moreover, alienation, as during his years of retreat with Yerko, had tangled up his tongue and crumpled his speech. Now, he could converse only with O Del, Honeypaw or himself. Even with Lumnia and Omar, he was either monosyllabic or he spoke with his eyes and nostrils.

No matter. Words acquired substance only when written down. Even then, unless they were engorged with destiny, they had little meaning.

I gave them the Book. I am preparing them for Romanestan. What more do they want?

He came out of the yurt.

Honeypaw was waiting for him.

They wrestled as they did every morning.

Then Honeypaw resumed his guard duty.

Branko stood at the edge of the escarpment and firmly planted his feet on the ice. Succumbing to the favourite fantasy of his youth – strange how the past kept surfacing these days – he imagined he was Tensing, the Sherpa, standing on Everest's summit. A man who could ascend no further, save into Heaven itself.

And his mind went to the man who could sink no further: Leo Leo.

The assimilationist had been stalking him for ages . . .

How long was that?

Almost since the time I took my children into the wilderness!

That long?

Yes. Well, finally he had come out into the open and was labouring surreptitiously to ingratiate himself with the people. Tall, upright, paternal, hair riding the wind in the manner of an ensign, he appeared to have acquired, between one season and the next, a vast reservoir of confidence and zeal. Dangerous qualities both. And he talked with enviable grandiloquence. He was not to be underestimated.

In Eastern Europe, the spirit of revolution had kept its momentum. Every communist country had overthrown its rulers. Romania had executed the Ceauşescus.

Freedom, however, had unleashed nationalism and bigotry as had been foretold at the special *kriss* that had started this movement. Almost overnight, ethnic identities, delineated by arcane interpretations of name, ancestry, religion and historic claims, had turned yesterday's friends into avowed foes.

Demagogues who had never known where east, west, north and south lay had appointed themselves cartographers to the gangs of cut-throats masquerading as militias. Any one of the countless sparks flying around could cause this hatred to conflagrate.

Even these sparks had singed the Gypsies.

In Yugoslavia, both the Serb and the Croat Republics, determined to conceal their military strength and political aims, had stage-managed some meaningless skirmishes by fielding their Gypsy conscripts as cannon-fodder. In Romania itself, Gypsies were being hounded by both Romanians and Transylvanian Hungarians even as these traditional enemies spewed hatred at each other. Consequently, waves of Gypsies had surged to the wilderness to join Branko.

As the ranks had filled, Leo Leo, trying to keep behind the wind so that his smell would not carry, had edged nearer the encampment.

And I, Branko, Saviour, keen to assess his strategy, allowed him to find stones to sleep upon.

Lumnia's divinations had been confirmed. Before infiltrating the camp, Leo Leo had been campaigning in Eastern Europe, urging the Gypsies to disregard Branko's movement and embrace the *gadje* world – 'the real world', as he had come to call it – and defeat persecution through assimilation. Arguing that the *gadje* were not all bad, that the new Europe upheld human rights and was, therefore, enlightened and heroic, he had advised them to seek refuge and jobs in the West.

And the weak had been seduced. Running in the direction Leo Leo had pointed, chasing jobs that did not exist or were kept out of their reach, they had ended up as refugees – most of them in Germany! Today, they lived in camps – camps! And waited for the *gadje* to conceive miraculously the inclination to accept them as human beings.

Recently, however, Leo Leo had modified his strategy. Though he still moved in and out of tents as if he were a stork delivering babies, he seldom referred to assimilation. For good reason. Deterioration in the political climate in Europe had frightened him.

The West had shifted its outlook. The collapse of the Eastern bloc, initially welcomed as the great leap towards universal peace, was now seen as a victory for capitalism; promises of instant democracy and prosperity for masses hungry for these rights had been abandoned or 'postponed'.

Afraid that the unrest and the economic chaos in the Soviet Union and the Balkan states might goad their own underclasses to discontent, the West had come to see the Gypsy refugees either as bands of subversive activists or as hordes of barbarians bent on ravaging democracy's stately mansions and snow-white women. Indeed, in yet another repetition of history, the demonization of the refugee – which, these days, included Mediterraneans, Blacks and Asians – echoed the reception given to the first Gypsy immigrants in the Middle Ages. Swarthy strangers – some, disturbingly dark-skinned – dangerously lustful of life: could they be anything but Satan's brood?

What Europe really wanted was a white commonwealth; one stripped of the richness and beauty of racial and cultural diversity – a commonwealth bled of its future life, in effect; a latter-day Third Reich.

Whether Leo Leo had noted this reality was unclear. But, nowadays, he urged the people to mark time. Get the *gadje* to like us, he told them, get them to see what good people we are, make them want us as neighbours.

Why does he cling to such naivety? Why won't he see there will never be a place for Gypsies until the Gypsies themselves create it?

He is an idealist. A romantic. That's why. That's how he seduces my children!

Many of his followers will die in destitution in waysides. Others will be shunted from dung-heap to dung-heap until their existence is forgotten. Those seeking asylum in the West will be sent back. They'll find the homes they had left behind razed to the ground. And as they grieve, they'll be put to the torch. Fire is what the *gadje* use for 'ethnic cleansing' – that's the new euphemism for 'extermination', coined in Yugoslavia.

Branko sat on 'the prophet's seat', the rock Omar had hewn for him. He gazed down at the mesa.

Melchior tried to jump into the void. He wanted to fall into infinity. But I peeled him off the ice.

I wouldn't today. I'd honour his wish. Gently drop him into the abyss.

Music rose from the encampment. There was always someone playing or singing. No sooner did an instrument sound than people ran out of their tents. Dancing was the Gypsies' lotus flower. It provided the fugue which blotted out time. Thus they forgot all they had endured and dismissed all they could see lying in wait.

But, latterly, the music had lost its sorcery. The trances the women wove, as they clapped hands and whirled, were full of perforations; the men failed to defy gravity as they shuffled the *hora*. Even the children, dogs, horses stomped as if frightened of breaking the earth's skin.

What has happened to my children? Why can't they delight in the wilderness? Yesterday they were still irrepressible. They would burgeon out of the earth, shoot out of the rivers, dive from the sky, erupt out of camp-fires.

Now, they resent the need for endurance. They dream of soft houses and softer chairs. Of money and mindless pursuits. Of life as they remember seeing on television. Of skin and culture sandpapered to the *gadje's* pallor. Now, only the dead, in their suits of dust, are prepared to struggle for the promised land.

When we appear before a *kumpania*, as if we came down from Heaven, and I signal Omar to tell them who we are and where we are going, they shed tears of joy. But they refuse to join us. They give us food, music, animals, clothing, but not their hopes. Because Leo Leo has been there before us; and he has blighted their marrow with his misguided vision.

Branko undid his trousers and started masturbating. A male and his organ, labouring for manhood.

He tried to think of Lumnia's body; but, as happened regularly these days, his thoughts went to Xyris. He undressed the latter in his mind and surrendered to her opulent folds.

He ejaculated. Not without some joy. An improvement on the past.

But I can father a people. I am . . .

I fear O Del will turn against me. He sifts everything I do or say for signs of madness.

Signs are aplenty.

All kinds of anger, for a start: survivor's, orphan's, neuter's, victim's. Not to mention the anger of the prophet who is destined to fail because madness will make him unfit for success.

As if madness were not integral to prophethood.

As if O Del Himself were sane!

Lumnia ridicules my fears. Omar thinks I am paranoid – paranoia is one of those *gadje* words he picked up during his minstrel days. Neither appears to be concerned about my children. Ever since they glimpsed, in my retina, images of their footprints in Romanestan, complaisance rules them like lust.

Every forgotten stone marks my tomb. When I touch water it is as if I am washing my corpse. Every camp-fire foreshadows my funeral pyre.

It is not death that terrifies me; I fear I will never set foot in Romanestan. The *mule* of the men I killed have begun to haunt me.

Often, in a sun-spot, I see a preview of my end.

I cross a flimsy bridge over a burning river. An eye measures me. A mouth points to the left. The bridge breaks. I fall. And I burn.

Not in Romanestan. Not even at its gates. But an ocean away.

The encampment lifted its veils. Branko focused on the three tents at the centre.

The first was Lumnia's – his, too, even though he never slept there.

She was outside and busy as ever. People never give it a thought, but magic takes ages to prepare. All those finicky procedures. Doing everything in the prescribed order. Crushing herbs. Sprinkling libations. Chanting incantations. Blowing ash into the wind – that's how she has protected the encampment all these years – with shields of ash. Most powerful *drabarni* for generations. That's not me being biased. Ask the old-timers.

He waved at her.

She waved back without interrupting her ritual. As she moved about, he watched the see-saw of her buttocks. Despite the harsh conditions of these past years, her body had filled out. She now had a liquid texture and moved like a primal cradle.

To love her flesh so much. Yet not dare touch it. Even shy away from thinking about it. Understandable, given that he was a usurer. A woman's body is never exclusive to her man. It also belongs to the children demanding to be born of it.

Lumnia felt equally sad, he knew. Back when they used to make love, her breasts always wept.

The second tent was Ariana's. She shared it with Xyris. The latter had moved in, at Lumnia's request, to look after Ariana.

Ever since they had camped here, frailty had taken a stronger grip on Ariana. Moreover, she seemed to have developed a form of dermatitis which, with the exception of her face, was hardening and blackening her skin. The condition, given that it had proved immune to Branko's healing, was not a sarcoma, Lumnia had ascertained, but, like the stigmata on the palms, another one of Fate's mysterious implements. Perhaps, Xyris had mused, Ariana had incarcerated, inside her body, all the ills that Lumnia had chased away with her magic and thus prevented them from attacking the Gypsies ever again.

Ariana, too, was outside her tent, watching him. In fact, she watched him all day and all night. Often when he couldn't sleep and walked the peaks, he spotted her, sitting by a patient fire, scanning the heights.

The third tent was Omar's.

The youth had also been looking out for him; now he was waving. Parno, his wife, was making flat-bread. His sons, the triplets, Lupu, Mincu and Sandu, were blowing kisses in his direction. Five years old now. Beautiful children: flaxen and olive-skinned, like molten drops from the sun.

He wished he could love them. But Omar's luck in siring not one son, but three, with one embrace, kept mocking him.

No doubt, it also served as a focus for people's contempt. Who respects a man who has never rocked his own child, never moulded the son that will father him?

Look at the way Omar adores his boys! All that love spinning out and cocooning them, wiping away doubts and fears, leaving neither an exposed heel, nor an unprotected shoulder.

I, too, could have generated such love! I could have taught them about strength, patience, sadness, joy, music. And started the day, singing and dancing!

The barren man carries the original curse! Thus he emasculates his father, himself and his unborn sons of prowess, completion of self, hero worship and ancestorship.

Omar loves everybody. And everybody loves him. Dodo, his lieutenant – excellent fighter – worships him. So do all the *Manush*.

Whereas they steer clear of me . . .

And the women adore him. Remember them queuing up – married or not – when he decided to wed?

Had Lumnia wanted him, too? Was that why Ariana had urged us to find him a wife?

Poor, childless Lumnia. Would she end up like Xyris, a mother to all except to her own?

Xyris was still busy with the sheep at the pens.

Not young. But possessing the smile of a goddess. And so earthy.

It was she who had woven the iconostasis for the Yurt of the Book. Some surmised she was a druid sent by Mother Earth to turn the children into ripe young men and women. She not only taught the boys the secrets of sex, it was said, but also initiated the girls in the lunar mysteries. That such assumptions, given the Gypsies' strict sexual mores, could be tolerated by the community was further proof of the strange reverence she evoked.

Many men wanted Xyris – her name meant the flower iris – but she chose to remain single.

The only person she might favour, Lumnia had once told Branko, was Branko himself.

Omar, Branko noted, had started his rounds. Later, he would come up and report. He would arrive around midday. When it came to climbing mountains, Omar was a clodhopper.

Cold comfort.

A procession, led by Matheas, the tall, spindly youth whose godly hands breathed life into wood and stone, crossed Omar's path.

An odd procession. Some were pulling sledges loaded with timber, stones and saplings; others were carrying ladders, saws, shovels, spades, pickaxes, hammers, chisels.

Branko barked at Honeypaw. 'Stay alert!'

He streaked down the mountain.

The procession reached the camp's perimeter.

It included Dodo. And Lalo, known as 'the genie of the lamp', because he could procure anything. It even included Omar, striding like a sleepwalker.

Taking cover behind trees and rocks, Branko trailed the procession.

A man emerged and walked alongside Matheas.

Leo Leo.

Patriarchal. Prompting Matheas to put additional vigour into his chest and steps.

I thought so: treachery.

Did Leo Leo have offspring?

I heard rumours saying he has. He also claims he's a chieftain from Bukovina.

Childless, in all probability. Which would explain why he is competing with me for the people.

The procession stopped at a clearing at the edge of the mesa.

Matheas and some of the men unloaded the sledges. Others started shovelling the snow. Yet others began digging.

Branko watched, crouched behind a tree.

These people were about to transgress. Yet he wanted to join them. He could not stand idle when others were active.

Leo Leo summoned a few men; they began planting the saplings.

Matheas and the rest – Omar among them – started to build a cabin.

Branko slunk into Leo Leo's group and began planting, too.

The tempo of the work increased as if the two groups were racing each other.

On one occasion, as he showed his group how to train branches for an espalier, Leo Leo appeared to notice Branko; but, when their eyes engaged, he showed no sign of recognition. Branko, nevertheless, noted a triumphant twist to his mouth.

Eventually, the groups finished their labour and gathered to admire their work. They had built a slat-roofed cabin and laid out an orchard.

Some musicians gave voice to their instruments. The people danced.

Branko slipped away and ran up the mountain.

He stormed into the Yurt of the Book. 'O Del!'

The iconostasis swayed. 'Here.'

'Your Romanies. Built a hut. Planted an orchard.'

'Weren't you planting also?'

'Had to do something. I was spying. The point: the people want to spread roots. Seduced by soil. They're rejecting You! And me!'

'They're being human. Wavering . . .'

'They should be punished!'

'I am not an angry God, Branko.'

Branko was shocked. 'You won't intervene?'

'No.'

'Then I will!' Hurriedly, Branko put on his chieftain's regalia.

'Branko, beware!'

Branko pushed past the iconostasis and burst into the Holy of Holies.

'Beware, Branko, beware!'

Carrying the Scrolls of the Book, Branko hurtled out of the Holy of Holies.

This time, he came down the mountain like a titan. The horizon turned grey as if his temper had banished the sun.

Honeypaw followed him with thunderous footsteps.

Branko materialized before the newly erected cabin. The laughter and the dancing died as his rage flayed word and music.

He summoned Omar. 'What's this?'

Bravely, the youth kissed his hands, then stood to attention. 'Don't be angry with me. I couldn't stop it. I was captivated.'

'Hut! Orchard! You know what they represent?'

'They represent sanity.'

The reply had come from Leo Leo.

Holding the Scrolls of the Book like javelins, Branko spun round. 'You dare! At last!'

Leo Leo pushed forward. 'Yes! At last! At last!'

'Sanity? How?'

Leo Leo scaled to his full height. 'I asked these people: where is this man, Branko, your chieftain? Transcribing the Book, they said. I asked: what Book? The one where our destiny is written, they said. I asked: what is your destiny? Liberation, reunification, Romanestan, they said. I asked: what is Romanestan? The Promised Land, they said. I asked: where is it? Beyond the seas, they said. I asked: why so far away? It is so decreed, they said. I asked: would you rather not stop here and put up a house and tend a field? Yes, but how, they asked. I will show you, I said. And we built this cabin and laid out this orchard.'

Branko felt like a child before an adult: he could not engage the renegade's eyes or wipe out his smile without standing on tiptoe.

So he squatted. He was tempted to send Leo Leo – and all the Gypsies – back to slavery and slaughter.

The people, motionless and silent, watched them.

Suddenly, Branko whipped at Leo Leo's ankles and felled him. Springing up, he lifted Leo Leo in a tight grip and smashed him down. Then, putting his foot on Leo Leo's face, he turned to the people. 'Look! Your false prophet!'

The people retreated before his wrath.

Branko shouted. 'He loves questions. You heard how he kept asking! Now, I've got some questions for him!'

The people edged further back.

Leo Leo strained to get up. 'Let me go . . .'

Branko stamped on chest, winding him. 'Question: which of O Del's many testicles produces the seed that conceives Romanies?'

Leo Leo groaned. 'What?'

'Answer: none. We are born of His marrow.'

Leo Leo struggled to straighten up.

Branko stamped on him again. 'Question: which rain falls from the ninth sky?'

Leo Leo muttered. 'I don't know.'

'Answer: the Word. Our Book.'

Leo Leo strained to get up.

'Question: what lives forever in seven seas and seven continents?'

'I don't know. Let me go!'

Branko stamped on him once again. 'Answer: Romanestan.'

Leo Leo tried to get his breath back.

'Question: what can the blind see and the deaf hear?'

Leo Leo attempted to crawl away.

Branko's foot, poised to kick, stopped him. 'Answer: Romanies liberated from the *gadje*.'

Leo Leo whined. 'Will you let me go!'

'Question: what should we do when we are ill?'

Leo Leo touched Branko's feet. 'For God's sake, man! Let me go, please!'

In disgust, Branko kicked him aside. 'Fight to be healthy. If need be, die standing up.' He turned to Omar. 'Tell the people: this man, Leo Leo, knows only how to make fool's gold.'

Leo Leo protested. 'And this man has not tempered his weakness for violence. Fighting means killing. Killing means having the dead sitting on your shoulders. Can the people accept that?'

For a moment Branko wavered. Killing also barred entry to Romanestan. Could he accept that?

He roared. 'Tell the people. If there's any killing to be done, I will do it! No one else!'

Omar hurried over to the gathering.

Branko squatted by the camp-fire and listened to Omar talking to the people. The people deliberated, shouting. The people always argued.

All conflicts end in defeat. For both sides. What was the use?

With a cry of despair, Branko rammed the Scrolls of the Holy Book into the camp-fire. When they caught fire, he hurled them into the newly built cabin.

Dodo sprang forward to attack Branko, but, seeing Honeypaw by Branko's side, he drew back.

Branko directed his fury at him. 'You are fickle! Weak! You don't deserve to be a people!'

The cabin went up in flames.

Matheas, distraught, ran towards the burning hut. 'The Book! The Book!'

A tongue of fire caught his hair. He bolted away, screaming, tearing at his head.

Omar took off his jacket and ran after him.

Matheas reached the edge of the mesa. Seeing the chasm before him, he tried to stop. But he slipped and tumbled over.

The people wailed.

The fire spread to the saplings.

Branko turned to Leo Leo. 'Another question: how long is eternity . . .'

Leo Leo cowered. His mane had lost its lustre.

'. . . And how long a moment?'

Leo Leo retreated.

Branko thundered. 'Answer: an eternity is the time it took to create Creation . . .'

Leo Leo began to shrink.

Branko pounced on him. '. . . A moment is all it takes to destroy it.'

Leo Leo evaded Branko and slithered away.

Branko chased him.

Leo Leo disappeared down the slope.

Branko raged. 'You call yourself a lion – running away like that?'

The mountains echoed him.

When the fires died down, Branko caught a glimpse of Leo Leo, way down in the valley, huddling by a bush. Shrunken to a scrawny frame, he looked like a foetus aborted in the wild. Suddenly, Branko pitied him.

Branko fetched a cauldron. He filled it with melted snow then mixed in the ashes of the cabin and the saplings.

He summoned Omar and Dodo. 'Drink this. See how fool's gold tastes.'

Omar and Dodo hesitated.

Branko thundered. 'Drink it!'

Omar drank it. Dodo still hesitated.

Branko glared at Dodo. 'Disobeying me, are you?'

Dodo, trying to hold on to his defiance despite his humiliation, drank the liquid.

Branko dismissed them. 'Now, take it round. I want everybody to drink it.'

Branko, heading towards the mountain, strode past the tents in the centre of the encampment.

Lumnia, Xyris and Parno, he could see, had gathered around Ariana and were listening to her solemnly interpret the stigmata on her palms.

For a moment, he was tempted to join them. But that would be pointless. He knew what needed to be known.

O Del's voice resonated from the Holy of Holies. 'You've burned the Book. You've succeeded where the Hitlerites failed. Do you still expect to see Romanestan?'

Branko outfaced Him. 'I know the Book by heart. I'll transcribe it again.'

'No need. A prophet maddened by his prophecy – I foresaw it. I made sure there would be another copy.'

'What copy?'

'Strike camp now – before Leo Leo informs the world where you are!'

Omar was waiting outside the Holy of Holies.

Honeypaw was watching him.

From a cloth bag, Omar brought out nine scrolls of vellum and offered them to Branko. 'I made a copy of the Book. O Del told me.'

Branko hit him across the face. 'Liar!'

Omar's arm jerked, ready to retaliate. But he controlled himself. Tears flooded his eyes. 'I have never lied to you.'

'O Del – telling you what to do! Since when?'

'A year now.'

'Where do you speak to him?'

'He summons me to audience. In my dreams.'

Branko smiled bitterly. 'I see. Yes. He would.' He hugged Omar, appalled by his violence. 'Forgive me.'

Omar nodded and kissed Branko's hands.

'Strike camp. We leave today.'

Omar's eyes lit up. 'For Romanestan?'

'Not yet – not after today's antics.'

'Where is it, chief – Romanestan?'

'Go on, get a move on!'

Omar hurried away.

Branko shouted at the Holy of Holies. 'Whore, aren't you? Summoning others to audience!'

O Del did not answer.

'What was it you said about seeing Romanestan?'

Again O Del did not answer. He had either left the yurt or was keeping silent.

i

branko

saviour

brood like an eye which sees all but not itself

i am immured in my mind with middle-yard worms

i rule with vexation

i use the rod not as something i can transform into a snake to render the gadjo harmless but as a stick with which to chastise the rock for withholding water

to appease me

o del has sent the first four creatures he kneaded out of chaos

but

the dolphin cannot raise me from my despair

the lion cannot protect me from my destiny

the eagle cannot fly me to another existence

and the woman cannot revive my dead seeds

some ask o del why have you perforated branko's testicles

he replies if branko had not been barren he would not have sired a people

i ask can o del be trusted might he abandon me

i need to know soon

on the shores of darkness i must confront vut-oza the eater of souls

he has already ambushed me twice

first time i was grazing my horses in a valley vut-oza stole all the water that farmers had put aside for hospitality and turned it into a deluge as the flood rushed at me i fired arrows into the air embedding each into the other so forming a herringbone ladder and i led my horses to the milky way

the second time vut-oza approached me in the highlands in the guise of fravashi the guardian angel and pushed me off the mountain but the spider nymph who always watches over saviours arrested my fall i climbed back and confronted vut-oza by exposing my feet and the eater of souls promptly fled he dares not show his feet which are those of a hen

the next encounter will be decisive.

can i trust o del

or will he abandon me

and reduce me

to the saviour of naught

save of my death

Twenty-Five

The false dawn stippled the darkness.

Branko ran his dinghy on to the bank and scrambled out. He always led, not the *false chief*. That was his rule.

Honeypaw followed.

They took cover behind clusters of bulrushes.

Branko listened to the night. When he ascertained that the area was deserted, he turned to the river and lilted like a warbler.

The mist, so effervescent in the Danube basin, magnified the boats as they emerged from the brume.

Branko climbed on to a mound to survey the disembarkation.

Discipline and an expertise achieved by hard training made the complex operation seem effortless. The people numbered nineteen thousand, three hundred and forty-seven souls; but they appeared to be a mere handful.

Lumnia, Ariana and Xyris, among the first to land, picked up a sheltered patch on the strand and began erecting their tents.

Omar, sculling back and forth in his canoe, managed to be everywhere. As ever, his ability to pre-empt problems inspired the people.

Despite the constant exchange of orders and responses, the only sound heard was the perennial dialogue of land and water. Not only had the people adapted to riverine existence resourcefully, but they had also mastered the art of travelling invisibly. They handled the boats – an assortment of punts, dinghies, coracles, kayaks, canoes, dugouts and rafts which they had built, stolen or acquired – as expertly as, once upon a time, they had handled horses. They had learned to hide their voices beneath Nature's babel. And to avoid the *gadje*, they had developed the skill of finding twin streams which were born of the same source, but which having constantly sought dominion over each other, had been condemned, by water deities, to run separate courses in order never to cross paths; thus whilst the *gadje* favoured one such river, for instance, the Mureş, the Gypsies plied its double, the Olt.

Having set up her tent, Lumnia joined Branko.

She had understood, right from the time they had first taken to the rivers, that operations on this scale had to be executed with exceptional military competence; of course, her armoury of defensive spells helped, but it was best to keep them as back-up: magic, if overused, lost its efficacy; besides, against some disasters, invariably caused by laxity, even magic was helpless. Thus, during each deployment, she had stood by Branko and learned the drills.

Now she watched him oversee the landing. She noted that at every delicate manoeuvre, his heart chewed its walls. She wondered, as she always did, how a man of such innate fragility could carry on his shoulders all the doubts, fears and frustrations of a reawakening people. At least, in the past, he could be sustained with joy; then she used to be able to transform him, just with a touch, into a lusty, ardent youth.

But since his retreats on the mountains and his endless communions with O Del, his mind had cast aside all attachments to life. He still did not touch her. Even during such operations, when they stood together as the people's wellspring, he kept his distance.

These days he only touched visions of a land that did not as yet exist.

And rage.

These days he also shivered pitiably like an injured swallow.

One day, she had asked him why he had stopped making love to her. Busying himself with the Auschwitz fragments, he had pretended he had not heard her. Later she had heard him shouting at the Holy of Holies. 'Why don't you kill me, O Del! I'd rather die than usurp her womb!' On another occasion, she had espied him throwing stones at his shadow on a rock-face.

She had given up telling him that she did not blame him. He would not believe her. He preferred his pain to her pride in being his woman. He did not wish to forgive himself – though the Book listed forgiveness as the third commandment.

Now, he faced desolation. He had perceived it in Ariana's stigmata and seemed to be impatient for it.

And the Angels of Destiny were abandoning him. Not just Luck, but all the sisters. For them, a man impatient for the end of the road is a weak man. Add to that his anger, his craving for fulfilment . . .

335

Can I still save him? What if I defied Fate? Disregarded the dead children? Made him stay with me tonight?

Hesitantly, Lumnia edged forward.

Sensing her approach, Branko muttered an exaggerated approval of someone's deftness and moved further away. Definitely beyond reclamation.

All the people were ashore now.

Still supervised by Omar, the men buried the rafts in the sand, anchored the punts and dugouts deep in the water and covered the rest with camouflage netting made of wicker and moss.

The women went in search of shelter. They scoured the elevations, the woods, the high grass, the scrub, the mud-shoals and the spread of bulrushes for caves, lees, lairs, quags and folds.

Young girls patched up damaged tents and attended to other mishaps.

Dodo assigned some *Manush* to the defences.

A platoon erected the new Yurt of the Book. Designed as a portable repository for both the Holy of Holies and the Scriptorium, this goatskin tent could be distinguished from the others by its colour: the green of a clement forest.

Honeypaw took up position as its principal guard.

Other *Manush* went to assist the bereaved. They would ensure that the lamentations would be conducted softly, out of the *gadje*'s hearing.

Ariana and Xyris went with them. They would wash the corpses and scent them with special herbs as prescribed by the Holy Book.

The rest collected driftwood for the cremations that would take place during the night. To prevent the *gadje* from detecting the fires, these would burn invisibly, sinking their smoke into the earth like ground mist – another skill Branko had taught them.

The dead – seventeen infants – had been struck by some sort of influenza.

Branko shivered and chased away the air.

Lumnia tried to soothe him. 'Malign spirits, my Rom. I'll deal with them later.'

'I thought you had . . .'

He was referring to the *wodne muzy*, the nixes that lurked in rivers and coastal waters and were said to attack sailors and voyagers as ferociously as sharks. In the past, it had been fear of these monsters that had stopped the Gypsies from travelling the seven seas, not, as some old songs claimed, memories of penal servitude in war galleys or distant colonies.

In fact, she had not needed to fight the nixes. No sooner had she confronted them with her magic than she had seen that they were, in reality, noble spirits. Their reputation for perpetrating evil, they had revealed, had been infamies disseminated by the *gadje* who had designated water and all the spirits living in it as enemy because water, being a life-giver, had refused to wash the blood off their murderous hands.

But there were other spirits. Spectres that extinguished light. Unburied spirits like the nine lemurs – Melalo, Lilyi, Tculo, Tcaridyi, Schilalyi, Bitoso, Lolmicho, Minceskro and Poreskoro – whom the Devil had made his own by stealing, from the Spinner of Life, their rights to interment. These fiends had been chasing Branko ever since he had slipped out of their hands in Auschwitz. Even after despoiling his seed, they had not been appeased.

He wailed. 'What does death want with children?'

Lumnia hesitated before replying. 'It's telling us something.'

There had been other deaths. That time when spring had slid back into winter and meltwater had turned into floe, many had died of exposure.

And more deaths before that.

But since they had come down to the rivers, only children had died.

Every day a few.

All his ministrations had failed. His miraculous powers had left him as suddenly as they had come. Save for these deaths, they might have numbered twenty thousand souls.

'Did we transgress?'

'I don't know – yet.'

'Can you find out?'

'I'm trying.'

'Should we have travelled across the mountains?'

'Not according to the prophecy.'

'What then?'

What did transgression mean, anyway? Admission of fear by those who denied fear? The prophecy to sail the rivers had been pronounced at the beginnings of time. The Holy Book had given it the purchase of a commandment: *hope will run down the mountains and stream to the sea.*

There were practical reasons, too, for plying the rivers. Primarily, they needed to avoid Leo Leo; like every dog, his sense of scent would flounder on water. Secondly, he, Branko, Saviour, had to cure his people of their fear of sailing and get them to acquire sea legs; otherwise they would never be able to live in Romanestan. Thirdly, his children had the obligation to signpost the seas with aquatic *patrin* so that other Gypsies could find their homeland. This task could only be accomplished by living on water.

The sun began to rise.

Omar boomed like a bittern.

The people dispersed.

Branko watched as Omar joined Parno and the triplets.

Almost every family had lost a child, yet Death had kept away from Omar's sons. Naturally, he was happy for Omar. But there was no denying: Luck always blessed a person at other people's expense.

Still, Luck could be fickle, too. Take me. I survived Auschwitz. I was chosen as Saviour. But who can be more luckless than a proud man begging for a lineage? Not even the labour of bringing forth a whole people compensates for that. Omar should be wary. Sooner or later, Luck extracts a high price.

The people went into their shelters.

Lumnia started walking away. 'Like clockwork. Well done. I'll be off, too.'

Branko waved a hand, without taking his eyes off the riverbank.

It was deserted now. Everybody, even the *Manush* who would keep watch, were well concealed. There were no indications that thousands of people had just sailed to this waterside in a makeshift armada.

He became aware of someone staring at him: Dodo, Omar's lieutenant. At his post. On a hillock. Glazed eyes reflecting the dawn's sheen.

He shouted. 'You want me?'

But Dodo did not hear him.

Puzzled, Branko moved down to the strand to keep vigil. He never slept when they were on the move.

Branko stared at Ariana's stigmata. 'Did we transgress? Did I?'

Ariana, looking troubled, extricated her hands from his grip. 'Saviours never transgress.'

'Is that true, Dei? Has that been revealed?'

Xyris looked up from her work. 'Doesn't the Book say so?' As if confirming an impression Branko had once had of her, she was sewing shrouds.

'I haven't come across it.' He turned to Lumnia. 'Have you?'

Lumnia, staring into the darkness by the flap of the tent, shook her head. 'No.'

Branko pondered. 'Maybe a portion I haven't worked on yet.'

Xyris latched on to the idea. 'Maybe.'

Branko sipped his tea uneasily. He felt distressed sitting in Lumnia's tent; though practically empty, it was suffused with her beauty. He would never have come in, but, having failed to find Ariana and Xyris in their tent, during his vigil, he had tracked them here. They had been engaged in a ritual; but no sooner had he appeared than they had stopped.

And Lumnia had insisted on giving him tea, which these days was offered only on very special occasions.

What were they doing?

He glanced at the table which Lumnia used as an altar and where her implements – her most formidable implements, if he remembered right – were still laid out: the mother-of-pearl hand mirror, the chunk of obsidian and the antique silver inkwell into which no one had ever dipped a pen – not even he who had wanted to use it for his transcriptions.

He noted that a set of figurines, sculpted from bat bones, was placed in an intricate formation on the mirror. A similar set, fashioned out of wax, lay on the obsidian. A third set, carved out of cork, floated in identical configurations on the ink.

He remembered Lumnia's words as he had approached the tent. 'That's you, Dei . . . There's Parno . . . Over there – the triplets . . . There – Branko and Xyris . . . And here: Omar and . . .'

Omar and who?

Was Lumnia, contrary to her normal practice, indulging in prophecy?

'If we've transgressed – will we see Romanestan . . .?'

Ariana responded firmly. 'Yes, we will.'

'Look into the future, Dei. Does it show that?'

Lumnia interjected impatiently. 'The future is never entirely visible, my Rom. That way we can't tamper with our destinies.'

Xyris glanced at Lumnia, her subdued regard urging indulgence.

Branko, catching Xyris' look, took her for an ally and laughed grimly. 'In other words, no clairvoyance among Gypsies . . .?'

Xyris, rolling her head in that ancestral way which gave no indication whether she agreed or not, resumed her work.

The shrouds she was sewing were for the dead children. All of them less than three years old. Infants born in the wilderness. Moulded as new Gypsies. Endowed with the birthright to live in Romanestan. What had gone wrong?

Branko barked. 'What if destiny needs changing?'

Lumnia stared into the night, pointedly ignoring the remark.

Branko turned to Xyris. 'What do you say, sister? Can destiny be changed?'

'Only by someone like you, chief.'

Lumnia glanced at Ariana. Xyris' presence, she had known from the moment of her arrival, had been predestined. But watching her unfold her petals, like a woman who knew love and had drunk of it regularly, every time Branko opened his mouth, made her indignant – jealous, if she were to be honest. But then, where was the woman, *drabarni* or otherwise, who could turn a blind eye when a matronly sister changed into a voluptuous temptress in front of her husband?

Ariana offered Lumnia a sympathetic smile.

Did she also see Xyris as another wife for Branko? One with more substance? One who could serve him better and become his favourite?

Branko grinned provocatively. 'Xyris thinks destiny can be changed.'

Lumnia regained her impassivity. What was the use of jealousy? She had sat opposite Calamity every day and broken bread with it! The future was clear. 'Xyris has seen much.'

Xyris' expression offered a variety of meanings.

Suddenly weary, Branko gulped down his tea and rose. 'I have to go.' As he moved to leave the tent, he turned to Lumnia and pointed at the implements on her altar. 'What do they say?'

Lumnia spoke softly, reassuringly, lovingly. 'Nothing about destiny. Plenty about Fate. That never changes. And so, those chosen by it are able to exchange mortality for immortality.'

Her response soothed Branko. I'm wallowing in Prophet's disease. I'll accept any opium to escape pain, doubt and recrimination.

He left, his face glowing, perhaps for the first time in years.

Lumnia moved to the altar.

Ariana and Xyris approached her.

Lumnia gazed at her implements. The same picture. In the mirror. On the obsidian. On the ink. Calamity, having finished the bread she had been given, was now rummaging the tent, picking up Branko's personal effects and loading them into a sack. Finally, It snatched the last of his belongings: the silhouette of his head that had been imprinted on their pillow during their years of happiness.

The picture misted over. The faces reappeared.

Lumnia pointed: 'That's you, Dei . . . There is Parno . . . Over there – the triplets . . . There – Branko and Xyris . . . And here: Omar and me . . . And may O Del forgive me for abusing my powers and looking into the future . . .'

Xyris shut her eyes, seemingly in a trance.

340

Ariana stuttered as if her heart had fallen on ice. 'Omar . . .? You . . .? I knew . . . I knew . . .'

Lumnia began to weep. How could she let Branko go – sever herself from that soul that once had been her own? Would Xyris be able to patch him up? Would she give him good breast? Open herself to him?

Dodo, turning slowly, like the hand of a clock, was keeping watch on every compass point from a hillock dominating the river.

Branko came and squatted by his side. 'You wanted to see me?'

Dodo straightened up. Nervously, he lit a cigarette and held it cupped in his hand.

Branko studied him. Cold fish. Not one of his favourites. 'What's on your mind?'

Dodo tried to sound casual, but betrayed both timidity and aggression. 'We've turned east. Heading for the Black Sea?'

Branko noted that he didn't impress Dodo either. Only Omar did. 'Yes.'

'Our boats aren't seaworthy.'

'Don't worry about that.'

A drone broke the silence.

Dodo, welcoming the intrusion, stubbed out his cigarette and scanned the sky.

An ancient biplane, used for spraying crops, appeared from the north.

Dodo spat. 'That damned wasp! I've seen it every day.'

Branko gave the aeroplane a cursory look. 'It's Leo Leo.'

'What?'

'He's searching for us.'

'How do you know?'

Branko looked up again. Though he had to stare at the sun, he spotted Leo Leo easily: in the second cockpit, behind the pilot, looking, in his leather headgear and goggles, like a First World War gunner. 'I can see him.'

'Then he can see us, too!'

'He doesn't have the eyes. He'll see us when we make ourselves visible. When we reach the sea.'

The biplane proceeded south and disappeared in the clouds.

'Won't that be dangerous . . .?'

'Like every birth.'

More at ease now, Dodo lit a fresh cigarette. 'I want to ask you something. Why are the children dying?'

Branko looked into the distance as if the answer were visible there. 'We've been transgressing . . .'

Dodo was almost in tears. 'That's what I think, too. But what merits such a terrible punishment?'

'I don't know . . .' Branko craned as he caught sight of two figures. One was Lumnia, climbing up to their position; the other, Ariana, standing by her tent, watching over him as she always did. And, suddenly, the answer dawned on him. 'None of you! None of you transgressed! I did. It can only be me – the transgressor. I am the *Vataf*.'

Dodo deliberated for a while, then responded humbly. 'We can't be without blame. Maybe we let our children die. To make ourselves childless – like you. Maybe we wanted to appease you.'

'I am not childless. You are my children.'

'We've grown up.'

'I am still your father.'

'We don't need a father any more. We need brothers.'

'Meaning . . .?'

Dodo, dragging on his cigarette, gathered all his courage. 'The Book says: *go with the man whom Luck favours*. An infertile man isn't lucky. We need a new chief.'

'When you say "we" . . .?'

'I speak for the people . . .'

Branko's mind went into spasms as if Dodo had switched on the electricity that had ravaged his youth. 'Who can fill my shoes?'

'Omar.'

The electricity abated. He felt shrivelled. 'Omar. Of course. Luck incarnate.'

Dodo ground out his cigarette and lit a new one.

Branko looked down the hill. Ariana was still watching. Lumnia was approaching. The electricity had churned a distant memory: a young mountaineer pissing on the naked corpse of an old man. 'What will you do with me? Leave me behind?'

'We need the Book. You have to finish it.'

'It's my Book!'

'It belongs to the people.'

'Writing it – it takes time . . .'

'Restoring it, you mean . . .'

'Is that what I mean?'

Dodo looked disconcerted. 'You're coming to the end.'

'Am I?'

'That's what you've been telling us.'

'Yes. Well. Endings. So many things can go wrong with endings . . .'

Dodo retorted angrily. 'Well, get a move on!'

'And then what?'

'That's it.'

Lumnia, Branko noted, had almost reached the top of the hill. 'How do I get to Romanestan?'

'Same way we will. Providing you tell us how.'

Branko gave him a distrustful look. 'How do I earn my passage?'

'As an elder.'

'A doused fire . . .?'

A hint of menace shaded Dodo's voice. 'You want to see Romanestan, don't you?'

'Maybe I'm not entitled.'

'Maybe not – given your luck.'

Branko grinned. 'On the other hand, I've been there already! Walked from one end to the other.'

Dodo looked at him sharply. 'Where is it?'

Branko jabbed his heart with his finger. 'In here!'

Dodo glared at him.

The biplane reappeared.

Dodo kept an eye on it. 'How come Leo Leo knows where to look?'

'He's guessing. He's no fool.'

'I'd like to see the end of him.'

Branko waited for the plane to disappear. 'And the end of me.'

'Only as chief.'

'You'll have to kill me first.'

Dodo unleashed his hostility. 'Don't tempt me!'

Branko punched Dodo viciously and knocked him down. 'I'm not easy prey! Remember that!'

Dodo, mouth and nose bleeding, pulled himself up. Then he burst into tears.

Branko, ready to hit again, suddenly became aware of Lumnia, staring at him reprovingly. Still seething, he barked. 'What do you want?'

Lumnia pulled Branko by the arm. 'Come with me!' She turned to Dodo. 'You, too!'

Branko, yielding to Lumnia's authority, allowed her to lead him; Dodo followed.

Lumnia led them to a burrow by the side of the hillock. 'This is your place, Dodo – right?'

Dodo nodded.

Lumnia went in. 'Come in – both of you.'

Inside the burrow, which was lit by a single candle, Branko noted the occupants, huddled on a pallet: Notarka, Dodo's wife, and their four children. Two of the children were breathing with difficulty.

Lumnia pointed out the latter. 'Dodo's youngest daughters. Rosa. Keja. Not yet three. Dying, as you can see. The so-called influenza.'

Branko, remembering that Dodo had already lost a child the previous week, felt deeply sorrowful.

'The illness is immune to magic. I can't cure them. But you can.'

Branko protested. 'My healing powers have gone. You know that!'

Lumnia beckoned him. 'You see how they're breathing? Watch.'

Gently, Lumnia spoke to the children. 'Rosa. Keja. There will be a new chief. Branko will hand over.'

Branko felt his rage rise. But instead of erupting, it paralysed him. He turned to look at Dodo, but saw only grief on the man's face. Then he confronted Lumnia. 'Since when have you been scheming all this?'

Lumnia held his look. Her eyes were tender, loving. 'I don't scheme. The *Urme* do.'

'You were looking into the future – breaking the rule. I saw – in your tent!'

'You asked me to find out why the children were dying.'

Branko noted that the breathing of the children had eased.

Lumnia took Branko's hand. 'You see. It's helping.'

Branko did not shirk from the touch and held on to her hand. 'Yes.'

'Save them.'

Branko, barely controlling his tears, approached the children and took their hands and held them against his cheeks.

As she left the burrow, Lumnia turned to Dodo. 'Nobody will know, but there'll never be a better father than Branko.'

Branko lumbered back to the hillock.

Here it was. The fall! Work unfinished. The fate of every prophet. Not a safe calling, prophethood. But, naturally, he had known, in his bones, this was how it would end. A man wizened by electricity could never seriously believe that prophecies would eradicate suffering, heal wounds, render people whole, reassure children who had been deprived of mother and father that they, too, were loveable and lights unto their people and the whole world.

Branko roared at the skies. 'I, Branko, Saviour, have become a plague, O Del! The innocent has been transformed into the transgressor! Have you no shame, you bastard!'

The skies remained silent.

Branko turned to Dodo and growled. 'I yield.'

Here it was then. End of prophethood. But not the end of destiny or fate – which, for a prophet, were one and the same. There was still an apotheosis to come.

Dodo muttered awkwardly. 'There's something else . . .'

'What?'

'You must give up Lumnia, too.'

Branko gaped at him. 'What?'

'Omar has luck. But she has magic. Without her we would not survive.'

Branko was ready to pounce on Dodo again. 'You survived because of me! I forged you! Protected you!'

'She did her share.'

'If you leave everything to luck and magic – you'll end up losing your steel.'

'We won't. We'll never forget all that you taught us.'

'She's not a nun! She can't renounce life!'

'She'll marry Omar.'

Branko was shocked. 'Omar. Again?'

'A good combination.'

'What about Parno? The triplets?'

'He'll leave them.'

'Has he agreed?'

'We haven't told him yet.'

'How do you think he'll respond to decisions taken behind his back?'

'He will see the point.'

'What if he refuses?'

Dodo lit a fresh cigarette. 'The chance of leadership, of a *drabarni* for a wife, are further examples of his good fortune. If he refuses, he'd be insulting Luck. He'd lose everything – including his family.'

'That's superstition!'

'Would you risk it?'

'When will I be deposed?'

Dodo hesitated before answering. 'Soon.'

Branko took a deep breath. 'Now is better than soon.'

Dodo, taken aback, became hesitant. 'If – you think so . . .'

'But I'll be *false chief* – not an elder.'

Dodo shifted uneasily. 'On what grounds . . .?'

'*False chief* defends the real chief. Serves the people. I'll still be doing that.'

'I was hoping to be . . .'

'When I'm dead.'

Branko sat in a corner. Two of the triplets had snuggled into his arms; the third lay with his head on his lap.

Parno stood in the opposite corner, her head bowed.

Omar paced the tent.

Dodo squatted on his haunches and waited.

An otherworldly tranquillity cocooned Branko. Now that he had been freed from leadership, emotions received the time and consideration they deserved. At this moment, for instance, he relished the joy of cuddling Omar's sons, savoured the warmth their need for him generated.

The boys had always been affectionate; but now, waiting for Omar's decision, wondering whether he would or would not abandon them, they had naturally come to Branko.

Victims mimicking lambs and begging for acceptance. As, all those years back, in an austere Pro Juventute office, he himself had begged Melchior and Eloïse . . . and as Melchior and Eloïse had begged him . . .

He no longer envied Omar. In any case, now that he had been deposed, his luck was bound to change.

In fact, Omar should be envying him. Even if he sired a dozen sons with Lumnia, he would never regain the full grace of fatherhood: neither the triplets, nor his new offspring, would own him completely. That would be bad luck.

Omar towered above Branko. 'Why don't you object? Resist? Refuse?'

Branko noted the triplets avoided looking at their father. But Parno had raised her head and was staring at him, the same question marking her expression.

Poor Parno. Earlier she had asked if such a momentous decision should not be taken at a *kriss*. Dodo had dismissed the idea, telling her that agreement between the principals would make the transfer of power easier. She had not spoken since.

Branko offered a long sigh. 'Resist – a whole people?'

Omar gazed out of the tent's opening. 'When I was a child – in Skopje, I kept going to places the earthquake had devastated. I wanted to remember what it had been like when it had struck, whether I had wanted to die with my mother and father. Naturally, I couldn't remember that far back. But I always felt something worse was to come. Worse than the earthquake. Worse even than orphanhood. I was right. This is it.' He looked at Parno, then at the triplets.

Pointedly they looked away from him.

Omar started weeping.

Dodo shook his head. 'I don't understand . . .'

Branko interjected. 'He means: good luck always carries a curse.'

Dodo protested. 'He'll be chief!' He held Omar's arm. 'Won't you accept?'

'Have I the choice?'

'Yes.'

Again Omar looked at his wife and sons. This time they faced him, sombre yet hopeful. Omar dropped his eyes and mumbled. 'I accept.' He turned to Branko, seeking his approval. 'I can't refuse, can I . . .?'

Branko stared at him impassively.

The triplets snuggled up closer.

Parno, numbed, fetched a bottle of *rakia* and some glasses and served the men with drinks.

Branko, Omar and Dodo found Lumnia in her tent, sitting silently with Ariana and Xyris.

Dodo thought the three women looked like owls appraising the night. The image disturbed him: the owl was the bird of death.

Lumnia got up and faced the men. 'I know why you're here.'

Branko took her hand. 'Let me explain . . .'

'No need.'

Omar interjected. 'We can't force you . . .'

She turned to him. 'Go now. Take Dodo with you. I'll be yours tomorrow. Today, I'm still my husband's.'

Acquiescing instantly, Omar led Dodo away.

Lumnia turned to the women. 'You, too, Dei. And you, Xyris – you'll have Branko tomorrow.'

Xyris ran her hand tenderly over Lumnia's face, then hurried out.

347

Ariana displayed her stigmata. 'It's not the end, son. You can see here –
it's not the end.'

Gently, Branko guided her out. 'I know, Dei.'

Branko and Lumnia faced each other.

Someone, in the distance, began to sing. Parno, Branko thought. One of
Omar's songs.

'I have reached an age
when
I love
in fear.
How many partings
can a soul survive?'

When the singing stopped, Lumnia started screaming.

Lumnia had screamed an eternity.

When she could scream no longer, she had collapsed into Branko's arms.

They had found themselves making love. At first, tentatively. Then
desperately. Finally, languidly, as on their first coupling on that mysterious
summit in Macedonia.

Now, lying side by side, listening to their bodies, determined to store
within secret chambers of memory all that belonged exclusively to their
eternal love, they caressed each other obsessively.

And Lumnia placed Branko's hand on her abdomen. Might they detect a
movement beneath the annulet of her belly, maybe a pulse, maybe even
astounding tremors announcing conception. Reprieve at the last second! A
seed, alive and prodigious! Why not?

He read her thoughts. 'You'll conceive with Omar.'

She wanted to scream again, but managed only a raucous yelp. Her fingers
tightened around his throat. 'Why do you yield? We can still be together!
Defy Destiny! Kill Omar! Abandon the movement! Abduct me!'

He prized her fingers loose and rose. 'I am yielding for my children.'

'Your children don't want you.'

He smiled wryly. 'How else will they find freedom?'

'Then let them go their own way! You and I – let's run off!'

'I promised them Romanestan. They still need me to get there.'

She remembered one of the stories he had transcribed.

A mighty Rom summoned his people in order to lead them to

348

Romanestan. Millions heeded his call and assembled along the rivers, mountains and steppes that divided Europe from Asia. The ingathering took forty years. But when they finally set out for Romanestan, nobody, not even the mighty Rom, could remember its whereabouts. And so the people dispersed once again.

'If there really is a Romanestan.'

'There is.'

'Where is it?'

'Where the Book says it is.'

'The Book does not say.'

'I haven't got to that portion yet. I will. Soon.'

'Do you really know where?'

He smiled. 'Yes.' He picked up his clothes. 'But you're wise to doubt me. We're no longer two souls in one body. It should be easier to push me out of your heart!'

She contemplated his body as he dressed. Still heavily muscled. And because it was now weather-beaten, even more manly. Tomorrow, that godly flesh would go to Xyris. And the repairer of broken people would enfold him with her earthy arms, suck him into her overripe peach and welcome his dead sperm as if it were full of live seeds. Then, in no time at all, she would give him the last rites.

O Del! Unsex Xyris! Wither her big thighs so that she can't entrap my Rom. Transform her into a mother! Another Ariana! Though a mother always wins, her victory is like defeat; because other women, younger women, unknown women, have feasted on her son's manhood and left her nothing but his obligatory respect.

Having dressed, he leaned over and kissed her eyes. 'I pronounce you free.'

She pushed him away. 'Free like a corpse. From which even the lice decamp.' She scrambled to her feet and started punching him. 'Where is your defiance?! How can you abandon me . . .'

He ignored the blows. 'You're abandoning me, too!'

'I'm ready to defy Fate!'

'You can't change Fate, remember?'

She punched him harder. 'Tomorrow I'll have another man's child! You should feel murderous!'

He pulled out his knife and held it between their throats. 'Shall I kill us both?'

She shouted. 'Yes! With my blessing!'

'But that would be killing a whole people.' He pocketed the knife and left. And it was as if he had dematerialized.

ketu the purveyor of pestilences rides his owl
    the mouth like a disembowelment grins
    the suppurating eye twitches to the left
    ketu's spear smeared in every poison impales me
    o del don't forsake me send hino the thunderbird to whisk me to the holy mountain himavata there to heal me with lightning-stones
    I maim My favourite son because mortals best hear gods through impaired bodies I afflict him with madness because only a crazed hero would seek patriarchy over a whole people.
    the poisons make me grotesque the people are deserting me i know a saviour must endure humiliation ugliness and abandonment he must even die so that he can live but the pain o del the pain
    o del you whore why have you forsaken me

Twenty-Six

The people had insisted that Omar and Lumnia should marry without delay. Luck and Magic, they had asserted, had kept out of each other's bed for too long.

But they had failed to find a site for the wedding. None of the clearings along the river could accommodate, in seclusion, the celebrations of a whole people.

So they had come to Branko for counsel.

He had directed them to build a floating islet.

First they had collected driftwood, logs, reeds, bulrushes and algae; then they had compacted these into a buoyant, but sizeable mass – about three acres in dimension – with the array of rubbish that litters the waterways; thereafter, cohering the agglomeration with sand, grass and moss, they had given it a good measure of malleability and attached it to their boats with tractable hawsers woven from twiners and lianas.

The result was an island that could be towed like a barge. Moreover, by bracing or slackening its hawsers, it could be adjusted both in length and width and manoeuvred through even the narrowest bends of the river.

Now, at the end of the sixth, and final, day of labour, Branko sat on the riverbank and watched the people dress the island with flowers.

His thoughts flew back to the floating islets of Lake Titicaca. Those holms, often no more than a few square metres in size, formed by stray reeds, had an existence that was at the mercy of the lake's currents. Yet, they had been settled, since the birth of the sun, by the Aymara people.

Branko remembered telling Melchior that the Aymara had a close resemblance to the Gypsies; that, given their musical virtuosity, artisanship and delight in colourful textiles, they could be taken for genuine Romanies; and that, therefore, they could well be a lost ancestral tribe.

Was that memory or hallucination?

Memory, surely. The trip to Bolivia had been a present from Melchior. Twenty-first birthday, was it? The old man, musingly, had related that the Gypsy Bible had contained a legend about a Romany tribe lost somewhere in South America. Or had it been Dr Kalderon who had told him that?

Nowadays, confusion permeates my mind.

Am I fumbling for a new focus because Omar deposed me and robbed me of my Lumnia?

Or am I collecting the shards that are all that remain of me in the hope that I can paste them together and recreate myself?

Why do I keep staring at Xyris' big thighs? Or imagine standing behind her every time she bends down?

The Sacred Book does mention a lost Gypsy tribe.

By the morning, the island will look like a fairground.

Tomorrow evening, Omar – one has to pity him: his eyes, forever seeking glimpses of Parno and the triplets, are like trapped bees – will possess Lumnia.

Let wild dogs tear you to pieces, Omar! Testicles first!

Branko strode back to the camp-fire. He, too, would finish his work that night. He would complete the Bible. Only one section remained. He would have it done by sunrise.

Xyris was waiting to serve the soup. Firmly planted on columnar legs, her skirt clinging to her in the breeze, her nipples pushing hard against her blouse in stubby tumescence, she looked like the priestess of a lusty goddess.

I suckled at the breasts of Sudolina, the goddess of wisdom.

Parno had set up the plates.

Ariana sat sorrowfully as if she were the one who had lost wife and sceptre.

Honeypaw was at his post, guarding the tent that served as the Yurt of the Book. Scandinavian Gypsies called the bear 'God's Dog'; here was proof of it.

The triplets were huddling against Honeypaw. These days they avoided

Parno. According to Xyris, they did not have the heart to witness her suffering. For Parno's pain was all too visible. Branko had seen it even on her shadow.

On Branko's approach, Honeypaw extricated himself from the triplets, reared up on his hind legs and yelped with delight. Branko hugged the bear, then ruffled the triplets' hair.

He noted that Parno's nipples, too, were pouting through her blouse. Like crocuses breaking out of the earth. Should he ask her to suckle him? Make Lumnia jealous. Omar, too. In revenge, if for nothing else.

He sat by the fire.

Xyris served the soup, then squatted opposite him. Her thighs bulged; her crotch collected light from the darkness. Branko could see the indentation of her vagina. He hungered for her. Had Xyris had children?

One of the triplets turned to him. 'Is everyone at the wedding?'

'Everyone, except us.'

The second triplet joined in. 'But we've seen some men . . .'

Branko glanced at Honeypaw. The latter had pricked up his ears. 'Where?'

The third triplet pointed at the trees. 'One was here this morning. We thought he might be our Dadoro. We ran after him. He disappeared.'

Parno, biting her lips, got up and emptied her soup – barely touched – back into the pot. She lay down by a fallen tree and put her arms around the trunk. Pressing her loins against it, she went to sleep.

Ariana covered her with a blanket.

Honeypaw gobbled up the rest of his food. He licked the triplets one by one, nuzzled Branko's arm, then lumbered back towards the Yurt of the Book.

Images invaded Branko. Abandoned men. Abandoned children. Abandoned women. Electricity! All this pain – for what?

Could Leo Leo be right? Should we assimilate? Would the *gadje* accept us? When? In another millennium? Would they let us survive all that time?

He turned to the triplets. 'These men – if you see them again, let me know'

They all answered, excitedly. 'Right!'

Ariana beckoned them. 'Time to sleep. Come on!' She led them into the foliage.

Branko shut his eyes. Xyris came across. She had removed her clothes. Her belly shone like water lit by the moon. An undulating path, strewn with lotus flowers, led to her recesses. She was saying something. He could not hear the words. But her hands were divesting him of his chief's raiment. So good to surrender. So easy.

He leapt up, flustered. Man had no respite from madness, not even if he made himself eyeless.

Xyris, who had curled up by his feet, sprang up also, ready to attend to him.

He smiled wanly. 'I must finish the Book.' He strode away.

He prepared his tools: wood alcohol, magnifying glass, pen, ink, scroll.

He felt elated. The usual butterflies in his guts had multiplied to swarms. But then this was the last section. Natural to feel nervous.

Hands steady. He was an expert now. He had spent months teaching himself the various processes for dissolving ambery matter.

He had soon decided against the simpler course of melting the hard resin. The required temperature for that process was in excess of 300° Celsius; building a hearth that would provide such heat was beyond the means of a wandering people. Besides, without sophisticated safeguards, the process would destroy the pathetic assortment of scraps on which the text had been written.

So he had had to use a solvent. Since it was impossible to acquire commercial solutions in the wilderness, he had decided to use wood alcohol. This product, which was the basic compound for methanol, a standard solvent for amber, could be bought or stolen from villagers or, at a pinch, distilled by the Gypsies themselves.

Wood alcohol, though rather a crude solvent, would not disintegrate the fossilized core because, like most solvents, it dissolved the resin only partially. Consequently, when applied to the Bible cakes, it removed only the darker top layer and left the text on the fossilized material legible through the lighter resin. In fact, the process proved so successful that, on occasions, the undissolved resin assumed the properties of a lens and magnified the text it contained.

Branko took the last slab of ambery ash and applied the wood alcohol.

The resin dissolved.

The Word emerged.

It crossed deserts, mountains and plains. None in its ranks was left behind; even those who had died or were killed rose up and followed It.

The Word reached land's end.

There, on ancient clay, It saw Its reflection. It recognized Itself as primal matter. Indivisible.

It distilled Itself and became the sea.
The people waded into it and found Romanestan.
All this Branko wrote.

Having well absorbed Branko's rule that strangers who hide in the bush invariably produce flowers of death, Honeypaw threaded his way through the woods silently and invisibly.

Branko followed, providing cover.

The *gadjo*'s odour was faint, barely detectable, just a whiff of well-oiled weapons, not dissimilar to the stale breath of the humus after a winter's slumber.

It had been the triplets – with the sixth sense of the innocent – who had picked up the scent early that morning.

Sadly, that meant that the *gadjo* had found a Gypsy who had taught him how to camouflage smell. Using turncoats was the *gadjo*'s favourite strategy; that was how he had conquered the five continents. But the turncoat – it could only be Leo Leo – had arrived too soon. He had to be chased away. Premature incidents had been known to sabotage history.

Honeypaw, slowing down, drew himself on to his haunches and listened to the air carefully.

Branko left the initiative to him. A bear, being cannier than twenty-four foxes, was the supreme hunter, so Yerko had instructed him.

Honeypaw darted forward; massive brown frame streaking on hind legs, he looked like an oak running. He bellowed short, sharp roars that sent the birds flying in terror.

Branko spotted Honeypaw's targets: five men; strongly built; brutal faces; dressed as peasants, but bearing the sulphur of cities; armed with machine-pistols – Czech – and comfortable with them.

The men, reacting to Honeypaw's roars, lost their bluster. Trying to sight the bear, they spun on their heels in panic. Even their guns, which they had held like proud, iron penises, appeared to wilt.

Branko took cover.

Honeypaw broke through the trees.

The men twisted round, tried to take aim.

Honeypaw ploughed into them and knocked them down like skittles. As they lay unconscious, he swept their guns into the undergrowth.

Branko held back. He had sensed another presence. Then he saw the rifle protruding from the foliage; a mane of white hair was aiming at Honeypaw.

He catapulted forward and hurled himself at Leo Leo, striking him, feet first, on the chest.

Leo Leo's companions were regional officials of the National Salvation Front, the party that had replaced the Ceauşescu regime. But as the NSF, though boasting to be the torch-bearer of democracy, was, in reality, a crude revamp of the old Communist Party, these officials were nothing more than ex-Securitate reconditioned. Now that they were trying to moderate their swagger, they looked even more sinister: fat, slimy sewer rats passing off as trim rodents.

One of them had a formidable reputation. Known simply by his nickname Hospodar – the title of the Phanariot princes whose reign, under the aegis of the Ottoman empire, was heinous even by the despotic standards of Romanian history – he was the old Securitate chief of Transylvania. During his time in office, he had often been heard threatening to put all the country's enemies – starting with the Gypsies – to the spear in emulation of Vlad the Impaler.

Branko and Yerko had made a point of never crossing his path.

Whilst Honeypaw watched over the men – a plight that plunged Hospodar into raging impotence – Branko hauled up Leo Leo. 'I wasn't expecting you yet. You've mistimed it.'

'Mistimed it? I've been trying to track you . . .'

'You're meant to turn up at the delta – when we approach the sea. That's what the Book says.'

'Does it? Well, I don't go by the Book. The sooner I stop your crazy caper, the better! Where are the people?'

'Around.'

'Still living like ghosts? Invisible by day, bats at night?'

Branko nodded.

Leo Leo bristled with hostility. 'Still hoping to get to Romanestan?'

'Where else?'

'How long can you keep up the lie?'

'Come with us. See for yourself.'

'If you reach the delta – if – that's the end. Nowhere else to go.'

'There's the sea.'

'Dive in – like lemmings? Or are you thinking of walking on it?'

356

'Sailing.'

'Sailing? You'll need a fleet.'

'O Del will provide.'

'You're crazy.'

Branko felt someone watching him; he spun round. It was Hospodar, looking him over with suppurating eyes.

Each turn of the Samsara demands a sacrifice.

Leo Leo resumed in a softer voice. 'Branko, listen. Whether you sail, swim or walk on water, you're heading for disaster. Any move you make will be treated as an uprising. It will end up in a blood-bath.'

'That's not our destiny.'

'Have some sense, for God's sake! They'll stop you! Come what may!' Leo Leo pointed at Hospodar. 'Ask him!'

Branko met Hospodar's eyes – still suppurating. 'What do *you* say?'

Hospodar's gaze slithered over him. 'Time's running out.'

'And when it does?'

Hospodar spat. 'I'll be there.'

Branko smiled. 'I'll look out for you.'

Leo Leo grabbed Branko's hands. 'Branko! Please! Join me! Assimilation – that's the answer. The only answer.'

'Nothing will stop us.' Branko turned to Hospodar. 'Did you hear that? Nothing will stop us. Tell your masters that.'

As Leo Leo tried to think of fresh arguments, Branko nodded at Honeypaw.

The bear reared up, growling.

The men, with Hospodar outpacing them all, ran into the woods.

Leo Leo screeched. 'Branko, listen!'

Honeypaw lumbered towards Leo Leo.

Leo Leo's defiance expired. He ran off shouting. 'You're mad! You'll all be killed!'

Branko stroked Honeypaw. 'I am mad! That's as it should be. But doubt and fear . . . Can I conquer them?'

Honeypaw nuzzled him as if to reassure him. Branko climbed on to his back. Honeypaw ambled away. Branko clasped his neck. Noble animal. Had Honeypaw been human, he would have outshone Omar. Then Omar's luck would not have appeared so prodigious and he, Branko, would still have been chief and Lumnia would still have been his wife.

357

During the years in the wilderness, on long winter nights, Yerko had often reminisced about old Orşova. And he had related that in that town on the Danube, and on its equally famous island, Ada Kale, the legendary site of the first olive tree, a Gypsy would invariably be seduced by two contradictory dreams.

In the first, featuring old Orşova, which had seen the ebb and flow of many peoples – until 1918 it had been a busy frontier between Romania and Hungarian Transylvania – there would be reflections of a world where the intercourse of diverse cultures had banished nationalistic, religious and ethnic conflicts.

In the second, featuring Ada Kale, where a community of Turks, living as artisans and healers, had enjoyed all the creative forces that put marrow into a people, the spirit of the Gypsy homeland would be manifest.

But time and politics had eventually caught up with both Orşova and Ada Kale. The construction of the Iron Gates Dam, altering the course of the Danube and raising its waters, had submerged them and their respective dreams, several fathoms deep.

Officialdom had promised that the new Orşova, built a few kilometres downstream, would soon outshine its predecessor. The promise was still awaiting fulfilment.

It was to a point above the sunken city of old Orşova that Branko rowed his dinghy to contemplate the nuptials of Lumnia and Omar.

When the sun burrowed into the Danube and the clouds of vapour it had raised dispersed, the people's island rose like a leviathan.

Branko recognized the smell of blood and vital fluids – of afterbirth, in fact. Perhaps it had been born of old Orşova and formed the embryo of two ancient dreams: a Gypsy homeland and a world without frontiers.

And night fell. And the elements burst into song. Exhorting Omar and Lumnia as Fate's favourites, they promised them many children, and many again unto their children and yet many more unto their children's children.

Out on the Milky Way, O Del harvested new stars for the newly weds.

Branko spat at his useless genitals and wept.

The moon climbed to her apogee.

Omar and Lumnia left the festivities and withdrew to their tent. They shed their clothes and conjoined.

They quickened.

In the forest, tears sprouted from Ariana's palms.

By the riverbank, Branko espied a drop of blood running down Lumnia's thigh.

At first, he thought her hymen, having been made whole as a symbolic gift from O Del, had been perforated. Then he saw that the blood was his own, the blood that had mingled with hers when they had married.

And as the vaginal fluids carried his blood to the earth, there to render it into dust, Branko espied an image on Lumnia's thigh. It was the reflection of her impregnated egg. Lucky Omar had achieved conception at his first attempt!

Branko howled and beat his head.

Ariana and Xyris heard him and came running.

Xyris, wrapping Branko in her shawl, took him in her arms. Branko's howling subsided. Xyris faced Ariana as if wanting her permission.

Ariana nodded a hasty consent.

Xyris took Branko to his shelter.

In her tent, Lumnia, who had also heard Branko's howls, now shut off her perceptions in order not to perceive Xyris attending to Branko.

Branko pressed himself against Xyris' surging breasts and sucked her nipples. Her giant legs entwined him. He sank into her loins, the softest of sources, and frolicked like a dolphin in her warm waters. When he spent himself, he laughed – for the first time in an eternity.

And also for the first time in years, he did not curse his barrenness. He imagined he was like old Orşova. A seed whose future had been cancelled, but a seed that had lived; of greater importance, a seed that had contained a whole people. And, for those who might doubt its existence, a seed whose harvest could be seen, dead but preserved, at the bottom of Xyris' lake.

And, draining his soul of self-hatred, he forgave himself.

Before the beginning, there was the Word, written with black fire upon white fire.

Such was its size that its ankles rested on the sea whilst its head reached the sky.

And still before the beginning, there was also the Book, the yoni to the Word's lingham.

And so that it could contain the Word, the Book was immense in size; Chrysor, the Phoenician, who taught mankind how to sail the oceans, would take a hundred years to navigate just one page.

359

And when the beginning came, O Del discovered both the Word and the Book.

And with them He created Creation.

And He said: 'May it always be My will that My mercy precedes My wrath and so prevents me from creating an End.'

And the Word and the Book took note of His wisdom and never wrote the End.

Twenty-Seven

Branko had briefed the people.

This final stretch of the Danube was the busiest.

For most of its eastward run, the river served as Romania's southern border first with Yugoslavia, then with Bulgaria. But it did not drain into the Black Sea in the vicinity of Constanţa, as might have been expected from its relatively straight course. At Silistra, on the Bulgarian border, about one hundred and thirty kilometres from the coast, it turned sharply to the north to bypass the mountains of Dobrogei. Thence, for some one hundred and fifty kilometres, it flowed parallel to the Black Sea. Finally, in the wake of its confluence with the River Prut, near Galaţi, it veered east and, about fifty kilometres further on, commenced its delta. On this last stretch, along the delta's northernmost branch, the Braţul Chilia, it served as a frontier also, this time, with Ukraine and Moldova – a frontier that had been imposed on Romania by an implacable Stalin at the end of the Second World War.

The Gypsies had to evade not only Leo Leo and the Romanian authorities, but also the river patrols of neighbouring countries.

The journey to the delta took nine months.

True to expectations, Omar carried the leadership as if born to it.

The elders approved particularly his decision to continue travelling invisibly at night. This leader, they agreed, did not seek self-aggrandizement with unwarranted or unsafe changes of policy.

But he was most impressive, everybody agreed, in the way he kept watch over the triplets and, to some extent, over Parno. Though the triplets, especially, tormented him daily by pointedly avoiding him, he never retaliated. He had been heard saying to them: 'Spit on me all you want, my heart will always embrace you.'

One reason for the slow pace was the intensification of the aerial search by Leo Leo's masters. Sometimes, to avoid aircraft with infrared, night-vision cameras, Omar would be forced to divert his fleet on to small tributaries where the banks were lushly strewn with weeping trees.

Another reason was Lumnia's pregnancy. A bard's jubilant pronouncement that the infant would portray the people the way a strand of hair represents a person had gained ground and, predictably, led to the conviction that the date of the child's birth would mark the inception of Gypsy sovereignty. Consequently, Lumnia was kept as pampered as a mare impregnated by a prize stallion.

For Branko, the journey felt interminable. He soon ceased to distinguish between day and night, sun and moon, rain and snow.

Mostly, he did little else than suckle at Xyris' ever-flowing fount. At times, he wrestled obsessively with Honeypaw as if only trials of strength could nourish his spirit. At other times, frustrated by the ambiguities in Ariana's stigmata, he sought out birds and flowers, insects and trees, and questioned them about reincarnation.

Occasionally, he hovered around Parno and tried to console her.

Poor, beautiful Parno, Luck's erstwhile consort! Whilst her sons, abandoned by her eyes, mouth and arms, sought shelter and affection under Branko's wing, she shed hair, shape and complexion. And on the day she became totally bald, she took up carving ornamental combs. She honed their teeth, obsessively, to a sharpness that could pierce stone and metal.

At Pătlăgeanca, where the Danube begins to deliver its delta, Branko took a census.

The Gypsies numbered half a million souls.

Most of the newcomers had come from Romania. Captivated by the promise of a homeland, they had finally left the towns and villages that had persecuted them for centuries. Others, a generation that had been rotting on the scrap-heaps of Europe, had been recruited by Dodo's agents and collected at various rendezvous points. Peaceable people.

Branko exulted: his children. He watched over them, kissed them if they had nightmares, then tucked them into their boats.

The old vision visited him regularly. It had acquired great clarity.

The people reach a river of molten metal.

There are viscera paddling in it.

And a mouth, like a disembowelment.

And a suppurating eye.

A bridge, the width of a single hair, spans the river.

The mouth and the eye select those who cross the bridge; the condemned fall into the molten river.

Branko, Saviour, goes first.

The mouth sneers.

The suppurating eye twitches to the left.

The bridge breaks.

He plummets down, smiling contentedly.

Above him the bridge restructures itself.

The people cross without mishap and emerge, at the other end, like first mortals.

He closes his eyes contentedly as the molten river consumes him.

Branko transported himself to the coast. He waded into the surf and reminded the Black Sea that, a long time ago, when the future had not been imminent, when he and Yerko had surveyed the entire region, he had asked it to be clement towards the Gypsies. They had negotiated at length and the brine had agreed to accommodate them.

Will you honour the agreement?

The Black Sea, pounding the beach with waves, affirmed that it would.

Branko embraced the water.

The ancient Greeks had called this sea '*Axeinos*', 'inhospitable', for its paucity of safe harbours. Later, seeking to propitiate its sudden storms, they had renamed it '*Euxine*', meaning 'hospitable'. The epithet 'black', it had been suggested, referred to the melanistic sheen caused by the vast deposits of hydrogen sulphide in its depths. The Turks called the sea, '*kara*', 'dark', which, according to one legend, had been coined by Attila the Hun as he had watched the swell reflect the sombre, undulating plains of his native cloud-hidden Central Asia.

There's unsurpassable beauty in all things black! Sleep is black. So is tenderness. So, too, the end of a journey; and the fulfilment of a prophecy. Gypsies are every shade of black. Honeypaw passes as black. Xyris is glorious ebony; and her cove: the sloe of oblivion. And I am black. And death, according to Yerko who wished to die here, is pure black.

Perhaps I am the one who will die here. Is that part of the deal? – I can't remember.

Omar convened a *kriss* so that all the questions that loomed when fires were lit – and all those that returned in dreams – could be addressed.

He presented his own first. Qualms of a new chief. For though he was still Luck's favourite, no prophecy had come to sit on his shoulders. Why are we delivering ourselves to the Black Sea, which, but for one narrow strait, is a closed sea? Why not the Mediterranean, or the Baltic, or, best of all, the Atlantic?

Then Dodo. Questions weighted down by remorse. Will the people suffer for deposing the Chosen One?

From the *Manush*. Fear counterpointed by lack of confidence. Will there be cover in the delta? Will we be able to keep the people safe?

From the elders. Carrying the apprehensions of age. Why must we sail to Romanestan? Why not travel overland?

From women. Practical questions. Where will we find boats? How will we feed our families?

Long deliberations, some considered and some impetuous, ensued. None satisfied.

Then Branko, still coated with the Black Sea's tangy salt, took the floor. Surprisingly unaffected, on this occasion, by the saviour's inarticulate delivery, he addressed all the questions. He spoke for forty hours.

First: a Chosen One is dispensable. His task is to forge his people. When he achieves that, he has served his purpose and must be cast aside. Moreover, a Chosen One always turns unstable, becomes a liability; you were right to depose me. I have forgiven you for reaching maturity. I have also forgiven myself for striving to be your father.

The Black Sea has been chosen because it is like us. Brave and defiant. So is the Danube delta.

I know water. I was an engineer. A professional. Nature is not kind to rivers. Not only does it expend them as fodder for seas, it also forces them to prostrate themselves in meek deltas before their immersion. The Danube does not accept this destiny. When it deviates sharply to the north, near Constanţa, it does not do so because it has to skirt round the Dobrogei range. That's geographers' talk. Geographers see only the external reality, never the mysteries. In that respect, they are like the gadje who know everything about killing, but nothing about the regeneration that death brings. The Danube diverts to the north for strategic reasons: to prepare for its confrontation with the sea. It fortifies itself with every available stream, and, at the same time, scouts for a terrain that loves water and will welcome its delta.

Consequently, no sooner does the Danube open its arteries – one here, at Pătlăgeanca, the other two at Tulcea – than it feverishly carves countless *ghiols*. It secretes, into these hidden channels, the contents of its minor veins so that for every volume of water it yields to the Black Sea, it saves an equal portion. Thus it is reborn perpetually.

Why does the Black Sea tolerate such defiance?

Because it is of Romany hue. It does not practise injustice. It upholds the Danube's right to life. It knows there can be no freedom unless there is freedom for all. That explains why most of us have lived near it or around it or along byways and waterways that led to it. Why even those brothers and sisters, scattered to other continents, still paint their stories, songs and dreams with its dark hues. Naturally, then, it is the perfect sea to give birth to Romanestan.

The delta ahead is a water-land of some four thousand, five hundred square kilometres which changes constantly, where the primal dualities of life, chaos and order, amorphousness and configuration, deformity and form, rule side by side.

Each moment brings a different mood and a new guise. When the *ghiols* feel sluggish, they congregate as marshes or lakes; when they turn energetic, they shunt the silt around and build up strings of islands and promontories which they then emblazon with willows, poplars, even oaks; and when they turn ebullient and scamper aimlessly across the wilderness, they emboss vast expanses with the floating reed islets which, the Holy Book tells us, once drifted as far as South America.

The water is sweet and clean. The buffalo that spend whole summers submerged vouchsafe that. So do the abundant fish. Countless birds – herons, pelicans, ibises, swans, mandarin ducks, polar grebes, falcons and fishing eagles – flourish here either as privileged residents or as migrants. So do predator minks, polecats, boars, wolves. In summer, when the giant horseflies drive them mad, you can hear them yelping. You can also hear them howling in winter, as their Eden turns into an icy waste.

It is time to emerge. To show ourselves to the world. To be reborn.

I hear Omar, Dodo and the *Manush* protesting. Why do we have to emerge here?, you ask. Ahead, at the delta, conditions favour us; the streams can close behind us and trap the enemy, you say. True. Few places on earth provide better protection than this wilderness. Throughout history numerous tribes have found refuge in these labyrinthine backwaters and lived unseen and unknown.

But we are no longer a people that needs to hide. We are now a people ready for sovereignty. It is time to prove – to ourselves, above all – that we have become whole, that, therefore, we are indestructible. We can keep under cover anywhere – we have shown that. We remained invisible for months on end, not in a region where concealment is easy, but on a major river running through open country. Now, it is time to burst forth, like sunrise, with all our colours.

If you doubt my word, look to Lumnia. The *drabarni*'s fruiting belly carries the message. Destiny does not hide in the bushes; it unfolds in the open so that both friend and foe can see its splendour.

We will attain Romanestan because that which is written in the Holy Book cannot be erased.

We will sail because when we last travelled on land, the gadje sought to destroy us on asphalt and cobblestones, on mountain passes and in secluded valleys, in picture-card villages and forest clearings, in the surgeries and crematoria of death camps.

The boats will come from everywhere. All the peoples of the world will watch us set foot in Romanestan.

All that is written in the Holy Book.

And so, at Pātlāgeanca, on a sunny, balmy day in June, the myriad small craft of the Gypsies appeared on the Danube like tidal spume.

As they conducted final preparations on the beach, Branko, accompanied by Ariana, met with Omar and Lumnia.

He spoke, darting his eyes everywhere except Lumnia's globed belly. 'I have a recurring vision . . .'

Lumnia looked up sharply. 'A bridge of hair over a molten river?'

Branko was surprised. 'How did you know?'

Lumnia muttered solemnly. 'It's been haunting me, too.'

'It's now imprinted on Dei's palm.'

Lumnia became troubled. 'Already?'

Ariana, displaying the stigma that depicted Branko's portrait, remarked portentously. 'A vision seeking to become reality . . .'

Lumnia, averting her eyes, nodded.

Omar looked at the women. 'What's that mean? What are you talking about?' He turned to Branko. 'Are you in danger?' He turned to the women again. 'Is he in danger?'

Branko sat on the ground. 'Nothing to worry about.'

Omar became all the more concerned. 'Are you in danger? Tell me!'

'It's not important! Listen! It's time you knew about Romanestan . . .'

Lumnia faced him, perturbed. 'Yes. I understand.'

Omar stared at them, confused. 'Understand what?'

Branko smiled. 'Listen! Think of crannogs – there's a reference in the Book . . .'

Omar nodded. 'Yes. Artificial skerries. Erected in lochs. Conceived by ancient Scots to defend themselves.'

Branko piled together some twigs. 'Remember the island we assembled for your wedding? We'll build a similar one on the sea. Then multiply it a million fold. And, when the need arises, multiply it again. There you have it . . . A mass as bountiful as any continent. Able to take any shape. Capable of sailing anywhere, of riding any storm, of coping with any current . . .'

Omar stared at him, stunned. 'That . . . That's going to be . . . Romanestan?'

Branko rose. 'That will be Romanestan.' He walked away.

Omar started laughing uproariously. 'Of course. Of course . . .' He turned to the women. 'Do you see? A travelling land! Perfect – don't you think?'

Ariana and Lumnia, offering token smiles, watched Branko as he ran, like a carefree youth, and joined Xyris.

On Branko's advice, they avoided Bratul Chilia, the branch that formed the border with the Ukrainian and Moldovan Republics.

Branko had offered two reasons. The nationalists in Moldova were seeking to secede from the Commonwealth of Independent States, the newfangled Soviet Union, and rejoin Romania; travelling through such a volatile region would expose the Gypsies to harassment, perhaps even to crossfire. Secondly, the borders, as redrawn after the Second World War, had placed the mouth of Bratul Cilia in Ukrainian territory; this would expose the Gypsies to yet another disputed terrain. Any trespass would provoke military action from the Ukraine – probably from Russia, too – both of which, destabilized by the Soviet Union's fragmentation, sought just that kind of excuse to distract their dissatisfied people.

They made for the river port of Tulcea, one of the oldest cities in Europe.

They sailed in formation.

Branko, as is incumbent on the *false chief*, led the vessels. Ariana and Xyris travelled with him in his rowing boat.

Branko's liaison with Xyris had become common knowledge; but the people, normally intolerant of concubinage, expressed no disapproval. Their respect for Xyris had increased. They could see she was nursing Branko's torn spirit in the only way possible, by keeping him ensconced in her flesh.

The fact that, as Branko rowed, Xyris sat in front of him, at the bow, unlike Lumnia who had always sat at the stern – as Ariana did now – also impressed the people. By so doing, Xyris not only inspired Branko with the horizons of her thighs, but also affirmed that she knew her place: for a man must expose his back to no one save his mother and wife.

The vessel carrying the Yurt of the Book followed Branko's boat. It was the flotilla's largest craft and had been built to emulate Cleopatra's barge. Lumnia, who, as she had once disclosed to Branko, had been that Gypsy queen's handmaiden in a previous incarnation, had provided the specifications to the builders.

The barge was manned by a select band of *Manush* and guarded by its loyal sentry, Honeypaw. The yurt itself, redesigned, for full visibility, as a soft hemispherical tent, squat like an igloo and woven of the warmest yellow silk, stood at the centre. Those who saw it float past thought the Gypsies possessed a sun of their own.

Behind, under the watchful eyes of Omar and Lumnia, coursed the people.

At daylight, in their small craft and colourful attire, they looked like flowering gardens on a journey. At night, as they sat around their fires, they rippled on the water's surface like moonbathing mer-folk.

Upon their emergence, Leo Leo reappeared, manning a patrol boat.

Hospodar, his commander, advised him to bring matters to a speedy close. 'Sink the principal boats. The rest will surrender immediately.'

But Leo Leo, knowing that he was incapable of firing on his own people, convinced Hospodar that such an action against a non-violent and defenceless multitude would incur opprobrium from the civilized world.

And so, for days on end, he tacked along the Gypsy flotilla with a loudspeaker. Mustering all his authority, he reproved the Gypsies for abusing the benevolence of the host nation and urged them to disband. If they did not, he warned them, the consequences would be severe.

He listed the forces commissioned to deal with them. Six helicopter gun-ships. Three hundred marines. Two motorized infantry brigades. A battalion of infantry. And five Russian-built, P-4 torpedo boats.

The Romanians rushed to the riverbanks.

At first, they pelted the Gypsies with trash, stones and other missiles. They exhorted them not to disband. They exulted that, having entreated God for centuries for deliverance from the Gypsy plague, now, at last, their prayers were being answered.

Later, spellbound by the Gypsies' dignity, they became silent. Some lit candles in churches. Others knelt by the water and prayed that all mankind, even Gypsies, be spared suffering and misfortune.

Later still, full of good will, they took to their boats and sailed out to the Gypsies. Shouting abuse at the helicopters, patrol boats and the soldiers, they pressed upon the Gypsies bread, cheese, hens, pigs and fruit. Some even gave their own boats so that those sailing on rafts or dugouts would have better craft. They asked nothing in return, save blessings.

And more and more Gypsies joined the exodus.

Here and there, small units under Leo Leo's command tried to stop this influx.

But the Romanian people intervened. Standing as a human shield in front of the troops, they enabled the newcomers to join the Gypsy flotilla.

Gadje and Gypsy shook hands in friendship. Old neighbours apologized for past offences.

Many asked: 'Who will colour our world after you've gone?' Farmers wailed that the countryside would look as if it had been denuded of topsoil. And village after village, hoping to change the Gypsies' minds at the last hour, offered them sons and daughters in marriage; partnerships in flocks, fields, orchards and fisheries.

The Gypsies began to waver. Some, remembering Leo Leo's dreams of assimilation, started to speak again of the need to put down roots.

But Branko, acting as Omar's spokesman, went from boat to boat and persuaded them to push forward.

Earthy-voiced women sang farewells. Men trilled with verses of fire and hope. Bards composed new ballads and gave them as gifts to those who wished them safe seas and good fortune.

The Gypsies arrived at Tulcea.

The city's people – harbour folk – followed the example of their countrymen. They offered the Gypsies tools and bolts, sea-charts and meteorological reports. They gave them the names of agents in foreign ports from whom provisions could be bought. And, in the event that they might need to circumvent maritime regulations, they instructed them on how to manipulate officialdom's greed, a finer art than straightforward bribery.

Twelve kilometres downstream from Tulcea, the Gypsies reached the bifurcation where the delta debouched its other principal arms.

Here, they took the southern and older branch, Braţul Sfîntu Gheorghe, in preference to the central one, Braţul Sulina, though the latter, developed as a deep-water canal for freighters, offered a more direct route to the sea. Ships, Branko argued, were cavalier with small craft.

Bratul Sfîntu Gheorghe brought its own perils.

Past the small village of Mahmudia, where the branch begins its serpentine course, the crowds lost their cohesion. Suddenly, these well-wishers could no longer move in a single wave; the sharp bights, the various elbows and oxbows of the river, divided them into a spate of small groups.

This allowed the authorities to surround and isolate the groups at various bends and expel them from the delta.

Thus the Gypsies lost their shield.

And the authorities, in need of scapegoats for their misrule, seized their chance. They recruited gangs and sent them in.

First, the politicians. Of every species: in office; in opposition; in the wilderness; in delusion. Strutting like revolutionaries.

And they brought with them those who had been fed on their lies: the landless, the unemployed, the hungry, the confused. All armed with iron bars, pickaxes, spades, hammers – the traditional weapons of uprisings – generously supplied by the politicians.

Together, they shook their fists at the world.

'The Gypsies stole our birthright!'

'Our food!'

'Our gold!'

'Our children!'

'They must not escape!'

'They must be crushed!'

Then came the fascists. Native ones as well as those from Bulgaria, Poland, Hungary, Ukraine, Russia, Serbia, Greece, Macedonia, Albania, Italy, Croatia, Austria, Czechoslovakia, Germany, France, even England.

They howled their venom into the wind.

'Gypsies sucked history dry!'

'Gypsies will destroy civilization!'

'They are vermin who rule the world!'

'Destroy them to survive!'

And in their wake came the racists. From all over Europe. Equally inflamed.

'The Gypsy contaminates our blood!'

'Weakens our race!'

'Plagues our future!'
'Unsex them!'
'Complete the job Hitler left unfinished!'

They were followed by the religious fundamentalists. Of all denominations.
'The last of days are at hand!'
'Submit to the true faith!'
'Join us – and life everlasting awaits you!'

Last to come were the so-called 'closet Gypsies', Gypsies who had buried their identities under wherever they could – the sort that the white-skinned amongst Leo Leo's assimilationists might become one day.

Frenetic with fear, they spoke in whispers and in darkness so that no *gadje* would hear them.
'Freedom brings destruction!'
'A culture of invisibility – that's the answer!'
'Forget Romanestan!'
'Live where you can!'
'Live where the *gadje* can't see you!'
'Live as if you don't exist!'

Some of the rabble seized boats and tried to scuttle the Gypsy craft. But the *Manush* repulsed them.
A few died of knife wounds and smashed heads.
They lost their courage and retreated in panic. Many had to swim back.
A number drowned.

The deaths further goaded the authorities. They pushed their tanks and cannon to the riverbanks; they hung their helicopters in the sky.
Leo Leo begged the Gypsies. 'Surrender – or they'll fire!'
Branko went to Lumnia and asked her. 'What happens to a *drabarni*'s powers when she is pregnant? Do they change? Do they still serve the people? Or does the foetus commandeer them?'
Lumnia affirmed. 'They do not change. They continue to serve the people – of whom the foetus is one.'
Branko commanded her. 'Then smash those weapons!'
Lumnia summoned high winds and torrential rains.

The helicopters were flung back into their hives; the tanks sank into the mud.

Lumnia requested help from the mosquitoes.

They obliged.

The soldiers, bitten mercilessly, became demented and sprayed their bullets into the air.

The authorities, noting the Gypsies' immunity to the mosquitoes, pronounced them Satan's children.

And they decided to deploy the torpedo boats.

Leo Leo pleaded that he be allowed to negotiate one last time.

Leo Leo ploughed up and down Braţul Sfîntu Gheorghe for a whole week. This time, Hospodar went with him.

Night and day, he begged the Gypsies to come to their senses, to return to their respective countries. He swore that the world was changing; that, above all, the *gadje* were changing; that peoples of different nations, races and religions were getting to learn to live together; that assimilation was the currency of the future; that, indeed, in two or three generations all national, racial and religious divisions would be eradicated.

Branko, listing the genocidal conflicts raging in four continents, refuted Leo Leo's claims.

These conflicts, too, would be resolved, Leo Leo stated. But nobody heard him; he had been struck mute for hitching his life to false hopes. He withdrew from the river, knowing that his misguided spirit would never find peace.

And as Hospodar enumerated, with relish, the desolations that awaited the Gypsies, he wept.

Then he experienced a revelation. He saw that Branko had been right all along: that, in order to survive, the Gypsy must distance himself from the gadje.

And he rejoiced: he would help in that salvation; he would emulate Branko and destroy his people's enemies.

And he picked up a gun.

And he burst into Hospodar's office.

And, pointing the gun at Hospodar, he thundered. 'Stop hounding my people! Send the soldiers back!'

Hospodar began to laugh.

Leo Leo placed his finger on the trigger. 'If you don't, I will kill you!'

Hospodar's laughter became demented.

Leo Leo tried to fire; but he could not.

Killing means being haunted by the dead – so Branko had said, once upon a time . . .

And as Leo Leo lowered the gun, Hospodar stopped laughing . . .

The six torpedo boats were ordered to blast the Gypsies off the delta. But the new day, washed clean by a stormy night, intervened.

To start with, the torpedo boats found the entrance to Braţul Sfîntu Gheorghe blocked by packed reeds torn up by the rains.

Then the horizon suddenly filled with a number of flagless ships.

When Romanian coastguards duly intercepted these, the captains declared that they had come to collect the Gypsies.

Further astonishing news followed.

Istanbul radio announced that an unprecedented number of vessels, with Romania as their destination, were passing through the straits of the Bosporus; an even greater influx was queuing up in the Sea of Marmara.

A CNN broadcast disclosed that countless other boats were steaming up the Aegean towards the Dardanelles.

The Gypsies, even as they realized that these were the ships Branko had promised them, were as surprised as the Romanian authorities. Where had they come from? Who was manning them? How had Branko summoned them?

Branko provided no explanations. Instead, he unfurled for them the Gypsy standard: a tricolour of blue, green and red, representing the sky, the earth and the camp-fire, embossed, at the centre, with the sketch of a wagon wheel.

And he commissioned the people to make hundreds of flags; they would need them all.

The media succeeded in unearthing a few answers.

Some of the boats had been built, over the years, in small shipyards by wealthy Gypsies.

Others had been bought by Gypsy communities which, like horses catching a whiff of their stables after a day in the field, had come to join the hegira to Romanestan.

Yet others had been chartered by Gypsies who, having concealed their identities for generations, had finally found the courage to reveal themselves.

And some – like the four rusty hulks in Tulcea's harbour, the *Ieser*, *Mindra*, *Clabucet* and *Marea Negra*, waiting to be sold for scrap – had been requisitioned by old Gypsy sea-dogs.

The rest of the boats were either chartered by or belonged to *gadje* sympathizers determined to prevent another genocide – among them many individuals from every persecuted people.

There were rumours that all these groups had links with Pablo Sanchez, the shipping mogul, himself a Gypsy.

One ship's captain, bearing an uncanny resemblance to this Sanchez, reported in an interview that Branko had recruited him in 1988 – he had been a woodcutter then – and instructed him to study everything about shipping, trade and holiday routes, tariffs, insurance, flags of convenience, *lex mercatoria*, national, international and maritime laws.

A few hours after the sighting of the boats, the *Manush* spotted Leo Leo's cutter drifting on the current.

They went to investigate and found him dead.

He had been impaled, with a spear, through the heart.

Branko prevailed that his old adversary should have a Gypsy funeral. Though Leo Leo's dreams of assimilation had been misguided, they had been the dreams of a man who had loved his people. That made him a good Rom.

And so they erected a funeral pyre and cremated him.

The Gypsies reached the mouth of Bratul Sfîntu Gheorghe.

The journey from Tulcea to the sea had taken exactly forty days.

Ideally, they should have disembarked on the southern beaches which, curving towards Lake Razim, were well sheltered.

But Branko, deciding that the islands of Sacalinul, lying immediately opposite that stretch, would restrict the ships' manoeuvrability, had urged the need for a more open coastline.

So they landed on the northern beaches.

This terrain, stretching north to Sulina in a straight line, was fully exposed to the sea and, consequently, unprotected from storms. It was also a mosquito-infested marshland where the demarcation between delta and sea barely existed.

The following day, the first ships cast anchor five kilometres off the townlet of Sfîntu Gheorghe.

And Lumnia gave birth to a boy.

Branko, who was supervising the disembarkation at the time, howled as dolorously as in old Orşova when Omar had impregnated her.
    This time, too, Lumnia heard him.

Omar wished to call his son Branko.
    But Branko reminded him that with a new history awaiting the people, the need for that name had ended. The newly born should be named after the first patriarch, he on whom O Del's favour fell.
    Thus the boy was named Rom.
    Two portentous events accompanied the birth. Rom was born with a golden tooth. And Lumnia's breasts produced so much milk that she suckled comfortably both her son and her husband.

Upon hearing Rom's vigorous first yell, Parno abandoned herself to that interminable dance which the Holy Book calls *the reel of the inconsolable heart*. Juggling her sharp, sculpted combs as if they were swords, she ran up and down the beach and leapt from dune to dune.
    Thereafter, she reeled from sunrise to sunset and from sunset to sunrise. She always wore red clothes. Thus, on dark nights, she was thought to be a squall of anger; and on clear nights, against the snow of the Milky Way, she was taken for a comet.
    The triplets, now totally bereft of her, asked Branko to adopt them.
    But Branko, knowing that he would soon have to cross the bridge of hair, took the boys to Omar.
    Omar and Lumnia, having fulfilled the people's wishes with Rom's birth, welcomed the triplets with tears and open arms. And Omar reclaimed his sons.

376

Given the inhospitable terrain, the Romanian marines and infantry took up positions on the relatively drier ground around Sfîntu Gheorghe.

The waves rode the beach. The gale penetrated even the interstices of the dunes where the Gypsies had secured their boats.

Within days these small craft lay askew, like ancient tombstones. They had borne valiantly all that the Danube had inflicted on them, but had had little resistance against a sea which obeyed its Siberian lover, the north wind, unquestioningly.

The people set up tents behind palisades of woven reed and remained patient and in good cheer. Having waited several centuries for freedom, they refused to fret over a few more weeks.

Another forty days passed.

'The Gypsy Dunkirk', a term coined by the British newspaper *The Guardian*, captured the imagination of the world.

Aerial and satellite intelligence reports – as well as estimates from the swarms of newsmen covering the event – put the number of Gypsies as approaching a million. Other reports claimed that still more Gypsies – some from such far reaches as Argentina, the US and Canada – were making their way to the nearest ports in order to join their brethren.

Though liberal activists, despite their small numbers, urged and organized immediate humanitarian aid for the Gypsies, governments of Europe viewed these developments with growing panic.

Right-wing parties denounced 'The Gypsy Dunkirk' as a pantomime from a criminal race. Through this devilish ruse, they maintained, a breed of free-loaders sought to gain entry into the wealthy EC countries as refugees.

As always, bigotry triumphed. One by one, countries put their navies on alert. Poorer countries, fearing that their wealthier neighbours might divert the Gypsies to their ports, lined their shores with assault troops and cannon.

When these measures brought outcries from human rights organizations, the said countries changed tack. As proof of their compassion, they announced that, much as they deplored the Gypsies' desperate tactics, they would nevertheless open their doors to a percentage of them.

Le Monde of France listed some of these countries and the numbers they offered to admit: Canada: 100,000; Germany: 90,000; US: 60,000; France: 40,000; Denmark, Sweden and Norway: 20,000 each; Holland: 15,000; Italy and Japan: 10,000 each; Belgium, Spain, Portugal and Israel: 5,000 each; Eire: 1,000; UK: 250.

In response, the Gypsies arranged a press conference.

Branko acted as their spokesman. Standing on the brow of a dune, his eyes fixed on the horizon where the ships were gathering, he addressed the assembly.

'We, Gypsies, are not trying to sneak into *gadje* countries. On the contrary. We're getting out of them.

'We have good reason: you *gadje* don't respect the land you live on. You treat it as spoils. You have done so throughout history. You refuse to understand that the earth is as fragile as its inhabitants. You refuse to accept that land belongs to all creation, that it is indivisible, that it is not yours to do with as you please.

'In your obsession to possess it, you neuter the land with names like "motherland" or "fatherland". Then, instead of mixing and strengthening your blood with peoples of all races and faiths, you inbreed with your own. Thus you are permanently sick.

'So you choose to worship killing. At least once every generation, you seek to annihilate yourselves – and the world.

'Today, the planet, devastated by your poisons, is close to death. People, plundered of birthright and drained of soul, can be seen rotting in waste lands, begging for the bread they can smell but cannot have.

'Given this desolation, our exodus is overdue.

'Hereafter, until you *gadje* learn to love life, no Gypsy will set foot on land again. Instead we shall live in Romanestan!

'I expect you wonder where Romanestan is and ask yourselves when you last invaded, sacked, colonized and despoiled it.

'The answer is: you haven't.

'No doubt, this puzzles you. I can hear you say: there is no place on earth which has escaped our devastation!

'Scan the seas. One day you may sight Romanestan.'

One September evening, Branko, squatting by the sea, felt his spine shiver. He stood up, expecting another visitation from his recurrent vision. Leaning on a walking-stick which he sometimes imagined was Ilyas' silver sceptre – that, too, had gone to Omar – he searched the horizon for the bridge of hair.

The skyline was clear, save for a bloom of ships. These had switched their lights on and looked, in the aura of the dusk, like a field of sunflowers. Dodo, who claimed that the ships stretched as far as the Crimea, had given up counting them.

How many ships had he and Pablo estimated in Les Saintes Maries de la Mer? Hundreds? Thousands? He could not remember.

They had all come. And they had brought whole tribes of Gypsies with them. Another eighteen ships – the last batch – were due the next morning. Then, they would begin embarking.

Would it be then that he would cross the bridge of hair?

The sun began to set.

He challenged Honeypaw to race him to the tents.

As they ran, he caught sight of Parno, leaping from dune to dune, juggling her sharp combs. In her red clothes she appeared to be drenched in blood.

Suddenly she fell from a high dune.

Children screamed.

Branko ran to her.

Honeypaw reached her first.

She looked like a deer killed by arrows.

In her fall, she had impaled herself on her combs.

The embarkation began at first light.

The ships' captains informed the Romanian coastguard that they were sending lifeboats to pick up the Gypsies.

The coastguard refused permission, stating that only Bucharest could give them clearance.

The captains retorted that the lifeboats were going in anyway. Since they were on a humanitarian mission, the Romanian authorities would do well to consider the sort of outrage they would provoke should they try and stop them.

On sighting the lifeboats, four sturdy *Manush*, carrying the Yurt of the Book on a float, came out of the dunes and moved to the sea.

The Gypsies followed. They lined up on the beach by the yurt and brandished their tricolours.

This prompted the Romanian forces to push forward from Sfîntu Gheorghe to the dunes. Simultaneously, coastguard MTBs and helicopter gun-ships deployed to the area.

But they desisted from action.

For, by then, hordes of reporters had swarmed the sea and the sky with their cameras.

By noon of the first day, when it became evident that the Romanian authorities had prudently decided to allow the evacuation, tension eased. The atmosphere turned festive.

Almost every Gypsy, reporters unanimously claimed, either coaxed miraculous sounds from an instrument or burst into song or churned the sand in uninhibited dancing.

There were four exceptions: Branko, Honeypaw, Ariana and Xyris.

Branko, a marmoreal figure, stood between the soldiers on the dunes and the Gypsies on the beach. Honeypaw, no longer needed to guard the Book, remained by his side. Everyone, even the soldiers, saw that the two formed an unassailable barrier.

Nearby, Ariana and Xyris kept watch over them. Ariana, some people noted, kept looking at her palms.

At dusk on the third day, all the Gypsies, save Honeypaw, Branko, Dodo, some *Manush*, Ariana and Xyris, had been evacuated. During this time Branko and Honeypaw had not shifted from their position.

Now, as Dodo and the warriors began boarding the lifeboats, Branko scanned the dunes for the last time.

He caught sight of an object on the sand. He identified it as a mouth. One without any lips. He hated lipless mouths. The doctors who had administered the electricity in the Pro Juventute orphanages had had lipless mouths. Strange how that memory suddenly surfaced with such clarity.

A mouth is like a womb. It produces words. Words are like children. They grow up. Most retain their goodness; some turn evil.

The people in his life passed before his eyes. Eloïse. Melchior. Nettie.

Young Glanz. Leo Leo. Dr Kalderon. Ilyas. Ramzi. Yerko. Lumnia. Omar. Ariana. Xyris. The mutilated man. Dei. Dadoro. A procession. Memories of a drowning man?

He focused on the mouth again. Like a disembowelment. Paddling in the river of molten metal.

He looked beyond and saw the suppurating eye.

And the bridge of hair loomed before him.

He began to shake. It was time to be judged. Time to see whether he was destined to exchange the victim's mantle for that of the survivor. The mouth and the eye, perhaps those of a Romanian soldier on the dunes or of an angel of death, maybe even of a Hitlerite – would select him for life or death.

'Ariana! Xyris!'

'Honeypaw! Branko!'

He turned. Dodo and a few *Manush* were calling them, pointing at the space they had reserved for them in the lifeboat.

Branko scanned the beach. It was empty. He, Honeypaw, Ariana and Xyris were the only Gypsies left. Exactly one million Gypsies had embarked.

Branko turned to Ariana and Xyris; Ariana, he noted, still staring at her stigmata, was swaying as if buffeted by a hurricane. 'The two of you – go!'

The women did not move.

Branko turned to Honeypaw and ruffled its fur. 'You go! Set them an example.'

But the bear waited for him.

'Branko!'

This time the call had come from the Romanian lines.

Branko spun round. The mouth and the eye loomed larger, as if magnified. He felt hot. He noticed there was smoke around. Then he saw, below him, the great stream of molten metal. He was crossing the bridge of hair. As he inched forward, he saw the mouth sneer, the eye twitch to the left.

He heard the retort of a rifle. He felt the bridge break beneath him.

All saviours must be victims.

As he plummeted down, he felt joyous. Death was a completion, hence, a great relief. It was also a beginning where all other beginnings could be forgotten, therefore, a purveyor of hope. He remembered the last words of Branko, the Scribe: 'In death, we are reborn!'

At that moment, the bullet hit him in the eye.

I, Branko, Bear-Tamer, Saviour, attest:

In the dark days of the Porajmos, Rom, the Patriarch, and St George, our protector, saved a boy and a girl and hid them in the mountains.

After the Porajmos, Adam's brood became dejected; for by killing the Gypsies, they had also killed colour, myth, poetry, song, dance – everything that induced happiness.

So they went to St George and begged him to bring the Gypsies back to life.

St George fetched the boy and the girl from the mountains.

For a time, as the youngsters enlivened the world, Adam's brood congratulated themselves for having failed to destroy happiness entirely.

But the nature of Adam's brood is to kill.

Before long, they resented the Gypsy boy's manliness and envied his gifts.

Then one day, they went hunting for him.

Now, when St George had saved the boy, he had decided to make him indestructible. He had dipped him in dragon's saliva which, as is known, forms an impregnable skin. But, deciding that a full sheath would impede his vision and so handicap him, he had left the boy's eyes untreated, therefore, vulnerable.

And so when Adam's brood ambushed Rom and discharged their weapons on him, the indomitable youth routed them; and even as they fled, one among them, Grylli by name, a viper who had always hated the Gypsies' sultry gaze, fired at the boy's eyes and killed him.

I, Branko, Bear-Tamer, Saviour, was that boy.

And knowing that one day O Del would abandon me, I took advice from Zoroaster, the sage.

Thus, during my unknown years, when I was as fecund as forty thousand pomegranates, I stole down to the sea and deposited my seed therein.

And, promptly after my death, on St George's advice, Lumnia – so the Gypsy girl was named – went to the ocean to bathe.

And seeing my semen shining, like eternal fire, at the bottom of the sea, she swam to it and was duly impregnated.

Now her loins are bringing forth a whole great people.

My people.

My children.

These new Gypsies, finally rebelling against Adam's evil, will refuse to set foot on land again.

Out on the oceans, they will create Romanestan.

Twenty-Eight

As Branko fell, Ariana and Xyris ran to his side.

Simultaneously, Honeypaw charged towards the dunes.

A burst of automatic fire riddled him with bullets.

Dodo and the few *Manush* waiting for them in a lifeboat, scrambled on to the beach.

Whilst the *Manush* used whatever cover was available, Ariana and Xyris strode like houris, indifferent to the fact that they presented easy targets to snipers.

They reached Branko and knelt by his side.

Wailing, Ariana stroked his torn face.

Xyris folded Branko's arms across his chest, covered his head in her shawl and lifted him up.

As Xyris, carrying Branko in her arms like a child, hurried to the lifeboat, Ariana called to Dodo to attend to Honeypaw.

The Gypsies cast off before nightfall, still within Branko's original schedule.

Branko's death, witnessed by billions of viewers on television, provoked universal revulsion.

People everywhere felt they had lost their own saviour.

To avoid further censure, the Romanian authorities tracked down the 'culprit' and consigned him to the mercy of the media.

This person, Grigore by name, a young, soft-spoken university graduate, answered the questions solemnly. He claimed that Branko's death had been accidental. He had been fiddling with his gun in boredom and had pulled the trigger inadvertently. For killing Honeypaw, however, he took full responsibility. No soldier, he insisted, would have hesitated to shoot a charging bear.

This statement became the official version.

But not everybody believed it.

A Swedish reporter discovered that Grigore's army file had marked him down as a poor shot. His chances of hitting a distant target were negligible. Branko had been killed by a sharpshooter.

A French journalist stumbled upon the truth. This person, being of Romanian origin, had happened to eavesdrop on off-duty soldiers. According to their gossip, the sniper had been none other than Hospodar, the ex-Securitate regional chief – reputedly a top marksmen – who, allegedly, had also killed Leo Leo.

Some soldiers had even heard Hospodar say, somewhat bewildered, that Branko's eyes had pleaded for a bullet.

But Hospodar was never questioned on this matter.

Branko's funeral was held at sea.

The line of ships, lying at anchor side by side, stretched for kilometres.

A barge, painted in traditional motifs and containing Branko's few possessions, served as a caravan.

Immense quantities of food and drink were prepared for the *pomana*, the ritual feast.

Branko and Honeypaw were washed, then laid out, side by side, on pallets.

On Lumnia's instructions, the water used for washing the bodies had been stored. It would provide deadly magic should the *gadje* choose to attack.

Countless Gypsies – Omar and Dodo among them – composed poems and songs and recited and sang them.

Lumnia danced and, with the movements of her feet and hands, related how Branko had redeemed the Holy Book.

Often, during the general lamentation, the triplets could be heard addressing Branko as 'Dadoro'.

When alcohol brought their grief into full focus, fights broke out between the men. That was good, too, because after bruising each other, they embraced and became better friends.

Ariana and Xyris kept vigil by Branko's side.

Ariana, now relieved of her stigmata – they had disappeared the moment Branko had died – occasionally bent down and whispered into his ear. 'I would burn with you, my son. But I gave you my word I would see Romanestan. I will keep that promise.'

Xyris spoke only once – to Ariana and Lumnia. 'Thank you for summoning me as his *Suvetar*. He will be fine now.'

The *pomana* lasted three days and nights.

At dawn, on the fourth day, the corpses were washed again. And again, the used water was stored for magic.

The Gypsies wrapped Branko and Honeypaw in shrouds and laid them out on the barge. To remind them that one day they would return to life, they placed stones beneath their heads. Then they set fire to the barge and let it drift out to the open sea.

Xyris took a small boat and returned to the land.

Lumnia and Ariana saw her change into an ibis and fly to the east.

The barge burned.

Flames engulfed Branko and Honeypaw. They had a gentle, shaky quality, Branko felt, like the hands of old people. They belonged, he realized, to an old fire: Auschwitz's fire. They were clasping and hugging him because he was the prodigal who had returned. He wondered whether he should surrender to them.

But this fire produced smoke. Therefore, it was imperfect. This fire had cremated millions. But it had not cremated all – neither all the Gypsies, nor all the Jews, nor all the others. This fire had failed.

Whereas *he* had succeeded.

The barge began to sink. He linked arms with Honeypaw.

He could see the Gypsies watching from their ships. And he could see the *gadje*. Also watching. On the beaches and in the sky. With their cameras.

The barge sank.

He and Honeypaw drifted as ash.

Voices converged.

385

'Hello, son.'

'Hello, Honeypaw.'

His Dei and Dadoro. And all the Ursari. And Branko, the Scribe. Coming towards them. Arms wide open.

The arms embraced them.

Gently, they streamed into life.

And it was time to separate the existent from the non-existent.

I became fire and entered the Universe.

In the starry depths, I reconstituted my ashes and impregnated the cosmic dust.

And I, Branko, Bear-Tamer, Saviour, was reborn.

I am a giant with a thousand testicles. Each one of my arms and legs are the size of ten oaks. And within my frame shelter both man and god.

EPILOGUE

The Gypsies assembled a pliable, floating islet and secured it to their ships with tractable hawsers woven from twiners and lianas.

Thus by bracing or slackening these hawsers, they could adjust the islet's length or width and manoeuvre it safely even through the narrowest straits.

And so they sailed.

And offering libations of wine and rice to the elements, they set sail with all that they had created for the world: music, colour, joy, love and dignity.

The elements, in turn, commissioned the winds, the clouds and the rainbows to collect all that the Gypsies needed – topsoil, grass, seeds, rain, dew, animals . . .

In nine months, the islet grew to an island.

In nine years, the island grew to a continent.

Fields and orchards flourished and herds lived openly and unthreatened.

But elsewhere disasters compounded.

Nature, in the absence of her custodians, the Gypsies, succumbed to disease. The sun became inflamed; the land erupted with sores; the air festered with poison; the bones of mountains withered and rivers ebbed sickly water.

Forty years later, the Earth spun deathward.

And Adam's brood finally realized that their war against life now threatened their own lives.

And they went to the Gypsies and begged them to return to the land and save the planet . . .